D0022653

INTERNATIONAL MARKETING

Sak Onkvisit
SAN JOSE STATE UNIVERSITY

John J. Shaw
PROVIDENCE COLLEGE

INTERNATIONAL MARKETING
Analysis and Strategy
Second Edition

Macmillan Publishing Company
New York

Maxwell Macmillan Canada
Toronto

Maxwell Macmillan International
New York Oxford Singapore Sydney

Editor: Charles E. Stewart, Jr.
Production Supervisor: Publication Services
Production Manager: Linda Greenberg
Cover photograph: C000-08132-100 COMSTOCK INC.

This book was set in Garamond Light by Publication Services and was printed and bound by
R.R. Donnelley & Sons Company.
The cover was printed by The Lehigh Press, Inc..

Copyright©1993 by Macmillan Publishing Company, a division of Macmillan, Inc.

Printed in the United States of America

All rights reserved. No part of this book may be reproduced or transmitted in any form or by any
means, electronic or mechanical, including photocopying, recording, or any information storage and
retrieval system, without permission in writing from the Publisher.

Earlier edition copyright © 1989 by Merrill Publishing Company

Macmillan Publishing Company
866 Third Avenue, New York, New York 10022

Macmillan Publishing Company is
part of the Maxwell Communication
Group of Companies.

Maxwell Macmillan Canada, Inc.
1200 Eglinton Avenue East
Suite 200
Don Mills, Ontario M3C 3N1

Library of Congress Cataloging Card Number: 92-083811
International Standard Book Number: 0-02-389343-5

Printing: 1 2 3 4 5 6 7 Year: 3 4 5 6 7 8 9

To my grandmother and Lawrence X. Tarpey, Sr.
and
Ann, Jonathan, and Rebecca and Dennis M.
Crites

Preface

From an academic perspective, international business provides insights for the understanding of the business process and discipline. From a nation's perspective, international business allows a nation to survive and gain a higher standard of living by trading its resources for what it lacks, while moderating the inflation rate and generating employment. From the company's perspective, many foreign markets offer growth, sales, profits, and risk diversification; they enable a company to discover new ideas that may lead to new products and applications.

International experiences are not luxuries; they are requisite to understanding the interdependence of nations and markets as well as the concepts of the various disciplines. Without the comprehension of global issues, education is not complete. Educators and students alike have a basic obligation to take advantage of the opportunities to transmit and learn the knowledge of the world.

Business schools are in an excellent position to play an important part in educating future managers to meet international challenges. A key ingredient in this process is that the student's frame of reference must be extended to the global market. Since 1980, the AACSB (American Assembly of Collegiate Schools of Business) has begun to require a new accreditation standard based on the international concern by stating that "every student should be exposed to the international dimension through one or more elements of the curriculum." The AACSB wants the curriculum to include a worldwide dimension and encourages efforts to internationalize the curriculum accordingly.

One of the problems in teaching international marketing is the scarcity of relevant textbooks, especially compared to the considerable number available in other areas of management and marketing. To compound the problem, several texts consist mainly of a collection of business cases with little or no decision-making framework. Furthermore, because of the dearth of theories developed for the discipline, most international marketing textbooks are more descriptive than theoretical or empirical in nature. Such descriptive contributions, though useful, merely report anecdotes based more on casual and personal observation than on rigorous investigation. Moreover, descriptive materials can become obsolete very rapidly.

We do want to acknowledge the contribution made by the pioneering books. Whereas our book builds on what they have accomplished, we feel that it is critical for the new generation of international marketing texts to offer theoretical and conceptual foundations that are useful for explanation, prediction, and control. This approach, as the basis of the first edition, has been very well received. One major and unique strength of the second edition of *International Marketing: Analysis and Strategy,* like that of the first edition, is a serious and comprehensive attempt to use theories to provide an analytical framework for understanding and predicting business incidents.

We have designed the book primarily for marketing majors and MBA students. Upper-level or graduate-level students should have completed introductory courses in marketing and management before reading this text.

FEATURES OF THIS BOOK

Unlike many texts that loosely tie concepts to isolated business incidents, this text provides fundamental principles and solid background necessary to do research and/or pursue a career in international marketing. Instead of relying mainly on nonacademic sources (i.e., newspapers and magazines), we extensively use scholarly journals for theory and business publications for pragmatism. We do not believe that the revision should merely update the examples. Furthermore, it is inappropriate to simply list a few new references. We feel that it is essential that the references are both current and that they are also integrated with other text materials.

Each chapter includes discussion assignments, minicases, and cases. As a result, the instructor and students are not restricted to only review questions. Instead, they can select from numerous assignments for active classroom discussion. The second edition has added several new cases and minicases. Furthermore, there is an abundance of chapter-opening vignettes, advertisements, figures, tables, and other illustrations that highlight the discussion and show how the business concepts are used in practice.

Although our book includes all the basic topics of the mainstream texts, it differs in many respects. First of all, it is more analytical. It goes beyond the customary descriptive technique, placing more emphasis on the integration of theories, applications, and managerial implications.

Another innovative feature is the inclusion of several relevant but relatively ignored topics. There are chapters on marketing barriers, financing, foreign exchange, consumer behavior, branding and packaging, and physical distribution. Furthermore, other topics are accorded more breadth and depth of coverage than is usually the case. Discussed in detail are U.S. export failure, export planning, financial strategies, analysis and management of political risks, bribery, jurisdiction, counterfeiting, gray markets, subcultures, services, free-trade zones, representation agreements, dumping, and countertrade.

A unique feature of the book is the inclusion of two simulation games: one involving culture and another focusing on foreign exchange. These games are easy to follow; they do not require the use of a computer. They teach students about common international marketing problems. Although the games can begin at almost any point during the first half of the semester, they should be started early in order to maximize the potential benefits. Students should find them interesting and challenging.

We feel that international marketing is a dynamic, exciting, and challenging discipline. Our approach in this text reflects this belief. We have provided the theoretical/conceptual foundations that are essential for understanding and integrating ideas, and we have made every effort to ensure that the material is readable and lively.

LEARNING AIDS

Each chapter in the book includes a number of pedagogical aids. The *questions* at the end of each chapter ask students to review or explain the concepts. In addition, *discussion assignments and minicases* require students to apply what they have learned in actual situations. In order to further stimulate ideas and debate so that students can become actively involved in applying the concepts, there are *cases* of varying length for each chapter. These cases were specifically written to address concepts and issues introduced in the chapter.

The instructor's manual accompanying the text was completely written by us to ensure the quality and relevance of the materials.

It is a pleasure to acknowledge the contribution of many individuals. First, we are grateful for the support, assistance, and encouragement of Dean Marshall Burak, Curtis Cook, Richard Werbel, Jim Stull, and Jeff Fadiman, all of San Jose State University. Second, we want to thank Malcolm Morris, James Kenderdine, James Constantin, and Rodney Evans. We really appreciate the encouraging comments from the students and adopters of the book; this is a great reward for our efforts. We also want to thank Dirk Wassenaar, Mary Brooks, and other colleagues who have written cases for this book. Next, for those reviewers who have given us their useful and insightful comments, we are thankful. The reviewers of the first and second editions include Keri Acheson, Northwestern University; Betsy Boze, Centenary College; Roger Calantone, University of Kentucky; Newell Chiesl, Indiana State University; Neil Ford, University of Wisconsin-Madison; P. Renee Foster, Delta State University; Jac L. Goldstucker, Georgia State University; Kemal Kurtulus, Dublin, Ohio; Ivor S. Mitchell, Atlanta University; Charles R. Patton, Pan American University; C. P. Rao, University of Arkansas; Allan C. Reddy, Valdosta State College; Dale Shook, Capital University; and John Thanopoulos, University of Akron. We are also indebted to a number of companies and organizations for their permission to use their advertisements and materials. Last but foremost, we appreciate the patience and understanding of our families.

S. O.
J. J. S.

Contents

6   Culture   255

7   Consumer Behavior in the International Context: Psychological and Social Dimensions   311

□ PART THREE   PLANNING FOR INTERNATIONAL MARKETING   357

8   Marketing Research and Information System   359

11 Product Strategies: Branding and Packaging Decisions   529

12 Distribution Strategies: Channels of Distribution   567

PART ONE
OVERVIEW OF WORLD BUSINESS

The first order of business for decision-makers—in both the public and private sectors—is to think beyond national borders and to embrace a mindset that says all world markets constitute one economy.

Fred Smith, president and CEO, Federal Express Corporation

Nature of International Marketing
Challenges and Opportunities

1

CHAPTER OUTLINE

PROCESS OF INTERNATIONAL MARKETING

INTERNATIONAL DIMENSIONS OF MARKETING

THE APPLICABILITY OF MARKETING

CHARACTERISTICS OF MULTINATIONAL CORPORATIONS (MNCs)

BENEFITS OF INTERNATIONAL MARKETING

THE WORLD'S MOST INDIFFERENT EXPORTER

CASE 1–1: Arizona Sunray, Inc.

CASE 1–2: Beautiful Vision, Inc.

MARKETING ILLUSTRATION
A New Breed—Denationalized Corporations

Consolidated Foods Corp. found that its corporate name failed to communicate the fact that the firm had evolved into a consumer products operating company. Many in the financial community did not know enough about Consolidated Foods; they thought that Consolidated's Sara Lee brand was owned by General Foods. As a result, the corporation decided to search for a new name. Among 200 major consumer companies, those using brand names as corporate names have received higher price-earning ratios than those using generic or founder names. After looking at 1,500 names, Consolidated chose *Sara Lee* because it came out on top in awareness, price for value, and quality (see Exhibit 1–1).

Sara Lee Corp., world-renowned for its pound cakes and brownies, is more than just a food corporation. Profits from the company's bakery business have been used to help Sara Lee enter the hosiery, socks, and underwear markets. The company's strategy is to select products that have spotty competition, extremely predictable demand, and less fleeting tastes. The next step is to buy an existing manufacturer for quick economies of scale while improving productivity. Then Sara Lee uses marketing to create a strong brand image so as to turn these near-commodity items into powerful brands. Sara Lee's nonfood brands include Hanes men's underwear, Hanes Her Way women's and girls' underwear, Champion sweatclothes, L'eggs nylons, Bali bras, and Coach leather goods.

Sara Lee is also more than a U.S. firm; it has global ambitions. According to the conglomerate's chairman, "our mission is to be a premier global, branded consumer packaged-goods company." There is plenty of evidence to assert that Sara Lee has become much more international. The company's international business includes: Douwe Egberts (a Dutch producer of coffee, tea, and tobacco products)—$1 billion in sales; Nicholas Kiwi (a multinational but Australia-based company of personal households, shoe care products, and home medicines)—$330 million; Intradal (personal care products)—$125 million; Sara Lee Australia (baked goods)—$40 million; and Sara Lee U.K. (baked goods)—$13 million. In 1974 the company was 5 percent international as compared with the 25 percent in 1985.

Sara Lee has used acquisitions to build up a $3.2 billion business in Europe, ranking the firm number 4 among U.S.-based consumer products companies with European operations. The firm's European food operation sells coffee, tea, nuts, and snack foods, and the Douwe Egberts and Van Nelle brands have helped the company become Europe's number 2 coffee company. After acquiring Dim, France's leading hosiery manufacturer, Sara Lee has extended the Dim brand to men's underwear and T-shirts. Sara Lee's Playtex and Bali brands are also a major force in Europe. In addition, the firm has planned to buy several Asian hosiery companies to help it achieve its goal of doubling Far East sales to $1 billion by 1995. Sara Lee's commitment to its overseas businesses is also supported by the fact that the company's president is the one who oversees the foreign operations. Furthermore, because coffee is one major part of the company's international business, the chairman and CEO has taken to drinking coffee instead of colas.

Sources: "This Marketing Effort Has L'eggs," *Business Week,* 23 December 1991, 50–51; "CFC Changes Name to Sara Lee," *Food & Beverage Marketing,* June 1985, 25; and Tamara Goldman, "CFC Kneads Sara Lee Name," *Food & Beverage Marketing,,* June 1985, 22–25

*Consolidated Foods
announces
its new name*

SARA LEE CORPORATION

*Of all the Consolidated Foods brands
today, Sara Lee was the first. Now our first
brand name is our brand new first name.
Because Consolidated Foods Corporation
is now Sara Lee Corporation.*

*Over the years, we've evolved into a
consumer products company marketing
many leading brands. And our best known
brand name reflects our commitments to
quality and leadership shared by every
company in our corporate family.*

*So it's with great pride that Consolidated
Foods adopts the name everybody knows.
Our name may have changed, but our
commitments never will.*

EXHIBIT 1–1   A corporate name change

Source: Courtesy of Sara Lee Corporation

The Sara Lee case exemplifies the importance of international marketing and the desirability of transforming a national company into a multinational firm. Worldwide competition has been intensifying, and in time companies that are not internationally inclined will be adversely affected. Rather than being reactive or defensive, a wise marketer must shed a rigid mentality and embrace a more progressive and flexible view of the world market. Potential problems can thereby be transformed into challenges and opportunities.

The emphasis of this text is on the planning, execution, and control of corporate resources with the ultimate goal of maximizing global market opportunities. The text examines the importance of international marketing, both to individual countries and to the world. It develops an appreciation of different cultures and their influence on international marketing. It provides a clear and complete treatment of the basic concepts and issues of international business in general and international marketing in particular. Finally, it extends basic marketing concepts and techniques into the framework of the world marketplace, directly tying them to international marketing decisions with an emphasis on the marketing mix.

The approach of the book is to move from the general to the specific. As such, Parts I and II constitute an overview of world business and the world market environment. Part III focuses on the planning of market entry, with emphasis on marketing information, market analysis, and entry strategies. Part IV, the greatest portion of the book, is devoted to marketing decisions. Part V, which examines international finance, can be optional, though this material should not be completely ignored because financial markets throughout the world are closely linked and because marketing decisions cannot be made without consideration of their financial implications.

Each chapter begins with a marketing illustration, a brief study from the business world that helps introduce the content of the chapter. Throughout a chapter, advertisements and other actual marketing examples are used for illustrative purposes. Each chapter ends with a summary, a set of questions about the concepts covered, a set of discussion assignments to stimulate ideas and debate, and a case or cases for analysis. Notes that correspond to the reference numbers scattered throughout the text are printed at the end of each chapter, providing documentation for facts and quotations.

This chapter addresses the who, what, why, and how of international marketing by giving an overview of the nature of international business. The discussion begins with an examination of how marketing in general is defined and how that definition works for international marketing. The role of marketing in other kinds of economies is considered. To dispel some popularly held misconceptions, there is an explicit and comprehensive treatment of the benefits of international trade. The chapter examines the criteria that determine when a company has successfully transformed itself into a multinational firm. Finally, it investigates the causes and implications of U.S. firms' failure to market actively abroad.

PROCESS OF INTERNATIONAL MARKETING

A study of international marketing should begin with an understanding of what marketing is and how it operates in an international context. Because of the large number of marketing textbooks, a variety of definitions of marketing are currently in use. Yet most of these definitions are convergent in the sense that they all describe the basics of marketing in much the same way. Any definition is acceptable as long as it captures the essential idea and as long as the strengths and limitations associated with the definition are acknowledged.

One of the most widely accepted definitions of marketing is the one used for decades by the American Marketing Association (AMA): marketing is "the performance of business activities that direct the flow of goods and services from producer to consumer or user."[1] To define international marketing, some authorities simply add the phrase "in more than one country" at the end of that definition of marketing. Although the AMA's definition is useful in some contexts, it suffers from several implicit assumptions.[2] And these weaknesses are greatly amplified when the definition is extended to international marketing.

One weakness is that the definition limits marketing only to "business activities." Another is that it assumes that there is a finished product ready for sale to consumers when, in many cases, a firm must determine consumer needs before creating a product to satisfy those needs. That is, the definition's orientation is to "we sell what we make" when it should be to "we make what we sell." The marketing function is not complete just because the product has been sold, because consumer satisfaction after the sale is critical for repeat purchases. For example, a frequent complaint voiced by Asian importers and users is the failure of U.S. firms to provide spare parts and after-sales service for the equipment sold.

Another weakness of the definition is that it overemphasizes place or distribution at the expense of the other aspects of the marketing mix. Accepting this narrow definition at face value has caused many U.S. firms to understand their international function as simply to export (i.e., move) available products from one country to another.

The addition of "in more than one country" does nothing to eliminate the definition's weaknesses. Furthermore, the phrase overstates similarities among countries and oversimplifies the nature of international marketing by implying that the marketing process is a mere repetition of using identical strategies abroad.

A new definition adopted by the AMA in 1985 overcomes most of these criticisms.[3] Thus, it is used as a basis for the definition of international marketing given here: **international marketing** is the multinational process of planning and executing the conception, pricing, promotion, and distribution of ideas, goods, and services to create exchanges that satisfy individual and organizational objectives. Only the word **multinational** has been added to the definition adopted by the AMA. That word implies that marketing activities are undertaken in several countries and that such activities should somehow be coordinated across nations.

This definition is not completely free of limitations. By placing individual objectives at one end of the definition and organizational objectives at the other, the definition stresses a relationship between a consumer and an organization. In effect, it excludes industrial marketing, which involves a transaction between two organizations. In the world of international marketing, governments, quasi-government agencies, and profit-seeking and nonprofit entities are frequently buyers. The definition also fails to do justice to the significance of industrial purchases.

Nonetheless, the definition does offer several advantages. It closely resembles the AMA's widely and easily understood definition. In several ways, it carefully describes the essential characteristics of international marketing. First, it makes it clear that what is to be exchanged is not restricted to tangible products (goods) but can include concepts and services as well. When the United Nations promotes such concepts as birth control and breast feeding, this should be viewed as international marketing. Exhibit 1–2 shows how one organization promotes the concept of preserving tropical forests. Likewise, services or intangible products are just as relevant to the definition, because airline flights, financial services, advertising services, management consulting, marketing research, and so on all play a very significant role in affecting trade balance.

Second, the definition removes the implication that international marketing applies only to market or business transactions. International nonprofit marketing, which has received only scant attention, should not be overlooked. The marketing of state governments and of religion underscores this point. State governments are very active in marketing in order to attract foreign investment. The state of Illinois, for instance, offered a package of tax incentives and direct aid worth $276 million for a Chrysler/Mitsubishi plant. To lure Mazda, Flat Rock (Michigan) offered a fourteen-year tax holiday; Toyota received a $150 million incentive package from the state of Kentucky. Exhibit 1–3 shows a highly successful campaign by the state of California to attract investors. Religion is also a big business, though most people prefer not to view it that way. Religion has been marketed internationally for centuries. Well-known exporters of religion have included Billy Graham and Jimmy Swaggart. Their television programs have been shown in many countries. Overseas trips by such figures can generate a great deal of publicity at home and abroad.

Third, the definition recognizes that it is improper for a firm to create a product first and then look for a place to sell it. Rather than seeking consumers for a firm's existing product, it is often more logical to determine consumer needs before creating a product. For overseas markets, the process may call for a modified product. In some cases, following this approach may result in foreign needs being satisfied in a new way (i.e., a brand new product is created specifically for overseas markets). Mazda, for example, understands that it is no longer adequate to simply adapt a Japanese care to the U.S. market, and its product strategy involves designing a car to meet U.S. buyers' desires. Mazda's widely acclaimed Miata was conceived and styled in Southern California and was engineered and built in Japan.

Fourth, the definition acknowledges that place or distribution is just part of the marketing mix and that the distance between markets makes it neither more nor less important than other parts of the mix. Place, product, promotion, and price—the *4 Ps* of marketing—must be integrated and coordinated in order to bring about the most effective marketing mix.

INTERNATIONAL DIMENSIONS OF MARKETING

One way to understand the concept of international marketing is to examine how international marketing differs from such similar concepts as domestic marketing, foreign marketing, comparative marketing, international trade, and multinational mar-

Some Of The Reasons For Saving Tropical Forests Are Disappearing.

Catharanthus roseus.
Rosy periwinkle, of Madagascar, is used to treat Hodgkins disease, leukemia, other cancers, and diabetes.

Zea diploperennis.
Teosinte of Mexico is a perennial disease resistant wild corn that may make it possible to raise corn without yearly plowing or sowing.

Cacao species.
Wild cocoa plants (on which the future of chocolate depends) grow in the threatened rain forests of South America.

Vermivora chrysoptera.
Golden-Winged Warbler, which winters in Cuba and the Bahamas, is now dangerously close to extinction.

Dioscorea species.
This Mexican yam has yielded numerous pharmaceutical treatments for arthritis, rheumatic fever, allergies and skin diseases.

Rauwolfia verticillata.
Native to China, this plant yields reserpine, used to produce tranquilizers and drugs to treat both hypertension and schizophrenia.

Phyllotreta species.
The South America flea beetle destroys alligator weed, which clogs U.S. waterways and costs millions of dollars to control.

Amaranthus species.
Native to Central and South America, fast-growing amaranths are promising, protein-rich food crops.

When an ax rings in some remote tropical forest, it strikes all too close to home. When the habitat of half the world's plant and animal species is destroyed at a rate of 50 acres every minute, we all pay the price.

Tropical forests have yielded precious medicines, food crop varieties and much more. They are habitat for many rare birds and other wildlife. And the lives of hundreds of millions of people depend on these forests for survival.

Continued deforestation at the current pace—which will lay waste to an area as large as one third of the continental U.S. by the year 2000—will rob us of these and other as yet undiscovered benefits.

But it need not continue. Write in order to find out how you can help keep tropical forests alive, before the reasons disappear.

Keep Tropical Forests Alive.

Tropical Forest Project, World Resources Institute, 1735 New York Avenue, N.W. Washington, D.C. 20006 / Prepared by Richardson, Myers & Donofrio, Inc.

EXHIBIT 1–2   Idea marketing

Source: Reprinted with permission of the Tropical Forest Project, World Resources Institute

One of the world's leading economic powers doesn't have its own currency, army or Olympic Team.

EXHIBIT 1–3   Nonprofit marketing

Source: ©1989 California Department of Commerce. Reproduced by permission. All rights reserved. ®Registered trademark of the State of California

© 1989 California Department of Commerce. All rights reserved.

CALIFORNIA REPUBLIC

Welcome to The Californias, the sixth largest economy in the world. Just behind France, West Germany, Japan, Soviet Union and the United States.

One of the most durable myths about this part of the world is that it's on the edge—the edge of the continent, the edge of the Pacific, the edge of change.

That's very romantic and very, very misleading. The Californias are the center, not the edge. If you want to be in the middle of things, you have to be here.

The Californias are the wealthiest, fastest-growing market. Six hundred billion dollars last year. And growing.

The Gross State Product has increased steadily—40% over the past four years.

Since 1983, over 2000 companies have located or expanded their operations here. Fully one-third of United States' high-tech companies are here.

U.S. trade with Asia now surpasses trade with Europe. One hundred billion dollars of foreign trade passes through The Californias each year.

Remember that saying about the right place at the right time? Forget it.

If you're in the right place, it doesn't matter what time it is.

The Californias®

California Department of Commerce
1121 L Street, Suite 600, Sacramento, CA 95814 • (916) 322-5665.

EXHIBIT 1–3   continued

keting. **Domestic marketing** is concerned with the marketing practices within a researcher's or marketer's home country. From the perspective of domestic marketing, marketing methods used outside the home market are foreign marketing. Therefore, **foreign marketing** encompasses the domestic operations within a foreign country. A U.S. company considers marketing in the United States as domestic marketing and marketing in Great Britain as foreign marketing. To a British firm, the opposite is true—British marketing is domestic, and American marketing is foreign.

A study becomes **comparative marketing** when its purpose is to contrast two or more marketing systems rather than examine a particular country's marketing system for its own sake. Similarities and differences between systems are identified. Thus comparative marketing involves two or more countries and an analytical comparison of marketing methods used in these countries.

International marketing must be distinguished from international trade. **International trade** is concerned with the flow of goods and capital across national borders. The focus of the analysis is on commercial and monetary conditions that affect balance of payment and resource transfers. This economics approach provides a macro view of the market at the national level, with no specific attention given to companies' marketing intervention. The study of international marketing, on the other hand, is more concerned with the micro level of the market and uses the company as a unit of analysis. The focus of the analysis is on how and why a product succeeds or fails abroad and how marketing efforts affect the outcome.

Some marketing authorities differentiate international marketing from multinational marketing because international marketing in its literal sense signifies marketing between nations (*inter-* means *between*). The word *international* can thus imply that a firm is not a corporate citizen of the world but rather operates from a home base. For these authorities, **multinational** (or **global,** or **world**) **marketing** is the preferred term, since nothing is foreign or domestic about the world market and global opportunities.

One might question whether the subtle difference between international marketing and multinational marketing is significant. For practical purposes, it is merely a distinction without a difference. As a matter of fact, multinational firms themselves do not make any distinction between the two terms. It is difficult to believe that International Business Machines will become more global if it changes its corporate name to Multinational Business Machines. Likewise, there is no compelling reason for American Express and American Telephone & Telegraph to change their names to, say, Global Express and Multinational Telephone & Telegraph. For purposes of the discussion in this text, *international* and *multinational marketing* are used interchangeably.

This text will use the United States, Japan, and the European Community as points of reference from which discussions of various issues will be made. This approach should not be interpreted as emphasizing a "home country" orientation; rather, it is a matter of necessity for purposes of discussion. Furthermore, this powerful triad dominates world trade, and the primary users of this text are familiar with these three markets.

It would beg the question to say that life and death are similar in nature, except in degree. As pointed out by Lufthansa (see Exhibit 1–4), it would be just as incorrect to say that domestic and international marketing are similar in nature but not in

Why flying to Munich is considerably different than flying to Muncie.

Many domestic airlines have begun to fly across the Atlantic. But an airline used to shorter flights still has much to learn about travelling overseas. On longer flights, passengers expect not just more service, but a different level of service. Food becomes far more important: ordinary airline meals just won't do. The environment has to be equally comfortable for working or sleeping, and cabin attendants must be consistently sensitive to every passenger's needs, for every hour of the trip.

In short, a trip to Munich shouldn't feel like a long trip to Muncie.

That's why we suggest, when you're flying to Germany and beyond, take the airline that understands longer flights.

People expect the world of us.   **Lufthansa**

Lufthansa is a participant in the mileage programs of United, Delta, USAir and Continental/Eastern. See your Travel Agent for details.

EXHIBIT 1–4   Domestic marketing versus international marketing

Source: Courtesy of Lufthansa German Airlines

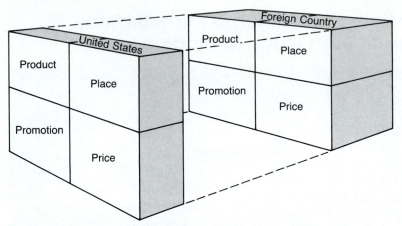

EXHIBIT 1–5   Extension of the U.S. marketing mix

scope, meaning that international marketing is nothing but domestic marketing on a larger scale. This kind of fallacious thinking can be the cause of a simple extension of the U.S. marketing mix into other markets, as shown in Exhibit 1–5.

Domestic marketing involves one set of uncontrollables derived from the domestic market. International marketing is much more complex because a marketer faces two or more sets of uncontrollable variables originating from various countries. The marketer must cope with different cultural, legal, political, and monetary systems. For example, American firms doing business in South Africa have contended with both black unions there and domestic protests within the United States. Further complicating the issue have been some city and state laws that require investments of public pension funds to be withdrawn from companies that operate in South Africa.

As shown in Exhibit 1–6, the two or more sets of environmental factors overlap, indicating that some similarities are shared by the countries involved. It is reasonable to expect a large degree of overlap between the United States and Western Europe, and this overlap would be relatively greater than an overlap between the United States and other continents or countries.

A firm's marketing mix is determined by the uncontrollable factors within each country's environment as well as by the interaction between the sets (see Exhibit 1–7). For optimum results, a firm's marketing mix may have to be modified to conform to a different environment, though wholesale modification is not often necessary. The degree of overlap of the sets of uncontrollable variables will dictate the extent to which the 4 Ps of marketing must change—the more the overlap, the less the modification. In any case, the varying environments within which the marketing plan is implemented may often rule out uniform marketing strategies across countries.

THE APPLICABILITY OF MARKETING

One interesting question often raised is whether marketing is needed in socialist/communist countries and in less-developed countries (LDCs). Implied in the question is that basic consumer needs in such countries are known but not met, and thus

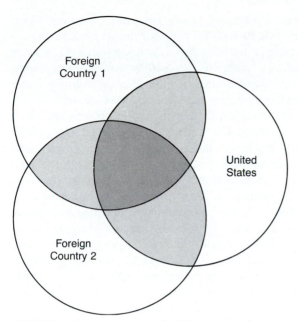

EXHIBIT 1–6   Environmental divergence and convergence

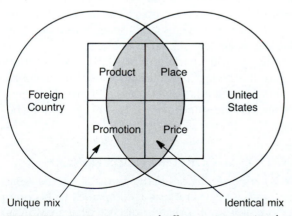

EXHIBIT 1–7   Environmental effect on international marketing mix

demand stimulation (which is usually a primary task of marketing) is not necessary. According to the conclusion of one study, there is no need for multinational corporations to stress marketing in developing countries.[4] Superior products alone provide sufficient advantage for such companies to compete successfully without emphasizing marketing functions. Under such circumstances, the action problem is supply—or the lack of it—and this problem is solvable by improving production efficiency.

This view is too narrow an interpretation of the marketing process and does not offer a complete picture. First, communist countries such as China allow some kind of private business and independent business action.[5] The former Soviet Union and Eastern Europe have begun to move in that same direction. Second, the goal of marketing is usually to maximize profit and not necessarily sales or demand. Marketing can thus be used to curb demand while maintaining the same level of profit when such a strategy is desirable. Third, marketing can alleviate the supply problem by manipulating the components within the marketing mix. The mix can be adjusted (e.g., less advertising, more selective distribution, higher price) so as to bring demand down to a level more closely matching supply. Finally, the marketing process stimulates innovations, which provide new and better ways to satisfy consumer needs more efficiently and effectively. Consequently, marketing is a desirable activity even in economies different from the advanced ones, such as in the United States.

Marketing is a universal activity that is widely applicable, but that does not mean that consumers in all parts of the world must or should be satisfied in exactly the same way. Consumers from various countries are significantly different because of varying culture, income, level of economic development, and so on. Therefore, consumers may use the same product without having the same need or motive and in turn may use different products to satisfy the same need. For example, different kinds of foods are used in different countries to satisfy the same hunger need. Further, Americans may use gas or electric heat to keep warm, whereas people in India may meet the same need by burning cow dung.

On the way to overseas markets, most U.S. firms prefer to take the path of least resistance. As a result, they tend to adopt the "**big car syndrome,**" which means that American consumers' preference for big cars should dictate what is to be exported. But the taste of American consumers is not the same as superiority in taste. It is this erroneous belief that makes many U.S. firms take the easy and usually misguided way of simply extending their U.S. marketing strategies to foreign markets.

Too often, marketing mix is confused with marketing principles. Sound marketing principles are universal and can thus be applied internationally. But universal principles in no way imply a uniform marketing mix for all markets. To be customer-oriented, for example, does not mean that the same marketing strategy should be repeated in a different environment.

CHARACTERISTICS OF MULTINATIONAL CORPORATIONS (MNCs)

Multinational corporations (MNCs) are major actors in the world of international business. As shown by the Sara Lee case, it is desirable for companies to become more internationally inclined. Therefore, it is appropriate to discuss what an MNC is and the role it plays.

The mention of MNCs usually elicits mixed reactions. On the one hand, MNCs are associated with exploitation and ruthlessness. They are often criticized for moving resources in and out of a country, as they strive for profit, without much regard for the country's social welfare. Varity Corp., a well-known Canadian multinational firm, was criticized for its action in 1991 to relocate its headquarters from Toronto to the United States (Buffalo) in order to take advantage of the U.S.-Canadian Free Trade Agreement. For a long time, India referred to MNCs as "agents of neocolonialism." It was not until 1991 that socialist India began wooing multinational companies.

On the other hand, MNCs have power and prestige; additionally they create social benefit by facilitating economic balance. As explained by Miller, "with resources, capital, food, and technology unevenly distributed around the planet, and all in short supply, an efficient instrument of quick and effective production and distribution of a complex of goods and services is a first essential."[6] This instrument is, of course, the MNC. Regardless of whether MNCs are viewed positively or negatively, they are here to stay, and the important point is to understand when a company becomes a member of this elite group.

The term implies bigness. The top ten multinational giants based on market value are the following: (1) Nippon Telegraph & Telephone, (2) Royal Dutch/Shell Group, (3) Exxon, (4) General Electric, (5) Industrial Bank of Japan, (6) Philip Morris, (7) International Business Machines, (8) Fuji Bank, (9) Mitsubishi Bank, and (10) Dai-Ichi Kangyo Bank.[7]

It is not unusual for corporate size in terms of sales to be used as a primary requirement for judging whether or not a company is multinational. As a matter of fact, according to the United Nations Department of Economic and Social Affairs, companies "with less than $100 million in sales can safely be ignored."[8] Based on this definition, some 300,000 small and midsize German companies do not qualify even though these firms (called the *Mittelstand,* or midranking) contribute mightily to Germany's export success. These midsize firms account for two-thirds of the country's gross national product and four-fifths of all workers.[9]

Most multinational corporations are large, but corporate sales should not be used as the sole criterion for multinationalism. As noted by one IBM executive, IBM did not become multinational because it was large; rather, it became large as a result of going international. There are empirical findings that support this view. "Size as currently developed in the literature is not useful as an indicator of export attitudes or needs, and activities. Thus it should not serve as a policy instrument for export development purposes."[10]

There is no single criterion that proves satisfactory at all times in identifying an MNC because the concept of an MNC is not unidimensional. Varying explanations have been used to define a multinational corporation, but these definitions are not necessarily convergent. As a result, whether a company is classified as an MNC or not depends in part on what set of criteria is used. According to Aharoni, an MNC has at least three significant dimensions: structural, performance, and behavioral.[11]

Definition by Structure

Structural requirements for definition as an MNC include the number of countries in which the firm does business and the citizenship of corporate owners and top managers. Singer Corporation, for instance, sells its sewing machines in 181 countries, thus satisfying the requirement with regard to the number of countries. Exhibit 1–8 shows how American Re-Insurance Company boasts of its doing business in a number of countries worldwide. Coca-Cola quite easily satisfies the requirement for multinationalism through the citizenship of members of its top management. Its chairman and chief executive officer is Cuban, and its other four top officers are Mexican, Argentina, Egyptian, and an American from Iowa.[12]

Definition by Performance

Definition by **performance** depends on such characteristics as earnings, sales, and assets. These performance characteristics indicate the extent of the commitment of corporate resources to foreign operations and the amount of rewards from that commitment. The greater the commitment and reward, the greater the degree of internationalization. Parker Pens, with 80 percent of its sales coming from overseas, is more multinational (at least on the basis of foreign sales) than A. T. Cross, whose overseas sales account for only about 20 percent of overall sales. As stated by Inco, it has balanced sales—in Europe, North America, and Asia (see Exhibit 1–9).

Japanese multinationals have shown willingness to commit their corporate resources to overseas assets. NEC has twenty-five manufacturing and forty-four marketing and service subsidiaries overseas, which employ 22,000 people. Half of Ricoh's cameras are made outside Japan, whereas nearly 100 percent of the firm's copiers sold in North America and Europe are made there as well. Hitachi, a worldwide giant, has forty-seven manufacturing subsidiaries and 130 sales and service companies worldwide. Hitachi makes TVs, automobile parts, PBXs, computer products, and large-capacity magnetic disks in the United States; TV tubes in Singapore; and CD players and room air conditioners in Taiwan; refrigerators in Thailand; and parts for turbine generators in Canada.

Human resources or overseas employees are customarily considered as part of the performance requirements rather than as part of the structural requirements, though the desirability of separating lower-level employees from top management is questionable. A preferable analysis would be to treat the total extent of the employment of personnel in other countries as another indicator of the structure of the company. In any case, the willingness of a company to use overseas personnel satisfied a significant criterion for multinationalism. Avon, for example, employs 370,000 Japanese women to sell its products house to house across Japan. Siemens, well known worldwide for its consumer and industrial products, has some 300,000 employees in 124 countries.

Definition by Behavior

Behavior is somewhat less reliable as a measure of multinationalism than either structure or performance, though it is no less important. This requirement concerns the behavioral characteristics of top management. Thus, a company becomes more multinational as its management thinks more internationally. Such thinking, known as geocentricity, must be distinguished from two other attitudes or orientations, known as ethnocentricity and polycentricity.

American Re's products and services are only available at the above location.

Today you need a reinsurer with financial stability, innovative products and services, and a strong international presence in order to respond to your clients' global needs. American Re has been in business for 75 years, and we have offices in 27 locations worldwide staffed by local experts. We have the capability to create customized programs that keep you current in a changing world. Update your global strategy. Talk to American Re.

AMERICAN
RE-INSURANCE COMPANY
555 College Road East, Princeton, N.J. 08543-5241 (609) 275-2000

Atlanta, Bermuda, Bogota, Boston, Brussels, Cairo, Chicago, Columbus, Dallas, Hartford, Kansas City, London, Los Angeles, Melbourne, Mexico City, Minneapolis, Montreal, New York, Philadelphia, Princeton, San Francisco, Santiago, Singapore, Sydney, Tokyo, Toronto, Vienna

EXHIBIT 1–8   MNC based on the country criterion

Source: Courtesy of American Re-Insurance Company/Greengage Associates

EXHIBIT 1–9   MNC based on performance

Source: Courtesy of Inco U.S., Inc.

Ethnocentricity is a strong orientation toward the home country. Markets and consumers abroad are viewed as unfamiliar and even inferior in taste, sophistication, and opportunity. Centralization of decision making in thus a necessity. The usual practice is to use the home base for the production of standardized products (i.e., without significant modification) for export in order to gain some marginal business. Detroit's big car syndrome is a reflection of the attitude of ethnocentricity. At one time, General Motors viewed its foreign subsidiaries' cars as "foreign." More recently, internationalism is apparently replacing nationalism at GM, as evidenced by a reorganization of the company's international operations and the upgrading of the heads of GM's foreign subsidiaries to the level of vice-president (as in the case of domestic car divisions).

Polycentricity, the opposite of ethnocentricity, is a strong orientation to the host country. The attitude places emphasis on differences between markets that are caused by variations within, such as in income, culture, laws, and politics. The assumption is that each market is unique and consequently difficult for outsiders to understand. Thus, managers from the host country should be employed and allowed to have a great deal of discretion in market decisions. A significant degree of decentralization is thus common across the overseas divisions.

Hout, Porter, and Rudden use the term *multidomestic industry,* which is essentially the same as polycentricity.[13] According to them, a company in a multidomestic industry "pursues separate strategies in each of its foreign markets while viewing the competitive challenge independently from market to market." Although some research and development and some component production may be centralized, strategy and operations are as a rule decentralized. These authors cite Procter and Gamble, Honeywell, Alcoa, and General Foods as examples of multidomestic industries.

A drawback of polycentricity is that it often results in duplication of effort among overseas subsidiaries. Similarities among countries might well permit the development of efficient and uniform strategies.

Geocentricity is a compromise between the two extremes of ethnocentricity and polycentricity. It could be argued that this attitude is the most important of the three. Geocentricity is an orientation that considers the whole world rather than any particular country as the target market. A geocentric company might be thought of as denationalized or supranational. As such, "international" or "foreign" departments or markets do not exist because the company does not designate anything international or foreign about a market. Corporate resources are allocated without regard to national frontiers, and there is no hesitation in making direct investment abroad when warranted. According to Colgate-Palmolive's chief financial officer, there is no mind-set within the company directing that the United States has priority or an automatic call on the company's resources.[14] As shown in Exhibit 1–10, Occidental Petroleum Corporation appears to have this kind of commitment.

There is a high likelihood that a geocentric company does not identify itself with a particular country. Therefore, it is often difficult to determine the firm's home country except through the location of its headquarters and its corporate registration. According to Ohmae, business is "nationalityless," and companies should attempt

EXHIBIT 1–10   MNC based on the geocentricity criterion

Source: Courtesy of Occidental Petroleum Corporation

to lose their national identity. As such, a corporation should not mind moving its headquarters to a more hospitable environment.[15] The chairman of Japanese retail giant Yaohan International Group, for example, moved the firm's headquarters as well as his family and personal assets to Hong Kong to take advantage of Hong Kong's low taxes and hub location in Asia. To reward his faith in China, which will take over Hong Kong in 1997, the Chinese government permitted Yaohan to build shopping malls in China.[16]

Geocentric firms take the view that, even though countries may differ, differences can be understood and managed. In coordinating and controlling the global marketing effort, the company adapts its marketing program to meet local needs within the broader framework of its total strategy. The approach combines aspects of centralization and decentralization in a synthesis that allows some degree of flexibility.

The term "global" industry as used by Hout, Porter, and Rudder in essence describes geocentricity.[17] Their examples of global industries include Caterpillar, Komatsu, Timex, Seiko, Citizen, General Electric, Siemens, and Mitsubishi. These companies' "various country strategies are highly interdependent in terms of operations and strategy. A country subsidiary may specialize in manufacturing only part of its product line, exchanging products with owners in the system.... A company may set prices in one country to have an intended effect in another." The strategy is a centralized one, though various aspects of the operations may or may not be so. A global company "seeks to respond to particular local market needs, while avoiding a compromise of efficiency of the overall global system." In effect, companies compete on a systemwide (i.e., worldwide) basis rather than a local level.

The case of European Silicon Structures illustrates the practice of geocentric marketing. In order to attract customers from around the continent, European Silicon Structures has decided to become a company without a country. Although incorporated in Luxembourg, the firm's headquarters is in Munich. The company has research facilities in England and a factory in southern France. With regard to its board of directors, the eight members come from seven countries. Furthermore, European Silicon Structures is among the few companies that do their accounting in ECUs (European currency units).[18]

Swedish firms generally have adopted the international orientation. Being a small country, Sweden has a limited number of domestic suppliers, and the constraint makes it necessary for Swedish firms to use foreign suppliers. It is thus natural for Swedish firms to have low "national myopia" and to exhibit a more favorable attitude to foreign suppliers than companies in some larger European countries.[19]

BENEFITS OF INTERNATIONAL MARKETING

International marketing daily affects consumers in many ways, though its importance is neither well understood nor appreciated. Government officials and other observers seem always to point to the negative aspects of international business. Many of their charges are more imaginary than real. The benefits of international marketing must be explicitly discussed in order to dispel such notions.

Survival

Because most countries are not as fortunate as the United States in terms of market size, resources, and opportunities, they must trade with others to survive. Hong Kong has historically underscored this point well, for without food and water from China proper, the British colony would not have survived long. The countries of Europe have had similar experience, since most European nations are relatively small in size. Without foreign markets, European firms would not have sufficient economies of scale to allow them to be competitive with U.S. Firms. Nestlé mentions in one of its advertisements that its own country, Switzerland, lacks natural resources, forcing it to depend on trade and adopt the geocentric perspective (see Exhibit 1–11). The United States, a country blessed with resources, population, and the highest level of consumption, is not immune from slowdowns of the national economy. The United States also needs trade, just as other nations do, in order to survive and thrive.

Growth of Overseas Markets

In 1989 the value of products traded globally exceeded $3 trillion for the first time, whereas world merchandise trade totaled less than $2 trillion five years earlier. Exhibit 1–12 shows world trade in terms of merchandise export shares and composition.

The Conference Board is a business information service that assists senior executives and other leaders in arriving at sound decisions, and more than three thousand organizations in over fifty nations participate as Associates. The Conference Board's study of some fifteen hundred companies found that U.S. manufactures with factories or sales subsidiaries overseas outperformed their domestic counterparts during the 1980s in terms of growth in nineteen out of twenty major industry groups and higher earnings in seventeen out of twenty groups.[20]

American marketers cannot ignore the vast potential of international markets. The world market is more than four times larger than the U.S. market. In the case of Amway Corp., a privately held U.S. manufacturer of cosmetics, soaps, and vitamins, Japan represents a larger market than the United States. A slowing of the growth of the U.S. population and changing lifestyles explain why the growth of other markets should be viewed with a critical eye. The fitness craze has contributed mightily to the leveling of U.S. sales of cigarettes and liquor. Without outside markets, executives of U.S. distillers and tobacco firms probably would be driven to drink and smoke to forget their troubles.

Sales and Profits

Foreign markets constitute a large share of the total business of many firms that have wisely cultivated markets abroad. Many large U.S. companies have done very well because of their overseas customers. The following companies, with non-U.S. income as percentage of 1988 total income in parentheses, earn more abroad than at home: Colgate-Palmolive (68 percent), Gillette (64.1 percent), Goodyear (56.2 percent), and

EXHIBIT 1–11   MNC based on the geocentricity criterion

Source: Reprinted with permission of Nestlé Foods Corp.

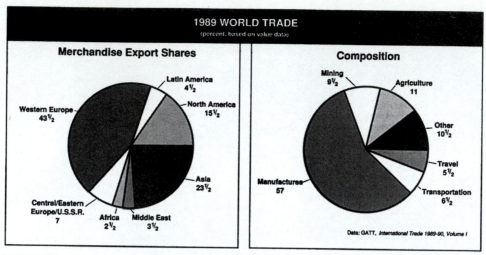

EXHIBIT 1–12   1989 world trade (percent, based on value data)

Source: IMF Survey, 10 December 1990, 377

General Motors (52.9 percent). Goodyear's plunge in domestic profits was more than offset by its excellent foreign earnings. Similarly, although General Motors barely broke even in the United States, it was still able to post a profit increase because its non-U.S. operating income jumped by 83.9 percent. Likewise, H. J. Heinz Co.'s profit margin of 5 percent in the United States on its baby-food sales is skimpy compared to the profit margins of up to 20 percent in Italy.[21]

In many cases, foreign operations may contribute disproportionately to the profit of the company when measured against the sales generated. A loss of 5 percent in sales from overseas business can mean more than a loss of 5 percent in profit. This phenomenon is caused by fixed costs already accounted for at home, lower labor and material costs abroad, less intense competition overseas, and so on. The after-tax return on assets of foreign affiliates of U.S. nonfinancial companies is 14.5 percent, far greater than a return of less than 2.5 percent for such companies in the United States.[22]

The case of Coca-Cola clearly emphasizes the importance of overseas markets. Coca-Cola's overseas operating income has risen from 53 percent in 1985 to 77 percent of the company's total in 1990. In terms of operating profit margins, they are less than 15 percent at home but twice that amount overseas. For every gallon of soda that Coca-Cola sells, it earns 37¢ in Japan—a marked difference form the mere 7¢ per gallon earned in the United States. The Japanese market contributes about $350 million in operating income to Coca-Cola (vs. $324 million in the U.S. market). With consumption of Coca-Cola's soft drinks averaging 283 eight-ounce servings per person per year in the United States, the U.S. market is clearly saturated. Non-U.S. consumption, on the other hand, averages only about 56 servings and offers great potential for future growth. The comparable figures for other markets are Australia (177), Germany (155), Japan (89), Great Britain (63), Thailand (26), and Indonesia (3.2). China, with annual consumption of just 0.2 serving for each of its 1.1 billion people, obviously offers ample room for growth.[23]

Diversification

Demand for most products is affected by such cyclical factors as recession and such seasonal factors as climate. The unfortunate consequence of these variables is sales fluctuations, which can frequently be substantial enough to cause layoffs of personnel. One way to diversify a company's risk is to consider foreign markets as a solution for variable demand. Such markets even out fluctuations by providing outlets for excess production capacity. Cold weather, for instance, may depress soft drink consumption. Yet not all countries enter the winter season at the same time, and some countries are relatively warm year-round. Bird, USA, Inc., a Nebraska manufacturer of go-carts and minicars for promotional purposes, has found that global selling has enabled the company to have year-round production. "It may be winter in Nebraska but it's summer in the Southern Hemisphere—somewhere there's a demand and that stabilizes our business."[24]

A similar situation pertains to the business cycle: Europe's business cycle often lags behind that of the United States. That domestic and foreign sales operate in differing economic cycles works in the favor of General Motors and Ford but not in the favor of Chrysler Corp., which does not have overseas operations to help smooth out the business cycles of the North American market.

Inflation and Price Moderation

The benefits of export are readily self-evident. Imports can also be highly beneficial to the U.S. market, because they constitute reserve capacity for the U.S. economy. Without imports (or with severely restricted imports), there is no incentive for domestic firms to moderate their prices. The lack of imported product alternatives forces consumers to pay more, resulting in inflation and excessive profits for local firms. This development usually acts as a prelude to workers' demand for higher wages, further exacerbating the problem of inflation. Import quotas imposed on Japanese automobiles saved 46,200 U.S. production jobs but at a cost of $160,000 per job per year. This huge cost was a result of the addition (in 1983) of $400 to the prices of U.S. cars and $1,000 to the prices of Japanese imports.[25] This windfall for Detroit resulted in record-high profits for U.S. automakers.

The short-term gain derived from artificial controls on the supply of imports can in the long run return to haunt domestic firms. Not only do trade restrictions depress price competition in the short run, but they can also adversely affect demand for years to come. In Europe, when prices of orange juice were driven upward, consumers switched to apple juice and other fruit drinks. Likewise, Florida orange growers found to their dismay that sharply higher prices turned consumers to other products. After the 1962 freeze, it took the citrus industry ten years to win back these consumers. United States orange growers finally learned to live with imports because they found that imported Brazilian juice, by minimizing price increases, is able to keep consumers.

Employment

Trade restrictions, such as the high tariffs caused by the 1930 Smoot-Hawley Bill, which forced the average tariff rates across the board to climb above 60 percent, contributed significantly to the Great Depression and have the potential to cause widespread unemployment again. Unrestricted trade, on the other hand, improves the world's GNP and enhances employment generally for all nations.

Importing products and foreign ownership can provide benefits to a nation. According to the Institute for International Economics—a private, nonprofit research institute—the growth of foreign ownership has not resulted in a loss of jobs for Americans, and foreign firms have paid their American workers the same as have domestic firms. As revealed by a benchmark survey of foreign direct investment in the United States conducted by the Commerce Department's Bureau of Economic Analysis, U.S. affiliates of foreign companies are responsible for 3,160,000 jobs. Affiliates of British and Canadian firms lead in job creation.

In 1990 more than seven million Americans owed their jobs to merchandise exports, and exports were responsible for about one in six U.S. manufacturing jobs. Furthermore, *Business Week* found that, unlike those who are employed in the import-competing and domestic sectors, those working in an exporting industry are more likely to be college-educated, to earn higher wages, and to be in a good position to benefit from worldwide growth.[26]

The employment benefit is confirmed by the Conference Board's analysis of the data from U.S. government agencies and its input-output model of the U.S. economy.[27] Exports of $10 billion created about 193,000 new jobs, with 82,600 jobs for laborers. Imports of the same amount destroy some 179,000 jobs, and 100,600 being laborers' jobs. More than half of new jobs resulting from increased exports are white-collar jobs, with sales and marketing positions making the greatest gain.

Standards of Living

Trade affords countries and their citizens higher standards of living than otherwise possible. Without trade, product shortages force people to pay more for less. Products taken for granted, such as coffee and bananas, may become unavailable overnight. Life in the United States would be much more difficult were it not for the many strategic metals that must be imported. Trade also makes it easier for industries to specialize and gain access to raw materials, while at the same time fostering competition and efficiency. A diffusion of innovations across national boundaries is a useful by-product of international trade. A lack of such trade would inhibit the flow of innovative ideas.

Understanding of Marketing Process

International marketing should not be considered a subset or special case od domestic marketing. As commented by the chairman of the supervisory board of N. V. Philips's Gloeilampen-fabrieken, "American managers should really understand, not just say they understand, that there are other parts of the world beside the United States. If Americans started doing business with other countries, they would develop greater understanding as well as more trade. And that is the most important thing, after all—that societies be open to each other. To close yourself off is the worst thing that can happen."[28] Thorelli and Becker echo the same sentiment: "By observing marketing in other cultures the executive (or the student) frequently gains a better understanding of marketing in his own."[29] The study of international marketing thus can prove to be valuable in providing insights for the understanding of behavioral patterns often taken for granted at home.

THE WORLD'S MOST INDIFFERENT EXPORTER

Table 1-1 provides a list of the world's leading exporting countries. The United States, once the world's greatest exporter until being replaced by Germany in 1986, somehow managed to regain the top spot in 1989 and 1991—in spite of the fact that it

TABLE 1–1 Leading exporting countries in world merchandise, 1989

Rank 1979	Rank 1989	Country	Share of World Exports (Percent)	1989 Value (US$ Billions)	Percentage Change 1989/88	Percentage Change 1989/79
1	1	United States	11.8	364	13	95
2	2	Germany, Federal Republic of	11.0	341	5	99
3	3	Japan	8.9	275	4	169
4	4	France	5.7	177	5	76
5	5	United Kingdom	4.9	153	5	77
6	6	Italy	4.6	141	9	95
10	7	Canada	3.9	120	2	107
7	8	U.S.S.R.	3.5	108	−2	68
8	9	Netherlands	3.5	107	3	68
11	10	Belgium-Luxembourg	3.2	98	6	72
25	11	Korea, Republic of	2.0	62	2	314
32	12	China	1.7	53	10	286
12	13	Sweden	1.7	52	4	88
13	14	Switzerland	1.7	52	2	94
28	15	Singapore[a]	1.4	45	13	214
19	16	Spain	1.4	43	6	136
16	17	Australia	1.2	37	13	100
33	18	Mexico[a]	1.2	36	17	192
24	19	Brazil	1.1	34	2	126
23	20	Austria	1.0	32	4	108
20	21	German Democratic Republic	0.9	29	3	74
9	22	Saudi Arabia	0.9	28	20	−55
26	23	Denmark	0.9	28	1	91
		Total of above	78.2	2,411	—	—
		Average	—	—	6	102
		World total	100.0	3,090	—	—
		Average	—	—	7	86

Note: Details may not add to totals because of rounding. Data from Taiwan, China, and Hong Kong are excluded.
a. Includes substantial reexports and estimated exports from free processing zones.
Source: The World Bank Annual Report 1990, 36.

is the world's most indifferent exporter. For years, the United States was a dominant force in world trade because of a circumstance that is not likely to recur: other countries' poor position as a result of World War II. Those countries have worked hard in making their way back to a more competitive position. Somehow, the United States seems to have worked just as hard to erode its competitive power.

Fooled by absolute increases in export volume and GNP, U.S. firms have taken trade for granted and thus have failed to see the erosion of the U.S. trade position (see Exhibit 1–13). In relative terms, Japan and Western Europe have made sizable gains while the United States has slipped in its share of the world's export. To compound the problem, the United States has borrowed heavily to finance its deficits, making it a net debtor for the first time in 71 years in 1985. In addition to the change from

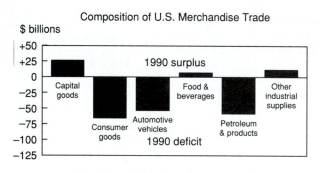

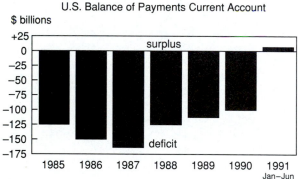

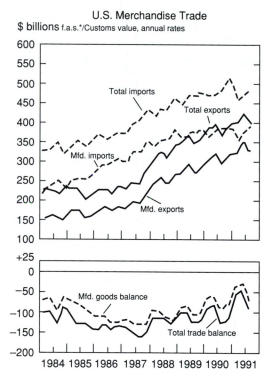

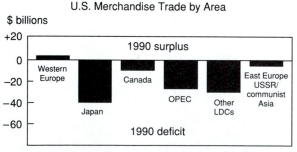

EXHIBIT 1–13   Trade position of the United States

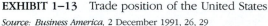

Source: Business America, 2 December 1991, 26, 29

creditor to debtor, the United States has also moved from a society of production to one of consumption. Exhibit 1–14 provides some pertinent U.S. trade facts.

Causes and Consequences

Not all U.S. companies are responsible for the decline of the U.S. prowess in world trade. Several American firms have done quite well abroad and should be able to continue to do so. Even in the difficult Japanese market, several U.S. companies have found remarkable success: Schick (possessing 70 percent of the razor blade market), McDonald's (30 percent of fast foods), Coca-Cola (30 percent of the soft drink market), NCR (26 percent of the point-of-sale equipment), and Sun Microsystems (30 percent of the computer workstations). The problem is that a majority of American companies cannot duplicate this kind of strength overseas.

It is not surprising that no one wants to accept the blame for the poor performance of the United States. Management blames labor and the government, labor blames the government and management, and so on. Actually, there is enough blame to go around from everyone, including management, academia, labor, the public, and the government.

Management *National myopia* is one likely reason that the United States has experienced persistent trade deficits.[30] Exhibit 1–15 clearly shows that, compared to other industrial countries, the United States has, for years, adopted domestic orientation.[31]

Why have so many firms failed to expand the market through exporting and what is the cause of their reluctance? The problem is often management's shortsightedness. The standard excuses include (1) foreign markets are too small, (2) foreign markets are too far away, (3) export profits are marginal, (4) exporting is too difficult, and (5) things are all right at home. These excuses lose legitimacy when one considers that Japan and Germany do so well in international trade.

Morita and Ishihara, in their highly controversial book, portray the United States as being poorly managed and badly governed. They blame the U.S. government's chronic budget deficits for high U.S. interest rates, low savings, low investment rates, and trade imbalances. They fault U.S. corporations for being more concerned with mergers and acquisitions and with short-term profit than with investment in long-term product development and improvement. According to them, the problem is not that Japan is exporting too much, because trade imbalances, after all, are a result of commercial transactions based on preferences.[32]

One discouraging fact is that the overseas experience of American chief executives is quite limited. Of the 1,000 largest U.S. corporations, only 13 percent of the chief executives have had overseas assignments during their careers. One slightly positive note is that 20 percent of those who became CEOs in 1990 had worked outside the United States. On the negative side, most CEOs with overseas experience acquired it in Canada and Europe and not in the Far East or Latin America.[33] Based on a study by the MIT Commission on Industrial Productivity, U.S. firms need a global outlook and should make a stronger effort to understand foreign languages, culture, and business practices.[34]

Academia As explained by Christensen, "an internationalized curriculum can provide students with a strong awareness of cultural and economic differences among

The United States is the world's largest economy and the largest market. In 1990 merchandise exports contributed almost 90 percent of real U.S. GNP growth.

MERCHANDISE TRADE

☐ U.S. two-way trade totaled $889 billion in 1990, with exports of $394 billion and imports of $495 billion.

☐ The 1990 U.S. trade deficit shrank to $101 billion, 34 percent below the 1987 deficit peak.

☐ U.S. merchandise exports rose to 7.3 percent of the nation's GNP in 1990 from 7.1 percent in 1989. That compares with 1989 shares for West Germany of 28.3 percent; Canada, 22.5 percent; the United Kingdom, 18.1 percent; and Japan, 9.7 percent.

☐ In the first half of 1990, the United States accounted for 13.0 percent of the world's merchandise exports and an estimated 16.5 percent of the world's merchandise imports.

☐ In 1990 total U.S. merchandise exports were composed of 80 percent manufactured goods, 11 percent agricultural goods, and 9 percent primarily of mineral fuels and crude materials.

☐ Total U.S. merchandise imports in 1990 were composed of 79 percent manufactured goods; 13 percent mineral fuels; and 8 percent agricultural and other goods.

☐ Merchandise exports accounted for more than seven million jobs in the United States in 1990.

☐ About one in six U.S. jobs in manufacturing was probably due directly and indirectly to exports in 1990.

☐ From 1891 through 1970, the United States had an unbroken string of trade surpluses. After 1970, it had deficits in every year except 1973 and 1975.

☐ Canada was by far the leading foreign market for exports from the United States in 1990, followed by Japan, Mexico, the United Kingdom, and West Germany. Canada was the leading import supplier to the United States, followed closely by Japan, and then by Mexico, West Germany, Taiwan, the United Kingdom, and South Korea.

☐ Capital goods—including aircraft—lead U.S. exports, followed by industrial supplies and materials; then nonautomotive consumer products; automotive products; and collectively—foods, feeds, and beverages.

☐ The Commerce Department estimates that roughly one-third of U.S. manufacturing companies, slightly more than 100,000 such companies, export manufactured goods.

☐ Two-thirds of U.S. merchandise exports are by U.S.-owned multinational corporations; more than one-third of these exports are shipped by the U.S. parent corporation to their foreign affiliates.

(continued)

EXHIBIT 1–14 U.S. trade facts

Source: Business America, 6 May 1991, 10

BUSINESS SERVICES EXPORTS

□ Exports of U.S. business services are almost one-third as large as U.S. exports of merchandise.

□ Exports and imports of business services totaled about $120 billion and $81 billion, respectively, in 1990.

□ In 1990 U.S. exports of business services accounted for about 2.8 percent of the nation's GNP. Travel service receipts and passenger fares accounted for about one-third of the total.

EXHIBIT 1–14 U.S. trade facts (*continued*)

nations, a deep appreciation of how professions operate on an international basis, and a burning desire to interact with colleagues on a worldwide basis. Hopefully, graduates of professional curricula will recognize that there are no geographical borders between them and their professional counterparts."[35] Unfortunately, based on a study of the reviews of 122 major Canadian corporations on the importance of various management skills and international courses, corporations felt that academia was not adequately responding to their international needs.[36]

Sadly, as commented by Porter and McKibben, "it is our impression from our extensive interviewing that business schools, collectively, have not yet become really serious about the international dimension of management."[37] There is definitely a need to teach students to be more aware of the world and less inclined to consider only the United States. Several well-known business schools offer no international courses, with the rationale that basic disciplines and principles of marketing, management, and so on are universal.

Part of the problem is that most business professors failed to take any graduate courses related to international business. As noted by the AACSB, during their graduate studies, only 17 percent of the 1984 business doctoral candidates had taken any international courses. Given the fact that it was 25 percent in 1976, the new figure was discouraging. In all likelihood, the next generation of faculty members will encounter difficulty in introducing international content into the courses they teach. Consequently, "most of our new teachers are entering the profession knowing only a subset (the domestic U.S. portion) of their fields, and that's all they are likely to teach."[38] As can be expected, their lack of interest is manifested in the material they choose to teach.

Labor Organized labor has made a significant contribution in protecting workers' welfare. But in many cases, the work rules and job classifications secured by labor tend to restrict productivity. Historically, management gave in to labor unions' demands based on the assumption that the U.S. economy was strong enough to absorb the costs of inefficient work rules. Another assumption was that other companies within the same industry would all accept these costly rules. Yet now consumers have cheaper foreign products as alternatives. Exhibit 1–16 is a typical example of organized labor's viewpoint, which has both merits and flaws. In any case, imports

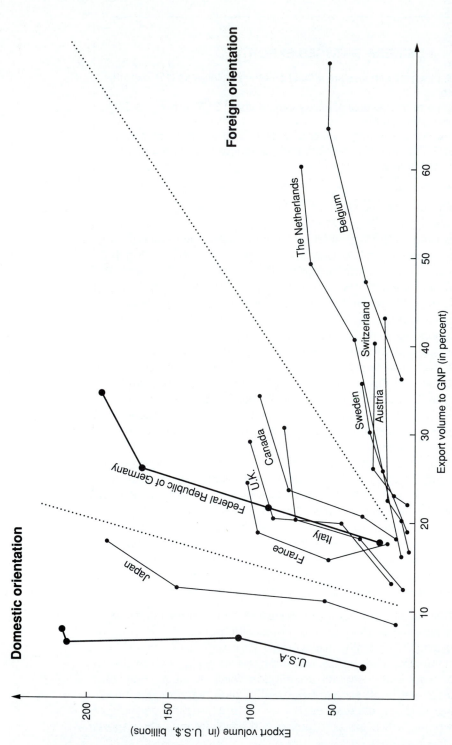

EXHIBIT 1–15 Domestic orientation and foreign orientation of the leading industrial countries as reflected by the years 1967–1975–1983–1987

Source: Erwin Dichtl, Hans-Georg Koeglmayr, and Stefan Mueller, "International Orientation as a Precondition for Export Success," *Journal of International Business Studies* 20 (no. 1, 1990): 25

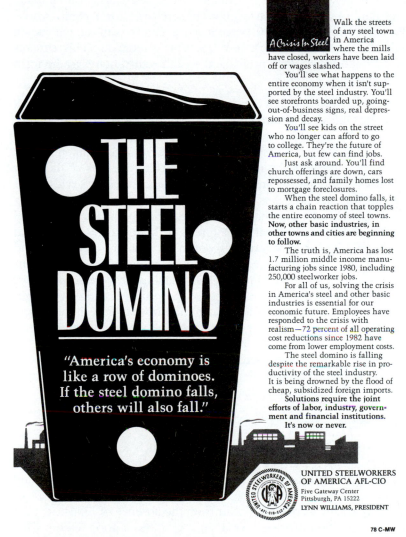

Walk the streets of any steel town in America where the mills have closed, workers have been laid off or wages slashed.

You'll see what happens to the entire economy when it isn't supported by the steel industry. You'll see storefronts boarded up, going-out-of-business signs, real depression and decay.

You'll see kids on the street who no longer can afford to go to college. They're the future of America, but few can find jobs.

Just ask around. You'll find church offerings are down, cars repossessed, and family homes lost to mortgage foreclosures.

When the steel domino falls, it starts a chain reaction that topples the entire economy of steel towns. **Now, other basic industries, in other towns and cities are beginning to follow.**

The truth is, America has lost 1.7 million middle income manufacturing jobs since 1980, including 250,000 steelworker jobs.

For all of us, solving the crisis in America's steel and other basic industries is essential for our economic future. Employees have responded to the crisis with realism—72 percent of all operating cost reductions since 1982 have come from lower employment costs.

The steel domino is falling despite the remarkable rise in productivity of the steel industry. It is being drowned by the flood of cheap, subsidized foreign imports.

Solutions require the joint efforts of labor, industry, government and financial institutions. It's now or never.

UNITED STEELWORKERS OF AMERICA AFL-CIO
Five Gateway Center
Pittsburgh, PA 15222
LYNN WILLIAMS, PRESIDENT

78 C-MW

EXHIBIT 1–16   A labor view on international trade
Source: Reprinted with permission of the United Steel Workers of America

and overseas investments, according to available evidence, are not necessarily bad for U.S. employment.

Public   The U.S. public unknowingly contributes to the U.S. trade woes. A 1985 poll by the *Wall Street Journal* and "NBC News" provided some evidence. Of the Americans polled, 51 percent were in favor of restricting imports for the purpose of protecting U.S. industries. This sentiment is supported by many union officials and politicians. They fail to appreciate the enormous costs associated with trade restrictions. Ironically, because of spending patterns, those who will be most adversely affected by import barriers are moderate- and low-income consumers. Trade restrictions on clothing, sugar, and cars resulted in a 23 percent income tax surcharge for a family whose income was below $10,000 but only 10 percent for a family with an income of $23,000.[39] It should also be pointed out that even U.S. firms' foreign direct investments actually benefit the United States since profits and wealth return home in the form of dividends to shareholders.

Government   The U.S. government has developed numerous regulations that result in export disincentives. One study showed that, when compared to tax laws of other industrialized nations, U.S. tax laws may put U.S.-owned foreign affiliates at a cash flow disadvantage, thus acting as an economic impediment to U.S. competitiveness internationally.[40] U.S. policymakers should consider the consequences of the early reporting of unrepatriated foreign earnings and the raising of corporate taxes.

In defense of a government's actions, trade cannot be considered in isolation, because the country has national interests other than economic well-being, such as national security, foreign policy, and so on. These varying interests are bound to interact with and affect each other. The problem arises when the government arbitrarily uses trade and economic/military aids to achieve these goals. When noncommunist, friendly nations such as Israel and Pakistan committed human rights violations or were suspected of having plans to manufacture nuclear weapons, the U.S. government looked the other way. However, when India was accused of acquiring nuclear-weapon technology and Nicaragua and Poland were accused of committing human rights violations, the U.S. government cut off aid and/or imposed export controls—not so much because of the validity of the charges but rather because of the perception that these countries, having been unduly influenced by the Soviet Union, were not "friends" of the United States. Aid and trade sanctions, when applied selectively, are counterproductive.

Some Competitive Steps

The recognition of export problems is a good start, but such recognition must be followed by corrective steps. To ensure that these steps enhance competitiveness, it is a good idea to use the rivals of the United States as a basis for analysis and comparison.[41]

That Japan and Germany were able to start from the absence of industrial base after World War II to a position of trade prominence provides a good lesson. What do they have in common that enables them to achieve this extraordinary success? The common trait is that in each country the various segments of society have shown a willingness to work together for the interests of the nation. Japanese and German consumers are willing to conserve both resources and cash while living with high prices for essentials. The paternalistic style of management in Japan and the system of codetermination in Germany have fostered worker loyalty. At the same time, each government is quite active in promoting exports while coordinating the activities of the various sectors. As a result, there is a great deal of sacrifice and cooperation. This does not mean that both countries have employed the identical approach. Japan, for example, is active in economic planning in order to allocate resources and select industries for promotion. Germany, in contrast, relies more on market forces to do the same thing.

The United Kingdom provides another useful comparison. Once the most prosperous and technologically advanced country, Great Britain has gone through tremendous economic turmoil. At one time it faced problems similar to those faced by the United States today. Common to both the United States and Great Britain is the negative regard that the various segments of each society have of one another. Management and labor simply do not trust each other and often blame the government for difficulties.

The basic difference between the two countries is the United Kingdom's system of national economic planning, which has proved ineffective in the absence of the cooperation of labor and management. The United States, in contrast, generally allows the various groups to make business decisions on their own. This hands-off approach, however, results in a lack of coordination.

The United States has a choice. It can follow the path taken by the United Kingdom, or it can go in the direction of Germany and Japan. Perhaps U.S. society is so open that government intervention to the extent of Japan or Germany is neither possible nor desirable. Still, it is clear that cooperation and commitment from all parties are necessary. The U.S. government can play a major role in developing broad consensus in policymaking among representatives of government, business, academia, consumers, and labor. There have been several bills in Congress that propose the creation of an independent, national council of cooperation to provide a forum for representatives of labor, business, and governments to identify national economic problems and to develop strategies and policies for dealing with such problems.[42] Exhibit 1–17 lists several proposals of Mobil that should be examined.

All parties may need to reexamine their roles in trade. Management should question how it can pursue profit without unduly alienating workers. Organized labor needs to keep in mind that wages, benefits, and job security cannot be increased without an exchange for higher productivity if layoffs are to be prevented during bad economic times. Universities need to commit resources to international studies. The academic world also has a role in educating consumers of the horrendous costs of trade protectionism, so that consumers will better understand the justification (or the lack of it) of the various protectionist measures proposed by U.S. manufacturers, politicians, and labor leaders. The U.S. government needs a coherent and consistent trade policy. At present, its policies are confusing and unpredictable, and its half-hearted effort in trade promotion has inevitably resulted in a less-than-desirable outcome. In the end, all parties need to understand that their interests are mutually linked and that the others are partners rather than adversaries.

In addition to pride, commitment, determination, and sacrifices, companies must adhere to the marketing concept—not just at home but also abroad. As discovered by Cooper and Kleinschmidt, companies that are marketing-oriented, in the sense that they segment the world market and design suitable products for the various segments, tend to experience strong export growth.[43] U.S. companies must be more marketing-oriented overseas if they want to be more competitive.

Protectionism: A persistent threat—III

A sound trade policy for America

Over the last two weeks, we've warned against the dangers a protectionist trade policy would pose to the American economy, and cited our specific concerns with H.R. 4800, the House-passed bill that would tilt the nation's trade laws toward protectionism.

If the Senate decides that it too must act this year, we respectfully suggest that it first establish some broad objectives a trade bill ought to achieve. In our view, such a bill should:

• Provide the Administration—and future administrations as well—with a solid base for negotiating improvements in international trade agreements. America has a long history of successful trade negotiations, and no President's hands should be tied before negotiations begin.

• Reinforce the importance of reciprocity. Trade is always a multilateral process, and for the long term, a successful trade arrangement cannot be imposed unilaterally.

• Broaden the access to foreign markets of American goods, services and investments. Here, too, negotiation works better than coercion; access cannot be won by the unilateral stroke of a pen in Washington, D.C.

• Assure U.S. trade officials the flexibility to deal effectively with a spectrum of foreign economic systems and cultures. People everywhere are not just like us. If we want to sell them things, and buy things from them, we have to recognize the differences and adapt to them.

• Signal our trading partners that the U.S. sees world trade as a means of fostering worldwide economic growth. U.S. trade policy mustn't be perceived as a way to gain for ourselves a bigger piece of the economic pie.

• Foster the recognition that world trade is too important to consider only in certain specific bills. Congress should recognize that most of the bills it enacts impact on trade in one way or another, and the effects on world trade should always be considered.

There's nothing mysterious or even very sophisticated about the points we've raised. Economists and those engaged in international commerce would probably regard them as obvious and self-evident. But few American politicians are economists, and few of them focus on foreign trade. (When the Congress passed the Smoot-Hawley tariff in 1930, it did so over the objections of more than 1,000 American economists.)

Instead, our political leaders often seek painless panaceas and quick fixes; hence the lure of protectionism as the "cure" for our trade deficit. It's easier to raise a tariff than to lower the value of the dollar overseas, or to reduce the budget deficit and bring down real interest rates at home.

What's often lost on American lawmakers is the importance of foreign trade to the American economy. Historically, our leaders haven't had to focus on foreign trade. In its early years, America devoted its energy to expanding westward. When the industrial age began, America found itself rich enough in raw materials to concentrate on filling its domestic needs.

But today, America has outgrown economic parochialism. American workers and American farmers produce within a global context. There's no going back to an earlier world of economic isolation. Nor should world trade be considered only when a so-called trade bill is being debated. The trade implications must be considered whenever Congress weighs any action that has economic implications.

Protectionism has been a failure whenever it's been tried. A trade bill like H.R. 4800 would add to the list of failures, precisely when America and its trading partners need some economic successes. We sincerely hope the Senate will act accordingly, and wisely.

Mobil®

EXHIBIT 1–17   Trade policy

Source: Reprinted with permission of Mobil Corporation. ©1986 Mobil Corporation

CONCLUSION

The plan of this book will be to divide the content into uncontrollable and controllable variables. The first half of the book (Chapters 1–9) is devoted primarily to a discussion of the domestic and foreign uncontrollable variables. The second half (Chapters 10–19) will largely concentrate on the controllable variables consisting of the 4 Ps of marketing.

The first chapter has provided an overview of the process and of the basic issues of international marketing. Similar to domestic marketing, international marketing is concerned with the process of creating and executing an effective marketing mix in order to satisfy the objectives of all parties seeking an exchange. International marketing is relevant regardless of whether the object of exchange is a product, service, or idea and regardless of whether the activities are for profit or not. It is also of little consequence whether other countries have the same level of economic development or political ideology, since marketing is a universal activity that has application in a variety of circumstances.

The benefits of international marketing are considerable. Trade moderates inflation and improves both employment and the standard of living, while providing a better understanding of the marketing process at home and abroad. For many companies, survival or the ability to diversify depends on the growth, sales, and profits from abroad. The more commitment a company makes to overseas markets in terms of personnel, sales, and resources, the more likely it will become a multinational corporation (MNC). This is especially true when the management is geocentric rather than ethnocentric or polycentric. Since many view MNCs with envy and suspicion, the role of MNCs in society, their benefits as well as their abuses, will continue to be debated.

In spite of its export volume, the United States is the world's most indifferent exporter. This is illustrated by the concomitant absolute growth in U.S. exports and the decline in U.S. market share. There is likely no one element that is responsible for this problem, but better cooperation is needed from management, academia, labor, consumers, and the U.S. government. Without an improvement of attitude toward exports, the probability for any significant improvement in trade performance appears bleak.

U.S. firms must understand that the practice of the marketing concept does not stop at the U.S. border. International marketing is more than the task of shipping products overseas (i.e., place). Product, promotion, and pricing must also be considered. Furthermore, the 4 Ps of marketing may have to be modified for the varying environment. Foreign consumers must be understood. It is thus peculiar for American firms to be customer-oriented only in the United States but management-oriented overseas. The marketing principles may be fixed, but the marketing mix is not. Domestic U.S. marketing practices may or may not be appropriate elsewhere, and the degree of appropriateness cannot be determined without careful investigation and consideration of the market in question.

QUESTIONS

1. What are the limitations of the AMA's old definition of marketing as adapted for the purpose of defining international marketing?
2. What are the strengths and limitations of the AMA's new definition of marketing as adapted for the purpose of defining international marketing?
3. Distinguish among (a) domestic marketing, (b) foreign marketing, (c) comparative marketing, (d) international trade, (e) international marketing, (f) multinational marketing, (g) global marketing, and (h) world marketing.
4. Are domestic marketing and international marketing different only in scope but not in nature?
5. Explain the "big car syndrome." Cite some nonautomobile industries or companies that seem to adopt this attitude.
6. Explain the following criteria used to identify MNCs: (a) size, (b) structure, (c) performance, and (d) behavior.
7. Distinguish among (a) ethnocentricity, (b) polycentricity, and (c) geocentricity.
8. What are the benefits of international marketing?
9. What are the causes of the U.S. export failure?

DISCUSSION ASSIGNMENTS AND MINICASES

1. According to a former vice-chairman of American Express, "The split between international and domestic is very artificial—and at times dangerous." Do you agree with the statement? Offer your rationale.
2. There are three distinct types of organizational orientation: production orientation, selling orientation, and marketing (customer) orientation. Which type of orientation seems to be predominant among a majority of U.S. exporters?
3. Do you feel that marketing is relevant to and should be used locally as well as internationally by (a) international agencies (e.g., the United Nations); (b) national, state, and/or city governments; (c) socialist/communist countries; (d) LDCs; and (e) priests, monks, churches, and/or evangelists?
4. Some of the best-known business schools in the United States want to emphasize discipline-based courses and eliminate international courses, based on the rationale that marketing and management principles are applicable everywhere. Is there a need to study international marketing? Discuss the pros and cons of the discipline based approach as compared to the international approach.
5. Do MNCs provide social and economic benefits? Should they be outlawed?
6. As reported by *Business Week,* Jardine, Matheson & Co., despite its role in the founding of Hong Kong a century and a half ago, has transferred its legal domicile to the British colony of Bermuda, thus anticipating the expiration of the British lease for Hong Kong from China in 1997. The change in the country of incorporation for Jardine provides both tax and security benefits. The company gains tax advantages because Hong Kong has raised corporate income tax from 17 percent to 18.5 percent. In terms of security, Jardine's business interests outside Hong Kong, which account for 28 percent of the company's earnings, are protected from adverse changes in business climate because any disputes must be arbitrated under Bermuda rather than Hong Kong law. Should Jardine be viewed as an MNC? Also do you agree with the actions taken by the company?
7. Colgate-Palmolive and Procter & Gamble are competitors in many markets. Which company appears to be more international?
8. Do you consider General Foods and Sony to be MNCs?
9. American consumers seem to favor less international marketing. According to a 1987 poll, 70 percent of residents in the state of Iowa are in favor of *buy American* restrictions on purchases made by the state. Discuss this finding by

considering the probable perceptions of Iowans as consumers/workers. Then discuss it again from the perspective of real (i.e., not perceived) economic impact.

10. Like Japan, most LDCs and communist/socialist countries (e.g., the Commonwealth of Independent States) have some kind of industrial plan-

ning. Discuss why, unlike Japan's success, economic progress in these countries has been generally unsatisfactory.

11. What should the U.S. government do (or not do) in order to encourage and facilitate U.S. export activities?

CASE 1–1
ARIZONA SUNRAY, INC.
Buy American or Look Abroad?

JEFFREY A. FADIMAN
San Jose State University

Arizona Sunray is one of the pioneering companies in solar energy within that state. Its founding generation consisted of third-generation Arizonans, descendants of the state's earliest pioneers. The founders took great pride in that pioneering heritage, often boasting that the family's rise to relative prosperity was a result of "thinking Arizona." To them, the phrase meant a ceaseless search for business opportunities within the state.

In the late 1950s, one member of this generation emerged as a new type of pioneer—one of a cluster of scientists and businessmen who hoped to develop the first practical applications of solar energy on a scale available to home owners. In the early 1960s, he pioneered the use of solar energy in offices and homes, incorporating, with other members of his family, into what proved to be a surprisingly successful firm, eventually named Arizona Sunray. After some experimentation, the firm chose the slogan "Follow the Sun: It's Arizona's Way." reasoning that the way to acquire new business was to follow the sun, the firm expanded into every area of Arizona, and then into Nevada and New Mexico.

The next generation took control of the business in 1965. As a result, a decision was made to redirect expansion away from the relatively unpopulated states of the Southwest and move due west into the larger urban population centers of coastal California. The Los Angeles/Orange Country area was considered particularly favorable for potential expansion, with relatively affluent target populations that might show considerable interest in the use of solar energy within their homes. Several aspects of the marketing program were reshaped to appeal more directly to coastal Californians, including a change in the firm's slogan, which became "Catch the Rays:

It's California's Way." The concept proved quite successful, and the firm continued to expand.

By 1986, members of the next generation were just beginning to reach positions of influence and authority within the firm. Their relative affluence, however, had permitted them to acquire both travel experience and education abroad. As a consequence, they proposed a further expansion, seeking to "follow the sun" on a scale undreamed of by their elders. They argued that Arizona Sunray should spread around the entire Pacific Rim, taking appropriate advantage of new techniques in miniaturization to fulfill an entire range of solar-powered needs—from solar-powered calculators to rural solar cookers—permitting Arizona Sunray (to be renamed Pacific Sunray) to take maximum advantage of both current opportunity and long-range planning for expansion.

Surviving members of the founding generation instantly rejected the proposal, refusing to contemplate such radical ideas. "Why even bother?" the firm's first president asked. "We're doing fine right in America. We know our product, we know our clientele, we know the West. This market's huge! We're making steady profits. Every member of this family and every worker in this firm is doing fine. Why would we want to dissipate our capital in marketing to places we know next to nothing about? The money's in America; why look abroad?"

Members of all three generations met to thrash out the issue. The oldest, though now retired, held considerable influence. The youngest, though lacking power, felt they held a wider and more flexible perspective. The middle generation, though holding formal decision-making powers, felt pulled both ways and wondered if there might be ways to satisfy both sides.

Questions

1. As a member of the youngest generation, present your case. What advantages could Arizona Sunray derive from an attempt to expand its goods and services abroad?
2. As a member of the oldest generation, present your case. Why should the firm remain within America? What hard questions could you ask of members of the youngest generation that might suggest weaknesses in their proposal?
3. As a member of the middle generation, what compromise can you propose that might prove acceptable to both sides?

CASE 1–2
BEAUTIFUL VISION, INC.

DIRK WASSENAAR
San Jose State University

Beautiful Vision, Inc., is a 3-year-old company engaged in the development, design, and production of extended-wear contact lenses. The company started as a developer and recently patented the Extended Vision Model 12 lens. This lens was truly for extended wear, which means that it could be worn continuously for 30 days or more. The production cost for the new material was well below that for competing products. To capitalize on this technological breakthrough, the company quickly raised substantial equity capital, built production capacity, and set up distribution throughout the United States. It also started an extensive advertising program. This program was mainly directed at the trade but did include some advertisements in selected consumer publications. Sales during the first year of production were $12 million, which exceeded forecasts.

Although the company was kept busy developing the U.S. market, it realized that certain foreign countries might also represent significant potential. Jack Brown, one of the company's founders and its president, recently read an article in which it was reported that a well-known Swiss contact lens firm was about to come out with a new lens that would be highly competitive with the Model 12. Mr. Brown had received an inquiry from the Russian Ministry of Health concerning Model 12 and had received a few orders from the United Kingdom, Brazil, and Nigeria.

Suppose that he has asked you, his assistant, to prepare a preliminary report on the foreign market potential for your company's product. Specifically, he has asked you to address the following questions.

Questions

1. Select and rank, in order of importance, the ten most promising foreign markets for the Model 12 contact lens.
2. Which factors did you consider in selecting the above countries? List as many as you can and rank them in order of importance.
3. List some of the major obstacles you may encounter in trying to market the Model 12 lens in foreign countries.

Source: Dirk Wassenaar, San Jose State University. © 1990. Adapted with permission.

NOTES

1. American Marketing Association, *Marketing Definitions: A Glossary of Marketing Terms* (Chicago: American Marketing Association, 1960), 15.
2. Thomas A. Staudt, Donald A. Taylor, and Donald J. Bowersox, *A Managerial Introduction to Marketing,* 3rd ed. (Englewood Cliffs, NJ: Prentice-Hall, 1976), 31.
3. "AMA Board Approves New Marketing Definition," *Marketing News,* 1 March 1985, 1.
4. Nizam Aydin and Vern Terpstra, "Marketing Know-how Transfers by Multinationals: A Case Study in Turkey," *Journal of International Business Studies* 12 (Winter 1981): 35–48.
5. See John A. Reeder, "Entrepreneurship in the People's Republic of China," *Columbia Journal of World Business* 19 (Fall 1984): 43–51. Also see Jacob Naor, "Towards a Socialist Marketing Concept—the Case of Romania," *Journal of Marketing* 50 (January 1986): 28–39.
6. J. Irwin Miller, "Future of the Multinationals," *The Management of International Corporate Citizenship* (September 1976): 4.
7. "The Global 1000," *Business Week,* 15 July 1991, 56.
8. United Nations, *Multinational Corporations in World Development,* Document No. ST/ECA/140 and Corr. 1, pp. 6–23, Department of Economic and Social Affairs.
9. "Think Small," *Business Week,* 4 November 1991, 58 ff.
10. Michael R. Czinkota and Wesley J. Johnston, "Exporting: Does Sales Volume Make a Difference?" *Journal of International Business Studies* 14 (Spring/Summer 1983): 147–53; See also Stan D. Reid, "Exporting: Does Sales Volume Make a Difference?—Comment," *Journal of International Business Studies* 16 (Summer 1985): 153–55; Michael R. Czinkota and Wesley J. Johnston, "Exporting: Does Sales Volume Make a Difference?—Reply," *Journal of International Business Studies* 16 (Summary 1985): 157–61.
11. Yair Aharoni, "On the Definition of a Multinational Corporation," *Quarterly Review of Economics and Business* (October 1971): 28–35.
12. "New Top Executives Shake Up Old Order at Soft-Drink Giant," *The Wall Street Journal,* 6 November 1981, 1.
13. Thomas Hout, Michael E. Porter, and Eileen Rudden, "How Global Companies Win Out," *Harvard Business Review* 60 (September–October 1982): 98–108.
14. Louis Uchitelle, "Going Global," *New York Times,* 28 May 1989.
15. Kenichi Ohmae, *The Borderless World* (London: Collins, 1990). Also see Kenichi Ohmae, *Triad Power: The Coming Shape of Global Competition* (New York: Free Press, 1985).
16. "Kazuo Wada's Answered Prayers," *Business Week,* 26 August 1991, 66–67.
17. Hout, Porter, and Rudden, "Global Companies."
18. "Firm without a Country," *San Jose Mercury News,* 17 August 1988.
19 Lars Hallen, "International Purchasing in a Small Country: An Exploratory Study of Five Swedish Firms," *Journal of International Business Studies* 13 (Winter 1982): 99–112.
20. "Economic Trends," *Business Week,* 23 December 1991, 20.
21. "The Quest for Profits Is Taking Some Surprising Turns," *Business Week,* 1 May 1989, 28.
22. "Economic Trends," *Business Week,* 6 November 1989, 34.
23. "The Real Thing Is Getting Real Aggressive," *Business Week,* 26 November 1990, 94, 96; "The Quest for Profits Is Taking Some Surprising Turns," *Business Week,* 1 May 1989, 28; "Coke Savors Foreign Markets," *San Jose Mercury News,* 15 May 1988.
24. "Exporters Cite Benefits in International Sales," *Business America,* 112 (no. 2, 1991): 7.
25. Michael Edgerton, "Politics Rules in 'Voluntary' Trade Curbs," *Chicago Tribune,* 26 December 1984.
26. "A New Way to Look at the U.S. Economy," *Business Week,* 17 December 1990, 70.

27. "Exports Create More Jobs Than Imports Lose," *Marketing News,* 9 October 1987, 13.

28. Nan Stone, "The Globalization of Europe: An Interview with Wisse Dekker," *Harvard Business Review,* 67 (May–June 1989), 90–95 at 95.

29. Hans Thorelli and Helmut Becker, *International Marketing Strategy,* rev. ed. (New York: Pergamon Press, 1980), xiv.

30. Sak Onkvisit, John J. Shaw, and Gerald Sussman, "National Myopia: A Cause of the U.S. Trade Failure," *Proceedings of the World Marketing Congress,* 1989, 51–56.

31. Erwin Dichtl, Hans-Georg Koeglmayr, and Stefan Mueller, "International Orientation as a Precondition for Export Success," *Journal of International Business Studies* 20 (no. 1, 1990): 23–40.

32. Akio Morita and Shintario Ishihara, *The Japan That Can Say "No": The New U.S.-Japan Relations Card* (Tokyo: Kobunsha, Kappa-Holmes, 1989).

33. "The Corporate Elite," *Business Week,* 25 November 1991, 182.

34. Michael L. Dertouzos, Richard K. Lester, and Robert M. Solow, *Made in America: Regaining the Productive Edge* (Cambridge, MA: MIT Press, 1989).

35. George C. Christensen, "International Curriculum for the Professions," *National Forum,* 68 (Fall 1988), 27–30 at 30.

36. Paul W. Beamish and Jonathan L. Calof, "International Business Education: A Corporate View," *Journal of International Business Studies* 20 (Fall 1989): 553–64.

37. Lyman W. Porter and Lawrence E. McKibben, *Management Education and Development: Drift or Thrust into the 21st Century?* (New York: McGraw-Hill, 1988), 319.

38. Lee C. Nehrt, "The Internationalization of the Curriculum," *Journal of International Business Studies* 18 (Spring 1988), 83–90 at 90.

39. Paul Magnusson, "Trade War Claims Innocent Victims," *San Jose Mercury News,* 24 May 1987.

40. B. Anthony Billings, Larry Bajor, and Al Gourdji, "Competitive Tax Disadvantages Faced by US Multinationals: How to Address Them," *Columbia Journal of World Business* 25 (Winter 1990): 28–39.

41. "What the U.S. Can Learn from Its Rivals," *Business Week,* 30 June 1980, 138.

42. Bruce R. Scott, "National Strategy for Stronger U.S. Competitiveness," *Harvard Business Review* 62 (March-April 1984): 77–91.

43. Robert G. Cooper and Elko J. Kleinschmidt, "The Impact of Export Strategy on Export Sales Performance," *Journal of International Business Studies* 16 (Spring 1985): 37–55.

It is the maxim of every prudent master of a family, never to attempt to make at home what it will cost him more to make than to buy. The tailor does not attempt to make his own shoes, but buys them of the shoemaker.

Adam Smith

Trade Theories and Economic Development

2

CHAPTER OUTLINE

BASIS FOR INTERNATIONAL TRADE

EXCHANGE RATIOS, TRADE, AND GAIN

FACTOR ENDOWMENT THEORY

A CRITICAL EVALUATION OF TRADE THEORIES

ECONOMIC COOPERATION

SYSTEMATIC PLANNING TO DETERMINE EXPORT OPPORTUNITIES

CASE 2–1: Trade Strategies: Inward or Outward?

CASE 2–2: The New Europe

CASE 2–3: The New North America

MARKETING ILLUSTRATION
Hong Kong—A Trader by Necessity

Because of their rapid growth in the late 1970s and their aggressive pursuit of exporting opportunities, Hong Kong, South Korea, Singapore, and Taiwan are called the four tigers of Asia. Hong Kong, a dependent territory of the United Kingdom, has few natural resources. Government policies based on *positive nonintervention* aim at fostering economic growth and development in an environment favorable to private initiative. During the 1970s and 1980s, the emergence of Hong Kong as a major international financial center was encouraged by the territory's low level of taxation and regulation, by the absence of exchange controls or restrictions over capital movement, by a trained work force, by the modern communication facilities, and by the well-established legal structures.

The financial services sector now comprises more than 10,000 establishments, employs over 100,000 people, and accounts for about 17 percent of the GDP (gross domestic product), or slightly less than the manufacturing sector. Foreign banks in Hong Kong include forty-four of the world's fifty largest, and they tend to concentrate more on international banking activities and less on local business than do their Hong Kong–based counterparts.

As a strong advocate and practitioner of free trade, the Hong Kong government imposes no import tariffs and provides no subsidies or other direct assistance to companies exporting goods. Hong Kong's economic development has been a result of adaptability, entrepreneurial skills, and its population's strong propensity to save money.

The external orientation of Hong Kong's economy and its exposure to changing international circumstances have made flexibility necessary, and Hong Kong's manufacturing industries have been very successful in adapting quickly to changes in market conditions. The structure of businesses in Hong Kong reflects this characteristic. Flexibility is evident by the continued preponderance of small-scale establishments, the extensive use of subcontracting with both domestic and foreign suppliers, and the freedom and willingness of firms to make adjustments that affect products, inputs, wages, and employment in response to market shifts.

Source: Roger Kronenberg, "Hong Kong Fosters Rapid Economic Development," *IMF Survey,* 15 April 1991, 114–16

The case of Hong Kong illustrates quite well the necessity of trading. Hong Kong must import in order to survive, and it must export in order to earn funds to meet its import needs. Hong Kong's import and export needs are readily apparent; not as obvious is the need for other countries to do the same. For example, there must be a logical explanation for a well-endowed country such as the United States to continue to trade with other nations.

This chapter explains the rationale for international trade and examines the principles of absolute advantage and relative advantage. These principles describe what and how nations can make gains from each other. The validity of these principles is discussed, as well as concepts that are refinements of these principles. The chapter includes a discussion of regional integration and its impact on international trade. The chapter concludes with a discussion of export planning.

BASIS FOR INTERNATIONAL TRADE

Whenever a buyer and a seller come together, each expects to gain something from the other. The same expectation applies to nations that trade with each other. It is virtually impossible for a country to be completely self-sufficient without incurring undue costs. Therefore, trade becomes a necessary activity, though in some cases trade does not always work to the advantage of the nations involved. Virtually all governments feel political pressure when they experience trade deficits. Too much emphasis is often placed on the negative effects of trade, even though it is questionable whether such perceived disadvantages are real or imaginary. The benefits of trade, in contrast, are not often stressed, nor are they well communicated to workers and consumers.

Why do nations trade? A nation trades because it expects to gain something from its trading partner. One may ask whether trade is like a zero-sum game, in the sense that one must lose so that another will gain. The answer is no, because though one does not mind gaining benefits at someone else's expense, no one wants to engage in a transaction that includes a high risk of loss. For trade to take place, both nations must anticipate gain from it. In other words, "trade is a positive sum game."[1]

In order to explain how gain is derived from trade, it is necessary to examine a country's **production possibility curve.** How absolute and relative advantages affect trade options are based on the trading partners' production possibility curves.

Production Possibility Curve

Without trade, a nation would have to produce all commodities by itself in order to satisfy all its needs. Exhibit 2–1 shows a hypothetical example of a country with a decision concerning the production of two products, computers and automobiles. This graph shows the number of units of computer or automobile the country is able to produce. The production possibility curve shows the maximum number of units made when computers and automobiles are produced in various combinations, since one product can be substituted for the other within the limit of available resources. The country may elect to specialize or put all its resources into making either computers (point A) or automobiles (point B). At point C, product specialization has not been chosen, and thus a specific number of each of the two products will be produced.

There is a cost involved in substituting one product for another. The cost of substitution depends on the production value of one commodity foregone (given up)

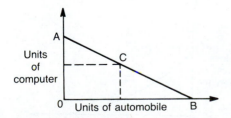

EXHIBIT 2–1 Production possibility curve: constant opportunity cost

for the production value of another product. Exhibit 2–1 shows a situation of constant opportunity cost—the country gives up one unit of computer in order to make one unit of automobile. In such a situation, the factors of production are in the same proportion throughout, meaning that the exchange ratio between these two products is constant. However, this assumption is objectionable for several reasons.[2] Theoretically, an individual industry (e.g., producing computers) may experience diminishing returns as it expands at the expense of another industry (e.g., producing automobiles). Furthermore, rising opportunity costs may result because one commodity uses production inputs in proportions different from another. Eventually, many industries experience rising marginal costs, resulting in larger and larger numbers of other commodities having to be given up to produce each succeeding extra unit of a particular commodity. This may serve to explain why no country completely specializes in the production of just one single product.

Exhibit 2–2 shows a production possibility curve with increasing opportunity costs—the curve shows that it becomes more and more expensive to substitute the production of one product for the production of another. The proportion of gain is increasingly lower as the volume of one product is reduced in order to increase the volume of the second product. Exhibit 2–3 shows the opposite result, a declining opportunity cost. With a shift from one product to another, producing a substitute product becomes less expensive as increases in substitution are implemented.

Another possibility is that the opportunity cost will vary with the volume of production; that is, for any two given products, opportunity cost may both increase and decrease as each succeeding level of production is reached. For instance, marginal costs may initially decline because of specialization and better economies of scale. But at a certain point, continued production may cause inefficiencies to occur, and the marginal costs will begin rising again.

Because each country has a unique set of resources, each country possesses its own unique production possibility curve. This curve, when analyzed, provides an explanation of the logic behind international trade. Regardless of whether the opportunity cost is constant or variable, a country must determine the proper mix of any two products and must decide whether it wants to specialize in one of the two. Specialization will likely occur if specialization allows the country to improve its prosperity by trading with another nation. The principles of absolute advantage and relative advantage explain how the production possibility curve enables a country to determine what to export and what to import.

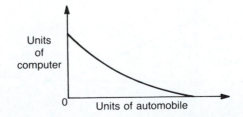

EXHIBIT 2–2   Production possibility curve: increasing opportunity cost

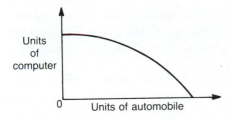

EXHIBIT 2–3 Production possibility curve: decreasing opportunity cost

Principle of Absolute Advantage

Adam Smith may have been the first scholar to investigate formally the rationale behind foreign trade. In his book *Wealth of Nations,* Smith used the **principle of absolute advantage** as the justification for international trade.[3] According to this principle, a country should export a commodity that can be produced at a lower cost than can other nations. Conversely, it should import a commodity that can only be produced at a higher cost than can other nations.

Consider, for example, a situation in which two nations are each producing two products. Table 2–1 provides hypothetical production figures for the United States and Japan based on two products, the computer and the automobile. Case 1 shows that, given certain resources and labor, the United States can produce 20 computers *or* 10 automobiles *or* some combination of both. In contrast, Japan is able to produce only half as many computers (i.e., Japan produces 10 for every 20 the United States produces). The disparity might be the result of better skills by American workers in making this product. Therefore, the United States has an absolute advantage in computers. But the situation is reversed for automobiles: the United States makes only 10 cars for every 20 units manufactured in Japan. In this instance, Japan has an absolute advantage.

In this instance, it should be apparent why trade should take place between the two countries. The United States has an absolute advantage for computers but an absolute disadvantage for automobiles. For Japan, the absolute advantage exists for automobiles and an absolute disadvantage for computers. If each country specializes in the product for which it has an absolute advantage, each can use its resources more effectively while improving consumer welfare at the same time. Since the United States would use less resources in making computers, it should produce this product

TABLE 2–1 Possible physical output

	Product	United States	Japan
Case 1	Computer	20	10
	Automobile	10	20
Case 2	Computer	20	10
	Automobile	30	20
Case 3	Computer	20	10
	Automobile	40	20

for its own consumption as well as for export to Japan. Based on this same rationale, the United States should import automobiles from Japan rather than manufacture them itself. For Japan, of course, automobiles would be exported and computers imported.

An analogy may help demonstrate the value of the principle of absolute advantage. A doctor is absolutely better than a mechanic in performing surgery, whereas the mechanic is absolutely superior in repairing cars. It would be impractical for the doctor to practice medicine as well as repair the car when repairs are needed. Just as impractical would be the reverse situation, for the mechanic to attempt the practice of surgery. Thus, for practicality each person should concentrate on and specialize in the craft that person has mastered. Similarly, it would not be practical for consumers to attempt to produce all the things they desire to consume. One should practice what one does well and leave the production of other things to people who produce them well.

Principle of Relative Advantage

One problem with the principle of absolute advantage is that it fails to explain whether trade will take place if one nation has absolute advantage for all products under consideration. Case 2 of Table 2–1 shows this situation. Note that the only difference between Case 1 and Case 2 is that the United States in Case 2 is capable of making 30 automobiles instead of the 10 in Case 1. In the second instance, the United States has absolute advantage for both products, resulting in absolute disadvantage for Japan for both. The efficiency of the United States enables it to produce more of both products at lower cost.

At first glance, it may appear that the United States has nothing to gain from trading with Japan. But nineteenth-century British economist David Ricardo, perhaps the first economist to fully appreciate relative costs as a basis for trade, argues that absolute production costs are irrelevant.[4] More meaningful are relative production costs, which determine what trade should take place and what items to export or import. According to Ricardo's **principle of relative** (or **comparative**) **advantage,** a country may be better than another country in producing many products but should only produce what it produces best. Essentially, it should concentrate on either a product with the greatest comparative advantage or a product with the least comparative disadvantage. Conversely, it should import either a product for which it has the greatest comparative disadvantage or one for which it has the least comparative advantage.

Case 2 shows how the relative advantage varies from product to product. The extent of relative advantage can be found by determining the ratio of computers to automobiles. The advantage ratio for computers is 2:1 (i.e., 20:10) in favor of the United States. Also in favor of the United States, but to a lesser extent, is the ratio for automobiles, 1.5:1 (i.e., 30:20). These two ratios indicate that the United States possesses a 100 percent advantage over Japan for computers but only a 50 percent advantage for automobiles. Consequently, the United States has a greater relative advantage for the computer product. Therefore, the United States should specialize in producing the computer product. For Japan, having the least comparative disadvantage in automobiles indicates that it should make and export automobiles to the United States.

Consider again the analogy of the doctor and the mechanic. The doctor may take up automobile repair as a hobby. It is even possible, though not probable, that the doctor may eventually be able to repair an automobile faster and better than the mechanic. In such an instance, the doctor would have an absolute advantage in both the practice of medicine and automobile repair, whereas the mechanic would have an absolute disadvantage for both activities. Yet this situation would not mean that the doctor would be better off repairing automobiles as well as performing surgery, because of the relative advantages involved. When compared to the mechanic, the doctor may be far superior in surgery but only slightly better in automobile repair. If the doctor's greatest advantage is in surgery, then the doctor should concentrate on that specialty. And when the doctor has automobile problems, the mechanic should make the repairs because the doctor has only a slight relative advantage in that skill. By leaving repairs to the mechanic, the doctor is using time more productively while maximizing income.

EXCHANGE RATIOS, TRADE, AND GAIN

Although an analysis of relative advantage can indicate what a country should export and import, that analysis cannot explain exactly how a country will gain from trading with a partner. In order to determine the extent of trading gain, an examination of the **domestic exchange ratio** is required. Based on Case 2 of Table 2–1, Japan's domestic exchange ratio between the two products in question is 1:2 (i.e., 10 computers for every 20 automobiles). In other words, Japan must give up 2 automobiles to make 1 computer. But by exporting automobiles to the United States, Japan has to give up only 1.5 automobiles in order to get 1 computer. Thus, trading essentially enables Japan to get more computers than feasible without trading.

The U.S. domestic exchange ratio is 1:1.5 (i.e., 20 computers for every 30 automobiles). The incentive for the United States to trade with Japan occurs in the form of a gain from specializing in computer manufacturing and exchanging computers for automobiles from Japan. The extent of the gain is determined by comparing the domestic exchange ratios in the two countries. In the United States, 1 computer brings 1.5 automobiles in exchange. But this same computer will result in 2 automobiles in Japan. Trading thus is the most profitable way for the United States to employ its resources.

Theoretically, trade should equalize the previously unequal domestic exchange ratios and bring about a new ratio, known as the **world market exchange ratio,** or **terms of trade.** This ratio, which will replace the two different domestic exchange ratios, will lie between the limits established by the pretrade domestic exchange ratios.

Such benefits derived from trade do not imply that trade must always take place and that all nations will always gain from trade. Carrying the hypothetical example a step further, in Case 3 of Table 2–1, the United States now makes 40 automobiles (instead of 10 as in Case 1 and 30 as in Case 2). Not only does the United States have absolute advantage for both products, but it also has the same domestic exchange

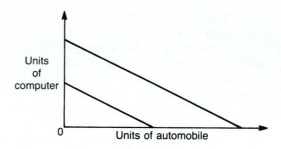

Units
of
computer

0   Units of automobile

EXHIBIT 2–4   Absolute advantage without relative advantage (identical domestic exchange ratios)

ratio as that of Japan. This situation is graphically expressed by two parallel production possibility curves (Exhibit 2–4).

Under these circumstances, trade probably will not occur for two principal reasons. First, since the United States is 100 percent better than Japan for each product, the relative advantage for the United States is identical for both products. Second, since both countries have the identical domestic exchange ratio, there is no incentive or gain from trading for either party. Whether in the United States or in Japan, 1 unit of computer will fetch 2 automobiles. When such other costs as paperwork and transportation are taken into account, it becomes too expensive to export a product from one country to another. Thus, international trade is a function of the varying domestic exchange ratios, and these ratios cause variations in comparative costs or prices.

FACTOR ENDOWMENT THEORY

The principles of absolute and relative advantage provide a primary basis for trade to occur, but the usefulness of these principles is limited by their assumptions. One basic assumption is that the advantage, whether absolute or relative, is solely determined by labor in terms of time and cost. Other factors of production are assumed to be (1) insignificant, (2) so evenly spread over all labor inputs that they always work in a fixed proportion with labor, or (3) merely representative of stored-up labor.[5] Labor, then, determines comparative production costs and subsequent product prices for the same commodity.

If labor is indeed the only factor of production or even a major determinant of product content, countries with high labor cost should be in serious trouble. American workers have been replaced as the highest paid workers in the world. In 1988 hourly wages and benefits in manufacturing in West Germany and Sweden were 30 percent and 21 percent higher than those in the United States, while Japan's wages and benefits were 95 percent of the U.S. level. On the other hand, manufacturing wages and benefits in Asia, Latin America, and other parts of the developing world have remained far below the U.S. level. For example, South Korean and Mexican wages were only 20 percent and 10 percent of those of U.S. workers.

An interesting fact is that the Japanese semiconductor industry has remained competitive even though the wages in Japan are higher than those in California or Texas. West Germany, in spite of its high labor cost (especially after the deutsche mark's phenomenal appreciation in the mid-1980s), has performed well in trade, and it suggests that absolute labor cost is only one of several competitive inputs that determine product value.

It is misleading to analyze labor cost without also considering the quality of that labor. A country may have high labor cost on an absolute basis, yet this cost can be relatively low if productivity is high. According to government figures, the United States leads other industrialized nations in worker productivity. In 1988 the average French worker and the West German worker respectively produced 86 percent and 81 percent as much as the American worker. The figures are 72 percent for British and Japanese workers and 40 percent in the case of South Korean workers.[6]

Furthermore, the price of a product is not necessarily determined by the amount of labor it embodies, regardless of whether the efficiency of labor is an issue or not. Since product price is not determined by labor efficiency alone, other factors of production must be taken into consideration, including land and capital (i.e., equipment). Together, all of these production factors contribute significantly to the creation of value within a particular product.

One reason for the importance of identifying other factors of production is that different commodities require different factor inputs and that no country is well-endowed in all production factors. The varying proportion of these factors embodied in various goods has a great deal of impact on what a country should produce. Corn, for instance, is best produced where there is an abundance of land (relative to labor and capital), even though corn can be grown in most places in the world. Oil refining, in contrast, requires relatively more capital and relatively less labor and land because of expensive equipment and specialized personnel. In clothing production, the most important input factor is that the economy is labor-intensive.

The varying factor inputs and proportions for different commodities, together with the uneven distribution of such factors of production in different regions of the world, are the basis of the Heckscher-Ohlin **theory of factor endowment.**[7] This theory holds that the inequality of relative prices is a function of regional factor endowments and that comparative advantage is determined by the relative abundance of such endowments. According to Ohlin, there is a mutual interdependence among production factors, factor movements, income, prices, and trade. A change in one affects the rest. Prices of factors and subsequent product prices in each region depend on supply and demand, which in turn are affected by the desires of consumers, income levels, quantity of various factors, and physical conditions of production.

Since countries have different factor endowments, a country would have a relative advantage in a commodity that embodies in some degree that country's comparatively abundant factors. A country should thus export that commodity that is relatively plentiful (i.e., in comparison to other commodities) within the relatively abundant factor (i.e., in comparison to other countries). This exported item can then be exchanged for goods that would use large quantities of the country's scarce factors if domestically produced. Exhibit 2–5 lists the Netherlands's well-endowed factors, for example.

Therefore, a country that is relatively abundant in labor but relatively scarce in capital is likely to have a comparative advantage in the production of labor-intensive goods and to have deficiencies in the production of capital-intensive goods. This con-

INFRASTRUCTURE

Medtronic Prospers In the Netherlands, The Heart of Europe

Medtronic, Inc. develops, manufactures and markets therapeutic medical devices designed to improve cardiovascular and neurological health in patients around the world. A leading producer of cardiac pacing technology for more than three decades, Medtronic today also produces heart valves, angioplasty catheters, membrane oxygenators, blood pumps, drug pumps, and nerve and muscle stimulation devices. Chairman and CEO Winston R. Wallin explains the importance of the company's long-standing investment in the Netherlands:

Medtronic ▨

Winston R. Wallin
Chairman and
Chief Executive Officer
Medtronic, Inc.

"Medtronic has had a long and happy relationship with Holland, dating back to 1967 when we opened a European Service Center in Amsterdam. In 1969, when we were ready to open our first international manufacturing site, we selected Kerkrade.

"Today we employ nearly 800 people in five locations in Holland. We have a major pacemaker manufacturing operation and a cardiopulmonary custom tubing pack facility in Kerkrade, a research center in Maastricht and a sales office in Eindhoven. In 1986 we acquired Vitatron, a leading Dutch pacemaker company with locations in Dieren and Velp.

"In the beginning, tax incentives played a major role in our decision to invest in Holland. Through the years there have been many other factors—not the least of which is the stability of the Dutch Government.

"In addition, the working conditions are excellent. The workforce we find in Holland is highly skilled, very loyal and highly educated. We don't have to worry about the quality of products they are producing. The Dutch schools provide excellent technical training, and they produce bilingual students, so there is no language barrier for us to overcome.

"Our long relationship with leading cardiologists and electrophysiologists in Holland and the central location of our facility make it easy for experts to interface with us. Indeed, the location of Holland as the Gateway to Europe gives us access to key medical facilities.

"Our first dual chamber pacemaker was created in Holland—as was our heart wire, our first custom tubing pack operation and a new custom catheter that is in the development stage.

"Through the years the government of Holland has been helpful in providing monetary incentives that have allowed us to conduct extensive research through our Bakken Research Center in Maastricht. An exciting new cardiovascular study is currently being led by the Bakken researchers. Clinical studies for many of our devices also often begin in Europe, another reason this area is so important to us.

"We currently are pursuing two major applications: cardiomyoplasty—or direct wrapping of the heart with transformed muscle—and cardiac assist—where the muscle powers a supplemental hydraulic system to augment cardiac output.

"Over the past 20 years we have had a very positive experience in the Netherlands, and we've never been sorry we decided to expand in Holland."

HIT THE GROUND RUNNING

For more information, please call:
Netherlands Foreign Investment Agency
New York: (212) 246-1434
San Mateo: (415) 349-8848
Los Angeles: (213) 477-8288
Ottawa: (613) 237-5030

This material is published by Ogilvy Public Relations Group, which is registered as an agent of the Government of the Netherlands. It is filed with the Department of Justice, where the required registration statement is available for public inspection. Registration does not indicate approval of the contents by the United States Government.

EXHIBIT 2–5 The Netherlands's relatively well-endowed factors

Source: Courtesy of Netherlands Foreign Investment Agency and Ogilvy Adams & Rinehart (Artist: Nancy Januzzi)

cept explains why China, a formidable competitor in textile products, has to depend on U.S. and European firms for oil exploration within China itself. In another example, in 1987 when Japan faced a dwindling supply of veneer-quality wood as well as a labor-intensive method for manufacturing top-quality chopsticks, Japan began importing many million pairs of chopsticks from the United States. The chopstick market is huge. It is believed that the Japanese alone discard 130 million pairs of chopsticks daily. While investigating the possibility of selling logs to a Korean chopstick factory, Lakewood Industries found that it could make chopsticks more cheaply in Minnesota by modifying machines used to make Popsicle sticks. In Minnesota, where aspen wood is abundant, the company is able to achieve a raw-material cost advantage of $4 million annually. This advantage enables the firm to make chopsticks at 0.3¢ a pair and more than adequately covers the higher labor expenses and transportation costs. Ironically, the relatively more capital-intensive plant represents an effort of a U.S. firm trying to become a supplier of low-cost goods to a newly industrialized market.[8]

The United States has a relative advantage in such temperate-zone agricultural commodities as wheat, corn, and soybeans as well as in high-technology manufactured goods (e.g., capital goods). These advantages are not surprising in a country that has a great deal of land and capital. On the other hand, the United States is a net importer of such low-technology manufactured goods as consumer products. The United States also imports mineral fuels (e.g., oil), even though it exports other crude materials.[9]

A CRITICAL EVALUATION OF TRADE THEORIES

The Validity of Trade Theories

Several studies have investigated the validity of the classical trade theories. The evidence collected by MacDougall shortly after World War II showed that comparative cost was useful in explaining trade patterns.[10] Other studies using different data and time periods have yielded results similar to MacDougall's. Thus there is support for the claim that relative labor productivities determine trade patterns.[11]

These positive results were subsequently questioned.[12] The studies conducted by Leontief revealed that the United States actually exports labor-intensive goods and imports capital-intensive products.[13] These paradoxical findings are now called the **Leontief Paradox.** Thus, the findings are ambiguous, indicating that in its simplest form the Heckscher-Ohlin theory is not supported by the evidence.[14]

A study conducted by Maskus showed that for the United States the Heckscher-Ohlin-Vanek (HOV) theorem was not consistent with available data on factor endowments, factor intensities, and trade. But "these conclusions do not necessarily imply that differences in relative factor endowments across countries do not play an important role in the determination of world trade patterns. The empirical literature has clearly demonstrated the fairly consistent and suggestive links between trade performance and factor intensities, for example. Rather, the most reasonable interpretation is that the HOV assumptions are simply too restrictive for that version of the factor endowments theory to hold in an empirical context."[15]

In theory, the more different two countries are, the more they stand to gain by trading with each other. There is no reason why a country should want to trade with another that is a mirror image of itself. However, a look at world trade also casts some doubt on the validity of classical trade theories. Trade among developed countries has increased much faster than overall world trade and accounts for the largest part of the world trade. In 1990 developed countries' exports to developing countries were \$527.6 billion, and imports from developing countries were \$614.8 billion.[16] Yet developed countries' exports to and imports from one another totaled \$1,867.1 billion and \$1,906.9 billion respectively (see Table 2–2). Thus developed countries tend to trade among themselves rather than with developing countries.

Furthermore, as shown in Exhibit 2–6, it is interesting to note that industrial countries have done quite well in the area of farm exports.

During the past two decades, there have been substantial changes in the pattern of U.S. merchandise trade as related to (1) the composition of trade with regard to the type of goods, (2) the regions with which trade is conducted, and (3) the type of goods traded by specific region.[17] First, the traditional primary market sources (Canada and Western Europe) for U.S. imports have shown significant declines in import share and yet remain at or near the top as sources of U.S. imports. Second, despite a decline in the importance of Western Europe as a market for U.S. export goods, Western Europe and Canada remain the dominant markets for U.S. exporters. Third, Southeast Asia (Japan as well as the Asian newly industrialized countries) has

TABLE 2–2 World trade flows

	With Industrial Countries		With Developing Countries		With U.S.S.R. and Selected Other Countries[a]		Total	
	Exports	Imports	Exports	Imports	Exports	Imports	Exports	Imports
Industrial countries (US\$ billions)								
1984	871.9	903.2	313.1	388.5	26.7	29.7	1,224.5	1,326.3
1985	921.7	965.5	307.6	380.9	26.0	26.8	1,268.4	1,378.3
1986	1,110.7	1,155.6	325.5	364.1	26.4	24.2	1,475.7	1,550.2
1987	1,323.5	1,358.7	369.5	435.0	26.8	27.0	1,733.8	1,828.7
1988	1,503.3	1,542.6	432.1	487.0	31.5	28.0	1,984.1	2,070.3
1989	1,611.7	1,651.6	463.4	544.2	35.1	30.0	2,127.5	2,238.9
1990	1,867.1	1,906.9	527.6	614.8	37.2	35.3	2,452.4	2,570.7
Developing countries (US\$ billions)								
1984	345.9	321.5	169.5	172.4	26.3	24.3	565.7	529.8
1985	330.2	312.7	162.8	162.8	28.9	24.9	542.7	511.9
1986	314.5	323.2	150.9	153.5	27.8	27.2	513.8	514.6
1987	381.2	365.5	186.3	185.7	28.3	27.6	619.7	592.2
1988	428.9	437.6	226.9	222.6	30.7	29.0	709.3	703.5
1989	478.0	469.5	251.2	250.0	32.2	28.4	785.3	763.3
1990	550.3	552.0	283.9	289.0	28.1	23.8	887.3	880.0

[a] Albania, Bulgaria, Cuba, Czechoslovakia, former German Democratic Republic, Democratic People's Republic of Korea, and Mongolia.
Data: IMF, *Direction of Trade Statistics* Yearbook, 1991
Source: IMF *Survey,* 26 August 1991, 226

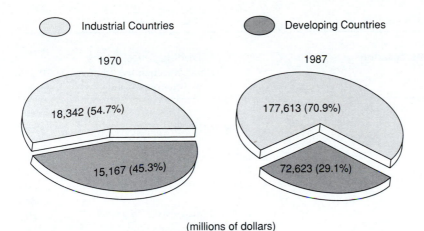

EXHIBIT 2–6 Industrial countries' soaring share of world farm exports
Source: IMF Survey, 18 June 1990, 188

increased dramatically as a market for exports and as a source of imports. Tables 2–3 and 2–4 show the top customers and suppliers of the United States.

The trade pattern shown is surprising theoretically, because advanced economies have similar climate and factor proportions and thus should not trade with one another since there are no comparative advantages. Apparently, other variables in addition to factor endowment play a significant role in determining trade volume and practices because much trade does occur between developed nations. Based on his analysis of over one hundred case studies of industries in ten leading developed nations, Porter has identified four major determinants of international competitiveness: factor conditions (i.e., factors of production); demand conditions; related and supporting industries; and firm strategy, structure, and rivalry. Chance and government policy are minor determinants.[18]

Limitations and Suggested Refinements

Trade theories provide logical explanations about why nations trade with one another, but such theories are limited by their underlying assumptions. Most of the world's trade rules are based on a traditional model that assumes that (1) trade is bilateral, (2) trade involves products originating primarily in the exporting country, (3) the exporting country has a comparative advantage, and (4) competition primarily focuses on the importing country's market. However, today's realities are quite different. First, trade is a multilateral process. Second, trade is often based on products assembled from components that are produced in various countries. Third, it is not easy to determine a country's comparative advantage, as evidenced by the countries that often export and import the same product. Finally, competition usually extends beyond the importing country to include the exporting country and third countries.[19]

In all fairness, virtually all theories require assumptions in order to provide a focus for investigation while holding extraneous variables constant. But controlling the effect of extraneous variables acts to limit a theory's practicality and generalization.

TABLE 2–3   Top U.S. markets and suppliers

Top 25 U.S. Markets U.S. Domestic and Foreign Merchandise Exports, 1990 (f.a.s.* value)		Leading U.S. Suppliers U.S. General Merchandise Imports, 1990 (customs value)	
Total Exports	(US$ billions) **393.3**	**Total Imports**	(US$ billions) **494.9**
1. Canada	83.9	1. Canada	91.4
2. Japan	48.6	2. Japan	89.7
3. Mexico	28.4	3. Mexico	30.2
4. United Kingdom	23.5	4. Germany	28.2
5. Germany	18.8	5. Taiwan	22.7
6. South Korea	14.4	6. United Kingdom	20.3
7. France	13.7	7. South Korea	18.5
8. Netherlands	13.0	8. China	15.2
9. Taiwan	11.5	9. France	13.1
10. Belgium-Luxembourg	10.4	10. Italy	12.7
11. Australia	8.5	11. Saudi Arabia	10.0
12. Singapore	8.0	12. Singapore	9.8
13. Italy	8.0	13. Hong Kong	9.5
14. Hong Kong	6.8	14. Venezuela	9.4
15. Spain	5.2	15. Brazil	8.0
16. Brazil	5.1	16. Nigeria	6.0
17. Switzerland	4.9	17. Switzerland	5.5
18. China	4.8	18. Thailand	5.3
19. Saudi Arabia	4.0	19. Malaysia	5.3
20. Malaysia	3.4	20. Netherlands	5.0
21. Sweden	3.4	21. Sweden	4.9
22. Israel	3.2	22. Belgium-Luxembourg	4.6
23. Venezuela	3.1	23. Australia	4.4
24. U.S.S.R.	3.1	24. Philippines	3.4
25. Thailand	3.0	25. Indonesia	3.3

*Free alongside ship (see Chapter 17)

Source: Business America, 22 April 1991, 5

This problem applies especially to trade theories. As explained by Heller, "international trade theory has to deal with a greater number of variables at any given time than do most other fields of economics. In order to keep the theories manageable and compact, certain simplifying assumptions are usually made in the first stage of the analysis. All these assumptions can be removed, one by one, but only at the cost of increasing the complexity of the models."[20]

One limitation of classical trade theories is that the factors of production are assumed to remain constant for each country because of the assumed immobility of such resources between countries. This assumption is especially true in the case of land, since physical transfer and ownership of land can only be accomplished by war or purchase (e.g., the U.S. seizure of California from Mexico and the U.S. purchase of Alaska from Russia). At present, however, such means to gain land are

TABLE 2–4   U.S. trade balances

U.S. Trade Balances, 1990
Listing of U.S. Merchandise Trade Balances
General Imports, Customs Value; Domestic and Foreign Exports, f.a.s. value

U.S. Surplus Positions		U.S. Deficit Positions	
	(US$ billions)	**Total**	**−101.0**
1. Netherlands	+8.0	1. Japan	−41.1
2. Belgium-Luxembourg	+5.9	2. Taiwan	−11.2
3. Australia	+4.1	3. China	−10.4
4. United Kingdom	+3.2	4. Germany	−9.4
5. U.S.S.R.	+2.0	5. Canada	−7.5
6. Spain	+1.9	6. Venezuela	−6.3
7. Egypt	+1.9	7. Saudi Arabia	−5.9
8. Turkey	+1.1	8. Nigeria	−5.4
9. Ireland	+0.8	9. Italy	−4.7
10. Bahrain	+0.6	10. South Korea	−4.1
11. Panama	+0.6	11. Brazil	−2.9
12. Pakistan	+0.5	12. Hong Kong	−2.6
13. France	+0.5	13. Thailand	−2.3
14. Morocco	+0.4	14. Iraq	−2.3
15. Jamaica	+0.4	15. Malaysia	−1.8
16. Chile	+0.4	16. Singapore	−1.8
17. Netherlands Antilles	+0.3	17. Angola	−1.8
18. El Salvador	+0.3	18. Mexico	−1.8
19. Leeward & Windward Is.	+0.3	19. Algeria	−1.7
20. Jordan	+0.3	20. Sweden	−1.5
21. Bahamas	+0.3	21. Indonesia	−1.4
22. French Guiana	+0.3	22. Colombia	−1.1
23. Greece	+0.3	23. Philippines	−0.9
24. Paraguay	+0.3	24. India	−0.7
25. Bermuda	+0.2	25. Ecuador	−0.7

Source: Business America, 22 April 1991, 5

less and less likely. As a matter of fact, many countries have laws that prohibit foreigners from owning real estate. Thus, Japan and many other countries remain land-poor.

A significant difference exists in the degree of mobility between land and capital. In spite of the restrictions on the movement of capital imposed by most governments, it is possible for a country to attract foreign capital for investment or for a country to borrow money from foreign banks or international development agencies. Not surprisingly, U.S. banks, as financial institutions in a capital-rich country, provide huge loans to Latin American countries. Yet at the same time, a favorable U.S. business climate makes it possible for the United States to attract capital from abroad to help finance its enormous federal deficits. Therefore, capital is far from being immobile.

Labor as a factor is relatively immobile. Immigration laws in most countries severely limit the freedom of movement of labor between countries. In China, people (i.e., labor) are not even able to select residence in a city of their choice. Still, labor can and does move across borders. Western European nations allow their citizens to pass across borders rather freely. The United States has a farm program that allows Mexican workers to work in the United States temporarily. For Asian nations, most are so well-endowed with cheap and abundant labor that such countries as South Korea and Thailand send laborers to work in Saudi Arabia. China, likewise, would like to export its labor because it is the most well-endowed nation in the world in terms of this resource. In the midnineteenth century, many Chinese peasants were brought to the United States for railroad building. When wages in South Korea jumped, Goldstar Co. minimized the labor problem by importing goods from its overseas facilities back into South Korea.

Because workers cannot easily emigrate to another country possessing better wages and benefits, wages have not been equalized across countries. Conceivably, computer workstations and communications technology could lessen this problem by allowing a portion of the work force to work for any company in any part of the world. Theoretically, if developments continue along these lines, a worldwide labor market is possible.

Production factors are now considered more mobile than previously assumed, but their mobility is still considerably restricted. As a result, production costs and product prices are never completely equalized across countries. The small amount of mobility that does exist serves to narrow the price/cost differentials. In theory, as a country exports its abundant factor, that factor becomes more scarce at home and its price rises. In contrast, as a country imports a scarce factor, it increases the abundance of that factor and its price declines. Therefore, a nation is usually interested in attracting what it lacks, and this practice will affect the distribution of production factors.

Since a country's factors of production can change owing to factor mobility, it is reasonable to expect a shift in the kind of goods a country imports and exports. Japan, once a capital-poor country, has grown to become a major lender/supplier of money for international trade. Its trade pattern seems to reflect this change. A cross-section regression analysis in which capital, human capital, labor, and energy were regressed shows drastic changes in the Japanese trade structure between 1967 and 1975. "Japanese exports shifted from the unskilled labor-intensive goods to capital-intensive goods while her imports shifted from capital-intensive goods to unskilled labor-intensive goods."[21]

Immobility is not the only item of relevance when considering the factors of production. Another item that is very significant involves the level of quality of the production factors. It is important to understand that the quality of each factor should not be assumed to be homogeneous worldwide. Some countries have relatively better-trained personnel, better equipment, better-quality land and climate. Some studies support the human-skills theory in explaining the Leontief Paradox. According to these studies, the United States has a relative advantage in the manufacturing of those products that require a high level of skills.[22] Such variations in the quality of the factors of production across countries result in variations of product quality.

Although a country should normally export products that utilize its abundant factors as the product's major input, a country can substitute one production factor for another to a certain extent. Cut-up chicken fryers are a good example. Japan imports chicken fryers because a scarcity of land forces it to use valuable land for products of relatively greater economic opportunity. Both the United States and Thailand sell cut-up chicken fryers to Japan. The two countries' production strategies, however, differ markedly. The United States, because of its high labor costs, depends more on automation (i.e., capital) to keep production costs down. Thailand, on the other hand, has plentiful and inexpensive labor and thus produces its fryers through a labor-intensive process. Therefore, the proportion of factor inputs for a particular product is not necessarily fixed, and the identical product may be produced with alternative methods or factors.

The discussion so far has dealt with an emphasis of trade theories on the supply side. But demand is just as critical, and demand reversal (when it occurs) may serve to explain why the empirical evidence is mixed. Tastes should not be assumed to be the same among various countries. A country may have a scarcity of certain products, and yet its citizens may have no desire for those products. Frequently, LDCs' products may not be of sufficient quality to satisfy the tastes of industrial nations' consumers. Yugo, for example, tried to convince American consumers that its automobiles, despite their very low prices, were not a bad value or of poor quality.

In some market situations, it is possible for product quality to be too high. Companies in developed countries, for example, sometimes manufacture products with too many refinements, which make the products too costly for consumers elsewhere. German machineries, for instance, have a worldwide reputation for quality. Nonetheless, many LDCs opt for less-reliable machinery products from Taiwan because Taiwan's products are less costly. Such circumstances explain why nations with similar levels of economic development tend to trade with one another, since they have very similar tastes and incomes.

Perhaps the most serious shortcoming of classical trade theories is that they ignore the marketing aspect of trade. These theories are primarily concerned with commodities rather than with manufactured goods or value-added products. It is assumed that all suppliers have identical products with similar physical attributes and quality. This habit of assuming product homogeneity is not likely to be made among those familiar with marketing.

More often than not, products are endowed with psychological attributes. Brand-name products are often promoted as having additional value based on psychological nuance. Tobacco products of Marlboro and Winston sell well worldwide because of the images of those brands. Also, firms in two countries can produce virtually identical products in physical terms, but one product has different symbolic meaning than the other. LDCs are just as capable as the United States in making good cosmetic products, but many consumers are willing to pay significantly more for the prestige of using an American brand such as Estee Lauder. Trade analysis, therefore, is not complete without taking into consideration the reasons for *product differentiation*. Exhibit 2–7 is an advertisement for Mercedes-Benz automobiles, which are highly differentiated from other cars. Although the United States is a major automobile manufacturer and the U.S. market is dominated by three American firms (GM, Ford, and Chrysler), there are more than twenty foreign automakers selling cars in the United States. This profusion of products clearly shows that automobiles are far from being homogeneous—they come in a great variety of product forms and brands.

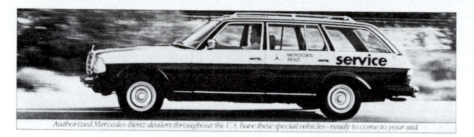

Authorized Mercedes-Benz dealers throughout the U.S. have these special vehicles—ready to come to your aid.

Mercedes-Benz Roadside Assistance: a commitment to roadside service unprecedented in the automotive world.

Automotive service takes an extraordinary step. Introducing the first national program of on-the-road assistance ever offered by an automobile maker.

Mercedes-Benz Roadside Assistance: A national toll-free hotline, staffed by Mercedes-Benz experts. A nationwide fleet of specially equipped Mercedes-Benz vehicles, in the exclusive service of Mercedes-Benz owners.

It is a commitment to Mercedes-Benz automobiles and owners far beyond convention. A commitment to service at night, on weekends, on holidays. A commitment made only by Mercedes-Benz.

A SPECIAL VEHICLE

Should your Mercedes-Benz need service on the road *anywhere* in the United States, Roadside Assistance stands ready Monday–Friday, 5 p.m. to midnight; Saturdays, Sundays, holidays, 8 a.m. to midnight. One toll-free 800 phone call

© 1984 Mercedes-Benz of N.A., Inc., Montvale, N.J.

connects you with a Mercedes-Benz technical advisor. His over-the-phone instruction can often put you promptly back on the road. If your car requires further attention, a specially equipped Mercedes-Benz station wagon, manned by a skilled technician, can be dispatched from a nearby authorized Mercedes-Benz dealership. Across the United States,

hundreds of such vehicles are poised for service.

Swift, expert help. Just a toll-free phone call away.

On highways, back roads, at night, in driving rain. For whichever member of the family is behind the wheel. The phone number is affixed to the inside of the glove compartment. You'll probably never need it. But you'll know it's always there. The 800 number and a full information package are available from your participating authorized dealer.

Roadside Assistance works. It has been operating successfully for over a year throughout Southern California and the Northeast (California and Northeast residents, please note: There is a new national Roadside Assistance number.)

WIDE-RANGING COMMITMENT

Extraordinary though it is, Roadside Assistance is but one component of Mercedes-Benz Signature Service: a range of programs that fosters a personal commitment from Mercedes-Benz dealers, managers, advisors, and technicians to their customers.

Mercedes-Benz and its authorized dealer network stand behind their automobiles.

Not with mere words. But with an ever-ready fleet.

Engineered like no other car in the world

EXHIBIT 2–7   A differentiated product

Source: Reprinted permission of Mercedes-Benz of North America, Inc.

A further shortcoming of classical trade theories is that the trade patterns as described in the theories are in reality frequently affected by *trade restrictions*. The direction of the flow of trade, according to some critics of free trade, is no longer determined by a country's natural comparative advantage. Rather a country can create a relative advantage by relying on out-sourcing and other trade barriers, such as tariffs and quotas. Japan's superiority in basic industries can be attributed in part to its "selective protectionism" to achieve "strategic reversals."[23] The process involves the initial importation of a technology from the West (e.g., steel or television technology). The new domestic industry using the imported technology is then protected in order to gain economies of scale, experience, cost parity, and momentum. Then the product is aggressively exported to enhance the cost position. That exportation in turn allows Japan to improve product quality. A complete reversal occurs, and Japan is able to manufacture profitably a better product at a lower price. After the reversal, the protection is shifted to a new or advanced technology.

The U.S. trade pattern is also distorted by trade restrictions and regulations. The U.S. automobile emission control standards have effectively prevented Brazilian cars from entering the U.S. market. It is also interesting to observe that the United States has no desire to allow Asian countries to maximize their comparative advantage in the manufacturing of textiles, which are labor-intensive. While allowing high-cost European manufacturers to ship unlimited numbers of garments to the U.S. market, the United States restricts those from low-cost Asian countries. To circumvent these trade barriers, Peninsula Knitters, a large Hong Kong sweatermaker, takes a more cumbersome and expensive step that involves shipping its sweaters to the United States from the company's British factory.[24] These examples show that protectionism can alter the trade patterns as described by trade theories.

The "new trade theory" states that trade is based on increasing returns to scale, historical accidents, and government policies. Japan's *targeted industry* strategy, for example, does not adhere to free-market principles. Therefore, a moderate degree of protection may promote domestic output and welfare. However, as pointed out by Jagdish Bhagwati, it is not easy to differentiate fair trade based on comparative advantage from what may be considered unfair trade. Are trade practices based on work habits, on infrastructure, and on differential saving behavior to be considered unfair? If so, all trade could possibly be considered unfair.[25]

In spite of the benefits to be derived when trading partners adhere to their comparative advantage, nations are tempted to solve economic problems by limiting imports. The cost of ignoring comparative advantage is very high. Textiles and apparel are the most heavily protected U.S. industries. According to the Institute for International Economics, for selected industries, the cost per job saved is $1 million (benzenoid chemicals and specialty steel), $750,000 (carbon steel), $240,000 (orange juice), and $150,000 (motorcycles).

ECONOMIC COOPERATION

Given inherent constraints in any system, conditions for the best policy rarely exist. A policymaker must then turn to the second-best policy. This practice applies to international trade. Worldwide free trade is ideal, but that cannot be attained. The **theory of second best** suggests that the optimum policy, then, is to have economic cooperation on a smaller scale.[26] In an attempt to reduce trade barriers and improve trade, many countries within the same geographic area often join together to establish various forms of economic cooperation. Major regional groups are shown in Exhibit 2–8.

Levels of Economic Integration

Trade theorists have identified five levels of economic cooperation. They are free trade area, customs union, common market, economic union/integration, and political union. Table 2–5 shows a concise comparison of these cooperation levels.

Andean Group (the Cartagena Agreement)   Bolivia, Colombia, Ecuador, Peru, and Venezuela

Arab/Middle East Arab Common Market   UAR, Iraq, Jordan, Sudan, Syria, and Yemen

ASEAN (Association of Southeast Asian Nations)   Brunei, Indonesia, Malaysia, the Philippines, Singapore, and Thailand

Benelux Customs Union   Belgium, the Netherlands, and Luxembourg

CARICOM (Caribbean Common Market)   Antigua and Barbuda, Bahamas, Barbados, Belize, Dominica, Grenada, Guyana, Jamaica, Montserrat, Saint Christopher-Nevis, Saint Lucia, Saint Vincent and the Grenadines, and Trinidad and Tobago

Central American Community   Costa Rica, El Salvador, Guatemala, Honduras, Nicaragua, and Panama

East Africa Customs Union   Ethiopia, Kenya, Zimbabwe, Sudan, Tanzania, and Uganda

ECOWAS (Economic Community of West African States)   Benin, Cape Verde, Dahomey, Gambia, Ghana, Guinea, Guinea-Bissau, Ivory Coast, Liberia, Mali, Mauritania, Niger, Nigeria, Senegal, Sierra Leone, Togo, and Upper Volta

EC (European Community)   Belgium, Denmark, France, Greece, Ireland, Italy, Luxembourg, the Netherlands, Portugal, Spain, the United Kingdom, and Germany

EFTA (European Free Trade Association)   Austria, Finland, Iceland, Liechtenstein, Norway, Sweden, and Switzerland

LAIA (Latin American Integration Association)   Argentina, Bolivia, Brazil, Chile, Colombia, Ecuador, Mexico, Paraguay, Peru, Uruguay, and Venezuela

Mahgreb Economic Community   Algeria, Libya, Tunisia, and Morocco

NAFTA (New Zealand–Australia Free Trade Agreement)   Australia and New Zealand

OECD (Organization for Economic Cooperation and Development)   EC members, Austria, Australia, Canada, Finland, Iceland, Japan, New Zealand, Norway, Sweden, Switzerland, Turkey, and the United States

RCD (Regional Cooperation for Development)   Iran, Pakistan, and Turkey

---

EXHIBIT 2–8   Regional groupings and their member nations

TABLE 2–5 Levels of regional cooperation

Characteristic of Cooperation	Free Trade Area	Customs Union	Common Market	Economic and Monetary Union	Political Union
Elimination of internal duties	yes	yes	yes	yes	probably
Establishment of common barriers	no	yes	yes	yes	probably
Removal of restrictions on factors of production	no	no	yes	yes	probably
Harmonization of national economic policies	no	no	no	yes	probably
Harmonization of national political policies	no	no	no	no	yes

In a **free trade area,** the countries involved eliminate duties among themselves, while maintaining separately their own tariffs against outsiders. Free trade areas include the EFTA (European Free Trade Association) and the defunct LAFTA (Latin-American Free Trade Association). The purpose of a free trade area is to facilitate trade among member nations. The problem with this kind of arrangement is the lack of coordination of tariffs against nonmembers, enabling nonmembers to direct their exported products to enter the free trade area at the point of lowest external tariffs. The first free trade agreement signed by the United States was with Israel. It should be apparent that countries forming a free trade area do not need to have joint boundaries. On January 1, 1989, the United States and Canada formed the world's largest free trade area, stretching from the Arctic Circle to the Rio Grande. By 1998 all tariffs between the United States and Canada will have been eliminated (see Exhibit 2–9).

A **customs union** is an extension of the free trade area in the sense that member countries must also agree on a common schedule of identical tariff rates. In effect, the objective of the customs union is to harmonize trade regulations and to establish common barriers against outsiders. Uniform tariffs and a common commercial policy against nonmembers are necessary to prevent them from taking advantage of the situation by shipping goods initially to a member country that has the lowest external tariffs. The uniformity of tariff rates is critical when member nations have joint boundaries. The world's oldest customs union is the Benelux Customs Union.

A **common market** is a higher and more complex level of economic integration than either a free trade area or a customs union. In a common market, countries remove all customs and other restrictions on the movement of the factors of production (such as services, raw materials, labor, and capital) among the members of the common market. As a result, business laws and labor laws are standardized to ensure

- All *bilateral tariffs* will be eliminated by January 1, 1998. Duties on some goods were eliminated when the Agreement went into effect in January 1989; duties on other goods will be phased out in five or ten equal annual steps, depending on the good in question. Duty drawbacks and similar programs for goods imported from other countries will be eliminated from bilateral trade within five years.
- The Agreement provides for a two-track system of *safeguard actions* in the future. Under the bilateral track during the transition period, if imports from one part alone are a substantial cause of injury, the other party may suspend duty reductions provided by the Agreement for a maximum of three years. Under the global track, both countries retain their Article XIX rights under the General Agreement on Tariffs and Trade (GATT).
- *Quantitative restrictions* on imports and exports will not be maintained or introduced except in accordance with GATT provisions. Existing quantitative restrictions, with a few exceptions, will be eliminated or phased out according to an agreed timetable.
- A *binational dispute settlement panel* will be established to review and determine, at either government's request, whether antidumping and countervailing duty decisions are in accordance with applicable laws. Decisions of the panel will be binding.
- *Sectoral trade* in agriculture, wine, distilled spirits, and energy will be liberalized according to a number of specific agreements, while the existing free trade arrangement in automobiles (the Auto pact) will be left essentially intact. The two countries agreed to limit duty-free entry privileges under the Auto pact to current participants.
- Trade in *services* will be covered by a set of disciplines based on the principle of national treatment, right of commercial presence, and right of establishment. With regard to financial services, the two countries agreed to grandfather existing privileges in each other's market and to improve access and competition for financial institutions consistent with each country's supervisory and regulatory requirements.
- On direct *investment,* the two countries agreed to provide each other's investors with national treatment with respect to the establishment of new businesses, and the conduct, operation, and sale of established businesses. The Agreement prohibits the introduction of new policies setting minimum national equity participation or forced divestitures, establishes standards for expropriation and compensation, and provides for the free transfer of profits and proceeds from asset sales.
- With regard to *government procurement,* the two countries agreed to expand access to purchases by governments by building on the GATT Government Procurement Code. Improvement of the GATT code will be achieved by establishing a common rule of origin, an effective challenge system for all potential suppliers, and improved transparency in the procurement process.
- The Agreement establishes a *Canada-U.S. Trade Commission* to supervise its implementation and administration and to resolve disputes.

EXHIBIT 2–9 Principal provisions of the Canada-U.S. Free Trade Agreement

Source: IMF Survey, 15 May 1989, 149

undistorted competition. For an outsider, the point of entry is no longer dictated by member countries' tariff rates since those rates are uniform across countries within the common market. The point of entry is now determined by the members' nontariff barriers. The outsider's strategy should be to enter a member country that has the least nontariff restrictions, because goods can be shipped freely once inside the common market.

The European Community (EC), often known as the European Common Market, is a prime example of this level of economic cooperation. Formed by the 1957 Treaty of Rome, the EC has grown from six to twelve members. Exhibit 2–10 lists the EC's milestones, and Exhibit 2–11 compares the EC with other economies.

The EC member states have ceded substantial sovereignty to the EC. The EC's institutions that function as the three traditional branches of democratic government are the European Parliament (as the legislative branch), the Court of Justice (as a judiciary), and the Council of Ministers of the European Communities (as the executive branch). The Council appoints members of the Commission of the European Communities, which initiates legislative proposals (regulations or directives) for the Council (see Exhibit 2–12).

The passage in 1985 of the Single European Act (SEA), an amendment to the Treaties of Rome, was largely responsible for the development of the EC Single Internal Market. Taking effect in 1987, this legal instrument makes it possible for the Council of Ministers to adopt an Internal Market directive or regulation on the strength of a qualified majority (fifty-four of seventy-six votes). Council votes are assigned by a weighted average. The Council of Ministers thus no longer has to reach unanimous agreement for a directive to pass. However, unanimity is still required for fiscal matters (e.g., taxation), decisions on the free movement of persons, and directives or regulations on the rights and interests of employed persons. As of mid-1991, the EC Commission reported that the EC Council of Ministers had adopted 70 percent of 282 directives and regulations. Once adopted, the provision must be implemented by member states within a period of from eighteen months to two years. However, only thirty-seven measures were fully implemented by all twelve member countries.

In 1993 the twelve-nation EC and the seven-member EFTA formed the world's largest and most lucrative common market—the European Economic Area. The European Economic Area eliminates nontariff barriers between the EFTA and EC countries to create a free flow of goods, services, capital, and people in a market of some 380 million people.

The cooperation among countries increases even more with an **economic and monetary union (EMU)**. Some authorities prefer to distinguish a monetary union from an economic union. In essence, monetary union means one money (i.e., a single currency). The Delors Committee, chaired by Jacques Delors, who is the President of the European Commission, has issued a report entitled *Economic and Monetary Union in the European Community* that defines monetary union as having three basic characteristics: total and irreversible convertibility of currencies; complete freedom of capital movements in fully integrated financial markets; and irrevocably fixed exchange rates with no fluctuation margins between member currencies, leading ultimately to a single currency.[27] The economic advantages of a single currency include the elimination of currency risks and lower transaction costs.

Milestones

1950
French Minister of Foreign Affairs, Robert Schuman, proposes the first European Community (dealing with coal and steel) on May 9, celebrated as the official "birthday" of the Communities.
1951
Paris Treaty of April 18 sets up the European Coal and Steel Community.
1957
The Treaties of Rome, signed on 25 March, establish the Common Market and Euratom.
1958
The Councils and Commissions to manage the Common Market and Euratom are set up.
1961
Greece signs an association agreement.
1962
The common agricultural policy is born in January, based on the principle of a single market and common prices for most agricultural products.
1963
The Yaoundé Convention, valid for five years, is signed in January, associating 18 African states with the Community.
Turkey signs an association agreement in September.
1964
A common agricultural market is set up, with supporting marketing organizations, and uniform prices for cereals, to go into effect in 1967. The European Agricultural Guidance and Guarantee Fund begins operations.
1967
The Treaty establishing a single European Commission and one Council comes into force.
1968
The customs union is completed, abolishing all duties on trade between members. A common external tariff is set up.
1972
To control wildly diverging exchange rates among currencies of member countries, the Community establishes the "snake" to maintain the relative values of currencies within an agreed margin of 2.25 percent.
1973
Denmark, Ireland, and the United Kingdom become members, enlarging the Community to nine members.
A free-trade agreement comes into force with some members of the European Free Trade Association that are not members of the EC.
1974
The European Council is born, to supplant earlier irregular summit meetings. It is decided to hold elections to the European Parliament by direct universal vote.
1975
The Community signs the Lomé Convention with 46 countries of Africa, the Caribbean, and the Pacific (ACP) to foster commercial cooperation by giving the ACP countries free access to the Community market, and guaranteeing stable earnings for 36 commodities from those countries.
1979
The Council, meeting in Paris on March 9–10, brings the European Monetary System into operation. The EMS comprises the European currency unit (ECU), an exchange and information mechanism, credit facilities, and transfer arrangements. The United Kingdom does not fully participate in the EMS.
First direct elections to the European Parliament take place.
A new Lomé Convention is signed (Lomé II), this time with 58 ACP countries.
1981
Greece becomes the tenth member of the Community.
The ECU replaces the European Unit of Account in the Community's general budget.
Greenland, an "autonomous region" of Denmark, opts out of the Community but is granted the same associate status as overseas countries and territories governed by member nations.
1984
Lomé III is signed, this time with 65 partners in Africa, the Caribbean, and the Pacific regions.
1986
Portugal and Spain become members.

EXHIBIT 2–10 Milestones of the European Community

Source: Finance & Development, September 1986, p. 31

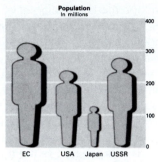

Population
In millions

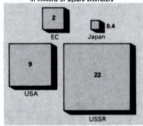

Area
In millions of square kilometers

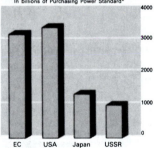

Gross domestic product at market prices[1]
In billions of Purchasing Power Standard[2]

[1]1983 figures.
[2]Purchasing Power Standard: a common unit representing an identical volume of goods and services for each country.
1 PPS = BF 37.2, DM 2.27, DKr 8.36, Ptas 78.1, F 6.17, £ 0.520, Dr 53.6, Lit 1036, £Ir 0.585, Lux F 37.7, f. 2.45, Esc 48.0, US$0.947

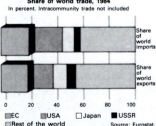

Share of world trade, 1984
In percent. Intracommunity trade not included

☐EC ☐USA ☐Japan ☐USSR
☐Rest of the world   Source: Eurostat.

EXHIBIT 2–11 The EC compared with other economies

Source: Finance & Development, September 1986, p. 31

70

Following is a brief guide to the main institutions involved in the integration efforts of the European Community.

European Community. The Community comprises twelve members: Belgium, Denmark, France, Germany, Greece, Ireland, Italy, Luxembourg, the Netherlands, Portugal, Spain, and the United Kingdom. The treaty establishing a single Council of Ministers and a single Commission of the European Communities was signed by the members of the three Communities—the European Coal and Steel Community, the European Economic Community, and the European Atomic Energy Community—in April 1965; it entered into force in July 1967. Although the three Communities share common institutions, they were established by different treaties and remain legally separate.

Council of Ministers of the European Communities. The Council is responsible for coordinating economic policies and adopting decisions to carry out the treaties of the Communities. The Council represents the governments of the member states and usually meets at the ministerial level. The European Council meets two or three times a year at the level of heads of state or government. The President of the Commission of the European Communities also attends meetings of the Council.

Commission of the European Communities. The Commission formulates and implements policies of the European Communities. Members of the Commission are appointed by member governments for a four-year term, but they do not represent their governments. No more than two members of the Commission may have the same nationality.

European Parliament. The Parliament advises and supervises the work of the executive bodies, the Commission, and the Council. The Parliament's 518 members are apportioned among the member states and are directly elected by citizens of member states.

Court of Justice. The Court rules on the interpretation and application of the treaties.

EXHIBIT 2–12 European Community institutions

Source: IMF Survey, 29 May 1989, 167

The European Commission's *One Market, One Money* report defines an economic union as a single market for goods, services, capital, and labor, complemented by common policies and coordination in several economic and structural areas.[28] Economic union provides a number of benefits. In terms of efficiency and economic growth, the transaction costs associated with converting one EC currency into another are eliminated, and the elimination of foreign exchange risk should improve trade and capital mobility. In addition, stronger competition policies should promote efficiency gains. In terms of inflation, the implementation of an economic union is a demonstration of a credible commitment to stable prices.

According to the Delors Committee, the basic elements of an economic union include the following: a single market within which persons, goods, services, and capital could move freely; a joint competition policy to strengthen market mechanisms; common competition, structural, and regional policies; and sufficient coordination of macroeconomic policies, including binding rules on budgetary policies regarding the size and financing of national budget deficits. Under the EC members' Economic and Monetary Union (EMU) agreements, the EC will move toward adoption of a single currency and a central bank by 1999.

A good example of an economic and monetary union is the unification of East Germany and West Germany. The terms of the monetary union called for an average currency conversion rate of M 1.8 to DM 1 and a conversion of East German wages at parity into deutsche marks. The July 1, 1990 German Economic and Monetary Union has resulted in one Germany. In addition to sharing a common, freely convertible currency (the deutsche mark), the legal environment, commercial code, and taxation requirements in the German Democratic Republic (East Germany) are now the same as those of the Federal Republic of Germany (West Germany). Because of German economic unification, East Germany has become a fully integrated member of the EC, thus sharing the common EC external tariff in trade with non-EC countries.

Because an EMU envisages total fiscal and monetary integration, nations that agree to join the union must work out an economic arrangement in which the trade between member countries directly benefits each of the countries' economic objectives. The features of an EMU require a common monetary policy, formulated by a single institution; highly coordinated economic policies; and adequate, consistent constraints on members' public sector deficits and their financing.

It should be readily apparent that the formation of an economic and monetary union is a complex and exceedingly difficult task, because this level of cooperation requires the harmonization of the national economic policies—especially in the monetary and fiscal areas. A member country must give up the prospect of currency devaluation as a short-term instrument for solving economic problems. For an EMU to function effectively, member countries should have similar economic conditions. In the case of the EC, economic disparities are highly evident. Per capita income differs from 4,500 pounds in Greece to 9,400 pounds in Germany. Unemployment varies from 1 percent in Luxembourg to 16 percent in Spain. Inflation rates vary from 2 percent to more than 20 percent. Short-term interest rates range from 9 percent to 19 percent. If the central bank pursues tight monetary policies, the weaker European countries would be hurt. If easier monetary policies are pursued to accommodate weaker countries, it would be a backward step.[29]

A **political union** is the ultimate type of economic cooperation because it involves the integration of both economic and political policies. With France and Germany leading the way, the European Community has been moving toward social, political, and economic integration. The EC's goal is to form a political union similar to the one created by the United States. The EC's debate over political union involves issues such as having common defense and foreign policies; strengthening the role of the EC Parliament, and adopting an EC-wide social policy. In late 1991 the member countries of the EC reached agreement on an EMU and political union. The agreement on political union has given the EC authority to act in defense, in foreign, and in social policies. Although unanimous approval by the twelve member states is required for an agreement on the EMU and Political Union, Britain was exempted from certain parts of both agreements.

A regional economic grouping does not always fall neatly into one of these five levels. ASEAN, which encompasses more than 250 million people in the fastest growing region in the world, is an organization for economic, political, social, and cultural cooperation (see Exhibit 2–13). It is not quite a free trade association because tariffs are reduced but not completely eliminated among the members. It is similar to an economic union because the member nations agree on production quotas for certain commodities. Furthermore, ASEAN has political objectives as well since all members have market-oriented economies and oppose communist Vietnam's aggression in the region.

It is doubtful that pure forms of economic integration and political union can ever become reality. Even if they did, they would not last long because different countries eventually have different goals and inflation rates. More important is that no country would be willing to surrender its sovereignty for economic reasons. The EC, despite great strides, has been plagued by infighting among member states with conflicting national interests.

Although the Treaty of Rome calls for a free internal market and permits market forces to equalize national economic differences, Germany, France, and the Netherlands—which have expensive social-welfare programs—argue that the *social dimension* must be taken into account in order to prevent "social dumping." In other words, they seek to prevent a movement of business and jobs away from areas with high wages and strong labor organizations to areas with low wages, less organized labor forces, and weak social-welfare policies. As a result, the EC Commission adopted the Social Charter in 1989 to establish workers' basic rights and to equalize European Community social regulations (e.g., a minimum wage, labor participation in

---

WHAT IS ASEAN?

The Association of Southeast Asian Nations (ASEAN) is an organization for economic, political, social, and cultural cooperation among its six member countries: Brunei, Indonesia, Malaysia, the Philippines, Singapore, and Thailand.

ASEAN was established on August 8, 1967, with the signing of the Bangkok Declaration by five of the countries. Brunei joined in 1984, shortly after its resumption of full independence from Britain.

ASEAN's original purpose was to preserve peace among its member countries and to respond to the communist threat in the region. During the first nine years of its existence, ASEAN's primary focus was political.

Economic cooperation only began at the first ASEAN Summit in Bali in 1976, when the Declaration of ASEAN Accord was signed. Under the Accord, ASEAN member countries agreed to cooperate in the supply and purchase of basic commodities, the establishment of preferential trading arrangements, and the stabilization of prices and promotion of export earnings from production of regional commodities.

EXHIBIT 2–13 ASEAN

Source: Business America, 17 June 1991, 16

management decisions, and paid holidays for educational purposes). Member countries accused of "social dumping" must subject their products to sanctions. European socialists believe that the Social Charter is necessary to prevent countries with the lowest social benefits from gaining a comparative advantage.[30]

Countries with lower labor costs (e.g., Portugal, Spain, and Greece), however, view the Social Charter as something that forces capital-poor countries to adopt the expensive social-welfare policies, in effect increasing the cost of labor and unemployment. To them, the Social Charter is nothing more than protectionism in the guise of harmonization. Such expensive policies are also a major concern to European industry. As can be expected, several initiatives are the subject of heated debate.

The history of Comecon, or CMEA (Council for Mutual Economic Assistance), gives another example of the difficulty related to the formation of a pure economic or political union. CMEA, an intergovernmental organization, was established in 1949 to coordinate the economies of the Soviet Union, the communist countries of Eastern Europe, and their allies. Pursuing its political goals, the U.S.S.R. wanted to push the CMEA in the direction of economic and political integration while restricting the bloc's trade with the West. This would involve more unified trade and economic planning so that the East-bloc market could be divided along industry lines. Although the Soviet Union dominated its East-bloc allies, it had troubles getting them to accept its trade and economic decisions, demonstrating the difficulty in creating a supranational authority that would decide who should produce what, where trade is to take place, and where factories are to be built. Subsequently, as the centrally planned economies were moving to join the world economy, CMEA disbanded in 1991 and has been replaced by the Organization for International Economic Cooperation, whose members trade with each other and other countries on an open market basis. In 1991 the members began trading among themselves with a convertible currency, thus removing a major barrier to freer trade with the rest of the world.

Economic and Marketing Implications

Marketers must pay attention to the effects of regional economic integration or cooperation because the competitive environment may drastically change over time. As in the case of the EC, although EC member countries still maintain their national identities, national borders are no longer trade barriers. Marketers must treat the EC as a single market rather than as twelve separate and fragmented markets while they rethink their marketing, finance, distribution, and production strategies. Foreign businesses need to make an effort to become familiar with new regulations so as to take full advantage in the changing market. For example, even though standard harmonization may exclude some U.S. firms from the EC markets, the United States should work to influence the process in order to turn the potential barrier into an advantage.[31]

Whereas countries that are not members of the EC view the EC's ambitious goals with some concern, outsider firms can still successfully cope with the *Europe 1992* program. Instead of viewing the EC's developments as obstacles, marketers should regard them as both challenges and opportunities. Not unlike coping with a single country's protectionist measures (except on a larger scale), the key to competing effectively in the EC is for an external firm to become an insider. General Electric Co. has formed joint ventures in major appliances and electrical equipment with Britain's largest electronics firm, has acquired France's largest medical equipment maker, and has planned to build a plastics factory in Spain. Coca-Cola has terminated some licensing agreements and has consolidated its European bottling operations to cut costs and prices. Using acquisitions to build up its European position, Sara Lee Corp. purchased a Dutch coffee and tea company and took control of Paris-based Dim, Europe's largest maker of pantyhose. In addition, Sara Lee has experimented with the "Euro-branding" strategy by putting several languages on a single package and distributing it to several countries.[32]

Initially, new trade policies generally tend to favor local business firms. For example, IBM encountered problems in Europe, where the EC members wanted to protect their own computer industry. Alternatively, outsider firms may be able to take advantage of the situation to overcome the barriers erected by a particular member of a regional economic cooperation. Facing France's troublesome entry procedure, Japan could first ship its VCRs into Germany before moving them more freely into France.

Because of the favorable economic environment in a cooperative region, additional firms desire entry and the competitive atmosphere intensifies. Firms inside the region are likely to be more competitive owing to the expansion of local markets, resulting in better economies of scale. External firms (those outside the area) are faced with overcoming trade barriers, perhaps through the establishment of local production facilities. For example, Ireland tried to attract foreign investment by mentioning in its advertisements that it is a member of the EC. Nike, a U.S. firm, was able to avoid the EC tariffs by opening a plant in Ireland. Foreign brands of sneakers that did not have local production facilities soon found that their products were too expensive in the EC. Exhibit 2–14 mentions business opportunities in Ireland.

Over time, a region will grow faster than before owing to the stimulation caused by trade creation effects, favorable policies, and more competition. But economic cooperation can create problems as well as opportunities within international markets. The expanded market offers more profit potential, but it may create an impression of collusion when subsidiaries or licensees are granted exclusive rights in certain member countries. The long-term result may be an areawide antitrust among new firms or nonmember countries wishing to trade within the economically integrated region.

Economic cooperation may either improve or impede international trade, depending on how the result of the cooperation is viewed. Economic integration encourages trade liberalization internally, while it promotes trade protection externally. An examination of eight FTAs and customs unions established over the past three decades reveals that those with stronger growth of internal trade had a similar economic structure and had substantially liberalized all trade.[33]

The tendency is for a member of an economic group to shift from the most efficient supplier in the world to the lowest supplier within that particular economic

DUBLIN, EUROPE'S NEW FINANCIAL SERVICES CENTER.

POWERED BY PEOPLE.

Irish people, educated, flexible, skilled, the main attraction for companies operating from Dublin's new International Financial Services Center.

Ireland with half it's population under 28 is rich in the resource that matters most in business today – skilled people. Furthermore, 55% of students in third level education choose engineering, science or business studies.

Add the most advanced digital telecommunications system in Europe and you will understand why the Dublin International Financial Services Center has already attracted more than 50 of the world's leading financial companies.

Companies like:
Alexander & Alexander Inc
American International
  Group
Chase Manhattan Bank
Citicorp
Scotia Bank

LEADING IRISH COMPANIES
SPONSORING THIS
ADVERTISEMENT INCLUDE;

Allied Irish Bank
Amdahl
Analog Devices B.V.
A.T. Cross Ltd
Bank of Ireland
Digital Equipment Corporation
L.M. Ericsson Holdings Ltd
GE Superabrasives
Janssen Pharmaceutical Ltd
Telecom Eireann
Wessel Industries Holdings Ltd

IDA Ireland
INDUSTRIAL DEVELOPMENT AUTHORITY

For information about business opportunities in Ireland contact IDA Ireland at:
NEW YORK: 2 Grand Central Towers, 140 East 45th Street, New York, NY 10017.
Tel: (212) 972 1000.
BOSTON: (617) 367 8225
ATLANTA: (404) 351 8474
CHICAGO: (312) 236 0222
LOS ANGELES: (213) 829 0081
SAN JOSE:(Calif.)(408) 294 9903

Head Office: Wilton Park House, Wilton Place, Dublin 2, Ireland.
Tel: (01) 686633

EXHIBIT 2–14   Ireland's comparative advantage

Source: Courtesy of IDA Ireland

region. Spain, upon joining the EC, was required to raise tariffs from 20 to 150 percent on feed grains grown outside the economic region. In effect, the action stopped Spain's imports of U.S. corn and sorghum. As such, trade creation among the partners is offset by trade diversion from the rest of the world, and the net effect may be either positive or negative.

Whether economic cooperation can improve the overall international marketing environment is somewhat debatable. On the one hand, trade among member nations flows more freely. On the other hand, trade between outsiders and members is more restricted because outsiders find the trade area much more difficult to pierce because of the trade barriers. In the balance, however, regional cooperation is seen as a hopeful sign that in the long run additional trade stimulation is likely to occur worldwide.

SYSTEMATIC PLANNING TO DETERMINE EXPORT OPPORTUNITIES

Because of the limitation of trade theories, a trade theory should be considered as a broad framework that merely describes trade in an ideal situation. For trade theories to be useful to those who investigate export opportunities, the framework must be modified to take into account more specific performance variables.

A good starting point for the determination of export opportunities is the identification of export barriers. Using factor analysis, Bauerschmidt, Sullivan, and Gillespie have identified five factors associated with export barriers, as perceived by executives of the U.S. paper industry: national export policy, comparative marketing distance, lack of export commitment, exogenous economic constraints (e.g., high value of U.S. dollar, high transportation costs), and competitive rivalry.[34] Table 2–6 shows mean responses for each type of export barrier. United States firms are least concerned with competitive rivalry. Their high appreciation of the importance of exogenous economic constraints, however, seems to imply that they believe there is nothing much they can do to affect their export performance. Not surprisingly, there is a lack of commitment to export activity.

It is incorrect for American executives to take the view that they cannot affect their firms' export performance. Another research study has identified German firms' export constraints (see Exhibit 2–15). By focusing on the foreign orientation of business managers, the study found that many small- and medium-sized firms with a primarily domestic focus could be turned into successful exporters.[35]

It is useful to identify the characteristics that differentiate export-oriented firms from those that are not so inclined. According to one study, systematic and nonsystematic exporting firms differ in terms of organizational, export marketing, and managerial characteristics.[36] In another study, sporadic exporters and regular exporters are similar in terms of size, age, and size of export orders. Differences exist in the areas of initial market-entry influences, export profit margins, export distribution channels, and information use. In addition to deriving a much higher proportion of their revenues in international markets, regular exporters have greater management involvement in export marketing. Also regular exporters are less likely than sporadic exporters to use domestic intermediaries, and they are more likely to exercise greater control in overseas marketing.[37]

TABLE 2–6 Responses to the questions concerning the importance of barriers affecting foreign trade

Barriers Affecting Foreign Trade	Number Responding	Not at all Important	Not very Important	Somewhat Important	Very Important	Extremely Important	Mean Response
Lack of U.S. government assistance in overcoming export barriers	114	22.8	33.3	24.6	11.4	7.9	2.5
Lack of U.S. tax incentives for exporters	113	22.1	30.1	23.9	18.6	5.9	2.5
High value of U.S. dollar relative to foreign currency	117	6.8	2.6	15.4	29.9	45.2	4.0
Aggressive enforcement of the U.S. Foreign Corrupt Practices Act	111	43.2	29.7	27.4	16.2	5.4	2.0
Risks involved in selling abroad	117	16.2	29.9	27.4	16.2	10.3	2.7
Management emphasis on developing domestic markets	113	15.9	23.9	14.2	37.2	8.9	3.0
Lack of available capital for expansion into foreign markets	113	36.3	35.4	17.7	8.6	1.8	2.0
Lack of productive capacity dedicated to sustain foreign markets	114	42.1	28.1	19.3	7.9	2.6	2.0
Language and cultural differences	113	37.2	32.7	16.8	10.6	2.7	2.1
Differences in product usage in foreign markets	112	25.9	26.8	32.1	12.5	2.7	2.4
Lack of foreign channels of distribution	114	21.9	25.4	23.7	24.6	4.4	2.6
Competition from local firms in foreign markets	114	32.5	25.4	19.3	15.8	7.0	2.4
Competition from U.S. firms in foreign markets	113	31.0	31.9	23.9	9.7	3.5	2.2
High transportation costs to reach foreign markets	116	8.6	6.0	22.4	40.5	22.4	3.6
Product specifications in foreign markets are different	117	23.1	26.5	31.6	14.5	4.3	2.5
High foreign tariffs on imported products	113	12.4	19.5	30.1	27.4	10.6	3.0
Confusing foreign import regulations and procedures	112	22.3	22.3	31.3	20.5	3.6	2.6

Source: Alan Bauerschmidt, Daniel Sullivan, and Kate Gillespie, "Common Factors Underlying Barriers to Export: Studies in the U.S. Paper Industry," Journal of International Business Studies 16 (Fall 1985): 116; reprinted with permission

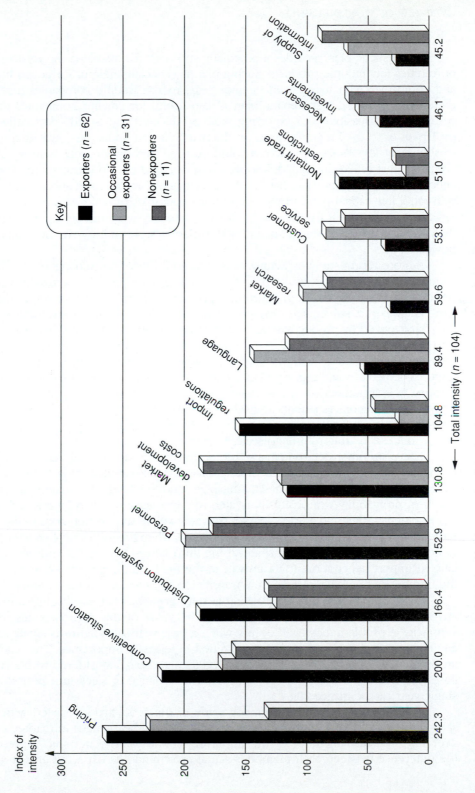

EXHIBIT 2–15 Export constraints perceived by German respondents

Note: The length of the columns is determined by the sum of weighted ranks, with no. 1 being awarded five points, rank no. 2, four points, and so forth. For comparison's sake, the resulting scores were standardized (n/N).

Source: Erwin Dichtl, Hans-Georg Koeglmayr, and Stefan Mueller, "International Orientation as a Precondition for Export Success," *Journal of International Business Studies* 20 (no. 1, 1990): 35

A systematic plan provides a pragmatic approach for assessing the relative opportunities for multiple products. Such a plan is especially helpful for governments and companies with many product lines (e.g., export trading companies and big multinational firms). A systematic plan is also useful for smaller companies in investigating the feasibility of exporting their products. Based on the data collected on Israeli exports of manufactured products in sixty-five industries, Ayal attempted to show that Israel's export success could be predicted by inherent industry characteristics that reflect another developed country's database (in this case, the United States). The findings indicate that the determinants of Israeli export success are high skill ratio, low capital per employee, and low economies of scale. The relationships indicated for low tariff barriers and low labor intensity were not strong, but nevertheless in the predicted direction, and both variables serve to improve the predictive power.[38]

A more recent study by Schneeweis focused on the determinants of U.S. trade patterns. According to the results, patents, research and development, and value added per employee are important in affecting export and import percentage within industries. High export percentage business units, especially in nonconsumer industries, are characterized by productivity and product development. On the other hand, import percentage is negatively related to value added per employee, patents, and capital intensity. Thus, business units with higher employee or capital productivity have lower import competition and higher relative export sales. Furthermore, research and development is accompanied by advertising and a temporary monopoly. Likewise, such market imperfections as patents and subsidies encourage export while insulating the units from import. Finally, economies of scale favor the export of products manufactured under increasing returns to scale.[39]

There are other determinants of the performance. Lecraw analyzed certain determinants of 153 transnational companies in six light-manufacturing industries in Indonesia, the Philippines, Malaysia, Singapore, and Thailand. The analysis revealed that firm profitability was positively related to advertising, intensity of research and development, tariffs, and a firm's market share, as well as the market share of the two largest firms in the industry. Profit tends to decline when the following characteristics exist: (1) an increase in market share of the third largest firm in the industry, (2) a gain in import penetration, (3) a growth in the firm's sales, and (4) an increase in the number of home countries of the transnational companies in the industry.[40]

Another approach involves looking at **sales growth**, whether absolute and relative, as an indicator of trade opportunity. The value of this approach lies in its simplicity. A problem, however, occurs when a base-year sales figure is small, since any increase is almost certain to be magnified in terms of importance. The result is an overstated opportunity for those products that are being considered with a small base-year figure. Thus, a heavy reliance on a net change in sales in a period of a single year can be misleading.

Shift-share analysis can remedy some of the problems associated with the sales growth method. A shift-share analysis emphasizes the changes in market share over time for each member of the importing countries. The net shift represents the difference between each member's actual growth and its expected growth (i.e., whether or not a member's growth rate had been equal to the entire group's average growth). Generally, a shift-share analysis tends to eliminate products with slow growth rates, mature or saturated market conditions, existing supplier-buyer relationships, and increased competition for an existing market, even though these products may seem promising under the sales growth method.[41]

Although each of these approaches is useful in identifying export opportunities, some caveats are in order. Each does have limitations, and the predictive power of one or another approach may only apply to the historical data under the time frame being considered. When possible, these approaches should be used in conjunction with one another, since the convergent results will serve to increase the confidence in the prediction of potential trade performance.

Policymakers should attempt to understand factors that affect trade performance. One study found that export knowledge, commitment, and the technological intensity of the exported product contribute to export success but that external support programs are viewed as a negative influence.[42] A study of 200 U.S. manufacturing industries found that high labor productivity and skill positively affects trade performance and that high labor content adversely affects such performance. The relative export success of those industries having a high level of capital outlays implies that government policies should encourage such expenditures. Investment tax credits and the liberalization of depreciation allowances should be implemented to foster modernization and replacement of obsolete plants and equipment. Because the United States does not fare well internationally in industries that have high labor content except when high-quality labor is involved, trade performance may be enhanced by converting to technologies that are less reliant on large numbers of unskilled workers. Conceivably, good educational policies, tax credits for on-the-job training, and retraining programs for displaced low-skill workers may improve U.S. export performance.[43]

Matsushita Electric Industrial Co. decided against locating a $400 million consumer electronics complex in Thailand because of the country's poorly developed infrastructure (e.g., inadequate port facilities at Bangkok).[44] Because of a lack of planning as well as Bangkok being the center of government and business activities, Thailand's traffic congestion is among the worst in the world. Hosting the annual meetings of the World Bank and the International Monetary Fund in Bangkok in October 1991, the Thai government wanted to impress delegates from all over the world as well as to make certain that they could get to meetings on time. The government thus solved the traffic problems, at least temporarily, by declaring the meeting dates as legal holidays and by ordering banks, schools, and government offices to close.

There is a positive relationship between public works expenditures and productivity. Exhibit 2–16 shows that countries sustaining a high level of public investment relative to output experience higher productivity growth than countries that do not invest in infrastructure. Japan has invested about 5.1 percent of output in public facilities and was awarded with a productivity growth of 3.3 percent. The United States, at the other end of the spectrum, has had a low public investment of 0.3 percent per year, which has been accompanied by a low productivity growth of 0.6 percent per annum. "Thus, a root cause of the decline in the competitiveness of the United States

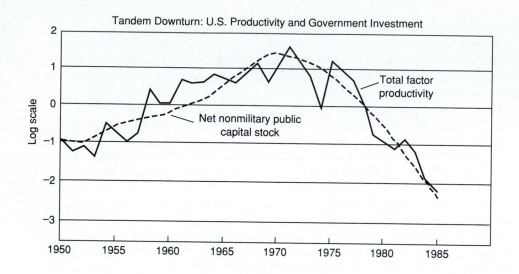

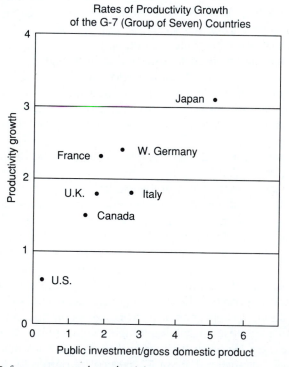

EXHIBIT 2–16 Infrastructure and productivity

Source: David Alan Aschauer, "Rx for Productivity: Build Infrastructure," *Chicago Fed Letter,* September 1988

in the international economy may be found in the low rate at which our country has chosen to add to its stock of highways, port facilities, airports, and other facilities which aid in the production and distribution of goods and services. Just as thoughtful athletes would not think of neglecting their health for fear of failing to compete well on the playing field, we as a country should be vitally concerned with the viability of our economic lifelines that enable us to meet the challenge of an increasingly competitive world marketplace."[45]

CONCLUSION

For countries to want to trade with one another, they must be better off with trade than without it. The principles of absolute and relative advantage explain how trade enables trading nations to increase their welfare through specialization. Trade allows a country to concentrate on the production of products with the best potential for its own consumption as well as for export, resulting in a more efficient and effective use of its resources.

Absolute production costs are not as relevant as relative costs in determining whether trade should take place and what products to export or import. Basically, a country should specialize in making a product in which it has the greatest comparative advantage. If no comparative advantage exists, there will be no trade, since there is no difference in relative production costs between the two countries (i.e., a situation of equal relative advantage).

Comparative advantage is not determined solely by labor but rather by the required factors of production necessary to produce the product in question. This advantage is often determined by an abundance of a particular production factor in the country. Thus, it is advantageous for a country to export a product that requires an abundant factor as a major production input.

Trade theories, in spite of their usefulness, simply explain what nations should do rather than describe what nations actually do. The desired trade pattern based on those theories related to comparative advantage and factor endowment often deviates significantly from the actual trade practice. It is thus necessary to modify the theories to account for the divergence caused by extraneous variables. Industrial nations' high income levels for instance may foster a preference for high-quality products that LDCs may be unable to supply. Furthermore, trade restrictions, a norm rather than an exception, heavily influence the extent and direction of trade, and any investigation is not complete without taking tariffs, quotas, and other trade barriers into consideration.

Perhaps the most serious problem with classical trade theories is their failure to incorporate marketing activities into the analysis. It is inappropriate to assume that consumers' tastes are homogeneous across national markets and that such tastes can be largely satisfied by commodities that are also homogeneous. Marketing activities such as distribution and promotion add more value to a product, and the success of the product is often determined by the planning and execution of such activities.

QUESTIONS

1. Is trade a zero-sum game or a positive-sum game?
2. Explain (a) the principle of absolute advantage and (b) the principle of relative advantage.
3. Should there be trade if (a) a country has an absolute advantage for *all* products over its trading partner and (b) if the domestic exchange ratio of one country is identical to that of another country?
4. What is the theory of factor endowment?
5. Explain the Leontief Paradox.
6. Discuss the validity and limitations of trade theories.
7. Distinguish among (a) free trade area, (b) customs union, (c) common market, (d) economic and monetary union, and (e) political union.
8. Does economic cooperation improve or impede trade?
9. Briefly explain these methods to determine export opportunities: (a) sales growth method and (b) shift-share analysis.

DISCUSSION ASSIGNMENTS AND MINICASES

1. Name products or industries in which the United States has a comparative advantage as well as those in which it has a comparative disadvantage.
2. Why is it beneficial for the well-endowed, resource-rich United States to trade with other nations?
3. For a country with high labor cost, how can it improve its export competitiveness?
4. Explain how the United States should cope with the shift in comparative advantage.

CASE 2–1
TRADE STRATEGIES
Inward or Outward?

SARATH RAJAPATIRANA
The World Bank

Economists and policymakers in the developing countries have long agreed on the role of government in providing infrastructure, promoting market efficiency, and maintaining stable macroeconomic policies. But they have disagreed on trade strategies that have enabled countries to attain high growth and develop their industrial potential.

OUTWARD- AND INWARD-ORIENTED POLICIES

Trade policies can be characterized as outwardly oriented or inwardly oriented. An outward-oriented strategy provides incentives that are neutral between production for the domestic market and exports. Because international trade is not positively discouraged, this approach is often, though somewhat misleadingly, referred to as export promotion. In fact, the essence of an outward-oriented strategy is neither discrimination in favor of exports nor bias against import substitution. An inward-oriented strategy, on the other hand, is one in which trade and industrial incentives are biased in favor of domestic production and against foreign trade. This approach is often referred to as an import-substitution strategy.

An inward-oriented strategy usually involves overt and high protection. This makes exports uncompetitive by raising the costs of the foreign inputs used in their production. Moreover, an increase in the relative costs of domestic inputs may also occur through inflation—or because of an appreciation of the exchange rate—as the quantitative import restrictions are introduced. Industrial incentives are administered by an elaborate and extensive bureaucracy.

Outward-oriented policies favor tariffs over quantitative restrictions. These tariffs are usually counterbalanced by other measures, including production subsidies and the provision of inputs at free trade prices. Governments seek to keep the exchange rate at a level that maintains equal incentives to produce exports and import substitutes. Overall protection is lower under an outward-oriented strategy than under inward orientation; equally important, the spread between the highest and lowest rates of protection is narrower.

Exhibit 1 is a classification of forty-one developing countries based on trade orientation.

EXHIBIT 1   Classification of developing economies by trade orientation

Outward-oriented		Inward-oriented	
Strongly	Moderately	Moderately	Strongly
		1963–73	
Hong Kong	Brazil	Bolivia	Argentina
Korea,	Cameroon	El Salvador	Bangladesh
Rep. of	Colombia	Honduras	Burundi
Singapore	Costa Rica	Kenya	Chile
	Ivory Coast	Madagascar	Dominican Rep.
	Guatemala	Mexico	Ethiopia
	Indonesia	Nicaragua	Ghana
	Israel	Nigeria	India
	Malaysia	Philippines	Pakistan
	Thailand	Senegal	Peru
		Tunisia	Sri Lanka
		Yugoslavia	Sudan
			Tanzania
			Turkey
			Uruguay
			Zambia
		1973–85	
Hong Kong	Brazil	Cameroon	Argentina
Korea,	Chile	Colombia	Bangladesh
Rep. of	Israel	Costa Rica	Bolivia
Singapore	Malaysia	Ivory Coast	Burundi
	Thailand	El Salvador	Dominican Rep.
	Tunisia	Guatemala	Ethiopia
	Turkey	Honduras	Ghana
	Uruguay	Indonesia	India
		Kenya	Madagascar
		Mexico	Nigeria
		Nicaragua	Peru
		Pakistan	Sudan
		Philippines	Tanzania
		Senegal	Zambia
		Sri Lanka	
		Yugoslavia	

Questions

1. Which trade policy (inward-oriented or outward-oriented) has fostered greater economic success? Base the answer on actual performance and pragmatic considerations, not just theoretical criteria.
2. Offer an explanation why governments of developing countries are usually hesitant to undertake trade policy reforms to achieve outward-oriented strategies.

Source: This case was abbreviated and adapted from Sarath Rajapatirana, "Industrialization and Foreign Trade," *Finance & Development* (September 1987): 2–5.

CASE 2–2
THE NEW EUROPE

Owing to the political and economic changes that will characterize Europe through-out the 1990s, doing business in Europe will never be the same. Consider the follow-ing facts. First, Eastern European countries have begun to introduce market opening mechanisms as well as Western-style commercial relationships. Second, the European Community (EC) grew by 17 million Germans in October 1990. Third, just like U.S. and EC businesses, Japan and the European Free Trade Association countries doubled their acquisitions in the EC in 1989 and 1990 relative to 1985. Fourth, four countries applied in 1990 to join the EC, and several more countries are expected to become part of the bloc in the 1990s.

The EC's 1992 program is an ambitious attempt to achieve a unified European market with the free movement of goods, capital, and people. The program will har-monize market conditions on an EC-wide basis, resulting in a more open, competitive marketplace. The elimination of national frontiers should provide the impetus for Eu-ropean economic growth. Toward this goal, the EC has worked to eradicate all the national legal barriers to trade and create a single market of 345 million people, thus deregulating many national and product markets.

In the past, the EC was marked by a set of distinct national markets dominated by local producers. For European consumers, the elimination of national barriers and stronger European competition will mean better access to a wide range of products at lower prices. To capitalize on new market opportunities, European businesses will initially move from their traditional national bases across borders into new national markets—previously closed to outside competition by trade barriers. Responding to the opening of new markets, the European private sector is developing new business strategies, new distribution systems, new computerized support systems, and new business alliances.

The United States worked to ensure that the EC's 1992 program would result in a more open market—not just internally to European companies but also externally. As pointed out by the United States, Europe can prosper in the evolving world economy by opening itself to global competition in a way that forces European companies to become leaner and more effective.

The EC is now the largest market in the world for American products (see Exhibit 2). Exports from the United States to the EC in 1990 totaled close to $100 billion, an amount considerably ahead of the roughly $85 billion of American exports to Canada. Four-fifths of U.S. exports to the EC are manufactured goods, valued at approximately $80 billion for 1990; this amount was more than two and a half times as much as American manufacturers exported to Japan. Actually, just the growth of U.S. manufactured goods exports to the EC since 1987 exceeded the United States's total exports of manufactured goods to Japan in 1990. American firms in 1990 exported more than $8 billion in aerospace equipment to the EC, over $6 billion of automated data processing equipment, over $2 billion of coal, and over $1.5 billion of medical equipment. More than 80 percent of all U.S. companies exporting to the EC are small- and medium-sized firms. Because the single market makes it easier to sell throughout the nearly $5 trillion Community economy, the outlook is for continued growth in U.S. exports to the EC.

American exporters and investors in Europe will be affected as EC markets adjust to a changing business environment, stronger competition, and the development of EC companies capable of competing not only in the single continental market but also in the U.S. and other third-country markets. For U.S. businesses, these changes mean new commercial opportunities as well as sharper competition from new players; U.S. businesses need to realize that the opportunities and challenges in Europe require close attention and new Europe-wide business strategies.

Questions

1. Discuss the obstacles and opportunities presented by the European Community market.
2. Although the EC has denied that there is any intent to create an economic "Fortress Europe," how should Japanese and American firms adjust their marketing strategies to meet the challenges?
3. Assess the likelihood that the EC will be able to establish a political union.

Source: This case was adapted from the following sources: J. Michael Farren, "Opportunities and Challenges in the New European Market," *Business America,* 25 February 1991, 6–7; Thomas J. Duesterberg, "Prepare Now for the 1992 Export Market," *Business America,* 25 February 1991, 8–9; and Don Linville, "Marketing in Europe in 1992," *Business America,* 15 January 1990, 14–15.

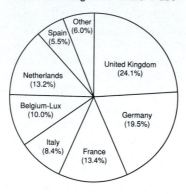

U.S. Exports to EC Countries
As a Percentage of U.S.-EC Trade

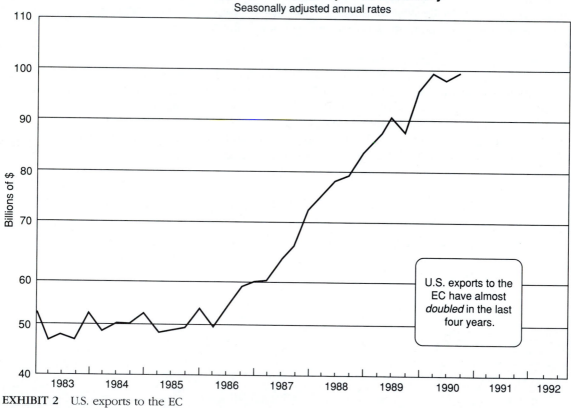

U.S. Exports to the European Community

Seasonally adjusted annual rates

U.S. exports to the
EC have almost
doubled in the last
four years.

EXHIBIT 2 U.S. exports to the EC

Source: Thomas J. Duesterberg, "Prepare Now for the 1992 Export Market," *Business America,* 25 February 1991, 9

CASE 2–3
THE NEW NORTH AMERICA

Based on 1989 data, the new North America is a market of 362 million consumers, a GNP of $5.9 trillion, and total trade of $225 billion: in terms of *population*, the figures are 250 million for the United States, 26 million for Canada, and 86 million for Mexico. In terms of *GNP*, the figures are $5.23 trillion for the United States, $463 billion for Canada, and $201 billion for Mexico. The *trade figures* are $171 billion for U.S.-Canada, $52 billion for U.S.-Mexico, and $2.3 billion for Canada-Mexico.

Canada's locus of economic activity has always been along the U.S. border, which stretches some four thousand miles. It is not too surprising that the natural axis of trade has always been from north to south rather than east to west (see Exhibit 3). The Free Trade Agreement (FTA), having taken effect on January 1, 1989, provides further stimulus for cross-border trade and investment.

U.S.-Mexican Trade

The United States is Mexico's most important trading partner, absorbing about two-thirds of total Mexican exports worldwide. Mexico was the third largest U.S. trading partner in 1989, ranking after Canada and Japan. Mexico supplied 6 percent of total U.S. imports and accounted for 7 percent of total U.S. exports.

The U.S. trade balance with Mexico was in deficit for most of the 1980s. The deficit reached a peak of $7.7 billion in 1983. Since then, the deficit has been on a downward trend, falling to $2.2 billion in 1989—the lowest annual deficit in the decade. The U.S. trade balance with Mexico has yet to return to the modest U.S. surpluses of the 1970s and early 1980s.

By far, Mexico is the largest U.S. trading partner in Latin America. Mexico accounts for about one-half of U.S. exports to and imports from the region. In 1989 the

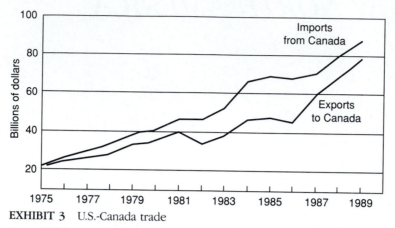

EXHIBIT 3   U.S.-Canada trade

Source: William A. Testa, "Two Good Neighbors Lower Their Fences," *Chicago Fed Letter* (September 1990), 3

$2.2 billion U.S. trade deficit with Mexico—accounting for about one-fifth of the U.S. deficit with the region—ranked behind the deficits with Venezuela ($3.8 billion) and Brazil ($3.6 billion).

Recent Aggregate Trade Trends

The United States's exports to Mexico reached a peak of $25 billion in 1989, making it the third largest U.S. export market (behind Canada and Japan). Export growth was particularly robust in 1989, showing a 21 percent gain over the 1988 level. However, it had been uneven in the 1980s and did not surpass the previous peak of $17.7 billion in 1981 until 1988 (and was then only 16 percent higher), largely because of the Mexican debt crisis.

In contrast, U.S. imports from Mexico more than doubled over the decade, hitting a peak of $27.2 billion in 1989. As in the case of exports, imports showed strong growth in 1989, increasing 17 percent over the 1988 level. Mexico ranks as the third largest foreign supplier to the U.S. market (behind Japan and Canada).

An important stimulus to the growth of U.S.-Mexican trade in the 1980s was U.S. and Mexican programs that encourage cross-border sharing of production. On the U.S. side, production-sharing provisions under Harmonized Tariff Schedule (HS) subheadings 9802.00.60 and 9802.00.80 (formerly TSUSA items 806/807) suspend the duties on the U.S. content of imported goods, applying duties only on the foreign value-added. In 1989 nearly $12 billion, or almost one-fourth of U.S. bilateral trade with Mexico, took place under HS 9802 provisions. Virtually all of this trade was in the manufactures sector, especially the automotive and electrical equipment sectors. On the Mexican side, the maquiladora program effectively suspends Mexican import duties on production-related intermediate goods (e.g., machinery and components) incorporated into exports. Factors that have led to the growth of U.S.-Mexican exports more recently have been relatively fast Mexican economic growth, Mexico's economic and trade liberalization, and a favorable exchange rate for the Mexican peso.

Mexican exports to the United States have also benefited from provisions of the Generalized System of Preferences (GSP) program, which provides for duty-free treatment for selected imports from developing countries. In 1989 about 10 percent of Mexican exports to the United States—primarily manufactures—benefited from GSP treatment. Major U.S. imports from Mexico receiving GSP include furniture, household electrical appliances, float glass, toys, games, and sporting goods.

Expanded U.S. market access has been given to some Mexican exports in recognition of Mexico's market liberalization measures. U.S.-Mexican bilateral steel trade is governed by the Agreement on Steel Trade Liberalization. Textile and apparel trade is regulated by bilateral agreement and the Multifiber Arrangement (MFA). Bilateral agricultural trade also has been affected by U.S. quotas and other constraints as well as Mexican trade barriers.

Given the proximity of the U.S. and Mexican markets, a large degree of trade occurs between U.S. firms and their affiliates in Mexico. Nearly 40 percent of U.S. manufactures trade with Mexico in 1987 was between related parties. Moreover, about 70 percent of all bilateral trade is intra-industry—that is, exports and imports tend to be in the same product category.

Commodity Trade

Manufactures predominate in U.S.-Mexican trade, comprising over 80 percent of U.S. exports to Mexico and 74 percent of total U.S. imports. In contrast to exports, the importance of manufactures in U.S. imports from Mexico has grown dramatically since 1980, when manufactures accounted for only 35 percent of U.S. imports. The share of manufactures in U.S.-Mexican trade is substantially higher than the share of manufactures in U.S. trade with other countries at Mexico's level of development. A peak manufactures trade surplus of $9.2 billion in 1981 declined in subsequent years, turning into a small deficit in 1986. By 1989 U.S. manufactures trade posted a $0.9 billion surplus.

Within manufactures, trade in high-technology products with Mexico accounted for about 20 percent of both U.S. exports to and imports from Mexico in 1988 (latest available data). By far, communications equipment and electronic components are the largest category of U.S. high-tech trade with Mexico—about 50 percent of U.S. high-tech exports and 70 percent of U.S. imports. Automatic data processing equipment and parts are also important, accounting for 14 percent of high-tech exports and 12 percent of imports in 1988. The U.S. balance in high-tech trade with Mexico deteriorated in the 1980s, swinging from a $1.5 billion surplus in 1980 to a $0.4 billion deficit in 1988.

In recent years, the largest bilateral trade category has been electrical and non-electrical machinery (both high-tech and non-high-tech), primarily electrical switches, cable and optical fibers, ADP equipment and parts, pipe valves, and TV and radio receivers.

About one-third of U.S. exports and almost 40 percent of U.S. imports in 1989 fell into this grouping. Much of the growth in this trade is due to U.S. and Mexican incentives for cross-border production sharing.

In 1989 auto parts were the single largest U.S. export item to Mexico and the fourth largest import item (see Exhibit 4). In the 1980s Mexico consistently was the second biggest (after Canada) and the fastest growing market for U.S. auto parts. On the more inclusive end-use basis, Mexico bought $646 million worth of auto

Manufactures Account for Over 80 Percent
Of U.S. Exports to Mexico

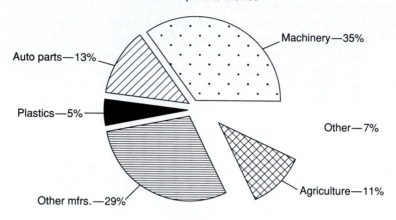

Machinery—35%

Auto parts—13%

Plastics—5%

Other—7%

Agriculture—11%

Other mfrs.—29%

1989 U.S. exports
$25.0 billion

Machinery, Petroleum, and Auto Parts Are
Prominent in U.S. Imports from Mexico

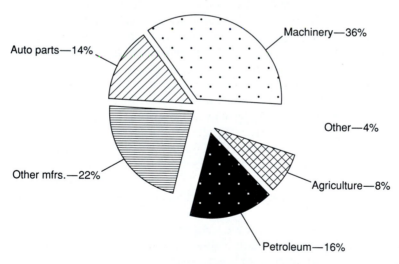

Machinery—36%

Auto parts—14%

Other—4%

Agriculture—8%

Other mfrs.—22%

Petroleum—16%

1989 U.S. imports
$27.2 billion

EXHIBIT 4   U.S. exports to Mexico and U.S. imports from Mexico

Source: Gary Teske, "U.S. Trade with Mexico in Perspective," *Business America,* 18 June 1990, 21–22

parts in 1983, a 7.2 percent export share, and $3.2 billion in 1989, a 19.5 percent export share. Mexico also is a major source of auto parts imports, ranking as the fourth largest supplier in 1989, with $3.8 billion in U.S. sales and a 12.3 percent import share. Again, the growth in bilateral auto parts trade has benefited largely from U.S. and Mexican incentives for cross-border production sharing. Maquiladora companies assemble U.S. parts and components into components and finished goods in Mexico, which are shipped back to the United States.

Petroleum consistently was the single largest U.S. import item from Mexico in the 1980s. In 1989 oil and petroleum products accounted for about 16 percent of total U.S. imports from Mexico, making Mexico the fourth largest supplier of petroleum to the United States. The importance of petroleum in U.S. imports from Mexico fell dramatically in the 1980s.

In 1989 Mexico was the third largest single market for U.S. agricultural exports, importing $2.8 billion of U.S. agricultural goods. At the same time, Mexico was the second largest supplier of U.S. agricultural imports, exporting nearly $2.3 billion of agricultural goods to the United States. The United States primarily exports bulk commodities to Mexico, such as corn, cereals, and soybeans, and imports tropical products and specialty crops, such as coffee, fruits, nuts, and tomatoes.

Importance of U.S. Trade to Mexico

Trade with the United States is vital to Mexico. Both imports to and exports from the United States in 1989 accounted for roughly two-thirds of Mexico's total trade with all countries. In terms of manufactures, the percentages are even higher. Although greatly reduced in 1989, Mexico's surplus in its trade with the United States—averaging almost 60 percent of its global trade surplus during 1985–88—has been indispensable in enabling Mexico to meet its debt-servicing obligations. Moreover, in 1988, Mexican exports to the United States contributed an estimated 13 percent of Mexican GNP.

Questions

1. Why do some U.S. economists and organized labor oppose the formation of the North American Free Trade Agreement (NAFTA) involving the United States, Canada, and Mexico? Why is it that they strongly object to the U.S.-Mexico Free Trade Agreement but not the U.S.-Canada Free Trade Agreement (CFTA)?
2. Discuss the merits and flaws of the arguments of those who oppose the U.S.-Mexico Free Trade Agreement.
3. What are the benefits of the North American Free Trade Agreement to the three participants?
4. In your opinion, should the United States implement the North American Free Trade Agreement?

Source: This case was largely based on Gary Teske, "U.S. Trade with Mexico in Perspective," *Business America*, 18 June 1990, 20–22

NOTES

1. Gerald M. Meier, *International Economics: The Theory of Policy* (New York: Oxford University Press, 1980), 57.

2. Peter H. Lindert and Charles P. Kindleberger, *International Economics,* 7th ed. (Homewood, IL: Irwin, 1982), 26.

3. Adam Smith, *Wealth of Nations* (1776; reprint, Homewood, IL: Irwin, 1963).

4. David Ricardo, *The Principles of Political Economy and Taxation* (1817; reprint, Baltimore: Penguin, 1971).

5. H. Robert Heller, *International Trade Theory and Empirical Evidence,* 2nd ed. (Englewood Cliffs, NJ: Prentice-Hall, 1973).

6. Bill Cunningham, "Don't Blame U.S. Uncompetitiveness on Wages," *The Wall Street Journal,* 29 November 1989.

7. Eli Heckscher, "The Effects of Foreign Trade on the Distribution of Income," in *Readings in the Theory of International Trade,* ed. Howard S. Ellis and Lloyd A. Matzler (Homewood, IL: Irwin, 1949); Bertil Ohlin, *Interregional and International Trade* (Cambridge, MA: Harvard University Press, 1933).

8. Christopher Knowlton, "The New Export Entrepreneurs," *Fortune,* 6 June 1988, 89 ff.

9. Wilfred Ethier, *Modern International Economics* (New York: Norton, 1983), 40.

10. G. D. A. MacDougall, "British and American Exports: A Study Suggested by the Theory of Comparative Costs," *Economic Journal* (December 1951); Robert Stern, "British and American Productivity and Comparative Costs in International Trade," *Oxford Economic Papers* (October 1962); Bela Balassa, "An Empirical Demonstration of Classical Comparative Cost Theory," *The Review of Economics and Statistics* (August 1963).

11. Ethier, *Modern International Economics,* 24.

12. Jagdish Bhagwati, "The Pure Theory of International Trade: A Survey," *Economic Journal* (March 1964).

13. Wassily W. Leontief, "Domestic Production and Foreign Trade: The American Capital Position Re-examined," *Proceedings of the American Philosophical Society,* September 1953; Wassily W. Leontief, "Factor Proportions and the Structure of American Trade: Further Theoretical and Empirical Analysis," *Review of Economics and Statistics* 38 (November 1956): 386–407.

14. Heller, *International Trade Theory,* 70.

15. Keith E. Maskus, "A Test of the Heckscher-Ohlin-Vanek Theorem: The Leontief Commonplace," *Journal of International Economics* 19 (November 1985): 201–12.

16. International Monetary Fund, *Direction of Trade Statistics,* 1991 Yearbook.

17. Jack L. Hervey, "Changing U.S. Trade Patterns," *Economic Perspectives* (March/April 1990): 2–12.

18. Michael Porter, *The Competitive Advantage of Nations* (New York: Free Press, 1990).

19. "Trade Specialist Calls Current Rules Outdated," *IMF Survey,* 15 July 1991, 209, 216.

20. Heller, *International Trade Theory,* 5.

21. Shujiro Urata, "Factor Inputs and Japanese Manufacturing Trade Structure," *The Review of Economics and Statistics* 65 (November 1983): 678–84.

22. Alex O. Williams, *International Trade and Investment: A Managerial Approach* (New York: Wiley, 1982), 40.

23. William L. Givens, "The U.S. Can No Longer Afford Free Trade," *Business Week,* 22 November 1982, 15.

24. "Hong Kong's End Run Around U.S. Protectionism," *Business Week,* 26 August 1985, 45.

25. "Economists Discuss Transition to Market-Oriented Economies," *IMF Survey,* 4 February 1991, 34–37.

26. J. E. Meade, *Trade and Welfare* (New York: Oxford University Press, 1955); R. G. Lipsey and K. Lancaster, "The General Theory of Second Best," *Review of Economic Studies* 24 (1956), 11–32; Meier, *International Economics.*

27. "Delors Report Suggests Step-by-Step Process of European Integration," *IMF Survey,* 10 July 1989, 209, 219.

28. "Report Highlights Benefits of Economic and Monetary Union in Europe." *IMF Survey,* 26 November 1990, 363–65.

29. Nancy Worth, "U.K. Official Urges Caution on Economic and Monetary Union," *IMF Survey,* 29 April 1991, 143–44.

30. See Paul Craig Roberts, "Europe 1992: Free Market or Free Lunch?" *Business Week,* 4 June 1990, 26; Don Linville, "EC Labor Policy—1992," *Business America,* 25 February 1991, 29.

31. Michael Dowling and Alfred Leidner, "Technical Standards and 1992: Opportunity or Entry Barrier in the New Europe?" *Columbia Journal of World Business* 25 (Fall 1990): 50–56.

32. Steven Greenhouse, "U.S. Companies See 1992 as Opportunity," *San Jose Mercury News,* 26 March 1989.

33. "Multilateral Negotiations Are Preferable to Free Trade Areas," *IMF Survey,* 14 November 1988, 362–64.

34. Alan Bauerschmidt, Daniel Sullivan, and Kate Gillespie, "Common Factors Underlying Barriers to Export: Studies in the U.S. Paper Industry," *Journal of International Business Studies* 16 (Fall 1985): 111–23.

35. Erwin Dichtl, Hans-Georg Koeglmayr, and Stefan Mueller, "International Orientation as a Precondition for Export Success," *Journal of International Business Studies* 21 (no. 1, 1990): 23–40.

36. Dimitris Bourantas and John Halikias, "Discriminating Variables between Systematic and Non-Systematic Exporting Manufacturing Firms in Greece," *Journal of Global Marketing* 4 (no. 2, 1991): 21–38.

37. Saeed Samiee and Peter G. P. Walters, "Segmenting Corporate Exporting Activities: Sporadic versus Regular Exporters," *Journal of the Academy of Marketing Science* 19 (Spring 1991): 93–104.

38. Igal Ayal, "Industry-Export Performance: Assessment and Prediction," *Journal of Marketing* 46 (Summer 1982): 54–61.

39. Thomas Schneeweis, "A Note on International Trade and Market Structure," *Journal of International Business Studies* 16 (Summer 1985): 139–52.

40. Donald J. Lecraw, "Performance of Transnational Corporations in Less Developed Countries," *Journal of International Business Studies* 14 (Spring/Summer 1983): 15–33.

41. Robert T. Green and Arthur W. Allaway, "Identification of Export Opportunities: A Shift-Share Approach," *Journal of Marketing* 49 (Winter 1985): 83–88.

42. Ven Sriram, James Neelankavil, and Russell Moore, "Export Policy and Strategy Implications for Small-to-Medium Sized Firms," *Journal of Global Marketing* 3 (no. 2, 1989): 43–60.

43. Michael Ursic and Clark Wiseman, "The Relation of Key Industrial Characteristics to Trade Performance," *Journal of Global Marketing* 3 (no. 1, 1989): 55–67.

44. Christopher Mead, "Asia Connection," *San Jose Mercury News,* 5 September 1988.

45. David Alan Aschauer, "Rx for Productivity: Build Infrastructure," *Chicago Fed Letter,* September 1988.

What protection teaches us is to do to ourselves in time of peace what enemies seek to do to us in time of war.

Henry George

Trade Distortions and Marketing Barriers

3

CHAPTER OUTLINE

MARKETING ILLUSTRATION
The Best Things in Life Are (Not) Free

South Korean buyers of high-priced foreign cars can expect special attention from the Korean tax unit. As a result, the sales of the Mercury Sable tumbled from between 200 and 300 per month to fewer than 100 per month. Korean customs officials frequently delay or reject imports of consumer items. One batch of U.S. cosmetics was held for eight months for "testing." Fresh foods (e.g., oranges and strawberries) often take five days and sometimes four months to clear customs. Consumer durables (e.g., refrigerators) are prohibitively expensive because of tariffs and taxes. Even dried peas are classified as luxury goods. Not surprisingly, consumer goods accounted for only 6 percent of U.S. exports to Korea in 1989.

A comic book titled *Our Body and Soul* was distributed in South Korea's primary schools. The book depicts a teacher telling his students to urge their mothers not to buy imports. Students were also told that farm products from abroad contain poisonous chemicals, antibiotics, and radioactivity. The government justified its campaign against imports by arguing that it was merely responding to a widely supported social movement against the consumption of luxury items, based on the traditional Confucian value of frugality. Korean officials claimed that the middle and lower classes were growing resentful of the increasingly obvious disparity between Korea's rich and poor and that its goal was to curb extravagant purchases and not necessarily imports.

Free trade makes a great deal of sense theoretically because it increases efficiency and economic welfare for all involved nations and their citizens. South Korea's trade barriers, however, do not represent an isolated case. In practice, free trade is woefully ignored by virtually all countries. Despite the advantages, nations are inclined to discourage free trade. The 216-page *1990 National Trade Estimate Report on Foreign Trade Barriers*, issued by the U.S. Trade Representative, defines trade barriers as "government laws, regulations, policies, or practices that either protect domestic producers from foreign competition or artificially stimulate exports of particular domestic products." Restrictive business practices and government regulations designed to protect public health and national security are not considered as trade barriers; The report classifies the trade barriers of thirty-five countries, the EC, and the Gulf Cooperation Council into eight categories: (1) import policies (e.g., tariffs, quotas, licensing, and customs barriers); (2) standards, testing, labeling, and certification; (3) government procurement; (4) export subsidies; (5) lack of intellectual property protection; (6) services barriers (e.g., restrictions on the use of foreign data processing); (7) investment barriers; and (8) other barriers. The report provides estimates of how much a country's particular barrier hurt U.S. exports. A more extensive listing, *Trade Policies and Market Opportunities for U.S. Farm Exports,* is published annually by the U.S. Department of Agriculture.

Sources: "Seoul's Crackdown on Imports May Be a Luxury It Can't Afford," *Business Week*, 21 January 1991, 46; Paul Blustein, "Korean Comic Book Is No Joke to U.S. Firms," *San Jose Mercury News,* 28 December 1990

This chapter catalogs the types and impact of marketing barriers. It examines trade restrictions and the rationale, if any, behind them. By understanding these barriers, marketers should be in a better position to cope with them. It would be impossible to list all marketing barriers because they are simply too numerous. Furthermore, governments are forever creating new import restrictions or adjusting the ones currently in use. For purposes of study, marketing barriers can be divided into two basic categories: tariffs and nontariff barriers. Exhibit 3–1 provides details for this division. Each category and its subcategories will be discussed in this chapter.

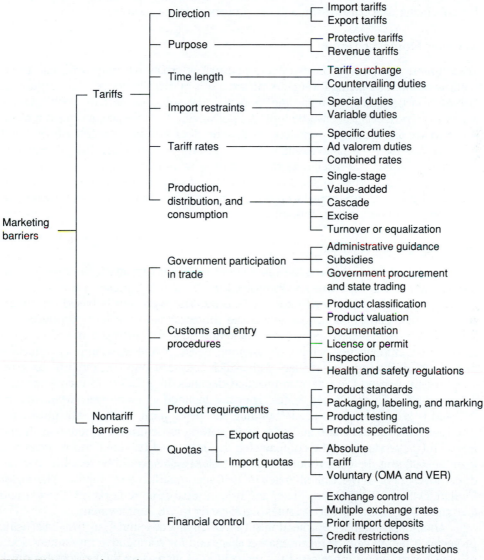

EXHIBIT 3–1 Marketing barriers

Source: Adapted from Sak Onkvisit and John J. Shaw, "Marketing Barriers in International Trade," *Business Horizons* 31 (May–June 1988): 64–72

PROTECTION OF LOCAL INDUSTRIES

Why do nations impede free trade when the inhibition is irrational? One reason why governments interfere with free marketing is to protect local industries, often at the expense of local consumers as well as consumers worldwide. Regulations are created to keep out or hamper the entry of foreign-made products. Arguments for the protection of local industries usually take one of the following forms: (1) keeping money at home, (2) reducing unemployment, (3) equalizing cost and price, (4) enhancing national security, and (5) protecting infant industry.

Keeping Money at Home

Trade unions and protectionists often argue that international trade will lead to an outflow of money, making foreigners richer and local people poorer. This argument is based on the fallacy of regarding money as the sole indicator of wealth. Other assets, even products, can also be indicators of wealth. For instance, it does not make sense to say that a man is poor just because he does not have much cash on hand when he has many valuable assets such as land and jewelry. Also, this protectionist argument assumes that foreigners receive money without having to give something of value in return. Whether local consumers buy locally made or foreign products, they will have to spend money to pay for such products. In either case, they receive something of value for their money.

Reducing Unemployment

It is a standard practice for trade unions and politicians to attack imports and international trade in the name of job protection.[1] Exhibit 3–2 presents this argument as made by the United Steelworkers of America. The argument is based on the assumption that import reduction will create more demand for local products and subsequently create more jobs. Most marketing analysts see this kind of thinking as one-sided, though not completely without merits. At the least, import reduction makes foreigners earn less dollars with which they can buy U.S. exports. As a result, foreign demand for American products declines. In addition, foreign firms may refuse to invest in the United States. They are inclined to invest only when import demand is great enough to justify building and using local facilities. Mitsubishi, for example, used market share and sales as its criteria to determine whether it should invest in U.S. production. The company felt that its annual U.S. sales had to exceed at least 240,000 units before production in the United States would be feasible. Foreign direct investment in the United States in 1990 amounted to $427 billion. The major foreign investors in the United States are: Britain, Japan, the Netherlands, Canada, and Germany. The investment contributes significantly to U.S. employment.

Another problem with protectionism is that it may lead to inflation. Instead of using protective relief to gain or regain market share and for competitive investment, local manufacturers often cannot resist the temptation of increasing their prices for quick profits. According to the Institute for International Economics, quotas enabled many U.S. industries in 1986 to earn extra profits from higher prices. These extra profits are substantial: apparel ($3.5 billion), steel ($2.8 billion), and automobiles ($2.5 billion).

THE TARGET IS YOU

Today, It's Steel. Tomorrow It Could Be Your Industry, Your Job.

U.S. Steel and British Steel plan to finish their negotiations by the end of November on a far-reaching plan to change the nature of the American steel industry.

Their decision, and our government's response to it, may be as important to you as it is to American steelworkers.

U.S. Steel has proposed to stop steel-making at its Fairless Works near Philadelphia, and import 3½ million tons of semi-finished steel slabs annually from the government-owned British Steel Company. Other East Coast and midwestern steel mills would soon be forced, by competitive pressure, to follow U.S. Steel's lead.

The United States would immediately lose 3,000 steel-making jobs at Fairless Works – and would soon lose 75,000 to 100,000 other steel-making jobs in other steel mills. Jobs in iron ore and coal mining would disappear too, as would jobs in the service industries which supply steel mills, steelworkers, coal and iron ore mines.

The British steel mills produce these slabs with huge government subsidies. Ironically, U.S. Steel in the past has been an outspoken critic of the dumping of subsidized foreign steel on the American market. Now, the company is saying that even if the British deal falls through, it will seek similar arrangements with other countries.

Since foreign steel facilities are usually government-owned and highly subsidized, American workers and companies find themselves in the position of trying to compete with a foreign government.

It can't be done. Take wages, for example. While some people seem to think American steel-workers make far more than we actually do, workers in steel-making facilities in many foreign countries make barely enough to survive.

Anything approaching such a wage scale in this country would result in a severe depression for everyone. Nobody could afford to pay American-style medical bills, taxes, home payments or food bills on such wages. Neither could they afford American automobiles, consumer goods or educations for their children. The result of such a low-wage policy would be devastating, not only for hourly workers, but for business and professional people and all others in our society.

We're doing everything we can to resist the U.S. Steel-British Steel deal. We're convinced it would open the way to the destruction of the American basic steel industry. But beyond that, we want to help make the American people aware of the dangers of foreign industrial targeting and dumping to all of us.

All of us are the targets.
Including you.

UNITED STEELWORKERS OF AMERICA

IF YOU WOULD LIKE MORE INFORMATION ON INDUSTRIAL TARGETING AND WHAT YOU CAN DO TO DEAL WITH THE PROBLEM, PLEASE MAIL THIS COUPON TO:

Lloyd McBride, President
United Steelworkers of America
Five Gateway Center
Pittsburgh, PA 15222

NAME

ADDRESS

EXHIBIT 3–2 Protectionism—labor's view

Source: Reprinted with permission of the United Steelworkers of America

With higher prices at home, consumers become poorer and buy less, and the economy suffers. To make matters worse, other countries will often retaliate by refusing to import U.S. products. When U.S. tariffs were imposed in 1986 on Canadian red cedar shingles worth $250 million, Canada immediately retaliated by imposing import duties on U.S. books, periodicals, computer parts, semiconductors, Christmas trees, rolled oats, cider, and teabags.

Not all labor groups have a favorable view on import restrictions. The International Longshoremen's Association viewed the domestic content bill negatively. It believed that the bill would cost from 7,500 to 11,600 longshore jobs, as well as more than 60,000 jobs when backup industries were included. The increase in the number of jobs in one industry would come at the expense of another.

The impact of imports and trade restrictions on jobs cannot be precisely ascertained. There is no agreement on the potential loss of jobs in the automobile and related industries if the restrictions on Japanese automobile imports were lifted. The various estimates of the number of jobs likely to be lost are in each case suspect because of the biases of the various parties offering such estimates. These parties and their estimates are as follows: Chrysler, 750,000 jobs; the United Auto Workers, 200,000; Chase Econometrics, a minimum of 150,000; Merrill Lynch, 50,000; and the Federal Trade Commission, 15,000.[2] Although the estimates of the cost of protection vary, they all point to the same conclusion: the costs to consumers are enormous. Quotas on auto imports in the early 1980s increased car prices by $1,300 (or about 30 percent) and contributed $460 million in windfall profit to American automakers. Overall, the four years of quotas resulted in $15.7 billion in higher prices. With 44,000 jobs being saved, the cost came to some $357,000 per job.[3] Exhibit 3–3 examines the cost of trade protectionism for various jobs.

On a related subject, note that the establishment of foreign operations is not necessarily harmful to employment at home. In fact, jobs are often created rather than lost. "Statistics show that U.S. companies with overseas subsidiaries export 32 percent more goods and services than do firms without foreign operations and create 38 percent more employment in the United States."[4]

Equalizing Cost and Price

Some protectionists attempt to justify their actions by invoking economic theory. They argue that foreign goods have lower prices because of lower production costs. Therefore, trade barriers are needed to make prices of imported products less competitive and local items more competitive. This argument is not persuasive to most analysts for several reasons. First, to determine the cause of price differential is unusually difficult. Is it caused by labor, raw materials, efficiency, or subsidy? Furthermore, costs and objectives vary greatly among countries, making it impossible to determine just what costs need to be equalized. In the case of the lumber industry, U.S. softwood-lumber producers and several industry trade associations charged that they lost nearly one-third of the market to subsidized Canadian timber. Their demand for 65 percent countervailing duty was nonetheless rejected by the U.S. Commerce Department, which determined that the actual subsidy was only 0.5 percent, an amount too small to justify the action. According to the Commerce Department, different prices were caused not so much by subsidy but rather by Canada's different approach to the management of national resources. That is, Canada's goal is to create jobs rather than make profits. In this particular case, however, the Commerce Department reversed its own decision a few years later.

Second, even if the causes of price differentials can be isolated and determined, it is hard to understand why price and cost have to be artificially equalized in the first place. Trade between nations takes place because of price differentials; otherwise, there is no incentive to trade at all.

Third, protectionism forces U.S. consumers to support local industries that prove unable to control costs and wages. Without imports, many domestic products would cost a great deal more.

If cost/price equalization is a desired end, then international trade may be the only instrument that can achieve it. For example, if wages are too high in one country,

---

Even though the lessons from trade policy reforms show that the process is manageable under certain conditions, the benefits from trade liberalization can be increased if the world trading environment is free. Such an environment will also make it politically viable for developing countries to undertake trade reforms. But in recent years there has been a resurgence of protection in the form of nontariff barriers. The proportion of North American and European Community imports affected by various nontariff restrictions has risen by more than 20 percent from 1981 to 1986. These restrictions cover large volumes of imports and particularly affect exports of developing countries. Nontariff barriers in clothing and footwear have proved porous, so some developing countries have been able to increase their exports to the industrial economies even as gaps in these barriers are being plugged.

COSTS OF PROTECTION TO INDUSTRIAL COUNTRIES

There are several ways of measuring the costs of protection. These methods generally underestimate the costs that are due to the negative effects of restraining competition on managerial efficiency, acquisition of new techniques, economies of scale, and savings and investments.

- □ *Costs to the consumers.* Protection of apparel in the United States is estimated to have cost U.S. companies in 1984 between $8.5 billion and $18.0 billion; of steel, between $7.3 billion and $20 billion; and of automobiles, around $1.1 billion.
- □ *Welfare costs.* This concept covers the extra cost to the economy as a whole of producing more of the goods domestically rather than importing them. Normally the welfare cost is considerably less than the consumer cost—particularly for tariffs or quotas. Even so, the estimates for textiles and apparel range from $1.4 billion to $6.6 billion in the European Community and the United States and nearly $2 billion for steel in the United States.
- □ *The cost of preserving a job.* Each protected job often ends up costing consumers more than the worker's salary. For example, each job preserved in the automobile industry in Britain is estimated to have cost consumers between $19,000 and $48,000 a year. In the United States the cost was between $40,000 and $108,500 a year. Looked at another way, the cost to consumers of preserving one worker in automobile production in the United Kingdom was equivalent to four workers earning the average industrial wage in other industries. In the U.S. automobile industry, the equivalent cost would be the wages of six ordinary industrial workers. The voluntary export restraints by foreign steel producers cost U.S. consumers $114,000 per protected job each year.

(continued)

EXHIBIT 3–3 The cost of protection

Source: Sarath Rajapatirana, "Industrialization and Foreign Trade," *Finance & Development* (September 1987): 5

COSTS TO DEVELOPING COUNTRIES

Developing countries bear heavy costs emerging from their own highly protective policy environments. But they also suffer costs from the protection in industrial countries.

Few studies exist of the latter. The available studies attempt to measure only the increase in export earnings for developing countries that would arise from reductions in the tariffs and nontariff barriers that face them. Studies by the World Bank, the Fund, and the Commonwealth Secretariat show that the result would be substantial export gains—worth several billion dollars a year. More detailed studies have been made for individual countries such as the Republic of Korea (South Korea). Restrictions on Korean exports of carbon steel cut sales to the United States by 33 percent, or $211 million; but Korea had offsetting gains in the form of higher prices and increased sales to other markets.

The costs of protection are high for both industrial and developing countries. They bear heavily on the latter, however. Protection structures in industrial countries discriminate more against developing countries than each other.

THE INTERNATIONAL ENVIRONMENT

Given their high unemployment, slowing growth, and the increased competition that they face from developing countries' manufacturers, there is the danger that industrial countries will increase barriers to manufactures from developing countries. This may mean more discriminatory nontariff barriers, more effectively administered. Such steps would further undermine the integrity of the GATT system and would restrict the growth of exports from developing countries. Many developing countries are already heavily in debt, so a reduction in their export earnings would aggravate the problems of world debt. Protectionist acts will have very serious implications for resource growth and maintaining orderly foreign exchange and capital markets in the world. These developments could produce widespread disillusionment with the outward-oriented trade strategies that have proved so successful for the newly industrializing countries in recent years.

If industrial countries become more protectionistic, developing countries would be forced into exploring other, second-best options. These would include trying to expand trade with the centrally planned economies and with other developing countries on a discriminatory basis. But the prospects of greatly improved trade in either of these directions are not good. Neither could replace trade with the industrial market economies.

EXHIBIT 3–3   *continued*

that country will attract labor from a lower-wage country. That process will increase the labor supply in the high-wage country, driving the wages down. On the other hand, the labor supply in the lower-wage nation will decrease, driving up the wages. Thus, equalization is achieved.

Enhancing National Security

Protectionists often present themselves as patriots. They usually claim that a nation should be self-sufficient and even willing to pay for inefficiency in order to enhance

THE KISS OF DEATH?

We now import more than 40 percent of all the oil we use, and that percentage continues to grow. This excessive dependence on foreign oil could poison America's economy and our national security if our supply were ever disrupted.

But the more we use nuclear energy, instead of imported oil, to generate our electricity, the less we have to depend on uncertain foreign oil supplies.

America's 112 nuclear electric plants already have cut foreign oil dependence by 4 billion barrels since the oil embargo of 1973, saving us $115 billion in foreign oil payments.

But 112 nuclear plants will not be enough to meet our rapidly growing demand for electricity. We need more plants.

Importing so much oil is a danger America must avoid. We need to

rely more on energy sources we can count on, like nuclear energy.

For a free booklet on nuclear energy, write to the U.S. Council for Energy Awareness, P.O. Box 66080, Dept. SK01, Washington, D.C. 20035.

U.S. COUNCIL FOR ENERGY AWARENESS

Nuclear energy means more energy independence.

© 1990 USCEA

As seen in May 1990 issues of The New York Times, The Washington Post, Natural History, The Leadership Network, The Economist, and Barron's; the May/June 1990 issue of State Legislatures; June 1990 issues of Reader's Digest, National Geographic, TIME, Sports Illustrated, Newsweek, U.S. News & World Report, Smithsonian, Business Week, Scientific American, Governing, and National Journal; July 1990 issues of Forbes and The Wall Street Journal; the July/August 1990 issue of American Heritage.

EXHIBIT 3–4 National security

Source: Courtesy of the U.S. Council for Energy Awareness

national security (see Exhibit 3–4). Section 232 of the Trade Expansion Act of 1962 allows the United States to protect those industries that are vital to national security. A secretary of commerce during the Reagan administration asked President Reagan to impose quotas on imported computer-numerically controlled (CNC) lathes and machinery centers, reasoning that strong domestic suppliers of advanced machine tools were critical to national security. The problem with such a law would be that American suppliers would gain benefits without having to address fundamental problems in their production and pricing.

Opponents of protectionism dismiss appeals to national security. A nation can never be completely self-sufficient because raw materials are not found in the same proportion in all areas of the world. The United States itself would be vulnerable if the supply of certain minerals were cut off. Moreover, national security is achieved at the cost of higher product prices, and money could be used for something more productive to the national interest. Also, in the case of such scarce resources as oil, if the United States were to try to be self-sufficient, it would quickly use up its own limited resources. The country may be better off exploiting or depleting the resources of others.

Most nations have some kind of cargo reservation or cargo preference. The policy requires some or all goods to and from a country to be shipped on carriers from that country. The primary rationale behind this practice is invariably considerations of national security.[5] Advocates of such forms of flag discrimination argue that the merchant fleet must be supported because it serves as a military transport auxiliary in times of national emergency. For the United States, cargo preference is supposed to be critical economically and strategically because 95 percent or more of a number of strategic materials needed for U.S. consumption is imported on foreign-flag vessels. Critics think that if national security is indeed necessary, it would be better for the government to provide direct financial assistance in order to remind its carriers of the reasons for the granting of economic benefits.

Protecting Infant Industry

The necessity to protect an infant industry is perhaps the most credible argument for protectionist measures. Some industries need to be protected until they become viable. South Korea serves as a good example. It has performed well by selectively protecting infant industries for export purpose. Note that "a pronounced difference in growth performance is associated with a strategy of export promotion as contrasted with one of import substitution." As a result, "a strong case can thus be made that the promotion of infant industry exports provides an effective means to hasten the achievement of international competitiveness."[6]

Even then, there is a question of how long an "infant" needs to grow up to be an "adult." A spoiled child often remains spoiled. A person taught to be helpless often wants to remain helpless or does not know how to stop being helpless. In a practical sense, there is no incentive for an infant industry to abandon protection and eliminate inefficiency. The Canadian shoe manufacturing industry provides a good illustration. Canadian manufacturers asked for and received quotas on shoe imports in 1972. Import restrictions made them complacent. Canadian shoe manufacturers failed to improve their operations and their market share subsequently slipped further from 40 to 38 percent.[7]

Furthermore, this kind of protection allows a protected industry to unjustifiably stretch its delivery times in spite of complaints from buyers. As such, the protection may actually serve to encourage local buyers to seek foreign suppliers who are more reliable, and this action will defeat the purpose of the protection.

Overview of Local Protection

Protectionist policies rarely achieve their objectives. As noted by a deputy U.S. trade representative, "the price you pay for protection is inefficiency." According to a 1986 study by the Congressional Budget Office, the clothing and steel industries failed to use import relief for investment in order to increase competitiveness. The findings were inconclusive in the case of the automobile industry. The study did show that the shoe industry's increased investment was not enough to become competitive with imports. These results mean that protection was not effective to revitalize the protected industry. As confirmed in a study by Canto, Eastin, and Laffer, the imposition of quotas on foreign steel "will not increase significantly domestic steelmakers' market share, profitability, employment, or investment."[8]

No nation can dominate all industries. "Efforts to preserve all industries will lower the national standard of living."[9] According to recent research, the protection of domestic economies against international competition is responsible for major economic losses for most sub-Saharan African countries. These countries need to open their economies, and structural adjustment programs should include more flexible exchange rate policies and price reform.[10]

Most politicians are shortsighted; they simply desire to keep wealth within the home country. The possibility of retaliation is not fully considered. They want the best of both worlds. Exhibit 3–5 presents one company's questions about the wisdom of certain trade provisions. In this view, artificial trade barriers reduce the world output of goods and services and subsequently the world economic welfare; in the end, everyone suffers.

GOVERNMENT: A CONTRIBUTION TO PROTECTIONISM

Government can be considered the root of all evils—at least as far as international trade is concerned. A government's mere existence, even without tariffs or any attempt to interfere with international marketing, can distort trade both inside and outside of its area.

At the international level, different governments have different policies and objectives, resulting in different rates for income and sales taxes. Tax laws vary widely from country to country. The United States has a social security tax but allows tax deductions for mortgage and interest payments. Many countries do exactly the opposite.

Taxation is not the only cause of tax and income differences. Some governments allow cartels to operate. A *cartel* is an international business agreement to fix prices and divide markets, in addition to other kinds of cooperation. Such an arrangement is illegal in the United States, but it is permissible and even encouraged in many countries. Australia and New Zealand, for example, allow livestock firms to cooperate with each other in exporting beef to the United States. Japanese computer makers are believed to make secret agreements in dividing foreign markets among themselves. There are almost 500 legal cartels in Japan, though Japan claims that most are for restraining exports. Governments themselves may form cartels, as in the case of the Organization of Petroleum Exporting Countries (OPEC). Malaysia wants

Protectionism: A persistent threat—II

What's wrong with H.R. 4800

The House-passed omnibus trade bill—H.R. 4800—is 458 pages long and quite complex. It would shift the U.S. sharply toward protectionism and away from its current emphasis on free trade. And in the fine print, it would do even more. It would attempt to extend U.S. law to sovereign foreign nations, and open the door to a federally planned economy at home.

Here are some of the bill's protectionist provisions we found most troubling:

● The bill would, under certain circumstances, weaken the President's long held discretion in trade matters and force him to impose quotas and raise tariffs, shifting the balance from negotiation to confrontation. This would soon trigger retaliation from the nations involved.

● Some provisions clearly violate the rules of the General Agreement on Tariffs and Trade, which the U.S. first signed in 1947 and which the U.S. intends to help amend and update again at international meetings beginning this fall. How much clout will this country have in treaty negotiations if its trade policies are governed by a law that is inconsistent with the treaty?

● The bill is sometimes vague, sometimes overly specific. For example, it would allow special import quotas against countries whose exports to the U.S. are 175 percent of its imports from the U.S. At present, this provision would apply only to Japan, West Germany and Taiwan. It would not answer the need to broaden those markets to U.S. exports, and thereby create jobs in the U.S. Besides, in the normal course of business, trade balances are never equal; they rise and fall in accordance with the shifting tastes and needs of both parties.

Equally onerous are those fine-print provisions guaranteed to make our trading partners wince.

For example, the bill defines as an "unreasonable" trade practice by a foreign nation the denial of collective bargaining, the absence of laws protecting child labor, and the lack of health and safety regulations. These are termed "internationally recognized workers' rights," but to the governments of many nations that trade with the U.S., the provision will doubtlessly be seen as an attempt to impose American law on their people. What do we know of worker protection in a country like China, say, where trade with the U.S. is growing and welcomed by both parties?

We're also particularly wary of provisions that open the back door to the discredited belief that government should plan the economy. The House measure would establish agencies called Industry Adjustment Advisory Groups. With members drawn from business, labor, government and public interest organizations, the groups could review the requests for help not only from companies, but also from trade associations and employee groups that say they're in trouble from foreign competition.

The groups would define the problem and provide advice on the type of federal help needed, and then monitor the industry to see that the "readjustment plan" was being followed. The bill would also create a Council on Industrial Competitiveness with subcouncils for specific industries to develop long-term strategies for those industries. In other words, whether a company said it wanted help or not, a request by an outside organization could suddenly find the company knee-deep in unwanted and unsought "advice."

For a long time, those who would restructure American society along collective lines have advocated exactly this sort of central planning. They haven't gotten very far because Americans have seen no reason to impose central government planning on their industries when even the Socialist countries are abandoning grandiose central plans in favor of free-market solutions to their economic problems.

Perhaps, for political reasons, the Senate feels it will have to pass a trade bill this year. If it does, it ought to recognize how central to America's well-being is the free flow of goods and services all over the world. To curtail America's trade is to cost Americans jobs, and punish the American economy.

But if the Senate follows the route taken by the House, the promised presidential veto would be the best trade relief we can think of.

Next: A sound trade policy for America.

Mobil®

EXHIBIT 3–5   On protectionist provisions

Source: Reprinted with permission of Mobil Corporation. ©1986 Mobil Corporation

to have a cartel with tin, whereas Peru wants one for silver. Without a doubt, all these arrangements affect price and trade.

Economic cooperation among governments yields economic benefits and problems by significantly affecting internal and external trade patterns. The EC's CAP (Common Agricultural Policy) is a good example. The CAP, with more than twenty price systems, was adopted to satisfy France's demand to protect its farmers as a condition for joining the EC. The practice requires the EC to impose variable-levy tariffs on many imported farm products in order to raise prices to European levels so that EC farmers will not be undersold at home regardless of world prices. Furthermore, authorities agree to buy surplus produce to maintain high target prices. The practice encourages EC farmers to overproduce products, which are later often sold abroad at lower prices. Not surprisingly, this expensive policy causes some conflict between France, which is a beneficiary, and the United Kingdom and Germany, which are net losers.

Based on the results of a number of studies, because of the Common Agricultural Policy (CAP), the EC has experienced an average loss of GDP of about 1 percent as well as a large redistribution of income to farmers from consumers and taxpayers. The distribution of costs is also uneven among member countries.[11] The CAP, while having failed to ensure adequate income levels for small-scale farmers, has produced windfall gains for large-scale producers and costly distortions in the EC economies as a whole.[12] Table 3–1 shows the costs of agricultural support policies of some industrial countries.

Many believe that the United States is the most liberal nation in promoting free trade. This notion is debatable because the government often yields to powerful lobbies. The 1930 Smoot-Hawley Bill, which contributed to the Great Depression, for instance, contained 2,000 amendments benefiting special interests. Actually, the U.S. government's many and bureaucratic regulations not only affect its own corporate citizens but also foreign firms. For example, U.S. farm operators' financial difficulties could be traced to the U.S. government's price-support loans. By removing U.S. grains from the market to maintain price supports, production abroad was encouraged and consumption discouraged by artificially high prices.[13]

TABLE 3–1 Costs of agricultural support policies

	Direct Cost to:			Producer Subsidy Equivalent[b]
	Taxpayers[a]	Consumers	Total	
	(US$ billions)			(percentage)
United States	49.1	17.1	66.3	28.3
Canada	3.0	2.7	5.7	39.1
Australia	0.6	0.7	1.3	14.5
New Zealand	0.4	0.1	0.5	22.5
Japan	7.4	34.9	42.3	68.9
Austria[c]	0.6	1.0	1.6	35.3
European Community	25.2	42.0	67.2	40.1
Total	86.3	98.5	184.9	38.4

[a]Taxpayer cost is net of budgetary receipts from tariff and includes data for all levels of government except local government. "Cost" assumes no change in other tax rates.

[b]The subsidy that would be required to maintain producers' incomes at the current level if all support policies were removed; measured as a percent of the gross value to agricultural producers.

[c]1984–85.

Source: Margaret Kelly et al., "Issues and Development of International Trade Policy," IMF Occasional Paper No. 63, 1988

Contrary to popular belief, the United States has by design many nontariff barriers against foreign goods. The country has a higher proportion of imported manufactured goods subjected to nontariff barriers than many nations, with 34 percent of its manufactured products explicitly protected.[14] By comparison, only 7 percent of Japan's manufactured goods are protected. In spite of some problem areas, the evidence indicates that access to the Japanese market definitely increased between 1979 and 1986.[15]

The United States achieves its protection goals through a variety of means. It has quotas on sugar, processed diary products (e.g., cheese), and clothespins. Voluntary quotas have been sought and obtained for steel, shoes, textiles, televisions, and so on. For a foreign author to gain copyright protection in the United States, a book must be printed in the United States as well as abroad. About half of all states in the United States place restrictions on the purchase of foreign-made goods for public projects. Imports must deal with an array of arbitrary and nonuniform bureaucratic practices.

In conclusion, governments everywhere seem to be the main culprits in distorting trade and welfare arrangements in order to gain some economic and political advantage or benefit. These governments use a combination of tariff and nontariff methods. Table 3–2 lists selected countries' barriers to agricultural imports. A discussion of the various kinds of tariff and nontariff barriers and their marketing implications follows.

MARKETING BARRIERS: TARIFFS

Tariff, derived from a French word meaning rate, price, or list of charges, is a customs duty or a tax on products that move across borders. Tariffs can be classified in several ways. The classification scheme used here is based on direction, purpose, length, import restraint, rate, and distribution point. These classifications are not necessarily mutually exclusive.

Direction: Import and Export Tariffs

Tariffs are often imposed on the basis of the direction of product movement, that is, on imports or exports, with the latter being the less common one. When export tariffs are levied, they usually apply to an exporting country's scarce resources or raw materials (rather than finished manufactured products). Chile has an export tax on copper, whereas Brazil uses it for coffee. Sometimes, the reason an exporting country resorts to export tariffs is that it is pressured into doing so. Based on the International Trade Commission's findings related to Florida Citrus Mutual's 1982 complaint about Brazil's unfair subsidy, Brazil agreed to impose an export duty of $38.50 per metric ton on frozen concentrate. Japan also thought of imposing an export surcharge, because an export tax by Japan was considered more desirable to improve the U.S. trade deficit than an import tax charged by the United States for the same purpose. Argentina was asked by the World Bank to drop its 16 percent export tax so that its trade balance could improve. The United States has no export tax.

Purpose: Protective and Revenue Tariffs

Tariffs can be classified as protective tariffs and revenue tariffs. The distinction is based on purpose. The purpose of a **protective tariff** is to protect home industry, agriculture, and labor against foreign competitors by trying to keep foreign goods out of the country. The South American markets, for instance, have high import duties that hinder the import of fully built cars. Brazil, for example, has a 50 percent import tax on imported "flyaway" planes.

The purpose of a **revenue tariff,** in contrast, is to generate tax revenues for the government. Compared to a protective tariff, a revenue tariff is relatively low. When Japanese and other foreign cars are imported into the United States, there is a 3 percent duty. On the other hand, American cars exported to Japan are subject to a variety of import taxes. Japan has a 23 percent commodity tax on imported cars and an 18.5 percent tax on air-conditioning components. Even the cost of shipping is taxed, since Japan considers that the shipping cost adds value to a car. As a result, a U.S. car sold in Japan can easily cost twice as much as its price in the United States. The U.S. tax is a revenue tariff, whereas the Japanese tax is more of a protective tariff.

Length: Tariff Surcharge versus Countervailing Duty

Protective tariffs can be further classified according to length of time. A **tariff surcharge** is a temporary action, whereas a **countervailing duty** is a permanent surcharge. When Harley Davidson claimed that it needed time to adjust to Japanese imports, President Reagan felt that it was in the national interest to provide import relief. To protect the local industry, a tariff surcharge was used. The tariff on heavy motorcycles jumped from 4.4 percent to 45 percent for one year and then declined to 35 percent, 20 percent, 15 percent, and finally 10 percent in subsequent years.

Countervailing duties are imposed on certain imports when products are subsidized by foreign governments. These duties are thus assessed to offset a special advantage or discount allowed by an exporter's government. Usually, a government provides an export subsidy by rebating certain taxes if goods are exported. Japan provides rebate of manufacturers' excise taxes for exported TV sets and other electronic goods. The EC rebates the value-added taxes on steel exports to the United States.

The United States has an almost century-old law whose terms require a U.S. penalty duty to offset a subsidy. The law focuses on payments of bounties or grants on products exported to the United States, and it applies regardless of the party making such a payment (e.g., country, group, individual), time of payment (e.g., production, exportation), and manner of payment (direct or indirect). Duty-free articles may be included if their imports can injure a U.S. industry. The U.S. secretary of the treasury is empowered to issue a countervailing duty order requiring an additional duty equal to the net amount of the ascertained bounty. U.S. Steel asked for the imposition of countervailing duties on steel imports from the EC. The EC's position was that a value-added tax was an exact refund of taxes paid and thus was not a bounty (i.e., a reward or allowance given by a government for taking certain actions, such as exporting or raising certain crops). The Treasury Department imposed countervailing duties in 1982.

TABLE 3–2 Barriers to agricultural imports

| Country | Commodity Division | Tariffs[a] | | Bilateral negotiation possibilities |
		Frequency	Average level	
Japan (JA)[b]	All	. . .	11	
	Foods		15	
	Raw mat.		7	
South Asia				
Bangladesh (BA)	All	97	62	PA, IO, MA, PH, TH
	Foods	98	66	
	Raw mat.	94	57	
India (IN)	All	99	106	MA, PH, TH
	Foods	99	119	
	Raw mat.	98	92	
Pakistan (PA)	All	93	59	BA, MA, PH, TH
	Foods	93	75	
	Raw mat.	94	21	
Sri Lanka (SR)	All	95	34	IO, MA
	Foods	95	48	
	Raw mat.	94	43	
Southeast Asia				
Indonesia (IO)	All	80	14	BA, SR, KO
	Foods	75	19	
	Raw mat.	100	10	
Malaysia (MA)	All	77	9	BA, IN, PA, SR
	Foods	68	8	
	Raw mat.	97	9	
Philippines (PH)	All	100	28	BA, IN, PA, KO
	Foods	100	35	
	Raw mat.	100	21	
Thailand (TH)	All	88	29	BA, IN, PA, KO
	Foods	86	36	
	Raw mat.	95	22	
East Asia				
Hong Kong (HK)	All			
	Foods			
	Raw mat.			
Korea (KO)	All	100	21	IO, TH
	Foods	100	29	
	Raw mat.	100	13	
Singapore (SI)[c]	All			
	Foods			
	Raw mat.			

[a] The data refer to general or statutory ad valorem tariff rates.

[b] The tariff data for Japan refer to Tokyo Round-bound rates. The nontariff barriers data do not include information about Japan's state trading and entry regulations.

[c] Singapore is grouped with the East Asia countries for analytical purposes.

Notes: The data refer to the following years: 1985 (Pakistan, Thailand), 1986 (Bangladesh, Japan, Korea, Singapore, Sri Lanka), and 1987 (Hong Kong, India, Indonesia, Malaysia, the Phillippines)

Source: Dean A. DeRosa, "Agricultural Trade and Protection in Asia," *Finance & Development* (December 1988): 52

TABLE 3–2 Barriers to agricultural imports

			Nontariff Barriers		
	Quantitive Restrictions		Bilateral		
Rest. licensing	Quotas	Prohibitions	negotiation possibilities	State trading	Entry regulations
24	12	3	KO	...	...
31	15	2			
1		6			
36		37	PA, KO, SI	1	2
44		30		1	3
18		56		3	
40		71	IO, PH	19	3
47		65		20	4
26		83		18	
43	2	39	BA, MA	5	
33	3	55		7	
70		5			
9			KO	4	
9				4	
9				1	
26	23	50	IN, MA	2	4
28	29	63		3	5
98					
8		1	PA, IO, PH, TH		20
8		2			29
10					1
49	6	9	IN, MA, TH	3	71
53	4	13		5	96
39	10				11
35	1	24	MA, PH	1	20
40	0	32		1	24
23	1				7
8	1		KO		3
8	2				4
7					
30			JA, BA, SR, HK		
38					
7					
22			BA		9
26					12
13					

115

To seek relief, U.S. firms can file petitions under the escape clause **(Section 301)** of the 1974 Trade Act with the International Trade Commission (ITC). Created as the U.S. Tariff Commission in 1916, the ITC is a fact-finding and quasijudicial agency. Its job is to determine whether imports have injured domestic producers. The ITC does not have to prove a causal relationship between imports and local industries' injuries. As a result, the industry has only to show that it is hurt by imports without having to prove that imported products are dumped or sold below production costs. Exhibit 3–6 is a flow chart showing the procedures in a countervailing-duty investigation.

The ITC caseload rose significantly in the 1980s. Among the industries seeking protection are steel, copper, canned tuna, footwear, stainless steel flatware, and automobile. The ITC determined that steel and copper producers were injured by imports and rejected escape clause petitions from the footwear, lumber, and stainless steel flatware industries.

Over a ten-year period the ITC recommended relief in thirty-one of fifty-two escape clause cases. A recommendation, however, does not guarantee that actual relief is granted. In the end, it is up to the President whether to go along with the recommendation or to overrule it. For example, Presidents Ford, Carter, and Reagan followed the ITC's advice in only eight cases. The automobile industry's petition was rejected by the ITC, but President Reagan still sought and secured voluntary quotas from Japan.

Subsidies and countervailing duties are a highly controversial issue. Exporting nations are unhappy if any countervailing duties are imposed on their products, and trade conflict and retaliation can quickly follow. Claiming that Canadian provincial governments' low stumpage fees (for the right to cut timber in government-owned forests) constituted an illegal subsidy, the U.S. government announced a 15 percent surcharge on imported softwood lumber. The dispute was settled and a trade war averted only after intensive bargaining. Canada agreed to impose a 15 percent tax that would be phased out once the provinces raised their stumpage fees.

Import Restraint: Special Duties and Variable Duties

Protective tariffs can also be classified as either import charges or import restraints. These tariffs include special duties and variable levies, which are imposed in addition to import tariffs. **Special duties** are extra duties for certain items. The purpose is to make it difficult to import and to sell those products. Usually, special duties are applied to products deemed unnecessary because they are either luxury items or can be produced locally. Automobiles and stereo equipment are examples.

The rationale behind variable duties is basically the same as that for special duties. As the name implies, **variable duties** mean different rates for different product categories, depending on how much the products have been processed and how much more processing they will undergo. For exports, there is one rate for semimanufacturers of raw materials and another, lower, rate for finished products. Finished products have more value-added content and are able to earn extra income for the nation.

Variable duties can be used for imports as well, except that in this case rates are reversed. That is, a country may encourage imports of raw materials or natural

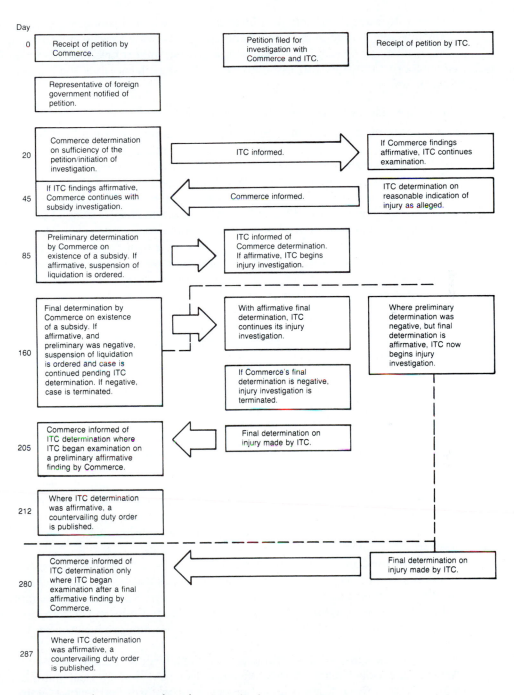

Day

0 — Receipt of petition by Commerce.

Petition filed for investigation with Commerce and ITC.

Receipt of petition by ITC.

Representative of foreign government notified of petition.

20 — Commerce determination on sufficiency of the petition/initiation of investigation.

ITC informed.

If Commerce findings affirmative, ITC continues examination.

45 — If ITC findings affirmative, Commerce continues with subsidy investigation.

Commerce informed.

ITC determination on reasonable indication of injury as alleged.

85 — Preliminary determination by Commerce on existence of a subsidy. If affirmative, suspension of liquidation is ordered.

ITC informed of Commerce determination. If affirmative, ITC begins injury investigation.

160 — Final determination by Commerce on existence of a subsidy. If affirmative, and preliminary was negative, suspension of liquidation is ordered and case is continued pending ITC determination. If negative, case is terminated.

With affirmative final determination, ITC continues its injury investigation.

Where preliminary determination was negative, but final determination is affirmative, ITC now begins injury investigation.

If Commerce's final determination is negative, injury investigation is terminated.

205 — Commerce informed of ITC determination where ITC began examination on a preliminary affirmative finding by Commerce.

Final determination on injury made by ITC.

212 — Where ITC determination was affirmative, a countervailing duty order is published.

280 — Commerce informed of ITC determination only where ITC began examination after a final affirmative finding by Commerce.

Final determination on injury made by ITC.

287 — Where ITC determination was affirmative, a countervailing duty order is published.

EXHIBIT 3–6 Countervailing-duty investigation

Source: U.S. Department of Commerce, *Subsidies and Countervailing Measures* (Washington, D.C.: Department of Commerce, 1980)

resources by taxing them less than finished or value-added products. Countries generally impose the highest tariff on finished products ready for sale and consumption. The practice provides an incentive for local firms to import raw materials or semifinished goods for further processing domestically, since local labor and materials will then be utilized.

Rates: Specific, Ad Valorem, and Combined

How are tax rates applied? To understand the computation, three kinds of tax rates must be distinguished: specific, ad valorem, and combined.

Specific duties are a fixed or specified amount of money per unit of weight, gauge, or other measure of quantity. Based on a standard physical unit of a product, they are specific rates of so many dollars or cents for a given unit of measure (e.g., $1/gallon, 25¢/square yard, $2/ton, etc.). Imported wines, for example, are taxed at 37.5¢ per gallon, down from $1.25 in 1936. Product costs or prices are irrelevant in this case. Because the duties are constant for low- and high-priced products of the same kind, this method is discriminatory and effective for protection against cheap products because of their lower unit value. That is, there is a reverse relationship between product value and duty percentage. As product price goes up, a duty when expressed as a percentage of this price will fall. On the other hand, for a cheap product whose value is low, the duty percentage will rise accordingly.

Ad valorem duties are duties "according to value." They are stated as a fixed percentage of the invoice value and are applied as a percentage to the dutiable value of the imported goods. The United States has a 3 percent duty applied to the value of an imported car. Japan's ad valorem tariffs on beef and processed cheese are 25 percent and 35 percent, respectively. This is the opposite of specific duties since the percentage is fixed but the total duty is not. Based on this method, there is a direct relationship between the total duties collected and the prices of products. That is, the absolute amount of total duties collected will increase or decrease with the prices of imported products. The strength of this method is that it provides a continuous and relative protection against all price levels of a particular product. Such protection becomes even more critical when inflation increases prices of imports. If specific duties were used, their effect lessens with time because inflation reduces the proportionate effect. Another advantage is that ad valorem duties provide an easy comparison of rates across countries and across products.

Combined rates (or **compound duty**) are a combination of the specific and ad valorem duties on a single product. They are duties based on both the specific rate and the ad valorem rate that are applied to an imported product. For example, the tariff may be 10¢ per pound plus 5 percent ad valorem. Under this system, both rates are used together, though in some countries only the rate producing more revenue may apply.

Since the duties paid according to both the ad valorem and combined systems depend on product value, there is often a question of how product value is determined. Frequently, a customs appraiser depends on furnished invoices. Obviously, the duties can be less if an importer can reduce product valuation. Exporters and importers may resort to phony invoices, a common practice in international business. An exporter can thus be caught in a dilemma: not submitting phony invoices means losing sales, but yielding to the practice means breaking the law. Such fraud was what Mitsui was charged with when it pleaded guilty to violating import laws in 1979. Amway and its Canadian subsidiary were accused of falsely declaring the value of their imports into Canada. The Canadian government filed criminal charges against Amway for cheating the country out of $22.7 million in customs duty over a fifteen-year period between 1965 and 1980.

Distribution Point: Distribution and Consumption Taxes

Some taxes are collected at a particular point of distribution or when purchases and consumption occur. These indirect taxes, frequently adjusted at the border, are of four kinds: single-stage, value-added, cascade, and excise.

Single-stage sales tax is a tax collected only at one point in the manufacturing and distribution chain. This tax is perhaps most common in the United States, where retailers and wholesalers make purchases without paying any taxes simply by showing a sales tax permit. The single-stage sales tax is not collected until products are purchased by final consumers.

A **value-added tax (VAT)** is a multistage, noncumulative tax on consumption. It is a national sales tax levied at each stage of the production and distribution system, though only on the value added at that stage. In other words, each time a product changes hands, even between middlemen, a tax must be paid. But the tax collected at a certain stage is based on the added value and not the total value of the product at that point. For example, a manufacturer initially pays taxes on raw materials worth $100. By transforming these materials into a finished product, the manufacturer adds another $50 to the product value. If the product is then sold to a wholesaler, the wholesaler pays taxes on the $50 (i.e., the value added) and not on the total value of $150. Value-added tax is very common in Europe, resulting in the tax being built into a product's retail price. In Korea, it is levied on most goods and services in hotels, tourist facilities, and major restaurants at a standard rate of 10 percent. In the United States, talks of abolishing a single-stage sales tax and replacing it with a value-added tax periodically surface. The importance of the value-added tax is due to the fact that GATT allows a producing country to rebate the value-added tax when products are exported. The United States, which depends more on income tax for its revenue, is put in a disadvantageous position because the income tax cannot be refunded.

Cascade taxes are collected at each point in the manufacturing and distribution chain and are levied on the total value of a product, including taxes borne by the product at earlier stages. A cascade tax is thus a combination of a single-stage sales tax and a value-added tax. It is similar to a single-stage sales tax in the sense that the tax is based on the total value of the product at that stage (not just the value added). On the other hand, it is like a value-added sales tax because the tax is collected at every point (not just at one point) in the production and distribution chain. Of the tax systems examined, this appears to be the most severe of them all. For over thirty years, a now-defunct cascade system of taxation in Italy (the IGE) hurt the development of large-scale wholesale business there.[16] Since the IGE was imposed each time the goods changed hands, Italian manufacturers minimized transfers of goods by selling products directly to retailers. The IGE was replaced by a value-added tax in 1973, and it was hoped by foreign manufacturers that the revival of

TABLE 3–3   A comparison of distribution taxes

Point in Chain (seller)		Price Charged	
Farmer		$ 4	
Manufacturer		$ 5	
Wholesaler		$ 7	
Retailer		$10	

Payer of Tax	Single-stage Sales Tax	Value-added Tax	Cascade Tax
Manufacturer	none	on $4	on $4
Wholesaler	none	on $(5 − 4)	on $(5 + previous tax)
Retailer	none	on $(7 − 5)	on $(7 + previous taxes)
Consumer	on $10	on $(10 − 7)	on $(10 + previous taxes)

wholesale organizations might facilitate imports of foreign consumer goods. Table 3–3 shows how the tax varies among the three systems.

An **excise tax** is a one-time charge levied on the sales of specified products. Alcoholic beverages and cigarettes are good examples. In the United States, the federal government collects a 3 percent excise tax on telephone services and collects 16¢ for each pack of cigarettes. State, county, and city governments may have their own excise taxes.

These four kinds of indirect taxes are often adjusted at the border. Border taxes can be used to raise prices of imports or lower prices of exports. Prices of imports are raised by charging imported goods with (in addition to customs duties) a tax usually borne by domestic products. For exported products, their export prices become more competitive (i.e., lower) when such products are relieved of the same tax that they are subject to when produced, sold, and consumed domestically. The rebate of this tax when the goods are exported, in effect, lowers their export prices.

The United States also has border taxes. To protect bourbon, for example, the United States imposes an average tax of $2.68 per fifth on Scotch whiskey, in addition to an import tariff to pay federal, state, and local excise taxes. Canada replaced its Federal Sales Tax (FST), which had been 13.5 percent for most products. The FST was collected at the manufacturing stage of production on domestic goods. On imports, the tax was collected by Canada Customs. Because of the hidden nature of the FST, many foreign marketers selling into the Canadian market did not realize that Canadian manufacturers had already built the 13.5 percent FST into their prices. As a result, foreign firms found that they were not as price competitive as they had assumed. The new tax is a more broadly based Goods and Services Tax (GST); it is a value-added tax similar to those found in most European countries. The GST taxes both goods and services and curbs exemptions. U.S. exporters should benefit from the more transparent nature of the new GST and find it easier to plan export pricing.[17]

Many countries have a **turnover,** or **equalization, tax.** This is a tax "intended to compensate for similar taxes levied on domestic products." Any critical examination of this tax would demonstrate that the tax does not equalize prices at all. "While the rate of the tax on the imported and domestic product may be the same, the effect on the import is greater in that the tax is usually levied on the full c.i.f., duty-paid value, rather than on the invoice alone."[18]

Normally, travelers making purchases in foreign countries are eligible to receive a refund of the value-added tax if the purchased items are to be used outside the countries where they are bought. The value-added tax varies from country to country and from product to product and so do the refund procedures. There is a waiting period apart from the paperwork time, and U.S. banks charge a fee for handling the exchange or a refund check in a foreign currency.

This section has examined the various types of tariffs, all of which distort market prices. The question remains whether tariffs are effective in improving a country's trade position. According to one model, the effectiveness depends on whether the tariff is temporary or permanent. If it is temporary—whether real or perceived—the country's trade account will improve "at the expense of a reduction in employment, output, and gross exports" because consumers save resources for the future, when foreign goods will be less costly. But if the tariff is permanent, the balance of payments is not affected because foreign goods are equally expensive across time. For a permanent tariff, consumers thus see no need to save and shift resources for future periods. Therefore, for the purpose of policymaking, "if tariff policy is to be successful in reducing the trade deficit it is essential that tariff legislation be such as to leave the perception that the imposed taxes on foreign goods will be of only short duration and not induce retaliation by foreign governments."[19]

MARKETING BARRIERS: NONTARIFF BARRIERS

Tariffs, though generally undesirable, are at least straightforward and obvious. Nontariff barriers, in comparison, are more elusive or nontransparent. Tariffs have declined in importance, while nontariff barriers have become more prominent. Often disguised, the impact of nontariff barriers can be just as devastating, if not more, as the impact of tariffs. Laird and Yeats have documented the spread of nontariff barriers from 1966 to 1988 that have been applied unevenly across countries and industrial sectors.[20] Exhibit 3–7 describes how one U.S. firm, Allen-Edmonds Shoe Corporation, intended to overcome frustrating Japanese import barriers.

By industry, U.S. exports of ferrous metal products and pharmaceuticals are affected the most by nontariff barriers. By country, "Japan is the most stringent country to U.S. manufactured exports, followed by the EEC countries."[21] Anaheim Manufacturing Inc.'s sales of garbage disposers in Japan went from zero to 15,000 units in 1985. Just as quickly came a steep decline in sales. The Ministry of Construction suddenly issued advisories the following year to the news media and local water agencies, warning that the ground-up garbage could harm the environment by overwhelming their sewers and polluting their rivers. The news media ran the stories and then refused advertisements for the product. When department stores stopped displaying the disposers, the company had to turn to door-to-door selling and pay a 40 percent commission, which increased the price to $1,600 or 10 times the U.S. price. To buy the product, Japanese buyers had to take out loans. Soon loan companies refused making loans for such purchases.[22]

WHEN THE JAPANESE TOLD US IT WAS CUSTOMARY TO LEAVE OUR SHOES AT THE DOOR, THIS IS THE DOOR THEY HAD IN MIND.

Keep your shoes to yourself. That's the clear message the Japanese government has given Allen-Edmonds and other U.S. shoe manufacturers. Tough licensing, even tougher tariffs and various other obstacles are making it nearly impossible to do business in Japan.

There is a market for our shoes there. The people have shown great interest in our classic styles and our superior quality. But the duty makes them terribly expensive. Fact is, U.S. shoes sold in Japan are taxed up to 60% higher than Japanese shoes sold in this country.

Don't misunderstand. We're not looking for help or sympathy. In fact, we're making headway with some good old-fashioned pushiness. Just recently our president literally crashed a Tokyo trade show we had been excluded from—and promptly sold over 300 pairs of shoes.

The point is this. A company—even a small one like our own—can't wait for political solutions to unfair trade barriers. Manufacturers must initiate action in a friendly but firm manner. Whether it's the Japanese market or any other, for now it's the best way we know to get a foot in the door.

ALLEN EDMONDS
The Handcrafted World of Allen-Edmonds.

Allen-Edmonds Shoe Corporation
Port Washington, WI 53074 U.S.A.
(414) 284-3461   Telex 229715
FAX (414) 284-3462

EXHIBIT 3–7 Japanese import barriers

Source: Reprinted with permission of Allen-Edmonds Shoe Corporation

There are several hundred types of nontariff barriers. These barriers can be grouped in five major categories. Each category contains a number of different nontariff barriers.

Government Participation in Trade

The degree of government involvement in trade varies from passive to active. The types of participation include administrative guidance, state trading, and subsidies.

Administrative Guidance   Many governments routinely provide trade consultation to private companies. Japan has been doing this on a regular basis to help implement its industrial policies. This systematic cooperation between the government and business is labeled "Japan, Inc." To get private firms to conform to the Japanese government's guidance, the government uses a carrot-and-stick approach by exerting the influence through regulations, recommendations, encouragement, discouragement, or prohibition. Many suspect that the Japanese government advises its traders on how to buy, sell, and hedge currencies in order to manipulate the value of the yen, thus making it favorable for Japanese exports. Japan's government agencies' administrative councils are influential enough to make importers restrict their purchases to an amount not exceeding a certain percentage of local demand. The Japanese government denies that such a practice exists, claiming that it merely seeks reports on the amounts purchased by each firm.

It is interesting to note that the guidance is used from time to time, albeit reluctantly, to encourage imports. In 1981 the Japanese Fair Trade Commission forced the Ministry of International Trade and Industry (MITI) to drop "guidance" to the paper industry. The Semiconductor Industry Association filed a complaint under Section 301 of the 1974 Trade Act, charging that the Japanese government limited U.S. firms' market share in Japan to only about 10 percent. The association dropped the complaint when Japan agreed to use "administrative guidance" to increase imports of U.S. semiconductors.

Government Procurement and State Trading   State trading is the ultimate in government participation, because the government itself is now the customer or buyer who determines what, when, where, how, and how much to buy. In this practice, the state engages in commercial operations, either directly or indirectly, through the agencies under its control. Such business activities are either in place of or in addition to private firms.

Although government involvement in business is most common with the communist countries, whose governments are responsible for the central planning of the whole economy, the practice is definitely not restricted to those nations. In Thailand, many of the petroleum production facilities are owned by such multinational oil companies as Exxon and Shell, but the Thai government also owns and operates its own petroleum facilities and gas stations. The U.S. government, as the largest buyer in the world, is required by the Buy American Act to give a bidding edge to U.S. suppliers in spite of their higher prices.

The problems caused by the practice of government procurement and trading are serious, and Japan perhaps illustrates these problems best. Tokyo's "buy Japanese" barriers are virtually impenetrable, especially in the huge communications equipment market. For example, only 1 percent of the equipment purchased by NTT (Nippon Telephone & Telegraph Company) is foreign made, even though Japanese products cost more. When the government is further involved in reselling imported products, matters become even more complicated. American tobacco companies complained that Japan's Tobacco and Salt Agency kept prices of their products artificially high and that salesmen from this government tobacco monopoly participated in discrediting the advertising of American products.

The Government Procurement Code requires the signatory nations to guarantee that they will provide suppliers from other signatory countries treatment equal to that which they provide their own suppliers. This guarantee of *"national treatment"* means that a foreign government must choose the goods with the lowest price that best meet the specifications regardless of the supplier's nationality. The Code requires that technical specifications not be prepared, adopted, or applied with a view to creating obstacles to international trade. The purchasing agency must adopt specifications geared toward performance rather than design and must base the specifications on international standards, national technical regulations, or recognized national standards, where appropriate.[23]

Subsidies   Government participation can take the form of subsidies to protect local industries or to push exports. Subsidies can take many forms—including cash, interest rate, value-added tax, corporate income tax, sales tax, freight, insurance, and infrastructure. Subsidized loans for priority sectors, preferential rediscount rates, budgetary subsidies, credit floors, and credit ceilings are among the various subsidy policies of several Asian countries.[24] One common subsidy method is for the government to provide *concessionary financing* (lower-than-market interest rates). Foreign grain buyers can get government financing from Canada at a rate close to the prime rate. The United States, likewise, made several hundred million dollars available to subsidize interest rates to foreign grain buyers.

Some countries may choose to be open about subsidies, simply by granting *cash subsidies*. The EC reduced its export price of grain by 35 percent from its internal price. Argentina, unable to finance exports, also resorted to heavy discounting in Asian markets.

Subsidy can take the form of a *favorable foreign exchange conversion rate*. The American Textile Manufacturers Institute, Amalgamated Clothing and Textile Workers Unions, and International Ladies Garment Workers Union claimed that Chinese exporters received a subsidy of more than 40 percent in the form of a more favorable foreign exchange conversion rate. These labor organizations thus filed a countervailing duty petition.

There are several other kinds of subsidies that are not so obvious. Brazil's *rebates of the various taxes*, coupled with *other forms of assistance*, can be viewed as subsidies. Tennessee, Ohio, Michigan, and Illinois, in order to attract foreign automakers to locate their plants in those states, provided such services as highway construction, training of workers, and tax breaks, which are simply subsidies in disguise.

Sheltered profit is another kind of subsidy. A country may allow a corporation to shelter its profit from abroad. The United States in 1971 allowed companies to form domestic international sales corporations (DISCs) even though they cost the U.S. treasury more than $1 billion a year in revenue. GATT, the multilateral treaty, eventually ruled that a DISC was an illegal export subsidy. A new U.S. law allows companies that meet more stringent requirements to form foreign sales corporations (FSCs), which have the same purpose as DISCs.

The extent of subsidies is great—worldwide farm-support payments alone exceed $100 billion a year, with $26 billion accounted for by the United States. As can be expected, the costs of agricultural support policies and protection are heavy. Liberalization can bring great rewards.[25]

The subsidy problem is difficult to resolve because so many issues are ambiguous. It has not determined, for example, whether foreign-government aid to cover operational deficits generated by state-run companies are considered export subsidies under the U.S. law. The French government decided to write off 14 billion French francs of Renault's debt in the process of converting Renault from a state agency into a state-owned company. The action led to an investigation by the European Community Commission to determine whether this aid distorted competition and whether it was legal under EC competition rules.

The **Subsidies Code,** technically named the Agreement on Interpretation and Application of Article VI, XVI and XXIII of the General Agreement on Tariffs and Trade, recognizes that government subsidies distort the competitive forces at work in international trade. The rules of the international agreement negotiated during the Tokyo Round of Multilateral Trade Negotiations (MTN) differentiate between *export subsidies* and *domestic subsidies*. The Code's rules also differentiate between subsidies paid on *primary products* (e.g., manufactures) and those paid on *nonprimary products* and primary minerals. A primary product is any product of farm, forest, or fishery in its natural form or that has undergone such processing as is customarily required to prepare it for transportation and marketing in substantial volume in international trade (e.g., frozen and cured meat). The Code prohibits the use of export subsidies on nonprimary products and primary mineral products.

Before countervailing duties can be imposed, the Code requires a ruling that subsidized imports are causing material injury to a domestic industry. Under the Code, for a government to investigate into the existence of a subsidy, it must have sufficient evidence of the likelihood that (a) a subsidy exists, (b) there may be material injury to a domestic industry, and (c) there is a causal link between the alleged subsidy and the injury to the industry. It is important to note that the entire industry must be found to be injured or threatened with injury and that the injury must be the direct result of the subsidized imports—not all imports taken together and not by reason of other factors that might be posing injury to the industry in question, such as a change in the pattern of consumption within a market.

There is considerable debate over what should be considered manufactured products, since such products are not entitled to any subsidies. For instance, according to the United States, the EC's export subsidies for such manufactured products as pasta and wheat flour are banned by the international subsidies code. The EC's position is that pasta and wheat flour are not manufactured products.

To combat subsidies, the United States has proposed the adoption of the "traffic light" approach to provide a framework for the classification of all subsidy programs.

There are three categories: prohibited (red light) subsidies; permissible but actionable (yellow light) subsidies; and permissible but nonactionable (green light) subsidies. The hallmark of the U.S. proposal is its treatment of the red light category. The United States has proposed eliminating the artificial distinction between primary and nonprimary products with respect to prohibited export subsidies. Moreover, the U.S. proposal recommends expanding the list of prohibited subsidies to include certain trade-related subsidies (e.g., subsidies contingent on local content requirements), subsidies to firms that are predominantly engaged in exporting, and domestic subsidies to firms if the amount of subsidy exceeds a certain percentage of the firm's sales.[26]

Customs and Entry Procedures

Customs and entry procedures can be employed as nontariff barriers. These restrictions involve classification, valuation, documentation, license, inspection, and health and safety regulations.

Classification   How a product is classified can be arbitrary and inconsistent and is often based on a customs officer's judgment, at least at the time of entry. The U.S. Customs reclassified Nissan's imported truck cabs and chassis from "parts" with 4 percent duty to "assembled vehicles" subject to 25 percent levies instead. When the U.S. government classifies a foreign film as propaganda instead of a work of art, that film will be subject to import duties on entry.

Product classification is important, because the way in which a product is classified determines its duty status. A company can sometimes take action to affect the classification of its product. For example, a ruling of the U.S. Customs resulted in a 100 percent punitive tariff on certain Japanese computers. Toshiba and NEC, however, took advantage of the ruling's loophole by importing boards without microprocessor chips. The boards were not classified as computers and were thus allowed to enter the United States duty-free. The microchips were then installed after entry.

In the United States, if an imported product is determined to have the acceptable minimum percentage of materials produced in a designated country, it can be classified by a customs officer as having duty-free status. Classification thus determines if certain product categories are qualified for a special treatment, but it also determines whether some products should be banned altogether. Most countries ban obscene, immoral, and seditious materials, as well as imports of counterfeit coins, bills, securities, postage stamps, and narcotics. In South Korea, prohibited articles include books, printed matter, motion pictures, phonograph records, sculptures, and other like articles that are deemed subversive or injurious to national security or detrimental to the public interest, as well as articles used for espionage or intelligence activities. Radio Shack was prohibited from selling citizens-band radios in the United Kingdom, Belgium, and Holland. This product, taken for granted in the United States, is banned in most countries because of the possibility that it might be used by terrorists or spies.

Valuation   Regardless of how products are classified, each product must still be valued. The value affects the amount of tariffs levied. A customs appraiser is the one who determines the value. The process can be highly subjective, and the valuation of a product can be interpreted in different ways, depending on what value is used (e.g., foreign, export, import, or manufacturing costs) and how this value is constructed. In Japan, a commodity tax of 15 percent is applied to the FOB factory price of Japanese cars. Yet U.S. cars are valued on the CIF basis, adding $1,000 more to the final retail price of these cars.

The United States relies on the *deductive value* for valuation purpose when the *transaction value* (of identical or similar merchandise) cannot be determined. Deductive value is the resale price in the United States with deduction for such items as commission, general expenses, transportation/insurance costs, duties, and values of further processing. If valuation under the first two methods is not possible, the *computed value* can then be used. Computed value consists of the sum of (1) materials, fabrication, and other processing used in producing the imported merchandise; (2) profit and general expenses; (3) any assist, if not included in items 1 and 2; and (4) packing costs.[27] An assist is an item provided by the buyer free of charge or at a reduced cost for use in the production of merchandise.

Documentation   Documentation can present another problem at entry because many documents and forms are often necessary, and the documents required can be complicated. Japan held up Givenchy's import application because the company left out an apostrophe for its I'Interdit perfume.

Documentation requirements vary from country to country. Usually, the following shipping documents are either required or requested: commercial invoice, *pro forma* invoice, certificate of origin, bill of lading, packing list, insurance certificate, import license, and shipper's export declarations. Without proper documentation, goods may not be cleared through customs. At the very least, such complicated and lengthy documents serve to slow down product clearance. France, requiring customs documentation to be in French, even held up trucks from other European countries for hours while looking for products' non-French instruction manuals which were banned.

License or Permit   Not all products can be freely imported; controlled imports require licenses or permits. For example, importations of distilled spirits, wines, malt beverages, arms, ammunition, and explosives into the United States require a license issued by the Bureau of Alcohol, Tobacco, and Firearms. India requires license for all imported goods.[28] An article is considered prohibited if not accompanied by a license. It is not always easy to obtain an import license, since many countries will issue one only if goods can be certified as being necessary.

Japan simplified its licensing procedure in 1986. Previously, a separate license application had been required for any new cosmetic product, even when only a change in shade was involved. The new requirements categorize cosmetics into seventy-eight groups and list permitted ingredients. A marketer simply notifies the government of any new product using those ingredients.

Inspection   Inspection is an integral part of product clearance. Goods must be examined to determine quality and quantity. This step is highly related to other customs and entry procedures. First, inspection classifies and values products for tariff purposes. Second, inspection reveals whether imported items are consistent with those specified in the accompanying documents and whether such items require any licenses. Third, inspection determines whether products meet health and safety regulations in order to make certain that food products are fit for human consumption or that the products can be operated safely. Fourth, inspection prevents the importation of prohibited articles.

Marketers should be careful in stating the amount and quality of products, as well as in providing an accurate description of products. Any deviation from the statements contained in invoices necessitates further measurements and determination, more delay, and more expenses.

Inspection can be used intentionally to discourage imports. Metal baseball bats from the United States, for instance, have a potential for selling very well in the Japanese market. But a major obstacle is that every single bat must carry a stamp of consumer safety, and this must be "ascertained" only after expensive on-dock inspection.

Not long ago, American firms wanting to export to Japan had to endure lengthy and costly inspections of each shipment. Their crates had to be opened at ports for lot-by-lot testing. This certification problem forced U.S. companies to manufacture in Japan, license their products, or give up. Complaints subsequently led to the amendment of regulatory statutes to permit the Ministry of International Trade and Industry (MITI) officials to inspect U.S. factories for certification. Because of the enormous costs, however, the visit by MITI officials was out of reach for small- and medium-sized companies. The problem was solved when the MITI authorized Applied Research Laboratories, Inc., a U.S. firm, to inspect electronics and electrical-appliance factories in the United States. The whole procedure can be completed within a few months for only $2,500.[29]

Health and Safety Regulations   Many products are subject to health and safety regulations, which are necessary to protect the public health and environment. For example, U.S. importation of eggs must be accompanied by a certificate, signed by a veterinary officer of the national government of the country of origin, stating that the eggs were washed, sanitized, and packed as prescribed by the regulations of the Animal and Plant Health Inspection Service and that the eggs were produced by flocks known to be free of Newcastle disease. Health and safety regulations are not restricted to agricultural products. Many other products (and applicable laws or regulations) include TV receivers, microwave ovens, X-ray devices, laser products, and other electronic products related to radiation (Radiation Control for Health and Safety Act of 1968); food, beverages, drugs, devices, and cosmetics (Federal Food, Drug, and Cosmetic Act—enforced by the FDA); chemical substances (Toxic Substances Control Act); and wearing apparel (Hazardous Substance and Flammable Fabrics Act—enforced by the Consumer Product Safety Commision).

Concern for safety was used by Japan against aluminum softball bats from the United States. The manufacturing process leaves a small hole in the top filled with a rubber stopper. Japan thus bans the bats on the ground that the stopper might fly out and hurt someone. According to U.S. manufacturers, this fear is unfounded.

Product Requirements

For goods to enter a country, product requirements set by that country must be met. Requirements may apply to product standards and product specifications as well as to packaging, labeling, and marking.

Product Standards Each country determines its own product standards to protect the health and safety of its consumers. Such standards may also be erected as barriers to prevent or to slow down importation of foreign goods. Because of U.S. grade, size, quality, and maturity requirements, many Mexican agricultural commodities are barred from entering the United States. Japanese product standards are even more complex, and they are based on physical characteristics instead of product performance. Such standards make it necessary to repeat the product approval process when a slight product modification occurs (such as color), even though the performance of the product in question remains the same. Furthermore, these standards are frequently changed in Japan in order to exclude imports.

Packaging, Labeling, and Marking Packaging, labeling, and marking are considered together because they are highly interrelated. Many products must be packaged in a certain way for safety and other reasons. Canada requires imported canned foods to be packed in specified can sizes, and instructions contained within packages or on them must be in English and French. The Canadian Labeling Act also requires all imported clothing to have labels in both languages.

Products must also be properly marked and labeled, and marking and labeling may apply either to products themselves or to their packages. An Italian judge ordered a seizure of bottled Coke because he felt that the ingredients listed on the bottle cap were not properly described and labeled. France requires all imported goods to carry labels of origin, and so does the United States. For identification and transportation purposes, packages should bear a consignee's mark, port mark, and package numbers. In general, the rule is that packaging, marking, and labeling must be accurate and informative without inducing any false impression.

Product Testing Many products must be tested to determine their safety and suitability before they can be marketed. This is another area in which the United States has some troubles in Japan. Although products may have won approval everywhere else for safety and effectiveness, such products as medical equipment and pharmaceuticals must go through elaborate standards testing that can take a few years—just long enough for Japanese companies to develop competing products. Moreover, the reviews take place behind the Health and Welfare Ministry's closed doors.

The EC's Global Approach to testing and certification for product safety provides manufacturers with one set of procedures for certifying product compliance with EC health, safety, and environmental requirements. The various means by which manufacturers can certify product conformance include manufacturer self-declaration of conformity, third-party testing, quality assurance audit, and/or approval by a body authorized by an EC member state and recognized by the EC Commission. The mark *CE* on the product signifies that all legal requirements have been met.[30]

Product Specifications Product specifications, though appearing to be an innocent process, can wreak havoc on imports. Specifications can be written in such a way as to favor local bidders and to keep out foreign suppliers. For example, specifications can be extremely detailed, or they can be written to closely resemble domestic products. Thus, they can be used against foreign suppliers who cannot satisfy the specifications without expensive or lengthy modification. Japan's Nippon Telephone & Telegraph

Company (NTT) was able to use product specifications as a built-in barrier when it was forced to accept bids from foreign firms. At one time, it did not even provide any specifications and bidding details in any language but Japanese. Its specifications are highly restrictive and written with existing Japanese products in mind.[31] Instead of outlining functional characteristics, NTT specifies physical features right down to the location of ventilation holes, the details of which are almost identical to those of Nippon Electric. For example, NTT requires metal cabinets for modems, whereas most U.S. makers use plastic. Parts must be made by the Japanese to qualify for bidding. In general, NTT goes well beyond specifications for performance. GATT has established procedures for setting product standards using performance standards rather than detailed physical specifications.

Quotas

Quotas are a quantity control on imported goods. Generally, they are specific provisions limiting the amount of foreign products imported in order to protect local firms and to conserve foreign currency. Quotas can be used for export control as well. An export quota is sometimes required by national planning to preserve scarce resources. Thailand, for example, limits the export of teak in its raw form but allows the export of the final, manufactured products based on it. From a policy standpoint, a quota is not as desirable as a tariff since a quota generates no revenues for a country. According to the Institute for International Economics, quotas and tariffs cost American consumers $56 billion in 1984. There are three kinds of quotas: absolute, tariff, and voluntary.

Absolute Quotas   An **absolute quota** is the most restrictive of all. It limits in absolute terms the amount imported during a quota period. Once filled, further entries are prohibited. Some quotas are global, but others are allocated to specific foreign countries. Japan imposes strict quotas on oranges and beef. To appease the EC, it has lifted quotas on skimmed milk powder and tobaccos from Europe. The most extreme of the absolute quota is an embargo, or a zero quota, as shown in the case of the U.S. trade embargoes against Iraq, Vietnam, and North Korea.

Tariff Quotas   A **tariff quota** permits the entry of a limited quantity of the quota product at a reduced rate of duty. Quantities in excess of the quota can be imported but are subject to a higher duty rate. Through the use of tariff quotas, a combination of tariffs and quotas is applied with the primary purpose of importing what is needed and discouraging excessive quantities through higher tariffs. When the United States increased tariffs on imported motorcycles in order to protect the U.S. motorcycle industry, it exempted from this tax the first 6,000 big motorcycles from Japan and the first 4,000–5,000 units from Europe. Exhibit 3–8 lists products that are subject to tariff-rate and absolute quotas.

Voluntary Quotas   A **voluntary quota** differs from the other two kinds of quotas, which are unilaterally imposed. A voluntary quota is a formal agreement between nations or between a nation and an industry. This agreement usually specifies the limit of supply by product, country, and volume.

Two kinds of voluntary quotas can be legally distinguished: **VER (voluntary export restraint)** and **OMA (orderly marketing agreement)**. Whereas an OMA

TARIFF-RATE QUOTAS

☐ Milk and Cream, not concentrated nor containing added sugar or other sweetening matter, of a fat content—by weight—exceeding one percent but not six percent
☐ Anchovies, in oil, in airtight containers
☐ Mandarins (Satsumas) in airtight containers
☐ Tuna fish
☐ Whiskbrooms wholly or in part of broom corn
☐ Other brooms wholly or in part of broom corn
☐ Certain textiles assembled in Guam
☐ Certain textiles from Canada

ABSOLUTE QUOTAS

☐ Certain candy and other confectionary

Chocolate, sweetened, in bars or blocks weighing 4.5 kg or more each

Apple or pear juices, not mixed and not containing over 1.0 percent of ethyl alcohol by volume

Ale, porter, stout, and beer, in containers other than glass each holding not over 3.8 liters

Ale, porter, stout, and beer, in containers other than glass each holding over 3.8 liters

White still wines produced from grapes, containing not over 14 percent of alcohol by volume, in containers each holding not over 3.8 liters, valued over $1.05 per liter

☐ Certain tungstic acid and ammonium paratungstate
☐ Milk and cream, condensed or evaporated
☐ Butter substitutes, containing over 45 percent of butterfat
☐ Animal feeds containing milk or milk derivatives
☐ Buttermix containing over 5.5 percent but not over 45 percent by weight of butterfat
☐ Chocolate, containing 5.5 percent or less by weight of butterfat
☐ Chocolate crumb and other related articles containing over 5.5 percent by weight of butterfat
☐ Ice cream
☐ Certain cheddar cheese
☐ Cotton, not carded, not combed, and not otherwise processed:

Having a staple length under 28.575 mm; and

Having a staple length 28.575 mm or more but under 34.925 mm; and

Having a staple length 34.925 mm or more

☐ Card strips made from cotton having a staple length under 30.1625 mm, and cotton comber waste, lap waste, silver waste, and roving waste
☐ Fibers of cotton processed but not spun
☐ Upland cotton
☐ Certain sugars, syrups, and molasses derived from sugarcane or sugar beets, except those entered pursuant to a license issued by the Secretary of Agriculture
☐ Fluid milk and sweet or sour cream of a fat content by weight exceeding six percent but not 45 percent
☐ Textiles from certain countries

EXHIBIT 3–8 U.S. import quotas

Source: Importing into the United States, U.S. Customs Service, Department of the Treasury, 1990, 60

involves a negotiation between two governments to specify export management rules, the monitoring of trade volumes, and consultation rights, a VER is a direct agreement between an importing nation's government and a foreign exporting industry (i.e., a quota with industry participation). Both enable the importing country to circumvent the GATT's rules (Article XIX) that require the country to reciprocate for the quota received and to impose that market safeguard on a most-favored-nation basis. Because this is a gray area, the OMA and VER can be applied in a discriminatory manner to a certain country. In the case of a VER involving private industries, a public disclosure is not necessary.

The largest voluntary quota is the Multi-Fiber Arrangement (MFA) for 41 export and import countries. This more than two-decade-old international agreement on textiles allows Western governments to set quotas on imports of low-priced textiles from the Third World. The treaty has been criticized because advanced nations are able to force the agreement on poorer countries. Furthermore, the MFA costs American consumers $369.4 million a year.

As implied, a country may negotiate to limit voluntarily its export to a particular market. This may sound peculiar because the country appears to be acting against its own self-interest. But a country's unwillingness to accept these unfavorable terms will eventually invite trade retaliation and tougher terms in the form of forced quotas. It is thus voluntary only in the sense that the exporting country tries to avoid alternative trade barriers that are even less desirable. For instance, Japan agreed to restrict and reprice some exports within Great Britain. The United States, because of its unwillingness to raise tariffs directly or to impose import quotas, has turned to voluntary quotas. In the early 1980s Japan agreed to limit its annual auto exports to the United States to 1.68 million units. Japan's voluntary quotas added $1,650 to the average price of an automobile sold in the United States in 1984, amounting to a 17 percent increase.[32]

Quotas are still quotas regardless of what they are called. They always inhibit free trade, and frequently they fail to achieve the desired goal. The example set by U.S. automakers is instructive. After arguing for quotas and price increases to gain extra monies to improve productivity and competitiveness, the automakers ended up using record profits to pay big bonuses to their executives. According to a vice-president of Drexel Burnham Lambert, "quotas screw the consumer." As reviewed and concluded by Boonekamp, voluntary quotas "are often not voluntary; they are costly and discriminatory; but they can be a tempting form of protection relative to other measures."[33]

Financial Control

Financial regulations can also function to restrict international trade. These restrictive monetary policies are designed to control capital flow so that currencies can be defended or imports controlled. For example, to defend the weak Italian lira, Italy imposed a 7 percent tax on the purchase of foreign currencies. There are several forms that financial restrictions can take.

Exchange Control   An **exchange control** is a technique that limits the amount of the currency that can be taken abroad. The reason exchange controls are usually applied is that the local currency is overvalued, thus causing imports to be paid for in smaller amounts of currency. Purchasers then try to use the relatively cheap foreign exchange to obtain items either unavailable or more expensive in the local currency. This is the reason why Mexican consumers before the 1982 economic crisis regularly did their shopping across the border in Texas and California. When these conditions occur, exchange control is necessary to limit the amount of foreign currency an importer can obtain to pay for the goods purchased.

Exchange controls also limit the length of time and amount of money an exporter can hold for the goods sold. French exporters, for example, must exchange the foreign currencies for francs within one month. By regulating all types of the capital outflows in foreign currencies, the government either makes it difficult to get imported products or makes such items available only at higher prices.

Japan allocates foreign exchange in such a way as to encourage imports of sophisticated, innovative technologies but not of consumer goods. China requires joint ventures to export enough to pay for imports.[34] American Motors (AMC) spent more than $23 million for imports of machinery and other items to assemble Jeep Cherokees for sale in China. Subsequently, it ran out of dollars for import kits or parts because China paid AMC mostly with Chinese yuan, which were not convertible.

Multiple Exchange Rates   **Multiple exchange rates** are another form of exchange regulation or barrier. The objectives of multiple exchange rates are twofold: to encourage exports and imports of certain goods and to discourage exports and imports of others. This means that there is no single rate for all products or industries. But with the application of multiple exchange rates, some products and industries will benefit and some will not. Spain once used low exchange rates for goods designated for export and high rates for those it desired to retain at home. Multiple exchange rates may also apply to imports. The high rates may be used for imports of particular goods with the government's approval, whereas low rates may be used for other imports. Table 3–4 lists countries with multiple exchange rates.

TABLE 3–4   Countries with multiple exchange rates (end of 1985)[a]

Country	Number of Exchange Rates[b]	Country	Number of Exchange Rates[b]
Afghanistan	3	Lao People's Democratic	4
Bahamas	2	Republic	
Bangladesh	2	Mexico	5
Chile	2	Nicaragua	3
China	2	Paraguay	3
Costa Rica	2	Peru	2
Dominican Republic	2	Romania	4
Ecuador	3	Sierra Leone	2
Egypt	3	Somalia	2
El Salvador	3	Sudan	2
Guatemala	3	Syrian Arab Republic	3
Iran	2	Venezuela	4
Kuwait	2	Vietnam	2

[a]Excluding subsidies, taxes, discounts, and premiums resulting in implicit multiple exchange rates.
[b]Excluding illegal parallel rates that are not officially recognized by the authorities.
Source: IMF Survey, 24 June 1985, 197

The severity of Mexico's near-collapsed economy in 1982 forced the government to nationalize banks and to adopt a two-tiered system, with a lower preferential exchange rate for transactions involving imports of necessities (e.g., food) and in the interest payments on new public and private foreign credits. The free-market rate is used in tourism and for most border and private transactions, while the regulated rate, which makes the peso relatively expensive, is used in about 80 percent of all transactions. The result is that the rates used by the government and the black market differ widely.

Because multiple exchange rates are used to bring in hard currencies (through exports) as well as to restrict imports, this system is condemned by the IMF. According to the IMF, any unapproved multiple currency practices are a breach of obligations, and the member may become ineligible to use the Fund's resources. The IMF "is prepared to approve multiple currency practices of a member for balance of payments reasons and other reasons under the following conditions: (1) the measures are temporary and do not impede adjustment of its balance of payments, (2) the practices do not give it unfair trade advantage over other members, and (3) they do not discriminate among members."[35]

Prior Import Deposits and Credit Restrictions   Financial barriers can also include specific limitations or import restraints, such as prior import deposits and credit restrictions. Both of these barriers operate by imposing certain financial restrictions on importers. A government can require **prior import deposits** (forced deposits) that make imports difficult by tying up an importer's capital. In effect, the importer is paying interest for money borrowed without being able to use the money or get interest earnings on the money from the government. Importers in Brazil and Italy must deposit a large sum of money with their central banks if they intend to buy foreign goods. To help initiate an aircraft industry, the Brazilian government has required an importer of "flyaway" planes to deposit the full price of the imported aircraft for one year with no interest.

Credit restrictions apply only to imports; that is, exporters may be able to get loans from the government, usually at very favorable rates, but importers will not be able to receive any credit or financing from the government. Importers must look for loans in the private sector—very likely at significantly higher rates, if such loans are available at all.

Profit Remittance Restrictions   Another form of exchange barrier is the **profit remittance restriction**. ASEAN countries share a common philosophy in allowing unrestricted repatriation of profits earned by foreign companies. Singapore, in particular, allows the unrestricted movement of capital. But many countries regulate the remittance of profits earned in local operations and sent to a parent organization located abroad. Brazil uses progressive rates in taxing all profits remitted to a parent company abroad, with such rates going up to 60 percent. Other countries practice a form of profit remittance restriction by simply having long delays in permission for profit expatriation. To overcome these practices, MNCs have looked to legal loopholes.[36] Many employ the following tactics:

Switch trading   This tactic requires that goods are sold for credit or for other products, which can later be sold for conversion into the desired currency. For example, assume that Russia has $1 million credit for Italian pasta, which Russia does not want. A U.S. firm may agree to sell its product to Russia at a premium in return for the $1 million credit for pasta. Subsequently, the U.S. firm can sell the pasta to Germany for deutsche marks, which are fully convertible to dollars.

Moving up the priority queue   A company can negotiate its way up the government's queue for permission to expatriate profits by bribing officials, refusing to service and repair the product sold, and so on.

Currency swaps   This tactic matches a multinational firm that wants to repatriate a currency with another firm that needs that currency and is willing to acquire it by offering to take it at a discount.

Netting   In this tactic, a subsidiary's blocked funds are utilized to cover affiliation costs within a country, such as the legal fees of the parent company.

Parallel loans   This variation of netting involves a back-to-back transaction. For example, a British subsidiary of a U.S. corporation lends British pounds to a British multinational firm whose U.S. subsidiary lends the same amount in dollars to the U.S. corporation.

Another tactic is to negotiate for a higher value of an investment than the investment's actual worth. In effect, this tactic increases the equity base from which dividend repatriations are calculated. Some techniques for effecting this purpose are:[37]

Invoicing   raising markup on intracompany shipments

Royalties   increasing royalties charged to subsidiaries on parts designed in the United States

Management fees   charging subsidiaries for the time managers at the parent company spend on international business

Engineering fees   charging subsidiaries for the time engineers develop and refine products made overseas

GATT

Virtually all nations seek to pursue their own best interests in international trade. The result is that sooner or later international trade and marketing can be disrupted. To prevent or at least alleviate any problems, there is a world organization in Geneva known as the **General Agreement on Tariffs and Trade (GATT).** GATT is a multilateral trade agreement with over 100 signatories, and it has been labeled the locomotive that powers international commerce.

Created in January 1948, the objective of GATT is to achieve a broad, multilateral, and free worldwide system of trading. For example, its code requires international bidding on major projects. GATT provides the forum for tariff negotiations and the elimination of trade discrimination. Its members account for some 90 percent of world trade. Those who are not GATT's members include some Latin American and African countries as well as many others in southern Asia and the Middle East.

The four basic principles of GATT are

1. Member countries will *consult* each other concerning trade problems.
2. The agreement provides a framework for *negotiation* and embodies results of negotiations in a legal instrument.
3. Countries should protect domestic industries *only through tariffs*, when needed and if permitted. There should be no other restrictive devices such as quotas prohibiting imports.
4. Trade should be conducted on a *nondiscriminatory* basis.

Reductions of barriers should be mutual and reciprocal because any country's import increases caused by such reductions will be offset by export increases caused by other countries' reduction of restrictions. This concept is the basis of the principle of the **most favored nation (MFN),** which is the cornerstone of GATT. According to this principle, countries should grant one another treatment as favorable as treatment given to their best trading partners or any other country. For example, reductions accorded France by the United States should be extended to other countries with which the United States exchanges the MFN agreement (e.g., to Brazil). Likewise, if a country decides to temporarily protect its local industry because that industry is seriously threatened, then the newly erected barriers must apply to all countries even though the threat to its industry might only come from a single nation. The MFN principle thus moves countries away from bilateral bargaining to multilateral (or simultaneous bilateral) bargaining. Each country must be concerned with the implications that its concessions for one country would mean for other countries. The only exception is that an advanced country should not expect reciprocity from less-developed countries.

The United States does not accord MFN status to communist countries that restrict emigration, but this requirement can be waived by the President. After China first received MFN status from the United States in 1980, mushroom imports from China jumped from nothing to nearly 50 percent of all U.S. mushroom imports. This increase owed much to the decline of canned mushroom duties, from 45 percent to 10 percent. The granting of MFN status to China was done largely for political reasons. The Soviet Union, despite having traded with the United States longer than China, remained unable to gain MFN status and denounced the U.S. action. In 1990 the U.S. Congress approved legislation extending most-favored-nation treatment to Czechoslovakia. In contrast, the United States required Romania to make substantial progress toward democratic change and the rule of the law before the MFN to Romania could be restored.

According to GATT, the only valid reason for tariffs in world business is for the protection of an infant industry. Other understandable reasons include defense or noneconomic concerns, such as some revenue raising. Three other noneconomic reasons are improvements in terms of trade, income, and balance of payments. These "beggar-thy-neighbor" policies create gains at the expense of others and are not considered by GATT to be valid reasons for refusing to reduce tariffs.

Seven successive rounds of multilateral trade negotiations under GATT auspieces produced a decline in average tariff on industrial products in industrial countries from more than 40 percent in 1947 to about 5 percent in 1988. In the meantime, global trade greatly expanded as the volume of trade in manufactured goods increased twentyfold.

Although GATT was formed to moderate tariff processes, it now handles nontariff processes such as export subsidies, quotas, packaging rules, government purchasing practices, and product standards. Under the sponsorship of GATT, and after five years of negotiations among ninety-eight nations at Geneva, the so-called Tokyo Round yielded agreements to lower both nontariff barriers and tariffs by 35 percent. The pacts covered 80–90 percent of world trade and established a broad legal framework for monitoring, notification, complaint procedures, and ongoing negotiations to extend the coverage. Details of the Tokyo Round are given in Exhibit 3–9.

GATT has also set the rules of conduct for trade, though basic enforcement is anything but easy. Because of Japanese resistance to open to free trade, the Tokyo agreement allows a country to retaliate against another on an individual basis. In effect, the GATT's safeguard rule (i.e., the MFN principle) can be violated. This practice, if allowed to continue unrestricted, will undoubtedly weaken the MFN principle over the long run.

The success after Tokyo proved limited. Tariffs, being both obvious and undesirable, were relatively easy to eliminate or reduce. In the 1980s, the major trade obstacles have shifted to the invisible nontariff barriers, which unevenly affect trading

---

Since the Second World War there have been seven rounds of multilateral trade negotiations:

1. Geneva negotiations, 1947
2. Annecy negotiations, 1949
3. Torquay negotiations, 1950–51
4. Geneva negotiations, 1955–56
5. Geneva negotiations ("Dillon Round"), 1959–62
6. Geneva negotiations ("Kennedy Round"), 1963–67
7. Geneva negotiations ("Tokyo Round"), 1973–79

The first six rounds were concerned almost exclusively with multilateral reduction of tariffs. With the successful and progressive lowering of tariffs, nontariff barriers to trade became the subject of greater concern. The Tokyo Round was a comprehensive effort to deal with tariff and nontariff measures. In addition to tariff reductions of about one-third in the major industrial markets, the Tokyo Round produced a series of new or reinforced codes dealing with a variety of nontariff practices, including codes on subsidies and countervailing duties, technical barriers to trade, import licensing procedures, antidumping, government procurement, and customs valuation. In addition, agreements dealing with dairy products, meat, and civil aircraft were also reached.

EXHIBIT 3–9   GATT trade negotiations

Source: S. J. Anjaria, "A New Round of Global Trade Negotiations," *Finance & Development* 23 (June 1986): 4

partners, making it difficult to achieve multilateral tradeoffs. Moreover, LDCs, embittered by the West's import restrictions on textiles, are reluctant to lower barriers for services and for high technology, because such new trade fields benefit advanced countries. Exhibit 3–10 examines a few issues of concern to GATT.

The Uruguay Round of multilateral trade negotiations, launched in Punta del Este, Uruguay, in September 1986, aims to liberalize trade further, to strengthen GATT's role, to foster cooperation, and to enhance the interrelationships between trade and other economic policies that affect growth and development. The Uruguay Round attempted to deal with new areas such as services, intellectual property rights, and trade-related investment. Although the Uruguay Round continued beyond the termination date of 1990, countries were unable to make difficult political decisions. Subsequently, trade ministers of the member countries of GATT finally agreed in Brussels on December 7, 1990, to suspend their negotiations in the Uruguay Round as a result of the failure to resolve differences on farm subsidies between the United States, the Cairns Group of food exporters, and the European Community. In particular, the EC, Japan, and Korea were unwilling to reform significantly their agricultural policies.

Without a successful Uruguay Round, bilateral and regional trading agreements are likely to increase at the expense of the growth of global trade. Production decisions within a country based on regional rather than on general market signals could fall short of potential. "It would be ironic if the virtually worldwide trend toward allowing national economies to be guided by market signals were to be frustrated by an inability to allow these same signals to guide the complex workings of the multilateral trading system."[38]

PREFERENTIAL SYSTEMS

Generalized System of Preferences (GSP)

Although the benefits derived from the creation of GATT are rarely disputed, LDCs do not necessarily embrace GATT because those countries believe the benefits are not evenly distributed. Tariff reduction generally favors manufactured goods rather than primary goods. LDCs rely mainly on exports of primary products, which are then converted by advanced nations into manufactured products for export back to LDCs. As a result, an LDC's exports will usually be lower in value than its imports, thus exacerbating the country's poverty status.

In response to LDCs' needs, the United Nations Conference on Trade and Development (UNCTAD) was created as a permanent organ of the UN General Assembly. Efforts by UNCTAD led to the establishment of the New International Economic Order (NIEO) program. The program seeks to assist LDCs through the stabilization of prices of primary products, the expansion of LDCs' manufacturing capabilities, and the acquisition by LDCs of advanced technology.

The goal of UNCTAD is to encourage development in Third World countries and enhance their export positions. This goal led to the establishment of a tariff preference system for LDCs' manufactured products. In spite of GATT's nondiscrimination principle, advanced nations agreed to grant such preferences to LDCs' goods.

In November 1983, the Director-General of the GATT appointed an independent study group on the international trading system. The group, headed by Dr. Fritz Leutwiler of Switzerland, consisted of seven distinguished persons from developed and developing countries, participating in their personal capacities. In March 1985 the group, generally referred to as the *Leutwiler Group* issued a report entitled "Trade Policies for a Better Future: Proposals for Action." The report, containing fifteen principal recommendations, summarized below, indicates the scope of potential trade policy reform that governments may need to address in the coming years:

1. Open formulation and monitoring of trade policy and actions; analysis of the costs and benefits of trade policy actions through a "protection balance sheet."
2. Clearer and fairer rules for agricultural trade, with no special treatment for particular countries or commodities.
3. A timetable and procedures to bring into conformity with GATT rules in all countries all measures that are currently inconsistent with the GATT, including voluntary export restraints and discriminatory import restrictions.
4. Trade in textiles and clothing should be fully subject to ordinary GATT rules.
5. Rules on subsidies need to be revised, clarified, and made more effective.
6. Improvement and vigorous application of GATT codes governing nontariff distortions of trade.
7. Clarify and tighten rules permitting customs unions and free trade areas to prevent their distortion and abuse.
8. Regular oversight or surveillance of country trade policies and actions by the GATT Secretariat, which should collect and publish information.
9. Greater security and limitations on application of emergency "safeguard" protection for particular industries that should continue to be nondiscriminatory.
10. Greater integration of developing countries into the trading system, with all the accompanying rights and responsibilities.
11. Expansion of trade in services and discussion of multilateral rules for this sector.
12. GATT's dispute settlement procedures should be reinforced by building up a permanent roster of nongovernmental experts to examine disputes and by improving the implementation of panel recommendations.
13. A new round of GATT negotiations should be launched to strengthen the multilateral trading system and further open world markets.
14. Establishment of a permanent, ministerial-level body in GATT to ensure high-level attention to trade issues.
15. A satisfactory resolution of the world debt problem, adequate flows of development finance, better international coordination of macroeconomic policies, and greater consistency between trade and financial policies.

EXHIBIT 3–10   The "Leutwiler Group"—trade policy reform

Source: S. J. Anjaria, "A New Round of Global Trade Negotiations," *Finance & Development* 23 (June 1986): 6

The U.S. preferential system system is known as the **Generalized System of Preferences (GSP).** Congress passed the Trade Act of 1974, authorizing the initiation of the GSP. The purpose of the act is to aid development by providing duty-free entry on 4,000 products from more than 130 developing countries. Products manufactured wholly or substantially (at least 35 percent for single country products) in the designated countries are permitted to enter the United States duty-free as long as a particular item does not exceed $50.9 million in sales or 50 percent of all U.S. imports of this product. Not all products qualify for such preferential treatment, however, and one should consult the Harmonized Tariff Schedule of the United States to determine whether a product may enter duty-free.

Exhibit 3–11 lists the designated beneficiary developing countries, as well as dependent countries and territories. For a country to qualify, a number of economic variables are considered, such as per capita GNP and living standard. Mexico, receiving some $2.2 billion in benefits, is the primary GSP beneficiary. Burma and the Central African Republic had their benefits suspended under the U.S. GSP for failing to meet the labor requirements. Venezuela was challenged as a result of a claim by Occidental Petroleum that its assets were expropriated without compensation. The four tigers (Hong Kong, Taiwan, Singapore, and South Korea), once receiving almost 60 percent of the benefits under GSP, were permanently graduated from the program in the beginning of 1989 as a result of their high degree of economic development and export competitiveness. Therefore, Black & Decker, which makes electric irons in Singapore, lost more than $3 million a year because of the new duties. Clearly, foreign exporters and American importers can find the GSP system highly advantageous, and it is inexcusable not to take advantage of it.

Caribbean Basin Initiative (CBI)

Another U.S. preferential system is the **Caribbean Basin Initiative (CBI).** The Caribbean Basin Economic Recovery Act of 1983 provides trade and tax measures to promote economic revitalization and expanded private-sector opportunities in designated countries in the Caribbean Basin region. The beneficiary countries are Antigua and Barbuda, Bahamas, Barbados, Belize, British Virgin Islands, Costa Rica, Dominica, Dominican Republic, El Salvador, Grenada, Guatemala, Haiti, Honduras, Jamaica, Montserrat, Netherland Antilles, Panama, Puerto Rico, St. Christopher-Nevis, St. Lucia, St. Vincent and the Grenadines, Trinidad and Tobago, and the U.S. Virgin Islands.

The main provision of the CBI eliminates U.S. duties on almost all products entering from qualified countries in the Caribbean Basin. The law, however, excludes important products (textiles, apparel, footwear, and leather goods) from duty-free status as a safeguard for domestic (U.S.) industry.

Although most products have already enjoyed low tariffs under the GSP, CBI has several unique features:

> CBI differs from GSP in several important ways. Whereas GSP applies worldwide, the CBI is limited to 27 Caribbean Basin countries. The product coverage under CBI is much broader, with most of the 7,350 TSUS items included.
>
> Direct importation, substantial transformation and rules-of-origin requirements apply for both GSP and CBI, but CBI is more liberal in several respects. First, GSP requires

INDEPENDENT COUNTRIES

Angola	Equatorial Guinea	Malta	Sierra Leone
Antigua and Barbuda*c*	Fiji	Marshall Islands	Solomon Islands
Argentina	Gambia	Mauritania	Somalia
Bahamas*c*	Ghana	Mauritius	Sri Lanka
Bangladesh	Grenada*c*	Micronesia	Sudan
Barbados*c*	Guatemala	Mexico	Surinam
Belize*c*	Guinea	Morocco	Swaziland
Benin	Guinea-Bissau	Mozambique	Syria
Bhutan	Guyana*c*	Nauru	Tanzania
Bolivia*a*	Haiti	Nepal	Thailand*b*
Botswana	Honduras	Niger	Togo
Brazil	Hungary	Oman	Tonga
Burkina Faso	India	Pakistan	Trinidad and Tobago*c*
Burundi	Indonesia*b*	Panama	Tunisia
Cameroon	Israel	Papua, New Guinea	Turkey
Cape Verde	Ivory Coast	Peru*a*	Tuvalu
Chad	Jamaica*c*	Philippines*b*	Uganda
Colombia*a*	Jordan	Poland	Upper Volta
Comoros	Kenya	Rwanda	Uruguay
Congo	Kiribati	Saint Kitts and	Vanuatu
Costa Rica	Lebanon	Nevis*c*	Venezuela*a*
Cyprus	Lesotho	Saint Lucia*c*	Western Samoa
Djibouti	Liberia	Saint Vincent and	Yemen Arab Republic
Dominica*c*	Madagascar	the Grenadines*c*	(Sanaa)
Dominican Republic	Malawi	Sao Tome and Principe	Yugoslavia
Ecuador*a*	Malaysia*b*	Senegal	Zaire
Egypt	Maldives	Seychelles	Zambia
El Salvador	Mali		Zimbabwe

NONINDEPENDENT COUNTRIES AND TERRITORIES

Anguilla	French Polynesia	Norfolk Island
Aruba	Gibraltar	Pitcairn Islands
British Indian	Greenland	Saint Helena
Ocean Territory	Heard Island and	Tokelau
Cayman Islands	McDonald Islands	Trust Territory of the
Christmas Island	Macau	Pacific Islands (Palau)
(Australia)	Montserrat*c*	Turks and
Cocos (Keeling) Islands	Netherlands Antilles	Caicos Islands
Cook Islands	New Caledonia	Virgin Islands, British
Falkland Islands	Niue	Wallis and Futuna
(Islas Malvinas)		Western Sahara

EXHIBIT 3–11   Beneficiary developing countries for purposes of the GSP

[a]Member countries of the Cartagena Agreement—Andean Group (treated as one country)
[b]Association of South East Asian Nations—ASEAN (GSP-eligible countries only) treated as one country
[c]Member countries of the Caribbean Common Market—CARICOM (treated as one country)
Source: U.S. Customs Service, *Importing into the United States* (Washington, D.C.: Department of the Treasury, 1990), 26.

that the 35 percent value added be from a single beneficiary country in most cases. For CBI, the 35 percent test can be met through processing in several beneficiary countries. Secondly, under CBI up to 15 percent of the 35 percent value added requirement can be accounted for by U.S. source materials. Finally, valued added in U.S insular possessions such as Puerto Rico and the U.S. Virgin Islands may count as beneficiary country input when computing value added under CBI.[39]

The Customs and Trade Act of 1990 makes the Caribbean Basin Initiative permanent and provides additional trade benefits for the Caribbean countries. The act provides a significant advantage to import from the region. The products will benefit by cost reductions through tariff elimination compared with imports from non-CBI countries. American firms producing products in the Caribbean may further profit from exporting to Europe, Canada, and South America, because many Caribbean Basin countries have preferential access to one or more of these other markets. The act thus encourages U.S. firms to open more labor-intensive assembly plants that export back to North America.

SOME REMARKS ON PROTECTIONISM

A country has a choice of opening or closing its borders to trade. If it adopts the open system, it has a much better chance of fostering economic growth and maximizing consumer welfare (see Exhibit 3–12). By adopting this approach, Hong Kong has been doing well economically. Albania, in stark contrast, has chosen to discourage almost all forms of contact with the rest of the world. As pointed out by Farmer, no nation, the United States included, can do everything by itself.[40] The United States has a choice, and it can choose between being more like Hong Kong or Albania.

Nations usually take a shortcut and try to have a quick fix for their trade problems. Preoccupation with immediate problems often makes them lose sight of the long-term objectives. Without proper perspective, they can easily end up with more serious problems later.

The problem facing the world is that most nations, developed and developing, are moving toward Albania's closed system. The United States and its trading partners have failed to reduce protectionist measures. Developed countries actually seem to have strengthened their nontariff measures affecting trade. Trade barriers have also remained high in LDCs.

The crowbar theory states that foreign markets do not open except under threat, and the theory appears to guide U.S. trade policy. According to Jagdish Bhagwati, similar to that experienced by the United Kingdom in the past, the United States has experienced a "diminished giant" syndrome. As a result, it has taken unilateral action to pry open foreign markets to U.S. exports. But the use of threats is likely to be ineffective as well as damaging to multilateral trading. The 1988 U.S. Trade and Competitiveness Act attempts to determine unilaterally what constitutes unfair trade based on the assumption that "we are fairer than thou and that we are more open than thou." However, the evidence is weak that the United States is less unfair in trade than other countries.[41]

According to Anjaria, Kirmani, and Petersen, the rise in protectionism is concentrated in sectors where comparative advantage is shifting, and the practice impairs the

The Beginning Of Mexico's New Foreign Trade Policy.

Mexico is tearing up its tariffs. And tearing down the barriers to trade.

Which means greater opportunities for you.

Suppose, for example, you seek access to the burgeoning Mexican market. Now your products can compete fairly with local goods. And should you own a subsidiary in Mexico, you can import components more cheaply than before. Thus making your manufactured items more competitive on the world market.

The end of restrictive trade policies is yet another example of how Mexico is now, shall we say, open for business.

Which brings us to Banca Serfin.

We've helped foreign companies do business in our country for more than 125 years. Becoming Mexico's trade finance leader in the process. As well as the bank offering the most comprehensive array of financial services in all Mexico.

If you'd like to learn how Mexico's new foreign trade policy can work to your advantage, talk with Banca Serfin.

And let the gains begin.

 BANCA SERFIN

EXHIBIT 3–12 Mexico's new trade policy

Source: Courtesy of Banca Serfin, S.N.C.

functioning of the international price mechanism. The practice also undermines trade liberalization. It is in conflict with the principle of comparative advantage, which is the basis for efficient trade growth. The Multi-Fiber Arrangement, by allowing discriminatory restrictions against LDC exporters, prevents them from fully exploiting their comparative advantages in textile and clothing manufacture. Trade barriers slow specialization, diversification, investment efficiency, and growth. As concluded by these authors, "insufficient political will to resist protectionist and bilateral measures is the major explanation" for the rise in protectionism.[42] Governments must make concerted and determined efforts to publicize the costs of protectionism. Trade policy should include a systematic consideration of such costs.

CONCLUSION

This chapter has discussed various trade barriers than can inhibit international marketing and, in turn, the world economic welfare of all consumers. It is important to understand that these are only some of the many trade barriers—others are not discussed. For example, more and more countries have now turned to "performance requirements" in order to gain trade advantage. Foreign suppliers are required to use local materials or to do exporting on behalf of an importing nation before they are allowed to sell their products there.

Regardless of the inappropriateness or injustice of many of these practices, they are part of international marketing. Although nations have used GATT to lessen many of these restrictions, many restrictions will undoubtedly remain. In fact, most countries in recent years have initiated more protective measures. Since an international marketer has no control over these wide-reaching forces, the best defense is to understand and to be knowledgeable of these trade practices. These barriers may be frustrating but are not necessarily insurmountable. By understanding them, the marketer can learn what to expect and how to cope. One must always remember that additional problems are often accompanied by additional opportunities—for additional profits.

QUESTIONS

1. Explain the rationale and discuss the weaknesses of each of these arguments for protection of local industries: (a) keeping money at home, (b) reducing unemployment, (c) equalizing cost and price, (d) enhancing national security, and (e) protecting infant industry.
2. Distinguish between these types of tariffs: (a) import and export tariffs, (b) protective and revenue tariffs, (c) surcharge and countervailing duty, and (d) specific and ad valorem duties.

3. Explain how these distribution/consumption taxes differ from one another: single-stage, value-added, cascade, and excise taxes.
4. Explain these various forms of government participation in trade: administrative guidance, subsidies, and state trading.
5. Other than cash, what are the various forms of subsidies?
6. Explain these customs and entry procedures and discuss how each one can be used deliber-

ately to restrict imports: (a) product classification, (b) product valuation, (c) documentation, (d) license/permit, (e) inspection, and (f) health and safety regulations.

7. Explain these various types of product requirements and discuss how each one can be used deliberately to restrict imports: (a) product standards; (b) packaging, labeling, and marking; (c) product testing; and (d) product specifications.

8. What is the rationale for an export quota?
9. Distinguish these types of import quotas: (a) absolute, (b) tariff, (c) OMA, and (d) VER.
10. Discuss how these financial control methods adversely affect free trade: exchange control, multiple exchange rates, prior import deposits, credit restrictions, and profit remittance restrictions.
11. What is GATT? What is its purpose?
12. What is GSP?
13. What is CBI?

DISCUSSION ASSIGNMENTS AND MINICASES

1. If simple existence of government can distort trade inside and outside its area, should governments be abolished in order to eliminate trade distortion?
2. Several U.S. government officials and elected officials have advocated the adoption of the European VAT system. What is their reasoning? Do you agree with their position?
3. Will tariffs play a more significant role than nontariff barriers during the 1990s in affecting world trade?

4. Discuss how you can overcome the financial control imposed by the host country.
5. Do you agree that GATT has served a useful purpose and has achieved its goals?
6. Should the United States continue the GSP system?
7. How should MNCs generally cope with trade barriers?

CASE 3–1
PARTNER OR ENEMY?

The Japanese automobile market is large but perceived to be closed to foreign automakers. In 1985 some 2.2 million Japanese cars were sold in the United States, but only 1,816 American cars were sold in Japan. To put it the other way, the United States exported one car to Japan for every 1,200 Japanese cars it imported. In 1990 some 3.3 million Japanese cars and trucks were sold in the United States, while total imports to Japan were 221,706 cars, with BMW, Daimler-Benz, and Volkswagen-Audi accounting for 128,832 cars.

In many ways, the automobile industry is typical in terms of the difficulties faced by foreign companies in selling their products in Japan. There are many legal, bureaucratic, and socio-cultural barriers to overcome. Foreign automakers must have their cars and documents physically inspected by Japanese officials. New dealers must be recruited since existing ones are not allowed to share facilities. Tariffs on automobiles are high by U.S. standards and apply even to the transportation costs.

In asking the U.S. government to continue the use of quotas on Japanese cars, Lee Iacocca, Chrysler's chairman, asserted that Japan's imports of raw materials from the United States and exports of such manufactured products as automobiles are "a classic definition of a colony. All we're missing are the Redcoats." Incidentally, Chrysler's sales in Japan in the first three quarters of 1987 were 214 units. The company did quite well, however, in the U.S. market, where quotas on Japanese imports were in effect.

The Japanese government, in defending its trade practices, pointed out that Japan's tariff rates were among the lowest in the world. Japan argued that U.S. automakers only had themselves to blame because American vehicles were perceived by Japanese buyers as gas guzzlers. Indeed, according to a survey published by

Nihon Keizai Shimbun, a leading business newspaper in Japan, only 5 of 1,000 Japanese businesspeople were interested in buying an American car. Among the negative reasons were fuel inefficiency (cited by 72 percent), poor after-sales service (49 percent), and frequent breakdowns (49 percent). In August 1991 the total market, excluding minicars, was 344,740. Sales of U.S. imported vehicles totaled 2,238 or 0.6 percent.

Moreover, U.S. firms may lack marketing aggressiveness, and they are slow at building dealer networks in Japan. The evidence is that the Americans have been greatly outsold by British, Swedish, and German automakers, whose sales were generally up. Since 1981 BMW has spent $100 million in building a network of 122 exclusive dealers. Likewise, Mercedes and Volkswagen have been setting up their own dealerships, and they have spent $200 million each on new service centers to make certain that their cars meet buyers' expectations. In addition, Mercedes and Volkswagen have contracted with Mitsubishi and Toyota, respectively, to sell some of their cars. Meanwhile, U.S. automakers have taken only modest steps, with Ford having made the most serious effort.

Of all foreign firms, German automakers were the clear leaders. As reported by the Japan Automobile Importers Association, the top ten imports in Japan in 1991 were the following: Mercedes-Benz (34,187 units), BMW (33,798), Volkswagen (30,195), Audi (14,367), Honda USA (14,302), Volvo (10,127), General Motors (9,261), Mini (6,763), Rover (5,357), and Peugeot (4,651). It should be noted that the top four were German automakers. General Motors, in spite of its various makes and models, did no better than seventh place, and Ford came in fourteenth. It is interesting that made-in-U.S.A. Honda cars were the best-selling American-made cars in Japan.

Japanese automakers have pointed out that they too faced trade barriers in the United States. They were forced to adhere to an OMA limiting the number of units they could export to the United States. Japan first started limiting its car exports to the United States to 1.68 million units in 1983. The limit was subsequently raised to 1.85 million units in 1984. The voluntary limits on auto exports to the United States continued into the 1990s. Automakers from most other countries did not face this quota problem when selling to and in the United States. In part to avoid such trade barriers, Nissan, Honda, Toyota, and Mazda established plants in Tennessee, Ohio, California, and Michigan, respectively.

In recent years, General Motors has annually shipped to Japan about 3,000 Cadillacs, Camaros, Corvettes, and other high-priced models aimed at affluent buyers. GM wanted to increase exports by shipping about 1,000 units of its sporty Pontiac Grand Am, as well as its Chevrolet Corsica and Beretta compact models. These cars were to be distributed by Suzuki, a company partially owned by GM.

The best year for U.S. automakers in the Japanese market was 1979, when the Americans sold 16,739 vehicles there. The Americans have been hopeful that the 1990s would be better than the 1980s.

Questions

1. Does Japan's trade success owe more to its manufacturing superiority or to its mercantilistic trading philosophy (i.e., import barriers)? Does the Japanese government use nontariff barriers unreasonably to restrict imports?

2. Given the huge trade deficit the United States has with Japan, should the United States continue to trade with Japan?

3. Some claim that U.S. trade deficits are caused by U.S. adoption of a free-trade philosophy. Do you think that the United States has fewer import barriers than its trading partners?

4. Will protectionist measures adopted by the U.S. government be effective in increasing employment in the United States? Do you think that the U.S. government's use of OMAs against Japanese auto imports benefits the United States?

5. What can U.S. firms (including automakers) do to overcome Japanese trade barriers and improve their performance?

NOTES

1. See, for example, Douglas A. Fraser, "Domestic Content of US Automobile Imports: A UAW Proposal," *Columbia Journal of World Business* 16 (Winter 1981): 57–61.

2. "More Japanese Cars: How Much Will They Hurt?" *Business Week,* 18 March 1985, 117, 120.

3. "End Japanese Auto Quotas Now," *Business Week,* 4 March 1985, 130.

4. OPIC, *Topics* (Winter 1986); 4.

5. Reuben Kyle and Laurence T. Phillips, "Cargo Reservation for Bulk Commodity Shipments: An Economic Analysis," *Columbia Journal of World Business* 18 (Fall 1983): 42–49.

6. Larry E. Westphal, "Fostering Technological Mastery by Means of Selective Infant-Industry Protection," in *Trade, Stability, Technology, and Equity in Latin America,* ed. Moshe Syrquin and Simon Teitel (New York: Academic Press, 1982), 255–79.

7. "Apparel Manufacturers Face Extinction Because of Their Failure to Assume a Marketing Orientation, Consultant Says," *Marketing News,* 18 January 1985, 1, 3.

8. Victor A. Canto, Richard V. Eastin, and Arthur B. Laffer, "Failure of Protectionism: A Study of the Steel Industry," *Columbia Journal of World Business* 17 (Winter 1982): 43–57.

9. Michael Porter, *The Competitive Advantage of Nations* (New York: Free Press, 1990).

10. Dean DeRosa, "Protection in Sub-Saharan Africa Hinders Exports," *Finance & Development* (September 1991): 42–45.

11. "Europe's Agricultural Policy Is Costly, Distorts World Trade and Prices," *IMF Survey,* 20 February 1989, 49.

12. Sanjeev Gupta, Leslie Lipschitz, and Thomas Mayer, "The Common Agricultural Policy of the EC," *Finance & Development* (June 1989): 37–39.

13. Peter F. Heffernan, "Nothing Is Forever: Boom and Bust in Midwest Farming," *FRB Chicago Economic Perspectives* 11 (September/October 1987): 27–31.

14. James O'Shea, "U.S. Is Far from Barrier Free," *Chicago Tribune,* 6 January 1983.

15. Joseph A. McKinney, "Degree of Access to the Japanese Market: 1979 vs. 1986," *Columbia Journal of World Business* 24 (Summer 1989): 53–59.

16. *International Trade Reporter: Export Shipping Manual* (Washington, D.C.: The Bureau of International Affairs).

17. Joseph E. Payne, Jr., "Canada's New Goods and Services Tax Has Implications for U.S. Exporters," *Business America,* 13 August 1990, 12.

18. Market Expansion Division, Office of Textiles and Apparel, *Foreign Regulations Affecting U.S. Textile/Apparel Exports* (Washington, D.C.: Department of Commerce, 1986), preface.

19. David Alan Aschauer, "Some Macroeconomic Effects of Tariff Policy," *FRB Chicago Economic Perspectives* (November/December 1987): 10–18.

20. Sam Laird and Alexander Yeats, "Nontariff Barriers of Developed Countries, 1966–86," *Finance & Development* (March 1989): 12–13.

21. A. D. Cao, "Non-tariff Barriers to U.S. Manufactured Exports," *Columbia Journal of World Business* 15 (Summer 1980): 93–102.

22. Teresa Watanabe, "Americans Say *This* Trade Battle Stinks," *San Jose Mercury News,* 10 July 1988.

23. Catherine A. Novelli, "Procurement Code Gives U.S. Suppliers 'Level Playing Field,' " *Business America,* 21 November 1988, 6–7.

24. Michael P. Dooley and Donald J. Mathieson, "Financial Liberalization in Developing Countries," *Finance & Development* (September 1987): 31–34.

25. Peter Winglee, "Agricultural Trade Policies of Industrial Countries," *Finance & Development* (March 1989): 9–11.

26. Susan Kuhbach, "Subsidies and Countervailing Measures," *Business America,* 10 September 1990, 10.

27. U.S. Customs Service, *Importing into the United States* (Washington, D.C.: Department of the Treasury, 1990), 34–42.

28. *International Trade Reporter.*

29. "A Short Cut Through the Red Tape," *Business Week,* 11 June 1984, 57, 60.

30. Mary Saunders, "EC Testing and Certification Procedures: How Will They Work?" *Business America,* 25 February 1991, 27–28.

31. "Japan Opens a Door with a Built-in Barrier," *Business Week,* 8 November 1982, 41.

32. Charles Collyns and Steven Dunaway, "The Cost of Trade Restraints," *IMF Staff Papers* (March 1987).

33. Clemens F. J. Boonekamp, "Voluntary Export Restraints," *Finance & Development* (December 1987): 2–5.

34. "China's Tight Fist May Squeeze Foreign Companies Out," *Business Week,* 7 April 1986, 50.

35. Joseph Gold, *SDRs, Currencies, and Gold. Sixth Survey of New Legal Developments* (Washington, D.C.: International Monetary Fund, 1983), 28, 30.

36. "Ways to Beat Exchange Rules," *Business Week,* 26 October 1981, 106ff.

37. "U.S. Business Starts to Repatriate its Cash," *Business Week,* 31 March 1980, 83–84.

38. H. B. Junz and Clemens Boonekamp, "What Is at Stake in the Uruguay Round?" *Finance & Development* (June 1991): 11–15.

39. International Trade Administration, *1986 GuideBook: Caribbean Basin Initiative* (Washington, D.C.: U.S. Department of Commerce, 1986), 6–7.

40. Richard N. Farmer, "Hong Kong or Albania: Which Trade Strategy Should the U.S. Adopt?" *Business Horizons* 28 (November/December 1985): 2–8.

41. "Bhagwati Examines Growing Unilateralism in U.S. Trade Policy at Fund Seminar," *IMF Survey,* 26 June 1989, 196–97.

42. Shailendra J. Anjaria, Naheed Kirmani, and Arne B. Petersen, *Trade Policy Issues and Developments,* occasional paper no. 38, International Monetary Fund, 1985.

PART TWO
WORLD MARKET
ENVIRONMENT

☐ **PART OUTLINE**

The economist as such does not advocate criteria of optimality. He may invent them....
But the ultimate choice is made, usually only implicitly and not always consistently, by the
procedures of decision making inherent in the institutions, laws, and customs of society.

Tjalling C. Koopmans, economist and Nobel laureate

Political Environment

4

CHAPTER OUTLINE

MULTIPLICITY OF POLITICAL ENVIRONMENTS

TYPES OF GOVERNMENT: Political Systems

TYPES OF GOVERNMENT: Economic Systems

POLITICAL RISKS

INDICATORS OF POLITICAL INSTABILITY

ANALYSIS OF POLITICAL RISK OR COUNTRY RISK

MANAGEMENT OF POLITICAL RISK

MEASURES TO MINIMIZE POLITICAL RISK

POLITICAL INSURANCE

CASE 4–1: Not Necessarily the Welcome Wagon

CASE 4–2: Big Brother

CASE 4–3: Marketing to Apartheid: Should U.S. Business Invest in South Africa?

MARKETING ILLUSTRATION
How to Win Friends and Influence People

Despite a growing sentiment for trade protectionism in the U.S. Congress, Japan has been relatively successful in influencing U.S. lawmakers' trade decisions. Japan's effectiveness can be attributed to its philanthropy and long-term, systematic, and coordinated "soft-side" activities, which added up to $310 million in 1988. These activities include channeling tens of millions of dollars into American education at all levels and donating money for museums and public TV stations. Japan Foundation spends $5 million a year on exchange programs, education, and libraries. To foster goodwill while gaining research ideas, Japanese companies have endowed sixteen chairs at $1.5 million each at MIT while spending $4 million a year for research access. Hitachi's grant of $12 million offers the firm the right to use two-thirds of the space at the biotech laboratory of the University of California-Irvine. The University of California-Berkeley received $4 million to build a computer lab. As evidenced by their donations to minority groups (e.g., United Negro College Fund, NAACP), Japanese firms have learned the U.S. concept of private citizens working for the public cause.

To promote "intercultural communications" to make Japan better understood, there are Japanese-American Societies in some twenty U.S. cities and Japanese Chambers of Commerce in many others. There are consuls in fifteen U.S. cities to monitor American attitudes. Japan's Washington representatives (lobbyists) received $50 million in 1988, and they were responsible for getting customers to bombard congressmen with warnings that cutoff of imported components would harm them. These lobbyists were so effective that they were able to delay major trade bills while prevailing over registration of foreign investments. At the state level, Japan beat back unitary taxes in twelve states, and U.S. governors saw fit to make thirty-six visits to Japan in a single year.

At the company level, Toyota received help from the Republican party chairman to obtain approval for a special trade zone in Kentucky where auto parts can be shipped duty-free. Hitachi, with the aid of an Oklahoma Representative, was able to get disk drive components deleted from the tariff list requiring 100 percent punitive tariffs for Japan's violation of 1986 semiconductor agreement. To overcome its negative image, Hitachi's strategy includes setting up the philanthropic Hitachi Foundation, a promise to use $350 million worth of U.S. capital goods and increase U.S. production, the Americanization of its U.S. operations by promoting American managers, and taking out full-page advertisements to proclaim the company as a "citizen of the world." Similarly, Toshiba managed to defeat efforts to impose harsh sanctions related to its sale of restricted propeller technology to the Soviet Union by mounting a $3 million campaign that enabled it to buy and gain access to Secretary of State Shultz and Secretary of Defense Weinberger.

Source: "Japan's Clout in the U.S.," *Business Week,* 11 July 1988, 64–70, 72–75

Whether political interests precede or follow economic interests is debatable, but certainly the two are highly interrelated. One study investigated the effects of the U.S. embargo on Occidental's shipment of superphosphoric acid to the Soviet Union: "the embargo had a minimal effect on the Soviet Union but significant cost on Occidental and on the U.S. economy."[1] Politics and economics did not mix well in that instance.

The economic interests of MNCs can differ widely from the economic interests of the countries in which these firms do business. A lack of convergent interests often exists between a company's home country and its various host countries. In the absence of mutual interests, political pressures can lead to political decisions, resulting in laws and proclamations that affect business. The example of Japan's lobbying efforts in the United States provides an introduction to the political and legal dimensions of international business. Japan's efforts also show that political risks, thought to be largely uncontrollable, can nevertheless be reasonably managed. It is thus important to understand the role of political risk in international marketing and its impact on each of the four Ps of marketing.[2]

This chapter examines the interrelationships among political, legal, and business decisions. The discussion will focus on how the political climate affects the investment climate. Among political topics covered are forms of government, indicators of political instability, and political risks. The chapter ends with the investigation of strategies used to manage political risks.

MULTIPLICITY OF POLITICAL ENVIRONMENTS

The political environment that MNCs face is a complex one because they must cope with the politics of more than one nation. That complexity forces MNCs to consider that environment as composed of three different types of political environment: foreign, domestic, and international.

Foreign Politics

Foreign politics are the politics of a local or *host country*. This part of the international business environment can range from being favorable and friendly to being hostile and dangerous. The host country's political and economic circumstances determine the kind of political climate a company faces.

A company doing business across national boundaries should understand that no nation allows goods to flow across national borders unregulated. When the company decides to import a product from its home-base country, it may quickly discover that the host country's political environment is not always hospitable. The host government, as a rule, views imports negatively because of imports' adverse contribution to the host country's balance of payments. This is generally true with luxury and nonessential products, especially when those items can be or are already produced locally. A case in point involves the huge $11.4 billion tobacco market in Japan. Despite the growing popularity of U.S. brands in Japan, their growth is severely hampered by local regulations that are designed to protect Japan's 113,000 tobacco growers. Japanese tobacco growers oppose any further relaxation in import rules. Members of the agriculture sector are the most active and influential of Japanese lobby groups. The some 5 million Japanese farmers account for only 9 percent of the country's work force, but they have great political power because the allocation of parliamentary seats favors rural areas.[3] Redrawing of district lines for the Diet (the national assembly) is slow to reflect the population change. As a result, an urban vote constitutes merely one-third the weight of a rural vote. Consequently, the penetration rate of American tobacco firms is less than 3 percent.

The host country's political atmosphere tends to improve if the company decides to invest in local production facilities, instead of importing finished products from outside to sell in the host country. Local production facilities improve the host country's balance of payments and create jobs. But a company should not assume that the host country will always welcome foreign capital. When IBM proposed building a personal computer plant in Mexico, the plan was rejected by the Mexican government. The government's principal objection involved IBM's policy of having 100 percent ownership of the company's foreign factories.

LDCs often view foreign firms and foreign capital investment with distrust and even resentment, owing primarily to a concern over potential foreign exploitation of local natural resources. Matters of concern to LDCs involving the location of facilities by foreign firms within a host country include excessive profits, acquisitions of local firms, inadequate personnel training, ignorance of social customs, loyalty to a foreign government, and use of obsolete technologies.[4]

Developed countries themselves are also concerned about foreign investment. Many Americans have expressed their concern that the increasing foreign ownership of American assets poses a threat to the United States' national security, both politically and economically. It should be pointed out that inflows of foreign capital add to the domestic capital stock. This activity contributes to the American standard of living and enhances the country's ability to service its international indebtedness. As a result, the benefits of foreign investment far outweigh the costs.[5]

A government's encouragement or discouragement of foreign investment is usually dictated by considerations of balance of payments, economic development, and political realities. Balance-of-payments problems result in policies favoring investments that improve the country's exports, whereas economic development concerns result in policies favoring investments in industries that stimulate employment, either directly through manufacturing or indirectly through use of locally produced parts. Sensitive political situations usually result in policies that prohibit the foreign ownership of vital or sensitive businesses, such as utilities, transportation, communications, and broadcasting.

Thus, the climate for foreign investment varies greatly from country to country. An investment climate depends on both the type of investment involved and the political mood at the time. In general, local manufacturing is preferred over imports and over exports of natural resources for manufacturing elsewhere. Business investments in economic sectors with high unemployment rates are usually welcomed, as is the introduction of sophisticated technologies, provided that those technologies do not displace existing jobs.

One problem often encountered with foreign politics is the conflicting signals sent by the host country to foreign firms. On one hand, the host country actively woos MNC investment. To win foreign capital and new technology, the country pledges cooperation and various tax and financial incentives. On the other hand, the host country is often quick to accuse foreign firms of not providing the latest technology and expertise in local operations. It may also criticize these companies for making excessive profits and draining the nation of its wealth. To indicate displeasure, the host government may restrict the repatriation of profits to corporate headquarters abroad.

Domestic Politics

Domestic politics are the politics that exist in the company's *home country,* also known as the parent or source country. At first glance, it would seem that domestic politics should pose no threat and that a company should have minimal problems at home. This is often not the case. Although a company's major political problems usually derive from political conditions overseas, it must still pay close attention to political developments at home.

Domestic criticism of the company's international activities comes largely from labor and political organizations, which frequently accuse the company of exporting capital and jobs. Although these organizations usually have no objection to the exportation of goods, they often strongly oppose the export of capital as well as the import of goods and services. They feel that imports and direct investment abroad create unemployment at home. To discourage such activity, organizations may advocate a requirement of local content for products that are sold in their country.

In some cases, the opposition to imported goods and foreign investment is based on moral principle. For example, the citizens of many nations want to prohibit the importation of gold from South Africa, and they pressure companies in their countries not to invest in South Africa because of that country's policy of apartheid. In the mid-1980s, the pressure became so great that the South African government ran advertisements in the United States in an attempt to minimize damage, as shown in Exhibit 4–1.

The government of the home country, instead of providing support for international trade, can turn out to be a significant hindrance. There may be many government regulations that interfere with the free flow of trade, and the actions taken by a home country may be motivated more by political considerations than by sound economic reasoning. For decades Taiwan has refused to trade with China, even though Taiwan has what China needs: capital and know-how. China, on the other hand, offers cheap labor to counteract Taiwan's rising wages.

International Politics

International politics are the interaction of the overall environmental factors of two or more countries. The complexity of the political environment increases significantly when the interests of the company, the host country, and the home country do not coincide. It may even be likely that the complexity can become so great that no reasonable solution exists. Dresser, a U.S. corporation, became involved in such a problem when trying to supply materials for a Soviet gas pipeline. Because of the Reagan administration's ban on American firms' participation in the project, Dresser was threatened by the United States with a civil suit and a loss of export license

South Africa
" I don't know much about it... "

South Africa arouses more controversy than almost any other country in the world. People tend to have a view about South Africa whether they have been there or not. Quite often, these views are not based on fact.

SHARING A BETTER QUALITY OF LIFE

South Africa is involved in a remarkable process of providing fair opportunities for all its population groups. The South African Government is committed to ensuring that each of South Africa's many nationalities has the ability and resources to realize its social, economic and political aspirations.

Developing the financial base on which so many other forms of progress depend, is a leading example of South Africa's development process. The recent establishment of the Development Bank of Southern Africa underlines progress and Government participation in this area.

Modelled on the World Bank, the Development Bank of Southern Africa is possibly the most ambitious development agency that has been created for Africa.

MEETING THE ECONOMIC CHALLENGE

The Bank's main objective is to achieve a more balanced geographical distribution of economic activity in Southern Africa while providing maximum scope for private sector participation. The Development Bank of Southern Africa is expected to more than double the flow of development capital to Black underdeveloped areas over the next five years.

The Small Business Development Corporation was formed as a partnership between South Africa's leading industrial and consumer groups and the Government to stimulate and develop entrepreneurial skills among all population groups. Already more than $100 million has been invested in general programs of the Corporation and its associates, and more than 33 000 new jobs have been created in the process.

THE FUTURE – BETTER PROSPECTS FOR ALL

The facts on the economy present only part of the picture. Many aspects of South African life have changed – and are changing at an ever-increasing rate. The future is exciting because we have the people, the dedication and a buoyant economy to enable us to keep on providing opportunities and improving the quality of life of all our people.

Because South Africa is a microcosm of so many of the world's sensitivities, it is often a contentious subject. If you are faced with a decision regarding South Africa, make sure you have all the facts.

For more information, simply complete the coupon below.

To: The Minister (Information),
The South African Embassy,
3051 Massachusetts Avenue,
Washington D.C., 20008 N.W.
Please send me more information on socio-economic and political developments in South Africa.
Name ....
Address ....
....Code ....

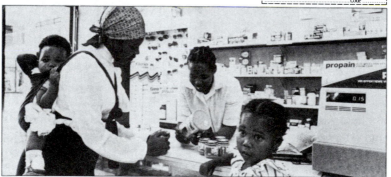

We're looking forward to the future.

EXHIBIT 4–1   Dealing with political pressure

Source: Reprinted with permission of the South African Consulate General

if it allowed Dresser-France (its French subsidiary) to ship three compressors to the Soviet Union. France, on the other hand, was just as adamant in its decision to go ahead with the project. Calling upon its 1938 war emergency rules to override corporate decisions to protect national interests, the French government threatened

Dresser-France with fines, jailing of executives, and seizure of the items in question. Dresser-France was put in the position of abiding by French laws that would cause its parent company to violate U.S. law.

Regardless of whether the politics are foreign, domestic, or international, the company should keep in mind that political climate does not remain stationary. The political relationship between the United States and a long-time adversary, China, is a prime example. After decades as bitter opponents, both countries became very interested in improving their political and economic ties.

Although most companies have little control in affecting changes in international politics, they must be prepared to respond to new developments. Companies can derive positive economic benefits when the relationship between two countries improves. Relations between the United States and Jamaica were strained until the election of Prime Minister Edward Seaga, who was strongly anti-Cuban. Jamaica suddenly gained favors because of Seaga's close relationship with President Ronald Reagan. The United States granted special tariff breaks on Jamaican goods and bought Jamaican bauxite solely for political reasons.

On the other hand, serious problems can develop when political conditions deteriorate. A favorable investment climate can disappear almost overnight. In one case, the United States withdrew Chile's duty-free trade status because of Chile's failure to take "steps to afford internationally recognized worker rights." Chile thus joined Romania, Nicaragua, and Paraguay in being suspended from the GSP (Generalized System of Preferences).

TYPES OF GOVERNMENT: POLITICAL SYSTEMS

A knowledge of the form governments can take can be useful in appraising the political climate. One way to classify governments is to consider them as either parliamentary (open) or absolutist (closed). **Parliamentary** governments consult with citizens from time to time for the purpose of learning about opinions and preferences. Government policies are thus intended to reflect the desire of the majority segment of the society. Most industrialized nations and all democratic nations can be classified as parliamentary.

At the other end of the spectrum are absolutist governments, which include monarchies and dictatorships. In an **absolutist** system, the ruling regime dictates government policy without considering citizens' needs or opinions. Frequently, absolutist countries are newly formed nations or those undergoing some kind of political transition. Absolute monarchies are now relatively rare. The United Kingdom is a good example of a constitutional hereditary monarchy; despite the monarch, the government is classified as parliamentary.

Many countries' political systems do not fall neatly into one of these two categories. Some monarchies and dictatorships (e.g., Saudi Arabia and South Korea) have parliamentary elections. The former Soviet Union had elections and mandatory voting but was not classified as parliamentary because the ruling party never allowed an alternative on the ballot. Countries such as the Philippines under Marcos and Nicaragua under Somoza held elections, but the results were suspect because of government involvement in voting fraud.

Another way to classify governments is by number of political parties. This classification results in four types of governments: two-party, multiparty, single-party, and dominated one-party. In a **two-party** system, there are typically two strong parties that take turns controlling the government, although other parties are allowed. The United States and the United Kingdom are prime examples. The two parties generally have different philosophies, resulting in a change in government policy when one party succeeds the other. In the United States, the Republican party is often viewed as representing business interests, whereas the Democratic party is often viewed as representing labor interests, as well as the poor and disaffected.

In a **multiparty** system, there are several political parties, none of which is strong enough to gain control of the government. Even though some parties may be large, their elected representatives fall short of a majority. A government must then be formed through coalitions between the various parties, each of which wants to protect its own interests. The longevity of the coalition depends largely on the cooperation of party partners. Usually, the coalition is continuously challenged by various opposing parties. A change in a few votes may be sufficient to bring the coalition government down. If the government does not survive a vote of no confidence (i.e., does not have the support of the majority of the representatives), the government is disbanded and a new election is called. Countries operating with this system include Germany, France, and Israel. In the 1991 elections in Poland, 29 parties (including the Polish Beer Lovers' Party) won seats, and no party got more than 13 percent of the vote.

In a **single-party** system, there may be several parties, but one party is so dominant that there is little opportunity for others to elect representatives to govern the country. Egypt has operated under single-party rule for more than three decades. This form of government is often used by countries in the early stages of the development of a true parliamentary system. Because the ruling party holds support from the vast majority, the system is not necessarily a poor, especially when it can provide the stability and continuity necessary for rapid growth. But when serious economic problems persist, citizens' dissatisfaction and frustration may create an explosive situation. For example, Mexico has been ruled since its revolution by the Institutional Revolutionary Party (PRI), but economic problems caused dissatisfaction with the PRI in the 1980s. The National Action Party (PAN), Mexico's main opposition party, began gaining strength, possibly foreshadowing a transition away from a single-party system.

In a **dominated one-party** system, the dominant party does not allow any opposition, resulting in no alternative for the people. In contrast, a single-party system does allow some opposition party. The former Soviet Union, Cuba, and Libya are good examples of dominated one-party systems. Such a system may easily transform itself into a dictatorship. The party, to maintain its power, is prepared to use force or any necessary means to eliminate the introduction and growth of other parties. For example, the Soviet Union had repeatedly shown a willingness to quell any opposition within its satellite countries.

One should not be hasty in making generalizations about the ideal form of government in terms of political stability. It may be tempting to believe that stability is a function of economic development in the sense that a more developed nation should also have more political stability. South Africa, a developed nation, has been beset with internal and external problems that seem to get worse each day. Italy is another politically unstable developed country. Its political atmosphere is marred by a weak economy, recurring labor unrest, internal dissension, and a constant threat that the Communist party may gain political control. Such reasons were partly responsible for Fiat's decision to seek out and emphasize business opportunities outside of Italy. In contrast, it can be argued that Burma, despite being a developing economy, was (until 1988) politically more stable than Italy. This stability is due in part to Burma's relatively closed society.

It may be just as tempting to conclude that a democratic political system is a prerequisite for political stability. India, the largest democracy in the world, possesses a solid political infrastructure and political institutions that have withstood many crises over time. The democratic system is strongly established in India, and it is almost inconceivable that the Indians would choose any other system. Yet India's political stability is hampered by regional, ethnic, language, religious, and economic problems. Unlike such other democratic nations as Australia, where such problems have largely been resolved, India's difficulties remain. These geographic, ideological, and ethnic problems inhibit the government's ability to respond to one sector's demands without alienating others.

Belgium, a democratic and economically developed country, has had language disputes between Flemings and Walloons that have led to several political crises. The country is linguistically divided, with the 5.5 million people in the northern territory of Flanders speaking Dutch and the 4.5 million people in the southern region of Wallonia speaking French. A failure to resolve a language dispute in a remote farming hamlet led to the resignation of Belgium's interior minister in late 1986.

Dictatorial systems, monarchies, and oligarchies may be able to provide great stability for a country, especially one with a relatively closed society, which exists in many communist countries and Arab nations. If a country's ruler and military are strong, any instability that may occur can be kept under control. The problem, however, is that such systems frequently exist in a divided society where dissident groups are waiting for an opportunity to challenge the regime. When a ruler suddenly dies, the risk of widespread disruption and revolution can be quite high.

To foster democratic pluralism, the Support for East European Democracies Act (SEED) of 1989 provides more than $900 million in support to Poland and Hungary in the form of GSP duty-free tariff treatment, financing and insurance coverage, broad technical assistance, and Enterprise Funds. However, because of the continuing warfare in Yugoslavia, the United States imposed economic sanctions against all six Yugoslav republics by suspending U.S. assistance under the SEED program, the U.S. GSP, and the bilateral textile agreement.

TYPES OF GOVERNMENT: ECONOMIC SYSTEMS

Economic systems provide another basis for classification of governments. These systems serve to explain whether businesses are privately owned or government owned, or whether there is a combination of private and government ownership. Basically, three systems can be identified: **communism, socialism** and **capitalism.** Based on the degree of government control of business activity, the various economic systems can be placed along a continuum, with communism at one end and capitalism at another. A movement toward communism is accompanied by an increase in government interference and more control of factors of production. A movement toward capitalism is accompanied by an increase in private ownership.

Communist theory holds that all resources should be owned and shared by all the people (i.e., not by profit-seeking enterprises) for the benefit of the society. In practice, it is the government that controls all productive resources and industries, and as a result the government determines jobs, production, price, education, and just about anything else. The emphasis is on human welfare. Because profit making is not the government's main motive, there is a lack of incentive for workers and managers to improve productivity.

The term *centrally planned economies* is often used to refer to the former Soviet Union, Eastern European countries, China, Vietnam, and North Korea. These economies tend to have the following characteristics: a communist philosophy, an active government role in economic planning, a nonmarket economy, a weak economy, large foreign debt, and rigid and bureaucratic political/economic systems. Burma and Argentina are similar in one respect; they have both gone from being wealthy countries to being impoverished through mismanagement. Burma's authoritarian government, for example, has so tightly regulated the economy that production has greatly suffered.

Despite communist countries' preoccupation with control of industries, it would be an error to conclude that all communist governments are exactly alike. Although the former Soviet Union and China adhered to the same basic ideology, there was a marked difference between these two largest communist nations. China has been experimenting with a new type of communism by allowing its citizens to work for themselves and to keep any profit in the process, as explained in Exhibit 4–2. By unleashing the largest labor force in the world, Chinese leader Deng Xiaoping earned the distinction of Man of the Year by *Time* magazine in 1985. Yet one must remember that "free markets" can exist in China only with the state's permission, and the operations of such markets are still overseen by government officials.[6] China's deviation from the basic ideology of communism initially proved quite unsettling to the Soviet Union, though in 1986 the Soviets decided to start allowing families and some small private entities to do business for profit.

The degree of government control that occurs under socialism is somewhat less than under communism. A socialist government owns and operates the basic, major industries but leaves small businesses to private ownership. Socialism is a matter of degree, and not all socialist countries are the same. A socialist country such as Poland leans toward communism, as evidenced by its rigid control over prices and distribution. France's socialist system, in comparison, is much closer to capitalism than it is to communism.

At one time Sweden was a role model of what socialism could be, but a middle road between communism and capitalism may now produce stalled economic growth.[7] Sweden's economic decline is due in part to a rapid expansion in regula-

Progress, intelligently planned. That's how the dictionary defines telesis. Today, one of history's most dramatic examples of telesis is unfolding, as China—under the leadership of Deng Xiaoping—makes its greatest leap yet towards a free market.

His goal: to bring China into the 20th century—before the 21st. In a nation that holds nearly one-quarter of the world's population, the sheer magnitude of this task is overwhelming. But, at 81, Deng Xiaoping is digging in, creating his own blend of communism and private enterprise.

The "responsibility system," as Deng calls his new program, is sending ripples throughout China's once stagnant economy. In the countryside, peasants now decide what and when to plant, and are free to sell their surplus in the open market once state quotas have been met. Since 1979, when government controls were eased, rural living standards have more than doubled, and once-drab villages have become diverse centers of local trade.

In the cities, Deng's new strategy penalizes workers for their company's losses and rewards them for profits. Not surprisingly, profits are up.

And everywhere, for the first time, the Chinese have money to spend. To keep up with the growing demand, privately-owned businesses are springing up all over—from motorcycle factories and appliance stores to restaurants and even banks.

Many call Deng's program of economic reform the "second revolution."

For the little man once denounced by Mao as a "capitalist roader," however, it is simply a matter of pragmatics: "It doesn't matter whether a cat is black or white," says Deng, "as long as it catches mice."

At Pacific Telesis, we salute the special kind of progress made by those who don't look back at what was, but forward at what can be.

Two years ago, the breakup of the Bell System presented us with the massive task of restructuring our own business. After careful consideration, we determined that real opportunities for long term growth lie in our ability to compete in new lines of business where our skills and experience give us a competitive edge. For example, through Pacific Telesis International, we're marketing our telecommunications know-how to developing nations, like China, where building better communications systems is a key priority.

At Pacific Telesis, we're committed to progress, intelligently planned in everything we do. That's why an investment in Telesis is an investment in progress.

To find out more about us, write Michael McGreevy, Director, Investor Relations, 140 New Montgomery, San Francisco, CA 94105.

PACIFIC ⊠ TELESIS ℠
Group

Pacific Bell   PacTel InfoSystems   Nevada Bell
Pacific Telesis International   PacTel Mobile Companies
PacTel Communications Systems   PacTel Spectrum Services
PacTel Publishing   PacTel Finance   PacTel Properties

EXHIBIT 4–2   Communism and capitalism

Source: Reprinted with permission of Pacific Telesis

tions and in the rising share of national income spent by central and local governments, which changed from about 45 percent during the early 1960s to 67 percent in 1986. Until recently, Sweden's marginal income tax rate exceeded 60 percent for most middle-class families, and many others must contend with a tax rate of over 80 percent. During the 1970s and 1980s, Sweden introduced very generous retirement and health benefits, lengthy paid leaves for parents, liberal rules for sick workers on taking days off, and many other types of transfer payments. Not surprisingly, on an average day, almost one in four employees is absent from work because of reported illness, parental responsibilities, study leave, and other reasons that allow a worker to stay home. In 1988, the average Swedish worker was out sick for almost a month of the year while receiving full salary. Moreover, differences in pay by education level, job experience, and other measures of worker productivity have largely disappeared. Over the long run, there is no incentive to work hard when one can get paid for staying home, when education and better jobs do not offer much higher wages, and when taxes offset any increase in pay. During the past 15 years, Sweden's growth in per capita income has been far less than the Organization for Economic Cooperation & Development average.

At the opposite end of the continuum from communism is capitalism. The philosophy of capitalism provides for a free-market system that allows business competition and freedom of choice for both consumers and companies. It is a market-oriented system in which individuals, motivated by private gain, are allowed to produce goods or services for public consumption under competitive conditions. Product price is determined by demand and supply. This system serves the needs of society by encouraging decentralized decision making, risk taking, and innovation. The results include product variety, product quality, efficiency, and relatively lower prices.

As with the other two economic systems, there are degrees of capitalism. Japan, when compared to the United States, is relatively less capitalistic. Although practically all Japanese businesses are privately owned, industries are very closely supervised by the state. Japan has the MITI and other government agencies that vigorously advise companies what to produce, buy, sell, and so on. Japan's aim is to allocate scarce resources in such a way as to efficiently produce those products that have the best potential for the country overall.

In search of the common characteristics of successful corporations, Chandler examined the 200 largest companies in the United States, Britain, and Germany from the 1880s through the 1940s and found that capitalism took a different form in each country.[8] It was *"managerial capitalism"* in the United States, where managers with little ownership ran companies and competed fiercely for markets and products. In Britain, *"personal capitalism"* took place as owners managed their companies. In Germany, it was *"cooperative capitalism"*; professional managers were in charge, and companies were urged to share markets and profits among themselves. However, successful companies in all countries invested in three areas: management, production processes, and distribution techniques. In general, the first companies to make and sustain these investments grew to dominate their industries domestically while sharing markets with only a few similar corporations globally. As an example, the U.S. tire industry was dominated by Firestone, Goodyear, Goodrich, and U.S. Rubber, which competed with Britain's Dunlop, France's Michelin, Germany's Continental, and Italy's Pirelli.

No nation operates under pure communism or pure capitalism, and most countries find it necessary to make some compromise between the two extremes. Even Eastern Bloc countries provided incentives for their managers, and China allows farmers to sell directly to consumers in local markets. Western European countries encourage free enterprise but intervene to provide support and subsidies for steel and farm products. The United States is also not a perfect model of capitalism. It has support prices for many dairy and farm products and has imposed price controls from time to time. Furthermore, the U.S. economy is greatly affected by the Federal Reserve Board's control of the money supply and interest rates. *Laissez faire,* the purest form of capitalism, is rare. In any case, there are no nations that allow businesses to be completely controlled by either the private or public sector.

Perhaps the only place that bears a great resemblance to an ideal free-trade market is Hong Kong, which does not even have a central bank. The China-U.K. Joint Declaration of 1984 contains the principles and conditions governing the transfer of authority over Hong Kong. In mid-1997, the United Kingdom will relinquish its authority and Hong Kong will become a Special Administrative Region (SAR) of the People's Republic of China. The Hong Kong SAR will retain a high degree of autonomy, and its capitalist system, for at least 50 years. Continuing to formulate its own monetary and financial policies, the Hong Kong SAR will maintain an independent tax system while not being subject to taxation by the central government. The Hong Kong dollar, as the legal tender, will remain freely convertible. In addition, Hong Kong will pursue a policy of free trade and will safeguard the free movement of goods, intangible assets, and capital.[9]

It would be presumptuous to say that capitalism, a system that encourages competition and efficiency, is the ideal system for all countries. It is true that Poland, for example, sets prices artificially low and thus has a great deal of difficulty in solving a supply dilemma. As a result, citizens are forced to stand in long lines for a small ration to meet their needs. But capitalism may be inappropriate for such countries as China because the system would allow wealth to be concentrated in the hands of a few people and subsequently leave the majority poor and hungry. Market action does not always serve the nation's best interests, particularly in areas of social need. Efficiency may be derived at the expense of jobs for the people, and the profit motive may intensify the inflation problem.

According to President Bush's economic report, "the massive historical experiment conducted throughout the 20th century that contrasted market-oriented and centrally planned economies has ended with the economic failure of communism."[10] In Eastern Europe and to a lesser but still significant extent in Latin America, widespread government interference and reliance on inefficient public enterprises have obstructed the normal operation of markets. After decades of state control and ownership, the worldwide movement toward market reliance and political freedom has forced both regions to replace their command systems with thriving private enterprises, which should allow producers to efficiently make the goods that consumers want.

Successful economic reform requires several critical policy principles, including establishing private property rights and privatization of public enterprises, promoting domestic competition, and reducing and reforming the role of government. The Polish program involves establishing competitive industries and independent financial institutions. In 1990 Yugoslavia attempted to stop soaring inflation by devaluing and fixing the nominal exchange rate of Yugoslavia's currency, temporarily freezing

TABLE 4–1   Overview of reforms

	Bulgaria	Czechoslovakia	Hungary	Poland	Romania	Yugoslavia
Price reform	All prices except energy freed in Feb. 1991.	Prices freed in sectors believed to be competitive.	Domestic pricing freed since 1988. More than 92% now free.	Most price restrictions ended Jan. 1990. 10% of prices now controlled.	Most prices still controlled.	75% of prices freed by Dec. 1989.
Privatization	Planning to privatize state firms. No timetable set.	Started privatizing small businesses. Foreigners can bid only if citizens don't buy.	National Property Agency set up. 130 of 3,000 salable firms privatized in 1990.	8,000 firms to be privatized. Eight sold so far. Foreign share limited to 10% without permission.	Privatization bill sent to Parliament. Plans to privatize 50% of capital stock of economy over 3 years.	Ownership issue difficult because of decentralized nature of worker self-management system.
Foreign trade	As of Jan. 1989, all firms free to conduct foreign trade. Decree of Feb. 1990 liberalized importation of all goods. 300% duty imposed on all exports except art.	As of Feb. 1991, exporters of goods in short supply must have licenses, as must importers of petroleum products and munitions.	90% of imports free from control.	No restrictions on imports. Export restrictions on 15 items accounting for 1% of total exports.	All citizens and foreigners can now conduct hard-currency trade.	All public and private firms can conduct foreign trade. 87% of imports free from restriction as of Feb. 1990. Tariffs low, uniform; quota restrictions on some imports.

Data: Group of Thirty, *Financing Eastern Europe: A Study Group Report*
Source: *IMF Survey,* 29 July 1991, 237

wages, allowing most prices to adjust freely, and lowering import barriers. In the same year Czechoslovakia implemented a comprehensive economic reform effort involving privatization, decontrolling about 85 percent of all prices, cutting subsidies to consumers and producers, eliminating its state planning and price-setting bodies, establishing partial convertibility for the international trade of goods, devaluing its currency, and tightening fiscal policy. As a result, the country's federal budget became a surplus. Table 4–1 lists the reforms taken by selected Eastern European countries.

In order to make a successful transition from socialism to capitalism and enjoy economic affluence and stability, Eastern Europe must become a full-fledged member of the global trade and payments system. The early results of reform in Poland, Hungary, and Czechoslovakia are encouraging. By giving a high priority to making their currencies convertible on current account, liberalizing their import regimes, and establishing competitive exchange rates, these countries have created the conditions for a rapid integration into the world economy. On the other hand, the outlook is

TABLE 4–1   Overview of reforms (*continued*)

	Bulgaria	Czechoslovakia	Hungary	Poland	Romania	Yugoslavia
Convertibility	Importation and exportation of leva prohibited (nonconvertible).	Liberalized in 1991, but local currency not necessarily convertible.	Net export earnings held until year-end in forint accounts with National Bank.	Resident convertibility for current transactions. Profit repatriation limited; use of net hard-currency earnings controlled.	Started phased transition to convertibility.	Convertibility for commercial transactions since Dec. 1989. Government suspended convertibility into US$ for repatriation at end of 1990.
Exchange rate policy	Since Feb. 3, 1991, leva has floated. Rates agreed daily by commercial banks and clients posted by National Bank on following day. One rate for all types of transactions.	Crown fixed against US$, subject to periodic adjustment. In Dec. 1990, devalued 17% to 28 crowns/US$1. One rate for all types of transactions.	Forint is fixed against a basket of currencies, subject to periodic adjustments.	In Jan. 1990, zloty devalued from Zl 6,000/US$1 to Zl 9,500/US$1, bringing official rate in line with street rate, legalized at same time. Exchange rate set against US$ for all kinds of transactions.	In Feb. 1991, dual exchange rate system introduced. In Nov. 1990, leu devalued to leu 35/US$1. Devalued on Apr. 1, 1991 to leu 60/US$1.	Dinar pegged to deutsche mark subject to periodic adjustments. Rate of Din 7/DM 1 set Jan. 1990, revised to Din 9/DM 1 in 1991 for all transactions.

not as promising for Bulgaria, Romania, the Commonwealth of Independent States, and Yugoslavia. The West faces policy dilemmas that accompany the entry of Eastern Europe into the global economy. The economic gap between East and West can be closed either by capital flows from the West or by labor migration from the East. To prevent a major migration problem, it makes sense for Western Europe to offer generous capital flows, including debt reduction and technical assistance, to the East.[11]

POLITICAL RISKS

There are a number of political risks with which marketers must contend. Hazards based on a host government's actions include confiscation, expropriation, nationalization, and domestication. Such actions are more likely to be levied against foreign investments, though local firms' properties are not totally immune. Charles de Gaulle, for example, nationalized France's three largest banks in 1945, and more nationalization occurred in 1982 under the French Socialists.

Confiscation is the process of a government's taking ownership of a property without compensation. An example of confiscation is the Chinese government's seizure of American property after the Chinese Communists took power in 1949. The U.S. Congress did not approve the normalization of economic relations with China until a satisfactory claims settlement had been negotiated. A more recent example involves Occidental Petroleum, which wanted the United States to review Venezuela's GSP eligibility after the country confiscated the firm's assets without compensation.

Expropriation differs somewhat from confiscation in that there is some compensation, though not necessarily just compensation. More often than not, a company whose property is being expropriated agrees to sell its operations—not by choice but rather because of some explicit or implied coercion.

After property has been confiscated or expropriated, it can be either nationalized or domesticated. **Nationalization** involves government ownership, and it is the government that operates the business being taken over. Burma's foreign trade, for example, is completely nationalized. Generally, this action affects a whole industry rather than just a single company. For example, when Mexico attempted to control its debt problem, President Jose Lopez Portillo nationalized the country's banking system. In another case of nationalization, Libya's Colonel Gadhafi's vision of Islamic socialism led him to nationalize all private business in 1981. Some countries permit nationalization—Germany, for example—but such action is not anticipated by either the public or private sectors. Unlike Communists in Hungary and Poland, Czech Communists nationalized 100 percent of their economy. As a result, rebuilding private markets in Czechoslovakia will be both slow and difficult.

In the case of **domestication,** foreign companies relinquish control and ownership, either completely or partially, to the nationals. The result is that private entities are allowed to operate the confiscated or expropriated property. The French government, after finding out that the state was not sufficiently proficient to run the banking business, developed a plan to sell thirty-six French banks.

Domestication may sometimes be a voluntary act that takes place in the absence of confiscation or nationalization. Usually, the causes of this action are either poor economic performance or social pressures. When situations worsened in South Africa and political pressures mounted at home, Pepsi sold its South African bottling operations to local investors, and Coca-Cola signaled that it would give control to a local company. Both companies seemed to share the same idea: neither wanted to spend time worrying about a mere 1 percent of its business. General Motors followed suit by selling its operations to local South African management in 1986. Shortly thereafter, Barclays Bank made similar moves.

Another classification system of political risks is the one used by Root.[12] Based on this classification, four sets of political risks can be identified: general instability risk, ownership/control risk, operation risk, and transfer risk.

General instability risk is related to the uncertainty about the future viability of a host country's political system. The Iranian revolution that overthrew the Shah is an example of this kind of risk. In contrast, **ownership/control risk** is related to the possibility that a host government might take actions (e.g., expropriation) to restrict an investor's ownership and control of a subsidiary in that host country.

Operation risk proceeds from the uncertainty that a host government might constrain the investor's business operations in all areas, including production, marketing, and finance. Finally, **transfer risk** applies to any future acts by a host government that might constrain the ability of a subsidiary to transfer payments, capital, or profit out of the host country back to the parent firm.

Estimates vary about the extent to which governments have nationalized businesses within the past few decades. *Business Week* reported 563 acts of expropriation involving 1,660 companies in seventy-nine LDCs from 1960 to 1979.[13]

Governments' rationale for nationalization varies widely and includes national interests, vote getting, prevention of foreigners' exploitation, and an easy, cheap, and quick way of acquiring wealth. Although the number of incidents may seem high, it is encouraging to note that the trend may have reversed. The risk of nationalization will likely be less in the future for several reasons. Many governments have experienced very poor records in running the businesses nationalized and have found that their optimistic projections have not materialized. Furthermore, many nations have realized that such actions have created difficulties in attracting new technology and foreign investment as well as in borrowing from foreign banks. There is also the possibility of open retaliation by other governments.

Although the threat of direct confiscation or expropriation has become remote, a new kind of threat has appeared. MNCs have generally been concerned with coups, revolutions, and confiscation, but they now have to pay attention to so-called creeping expropriation. The Overseas Private Investment Corporation (OPIC) defines **creeping expropriation** as "a set of actions whose cumulative effect is to deprive investors of their fundamental rights in the investment."[14] Laws that affect corporate ownership, control, profit, and reinvestment (e.g., currency inconvertibility or cancellation of import license) can be easily enacted. Because countries can change the rules in the middle of the game, companies must adopt adequate safeguards. Various defensive and protective measures will be discussed later.

INDICATORS OF POLITICAL INSTABILITY

To assess a potential marketing environment, a company should identify and evaluate the relevant indicators of political difficulty. Potential sources of political complication include social unrest, the attitudes of nationals, and the policies of the host government.

Social Unrest

Social disorder is caused by such underlying conditions as economic hardship, internal dissension and insurgency, and ideological, religious, racial, and cultural differences. Lebanon has experienced conflict among the Christians, Muslims, and other religious groups. The Hindu-Muslim conflict in India continues unabated. A company may not be directly involved in local disputes, but its business can still be severely disrupted by such conflicts. A good example is the Philippines just before the fall of the Marcos regime. In 1984, there were 274 strikes and a loss of 1.8 million work-hours, twice the level in 1981.[15] The growing labor unrest, supported by left-wing groups, was so great that several MNCs decided to leave the country. Baxter Travenol wound up its operations and wrote off an investment of nearly $10 million. Ford closed down its assembly operations, and the Bank of America moved its regional data-processing center to Hong Kong.

The breakup of the Soviet Union should not come as a surprise. Human nature involves **monostasy** (the urge to stand alone) as well as **systasy** (the urge to stand together), and the two concepts provide alternative ways of utilizing resources to meet a society's needs.[16] Monostasy encourages competition, but systasy emphasizes competition. As explained by Alderson, "a cooperative society tends to be a closed society. Closure is essential if the group is in some sense to act as one." Not surprisingly China, although wanting to modernize its economy, does not fully embrace an open economy, which is likely to encourage dissension among the various groups. For the sake of its own survival, a cooperative society may have to obstruct the dissemination of new ideas and neutralize an external group that poses a threat. China apparently has learned a lesson from the Soviet Union's experience.

The breakup of the Soviet Union underscores the point that a shift toward monostasy to encourage modernization and competition is inevitably accompanied by the desire of ethnic groups to seek autonomy and freedom. Thanks to *glasnost'*, one group after another of the country's 100 national groups wanted official restoration of their native language or reexamination of their ethnic history. Estonia, Latvia, and Lithuania, before being annexed by Stalin, were all independent states with free-market economies from 1918 to 1940. Even before the breakup, these states demanded greater economic and political independence from Moscow and sought secession and total autonomy.

A liberated political climate may easily lead to a call of the long-suppressed national minority groups for cultural and territorial independence. The groups' past conflicts, unsettled but subdued during the Communist period, are likely to escalate. Three kinds of conflict may result.[17] First, a domestic dispute may escalate into violence that is confined within the boundaries of the country in question. The civil war that started in 1991 between Serbs and Croats in Yugoslavia is a good example. Another example is the centuries-old ethnic animosity between Christians in Armenia and Muslims in neighboring Azerbaijan, which led some 600 Armenian nationalists to clash with Soviet soldiers during earthquake rescue efforts in Armenia. Second, an internal dispute may draw interested parties outside the country in question into the conflict. For example, problems in Yugoslavian Macedonia may force Bulgaria and Greece to intervene. Finally, the third form of conflict, resulting either from the first two kinds of conflict or from an international dispute, may lead to a direct confrontation between two countries. Romania and Hungary, which have deep-rooted grievances against each other, could become involved in this form of conflict.

Attitudes of Nationals

An assessment of the political climate is not complete without an investigation of the attitudes of the citizens and government of the host country. The nationals' attitude toward foreign enterprises and citizens can be quite inhospitable. Nationals are often concerned with foreigners' intentions in regard to exploitation and colonialism, and these concerns are often linked to concerns over foreign governments' actions that may be seen as improper. Such attitudes may arise out of local socialist or nationalist philosophies, which may be in conflict with the policy of the company's home-country government. Any such inherent hostility is certain to present major problems because of its relative permanence. Governments may come and go, but citizens' hostility may remain. This kind of problem may explain why twelve U.S. firms decided to leave El Salvador in the 1980s. Their departure meant the departure of some 20 percent of U.S. capital investment in that country.

Policies of the Host Government

Unlike citizens' inherent hostility, a government's attitude toward foreigners is often relatively short-lived. The mood can change either with time or change in leadership, and it can change for either the better or the worse. The impact of a change in mood can be quite dramatic, especially in the short run.

Government policy formulation can affect business operations either internally or externally. The effect is internal when the policy regulates the firm's operations within the home country. The effect is external when the policy regulates the firm's activities in another country. An example of an internal policy is Quebec's Bill 101. The bill requires all business to be conducted entirely in French and dictates where the investments of insurance and trust companies will be placed. When this bill was passed, the reaction was a massive capital flight of some $57 billion. One major investment company alone moved its $19.2 billion portfolio from Montreal to Ottawa.

Although an external government policy is irrelevant to firms doing business only in one country, such a policy can create complex problems for firms doing business in countries that are in conflict with each other. Disputes among countries often spill over into business activities. A company in one country, for example, may be prohibited from doing business with other countries that are viewed as hostile. A dispute over the boundary between Chile and Argentina prompted Argentina to restrict traditional exports to Chile, including petrochemicals, pharmaceuticals, vehicles, and vehicle replacement parts. The restriction disrupted the marketing plans of General Motors, Peugeot, and Renault, all of which supplied Chile with automobile parts from Argentine plants.

A company should pay particular attention to election time. Elections pose a special problem because of many candidates' instinctive tendency to use demagoguery to acquire votes. Candidate activities and tactics can very easily create an unwelcome atmosphere for foreign firms. When French politicians cited the fact that one French worker became unemployed for every five to ten Japanese cars imported, the government held up imported cars when the election was a few weeks away. The industry minister used every conceivable excuse to avoid signing the required certificates.

The use of unfriendly rhetoric before an election may be nothing but a smoke-screen, and the "bark" will not necessarily be followed by a "bite." In such a case, a company need not take drastic action if it is able to endure through the election. Ronald Reagan, long an advocate of free trade, became much more of a protectionist just before his reelection in 1984. After the election, a policy of free trade was re-instituted. Therefore, a company must determine whether early threats are just that and nothing more or whether such threats constitute the political candidates' real intention and attitude for the future.

ANALYSIS OF POLITICAL RISK OR COUNTRY RISK

Although political scientists, economists, businesspersons, and business scholars have some ideas about what political risk is, they seem to have difficulties agreeing both on its definition and on methods to predict danger. Perhaps because of this lack of agreement on the definition, many different methods have been employed to measure, analyze, and predict political risks. Simon provides a good overview of political risk assessment in terms of definition, approach, data bases, and variables.[18]

Some assessment methods are country specific in the sense that a risk report is based on a particular country's unique political and economic circumstances. As such, there is a lack of a consistent framework that would allow comparison across countries. Because an MNC must decide to allocate resources based on potential opportunities and risks associated with each country, a common methodology is essential.

Even when a systematic attempt is made for crossnational comparisons, the methods used vary greatly. Some are nothing more than checklists consisting of a large number of relevant issues that are applicable to each country. Other systems rely on questionnaires sent to experts or local citizens in order to gauge the political mood. Such scoring systems, which permit numerical ratings of countries, have gained acceptance. Some institutions have turned to econometrics for this purpose. Marine Midland Bank, for example, uses econometrics to rate various countries in terms of economic risk. The method, however, is not perfect. "This method has the disadvantages that it deals only with economic data, that relationships that are true on average for many countries are used to predict individual country results, and that the statistical significance is not as high as might be desired."[19]

Simon has pointed out that the variables used to assess political risk can be classified along several dimensions.[20] The variables may thus be either societal-related or government-related, either external or internal (based on the origins of risks), and either macro or micro (based on whether government actions are directed at all foreign companies or only at selected industries in the host country).

The level of economic development and the type of political system can be used as additional dimensions. Countries may be either industrialized or developing, with either open or closed political systems. A society is open when nongovernmental actors can shape events by voicing their approval or discontent in the forms of voting, protests, boycotts, and so on. In closed societies a government does not allow these forms of expression publicly, and the repression of the populace can lead to violent encounters. Table 4–2 shows a political risk framework based on such variables.

Douglas and Craig, in comparison, propose four distinct dimensions for the assessment of political risk, each of which can be "objectively" measured.[21] The four

TABLE 4–2 A Political Risk Framework

	Industrialized		Developing	
	Internal	**External**	**Internal**	**External**
Open Direct	Host government licensing, price controls, taxation Adverse legal rulings Negative media reports	Home government licensing, taxation policies Regional and global organizations, monitoring of MNC operations	Local content rules, joint venture pressure, technology transfer, and import/export regulations Strikes, protests, boycotts, negative public opinion Adverse legal rulings Negative media reports	Home government licensing, taxation policies Regional and global organizations' code of conduct for MNC
Indirect	Bureaucratic delays and procedures Elections, public pressure for environmental controls Local business pressure for subsidies, favorable treatment	Host–home country trade disputes Bilateral/multilateral trade agreements detrimental to MNC Global economic developments	Intragovernmental friction General strikes, elections Local business pressure for subsidies, favorable tax rates	North-South issue disputes Anti-MNC public sentiment owing to home country's foreign/military policy Regional/border wars High external debt, default Commodity price fluctuations
Closed Direct	Restrictions on remittances Strikes, terrorism, violent demonstrations, protests	Home government restrictions on operations Negative home and international public opinion, disinvestment pressure	Nationalization, expropriation Terrorism, riots, strikes	Home government restrictions on operations Negative home and international public opinion, disinvestment pressure
Indirect	Coups, radical regime change, leadership struggles Revolution, guerrilla war, riots	Deteriorating host-home relations International economic sanctions/boycott International protests Global economic developments	Coups, radical regime change, leadership struggles Revolution, guerrilla war, riots	North-South issue disputes Anti-MNC public sentiment owing to home country's foreign/military policy Regional/border wars High external debt Commodity price fluctuations

Source: Jeffrey D. Simon, "A Theoretical Perspective on Political Risk," *Journal of International Business Studies* 14 (Winter 1984): 132–133

dimensions (and some indicators or variables associated with each) are as follows: (1) domestic stability (e.g., riots, purges, and assassinations), (2) foreign conflict (e.g., diplomatic expulsions and military violence), (3) political climate (e.g., size of the country's communist party and number of socialist seats in the legislature), and (4) economic climate (e.g., GNP, inflation, external debt levels, and frustration level).

Among U.S. firms, Amoco Corp. is unique because it has a separate five-person foreign intelligence office which scrutinizes about 50 countries. To many small- and medium-sized firms, doing their own country-risk analyses is out of the question because of the cost, expertise, and resources required. However, there are some alternatives that can provide a useful assessment of political risk. One is to interview people who have some knowledge or experience with the countries of interest, including businesspersons, bankers, and government officials. Molex Inc., a manufacturer of high-technology electrical products, has been able to protect itself by listening to international bankers, lawyers, and accounting firms. Another method is to rely on the advice of firms specializing in this area. Controlled Risks, a Washington area firm, advises about 400 U.S. companies on the danger of doing business in seventy countries. For fees that can total $9,000 a year, the firm offers information and provides training for executives on how to protect themselves, cope with kidnapping and extortion, and guide their employees in political crises.[22]

Another alternative is to subscribe to reports prepared for this purpose. One valuable report is the country credit rating prepared by *Institutional Investor* magazine. Based on a survey of approximately 100 leading international banks concerning a country's creditworthiness and the chance of payment default, rankings are assigned to 100 countries every six months. Greater weight is given to the responses of those banks that have the largest global exposures and possess the most sophisticated systems of risk analysis. Yet the loan problems encountered by the Bank of America and Citicorp make it clear that the risk-analysis systems used by some of the world's largest banks are anything but foolproof.

Another relatively simple method is based on LIBOR (London Interbank rate). The LIBOR rate, relatively risk-free, is the interest rate charged for loans between banks. Nonbank borrowers, of course, have to pay a premium over LIBOR, with the premium (i.e., the spread between the loan rate and LIBOR) indicating the extent of risk involved. A borrower from a country with a high risk of default must expect a high premium. The premium is thus a good indicator of risk because it reflects a lender's assessment of the country in terms of debt levels and payment records. Because all loans are not comparable, adjustment must be made for volume and maturity. *Euromoney* magazine has devised a formula to allow for this adjustment, and its formula to compute a country's *spread index* is the following:

$$[(\text{volume} \times \text{spread}) \div Euromoney \text{ index}] \div (\text{volume} \times \text{maturity})$$

By simply examining the spread index of a particular country and comparing it with those of other countries, an investor can arrive at the conclusion of a degree of risk associated with the country of interest.

Although *Euromoney*'s and *Institutional Investor*'s country risk ratings are derived in different ways, the two measures are highly correlated and strongly agree on the creditworthiness of the assessed countries. Both magazines' ratings can be replicated to a significant degree with a few economic variables. "In particular, both the level of per capita income and propensity to invest affect positively the rating of a country. In addition, high-ranking countries are less indebted than low-ranking countries."[23] Table 4–3 describes the variables used.

As assessment methods of political risks have become more sophisticated, there has been a shift from the earlier conceptual and qualitative approaches to the approaches that are quantitative and derivative of applied research. There is a need, however, to integrate these two major kinds of approaches. As explained by Simon,

TABLE 4–3   Description of the explanatory variables

Variable	Motivation	Expected Sign
Gross National Product (GNP) per capita	Poorer countries may have less flexibility to reduce consumption than richer countries. Countries with low GNP per capita may thus be less able to solve debt service difficulties by implementing austerity programs.	+
Propensity to invest	This variable captures a country's prospects for future growth. The incentive to default is a decreasing function of the propensity to invest since the cost of default (e.g., an embargo on future borrowing or a higher cost of future credit) increases with future output.	+
Reserves-to-imports ratio	The larger reserves are relative to imports, the more reserves are available also to service external debt and the lower is the probability of default.	+
Current account balance on GNP	This variable is negatively related to the probability of default since the current account deficit broadly equals the amount of new financing required (aside from the amount of capital provided by direct foreign investment).	+
Export growth rate[a]	Since for most countries exports are the main source of foreign exchange earnings, countries with high export growth rates are more likely to service debt.	+
Export variability[b]	Traditionally the literature has argued that countries with volatile exports are more vulnerable to foreign exchange crises and are less creditworthy. In contrast, Eaton and Gersovitz show that default risk will be smaller, the larger exports fluctuations. The underlying rationale is that countries with more volatile exports are more frequently in need of borrowing to smooth consumption across periods of varying income and are therefore incited to maintain a good credit record.	?
Net foreign debt to exports	A country with a high net foreign debt (foreign debt minus nongold reserves) to exports ratio is more vulnerable to foreign exchange crises and more likely to default.	−
Debt service difficulties dummy variable[c]	When a country is known to have asked some of its creditors for debt relief, other creditors are apprehensive of default and the credit rating is likely to fall.	−
Political instability indicator[d]	Aliber shows that political instability can reduce a country's willingness to service debt.	−

Notes:

[a] Export growth rate is measured as the average of the annual growth rates over a five-year (1982–1986) period.

[b] Export variability is measured as the average absolute percentage deviation from a five-year (1982–1986) trend.

[c] This dummy variable took the value of 1 for the countries which renegotiated their foreign debt in 1986 and 0 for the other countries.

[d] We consider two types of political instability indicator: (1) political protest (e.g., protest demonstrations, political strikes, riots, political assassinations) and (2) successful and unsuccessful irregular executive transfers (e.g., coups d'etat, coup attempts). We record the number of these disruptive events over a five-year period (1982–1986).

Source: Jean-Claude Cosset and Jean Roy, "The Determinants of Country Risk Ratings," *Journal of International Business Studies* 22 (no. 1, 1991): 137

"within this atmosphere of increased pressure for applied results, it is not surprising that theoretical concerns have laid dormant. Without theory, each new risk situation tends to be viewed as unique to the particular country involved, and no attempt is made to identify recurring patterns and trends across nations. Because host countries are part of an interdependent international and global system, in-depth country analyses often miss some of the key determinants of political risk."[24] Therefore, a general framework should take into account the four basic environments (host country, home country, international arena, and global arena) in which an MNC must operate.

MANAGEMENT OF POLITICAL RISK

To manage political risk, there are four policies that an MNC can pursue: avoidance, insurance, negotiating the environment, and structuring the investment.[25] *Avoidance* means screening out politically uncertain countries. In this, measurement and analysis of political risk can be useful. *Insurance,* in contrast, is a strategy to shift the risk to other parties (e.g., private insurers, FCIA, and OPIC). This strategy will be covered in detail later.

In *negotiating the environment,* the idea is to develop an explicit concession agreement before committing the company to direct investment abroad. Such an agreement is used to define the rights and responsibilities of the MNC, the MNC's foreign partner, and the host-country government.

In *structuring the investment,* the objective is to minimize potential threats by adjusting the firm's operating and financial policies. Once an investment is made, there are several operating policies that can deal with uncertainties. Such policies range from having local stakeholders and planned divestiture to short-term profit maximization and a change in the benefit/cost ratio. Financial techniques include

> Keeping the affiliate company or subsidiary dependent on sister companies for markets or supplies or both.
>
> Concentrating research and development affiliates and proprietary technology in the home country.
>
> Establishing a single, global trademark so that the host country could, at best, take away only physical facilities and not a product's intangible assets.
>
> Controlling transportation.
>
> Sourcing production in multiple plants.
>
> Developing external financial stakeholders.

Political risks are affected by the company's bargaining power. A subsidiary has little such power when its technical, operational, and managerial complexity requirements are within reach of a host country's abilities. When this is the case, government intervention is likely to increase.[26] To increase its bargaining power, the company may want to take certain actions. As the sales of the subsidiary to affiliated companies climb, the MNC exerts a greater control over sales and is able to deter intervention. Similarly, as the subsidiary engages more and more in exporting, the same effect can be achieved.

A study by Fagre and Wells seems to confirm that the extent of foreign ownership of subsidiaries in a host country is a function of "the level of technology of the multinational, the degree to which a multinational attempts to differentiate its products, the extent to which a subsidiary's output is exported to other parts of the multinational, the diversity of products offered by the multinational, and the extent of competition by other multinationals."[27] Size of the investment does not appear to significantly affect government policies toward ownership.

To cope with uncertainties, Mascarenhas suggests the use of strategies for exerting control and flexibility.[28] Strategies for *exerting control* are used to keep the environment from adversely changing. Techniques include

Using backward integration to control supply sources and forward integration to control markets, especially when some or most of the sources of supply and markets are outside a host country.

Lobbying the government for favorable legislation.

Making questionable payments.

Using promotion to influence consumers.

Entering into contracts with suppliers for inputs and buyers for outputs.

Forming cartels with competitors.

It should be noted that some of these strategies are probably illegal in a number of countries.

Increasing flexibility — usually done at a cost — increases a company's adaptability to a changing environment. Strategies include

Using general-purpose equipment to produce multiple products so as to reduce dependence on a single product.

Selling each product in a number of markets.

Undertaking more exporting, leasing, licensing, franchising, and subcontracting to reduce committing resources into fixed and durable assets abroad.

Decentralizing decision making so that decisions can be made quickly.

Avoiding long-term commitments by having short-notice termination clauses.

Maintaining a financial cushion (liquid assets, emergency borrowing, and stock issuing power) for a quick response to environmental changes.

Installing an intelligence system to assess environmental developments.

Table 4–4 lists the varying methods to reduce uncertainty and the conditions that are appropriate for each method.

The rapid changes in Eastern Europe present both challenges and opportunities. In the former days of centralization, a trade minister in the capital could speak for the entire nation. But with decentralized decision making, an MNC has to go to the fifteen republics for information and approval. As an example, McDonald's Restaurants of Canada, Ltd. spent 14 years setting up its joint venture and does business only in rubles. Exhibit 4–3 provides some tips for doing business in Eastern Europe.

TABLE 4–4 Some conditions under which methods of uncertainty reduction are likely to be used

Methods	Conditions	Examples
Prediction	a. When the uncertainty can be confidently reduced using available forecasting techniques. b. When markets are large and investigation costs can be amortized over a large volume. c. When data are available and reliable. d. When amount at stake is large and can easily absorb the investigation costs. e. When managers understand and feel comfortable with forecasting techniques.	Prediction of the consumption of a staple food item (dairy products) based on demographic trends. Political and geological risk forecast before making large investment in oil production.
Control	a. When there are no ethical or government constraints that prohibit questionable payments. b. When there are no restrictions on advertising. c. When integration is not prohibited by antitrust action. d. When integration is not precluded by the existence of many inputs and many outputs. e. When forward contracts are available for the time period, currency, or commodity desired. f. When contracts are likely to be honored.	Retailer with many suppliers and many customers cannot easily integrate backward or forward. Company that markets clothes in Mexico not knowing exactly what sales and profits will be in the future is not likely to use a forward contract.
Insurance	a. Theoretically, only uncertainties whose historical probabilities and outcomes are known are insurable. Uncertainty must not involve moral hazard. b. When deductibles and premiums are reasonable.	Political risk insurance is available only for some countries, some industries, and for some types on uncertainties.
Flexibility	a. When the technical nature of the business permits the investment to be broken up into smaller, viable parts. b. When there are parties that are able to be lessors and fulfill the subcontracted obligation. c. When there are many sources of supply and many buyers for the firm's activities. d. When the need for effectiveness outweighs the benefits of economies of scale and specialization. e. When subcontracting is not likely to create a competitor. f. When licensing, franchising, and exporting are feasible.	Clothing company was able to subcontract out the stitching of jeans because the required expertise was basic and readily available. Firms used duplication in system to reduce impact of political and production uncertainty.
Avoidance	a. When the bargaining power of the firm, or existence of government guarantees, permit the firm to transfer the uncertainty to others. b. When the perceived uncertainty relative to the expected return is too high.	Acceptance of payment only in hard currencies.

Source: Briance Mascerenhas, "Coping with Uncertainty in International Business," *Journal of International Business Studies* 13 (Fall 1982): 95–96

- Enter the market with a clear idea of what you want to achieve from the beginning. Decide in advance which of your company's products or services fit each country or countries in the region. Avoid an unfocused approach.
- Do not expect short-term successes. Most successful companies prepare to enter the market for the long term.
- Start small; enter the market first through sales, cooperation, or licensing. Joint ventures and long-term investment need research, planning, and preparation.
- Be prepared to *reinvest* profits in the short term, and to *recoup* profits over the long term.
- Be creative in approaching the Eastern European market. Creative financing, cooperation, sales, and investment are keys to getting the deal.
- Be aware that creativity includes long-term thinking. Sell a planned quantity of units this year, but agree to cooperate to conduct research and development, pool your expertise, and together develop a better product to beat the competition next year.
- Learn all of the needs of the company or enterprise you are dealing with. What are the labor, capital, equipment, social, and ecological needs of your potential partner?
- Prepare well for entry into the Eastern European market. Contact the Department of Commerce and other information sources before considering a market. Do the necessary homework, but do not substitute research for traveling to the region to examine the countries firsthand.
- Participate in trade fairs, trade missions, and business councils. The Department of Commerce schedules a number of trade promotion activities by industry sector each year.
- If your company lacks experience in the area, consider hiring a consultant to assist you. Hiring a lawyer with expertise in Eastern European law is also helpful.
- Although English is widely understood by business and technical personnel in Eastern Europe, be prepared to use the services of interpreters and translators familiar with technical and business language for serious marketing and negotiation activities.
- Be prepared for strong competition from European firms. Europeans have had more experience and proximity to Eastern Europe, but American firms have competitive products.
- Consider using the extensive experience of a Western European company or subsidiary.

EXHIBIT 4–3 Tips for doing business in Eastern Europe

Source: Business America, 18 June 1990, 6

MEASURES TO MINIMIZE POLITICAL RISK

Political risk, though impossible to eliminate, can at the very least be minimized. There are several measures that MNCs can implement in order to discourage a host country from taking control of MNC assets.

Stimulation of the Local Economy

One defensive investment strategy calls for a company to link its business activities with the host country's national economic interests. Brazil expelled Mellon Bank because of the bank's refusal to cooperate in renegotiating the country's massive foreign debt.

A local economy can be stimulated in a number of different ways. One strategy may involve the company's purchasing local products and raw materials for its production and operations. By assisting local firms, it can develop local allies who can provide valuable political contacts. A modification of this strategy would be to use subcontractors. For example, some military tank manufacturers tried to secure tank contracts from the Netherlands by agreeing to subcontract part of the work on the new tanks to Dutch companies.

Sometimes local sourcing is compulsory. Governments may require products to contain locally manufactured components because local content improves the economy in two ways: (1) it stimulates demand for domestic components, and (2) it saves the necessity of a foreign exchange transaction. Further investment in local production facilities by the company will please the government that much more. IBM is the only foreign company allowed to sell switchboards in France because the firm's PBXs are made there.

Finally, the company should attempt to assist the host country by being export oriented. Exhibit 4–4 shows how Marubeni, a Japanese firm, emphasizes this strategy in its advertisement aimed at the U.S. market. Both United Brands and Castle and Cooke were able to survive the Sandinista revolution in Nicaragua by implementing this strategy. Their export dollars became vital to the Nicaraguan government, thus shielding their Latin American operations from expropriation. AT&T was able to enter the French telephone switch market by agreeing to assist Compagnie Générale d'Electricité (CGE), a French nationalized switchmaker, in selling smaller digital switches in the United States.

Employment of Nationals

Frequently, foreigners make the simple but costly mistake of assuming that citizens of LDCs are poor by choice. It serves no useful purpose for a company to assume that local people are lazy, unintelligent, unmotivated, or uneducated. Such an attitude may become a self-fulfilling prophecy. Thus, the hiring of local workers should go beyond the filling of labor positions. United Brands's policy, for example, is to hire only locals as managers.

Firms should also carefully weigh the impact of automation in a cheap-labor, high-unemployment area. Automation does not go over well in India, where job creation, not job elimination, is national policy. Technology is neither always welcomed nor always socially desirable. An inability to automate production completely does not necessarily constitute a negative for MNCs. MNCs may gain more in LDCs by

WE EXPORTED

$3.3 Billion

TO JAPAN LAST YEAR FROM AMERICA

Marubeni has built some big markets for the U.S.A. in Japan, in close tie with its subsidiary Marubeni America. And not by chance. Success like this takes more than sales skills: it requires deep insight into the realities that create the Japanese marketplaces, and investment to help shape them. We're the kind of "hands on" trading companies that are geared to meet these challenges squarely.

Consider our record with American high-tech products. Marubeni's had tremendous success marketing sophisticated computers and semiconductor manufacturing equipment from the U.S.A. in Japan. The reason: we've built a complete subsidiary, Marubeni HYTECH, and staffed it with specialists and engineers who know these products inside out. Far beyond sales, our people provide a brand of on-call support and service to customers that's much better than what other importers can do. We even feed back user comments to makers, for product improvement.

Right now, HYTECH is handling sales and support of electronic-industry design systems from such U.S. companies as ECAD, Zycad, Viewlogic and others. Sales of these systems to Japan's IC manufacturers are growing rapidly.

Of course we handle a great many more "Made in U.S.A." goods, too: we export America's agricultural produce and consumer products, we license its services and sell its high-fashion clothing, and we introduce partners for the venture businesses that build the future. Marubeni America Corp. is today, in fact, one of the leaders in increasing U.S. exports, as its $3.3 billion in sales to Japan and $2.2 billion elsewhere attest.

We build world trade in other ways as well. By providing customized financing, investment, leasing, supply of natural resources—even turnkey plant or infrastructure project management.

Take advantage of our skills. Marubeni's 192 offices worldwide are on-line channels of business opportunity, linked by 24-hour satellite telecommunications. Our 13 offices in America are waiting and willing to talk over the business potentials in Japan, or anywhere, any time you'd like.

Always with and for you.

Marubeni

C.P.O. Box 595, Tokyo 100-91, Japan

Marubeni America Corporation Head Office:
42nd Fl., Pan American Bldg., 200 Park Avenue, New York, N.Y. 10166 Tel. 212-599-3700

Los Angeles Tel. 213-972-2700 **San Francisco** Tel. 415-954-0100 **Chicago** Tel. 312-222-6211 **Houston** Tel. 713-654-4000 **Seattle** Tel. 206-624-5850 **Portland** Tel. 503-224-3760 **Dallas** Tel. 214-880-9001 **Detroit** Tel. 313-353-7060 **Boston** Tel. 617-273-4940 **St. Louis** Tel. 314-291-1127 **Washington D.C.** Tel. 202-331-1161 **Nashville** Tel. 615-885-2530

EXHIBIT 4–4 Export orientation to benefit the host country

Source: Reprinted with permission of Marubeni America Corporation

using "intermediate technology" instead of the most advanced equipment. Intermediate technology, accompanied by additional labor, is less expensive, and it promotes goodwill by increasing employment.

Sharing Ownership

Instead of keeping complete ownership for itself, a company should try to share ownership with others, especially with local companies. One method is to convert from a private company to a public one or from a foreign company to a local one. Dragon Airline, claiming that it is a real Chinese company, charged that Cathay Pacific Airways' Hong Kong landing rights should be curtailed because Cathay Pacific was more British than Chinese. The threat forced Cathay Pacific to sell a new public issue to allow Chinese investors to have minority interests in the company. The move was made to convince Hong Kong and China that the company had Chinese roots.

One of the most common techniques for shared ownership is to simply form a joint venture. Any loss of control as a result can, in most cases, be more than compensated for by the derived benefits. United Brands's policy in South America is not to initiate any business unless local joint venture partners can be found to help spread the risk.

In some overseas business ventures, it is not always necessary to have local firms as partners. Sometimes, having co-owners from other nations can work almost as well. Having multiple nationality for international business projects not only reduces exposure; it also makes it difficult for the host government to take over the business venture without offending a number of nations all at once. The political situation in South Africa was one of the reasons Ford chose to merge its automobile operations there with Anglo American. The merger reduced Ford's exposure to a 40 percent minority position.

Sometimes multiple nationality backfires. This can be a problem when a member of the project is from a nation that is unfriendly to the host country. Fiat, partially owned by the state-owned Libyan Arab Foreign Investment Company, saw the awarding of a bulldozer contract to its Fiatallis North America, Inc., subsidiary being suspended by the U.S. Department of Defense because of Fiat's financial ties with Libya. To solve the problem, Fiat requested to buy back its shares from Libya. The Libyan government initially refused to sell its holdings before agreeing to accept Fiat's attractive price offer.

Another strategy may include voluntary domestication. A case in point involves India's Foreign Exchange Regulation Act, which was passed in 1973 to protect domestic industry. The act forbids expatriate companies from holding more than 40 percent in Indian operations, unless the company is high-technology- or export-oriented. Both IBM and Coca-Cola chose not to give up their independence and left in 1978. Pharmaceutical firms such as Warner-Lambert and Parke Davis, in contrast, agreed to cut their equity.

Voluntary domestication, in most cases, is not a desirable course of action because it is usually a forced decision. The company should therefore plan for domestication in advance instead of waiting until it is required, because by that time the company has lost much of its leverage and bargaining power. This strategy is also likely to be perceived as a gesture of goodwill, an accomplishment in addition to the desired reduction of exposure. A wise strategy may be for the company to retain the marketing or technical side of the business while allowing heavy local ownership in the physical assets and capital-intensive portions of the investment.

Being Civic Minded

MNCs whose home country is the United States often encounter the "ugly American" label abroad, and this image should be avoided. It is not sufficient that the company simply does business in a foreign country; it should also be a good corporate citizen there. To shed the undesirable perception, multinationals should combine investment projects with civic projects. Corporations rarely undertake civic projects out of total generosity, but such projects make economic sense in the long run. It is highly desirable to provide basic assistance because many civic entities exist in areas with slight or nonexistent municipal infrastructures that would normally provide these facilities. A good idea is to assist in building schools, hospitals, roads, and water systems because such projects benefit the host country as well as the company, especially in terms of the valuable goodwill generated in the long run.

There are many examples of U.S. global philanthropy.[29] American Express spent $500,000 to develop an academic course to educate secondary school students on travel and tourism issues. At a cost of $400,000, Du Pont sent 1.4 million water jug filters to eight African nations, and its synthetic fabric removes debilitating parasitic worms from drinking water. Alcoa and local authorities in southern Brazil built a sewage plant for $112,000 to serve 15,000 rural residents. In China and Thailand, through its Institute of Nutritional Sciences in Chengdu, China, H. J. Heinz spent $94,000 to fund infant nutrition studies. IBM donated computer equipment and expertise worth $60,000 to Costa Rica's National Parks Foundation to find ways to preserve rain forests. Japanese foreign contributions of $500 million in 1991 resulted from a new law that doubled a corporate tax deduction for foreign charitable giving of up to 2.5 percent of pretax income. It is wise to remember that in many less developed countries, a small sum of money can go a long way.

Political Neutrality

For the best long-term interests of the company, it is not wise to become involved in political disputes among local groups or between countries. A company should clearly but discreetly state that it is not in the political business and that its primary concerns are economic in nature. Brazilian firms employ this strategy and keep a low profile in matters related to Central American revolutions and Cuban troops in foreign countries. Brazilian arms are thus attractive to the Third World because those arms are free of ideological ties. In such a case, a purchasing country does not feel obligated to become politically aligned with a seller, as when buying from the United States or China.

Each country probably has certain matters deemed critical to its pride. As such, a company must be sensitive to these issues. The U.S. Department of Commerce warns that proper nomenclature is a matter of particular concern in China: "It is important to avoid references to 'Red,' 'Communist,' or 'mainland' China. It is also important not to refer to Taiwan as a country or as 'the Republic of China,' or 'nationalist China.' Likewise, Hong Kong should not be identified as 'HMCC' or 'Her Majesty's Crown Colony.' The appropriate terminology is 'People's Republic of China' or 'China,' 'Taiwan,' and 'Hong Kong.' "[30]

Behind-the-Scenes Lobby

Much like the variables affecting business, political risks can be reasonably managed. Companies as well as special interest groups have varying interests, and each party will want to make its own opinion known. When the U.S. mushroom industry asked for a quota against imports from China, Pizza Hut came to China's rescue by claiming that most domestic and other foreign suppliers could not meet its specifications. As one of China's largest customers and as a user of half of some 9 million pounds of mushrooms for pizzas, Pizza Hut had a great deal at stake. Furthermore, its parent, PepsiCo, hoped to open a factory in southern China. Because the U.S. government also wanted to strengthen its relationship with China, the petition of the U.S. mushroom industry was denied.

When practical, firms should attempt to influence political decisions. Exhibit 4–5 shows how Mobil tried to affect a decision that would benefit its partner, Saudi Arabia. Even though a firm's operation is affected by the political environment, the direction of the influence does not have to flow in one direction only. Lobbying activities can be undertaken, and it is wise to lobby quietly behind the scenes in order not to cause unnecessary political clamor. In explaining the intensity of foreign corporate representation in Washington, the level of U.S. imports from the home country of the MNC is the most important variable, as it outranks U.S. exports to the home country and foreign direct investment in the United States from the home country.[31]

Importers must let their government know why imports are critical to them and their consumers. For example, many U.S. clothing retailers complained vigorously when trade barriers were erected against the importation of clothes. U.S. computer makers, likewise, voiced their objection to a government action designed to protect the prices of U.S.-made semiconductors because those firms would have to absorb any price increase.

Companies may not only have to lobby in their own country, but they also may have to lobby in the host country. Companies may want to do the lobbying themselves, or they may let their government do it on their behalf. Their government can be requested to apply pressure against foreign governments.

Observation of Political Mood and Reduction of Exposure

Marketers should be sensitive to changes in political mood. A contingency plan should be in readiness when the political climate turns hostile, when measures are necessary to reduce exposure. Some major banks and MNCs took measures to reduce their exposure in France in response to a fear that a Socialist-Communist coalition might gain control of the legislature in the elections of 1978. Their concern was understandable, as most of these companies were on the left's nationalization list. Their defensive strategy included the outflow of capital, the transfer of patents and other assets to foreign subsidiaries, and the sale of equity holdings to foreigners and French nationals living abroad. Such activities once concluded made it difficult for the Socialist government to nationalize the companies' properties. Prudence required that these transactions be kept quiet so as to avoid reprisals. As events developed, the fears were partially realized. Although the coalition did win, the new government was pragmatic and did not actively pursue expropriation in a broad sense. Nevertheless, in a time of uncertainty and under such circumstances, what these companies did was logical.

Selling missiles to the Saudis serves <u>America's</u> best interests

Even before President Reagan vetoed the Congressional resolution to block the sale of defensive missiles to Saudi Arabia, commentators from across the political spectrum agreed the sale should proceed. They reasoned that the sale would serve not only Saudi Arabia's interests, but, more important, vital American interests in the strategic Middle East.

For example, *The New York Times,* certainly no knee-jerk supporter of the Administration, said in an editorial on May 7: "Congress is wrong to try to block the proposed sale of $354 million worth of arms, mostly antiaircraft missiles [to the Saudis]." The *Times* editorial writer noted that the Saudis "…counteract the influence of Iran and Syria by assisting Iraq and Jordan. And they invest their fortunes in the West, notably the United States. They are not conspicuous allies, but they are friends, and useful ones."

The same editorial noted that if the sale is killed, the Saudis would be pushed into buying arms from other nations. Said the *Times*: "The Saudis have faithfully protected American weapons against unauthorized transfer, a safeguard that is lost if we keep pushing them to buy elsewhere." The *Times*' conclusion: "The new deal…is diplomatically desirable for America."

John M. Poindexter, assistant to the President for national security affairs, pointed out the strategic role of the Saudis in an article published in *The Washington Post.* Citing the turmoil in the region—a war "prolonged by Iranian fanaticism,…Soviet support for radical extremists in South Yemen and elsewhere," and Soviet intervention in Afghanistan—Poindexter called it fortunate that "America has many friends in the region who are helping maintain regional security and whose security in turn it is in our own interest to support. Saudi Arabia is among the most important of these."

Wrote Poindexter: "Completion of the sale at this time, even though the missiles will not be delivered for several years, provides a clear and important political demonstration of U.S. commitment to Saudi self-defense. It helps deter Iran from expanding the Gulf war, bolsters the resolve of other Arab moderates, and diminishes the possibility that U.S. troops may eventually have to be used to protect our interests in the Persian Gulf."

The *Post* itself was convinced. In an editorial on May 9, two days after the Poindexter article appeared, the *Post* wrote: "For the Saudis, open to a host of perils, defense is central. There lies the reason for American support of Saudi defense, by displays of constancy and the provision of arms. This is the connection that Congress would now casually break."

The *Post* added that "Congress should examine the implication of its effective position that all Arabs, whether they be designated moderate or radical, are alike under the skin, and are unreliable. This is a simplistic and self-defeating judgment with more than a touch of condescension to it. It writes off 20-odd countries, and invites radicals, fundamentalists, and Russians to dominate a major region of the world."

President Reagan reinforced that view in his veto message, saying "the Saudis have proven their friendship and good will," and have "worked quietly" to improve the climate in the region.

This week, the Senate will attempt to override President Reagan's veto, and kill the sale. When the crucial roll call is taken, members should remember a simple fact: They <u>aren't</u> voting on just an arms bill for Saudi Arabia. They <u>are</u> voting on an arms bill for America, and for American interests. Against such a yardstick, we trust the presidential veto will be sustained.

Mobil®

EXHIBIT 4–5   Corporate effort and political decision

Source: Reprinted with permission of Mobil Corporation. ©1986 Mobil Corporation

Other Measures

There are a few other steps that MNCs can undertake to minimize political risk. One strategy could involve keeping a low profile. Because it is difficult to please all the people all the time, it may be desirable for a company to be relatively inconspicuous. For example, in the 1980s Texas Instruments removed identifying logos and signs in El Salvador.

Another tactic could involve trying to adopt a local personality. A practical approach may require that the company blend in with the environment. There is not much to be gained by a company being ethnocentric and trying to Westernize the host country's citizens. A veteran of international business would very likely realize that it is far better to be flexible and adaptable. Such a firm would know that it should behave like a chameleon, adapting itself to fit the environment. The main reason that McDonald's uses local corporate staff is to look like a local company. This is also the goal of Hawley Group. That company is thought to be American in the United States, British in the United Kingdom, and Australian in Australia.

After years of being the ugly American, IBM wants to be a good European citizen, striving to show that it is as European as its competitors. Whenever possible, IBM gave the message to EC officials and more than 200 European journalists: (1) the company locally produces 92 percent of what it sells in Europe, (2) it is France's sixth-biggest taxpayer and Britain's fifth-biggest exporter, and (3) its research facilities in Europe create high-technology jobs. Regarding the politically sensitive area of telecommunication services, in which local telephone monopolies have traditionally reigned, IBM is in joint data network ventures with Fiat in Italy, Crédit Agricole and Banque Paribas in France, and Copenhagen Telephone. In addition, the company has networking-development accords with Siemens and Sweden's Ericsson.[32]

Finally, various defensive precautions can be implemented. Automobile drivers should be trained in how to react to a kidnapping attempt, and managers themselves should be instructed in how to deal with the unexpected and taught especially to avoid driving routine routes. Very basic precautions might be undertaken. For example, in El Salvador, Texas Instruments erected protective walls for its facilities and employed extra guards. It is better to be safe than sorry.

POLITICAL INSURANCE

In addition to the strategies of risk avoidance and risk reduction, MNCs can employ the strategy of *risk shifting*. Insurance coverage can be obtained from a number of sources. For U.S. firms, the three primary ones are private insurance, OPIC, and FCIA.

Private Insurance

Through ignorance, a large number of companies end up as self-insurers. A better plan would be to follow Club Med's example by shifting political risk to a third party through the purchase of political insurance. NBC was handsomely compensated by its insurers when it had to cancel its telecast of the 1980 Moscow Olympic Games when President Carter prohibited U.S. athletes from participating as a protest against the Soviet Union's invasion of Afghanistan.

Although property expropriation seems to be the most common reason for obtaining political insurance, the policy should include coverage for kidnapping, terrorism, and creeping expropriation. Information about most companies' coverage is rather scarce, because it is both imprudent and impermissible for companies to reveal that they are carrying such a thing as kidnap insurance. Revelation of such coverage would only serve to encourage such activity.

Premium rates for noncatastrophic political insurance are typically five to ten times higher than conventional commercial insurance. The high prices reflect the small number of private insurers in the United States as well as a lack of actuarial experience to calculate rates scientifically.[33] A few crude formulas do exist. For a U.S. contractor building a $200 million hospital abroad, the rate charged will depend on the location of the construction. If the project is located in Spain, the premium may only be $1.6 million, but this amount will more than double for Saudi Arabia, a medium-risk country, and quadruple for Libya, a high-risk country. The rate can be discounted and reduced by almost 50 percent if the company uses the same insurer for all of its worldwide business operations.

OPIC

MNCs do not have to rely solely on private insurers. There are nonprofit, public agencies that can provide essentially the same kind of coverage. One such organization is the Overseas Private Investment Corporation (OPIC). OPIC is a U.S. government agency that assists economic development through investment insurance and a credit financing program. Unlike AID (Agency for International Development), which provides government-to-government assistance, OPIC is a business-oriented agency whose purpose is to support U.S. private investments. Chartered by Congress in 1981, OPIC is a financially self-sustaining, independent corporation that receives no public funds. Its contracts, however, are fully backed by the U.S. government, a sole owner of the corporation. The Insurance and Finance Departments are the agency's two principal operating units.[34] Exhibit 4–6 explains the eligibility requirements for the programs of these two departments.

OPIC has multiple objectives, one of which is to promote overseas investment that will contribute to the economic development of Third World countries. These objectives require OPIC to review carefully each project to ensure consistency with host country aims (i.e., jobs, import savings, export earnings, training, tax revenues, and so on). Approved projects must also serve U.S. interests in terms of expanded trade, protection of U.S. market position, employment, access to needed materials, investor earnings, and assistance to friendly nations. Therefore, OPIC is prohibited by its governing legislation from supporting any U.S. private investment that could hurt the U.S. economy. In fiscal 1985 OPIC rejected 20 of 147 projects because of possible adverse U.S. effects. Most rejected projects were related to such economically sensitive sectors as textiles, footwear, work gloves, electronics, and ornamental flowers.[35] One such project involved a footwear operation in which U.S.-made-and-cut fabric was to be sent abroad to be sewn and returned to the United States for attachment to synthetic

OPIC programs are available only if

☐ The investor's project is a new venture or an expansion of an existing enterprise, and
☐ The project is located in a developing country where OPIC operates, and
☐ The project will assist in the social and economic development of the host country, and
☐ The project is approved by the host government, and
☐ The project is consistent with the economic interests of the United States and will not have a significant adverse effect on the U.S. economy or U.S. employment.

OPIC will not support a "runaway plant" project (i.e., the closing down of a U.S. facility to open a foreign facility where the same products or services will be produced for the same markets as before). OPIC cannot support certain other types of projects, including gambling facilities, distilleries, military projects, and projects posing serious environmental hazards.

SPECIFIC PROGRAM ELIGIBILITY

In addition, the following general restrictions and guidelines should be kept in mind when considering specific OPIC programs:

Insurance

☐ OPIC can only issue insurance to "eligible investors," who are defined as

citizens of the United States, or

U.S. corporations, partnerships, or other business organizations of at least 50 percent U.S. ownership, or

foreign corporations, partnerships, or other business organizations at least 95 percent owned by investors eligible under the above.

☐ OPIC generally will cover no more than 90 percent of an investment plus attributable earnings. Therefore, the investor typically must bear the risk of loss of at least 10 percent of any investment insured by OPIC.
☐ OPIC insurance is not available retroactively. Investors must obtain an OPIC insurance registration letter before the investment has been made or irrevocably committed. Investors are thus encouraged to contact OPIC in the early stages of investment planning.
☐ There is no fixed form that an investment must take in order to be eligible for OPIC insurance coverage. Conventional equity investments and loans; investment or exposure of funds; goods or services under contractual arrangements; and production-sharing agreements are among the investment forms commonly insured.

Finance

☐ Direct loans are issued only for investment projects sponsored by, or significantly involving, U.S. small businesses or cooperatives.
☐ Loan guarantees are issued to

U.S. lenders having over 50 percent U.S. ownership, or

Foreign lending institutions that are at least 95 percent U.S. owned.

☐ OPIC will not purchase equity in a project, but may purchase convertible notes and debt instruments with equity participation features.

EXHIBIT 4–6   OPIC overall eligibility

Source: Overseas Private Investment Corporation (Washington, D.C.: OPIC), 12

soles. The investor argued that the method would allow him to stay in business to compete with imported shoes so that he could retain his American employees. OPIC, however, saw it differently. Concluding that the project would hurt other U.S. shoe manufacturers, OPIC turned down the request for assistance.

OPIC provides several forms of assistance, with political risk insurance as its primary business. Other types of assistance include loan guarantees, direct loans, local currency loans, special project grants, and reconnaissance survey and feasibility study findings. It has made nearly $1 billion in direct loan and loan guarantee commitments.

OPIC has three types of insurance protection to cover the risks of (1) currency inconvertibility, (2) expropriation (including creeping expropriation), and (3) loss or damage caused by war, revolution, or insurrection. Exhibit 4–7 describes these risks and the premium cost for each type of coverage. A typical insurance contract runs up to twenty years at a combined annual premium of 1.5 percent for all three coverages. Considering that private insurers issue a three-year policy, OPIC's coverage is a positive feature.

Almost all types of investor exposure can be insured. They include "equity, loans, both the interest and principal, guaranty of repayment of a loan made by another lender, earnings retained in the foreign enterprise; earnings reinvested in new or expanded capacity, royalties and fees, recoupment of investor costs under production-sharing contracts with foreign governments, all other normal and accepted forms of income associated with investor activities.[36] For construction and engineering firms, OPIC offers protection for contract cancellation and provides insurance for bid and performance guarantees by covering letters of credit that U.S. contractors are required to post in many countries for this purpose.

Since OPIC's inception, the agency has issued more than $28 billion in political risk insurance coverage. OPIC's services are valuable. Many low-income or less developed countries have signed agreements making OPIC programs available to them. So far, eighty-seven developing countries and 2,000 investment projects have utilized OPIC's services. For example, OPIC has issued more than $225 million in expropriation and political violence coverage to twenty American firms operating in China.

Scores of industries have benefited from OPIC programs, ranging from agricultural production and chemicals to branch banking and heavy construction. Companies whose successful overseas ventures were assisted by OPIC include Ford in India (insurance), Hormel in the Philippines (insurance), Black and Decker in Yugoslavia (insurance), Dresser Industries in China (insurance), Owens-Illinois in Egypt (insurance), Union Carbide in Sudan (insurance), Squibb in Pakistan (local currency, insurance), and Agro-Tech International in the Dominican Republic (direct loan). In 1990 OPIC signed its first political risk insurance contract with a company doing business in Hungary. It insured General Electric Co.'s $150 million investment in a joint venture with Tungsram Co. of Budapest, an electric bulb manufacturer.

Hormel provides good illustrations of how OPIC operates.[37] By the early 1970s agricultural production in the Philippines was approaching a level that demanded the establishment of new processing, storage, and distribution facilities to create a "food chain" linking agricultural and urban areas. Hormel International and the Pure Foods Corporation of the Philippines began a joint operation for processing meat

While private investors generally have the capability to assess the commercial aspects of doing business overseas, they may be hesitant to undertake long-term investments abroad, given the political uncertainties of many developing nations. To alleviate these uncertainties, OPIC insures U.S. investments against three major types of political risks:

INCONVERTIBILITY

This coverage protects an investor against the inability to convert into U.S. dollars the local currency received as profits, earnings, or return of capital on an investment. OPIC's inconvertibility coverage also protects against adverse discriminatory exchange rates. Conversion of local currency into dollars is ensured only to the extent that such currency could have been exchanged for dollars at the time the insurance was issued. The coverage does *not* protect against the devaluation of a country's currency.

EXPROPRIATION

This coverage protects an investor against confiscation or nationalization of an investment without fair compensation. Expropriation coverage also protects U.S. investors against losses due to a variety of situations described as "creeping expropriation;" that is, a set of actions whose cumulative effect is to deprive investors of their fundamental rights in the investment. Expropriatory actions provoked or instigated by the investor are not covered.

WAR, REVOLUTION, INSURRECTION, AND CIVIL STRIFE

This coverage protects an investor against losses as a result of war (declared or not), revolution, or insurrection. In addition, coverage is available against losses resulting from "civil strife"—politically motivated violent acts including terrorism and sabotage. Civil strife coverage can only be obtained as a rider to OPIC's war, revolution, and insurrection coverage. Losses caused by an individual or group acting primarily to achieve nonpolitical ends, such as student- or labor-related objectives, are not covered.

Premiums for OPIC's insurance coverages are based on the nature of the investor's undertaking and the project's risk profile, not the country where the project is located. Although different rates may apply to specialized coverages, the following rates are typical for most projects.

Coverage[a]	Annual Base Rate per $100 of Coverage
Inconvertibility	30¢
Expropriation	60¢
War, Revolution, Insurrection,	60¢
Civil Strife Rider	15¢

[a]All OPIC insurance is backed by the full faith and credit of the United States of America.

Since its inception, OPIC has settled approximately 150 insurance claims totalling more than $400 million; it has denied only 8 percent of the claims received.

EXHIBIT 4–7 OPIC insurance coverage

Source: Overseas Private Investment Corporation (Washington, D.C.: OPIC), 2

and various food products. Hormel served as a technical supervisor for training and production, and later acquired an interest in the project as operations expanded. By 1985 production output served a market of more than 20 million people. Much of the major equipment used in the venture was purchased in the United States. OPIC insurance was issued for the original project and subsequent expansions.

Overall, OPIC has been relatively successful. The number of countries and companies utilizing its program has been increasing, and OPIC's insurance volume continues to grow. The success of the agency was confirmed by Mandel's study.[38] But OPIC's multiple objectives do not necessarily converge. A foreign aid program may or may not increase U.S. firms' overseas market share or stimulate the U.S. economy. Also, OPIC will inevitably encounter some conflicts between its political and economic goals. Some explicit prioritization of its objectives may thus be necessary.

FCIA

Another agency that U.S. firms can turn to is the Foreign Credit Insurance Association (FCIA), an association of some fifty leading U.S. companies in the marine and casualty insurance field. Created in 1961, FCIA makes it possible for U.S. firms to become internationally competitive by insurance U.S. exports of both goods and services against commercial and political risks. Such risks are numerous. As explained by FCIA, they "may result from economic deterioration in the buyer's market area, fluctuations in demand, unanticipated competition, shifts in tariffs, or technological changes. One of the principals or key management members of the buyer's company may die or become inactive—causing the company to close. A buyer's own government or one of his major customers may alter purchasing patterns. Or the buyer may be subject to an unexpectedly sharp increase in operating expenses. Natural disasters, such as floods and earthquakes, can also affect the ability of a buyer to operate in a market."[39]

The benefits of FCIA coverage are as follows:

It protects the exporter against the buyer's failure to pay.

It encourages the exporter to offer reasonable terms of payment or longer repayment terms to foreign buyers.

It supports the exporter's prudent attempt to broaden and penetrate higher-risk foreign markets.

It provides the exporter greater financial liquidity, leverage, and flexibility in managing his foreign receivables portfolio.

In short, the coverage helps the exporter make competitive offers by extending credit terms and obtaining financing of foreign receivables. Over 8,000 firms have taken advantage of FCIA insurance services. An exporter can apply for export credit insurance through either a national insurance broker or FCIA regional offices. Table 4–5 lists the various assistance programs for specific transactions. In fiscal year 1990 FCIA insured over 1,100 companies' shipments of almost $4 billion.[40]

FCIA operates in cooperation with Eximbank. Acting as a partner, Eximbank governs FCIA. Whereas private insurance companies underwrite and cover the normal commercial credit risks, Eximbank covers the political risks and reinsures certain

TABLE 4–5   Eximbanks and FCIA programs

SHORT-TERM (Up to 180 days)	
Product Examples	**Appropriate Program**
Consumables	FCIA policies
Small manufactured items.	
Spare parts	
Raw materials	
Farm products	

MEDIUM-TERM (181 days to 5 years)	
Product Examples	**Appropriate Programs**
Mining and refining equipment	FCIA policies
Construction machinery	Commercial bank
General aviation aircraft	Switch cover for foreign distributors
Agricultural machinery	
Communications equipment	Discount loans
Planning and feasibility studies	Bank-to-bank guaranteed lines

LONG-TERM (Over 5 years)	
Product Examples	**Appropriate Programs**
Cement plants	Direct loans
Chemical facilities	Financial guarantees to commercial banks
Power plants—hydro, thermal, nuclear	
LNG, and gas processing facilities	PEFCO loans
Commercial jet aircraft	
Locomotives	

Source: A Basic Guide to Exporting (Washington, D.C.: U.S. Department on Commerce, 1981), 60

excess commercial risks. Its liability for political risks include "exchange transfer delay, such hazards as war, revolution, or similar hostilities; unforeseen withdrawal or non-renewal of a license to export or import; requisition, expropriation, confiscation, or intervention in the buyer's business by a government authority; transport or insurance charges caused by interruption or diversion of shipments; and certain other government acts that may prevent or unduly delay payment beyond the control either of the seller or buyer.[41]

Among FCIA's products is the Master Policy, which provides an automatic and blanket protection for an attractive price under one policy for all sales. The Master Policy is written for shipments during a one-year period and insures all of an exporter's eligible sales (i.e., the exporter's various products shipped to a number of different markets). Both short-term and medium-term sales can be insured under this policy. Usually, 90 percent of a commercial loss and 100 percent of a political loss are covered. The Master Policy's advantages include lower premiums, faster service, and less paperwork.

FCIA also provides a number of special coverages. For example, its "preshipment coverage" offers protection from the sales contract date instead of the shipment date. Goods on consignment can also be insured. In addition, companies that are new in the export area or have limited volume can apply for the Small Business Policy, which is patterned after the Master Policy but provides added flexibility and benefits.

CONCLUSION

The international marketer's political environment is complex and difficult because of the interaction among domestic, foreign, and international politics. If a product is imported or produced overseas, political groups and labor organizations accuse the marketer of taking jobs away from people in the home country. On the other hand, foreign governments are not always receptive to overseas capital and investment because of suspicions about the marketer's motives and commitment. When both the host country and the home country have different political and national interests, their conflicting policies can complicate the problem further.

This chapter has covered the political dimension of international trade. Because of the diversity of political and economic systems, governments develop varying philosophies. In some circumstances, their political motives overshadow their economic logic. The result is often that political risks—such as expropriation, nationalization, and restrictions—are created against exports and/or imports and are likely inevitable.

Marketing decisions are thus affected by political considerations. When investing in a foreign country, companies must be sensitive to that country's political concerns. Because of the dynamic nature of politics in general, companies should prepare a contingency plan to cope with changes that occur in the political environment. To minimize political risk, companies should attempt to accommodate the host country's national interests by stimulating the economy, employing nationals, sharing business ownership with local firms, and being civic-oriented. On the other hand, to protect their own economic interests companies should maintain political neutrality, quietly lobby for their goals, and shift risks to a third party through the purchase of political insurance. Finally, a company should institute a monitoring system that allows it to systematically and routinely evaluate the political situation.

Some companies view politics as an obstacle to their effort to enter foreign markets and as a barrier to the efficient use of resources. For other companies, political problems, instead of being perceived as entry barriers, are seen as challenges and opportunities. According to firms with the more optimistic view, political situations are merely environmental conditions that can be overcome and managed. Political risks, through skillful adaptation and control, can thus be reduced or neutralized.

QUESTIONS

1. Explain the multiplicity of political environments.
2. Distinguish between parliamentary (open) and absolutist (closed) governments.
3. Distinguish among these types of governments: two-party, multiparty, single-party, and dominated one-party.
4. Distinguish among these economic systems: communism, socialism, and capitalism.
5. Is country stability a function of (a) economic development, (b) democracy, and (c) capitalism?
6. Explain confiscation, expropriation, nationalization, and domestication.
7. What is creeping expropriation? What is its economic impact on foreign investors?

8. What are the potential sources and indicators of political instability?
9. How can a company do country risk analysis for investment purposes?
10. Explain these methods of political risk management: avoidance, insurance, negotiating the environment, and structuring investment.
11. What are measures that can be undertaken to minimize political risk?
12. What is OPIC and how can it assist U.S. investors abroad?
13. What is FCIA and how can it assist U.S. investors abroad?

DISCUSSION ASSIGNMENTS AND MINICASES

1. According to Harvey E. Heinbach, a vice-president of Merrill Lynch, "You're better off making any car in Japan than in the U.S. But the political realities don't allow that." Discuss this comment from both economic and political perspectives and as related to the United States and Japan.
2. Why is a host country (including the United States) not always receptive to foreign firms' investment in local production facilities?

3. Once viewing each other with great distrust, the United States and China have dramatically improved their economic and political ties. What are the reasons for this development?
4. How likely is it for a country to adopt a system of either 100 percent capitalism or 100 percent communism?
5. Is capitalism the best system—economically as well as socially—for all countries?

CASE 4–1
NOT NECESSARILY THE WELCOME WAGON

In 1987 Tsuneo Sakai, an employee of Fuji Photo Film, was admitted to the Simon School of Business at the University of Rochester only to have that admission rescinded a few months later with no explanation given. Later it was revealed that the instigator of the change of heart was Eastman Kodak, whose headquarters are located in Rochester. Kodak had complained to the University that Sakai might learn of Kodak's trade secrets from its many employees who attend the university's business classes, as these secrets might be inadvertently divulged during classroom discussions. That Kodak is the university's major contributor apparently had something to do with the university's about-face. William E. Simon, a former Treasury secretary who has also been associated with Rochester's graduate business school, was highly critical of both the university and Kodak, calling the action "corporate bribery." Kodak's defense was that "what we did was to try to protect our business interests." Kodak insisted that its action was quite reasonable.

Questions

1. Do you agree with Kodak's decision to influence the university?
2. Do you agree with the university's decision to rescind the admission?
3. Kodak and the University of Rochester eventually arranged for Sakai to be admitted to M.I.T.'s Sloan School of Management, and the faculty of Rochester subsequently invited Sakai to attend the Simon School of Business, an offer that was declined. Should these developments affect your answers?

CASE 4–2
BIG BROTHER

In 1987 the Massachusetts Institute of Technology planned to buy or rent a super-computer and solicited bids for the $7.5 million contract. Among those submitting proposals were Cray Research, IBM, E.T.A. Systems, Amdahl (46 percent owned by Fujitsu), and Honeywell-NEC (50 percent owned by Nippon Electric Corp.).

Learning of M.I.T.'s preference for Japanese-made machines, the U.S. government intervened. The acting Secretary of Commerce formally informed M.I.T.'s president that "imported products may be subject to U.S. antidumping duty proceedings." Informally, despite a denial of the Commerce Department of the government's threat, it was made clear to M.I.T. that in light of Japan's barriers preventing U.S. supercomputer firms from entering the Japanese market, it would not be in the interest of the United States to purchase Japanese units.

M.I.T. reacted to the U.S. government's intervention by cancelling its procurement and announcing that it planned to apply for federal funds for a research center that would use several U.S.-made supercomputers.

Questions

1. Is it appropriate for the U.S. government to pressure M.I.T. to reject Japanese supercomputers in spite of lower prices? Note that the M.I.T. research projects that would use the supercomputers were federally funded.
2. Did M.I.T. react properly in cancelling its procurement plan?

CASE 4–3
MARKETING TO APARTHEID
Should U.S. Business Invest in South Africa?

JEFFREY A. FADIMAN
San Jose State University

Navazuni, Inc. (a hypothetical but representative Southern California firm) produces luxury clothing for both men and women, either cut from softened lamb and kidskin or knitted from the highest grades of wool or mohair (from goats). Their product line is distinctive because of the use of highly sophisticated variations of AmerIndian tribal designs, originally developed by Zuni and Navajo peoples of the American Southwest. The designs, whether machine produced or handmade, proved quite popular with trendy younger people in urban areas, to the point where by 1980 the firm began to consider expansion overseas.

In 1981 orders for Navazuni products were received unexpectedly from the Republic of South Africa, a country whose pioneer past—similar to that of the American West—has created consumer interest in American Indians among its European (white) community. Large numbers of whites visit California as tourists, where they show a fascination for AmerIndian designs, which are similar to those used by Bantu peoples in southern Africa. Initial requests, once filled, were followed by larger orders throughout the year. In 1982 volume continued to expand, causing Navazuni executives to consider exploration of the South African market.

In 1983 Navazuni's president was visited by a member of the South African Consulate, based in Los Angeles. Would the firm be willing, he asked, to examine the possibility of establishing a wholly owned subsidiary production facility in South Africa? The site would be located within a preestablished "white" industrial zone, on the edge of Kwazulu (Zululand), one of the so-called Bantustans or Independent Tribal Homelands established by the government for the Bantu peoples.

Kwazulu, the consul explained, is home to over 2.1 million members of the former Zulu confederation of tribes; the homeland also contains some 2.8 million sheep and goats, for which too few commercial outlets existed. Recent research has suggested, however, that the quality of the highest grades of skins, mohair, and wool would meet the standard required by Navazuni. The Amazulu people—noted for both intelligence and industry—could serve as labor.

The South African government was also prepared to provide European (white) expertise. The proposed Navazuni facility would be one of a continuously expanding number of similar enterprises—small and medium-sized "cottage-type" industries, intended to encircle the entire Kwazulu Homeland by 1999, thereby providing employment to its people. During each stage of Navazuni operation, therefore, from initial construction to on-line operations, the government would offer whatever assistance was required in organizing, training, and managing the work force. Specifically, it was prepared to assist in recruiting whatever type of worker that was required from within Kwazulu itself. Those workers selected would be transported by subsidized public transport to the worksite each morning. At day's end, the government would return the workers to their respective locations within the homeland.

Navazuni, for its part, would be required to pay employee wages at a rate it would find substantially lower than that of American workers in comparable employ. (A 1979 survey of U.S. firms that had invested in South Africa found that 95 percent of those responding paid Bantu workers between $192 and $238 per month.) In addition, the firm would be expected to provide an on-site medical dispensary for treatment of routine work-related injuries. There would be no need, however, to pay any of the employee benefits customary in America, unless white South Africans were hired.

The consul also spoke briefly of the South African domestic market. In 1980 South Africa's whites numbered just under 5 million, densely clustered within the three urban areas of Durban (adjacent to Kwazulu), Johannesburg, and Cape Town. By the year 2000, assuming that present rates of population growth continued, their number would almost double, especially if supplemented by immigration from the United Kingdom and Western Europe. Present immigration remained relatively stable at 300,000 per year, drawing from Belgium, Holland, Denmark, Norway, and France, as well as England and Ireland.

White workers in South Africa enjoy full employment. Their living standards, easily the highest in Africa, equal or surpass those of many areas in the United States, an affluence that has generated consistent interest both in luxury items (such as clothing) and current fashion trends in Europe and the United States. This affluence, considered in context with continued white interest in America's cowboy-and-Indian past (stimulated perhaps by American cinema), suggested considerable market potential for Navazuni's product line.

The consul also felt that the Bantu domestic market justified exploration. In 1960 people of wholly African descent within South Africa numbered some 11 million, with an estimated population growth rate of 2.53 percent. By 1980 the number approached 20 million, with a growth rate of 3 percent. By 2000 demographers predicted a Bantu population of 37 million; in 2020, 62 million.

Contrary to popular belief, these people were not impoverished and starving, as was the case in areas of tropical Africa. In the 1960s most Bantus worked the land and per capita annual income averaged $128. During the 1970s, however, the increasing technological level of many industries, especially manufacturing, produced a demand for both skilled and semiskilled workers that neither whites, Asians, nor "coloreds" (people of mixed racial heritage) could fill. In consequence, industries began to employ greater numbers of Bantus as clerks, drivers, low-level supervisors, and—as would be the case with Navazuni—operators of increasingly complex machines. Between 1969 and 1972, for instance, the number of Bantus holding skilled jobs increased by 175 percent, whereas the average industrial worker earned three to twenty times more than a comparable worker in Sierra Leone, Zambia, Zaire, or anywhere else in industrial Black Africa.

The consul mentioned that many other American firms had benefited from South Africa's favorable economic climate. In 1977, for instance, direct U.S. investments reached $1.8 billion; 17 percent of all foreign investment within the country. Out of the top 100 American corporations, no less than 55 had South African investments that year, including such corporation heavyweights as ITT, General Electric, General Motors, Caterpillar, Goodyear, and Ford.

One reason for this trend, the consul believed, was government insistence that no unreasonable restrictions be placed on U.S. commercial operations. Unlike firms that launched commercial ventures in other Third World regions, Navazuni would not be forced into any form of partnership, either with the government or private interests. Licensing and tariff requirements, where applicable, would be minimal. Nor would unreasonable restrictions be placed on remission of profits to the United States. Industrial security would be guaranteed by South Africa's 40,000-member police force, and national security lay with a 494,000-person army, supported by a billion-dollar defense industry able to provide armament equal in quality to any in the world.

In addition, he concluded, the government would be prepared to explore the possibility of providing certain additional incentives, whether in the form of limited subsidies or other practical considerations during initial stages of the operation, should specific circumstances warrant mutual consultation.

The reason for these policies, he explained, is to serve the long-term commercial and economic interests of both South Africa and the United States. "Our hope is that your firm—and others like you—will thrive and expand over the coming decades, and in so doing provide gainful subsistence employment to ever larger numbers of Bantu. By the year 2000 we plan to completely encircle each of the eleven black Homelands with a white ring of small and medium-sized European-owned industries, able to provide gainful work to everyone within the Bantustans. Our hope is to create an affluent Bantu working class, capable of providing the goods and services needed to sustain both black and white South Africa. We will live separately, but work together to maintain our leading role in Africa. We invite you to take part."

The Navazuni board of directors convened to study the proposal. Simultaneously, the South African Bureau of Public Affairs, a division of the Los Angeles consulate, released a feature story in the *Los Angeles Times* describing the proposed Navazuni project as an example of potential South Africa–U.S. cooperation in bringing employment to black Africans.

Two days later, the president of Navazuni received a delegation of distinguished African-American ministers, lawyers, and educators. The delegation courteously asked

TABLE 1　The Sullivan Principles

I.	Nonsegregation of the races in all eating, comfort, and work facilities
II.	Equal and fair employment practices for all employees
III.	Equal pay for all employees doing equal or comparable work for the same period of time
IV.	Initiation of and development of training programs that will prepare, in substantial numbers, blacks and other nonwhites for supervisory, administrative, clerical, and technical jobs
V.	Increase in the number of blacks and other nonwhites in management and supervisory jobs
VI.	Improvement in the quality of employee's lives outside the work environment in such areas as housing, transportation, schooling, recreation, and health facilities

Source: Stratford P. Sherman, "Scoring Corporate Conduct in South Africa," *Fortune,* 9 July 1984, 168

the company to abandon the entire project in the name of their common humanity, as it was based on the continued economic exploitation of a black majority that was denied every civil and political right.

The delegation also mentioned and asked Navazuni to adhere to the Sullivan Principles (see Table 1). Established by the Reverend Dr. Leon Sullivan from Philadelphia, the code emphasizes the need for equal treatment, socially and economically, for blacks and other nonwhites and advocates employment of blacks and nonwhites in management and supervisory positions. These principles have been embraced and adopted as operating policies by several MNCs as well as many U.S. companies doing business in South Africa. As a result, Navazuni gave these principles some serious consideration.

Questions

1. Should Navazuni abandon or continue to explore the South African proposal? Why?
2. Does an alternative exist that might partially satisfy both sides?
3. How should U.S. firms deal with investment in nations to which Americans are ideologically opposed?

NOTES

1. Victor A. Canto and Arthur B. Laffer, "The Incidence of Trade Restriction," *Columbia Journal of World Business* 17 (Spring 1982): 60–66.

2. See Roberto Friedmann and Jonghoon Kim, "Political Risk and International Marketing," *Columbia Journal of World Business* 23 (Winter 1988): 63–74.

3. Chikara Higashi, *Japanese Trade Policy Formulation* (New York: Praeger, 1983), 73–74; "U.S. Cigarette Makers Try to Open a Market," *Business Week,* 22 March 1982, 42.

4. R. Hal Mason, Robert R. Miller, and Dale R. Weigel, *International Business,* 2nd ed. (New York: Wiley, 1981), 392.

5. Badiul A. Majumdar, "Foreign Ownership of America: A Matter of Concern," *Columbia Journal of World Business* 25 (Fall 1990): 13–21.

6. John A. Reeder, "A Small Study of a Big Market in the People's Republic of China—The 'Free Market,'" *Columbia Journal of World Business* 18 (Winter 1983): 74–80.

7. Gary S. Becker, "As Role Models Go, Sweden Is Suspect," *Business Week,* 9 July 1990, 14.

8. Alfred D. Chandler, Jr., *Scale and Scope: The Dynamics of Industrial Capitalism* (Cambridge, MA: Belknap Press, 1990).

9. Roger Kronenberg, "Hong Kong Fosters Rapid Economic Development," *IMF Survey,* 15 April 1991, 114–16.

10. "Economic Report of the President: Economies in Transition around the World," *Business America,* 11 March 1991, 2–5.

11. "Selected Topics," *IMF Survey,* 10 June 1991, 178–80.

12. Franklin R. Root, *Foreign Market Entry Strategies* (New York: AMACOM, 1982), 146.

13. "Insuring Against Risk Abroad," *Business Week,* 14 September 1981, 59.

14. *Overseas Private Investment Corporation* (Washington, D.C.: OPIC), 2.

15. "Baxter Travenol Calls It Quits—and Others May Follow," *Business Week,* 11 February 1985, 42.

16. Wroe Alderson, *Dynamic Marketing Behavior* (Homewood, IL: Richard D. Irwin, 1965); Sak Onkvisit and John J. Shaw, "Myopic Management: The Hollow Strength of American Competitiveness," *Business Horizons* 34 (January–February 1991): 13–19.

17. Janusz Bugajski, "Eastern Europe in the Post-Communist Era," *Columbia Journal of World Business* 26 (Spring 1991): 5–9.

18. Jeffrey D. Simon, "Political Risk Assessment: Past Trends and Future Prospects," *Columbia Journal of World Business* 17 (Fall 1982): 62–71.

19. James Merrill, "Country Risk Analysis," *Columbia Journal of World Business* 17 (Spring 1982): 88–91.

20. Simon, "Risk Assessment."

21. Susan P. Douglas and C. Samuel Craig, *International Marketing Research* (Englewood Cliffs, NJ: Prentice Hall, 1983), 83.

22. Stephen Franklin, "Keeping an Eye on the World," *San Jose Mercury News,* 19 August 1990.

23. Jean-Claude Cossett and Jean Roy, "The Determinants of Country Risk Ratings," *Journal of International Business Studies* 22 (no. 1, 1991): 135–42.

24. Jeffrey Simon, "A Theoretical Perspective on Political Risk," *Journal of International Business Studies* 14 (Winter 1984): 123–43.

25. Alan C. Shapiro, "Managing Political Risks: A Policy Approach," *Columbia Journal of World Business* 16 (Fall 1981): 63–69.

26. Thomas A. Poynter, "Government Intervention in Less Developed Countries: The Experience of Multinational Companies," *Journal of International Business Studies* 13 (Spring/Summer 1982): 9–25.

27. Nathan Fagre and Louis T. Wells, Jr., "Bargaining Power of Multinationals and Host Governments," *Journal of International Business Studies* 13 (Fall 1982): 9–23.

28. Briance Mascarenhas, "Coping with Uncertainty in International Business," *Journal of International Business Studies* 13 (Fall 1982): 87–98.

29. "Charity Doesn't Begin at Home Anymore," *Business Week,* 25 February 1991, 91.

30. International Trade Administration, *Doing Business with China* (Washington: D.C.: Department of Commerce, 1983), 12.

31. William F. Averyt, "Managing Public Policy Abroad: Foreign Corporate Representation in Washington," *Columbia Journal of World Business* 25 (Fall 1990): 32–41.

32. "IBM Is More European Than…Well, Most Anybody," *Business Week,* 19 September 1988, 148.

33. "Insuring Against Risk Abroad."

34. See *The Overseas Private Investment Corporation 1985 Annual Report* (Washington, D.C.: OPIC, 1985); *Overseas Private Investment Corporation: A Guide to the Investment Services of the Overseas Private Investment Corporation* (Washington, D.C.: OPIC, 1978); *Investor Information Service* (Washington, D.C.: OPIC); *Opportunity Bank* (Washington, D.C.: OPIC).

35. "Development OK, But Not at U.S. Expense," *Topics* (Fall 1985): 3.

36. *Guide to the Investment Services,* 6.

37. *1985 Annual Report,* 10, 20.

38. Robert Mandel, "The Overseas Private Investment Corporation and International Investment," *Columbia Journal of World Business* 19 (Spring 1984): 89–95.

39. FCIA, *FCIA Export Credit Insurance: Your Competitive Edge* (Washington, D.C.: FCIA, 1983).

40. See Rob Garverick, "FCIA Insurance Can Reduce the Risk of Exporting," *Business America,* 3 June 1991, 12–15.

41. International Trade Administration, *A Basic Guide to Exporting* (Washington, D.C.: U.S. Department of Commerce, 1981), 59.

The merchant will manage commerce the better, the more they are left to manage for themselves.

Thomas Jefferson, 1800

Legal Environment   5

CHAPTER OUTLINE

MARKETING ILLUSTRATION
The Long Arm of the Law

German laws forbid showering after 10 P.M. and mowing the lawn between noon Saturday and Monday. The intent of the laws is to protect against noise that could disturb others. The prohibition against a telephone extension in one's home is part of modern Germany's extensive privacy protection. City officials even have the power not to approve a child's name. One couple was not allowed to name their child Schroder after the beloved comic character because the name was not sex-specific.

A consumer affairs court in Helsinki charged McDonald's with using a TV commercial to exploit the loneliness of a child in order to promote its business. The commercial shows a depressed boy walking around in an empty apartment. His depression was gone when he looked out the window and saw a McDonald's at the opposite corner. The Finnish court ruled that the advertisement implied that McDonald's could eliminate loneliness or serve as a substitute for friends. The court banned the commercial and threatened to fine McDonald's $50,000 if such exploitation reoccurred.

Canada's 7 percent tax on goods and services (GST) took effect in 1991. Uncooked fish bought in markets is considered a grocery and is therefore exempt from the GST, but sushi in restaurants is "an arranged food" subject to the GST. Unlike a tax-free plain croissant, a chocolate croissant carries the tax because it is not as healthy. Although five chocolate rolls are taxable, a half dozen are tax-free because anyone buying six or more is likely to be taking them home.

Sources: Marc Fisher, "Germans Go by the Book When Picking Names," *San Jose Mercury News,* 28 March 1991; "Censorship in Finland," *Parade,* 1 July 1990, 11; "More May Be Less under Canada Tax," *San Jose Mercury News,* 11 January 1991.

The cases in the marketing illustration provide examples of the complexity of the legal environment. As can be expected, regulations can sometimes be ambiguous. Because regulations do not allow marketers to plead ignorance, they must themselves somehow try to take control of the situation. They must attempt to conform to the legal requirements for each of the product categories they are selling.

The purpose of this chapter is to discuss the impact of the legal environment on business decisions and to explain how the legal and political dimensions are interdependent. The chapter examines how countries' varying laws and interpretations affect imports, exports, and the marketing mix. The emphasis is on U.S. laws that inhibit U.S. exports. In addition to a look at the major legal systems, issues discussed include gray market goods, patents and infringement, counterfeiting, and bribery. A section is also devoted to the discussion of the various legal forms of business organizations.

LEGAL SYSTEMS

To understand and appreciate the varying legal philosophies among countries, it is useful to distinguish between the two major legal systems: common law and statute law.

There are some twenty-five common law or British law countries. A **common law system** is a legal system that relies heavily on precedents and conventions. Judges' decisions are guided not so much by statutes as by previous court decisions and interpretations of what certain laws are or should be. As a result, these countries laws are tradition-oriented. Countries with such a system include the United States, Great Britain, Canada, India, and other British colonies.

Countries employing a **statute law system,** also known as **code** or **civil law,** include most continental European countries and Japan. Most countries—over 70— are guided by a statute law legal system. As the name implies, the main rules of the law are embodied in legislative codes. Every circumstance is clearly spelled out to indicate what is legal and what is not. There is also a strict and literal interpretation of the law under this system.

In practice, the two systems greatly overlap, and the distinction between them is not clear-cut. Although U.S. judges greatly rely on other judges' previous rulings and interpretations, they still refer to many laws that are contained in the statutes or codes. For statute law countries, many laws are developed by courts and are never reduced to statutes. Therefore, the only major distinction between the systems is the freedom of the judge in interpreting laws. In a common law country, the judge's ability to interpret laws in a personal way gives the judge a great deal of power to apply the law as it fits the situation. In contrast, a judge in a civil law country has a lesser role in using personal judgment to create or interpret laws because the judge must strictly follow the "letter of the law."

MULTIPLICITY OF LEGAL ENVIRONMENTS

Much like the political environment discussed in an earlier chapter, there are a multiplicity of legal environments: domestic, foreign, and international. At their worst, laws can prohibit the marketing of a product altogether. To most businessmen, laws act as an inconvenience. Club Med's policy of rotating its international staff every six months, for example, is hampered by the U.S. immigration law, which makes the process of rotation both time-consuming and costly.

Domestic Legal Environment

In the domestic environment, a businessperson must abide by the laws of the home country. Such laws can affect both imports and exports. In the case of the United States, items that are "restricted" but not "prohibited" include automobiles, cultural treasures, more than $5,000 of cash, firearms, wildlife, and fish. Counterfeit products and illegal drugs cannot be imported. But other consumer products, although they may appear innocent enough, are also prohibited entry into the country. In addition to certain wildlife products, other prohibited items include most agricultural products; endangered species; monkeys and other primates; hazardous articles and substances (narcotics and dangerous drugs, toxic substances, and liquor-filled candy); books, records, and cassettes violating copyright laws; obscene articles and publications; seditious and treasonable materials; lottery tickets; and products made by forced labor.[1] Because U.S. law prohibits import of prison products, Customs Service agents searched the office of E. W. Bliss Co. and found evidence that the firm had imported machine presses manufactured in Chinese prison factories. The agents also seized thirty-one machines valued at $560,000.[2]

Foreign lottery tickets cannot be imported because they violate Title 18, U.S. Code, Section 1302, as well as Title 39, U.S. Code, Section 3001. The U.S. Postal Code defines this material as nonmailable matter.[3] As a result, it is illegal for Winshare Club of Canada and other agents to sell Canadian lottery tickets by mail and telephone at a markup in the United States, and Ontario Lottery Corp. even moved to disconnect these agents' terminals. Winshare argued that no American laws were broken because it only sent confirmation of ticket sales and other information through the mail.

Foreign Legal Environment

Once a product crosses a national border, it becomes subject to both an entirely different set of laws and a new enforcement system. In China, all joint ventures with foreigners must be audited by a Chinese CPA. This simple requirement is difficult to satisfy because there are only about 1,000 registered accountants in the country.[4] France bans all imports of live crawfish because of the risk of disease.[5] To comply with the requirements of this law, a marketer has two options. One option is to use the Economic Community's rules to his advantage. Turkey, for example, is able to avoid the French ban by trucking in crawfish live from Belgium, which is a member of the EC. The other option involves switching from live to frozen crawfish with some sacrifice in taste. Ecrevisse Acadienne, a U.S. firm, was able to overcome both the legal and marketing hurdles by developing its own exclusive cryogenic freezing technique, which uses nitrogen to retain taste.

International Legal Environment

In many cases, agreements between nations must be secured before marketers can enter a particular market. The airline business provides a good illustration of such agreements. International air routes are governed by treaties, and airlines cannot secure landing rights without treaties among nations. This reality explains why Texas Air attempted a buyout of TWA in an unsuccessful attempt to gain TWA's foreign air routes. United Airlines, likewise, had to postpone its inaugural flight to Japan after the purchase of Pan Am's routes. Japan, considering United as a new airline that was not included in its air treaties, maintained that Pan Am's landing rights could not be bought or transferred. Japan did, however, allow United to go ahead with a restricted schedule pending further negotiations with the U.S. government. The company was eventually cleared after it requested the U.S. government to intervene. This event underscores the importance of being able to have the home country's government apply some pressure on the host country.

The complexity of the international legal environment, combined with the international business network, can sometimes provide unexpected opportunities and solutions to various problems. Cuban nickel provides a good example. Despite the U.S. embargo against imports from Cuba, Cuban nickel has found its way into the U.S. market by disguising its origin. One route involved the Soviets' shipping Cuban nickel through Canada. Because Canadian nickel (imported under the Most Favored Nation clause) can enter the United States duty-free, the Soviets profited by not having to pay a tariff of 3 cents per pound. The other route used by the Soviet Union was through West Germany, where there were two import categories—one for internal use and another for reexport. The reexport category was used primarily for processing export business. Thus, the Soviets were accommodated in their preparation of the nickel for the U.S. market.[6]

There is no international law per se that prescribes acceptable and legal behavior of international business enterprises. There are only national laws—often in conflict with one another, especially when national politics is involved. This complexity creates a special problem for those companies that do business in various countries, where various laws may demand contradictory actions.

Although an international business law does not exist, several international organizations have increasingly been moving in that direction. The United Nations has become active in its attempt to regulate local and international business. Its Guidelines for Consumer Protection is a good example, although the effectiveness of those guidelines is questionable. Many countries, including the United States, oppose the UN's effort, holding that the UN has no role in intervening in business matters within the domestic jurisdiction of any country.

Among the most active organizations is GATT, whose role in the promotion of free trade was discussed in Chapter 3. The EC, representing its members' desire for economic integration, strives for the same goal. An EC ruling can strike down domestic laws that pose a barrier to the free movement of goods among member countries. Such is the case with the West German beer market, which was protected for almost 500 years from imported beers by the "purity of beer" law. This German law requires beer to contain only malted cereals, hops, water, and natural yeast, and no chemical additives (preservatives and stabilizers). The purity law applies to beers imported into Germany but not German beers exported to other countries.[7]

THE LAW AND MARKETING MIX

Government regulations are designed to serve societal interests by preserving business competition on the one hand and protecting consumers on the other. Such regulations not only increase a company's cost of doing business, but also affect its marketing strategies. Any one of the 4 Ps of marketing can be affected.

Product

There are many products that cannot be legally imported into most countries. Examples include counterfeit money, illicit drugs, pornographic materials, and espionage equipment. It is usually also illegal to import live animals and fresh fruit unless accompanied by the required certificates. Furthermore, many products have to be modified to conform to local laws before these products are allowed to cross the border. The modifications may be quite technical from an engineering standpoint or may only be cosmetic, as in the case of certain packaging changes.

A company's production strategy can also be affected by the legal environment. The United States bans the importation of the so-called Saturday night specials—

cheap, short-barreled pistols—because they are often used in violent crime. Curiously, the gun control legislation does not prohibit the sale of such inexpensive weapons; only the import of such weapons is banned. As a result, Beretta, an Italian gunmaker, is able to overcome the import ban by setting up a manufacturing operation in the state of Maryland.

Place

In the United States, a manufacturer has a number of distribution channels from which to choose as long as competition is not stifled in the process. In most other countries, the manufacturer does not have such freedom. In Europe, independent dealers handle personal computers, but EC regulations restrict IBM's control of the distribution for its midsize machines. As a result, IBM was forced to recruit commissioned independent sales agents, a less desirable channel. Direct marketers in Spain were frustrated by the prohibition to send a package to a house. Spanish consumers have to go to a central post office to pick up packages, thus defeating the main reason (i.e., convenience) of mail order.

In terms of retailing, not all types of sellers are available for distributing the product. For those who do distribute, effectiveness and efficiency may be severely limited. In Japan, small stores protected by law dominate the retailing industry. The Large-Scale Retail Store Law allows neighboring small stores to veto any proposed new stores of more than 27,000 square feet and proposed expansions of existing stores. This restriction on the growth of department and superstore chains forces manufacturers and importers to sell through small retailers, a more expensive channel. Many view the law as a major trade barrier as small retailers are much less likely than large retailers to stock and sell imported goods.

In France, feminine hygiene products can be distributed through either supermarkets or pharmacies but not both. As a result, Johnson & Johnson sells Tambrands products in supermarkets and the o.b. brand in pharmacies, which attract a smaller, older market.[8]

Retailing in a number of countries is also affected by ancient so-called blue laws, which bar many shops from being open on Sundays: "In England and Wales, it is legal to buy a pornographic book on Sunday but not a Bible; whiskey and gin, but not dried milk in cans; postcards, but not birthday cards; fodder for horses, mules and ponies, but not dog or cat food; fresh vegetables, but not canned ones; aspirin, but not cough mixture; a kippered herring, but not meat."[9] The issue of Sunday opening, with its religious and employment implications, is likely to produce emotional debate for some time to come.

Promotion

There is virtually no limit on how much an advertiser can spend for promotion in the United States, but free spending is usually regarded as improper elsewhere. Taking the view that advertising is not necessary for doing business, many countries have direct taxes on advertising billings, agencies, or media. Some governments use advertising taxes to discourage advertising so that demand and inflation can be curbed. Other governments use advertising restrictions as a nontariff barrier to foreign exports. For example, Japan does not allow foreign cigarettes to be advertised in the Japanese language.

Obstacles to overseas advertising can also take a less explicit form. Some countries do not allow advertising materials produced elsewhere to be shown in the native country. Australia requires all TV commercials to be filmed by local film producers.[10] South Africa and Mexico require that products sold in those countries be the ones used in advertisements. Such a requirement may have no impact on imported products but may create many problems for products produced and sold locally—commercials filmed outside the country (e.g., in the United States) cannot be used because the products used in the advertisements are also made outside of these countries.

If there is one law that virtually all countries have in common, it is the law banning the use of misleading or deceptive advertising. Germany requires information on goods, especially in advertising, to be true, correct, and unambiguous. Simpson-Sears, Canada's largest retailer, was fined $800,000 for its misleading advertisements in catalogs and newspapers. It ran advertisements that offered diamond rings at one-third or one-half off the "appraised value" with a certificate. Buyers were misled into believing that they were acquiring diamond rings at less than the normal retail price.[11] The court, however, ruled that the certificate was meaningless because it was impossible for the company to appraise each and every ring. The court also did not accept the company's defense that the price reduction from the appraised value was a "common trade practice at the time."

Another problem that a company must be prepared to deal with is the varying interpretations that occur with advertisements. What is acceptable in one country may be "misleading" in another. As noted by the Committee of Ministers of Council of Europe, the definition of *misleading* is so general as to be interpreted differently by each country. The chance of a uniform interpretation of a "misleading" advertisement is thus virtually none.

Price

The free-market system does not operate freely in many countries. As demonstrated by the drug industry in the EC, national health laws and government price controls can create a price differential of as much as 600 percent between one EC country and another. Price controls are common in many countries, and they are used in the United States from time to time. The general policy for using price controls is to protect consumers' interests or to control inflation. Generally, the company has no choice but to obey the wage and price controls imposed by the government.

Despite the need for price control from time to time, many countries also recognize the important role of price competition. As such, certain practices that can interfere with market prices are prohibited. In the case of Germany, the Federal Cartel Office may intervene in

1. "Resale price agreement" that recommends upper or lower price limits
2. "Concerted conduct" or "international parallelism" between firms
3. Discrimination and boycotts against competitors
4. Certain extensive restraints in connection with license agreements
5. Certain mergers and acquisitions[12]

One pricing practice that is unlawful in most countries is price discrimination. In the United States, the Robinson-Patman Act outlaws this practice. The European Commission has also been moving in this direction. It has introduced price-equality and cost-justification principles into the EC law. Discounts given must be commensurate with the tasks dealers perform and must be directly linked to genuine reductions in a manufacturer's costs.

LEGAL DYNAMICS

If laws were to stay unchanged, lawmakers would soon be out of business. There will always be new laws, changes in old laws, and new interpretations of existing laws. These changes can become serious roadblocks for some companies. American Express has been unhappy with the regulations of several European Postal Telephone and Telegraph administrations that outlaw the routing of data from private networks to public networks unless the data is administratively processed at the interconnection points. The regulations handicap the overseas transmission of credit card authorizations from the company's Phoenix office.

New laws often present both obstacles and challenges. As marketers, companies should be on the lookout for any new opportunities that new laws present. With rapid and frequent changes in social and economic norms and in regulatory assumptions about such norms, a market once closed may suddenly open. Until the early 1980s, West Germany and Continental Europe were reluctant to permit bank cards that extended rollover credit because they did not want to lose control over credit creation and the money supply, both of which affect inflation. As a result, only cards guaranteeing checks or travel-and-entertainment cards (e.g., American Express and Diner's Club) were permitted. Because of new laws, banks in the Netherlands and other Benelux countries, once prevented from issuing true credit cards by their central banks, are now able to issue Visa cards or other cards that extend credit.

LOOPHOLES AND LEGAL MANEUVERS

Although a company must comply with existing laws, it is not entirely at the mercy of one country's laws. U.S. marketers of certain kinds of sugar substitute, chemicals, and pesticides (e.g., DDT) can sell these products elsewhere in spite of the ban in the United States. Taiwan's "three no's" policy of no contact, no negotiations, and no compromise with China has not prevented Taiwan businesses from creating a $2 billion-a-year trade with China. They accomplish such trade by transshipping goods through Hong Kong and other third-country ports.

As a multinational enterprise, the multinational company has countervailing powers. It may simply choose to leave a country whose laws create too many problems to justify the costs of doing business there. If leaving is neither practical nor desirable, it can work toward affecting changes in those laws, perhaps with the threat of leaving as a negotiating ploy.

One example of how foreign exporters and local importers work together toward changing laws involves modern retailers in Japan. Japan's large retailers, hampered by a law protecting small retail stores, are unable to expand their floor space and business activities. The United States views the law as a barrier to imports. When the MITI asked Japanese companies to increase imports in response to U.S. pressure, big retailers seized the opportunity to ask for removal of restrictions that had prevented them from modernizing the distribution system. The big retailers wanted to add special import-only departments of up to 4,500 square feet without having to secure tedious approvals and inspections, which could take up to five years. They further wanted to hold import fairs outside their stores for up to two weeks instead of observing the required limit of three days.

In some cases, laws may have intended or unintended technical loopholes. MNCs, with their international network, are in a good position to exploit any legal loopholes to their advantage. The communication business provides a good illustration. In spite of deregulation in the United States, foreign communication is still largely operated by public agencies that are anything but eager to link up with U.S.-based common carriers.[13] The Postal Telephone and Telegraph of Japan has refused to accept messages from Western Union, a potential competitor. Unable to complete the delivery of messages, Western Union struck back by routing Japan-bound traffic through a third country, which acted as a middleman. Because Japan has a low-rate agreement with that country, Japan ended the year with $1 million less in revenues than it would have received directly from Western Union.

U.S. LAWS IMPEDING EXPORTS

Because the United States is a very legalistic society, it is not surprising that U.S. tort costs (legal and administrative expenses as well as jury awards and settlements) have always far exceeded those of other countries as a percent of total national output. Compared with an average 0.5 percent of gross domestic product for twelve other industrial nations, U.S. tort costs have soared to 2.6 percent of national output.[14] As commented by Vice-president Dan Quayle, the existence of far too many lawyers in the United States undermines U.S. competitiveness. The United States accounts for 70 percent of the world's lawyers. Compared with one Japanese lawyer for every 9,000 Japanese, there is one American lawyer for every 335 Americans. Rand Corp.'s studies showed that expensive product liability suits often force manufacturers to pull products off the market.[15] Naturally, American lawyers do not agree with this assessment.

As mentioned in Chapter 1, a contributing factor to the trade deficit of the United States is the lack of export awareness on the part of American firms. The same problem in a similar fashion applies to U.S. lawmakers. There are many laws that have made exports exceedingly difficult.[16] Although these laws may have been enacted with good intentions, their appropriateness depends on the criteria used to judge them. They may make sense from the standpoint of foreign policy. If trade is the criterion, however, these laws are clearly disadvantageous to U.S. firms. Exhibit 5–1 describes the new Trade Act.

On Aug. 23, when President Reagan signed the Omnibus Trade and Competitiveness Act of 1988, the White House issued the following "fact sheet" outlining principal features of the legislation.

Trade Negotiating Authority—Enables trade agreements negotiated by the President to be considered by the Congress on an expedited, non-amendable basis. Other provisions will facilitate successful conclusion of the Uruguay Round of multilateral trade negotiations.

Windfall Profits Tax—Repeals the Windfall Profits Tax, a counterproductive tax that imposed substantial and unnecessary administrative costs on our energy industry while raising little revenue.

Worker Readjustment Program (WRAP)—Creates a considerably expanded and newly-designed program and authorizes $980 million for retraining of workers who must shift jobs as the economy adjusts to competitive challenges. An estimated 700,000 dislocated workers will be served by the new program when fully implemented. WRAP greatly expands services to dislocated workers, emphasizes early intervention, and incorporates a number of innovative approaches for serving these workers. These include rapid response teams to assist communities impacted by major layoffs, labor-management committees to coordinate assistance to workers, and emphasizes high quality training to assist workers in the transition to emerging opportunities in the labor market.

Unfair Trade—Authorizes the U.S. Trade Representative to determine whether a foreign government's trade practice is unfair. Subject to specific direction of the President, allows the U.S. Trade Representative to decide what retaliatory action to take. Requires action in response to violations by foreign governments of trade agreements but provides exceptions, such as if the foreign government ends the practice. Provides new definitions of unfair trade practices and sets new deadlines for action. Under the so-called "Super 301," requires the U.S. Trade Representative in 1989 and 1990 to identify "priority countries" and to investigate those countries.

Intellectual Property—Requires the U.S. Trade Representative to identify priority countries that deny protection for U.S. patents and copyrights. Provides for expedited decisions.

Telecommunications—Provides for trade liberalizing negotiations. If the negotiations do not produce a satisfactory agreement, the President is required to take whatever action is appropriate and most likely to achieve the negotiating objectives.

Harmonized System—Implements the Harmonized System of tariff nomenclature, which creates a common tariff code system for all member nations.

Export Controls—Liberalizes the ability of U.S. exporters to obtain export licenses for products on the export control list.

Controlled Technology—Imposes sanctions against foreign firms that sell controlled technology in a manner that violates internationally agreed upon export controls and damages U.S. national security.

Anti-Dumping and Countervailing Duty—Enhances the authority of the Commerce Department to prevent circumvention through the practice of minor alteration

(*continued*)

EXHIBIT 5–1   Principal features of the Omnibus Trade and Competitive Act of 1988

Source: Business America, 26 September 1988, 6

of the merchandise covered by anti-dumping and countervailing duty orders or by additional minor assembly in the U.S. and third countries.

Foreign Corrupt Practices Act—Amends the Foreign Corrupt Practices Act so that only those businesses and persons who know of bribes and other illegal payments to foreign officials can be subject to civil and criminal liability.

Foreign Investment—Authorizes the President to halt the sale, merger or takeover of U.S. firms by foreign entities if such proposed transactions threaten the national security.

Government Procurement—Bans U.S. Government procurement of any or all goods/services from countries that have a significant and persistent pattern or practice of discriminating against U.S. products and services and whose products/services are acquired in significant amounts by the U.S. Government.

Agricultural Trade—Creates a marketing loan program for the 1990 crop of wheat, feed grains and soybeans, subject to Presidential waiver. Extends Export Assistance Program through FY 1990 and raises program ceiling to $2.5 billion. Increases funding for Targeted Export Enhancement Program to $215 million.

Trade Agreements—Implements recent trade agreements including the citrus and pasta agreement with the European Community and extends authority for U.S. participation in the international coffee agreement.

Nairobi Protocol—Implements Nairobi Protocol, which provides for duty-free imports of educational, scientific and cultural materials and articles for the handicapped.

EXHIBIT 5–1 Principle features of the Omnibus Trade and Competitive Act of 1988 (*continued*)

Export Controls

The United States has an embargo on exports to South Africa and Namibia of military equipment. U.S. law also restricts exports of products with potential military use to the communist nations, and it does not trade at all with such countries as North Korea, Kampuchea, Vietnam, and Cuba.

Because of the removal of the democratically elected constitutional government of Haiti, the United States imposed a total ban on all Haitian imports in 1991. Designating Libya as a nation that repeatedly supported acts of international terrorism, the United States imposed a trade embargo. After revocation of export licenses to Libya in 1986, Carpenter & Patterson, a Massachusetts firm, evaded the export embargo on Libya by falsifying commercial invoices and shipper's export declarations to ship an order to Libya via Belgium. The firm was fined $150,000.

The embargo is most understandable when high-technology equipment is involved. The Pentagon's rationale is that export controls save the country billions of dollars in defense costs. Although justifiable on political grounds, the embargo was questioned by businesses when the United States refused to sell grain to the Soviet Union and other communist countries.

It is also debatable whether some high-tech products are indeed high-tech in nature. For example, the Department of Defense wanted to block the sale of unsophisticated computers to Iran for printing even though such computers could even be sold directly to the Soviet Union. In another example, Emhart Corp. lost a $20 million order to repair railroad car wheels when restrictions were imposed on the sales of advanced technology to the Soviets. Emhart was unable to ship the necessary machinery because the machine used computer technology. The Soviet Union was forced to purchase the repair service from a German firm, which may have set a pattern for the future.

Sanctions often damage the reputation of the United States as a dependable supplier, in both the short run and the long run, directly and indirectly. According to the results of a study by the National Academy of Sciences, such export controls have not significantly improved national security and yet have cost more than $9 billion a year and a loss of 188,000 jobs.

One export problem is that foreign manufacturers have grown reluctant to use U.S. components subject to export restrictions, because those firms are required to seek U.S. approval before their products that use such components can be sold. As a result, many firms have chosen instead to design their products without U.S. parts and components. To overcome the problem, the U.S. Department of Commerce announced eleven initiatives in 1987. Among them were a reduction in processing time for export license, a reduction in the number of parts subject to control, and a permission for virtually all products sold to government agencies of Japan and NATO countries to move freely.

Nuclear Proliferation Treaty

Section 378.1 of the U.S. Export Administration Regulations applies to nuclear weapons and explosive devices. A concern over the use of nuclear weapons prompts the United States to limit exports of nuclear reactors and material to any countries that may produce a nuclear bomb. Israel, despite refusing to sign the Nuclear Proliferation Treaty, is able to substantially secure much of what it needs anyway. India, on the other hand, is unable to get the needed materials and technology from the United States in spite of its willingness to sign the treaty. Critics of the law believe that if a country wants nuclear materials it will find a source, and it is naive to believe that leaders would not consider using nuclear weapons just because a treaty has been signed. It is difficult to believe that a country would prefer to lose a war with dignity rather than "winning ugly." What is most bothersome to many Third World critics is the idea that only the superpowers or developed nations know how to use nuclear weapons "responsibly."

Human Rights Policy

The human rights policy of the United States at times interferes with American firms' business activities. For protection of human rights, there are regulations for export of crime-control and detection instruments and data to all countries except NATO members, Japan, Australia, and New Zealand. The strictest adherence to this policy occurred during the Carter years, which led to severe restrictions on trade with countries that violated the human rights code. Loans were withheld from South Africa, Uruguay, El Salvador, and Chile.

Critics charge that the United States has been arbitrary in the application of its sanctions. While criticizing rights abuses in Cuba, Czechoslovakia, Nicaragua, and the former Soviet Union, the United States has at times ignored or tolerated similar abuses in Haiti, Honduras, Kenya, South Africa, and Turkey. According to two private groups (Human Rights Watch and the Lawyers Committee for Human Rights), the Reagan administration "[applied] human rights standards inconsistently between perceived allies and foes."

Other questions related to the restrictions involve whether the end justifies the means and whether the restrictions are effective. Repeated pressures on El Salvador, for example, yielded few concrete results. Even when the sanctions are effective, they may not result in the accomplishment of the desired goal. There was overwhelming evidence of human rights violations in Iran and Nicaragua during the administrations of the Shah and President Somoza, respectively. Yet it has been widely debatable whether the new regimes, after overthrowing those dictators, have provided desirable alternatives. Nevertheless, the U.S. human rights policy has served a useful purpose in some instances.

Antiboycott Regulations

The U.S. Export Administration Act of 1977 has antiboycott provisions that establish a U.S. policy of opposing restrictive trade practices imposed by foreign countries against other countries friendly to the United States. The purpose of the law is not to challenge any country's sovereign right to boycott products from another nation, but rather to prevent U.S. citizens from being used as tools of another nation's foreign policy. American firms are urged to refuse any request to support such boycotts and are required to report such a request to the Office of Antiboycott Compliance (OAC), which administers the law.

The antiboycott provisions specifically prohibit U.S. persons from

Refusing to do business with blacklisted firms and boycotted countries friendly to the United States pursuant to foreign boycott demands.

Discriminating against other U.S. persons on the basis of race, religion, sex, or national origin to comply with a foreign boycott.

Furnishing information about another person's race, religion, sex, or national origin where such information is sought for boycott enforcement purposes.

Furnishing information about their business relationships with boycotted countries or blacklisted companies.[17]

In response to the Arab nations' boycott of Israeli-made goods, the United States has adopted anti-Arab boycott rules, which require U.S. exporters to forego Arab contracts that prohibit the inclusion of goods from Israel. Safeway Stores Inc. provides technical and management assistance to Arab-owned stores in Saudi Arabia and Kuwait, which refused to do business with companies on the anti-Israeli black-list. As a result, Safeway managers told customers and suppliers not to do business with Israel or with blacklisted companies. Safeway also furnished information about its dealings with Israel to the Israel Boycott Office of Kuwait. To settle the charges that

Safeway had illegally complied with the Arab boycott, Safeway paid the Department of Commerce $995,000. The previous largest antiboycott penalty was a $323,000 fine paid by Citicorp.

Foreign Corrupt Practices Act (FCPA)

This act greatly limits corporate payments of fees to obtain a foreign contract, and a violation of the act is punishable by fines and jail terms. But the law is ambiguous, and it increases delays as well as the cost of doing business. For example, a person associated with a company must certify that there is no bribe or immoral act practically every time business is transacted. The company's agent must get an expense account validated by the American Consular authority before receiving a payment for expenses as routine as a taxicab ride. According to one survey, the major concerns of the U.S. business community are these:

> The act has not achieved its intended purpose.
>
> Questionable practices have not declined.
>
> The act has put American MNCs at a competitive disadvantage.
>
> The act has contributed slightly to the unfavorable U.S. balance of payments.[18]

Still, the general feeling is that the act should be sustained even though it has not upgraded international confidence. Additional implications of the Foreign Corrupt Practices Act are examined in the section dealing with bribery.

Health, Safety, and Environmental Regulations

These regulations are based on the assumption that what is good for the United States is good for other nations. The health, safety, and environment rules thus enforce strict U.S. standards over American firms' overseas operations. The problem that some businesses see is that U.S. standards may make certain products either unavailable or too expensive for foreign consumers. Critics of the regulations contend that the United States should not make health, safety, and environmental decisions for citizens of other countries.

Export-Import Bank Restrictions

The problems related to U.S. Export-Import Bank regulations are quite numerous. First, the funding by Congress has been meager at best. Second, the rules govern and place tight restrictions on the amount of subsidized credit for financing exports. The Trade Act of 1974 bans the use of the Export-Import Bank's credit to most communist countries.

Antitrust Laws

U.S. antitrust regulations result in a reluctance on the part of American firms to form joint trading companies or to bid jointly on major overseas projects. In the 1980s, with a trend toward megamergers, the antitrust restrictions appeared to be relaxing. A 1982 law allowed exporters to form export trading companies so that they could pool resources under antitrust exemptions. Despite new rules, exporters must deal with varying definitions and interpretations of the law among the Treasury, Commerce, and Justice departments.

Tax Regulations

It is neither always possible nor always desirable for U.S. firms to run businesses abroad from their domestic headquarters. But the costs of having American managers in foreign markets can be very expensive because of fluctuating currencies, inflation, and the higher living costs overseas. In Japan, an apartment—if available at all—can easily cost a few thousand dollars a month, and private schooling can run roughly the same amount per child per year. Expatriates are usually compensated for extra housing and schooling expenses. Until 1976, the 1954 tax code also allowed them to exempt $20,000–25,000 of their income from income tax. In 1976 Congress cut the exclusion amount to $15,000.

The problem became more difficult with the passage of the Tax Reform Bill of 1978, which eliminated the exclusion and replaced it with a complex formula allowing deductions for basic living expenses. The tax burden was thus increased for Americans working abroad, forcing companies to reimburse their expatriates for the extra taxes.

A U.S. firm's employee in Saudi Arabia with a salary of $40,000 would need more than three times that amount to maintain the same level of benefits as in the United States. These increased costs have forced many companies to employ more local people. Local managers, in many cases, can function as well as American repatriates, except that they may be accustomed to buying materials locally or from Europe instead of from the United States. For labor-intensive construction and drilling companies, it is not easy to replace skilled engineers with foreign nationals. As a result, the increased tax burden has reduced U.S. exports and tax revenues for the United States.

The 1978 law was replaced by a set of much more reasonable laws in 1981. With a $70,000 exclusion, the cost of sending U.S. personnel has been reduced. The new law also has no tax effect when other countries have higher income tax rates. Because Western Europe, Latin America, and Japan all have taxes that are higher than the maximum U.S. tax, there is no U.S. income tax in such cases. More favorable tax rules have been able to reverse the reluctance on the part of U.S. companies to send American personnel overseas. Exhibit 5–2 illustrates the complexity and consequences of tax laws.

In addition to the federal tax laws, a number of states have a **"unitary tax,"** which is a highly controversial method of computing the state income tax. This tax allows the state to include the income of out-of-state and worldwide divisions of a company incorporated in that state for the purpose of computing the firm's tax bill, if the firm is considered to be a "unitary business." The formula tends to hurt a company that is already successful elsewhere before establishing itself in the state. Inversely, a company located in the state with this tax should receive a tax benefit from the loss incurred by the startup of a foreign operation. Several foreign governments have asked the U.S. government to eliminate these state laws. After losing companies to other states, Florida repealed such a law.

Eavesdropping in a foreign boardroom

Through the magic of modern imagination, we now travel to the board meeting of Allcircuits Inc., the giant (but mythical) foreign conglomerate based in Scandinasia. The conversation goes something like this:

Vice President/Manufacturing: "Gentlemen, we must increase our production runs. America is giving us a golden opportunity. I predict we can dominate the worldwide market for widgets simply by underselling the American manufacturers."

Chairman: "How so?"

Vice President/Finance: "Simple. America is, in effect, reducing our costs for us. If their new tax plan passes, we will have an extra edge."

Chairman: "Explain, please."

Vice President/Finance: "Of course. As you know, our tax laws shield us against double taxation. We do not pay double taxes here in Scandinasia on money earned overseas, because our government makes the proper allowance for the taxes we have already paid to those countries where the earnings originated. The United States has done the same for its companies, and has been doing so since 1918."

Vice President/Research: "Clever, those Americans."

Vice President/Finance: "Not so clever, really. Now they're proposing to change their tax code. Currently, they use an overall system which allows companies to total up all the foreign income taxes they've paid. If they've paid as much or more than the U.S. tax rate, they owe no taxes on their foreign-source income. If they've paid less, they owe the difference. Remember, we're talking only about foreign-earned income; any money earned in the U.S. is taxed by the U.S., as in Scandinasia."

Chairman: "And the proposed changes...?"

Vice President/Finance: "The proposed changes would switch to a per-country formula. The taxes paid in each country would be measured against the U.S. tax rate. It would be a most complicated system; generally, the result would be a higher tax burden for U.S. companies. The estimate is $13.3 billion more in revenue for the U.S. Treasury over the next five years."

Chairman: "And since our tax load doesn't go up, we gain a competitive advantage. The Americans can't even raise prices to recover the added taxes they'll pay. How could they, when we could undersell them, and act as the worldwide price-setter?"

Vice President/Planning: "The Americans may even have to pull out of certain countries. So we have to be ready to move into those markets they abandon."

Chairman: "Gentlemen, these glad tidings from America are a mixed blessing. Americans are already grumbling about foreign competition. When they start losing jobs at home because they're limited in where they can operate profitably overseas—and because of proposed changes in how exports are taxed—those cries will become even stronger. No doubt we will be blamed for the Americans' own follies, and there will be attempts to retaliate against us.

"But the good news outweighs the bad. On the day America does alter the foreign tax credit, we should declare a national holiday."

Moral: Other nations shield their companies against double taxation. Weakening the foreign tax credit weakens the shield U.S. companies now enjoy, and strengthens their foreign competitors. Ultimately, the effect is a weaker America. Should that be the purpose of tax reform?

Mobil

EXHIBIT 5–2   Tax laws—complexity and consequences

Source: Reprinted with permission of Mobil Corporation ©1985 Mobil Corporation

The unitary tax concept was first adopted in California in the early 1970s to prevent companies that do business in more than one state or nation from avoiding taxes by shifting profit across state or national borders. The unitary system requires the company to calculate the total value of its sales, payroll, and property worldwide and determine what percentage comes from California. If, for example, subsidiary A represents 10 percent of parent B's global sales, payroll, and property, A is assessed state income taxes against 10 percent of B's worldwide profit, regardless of whether B is making or losing money.

In 1984 the Supreme Court ruled that California could tax multinational corporations doing business in the state based on their worldwide performance. Because the 1984 ruling dealt only with MNCs with parent companies based in the United States, the California tax was later challenged by Alcan and Imperial Chemical, both of which have U.S. subsidiaries doing business in California. Subsequently, the U.S. Supreme Court ruled that foreign-based firms, such as U.S. companies, must pursue their state tax disputes in state courts before seeking relief at the federal level. ICI Americas Inc., a U.S. subsidiary of Imperial Chemical Industries, PLC, then challenged unitary taxation in California courts. The Third District Court of Appeals in Sacramento overturned unitary taxation in late 1990 and stopped the State from applying unitary taxation to corporations based outside the United States.[19] In the end, the U.S. Supreme Court ruled in favor of the State of California.

BRIBERY

At first thought, bribery is both unethical and illegal. A closer look, however, reveals that bribery in not really that straightforward an issue. There are many questions about what bribery is, how it is used, and why it is used. The ethical and legal problems associated with bribery can also be quite complex.

According to the Foreign Corrupt Practices Act of 1977, bribery is "the use of interstate commerce to offer, pay, promise to pay, or authorize giving anything of value to influence an act or decision by a foreign government, politician, or political party to assist in obtaining, retaining, or directing business to any person." A bribe is also known as a "payoff," "grease money," "lubricant," "little envelope," *mordida* or "bite" (Mexico), and "under-the-table payment," as well as by other terms. A bribe may take the form of cash, gifts, jobs, and free trips. Exhibit 5–3 describes a bribe as a transaction.

According to the Conference Board, about three quarters of seventy-three U.S. business leaders acceded to foreign officials' demands for unusual payments. The companies involved include Exxon, Lockheed, General Motors, Ford, United Brands, Grumman, Northrop, and McDonnell-Douglas. Payments ranged from those made

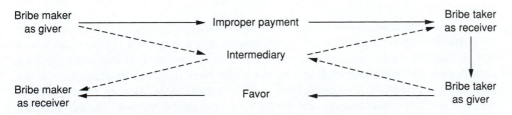

EXHIBIT 5–3   The anatomy of a bribe

Source: Sak Onkvisit and John J. Shaw, "International Corporate Bribery: Some Legal, Cultural, Economic, Ethical-Philosophical, and Marketing Considerations," *Journal of Global Marketing* 4 (no. 2, 1991): 6

to important people to those given to clerks. Goodyear International Corp. paid a $250,000 fine in 1989 after pleading guilty to paying nearly $1 million in bribes to obtain $19 million in Iraqi government orders for truck tires.

There are several reasons why a bribe is solicited, offered, and accepted. Low salaries of public officials is one reason; simple greed is another. The loyalties and commitments public servants have to their political parties, families, and friends can cause them to ask for favors that will benefit those groups. The proliferation of bureaucratic regulations seems to be another cause. Complex regulations create the opportunity for bribery because by paying a bribe a company can cut through bureaucratic red tape quickly. Brazil's governmental system is so complicated that it even has the Debureaucratization Ministry. Among reasons why some businesspersons are willing and even eager to offer a bribe are

To speed up the required work or processing.

To secure a contract.

To avoid the cancellation of the contract.

To prevent competitors from getting the contract.

Bribery is not always an absolute; rather it may be a matter of degree. What may seem like a bribe to one person may not be to another—especially to the one who accepts the payment. This problem of interpretation can perhaps be better understood by considering the tipping system that is so prevalent in the Western world. When considered in this light, there is a fine line between a bribe and a gratuity. The tip is given "to ensure promptness"—the same purposes for which a bribe is tendered. Those who provide services expect a tip, and this is true even when the service given may be routine and of poor quality.

In China, tipping is prohibited, though gifts of nominal value can be given to a group host. For non-Europeans and non-Americans, the tipping system makes no sense. Should patrons not expect good service when their patronage provides income for companies and jobs for employees? In the broad sense, a tip is often a bribe in disguise, and to call it a bribe by another name (i.e., tip) still does not make it any less of a bribe.

An interesting paradox is that countries that have no tipping system are often accused of being tolerant of bribery, whereas Western countries condemn bribery vigorously but tolerate and even encourage tipping. Just as interesting is that Japanese workers provide good services even when the government discourages them from taking a tip.

The determination of whether something is a bribe is not is complicated further by particular types of payments. When a businessperson gives a public employee a few dollars for extra services so that a delay can be avoided, is this payment a tip or a bribe? The same question in a broader sphere may be asked about compensation and commissions for middlemen. Lockheed paid large sums of money for the services of Prince Bernhardt of the Netherlands and Prime Minister Tanaka of Japan. Under normal circumstances, payments to middlemen pose no problem whatsoever. In the Lockheed case, however, the two middlemen happened to be well-known personalities—a prince and a prime minister—who were in the position of being able to secure favorable treatment for the company. The U.S. Securities and Exchange Commission (SEC) takes the position that payments made to low- and middle-level officials for tasks routinely performed by such officials are not illegal but that payments to high-level government officials for special favors are unlawful.

Another kind of questionable payment involves political contributions. When Gulf Oil was forced to contribute $4 million toward the reelection of Korea's President Park, this was viewed by the Koreans as a political contribution and by U.S. officials as extortion. It is rather ironic that U.S. senators and congressmen would be upset with Gulf's compliance of the Koreans' request when such politicians routinely solicit corporate contributions for their own reelection in the United States.

Special discounts present another ambiguous issue. In a celebrated case, a top White House aid, Michael Deaver, made news when he purchased a BMW sports car at diplomatic discount during an official trip to Germany. Yet his purchase was hardly a unique transaction; many other White House staff members have done much the same thing simply by sending a copy of their diplomatic passports to the company, without even setting foot in Germany.[20] As far as BMW is concerned, these special discounts make good marketing sense because the company is able to get opinion leaders to drive its cars and the result is free publicity. But to some observers the scheme does not differ greatly from a bribe, because the quid-pro-quo exchange allows each party to gain something from the transaction. There may additionally be a conflict of interest on the part of White House officials because the White House develops policy concerning imported cars.

There has also been debate about gifts. Traditionally U.S. firms provide Christmas gifts for their customers, employees, and those who have assisted the firm. In foreign countries, gifts may be given for other occasions, such as a new-year holiday or birthday. These gifts are often considered by Westerners as bribes when in reality they serve the same purpose as Christmas gifts.

To answer clearly the question of whether a bribe is illegal is difficult for two reasons. First, bribery is not an either/or proposition. There are several kinds of payments that fall on the borderline of legality and illegality. Second, the interpretation of legality and illegality depends on the particular laws of a particular country. What is illegal in one country is not necessarily so elsewhere. In the former Soviet Union, a simple gift—such as clothing for a public official—was considered a bribe. Unlike U.S. law, the laws of France, Japan, Germany, and Great Britain do not specifically deal with foreign bribery. Canada takes the position that Canadian firms should comply with the host country's law. Italy, in contrast, has gone one step further: that country has made it legal for Italian firms to pay foreign officials to acquire business orders.

The difficulty in determining the legality of bribery has long frustrated many businessmen. One survey revealed that 69 percent of the respondents who were members of the *Fortune* 500 firms thought that the Justice Department and the SEC have so far failed to establish clear guidelines.[21] As a result, companies have great problems interpreting whether they have "reason to know" that some payments will go to foreign officials and whether their accounting control systems provide "reasonable assurance" that they are in compliance with the law.

Sections 5001-5003 of the 1988 trade act amended the FCPA in many respects. The primary change concerns payments to third parties by a U.S. firm "knowing or having reason to know" that the third party would use the payment for prohibited purposes. Under the new law, the U.S. firm must have actual knowledge of or willful blindness to the prohibited use of the payment. The act also clarifies the types of payments that are permissible. For example, under the FCPA as originally enacted, although payments to low-level officials who exercise only "ministerial" or "clerical" functions were exempt, the provision provided little guidance to exporters in determining whether a given foreign official exercised discretionary authority. The fact that the Middle East and Africa have part-time officials complicates the matter even more. The trade act provides guidance by specifying the *types* of payments that are permissible rather than which individuals can receive them. A payment for a routine governmental action (e.g., processing papers, stamping visas, and scheduling inspections) may be made without subjecting the exporter to the worry of whether this type of payment may lead to criminal liability.[22]

Ethical considerations about bribery are even more ambiguous than legal definitions. Generally, ethics precede law. What is illegal is almost always considered unethical, whereas what is unethical may not be considered illegal. Whether bribery is unethical or not depends on the standards used. Morality exists only in the context of a particular culture. What is unethical in one culture is not necessarily so in another culture. Bribery may thus be acceptable in some countries. In many LDCs, the practice of providing bribes is so common that not to do so may be interpreted as an insult or a lack of respect. The Japanese, viewing payments to foreign officials to secure business deals as a normal practice, had a hard time understanding why there was such an uproar when an advisor to President Reagan, Richard Allen, accepted a watch as a gift from a Japanese magazine and why he had to resign over this common courtesy.

There is also another side to ethics. If a company tries to be ethical by refusing to make questionable payments, it may risk having its cargo left on the dock or in a customs warehouse where its goods can easily be damaged or stolen. Moreover, to refuse giving a bribe may result in the loss of a contract, thus hurting stockholders and employees. Generally, it is a good idea for a company to maintain its integrity. But this task is difficult if the company's efforts are adversely affected by competitors who routinely offer bribes and thus take advantage of the company's ethical conduct.

Although bribes often make the difference between securing or losing an order, the significance of bribery should not be overstated. "The macroeconomic data indicate that American executives have been wrong about the importance of bribery in international business."[23] Improper payments can prove both ineffective in the short run and damaging in the long run. Bribery thus should not be considered in isolation, without taking into account other export incentives and products' superior performance.

Despite the lack of agreement about what a bribe is and whether bribes are always undesirable, companies must nevertheless cope with the practice. A good rule of thumb may be to be discreet and not to pursue a bribe too aggressively. It may be prudent to wait for the other party either to bring up the issue or to provide a hint. Perhaps occasions for giving should be considered, and holidays can often provide an appropriate excuse. In fact, the absence of a gift at major holidays can be quite conspicuous. In some cultures, it is acceptable to give a gift upon being introduced or in first meeting someone. In other cultures, an occasion for gift giving is upon the consumption of a deal or when departing. If a U.S. firm decides not to comply with a request for bribe, it should cite the Foreign Corrupt Practices Act as a legitimate excuse. In any case, no matter how distasteful bribery may appear to be, marketers must realize that it is part of the international "game" that many businesspersons play.

International marketers need to develop strategies to deal with bribery problems. Good strategies should include having corporate codes of ethics, sensitization of ethics in managers through training and education, and conducting ethics audits.[24] A study of the usage and contents of corporate codes of ethics found that significantly fewer European firms than U.S. firms have adopted codes of ethics. In Europe, the large majority of codes have only been recently introduced, and such codes have made their way into Europe via subsidiaries of U.S. firms. There are also significant differences in content between U.S. and European codes of ethics. Although most ethical issues transcend national barriers, German companies stress a shared responsibility on the part of management and employees, whereas French and British companies promote a sense of belonging. U.S. firms, on the other hand, emphasize fairness and equity.[25]

It is encouraging that companies seem to take ethical behavior more seriously than before. As found by the Ethics Resource Centre, a Washington-based research group, codes of ethics were adopted by 73 percent of the United States' 500 largest firms, and the figure rose to 85 percent of the 2,000 largest firms in 1988. Only 3 percent of the companies in the survey had ethics training for their managers in 1980, but the figure has since risen to 35 percent.[26]

JURISDICTION AND EXTRATERRITORIALITY

There is no international law per se that deals with business activities of companies in the international arena. There are only national laws that vary from one country to another. In preparing a contract, a seller or buyer should stipulate a particular legal system that is to take precedence in resolving any contract dispute. The court to be used for legal remedy should also be specified. The company must keep in mind that to earn a legal victory in its home court is one thing, but to enforce a judgment against a foreign party is something else altogether. Enforcement is difficult unless that foreign party has the desire to continue to do business in the country where the judgment is obtained.

It is often necessary to file a lawsuit in the defendant's home country. To make certain that the foreign court will have **jurisdiction** to hear the case, the contract should contain a clause that allows the company to bring a lawsuit in either the home country or the host country.

A marketer should realize that a firm cannot easily escape responsibility in a foreign country simply by claiming that foreign courts lack jurisdiction. Take Duple Motor Body Works, Ltd., an English company, as an example. Duple furnished bus bodies to Vauxhall Motors, another British firm, which assembled the buses in England for its Hawaiian customer. When a personal injury case involving product liability was filed in Hawaii, there was no doubt that Vauxhall was subject to the Hawaiian court's personal jurisdiction. Duple, on the other hand, claimed a lack of jurisdiction by Hawaiian courts, arguing that it did no business or advertising there. But Duple knew that its bus bodies would eventually be used in Hawaii, which proved more than enough for the court there to assert jurisdiction over the company.[27]

Sometimes the jurisdiction criteria can be rather excessive. Section 14 of the French Civil Code allows a nonresident alien to be brought before a French court if the alien has incurred obligations in regard to a Frenchman.[28] A French company was thus able to sue an English shipping firm in a French court just because the French firm paid a damage claim to English-owned goods carried by that British company. The evidence is that domestic courts find little difficulty in obtaining personal jurisdiction over foreign defendants, especially in a product liability case.

Whenever possible and practical, companies should consider commercial **arbitration** in place of judicial trials. Arbitration proceedings provide such advantages as an impartial hearing, a quick result, and a decision made by experts. Both IBM and Fujitsu seemed satisfied with the ruling of their two arbitrators in settling a copyright dispute. Intel, in contrast, did not want arbitration and was frustrated by the pace of its copyright lawsuit against NEC. After hearing lengthy and time-consuming arguments, a U.S. District judge ruled that Intel held a legitimate copyright. The case became more complicated when higher courts took another year to decide whether the judge should disqualify himself. The judge finally had to step down and the arguments were ordered reheard because he happened to own Intel stock worth $80 through an investment club.

When the arbitration is voluntary rather than compulsory, there is one additional benefit related to the jurisdiction issue, one provided for by the 1958 UN Convention on Recognition and Enforcement of Foreign Arbitral Awards: "The Convention, which sets up uniform provisions under the contracting states, shall recognize and enforce under their rules of procedure, in their respective jurisdictions, arbitral awards that have been issued in other member countries."[29] It prohibits a court of a contracting state from taking jurisdiction of a matter submitted to arbitration.

Three important multilateral agreements on international arbitration address the enforcement of agreements to arbitrate and judicial assistance in the execution of arbitral awards. The **New York Convention** has received broad worldwide acceptance and is now in force in eighty-two countries. The **Inter-American Convention,** closely paralleling the framework of the New York Convention, states that parties that have agreed to arbitrate may be compelled to do so and that arbitral awards shall be recognized and enforced in the same manner as final judicial decisions. The **ICSID Convention** (The **Convention on the Settlement of Investment Disputes between States and Nationals of Other States**) has established the International Centre for the Settlement of Investment Disputes (ICSID) in Washington, D.C., to facilitate the arbitration of disputes between foreign investors and host governments. Over ninety nations have ratified the ICSID Convention.

Many Latin American countries adhere to the **Calvo Doctrine** (after the Argentine jurist Carlos Calvo), which is generally hostile to international arbitration. Under the Calvo Doctrine, disputes between foreign investors and a host government must be submitted to the domestic courts of the host government instead of an independent third party. The general inclination of Latin American countries against ratification or accession to the New York Convention or adoption of ICSID demonstrates the historical aversion those countries have had to arbitration as a substitute for judicial resolution of disputes.[30]

One aspect of the law that does not have universal acceptance involves **extraterritorial application** of the law. A nation wishing to protect its own interests often applies its laws to activities outside its own territory. Thus, an American firm doing business abroad must still observe U.S. laws. Not as clear-cut and much more controversial are the activities of its foreign subsidiaries and affiliates. Although owned by U.S. firms, foreign subsidiaries are non-American firms on foreign soil, and it is questionable whether these subsidiaries should comply with U.S. government's decrees. In response to President Reagan's 1986 prohibition of U.S. firms from doing business with Libya after terrorist attacks at the Vienna and Rome airports, American firms complied with the order but did not forbid their foreign subsidiaries from doing business as usual with Libya, as long as American personnel were not stationed there.

According to an Equal Employment Opportunity Commission (EEOC) lawyer, "employers can't go around discriminating, discharging, and harassing people simply because they're overseas." Ali Bouresland, a Lebanese-born naturalized U.S. citizen, claimed that his supervisor at the Arabian American Oil Co. harassed him, denied him time off for Muslim holidays, and fired him because of his race, religion, and national origin. But the Supreme Court stated that a provision of the 1964 Civil Rights Act barring employment bias based on race, sex, religion, and national origin does not apply to U.S. citizens working abroad for American firms. The ruling stressed a principle of American law that limits federal legislation to U.S. territory. As a rule, American courts will not apply laws beyond their border (i.e., **extraterritorially**) unless Congress expresses a different intent. John Pfeiffer, a high-ranking executive for Wrigley Corp. in the United States, was protected under U.S. law from discrimination based on his age. After his transfer to a high position in Wrigley's German office, Pfeiffer turned sixty-five and was immediately fired on the basis of his age. Because of the transfer, he had no recourse.

When a nation attempts to apply its laws extraterritorially, it may upset its trading or political partners. The United States has been placed in this awkward position a number of times in the past. The United States angered Canada when the U.S. government tried to prevent U.S. firms' Canadian subsidiaries from selling products to Cuba. The United States created another uproar in Europe when it prohibited European subsidiaries of American firms from participating in a Soviet pipeline project. Having learned from these costly lessons, the United States now attempts to avoid disputes over extraterritoriality. In the U.S. trade embargo against Nicaragua, the United States was careful not to create any unnecessary conflicts with its Central American allies, as Nicaragua has significant trade with the other four members of the Central American Common Market (i.e., Guatemala, El Salvador, Honduras, and Costa Rica). The United States did not want to cause trade disruptions that could injure the economies of those and other allies. As a result, Nicaragua could still acquire U.S. spare parts through Canada and Mexico. Thus, the U.S. embargo amounted to more of a political statement than an economic sanction.

LEGAL FORM OF ORGANIZATION

Firms doing business in Great Britain have three primary choices for the legal form of organization: British branch, limited company, or partnership. If a limited company is the choice, more decision is needed. A limited company may be either a *public limited company (PLC),* which can raise capital by selling securities to the public, or a *private company (ltd.),* which is not allowed to offer shares or debentures to the public. In general, a public company must meet a number of requirements in terms of registration and capital structure, subscription for shares, and profits and assets available for distribution.[31]

In the United States, a business is able to select from among these forms: sole proprietorship, partnership, and corporation. For firms involved in international trade, the most common choice is the corporation because of the limited liability associated with the corporate form, its relatively permanent structure, and its ability to raise money by selling securities. Most large U.S. firms have a *Corp.* or *Inc.* nomenclature as part of their trade names.

The nomenclature indicating incorporation is different in other countries. For most British Commonwealth countries, corporate names include *ltd.* or *ltd. co.* to indicate that the liability of the company is "limited." Equivalencies in civil law countries include the following: in France, *S.A. (société anonyme,* or *sociedad anónima)* for a "formal" corporation/stock company and *SARL (société a responsabilité limitée* or *sociedad de responsabilidad limitada)* for an "informal" corporation/limited liability company; in Germany and Switzerland, *AG (Aktiengesellschaft)* for a stock company and *GmbH (Gesellschaft mit beschrankter Haftung)* for a limited liability company; in Japan, *K.K. (kabushiki kaisha)* for a stock company; in Sweden, *A.B.:* and in the Netherlands, *N.V.* To eliminate confusion and to ensure some uniformity, European countries are now encouraging the use of *PLC* instead of other nomenclature to indicate that a company is incorporated.

BRANCH VS. SUBSIDIARY

One legal decision that an MNC must make is whether to use branches or subsidiaries to carry out its plans and to manage its operations in a foreign country. A **branch** is the company's extension or outpost at another location. Although physically detached, it is not legally separated from its parent. A **subsidiary,** in contrast, is both physically and legally independent. It is considered a separate legal entity in spite of its ownership by another corporation.

Marshall Field's, a well-known Chicago department store, can help in making this distinction clear. Field's has its main store in downtown Chicago and several branch stores in the suburbs of Chicago, as well as branches located as far away as Texas. That company, in turn, is a subsidiary of Batus, a U.S. holding company, which also owns Saks Fifth Avenue, Ivery's department stores, Breuners home furnishings and rental stores, Thimbles specialty stores, and Brown and Williamson Tobacco Corporation. The parent company of Batus is the London-based B.A.T. Industries, a British conglomerate.

Exhibit 5–4 shows how Bayer uses affiliated subsidiaries as an entry strategy for the U.S. market.

It's Bayer USA.

A group of progressive, dynamic, forward-looking companies like Miles Laboratories and Mobay Corporation.

Our businesses range from chemicals to health and life sciences to imaging and graphic information systems.

And those individual successes added up to make us #117 in our very first year!

Actually, if the sales of Agfa-Gevaert and Compugraphic, two affiliated companies, had been included, Bayer USA would have been ranked much higher on the *Fortune List*.

Given our commitment to research and development, our rise should be steady from here on. We have access to a worldwide R&D budget of more than $1 billion — one of the largest in the chemical industry — through our parent, Bayer AG of West Germany. And we devoted $200 million last year to research programs here in the U.S. alone.

So our dedication to growth in the years ahead is deep. And our perspective is worldwide.

For more information about Bayer USA, one of the most potent new factors on the American industrial scene, contact Bayer USA Inc., attn. Elliot Schreiber, Dept. 1B, One Mellon Center, Pittsburgh, PA 15219-2502.

Bayer USA INC.

MEETING A WORLD OF NEEDS.

EXHIBIT 5–4 Using affiliated subsidiaries as an entry strategy

Source: Reprinted with permission of Bayer USA Inc.

A subsidiary may either be wholly owned (i.e., 100 percent owned) or partially owned. GE receives $1 billion in revenues from its wholly owned and partially owned subsidiaries in Europe. The usual practice of Pillsbury, Coca-Cola, and IBM is to have wholly owned subsidiaries. Nevertheless, it is difficult to generalize about the superiority of one approach over the other. The only firm conclusion that can be made is that a parent company has total control when its subsidiary is wholly owned, but whether the total control is desirable or not is another issue altogether.

It appears from the figures available that a multinational, as a rule, prefers subsidiaries to branches. Fiat has 432 subsidiaries and minority interests within 130 companies in sixty countries. The question that must be asked is why Fiat, like other MNCs, would go through the trouble and expense of forming hundreds of foreign companies elsewhere. When compared to the use of branches, the use of subsidiaries adds complexity to the corporate structure. They are also expensive, requiring substantial sales volume to justify their expense.

There are several reasons why a subsidiary is the preferred structure. One reason may involve gaining quick access to a particular market by acquiring an existing company within the market and making it a subsidiary. The Swiss-based Ciba-Geigy Corporation acquired Airwick, a U.S. firm, with two goals in mind: gaining access to the U.S. consumer market and acquiring a well-known brand.

Merrill Lynch had its own reasons for forming a subsidiary to do business in Japan. Its problem had to do with Japanese law, which would not permit Merrill Lynch to incorporate its Tokyo branches into subsidiaries, although Japanese firms were allowed to create subsidiaries. Because titles mean a great deal in Japan, Merrill Lynch had a difficult time recruiting management. Its top administrator in Japan had to settle for being a "branch manager" instead of having a prestigious title of president or managing director.[32] To solve this problem the company created Merrill Lynch Japan in the United States, and was then able to attract Japanese management personnel to run its subsidiary in Japan.

Subsidiaries may also be preferred because of the flexibility created, which may allow the parent company to take advantage of legal loopholes or of the opportunity to circumvent certain government requirements. In response to a strong outcry against the huge grain purchase secretly arranged by the Soviet Union, which caused prices to go up after disclosure, the United States began requiring U.S.-based companies to report sales of grains and oilseeds of more than 100,000 tons to be made within 24 hours, and the Agriculture Department must publicly announce the information immediately. The aim of such a requirement is to protect bakers and other businesses that may be misled about supply and demand, therefore helping to reduce any market uncertainty that may cause consumers to pay higher prices. Most MNCs prefer to keep deals secret because they want the time to hedge their positions before speculators buy in, and also because the Chinese generally insist on secrecy in such deals. American MNCs are able to circumvent disclosure requirements routinely by handling a majority of their U.S. transactions through Swiss-based subsidiaries or affiliated trading companies elsewhere.

Such examples raise several issues. There is an inherent conflict between corporate interests and consumer welfare. A company must decide whether it should fully comply with the intention or spirit of the law designed to protect consumers or whether it should look after the interests of its stockholders. The grain example also illustrates that a company can often overcome legal obstacles, deliberately circumventing the law by using its foreign subsidiaries. In other circumstances, the system could not be circumvented if a company's operations abroad were structured as branches rather than subsidiaries. Laws could be changed to close loopholes—Congress can always require American firms' subsidiaries and foreign-owned operations to be included in the reporting system. But the effectiveness of such attempts is questionable, and there is the issue concerning the extraterritorial application of the law.

Another advantage in favor of maintaining subsidiaries is the tax benefits. When formed in a foreign country, a subsidiary is considered a local company, enabling it to receive tax benefits granted to other national companies. Moreover, a subsidiary provides the parent company with some flexibility in terms of when the parent has to pay tax on the income generated by its subsidiary. With a foreign branch, the income is immediately taxable through the parent firm, regardless of whether there is the remittance for the profit. Given this situation, there is no opportunity for the parent to defer any profit or loss.

It is important to keep in mind that a subsidiary does not have the tax advantage in all countries. Any tax benefit cannot be determined in advance without adequately studying the specific local laws. In Denmark, a case can be made for the establishment of a branch instead of a subsidiary. A branch's profit can be remitted with no restrictions to its head office, whereas a subsidiary's dividend to its foreign parent company is subject to a 30 percent withholding tax, as well as other restrictions.[33] Furthermore, any taxable loss in the Danish branch can be set off against the taxable profit in the home country, but the subsidiary's loss cannot be utilized in the same fashion by the parent firm.

Another point to keep in mind is that each legal form of organization has its own strengths and weaknesses. Therefore, any tax advantage must be considered with criteria that may offset this advantage. A branch may offer tax advantages over a subsidiary in Japan, but in Japan a branch has more difficulty getting financing, buying land, and adding manufacturing. As a result, branches are usually appropriate only when sales-and-service operations are involved.[34] Similarly, a branch's tax advantage in South Africa is offset by a disclosure requirement. The branch must lodge its own financial statements as well as those of its parent with the Registrar of Companies, whereas locally registered private companies are not required to make their parents' financial information public.[35] This is also true for Denmark.

The limited-liability advantage may be one of the most important reasons why a subsidiary is formed. With this organizational structure, the parent firm's liability is limited to its investment in the foreign subsidiary. That is, its maximum loss can be no greater than the assets invested in its subsidiary. Also, the formation of a separate company provides some protection against hostile acts. During World War II, for example, Philips formed North American Philips (N.A.P.) as a separate entity by placing its U.S. operations in a trust in order to protect the company from takeover attempts by the Nazis. The problem in this case was the N.A.P. eventually grew to be too independent and would not even buy the parent's video cassette recorders for sale in the U.S. market. Philips finally dissolved the trust in 1986, reclaiming the 58 percent interest in N.A.P. in order to have "one face to the world, one central policy."

MNCs generally believe that they are protected against their subsidiaries' actions and liabilities because of the separate incorporation of parent firms and subsidiaries, making them separate legal entities. This precept has recently come under severe test in a lawsuit filed by India against Union Carbide over an industrial disaster at Bhopal, India. A gas leak at a Union Carbide plant killed more than two thousand people and injured thousands of others. In addition to the lawsuit against Union Carbide, victims' lawyers, alleging plant design defects as a contributing factor, sued Humphreys &

Glasgow Consultants Pvt. Ltd., Union Carbide's prime contractor. This Bombay-based firm is affiliated with Humphreys and Glasgow Ltd., a London engineering firm, which in turn is owned by Enserch Corp., a Dallas diversified energy company.

The main legal issue in the Bhopal case was whether the parent company is also responsible for the damage caused by its subsidiary. The issue in most cases could probably be decided easily if the parent company owns 100 percent of its subsidiary's voting stock. With full control over a wholly owned subsidiary, there is little question about whether the parent and its foreign subsidiary are indeed independent and separate. In the Union Carbide case, the issue was complicated by the fact that Union Carbide India Ltd. is not a wholly owned subsidiary. Although theoretically and legally autonomous in terms of decision making and responsibility, the subsidiary does not function independently in practice, as its authority is granted by the parent. This is exactly the issue that was legally raised in India in regard to who was responsible for the disaster.

India's contention was that MNCs that are engaged in hazardous activities should not be insulated from their subsidiaries' actions. The liability issue hinged largely on the extent of Union Carbide's involvement in managing its Indian subsidiary. According to India, the two should not be considered legally separate because of their close links. Evidence included the Indian subsidiary's inability to spend large sums of money without authorization from the Connecticut headquarters. Union Carbide's defense was that, although it had the power to veto large outlays as a majority share-holder, the day-to-day operations were run locally.[36] A settlement between India and Union Carbide was finally reached, but many legal issues are yet to be resolved.

INTELLECTUAL PROPERTY

Individuals and firms have the freedom to own and control the rights to **intellectual property** (i.e., inventions and creative works). The terms patent, trademark, copyright, and trade secret are often used interchangeably. In fact, they are four basic forms of intellectual property and hold different meanings (see Exhibit 5–5).

A **trademark** is a symbol, word, or thing used to identify a product made or marketed by a particular firm. In the United States, it becomes a **registered trademark** when the mark is accepted for registration by the Trademark Office. A **copyright,** which is the responsibility of the Copyright Office in the Library of Congress, offers protection against unauthorized copying by others to an author or artist for his or her literary, musical, dramatic, and artistic works. A copyright protects the form of expression rather than the subject matter.

A copyright has now been extended to computer software as well. IBM did not copyright its software until 1978, and Congress amended copyright laws to extend protection to software in 1980. In the mid-1970s, when the extent of protection for operating-system software under U.S. and Japanese copyright laws was very unclear, Fujitsu introduced operating-system software that controls the operation of its main-frame computers. IBM accused Fujitsu of copying in 1982 and received a substantial undisclosed sum. The two firms' 1983 agreement provided that they resolve remaining differences through binding arbitration. The American Arbitration Association subsequently administered the resolution procedure.[37]

Intellectual Property is a general term that describes inventions or other discoveries that have been registered with government authorities for the sale or use by their owner. Such terms as patent, trademark, copyright, or unfair competition fall into the category of intellectual property.

A **patent** is a government grant of certain rights given to an inventor for a limited time in exchange for the disclosure of the invention. The most important of these rights is the one under which the patented invention can be made, used, or sold only with the authorization of the patent owner.

A **trademark** relates to any work, name, or symbol which is used in trade to distinguish a product from other similar goods (e.g., "Coke"). Trademark laws are used to prevent others from making a product with a confusingly similar mark. Similar rights may be acquired in marks used in the sale of advertising of services (service marks).

A **copyright** protects the writings of an author against copying. Literary, dramatic, musical, and artistic—and more recently computer software—works are included within the protection of copyright laws.

A **mask work** is a new type of intellectual property, protected by the Semiconductor Chip Protection Act of 1984. It is, in essence, the design of an electrical circuit, the pattern of which is transferred and fixed in a semiconductor chip during the manufacturing process.

Unfair competition is a very broad term defining legal standards of business conduct. It provides protection against such things as simulation of trade packaging, using similar corporate and professional names, misappropriation of **trade secrets,** and palming off one person's goods as those of another.

EXHIBIT 5–5 Definitions

Source: *Business America*, 25 September 1989, 2

The United States has finally joined the eighty-nation **Berne Convention for the Protection of Literary and Artistic Works,** allowing greater protection against foreign pirating of U.S. copyrighted works in 25 additional countries. In order to conform to the Berne Copyright Convention, changes in the copyright law in the United States were necessary. Under the new amendment, affixing a copyright notice is optional. For works created after January 1, 1989, mere publication and use are enough to obtain copyright protection.

As long as a computer program has been registered somewhere, failure to register in Brazil does not diminish the rights of the owner.[38] Still, copyright registration in Brazil may be advantageous because it establishes previous assumption of ownership and facilitates court proceedings in a court case involving copyright infringement. Even though the copyright notice is no longer required, it is still a good idea to place a ©, the author's name, and date of publication on the original work. Also, for only $10, an author can register his or her material with the Copyright Office. A clear notice entitles the author to obtain more effective remedies against infringers.

A **patent** protects an invention of a scientific or technical nature. It is a statutory grant from the government (the Patent Office) to an inventor in exchange for public disclosure giving the patent holder exclusive right to the functional and design inventions patented and excluding others from using those inventions for a certain period of time.

While America's annual share of new U.S. patents fell from 62 percent in 1978 to 53 percent in 1989, the Japanese share of U.S. patents soared from 10.5 percent to more than 20 percent (and even higher in several product categories). The development indicates that Japan is more than a copycat manufacturer and that foreign patents represent a desire to exploit the market. According to the Commerce Department's Patent and Trademark Office, the top four companies to receive the greatest number of U.S. patents in the 1989 fiscal year were Japanese: Hitachi, Toshiba Corp., Canon Kabushiki Kaisha, and Fuji Photo Film. Among U.S. companies in the top 10 were: General Electric (5th), IBM (9th), and Eastman Kodak (10th). The percentage of U.S. patents issued to foreigners was 46.7 percent in 1989.

The term **trade secret** refers to know-how (e.g., manufacturing methods, formulas, plans, and so on) that is kept secret within a particular business. This know-how, generally unknown in the industry, may offer the firm a competitive advantage.

Infringement occurs when there is commercial use (i.e., copying or imitating) without owner's consent, with the intent of confusing or deceiving the public. For example, Texas Instruments charged that eight Japanese firms made memory chips based on its patents after the expiration of license agreements, and the U.S. company was able to force the Japanese firms to pay nearly $300 million in royalties. Texas Instruments also obtained an International Trade Commission ruling to seize Samsung's DRAM (dynamic random access memory) chips, which infringed upon Texas Instruments' semiconductor patents. Samsung then joined the eight Japanese companies in agreeing to pay royalties.

Although patent, trademark, and copyright are distinctly different, they have a common sense in that all have something to do with the protection of an owner's property. All require applications to be filed—not at the same office, however. Although this section deals with patents more specifically, the same basic ideas apply as well to the trademarks and copyrights.

According to the 1990 Trade Policy Agenda and 1989 Annual Report of the President of the United States on the Trade Agreements Program, inadequate intellectual property rights protection and enforcement around the world costs U.S. companies $40 billion to $60 billion each year.[39] According to Business Software Association, a Washington-based group that represents the major U.S. software publishers internationally, the losses to French and U.S. software publishers in France because of illicit copying amounted to $950 million in 1988, or more than twice the actual sales of $400 million.

When a firm develops an innovation, a patent should be obtained. The purpose of a patent is to enable the company to exploit its invention commercially while preventing others from interfering. Not all new ideas are patentable. A patent is granted only if the item under consideration is able to satisfy certain criteria. In general, the item must be new, unobvious, and useful, and must also involve an inventive step. In South Korea, biotechnology companies must submit a local deposit of patentable microorganisms for consideration for product patent protection. Inventors in the Commonwealth of Independent States and the Eastern Bloc, however, have a special problem. Because of the former Soviet Union's so-called inventor style, all rights and control of a new invention must pass to the state. All that an inventor in those nations is granted is the designation as the originator and sometimes an inventor's fee. One argument for this system is that no single person owns the patent, and therefore the invention should quicken the spread of technology through the country. The system, however, does not provide much incentive for potential inventors to create something new.

The problem of getting a patent granted is often difficult in many communist countries and LDCs because patent laws do not exist or are ignored. China did not enact its first patent law until 1984. Such countries may refuse to recognize certain patents granted elsewhere, or they may refuse to approve foreign firms' patent applications in their countries. Items not covered by patents in China include computer software, animals, plants, food, beverages, and atomic-energy-related inventions. Also not fully protected are those items related to national defense, the economy, and public health. China does not give patents for chemicals and pharmaceuticals, reasoning that other countries at similar stages of economic development have not granted such patents.

Patent laws vary widely, and one should not jump to conclusions that patent problems are restricted only to communist or developing countries. Industrial nations may also exclude items from protection. Canada is the only industrialized nation requiring compulsory licensing of drugs. Smith Kline had success with Tagamet, a drug for treating ulcers, but Canada issued Novopharm a license for a generic version only four years after Tagamet first appeared on the U.S. market. As a result, Smith Kline sued the Canadian government for violation of patent rights.

An inventor should understand that the patent obtained in one country does not extend protection beyond that nation's territorial limits. For further protection, it is necessary for the inventor to file application in other important markets. A few international agreements help simplify this cumbersome process.[40] One such agreement is the **Patent Cooperation Treaty (PCT).** The PCT Union has forty-nine countries as members (see Table 5–1). The PCT is a multilateral treaty that makes it possible to file an international application simultaneously in member countries. It thus eliminates the need for separate applications.

Another international agreement is provided by the **Paris Union (Paris Convention)** or the International Convention for the Protection of Industrial Property of 1883. The Paris Union claims about eighty countries as its members (see Table 5–2). The most important provision is the **"priority right"**, which means that the registering of a patent in one member country gives the inventor one year from the filing date to do the same in other countries before losing the protection. In addition, the convention establishes other rules, principles, and rights. The **"national treatment"** rule prevents discrimination by requiring member countries to treat foreign applicants and their own nationals in the same manner. The principle of **"independence of patents"** provides further protection because the revocation or expiration in the country of original filing has no effect on its validity in other countries.

Centralized protection of trademarks is easier to accomplish than centralized protection of patents. One treaty for the purpose of international registration is the **Madrid Agreement for the International Registration of Marks.** Twenty-two countries, mostly in Europe, are signatories, though the United States is not one of

TABLE 5–1   International Patent Cooperation Union (PCT Union)

Member States (1980)	Starting date of membership in the Union
Australia	March 31, 1980
Austria	April 23, 1979
Brazil	April 9, 1978
Cameroon	January 24, 1978
Central Africa Republic	January 24, 1978
Chad	January 24, 1978
Congo	January 24, 1978
Denmark	December 1, 1978
Finland	October 1, 1980
France	February 25, 1978
Gabon	January 24, 1978
Germany, Federal Republic of	January 24, 1978
Hungary	June 27, 1980
Japan	October 1, 1978
Korea, Democratic People's Republic of	July 8, 1980
Liechtenstein	March 19, 1980
Luxembourg	April 30, 1978
Madagascar	January 24, 1978
Malawi	January 24, 1978
Monaco	June 22, 1979
Netherlands	July 10, 1979
Norway	January 1, 1980
Romania	July 23, 1979
Senegal	January 24, 1978
Soviet Union	March 29, 1978
Sweden	May 17, 1978
Switzerland	January 24, 1978
Togo	January 24, 1978
United Kingdom	January 24, 1978
United States of America	January 24, 1978

Source: Joseph M. Lightman, "Foreign Patent Protection: Treaties and National Laws," in *Foreign Business Practices* (Washington, D.C.: U.S. Department of Commerce, 1981), 57

them. The Madrid Arrangement provides an automatic extension of protection to all member countries when a company pays a single fee of about $300 for the period of protection of twenty years. After a trademark owner has registered a mark in a member country, the International Bureau of the World Intellectual Property Organization (WIPO) in Geneva will then issue and deposit an international registration with the trademark offices in member countries for examination in accordance with their own laws.

The **Trademark Registration Treaty (TRT)** simplifies the application process further by not requiring a prior home registration, as in the case of the Madrid Arrangement. If member countries designated in the application do not refuse reg-

TABLE 5–2   International Union for the Protection of Industrial Property (Paris Union)

Member States (1980)

Algeria	Hungary	Philippines
Argentina	Iceland	Poland
Australia	Indonesia	Portugal
Austria	Iran	Romania
Bahamas	Iraq	San Marino
Belgium	Ireland	Senegal
Benin	Israel	South Africa
Brazil	Italy	Southern Rhodesia
Bulgaria	Ivory Coast	Soviet Union
Burundi	Japan	Spain
Cameroon	Jordan	Sri Lanka
Canada	Kenya	Suriname
Central African Republic	Lebanon	Sweden
Chad	Libyan Arab Jamahiriya	Switzerland
Congo	Liechtenstein	Syria
Cuba	Luxembourg	Tanzania
Cyprus	Madagascar	Togo
Czechoslovakia	Malawi	Trinidad and Tobago
Denmark	Malta	Tunisia
Dominican Republic	Mauritania	Turkey
Egypt	Mauritius	Uganda
Finland	Mexico	United Kingdom
France	Monaco	United States of America
Gabon	Morocco	Upper Volta
German Democratic Republic	Netherlands	Uruguay
Germany, Federal Republic of	New Zealand	Vietnam
Ghana	Niger	Yugoslavia
Greece	Nigeria	Zaire
Haiti	Norway	Zambia
Holy See		

Source: Joseph M. Lightman, "Foreign Patent Protection: Treaties and National Laws," in *Foreign Business Practices* (Washington, D.C.: U.S. Department of Commerce, 1981), 58–60.

istration under their national laws in fifteen months, the mark is treated as being registered there.

There are other treaty arrangements. For example, the European Patent Convention (EPC) establishes a regional patent system for Western Europe. A person can thus file a single international application for a European Patent at the European Patent Office, which administers patent applications. For Latin America, there is the Inter-American Convention on Inventions, Patents, Designs, and Industrial Models.

The cost of preparing and registering patents can be quite high. Recently, Genentech and Biogen have been competing over parent rights for alpha interferon (human protein to treat some cancer and viral infections). Genentech has filed more than 1,400 applications worldwide and has received 80 patents.[41] Biogen spent more than $1 million in 1983 on patenting fees.

There are costs other than the initial filing fees as well. Periodic maintenance fees (i.e., annual taxes) must be paid during the life of the patent to keep it active. Other requirements must often be met for both the initial patent and the renewal of the patent. The required evidence in support of the application usually includes the use and continuous use of the patent.

Because of the high costs associated with patent application and maintenance, the costs must be weighed against the benefits. In England, illegal tape manufacturing is rampant because infringement penalties are less than $100. Even the police believe that the crime does not warrant their attention and are very lax at enforcing the law. As a rule of thumb, patent applications and registration are very important and needed in the most important markets (i.e., the United States, Great Britain, Germany, and Japan). For other industrialized countries, such as France, Italy, Sweden, and Switzerland, the potential benefits should justify the costs. In Eastern Europe and Taiwan, it may not be economically worthwhile to file for patents because patent enforcement there is so weak as to be practically nonexistent. Gucci and Rolex fought long and largely unsuccessful battles in those markets.

In spite of the costs, the marketer must realize that without a valid patent it can be more costly to do business in the long run. A manufacturer that takes legal action against patent violators is often faced with the burden of proof of ownership. The failure to obtain a patent encourages active infringement and increases the subsequent legal costs and difficulty of proving a case. The legal costs incurred in a single court case can easily exceed the registration costs in several countries.

The value of the patent is well illustrated by IBM's legal victories against its Japanese competitors. Charged with copying IBM software for its own machines, Fujitsu was forced to pay IBM many millions of dollars, $8 million a month until the year 2002. Likewise, Hitachi was required to pay IBM between $2 million and $4 million a month and to let IBM inspect all of Hitachi's new products to ensure that it was not infringing on IBM copyrights. The total cost to Hitachi for eight years would have amounted to anywhere between $194 million and $384 million, but IBM, in its aim to put pressure on Fujitsu, announced in 1986 that it would not collect anymore payment from Hitachi. In another case, Matsushita was fined about $2 million after being found by U.S. Customs to have infringed on IBM's BIOS (basic input output system) copyright.

Based on a review of cases over a fourteen-year period, the U.S. International Trade Commission was found to have performed its regulatory role, and a substantial portion of cases were settled through agreements.[42] Infringing foreign firms run a risk of being caught and excluded from U.S. markets. For example, Apple Computer Company filed a complaint in 1983 with the U.S. International Trade Commission against foreign firms that manufactured Apple IIe look-alikes. These machines, sold at much lower prices, contained duplicate operating systems and violated Apple's U.S. patents. The International Trade Commission issued a general exclusion order the following year barring infringing firms from competing in the United States. Nevertheless, U.S. firms using the International Trade Commission to defend markets from foreign competitors also run a risk of losing their patents or being reprimanded.

In the process of filing for patent protection, it is a good idea to make a distinction between common law countries and statute law countries. A common law country determines patent ownership by **priority in use.** In comparison, the ownership in a statute law country is determined by **priority in registration.** That is, the "first-to-file" is granted a patent even if an innovation was actually created or used earlier by someone else. China employs this system. The United States, as a common law country, relies on the "first-to-invent" system.

Europe and Japan have the first-to-file patent system, and they make patent applications public eighteen months after filing. The U.S. system's first-to-invent standard is unique, and the person who had the idea first receives a patent. Patent applications are secret, sometimes for years, until a patent is granted. The practice attempts to provide a balance between innovation and competition, patent holders receive a seventeen-year monopoly on their inventions. The U.S. system can and does result in redundant research.[43]

COUNTERFEITING

Counterfeiting is the practice of unauthorized and illegal copying of a product. In essence, it involves an infringement on a patent or trademark or both. According to the U.S. Lanham Act, a counterfeit trademark is a "spurious trademark which is identical with, or substantially indistinguishable from, a registered trademark." Section 42 of the U.S. Trademark Act of 1942 prohibits imports of counterfeit goods into the United States.

The Motion Picture Export Association of America (MPEAA) conducted a study of foreign film piracy in 58 countries and estimated that illegal copies cost the U.S. industry $740 million annually in lost revenues. Piracy was particularly troublesome in Saudi Arabia, Turkey, Egypt, South Korea, the Philippines, and Indonesia. In South Korea, police officials do not view the matter as a priority, resulting in sporadic police raids on video pirates.[44]

There are several levels of counterfeiting. At the top of the hierarchy is the true counterfeit product, which uses the name of the original and looks like it.[45] Next is a *look-alike* or *knock-off,* which duplicates the original's design but does not use its name. Apple computers' look-alikes include the Orange in New Zealand, Lemon in Italy, and Apolo II in Taiwan. Look-alike packages have been a big problem in the $3 billion U.S. market for counterfeit auto parts. For example, most consumers who glance at a Motorcare box see familiar colors, lettering, and logos, and they may easily mistake it for a Motorcraft box, without realizing that the word "replacement" is on the box and that the familiar racing car is going in the opposite direction.

The next level of counterfeiting is the *reproduction* or *replica*—a close but not exact copy. Chanel No. 6, a replica of Chanel No. 5, falls under this category. Finally, at the bottom of the counterfeiting rung is the *imitation* or *associative counterfeit,* which is a cheap but poor copy of the original. But it is the illegal use of the name and a product shape that differs little from the original which leads consumers to associate an imitation with the original.

Counterfeiting may be either direct or indirect (intermediate), depending on whether a counterfeiter steals product information directly. Each kind of theft can be broken down further into two subcategories, resulting in four typical counterfeiting strategies.[46] One direct strategy involves counterfeiting in a third country to reduce detection and legal remedies before shipping the product for sale in the counterfeiter's country. Another direct strategy is when the originating company's employee sells inside information to a foreign competitor, who uses the information to manufacture the product to be sold in the originator's country. In one indirect strategy, an agent/intermediary is used to steal product information in order to reduce potential legal consequence of the theft. Once manufactured in the counterfeiter's country, the product is then sold in some third country. A more complex strategy is to manufacture the product in a foreign market for sale in the originating company's country, the counterfeiter's country, and everywhere else.

The International Chamber of Commerce estimates that counterfeit goods account for nearly 5 percent of world sales. In addition to the direct monetary loss, companies face indirect losses as well. Counterfeit goods injure the reputation of companies whose brand names are placed on low-quality products. This is exactly the problem faced by G. D. Searle's Ovulen birth control pills, because the fakes in the market are not as good as the originals.

Products affected by counterfeiting cover a wide range. At one end of the spectrum are prestigious and highly advertised consumer products, such as Hennessy brandy, Dior and Pierre Cardin fashion apparel, Samsonite luggage, Levi's jeans, and Cartier watches. At the other end of the spectrum are industrial products, such as Pfizer animal feed supplement, medical vaccines, heart pacemakers, and helicopter parts. Counterfeits include such fashionable products as Gucci and Louis Vuitton handbags, as well as such mundane products as Fram oil filters and Caterpillar tractor parts. Although fakes are more likely to be premium-priced consumer products, low-unit-value products have not escaped the attention of the counterfeiter. Even Coke is not always the "real thing," as it is very easy for counterfeiters in LDCs to put something else that looks and tastes like Coke into genuine Coke bottles.

Fakes can come from anywhere, including the United States. Japan, the second largest country in the world in terms of gross national product, is accused of having more imitations than any other developed country. The MITI, one of the agencies with responsibilities in this case, was embarrassed when counterfeit Cartier products were offered for sale right in the building of its headquarters. Certain countries tend to specialize in counterfeiting certain products. The major sources of counterfeits come from Italy, Taiwan, Hong Kong, South Korea, and various Southeast Asian countries. The counterfeit goods entering the U.S. market from Italy alone amount to $3 billion a year.[47] The problem is severe in Taiwan, because so many local manufacturers pay no attention to copyrights and patents. The strong export potential for bogus merchandise makes the government there look the other way. In Mexico, one counterfeiter openly operated several "Cartier" stores in American-owned hotels. After many years in Mexican courts and at least forty-nine legal decisions against the retailer, Cartier was still unable to gain the cooperation of Mexican officials to close down this counterfeiter.

Controlling the counterfeit trade is difficult in part because counterfeiting is a low-risk, high-profit venture. It is difficult and time-consuming to obtain a search warrant. Low prosecution rates and minimal penalties in terms of jail terms and fines do not make a good deterrent. Moreover, there are many small-time counterfeiters who could just pack up and go to a new location to escape police. Just as critical, if not more so, is the attitude of law enforcement agencies and consumers. Many foreign consumers understand neither the seriousness of the violation nor the need to respect trademark rights. Law enforcement agencies often believe that the crime does not warrant special effort.

It is illegal to import into the United States a product bearing a trademark that "copies or simulates" a recorded U.S. trademark. At one time, the customs law in the United States—as in many other countries—only called for the obliteration or destruction of the trademark on counterfeit goods. An importer of such goods was thus only slightly inconvenienced because the goods could still be shipped to another country for resale. Such inconvenience was hardly a deterrent, as there was no economic penalty involved.

New U.S. Customs law and similar international laws have finally provided penalties that can really hurt counterfeiters and those who buy the fakes. These laws require the forfeiture of the bogus merchandise, and customs officials can confiscate and destroy such goods. Importers who insist that the items are genuine find that the burden of proof rests upon them. The Trademark Counterfeiting Act of 1984 makes it possible to fine and jail distributors of bogus goods. Counterfeiting is a federal crime punishable by fines of up to $1 million and prison terms of fifteen years.

Although the new U.S. law makes it easier to seize counterfeit goods, there is another way to fight the importation of these goods. Section 42 of the Trademark Act of 1946 prohibits entry of counterfeit goods or those articles that are confusingly similar to trademarks registered in the United States. The company can also protect itself against patent and copyright infringement through Section 337 of the Trade Act of 1974. The International Trade Commission has the power to exclude pirated imports. This exclusion is more valuable to companies than the monetary damages awarded by the courts. For the surveillance and confiscation to be effective, companies must work closely with the Customs Department. Apple, for example, has a cooperative arrangement with U.S. Customs in stopping Apple copies that enter the United States.

For $190, the U.S. companies can engage the Value, Special Programs, and Admissibility Branch of the U.S. Customs Service to be on the lookout for imported products that might violate their copyright and trademark rights. The U.S. Customs Service has developed a computerized system that allows a Customs officer to instantly scan thousands of government files on intellectual property violations and determine whether a U.S. firm's copyright, trade name, or trademark is being violated by a foreign producer. Furthermore, the Trademark Counterfeiting Act of 1984 allows firms to obtain a search warrant to raid pirates and take away merchandise and business records.

In order for U.S. Customs to be able to seize counterfeit goods, it needs good evidence that such goods are indeed fakes. One problem is that some of the counterfeit goods can appear to be just as good as the genuine merchandise. A trademark owner must therefore be able to offer concrete proof. G. D. Searle marks its pills using a number of covert methods. Other companies turn to technology, such as hidden magnetic or microchip tags, disappearing and reappearing inks, holographic images, and digitized fingerprints of labels.[48] Levi Strauss uses verifiable labels (i.e. labels with unique patterns of fibers). The label adds about one or two cents to the cost of each pair, and the cost increases when spot checks are conducted at stores. Allied Corp uses True Tag, which packs a magnetic tag containing a four-digit code number, and the company also prints the True Tag number on the outside of the box. It can then use a scanner to compare the tag and code number.

It is not sufficient for a company to fight counterfeiting only in its home country. The battle must be carried to the counterfeiters' own country and to other major markets. Apple has filed suits against imitators in Taiwan, Hong Kong, and New Zealand and has planned further legal action in Singapore, Japan, Australia, and Western Europe. The overall idea is to prevent bogus goods from entering the industrialized nations that make up the major markets. To make the tactic effective, it is necessary to go after the distributors and importers in addition to the manufacturers of counterfeit goods. Cartier, for example, has filed 120 lawsuits against retailers in almost every major city. Because it is difficult and time-consuming to shut down foreign counterfeiters in their home countries, major middlemen must be targeted so that they become aware of the risks in handling fakes.

The cooperation that a company receives from foreign governments in reducing the amount of counterfeiting varies greatly. Hong Kong has customarily done a credible job of enforcing court judgments against counterfeiters. Taiwan, in contrast, has been reluctant and unpredictable in going after counterfeiters. It has ignored most criticism because its economy significantly depends on the export of bogus goods. In a case such as this, the injured firm should request that its own government intervene by applying pressure on a country that harbors counterfeiters. The U.S. Tariff and Trade Act, passed in 1984, is intended to deal with this problem on an international basis. It allows the United States to deny tariff preferences and duty-free imports to LDCs that do not make a satisfactory attempt to control a counterfeit problem originating in their countries.

The threat of denial of the GSP status has shown results in the case of South Korea. South Korea, known as the "pirate kingdom," has weak intellectual property protection.[49] It has not joined any international copyright convention. As can be expected, there is widespread violation involving foreign publications, sound recordings, computer software, chemicals, and pharmaceuticals. The government's tolerance stems from its desire to protect local companies and employment, as some 700,000 jobs are affected. The pressure exerted by other governments, primarily the United States, has finally forced the Korean government to agree to offer better protection for foreign products. Still, there is skepticism about the government's actual enforcement.

Finally, the company must invest in and establish its own monitoring system. Its best defense is to strike back rather than relying solely on government enforcement. One computer firm in Taiwan allows consumers to bring in fakes that it then exchanges for the purchase of genuine computers at a discount. Chanel spends more than $1 million a year on security. It goes after counterfeiters by using a computer to keep track of protected names in various countries, the names of suspected counterfeiters, and their near names, such as Channel, Chabel, or Replica No. 5. Another innovative tactic has been employed by Cartier. It opened its own store directly across the street from the store selling fakes, forcing the retailer of the bogus merchandise to stop selling forgeries in return for a sole local distributorship in Mexico.

When the cost of surveillance is high, it may be more desirable to form an association for the purpose of gathering information and evidence. Apple, Lotus, Ashton-Tate, Microsoft, Autodesk, and Word Perfect formed the Business Software Association as an investigative team. The team was successful in providing information to authorities for the arrest of pirates. This strategy reduces costs while increasing cooperation and effectiveness.

GRAY MARKET

A **gray market** exists when a manufacturer ends up with an unintended channel of distribution that performs activities similar to the planned channel—hence the term **parallel distribution.** Through this extra channel, gray market goods move, internationally as well as domestically. In an international context, a gray market product is one imported by an unauthorized party. Products notably affected by this method of operation include watches, cameras, automobiles, perfumes, and electronic goods.

The size of the U.S. gray market has grown steadily and substantially, from 2 percent of imports in 1979 to 20 percent in 1981. The size of the gray market in 1984 was more than $7 billion. Of the $3–4 billion watch market in the United States, $100 million worth of merchandise are gray market goods. The problem is particularly acute for Seiko, because one out of every four Seiko watches imported into the U.S. market is unauthorized.

A gray marketer can acquire goods in two principal ways. One method is to place an order directly with a manufacturer by going through an intermediary, in order to conceal identity and purpose. Another method is to buy the merchandise for immediate shipment on the open market overseas. Asian countries in general and Hong Kong in particular are favorite targets because the wholesale prices there are usually much lower than elsewhere. The importance of the gray market even gets some countries to specialize in handling such goods for the third country, primarily the United States. Germany stimulates the practice by rebating all import duties and local VAT for reexports.[50] Paris' Roissy airport is popular with international brokers because of its duty-free warehouse space for transshipments, which are not taxed either. The airport also allows quick delivery because goods simply move through it without any intermediate delivery.

The existence of the gray market has stimulated a great deal of debate. Complaints are made, and responses to the charges are offered. At least four questions must be asked. First, why does the gray market exist? Second, are gray market goods illegal? Third, do gray marketers perform any useful functions? Fourth, are gray market goods inferior?

Gray marketing of a product within a market often takes place because of the channel structure and margins.[51] A manufacturer who wants to eliminate the potentially profitable gray marketing activity should restructure its pricing and discount policies. Parallel importation of trademarked products occurs for several reasons: (1) gray marketers can easily locate sources of supply because many trademarked products are available in markets throughout the world, (2) price differences among these sources of supply are great enough, and (3) the legal and other barriers to moving goods are low.

Although there are several causes, price differential is the only true reason for the gray market to exist. There is no justification for the existence of the gray market unless prices in at least two domestic markets differ to the extent that even with extra transportation costs reasonable profits can be made. This is a good example of the economic force at work. Gray market goods can be purchased, imported, and resold by an unauthorized distributor at prices lower than those charged by manufacturer-authorized importers/distributors. As a result, identical items can carry two different retail prices.

At one time, whether gray market goods are illegal or not could not be answered with a great degree of certainty. Unlike the black market, which is clearly illegal, the gray market, as its name implies, is neither black nor white—legality is in doubt. For the U.S. market, all U.S.-registered trademark owners are protected under the Tariff Act of 1930 and Section 42 of the Lanham Act. The law protects an independent American trademark owner who invests money in promoting a brand to the extent that the owner becomes identified with that brand in the United States. The protection is granted to protect the mark owner from unfair competition by those seeking to sell the same goods without authorization. If the owner of a U.S. trademark bought distribution rights from an "unrelated" foreign manufacturer, that owner is thus able to obtain an exclusion order from the Customs Service to forbid entry of goods bearing his brand name.

Thus, a trademark must first be registered with the Trademark Office. Second, this trademark must also be registered with the Treasury Department in order to bar unauthorized imports. A mark owner applies by sending a letter to the Commissioner of Customs, along with a fee of $190 and the Trademark Office's certified certificate of registration. Section 526 of the Tariff Act of 1930 requires the U.S. Customs Service to bar from entry imported goods bearing marks registered with the Treasury Department by a U.S. citizen or corporation. Third, only *independent* American firms are entitled to seek this protection. An exclusion order is not granted to foreign companies, and this includes those using their own U.S. subsidiaries to import their goods into the United States. As a result, Canon and Minolta were unable to register their trademarks with the U.S. Customs for the purpose of banning entry of gray market goods.

Confusion abounds because of inconsistent rulings. The International Trade Commission ruled for Duracell in its effort to ban imports of batteries manufactured by its Belgian plant for European consumption, but the International Trade Commission was subsequently overruled by President Reagan. North American Watch, on the other hand, was able to obtain a permanent injunction against Buchwald Seybold Jewelers to bar the sale of Piaget through unauthorized outlets. The court also prohibited 47th St. Photo from importing, buying, and selling illegally imported Piaget watches. Piaget won because the name is trademarked in the United States, and it has a government-authorized exclusion order stating that Piaget, a subsidiary of North American Watch, alone can import. In another case, however, the U.S. Court of Appeals in New York vacated the injunction prohibiting a parallel distributor from selling Japanese cameras to discount houses.

One interesting case involved J. Osawa, which is an authorized worldwide distributor for Bell & Howell: Mamiya. J. Osawa bought Bell & Howell: Mamiya, a U.S. firm distributing Osawa products in the U.S. market. J. Osawa then won a case that blocked Masel Supply, an international dealer based in Hong Kong, from distributing Osawa products in the United States. Masel fought back by arguing that Bell & Howell's exclusion order should never have been issued in the first place because of the lack of independence, as Bell & Howell, Mamiya, and Osawa are financially interlocked.[52]

At present, the law seems more on the side of parallel distributors. The U.S. Court of Appeals ruled that a trademark owner receives no injury to its reputation because there is no confusion about the product's origin and that a manufacturer is capable of labeling and advertising to inform the public of the lack of warranty of gray market merchandise. Courts in other countries often take the same position. Japanese judges repeatedly rule for gray market importers. The British Fair Trading Act allows wholesalers to sell to any retailers, who in turn can buy from any wholesalers. The 9th U.S. Circuit Court of Appeals held that "this country's trademark law does not offer (the manufacturer) a vehicle for establishing a discriminatory pricing scheme simply through the expedient of setting up an American subsidiary with nominal title to its mark."

The U.S. Supreme Court's rulings on two separate cases, though somewhat contradictory, appear to endorse gray marketing. Sharp Electronics Corp. stopped selling calculators to Business Electronics Corp., a Houston discount retailer, after receiving a complaint from a full-price retailer. The Supreme Court ruled that such a cutoff is not an automatic violation of federal antitrust law because Sharp did not explicitly set prices. The high court, arguing that higher prices lead to better service which benefits consumers, held that manufacturers can cut off "free riders" who take unfair advantage of the greater service provided by full-price firms. In a 5-to-4 vote in another case, however, the Supreme Court legitimized the gray market. The Tariff Act of 1930 allows imports to be blocked only when requested by a U.S. firm that is authorized by an unaffiliated foreign trademark owner to distribute its product. Foreign goods can be imported when the foreign and domestic trademark holders are "subject to common ownership or control."[53]

To manufacturers and authorized dealers, parallel distributors are nothing but freeloaders or parasites who take advantage of the legitimate owners' investment and goodwill.[54] Manufacturers also feel that these discounters deceive buyers by implying that gray market goods have the same quality and warranties as items sold through authorized channels.

Gray marketers naturally see the situation differently. They feel that manufacturers have treated them unfairly because "manufacturers will use us, abuse us, and call us names—when they don't need us."[55] Gray marketers accuse manufacturers of not wanting to be price competitive and view manufacturers' distribution restrictions as a smokescreen for absolute price control. Parallel distributors claim to align themselves more with consumers by providing an alternative and legal means of distribution, a means capable of delivering the same goods to consumers at a lower but fair price under the free enterprise system. Some parallel distributors have even sued Mercedes-Benz for restraint of trade, which is a violation of the Sherman and Clayton Acts. As pointed out by them, trademarks are designed to counter fraud rather than limit distribution.

With regard to the charge that gray matter goods are inferior, manufacturers and authorized dealers refuse to service such goods by pointing out that gray market goods are not for U.S. consumption. Therefore, such goods are adulterated, second-rate, or discontinued articles, and consumers may be misled into believing that they receive identical products with U.S. warranties. Gray marketers, however, do not buy this argument. According to them, there is really no proof that the products they handle are inferior. It is inconceivable that a manufacturer would stop a production line just to make another product version for the non-U.S. market. As such, gray market goods are genuine products subject to the same stringent product control. Concerning the inferior warranty and the manufacturer's refusal to service gray market goods under warranty terms, parallel distributors show no concern because they have their own warranty service centers that can provide the same, if not better, service. Their service offices are often closer to the market being served. Gray marketers also point out that they would not survive in the long run if they did not provide service and quality assurance.

The arguments used by both sides are legitimate and have merits. Only one thing is certain: authorized suppliers are adversely affected by parallel distribution. They lose market share as well as control over price. They may have to service goods sold by parallel competitors, and the loss of goodwill follows when consumers are unable to get proper repair.

Manufacturers and authorized suppliers definitely see the need to discourage gray marketing. There are several strategies for this purpose, and each strategy has both merits and problems. Although tracking down offenders costs money, disen-franchisement of offenders is a stock response. This move sends loud signals of commitment to distributors who abide by the terms of the franchise agreement. A one-price-for-all policy can eliminate an important source of arbitrage, but it ig-nores transaction costs and forecloses valid price discrimination opportunities among classes of customers who are buying very different benefits in the same product. An-other strategy is to add distributors (perhaps former gray market distributors) to the network, but this approach may create disputes among current distributors.[56]

There are both reactive and proactive strategies that can be employed (see Tables 5–3 and 5–4). Reactive strategies to combat gray market activity are strategic confrontation, participation, price cutting, supply interference, promotion of gray market product limitations, collaboration, and acquisition. Proactive strategies are product/service differentiation and availability, strategic pricing, dealer development, marketing information systems, long-term image reinforcement, establishing legal precedence, and lobbying.[57]

Certain strategies warrant further attention. When wanting to track the trail of gray market goods, manufacturers can use serial numbers on products and warranty cards to identify those who are involved in unauthorized distribution. There are two problems related to this strategy. First, using special model numbers or identifying

TABLE 5–3 Reactive Strategies to Combat Gray Market Activity

Type of Strategy	Implemented by	Cost of Implementation	Difficulty of Implementation	Does It Curtail Gray Market Activity at Source?	Does It Provide Immediate Relief to Authorized Dealers?	Long-term Effectiveness	Legal Risks to Manufacturers or Dealers	Company Examples
Strategic confrontation	Dealer with manufacturer support	Moderate	Requires planning	No	Relief in the medium term	Effective	Low risk	Creative merchandising by Caterpillar and auto dealers
Participation	Dealer	Low	Not difficult	No	Immediate relief	Potentially damaging reputation of manufacturer	Low risk	Dealers wishing to remain anonymous
Price cutting	Jointly by manufacturer and dealer	Costly	Not difficult	No, if price cutting is temporary	Immediate relief	Effective	Moderate to high risk	Dealers and manufacturers remain anonymous
Supply interference	Either party can engage	Moderate at the wholesale level; high at the retail level	Moderately difficult	No	Immediate relief or slightly delayed	Somewhat effective if at wholesale level; not effective at retail level	Moderate risk at wholesale level; low risk at retail level	IBM, Hewlett-Packard, Lotus Corp, Swatch Watch USA, Charles of the Ritz Group Ltd., Leitz, Inc., NEC Electronics
Promotion of gray market product limitations	Jointly, with manufacturer leadership	Moderate	Not difficult	No	Slightly delayed relief	Somewhat effective	Low risk	Komatsu, Seiko, Rolex, Mercedes-Benz, IBM
Collaboration	Dealer	Low	Requires careful negotiations	No	Immediate relief	Somewhat effective	Very high risk	Dealers wishing to remain anonymous
Acquisition	Dealer	Very costly	Difficult	No	Immediate relief	Effective if other grey market brokers don't creep up	Moderate to high risk	No publicized cases

Note: Company strategies include, but are not limited to, those mentioned here.

Source: Cavusgil and Sikora, "Counter Gray Market Imports," *Columbia Journal of World Business* 23 (Winter 1988): 78

TABLE 5–4 Proactive Strategies to Combat Gray Market Activity

Type of Strategy	Implemented by	Cost of Implementation	Difficulty of Implementation	Does It Curtail Gray Market Activity at Source?	Does It Provide Immediate Relief to Authorized Dealers?	Long-term Effectiveness	Legal Risks to Manufacturers or Dealers	Company Examples
Product service differentiation and availability	Jointly, with manufacturer leadership	Moderate to high	Not difficult	Yes	No; impact felt in medium to long term	Very effective	Very low risk	General Motors, Ford, Porsche, Kodak
Strategic pricing	Manufacturer	Moderate to high	Complex; impact on overall profitability needs monitoring	Yes	Slightly delayed	Very effective	Low risk	Porsche
Dealer development	Jointly, with manufacturer leadership	Moderate to high	Not difficult; requires dealer participation	No	No; impact felt in long term	Very effective	No risk	Caterpillar, Canon
Marketing information system	Jointly, with manufacturer leadership	Moderate to high	Not difficult; requires dealer participation	No	No; impact felt after implementation	Effective	No risk	IBM, Caterpillar, Yamaha, Hitachi, Komatsu, Lotus Development, insurance companies
Long-term image reinforcement	Jointly	Moderate	Not difficult	No	No; impact felt in long term	Effective	No risk	Most manufacturers with strong dealer networks
Establishing legal precedence	Manufacturer	High	Difficult	Yes, if fruitful	No	Uncertain	Low risk	COPIAT, Coleco, Charles of the Ritz Group, Ltd.
Lobbying	Jointly	Moderate	Difficult	Yes, if fruitful	No	Uncertain	Low risk	COPIAT, Duracell, Porsche

Note: Company strategies include, but are not limited to, those mentioned here.

Source: Cavusgil and Sikora, "Counter Gray Market Imports," *Columbia Journal of World Business* 23 (Winter 1988): 82

marks on products increases inventory cost and affects the manufacturer's flexibility in rerouting products quickly and cheaply to markets with a sudden surge in demand. Second, even when unauthorized dealers are identified, there is a question of whether anything can be done to rectify the situation. When Canon stopped shipments to the Netherlands, Dutch dealers simply imported Canon cameras from Germany instead. Furthermore, any overt and concerted action against gray market dealers may be construed as an illegal restraint of domestic and international commerce.

Another strategy involves educating consumers. Minolta ran advertisements to inform consumers that gray market cameras have inferior warranty. This strategy is risky because the message implies that something is wrong with the manufacturer's own product.

The most effective way to eliminate the gray market is to eliminate the cause — price discrepancy between markets. Price matching can put gray retailers out of business overnight. But this method requires the manufacturer to reduce prices in the most profitable markets. Another problem with this strategy is that it adversely affects the product's prestige image and brand value. Certain brands are successful because of the snob and exclusivity appeal, and they must be promoted as luxury articles that must be expensive. In the case of automobiles, price cutting would disrupt both insurance rates and resale values, creating a peculiar situation by making new cars less expensive than used ones.

To resolve some of the problems pointed out above, the strategy of product differentiation should be used. Porsche makes its cars for the U.S. market more powerful and better equipped in order to reflect the higher price. The assumption here is that the differences in features are noticeable and justify the price differential. Multiple brands can also be employed for the same product, with each brand assigned to a certain market. Like other strategies, however, the use of multiple brands affects the economies of scale and increases the production, inventory, and marketing costs.

CONCLUSION

This chapter has examined the various legal issues related to the conduct of international business activities. Because of the variety of legal systems and the different interpretations and enforcement mechanisms, the discussion must, of necessity, be somewhat general. Based on the same rationale, it is impossible for the top management and legal staff at corporate headquarters to completely master the knowledge of foreign law on their own.

To appreciate the problem and subtlety of foreign law, it is clearly necessary to consult local attorneys to find out how a company's operation may be constrained by particular laws. To deal with problems related to bribery, incorporation, counterfeiting, and infringement, the services of local attorneys are essential. Just as essential is the cooperation of the governments of both the host and home countries.

The legal environment is complex and dynamic, with different countries claiming jurisdiction (or a lack of jurisdiction) over business operations. The interaction among domestic, foreign, and international legal environments creates new obstacles as well as new opportunities. A host country may use an MNC's subsidiary in its country as a method of influencing the MNC and subsequently its home country's policies. Likewise, the home country may instruct the parent company to dictate its foreign subsidiary's activities. It is thus not uncommon to find a situation in which the firm is being pressured in opposing directions by two governments. Still the MNC can use its global network to counter such a threat by shifting or threatening to shift the affected operations to other countries, thus lessening the governments' influence on its behavior. It is this countervailing power that allows the company to have a great deal of freedom in adjusting its marketing mix strategies.

It is important to keep in mind that legal contracts and agreements can only be as good as the parties who create them and the countries that enforce them. In Indonesia, legal agreements are more of a reminder of moral obligations and may thus not be enforceable in court in the event of a dispute.[58] Therefore, a contract cannot be used as a substitute for trust and understanding between parties or careful screening of business partners.

QUESTIONS

1. Describe the multiplicity of the legal environments.
2. Distinguish between common law and statute law systems.
3. Cite examples of products that cannot be imported into the United States.
4. Explain how the legal environment can have an impact on an MNC's marketing mix.
5. What is the extraterritorial application of law?
6. Why do MNCs prefer to use corporate subsidiaries in foreign markets?
7. Distinguish among patent, trademark, copyright, and infringement.
8. Distinguish between priority in use and priority in registration.
9. What can trademark owners do to minimize counterfeiting?
10. What are gray market products? Are they legal?

DISCUSSION ASSIGNMENTS AND MINICASES

1. Consider the U.S. laws cited in the chapter. In one way or another, they impede U.S. exports. Do you agree with the rationale of these laws from the perspectives of national security and foreign policies?
2. Given that the various government agencies overseeing U.S. exports of high-tech products have conflicting objectives, what is your proposal to improve the situation?
3. Why is it so difficult for an MNC to deal with bribery?
4. Do gray marketers serve useful marketing functions—for consumers and manufacturers?
5. U.S. Customs regulations require watches to have a small inked stamp on the movement. Seiko thus

charged that the gray market Seiko watches imported into the United States were unfit because the opening for marking harmed dust- and water-resistant seals and contaminated the watch movement.

(a) Do you feel that gray marketers' marking to comply with customs regulations is harmful to the product?

(b) Because Seiko is a popular brand and gray market Seiko watches are carried by a number of discounters and catalog showrooms, what should Seiko do to alleviate the problem of unauthorized imports?

CASE 5–1
ENVIROWALL, INCORPORATED

PATRICK H. MCCASKEY
Millersville University

October 10, 1973

Ben Stone, president of Envirowall, and George Alexander, vice-president of marketing, were dismayed at the news. What had seemed like the start of a good week for Envirowall had turned into a disaster. Envirowall had hoped to begin signing some of the paperwork that would have led to the eventual establishment of a manufacturing facility in a free-trade zone in northern Egypt.

Company Background

Envirowall, Inc., had been formed in the early 1970s. It was the result of a reorganization and repositioning of Jersey Panelwall, a company founded in 1952 in New Jersey. The original company had concentrated on the mass production of standardized panel walls. Panel walls, widely used throughout the commercial/industrial construction industry, are aluminum-encased panels that serve as prefabricated walls. Panel walls are often found in motels and hotels where the upper portion of the panel is made of two or more layers of glass, and the bottom of metal or other facing on the outer side with an interior wall finish on the inner side. During construction the panels are inserted into a supporting framework. In a large building, the use of panel walls will speed the erection process and reduce the overall cost of materials because of their prefabrication off-site.

Jersey Panelwall, historically undercapitalized, experienced particularly tough times during cyclical downswings in the economy. The company's location on the East Coast, together with high transportation costs, had also limited their efforts to serve markets outside of the Middle Atlantic states. Ben Stone had worked for Jersey

Panelwall since finishing his MBA and had risen to the post of plant manager and vice-president of finance. George Alexander, with a master's degree in engineering, had worked in product design and sales. In 1971, at a particularly low point in the company's sales, Ben and George approached the firm's owners and offered to purchase Jersey Panelwall. The negotiations that followed led to the acceptance of long-term notes by the former owners. Ben and George also borrowed against their personal assets, which enabled them to purchase Jersey Panelwall.

The two men set out to redefine the company's products as "environmental control surfaces." They continued to manufacture the standardized panel walls, which provided a relatively steady cash flow, while George began to meet with architects about new products. Through variations in the thickness of the glass and the amount of air space between panels, as well as through judicious use of insulation, their new wall designs could control for sound and temperature. Such applications enabled the panels to be customized to a site's needs and yet still provided for substantial prefabrication savings over on-site construction. Eventually, R&D efforts led to the encasement of thin blinds between two layers of glass. Thus walls could also be produced that controlled light. To better reflect the company's products the company's name was changed to Envirowall, Inc.

Opportunity Knocks

Envirowall continued to suffer from undercapitalization. Although margins were much higher on their new customized products, working capital was already stretched to the limit by their ongoing business in standardized panels. Investor interest was piqued by a demonstration of George's design work in a building at the end of a jet runway—a person could sit watching the nearby jets rev their engines without hearing any of the engine noise. Several investors offered to fund the development of Envirowall's new products, but Ben and George were concerned about maintaining ownership and control.

Then a group of investors offered to fund an international expansion of Envirowall. And they were willing to do so for an interest in profits only! The investors suggested that the ability to control for light and heat would be of very high market value in construction in the Middle East. Also, recent increases in oil revenues had led to extensive growth and construction in the region. Envirowall's panels, if manufactured locally, would be very marketable. An aluminum extrusion plant had recently been built by an American firm in Turkey, and a factory that could produce the needed custom thicknesses of glass was located in Italy. The design of the product was technically complex, utilizing a computer program for analysis. But the actual manufacturing of the panels called only for careful unskilled labor. Egypt provided the ideal location for import of raw materials, labor force, and access to the market. In addition, Egypt had been aggressively pursuing foreign investment and had established a free-trade zone in an appropriate location.

Apparently successful negotiations with the investors and U.S.-based Egyptian representatives rapidly took place.

The Roof Falls In

George got the news. A routine background check by Egyptian representatives had revealed that Ben's father was Jewish. Ben was truly shocked at the investors' concern. His mother's family had been Catholic, and his upbringing had been devoid of any religious practice of either faith. The plans for a manufacturing facility were apparently to be cancelled.

Questions

1. What options are available to Envirowall, Inc., in 1973?
2. Had the year been 1979, after the Camp David Accords between Israel and Egypt, how might events be different?
3. What are your recommendations to Envirowall, Inc.?

CASE 5–2
BRIBERY
A Matter of National Perspective

JEFFREY A. FADIMAN
San Jose State University

U.S. executives may feel unsure, for example, of how to cope with foreign payoffs, especially when requests for "gifts" take on a form that most Americans consider bribes. Although payoffs obviously exist in the United States, they are detested in our culture. In consequence, this type of solicitation may suggest to even the most overseas-oriented executives that U.S. business values are morally superior to those used abroad.

This conviction, if sensed by foreign colleagues, can shatter the most carefully planned commercial venture. My own initial experience with Third World forms of bribery may serve as an example. It occurred in East Africa during the 1970s and began with this request: "Oh, and, Bwana, I would like [a sum of currency was specified] as Zawadi, my gift. And, as we are now friends, for Chai, my tea, an eight band radio, to bring to my home when you visit."

Both *Chai* (tea) and *Zawadi* (gift) can be Swahili terms for "bribe." These particular suggestions were delivered in tones of respect. They came almost as an afterthought, at the conclusion of negotiations in which details of a projected business venture had been settled one by one. I had looked forward to buying my counterpart a final drink, to symbolically complete the deal in American fashion. Instead, after every commercial aspect had been settled, he expected money.

The amount he suggested seemed huge at the time, but it was his specific request for a radio that angered me. Somehow, it added insult to my injury. Outwardly, I simply kept smiling. Inside, my stomach boiled. I was being asked for a bribe, a request my own culture would condemn. I didn't do it and didn't expect it of others. Beyond that, like most Americans, I expect all monetary discussion to precede the signing of contracts. In this instance, although negotiations were complete, I had been asked to pay once more. Once? How often? What were the rules? Where would it stop? My reaction took only moments to formulate. "I'm American," I declared. "I don't pay bribes." Then, I walked away.

That walk was not the longest of my life. It was, however, one of the least commercially productive. For in deciding to conduct international business by American rules, I terminated more than a commercial venture. I also closed a gate that opened into a foreign culture. Beyond it lay the opportunity to do business in a wholly local fashion, as well as an interpersonal relationship that could have anchored my commercial prospects in that region for years to come.

Questions

1. Do you agree with the author's rejection of the request for "gifts"?
2. If you were in a similar situation, how would you handle the situation while considering your own business needs?

Source: Jeffrey A. Fadiman, "Understanding Third World Business Practices," *Northern California Executive Review* 1 (Fall 1986): 17–22

NOTES

1. U.S. Customs Service, *Know Before You Go* (Washington, D.C.: Department of the Treasury, 1991).
2. "Bush Is Setting the Bloodhounds on Beijing," *Business Week,* 23 December 1991, 36.
3. Lucille de Saint-Andre, "Ontario to Halt MO Lottery Sales over Border after Suit by America," *DM News,* 15 April 1986, 1, 54.
4. Pauline Wallace, "Keeping the Books in the PRC: New J-V Accounting Regs and a Domestic Accountancy Law," *East Asian Executive Reports* 7 (August 15, 1985): 7–9.
5. Ray Moseley, "Crawfish Could Be Cajuns' Cash Crop," *Chicago Tribune,* 5 July 1984.
6. "How Cuban Nickel Sneaks into the U.S.," *Business Week,* 31 October 1983, 64.
7. William Tuohy, "West German Brewers Frothing over Threat to 'Purity' Law," *Los Angeles Times,* 2 November 1986.
8. Laurel Wentz, "J&J Plans European Tampon Blitz," *Advertising Age,* 25 September 1989, 14.
9. Ray Moseley, "Oh, Blimey! Shopping on Sunday," *Chicago Tribune,* 4 December 1985.
10. Dean M. Peebles and John K. Ryans, Jr., *Management of International Advertising: A Marketing Approach* (Boston: Allyn & Bacon, 1984).
11. "Misleading Ads Cost Firm $1 million Fine," *Jewelers Circular-Keystone* 154 (August 1983): D.
12. *Investment in Germany* (Peat Marwick, 1982), 62.
13. "U.S. Deregulation Has Common Carriers Slugging It Out," *Business Week,* 24 October 1983: 140, 144.
14. "Economic Trends," *Business Week,* 6 November 1989, 34.
15. Steve Kaufman, "Time to Cut Lawyer Ratio," *San Jose Mercury News,* 16 September 1991.
16. Sandra M. Huszagh, "Exporter Perceptions of the U.S. Regulatory Environment," *Columbia Journal of World Business* 16 (Fall 1981): 22–31.
17. International Trade Administration, *A Summary of U.S. Export Administration Regulations* (Washington, D.C.: U.S. Department of Commerce, 1985), 3–4.
18. Suk H. Kim and Sam Barone, "Is the Foreign Corrupt Practices Act of 1977 a Success or Failure? A Survey of Members of the Academy of International Business," *Journal of International Business Studies* 12 (Winter 1981): 123–26.
19. Mike Langberg, "Court Ruling Could Cost State Millions," *San Jose Mercury News,* 5 December 1990; "State Wins Round in Tax Battle," *San Jose Mercury News,* 11 January 1990.
20. George de Lama, "Deaver's BMW Deal Not First in D.C.," *Chicago Tribune,* 14 March 1985.
21. Suk H. Kim, "On Repealing the Foreign Corrupt Practices Act: Survey and Assessment," *Columbia Journal of World Business* 16 (Fall 1981): 16–21.
22. "The New Trade Act," *Business America,* 24 October 1988, 2–6.
23. John L. Graham, "Foreign Corrupt Practices: A Manager's Guide," *Columbia Journal of World Business* 18 (Fall 1983): 89–94.

24. Sak Onkvisit and John J. Shaw, "International Corporate Bribery: Some Legal, Cultural, Economic, Ethical-Philosophical, and Marketing Consideration," *Journal of Global Marketing* 4 (no. 2, 1991): 5–20.

25. Catherine C. Langlois and Bodo B. Schlegelmilch, "Do Corporate Codes of Ethics Reflect National Character? Evidence from Europe and the United States," *Journal of International Business Studies* 21 (no. 4, 1990): 519–39.

26. "Business Bribes," *The Economist,* 19 November 1988, 21–24.

27. John Siegmund, "Increasing Product Liability Impact on International Commerce," in *Foreign Business Practices,* International Trade Administration (Washington, D.C.: U.S. Department of Commerce, 1981), 99–108.

28. Ibid.

29. Ovidio M. Giberga, "Enforcement of Foreign Arbitral Awards under the U.N. Convention," in *Foreign Business Practices,* International Trade Administration (Washington, D.C.: U.S. Department of Commerce, 1981), 27–37.

30. Stephen D. McCreary, "International Arbitration in Latin America," *Business America,* 11 February 1991, 17–18.

31. *Investment in the United Kingdom* (Peat Marwick, 1985), 42–43.

32. "Now Japan Wants to Conquer Global Finance," *Business Week,* 8 April 1985, 58–59.

33. *Investment in Denmark* (Peat Marwick, 1985), 37–38.

34. *Investment in Japan* (Peat Marwick, 1983), 5.

35. *Investment in South Africa* (Peat Marwick, 1985), 19.

36. "India's Bhopal Suit Could Change All the Rules," *Business Week,* 22 April 1985, 38; "Carbide's Contractor in Bhopal," *Business Week,* 28 January 1985, 48; "Early Steps to a Carbide Settlement," *Business Week,* 28 January 1985, 48.

37. For a discussion regarding why computers are a copyright problem rather than trademark, patent, and/or trade secret problems, see Gunter Hauptman, "Intellectual Property Rights," *International Marketing Review* 4 (Spring 1987): 61–64.

38. "Copyright Protection for Software in Brazil," *Business America,* 5 June 1989, 14.

39. "Report Outlines President's Agenda and Review of U.S. Trade Policy" *Business America,* 26 March 1990, 8–13.

40. See Vincent Travaglini, "Protection of Industrial Property Rights Abroad," in *Foreign Business Practices.* International Trade Administration (Washington, D.C.: U.S. Department of Commerce, 1981), 39–44; William T. Ryan and Doria Bonham-Yeaman, "International Patent Cooperation," *Columbia Journal of World Business* 17 (Winter 1982): 63–66; "New Procedures Will Make It Easier to File and Process an International Patent Application," *Business America,* 23 September 1991, 19–20.

41. "Gene-Splicers Brace for a Brawl over Patents," *Business Week,* 12 March 1984, 28.

42. Robert J. Thomas, "Patent Infringement of Innovations by Foreign Competitors: The Role of the U.S. International Trade Commission," *Journal of Marketing* 53 (October 1989): 63–75.

43. "Is It Time to Reinvent the Patent System?"' *Business Week,* 2 December 1991, 110 ff.

44. Ernest Plock, "International Piracy of Motion Pictures," *Business America,* 25 September 1989, 7.

45. "The Counterfeit Trade," *Business Week,* 16 December 1985, 64–68, 72.

46. Michael G. Harvey and Ilkka A. Ronkainen, "International Counterfeiters: Marketing Success without the Cost and the Risk," *Columbia Journal of World Business* 20 (Fall 1985): 37–45.

47. "New U.S. Customs Anti-Fraud Program," *Jewelers' Circular-Keystone* 154 (November 1983): 70.

48. "How High Tech Foils the Counterfeiters," *Business Week,* 20 May 1985, 119.

49. "Executive Briefing," *East Asian Executive Reports* 7 (August 15, 1985): 5–6; Ronald E. Yates, "South Korea OKs Cigarette Imports, Curb on Patent Pirates," *Chicago Tribune,* 27 July 1986.

50. "Why Camera Prices Are Falling," *Business Week,* 6 September 1982, 61, 64.

51. Dale F. Duhan and Mary Jane Sheffet, "Gray Markets and the Legal Status of Parallel Importation," *Journal of Marketing* 52 (July 1988): 75–83.

52. "Fog Envelops the Law on 'Gray Market' Goods," *Chicago Tribune,* 3 November 1983.

53. See "A Ruling That Doesn't Do Discounters Justice," *Business Week,* 16 May 1988, 146; "A Red-Letter Day for Gray Marketers," *Business Week,* 13 June 1988, 30.

54. Mike Schwartz, "Jewelers Balance Profits against Problems," *Jewelers Circular-Keystone* 155 (February 1984): 186–88 ff.

55. "There's Nothing Black-and-White about the Gray Market," *Business Week,* 7 November 1988, 172–76.

56. Frank V. Cespedes, E. Raymond Corey, and V. Kasturi Rangan, "Gray Markets: Causes and Cures," *Harvard Business Review* 88 (July-August 1988): 75–82.

57. S. Tamer Cavusgil and Ed Sikora, "How Multinationals Can Counter Gray Market Imports," *Columbia Journal of World Business* 23 (Winter 1988): 75–85.

58. Market Expansion Division, *Foreign Regulations Affecting U.S. Textile/Apparel Exports* (Washington, D.C.: International Trade Commission, 1986), 78.

People are tyrannized by their culture.

Edward T. Hall, anthropologist

Culture

6

CHAPTER OUTLINE

CULTURE AND ITS CHARACTERISTICS

INFLUENCE OF CULTURE ON CONSUMPTION

INFLUENCE OF CULTURE ON THINKING PROCESSES

INFLUENCE OF CULTURE ON COMMUNICATION PROCESSES

CULTURAL UNIVERSALS

CULTURAL SIMILARITIES: An Illusion

COMMUNICATION THROUGH VERBAL LANGUAGE

COMMUNICATION THROUGH NONVERBAL LANGUAGE

AMERICAN CULTURE

JAPANESE CULTURE

SUBCULTURE

CASE 6–1: *Cultural Considerations in International Marketing: A Classroom Simulation*

CASE 6–2: *Beneath Hijab: Marketing to the Veiled Women of Iran*

MARKETING ILLUSTRATION
Innocent Abroad

One major reason attributed for the worldwide success of Singer is its acute respect for local customs. Yet this very successful international trader runs into unexpected problems from time to time. In one Islamic country, it "mohammedanized" its store mannequins in great detail only to be surprised by a mob shouting and smashing its display windows. Singer finally realized that it had made a grave mistake because the mannequins were not wearing veils.

One of Singer's great challenges was Japan, where the traditional kimono is sewn loosely with simple basting stitches for removal and replacement on washday. Because Singer machines at the time made only short, tight, and permanent stitches, the company had to develop a new machine that sewed a quarter-inch basting stitch. But the Japanese refused to trust the machine with their kimonos. The company had more success in promoting the acceptance of Western-style dresses. It owed this success to careful planning. The scheme called for Singer to start a sewing school in Tokyo for 1,000 day pupils and 500 boarders. The plan was implemented and was successful, and the company was able to get Western-style clothing to coexist with, but not to replace, the kimono.

Source: David P. Cleary, *Great American Brands* (New York: Fairchild, 1981), 275.

Singer's experience illustrates the importance of recognizing and appreciating varying cultures. Culture plays a significant role in influencing consumer perception, which in turn influences preference and purchase. The Singer case should serve to remind others that a good marketing plan can easily go awry when it clashes with tradition. A marketing mix can be effective only as long as it is relevant to a given culture. One should expect that a product may have to be modified, that a new distribution channel may have to be found, or that a new promotional strategy may have to be considered.

What is more surprising than the blunders that occur are the underlying causes for these mistakes. The most fundamental problem appears to be the indifferent attitude of many American firms toward international markets. The firms often enter foreign markets with a complete disregard for the customs and traditions there—something they would never do at home. In marked contrast, many Japanese firms have been highly successful in the United States and elsewhere because of their keen awareness and understanding of the local culture.

In order to develop an appreciation for the role of culture in society as well as the marketing implications of culture, this chapter will explore the following: (1) what culture is, (2) what its characteristics are, and (3) how culture affects consumer behavior. The varying methods of developing cross-cultural communication, verbally and otherwise, are discussed. To lend an understanding of how cultures vary, the chapter will compare American culture with that of Japan. Finally, because population homogeneity within a country is an exception rather than a rule, it is necessary to examine the relevance and bases of subcultural groups.

CULTURE AND ITS CHARACTERISTICS

Culture, an inclusive term, can be conceptualized in many different ways. Not surprisingly, the concept is often accompanied by numerous definitions. One study found that there are at least 164 definitions of culture.[1] Another research effort identified some 241 definitions. In any case, a good basic definition of concept is that **culture** is a set of traditional beliefs and values that are transmitted and shared in a given society. Culture is also the total way of life and thinking patterns that are passed from generation to generation. Culture means many things to many people because the concept encompasses norms, values, customs, art, and mores.

Culture is **prescriptive.** It prescribes the kinds of behavior considered acceptable in the society. As illustrated by Wacoal's early difficulties in Japan, certain behavior may not be acceptable. When Wacoal scheduled its first fashion show in 1952 for its line of ladies' lingerie, the company had to hire bar-room strippers because professional models refused to appear in the company's skimpy undergarments. Also, to maintain a Japanese norm of decency, Wacoal barred all men—even its own president—from attending the show.[2]

The prescriptive characteristic of culture simplifies a consumer's decision-making process by limiting product choices to those which are socially acceptable. This same characteristic creates problems for those products not in tune with the consumer's cultural beliefs. Smoking, for instance, was once socially acceptable behavior, but recently it has become more and more undesirable—both socially and medically.

Culture is **socially shared.** Culture, out of necessity, must be based on social interaction and creation. It cannot exist by itself. It must be shared by members of a society, thus acting to reinforce culture's prescriptive nature. For example, Chinese parents at one time shared the preference of wanting their girl children to have small feet. Large feet, viewed as characteristic of peasants and low-class people, were scorned. As a result, parents from the upper class bound a daughter's feet tightly so that her feet would not grow large. It did not matter to the parents that the daughter would grow up having difficulty walking about with distortedly small feet.

Culture **facilitates communication.** One useful function provided by culture is to facilitate communication. Culture usually imposes common habits of thought and feeling among people. Thus, within a given group culture makes it easier for people to communicate with one another. But culture may also impede communication across groups because of a lack of shared common cultural values. This is one reason why a standardized advertisement (i.e., a global advertisement prepared for many countries) may have difficulty communicating with consumers in foreign countries. How marketing efforts interact with a culture determines the success or failure of a product. Advertising and promotion require special attention because they play a key role in communicating product concepts and benefits to the target segment.[3]

Culture is **learned.** Culture is not inherited genetically—it must be learned and acquired. **Socialization** or **enculturation** occurs when a person absorbs or learns the culture in which he or she is raised. In contrast, if a person learns the culture of a society other than the one in which he or she was raised, the process of **acculturation** occurs. The ability to learn culture makes it possible for people to absorb new cultural trends. Asian countries have complained, sometimes bitterly, about how their cultures are being contaminated by rock-and-roll music and Western sexual and social permissiveness—foreign elements they consider undesirable and harmful. South Korea has been unsuccessful in banning rock-and-roll music, as was the former Soviet Union.

Culture is **subjective.** People in different cultures often have different ideas about the same object. What is acceptable in one culture may not necessarily be so in another. In this regard, culture is both unique and arbitrary. As a result, the same phenomenon appearing in different cultures can be interpreted in very different manners. It is customary in many cultures for a bridegroom's family to offer a dowry to a bride's family, either for the bride's future security or to compensate her family for raising her. In India, an entirely different set of cultural rules apply. A woman there is viewed as a burden to both her own family and her husband-to-be. When she marries, her family must offer a dowry to the bridegroom. Some men have been so unhappy with what they perceive as an inadequate dowry that they have set their new wives on fire. The problem is so acute that the government has come forward to condemn the practice publicly.

Culture is **enduring.** Because culture is shared and passed along from generation to generation, it is relatively stable and somewhat permanent. Old habits are hard to break, and a people tends to maintain its own heritage in spite of a continuously changing world. This explains why India and China, despite severe overcrowding, have a great deal of difficulty with birth control. The Chinese view a large family as a blessing and assume that children will take care of parents when grown old. They also have a great desire to have sons in order to preserve their family name. The modern Chinese government's mandate of one child per family has resulted in numerous deaths of firstborn daughters. The suspicion is that parents murder their daughters in order to circumvent the quota—they want to be able to have another child, hoping for a son.

In India, poverty can make some people very cruel and cold-hearted. Some parents there desire to have many children so that the kids can be sent out to beg for money. Like in China, children are perceived to be a form of "social security" for parents.

Because of the enduring aspect of culture, it is easier for marketers to make products consistent with the culture in which the products are marketed rather than to try to change the culture to fit the products. One U.S. firm took its domestically successful mixes for fancy, iced cakes to the British market. Because of an enduring preference there for dry sponge cake—served with tea rather than as a dessert after dinner—the company endured five years of an unsuccessful venture before giving up.

Culture is **cumulative.** Culture is based on hundreds or even thousands of years of accumulated circumstances. Each generation adds something of its own to the culture before passing the heritage on to the next generation. Therefore, culture tends to become broader based over time, because new ideas are incorporated and become a part of the culture. Of course, during the process, some old ideas are also discarded.

Culture is **dynamic.** Culture is passed along from generation to generation, but one should not assume that culture is static and immune to change. Far from being the case, culture is constantly changing—it adapts itself to new situations and new sources of knowledge. Length of hair serves as a good example of cultural change. In the United States, long hair for men was once the usual norm. Short hair became quite popular in the 1950s before going out of style in the early 1960s. In the 1980s, it has become very popular for men to have short hair again.

The dynamic aspect of culture can make some products obsolete and can usher in new buying habits. Japanese tastes, for example, have been changing from a diet of fish and rice to an accommodation of meat and dairy products.

Because values and ideas change over time, marketers must keep up with changes in tastes in order to capitalize on new cultural trends. In England, the beer market is undergoing significant change, and Anheuser-Busch fully intends to benefit from these changes. The decline in the sale of British ales and dark beers served at room temperature is being matched by an increase in the popularity of lighter, cleaner Continental and American beers, notably Carling Black Label, Heineken, Skol, Carlsbergs, and Fosters from Continental Europe and Australia. In addition to these changing tastes, changes in lifestyle have also offered a helping hand to Anheuser-Busch. The average beer-drinking Briton now consumes more beer out of cans at home, thus reducing the attractiveness of pubs as a gathering place to drink beer.

INFLUENCE OF CULTURE ON CONSUMPTION

Consumption patterns, living styles, and the priority of needs are all dictated by culture. Culture prescribes the manner in which people satisfy their desires. Not surprisingly, consumption habits vary greatly. The consumption of beef provides a good illustration. Some Thai and Chinese do not consume beef at all, believing that it is improper to eat cattle that work on farms, thus helping to provide foods such as rice and vegetables. In Japan, the per capita annual consumption of beef has increased to 11 pounds, still a very small amount when compared to the more than 100 pounds consumed per capita in the United States and Argentina.

The eating habits of many peoples seem exotic to Americans. The Chinese eat such things as fish stomachs and bird's nest soup (made from bird's saliva). The Japanese eat uncooked seafood, and the Iraqis eat dried, salted locusts as snacks while drinking. Although such eating habits may seem repulsive to Americans and Europeans, consumption habits in the West are just as strange to foreigners. The French eat snails. Americans and Europeans use honey (bee expectorate, or bee spit) and blue cheese or Roquefort salad dressing, which is made with a strong cheese with bluish mold. No society has a monopoly on unusual eating habits when comparisons are made among various societies.

Food preferences are affected by geography, nutrition, and economics.[4] Chinese adults lack lactase, which is an enzyme necessary for the digestion of lactose (the sugar in milk), making them unable to digest milk. This is the problem also for those of Japanese, African (south of the Sahara), and southern European descent. Generally, people of northern European descent can drink unfermented milk. For those cultures with inadequate supplies of such domesticated animals as cattle, sheep, goats, and pigs to provide animal protein and fat, insects can offer the same benefits efficiently. If you are what you eat, the French then are part horse, the Japanese part grasshopper, and the Greek part goat.

Food preparation methods are also dictated by cultural preferences. Asian consumers prefer their chicken broiled or boiled rather than fried. Consequently, the Chinese in Hong Kong found American-style fried chicken foreign and distasteful.

Not only does culture influence what is to be consumed, but it also affects what should not be purchased. Muslims do not purchase chickens unless they have been halalled, and like Jews, no consumption of pork is allowed. They also do not smoke or use alcoholic beverages, a habit shared by some strict Protestants. Although these restrictions exist in Islamic countries, the situation is not entirely without market possibilities. The marketing challenge is to create a product that fits the needs of a particular culture. Moussy, a nonalcoholic beer from Switzerland, is a product that was seen as being able to overcome the religious restriction of consuming alcoholic beverages. By conforming to the religious beliefs of Islam, Moussy has become so successful in Saudi Arabia that half of its worldwide sales are accounted for in that country.

INFLUENCE OF CULTURE ON THINKING PROCESSES

In addition to consumption habits, thinking processes are also affected by culture. When traveling overseas, it is virtually impossible for a person to observe foreign cultures without making reference, perhaps unconsciously, back to personal cultural values. This phenomenon is known as the **self-reference criterion (SRC).** Because of the effect of the SRC, the individual tends to be bound by his or her own cultural assumptions. It is thus important for the traveler to recognize how perception of overseas events can be distorted by the effects of the SRC.

Animals provide a good illustration of the impact of the SRC on the thinking processes. Americans and Europeans commonly treat dogs as family members, addressing the animals affectionately and even letting dogs sleep on family members' beds. Arabs, however, view dogs as filthy animals. Some in the Far East go so far as to cook and eat dogs—a consumption habit viewed as revolting and compared to cannibalism by Americans. Hindus, in contrast, revere cows and do not understand how Americans can eat beef—especially in large quantity.

In order to investigate a phenomenon in another country, a researcher or marketing manager must attempt to eliminate the SRC effect. The presence of the SRC, if not controlled, can invalidate the results of a research study. Lee suggests a multistep approach to remove the undue influence of the SRC. First, the problem should be defined in terms of the culture of the researcher's home country. Second, the same problem is defined again, except that it is defined in terms of the cultural norms of the host country. Third, a comparison is made of the two cultural composites. Any difference noted between the composites indicates an existence of the SRC, necessitating another look at the problem with the SRC removed.[5]

The value of this approach is that it forced the manager/researcher to make objective evaluations about assumptions. This, in turn, compels the marketing manager to examine the applicability of initial assumptions in terms of another culture. By being aware of the influence of the SRC, a manager can isolate the SRC, making it possible to redefine a problem from a more neutral viewpoint. An awareness of this undue influence should sensitize a person to think in terms of the host country's culture. The end result should be that the manager thinks in international terms and not in terms of his or her native culture.

Although African, Arab, and Asian business methods have endured for centuries, most American firms react to those methods in ethnocentric terms and prefer to conduct business along familiar Western lines. Project heads launching a venture in a less developed country should consider the following guidelines: (1) resist the tendency to conduct business immediately on landing, (2) resist the tendency to conduct business at all times, (3) consider doing favors as a business tool to generate allies, (4) contact, cultivate, and conduct fieldwork among at least one sample clientele to serve as an initial testing center for the firm's product, (5) introduce the product line into the sample group by local forms of cause-related marketing, and (6) extend product acceptance beyond the sample clientele into related market segments.[6]

An awareness of the influence of the SRC is valuable because such awareness can help a manager to prevent a transfer of personal cultural norms on a wholesale basis to an overseas market. This awareness should make a manager more customer-oriented, and the marketing strategy developed will more likely reflect true market needs. The marketing of fire insurance can be used to explain this rationale. For American consumers, the purchase of fire insurance is a sensible and practical acquisition. But it is difficult to encourage Brazilian consumers to purchase insurance because of superstition. In Brazil, many consumers hold the belief that by purchasing fire insurance they may somehow encourage a fire to occur. Therefore, they do not want to think about such an occurrence and avoid the discussion and purchase of fire insurance.

INFLUENCE OF CULTURE ON COMMUNICATION PROCESSES

A country may be classified as either a high-context culture or a low-context culture.[7] The context of a culture is either high or low in terms of in-depth background information. This classification provides an understanding of various cultural orientations and explains how communication is conveyed and perceived. North America and northern Europe (e.g., Germany, Switzerland, and Scandinavian countries) are examples of **low-context cultures.** In these types of society, messages are explicit and clear in the sense that actual words are used to convey the main part of information in communication. The words and their meanings, being independent entities, can be separated from the context in which they occur. What is important, then, is what is said, not how it is said and not the environment within which it is said.

Japan, France, Spain, Italy, Asia, Africa, and the Middle Eastern Arab nations, in contrast, are **high-context cultures.** In such cultures, the communication may be indirect, and the expressive manner in which the message is delivered becomes critical. Because the verbal part (i.e., words) does not carry most of the information, much of the information is contained in the nonverbal part of the message to be communicated. The context of communication is high because it includes a great deal of additional information, such as the message sender's values, position, background, and associations in the society. As such, the message cannot be understood without its context. One's individual environment (i.e., physical setting and social circumstances) determines what one says and how one is interpreted by others. This type of communication emphasizes one's character and words as determinants of one's integrity, making it possible for businesspersons to come to terms without detailed legal paperwork.

It is also possible that a subcontext can exist in a broader but different context of the culture. The United States, for example, is a low-context culture that consists of several subcultures operating within the framework of a much higher context. Therefore, communication strategy requires a proper adjustment if it is to be effective.

One common advertising method used by U.S. advertisers is to present a TV commercial as an illustrated lecture. In this low-context method, a product is discussed in the absence of its natural setting. Such a message is not easily understood in high-context cultures because of the omission of essential contextual detail.[8] One study tested six European commercials on five cultural groups, ranging from the high-context Asian group to the low-context Swedish group, and the evidence supported Wells' proposition. Compared to a low-context culture, high-context cultures perceive nonverbal communications elements as being more informative.[9]

According to Hall, cultures also vary in the manner by which information processing occurs.[10] Some cultures handle information in a direct, linear fashion and are thus **monochronic** in nature. Schedules, punctuality, and a sense that time forms a purposeful straight line are indicators of such cultures. Being monochronic, however, is a matter of degree. Although the Germans, Swiss, and Americans are all monochronic cultures, the Americans are generally more monochronic than most other societies, and their fast tempo and demand for instant responses are often viewed as pushy and impatient.

Other cultures are relatively **polychronic** in the sense that people work on several fronts simultaneously instead of pursuing a single task. Both Japanese and Hispanic cultures are good examples of a polychronic culture. The Japanese are often misunderstood and accused by Westerners of not volunteering detailed information. The truth of the matter is that the Japanese do not want to be too direct because by saying things directly they may be perceived as being insensitive and offensive. The Japanese are also not comfortable in getting right down to substantive business without first becoming familiar with the other business party. For them, it is premature to discuss business matters seriously without first establishing a personal relationship. Furthermore, American businesspersons consider the failure of the Japanese to make eye contact as a sign of rudeness, whereas the Japanese do not want to look each other in the eye because eye contact is an act of confrontation and aggression.

The cultural context and the manner in which the processing of information occurs can be combined to develop a more precise description of how communication takes place in a particular country. Germany, for example, is a monochronic and low-context culture. France, in comparison, is a polychronic and high-context culture. A low-context German may insult a high context French counterpart by giving too much information about what is already known. Or a low-context German becomes upset when he feels that he does not get enough details from the high-context Frenchman.

CULTURAL UNIVERSALS

The failure to consider cultural universals results in a tendency to overemphasize cultural differences. As human beings, regardless of race or religion, all have similar basic needs, it is reasonable to expect that certain cultural traits transcend national boundaries. For example, people everywhere have a love for music and a need for fun. Some of the cultural universals identified by Murdock are athletic sports, bodily adornment, calendar, cooking, courtship, dancing, dream interpretation, education, food taboos, inheritance rules, joking, kin groups, status differentiation, and superstition.[11]

According to a projection made by Backer Spielvogel Bates Worldwide, materialism is likely to continue to be a driving force in U.S. society as well as other major markets in the year 2000.[12]

Because of the universality of basic desires, some products can be marketed overseas with little modification. The need to have fun, for instance, makes it natural for people everywhere to accept video games such as Pac-Man. Likewise, culture is not a barrier to computer software dealing with engineering and scientific applications that manipulate schematic drawings and numbers rather than words. The homogeneous desire for beauty and diamonds also makes it possible to promote diamonds in basically the same way worldwide. When Yamazaki-Nabisco was considering selling Oreo cookies in Japan, many managers felt that no Japanese would eat "black food." The company introduced Oreo cookies in 1987, and it has become the number one cookie in the country.[13]

Note that shared values do not necessarily mean shared or identical behavior. The manner of expressing culturally universal traits still varies across countries. Music is a cultural universal, but that does not mean that the same kind of music is acceptable everywhere. Because musical tastes are not internationally uniform, the type of music used must be varied to appeal to a particular country. Likewise, all peoples admire the beautiful, but cultural definitions of beauty vary greatly.

Some cultural values remain unchanged over time. For products appealing to basic generic values, certain successful products need not be changed, in spite of the changing environment. Such is the case with *Reader's Digest*'s extraordinary success for more than three-quarters of a century. In the face of violent shifts in lifestyles and cultural tastes around the world, *Reader's Digest* magazine, founded in 1922, has maintained a bland, low-brow editorial formula. It continues to tell people that laughter is the best medicine, that difficulties can be overcome, and that the world is a good, though not perfect, place. The magazine provides people with spirit-lifting stories. These cultural traits are also quite universal, as evidenced by the fact that some 100 million people read the magazine's thirty-nine editions in fifteen languages. Its success should remind the marketer that, while cultural values may be constantly shifting, there are basic or generic values that are universal and constant. For some products, that market will always be there as a viable alternative in a fast-changing world.

CULTURAL SIMILARITIES: AN ILLUSION

Cultural universals, when they exist, should not be interpreted as meaning that the two cultures are very much alike. Too often, cultural similarities at first glance may in fact be just an illusion. A marketer must thus guard against taking any market for granted. For many Americans, Canada is merely a northward extension of the United States, a notion resented by most Canadians, who resist cultural absorption by the United States.

The perceived cultural difference, real or imagined, explains not only why some American products have been unsuccessful in Canada but also why some Canadian products have failed in the U.S. market. Repeated campaigns to sell the electric tea kettle, an indispensable part of Canadian homelife, in the U.S. market have yielded less than a 1 percent market penetration.[14] American consumers view the electric kettle as a strange device that might spoil their coffee. Likewise, Vegemite is the closest thing to Australia's national food, with 90 percent of Australian homes having it. Yet this black yeast spread has never been able to find its way into the American consumer's diet.

COMMUNICATION THROUGH VERBAL LANGUAGE

Language is a significant part of culture, and communication is impossible without it. The problem is that there are several thousand languages. Indonesia alone has 250 languages. In China, even though the written language is uniform, there are hundreds of local dialects. Putonghua ("common speech") or Mandarin, the national language, is used throughout the country. Unlike the English language, which is relatively straightforward, many languages are quite subtle. The Italian language allows several different ways of addressing someone that show a speaker's position and feelings. Likewise, the Japanese language has literary and conversational styles, male and female styles, young and old styles, and various degrees of politeness.

An observation made by Berlo explains in accurate terms the importance and influence of language. Because languages affect thought, "systems that employ different codes may well employ different methods of thought. A German's language is different from an American's language. It may follow that his methods of thinking are also different."[15] An incident that occurred during the 1984 Olympics illustrates this point. Some American female gymnasts had received relatively low scores from Eastern European judges. Bela Karolyi, a defector from Rumania who was coach of the eventual gold medal winner at the games, was so angry that he wanted those judges to be sent to the "farm." Many Americans were puzzled by his comment, as farmers are respected members of the U.S. society. But in many other countries, farmers are viewed as uneducated and unsophisticated peasants. With that cultural difference in mind, it is understandable that one farm equipment company's advertising campaign based on the testimonials of small farmers angered dealers in Europe.

A marketer must be careful even when the same language is used in two or more markets, such as Great Britain, and the United States. Although the two countries have a great deal in common, there are many differences important to a marketers. As noted by Oscar Wilde, "the English have really everything in common with the Americans except of course language."

There are significant differences between American English and British English. Different words are used to indicate the same thing, as shown in Table 6–1. For the American *apartment* and *elevator,* the British use *flat* and *lift,* respectively. People use *subways* in New York, but they use the *underground* in London.

TABLE 6–1 American English vs. British English

American	English	American	English
aisle	gangway	mezzanine	dress circle
baby carriage	pram	molasses	black treacle
bacon	gammon	monkey wrench	spanner
baggage	left luggage	moving van	pantechnicon
room	office	mutual fund	unit trust
balcony	gallery	newspaper stand	news agent
band-aid	elastoplast	one-way ticket	single ticket
bobby pin	kirby grip	orchestra seats	stalls
bookie	turf accountant	person-to-person	personal call
checkers	draughts	call	
chicory	endive	phone booth	telephone kiosk
coffee with or	black or white	pier	quay
without cream	coffee	popsicle	iced lolly
dessert	sweet	radio	wireless
diaper	nappy	raincoat	mackintosh
druggist	chemist	raisin	sultana
eggplant	aubergine	round-trip ticket	return ticket
electric cord	flex	Scotch tape	sellotape
elevator	lift	second floor	first floor
endive	chicory	sidewalk	pavement
flashlight	torch	soft rolls	baps
french-fried	chips	subway	underground
potatoes		superhighway	motorway
grade crossing	level crossing	suspenders	garters
installment buying	hire purchase	thumb tack	drawing pin
kerosene	paraffin	tic-tac-toe	naughts and
lady fingers	boudoir biscuits		crosses
lawyer	solicitor	toilet	W.C. or cloakroom
lease (rent)	let	trolley car	tram
leash	lead	truck	lorry
line	queue	two weeks	fortnight
liquor store	wine merchant	underwear	smalls
long distance call	trunk call	vacation	holiday
lost and found	lost property	vanilla pudding	blancmange
mail box	pillar box	yellow turnips	swedes

Citizens of the two countries may sometimes use the same word or phrase when they mean different things. A *billion* is a thousand million to the Americans but a million million to the Britons. When the Americans *table a motion,* the item is set aside without further discussion. But the British take this expression to mean that the item should be placed on the agenda for immediate discussion. A movie that *went like a bomb* was a success to the Briton but a failure to the American. An American *vacuums* the carpet, but the Briton *hoovers* or *bissels* it instead.

Even when the same word with the same meaning is used, the spelling may vary. For example, *color* and *theater* are used in the United States, whereas *colour* and *theatre* are used in Great Britain. The pronunciation can also be different, especially with the letter Z, which is pronounced as *zee* in the United States but *zed* in the United Kingdom. An American brand name such as E-Z is puzzling in England.

Such problems are not unique to the English language. When an American airline promoted its "rendezvous lounges" in Brazil, it did not realize that, in Portuguese, it was advertising a room for rent for lovemaking. Usage and meanings within the Spanish language also vary from one Spanish-speaking country to another. One can take a language for granted but only at one's peril.

Language differences often necessitate marketing strategy modification. Singer provides its salespeople with instruction books printed in more than fifty languages. Some of these books consist entirely of pictures. In many cases, more than a basic translation of the manual is needed. Computer marketers, for example, have to change software and hardware processes for use in a foreign language. One reason that Japanese computer makers still have difficulty breaking into the U.S. market is because of the problems encountered in exporting software written in Japanese. Accounting and financial programs must be completely rewritten because accounting rules and financial reporting systems vary greatly from country to country. Apple lost market share in Japan because it only had a U.S. model available in Japan with very little software adapted to the Japanese language. To overcome the problem, Apple IIe now comes in eighteen different national versions—each with a keyboard that displays a particular alphabet.

Less obvious than the variations in accounting and financial rules are the writing and reading rules in different countries. Americans take it for granted that when they read and write they should begin from left to right, one row at a time before going to the next lower row. The Chinese system requires the reader to go from top to bottom, one column at a time rather than row by row. The Chinese also read from right to left (i.e., they start with the column nearest to the right of the page before moving to the next column on the left). These differences usually require a product to be adjusted to some extent. Computer makers have also found that they must change their system for Arab countries, so that the computer can produce a printout reading from right to left.

Several studies have confirmed a widely held belief that the U.S. population in general has very low foreign language fluency. According to one study, "none of the 44 schools offering MBAs require foreign language fluency of the students."[16] Not surprisingly, many American managers believe that it is not necessary for them to learn another language. They prefer to believe that English is the universal language of business communication. Although this assumption is partially true, it can cause difficulty in carrying out business in parts of the world where English is not spoken.

Many U.S. firms complain that the Japanese market is closed to them, but Japanese officials and businessmen see the situation in another way. They feel that U.S. firms are at fault because U.S. managers do not try hard enough to understand the Japanese market. Japanese managers make a conscientious effort to learn the English language, but very few Europeans and Americans reciprocate. Western managers have difficulty in communicating with Japanese suppliers, distributors, and customers. In addition, such managers cannot lobby effectively for their causes in Japan.

Exhibit 6-1 describes language learning systems. Not all individuals can master a foreign language. There are, however, a few indicators that can predict a person's

Perestroika.

Sony's language learning systems are so flexible, they can be restructured to fit all your changing needs.

Like you, Sony believes that teaching and learning is an evolutionary process. That's why we build every one of our language learning systems to grow as your needs change. The modularity of design allows for easy adaptation as new technology and teaching techniques emerge.

With the technology explosion of the past decade, educators have been deluged with complicated systems to help them teach. Sony's philosophy has been to cut through the technology to bring the language instructor an advanced, user friendly system. Attention to detail and the integration of state-of-the-art technology allow Sony to offer the best value in learning labs. The new multimedia capabilities of the LLC-9000 and the digital audio ZL-10 language learning labs prove that Sony listens to your requirements and offers solutions.

"Perestroika" means "restructuring." The sweeping changes of world events will affect how we think and communicate for years to come. Sony will provide you with the best language learning systems now, next year, and well into the 21st century.

1-800-326-SONY

SONY.

Audio Visual Products
Business and Professional Group
A Division of Sony Corporation of America
10833 Valley View Street
Cypress, California 90630

EXHIBIT 6–1 Language learning systems

Source: Courtesy of Sony Corp.

ability to succeed at learning a language.[17] First, if a person has already learned one foreign language, the chances are good that another language can be mastered. It has been found that linguistic aptitude is quite constant across languages and that intelligence does not ensure success in learning a language. What seems to be important is self-confidence, as well as a disinclination to take oneself too seriously when making mistakes.

Flexibility and spontaneity also help, but being too analytical is not a positive attribute. Some individuals become discouraged when they want to find the reason why the German language puts its verb at the end of the sentence or why some letters in certain French words are silent. Patience is an absolute necessity, because months of repetition are needed before a payoff occurs. The language student should also have a long attention span because focusing attention for long periods of time is necessary to learn effectively.

Finally, one's background has a great deal to do with one's learning ability. Engineers, teachers, and Southerners, for various reasons, usually encounter learning difficulties in languages. Southerners are perhaps not sufficiently cosmopolitan because of their lack of exposure to immigrant groups. Engineers are likely too logical. Teachers may develop too strong a habit of giving out knowledge, making it difficult to accept new knowledge.

If a person wants to learn a foreign language, the person must attempt to become internationalized in the sense of thinking multilingually or thinking like a foreigner in that foreign language. In other words, one should be able to think in the foreign language without going through a translation process first.

When a marketing campaign is exported, careful translation is needed. It is critical to keep in mind that the thought, not the words, must be translated. Examples of careless translation abound. In order to stop people from wearing shorts into the court, a sign was installed outside Courtroom G in the city of Bakersfield in California. To many Hispanics, the *Se Prohiben...Calzon Corts...en la Sala de Corte* sign told them that "women's panties...prohibited in the courtroom."[18] The San Jose Public Library's huge multilingual welcome banner costs $20,000 and contains 27 languages. *Tuloy Po Kayo* means "welcome" in Tagalog, but what appeared on the banner was *Tuley Po Kayo*, which sounded like *circumcised*. Six more errors (including one in French) were later discovered. Both the Swedish and Dutch greetings were misspelled. It cost more than $9,000 to correct these mistakes. A St. Paul, Minnesota, liquor distributor used billboards to bid a friendly welcome to Mikhail Gorbachev. Instead of raising a toast to the Soviet leader's health (*Za Zdorové*) as intended, a one-letter error in the Russian phrase *Na Zdorové* implied either "sneezing is not a sign of illness" or "let this food be healthy for you."

Because differences in language go beyond differences in words, it is ineffective to have a word-for-word translation. Although dictionaries may help a person understand foreign words, dictionaries cannot include subtle differences in syntax, grammar, pitch, and pronunciation. As a result, advertising copy may have to be interpreted rather than translated.

Another practice that perplexes non-Americans is the system of dating used in the United States. Americans are taught to begin the date with the month, followed by the day and year. For much of the world, it is more logical to start out with the smallest unit (i.e., day). Therefore, a date written as February 3, 1994 by an American seems illogical to foreigners, who find more sense in 3 February 1994.

The confusion increases significantly when the written date consists solely of numerals. Consider 2/3/1994. Americans read that date as February 3, 1994, whereas others read that date as the second day of the third month (i.e., March) in the year 1994. One can easily imagine the difficulty that may result through a misunderstanding between an American firm and its foreign customer about delivery and payment dates.

When communicating with customers, it cannot be emphasized strongly enough that there is no place for slang, idioms, and unfamiliar phrases in business correspondence or negotiation. One American firm lost a contract with a Japanese company because of the remark "this is a whole new ball game."[19] The Japanese, who do not think of business as a game, cancelled the deal. There are many other words or phrases that when translated literally can be misunderstood or insulting. It is wise to avoid such American phrases as "call it a day," "big shot," "lay your cards on the table.," and "bottom line."

Safe rules of thumb in international communication are

When in doubt, overpunctuate.

Keep ideas separate, making only one point at a time.

Confirm discussion in writing.

Write down all figures using the style of the person you are talking to.

Adjust your English to the level of your foreign counterpart.

Use visual aids whenever possible.

Avoid technical, sports, and business jargon.

To put it another way, "Speak to the rest of the world as if you were answering a slightly deaf, very rich old auntie who just asked you how much to leave you in her will."[20]

COMMUNICATION THROUGH NONVERBAL LANGUAGE

People do not always communicate solely through the spoken or written word. Knowingly or not, people routinely communicate with one another in a nonverbal manner (see Exhibit 6–2). Body language includes movement, appearance, dress, facial expressions, gestures, posture, use of silence, use of touch, timing, distance between speakers and listeners, physical surroundings, tone, and rhythm of speech. Some body language "phrases" (e.g., a smile) are universal. But other phrases vary in meaning across cultural lines. Whereas the Japanese view prolonged eye contact as rude, Americans instead feel that avoidance of eye contact is impolite. In Latino cultures, it is also rude to sustain eye contact. In addition, nonverbal cues may vary with a person's gender and social or economic class. Sitting at a table around a corner signals cooperation and active listening. Sitting straight across from one another, on the other hand, may be perceived as being confrontational. But sitting side by side makes conversation awkward.[21]

EXHIBIT 6–2 Nonverbal communication and enduring culture

Source: Courtesy of Jim Beam Brands Co.

Beckoning someone with a wave of the hand with the palm up is fine in America, but very rude in Japan. Foreigners in Indonesia should also think about local nonverbal communication. "Indonesians are polite people....A business guest will often be served something to drink and should not reach for his drink until the host gestures to do so. It is polite to at least sample the drink or any food offered. Indonesians are not known for their punctuality, so offence should not be taken if events do not start on time or if your guest arrives late. Indonesians avoid the use of the left hand when offering food and other objects, as it is regarded as the unclean hand. It is also considered rude to point with a finger."[22]

Like words, nonverbal signs often convey different meanings in different cultures.[23] For example, signaling by forming a circle with the thumb and forefinger has more than one meaning. It means "OK" or "the best" to Americans and most Europeans, "money" to the Japanese, and "rudeness" to the Brazilians, while having a vulgar connotation in some Latin American countries. In contrast, when the forefinger and middle finger are raised, it may mean "two," "peace," or "victory."

Exhibits 6–3, 6–4, and 6–5 describe the impact of Asian cultures and how to do business in Japan, Korea, and Singapore.

In a popular and often-quoted article, "The Silent Language in Overseas Business," Edward T. Hall explains that there is a need to appreciate cultural differences in matters concerning the language of time, space, things, friendship patterns, and agreements. For the purpose of illustration, these languages are discussed here, modified but derived from work done by Hall and by Arning.[24]

Language of Time

Time has different meanings in different countries. An American and an Asian do not mean the same thing when they say, "Why don't you come over sometime?" In the United States, the statement takes a formal tone, implying that advance notice should be given if the visit is to take place. For an Asian, the meaning is exactly what is said—drop in any time without any appointment, regardless of how early or late it may be in the day. If a person has friends who are moochers, they might conveniently drop by at meal time so that they will be invited to partake in the food being served.

In Saudi Arabia, a Western-style calendar or daily appointment book is unsuitable as a gift because the first of January is already halfway into the Islamic year. In Jordan, an Islamic country, the official weekend is on Friday, and the new week begins on Saturday. Therefore, Fridays in Jordan and most of the Middle East are like Sundays in the West. As a result, the outside world can do business with Jordan and other Muslim countries only on Mondays, Tuesdays, Wednesdays, and half of Thursdays (when most businesses close down early).

In the United States, there is a direct relationship between time and the importance of a matter. When a matter is important, it requires immediate attention and action. In some countries, a reverse relationship exists. A matter of importance requires more time to ponder, and to declare a deadline is to exert undue pressure.

Perceptions of time are culture bound, and three different perceptions can be identified: linear-separable, circular-traditional, and procedural-traditional.[25] In the case of **linear-separable time,** common in most European and North American

Anyone who does business in Japan knows that aggression often leads to disaster.

The slightest hint of aggression can kill a business deal. Be sure to make your point but don't push it. Many Japanese find it difficult to say no—instead, they may say your request would be hard to fulfill. If you do not get a definite answer, just let the subject drop. Your wisdom should speak for itself.

Bathe in mud.
Or sand. Or sulfur. Or just plain water. You will find all kinds of hot-spring spas and baths throughout Japan. First wash yourself with a bathside basin, leaving no traces of soap, then slip gently into the bath. It's very hot at first, but once you get used to it, there's nothing more relaxing after a hard day's work.

Help!
No problem is too big or small for the Tokyo English Lifeline. They'll answer questions on everything from culture to medical emergencies. Telephone 03/264-4347.

Tipping tips.
There's no such thing as tipping in Japan. More expensive restaurants and hotels add a 10%-15% service charge to your bill, but don't tip cab drivers, waitresses, or bellhops. And do not count your change— it'll be considered a sign of distrust.

Northwest notes.
We now offer exclusive nonstop service from Los Angeles to Osaka and the only daily nonstops from Chicago to Tokyo. And, in addition to providing more service to Japan from the U.S. than any other carrier, we offer something no other airline can: the knowledge that comes from over 40 years of helping people do business in Asia. For international reservations, call your travel agent or Northwest at 1-800-447-4747. To find out more about doing business in Asia, call 1-800-553-2215, ext. 77.

© 1989 Northwest Airlines, Inc.

NORTHWEST AIRLINES
Asia Series

EXHIBIT 6–3   Doing business in Japan

Source: Courtesy of Northwest Airlines

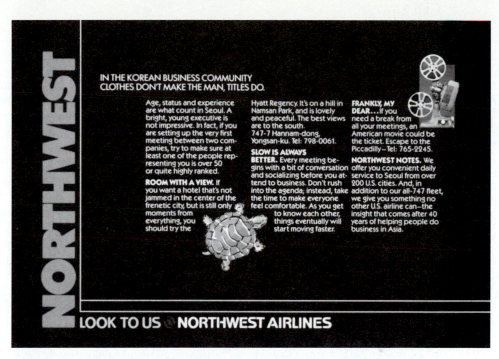

EXHIBIT 6–4 Doing business in Korea

Source: Courtesy of Northwest Airlines

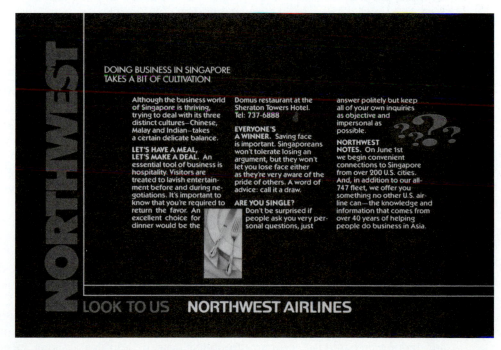

EXHIBIT 6–5 Doing business in Singapore

Source: Courtesy of Northwest Airlines

cultures, time is linear in the sense that it has a past, present, and future. There-fore, time is valuable—time spent in the past will make some contribution to the future. In the case of **circular-traditional time,** life is supposed to follow a cycle, and the future thus cannot be altered. As a result, the future is seen as the past repeated, and there is no need to plan because time is not valuable. Finally, in the case of **procedural-traditional time,** the activity or procedure is more relevant than the amount of time spent on it. Time and money are separate, and earnings are determined by task rather than time. When one activity ends, the next one can start.

Americans tend to value time highly—both work time and leisure time—because "time is money." They often feel that things need to be settled and com-pleted as soon as possible and that they have no time to waste or spare. Russians, in contrast, have formal classroom training in bargaining and chess. They are patient and careful before making a move, often taking extra time just to gain an advantage in the process of negotiation.

American impatience is not a virtue in dealing with foreign firms. Consider, for example, the four stages of business negotiations: (1) nontask sounding, (2) task-related exchange of information, (3) persuasion, and (4) concessions and agree-ment.[26] A typical American negotiator wants to skip the first two stages, or at least finish them quickly. But in Brazil, as in many other countries, much time is need-ed to develop a strong relationship of trust before any business matter can begin, primarily because Brazilians cannot trust a legal system to resolve future conflicts. Likewise, the Chinese are slow, thorough, and deliberate, and negotiation can some-times take weeks. They are not concerned with a Western businessperson's urgency and need to consider schedules the following day in another country.

Time takes a more "leisurely walk" in many non-Western societies, where people have ample time and see no need why any situation should be urgent. Whereas Latin American people are usually late, Swedish people are very prompt. Actually, lack of punctuality may even imply importance and status in some places. But any generalization about punctuality is risky. Asians, for instance, tend not to be punctual, but the Chinese observe strict punctuality for social occasions and appointments. In general, there is a lack of punctuality in Asian and Africa, and it is not uncommon for people to be half an hour or an hour late for an appointment. Usually, no excuse is offered to those who are kept waiting. But if an excuse is needed, it may sound something like this: "If I would have hurried through the traffic, I may have been involved in an accident that would have delayed me even more."

How late is late? According to one study, "being late" is 19 minutes to U.S. students and 33 minutes to their Brazilian counterparts.[27] Brazilian respondents were less likely to attribute tardiness to lack of caring, and they tended not to blame others harshly for being late. Rationalizing that their inability to be on time was due to unforeseen circumstances beyond their control, they were less likely than Americans to be apologetic.

Societies hold various views of urgency and punctuality. One study investigated time differences or pace of life in Japan, Great Britain, the United States, Italy, Taiwan, and Indonesia, based on accuracy of public clocks, pedestrians' walking speed, and speed of service in buying a stamp at the post office.[28] The results reveal that the Japanese walk fastest and keep the most accurate clocks. The United States comes in second. At the other extreme is Indonesia, which is last in all categories except for post office speed. Italy has the dubious distinction of having postal clerks who seem to take forever to accomplish a simple task, such as selling postage stamps.

Time may be important to non-Westerners in different ways. Astrologers and monks are frequently consulted in order to determine the proper time for personal and business matters. The beginning of a construction project, the ceremonial opening of a new building or business, and the right time to marry or to sign a contract are all affected by timing. In India, one should not travel in a time period determined to be unsafe or unlucky. This creates a dilemma for those who are traveling on a plane whose departure time is deemed to be inappropriate. The traveler can, however, circumvent the inappropriate departure time by being flexible. To accommodate both the modern world of travel and the traditional belief concerning the inappropriate departure time of his plane, a traveler may choose to view the departure from home, not from the airport, as the actual time of beginning the travel. If the departure time from home is also inappropriate, the traveler may leave home an hour earlier and drive around for an hour or two before going to the airport.

Language of Space

Space has its own special meaning. Its importance is most evident when people converse with one another. When the other party is nearby, such as in the same room, communication is easily facilitated. Difficulty of communicating severely increases when the distance between the receiver and the sender of a message is great (e.g., when one party is across the street, on another floor, or in another room). In such cases, people have to speak loudly or shout in order to be heard, and the other party still may not hear every word, if any words at all.

Space also has implications for personal selling. Latin Americans are comfortable with just a few inches of distance and repeated embracings. Asians, on the other hand, prefer substantial conversational distance and no physical contact. For Americans, a comfortable distance is something in between those extremes. An American can give the impression of crowding to an Asian and of running away to a Latin American.

Space is also relative: what is perceived as crowded in the United States may be perceived as spacious somewhere else. A small room with low ceilings, by U.S. standards, is not small to the Japanese. In U.S. department stores, executive suites are on the top floor and the budget store is in the basement. In Japan, top executives have offices on the ground floor, and the top floor is reserved for bargain-priced merchandise.

Language of Things

Americans are often accused as being materialistic, with an emphasis on working hard to acquire material possessions in order to make life comfortable and to impress others. Peoples of other countries may believe that wealth and possessions are positive attributes but may work only just hard enough to get by. In other cultures, life is to be enjoyed, and thus many will make a regular practice of quitting work after acquiring a small amount of money. When the money is exhausted they return to work, and this cycle is repeated. Such practice does not mean that foreign consumers are not materialistic—they may be, but they also may be more concerned with other things. For example, in the Middle East, relatively more emphasis is placed on family, friendship, and connections. To do business, it may thus be necessary to use an intermediary or "connector" who knows the right people. Such concerns can be just as meaningful, if not more so, than material concerns.

The relative emphasis on family provides a good basis for comparison between Americans and their counterparts overseas. In one survey, 71 percent of Japanese women feel that their lives after marriage should center on their husbands and children.[29] This sentiment, on the other hand, is shared by only 17 percent of American women.

There are various kinds of family responsibilities and obligations. An extended family goes beyond the traditional American nuclear family of husband, wife, and offspring, encompassing such relatives as aunts, uncles, cousins, nephews, nieces, and grandparents as interdependent family members. Respect for elders is expected. In some cultures, it is expected that the eldest son will carry on the family's business. He cannot simply get married and then move away to work for himself or someone else. Family obligation may make nepotism an acceptable practice. Although American business owners try to minimize nepotism, nepotism is expected in other countries by relatives and employees, and it takes precedence over competence.

Family concerns and interests vary in different parts of the world. Europeans do not like to talk about family at work, in keeping with their desire to preserve privacy. In Asia, the practice is exactly the opposite. Acquaintances, social or business, are supposed to show concern and deference at meetings by asking about the well-being of family members. In Mexico it is customary to inquire about one's wife and family, whereas it is inappropriate to inquire about one's wife in Saudi Arabia.

Language of Agreement

The United States is a very legalistic society. Americans are both specific and explicit in terms of agreement, making legal contracts common and indispensable. Not surprisingly, lawyers become partners in virtually all business deals. When Japan wanted clarification concerning AT&T's products, the company reacted in a typically American fashion by sending a lawyer instead of a manager. Per capita, the United States has more lawyers than any other country in the world. American lawyers earn good income and are accorded social status not found elsewhere.

According to an old saying in Thailand, "it is better to eat a dog's feces than to engage in a lawsuit." Such thinking explains why the Chinese abhor litigation and why they prefer to withdraw from a deal rather than be involved in potential legal disputes. In many cultures, written contracts are not as binding as one's word. According to people in these societies, if a person cannot be trusted as a friend, then it is futile to expect that person to live up to obligations—written or otherwise.

Even when an agreement is reached, the agreement may not necessarily be iron-clad because the agreement can be modified by changing circumstances. In South Korea, a businessperson considers a contract a loosely structured consensus statement that allows flexibility and adjustment.[30] In some societies, agreements merely signify intention and have little relation to capacity to perform.

Culture dictates how a disagreement is expressed and resolved. North Americans generally prefer a straightforward approach. Elsewhere, one must be careful in a disagreement never to make someone else lose face. Asians, in particular, are sensitive to affronts and can become violent when "loss of face" results. Public humiliation or criticism must thus be avoided in Asia, where politeness is valued over blunt truth. Even in California's Silicon Valley area, which is characterized by multiculturalism and diversity, unlike the white American male who gets attention by speaking up, Asian cultures do not teach workers to argue point-blank with immediate supervisors. As a result, an Asian engineer will include his argument in a written report.[31]

In Mexico, direct statements of criticism are considered rude, and thus Mexicans practice circumlocution, making it difficult to determine the true meaning. In Latin America, disagreements may be viewed as personal attacks against the individual. Subordinates are expected either to support their managers openly or to keep silent. Similarly, in Japan silence is perceived as a positive concurrence, and open exchanges and debates are considered inappropriate. Only the top decision maker can comment freely. Japanese stockholders are not allowed to question management critically; companies may hire "guards" to dissuade those who ask too many questions from asking more questions.

U.S. firms prefer to base decisions on objective criteria, or at least they make that claim. The system makes allowances for those who strongly criticize decisions. But such a process would be unacceptable in countries where it is inappropriate to question an executive's personal judgment. Managers often find themselves in a dilemma, as one one cannot consult with others on matters about which one is presumed to be the expert.

As might be expected, the different forms of disagreement may confuse American managers. When potential customers keep quite, nod their heads, or state that they will think about it, American managers may think a deal is developing. But foreign buyers may stay quiet even when the product in question is clearly unsuitable for their needs, because they do not want to offend the American by saying something critical.

Somewhat related to the expression pattern of agreement and disagreement are attitudes about authority. There are several types of authority and management styles, ranging from an autocratic style on the one hand to a laissez-faire style on the other. Somewhere between the two are such styles as patrimonial, paternistic, and democratic or participative.

It is impossible to pick one of the systems as an ideal authority system for all circumstances. In the United States, there is no agreement about which system is the best. In other countries, especially those with strong and extended family ties, paternistic management is relatively common. An owner/manager may treat employees as children. In other countries, there may be a high degree of centralization if authority is viewed as an absolute natural right of management. In any event, a marketer needs to find out if there is any delegation of authority in order to contact the person who is responsible for making a purchase decision.

Language of Friendship

Americans have the unique characteristic of being friendly, even at first meeting. Americans seem to have no difficulty in developing friendship in a very short time, and this trait is carried over into business relationships. American businesspersons are impatient to develop the deep personal ties that are critical in Japan, as well as in other countries. In many countries, friendship is not taken lightly—it involves real obligations such as providing financial and personal help when friends are down and out. Friendship is not developed as fast in these other countries, but when it is developed it tends to be deeper and longer lasting.

In India, it is an honor to be invited to have dinner at a private home—a sign of real friendship. Thus, any business discussion at dinner would be inappropriate. In Italy, Egypt, and China, dinner is a social event in itself, making it an all-evening affair, as exemplified by the ten-course meal in China. In the United States, people finish their meals in a hurry, as if eating were a mere necessity, and then quickly get on to the purpose or objective for having had the dinner.

Pillsbury is one company that owes its success in Japan to an ability to adjust to the radically different style of doing business there. The oriental values of old friends, long courtship, trust, and sincerity were all understood by Pillsbury's management, and those values were kept in mind when Pillsbury decided to conduct business in Japan. Pillsbury saw its joint venture as like a marriage in a society where divorce is frowned upon, and thus took great pains to learn the accepted way of doing business there.

Friendship is also an important ingredient in doing business in China. As explained by the U.S. Department of Commerce, "The emphasis placed on dealing with 'old friends' due in part to China's bad experiences with foreign commercial relationships in the 19th and 20th centuries. . . . Chinese culture predisposes trade officials to depend on personal and informal long-term relationships, in contrast to the Western stress on impersonal and formal legal mechanisms. While it is true that the Chinese sometimes use friendship to extract concessions in commercial negotiations, it also is true that successful long-term business relationships with the Chinese depend on the mutual trust and confidence developed between friends."[32] Still, the Chinese have many old friends and expect their friends to be competitive.

An Italian boot manufacturer considered expanding its business to include the U.S. market. Because it wanted to use direct mail to reach major retailers across the United States, a meeting was arranged for the manufacturer and a U.S. firm specializing in direct mail. After answering all the questions, the direct mail team concluded the meeting and made the appropriate parting gestures. At that point, it became apparent that the potential client was just settling in and wanted to start the serious questioning. The Italian firm wanted to know where the direct mail firm's vice president and her staff went to school, whether they were married and had children, and so on. To the client, personal questions were just as important as business questions. The meeting continued over dinner. The client appeared the next morning with the signed contract. The U.S. firm, although pleased, was surprised.[33]

The manner of addressing a friend can differ depending on the person being addressed, whether a colleague, a business acquaintance, or a customer. The quick friendship characteristic of the United States prompts Americans to use first names in social as well as business encounters soon after a first meeting. This informal approach, claimed to be used to make foreigners feel comfortable, actually makes Americans themselves comfortable at the expense of foreigners.

The American practice of using first names can be very offensive in other countries, where formality and respect are strongly established traditions. Foreigners find it distasteful for American children to address their parents by their first names. Prime Minister Margaret Thatcher was reported to have been very annoyed with President Jimmy Carter for calling her by her first name. The French as well as most northern Europeans find the practice to be offensive. Germans are also formal, and addressing each other by first names is reserved for relatives and close friends. Germans answer the telephone by announcing their last name only. First names, often considered a secret, are revealed only to good friends. In China, it must be understood that the name mentioned first is actually the family name, and thus it would be a mistake to assume that Chinese social customs permit addressing someone by the first or given name.

Addressing someone by a first name is not common outside of the Western hemisphere, unless the first name is accompanied by the proper pronoun or adjective (e.g., Mr. or Mrs.). This formal first-name approach is customary in Asia, Latin America, and the Arab world, whereas the formal last-name approach should be used in Europe. It is thus very important for a businessperson to remember to address foreign counterparts with formal pronouns unless or until being asked to do something else. When can one switch to first names? "In Australia and Venezuela the proper waiting time could be five minutes; in Argentina, Germany, and France one year; in Switzerland three years; and in Japan a decade."[34]

Language of Negotiation

Negotiation styles vary greatly. Hispanic businesspeople are surprised by Anglos' resistance to bargaining. In the United States, a lack of eye contact is usually viewed as an indication that something is not quite right. But the cultural style of communication negotiation in Japan requires a great deal less eye contact between speakers.[35] Furthermore, in Japan periods of silence are common during interactions, and a response of silence should not come as a surprise. Americans should learn to be more comfortable with this negotiating tactic, instead of reacting by quickly offering either more concessions or new arguments.

Americans' straightforward style may prove a handicap in business negotiations. Chinese negotiators are generally tough-minded, well prepared, and under no significant time constraints. They are prepared to use various tactics to secure the best deal. While proclaiming ignorance of foreign technology and foreign business practices, these negotiators may actually be willing to play off one competitor against another. In China, foreigners should expect repetitious and time-consuming negotiations. Concessions from the Chinese may not come until Western negotiators, after many days of unproductive negotiations, are ready to give up and head to the airport. Only then will they be called back for further negotiations.

The preliminary results of one exploratory study established varying negotiation patterns among the American, Japanese, and Brazilian executives.[36] The Japanese were found to be willing to turn to aggressive persuasive tactics, but such tactics were limited to buyers and to the later stages of negotiations, when all else had failed. Both facial gazing and the use of the word *no* were relatively infrequent.

Brazilian managers, in comparison, were aggressive, pushy, and rude. They frequently interrupted and disagreed with bargaining partners, while making relatively fewer commitments and more commands. There was more touching as well as gazing at partners' faces.

Language of Religion

In search of spiritual guidance, people turn to religion. The major religions are familiar to everyone. In some parts of the world, animism (the belief in the existence of such things as souls, spirits, demons, magic, and witchcraft) may be considered a form of religion. Regardless of the religion involved, it is safe to say, specific religious protocols are observed by the faithful (e.g., having evil spirits exorcised).

Religion affects people in many ways because it prescribes proper behavior, including work habits. The Protestant work ethic encourages Christians to glorify God by working hard and being thrifty. Thus, many Europeans and Americans believe that work is a moral virtue and disapprove of the idle. Likewise, Islam exalts work, and idleness is seen as a sign of person's lack of faith in the religion. As such, anyone who is able to work is not allowed to become voluntarily idle. Some religions, however, seem to guide people in the opposite direction. In Hinduism and Buddhism, the emphasis is on the elimination of desires because desires cause worrying. Not striving brings peace, and a person at peace does not suffer.

Marketers must pay attention to religious activities. Buddhists observe the days associated with the birth and death of Buddha and, to a lesser extent, those days of full moon, half moon, and no moon. The entire month of Ramadan is a religious holiday for Muslims, who fast from dawn to dusk each day during that month. Therefore, workers must use part of normal sleeping time for eating. Work productivity can be greatly affected. Furthermore, Muslims pray five times a day, and they stop all work to do so. The data of one study suggest that attitudes and religious and social values shape the text and visual images that appear in print advertisements in the Middle East.[37]

There is no doubt that international marketing is affected by religious beliefs. Saudi Arabian publications will not accept any advertisement that has a woman pictured in it. Sleeveless dresses are considered offensive to Islamic rules, and all advertisements that include pictures of such dresses are banned in Malaysia. Also, religious requirements may prohibit consumption of certain items. Religious taboos include pork and alcohol for Muslims, beef for Hindus, and pork and shellfish for Jews, and once included meat on Friday for Roman Catholics.

Because it is often difficult to separate religious activities from business activities, it is necessary to understand the logic of a particular religious rule. The Islamic economic system can be used to explain this point. This system is greatly influenced by the **Shariah** (i.e., the codification of injunctions given in the Koran and the prophet Muhammad's traditions). Islam holds that individual rights are gained only when obligations are fulfilled and not the other way around. That precept is the basis of the Koran's prohibition for the payment and receipt of all forms of interest. "Money represents the monetized claim of its owner to property rights created by assets that were obtained through work or transfer. Lending money, in effect, is a transfer of this right and all that can be claimed in return is its equivalent and no more. Thus, interest on money is considered as representing unjustified creation of instantaneous property rights: unjustified, because interest is property right claimed outside the legitimate framework of recognized property rights; instantaneous, because as soon as the contract for lending upon interest is concluded, a right to the borrower's property is created for the lender."[38] Once the rationale is understood, it is possible to make business operations conform to the religious rule. In this case, banks can replace an interest-based system with a service-charge and equity-based system (i.e., profit-sharing system). Exhibit 6–6 illustrates how business operations in Saudi Arabia are influenced by the country's Islamic heritage.

Staying in the game means playing by the rules.

In the 1984 Olympic Games, the Saudi soccer team emerged as a force to be reckoned with in the future. In much the same way, SABIC (Saudi Basic Industries Corporation) is emerging as a world-class supplier of petrochemicals, committed to the rules and conventions of international trade, now and in the future.

Part of the commitment stems from our Islamic heritage, with its strong code of friendship, fairness and honor. A code that has long been a stabilizing influence on the world oil scene. SABIC will abide by this code in marketing world petrochemicals. We consider it to be not only a matter of national pride, but the basis for good business.

In the other key areas of technology, quality control and a reliable source of supply and delivery, we offer the world petrochemical market a wide spectrum of products of the highest quality.

We see our role, both now and in the long-term, as best summed up in a statement by the President of SABIC Marketing Company, Ltd., Abdullah S. Al-Nojaidi: "We will play by the rules."

SABIC

World Class Petrochemicals. World Wide Cooperation.

Saudi Basic Industries Corporation
P.O. Box 5101, Riyadh 11422, Saudi Arabia
Telex: 201177 SABIC SJ

EXHIBIT 6–6 Religious code and business rules

Source: Reprinted with permission of Saudi Basic Industries Corporation

Language of Superstition

In the modern world it is easy to dismiss superstition as nonsense. Yet superstitious beliefs play a critical role in explaining personal as well as business behavior in all parts of the world. In Asia, fortune telling, palm reading, dream analysis and interpretation, phases of the moon, birthdate and handwriting analysis, communication with ghosts, and many other beliefs are parts of everyday life. Physical appearance is often used to judge a person's character. Long ears, for example, supposedly belong to those who have good fortune.

Some Westerners may be amused to see foreigners take superstition so seriously. They may not put much credence in animal sacrifices or other ceremonial means used to get rid of evil spirits. But they should realize that their own beliefs and superstitions are just as silly when viewed by foreigners. Americans knock on wood, cross their fingers, and feel uneasy when a black cat crosses their path. They do not want to walk under ladders and may be extra careful on Friday the 13th.

It must be remembered that people everywhere are human beings with emotions and idiosyncrasies. They cannot be expected to always behave in a rational and objective manner. Instead of belittling or making fun of superstition, one is prudent to show respect for local customs and beliefs. A show of respect will go a long way in gaining friendship and cooperation from local people. In 1972 when Hyatt Regency opened a hotel in Singapore, the facility was plagued by many problems, one of which was the low occupancy rate. Hyatt's local managers summoned a *feng shui* monk to inspect the hotel for harmful influences. The monk found that the problems were caused by sinister spirits, which according to ancient Chinese belief traveled only in straight lines. To ward those spirits off, he ordered the entrance doors to be repositioned at angles. After the doors were repositioned the business markedly improved.[39]

Language of Color

Colors have meaning, and preferences for particular colors are determined by culture. Because of custom and taboo, some colors are viewed negatively. A color deemed positive and acceptable in one culture can be inappropriate in another. The use of color in flowers can provide a good illustration. Those flowers associated with death or unhappy circumstances are purple flowers in Brazil; white lilies in Canada, Great Britain, and Sweden; white and yellow flowers in Taiwan; and yellow flowers in Mexico. Yellow flowers signify infidelity in France and disrespect for a woman in Russia. In Mexico, red flowers, according to the superstition, cast evil spells, and white flowers must be purchased to remove the spells.[40]

Other than flowers, colors by themselves have special meaning. Yellow is associated with disease in Africa. White is an appropriate color for a wedding gown in the United States, yet white is used alternately with black for mourning in India, Hong Kong, and Japan. Americans see red when they are angry, but red is a lucky color for the Chinese. It is customary for the Chinese to put money in red envelopes as gifts for employees and children on special occasions, especially on the Chinese New Year day.

Marketing managers should be careful in using certain colors with their products because using the wrong color can make or break a deal. A manufacturer of medical systems lost a large order for CAT (computerized axial tomography) scanners in one Middle Eastern country because of the whiteness of the equipment. Parker's white pens did not fare well in China, where white is the color of mourning. Its green pens suffered the same fate in India, where green is associated with bad luck.

Language of Gifts

Cultural attitudes concerning the presentation of gifts vary greatly across the globe. Because of varying perceptions of gifts and their appropriateness, good intentions can turn into surprises and even embarrassment when particular gifts violate cultural beliefs. Apparel is not commonly given in the United Kingdom, where it is considered too personal a gift, nor in Russia, where it is considered a bribe. In France, Russia, Germany, Taiwan, and Thailand, giving a knife as a gift is inappropriate because it may "cut" or "wound" a friendship. Although improper to be given, cutlery can be sold—for a small sum of money as token payment.

Handkerchiefs should never be given in Thailand, Italy, Venezuela, and Brazil because such a gift is akin to wishing a tragedy upon the recipient, implying that something distressful will happen in the near future which will necessitate the use of a handkerchief to wipe away the tears. Prudence requires one not to give potted plants for the sick in Japan because the illness may become more severe by taking deeper root. It is also wise to avoid giving four of anything or any item with *four* in the name to the Chinese and Japanese because the word sounds like *si* in these languages and means death. Likewise, clocks are a poor choice of gift in China and Taiwan, because the world for a clock sounds like the word for "terminate" or for a prefuneral visit to the dying.

Many Americans think of gift giving as a waste of time, yet they embrace Christmas gift buying and giving in spite of the excessive commercial overtones. In many parts of the world, a gift is a symbol of thoughtfulness or consideration, and one does not visit another person's home empty-handed. In Japan, the practice is extended to Japanese officials' overseas trips. This old tradition requires that the prime minister carry a gift *(miyage)* to a country being visited. The gift may take the form of trade policy concessions, as demonstrated by Prime Minister Nakasone's visit with President Reagan in Washington, D.C., in 1983. The prime minister brought with him the easing of quotas on farm products as well as a reduction of tariffs.[41]

Gift giving is, to a certain extent, an art. Gifts are given in Europe only after a personal relationship has developed, but they are given in Japan when persons first meet as well as when they part. In Japan, form is more important than content. As a result, wrapping *(tsutsumi)* has been an art in Japan for over ten centuries. Special rules apply to wrapping particular items, and the occasion dictates materials and style.[42] Because of obligations to others in society, the Japanese lose face if they are put in a position of not being able to reciprocate. Foreign businessmen should not "outgift" their Japanese acquaintances.[43] As for the Arabs, who pride themselves on being generous, they are not embarrassed when given even generous gifts. An

American businessperson should keep in mind that often a gift is most conspicuous by its absence. Therefore, a cardinal rule in international gift giving is that, when in doubt, one should study closely the customs of the society.

AMERICAN CULTURE

Culture exists in every part of the world, though cultural traits vary greatly from one country to the next. Consumer behavior can be better understood when basic cultural values of the country of interest are identified. In order to appreciate the significance of cultural diversity, consider two important but very different cultures: American and Japanese cultures.

American culture has several distinctive characteristics. First, it is *materialistic*. A great deal of importance is placed on material possessions and conspicuous consumption. American consumers are clearly the heaviest users of many product categories, with gasoline as a prime example. American consumers purchase all manner of goods and services to make life comfortable. Price is usually secondary to convenience, and planned obsolescense seems the rule rather than the exception, resulting in annual model changes and trade-ins for newer products. A nationwide survey involving 1,800 questions suggested that Americans are shallow and materialistic. About a quarter of those surveyed indicated that, for $10 million, they would abandon their families or become a prostitute for a week. Follow-up interviews found the results to hold until the price dropped below $2 million.[44]

American culture is also *individualistic*. U.S. high schools have flexible curricula to reflect students' individual interests. As noted by Education Secretary William Bennett, the curriculum of some U.S. high schools has been debased by such nonacademic courses as rock poetry and Baja whale watch. In contrast, the curriculum of virtually all schools anywhere else in the world is rigidly set and allows students no option.

Americans identify themselves either as individuals or by their occupations. In the Japanese culture, the Japanese define themselves by their work or by organizations, such as by the department and company with which they are associated. Instead of saying "I am an engineer," a Japanese worker will say "I am a manager" of a particular company. The Japanese "consider themselves members of corporate society and fulfill themselves through their companies."[45] In the United States, there is no lack of conformity, but freedom of expressions in terms of ideas and consumption is encouraged. A consumer has a choice of either conforming to the general public opinion or taking a view that is uniquely personal. In such countries as China, the choice or freedom to express a different view is much more limited.

American culture is *achievement-oriented*. Because of this characteristic, competition is emphasized at the expense of cooperation. In order to get ahead, one often shows disregard for friends or colleagues. The public may claim to root for the underdog, but how often do they remember a runner-up or a loser in a contest? In contrast, Japanese firms rarely lay off permanent employees because all people are supposed to be equally committed to the company through good and bad times. Koreans also emphasize cooperation rather than competition.

American culture is *time-oriented*. In the United States, people are usually prompt if they have scheduled an appointment. For Americans, time is valuable. Sometimes, Americans give the impression of always being in a hurry, trying to be on time for the next scheduled meeting. Many advertisements in the United States reflect this time-oriented value.

American culture is *youth-oriented*. In the United States, a high value is placed on being young. This attitude started a few decades ago and shows no sign of changing. Actual age sometimes does not matter as much as being "young at heart." This fear of growing old offers tremendous opportunities for hair-coloring products, face lifting, vitamins (e.g., Geritol), and mild detergents for keeping hands looking young.

American culture is *practical* and *efficient*. In a general sense, Americans tend to be less formal than other cultures, making informal lifestyles and products widely acceptable. For business firms, the emphasis is on efficiency—introducing products at the lowest production cost while maximizing sales. In contrast, the Indian government puts more emphasis on employment opportunities than on automation and efficiency. Because of this American characteristic of practicality, the Japanese have difficulties convincing their American partners that it is bad business relations to cut distribution costs by shortening the lengthy distribution system in Japan.

No one should misunderstand that these characteristics identified as American are unique to the culture of the United States. Actually, many of these characteristics are possessed to one degree or another by people in other parts of the world. Materialism, for example, is prominent in other cultures—to the extent that American materialism sometimes seems mild in comparison. For example, a Japanese man may willingly spend $8,000 for a Beretta shotgun because that object is considered a status symbol there, whereas in the United States such a purchase would be a very carefully weighed decision.

None of these characteristics should be considered inherently good or bad. Whether a characteristic is good or bad depends on the context or culture in which it is interpreted. What is appropriate in the United States may be inappropriate somewhere else. What is illogical to an American may be quite logical to someone from another country.

In marketing, it is useful to identify the cultural values of the target market because these values correlate with consumer behavior, suggesting their potential in predicting consumption.

Because cultural change and consumption change are related, the wise marketer should be aware of such trends and should attempt to reflect them in the products and advertisements being produced. Some of the currently held cultural values were identified in the 1950s and are still operative today.[46] Some of these important trends are:

A growing desire to be identified with youth.

The urge to be different or distinctive in taste, within certain limits of conformity, including the desire to be well-off in terms of personalization, physical health, and well-being.

A trend toward informality and casual living.

A greater sophistication in behavior.

Changed concepts of sex roles, of what is masculine and what is feminine, including increasing importance of women's roles and careers (see Exhibit 6–7).

An active search for adventure or new experiences.

An increased desire for leisure that provides an outlet for creativity.

The wish to be modern, or not to be old-fashioned.

EXHIBIT 6–7   Women's changing roles and needs

Source: Reprinted with permission of the New York Life Insurance Corporation.

To this list, some relatively new values might be added. One trend is an aversion to complexity, and this trend is accompanied by tendencies toward life simplification, a return to nature, and a rejection of bigness. Another trend is the adoption of an anti-Puritanical value system, which emphasizes pleasure for its own sake and living for the present. Finally, there is a growing trend toward more liberal sexual attitudes and the elimination of some social taboos.

As can be attested by any keen observer of American society, these trends are strongly supported and show no sign of weakening. It is also apparent that businesses are aware of these trends. Instead of trying to counter or reduce their impact, many firms have actually capitalized on them. Commercials have become more subtle in response to consumers' increased sophistication. Many new products and styles have emerged that offer comfort and an informal lifestyle, evidenced by blue jeans, sneakers, and the many kinds of informal clothing found in the marketplace. Women's liberated lifestyles have become more acceptable, as reflected in the Charlie perfume commercials. Many social taboos have been discarded, and women's magazines now freely and openly show advertisements for numerous birth control devices (including condoms) for young women and men, regardless of marital status. Night clubs are a prime example of a decline in puritan values, because the night club offers instant gratification as well as pleasure for its own sake. Back-to-nature products are to be found everywhere, ranging from yogurt to earth shoes. Youthfulness is emphasized in soft drink and fast-food commercials. These trends will, in all likelihood, continue into the foreseeable future.

JAPANESE CULTURE

Although Japan and the United States compete with each other in many product areas and industries, their methods of conducting business are markedly different. The variations that occur are derived from the differences found within the broader social systems of the two countries. An understanding of these variations is essential for an appreciation of Japanese industry. The unique experience of Japan as a non-Western industrial nation provides an excellent opportunity for an analysis of how the process of industrialization may take place in other Asian countries. Exhibit 6–8 shows how the Japanese culture influences the way the Japanese do business.

Putting aside exceptions and detail, it is possible to make a few generalizations regarding business and social practices in Japan.[47] Some general characteristics of the Japanese social system and Japanese business organizations are discussed in the following sections.

Permanent and Irrevocable Membership

Membership in a Japanese organization is permanent and irrevocable. It has been customary for workers to work for their entire lifetime for a single company. The process begins when a person first enters the labor force upon the completion of education, and it continues for an entire career despite possible advantages in moving to another firm.

IMPRESSIONS OF EACH OTHER

Americans talk too much, the Japanese are too polite. Americans are too time-conscious, the Japanese are too slow at making decisions.

These are just some of the perceived and real cultural differences between these two countries that can affect business decisions, according to Hiroki Kato, who spoke at the Pacific Rim Futures Conference on cultural differences. Kato, vice-president of Asian development at the Chicago Mercantile Exchange, listed top complaints Japanese and Americans have of each other from John C. Condon's book, "With respect to the Japanese: A guide for Americans."

Americans believe the Japanese are so polite that no one knows what they're thinking. The Japanese are so ambiguous, it's hard to know where they stand. They are conformists. They are always expressing thanks and appreciation and are always apologizing—sometimes for nothing. They put too much weight on certain actions and are too slow at making decisions. They are very ethnocentric, yet imitative, and they are overly impressed by status. The Japanese are too formal.

What do the Japanese think about Americans?

Besides talking too much, they constantly interrupt other people—even finish sentences. Americans don't listen enough and seem to think if they don't divulge something, no one will know it. Americans are too direct in asking questions, giving opinions and poking fun. They fail to express thanks sufficiently. They are reluctant to admit faults and limitations. American managers give more attention to individuals than to the entire group, which is very embarrassing to the Japanese. Americans do not appreciate the importance of certain formalities in Japan—even to the point of joking about them. Americans are too much in a hurry.

One point was clear in both cultural sessions: Know the proper business etiquette when doing a business. It could make or break the deal.

SIX Ps SPELL SUCCESS IN JAPAN

Forming a joint venture or partnership with a company from another country takes more than a good fit. Hiroshi Yokota, manager of marketing and systems development for Mitsubishi Corp. in Tokyo, calls his rules for success the "Six Ps."

1. *Performance.* When Mitsubishi was looking for a U.S. partner to develop futures funds, at least a dozen firms approached it. Baldwin Financial Corp was selected mainly because of performance, although the company also had "good experience, good knowledge, good (people) and a good name," Yokota says.
2. *Price.* "In any service industry, the price must be reasonable and fair," Yokota says.
3. *Participation.* Yokota says this is extremely important in the new emerging Japanese markets.

(continued)

EXHIBIT 6–8   Japanese culture and business practices

Source: Ginger Szala, "Are Joint Ventures Worth the Effort?" *Futures* (December 1991): 6. Reprinted from *Futures* magazine, 219 Parkade, P.O. Box 6, Cedar Falls, Iowa 50613

"When we were trying to sell this type of new financial component in Japan, it was a bit difficult to sell many U.S. ready-made package funds to the Japanese markets," he says. "The Japanese markets have their own special factors to consider, like regulatory (issues)."

Funds must be developed jointly to suit the needs of the Japanese market.

"More and more Japanese are trying to know what (this business) is all about," Yokota says. "They are no longer satisfied just to sell the packaged product."

4. *Philosophy.* There must be mutual respect on both sides and a sense of sharing.
5. *Personality.* "Sometimes personality is more important than money in terms of a long-term relation. It's the same as a marriage, isn't it?" he says.

He also contradicted the notion that Americans shouldn't joke with their Japanese colleagues.

"Japanese laugh twice when you make a joke. Once when they hear it and once when they understand it. Of course, you shouldn't try to be a Johnny Carson in Japan, so what you should do is make it simple. A human joke is a good way to smooth a relationship and show your natural personality."

6. *Patience.* "In terms of long-term relations, patience is very important," he cautions.

EXHIBIT 6–8   Japanese culture and business practices *(continued)*

Companies, likewise, take certain obligations and responsibilities very seriously. The risk of losing highly trained personnel to another firm is not great because companies do not want to upset their own employees by hiring outsiders in mid-career. The company may continue to provide workers with jobs and/or income, even at great cost to the company. "Dismissing employees is regarded as improper, against the socially accepted principle of paternalism, and the last resort before going bankrupt."[48] Japanese firms rarely lay off permanent employees because the Japanese view is that everyone is supposed to be in the "same boat," through the good and bad times. When Toyota's automobile demand and production were affected by the oil crisis, the company had to find work for many of its employees, especially its engineers. To solve the problem, it entered the construction business by seeking contracts to construct houses and commercial buildings. One reason why Sony has formed joint ventures with U.S. firms in marketing sporting goods, insurance, and phonograph records is because such ventures provide a dumping ground for electronics employees that Sony wants to replace. As an added benefit, these ventures also provide Sony with a testing ground for young executives.

Another important practice in Japanese business is that an employee's inadequacy or incompetence is not grounds for dismissal. The employee is simply transferred to a unit where the person is less likely to do serious damage. The worst that could happen is that a bonus is used to induce an unwanted employee to resign. Dismissals are thus rare. As explained by Sony's Akio Morita, "when I find an employee who turns out to be wrong for a job, I feel it is my fault because I made the decision to hire him. Generally, I would invest in additional training, education, or change of duty, even perhaps sending him overseas for additional experience. As a result, he will usually turn out to be an asset in the long run. Even if the positive return is only one out of every five, that one individual's productivity will cover the losses incurred by the other four. It is greater to lose that one productive person than to maintain the presence of the four incompetents."[49]

This characteristic of Japanese organizations does have limits. Lifetime employment is usually restricted to large firms or those in the upper echelon of industry. Among small- and medium-size companies, labor mobility is much more common. Furthermore, only "regular" and male employees are entitled to this benefit. Neither part-time workers nor women are part of the system. In addition, workers supplied by labor contractors also serve as a buffer for varying work loads. When business is slow, the employment problem is thus passed down to smaller companies or suppliers. One study found that "lifetime employment is offered within a rhetorical context of loyalty and benevolence based on cultural values." The impact allows managers to increase the control of employees.[50]

To appreciate the Japanese employment system, it is necessary to understand the culture in which it exists. "With a strong sense of obligation, it is a culture that is highly organized, harmony-oriented, hierarchical, self-effacing, ego-denying, and security-risking. Lifetime employment, Japanese style, cannot be indiscriminately transplanted to a culture that is ego-oriented, individualistic, and competitive, a culture where product quality and social welfare philosophies have become so intertwined that the price of the former often reflects the expense of the latter."[51]

Recruitment and Selection

Recruitment into an organization is based largely on personal qualities rather than on particular work skills or job requirements (i.e., professional qualifications). The same basis is also used to select employees for positions within an organization. General qualities such as a person's education, character, and background are primary screening criteria. Employees can be assigned to any task and location, depending on the need. University graduates tend to prefer working for large firms, and corporate relations with Japanese universities must be carefully nurtured. Although large companies attempt to discourage hiring close family relatives among employees, nepotism is often important in the Japanese employment system. In general, the recruitment and selection system as it exists is a reinforcement and extension of the basic system of the worker-firm relationship.

Status

Status acquired in an organization is a continuation and extension of the worker's status in the society at the time of initial employment. It is customary for a worker to be entitled to a particular status based on education. College education, when compared to high school education, enhances the employee's status. A graduate of a well-known public university, such as Kyoto University or Tokyo University or other prestigious private universities, is accorded a degree of respect that is not given to those who graduate from less prestigious colleges. Just as important is the worker's family background, as the parents' status is a large determinant in position as well.

It is this status system that determines an employee's initial position in the company and that poses either an opportunity or a limit on an employee's future movement within the organization.

Compensation

According to Japanese Ministry of Labor statistics, employees of giant firms (with more than 500 employees) have an average monthly pay of 315,000 yen, whereas the average for small companies (with 100 workers or less) is only 205,000 yen, resulting in a substantial wage gap. A worker's compensation only partly occurs in the form of money; thus, monetary pay is just one of many items that make up the total compensation package. Therefore, it is misleading to compare a Japanese employee's actual cash pay with that of an American counterpart and to include that Japan's competitive advantage is the result of its low wages. Other compensation items in the total package are housing, meal, medical insurance, commutation allowances, recreation facilities, and personal services.

The pay system is based primarily on broad social criteria rather than on production criteria. Promotion is decided on seniority. As a result, in addition to allowance for education background, the reward criteria include the worker's age, service length, and family size. Reward is thus a function of loyalty and fidelity to the organization and to the needs of the worker as husband and father. Occupying secondary importance are such criteria as job rank, competence, and productivity. Because such criteria appear to contradict good management principles in most other industrial nations, it may seem that there is little incentive for a worker to work hard, especially when the threat of being fired is minimal. But the high output rate makes it clear that employee loyalty and group identification can be important motivational factors. In fact, money and material rewards are viewed as secondary to the organization's success. During times of difficulty, all members of the organization are expected to suffer through the hard times together.

Corporate Responsibilities

Companies are substantially responsible not only for their workers' job-related activities but also with the employees' nonbusiness activities. The responsibility is so complete that intimate or personal matters are not exempted. Companies may advise workers on how to manage their personal lives, their spending, the education of their children, religious activities, and many other family matters. If a dispute arises between a male employee and his wife, the company may step in and become the referee. To monitor and to account for the well-being of the worker and his family, the company may use both formal personnel procedures and informal channels. The corporate philosophy requires the firm to make certain that its responsibility to its employees is complete. Note that the employees do not view the company's interference as an intrusion into their private affairs.

Authority and Responsibility

The organizational structure of an American firm is logically designed, and detailed job descriptions are both common and expected. It is no surprise to American employees that the authority and responsibility that come with each position are clearly delineated. The system ultimately promotes specificity as well as rigidity.

Japanese firms, in contrast, are less structured and thus tend to be more confusing. Formal positions, though well defined in terms of rank and title, are accompanied by very general and abstract descriptions. As a result, responsibility and authority are not well defined, and outsiders tend to have difficulties identifying the person who makes the decisions. The system, however, does promote flexibility in managing the functions of the firm.

Decision Making

Japanese organizations are characterized and managed by the "family head management system" (*kafuchoo sei*). Under this system, the male head of the family or organization has absolute power and authority.[52] It is common practice for the leader to act like a father with parental concerns (*onjo-shugi*). By being fatherly, he can attract followers and become more effective in motivating the employees and the people who surround him.

The negotiating style of the Japanese is dictated by the philosophy of risk minimization and confrontation avoidance. Partially because of the desire not to become individually responsible for the consequence of a decision, employees avoid making decisions on their own. It is thus unacceptable for an employee to blame another if a decision is incorrect. The approach also fosters the continuance of not having well-defined authority and responsibility for a formal business position. Thus, the group rather than the individual exercises the decision-making function.

The leadership style is usually quite open and democratic. Although most decisions must ultimately be made at the top, top management is not dictatorial in making decisions. Japanese management is characterized by a style of "middle-up consensus management"; decisions are initially made at the lower positions in the organization. Participation is encouraged, and the ideas of junior officials are carefully reviewed. Management at all levels is subsequently affected by the views of workers at lower levels. Although the system appears cumbersome, the implementation of a strategy, once agreed upon, can move swiftly toward the chosen objective in a coordinated fashion because all parties have already been involved and are in agreement. As noted by several observers, Japanese organizations are very effective in implementing strategies but not necessarily in formulating them.

One important outcome that is the result of the Japanese decision-making approach is that middle managers cannot be bypassed. Sterling Drug, for example, owes its success in Japan to its courting of middle managers behind the scenes.[53] Drafts of sales goals are formulated and sent to lower levels of the organization to gain support along the way before a formal proposal is delivered to top management. It is also critical to identify and consult with those who will make decisions, as well as to gain support for a plan before it reaches the top decision makers.

Marketing Practices

There are four related concepts that can shed some light on Japanese marketing practices and the process of how adjustments are made: pseudoharmonism, eclecticism, exceptionism, and economic nonfunctionality.[54] *Pseudoharmonism* stresses the maintenance of harmony while acknowledging the presence of underlying discord. *Eclecticism* also emphasizes human harmony in decision making but in addition recognizes a trade-off of economic costs. *Exceptionism* emphasizes exceptions to established policies and results in paradoxes and inconsistencies that allow for flexibility and adaptability. *Economic nonfunctionality* requires marketing decisions to be based on individual human factors in addition to economic efficiency and profit.

The Japanese idea of competition is to compete "hard but fair." This idea differs substantially from the competitive practices of the U.S. market. The Japanese resist the American practice of growth through merger and acquisition. In order to protect small Japanese companies from being driven out of business by excessive price competition, there are laws that limit the operational tactics of large firms. Yet the Japanese way does allow for such marketing practices as particular types of advertising discounts, which are illegal in the United States.

Sexual Discrimination

Many actions and policies that would be considered as expressions of sexual discrimination in the United States are willingly accepted in the Japanese culture, even by Japanese women. It is remarkable that Japanese women are willing to accept and endure so many disadvantages throughout their lives. As daughters, their chances of going to good schools and getting a good education are remote. The assumption is that they will marry early and move away and that married women at best work only part-time or not at all. Thus, a young girl's parents see no reason why they should invest in an education for their daughters.

As workers, Japanese women have to be content with an unwritten custom: the company will hire only young women who are absolutely well-mannered, obedient, and unambitious. These women are also expected to be sufficiently attractive to serve as part of the aesthetically pleasing features of an office.[55] To fulfill the duties for which they are employed, the young women are offered only menial jobs with low pay, often at half as much as their male counterparts are earning. Furthermore, chances for promotion are slight. Highly-skilled jobs and managerial positions are always reserved for men, regardless of whether these men are competent or not. Being used more or less in a reserve capacity, the young women are not protected by the traditional lifetime employment. As if to remind them constantly of this inequity, female employees are almost always required to wear company uniforms, whereas their male counterparts can go to work in street clothes.

As wives, Japanese women do not differ greatly from live-in maids. It is not unusual for them to arise well before their husbands and to go to sleep after their husbands have fallen asleep. Neither is it uncommon for a women to tie her husband's shoelaces when he dresses or to wave a fan to cool her husband's face while he sleeps. In Japan, childcare is the major responsibility of women. On balance, Japanese women are perceived to exist not to serve themselves but to serve others.

Tradition vs. Change

One change that has occurred in Japan is in the area of leisure time. Because of Japan's trade surplus and the lobbying pressure of its trading partners, the Japanese government has sought to minimize trade friction by pressuring companies to shorten the workweek. The idea is that if the Japanese work less, then they will have more leisure time, will increase spending, and will consume more products made by Japan and others.[56] The Ministry of Labor even used a poster that asked, "Workers, will you take your summer holiday with courage?" This is a significant change in attitude given these facts:

> Each Japanese employee works 2,180 hours a year (versus 1,898 in the United States and 1,613 in Germany).
> Only 7.8 percent of the Japanese work a five-day week.
> More than 30 percent prefer work to leisure and 60 percent would probably not take more leisure time, if made available.

Japan, much like other industrialized nations, has been undergoing changes. Those who welcome the new changes are people who have difficulties adapting to traditional Japanese society and organization. One group interested in making change is composed of the young Japanese who are urban reared and educated beyond the legally prescribed minimum of a middle school education. In addition to their disapproval of the traditional practice of arranged marriage, these young Japanese do not accept the one-company employment system and are willing to consider working for foreign firms. According to one survey conducted by the Ministry of Labor, a third of employees under age thirty said that they would consider changing jobs. Another group encouraging change is composed of young women who have been schooled in a newer pattern of relationships and role expectations.

With regard to organized labor, unions have been unable to gain power to improve their traditionally weak role in the decision-making process. Unions have been hindered in their efforts primarily by the surplus of labor and by employee fidelity, a tradition that they have been unable to overcome. As a result, management is unconcerned about the possibility that labor unions might pose a serious threat to the organization's autonomous functioning. As a matter of fact, strikes during a "spring break offensive," although not unusual, are very brief because they are a demonstration rather than an obstructive defiance. These strikes are carefully timed after consultation with management in order to minimize any disturbance of production and business schedules.[57]

In spite of some changes, the Japanese have been able to maintain many of the country's traditional values. The nation should thus be characterized as experiencing blending rather than cultural borrowing. The embracing of Western ideas has not radically altered Japanese fundamental values. The changes that have occurred could be characterized as the Japanization of American methods rather than the Americanization of Japanese practices.[58] By adjusting and adapting American ideas and practices to Japanese culture, the Japanese have been able to create a new approach that, although being uniquely Japanese, incorporates relevant American ideas. Despite the successful blending of the two culturally diverse approaches, the Japanese culture has remained largely intact.

Some Concluding Remarks

Japan and the West differ fundamentally in at least two ways relating to the nature of social organization of the company. First, the Japanese firm does not differ much in its operation from other organizations in the society. The Western view recognizes life segments, each serving a special end with differentiated relationships—the family, the association, the workplace—which results in a clear separation of activities and organization in each group. The second difference relates to the extent to which there is an individualization or impersonalization of relationships in the company. The Japanese firm develops and employs a flexible and human-oriented structure that is well understood by its employees.

Regarding policy toward dismissal and layoffs, an explanation from an economist's point of view is that Japan strives to maintain internal stability (i.e., full employment). The practice could also be explained in another way: instead of maximizing profits, the main objective of the firm is to satisfy the needs of all parties concerned. The economic ends take a secondary position to the maintenance of group integrity. This should not be viewed as an irrational approach because it has been shown to bring about voluntarily singular unity among the firm's employees. This point of view may substantially account for the powerless position of Japanese unions. In contrast, organized labor is powerful in the United States, where efficiency is emphasized and where motivation and group cohesiveness are major difficulties encountered. The absence of such problems in Japan may be because the Japanese company considers itself responsible for the total person.

Credit must be given to the Japanese for their very successful industrialization programs. Had their system not been successful, it may have been easy to conclude that the failure was the result of deviations from the standard industrial practices as found in the United States. It may have been further concluded that only Western assumption and practices are appropriate for all countries, regardless of culture and environment. The important point to be noted is that considerable success is possible under varying cultural and environmental circumstances. Although it may be true that the Western style of organization maximizes productivity, substantial industrial progress can be made within quite a different style of social organization.

The moral of the Japanese success is that interpersonal relationships determine economic activity in a given country, and these relationships depend on a country's culture. Marketing and management principles are not absolute but must be related and adapted to the culture of the society. There is more than one way to skin a cat, and there is more than one way to achieve efficiency and advance economically.

SUBCULTURE

Because of differing cultures, worldwide consumer homogeneity does not exist. Neither does it exist in the United States. Differences in consumer groups are everywhere. There are white, black, Jewish, Catholic, farmer, truckdriver, young, old, eastern, and western consumers, among other numerous groups. Communication problems between speakers of different languages is apparent to all, but people who presumably speak the same language may also encounter serious communication problems. Subgroups within societies utilize specialized vocabularies. Anyone listening to truckdrivers' conversation on a CB radio could easily verify this point.

In order to understand these diverse groups of consumers, particular cultures must be examined. As the focus is on a subgroup within a society, the more appropriate area for investigation is not culture itself by rather **subculture,** culture on a smaller and more specific level.

A **subculture** is a distinct and identifiable cultural group that has values in common with the overall society but also has certain characteristics that are unique to itself. Thus, subcultures are groups of people within a larger society. Although the various subcultures share some basic traits of the wider culture, they also preserve their own customs and lifestyles, making them significantly different from other groups within the larger culture of which they are a part. Indonesia, for instance, has more than 300 ethnic groups, with lifestyles and cultures that seem thousands of years apart.

Functions of Subculture

Subculture is important to a person because it serves at least three important functions: group identification, a network of groups and institutions, and a frame of reference.[59]

A subculture provides a psychological source of group identification. It offers a unique identity based on an association with the same kind of people. An individual will know if he or she is white, black, or Spanish, for instance. The subculture therefore lets the individual identify with other similar members in the society.

A subculture also offers a patterned network of communication. A subculture provides for the maintenance of primary relationships with others in the same subculture. Briefly speaking, it makes available the means of contact through a communication network.

Belonging to a subculture makes it easy for a person to understand a new environment by serving as a frame of reference for viewing the new culture. Comparisons can be made with previous experiences in the subculture. Understanding of a new situation or environment is thus achieved easier and faster.

Bases of Subculture

There are many different ways to classify subcultures. Although race or ethnic origin is one obvious way, it is not the only one. Other demographic and social variables can be just as suitable for establishing subcultures within a nation. As explained by Valentine, "the list only begins with (1) socioeconomic strata—such as the lower class or the poor. It goes on to include (2) ethnic collectives—e.g., Blacks, Jews; (3) regional populations—Southerners, Midwesterners; (4) age grades—adolescents, youth; (5) community types—urban, rural; (6) institutional complexes—education, penal establishments; (7) occupational groupings—various professions; (8) religious bodies—Catholics, Muslims, and even (9) political entities—revolutionary groups, for example. Yet this does not exhaust the catalog, for one also finds (10) genera of intellectual orientation, such as 'scientists' and 'intellectuals'; (11) units that are really behavioral classes, mainly various kinds of 'deviant'; and (12) what are categories of moral evaluation, ranging from 'respectables' to the 'disreputable' and the 'unworthy' poor."[60]

Some Subcultures

The degree of intracountry homogeneity varies from one country to another. In the case of Japan, the society as a whole is remarkably homogeneous. Although some regional and racial diversities as well as differences among income classes are to be found, the differentials are not pronounced. There are several reasons why Japan is a relatively homogeneous country. It is a small country in terms of area, making its population geographically concentrated. National pride and management philosophy also help to forge a high degree of unity. As a result, people work together harmoniously to achieve the same common goals. The need to work hard together was initially fostered by the need to repair the economy after World War II, and the lessons learned from this experience have not been forgotten.

Canada, in contrast, is a large country in terms of geography. Its population, though much smaller than that of Japan, is much more geographically dispersed, and regional differences exist among the provinces, each having its own unique characteristics. Furthermore, ethnic differences are clearly visible to anyone who travels across Canada.

Canada's social environment makes it possible for ethnic groups to be active members of the Canadian society while having the freedom to pursue their own native customs. The environment thus accommodates what is known as *ethnic pluralism*. Canadians not only tolerate but even encourage diversity in ethnic customs. Ethnically speaking, two prominent subcultures emerge: English-speaking and French-speaking subcultures. As noted by Yeates, the French-speaking consumer "has different motivations, a different cultural set, different living standards and different buying habits—different from other Canadians, different from Americans, different from the European French, different from any other consumer group in the world."[61]

Studies in Canada have repeatedly shown that the French-speaking and English-speaking households differ from each other significantly in terms of demographics, subculture, and consumption habits. According to the results of a study conducted by Schaninger, Bourgeois, and Buss, French-speaking Canadians are generally lower in income, social class, education, and occupation.[62] On the other hand, they "have more children, greater family stability, stronger father roles, and more extended kinship systems." One question that must be raised is whether the varying consumption habits between the two ethnic groups are caused by demographic differences or by subcultural diversities. Schaninger, Bourgeois, and Buss attempted to answer this question by using comparable subsamples from the same market area in order to control for the demographics. Despite the effort to hold market factors constant, significant differences were still found among French, bilingual, and English-speaking families in terms of consumption habits for many product categories, as well as for media habits. When compared to English-speaking households, French-speaking families use more staples associated with original cooking and more soft drinks, sweet instant beverages, beer, wine, and Geneva gin. They use less frozen vegetables, dietary beverages, and hard liquor and mixers, and their furniture is less valuable.

In spite of the notion that the United States is a "melting pot," it is less of a heterogeneous mixture than may otherwise be believed. The U.S. market actually consists of several distinct subcultures. In terms of the size of the ancestry groups, the leader is the English (50 million), followed by the German (49 million), the Irish (40 million), the African-American (21 million), the French (13 million), the Italian (12 million), the Scottish (10 million), the Mexican-American (8 million), the American Indian (7 million), and the Dutch (6 million).[63] An ethnic group may be small yet still be highly viable as a result of geographic concentration. California contains most of the various European ancestry groups. New York is first in population size for the peoples of Italian, Polish, Russian, and Hungarian ancestry. Minnesota has most of the Norwegians, whereas Illinois and Florida have more Czechs and Bahamians respectively.

Each ethnic group is a part of the larger U.S. culture and yet has its own unique cultural, demographic, and consumption characteristics. For example, black consumers are the largest so-called ethnic minority group in the country. This segment has a high number of families headed by women. Black females are relatively young, with the median age of 27.2 years as compared to 33.1 for white females. Blacks have begun recently to spend less on cigarettes, liquor, clothes, and food than previously and have begun to spend more on housing, recreation, travel, and education.

Another important subculture in the United States is the Hispanic group, which is significant because it is large; it will soon become the largest ethnic minority group in the nation. This should not be surprising because, in addition to the annual arrival of new immigrants, Latinos generally have larger families. With some $70 billion in annual spending power, this subcultural segment is much too important to be ignored.

Hispanics' tastes and purchasing habits are unique to that group. In terms of brand loyalty, there is an unusually strong tenacity, with an average of 9.5 years before brand switching occurs.[64] Hispanics generally take a great deal of pride in dressing their children well, thus making them important to the children's clothing market. Their strong family orientation serves to explain why they patronize fast-food restaurants twice as often as the national average. Chicken is a particularly popular dish, as evidenced by the consumption of fowl, which is three times the rate consumed by other American consumers.[65]

The Hispanic subculture poses special marketing challenges. Operating contrary to the usual assimilation process, Spanish-speaking consumers generally want to maintain a distinct identity. Moreover, Cubans, Puerto Ricans, and Mexicans even differ from one another in terms of language nuances, geographic location, demographics, and heritage. Stroh, in promoting its beer to these Hispanic subgroups, regionalizes radio spots by using different musical backgrounds, voice tones, and dialects to reach each group effectively. Miller Lite likewise features Tex/Mex music and El Pipporo (a Mexican artist) and Carlos Palomino (a Mexican-American boxer) in the Southwest region of the United States, while featuring Salsa-Caribbean music and such Caribbean ex-baseball players as Manny Mota and Camilo Pasqual in the East and Southeast.

To make contact with Latinos, a variety of media can be used, ranging from Spanish language newspapers and telephone directories to local TV and the Spanish-language TV network. The most effective medium, however, is probabaly radio, as

Hispanic consumers listen to it for more hours and more frequently than do non-Hispanics.

Firms attempt to attract Latinos in many different ways. Big city banks provide automatic teller machines (ATMs) that communicate in both English and Spanish. Many companies design products that focus on Hispanic tastes, ranging from L & M Superior and Dorado brand cigarettes to Que Guapa popular-priced cosmetics. Some companies, such as Kentucky Fried Chicken, have adapted advertising campaigns to the Hispanic market. Other firms, such as Kraft, Procter and Gamble, General Foods, Campbell, and Anheuser-Busch, create Spanish language commercials especially for this market.

As pointed out earlier, any translations must be carefully made, and this applies to the translation of English language advertisements for the Hispanic population. Beer (*cerveza*), for example, is a noun of the feminine gender. To literally translate Budweiser's "king of beers" slogan is to incorrectly use a Spanish gender, and the translation would connote "queen of beers" instead. To be effective, more than a simple translation of a standardized advertisement is usually needed. As explained by one account executive of Donnelly Marketing, "While you can translate the language, you can't translate cultural values. Language is just a mechanism for communication. What's actually important is the culture behind the language."[66] This explanation makes it clear why Maxwell House felt a necessity to change its campaign theme. While stressing "tradition in American kitchens" for its general U.S. market, the company learned that the product's tradition did not exist among Hispanics. As a result, some adaptation was needed, and the "Fernandez Family" tradition was introduced. The message theme states that "75 years ago, the Fernandez Family arrived in this country and found a tradition."

CONCLUSION

Culture prescribes acceptable beliefs, traditions, customs, and values that are then socially shared. Culture is subjective, enduring yet dynamic, and cumulative. It affects people's behavior in diverse ways through logic, communication, and consumption. Although some cultural traits are universal, many others are unique and vary from country to country. And in spite of national norms, cultural differences as a rule even exist within each country.

While there may be a tendency to misunderstand different cultures and sub-cultures, this temptation should be resisted. Being the force that it is, the culture of one country should not be judged as superior to the culture of another country. Each culture has its own particular values and social practices, and the international marketer will be much further ahead if he or she tries to walk in the other person's shoes in order to understand more clearly that person's concerns and ideas.

Because marketing takes place within a given culture, a firm's marketing plan takes on meaning or is appropriate only when it is relevant to that culture. A U.S. company should understand that foreign consumers are not obligated to take on American values—nor may those consumers desire to do so. Also, it is more important to know what a person thinks than what that person's language is. Because of the great differences in language and culture around the world, American firms need to adjust their approach to solving marketing problems in different countries. In a foreign cultural environment, the marketing plan that has worked well at home may no longer be effective. As a result, the firm's marketing mix may have to undergo significant adaptation and adjustment. Effective marketing in this environment will thus mandate that the company be culturally responsive.

QUESTIONS

1. What are the characteristics of culture?
2. Explain the impact of culture on consumption.
3. What is the SRC (self-reference criterion)?
4. Distinguish between high-context and low-context cultures.
5. Distinguish between monochronic and poly-chronic cultures.
6. Explain how the meanings of time, space, agreement/disagreement, and friendship can vary from one culture to another. Also discuss their business implications.
7. What are some of the unique characteristics of the U.S. culture?
8. What are some of the unique business characteristics of the Japanese culture?

DISCUSSION ASSIGNMENTS AND MINICASES

1. Which one of the following seems to better characterize the world: cultural commonality or cultural diversity?
2. Because English is the world language of business, is it necessary for U.S. managers to learn a foreign language?
3. Do you agree that the United States is a "melting pot"?
4. As Hispanic consumers in the United States are also American consumers, is it necessary for marketers to adjust their marketing mix for this market segment?
5. Explain how culture affects the ways people use eating utensils (e.g., fork, spoon, knife, chopsticks).
6. Explain why people in several countries are upset when they see (a) an advertisement showing an American crossing his legs at the reader or putting his legs on a table; and (b) Americans wearing shoes into their homes.
7. According to Edward T. Hall, a renowned anthropologist, Americans are more comfortable with Germans than with the Japanese because Germans generally make eye contact to indicate attention to a speaker. Still, the Americans feel that the Germans do not smile often enough. How do the Germans and Japanese regard the Americans' frequent smiles and eye contact?
8. According to William Wells of the DDB Needham Worldwide advertising agency, American TV commercials are usually shown either as an illustrated lecture or as a drama in which a product is a prop (or a mixture of both techniques). Why is the lecture approach (a low-context technique) inappropriate for high-context cultures? Why is the drama approach (a high-context technique) appropriate for Japan? Note that Japanese commercials go to great lengths to present cues that are not product-related before devoting only a few seconds to the product itself at the end. To American advertisers, this advertising approach is ambiguous and puzzling.

CASE 6-1
CULTURAL CONSIDERATIONS IN INTERNATIONAL MARKETING:
A Classroom Simulation

JAMES B. STULL
San Jose State University

With the constant increase of multinational companies (MNCs), foreign investments, and international negotiations, the need for smooth interpersonal transactions and business strategies also grows. Practices taken for granted in one country face varying degrees of probability of achieving desirable results in another. For example, if a Saudi Arabian host offers an American visitor a cup of coffee, the American stands a better chance of preserving friendly relations if he accepts the Saudi's offer. Politely refusing a cup of coffee may be acceptable behavior in the United States, but to a Saudi it may be an insult, as the offer of a cup of coffee is an expression of Saudi hospitality and a symbol of one's honor. An American visiting a Latin American country may arrive at his host executive's office for a 10 A.M. appointment at 9:55 A.M. However, the host may not appear until 11 A.M. While the American may be fuming at having to wait over an hour, his host may feel no need to apologize to the American as this is normal practice in this host's business environment.

This simulation is designed to illustrate how the sensitive businessperson may be the one who approaches another culture by attempting to adopt the viewpoint of that particular culture.

Components of Culture

Culture is a complex pattern of consistent behaviors which can be broken into components. For the purposes of this exercise, let's consider those proposed by Vern Terpstra in his first edition of *The Cultural Environment of International Business*: language, religion, attitudes and values, social organization, education technology, political systems, and legal systems.

Language

Language reflects the philosophy and lifestyle of a group of people. It also conditions people to think and behave in certain ways. Eskimos have more than 25 words for "snow," but no word for "war." Arabs have over 6,000 words for camel, its parts and equipment. The Arabic word for "citizen" translates roughly as "one who performs Allah's will." Nearly one-half of English is made of up scientific and technological terms. A clock "runs" in the United States, while it "walks" in some Spanish-speaking countries. People who study languages learn much more about other people than merely how they speak. Language may be the most reliable indicators of other components of a culture; it can tell us a great deal about how other people live and think as well.

Religion

If religion provides people with a sense of why they are on this earth, it may consciously and subconsciously dictate how they conduct their lives. Attitudes, values, and behavior can often be traced to religious philosophies. Although numerous religions exist, most of the world fits into six basic religious categories: animism (primitive religions), Hinduism, Buddhism, Islam, and Christianity. Judaism is found primarily in Israel.

Attitudes and Values

A people's attitudes and values about certain topics are important to that society's economic development and its people's behavior. Of particular concern are attitudes and values about time, work and achievement, wealth and material gain. Religions play a major role in their development. The tenets and canons followed by most religions often contain prescriptions and proscriptions about greed and the attainment of wealth and material items.

Social Organization

People organize activities and role relationships consistent with other cultural values and expectations. Important considerations include a culture's origin and history, family relationships, friendships, class structure, governmental powers, social and reference groups (including labor unions), gender roles, supervisor-subordinate relationships, and more.

Education

Educational systems are culture-specific, promulgating norms as a vein of cultural existence. Studies show a high correlation between educational enrollments in secondary and higher levels of education and a country's economic development. Diffusion of innovations into a culture depends heavily on literacy, which typically leads to better communication systems, new ideas, new ways to solve problems, increased technological development, improved labor forces, and more.

Technology

The artifacts, material symbols, problem-solving techniques, quantitative systems, managerial styles, and other intellectual tools reflect the educational and technological development of a culture. Studies show high positive relationships between per capita incomes and per capita energy consumption; high gross domestic products and manufacturing; and low gross domestic products and agriculture. Also characteristic of technologically developed cultures are more urban dwellers; high per capita expenditures on education; more cars, radios, televisions, and telephones; more scientists, engineers, and technicians; and higher expenditures for research and development. Technology determines how a country uses its land, labor, capital, and education. It also leads to further technological innovation.

Political Systems

Political environments both within and between countries are major considerations when conducting international business. Politicians exercise controls over resources and how people use them. Religious groups, labor unions, and multinational companies are also clearly political. Multinational corporations (MNCs) are always at risk politically when they enter a foreign arena to conduct business. The MNC may be forced to take severe action because of sudden changes in a host country's environment, including competing political philosophies, social unrest, lobbying independence, war, and new international alliances.

Legal Systems

Laws are rules of a culture established by authority, society, or custom. They reflect the attitudes of the culture; they may be written or unwritten. Most of the world fits into one of the following legal systems: common, civil, communism, Islam, or indigenous. Some of the legalities an MNC must consider include location, structure, finances, money, taxes, property, antitrust, and transportation. Additional considerations might involve controls over importing, exporting, patents, trademarks, competition, and controls over the host country imposed by still other nations.

Economic forces such as employment, income, gross national product, foreign exchange risk, balance of payments, and commodity agreements also affect international business. One must also look at the country's population, climate, geography, natural resources, ecological systems, and plant and animal life. You may wish to add these variables to the simulation, but they are not discussed in detail here.

Simulating International Business

This simulation was originally designed for a 15-week, two 75-minute sessions per week marketing class, with approximately forty students per section. It can easily be adapted to fit the needs of any group.

Simulations are a popular, widely used method of teaching and training people in the development of various skills. Discoveries about aircraft in flight have been made in wind tunnels. Astronauts train for space flight through simulations. Airplane pilots and automobile drivers learn on simulators. Law students experience trial conditions through moot courts. First aid personnel practice cardiopulmonary resuscitation on inflatable dummies. Security, safety, and medical personnel train to deal with various hazards and obstacles through fire, lifeboat, and air raid drills, disaster training, and other forms of simulation.

Simulations are also used widely in management training. Machine and interpersonal simulations have given trainees ideas about what to expect and how to react to probable leadership situations.

A simulation is an operating model of real life in which participants can experience much of what would happen without suffering many of the negative consequences.

Here is one way to successfully experience the benefits of this simulation:

Week 1: You will be assigned to a research group to find out as much as you can about *one* of the following variables: language, religion, attitudes and values, social organization, education, technology, political systems, and legal systems. An excellent source of information for this phase of the simulation is Vern Terpstra, *The Cultural Environment of International Business,* Cincinnati: South-Western, 1978.

Weeks 1–5: Your group should pace itself and prepare to present your research findings to the class sometime during weeks six through nine. You should develop ways for your audience to actually *experience* your concept or component as it is experienced in other cultures.

Weeks 6–9: Your group will present your findings during one class period. Plan for one concept to be presented each class period. Be sure to take notes and participate in this phase, as the information will be used during the next module, weeks 10–15.

Weeks 10–15: On the first day of this phase you will be assigned to a new group. One member from each of the research groups from the first nine weeks will be assigned to a culture group, so that each culture group has an expert on each of the separate components making up that culture. Each new group will function as a business organization representing one of the following five cultures: Bwana, Feliz, Leung, Koran, and Dharma.

Bwana   This African republic is slowly beginning to trade with the rest of the world. Its level of technology is far behind countries such as Japan, Germany, Great Britain, and the United States. Bwana is rich with gems, ivory, and precious metals, but its primary exports are coffee and textiles. The primary language is Swahili, although some English is spoken in the capital city, Zulu. Organized religion has made little impact on this tiny nation. Most of the people are animistic, believing that spirits inhabit everything; people worship volcanoes, the moon, rubber trees, and waterfalls. A very traditional, slowly emerging country, Bwana still relies on tribal laws that have been handed down through generations. Children can get a formal education in the capital city, but most of the people live in rural villages where tribal leaders determine what needs to be learned.

Feliz   This Central American country is constantly in the world news. Guerrilla warfare leaves Feliz politically unstable. Although the official language is Spanish, dozens of pre-Columbian dialects are spoken in rural villages. Catholicism is the primary religion; however, some pre-Catholic animism still exists as the local *brufo* or shaman is frequently seen waving incense pots and chanting at village churches. Some technological advancements have been made in the capital and two other large cities. Exports include rum, sugar, rice, lumber, and motor vehicles. Tourism is strong on the Caribbean cost, where fishing is extremely popular and politics seem not to exist. In the cities, many children complete their secondary education. Village children typically receive no formal education. Civil law is followed in Feliz.

Leung   Leung is located in Asia. Cantonese is spoken throughout the country. The Leungese people revere education and encourage their children to learn as much as they can, but the country's economy makes it virtually impossible for the education to be put to use. Most of the children receive a solid education, but formal training is limited to trade schools and technology centers. The average citizens believes in the country, but many Leungese leave to seek opportunities elsewhere. A significant number of those who have been educated and trained in Western countries are beginning to return to help develop their native land. Leung exports rice, wheat, corn, cotton, and textiles. It produces steel, iron, coal, and some machinery. Recent ventures have resulted in foreign-owned high-technology computer assembly plants being set up and operated near the port cities. The people follow the teachings of Confucius, Buddha, and Tao. Communism has been the main form of government since the 1920s, but the younger generation wants to see change soon. Some free trade zones have emerged in the past few years, allowing merchants to experience other countries' ways of doing business.

Koran   Koran is situated in the Middle East, in a very dry desert region. The country has produced and exported oil since 1938, and is also abundant with fertilizers, petrochemicals, and cement. Koran enjoys a strong fishing industry. Desalinization plants have helped Koran provide water for agriculture and industry. Because of its success with oil, the per capita income is one of the highest in the world. However, other levels of technology are low. Some areas of the country are run down and the people are extremely poor. Koran imports a great deal from the rest of the world. The primary language is Arabic. Islam is the only religion, with Muslims following the word from the holy book, *The Koran*. The oil industry has modernized part of the country, but Islam dictates that Muslims adhere to tradition.

Dharma   Dharma, a former British colony, is located on the Indian subcontinent. The people speak Hindi, though some 200 different dialects may be heard. Most Dharmese practice Hinduism. Education is very important to the Dharmese people, and they make great sacrifices to be sure that their children go to school. The economy is historically poor. The main exports are rice, legumes, tea, and tapioca. Children often leave Dharma to study in England, Canada, or the United States, and they tend not to return to their homelands except to visit their families. The government is primarily socialist, with strong ties to the English common law system.

Although these cultures are obviously fictitious, they are intentionally similar to real cultures so that you can make reasonable inferences that will help you succeed in this simulation.

Procedure for Weeks 10–15

You will need to go through the following steps to compete the phase of the simulation:

1. Each culture must consult its specialists to develop a clear understanding of its own identity regarding each component. Focus on developing specific verbal and nonverbal language norms which will be observed during negotiations with other cultures. This may take a few class days.

2. Study the other cultures to gain some familiarity with their cultural components. Research real cultures that you perceive as similar so that you can make reasonable inferences about life in the fictitious culture.

3. Your overall goal is to market a product, product line, service, or idea to the other culture. Your success will depend on how well you know the other culture and how well you adapt your business and marketing strategies to each.

4. You must identify a product, service, or idea that you believe is compatible with your own culture and that you could market successfully to the other culture. You don't have to invent something.

5. Develop business and marketing strategies that you believe will be sensitive to the idiosyncrasies of each other culture.

6. You will negotiate with each other culture, persisting until a contract has been settled or until you perceive that a stalemate has been reached.

7. Discuss the simulation, focusing on how you felt and what you learned while you were simulating international business.

8. Your instructor may modify this simulation to meet the needs of your particular class.

CASE 6–2
BENEATH HIJAB
Marketing to the Veiled Women of Iran

JEFFREY A. FADIMAN
San Jose State University

Hijab means modest dress, and that is how Muslim women cover themselves. To Muslim women wearing *hijab,* one of the most annoying questions asked by Western women is, "Why?"

In defense of the practice, *Mahjubah: The Magazine for Moslem Women* (an English-language journal published in Iran for foreign distribution) ran an article examining *hijab* from the perspective of Muslim women. According to the article, men and women are physically and psychologically different. Muslim women are equal to men but not the same as men. Each sex has its own rights and place in society. Women wear *hijab* not because they are weak but because of the high status given to them by Allah and because of their desire to adhere to Islamic morality. As such, *hijab* means more than an outer garment; the heart must be modest as well.

Muslim women, on the other hand, often wonder why Western women wear skimpy, skin-tight dresses that are impractical and uncomfortable. Why must Western women be slaves to appearance, forever listening to the media about how to be glamorous? Why must they have to look beautiful for strangers to ogle them in public places? Why do Western feminist groups want to turn women into men? Muslim women wonder whether such questioning of gender roles is a sign of strength or actually a sign of weakness.

Questions

Assume that Iran's new leaders now welcome U.S. businesses, requiring only that the members of each firm respect the religious, ethical, and moral beliefs of the nations. Consider that before the Ayatollah Khomeini's revolution, Iran's women showed enormous and increasing interest in a wide range of U.S. goods, often wearing them "beneath the *hijab,*" in deference to the opinions of Iranian men. Then came Khomeini, labeling the United States "the Great Satan." As a consequence, Western goods became equated with religious evil. Now the market has opened once more, after a drought of years.

How can you reawaken that demand? How can you stimulate the demand for Western goods (or services) among Iranian women without generating anxiety on the part of Iran's (all male) religious and secular authorities?

Your responses to this question should take the form of an essay, suggesting a number of specific measures that might be taken. The essay should include your responses to the following:

1. *Product selection* What type of product (goods or service) could you, as marketing director of a small U.S. firm, attempt to test market to the female population of Iran? Describe in detail. Justify your choice of product.

2. *Segment market* Which segment of the market should you target as an initial clientele? Describe in detail, including sex, age, social class, residential pattern (rural, suburban, urban), and so on. Justify your choice of segment.

3. *Product modification* In what ways should the product (or service) be modified to stimulate demand by women, particularly those who continue to wear the black *chadur,* thereby conforming to *hijab* either by preference or in deference to male authority? Justify your modifications.

4. *Product image* In what ways must the product image be modified to conform to Iranian religious, ethical, and moral norms, considering that these are entirely imposed by men. Justify your modifications. (Note: Although upper- and middle-class women often do their own shopping, lower-class and more traditional middle-class women do not. Their husbands, fathers, and other men shop for them, and the man involved selects what seems appropriate to him. The problem is how to market products or services that entice women, without thereby alienating their men.) Also consider media selection, potential distribution outlets, point-of-purchase strategies, and so on.

5. *On-site project head* Considering both the legacy of hostility that Iranians feel toward America and their long-range fascination with Western goods, what type of individual would you select to launch this first-time effort within the country? Assume his or her professional qualifications to be adequate, but describe those personal characteristics (sex, age, appearance, temperament, language potential, special skills, etc.) that the ideal candidate should possess to deal with Iranians. Once you have described your ideal candidates, consider this question: based on the data available to you at this moment, who among your classmates would appear to be the best selection? Justify your choice.

As you write your essay, you should consider specifics about Iranian distribution outlets. Iran's cities, like many in the Middle East, can be described as three communities in one:

Modern core   Department stores, specialty shops; luxury goods (pre-Khomeini) elitist, Western-oriented clientele; also patronized by middle class.

Traditional core   Middle Eastern marketing patterns—open bazaars, with separate sections for specialists (e.g., street of the silversmiths, etc.), family godowns, (small general stores) clustered along tiny streets; lower-middle-class, "traditional," and urban worker clientele.

Worker zones   Concentric circles around both cores, each less wealthy than its predecessor, extending outward until they blend into the rural villages, from which the cities draw their food.

NOTES

1. A. L. Kroeber and Clyde Kluckhohn, *Culture: A Critical Review of Concepts and Definitions* (New York: Random House, 1963).

2. "Japan's Latest Invasion: Ladies' Lingerie," *Business Week,* 19 August 1985, 71–73.

3. Hirokazu Takada and Dipak Jain, "Cross-National Analysis of Diffusion of Consumer Durable Goods in Pacific Rim Countries," *Journal of Marketing* 55 (April 1991): 48–54.

4. Marvin Harris, *Good to Eat: Riddles of Food and Culture* (New York: Simon & Schuster, 1985).

5. James A. Lee, "Cultural Analysis in Overseas Operations," *Harvard Business Review* 44 (March–April 1966): 106, 111.

6. Jeffrey A. Fadiman, "Should Smaller Firms Use Third World Methods to Enter Third World Markets: The Project Head as Point Man Overseas," *Journal of Business & Industrial Marketing* 4 (Winter/Spring 1989): 17–28.

7. Edward T. Hall, *Beyond Culture* (Garden City, New York: Anchor Press/Doubleday, 1976).

8. "Global Advertisers Should Pay Heed to Contextual Variations," *Marketing News,* 13 February 1987, 18.

9. Rita Martenson, "International Advertising in Cross-Cultural Environments," *Journal of International Consumer Marketing* 2 (no. 1, 1989): 7–18.

10. Hall, *Beyond Culture.*

11. George P. Murdock, "The Common Denominator of Cultures," in *The Science of Man in the World Crisis,* ed. Ralph Linden (New York: Columbia University Press, 1945), 123–42.

12. Jon Lafayette, "Backer Predicts Material World," *Advertising Age,* 29 July 1989, 79.

13. Damon Darlin, "Myth and Marketing in Japan," *The Wall Street Journal,* 6 April 1989.

14. Allan B. Yeates, "Americans, Canadians Similar but Vive la Différence," *Direct Marketing* (October 1985): 152ff.

15. David R. Berlo, *The Process of Communication* (New York: Holt, Rinehart, & Winston, 1960), 164.

16. Lee H. Radebaugh and Janice C. Shields, "A Note on Foreign Language Training and International Business Education in U.S. Colleges and Universities," *Journal of International Business Studies* 15 (Winter 1984): 195–99.

17. "How to Learn a Foreign Language," *Business Week,* 29 September 1980, 132ff.

18. "State Interpreting Rules Get Lip Service," *San Jose Mercury News,* 18 December 1989.

19. *The Tower of Business Babel: A Guide for the Correct Use of the English Language in International Trade* (Janesville, WI: Parker Pen Co., 1983).

20. Ibid.

21. "How to Make Body Language Work for You," *San Jose Mercury News,* 3 March 1991.

22. *Investment in Indonesia* (Kantor Akuntan Sudjendro and Peat Marwick, 1985), 15–16.

23. See David A. Ricks, *Big Business Blunders: Mistakes in Multinational Marketing* (Dow Jones-Irwin, 1983, 14–18); Roger E. Axtell, ed., *Do's and Taboos around the World* (New York: Wiley, 1985).

24. Edward T. Hall, "The Silent Language in Overseas Business," *Harvard Business Review* 38 (May–June 1960): 87–96; H. K. Arning, "Business Customs from Malaya to Murmansk," *Management Review* 53 (October 1964): 5–14.

25. Robert J. Graham, "The Role of Perception of Time in Consumer Research," *Journal of Consumer Research* 7 (March 1981): 335–42.

26. John L. Graham and Roy A. Herberger, Jr., "Negotiators Abroad—Don't Shoot from the Hip," *Harvard Business Review* 61 (July–August 1983): 160–68.

27. Robert Levine and Ellen Wolff, "Social Time: The Heartbeat of Culture," *Psychology Today* (March 1985): 28–35.

28. Ibid.

29. "Japan's Secret Economic Weapon: Exploited Women," *Business Week,* 4 March 1985, 54.

30. "Korea," *International Trade Reporter,* 29 May 1985 (no. 1580): 97:24.

31. "It's No More Mr. White Guy," *San Jose Mercury News,* 29 September 1991.

32. International Trade Administration, *Doing Business with China* (Washington, D.C.: U.S. Department of Commerce, 1983), 14.

33. Ellen Hotung, "New Opportunities for European DMers," *DM News,* 1 September 1988, 33, 39.

34. Erik Wiklund, *International Marketing: Making Exports Pay Off* (New York: McGraw-Hill, 1986), 150.

35. John L. Graham, "A Hidden Cause of America's Trade Deficit with Japan," *Columbia Journal of World Business* 16 (Fall 1981): 5–15.

36. John L. Graham, "The Influence of Culture on the Process of Business Negotiations: An Exploratory Study," *Journal of International Business Studies* 16 (Spring 1985): 81–96.

37. M. Kavoossi and J. Frank, "The Language-Culture Interface in Persian Gulf States Print Advertisements: Implications for International Marketing," *Journal of International Consumer Marketing* 3 (no. 1, 1990): 5–26.

38. Mohsin S. Khan and Abbas Mirakhor, "The Framework and Practice of Islamic Banking," *Finance & Development* 23 (September 1986): 32–36.

39. "Singapore Is Building Itself a Hotel Glut," *Business Week,* 20 May 1985, 113–14.

40. Bradley Hitchings, ed., "Personal Business," *Business Week,* 6 December 1976, 91–92.

41. Chikara Higashi, *Japanese Trade Policy Formulation* (New York: Praeger, 1983), 72.

42. John F. Sherry, Jr. and Eduardo G. Camargo, " 'May your Life Be Marvelous:' English Language Labelling and the Semiotics of Japanese Promotion," *Journal of Consumer Research* 14 (September 1987): 174–88.

43. Enid Nemy, "In International Business, Gift Giving Can Be a Package Deal," *Chicago Tribune,* 6 October 1983.

44. James Patterns and Peter Kim, *The Day America Told the Truth: What People Really Believe about Everything That Really Matters* (Prentice Hall, 1991).

45. Hiroshi Takeuchi, "Motivation and Productivity," in *The Management Challenge: Japanese Views,* ed. Lester C. Thurow (Cambridge, Massachusetts: The MIT Press, 1985), 18–30.

46. Pierre Martineau, *Motivation in Advertising* (New York: McGraw-Hill, 1957), 157–62.

47. For a summary of the literature on Japanese cultural differences, see Lane Kelly and Reginald Worthley, "The Role of Culture in Comparative Management," *Academy of Management Journal* 24 (1981): 164–73; for in-depth discussion, see James G. Abegglen, *The Japanese Factory: Aspects of Its Social Organization* (Glencoe, Illinois: Free Press, 1958); William Lazer, Shoji Murata, and Hiroshi Kosaka, "Japanese Marketing: Towards a Better Understanding," *Journal of Marketing* 49 (Spring 1985): 69–81; George Fields, *From Bonsai to Levi's* (New York: MacMillan, 1983); Mark Zimmerman, *How to Do Business in Japan* (New York: Random House, 1985); Higashi, *Japanese Trade Policy Formulation.*

48. Norihiko Suzuki, "Spin-out Employees in Japanese Business Society: Their Problems and Prospects," *Columbia Journal of World Business* 16 (Summer 1981): 23–30.

49. Akio Morita and Shintaro Ishihara, *The Japan That Can Say "No": The New U.S.-Japan Relations Card* (Tokyo: Kobunsha, Kappa-Holmes, 1989).

50. Jeremiah J. Sullivan and Richard B. Peterson, "A Test of Theories Underlying the Japanese Lifetime Employment System," *Journal of International Business Studies* 22 (no. 1, 1991): 79–97.

51. Thomas E. Maher, "Lifetime Employment in Japan: Exploding the Myth," *Business Horizons* 28 (November/December 1985): 23–26.

52. Higashi, *Japanese Trade Policy Formulation.*

53. Zimmerman, *Business in Japan.*

54. Lazer, Murata, and Kosaka, "Japanese Marketing."

55. "Exploited Women"; Evelyn Richards, "In Japan, It's a Man's World," *San Jose Mercury News,* 12 October 1986.

56. Ronald E. Yates, "Question: Will Leisure Play in Japan?" *Chicago Tribune,* 29 June 1986; Evelyn Richards, "Weekends Could Catch on in Japan," *San Jose Mercury News,* 19 October 1986.

57. *Investment in Japan* (Peat Marwick, 1983), 37.

58. Fields, *From Bonsai,* 14–15.

59. Milton M. Gordon, "The Subsociety and the Subculture," in *Sociology of Subcultures,* ed. David O. Arnold (Berkeley, CA: Glendessary Press, 1970).

60. C. A. Valentine, *Culture and Poverty* (Chicago: University of Chicago Press), 1968.

61. Yeates, "Americans, Canadians Similar."

62. Charles M. Schaninger, Jacques C. Bourgeois, and W. Christian Buss, "French-English Canadian Subcultural Consumption Differences," *Journal of Marketing* 46 (Spring 1985): 82–92.

63. Ed Burnett, "A Brief Note on Ethnic Lists and List Sources," *DM News,* 15 December 1984, 30–31.

64. Nino Noriega, "Cooperation Will Benefit Both Corporate America, Hispanics," *Marketing News,* 27 May 1983, 3.

65. Renee White Fraser, "Dispel Myths Before Trying to Penetrate Hispanic Market," *Marketing News,* 16 April 1982, 1.

66. Carol Wheelan, "Hispanics Respond to Quality Invites," *Food & Beverage Marketing* (March 1985): 40ff.

Let us all be happy and live within our means, even if we have to borrow the money to do it with.

Artemus Ward

Consumer Behavior in the International Context
Psychological and Social Dimensions

7

CHAPTER OUTLINE

MARKETING ILLUSTRATION
It's Not a Small World After All

To compete with Brazil and Mexico, the Federation of Colombian Coffee Growers needed an image (see Exhibit 7–1). Based on its composite Colombian coffee man, it wanted a Latin name that was both pronounceable and easy to remember for Americans. Thus, Juan was chosen as the first name because it is easy and rhymes with *one* (coffee beans are picked one by one). Because Rodriguez is too complicated a name for Americans, Valdez was picked as the last name. At first, the Federation cast a New York-based Cuban actor as Juan but decided not to renew his contract in 1969 because of his arrest for nonpayment of alimony. A nationwide search was arranged for a Colombian replacement who would fit the American conception of the Latin male. The screening led to Carlos Sanchez, a relatively impoverished, university-educated silk-screen artist and sometime actor. The Federation's marketing campaign has been very effective.

One foreign airline's commercials showed a Japanese stewardess, clad in a beautiful kimono, serving sushi to a delighted Japanese passenger. Japanese viewers, however, were not impressed, criticizing her kimono, manners, and the sushi. They did not realize that the stewardess was actually a professional Japanese model and that the sushi came from a famous restaurant in Tokyo. To them, the stewardess was tainted because she worked for a foreign firm. When the commercial was shown to a different group with the identity of the airline concealed, the audience showed no such objections and thought that the airline was Japan Air Lines.

Sources: David Schrieberg, "The Real Juan Valdez," *San Jose Mercury News,* 27 March 1989; George Fisk, "Scaling the Cultural Fence," *Advertising Age,* 13 December 1982, M-11, 12

As shown in the case of Japanese viewers' reactions to an airline's commercial, consumers' perceptions are highly subjective. Consumers can be quite unpredictable, and the complex nature of consumers makes the study and understanding of consumer behavior imperative. The Federation of Colombian Coffee Growers' creation of Juan Valdez represents an attempt to utilize a symbol to affect consumer perceptions. The Federation has been successful in creating a desirable image for its product and using it to communicate with consumers.

Domestically, marketing scholars have employed a variety of techniques, including the cultural approach, to study consumer behavior. Yet consumer study on an international basis has almost exclusively employed the cultural approach. Samli, Grewal, and Mathur felt that there was little attempt to understand variables other than culture that affect the international industrial buyer's behavior. They discussed three models of organizational buying behavior from an international perspective and found a host of factors that affected the models' credibility in the international arena.[1] As echoed by Wills, Samli, and Jacobs, consumer behavior is not just American consumer behavior, and consumer behavior research must include international dimensions. Such concepts as learning and involvement warrant attention.[2]

Culture undoubtedly affects the psychological and social processes and thus affects consumer behavior. But perhaps too much emphasis has been being placed

Some people can't wait for their next coffee break.

The richest coffee in the world."

EXHIBIT 7–1   Colombian coffee and product image

Source: Courtesy of the National Federation of Coffee Growers of Colombia

on a single concept (i.e., culture). It is a questionable practice to rely on culture as the sole determinant of behavior or as the only concept that largely, if not entirely, explains behavior.

Because the influence of culture has already been discussed in depth in Chapter 6, this chapter covers other relevant concepts. The focus is on the major approaches used to study consumer behavior. The basic purpose of the chapter is to acknowledge the role that determinants other than culture play in influencing consumer behavior. The chapter thus examines the psychological and social dimensions, and these include motivation, learning, personality, psychographics, perception, attitude, social class, group, and family.

PERSPECTIVES ON CONSUMER BEHAVIOR

Consumer behavior can be defined as a study of human behavior within the consumer role and includes all the steps in the decision-making process. The study must go beyond the explicit act of purchase to include an examination of less observable processes, as well as a discussion of why, where, and how a particular purchase occurs.

Consumer behavior is an area of study that draws on the work of scholars and practitioners from many diverse disciplines. Most studies of consumer behavior attempt to explain the so-called black box model, as shown in Exhibit 7–2. This is essentially a model of stimulus and response. The mind of a consumer is analogous to a black box in that the box, like the mind, does not permit the observation of processes within it. Mental activities between a stimulus and the resulting response cannot be observed, causing difficulty in comprehending why a person decides to take a particular action. Scholars have been attempting for many years to draw some conclusion, based on their observation of the input and output activity, about what takes place inside that black box. Part of the problem may be that investigators from diverse disciplines tend to make different assumptions and, subsequently, conflicting deductions.

There are four major perspectives employed to explain the internal operation of the black box. These four perspectives, as shown in Exhibit 7–3, include (1) economics, (2) social-biology, (3) behavioral sciences, and (4) marketing.

Economics Perspective

Economists were the first group of scholars to conduct formal studies of consumer behavior. According to them, consumer decision is based on a careful allocation of resources among various alternatives to maximize the utility within the constraints imposed by a financial budget. In Exhibit 7–4, the straight line *AB* is the budget line—the amount of disposable income that can be spent on one of the two alternatives or on a combination of them. The first so-called indifference curve (I_1) intersects the budget line at two points (*C* and *D*), implying that either combination will give this particular consumer equal satisfaction—the consumer is indifferent at either point because both points are on the same indifference curve and the utility obtained is held constant by simply adjusting the quantities of both alternatives. The third indifference curve (I_3), being higher, will yield more satisfaction. But that curve does not intersect the budget line at all, making it unattainable by the consumer. The optimum point,

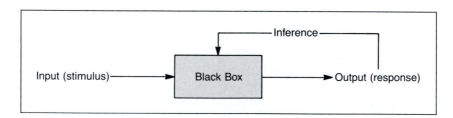

EXHIBIT 7–2   Black box model

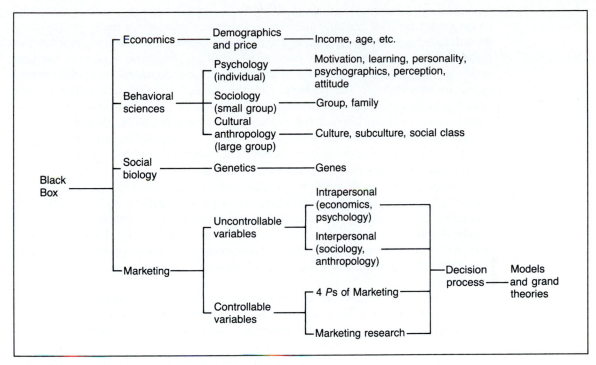

EXHIBIT 7–3 Perspectives on consumer behavior

then, is E on the second indifference curve (I_2), because it is attainable and because it is the only point of intersection of I_2 and the budget line, resulting in the maximum satisfaction within the available budget. Thus, rational consumption is almost solely a function of income—either present or future expected income—and the consumer will choose the total bundle of goods and services that yields the optimum satisfaction.

This economics framework, although useful, is inadequate because of its restrictive assumptions. First, it assumes that consumers want to maximize satisfaction when many actually seek only satisfactory purchase solutions rather than optimal ones.

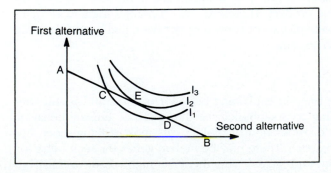

EXHIBIT 7–4 Economics perspective with indifference curves

Second, consumers are assumed to make careful measurements of the utility to be gained from all possible alternatives. In reality, consumers rarely get involved with detailed calculations of the satisfaction to be derived from each alternative. The measurement, assuming that it is done at all, would normally be imprecise. Because utility is subjective, any intrapersonal and interpersonal comparisons of the derived utility are very difficult. The problem with the subjective assignment of the amount of utility to an object is further compounded by the fact that consumers within different countries have different value systems, resulting in varying degrees of utility that can be derived from a given object. One study found that "the price-quality relationship shows different formations in different cultures based upon socioeconomic patterns, economic foundations, and value structure."[3]

Third, a rational decision is presumed to be made; that is, the consumer is presumed to have complete information about prices, markets, and products. This condition, however, does not exist in the real world because complete information is unavailable, too costly to obtain, or too technical to understand. This is especially true in countries where communication networks are underdeveloped or inadequate. When a foreign product is involved, the information may not be disseminated properly or effectively.

Fourth, the consumer, assumed to be rational, is actually influenced a great deal by emotions. Price and durability often become secondary to beauty and prestige.

Fifth, the basic assumption in economics is homogeneity: homogeneous products and homogeneous consumer preference. In the international context, supposing consumers across countries to be homogeneous is a very unrealistic assumption. Marketing, on the other hand, is based on the heterogeneity concept: both demand and supply are heterogeneous, thus approximating the real world much more correctly.

The economics perspective should be considered as being prescriptive or normative, and not descriptive, in nature—explaining what a consumer should do rather than what one actually does. In this regard, the correct consumption emphasis can be ascertained by the level of economic development in a country. Advanced nations, being more wealthy, are able to sustain a relatively higher level of consumption, whereas LDCs, because of lower per capita income, must limit local consumption. But the economics perspective is inadequate in explaining why consumers in countries with the same level of economic development have different preference patterns. Nor does it explain why members of the same income class in the same country do not necessarily prefer the same product. Therefore, the economics framework by itself does not provide a complete picture of consumer behavior, and other academic disciplines must be taken into account.

Social-Biology Perspective

This perspective involves the latest in explaining behavior patterns and is still very much in its infancy. According to sociobiologists, the study of human behavior makes no sense without the consideration of biology. "Its most striking tenet: human behavior is genetically based.... There may be human genes for such behavior as conformism, homosexuality, and spite."[4] This theory is highly controversial because it maintains that all other physical sciences and human sciences should become branches under one great discipline of social biology. Furthermore, "it may be used to show that some races are inferior, that male dominance over women is natural," and so on. One may then be tempted to ask, for example, whether the level of economic development is a result of genetic differences, or whether some countries become highly developed because their members gradually accumulate a separate and superior gene pool, or whether undeveloped countries remain largely undeveloped because their citizens are genetically inferior.

A firm conclusion with regard to the validity of the social-biology perspective is premature because there is little empirical evidence to support or refute this theory. In any case, it is highly unlikely that heredity or biological development can be used to explain brand choice behavior. Consumers are not dictated solely by their instincts, and their learning abilities certainly have a great deal to do with how they behave. Therefore, any contribution made by social biology to the understanding of consumer behavior in the near future is expected to be limited at best.

Behavioral Science Perspective

The major behavioral sciences relevant to consumer study are psychology, sociology, and cultural anthropology. Psychology, with the *individual* as its central unit of analysis, is the study of individual and interpersonal behavior. Behavior is governed by a person's cognitions, such as values, attitudes, experiences, needs, and other psychological phenomena. Purchase, then, becomes a function of the psychological view of products, and the consumer buys a product not only for consumption but also because of a perception of how a product can be used to communicate with other people. Some psychological concepts relevant to the study of consumer behavior are motivation, learning, personality, perception, and attitude.

Sociology is a study of groups and human interactions. The unit of analysis is not the individual but rather the *group*. The group, consisting of a set of individuals who interact over time, is important because it can exert a significant influence on a person's preferences and consumption behavior. In many instances, it may be useful for a marketer to think of consumers as a group. For example, a family, not an individual, often makes a purchase decision that affects all members of the family group. Important sociological concepts are reference group and family.

Cultural anthropology is the study of human culture. Thus, the analytic perspective may be quite large. Culture involves an aggregate, social category level (i.e., a *large* group), and the social categories are significant in the sense that they influence consumers' cognitive and personality development. The concepts from this discipline usually included in the analysis of consumer behavior are culture, subculture, and social class.

Marketing Perspective

Economics, sociobiology, and the behavioral sciences may provide a solid foundation for the study of consumer behavior, but they are of limited value for marketers because their objectives are to describe and explain behavior rather than to suggest specific solutions to decision problems. Furthermore, a particular discipline is not always adequate in providing complete insights into consumer behavior. The study of consumer behavior must thus be multidisciplinary, involving all relevant disciplines. The marketing perspective moves toward this end by attempting to integrate several disciplines together. Even though this approach is based on concepts and theories borrowed from other disciplines, marketing has now become a distinct applied field of its own. Based on this perspective, relevant variables are classified as either uncontrollable or controllable. **Controllable variables** are those variables that can be manipulated by marketers, namely the 4 Ps of marketing. **Uncontrollable variables,** in contrast, are those outside marketers' control, and such variables are divided into intrapersonal (psychological) and interpersonal (social and cultural) variables.

MOTIVATION

Motivation is fundamental in initiating consumer behavior. **Motivation** can be thought of as a drive that is directed by a motive formed in relation to a particular goal. Once the motive-drive relationship is developed, the consumer takes some forms of motivated behavior to satisfy a previously recognized need.

The motivation process has five components in the following sequence: unfilled need, drive, motive, goal, and motivated behavior (see Exhibit 7–5). These components may be visualized as occupying different locations on a motivation continuum. Moving from the left end of the continuum to the right end, motivation becomes more specific and observable. Therefore, movement in this direction indicates a change from generality to specificity, along with a correspondent increase in the likelihood of a more rigorous measurement.

Consumer motives are largely determined by buying habits, though motives can vary and it is important to recognize the various types of motives. Motives can be classified as rational and nonrational. Examples of **rational** motives are price, durability, and economy in operation. **Nonrational** appeals, in comparison, include prestige, comfort, and pleasure.

The problem with the conventional classification (i.e., rational vs. emotional) is that a consumer may not recognize emotional motives and may have the tendency to rationalize personal behavior by assigning only rational and socially acceptable motives. In addition, the process of classification is not always straightforward. Convenience, for instance, can be both rational and nonrational at the same time. Also, "many psychologists have studied the relative persuasive effects of rational and non-

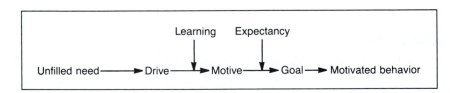

EXHIBIT 7–5 Motivational model

rational aspects of communication and have actually come up with little concrete evidence to support the superiority of one form over the other."[5]

In the end, the success of a product is greatly affected by whether its target customers are properly motivated. Whether a motive is rational or irrational is not particularly important. What is important is to identify specific motives relevant for marketing purposes. A critical task is to select, carefully and properly, a relevant motive for the purpose of product promotion. According to one study, Chinese consumers place greater emphasis than American consumers on convenience of location and salesperson's manner, and less emphasis on the store's return policy. American consumers, on the other hand, are more concerned with merchandise quality.[6] Exhibit 7–6 is an automobile advertisement that combines both emotional and logical motives.

The relevance of a particular buying motive often varies from country to country. Even when national groups have the same demographic and psychographic profile, they may drink mineral water for different reasons. French women use it to keep them svelte. For Germans, mineral water is a curative and preventative home remedy product that is healthful for the internal organs.[7] In the United States, it is common practice to treat pets as if they were children. In the non-Western world, people see no need to love or pamper their animals in this way. To humanize pets' needs thus may seem repulsive to non-Westerners, and the use of this wrong motive could result in a costly market failure.

LEARNING

Like all habits, food and drink habits are learned. Before World War II, the British were accustomed to drinking tea, not coffee. Then came the American troops, who brought the American taste for coffee—at first, a relatively light, almost blond coffee. Before long, Britons had learned to drink coffee too. In another example, a large lunch and wine presents no problem to a Swiss, but the same will put an American to sleep. On the other hand, American-style cocktails may prove to be too much for Europeans, who are accustomed to milder drinks. Marketers must take these habits into consideration.

Because motives, cultural norms, and consumption habits are all learned, a marketer should understand the learning process. **Learning** is a change in behavior that occurs over time relative to a given set of external stimulus conditions. Based on this definition, two important characteristics of learning can be identified: (1) There must be some change (or origination) in response tendencies (i.e. behavior), and (2) this change must be the result of some external stimulus condition (i.e., the effects of experience). Three types of learning explain such changes: classical learning, instrumental learning, and cognitive learning.

Classical Learning

Classical learning is the process in which (1) an unconditioned stimulus (UCS) known to elicit (2) a particular unconditioned response (UCR) is paired with (3) a

21 LOGICAL REASONS TO BUY A SAAB.

In each of us, there is a tough, cold, logical side that wants to have hard facts, data and empirical evidence before it will assent to anything.

So when your impulsive, emotional side saw the exciting photograph on the facing page and yelled "Hey, look at this!," your logical side immediately asked to see some solid and relevant information about the Saab.

Here, then, are some of the more significant hard facts about Saabs, facts that make a strong logical argument in favor of owning a Saab:

1) Front-wheel drive. Once, Saab was one of the few cars in the U.S. that offered this. Since then, most other carmakers have discovered the superior handling and safety of front-wheel drive and have followed Saab's lead.

2) Turbocharging. More power without more engine displacement. Saab's third generation of turbocharging, incorporating an intercooler and Saab's Automatic Performance Control system, is still a generation or two ahead of any competition.

3) Four-valve technology. Doubling the number of valves per cylinder improves engine efficiency enormously. Yet another group of manufacturers is beginning to line up behind Saab.

4) Advanced ergonomics. That's just a way of saying that all instruments, controls and functional elements are designed so that they will be easy and natural to use. A legacy of Saab's aerospace heritage. Saab is the only car manufacturer which also builds supersonic military jets.

5) Special steel underpanel. The Saab's smooth underside improves its aerodynamics and helps shed water to prevent rust.

6) Balance. 60% of the car's weight is borne by the front wheels, to maintain a consistent slight understeer and superior traction.

7) Rustproofing. A 16-step process that's designed to protect the car from the wetness and saltiness of Sweden's long winters.

8) Climate control. Your Saab is going to be comfortable inside, whatever is happening outside. Air conditioning is standard on all models, and effective insulation helps to control the temperature as well as the noise level inside.

9) High capacity electrical system. For reliable starts in subarctic cold.

10) Advanced Sound System. When you're in the Saab, the AM/FM cassette system sounds wonderful. When you get out, it can come with you, to provide the most theft deterrent possible.

11) One of the world's safest steering wheels. Heavily padded and designed to collapse in a controlled manner in case of heavy impact.

12) Safety cage construction. Last year, the U.S. Highway Loss Data Institute ranked the safety of cars based on actual damage and injury claims. Saab 900's were safer than any other midsize sedans.

13) Fold-down rear seats. This makes Saab the only performance sedan in the world that can provide up to 56 cubic feet of cargo space.

14) Large, 15-inch wheels. They permit good high-speed control with a very comfortable ride. They also permit larger disc brakes all around.

15) Price. It's modest, particularly when you see it against comparable Audi, BMW, Mercedes or Volvo models.

16) Side-cornering lights. These show you what you're getting into when you signal for a turn at night.

17) Front seats. Firmly supportive, orthopedically shaped and adjustable in practically every dimension you can imagine. They're even heated.

18) Saab dealers. They're all over the country, waiting to help you with specially trained mechanics and comprehensive stocks of Saab parts, and...

19) Saab accessories. These may be a bit too much fun for your logical side. They let you customize your Saab with factory-approved performance wheels, floor mats, fog lights and so on. And on. And on.

20) Saab's aircraft heritage. The first Saab automobile was designed by aircraft engineers who established a company tradition of carefully rethinking problems rather than just adopting the conventional solution.

21) The Saab driving experience. Best expressed on the facing page.

The most intelligent cars ever built.

EXHIBIT 7–6 Motives for buying

Source: Reprinted with permission of Saab-Scania of America, Inc.

neutral or conditioning stimulus (CS) to increase the tendency that the CS alone will produce the same response (UCR), which is then called (4) a conditioned response (CR). This process is shown in Exhibit 7–7. In order to cause the CS to produce the desired result, both the UCS and CS must be introduced together and repeatedly exposed to the respondent.

Consumer preference can be influenced by such advertising stimuli as background music, color, and other features that are not part of a product itself. For

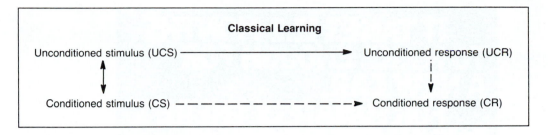

EXHIBIT 7-7   Classical learning

instance, listening to liked or disliked music in conjunction with the viewing of a product has been found to affect preference.[8] These findings may explain why Japanese TV commercials emphasize cues not related to advertised products in order to induce a positive mood.

Instrumental Learning

Instrumental learning is a type of learning that increases the frequency or probability of a particular response. Based on a process of trial and error, an individual selects an optimal alternative from a number of alternatives for a given problem situation. The alternatives (e.g., brands or stores) are tried at random until the most rewarding option gradually emerges as the most dominant or preferred choice, as shown in Exhibit 7-8.

A marketer can play a significant role in influencing the learning process by using a variety of rewards to encourage instrumental learning to occur for his market offering. Exhibit 7-9 shows how Northwest Airlines offered a special reward to its customers. Infant formula provides another example. The product is useful in many non-Western countries for well-to-do women who do not want to bother with breast feeding. Poor women seek the reward of using this status symbol and of having fatter babies—a benefit implied by this product. Furthermore, young mothers like the prestige of using American or European products.

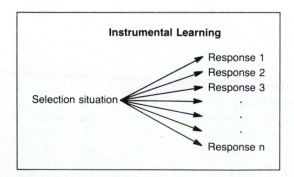

EXHIBIT 7-8   Instrumental learning

EXHIBIT 7–9   Learning and reward

Source: Courtesy of Northwest Airlines

Cognitive Learning

Classical learning and instrumental learning are both based on theories of stimulus-response and repetition. **Cognitive learning,** in contrast, functions very differently and goes beyond the process of stimulus-response and repetition. The theory of cognitive learning suggests that a consumer relies on personal analytical skills before making a response to a stimulus, as shown in Exhibit 7–10. The individual uses

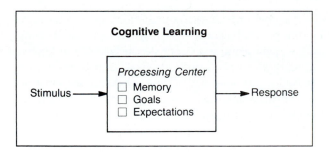

EXHIBIT 7–10   Cognitive learning

insight and problem-solving patterns based on memory, expectation, and goal seeking to provide an appropriate response. Whereas a stimulus is both a necessary and sufficient condition in stimulus-response theory for learning to take place, a stimulus is a necessary condition but not a sufficient condition in cognitive theories of learning. Cognitive learning acknowledges that the consumer is an intelligent information processor who constantly uses acquired information in an active manner to alter and modify responses to stimuli the consumer receives. The implication for marketers is that relevant information should be provided to potential customers so that they can intelligently draw their own conclusions.

It is inconceivable that a particular school of thought has a monopoly on describing learning behavior. In all likelihood, all three theories contain some truth about how a person learns. As the three kinds of learning are interrelated, a marketer must repeatedly provide information with regard to how a product is associated with the rewards potential customers are seeking. A product cannot succeed unless consumers understand what the product is for and what its advantages are.

The change of breakfast habits in Japan is probably a result of all three kinds of learning. On the one hand, it involves the cereal firms' repeated use of advertising stimuli to condition consumer responses while suggesting product benefits as buying motives. Consumers, on the other hand, need to process the information before making an informed decision. Breakfast used to be only rice before becoming rice and bread. Now the Japanese have discovered the benefits of cereal. Customers have a variety of reasons for switching from rice to cereal. Children eat presweetened cornflakes as a snack in the afternoons, whereas calorie-conscious young women want a lighter breakfast. Housewives who work tend to like cereal because they do not have time to cook rice, fish, and soup for breakfast. Old consumers find cereal and milk to be easy to digest and therefore good for ailments. Many adults have become convinced that cereals are real food rather than children's snacks. Still, sales of breakfast cereal are confined almost entirely to major Japanese cities.

Learned behavior does not change quickly or easily. Wacoal's early efforts to educate Japanese women in Western ways proved anything but easy. Initially, sales tended to drop in the winter, when customers reverted to the kimono for its warm layers of shapeless undergarments. Such cultural habits were eventually overcome, and Wacoal's sales took off in the late 1950s.

Long-standing conditioned habits that impede marketing effectiveness may have to be slowly replaced by new conditioned behavior. Direct marketing, a fast-growing activity in the United States, is only slowly gaining acceptance outside of the United States, where people distrust sending money to buy products from companies too far away to visit in person. The increased awareness of the value of direct response in terms of time and convenience, however, helps in conditioning non-U.S. consumers to become more responsive to offers from reputable companies.

PERSONALITY

Personality study has long been a subject of interest to marketers because of the assumption that product purchases are an extension of a consumer's personality. **Personality,** derived from a Latin word meaning "personal" or "relating to person," is the individual characteristics that make a person unique as well as consistent in adjustments to a changing environment. Personality is an integrated system that holds attitude, motivation, and perception together. To study a personality is to study the person as a whole—not just the separate, individual elements that make up a person.

Personality traits are relatively stable qualities, but they do vary in degree from person to person. Traits can be factor analyzed in order to determine the number of personality dimensions and the relationships among such traits. In one study, religious differences were found to affect Nigerians' acceptance of unfamiliar products, but the effects were moderated by personality. Furthermore, "the study also revealed the existence of meaningful personality differences between religious subcultural groupings, with the tendency being that Muslims were more likely to be closed minded (high dogmatic) vis-a-vis their Christian counterparts."[9]

Because personality study applies to a person rather than a group, it is difficult to make generalizations about personality traits among people of a particular country. Nevertheless, it is useful to consider the concept of *national character*, which states that "the people of each nation have a distinctive, enduring pattern of behavior and/or personality characteristics."[10] The English, for example, are highly impulse-restrained and unassertive.

Despite the difficulty, particular personality traits seem dominant in certain countries. In Japan, the ideal public official is oriented to the routine and traditional.[11] The virtues most admired are cooperation, fairness, and understanding of others. The personality type that has the characteristic of assertiveness or aggressiveness would be viewed by the Japanese as neurotic. As a result of this attitude, the Japanese hold an unfavorable view of personal drive, forcefulness, assertiveness, creativity, and individualism. It is common practice among Orientals to accede to a point in order to move a discussion forward in a peaceful, harmonious fashion. Korean businessmen view argumentative and adversarial exchanges as distasteful and thus avoid such confrontations at almost all cost. This apparent agreement is often mistaken by Americans as a true agreement, subject to contract terms.

Koreans see themselves as being driven by two complementary passions that are uniquely theirs: *han* (bitterness) and *jong* (devoted love). The interplay of the two explains Korea's ability to be at once intensely productive and violent, to both drive and stall a society, and to be capable simultaneously of love and hate.[12]

Some may emphasize that there appears to be a great difference between the American personality and the Japanese or Korean personality. Yet Canadians and Americans—despite geographic proximity and a common language—also have different personality characteristics.[13] Canadians are more conservative, philosophically and financially. They are more cautious, restrained, reserved, unimaginative, and collectivist in their approach.

Americans, when compared to Canadians, are more impulsive, self-confident, and risk-taking. Because Americans are more personally innovative, they tend to be much more receptive to new products. In a way, Gen. George S. Patton's statements seem to describe Americans' personality characteristics well. According to him, America loves a winner and will not tolerate a loser. "Americans traditionally love to fight! All real Americans love the sting of battle!" These characteristics seem to have served the United States well. Nevertheless, the same characteristics may be unsuitable for many countries, where the people may value other personality traits.

The differences in personality characteristics may explain why Canadians and Americans have different attitudes and buying habits. Americans, having less of an expressed need for law and order and being far more individualistic, favor personal ownership of handguns, something that Canadians strongly oppose. In contrast, Canadians' conservative nature may explain their tendency to borrow less and to make less use of credit cards. By the same rationale, a conservative nature may explain why Canadians own more life insurance per capita than anyone but the Japanese.

It is also possible to identify personality traits that vary from one region to another within the same country. Swanson delineates twelve major sociolinguistic "nations" of China, each having a language, local capitals, heroes, and characteristic behavioral traits and tastes.[14] These "nations," transcending political/provincial boundaries, represent distinctly different regions. The marketer may want to match the traits of the product with the audience's positive traits, which are stereotypical of the audience members themselves. For example, products marketed in the Gan nation and the Northern, Northwestern, and Southwestern Mandarin nations should perhaps use simple, conservative, frugal themes. The luxury theme may perform better in the Wu and Eastern Mandarin nations. For other groups, possible themes should be independence or manliness (Hakka), gentle humble images (Northern Mandarin), adventure (Minnan), athletic images (Minbei), and hard-working, pioneer virtues (Northwestern and Southwestern Mandarin, Yue, Wu, Minnan, and Hakka). Whereas the Northern Mandarin peoples are more conservative and resistant to change, the Yue, Wu, and Minnan peoples are generally innovative and aggressive, thus making them good markets for new products. It must be pointed out, however, that stereotyping, though being useful in terms of generalization, also has problems because it is a convenient but sometimes misleading method of grouping people.

Exhibit 7–11 makes a reference to a person's personality as a factor in choosing a car.

TEST DRIVE A SAAB. IT WILL TELL YOU A LOT ABOUT YOURSELF.

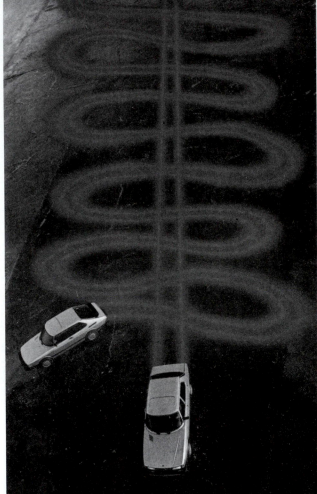

Thirty minutes in the driver's seat of a Saab 900 can be more revealing than a session on a psychiatrist's couch.

Will you look at Saab's front-wheel drive as a way to get through winter and the foul weather of the other seasons? You're ruled by your intellect.

Or will you look at front-wheel drive as the means to give a sedan the road-hugging, toe-curling, cornering ability of a sports car? You're ruled by your emotions.

But maybe you see front-wheel drive as both. You're ruled neither by your intellect nor your emotions. You are ruling them.

The ego and the id.

The id, the repository of your instinctual impulses, will want to know, on a test drive, how good a Saab is at, well, burning rubber. Don't repress that feeling.

All the practical considerations for buying a Saab (economy, the reasonableness of its price, the active and passive safety features, the durability in a world where disposability is a perverse virtue) are just as real and just as practical after testing its acceleration as they were before.

Sure, a car's reason for being is to get from Point A to Point B. But a Saab's reason for being is to do that as responsibly as possible without ignoring the romance in the possibilities of Points Q, R, S, T, not to mention X, Y, and Z.

An interpretation of your dreams.

Is the Saab 900 the car of your dreams? Who knows?

We do know it's the car of our engineers' and designers' dreams. There are, you know, seemingly disparate elements on a Saab.

Rack-and-pinion steering, disc brakes on all four wheels, front-wheel drive, 53 (!) cubic feet of cargo space, aerodynamic body, incredible fuel efficiency* considering its performance.

On a Saab, though, they add up to a whole greater than its parts. Saabs somehow feel better to Saab owners than other cars they've owned.

For the first time, they got the performance car they wanted with the responsible car they needed.

They found out the joy of not following the crowd, but of starting a crowd of their own.

Truth is, a 30-minute test drive may not be able to tell you all this. But we'll bet that three years owning one will.

SAAB 900

The most intelligent car ever built.

Saab 16-valve Turbo 5-speed: 19 EPA estimated city mpg, 25 estimated highway mpg. Use estimated mpg for comparison only. Mileage varies with speed, trip length and weather. Saabs range in price from $11,850 for the 900 3-door, 5-speed to $18,620 for the 900 4-door, 5-speed, 16-valve Turbo. Manufacturer's suggested retail prices. Not including taxes, license, freight dealer charges or options.

EXHIBIT 7–11   Personality and car ownership

Source: Reprinted with permission of Saab-Scania of America, Inc.

PSYCHOGRAPHICS

Because of the disappointing results in using personality to predict purchase behavior, marketers have turned to other meaningful purchase variables that might be used in conjunction with personality characteristics. This area of purchase behavior study is known as psychographics, also known as lifestyle or AIO (activities, interests, and opinions) study. **Psychographics** is a quantitative analysis of consumers' lifestyles and activities with the purpose of relating these variables to buying behavior. The analysis encompasses both the strength of the qualitative nature of Freud's psychoanalytic theory and the statistical and methodological sophistication of trait and factor theories. As a result, questions are well organized, and responses are subject to numerical representation and multivariate analysis.

Questions normally included in psychographic studies are those related to demographics, personality traits, and activities such as media habits, retail patronage, and general interests. People can be classified by their lifestyles and then be contrasted in terms of their consumption habits. Studies of Canadian women revealed the existence of five diverse lifestyle segments: contented striver, independent/self-confident, insecure, traditionalist, and career-oriented.[15] The largest segment proved to be the contented striver. A member of this group is usually more than forty years old and is content with her role as a homemaker. She reads grocery advertisements and saves and redeems coupons. Refusing to pay more in order to save shopping time, she shops around for bargains. In contrast, independent, self-confident women, the second largest segment, are not overly price-conscious or interested in coupons. This is the youngest group and they like to shop by catalog. Being ambitious and having initiative, these women want to be leaders.

The third largest group consists of insecure women who feel lonely and inadequate. Because of a lack of brand loyalty, these consumers are price-conscious and purchase private-label products. Next in line in the study was the traditionalist segment. Being older, its members are committed to traditional beliefs, and they value quality and convenience over price. Being cautious of unknown brands, they are store and brand loyal and pay cash for their purchases. Finally, the career-oriented women are members of the last and smallest group. They are similar to those in the independent, self-confident segment, except that this last group is older and more opinionated about the roles its members should play.

Because of varying lifestyles, marketers must adjust communications strategies accordingly. At the least, one campaign could be devised for the more traditional market consisting of the contented striver, insecure, and traditionalist groups, all of which focus on home life. Another kind of communication theme would be necessary for working women (i.e., independent/self-confident and career-oriented), who are interested in work and labor force involvement.

It is generally believed that Japan is so homogeneous that the market should not be segmented and that there will either be a mass response or little response. Still, psychographics—when used in conjunction with certain demographic variables such as age and sex—can yield useful information.[16] For example, there are greater lifestyle differences across age groups in Japan than there are in the United States.

Furthermore, there are differences between the two cultures. Japanese women are more home-oriented, are less inclined to eat out, are less price-sensitive, and are less likely to drive a car or attend movies. Also, older Japanese groups rely less upon advertising for shopping information.

Psychographics is also useful in explaining the diverse values and buying habits of consumers in different countries. A study conducted by Boote reveals that values and lifestyles vary significantly within as well as across countries (i.e., Germany, France, and the United Kingdom).[17] It is thus necessary to examine any standardized advertising message in light of varying lifestyles.

Marketers, in addition to identifying lifestyle variations within a country, may also identify lifestyle groups on a worldwide basis. According to Backer Spielvogel Bates Worldwide, there are five distinct groups of consumers worldwide: (1) strivers (26 percent)—relatively young people who work very hard and seek convenience and instant gratification, (2) achievers (22 percent)—affluent opinion and style leaders who pick brands that make statements about status and quality, (3) pressured (13 percent)—predominantly women who contend with economic and family pressures and have little room for pleasure or enjoyment, (4) adopters (18 percent)—older consumers who live comfortably in a changing world by respecting new ideas without losing sight of time-honored values, and (5) traditionals (16 percent)—those who embody the oldest values of their countries and cultures and resist change while preferring familiar products. However, 5 percent of the consumers did not fit into any of the categories.[18]

Lifestyle variations can dictate a product's success or failure. American consumers, for example, encompass several different lifestyles and consumption habits. Every day, Americans buy 120,000 new radios, 50,000 TV sets, 10,000 minks, 1,500 boats, and 12,000 refrigerators. Also each day, they spend $300 million on clothes, $3.6 million on toys and accessories for pets, and $700 million on entertainment and recreation. In a single day, 833,000 pairs of jeans are made, 60 million diapers are changed, and 100,000 Americans move to a different home.[19]

For some reason, U.S. lifestyles appear to create a great deal of social pressure, the result being that the United States has more people seeking psychiatric counseling than people of other countries. It is routine for Americans to use sedatives such as Valium and various pain relievers (52 million aspirins a day) for headaches very likely caused by stress. In Japan, the demand for such sedative drugs is small because the Japanese, after working hard all day, simply go to sleep and do not consciously dwell on anxieties and worries.

PERCEPTION

To learn, a person must perceive. Perception goes beyond sensation by providing meaning to sensory stimulations. It is the process of interpreting nervous impulses or stimuli received that the brain must organize and give meaning through cognitive interpretations. The Chinese, for instance, perceive Coke to look and taste like medicine.

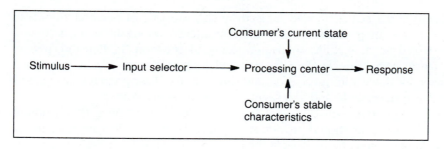

EXHIBIT 7–12   Model of perception

Exhibit 7–12 shows a simplified conceptual model of perception, a model based on the work of Warr and Knapper.[20] The process involves the selection by the input selector of certain aspects of a stimulus that will be processed by the processing center. This processing center is in turn influenced by a person's current state (e.g., mood) and stable characteristics (e.g., personality and culture). The result is a response that is internal and emotional.

One's culture greatly affects one's perception and behavior. Americans, for example, generally prefer steak on the "rare" side, in order to maintain moisture and flavor. Asians, on the other hand, would not dream of eating steak this way, believing that meat in that condition is raw and unsafe. Furthermore, Americans prefer to cook a big piece of meat, to be cut up or sliced on a serving plate at the dining table when they are ready to eat. The Chinese, however, prefer to cut the meat into small, bite-sized pieces before cooking and thus have no need for a knife at the dining table.

It is important to keep in mind that perceptions are formed through a highly subjective and selective process. The consumer's cognitive map of the environment is not a photograph of that physical environment. It is instead a partial and personal construction of a situation in which certain cues—selected and given emphasis—are perceived in an individual manner. More precisely, when one forms a perception, one is not a photographer but rather an artist who draws or paints an object in the way one thinks it is or should be. Therefore, no object or product is ever perceived exactly in the way it actually appears. One study, done in 1990, showed that the Japanese associated America with former President Reagan, great power/strong nation, and such products as cars, beef, oranges, wheat, and corn. However, California and New York recalled different associations.[21]

Because of a person's need for organization and stability, perception of an object tends to be stable over time in spite of the changes in that object. This was the problem encountered by Laker's Skytrain, which pioneered the concept of the walk-on, walk-off discount flight that charged for food and frills. The cut-rate strategy of "flying cheap and cheerful" worked until Laker in mid-1979 abandoned the original mission of price advantage in order to add frills. Passengers' perception of the airline's limited services, however, did not change, resulting in a blurred image. The downfall of the company followed when many customers deserted it for other better-known carriers that had better images.

Because of the selectivity and subjectivity characteristic of perception, people "seeing" the same thing can have vastly different interpretations. In Spain, accepting credit is viewed as an inability to pay—a shameful situation. In England, people perceive fancy, iced cakes as extra special, and such cakes are usually purchased from a bakery or made with great effort and care at home. Easy-prepared cake mixes are viewed as unacceptable and as a slight to a homemaker's role.

Whether a product will be successful or not depends significantly on how it is perceived. A marketer should provide some cues about a product in order to aid consumers in perceiving the product in the desired manner. Exhibit 7–13 shows how Ford uses the "quality" theme to affect consumer perceptions.

Another example concerns the acceptance problems encountered by Irish whiskey. Research has revealed that, though the word *Ireland* gets a favorable response, the word also conjures up images of fighting. To compound the problem, the word *whiskey* also has negative connotations, and thus Irish whiskey in particular has a reputation for being a harsh, strong drink. For this reason, the product possesses a strong double negative.[22] To overcome such a negative perception, the Irish promote their whiskey by brand names (e.g., John Power and Son, Dunphy's, and Jameson).

Americans generally have a positive perception of Canada. Research has shown that Canada conjures up images of "blue skies, snowcapped mountains, sparkling brooks, and green forests."[23] This positive perception is carried by Canadian beers as well. This is good news for Moosehead beer, which found from its focus group studies that the moose itself also had a positive image. The animal was perceived as "independence, strength, the king of the forest—a nice guy and friendly, but you don't cross him." Based on these images, the beer's advertising campaign carries such taglines as "head and antlers above the rest," "the moose is loose," and the beer being brewed "on the fringes of the Canadian wilderness." Exhibit 7–14 shows that Canadian Mist whiskey uses the same advertising approach.

Not only do consumers have general images about certain countries, but they also form specific attitudes about products made in those countries. This topic has received a great deal of interest and has been researched in great depth. Many empirical studies support the hypothesis that consumers have stereotyped opinions about specific products from particular countries. Among recent studies, one study found that a consumer's attitude about the quality of the automobile produced by a particular country created a "halo effect" that covered all products from that country.[24] Another study revealed that, although consumer perceptions of U.S. products and marketing efforts have improved over time, their corresponding perceptions of Japanese products have improved substantially more. Even in areas where U.S. firms had initial advantages, Japanese firms were able to surpass such advantages.[25]

A review of the literature reveals a number of interesting results.[26] Country of origin affects product evaluations. There is a positive relationship between countries' economic development levels and product evaluations; that is, products made in developed countries have better image than those made in LDCs. Still, products made in different developed countries are not perceived in the same manner; neither are those made in different LDCs. In any case, perceptions are also influenced by demographic and personality variables.

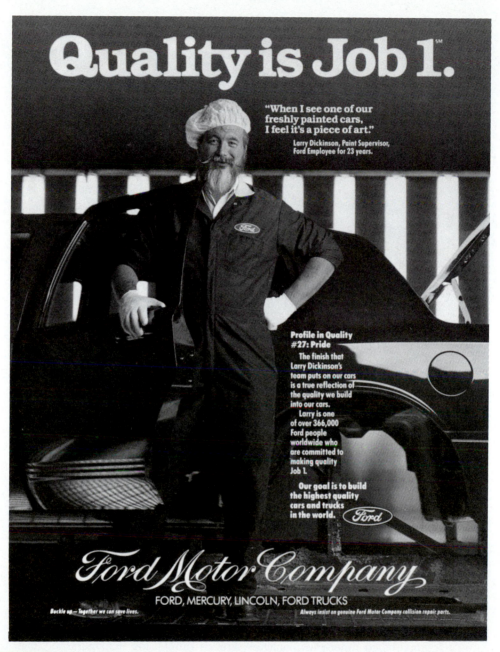

EXHIBIT 7–13 Creating a positive image

Source: Courtesy of Ford Motor Company

EXHIBIT 7–14   Perception of Canada and a Canadian product

Source: Courtesy of Brown Forman Beverage Co.

Although industrial users are supposedly more objective than consumers, they nonetheless have certain beliefs about products made in certain countries. When compared to American managers, French purchasing managers perceive American products as more expensive, having more unrecognizable brand names, and more concerned with performance.[27] American managers, in contrast, perceive French products as less reliable and more imitative. Furthermore, American managers view the Japanese and German products more favorably than do the French, whereas British products are better received by French managers than by their American counterparts.

One earlier study provided evidence that country of origin affects beliefs but not attitudes.[28] A more recent study, however, found that the country of origin directly influences product evaluations.[29] According to test results of another study, consumers not familiar with a country's products use country image as a halo from which they infer a brand's product attributes and develop their attitudes toward the brand indirectly through product attribute rating. On the other hand, when consumers become familiar with a country's products, country image may become a construct that summarizes consumers' beliefs about product attributes and directly affects their attitudes toward the brand.[30]

One experiment demonstrates that country of origin has a greater influence on product evaluation when this piece of information is presented one day before product-specific attribute information was provided. The effect is less when the country of origin information is conveyed at about the same time that attribute descriptions are given. It appears that, when subjects learn a product's country of origin an appreciable period of time before receiving other information, they form an initial evaluative concept of the product on the basis of its place of origin alone. This concept is used as a basis for judgment in its own right, and also influences the processing of attribute information presented later. It should be pointed out that, in the real world, it may not be practical to control the sequence and time interval of information.[31]

Consumer perceptions of the quality of products made in a particular country are sometimes product specific. Japanese consumers, for example, may prefer domestic origins for some products and foreign origins for other products. As a result, in Japan Warner-Lambert emphasizes the U.S. origins of its made-in-Japan chewing gums and candies but does not stress the origin of its U.S.-made razor blades.

The findings of these various studies have several marketing implications. When consumers seek a product with superior tangible attributes and when the financial risk is high, they are more wary of products from LDCs. Naturally, LDCs need to solve this marketing problem.[32]

When a "made in" designation is not favorably received, a marketer may want to deliberately conceal or not mention the product's origin. Many countries, however, including the United States, require proper origin identification in the form of tag, label, or other identification means before foreign products can be imported. Cattin, Jolibert, and Lohnes suggest two strategies: "The first one relies upon a communication campaign oriented toward the improvement of the national image; however, such a strategy cannot be undertaken by one company alone because of the cost involved. It can only be a concerted action by several firms with support from the national authorities. The second strategy involves the association of the corporation with local institutions (and little or no promotion about the country of origin). This may be achieved by using well-known local distributors, or by the 'domestication' of the firm through subsidiaries or joint ventures."[33]

It should be pointed out that there are separate country of design and country of assembly effects.[34] Credibility of attribute claims for products (TVs and stereos) made in a newly industrialized country (Korea) can be significantly improved if such products are manufactured in the United States. In addition, attribute claims become more credible when the products are distributed through a prestigious retailer.[35]

Because consumers continuously merge product information with country image, quality control is necessary. The industry association and the government should establish quality standards and provide such incentives as tax benefits and subsidies to exporters who meet the standards, while penalizing those who do not by imposing export taxes or withholding export licenses. To help consumers generalize product information over the country's products, individual marketers can benefit from favorable country image by highlighting products of superior quality from the same country. For example, Mitsubishi may claim that its TV sets are as good as those manufactured by Sony. Alternatively, to prevent consumers from using the country's negative image in product evaluation, marketers should dissociate their products from unsuccessful products from the country. As an example, Chrysler may stress that its Colt is a Japanese compact rather than an American car (see Exhibit 7–15).[36]

An international marketer should pay attention to the relationship between country of origin and the perception of product quality. Country-of-origin information is more important than price and brand information in affecting product quality assessments.[37] In general, engineering and technical products from Germany, electronics products from Japan, fashion products from France, and tobacco products from the United States are favorably received in most parts of the world. Also, consumers in LDCs usually prefer imported or foreign goods, believing that those goods are of higher quality and prestige.

A company must keep in mind that a product's image can change once its production facilities are moved from one country to a new location. Lowenbrau lost its image as a prestigious import beer once American drinkers became aware that the beer was licensed to be made by Miller in the United States. After years of disappointing sales, Miller attacked the problem head on with its campaign theme "this world calls for Lowenbräu," extolling the fact that the beer was made in many beer-loving countries.

Perception tends to be stable, but it can change, especially when the stimulus has changed significantly over a long period of time. Unfortunately for the United States, the perception of U.S. products has taken a turn for the worse. In the past, foreign consumers perceived American goods as big and expensive, but good and reliable. They still perceive these products as big and expensive but no longer of good quality.

International marketers should understand that their marketing practices have a great deal to do with how their products are perceived abroad, because consumer attitudes are conditioned by such practices. As explained by Piercy, "If an exporter competes primarily on price, there is a danger of becoming a 'bargain basement' supplier, with an image of cheapness and low quality, with a consequently low level of buyer loyalty. This may act to reinforce the buyer's national stereotype, and tie the exporter in to one segment of the market—which may not be the most attractive long-term prospect."[38]

Because of the constancy or stability of perceptions, a negative perception associated with a particular country tends to persist. But the problem can be overcome if a firm or country perseveres and is determined to improve its product quality.

EXHIBIT 7–15 Favorable country image

Source: Courtesy of Chrysler Corporation

A case in point is Japan. Its initial effort to penetrate the U.S. market after World War II was greeted with the perception that its products were cheap, imitative, and shoddy. Ironically, many consumers, including those in the United States, came to feel that Japanese products are superior to American goods, offering better value for the money. South Korea is presently striving to match Japan in this perception game. Both Yugoslavia's Yugo and South Korea's Hyundai automobiles have perception hurdles to overcome. Exhibit 7–16 shows how Jaguar Cars Inc. provides advertising cues related to the country of origin—the United Kingdom.

The 1989 Vanden Plas is the most exclusive and luxuriously equipped Jaguar sedan. Its sumptuous interior recalls a time when Vanden Plas was a builder of elegant custom carriages.

Hand-finished and meticulously inlaid walnut veneers lend lustrous warmth throughout the cabin. The rich feel and fragrance of supple leather abound. The front seats incorporate temperature-controlled heating elements.

For the rear seat passengers, burl walnut fold-down picnic tables and high-intensity reading lamps have been provided. Individual headrests on the rear seats offer added comfort and safety. An extended console brings air conditioning and heating vents within easy reach of rear seat passengers. A car of uncompromising luxury, the Vanden Plas is even furnished with fleecelike throw rugs in the passenger footwells.

To experience the elegance that is Vanden Plas, and for information on Jaguar's comprehensive three-year/36,000-mile warranty, see your Jaguar dealer. He can provide details on this limited warranty, applicable in the USA and Canada, and on Jaguar's Service-On-Site℠ Roadside Assistance Plan. For your nearest dealer, call toll-free: 1-800-4-JAGUAR. Jaguar Cars Inc., Leonia, NJ 07605.

ENJOY TOMORROW. BUCKLE UP TODAY.

The 1989 Jaguar Vanden Plas reflects an elegance that is as much a part of English life as afternoon tea.

JAGUAR
A BLENDING OF ART AND MACHINE

BLENHEIM, WOODSTOCK, ENGLAND

EXHIBIT 7–16 Product and country of origin

Source: Courtesy of Jaguar Cars Inc.

ATTITUDE

Attitude is the learned tendency to respond to an object in a consistently favorable or unfavorable way. Attitude is a complex and multidimensional concept. It consists of three components: cognition, affect, and conation (behavioral intention). Based on this definition, a few properties of attitude can be identified. First, the relationship between an individual and an object is not neutral: the reaction to the object is either favorable or unfavorable. Most people, for example, have favorable attitudes toward such automobiles as Mercedes-Benz, BMW, and Rolls-Royce, viewing them as status symbols. On the other hand, except for American consumers, who have long been conditioned to prefer large automobiles, most consumers have strong reservations about large cars because they look unsightly and are difficult to maneuver on the narrow roads found in most parts of the world.

Second, attitudes are relatively enduring and patterned and not temporary or transient. As a person becomes older, attitudes become more established. This becomes a challenge for international marketers who want to introduce change. A new product often involves a change in a long-held attitude. Finally, attitude is not innate—it must be learned. One's attitude about an object is formed by one's experience with the object, either directly or indirectly.

To achieve better measurement results, the standard attitude models may have to be modified for overseas markets. Confucian culture consumers (i.e., Koreans) have a fundamentally different cultural background from that which is dominant in the United States. Therefore, Lee modified the Fishbein behavioral intention model by incorporating the concepts of group conformity and face saving because of their pervasive influences over Confucian culture consumers' attitudes and behavior. The modified model improves the performance of the Fishbein model in explaining Korean consumers' behavioral intention formation process.[39] Commercials should show that many members of the target group purchased a product. Another study found that attitude-intention links were stronger than those found in similar tests in the West.[40]

Attitudes exist within an individual to serve four useful functions: instrumental, ego-defensive, value-expressive, and knowledge. The **instrumental function** results in the expression of an attitude in such a way as to maximize external rewards and minimize internal punishments. This function is also known as the utilitarian or adjustive function, because the individual adjusts an attitude in an acceptable and socialized manner in order to seek favorable responses from others. This type of attitude behavior is particularly strong in Japan, where people are willing to be shaped by group processes. Therefore, a marketer in Japan would be wise to show how a product can satisfy a consumer's need for group affiliation.

The **ego-defensive function** serves to protect a person against internal conflicts and external dangers. Wanting protection without acknowledging deficiencies, one forms an attitude to defend one's self-concept and to cover up one's weaknesses. Low-income American consumers, for example, are least likely to perceive American apparel as being superior to imported items. One possible explanation is that low-income buyers, having no choice but to purchase less expensive imported goods, may develop this type of defensive behavior.

Unlike Americans, who dare to be original and are accustomed to being criticized for their originality, people in Latin America and the Far East are particularly sensitive to any loss of face. It is thus distasteful to use aggressive advertisements that attack either competitors or consumers' beliefs directly. Japanese advertisers, when extolling the merits of their products, are very careful not to mention competitors' names in their TV commercials.

One study found that patriotic responses play a significant role in a choice between domestic and foreign products. An advertisement, instead of arousing consumers' guilt about not buying U.S. products, should emphasize consumers' patriotic obligation to buy domestic products and evoke their fears about the decline of the U.S. industry. Patriotic advertisements should be targeted to older, white, female, and blue-collar consumers.[41]

The **value-expressive function** is related to the individual's need to project worthy values into the open. The individual wants to be different or original and desires to maintain and express a self-identity. This function is very common in the Western world, especially in the United States. People elsewhere, however, view this function of attitude with distrust and resentment, fearing that their traditions will be diluted or destroyed by the permissiveness associated with the West. Their concern is the result of younger generations being so Americanized that they are preoccupied with self-expression rather than group welfare and respect for elders. The younger generation in the United States, as well as in other parts of the world, is generally receptive to products emphasizing symbolic attributes that provide for self-enhancement.

The **knowledge function** is also called the object-appraisal function because it is related to a person's need to understand an object. Based on a desire for clarity, predictability, and stability in perception, the individual seeks to have coherence and focus for experiences with an object. A marketer should thus take care to provide adequate information in order to familiarize potential customers with a product's benefits (see Exhibit 7–17). In Japan, some advertisements may seem to describe nothing about advertised products, but they are actually about products whose functions are well known. Japanese consumers want to know what a product is, and the Japanese do indeed demand product information, especially in the case of new products.

Attitude is greatly influenced by culture. Attitudes toward women, for example, vary from country to country. In many countries, women are still considered as a man's property, and a woman must seek her husband's approval before entering into a contract or being allowed to apply for a visa or passport. In Saudi Arabia, strict Muslim restrictions make it very uncommon for women to work. In Japan, working women are common but rarely have the opportunity to rise to a managerial position. Therefore, when women are portrayed in advertisements, the portrayal should be consistent with the expected role of women in that particular culture.

Attitude can affect marketing plans in other ways. Some countries have favorable attitudes toward foreigners, wealth, and change, making it relatively easy for MNCs to introduce new products. In fact, attitudes toward marketing itself should be considered. In India, marketing is viewed as unnecessary, annoying, and wasteful. Nestlé's infant formula received enormous adverse publicity because of the negative

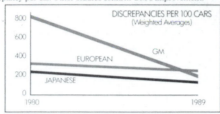

YOU ASKED US TO CHANGE MORE THAN JUST THE LOOKS OF OUR CARS AND TRUCKS. AND WE HEARD YOU.

We've introduced 77 new models since 1985, dramatically improving almost all the cars and half the trucks we make. The looks are new, of course, but the big improvements are in the heart of our cars and trucks—in the engines, transmissions, and electrical systems.

Quality That Lasts

According to one quality survey by Harbour & Associates, GM vehicles are better built than the average European import, and the difference between GM and the average Japanese import is less than one-half of one discrepancy per car. Other studies confirm GM's improvement.

DISCREPANCIES PER 100 CARS
(Weighted Averages)

GM — EUROPEAN — JAPANESE

1980 — 1989

You can count on GM cars for the long term. When J.D. Power studied the dependability of 1985 models, GM was ranked highest in vehicle dependability among all American manufacturers.* No other U.S. carmaker has done the job better in the last five years.

What does this kind of quality mean to our customers? Just ask. After six months of ownership, at least 95% of all Chevrolet, Pontiac, Oldsmobile, Buick, Cadillac, or GMC Truck owners would recommend a vehicle from that division to a friend.

(*J.D. Power and Associates Vehicle Dependability Index Study." In a ranking of the three domestic manufacturers, based on things gone wrong to 4-to-5-year-old 1985 model vehicles in the past 12 months.)

Dependable Engines

GM's engines are more dependable than those of all other domestic carmakers. Our 3800 V-6 is at the top in engine quality among engines from all makers, foreign or domestic, according to the most comprehensive customer-based survey in the auto industry.

In the latest evaluation of 1989 engine quality, the 2.3-liter Quad 4 was as problem-free as 2-liter engines from Toyota or Honda after 3 months' ownership. In the latest survey of a full year of ownership (for 1988 models), Cadillac owners reported fewer engine problems than Toyota or Mercedes-Benz owners, a tribute to the 4.5-liter V-8 engine. In 1990, we're dedicated to delivering the quality you demand.

Problem-free Transmissions

Any car or truck is only as reliable as its transmission. Our automatic transmissions are more problem-free than those of most imports, and more problem-free than any domestic competitor.

We Care About You

Today there is a new pride at GM. A new commitment to quality. A clear focus on our customers and on their needs.

People throughout General Motors, the GM Quality Network, are dedicated to continually improving our vehicles. Year after year. Until every model is as good as the best in the world.

All of GM going all out for you.

PUTTING QUALITY ON THE ROAD

GM
MARK OF EXCELLENCE

Chevrolet   Pontiac   Oldsmobile   Buick   Cadillac   GMC Truck

EXHIBIT 7–17   Knowledge function and product information

Source: Reproduced with permission of General Motors Corporation

view in LDCs about the company's marketing activities in poor countries. In contrast, Finnish consumers generally have a positive attitudinal response to the marketing activities and products of Finland, Sweden, and Germany.[42] Another study showed that consumers in six developed countries had varying attitudes toward government regulations of marketing.[43]

One problem firms have in marketing their products overseas involves the negative attitudes toward situations associated with their products and sometimes toward the products themselves. For example, customers may have favorable attitudes toward German machinery but not toward the purchase of such machinery because of the high cost, service, or availability of parts.

It is important for a marketer to distinguish between private and public attitudes, because an expressed public attitude can differ widely from a private attitude, especially when the private attitude contradicts the society's cultural norms. In Japan, attitudes can be used to divide consumers into two groups: conformists and nonconformists. At first glance, nonconformists are just a small minority. A more careful examination should reveal that salaried office workers, though conformist in appearance, working habits, and other public activities, may have different interests privately. Mail and phone ordering makes it possible for them "to make the buying decision free of conformity pressures associated with dealing with a sales clerk."[44]

SOCIAL CLASS

Social class implies inequality. Even in the United States, where all are supposed to be equal, some people seem to be much more equal than others. Social class exists because it provides for and ensures the smooth operation of the society. For a society to exist, many functions must be performed—some of which are not very pleasant. In this regard, members of society are not that different from the bees of a hive— different types of bees exist for different purposes (e.g., working bees, queen bees, soldier bees, and so on.). In Japan, even though the government long ago abolished the social caste system to allow for the mixing and reshuffling of people at all social levels, the selective access to higher education still impedes certain individuals from becoming career officials within the government.

Many societies see nothing wrong with the existence of a social hierarchy. In Indonesia, "inequalities and status differences tend to be seen positively. Senior levels of the hierarchy demand respect, and it is common for middlemen or go-betweens to be used when dealing with persons who are of lower status or not of Indonesian origin."[45] Moreover, status, position, and age are highly respected there. One must be polite and formal in the presence of elders and superiors. Connections with socially acceptable persons are often important in securing business.

The criteria used to assign people into social classes vary from country to country. A study of Chinese social classes found that income, occupation, education, residence, and family background, as components of class standing, affect purchase behavior.[46]

In the United States, relevant characteristics usually used in the construction of a social class index for classification purposes are occupation, source of income, house type, and dwelling area. Table 7–1 examines these characteristics. In other countries, occupation and/or amount of income (rather than source of income) are the dominant discriminating variables. In some societies, royalty affiliation is employed as well to distinguish one social class from another.

The U.S. social system differs from those of other countries in several respects. First, its greatest representation occurs approximately at the middle (i.e., the lower-

TABLE 7–1 U.S. social class descriptions

Social Class	Proportion (%)	Occupation	Income Source	House Type	Dwelling Area
Upper-upper	0.5	investments, civic work, law, professionals, owners of large businesses	inherited wealth in the second or third generation	excellent family mansion	older affluent areas (very high); Gold Coast, North Shore, etc.
Lower-upper	1.5	professionals, corporate heads	earned wealth: salary, profit, and fee	new and modern mansion	newer affluent areas
Upper-middle	10	professionals, business-persons	salary and dividends	new split or bilevel house house with a larger than average area	better suburbs, areas all residential
Lower-middle	33	white-collar workers	salary	tract house, duplex, modest row house, tidy apartment	suburbs, no deterioration in the areas
Upper-lower	40	blue-collar workers	wages	older frame house	areas of central city; older, more run-down, below average, deteriorating, businesses entering
Lower-lower	15	unskilled workers	wages and public relief	tenements, very poor and substandard house	slums

middle and upper-lower categories) of the social class scale. Many LDCs have a very large lower class, and the graphic composition of all social classes appears very much like a pyramid: the upper class is a small minority group at the top and the vast number of lower-class people occupy the large base at the bottom. Second, the U.S. system allows for social class mobility. The social caste system in India, in contrast, is extremely rigid. People there are born into a particular social class, and there is little opportunity to move from one social class to another.

Another difference can occur in the variation of the number of social classes across countries. The United States has three major classes (i.e., upper, middle, and lower), with each class further subdivided into two subcategories (i.e., upper and lower within each of the major classes). In Thailand, five classes are identified: (1) an aristocracy, composed largely of descendants of royalty and the old nobility, (2) an elite, comprising the top political, professional, and business leaders, (3) an upper middle class, made up of merchants, small businessmen, and white-collar workers, (4) a lower middle class, made up mostly of craftsmen and skilled laborers, and (5) a lower class, made up of unskilled laborers, domestic servants, peddlers, and so on.[47] There is also a large institution of the Buddhist Order, whose members are on a level with the top ranks of this social class structure but are not incorporated into the social class structure. The king, above all others in the social scale, is in a superior class by himself, as shown in Exhibit 7–18. Still, it should be noted that although Thai people are aware of their own status as well as general class distinctions, they do not have a strong sense of identity with other members of their own class. Because of the openness of the society and the general lack of both acute class consciousness and common class interests, Thailand does not have a class system in the traditional European sense of the term (i.e., rigid caste system). As a result, a person's social class is determined much more by wealth and education and less by family background.

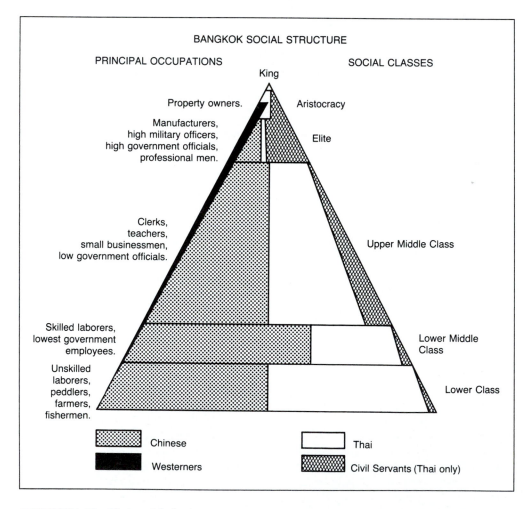

EXHIBIT 7–18   Thai social classes

Source: Wendell Blanchard, *Thailand: Its people, Its Society, Its Culture* (New Haven, CT: HRAF Press, 1966) 410. Reprinted with permission of HRAF Press (Human Relations Area Files, Inc.)

Even when the same distinguishing variable is used in different countries for classification, it may not have the same meaning and does not necessarily yield the same result. If the classification of occupation is considered, in the United States, financial considerations very likely explain why lawyers and attorneys are accorded the kind of status and prestige rarely found elsewhere. Engineering positions, on the other hand, are regarded much more highly in societies outside of the United States.

Social class has a great deal of relevance for marketing strategies. It influences store selection, product selection, media selection, advertising appeal selection, and sales promotion selection. Different motives may thus have to be employed for different social classes. The relevance of social class may extend to European automobiles as well. There is "a distinct pecking order for European cars. A Citroën does not pass an Audi. The Audi must let a Mercedes pass. The Mercedes bows to the Porsche. And the Porsche dares not pass a Lamborghini."[48]

Thresher, a British liquor store chain of 990 outlets, used the results of its marketing research to divide its shops into three designations: Drinks Stores, Wine Shops, and Wine Racks. The designations are based on the social status of a neighborhood. The down-market Drinks Stores are located in working-class areas, and they stock mostly beer. Wine Racks, offering a larger selection of wines and champagnes, are found in tonier locations and have a better-educated staff. The middlebrow Wine Shops are somewhere in between. Sheraton has inconsistent image. Although it looks grand and appeals to upper-class clientele overseas, that class image does not extend to its home market in the United States.

GROUP

A **group** consists of two or more persons who share a set of norms and have certain implicitly or explicitly defined relationships with one another in such a way that their behavior is interdependent. Originally formed for defense and survival, a group now serves its members more for needs of social and psychological satisfaction. An individual cannot operate well in isolation because all persons are biologically and socially interdependent. An individual needs to belong to a group to interact with those who can provide identification and help meet needs in a more efficient manner. The influence of a *reference group* is derived in part from its capacity to disseminate information.

The relevance and strength of influence of a reference group is not constant across product categories. Its influence is determined in part by the *conspicuousness* of the product in question. A product can be conspicuous in two ways: by having the qualities of visibility and by standing out. The more the product is visible and stands out, the more conspicuous it becomes. Product conspicuousness allows a reference group to operate in exerting its influence on consumer behavior. For example, Philip Morris's Galaxy brand was at one time perceived as a "diet" cigarette, and for that reasons Brazilians became ashamed to be seen with it because social and personal pressures were placed on those who smoked Galaxy.

The relevance of group appeal may be dictated by cultural norms. The Fishbein behavioral intentions model was found to reflect cultural differences (i.e., the collectivist culture of Korea and the individualistic culture of the United States). The greater importance of subjective norm in Korea and of attitude toward an act in the United States indicates that social pressures, while having a relatively weak influence on Americans, play a major role in the formation of Koreans' behavioral intentions. Therefore, international marketers operating in Confucian cultures should keep in mind that a product may not be evaluated independently of group conformity and face saving. A marketing mix program should take into account these social factors.[49]

In contrast to Americans, who are more individually oriented, the Japanese are more committed to group membership and are consensus-oriented. Group pressure is so great that Nippon Telegraph and Telephone has to offer outlets for stress, charging 40 cents a minute for a person to call a telephone number that offers a tape-recorded message. When the number for "dial-an-apology" is dialed, a caller can shout angrily and then hear a recorded voice simper in reply: "I'm sorry. It's all my fault. You are right." The "dial-a-sympathy" telephone number has a male voice reassuring the caller: "Even men have difficult times. It's OK (sniffle...sniffle)." The need to relieve stress is so great that each number receives 500 to 600 calls a day.[50]

The importance of group orientation is also illustrated by the experience of Hispanics in the United States. Having a tendency to buy as a group, Hispanics concentrate their influence on a few brands in a few markets.[51] This kind of highly concentrated buying power can operate to double a company's market share in some market areas. Libby's, for example, is a brand most often used by only 8 percent of non-Hispanics, in stark contrast to a 40 percent rate among Hispanics. This kind of brand loyalty can substantially account for the increase of the brand's market share in New York from 8 percent to 14 percent. There are several reasons why Hispanics "bloc vote" their dollars. On the one hand, buying diversity is constrained by such physical limitations as label deciphering, lower media exposure, and fewer products on the shelf. On the other hand, they feel that trying new brands is risky. As a result, their buying behavior opportunities are viewed as somewhat limited.

FAMILY

In the United States, the word **family** has a narrow meaning because it encompasses only the husband, wife, and their offspring (if any). This family is known as a nuclear or conjugal family. In the other parts of the world, the word has a much broader meaning because it is based on the concept of an extended or consanguine family. A family can be vertically extended when it includes several generations. It can also be horizontally extended when such family members as uncles, aunts, and cousins are included. Thus non-Americans count vertical and horizontal relatives of either the husband or wife or both as part of their family. It is not uncommon for a son to live in his parents' home even after getting married. When his parents become old, it will become his responsibility to take care of his parents, the home, and the business. In such a country, nursing homes are relatively rare, and the placement of elderly or ill parents in homes for the aged is disdained.

As a subset and special kind of reference group, the family can be distinguished by its characteristics. First, a family allows its members ample opportunity to interact with one another on a face-to-face basis. In effect, each member operates as both a counselor and an information provider. Second, the family is a consuming unit in the sense that most members share the consumption of many products, especially those that are durables or that affect family budget. Third, individual needs are usually subordinated to family needs. Finally, one member is often assigned the primary duty of buying products for other users, thus acting as a gatekeeper or purchasing agent.

American and non-American families raise their families in very different ways. Americans emphasize individual freedom, and children are taught to be self-sufficient and independent. In Japan and China, the family is the main focal point. Similar to the Hispanics' strong family orientation, the Japanese feel a strong sense of responsibility and obligation to their families, and these obligations predominate in family decisions.

One study manipulated ethnicity of models (Asian and Caucasian) and the advertised product's country of origin for the purpose of examining Singaporean students' cultural variables (i.e., traditional Eastern values about family and conformity). Culture appears to have a mixed effect because family orientation, but not conformity, affects advertising evaluation. The student sample used in the study, influenced by both traditional Eastern and modern Western cultures, preferred imported products to local products and also preferred Western models. The preferences expressed were product specific.[52]

Because of the emphasis on family orientation, nepotism is an expected and accepted practice in most parts of the world. The tradition may even be carried on to include business partners. In Japan, close bonds among all members of a manufacturer's distribution channel explain why unprofitable members are not dropped from the system. Pillsbury has to accommodate this different style of doing business in Japan, where the emphasis is on long courtship, trust, sincerity, and Asian "old friends." Joint ventures are akin to a marriage, and a divorce of this kind is strongly frowned upon. The family tradition also explains why Japanese corporate priorities are employees, suppliers, customers, community, government, bankers, and finally shareholders.

A family functions more efficiently when its members specialize in the roles they are most comfortable with or are capable of performing better than other family members. A marketer must determine the kind of decision making that is relevant to the product. Once that fact is known, the marketer can direct a promotional effort toward the party making the purchase decision. It is thus useful to consider and to assess the relative influence of each spouse in the decision-making process.

OPINION LEADERSHIP

Within each social group, there are some individuals who are able to exert a significant influence on other members in such a way as to affect their thinking and behavior in a desired direction. These individuals are known as **opinion leaders**. In the context of consumer behavior, their opinions about products can affect subsequent purchases made by others. In one focus group study of beer drinkers, 80 percent of Moosehead drinkers were introduced to this Canadian brand by a friend.

Becoming an opinion leader requires certain qualifications. In regard to social and psychological characteristics, the limited evidence indicates that opinion leaders are more self-confident, progressive, assertive, likable, emotionally stable, susceptible to change, outgoing, and less depressive.

Are opinion leaders born or created? The answer is that opinion leadership is not an all-or-nothing phenomenon. Just because an individual is an opinion leader for one product does not mean that he or she will also be an opinion leader for all other products. This situation poses problems in applying the concept to marketing, as opinion leaders' characteristics vary across products. It may be necessary to identify characteristics for each product before the appropriate marketing effort can be directed at the correct opinion leaders for that product. Kunnan, in promoting its Pro Kennex tennis rackets, relies on tennis instructors and pro shops in addition to endorsements from professional players.

In marketing products overseas, MNCs should attempt to appeal to opinion leaders. In general, these are likely to be people who command respect from others. In Ghana, government health workers gain better cooperation and reception by asking for village witch doctors' approval before inoculating people or spraying huts to fight malaria. In developing countries, it is a good strategy to market new ideas to teachers, monks, or priests first, because their opinions influence the acceptance of these ideas by others.

When it is doubtful who the opinion leaders are, marketers should try to identify those with influence and affluence. BMW, for example, sells its cars at a discount to diplomats, believing that its target consumers will take notice of the kind of cars driven by those in power. In foreign countries, business periodicals and English language newspapers are usually an effective means of reaching government and business leaders who are potential opinion leaders.

DIFFUSION PROCESS OF INNOVATIONS

The **diffusion process of innovations** is an acceptance over time of a product or idea by consumers, linked to a given social structure and a given system of values or culture. Innovators possess certain characteristics that distinguish them from noninnovators. Table 7–2 provides a comparison of general characteristics across adopter categories.

The diffusion process varies from culture to culture. The conservative business etiquette in South Korea is reflected in Korean firms' organizational structure as well as in their managerial approach, which emphasizes harmony and structure over innovation and experimentation.

Culture not only affects the diffusion process in general, but it also exerts a great deal of influence on the adoption of a product in particular. A product that is suitable in one culture may be totally inappropriate elsewhere. The Italian and Asian preference for fresh meat and vegetables has hampered the acceptance of frozen foods. In Italy and Southeast Asia, markets open and close early, and shoppers who wish to select the best items must get to market very early in the morning. By the early afternoon, the market is ready to be closed, with only a few poor items left for selection.

TABLE 7–2 Characteristics of adopter categories

Adopter Category	Description	Status	Opinion Leadership	Sources of Information
Innovators	venturesome	above average	some	impersonal
Early adopters	respectable	highest	greatest	impersonal & personal
Early majority	deliberate	slightly above average	some	personal
Late majority	skeptical	below average	little	personal
Laggards	traditional	lowest	very little	personal

Note: This table is based in part on Everett Rogers, *Diffusion of Innovations* (Glencoe, IL: Free Press, 1971)

Based on limited evidence, there seems to be a relationship between companies' export orientation and innovativeness. This is true in the case of Peru's adoption of process innovations.[53] "Exporting for textile producers in Peru is positively related to the use of capital intensive innovations." Further research is necessary to confirm that companies committed to export activities are likely to be innovative.

As explained by the international product life-cycle concept, a new product is not adopted at the same time or at the same rate in various countries. It is thus necessary to ask whether innovators should be classified on a national (local) or international (worldwide) basis. If innovators are defined as the first 10 percent of adopters, how should a consumer be classified if he is not in the first 10 percent internationally but well within the first 10 percent of purchasers within his home country? The answer is that the diffusion rate should be based on segmentation criteria for each target market. Special consideration must be given to certain ethnic groups, age levels, social classes, geographic areas, and so on. Therefore, innovators should be classified as the first 10 percent of a particular target market, regardless of the percentages of adoption in other countries or on a worldwide scale.

It must be pointed out that innovators are small in number and that their influence is not always positive in that they may reject a new product. Although innovators are important, the evidence suggests that "the basic strategy should be aimed at imitators in the market in order to stimulate demand for the new product. Furthermore, the product should be tailored carefully to the needs and wants of that segment."[54]

CONCLUSION

Consumer behavior, as a discipline of study, has been studied so extensively in the United States that it has been thoroughly researched at both the macro and micro levels. Surprisingly, it has not been rigorously and diligently investigated in the international context. Much too frequently, studies that compare consumers in various countries attribute differences in consumer characteristics and behavior to cultural differences. This convenient approach (i.e., culture) by itself is inadequate and does not enhance the understanding of consumption behavior overseas.

Instead of explicitly or implicitly attempting to use culture to explain most variations in consumption, researchers should redirect their attention toward smaller units of analysis. This requires a study of psychological concepts as well as social concepts which are not solely based on cultural determinants.

At the psychological level, relevant concepts such as motivation, learning, personality, psychographics, perception, and attitude should be closely examined. Because consumer needs vary across countries, as does the degree of importance attached to a particular need, it is unrealistic to expect consumers everywhere to be motivated in the same way. The varying motives that occur are due in part to individual personality traits and lifestyles. The learning and perception of a product and the attitude toward it will also affect consumers' motivations in acquiring the product. Although American firms pride themselves on manufacturing products of high quality, they need to realize that foreign consumers, middlemen, and competitors may not have the same kind of perception.

At the social level, it is redundant to state that consumer behavior is affected by the cultural environment. It is more important to list specifically the cultural norms in a country and to understand why those norms vary from country to country. It is thus important to appreciate how these norms are shaped by reference groups, social class, family, opinion leadership, and the diffusion process of innovation. Consumer preference depends in part on how well a product fits into the cultural circumstance and on whether the product will have the approval of a consumer's reference group, social class, and family.

In conclusion, marketers and researchers should guard against using culture as a catchall term and should not use it on a wholesale basis to explain overseas behavior. It is necessary to go beyond noticing cultural differences and instead to attempt to understand the underlying causes of cultural variations. This goal requires researchers to be more specific and rigorous in their investigation by extending the application of relevant psychological and social concepts to the international scene. It is time to move away from a vague and generic explanation of consumption behavior to a more precise and better-focused avenue of research.

QUESTIONS

1. Explain the economics approach to the study of consumer behavior. What are the assumptions and limitations of this approach?
2. Distinguish among these three disciplines in terms of the unit of analysis: psychology, sociology, and anthropology.
3. Are rational motives more effective than their emotional counterparts in motivating consumers to make a purchase?

4. Are consumers' perceptions of products affected by the information concerning the products' countries of origin?
5. Explain how attitudes toward (a) marketing and (b) women may vary across countries.
6. Do social classes exist in the United States, the so-called land of equality?

DISCUSSION ASSIGNMENTS AND MINICASES

1. Do you feel that consumer differences can be adequately explained by the all-encompassing concept of culture? Is it a waste of time to employ other psychological and social concepts to understand consumer behavior?

2. In your opinion, can cultural differences be accounted for by racial genetics?

3. Are the same buying motives effective worldwide?

4. Because personality is related to an individual person, is it possible for citizens of a country to have unique personality traits?

5. Compared to Americans, are Asians and Africans (1) more group-oriented, (b) more family-oriented, and (c) more concerned with social status? How might such orientations affect the way you market your product to Asian and African consumers?

6. Do you think it is worthwhile to appeal to opinion leaders and innovators in foreign markets?

CASE 7–1
BORN IN THE U.S.A.

One Day in Japan

A Japanese woman stopped inside Tokyo's giant Takashimaya department store. While examining a counter laden with U.S. kitchen appliances, she picked up an electric juicer and said, "Interesting. What about the quality?"

"This is a top product in America," a young saleswoman assured her.

"Yes, but what about in Japan? Is the quality comparable to Japanese products?" the customer asked.

Back in the U.S.A.

Half a world away, U.S. manufacturers seem to be unaware of the Japanese woman's skepticism about the quality of their products. They feel that their difficulties in selling to the Japanese are caused by Japan's import barriers and that their difficulties in selling to American consumers are caused by imports' unfair prices.

To fight against imports and to encourage American consumers to use American products, U.S. firms and labor organizations have tried to convince consumers that it is a good idea to "buy American." Using patriotism to appeal to Americans, U.S. manufacturers and organizations employ such well-known stars as Bob Hope as their spokespersons to advise consumers to look for merchandise with the Made-in-the-U.S.A. label. Surprisingly, U.S. consumers seem to favor import restrictions to preserve jobs, as long as they can still have the freedom to buy imported products. What they say and what they do are confusing and contradictory.

Questions

1. Is the Japanese woman alone in her perception of the quality of U.S. products? Do other Japanese as well as American consumers share her feeling?
2. Is the Made-in-the-U.S.A. campaign effective in stimulating consumer interest in U.S. products? If not or if the campaign is inadequate, what else should U.S. manufacturers do?

Source: The incident cited was adapted from Ronald E. Yates. "Japan's 'Buy American' Plan." *Chicago Tribune.* November 3, 1985

CASE 7–2
BIG SPENDERS

There is no question that the United States is the largest consumer nation in the world. Americans are widely known for their big cars, disposable products, and fascination with frills. With regard to spending and saving in general, Americans are perceived, correctly, as being big spenders and poor savers. Unlike Americans—who never seem to hesitate getting into debt to finance purchases—German workers do not believe in using credit except for an important purchase. When compared to Americans, Germans are thriftier and believe in capital accumulation for the future.

The U.S. savings rate, depressed by high social security taxes and already the lowest of major industrial countries, slid down further to a meager 4.6 percent after U.S. law allowed workers to open IRAs (individual retirement accounts). Exhibit 1 compares the private savings rate and other factors of the United States with those of Japan and OECD countries.

Markedly different from the emphasis on instant gratification and the consumption- and spending-oriented system of the United States is the fanatical saving habit of the Japanese. Encouraged by Japan's underdeveloped social security and pension system and reinforced by cultural and religious values, Japan's private savings rate rose to 22.7 percent. That society seems to have become preoccupied with postponing awards, spurred by a tax system encouraging personal saving and survival as well as by a 100-year tradition reinforcing the natural desire of the Japanese to save for "a rainy day." To the U.S. government, the saving habit of the Japanese poses a serious problem to trade and serves as a kind of import barrier.

Living in a small island nation with few natural resources, the Japanese feel vulnerable. As a result they believe, contrary to outsiders' perception, that their economic success and increases in personal wealth constitute only modest advances.

EXHIBIT 1   Comparative factors: Japan, the United States, and OECD

Factor[a]	Japan	United States	OECD mean[b]
Growth rates of per capita income	1.6	1.1	1.5
Ratio of aged to working-age population	15.0	20.0	22.6
Ratio of young to working-age population	50.7	54.5	54.4
Labor force participation rate of the aged	50.2	24.3	21.5
Consumer price inflation	4.9	7.8	11.5
GDP per square kilometer	2,555.1	278.4	1,023.5
Per capita income	5,946.2	8,268.7	6,165.6
Retirement age	60.0	65.0	63.9
Public pension benefits per person over 65 as a percent of per capita private national income	31.6	47.3	71.3
Private savings rate	22.7	10.4	15.6

Sources: OECD, IMF, UN, and ILO data
Table from Charles Yuji Horioka, "Why Is Japan's Private Savings Rate So High?" *Finance & Development* 23 (December 1986): 23
[a] All variables are expressed in percents except for GDP per square kilometer and per capita income, which are in U.S. dollars, and retirement age, which is in years
[b] All figures pertain to the full sample of 21 OECD countries except for those for public pension benefits, which exclude Iceland

Furthermore, Japan has conditioned its consumers to believe that exports are positive and imports are negative. Such an attitude causes difficulty in correcting the problem of trade imbalances.

As pointed out by Mikuni, the quite different systems of the two countries create a built-in trade barrier that operates against the United States. If the trade deficit of the United States is to be reduced, the Japanese government may have to tax savings and cut income taxes so that the Japanese economy can become more consumption driven. For the United States, savings and not consumption will have to be rewarded so that funds can be accumulated and made available for economic growth.

As one might expect, the saving tradition of the Japanese discourages credit use. To overcome this reticence, American Express emphasizes that its card does not provide credit, and the company insists on immediate payment of bills. American Express wants its card to be thought of as a charge vehicle that works worldwide to relieve cardholders of having to carry a large amount of cash.

Questions

1. What are the causes of high per capita consumption and low savings rates in the United States, as well as the opposites in Japan? Are these causes the result of economic, legal, psychological, or social factors?

2. Is it necessary for the United States to push Japan to save less and to consume more?

3. Do you agree with the strategy of American Express in Japan? Will this strategy help the Japanese learn new habits and change cultural attitudes?

Sources: Charles Yuji Horioko, "Why Is Japan's Private Savings Rate So High?" *Finance & Development* 23 (December 1986): 23; Akio Mikuni, "Time for a Trade: U.S. Tax Goals for Japan's," *Business Week,* 1 January 1986, 20

NOTES

1. A. Coskun Samli, Dhruv Grewal, and Sanjeev K. Mathur, "International Industrial Buyer Behavior: An Exploration and a Proposed Model," *Journal of the Academy of Marketing Science* 16 (Summer 1988): 19–29.

2. James Wills, A. Coskun Samli, and Laurence Jacobs, "Developing Global Products and Marketing Strategies: A Construct and a Research Agenda," *Journal of the Academy of Marketing Science* 19 (Winter 1991): 1–10.

3. Ugur Yucelt, "A Cross-Cultural Study of Buyers' Perception of Price-Quality Relationship: An Empirical Investigation," *Journal of International Consumer Marketing* 2 (no. 1, 1989): 55–81.

4. "Sociobiology: A New Theory of Behavior," *Time,* 1 August 1977, 54–63.

5. Stuart Henderson Britt, *Psychological Principles of Marketing and Consumer Behavior* (Lexington, MA: Lexington Books, 1978), 316.

6. Richard Ettenson and Janet Wagner, "Chinese vs. U.S. Consumer Behavior: A Cross-Cultural Comparison of the Evaluation of Retail Stores," *Journal of International Consumer Marketing* 3 (no. 3, 1991): 55–71.

7. Robert F. Roth, *International Marketing Communications* (Chicago: Crain Books, 1982), 5.

8. Gerald J. Gorn, "The Effects of Music in Advertising on Choice Behavior: A Classical Conditioning Approach," *Journal of Marketing* 46 (Winter 1982): 94–101.

9. Leon G. Schiffman, William R. Dillon, and Festus E. Ngumah, "The Influence of Subcultural and Personality Factors on Consumer Acculturation," *Journal of International Business Studies* 12 (Fall 1981): 137–43.

10. Terry Clark, "International Marketing and National Character: A Review and Proposal for an Integrative Theory," *Journal of Marketing* 54 (October 1990): 66.

11. Chikara Higashi, *Japanese Trade Policy Formulation* (New York: Praeger, 1983), 68.

12. Michael Shapiro, *The Shadow in the Sun: A Korean Year of Love and Sorrow* (New York: Atlantic Monthly Press, 1990).

13. Allan B. Yeates, "Americans, Canadians Similar But Vive La Difference," *Direct Marketing* (October 1985): 152ff.

14. Lauren A. Swanson, "The Twelve 'Nations' of China," *Journal of International Consumer Marketing* 2 (no. 1, 1989): 83–105.

15. "When Fragmenting Works Better Than Segmenting," *Marketing News,* 1 January 1986, 56.

16. David A. Aaker, Yasuyoshi Fuse, and Fred D. Reynolds, "Is Life-Style Research Limited in Its Usefulness to Japanese Advertisers?" *Journal of Advertising* 11 (no. 1, 1982): 31–36, 48.

17. Alfred S. Boote, "Psychographic Segmentation in Europe," *Journal of Advertising Research* 22 (December/January 1983): 19–25.

18. Jon Lafayette, "Backer Predicts Material World," *Advertising Age,* 29 July 1989, 79.

19. Tom Parker, *In One Day* (Boston: Houghton Mifflin, 1985).

20. Peter B. Warr and Christopher Knapper, *The Perception of People and Events* (London: Wiley, 1968).

21. Sadafumi Nishina, "Japanese Consumers: Introducing Foreign Products/Brands into the Japanese Market," *Journal of Advertising Research* 30 (April/May 1990): 35–45.

22. Ray Moseley, "Ireland's Distillers Whisk 'Water of Life' to America," *Chicago Tribune,* 25 April 1985.

23. Janet Cawley, "Moosehead Beer Bulls Its Way out of Woods," *Chicago Tribune,* 29 October 1985.

24. Donald G. Howard, "Understanding How American Consumers Formulate Their Attitudes about Foreign Products," *Journal of International Consumer Marketing* 2 (no. 2, 1989): 7–24.

25. John R. Darling and Van R. Wood, "A Longitudinal Study Comparing Perceptions of U.S. and Japanese Consumer Products in a Third/Neutral Country: Finland 1975 to 1985," *Journal of International Business Studies* 21 (no. 3, 1990): 427–50.

26. Warren J. Bilkey and Erik Nes, "Country-of-Origin Effects on Product Evaluations," *Journal of International Business Studies* 13 (Spring/Summer 1982): 89–99.

27. Philippe Cattin, Alain Jolibert, and Colleen Lohnes, "A Cross-Cultural Study of 'Made In' Concepts," *Journal of International Business Studies* 13 (Winter 1982): 131–41.

28. Gary M. Erickson, Johny K. Johansson, and Paul Chao, "Image Variables in Multi-Attribute Product Evaluations: Country-of-Origin Effects," *Journal of Consumer Research* 11 (September 1984): 694–99.

29. Sung-Tai Hong and Robert S. Wyer, Jr., "Effects of Country-of-Origin and Product-Attribute Information on Product Evaluation: An Information Processing Perspective," *Journal of Consumer Research* 16 (September 1989): 175–89.

30. C. Min Han, "Country Image: Halo or Summary Construct?" *Journal of Marketing Research* 26 (May 1989): 222–29.

31. Sung-Tai Hong and Robert S. Wyer, Jr., "Determinants of Product Evaluation: Effects of the Time Interval between Knowledge of a Product's Country of Origin and Information about Its Specific Attributes," *Journal of Consumer Research* 17 (December 1990): 277–88.

32. Victor V. Cordell, "Competitive Context and Price as Moderators of Country of Origin Preferences," *Journal of the Academy of Marketing Science* 19 (Spring 1991): 123–28.

33. Cattin, Jolibert, and Lohnes, " 'Made In' Concepts," 139.

34. Paul L. Sauer, Murray A. Young, and H. Rao Unnava, "An Experimental Investigation of the Processes behind the Country of Origin," *Journal of International Consumer Marketing* 3 (no. 2, 1991): 29–59.

35. Paul Chao, "The Impact of Country Affiliation on the Credibility of Product Attribute Claims," *Journal of Advertising Research* 21 (April/May 1989): 35–41.

36. Han, "Country Image: Halo or Summary Construct?"

37. Marjorie Wall, John Liefeld, and Louise A. Heslop, "Impact of Country-of-Origin Cues on Consumer Judgments in Multi-Cue Situations: A Covariance Analysis," *Journal of the Academy of Marketing Science* 19 (Spring 1991): 105–13.

38. Nigel Piercy, *Export Strategy: Markets and Competition* (London: George Allen and Unwin, 1982), 171.

39. Chol Lee, "Modifying an American Consumer Behavior Model for Consumers in Confucian Culture: The Case of Fishbein Behavioral Intention Model," *Journal of International Consumer Marketing* 3 (no. 1, 1990): 27–50.

40. Chin Tiong Tan and John U. Farley, "The Impact of Cultural Patterns on Cognition and Intention in Singapore," *Journal of Consumer Research* 13 (March 1987): 540–44.

41. C. Min Han, "The Role of Consumer Patriotism in the Choice of Domestic versus Foreign Products," *Journal of Advertising Research* 28 (June/July 1988): 25–32.

42. John R. Darling, "The Competitive Marketplace Abroad: A Comparative Study," *Columbia Journal of World Business* 16 (Fall 1981): 53–62.

43. Hiram C. Barksdale, et al., "A Cross-National Survey of Consumer Attitudes towards Marketing Practices, Consumerism and Government Regulations," *Columbia Journal of World Business* 17 (Summer 1982): 71–86.

44. Stan Rapp, "Copywriting Is Different in Japan," *DM News,* 15 November 1984: 13, 40.

45. *Investment in Indonesia* (Kantor Akuntan Sudjendro and Peat Marwick, 1985), 16.

46. John Mager and John F. Hulpke, "Social Class in a Classless Society: Marketing Implications for China," *Journal of International Consumer Marketing* 2 (no. 4, 1990): 57–88.

47. Wendell Blanchard, *Thailand, Its People, Its Society, Its Culture* (New Haven: HRAF Press, 1966).

48. A. F. Gonzalez, Jr., "When Europeans Take Road, Every Lane Is the Fast Lane," *Chicago Tribune,* 27 July 1986.

49. Chol Lee and Robert T. Green, "Cross-Cultural Examination of the Fishbein Behavioral Intentions Model," *Journal of International Business Studies* 22 (no. 2, 1991): 289–305.

50. "The High Price Japanese Pay for Success," *Business Week,* 7 April 1986, 52–54.

51. Carol Wheelan, "Hispanics Respond to Quality Invites," *Food & Beverage Marketing* (March 1985): 40 ff.

52. Chin Tiong Tan and John U. Farley, "The Impact of Cultural Patterns on Cognition and Intention in Singapore," *Journal of Consumer Research* 13 (March 1987): 540–44.

53. John D. Daniels and Fernando Robles, "The Choice of Technology and Export Commitment: The Peruvian Textile Industry," *Journal of International Business Studies* 13 (Spring/Summer 1982): 67–87.

54. Hirokazu Takada and Dipak Jain, "Cross-National Analysis of Diffusion of Consumer Durable Goods in Pacific Rim Countries," *Journal of Marketing* 55 (April 1991): 48–54.

PART THREE
PLANNING FOR
INTERNATIONAL MARKETING

□ PART OUTLINE

The faster and further you move information, the more valuable it becomes.

Glen McG. Renfrew, managing director, Reuters Holdings PLC

Marketing Research and Information System

8

CHAPTER OUTLINE

MARKETING ILLUSTRATION
Smoke Gets in Your Eyes

Brazil, the largest country in Latin America, is also one of the world's largest cigarette markets. Its impressive size is clearly evident: 120 million people in the population and 120 billion units or 6 billion packs in annual cigarette consumption. Philip Morris, with its competitors' brands well entrenched, encountered serious difficulties in attempting to penetrate the market. Learning from its market research that Brazilian smokers wanted cigarettes that had less nicotine and did not irritate the throat, the company decided to be first in a new market segment that preferred lower levels of nicotine, a unique product attribute. Amid much fanfare, Philip Morris introduced Galaxy, a brand with less nicotine than other brands sold in Brazil. This attribute was further supported by scientific findings mentioned in the promotional campaign. The results of the brand's campaign were almost enough to drive the managers of Philip Morris Brazileira to tears—the product proved a sensational flop.

Philip Morris's focus groups revealed a surprising piece of information. Smokers perceived Galaxy as a "diet cigarette" and were ashamed to be seen with it. After using scientific evidence to convince Brazilians of the nicotine attribute, that attribute had become a liability. Galaxy had presented the attribute without a relevant perceived benefit. To provide a link between the two, Philip Morris launched a new campaign to appeal to the intelligent minority. The new theme: switching to Galaxy is not merely a logical and emotional decision but also an intelligent one. The new campaign worked. Measurements made before and after the campaign showed a significant attitude change. The most convincing piece of evidence was that sales increased dramatically.

Source: "Marketing Research Helped Philip Morris Penetrate the 'Impenetrable' Brazil Market," *Marketing News*, 17 September 1982

The case of Galaxy illustrates the value of marketing information and how such information can make the difference between success and failure. The data helped Philip Morris make timely adjustments to gain acceptance for its product. The company's understanding of consumer habits was based on a variety of research activities, including desk research, sales analysis, store audits, group interviews, package and product tests, advertising pretest, on-air tests, and ongoing tracking studies. In short, Galaxy owed its success to marketing research.

Lack of knowledge and unfamiliarity with foreign markets usually heighten the risks for a company wanting to do business in a foreign land. The problem is further complicated by the fact that international marketing research is more difficult, more complex, and more subjective than domestic research. As explained by Cavusgil, the causes of less-than-accurate information being obtained from export marketing research include companies' limited experience in this kind of research and the difficulties involved in collecting information overseas. A company's international involvement and commitment as well as the degree of business risk determine the extent of its international marketing research. Foreign direct investment involves more risks and necessitates more elaborate research. In contrast, if a company is relatively uncommitted to international marketing, it tends to "make decisions on the basis of limited research, aided by 'judgment calls.' "[1]

Approximately two out of every three U.S. exporters do not have a formalized international marketing research plan, and 27 percent of these exporters do not do any international marketing research at all. Exporters that do international marketing research are greater in size and have higher export sales as a percent of total sales, and their export executives tend to have had a formal course in international business. Therefore, colleges and export workshops/conferences can play a role in stimulating marketers to undertake international marketing research.[2]

In terms of marketing research expenditures, the top three countries are the United States, the United Kingdom, and Germany. Japan ranks fourth.[3] According to "Market Statistics and Client Study" of ESOMAR (European Society for Opinion and Market Research), 1988 world marketing research was $5.42 billion, with Western Europe and the United States accounting for 40 percent and 39 percent respectively. Japan, in contrast, accounted for only 9 percent. Research in Europe was primarily conducted in Germany, the United Kingdom, France, Italy, and Spain, whereas Ireland accounted for only 1 percent of the total research volume.[4]

Given the complexity of today's fast-changing world and the unpredictability of consumer demands, the use of marketing research is essential if a company is to reduce the serious risks associated with marketing a product. Thus, the purpose of this chapter is to examine the nature and techniques of international marketing research. The chapter investigates such topics as types of data, types of data collection methods, sampling, and measurement. The discussion emphasizes the difficulties associated with cross-cultural research and the necessity for adapting marketing research techniques to international markets.

NATURE OF MARKETING RESEARCH

According to the American Marketing Association, **marketing research** involves the "systematic gathering, recording, and analyzing of data about problems relating to the marketing of goods and services." This definition provides a useful description of the nature of marketing research, but it fails to include preresearch analysis, which is an important aspect of the research process.[5] Before data collection, careful planning is required to specify both the kind of information needed and the purpose for such information. Without preresearch activities, there is a great danger that critical information may not be obtained and that what is obtained may turn out to be irrelevant or unsuitable. The letter in Exhibit 8–1 shows a lack of problem definition, research objectives, and preresearch activities.

Table 8–1 describes Japanese companies' attitudes toward marketing research.

Marketing research can be valuable in identifying opportunities as well as potential problems. Mack Trucks entered the Pakistan market in the late 1960s. The company's subsequent failure was attributed to ignorance of the fact that its chief competitor was the son of the country's president.[6]

The gathering of information can never be a substitute for good managerial judgment. A story about marketing to shoeless islanders illustrates this point. Two shoe salesmen from two companies visited the same island and came away with vastly different interpretations. One felt that a market opportunity was nonexistent, because

---

To: International Trade Administration
U.S. Department of Commerce
Washington, D.C.

Dear Sir/Madam:

I am in the process of planning the importation of a foreign product into the United States for wholesale distribution.

I have not yet determined the nature of the product. I am certain, however, that it is neither a food item nor automotive products. I am also undecided about the country of origin, even though I am leaning in the direction of the European or Asian manufacturing firms. These requirements should be able to minimize the research required to locate the research materials which I would like to receive from you.

Thank you for your assistance in providing me with the requested information.

Sincerely,

Potential Importer

EXHIBIT 8–1   Poorly formulated research

people there did not wear shoes. The other salesman, however, was enthusiastic, because in his determination no one as yet had sold shoes to these "customers." The moral of the story is that marketing research is only part of the equation, and proper analysis and judgmental decisions are important and required.

MARKETING INFORMATION SOURCES

Once a researcher has identified the marketing problem and has completed a preresearch analysis, the relevant information must be collected. The two major sources of information are primary data and secondary data.

Primary data can be defined as information that is collected firsthand, generated by original research tailor-made to answer specific, current research questions. The major advantage of primary data is that the information is specific, relevant, and up-to-date. The desirability of primary data is, however, somewhat moderated by the high cost and amount of time associated with the collection of this type of data.

Secondary data, in contrast, can be defined as information that has already been collected for other purposes and is thus readily available. Note that the advantages of primary data are the disadvantages of secondary data, and that the advantages of secondary data become the disadvantages of primary data.

TABLE 8–1 Japanese attitude toward marketing research

		Agree		Neither	Disagree	
Attitude		Definitely	Somewhat		Somewhat	Definitely
No.	**Statement**	**(A)**	**(B)**	**(C)**	**(D)**	**(E)**
1.	The marketing research department should become a strategic department and collect all necessary information for the company.	35%	38%	17%	9%	1%
2.	To fully understand consumer needs, it is necessary to develop new marketing-research techniques.	27	41	24	6	1
3.	Top management has a high interest in marketing research.	28	37	21	12	1
4.	Research to determine long-term basic trends is not conducted; only short-term research is conducted.	19	46	22	11	1
5.	It is not necessary for the manager of the marketing research department to be a marketing research specialist.	18	45	20	14	4
6.	Nowadays, qualitative research can help management understand the market better than quantitative research.	16	40	35	7	1
7.	Outside data such as government statistics and sales data are not fully analyzed.	7	42	22	25	4
8.	In many cases, marketing research results are not utilized for actual marketing decision making.	5	40	28	23	3
9.	The marketing research function should not necessarily be centralized.	10	33	27	22	7
10.	Many people in my company think that appropriate decision making can be done without marketing research.	6	35	27	26	6
11.	If money is available, it is better to use it for sales promotions rather than for marketing research.	0	7	22	41	30

Source: Kazuo Kobayashi and Peter Draper, "Reviews of Market Research in Japan," *Journal of Advertising Research* 30 (April/May): 17

As a rule, no research should be done without a search for secondary information first, and secondary data should be used whenever available and appropriate. To determine the suitability of the secondary data, a researcher should employ relevant criteria to evaluate the purpose, methodology, definitions of the concepts, and time period covered in the study yielding the secondary information. The evaluation

TABLE 8–2 Definitions of *urban*, by country

Country	Definition of Urban
Albania	Localities of 400 or more inhabitants
Argentina	Localities of 2,000 or more inhabitants
Bermuda	Entire country
Canada	Areas with 1,000 or more inhabitants and a population density of 400 or more per square kilometer
Congo	Localities of 5,000 or more inhabitants
Cyprus	Localities of 5,000 or more inhabitants
Denmark	Localities of 200 or more inhabitants
Iceland	Localities of 200 or more inhabitants
Japan	Cities (*shi*) having 50,000 or more inhabitants with 60 percent or more of the houses located in the main built-up areas and 60 percent or more of the population (including their dependents) engaged in manufacturing, trade, or other urban type of business. Alternatively, a shi having urban facilities and conditions as defined by the prefectural order is considered as urban.
Kuwait	Localities of 10,000 or more inhabitants
Lebanon	Localities of 10,000 or more inhabitants
Mauritius	Localities of 20,000 or more inhabitants
Nigeria	Localities of 20,000 or more inhabitants
Singapore	Entire country
Switzerland	Localities of 10,000 or more inhabitants
Uganda	Localities of 100 or more inhabitants
U.S.A.	Urbanized areas or places of 2,500 or more inhabitants outside of urbanized areas

Source: World Population 1983 (Washington, D.C.: U.S. Bureau of Census, 1983): 577–86

process becomes much more complicated if secondary data from various countries must be compared in order to analyze the business potential of each country.

A problem for marketers is that secondary data on international marketing may not be comparable for several reasons. First, countries may employ different data-collection methods. Second, there might be a problem with classification differences. Definitional differences are another common problem because countries tend to use various definitions in collecting the same kind of information. Table 8–2 lists the various definitions for the "urban" concept.

SECONDARY RESEARCH

There are many different ways to collect secondary data, and there are many information sources for this purpose.[7] Such sources can be grouped under either public or private sources.

Private Sources

A very basic method of finding business information is to begin with a public library or a university library. A library with a reasonable collection should contain standard reference guides, commercial and industrial directories, financial reference manuals, and other materials containing pertinent business information.

One source of information can be found in world trade centers and trade associations. Another good source of information is a community's chamber of commerce. Being well informed on local business, this organization is likely capable of providing helpful advice. In addition to the U.S. Chamber of Commerce, which publishes the *Foreign Commerce Handbook,* there are local chambers of commerce, which are often some of the best sources of information on trade and industry in specific localities. Larger organizations have city and general directories, specialized references, and trade journals covering industries of importance in the area. They may publish classified buyers' guides, manufacturers' guides, or lists of international traders in their areas. Finally, foreign chambers of commerce are in a position to provide a great deal of relevant information about their countries because they act as public relations offices. One researcher contacted the Taiwanese Chamber of Commerce and received in just one day the requested information on a manufacturing plant in that country, enabling him to learn of the plant's address, product, and capacity.[8]

Frequently, a researcher finds it necessary to contact the firms that are the potential customers or suppliers in order to acquire information. In this situation, directories are essential. In the United States, there are literally thousands of directories, and some of them are bound to meet the researcher's needs.

Foreign firms wishing to do business with U.S. manufacturers have several directories from which they can glean information. The best-known directory is perhaps *Thomas' Register of American Manufacturers.* This annual ten-volume comprehensive directory lists U.S. manufacturers, arranged geographically under product classifications, addresses, ratings, nature of products, and interest in export business. For information about manufacturers' agents, some general information sources include

Manufacturers' Agents National Association Directory of Members
Verified Directory of Manufacturers' Representatives (Agents)

In the case of exporters and importers, information can be obtained from local telephone directories or from

Export—Annual Buyers Guide to Export Products
American Export Register
Directory of United States Importers

If foreign firms wish to do business in the United States, the *Custom House Guide* contains tariff schedules and presents listings of some ten thousand U.S. port firms serving foreign trade in each American port.

For data on firms in specific areas outside of the United States, the following guides and directories are relevant:

The Latin American Market Guide
Pacific Islands Business Directory
The Caribbean Year Book

Concerning country information, Dun's Marketing Services offers *Exporter's Encyclopaedia*, which provides comprehensive country-by-country information for over 200 markets. Several large accounting firms also publish their own country-by-country books.

To start a search process, one useful source is the *Encyclopaedia of Business Information Sources,* which is a guide to help find information sources. It lists some sixteen hundred subject areas and five hundred geographic areas. One of the most complete all-purpose sources of information is the *Export Advisory Service.* This is a subscription service offered by Information Handling Services that provides a wealth of information in microforms (i.e., microfiche). Virtually all kinds of information about trade regulations, legislation, statistics, and related publications can be found in the *Export Advisory Service.* Subjects include antidumping duty, arms control, arms export control act of 1968, ASEAN, Australia, bamboo, bonds, carriers, customhouse brokers, and the IMF. It should be evident that the areas covered are quite diverse and that these are just a few of a large number of topics included in the *Export Advisory Service.* Because this advisory service is so complete, it is strongly recommended that a researcher try to consult this source early in an investigation by going through the subject index, numerical index, legislation index, periodicals listings, related publications listing, and addresses to find information that may be needed.

Public Sources

Public sources of market information are just as numerous as private sources. Foreign governments, their embassies and consulates, and trade promotion agencies either have the information desired or are in a position to guide the marketer to the proper sources of information. Germany, for example, has the Society for Information and Documentation, which promotes development of information science and exchanges scientific and technical data with other countries. France's Center for Information and Documentation offers services similar to those provided by U.S. information brokers. Furthermore, regional and international organizations, such as the World Bank and the IMF, routinely collect information on population and nation financial circumstances. GATT, for instance, publishes *Compendium of Sources and International Trade Statistics.*

The Organization for Economic Cooperation and Development (OECD) is the international organization of the industrialized, market-economy countries. It regularly gathers statistical information on the foreign trade of its member countries and makes the statistics internationally comparable by converting the information into uniform units. OECD publishes these statistics in six basic formats to meet the needs of a variety of users:

Monthly Statistics of Foreign Trade (Series A) is a monthly bulletin providing timely statistical data on the foreign trade of OECD member countries. The data cover overall trade by country as well as a number of seasonally adjusted series, volume and average value indices, and trade classified by the Standard International Trade Classification (SITC), which was established by the United Nations.

Foreign Trade by Commodities (Series C) is a bulletin providing annual summary information of the value in U.S. dollars of trade commodities broken down by partner country. The tables are arranged in matrix form and show data for each OECD country as well as for regional groupings of OECD countries. All commodities at the one- and two-digit SITC levels are shown.

OECD Microtables: Annual Foreign Trade Statistics by Country are sets of computer output microfiche for the imports and the exports of each OECD country, as well as for OECD Europe, EEC, and OECD total. These sets provide annual trade figures in value and, where possible, volume by SITC commodity classification to the five-digit level. With each SITC number, data are broken down by trading partner or country.

OECD Microtables: Annual Foreign Trade Statistics by Commodity is a set of approximately eighty computer output microfiche presenting import and export values and volumes by commodity. Each frame has a table listing OECD countries across the top and commodities down the side. Levels one through five of the SITC code are covered. The layout is similar to that used in *Foreign Trade by Commodities (Series C)* but is much more detailed.

Overall Trade by Country Monthly, Magnetic Tape is a monthly tape containing the same statistical files as *Monthly Statistics of Foreign Trade (Series A)*. It provides a currently available picture of recent developments in foreign trade in all OECD countries. There are approximately eight thousand monthly and quarterly series and the figures generally go back to 1960.

Detailed Foreign Trade by Commodity, Magnetic Tape deals with the imports and exports of each OECD country, with breakdowns by country of origin or destination, and by product according to SITC code at all levels of detail. The annual tapes contain cumulative quarterly data. It is a voluminous file because of the several million new items of information generated each year.

For U.S. firms, the most logical public source of information is the U.S. government and its agencies. A good starting point would be to contact the International Trade Division of the Department of Commerce. The International Trade Division maintains reference libraries in major cities where one can talk to trade experts and find statistical data and trade reports for each country. At its main office in Washington, D.C., there are experts assigned to cover a particular country. One U.S. company interested in selling microwave toilets to Nigeria avoided a costly mistake after being advised that what Nigeria really needed was basic sewage systems.

The U.S. Department of Commerce offers several kinds of services and information. Its publications include the following:

Business America (a biweekly periodical)
International Demographic Data
FT 410
U.S. Foreign Trade Statistics: Classification and Cross-Classification
Trade Information and Analysis Publications
Guide to Foreign Trade Statistics

One very good source for export information is the monthly *FT 410 (Foreign Trade Report)*. Listing commodity by country, *FT 410* provides statistical data of the shipments of all merchandise from the United States. The examination of such statistical records can provide ideas about some forty-five hundred U.S. products and some one hundred sixty buying countries. A company can learn what has been exported, in what amount, and to which country.

The Domestic and International Business Administration (DIBA) has several prepared reports that are useful for exporters. These reports include the following:

Market Share Reports

International Economic Indicators and Competitive Trends

Index to Foreign Market Reports

International Marketing Series

International Economic Indicators are quarterly reports providing economic data (e.g., GNP, industrial production, trade, prices, finance, and labor) of the United States and seven industrial countries. These reports assess the relative competitive position of the United States. *Market Share Reports*, on the other hand, are annual reports that evaluate market trends, changes in the import demand for specific products, and countries' competitive positions. One Ohio firm that manufactures process control equipment analyzed potential foreign markets by relying on *Market Share Reports* as well as the *Global Market Surveys*. It then proceeded to utilize the Department of Commerce's other services, such as the Department's overseas exhibitions and Agent/Distributor Service. The effort was so successful that the company now does business in twenty-two countries and exports account for more than 50 percent of its multimillion-dollar business.

Publications in the International Marketing Information Series include the following:

Overseas Business Reports (OBR)

Foreign Economic Trends and Their Implications for the United States (FET)

Global Market Surveys (GMS)

Country Market Sector Surveys

The *OBR* series discusses background data and marketing information on individual countries and products demanded by those countries. The *FET* series offers country-by-country reviews of business conditions and prospects. The *GMS* publishes extensive marketing research studies of specific U.S. products, and each *GMS* contains market summaries for individual countries. Finally, *Country Market Sectoral Surveys* are in-depth reports covering the most promising export opportunities in a single country.

The U.S. and Foreign Commercial Service has *Annual Worldwide Industry Review*. This annual multicountry survey examines export prospects for specific U.S. industries. Based on U.S. exports over the most recent five years to various countries, the review provides a worldwide profile of the industry's export trends in conjunction with country-by-country assessments in order to identify promising markets. The cost of each *Review* is $200.

Marketers should consider purchasing some of the various reports and information services, which are usually available at very reasonable prices. The reports available through the Department of Commerce include ESP, FTI, Export Contact List Services, and *Market Research Reports.*

Export Statistics Profiles (ESP) is a series of specially designed statistical tables showing the exports of specific U.S. products to individual countries. These profiles are based on export data compiled by U.S. and Foreign Commercial Services from Census Bureau statistics and United Nations foreign import and market share data. The price for each standard industry profile is $70, whereas custom orders at special request cost between $50 and $500.

Each profile contains three elements. First, it contains an Export Market Brief—a brief overview of the export market for a specific industry. Second, it includes a Trade Opportunity Frequency Report that shows the number of sales leads, by product category, received by the Department of Commerce. Third, each profile has statistical tables showing a five-year flow of exports. All tables rank countries and products in order for quick and easy comparisons. The profiles' special features are an Export Market Brief, which highlights the fastest growing markets, and an Export Potential Matrix, which rates the export potential country-by-country of the industry in question.

Each profile can be useful for decision making in several ways. It identifies best-selling products and best markets, determines export potential, measures overseas demand and growth, gives competitor country shares, spots key fluctuations from year to year, and analyzes and forecasts trends. The tables, which are the heart of the profile, rank exports product-by-product, country-by-country, and include a user guide for analysis.

As an alternative to standard ESP, companies may want to inquire about custom service. Custom service provides data on products not covered in standard ESP industries or specific countries not appearing in the standard ESP country rankings for the industry. A company can choose import data of specific products and countries and specify how the data should be displayed.

The Foreign Traders Index (FTI) is an automated file and database of foreign companies listed by product according to the five-digit Standard Industrial Classification (SIC) code and by country. The FTI is useful for an exporter looking for a list of prospective contacts in a foreign country. Information for the FTI is gathered by the Foreign Commercial Service through direct contact with representatives of firms that are the result of U.S. government trade promotion activities abroad (i.e., collection of information for *World Traders Data Reports,* foreign exhibitions, and other programs).

The FTI contains data on over 145,000 firms in 143 countries. Included in the FTI are manufacturers, service organizations, agent representatives, retailers, wholesalers/distributors, importers, exporters, and cooperatives. These can be retrieved singly or in any combination, relative to any given product group or industry. The FTI lists firms that import from the United States and firms that have high potential as purchasers of U.S. goods. The index also includes firms that have announced that they are interested in representing U.S. exporters.

The FTI file is available through Export Contact List Services in three forms: EMLS, Trade Lists, and DTS. *EMLS (Export Mailing List Service)* consists of specific data retrievals for requesters wishing to obtain lists of foreign firms in selected countries by commodity classification. Retrievals are provided on gummed mailing labels or in printout form. The cost in 1988 was $25 for access and 25 cents per company record. One small manufacturer in New York City developed a good export business for his electronic production equipment by using the EMLS as his initial source.

Trade Lists are printed booklets sold off the shelf. They contain all commercial data available in the automated FTI for selected developing countries as well as certain "target industries." The cost in 1988 ranged from $3 to $5 per retrieval or trade report.

Data Tape Service (DTS) contains FTI information on all firms in all or selected countries in magnetic tape form. The purpose of DTS is to make it possible for a user to retrieve various segments of data through the use of his or her own computer facilities. In 1988, the Data Tape Service cost was $5,000, though tapes containing all the information for a particular country could be purchased for $300 per country.

Market Research Reports are comprehensive reports covering single industries in selected countries or regions. They provide market access and trade barrier information; analyze market size and trends; forecast demand; and list market share figures, imports from the United States, best-selling products, and end-users. Each report also gives key buyers, potential agents, trade associations, and local publications suitable for advertising. A summary of the reports on a specific country can be found in Country Market Surveys, each survey costing $10.

Another source of information is *Trade Opportunities Program (TOP)*. A U.S. firm simply indicates its products, countries of interest, and the types of opportunities desired (i.e., direct sales, overseas representation, or foreign government tenders). Export opportunities are transmitted by U.S. Foreign Service Posts around the world to the TOP computer in Washington, D.C. If the product interests of a foreign buyer and those of a U.S. subscriber match, a "trade opportunity notice" is mailed to the subscriber, giving information about the foreign buyer, deadline dates, required quantities, and transaction requirements. As an alternative, American firms can subscribe to the *TOP Bulletin* for about $100 per year or to the TOP Datatape Service. The *TOP Bulletin,* published weekly, is a compilation of all export leads received and processed by TOP.

One relatively new service is *Automated Information Transfer System (AITS)*. On a timely basis, this system provides international data, including export sales leads and basic facts on foreign customers. An exporter can go to any of the offices of the International Trade Administration (ITA) to use the AITS computerized network. The main information file contains information on client companies that use ITA services and represent good prospects for the purchase of American goods.

A marketer who requires country-specific assistance can turn to the International Economic Policy (IEP) office of the International Trade Administration. This office offers professional business counseling and commercial information on a geographic basis for major marketing areas of the world. The IEP staff provides general briefings on how to do business in particular markets and also assists in resolving problems that U.S. firms encounter overseas. IEP's services are specifically designed to help U.S. companies develop their export trade. To assist companies in researching the market potential of their products in a selected country or geographical region,

IEP's country specialists provide basic statistical data on production, exports and imports, market share, and third-country competition. The specialists also analyze industrial-sector reports and growth projections for active and potential traders. The IEP staff identifies private overseas market research firms to assist companies in preparing an effective marketing strategy. Then, it helps in the selection of an appropriate agent or distributor.

There are many useful sources that provide data on demographics. *The World Bank Atlas* has demographic and growth rates for all countries. *World Population,* prepared by the Center for International Research of the Bureau of the Census contains population and demographic statistics for every country. The Central Intelligence Agency (CIA) annually publishes *World Factbook,* which contains maps, charts, and general demographic data for over 100 countries. *The U.N. Statistical Yearbook* provides comprehensive, single-volume sources of international statistics—economic and social data for its member countries and territories.

The U.S. government has access to a wealth of information. The Department of Commerce's Commercial Information Management System (CIMS) uses its worldwide network of offices to gather and electronically link all economic and marketing information. The Small Business Administration's Export Information System (XIS) provides data on some seventeen hundred product categories while listing the twenty-five largest markets that import these U.S. products. Overseas Private Investment Corporation (OPIC) has Country Information Kits for over 100 developing countries and sixteen regions worldwide. The U.S. government's *Inside Washington: The International Business Executive's Guide to Government Resources* contains market information resources and financial support programs. U.S. firms may also want to consult with the U.S. Department of Commerce's Foreign Commercial Service (US&FCS), which has commercial officers located in the commercial sections of U.S. embassies and consulates.[9]

Because there are numerous government agencies that provide a very large volume of data, marketers can be easily overwhelmed. Additionally, detailed trade data were previously available only on computer tape. To overcome these difficulties, the Omnibus Trade and Competitiveness Act requires the Commerce Department and thirteen other federal agencies to collect in one place the federal government's extensive offerings of information on international trade and export promotion. The result is the National Trade Data Bank (NTDB), which contains more than one hundred thousand documents. The NTDB makes international trade and economic information available in a consolidated convenient electronic format (laser discs for microcomputers). CD-ROM (compact disc–read only memory) is the medium used to store the data bank and serve as the vehicle for delivery. The NTDB is available as an annual subscription (twelve monthly CD-ROMs) for $360 or single-month CD-ROMs for $35 each.[10]

In conclusion, the U.S. government collects large amounts of relevant data that it makes available at reasonable cost. From this large database, several data products and services are produced, as shown in Table 8–3 and Exhibit 8–2. Many of these services differ only in terms of how the information is retrieved and packaged for sale. A marketer thus should consult the International Trade Administration before ordering too many services, some of which may turn out to be redundant.

TABLE 8–3 U.S. government data products and services matched with international business requirements

If you are seeking information or assistance regarding → Use	Potential Markets	Market Research	Direct Sales Leads	Agents/Distributors	Licenses	Credit Analysis	Financial Assistance	Risk Insurance	Tax Incentives	Export Counseling/Education
Foreign Trade Statistics (FT-410)	•	•								
Global Market Surveys	•	•								
Market Share Reports	•	•								
Foreign Economic Trends	•	•								
Commercial Exhibitions	•	•	•	•	•					
Overseas Business Reports (OBR)	•	•								
Overseas Private Investment Corp.		•					•	•		
New Product Information Service			•	•	•					
Trade Opportunities Program (TOP)			•	•	•					
Export Contact List Services			•	•	•					
Agent Distributor Service (ADS)				•						
World Traders Data Reports (WTDR)						•				
Export-Import Bank							•	•		
Foreign Credit Insurance Assoc. (FCIA)								•		
Domestic Int'l. Sales Corp. (DISC)							•		•	
U.S. Commercial Service	•	•								•
ITA Business Counseling	•	•								•
Export Seminars										•
U.S. Foreign Commercial Service	•	•	•	•		•				•
International Economic Indicators	•	•								
Country Market Sectoral Surveys	•	•								
Office of Country Marketing	•	•								
East-West Trade	•	•								
Office of Export Administration										•
Small Business Administration							•			•
Private Export Funding Corporation							•			
Major Projects (Overseas)										
Worldwide Information and Trade System	•	•	•	•	•					
Duties Drawback										
Webb-Pomerene Association										
Free Ports & Free Trade Zones										
International Chamber of Commerce										•
Product Marketing Service	•	•	•	•						

[a] Page numbers listed in table refer to pages in *A Basic Guide to Exporting*, from which this table was taken.
Source: A Basic Guide to Exporting (Washington, D.C.: International Trade Administration, U.S. Department of Commerce, 1981): 89

TABLE 8–3 *(continued)*

Export/Import Regulations	Major Overseas Contract Opportunities	Marketing Plans/Strategies	Trade Complaints	Customs Advantages	Carnet	See Page(s)[a]	Use
						5	Foreign Trade Statistics (FT-410)
						6–7	Global Market Surveys
						6	Market Share Reports
						6	Foreign Economic Trends
						74–77	Commercial Exhibitions
						6	Overseas Business Reports (OBR)
						61	Overseas Private Investment Corp.
						7	New Product Information Service
	●					7	Trade Opportunities Program (TOP)
						9	Export Contact List Services
						62	Agent Distributor Service (ADS)
						63	World Traders Data Reports (WTDR)
						58–60	Export-Import Bank
						59–60	Foreign Credit Insurance Assoc. (FCIA)
						54–55	Domestic Int'l. Sales Corp. (DISC)
●			●			1	U.S. Commercial Service
●			●			2	ITA Business Counseling
						2	Export Seminars
●	●					2–3	U.S. Foreign Commercial Service
						5	International Economic Indicators
						7	Country Market Sectoral Surveys
●	●	●				9–10, 81	Office of Country Marketing
●		●				10–11	East-West Trade
●						43–45	Office of Export Administration
						60–61, 83	Small Business Administration
						61	Private Export Funding Corporation
	●					80–81	Major Projects (Overseas)
	●					81	Worldwide Information and Trade System
				●		53–54	Duties Drawback
●						55	Webb-Pomerene Association
				●		55–56, 109–113	Free Ports & Free Trade Zones
					●	69–70	International Chamber of Commerce
						69	Product Marketing Service

EXPORT SERVICES OF COMMERCE'S ITA

The Commerce Department's International Trade Administration provides a number of services to help U.S. exporters penetrate foreign markets. The US&FCS overseas commercial officers play a key role in making these services possible. The US&FCS is setting up managers for each of these services who will be stationed at Commerce headquarters in Washington, D.C. For information on the services, call your nearest Commerce Department District Office (see listing on inside back cover).

Export counseling   Trade specialists are available at ITA district and branch offices for individualized export counseling. The Washington, D.C., Branch Office counsels visitors to the capital at the U.S. Department of Commerce headquarters; they also schedule appointments with Department officials.

Agent/Distributor Service   A customized search for interested and qualified foreign representatives will identify up to six foreign prospects who have examined the U.S. firm's literature and expressed interest in representing it.

Commercial News USA   A monthly magazine that promotes the products or services of U.S. firms to more than 110,000 overseas agents, distributors, government officials, and end-users. Exporters may submit a black-and-white photo and a brief description of their product or service.

Comparison Shopping   A custom-tailored service that provides firms with key marketing and foreign representation information about their specific products. Commerce Department staff conduct on-the-spot interviews to determine nine key marketing facts about the product, such as sales potential in the market, comparable products, distribution channels, going price, competitive factors, and qualified purchasers.

Foreign Buyer Program   Exporters can meet qualified foreign purchasers for their product or service at trade shows in the United States. The Commerce Department promotes the shows worldwide to attract foreign buyer delegations, manages an international business center, counsels participating firms, and brings together buyer and seller.

Trade Opportunities Program   Provides companies with current sales leads from overseas firms seeking to buy or represent their product or service. These leads are available electronically from the Commerce Department and are redistributed by the private sector in printed or electronic form.

Gold Key Service   A custom-tailored service restricted to U.S. firms planning to visit the country. The program combines several services into one package, including agent and distributor location, one-on-one counseling, and a schedule of appointments with local end-users, agents, and wholesalers. The service is not available in every country with a US&FCS post. It is called the Gold Key service in Spain and France, Cross Flags in Italy, and Rep Find in Mexico.

World Traders Data Report   Custom reports that evaluate potential trading partners. Includes background information, standing in the local business community, credit-worthiness, and overall reliability and suitability.

Overseas Catalog and Video-Catalog Shows   Companies can gain market exposure for their product or service without the cost of traveling overseas by participating in a catalog or video-catalog show sponsored by the Commerce Department. Provided with the firm's product literature or promotional video, the Department's U.S. and Foreign Commercial Service will send an industry expert to display the material to select foreign audiences in several countries.

Overseas Trade Missions   Officials of U.S. firms can participate in a trade mission which will give them an opportunity to confer with influential foreign business and government representatives. Commerce Department staff will identify and arrange a full schedule of appointments in each country.

(continued)

EXHIBIT 8–2   International Trade Administration's export services

Source: Business America, 4, June 1990, 5

Overseas Trade Fairs   U.S. exporters may participate in overseas trade fairs which will enable them to meet customers face-to-face and also to assess the competition. The Commerce Department creates a U.S. presence at international trade fairs, making it easier for U.S. firms to exhibit and gain international recognition. The Department selects international trade fairs for special endorsement, called certification. This cooperation with the private show organizers enables U.S. exhibitors to receive special services designed to enhance their market promotion efforts. There is a service charge.

Matchmaker Events   Matchmaker Trade Delegations offer introductions to new markets through short, inexpensive overseas visits with a limited objective: to match the U.S. firm with a representative or prospective joint-venture/licensee partner who shares a common product or service interest. Firms learn key aspects of doing business in the new country and meet in one-on-one interviews with the people who can help them be successful there.

U.S. Trade Centers   US&FCS Trade Centers in Tokyo, Seoul, Mexico City, and London are available for companies' promotions for a small fee. The Centers also organize specialized exhibitions on themes targeting special opportunities in the local marketplace.

EXHIBIT 8–2   International Trade Administration's export services *(continued)*

PRIMARY RESEARCH

When secondary data are unavailable, irrelevant, or obsolete, the marketer must then turn to primary research. One decision that must be made is whether to make or buy the information. In other words, the question to be decided is whether outside agencies such as marketing research firms should be used to collect the information needed or whether the firm should use its own personnel for this purpose.

A list of international marketing research firms can be found in the U.S. Department of Commerce's Trade List: Market Research Organizations Worldwide, the American Marketing Association's *International Directory of Marketing Research Houses and Services* (Green Book), and *Bradford's Directory of Marketing Research Agencies and Management Consultants in the United States and the World*. Exhibits 8–3 and 8–4 show that marketing research firms can help marketers obtain marketing data in Japan.

If outside personnel are to be used, the company should make distinctions among different types of information brokers. The information brokering industry has more than 200 companies, not counting some one thousand individuals working as independent consultants out of their homes. The industry can be segmented by the extent to which value is added to the information delivered.[11] At the low end of the value-added scale are document delivery firms, most of which are in Washington, D.C. Holding the largest market share, these firms are effective when their clients know what they want and when the materials are already available in printed form.

Next in line are those firms who do searches of published sources. These searching firms are used by clients who believe that the information is already printed somewhere but who have no knowledge of where to locate the particular document. Full-service research firms are even more sophisticated because, after searching existing data bases, these firms can proceed to conduct interviews. At the top of the value-added pyramid are firms that train clients to do their own research. It is

SUCCESS BREEDS SUCCESS

For over 25 years we at ASI-Japan have taken pride in helping our clients to grow, because their successes have contributed to ours. We have seen their families of new products and services—many from other countries —take root in Japan and prosper.

Our team of professionals is committed to working with yours to develop the Japanese marketplace for you. Our quarter century of bilingual and bi-cultural experience in market research in Japan, as well as the hands-on business experience of many of our Japanese and non-Japanese professionals, have aided hundreds of multinational companies in succeeding in Japan.

From idea generation to rollout, from trend analysis to expansion of your existing markets—whether you are new to this market or already well-established, ASI-Japan can be your partner in growth.

For more information call George Fields, Chairman, (03) 3432-3737 or Jim Conte, Executive Vice President, (03) 3432-2288, or send for the ASI-Japan capabilities brochure.

A member of the AGB International plc group

ASI MARKET RESEARCH (JAPAN), INC.
Yoneda Building, 17-20, Shimbashi 6-chome, Minato-ku, Tokyo 105, Japan
Tel: (03) 3432-1701, Fax: (03) 3433-3394

EXHIBIT 8–3   Marketing research in Japan

Source: Courtesy of ASI Market Research

possible that firms in each information segment may ensure their success by forming cooperative networks with other firms, which may include foreign affiliates. The network thus developed provides for greater efficiency while increasing the value of the services provided.

If a marketer decides to conduct his or her own research without hiring outside consultants or researchers, there are many alternatives available to collect primary information. First, the marketer should subscribe to the newspapers in the competitor's home country. These newspapers should include the local language papers and dailies with large circulation. Even a newspaper in a small town nearby the potential market area is useful, because that paper is likely to cover the news concerning a major company or employer in the area. Second, the marketer can learn about a

The Japanese market isn't closed

If you have the key.

And that key is information.

Accurate, complete, up-to-date information from A&S · MRS, the leading market research company in Japan.

Try our All-Japan Retail Store Audit, for instance. If you want to tap Japan's growing market for imported food products and household goods, we'll give you the latest data on sales, inventories, and prices. Our professional staff of 1,200 auditors regularly surveys over 6,500 grocery stores and super-markets throughout Japan.

Or if you need to know more about Japanese consumers, we'll design and run a comprehensive survey of their attitudes, shopping habits, and advertising awareness. We have over 800 well-trained interviewers ready to get the information you need.

Or if you aren't sure which way to go, we'll design a research package that's tailored precisely to your goals. Each of our research managers is an expert at assessing your requirements and providing incisive, practical anaylses.

A&S · MRS is a joint venture of Audits & Surveys, the largest privately-held research company in the United States, and Market Research Service, the oldest and most experienced market research firm in Japan. And our extensive coverage of the Japanese market is just the beginning. We can also open doors to markets in South Korea, Thailand, the Philippines, Singapore and Australia. In fact, we cover the entire Pacific basin.

So if you are feeling locked out, contact A&S · MRS,

We'll help you find the key.

For more information about what A&S · MRS can do for you, send us a letter by mail or fax.

A&S · MRS Co., Ltd.

2-2-3 Irifune, Chuo-ku, Tokyo 104, Japan
Fax 81-3-552-0743   Telephone 81-3-553-8461

EXHIBIT 8–4   Marketing research in Japan

Source: Courtesy of A&S MRS Co., Ltd.

foreign market by personally visiting it or by being a member of a trade mission. By attending trade fairs, the marketer can observe competitors' display booths and have the opportunity to talk with potential customers and distributors. If the marketer is interested in the cross-cultural aspects of the market, the marketer's questions and approach will be influenced by the type of study that is developed and conducted. Table 8–4 sets forth the various types of cross-cultural management research.

If consumers' attitudes are of interest, a marketer can conduct a survey called a *quantitative-descriptive study.* This kind of research is very common in marketing because of the need to understand consumer purchase habits and characteris-tics. If the marketer has difficulty in formulating the problem or is unsure of how to

TABLE 8–4 Types of cross-cultural management research

Title	Culture	Approach to Similarity and Difference	Approach to Universality	Type of Study
Parochial research	Single culture studies	Assumed similarity	Assumed universality	Domestic management studies
Ethnocentric research	Second culture studies	Search for similarity	Questioned universality	Replication in foreign cultures of domestic management studies
Polycentric research	Studies many cultures	Search for difference	Denied universality	Individual studies of organizations in specific foreign cultures
Comparative research	Studies contrasting many cultures	Search for both similarity and difference	Emergent universality	Studies comparing organizations in many foreign cultures
Geocentric research	International management studies	Search for similarity	Extended universality	Studies of multinational organizations
Synergistic research	Intercultural management studies	Use of similarities and differences as a resource	Created universality	Studies of intercultural interaction within work settings

Source: Nancy J. Adler, "A Typology of Management Studies Involving Culture," *Journal of International Business Studies* 14 (Fall 1983): 30–31

TABLE 8–4 *(continued)*

Primary Question	Main Methodological Issues
What is the behavior of people in work organizations? Study is applicable only to management in one culture, yet is assumed to be applicable to management in many cultures.	*Traditional methodologies:* All of the traditional methodological issues concerning design, sampling, instrumentation, analysis, and interpretation without reverence to culture.
Can we use home country theories abroad? Can this theory which is applicable to organizations in culture A be extended to organizations in culture B?	*Standardization and translation:* How can management research be standardized across cultures? How can instruments be literally translated? Replication should be identical to original study with the exception of language.
How do managers manage and employees behave in country X? What is the pattern of organizational relationships in country X?	*Description:* How can country X's organizations be studied without either using home country theories or models and without using obtrusive measures? Focus is on inductive measures methods and unobtrusive measures.
How are the management and employee styles similar and different across cultures? Which theories hold across cultures and which do not?	*Equivalence:* Is methodology equivalent at each stage? Are meanings of key concepts defined equivalently? Has the research been designed such that the samples, instrumentation, administration, analysis, and interpretation are equivalent with reference to the cultures included?
How do multinational organizations function?	*Geographic Dispersion:* All of the traditional methodological questions are relevant with the added complexity of geographical distance. Translation is often less of a problem since most MNOs have a common language across all countries in which they operate. The primary question is to develop an approach for studying the complexity of a large organization. Culture is frequently ignored.
How can the intercultural interaction within a domestic or international organization be managed? How can organizations create structures and processes that will be effective in working with members of all cultures?	*Interaction models and integrating processes:* What are effective ways to study cross-cultural interaction within organizational settings? How can universal and culturally specific patterns of management be distinguished? What is the appropriate balance between culturally specific and universal processes within one organization? How can the proactive use of cultural differences to create universally accepted organizational patterns be studied?

proceed, an *exploratory study* may be considered. Simulation, for example, can be a useful tool for this kind of study. Wanting to learn about British homemakers' baking habits, a U.S. company asked 500 homemakers to bake their favorite cakes. Most chose to bake a simple but popular dry sponge cake. This exploratory study enabled the company to gain some insight into a market opportunity. It then proceeded to introduce a similar easy-to-prepare mix, which gained a 30–35 percent share of the cake mix market.

A marketer should make an attempt to determine the effectiveness of the planned marketing mix. In many cases, neither the exploratory nor the quantitative-descriptive study is appropriate or adequate for the purpose. Instead, some type of *experimental technique* may be necessary to determine a cause-and-effect relationship.

One type of field experimentation often employed in marketing studies is **test marketing.** The technique can be used to test a planned national marketing program for a new product in a limited geographic area. A good test market should possess the following characteristics:

Representativeness
Self-contained media
Self-contained trading area

The concern about representativeness involves demographic comparability. The test market should be demographically similar to the country of which it is part and its population should portray the country's average characteristics. This market should be large enough to provide meaningful data and yet not be so large as to make the costs of the study prohibitive.

The market should be self-contained from a media standpoint in order to avoid media spillage out of the market. If the market is not isolated in terms of media coverage, communication costs are wasted because an audience is being contacted outside of the intended market. Media should also be available at a reasonable cost. A city such as Tokyo is unsuitable for test marketing because of the exorbitant prices charged for TV time—time not at all readily available.

Finally, the test market should be self-contained in terms of trading area. This is necessary in order to avoid transshipments into and out of the area. If the city gains population during the daytime because outside people travel into the city for work or if a distributor distributes the product in other nearby cities, it is difficult to achieve accurate readings of sales, because the sales figure is actually overstated given the normal residential population of the trading area. Cities such as Tokyo and New York are definitely not self-contained.

In North America, Winnipeg, the capital of the Canadian province of Manitoba, is considered a premier test market.[12] Its fairly cosmopolitan and conservative population displays the same characteristics as a larger target audience or general market. This city of 640,000 is favorably isolated because the nearest urban centers are Regina, Saskatchewan, and Minneapolis, Minnesota, both of which are approximately three hundred miles away. Thus, the market is controllable because its residents are not exposed to conflicting or competing information from outside sources. In terms of media, Winnipeg has its own newspapers and TV stations; their easy access eliminates any problems related to media availability and waste.

Winnipeg has been used to test several product concepts before those products were introduced and made available in the U.S. market. Champs Food Systems tested a variety of restaurant concepts ranging from a steak-and-lobster restaurant to a crepes restaurant. Its final product became Mother Tucker's, a restaurant with a specialty of prime rib and a sixty-item salad bar. McDonald's first tested its chicken product in Winnipeg by combining it with french fries. Consumers, however, considered chicken to be a diet food and preferred the product without a bun or fries. Subsequently, McDonald's Chicken and Chips became Chicken McNuggets. Other products successfully tested in Winnipeg include cherry-flavored Pepsi and Luvs disposable diapers. Another interesting point concerning the use of Winnipeg as a test market is that, if certain countries are demographically and psychologically similar, a firm can use a city in one country as a test market to research market conditions in another country.

Regardless of whether the research is exploratory, quantitative-descriptive, or experimental, there are certain steps that the researcher should follow. Table 8–5 lists several methodological techniques and their characteristics. The following sections examine certain steps in the research procedure, with an emphasis on some of the peculiarities that may be encountered in conducting international marketing research.

TABLE 8–5　Methodological issues in comparative management research *(continued next page)*

Methodological Issue	Description
Purpose of comparative management research	To develop equivalent theories of social behavior within work settings in cultures around the world.
Fundamental dilemmas confronted in all comparative management research	*What is culture?* —What is the definition of culture? —Can country be used as a surrogate definition for culture? —Should domestic (within a country) populations be assumed to be multicultural or culturally homogeneous? —Culture should be used as an independent or as a dependent variable, but not as a residual variable. *Culturally specific versus universal aspects of organizational behavior.* —Which aspects of organizational behavior vary across culture and which are constant regardless of culture? —When is culture a contingency? —When is culture—as an independent variable—not related to the dependent variable or theory of interest? When is a theory culture-free? *Mental programming of the researcher as a cultural being.* In order to design, conduct, and interpret research from each culture's perspective—and not strictly from a single culture or ethnocentric perspective—research teams should be multicultural. *Identical versus equivalent approaches to cross-cultural research.* At a sufficiently high level of abstraction, the research topics, concepts, and approaches should be identical. At lower levels of abstractions, the operationalization of the concepts and approaches should not be identical, but should be culturally equivalent. *Threats to interpretation.* Interaction between cultural variables and the research topic and approach.

TABLE 8–5 *(continued)*

Methodological Issue	Description
	—Cultural and research variables interact. The interaction can confound results and render them uninterpretable.
	—Multiple approaches and multiple methods are needed to understand interaction effects.
Research topic	At the highest level of abstraction, the research topic (that is, the research question or theory being tested) should be identical across cultures. The conceptual and methodological approaches to researching that topic should be equivalent across cultures. Across cultures, the topic should be
	—Conceptually equivalent. The definition of the concept should have the same meaning in each culture.
	—Equally important. The phenomenon should be equally modal or marginal in each culture.
	—Equally appropriate. For example, the topic should be equally appropriate regarding political and religious sensitivities in each culture.
Sampling	Sampling issues involve size of sample, selection of cultures, representative versus matched samples, and the independence of samples:
	—*Size of sample.* The number of cultures selected should be large enough to
	Randomize variance on nonmatched variables.
	Eliminate rival hypotheses.
	Studies with insufficient numbers (that is, two or three) should be treated as pilot studies.
	—*Selection of cultures.* The selection of cultures should be based on theoretical dimensions of the research, not on the opportunistic availability of access to particular cultures.
	—*Representative versus matched samples.* Is the research goal to have samples which are representitive of each culture or is it to have matched samples which are equivalent on key theoretical dimensions across cultures? Matched samples should be functionally, not literally, equivalent.
	—*Independence of samples.* Given the interrelatedness of the industialized world, culturally, politically, and geographically independent samples in management research are generally neither feasible nor desirable.
Translation	*Equivalence of language.* The language used in each version of the research—instrumentation and administration—should be equivalent across cultures, not literally identical.
	—*Wording.* The wording of items and instructions should
	Use a common vocabulary (i.e., high-frequency words).
	Avoid idiomatic expressions.
	Use equivalent grammar and syntax.
	Use plain, short sentences.
	Include redundancy.
	—*Method of translation.* Recognizing the Whorfian hypothesis, the translation technique should aim at equivalence, not at literal translations.
	—*Whorfian hypothesis.* Different cultural and linguistic backgrounds lead to different ways of perceiving the world. Unless their linguistic backgrounds are similar or can be calibrated, people who speak two different languages will not perceive the world in the same way.
	—*Translational techniques.* To achieve equivalent translations, the material should be

TABLE 8–5 *(continued)*

Methodological Issue	Description
	Back-translated. Translated and then back-translated into the original language using a good bilingual target population, or Translated by an expert. Translated independently by excellent bilingual translators who are (1) familiar with the linguistic and cultural backgrounds in both cultures, (2) familiar with the subject matter of the research, and (3) translating into his or her native language.
Measurement and instrumentation	*Equivalence of instrumentation.* Are the test items, scaling, instrumentation, and experimental manipulations equivalent across cultures?
	—*Equivalence variables.* Across cultures, are the items or measures conceptually equivalent, equally reliable and equally valid? Have indigenous measures been created to operationalize conceptually equivalent variables? Are variables based on equally salient conceptual dimensions?
	—*Equivalent scaling.* Differences in means are uninterpretable unless measured on equivalent scales which have been developed individually in each culture. Equivalent procedures. Researcher must use the same or equivalent procedures in each culture to develop scales, or Similar patterns of correlations. Items must have similar patterns of correlations within each culture.
	—*Equivalence of language.* See translation above.
	—*Equivalence of experimental manipulations.* Interaction between experimental and cultural variables can confound interpretation. Therefore experimental manipulations must be equivalent across cultures.
Administration	*Equivalence of administration.* The research settings, instructions, and timing should be equivalent, not identical across cultures.
	Equivalence of response. Given that observation changes that which is observed (Heisenberg effect), the influence of the research on the subjects should be equivalent across cultures. The research should be designed and administered in such a way that the responses to the stimuli and to the situation are similar across cultures on such dimensions as
	—*Familiarity.* Subjects should have equal familiarity with test instruments, format, and the social situation of the research.
	—*Psychological response.* Subjects should have similar levels of anxiety and other psychological responses in the test situation.
	—*Experimenter effect.* The extent to which the researchers communicate their preferred hypotheses to subjects—both verbally and nonverbally—should be equivalent across cultures.
	—*Demand characteristics.* The extent to which subjects attempt to discover the researcher's hypotheses and thereafter attempt to help (usually) or hinder the research varies across cultures based on such things as (1) sensitivity to various topics (sex, religion, politics) and (2) the courtesy bias.
	—*Characteristics of the person conducting the research.* Depending on the culture, there can be a difference in response (respectfulness, indifference, hostility) to such characteristics of the research aministrator as Gender Race Origin: from an economically developed or developing country Status relative to subjects: high versus low Foreigner versus citizen

TABLE 8-5   *(continued)*

Methodological Issue	Description
	—Characteristics of the presentation. The response of the subjects can vary in reaction to the Introduction of the research Introduction and characteristics of the presenter Task instructions Closing remarks Timing of the presentation and data collection Setting of the presentation and data collection The goal in comparative management research is to have the administration and experimental conditions equivalent, not standardized, in each culture. The approach to conducting the reasearch may be identical, but the ways in which it is operationalized will vary from culture to culture.
Analysis	*Multivariate techniques.* Comparative research studies are complex. Univariate statistical techniques are generally inappropriate. *Ecological fallacy.* The problem in comparative research is that cultures are often treated and categorized as if they were individuals. Cultures are not individuals; they are wholes, and their internal logic cannot be understood in terms used for personality dynamics of individuals. The ecological fallacy is the confusing of country or cultural level (ecological) correlations with individual correlations. The reverse ecological fallacy is the confusing of individual correlations with ecological/cultural correlations.

Source: Nancy J. Adler, "A Typology of Management Studies Involving Culture," *Journal of International Business Studies* 14 (Fall 1983): 37–40

RESEARCH DESIGN

If the purpose of the study is to learn about how consumers of a particular country respond to an experimental variable of interest (e.g., price) or to compare an experimental group with a control group, both from the same country, a researcher can use virtually all research designs. Such research designs could include the following:

One-shot case study

One group, pretest posttest

Static group comparison

Pretest/posttest control group

Solomon four-group, six-study

Posttest-only control group

Statistical designs such as the Latin square and factorial design can be used as well.

A problem arises when the purpose of the study is to compare responses to an experimental variable across countries, because such a sample does not lend itself to an experimental design. Respondents in different countries cannot simply be assigned to each national group by random procedure. That is, respondents are automatically preassigned to each group by nationality. It is thus difficult to have experimental and control groups that are comparable before a treatment is given.[13] The data then must be adjusted, perhaps subjectively, to account for built-in national or cultural biases.

SAMPLING

As with virtually all consumer market studies, it is neither feasible nor practical for a researcher to contact all the members of the population. What is usually done is to contact a select group of consumers considered to be representative of the entire population. This practice is known as **sampling.**

There are several kinds of sampling techniques, with probability and nonprobability sampling methods being the two major categories. In **probability sampling,** it is possible to specify in advance the chance that each element in the population will have of being included in that sample, though not necessarily in equal probability for every element. In **nonprobability sampling,** it is not possible to determine such probability or to estimate the sampling error.

The problem of poor sampling methods is not always under the control of the researcher. An ideal sampling method, for instance, may not be practical for many reasons when used in the various markets of the world. In the United States, it is possible to use virtually all types of probability and nonprobability sampling methods that closely reflect the population of a target market. The luxury of these options may not be available in other advanced countries. This problem is of a greater magnitude with sampling in LDCs.

Probability sampling methods, though theoretically superior, may be difficult to employ, and the temptation to use nonprobability methods becomes great. There are several reasons for this difficulty. A map of the country is often not available or out of date. Some cities in Saudi Arabia, for example, have no street names, and houses have no numbers. In Hong Kong, a large number of people live on boats. The unavailability of block statistics thus precludes meaningful stratification. Lists of residents may be nonexistent or inaccurate. Poor people may illegally build shacks and pay their neighbors to allow illegal hookups of electricity and water—thus, even utility companies' lists may not be as accurate as they might first appear.

Poor road systems can create another problem because they preclude the use of the dispersed sample. Even when a proper location is identified, it is still difficult to identify the selected sample element. For example, if the element is a homemaker of a particular housing unit, the researcher may be surprised upon arrival that that particular household has more than one homemaker. This can be a common situation in many parts of the world. The prevalence of extended families and joint tenancy makes it very easy for one housing unit to consist of several primary family units. In some countries, a husband may be a polygamist, and all of his wives may live together in the same house.

It is "advisable to pay appropriate attention to sampling design issues without getting unduly obsessed with them."[14] In Japan, it is difficult to apply sampling theory in a "real-world" situation. The official residential list was the most widely used list for random sampling, but many municipal governments have moved to restrict the use of those lists.[15] Mazda has listened to Japanese trend-setting students from the top universities. These upscale student groups represent a large segment of the automobile buyer market. Although the mini-car like the Carol has been targeted toward young women, young college women view the mini-car negatively as a "shopping car for housewives."

In cross-national studies, sampling procedures become even more complicated. A researcher may desire to use the same sampling method for all countries in order to maintain consistency. Theoretical desirability, however, often gives way to practicality and flexibility. Sampling procedures may have to vary across countries in order to ensure reasonably the comparability of national groups. For durable products, a random sample may work well in the United States, but a judgmental sample based on the more upscale segment of the population may be more meaningful in an LDC, because relatively affluent consumers there are more likely to purchase and use such products. Thus, the relevance of the sampling method depends on whether it will yield a sample that is representative of a country's population and on whether comparable samples can be obtained from the intended groups of different countries. Furthermore, a researcher may have to distinguish samples obtained from rural and urban areas because dual economies exist in many countries, resulting in rural and urban inhabitants being distinctly different.

Nonresponse is the problem of an inability to reach selected elements whereas *noncoverage* involves the problem of identifying proper elements for the sample. A good sampling method can only identify subjects who should be selected—there is no guarantee that such subjects will ever be included. Therefore, the selection of an appropriate sampling method does not necessarily solve the nonresponse problem. As a result, opinions of the subjects who do not respond are not obtained or properly represented.

The two main reasons given for nonresponse errors are (1) *refusal to respond* and (2) *not being at home* to be interviewed. In countries where males are still dominant in the labor force, it is difficult to contact a head of household at home during working hours. Frequently, only housewives or servants are at home during the day.

To solve the absentee problem, callbacks are necessary. Yet, in many countries, a callback may be quite difficult to make because of the poor road system, poor lighting, and high crime rate—all of which would discourage a research worker from making a callback. In LDCs, such impediments cannot be overcome by making telephone calls, because telephone service may be either inadequate or unavailable.

Even when individuals are at home or can be contacted, they may refuse to participate in the study. Such reluctance to cooperate is understandable. Women of the Middle East will not give interviews in the absence of their husbands. In most countries, people are suspicious of strangers, thinking that they may be tax inspectors, salesmen, or burglars. If the subjects are well-to-do, an interviewer may have a difficult time getting past their servants. In Thailand, a more unusual problem awaits any interviewer who is able to pass through the front door: Thai people are overly polite and may be too cooperative in an interview session. They will want to please their "guest" by serving beverages and will repeatedly ask whether there are any additional questions they may answer for the interviewer. Under such circumstances, a five-minute interview may easily expand to an hour.

In general, standard motivation methods such as incentives and personal pleas can be used to reduce the nonresponse rate. These methods may minimize the problem of not acquiring the opinions of certain kinds of subjects not properly represented in a survey. Still, the effectiveness of incentives may vary from country to country. A study conducted by Keown revealed that, with a $1 incentive, the response rate from Japanese businessmen increased, but that the response rate from Hong Kong respondents with the same incentive declined.[16]

Another study investigated the effects of an enclosed incentive (bookmark), a promised incentive (offer of free copy of the survey results), the target country, and the nationality of the parent company on response from a sample of American- and Japanese-owned foreign subsidiaries in Singapore, Malaysia, and Thailand. The results showed that

1. The psychological effect of a low-value nonmonetary incentive (bookmark) induced higher response.
2. A promise to send a free copy of the results (versus no offer) was not effective in cross-national mail surveys.
3. Regarding the destinations of the mail questionnaires, the country to which the questionnaires were sent had no effect on the response rate (probably because of the similarities among the three ASEAN countries).
4. In the case of the nationalities of the parent companies, the response from U.S. subsidiaries was higher than that of Japanese subsidiaries. "The major practical implication of the study is that the choice of incentive is critical to cross-national researchers wanting to improve response to mail surveys."[17]

BASIC METHODS OF DATA COLLECTION

There are two principal methods for the collection of primary data: (1) observation and (2) the administration of survey questions. In the case of observation, respondents are visually observed, regardless of whether they realize it or not. When the survey question method is used, respondents are asked certain questions relating to their characteristics or behavior.

Observation

The principal advantage of the observation method is that, on a theoretical basis, it is supposed to be more objective than the use of survey questions. When using observation, a researcher does not have to depend on what respondents say or are willing to say. Another reason the observation method tends to yield more objective information lies in the fact that there is no influence exerted by an interviewer, regardless of whether such influence would be real or imagined by respondents. The lack of social interaction eliminates the possibility of influencing the respondent.

In addition to consumer interviews, Toyota's product teams attended a cocktail party at a Houston country club and learned that car owners preferred a distinctive grille that made the car more impressive when brought to the door by a valet. The teams also measure how close cars were parked to one another at the ball parks, leading the company to implement sliding doors instead of swing-open doors in its minivans. By observing that adults take their children along when shopping and return to the car with their arms full, Toyota realized the need to have an easy-to-open door mechanism that also opens the trunk.[18]

In some cases (especially those involving sensitive, personal, or controversial issues), the observation technique may yield more information than could otherwise be obtained, because the method is independent of respondents' unwillingness or inability to answer. In some developing countries where certain classes provide no opinion, surveys should be complemented with observation methods.[19]

Individuals are usually reluctant to discuss personal habits or consumption, and observation avoids this problem. In the Middle East, Latin America, and Asia, interviewers are suspected of being tax investigators in disguise, making it difficult to obtain data about income and purchases. The degree of openness in a society may also vary. Because of the effectiveness of the observation technique, Edward T. Hall, an internationally known anthropologist, has replaced listening and asking with watching.

Although the personal or direct technique of observation is most commonly used, observation does not have to be done in person. Mechanical recording devices are often used to measure TV viewership, and cash register scanners can be used to keep track of consumer purchases and inventories. These devices, however, are not yet common in many countries because of the cost, especially if labor costs are low in those countries.

There are conflicting opinions about the kind of personnel that should be involved in direct observation. Some contend that local observers should be used because of their familiarity and understanding of the local culture. Others, on the other hand, believe that familiarity breeds carelessness. Local observers, by being familiar with local events, tend to take those occurrences for granted. Consequently, essential and rich detail may be left out of a report. For example, a local observer may fail to notice that students wear school uniforms if that is a common local practice. The failure to include this piece of information may be quite critical for an American firm wanting to sell clothing to school children. If an American observer were used in the same study, it would be unlikely that such information would be missing, since school uniforms are the exception in the United States. Of course the situation can also be reversed. An American observer may see nothing unusual about students' wearing blue jeans to school, but this kind of behavior might be very conspicuous to a non-U.S. observer.

Whereas familiarity may result in some details being left out, lack of familiarity may lead an inexperienced observer to draw a wrong conclusion. An American observer seeing two foreign males holding hands could draw a hasty conclusion that these men must be homosexual. But this conclusion could be based on an ignorance of the local culture. In many countries, there is nothing sexual or unusual about friends of the same sex holding hands. In such countries, what is unusual is for members of the opposite sex to hold hands in public.

The only safe conclusion that can be made about observers is that there is no substitute for careful training. Observers must be explicitly instructed about what they are supposed to notice. Training and practice are necessary if desired details are to be systematically noted and recorded. If bias cannot be completely eliminated through training, it may be necessary to use observers of various backgrounds to cover each other's blind spots.

Clearly, no company can learn about the competition by interviewing competitors. This is one situation where the observation technique can prove useful in gathering information. One common method used to gather data involves such traditional sources as media and business indexes. A marketer can learn about competitors by reading newspaper or magazine stories about those companies. Problems with such sources are that stories appearing in the print media may be too general and that standard business sources are often outdated. Furthermore, print media may not provide information on competitors' plant operations, capacity, sales force, management structure, and distribution.

To acquire information not available from traditional sources, other observation techniques must be devised for intelligence gathering.[20] If a marketer is interested in the size of a competitor's labor force, an observer can count the number of parking spaces at the competitor's plant. An alternative method is to count the number of people walking in or out while noting the number of production shifts. The Japanese have been known to send executives to a competitor's plant after business hours to measure the amount of rust accumulated on the rail siding next to the plant. With this observation, the company can tell how often a boxcar has been rolled up the siding during a period of a week or a month. This information in turn reveals the number of shipments the plant has received.

Another observation technique is scrutinizing competitors' help-wanted advertisements, because these may reveal information on the company's facilities, service networks, and new products. Even a corrugated box might yield information about a competitor's unit sales. The bottom of a box may have a stamp indicating who the box manufacturer is; if the manufacturer is contacted, it may reveal the number of boxes ordered by a competitor. Finally, a competitor's UCC (Uniform Commercial Code) filings can provide some information about commercial loans, which are often obtained for plant and equipment. Such loan figures can be used to estimate the competitor's asset value.

Questioning

Survey questions can be used more frequently than observation because of speed and cost. With questioning, data can be collected quickly and at a minimum cost because the researcher does not have to spend idle time waiting for an event to happen to be observed. The survey question method is also quite versatile, because it can be used to explore virtually all types of marketing problems. Survey questions can be employed to acquire information on the past, present, and future. They are even useful to learn about a consumer's internal workings—such as motives and attitudes—that are not observable. There are three basic ways of administering questions: the personal interview, the telephone interview, and the mail questionnaire.

The popularity of each questioning mode varies from country to country. In many developing countries, telephone and mail surveys are impractical for a variety of reasons. Unlike in the United States, where telephone interviewing is important, this questioning mode is relatively unimportant in the United Kingdom. Although personal, door-to-door, in-home interviews are the dominant mode for gathering research data in Great Britain and Switzerland, central location/street interviews are the dominant technique in France. Whereas mail and central location/street interviews are most popular in the Netherlands, telephone interviewing is dominant in

Sweden.[21] In Japan, personal door-to-door interviewing, accounting for 34 percent of total annual sales, is a major data collection method. Telephone surveys are not very popular even though 92 percent of Japanese households own a telephone.[22]

When the **personal interview** is used, an interviewer must know and understand the local language. This imperative can present a problem in a country such as India, where there are fourteen official languages. Also, a great deal of personal and social interaction occurs in a personal interview, and the appearance of the interviewer must thus be taken into account. If an interviewer is dressed too well, farmers and villagers may be intimidated and may claim to use expensive products just to impress the interviewer.

Personal interview style and technique may need to be adjusted from country to country. A researcher will not be able to ask too many questions in Hong Kong. People there, constantly in a hurry, will not tolerate lengthy interviews.

The use of the personal interview should not be restricted only to the individual interview. It can also be used with a group of respondents. One variation of the group interview is a **focus group.** This technique requires a moderator to lead a group discussion. The focus group was used successfully in Brazil by a major publisher who bought the distribution rights to a cooking series published by Time-Life Books.[23] The publisher formed several focus groups to critically evaluate brochures he was preparing to use in a marketing program. The groups told the marketer that the brochures contained too much information and that the brochures could be made simpler with more pictures and less text. A less complicated brochure booklet was thus produced and used as a promotional tool.

Telephone interviews pose a special challenge for international researchers. State-run telephone monopolies are usually associated with poor service, and it is therefore difficult and at times impossible to conduct a telephone survey. It is exceedingly difficult for residents in many countries to receive their own telephone lines—something Americans have always taken for granted. Consumers in other countries may have to pay several hundred dollars for the privilege of being put on a waiting list in the hope that new telephone lines and numbers become available. Often, a person waits several years before eventually receiving a telephone. Hungary even issued a government bond for the purpose of cutting down the waiting list.[24] Because citizens of Eastern bloc countries commonly wait ten or more years for telephone installation, Hungarian citizens snapped up the issue in spite of a low coupon rate. Their buying motive: the government promised bond buyers a telephone within two years.

The extent of telephone ownership varies greatly across countries. China, for instance, has only .038 telephone for each 100 city dwellers and .013 telephone per 100 among rural inhabitants.[25]

Assuming that private telephones are available, there remain several problems associated with a telephone interview. First, some cities do not have telephone books. Second, foreign telephone owners are much more likely than their U.S. counterparts to be members of the educated and higher-income groups, making them untypical of the larger population. Finally, telephone conversational habits can be vastly different, and an interviewer may experience great difficulty in obtaining information over the telephone. Some people, for example, may be reluctant to give any information over the telephone to an unknown person. Even in modern Japan, few office workers use telephones except to convey simple messages.

The **mail questionnaire** is a very popular survey method because of its low cost and high degree of standardization. Despite these advantages, its effectiveness is contingent on the country in which it is used. Unilever, for instance, will not use the mail questionnaire in Italy. Every marketer should understand the problems associated with the use of this method in the international arena.

One problem involves the scarcity of good mailing lists. In a sample taken of an Asian city, one of every four addresses was found to be nonexistent. No population is as mobile as the U.S. population, but people in most countries generally do not bother to report their new addresses, not even for the purpose of mail forwarding. As a result, a government's list based on the census report and household registration is, as a rule, woefully out of date.

Another problem is illiteracy. Without doubt, this is a significant problem in many LDCs; but the United States is hardly immune to this problem. Of the some sixty million American adults, more than a third are functionally illiterate. Out of the 158 members of the United Nations, the United States ranks 49th in terms of literacy.[26]

Lack of familiarity with the mailed survey question method should be given careful consideration, because many people are not used to responding by mail. This may be due in part to the low volume of mail received outside of the United States: the average number of units of internal mail received per capita per year in Thailand is only 4, and it is not really that high for more advanced countries, such as West Germany (202) and Greece (30).[27] Finally, poor postal service, especially in rural areas, is a cause for complaint in most parts of the world. In Brazil, approximately 30 percent of the mail sent is never delivered. This problem is far from being uncommon, and there are several reasons for unreliable mail delivery. Many postal workers are simply lazy or careless. Some take the stamps attached to the envelopes if stamps can be reused or if the pictures are beautiful. Others open envelopes to look for money. Postal carriers will rarely deliver letters that have been opened or that carry no stamp.

MEASUREMENT

The best research design and the best sample are useless without proper measurements. A measuring method or instrument that works quite satisfactorily in one culture may fail to achieve the intended purpose in another country. Special care must therefore be taken if the reliability and validity of the measurement are to be ensured. Questions and scales must be assessed in order to make certain that they perform the function properly.

A measuring instrument is considered **reliable** when it yields the same result repeatedly, assuming no change in the object being measured. If a bathroom weighing scale has been dropped on the floor a number of times, it may not function properly. If a person steps on it five times and gets five different results, then certainly something is wrong with the scale, because the person's weight does not change appreciably within a short span of time.

The same reliability problem applies to international marketing research. An American questionnaire, when used within foreign markets, increases the chance that misinterpretation, misunderstanding, and administration variation will occur. Respondents' inconsistent answers are likely to be an indicator of the possible unreliability of the instrument. There is empirical evidence showing that "the same research instrument used in a cross-national survey may lead to different levels of response reliabilities among the various country samples due to differences in the knowledge of products and/or brands; the perceptions of products and/or product attributes; the familiarity with the research instrument used; and the national propensity for certain response styles."[28]

Validity is an indication of whether a measuring instrument is able to measure what it purports to (i.e., whether the measure reflects an accurate representation of the object being measured). A thermometer has been universally accepted as being a valid instrument for measuring temperature. But its validity must be seriously questioned if it is used to measure something else, such as the length of a room or the amount of rainfall.

Reliability is a prerequisite for the existence of validity. If an instrument is not reliable, there are no circumstances under which it can be valid. Reliability, although a necessary condition for validity, is not a sufficient condition. Just because an instrument is reliable, the instrument is not automatically valid.

Linguistic and conceptual nonequivalencies in questionnaire instruments that are used in cross-national surveys could conceivably operate to produce differences in the reliabilities of measurements, thus affecting the validity of conclusions drawn about market similarities or differences. The occurrence of reliability differentials in cross-national samples varies according to the type of variable. The attainment of measure equivalence in cross-national surveys seems to be more difficult for soft variables (attitudinal and perceptual variables) than for hard variales (demographic variables).[29]

A study of a cross-national consumer research instrument found it to be sensitive to the nature of the attitudinal constructs, the nationality of the respondents, and the country-of-origin effects. The same scales, which may have different reliabilities in different cultures, may also, because of various levels of consumers' product knowledge, exhibit different reliabilities when used by the same individual in evaluating products from different cultures. Therefore, it may not be sound to simply compare research results in cross-national marketing. One way to minimize the problem is to pretest measures in each market of interest until they elicit similar and satisfactory levels of reliability. Another method is to develop a confidence interval around the values of the measure based on its reliability. As a result, the existence of the similarity of consumers in two markets depends on whether or not the spread on this parameter overlaps across markets.[30]

An instrument proven to be reliable and valid in one country may quite possibly not be so in another culture. International marketing research thus often necessitates some measurement adaptation to overcome this problem. The rest of this section on measurement is devoted to the problems and adjustments of measurement in terms of conceptual equivalence, instrument equivalence, linguistic equivalence (translation), response style, measurement timing, and external validity.

Conceptual Equivalence

Conceptual equivalence is concerned with whether a particular concept of interest is interpreted and understood in the same manner by people in various cultures. Such concepts as hunger and family welfare are universally understood and pose little problem. Other concepts, however, are culturally specific. The concept of dating between the sexes, which is taken for granted by Americans, is incomprehensible to citizens of countries where the arranged marriage is the norm and where a man can see a member of the opposite sex only in the presence of her family or a chaperon. Culture-specific concepts such as these can have implications for marketers. For example, Pizza Hut found that it could not do market research in Thailand because Thai consumers at the time did not know what a pizza was.

Demographics, in spite of being apparent and easily understood, should not be readily embraced in terms of conceptual equivalence without an examination of the varying frames of reference. A demographic variable such as sex is universal, and a question of this nature can be used in a cross-cultural study. Age, on the other hand, is not always considered in the same way—the Chinese include the time during pregnancy in their age. Educational level, likewise, does not have the same meaning everywhere. The meaning of primary school, grade school, secondary school, high school, college, and university varies greatly. A primary school can range from four years to eight years, depending on the country. In some countries, a college may be nothing more than a vocational school. A college education in one country may not at all be equivalent to that in another. It is thus wise in many instances to ask about the number of years of schooling attended by the respondent.

One kind of conceptual equivalence a researcher should pay close attention to is **functional equivalence.** A particular object may perform varying functions or may satisfy different needs in different countries. A bicycle is a recreation device in some countries and a basic transportation device in others. Antifreeze is used to prevent freezing of engine coolant in cold countries but to prevent overheating in countries with warm climates. A hot milk-based drink is perceived as having restful, relaxing, and sleep-inducing properties in the United Kingdom; Thai consumers, in contrast, view the same drink as stimulating, energy-giving, and invigorating. Thais consume hot milk as either a substitute or a supplement to breakfast. Therefore, a valid comparison requires the use behavior to have been developed in response to similar problems in different cultures. Use differences must be built into the measuring instrument if meaningless results are to be avoided.

Definitional or **classification equivalence** is another type of conceptual equivalence that requires careful treatment. This factor involves the way in which an object is defined or categorized—either perceptually by consumers or officially by law or government agencies. Beer is an alcoholic drink in northern Europe, a soft drink in Mediterranean countries, and a malt liquor in Thailand.

Additionally, even demographic characteristics are subject to the problem of definitional or classification equivalence. Age is one such example. Persons in the same age group in different countries are not necessarily at the same stage of life or family life. When a boy becomes a man or a legal adult depends on the definition used by a particular country. The age of legal adulthood may vary anywhere from the very early teens to twenty-one years. In India, a "boy" of only thirteen or fourteen years of age can legally marry a girl who is a few years younger. As a result, chronologically identical age groups within two or more countries do not necessarily lead to comparable equivalent groups. It is thus not possible to standardize age groupings and have the same definitional or classification equivalence on an international basis.

Instrument Equivalence

In devising and using a measure, a researcher should distinguish between two kinds of measuring instruments: emic and etic. **Emic instruments** are tests constructed to study a phenomenon within one culture only. **Etic instruments,** on the other hand, are those that are "culture universal" or "culture independent." As such, when properly translated, etic measuring instruments can be used in other cultures. Table 8–6 compares measurement terms that distinguish between culturally specific and culturally universal behaviors.

One area of concern is the use of **rating scales.** Many times during the course of an investigation, it is inadequate to determine only whether the object being investigated possesses a specific quality or characteristic. Frequently, the researcher must determine the quantity or degree of that quality. Furthermore, coding systems are needed to facilitate the recording and analysis of data. For this purpose, a researcher has to turn to rating scales. Rating scales allow an object to be rated and placed in one of an ordered series of categories, with a numerical value assigned to each category.

TABLE 8–6   Differentiating the universal from the particular

Terms Denoting Cultural Uniqueness	Terms Denoting Universality
Culturally specific	*Culturally general*
Emic: Sounds that are specific to a particular language	*Etic:* Sounds that are similar in all languages
Particular	*Universal*
Idiographic: Descriptive of the uniqueness of the individual	*Nomothetic:* Laws describing behavior of groups of individuals
Polycentric: Cultures must be understood in their own terms	*Geocentric:* Search for universal, pan-cultural laws of human behavior
Within culture: Studies behavior from within the culture to discover whatever structure it might have. Both the antecedents and the consequences of the behavior are found within the culture.	*Across cultures:* Emphasizes the most general description of social phenomena with concepts that are culture-free. Structure of observation is created by the scientists.
Culturally contingent: The studied behavior is dependent on the particular culture in which it is embedded.	*Culturally independent:* The student behavior is not related to or influenced by the particular culture in which it is embedded.
Difference emphasized	*Similarity emphasized*
Universality denied	*Universality central and accepted*
Unique	*Pancultural*

Source: Nancy J. Adler. "A Typology of Management Studies Involving Culture." *Journal of International Business Studies* 14 (Fall 1983): 36

In consumer research, the most popular rating scales are the Likert scale and the semantic differential scale. When a **Likert scale** is employed, a respondent is asked to respond by indicating agreement (or disagreement) and the relative intensity of such an agreement to each item or question. The degree of agreement (or disagreement) usually ranges from "strongly agree" to "strongly disagree." Table 8–7 shows the results of a study that employed the Likert scale to determine how exporters view potential trade barriers.

The **semantic differential scale** measures the meaning of an object to a respondent who is asked to rate that concept on a series of bipolar rating scales (i.e., the extremes of each scale employ adjectives of opposite meanings).

TABLE 8–7 Exporters' responses to potential barriers (n = number of firms)

Statement	Strongly Agree	Agree	Neither Agree nor Disagree	Disagree	Strongly Disagree
Transportation cost is a major obstacle to export to Japan (n = 110)	17	22	37	24	10
Product quality requirements in Japan are not major obstacles to exporting (n = 111)	27	23	14	22	25
Language and culture in Japan are major obstacles to exporting (n = 111)	17	21	28	24	21
Tariffs and quotas are not an important problem (n = 111)	17	12	39	24	19
The prices we can obtain in Japan do not make export particularly interesting (n = 111)	1	7	35	31	37
An important obstacle to exporting to Japan is the strong competition from other countries (n = 110)	11	24	35	25	15
Competition among Norwegian exporters in Japan is not an important problem (n = 110)	20	30	26	21	13
The distribution system for fishery products in Japan is an obstacle to exporting (n = 108)	0	10	64	15	19
The risk involved in exporting to Japan is higher than in other markets due to importer dependence (n = 108)	6	22	34	25	21
The long time necessary to achieve results in Japan is an obstacle to exporting (n = 106)	16	44	29	11	6

Source: Geir Gripsrud, "The Determinants of Export Decisions and Attitudes to a Distant Market: Norwegian Fishery Exports to Japan," *Journal of International Business Studies* 21 (no. 3, 1990): 479

A researcher must keep in mind that the Likert and semantic differential scales, though proven to be satisfactory in measuring behavior and opinion in the United States, may not be understood or may not elicit the same manner of response in other markets. Similarly, asking whether a particular object is a 10 on a scale of 1 to 10 may be meaningful to American respondents but may not be understood by respondents in most other countries, where this rating scheme is uncommon. It is imperative that scales be tailor-made and carefully tested in each culture in terms of relevance and appropriateness.

Another issue related to rating scales is the number of choices (possible answers) provided with each question. A seven-point scale, for example, may not yield more information than a five-point scale in the United States, but the former may prove useful elsewhere. In general, a higher-point scale is needed when a group is relatively homogeneous, since more information is required to distinguish among members of the group.

Researchers need to recognize the demographic and linguistic differences between American and Hispanic consumers. The following practices should be avoided: (1) translating rather than adapting a questionnaire, (2) relying on numerical scales (e.g., the 1 to 10 scale), and (3) using response scales that have a positive skew, because Hispanics tend to rate positively. To achieve discrimination, a researcher should offer a larger number of alternatives among the positive categories being used.[31]

Content validity should be routinely examined. Content validity is critical when a measuring instrument developed for one population is going to be used with another population. A test has content validity when it consists of items or questions judged to be representative of the specified universe of content. A test to measure the spelling ability of fifth-grade students should consist of words students at that level of education are supposed to have learned. If a test were to contain a relatively large number of sports terms, for example, if would not have content validity because it would be unfair to those not interested in sports.

Standardized tests, such as I.Q., ACT, and SAT tests, are somewhat controversial because of content validity or the lack of it. In the United States, such tests are criticized by the poor and various ethnic minorities for being biased because the questions purportedly reflect the experience of white, middle-class Americans. As such, the questions are not representative of the universe of content of interest. The problem is greatly amplified when U.S. colleges require foreign students to take these standardized tests to determine admission eligibility.

The problems encountered in one study provide a valuable lesson. To investigate Chinese managerial behavior, the researchers employed the Laurent Questionnaire, which was developed in the West and which has been used extensively in Europe and North America. The great amount of within-country variance indicated that the instrument failed to produce a valid and reliable description of Chinese managerial behavior, leading the researchers to conclude that "we know that we don't know" how to observe across such profound differences in culture, politics, history, and economic systems. They felt that their observations and interpretations might be too bound by culture, thus forcing them to question the research process. "We know that we cannot blindly apply western models, at least as measured by the Laurent Questionnaire. . . . Perhaps we will need to use grounded theory or similar anthropological techniques to create new instrumentation based directly on the Chinese managers themselves."[32]

Uniformity is usually desirable, but that should not be achieved at the expense of content validity. A researcher must keep in mind that some questions are culturally specific, making them difficult for foreigners, no matter how acculturated or smart they might be, to understand. Some of the questions in the Trivial Pursuit board game, for example, are meaningful to Americans but incomprehensible to Britons. A foreign language can complicate matters even more. It would be unreasonable to say that non–English-speaking children are unintelligent just because they cannot answer questions written in English.

A researcher must remember that the content validity of an instrument depends on the purpose of the study as well as on the groups of people under investigation. The universe of content can vary from group to group and culture to culture. Standardized tests, therefore, may not necessarily work. Identical questions do not guarantee comparable data from different countries, and some variations in questions may be necessary.

Linguistic Equivalence

Linguistic differences can easily invalidate the results of a study. One researcher translated nine scale terms into Arabic, Chinese, Farsi, French, German, Korean, and Spanish and asked respondents, who were native speakers of those languages, to place values on the translated terms. By comparing the average values of the translated terms to the average values of the English terms, the researcher was able to ascertain that there was a measurement equivalency problem. Therefore, intuitively developed scales are likely to result in poor comparability of research results.[33]

There is no question that poor translation works against sound research methodology. Particularly disadvantageous are imprecise literal translations made without regard to the intended purpose or meaning of the study. **Linguistic equivalence** must be ensured when cross-cultural studies are conducted in different languages.

The goal of linguistic equivalence requires the researcher to pay close attention to potential translation problems. According to Sekaran, translators should pay attention to idiomatic vocabulary, grammatical and syntactical differences in languages, and the experiential differences between cultures as expressed in language.[34] Vocabulary equivalence requires a translation that is equivalent to the original language in which the instrument was developed. Idiomatic equivalence becomes a problem when idioms or colloquialisms unique to one language cannot be translated properly to another. Grammatical and syntactical equivalence poses a problem when long passages must be translated. With regard to experiential equivalence, care must be taken that accurate equivalence of inferences in a given statement are drawn by respondents from various cultures.

There are several translation techniques that can be used: back translation, parallel-blind translation, committee approach, random probe, and decentering.[35] With *back translation,* the research question is translated by one translator and then translated back into the source language by another translator. Any discrepancy between the first and last research questions indicates translation problems. One Australian soft drink company planned to use in Hong Kong a translated version of its successful slogan "Baby, it's cold inside." The back translation revealed a translation error; in Chinese, the message turned out to be "Small mosquito, on the inside it is very cold." "Small mosquito" is a local colloquial expression for a small child, and it is hardly synonymous with the English slang word *baby* for a woman or loved one.

In a *parallel-blind translation,* the question is translated by several individuals independently, and their translated statements are then compared. The *committee approach* differs from the parallel-blind technique in the sense that the former permits committee members to discuss the research questions with one another during the translation.

A *random probe* involves placing probes at random locations in both the source and translated question during pretesting in order to ensure that the respondents understand questions in the same way. In *decentering,* both the source version and target version are viewed as open to modification. If translation problems are recognized for the source document, then it should be modified to be more easily translatable. Consequently, the source question becomes more lucid and precise. For example, the statement "I am an aerobic instructor" may be changed to "I am a dance-exercise teacher."

Regardless of the method of translation, there will always be concepts that cannot be translated into certain languages or that cannot be asked in a meaningful way in certain cultures. 7UP's "uncola" slogan is an example of such a concept. Some language purists may even contend that linguistic comparability is an unattainable goal. In any case, none of the translation methods can guarantee linguistic equivalence, but the recognition of potential translation problems should at least minimize problems.

Response Style

People from different cultures have different response styles when dealing with the same questions. Asian people, for example, are generally very polite and may avoid making negative statements about a product. In such a case, a researcher may have to employ an even number scale (e.g., yes/no) in order to receive an objective response. The even number scale, however, may create another problem in the sense that it may elicit an opinion that does not truly exist in that particular culture. A researcher may then want to consider whether to use an odd number scale so that respondents have an option of making a neutral response.

Another issue concerning response style variation is the willingness—or lack of it—on the part of a respondent to take an extreme position, especially when such a position is not a popular one. It may thus be appropriate to adjust for respondents' extreme positions and/or response style by using "normalized" scores rather than raw scores.

More often than not, one must be sensitive to the logic of a language. English-speaking people, for example, use the words *yes* and *no* in a manner that differs from the way non–English-speaking people do. Thus, "yes" is not always "yes," and sometimes "no" may mean "yes" instead. The English and Western languages require the answer to be "yes" when the answer is affirmative. It is "no" when the answer is a negative one. For other languages, however, "yes" or "no" refers to whether a person's answer affirms or negates the question asked. Consider the question, "Don't you like it?" An American who does not like the item in question would say "no." But a non-

Westerner would probably say "yes," indicating agreement with the question. For the non-Westerner, the statement "Yes, I don't like it" is perfectly logical. Therefore, it is a good idea to phrase questions in simple, positive terms. Questions with negatives should be avoided.

Measurement Timing

A cross-national study can be done simultaneously, sequentially, or independently. A researcher may initially think it advantageous for a study to be conducted simultaneously in the countries of interest. But simultaneous studies in different markets may present problems of data comparability, especially because of seasonal factors. Consider a study of soft drink consumption, which is generally highest in the summer. Winter in Canada occurs when it is summer in Argentina. Simultaneous studies in such a case would yield invalid results.

"History" can sometimes act as an extraneous variable, complicating cross-national studies. A specific event may affect the outcome or respondent behavior within a study. For example, an important election (i.e., history) held in one country and not in another can considerably affect the results of a study. Likewise, sales in the United States during the Christmas season are much higher than sales during the rest of the year, whereas sales in China and Hong Kong tend to be higher than normal during the period of the Chinese New Year. In another example, R. J. Reynolds was about to distribute cigarettes door-to-door in Lebanon, with a plan to return for interviews after consumers had sampled the brand. The whole program test, however, had to be halted when war broke out in Beirut.[36] To be impartial, significant events should be controlled for, since they can critically affect a study that is done sequentially or independently.

Another complicating factor can be a product's life cycle stage. The same product may be in different stages of its life cycle in different countries. Because of the phenomenon of an international product's life cycle, LDCs may lag behind more advanced nations in adopting the product. The sales of the product in two or more countries for the same period may not be comparable, casting doubt on the wisdom of conducting simultaneous studies. Because of this problem, it may be better in some cases to conduct "simultaneous" studies when the countries are in the same product-life-cycle stage. In addition, it may be prudent to conduct sequential studies for a particular stage in the product's life cycle when the product is not introduced at the same time in the countries of interest.

External Validity

There are two major types of validity: internal and external. This chapter has so far only discussed internal validity. A study is said to have **internal validity** when it accurately measures the characteristic or behavior of interest. But a researcher is prudent to ask whether the findings concerning a particular sample in a particular study will hold true for subjects who did not take part in the study. For example, American dog owners may be found to react favorably to a beef-flavored, premium dog food; but that finding does not indicate that either Americans who are not dog lovers or foreign dog owners will react in the same way to what may seem to them an excessive pampering of animals.

External validity is concerned with the generalization of research results to other populations. Ordinarily, there is a limit on how far research findings can be generalized. Consequently, the findings may not be applicable to other groups or populations, other products, other cities, or other countries.

Consider the health concerns about the use of saccharin. Many studies have provided evidence for a link between saccharin and cancer. The scientific evidence has shown that saccharin is a carcinogen (cancer-causing substance) and that it may act as a cancer catalyst in the sense that it assists the carcinogen to work. Internal validity has never been much of an issue, because studies have repeatedly proven that saccharin indeed causes cancer, at least in laboratory rats. Critics of this evidence have concentrated on the issue of external validity. According to the critics, producing a disease in rats is not a valid basis for predicting the effect of saccharin on humans. The Federal Drug Administration (FDA), however, has dismissed this criticism by pointing out that the analysis is not accompanied by any proof that the mechanism causing cancer in rats would be different in humans. As far as the FDA is concerned, the studies in question are both internally and externally valid.

The FDA, surprisingly, has reacted conservatively when test results submitted have used foreign subjects. Although the FDA has accepted results using rats (whether American or not) as surrogates for human beings, it had long shown great reluctance in accepting foreigners as being similar to Americans in terms of the impact of drug treatment. New FDA rules permit a drug company to submit the results of clinical studies done abroad to support claims of safety and efficacy. Such studies are permitted as long as they have been conducted by competent foreign researchers, can be validated, and are applicable to the U.S. population.

External validity is generally not a problem when the matter of concern is physiological in nature. The same cannot be said about psychological matters. Thus, people may have similar demographics but diverse attitudes and behavior. The behavior of one consumer group or the general behavior of the people in one country should not simply be extended to another group or people. It may not be reasonable to assume that a study of a marketing problem in one country or the results obtained within one culture will also be applicable to a marketing problem or people in other cultures. Because of differences between cultures, the problem of external validity is amplified when marketers engage in international marketing research.

MARKETING INFORMATION SYSTEM

A **Marketing Information System (MIS)** is an integrated network of information designed to provide marketing managers with relevant and useful information at the right time and place for planning, decision making, and control. As such, the MIS helps management identify opportunities, become aware of potential problems, and develop marketing plans. The marketing information system is an integral part of the broader management information system. For example, Benetton's stores around the world are linked by computer. When an item is sold, its color is noted. The data collected make it possible for Benetton to determine the shade and amount of fabric to be dyed each day, enabling the firm to respond to color trends very quickly.

In spite of computer and other advanced technologies, "dark age" methods of data collection and maintenance are still prevalent. In many parts of the world, a knowledge and application of modern management systems is nonexistent. In many offices, scores of desks are crammed together in the same room. Each employee may have his or her own unique and disorganized system for filing documents and information. New employees inherit these filing and accounting systems and modify them to fit their needs. The unindexed filing system, a long-honored custom, makes each employee practically indispensable since no one knows how to find a document that has been filed by someone else.

Such problems are not just confined to LDCs. Advanced nations such as some European countries and Japan, are still struggling with the automation of their information systems. The experience of Bank of America shows that U.S. firms are also not immune to this problem. Bank of America has traditionally organized customer information by product line, which is organized in separate data banks that cannot be linked.[37] It is thus impossible for the bank to have access to complete customer profiles in order to learn about the products and services purchased by its customers. Also, by treating its 950 California branches and international units as independent businesses, the bank has had to struggle with different reporting methods and incompatible systems, hampering its own systematic attempts at gathering data.

To overcome the problem, Bank of America took four years to develop a $200 million prototype information system for its international operations in Europe. The European unit's corporate lending officers became able to access an electronic file on a customer's balances, loans, foreign exchange positions, and other information in Europe. The bank plans to extend the system around the world eventually. The information allows the bank to have a total relationship with its client, making it possible to determine a customer's creditworthiness and the products or services in demand, along with other facts. In the process of establishing the information system, the bank has also created a better control system.

There is often a misconception that an MIS must be automated or computerized. Although many firms' systems are computerized, it is possible for a company to set up and utilize a manual system that can later be computerized if desired. With modern technology and the availability of affordable computers, it seems quite worthwhile for an international firm to install a computer-based information system. Yet no one should assume that the computer is a panacea for all system problems, especially if flaws are designed into the MIS. A poorly designed system, whether computerized or not, will never perform satisfactorily.

For the MIS to achieve its desired purpose, the system must be carefully designed and developed. Development involves the three steps of system analysis, design, and implementation. System analysis involves the investigation of all users' information needs. The relevant parties must be contacted to determine the kinds of information they need, when it is needed, and the suitable format through which the information is made available. Because information is not cost free, it may not be feasible to satisfy all kinds of information needs. The benefit of the information provided must be compared with the cost of obtaining and maintaining it. Only when the benefit is greater than the cost can a particular information need be accommodated.

System design should be the next major consideration. System design transforms the various information requirements into one or more plans that clearly specify the procedures and programs in obtaining, recording, and analyzing marketing data. Alternative or competing plans are developed and compared, and the most suitable one is ultimately selected.

The last step comprises system implementation. The chosen system is installed and checked to make certain that it functions as planned. Both those who operate the system and those who use it must be trained, and their comments should be evaluated to ensure the smooth operation of the system. Even after implementation, the system should continue to be monitored and audited. In this way, management can make certain that the system serves the needs of all users properly while preventing unqualified persons from gaining access to the system. Security Pacific Bank, for example, lost $10.3 million when a consultant was able to obtain an electronics fund transfer code and use it to deposit money into his Swiss bank account.

For the MIS to be effective and efficient, it should possess certain characteristics. According to Sweeney and Boswell, the system should be user-oriented, expandable, comprehensive, flexible, integrated, efficient, cost-effective, reliable, timely, and controllable.[38] The MIS should also be systematic and self-perpetuating. Marketing and environmental information should be routinely received, evaluated, and continuously updated.

A. C. Nielsen is the world's largest consumer market research company with operations in twenty-seven countries. Nielsen Europe has synchronized its continent-wide reporting periods and implemented pan-European databases. The databases, as defined by international standards, should enable marketers to efficiently access and compare data on their own products and those of their competitors. Although many key influencing factors such as language, consumption habits, retail trade structure, and TV advertising will continue to have distinct local character, the uniform methods allow for a quick examination of market situations across the entire continent.[39]

The MIS consists of several subsystems: internal reporting, marketing research, and marketing intelligence. The internal reporting subsystem is vital to the system because a company handles a great deal of information on a daily basis. The marketing department has sales reports. The consumer service department receives consumers' praises and complaints. The accounting department routinely generates and collects such information as sales orders, shipments, inventory levels, promotional costs, and so on. All of these types of internally generated information should be kept and made available to all concerned and affected parties.

For externally generated information, the MIS should consist of two subsystems. One of these is the marketing research subsystem. The activities of this subsystem have already been discussed extensively. The other subsystem is the marketing intelligence or environmental-scanning subsystem. The responsibility of this subsystem is to track environmental changes or trends. This subsystem collects data from salespersons, distributors, syndicated research services, government agencies, and from publications about technology, social and cultural norms, the legal and political climate, economic conditions, and competitors' activities.

The implementation of the MIS must conform to local laws. Many countries, concerned with citizens' privacy, have laws that restrict free flow of information. In

England, data users are required by the Data Protection Act to register with the Office of Data Protection Registrar; otherwise, heavy fines are levied. Computer users must state how personal information was obtained and how it will be used. Furthermore, British residents have the right to see personal data about themselves.

The EC's Privacy Directive, aiming to safeguard individual privacy, has a number of restrictions. Private companies need the consent of the subjects in order to collect or process personal data, and they must register all data bases containing personal information. The EC's Privacy Directive requires outside countries to have "adequate" levels of data protection before data on European citizens can be released across their borders. Conceivably, international banks and other institutions may not be allowed to pass financial information between Europe and the United States through telecommunications or other means. As a result, a European national may not be able to use credit cards in the United States, Asia, South America, Africa and parts of Eastern Europe because these locations do not have data protection legislation.[40]

The MIS should be designed to do more than data collection and maintenance. It should go beyond data collection by adding value to the data so that the information will be of most use to users. The MIS thus requires an analytical component that is responsible for conceptually and statistically analyzing the data. This component may even go a step further by offering conclusions and recommendations based on the analysis of the data.

CONCLUSION

To minimize risks, a company needs information. In general, U.S. firms fail to realize the significance of information on foreign markets. The Japanese are quite puzzled by this behavior of American companies. As noted by the director of MITI's international trade research office, the United States was able to defeat Japan in World War II because of the U.S. government's superior intelligence network. "Why can't American businessmen develop the same kind of superior intelligence and strategy to cope with Japan today and be victorious? Most Japanese can't understand why American businessmen cannot win this war."[41]

This chapter has discussed the need for information on the one hand and the difficulty of managing information on the other hand. The primary goal is to provide a basic understanding of the research process and the utilization of information. Special attention has been given to the information collection process and the use of marketing information. This coverage is far from being exhaustive, and the reader should consult marketing research textbooks for specific details related to particular research topics.

Regardless of where the intended market is, a company must understand the market and its consumers. Japan and the European countries are successful abroad because of their adoption of the marketing concept, a concept popularized and originated in the United States. Yet American firms often fail to implement the marketing concept overseas. Basically, the marketing concept requires companies to understand consumer needs, and marketing research is a necessary undertaking in making that determination. Although it may be true that foreign market information is frequently lacking or of poor quality, this general problem can be a blessing in disguise, because competitors do not have either adequate or reliable information. A company that does a better job in acquiring information can gain a competitive advantage.

A marketer should initiate research by searching first for any relevant secondary data. There is a great deal of information readily available, and the researcher needs to know how to identify and locate the various sources of secondary information both at home and abroad. Private sources of information are provided by general reference publications, trade journals from trade and business associations, syndicated services, and marketing research agencies. Government sources also have many kinds of information available in various forms for free or at reasonable costs.

When it is necessary to gather primary data, the marketer should not approach its collection from a perspective of the home country. A marketer should be aware of numerous extra constraints that exist overseas, since such constraints can affect virtually all steps of the research process. Because of these constraints, the process of data collection in the international context is anything but simple. One cannot simply replicate the methodology used in one country and apply it in all countries. The marketer should expect to encounter problems unique to a particular country, and some adaptation in research strategies may be necessary. In order to make certain that a study is reliable and internally and externally valid, it is important to have conceptual, instrumental, and linguistic equivalence.

A company should set up an MIS to handle the information efficiently and effectively. The system should integrate all information inputs from the various sources or departments within the company. For a multinational operation, this means the integration and coordination of all the information generated by the overseas operations as well. The system should be capable of being more than a compilation of data. It should routinely make meaningful outputs available in the desired format for its users in a timely fashion. With the advanced development of artificial intelligence (AI), it may be possible in the near future for a computer to perform all necessary functions, including the making of recommendations for marketing strategies. Still, in the final analysis, every marketer must keep in mind that information can never replace judgment. Remember, it is useless to have "data, data everywhere, and not a thought to think."

QUESTIONS

1. What are the difficulties in using and comparing secondary data from a number of countries?
2. What is the *Encyclopaedia of Business Information Sources?* How can it be useful to international marketers?
3. Describe these products of the U.S. Department of Commerce: *FT 410, OBR,* ESP, FTI, and TOP.
4. Why is it difficult to employ probability sampling techniques overseas?
5. Distinguish among: back translation, parallel-blind translation, committee approach, random probe, and decentering.
6. Distinguish between internal and external validity. What are the implications of external validity for international marketers?
7. What are the desirable characteristics of the MIS?

DISCUSSION ASSIGNMENTS AND MINICASES

1. Would Tokyo be a good test market? Why or why not?
2. Do you prefer observation or questioning in collecting overseas data?
3. Cite certain kinds of behavior so common in the United States that they are often taken for granted by Americans—but not by foreign observers.
4. Discuss the reliability and validity problems in conducting a cross-national comparison study with the use of a standardized questionnaire.
5. *Dieting* and *jogging* are concepts that Americans can easily relate to. Are they understood by non-Americans?
6. Do demographic variables have universal meanings? Is there a likelihood that they may be interpreted differently in different cultures?
7. After learning of no import barriers to its product, a U.S. manufacturer of processed food conducted marketing research in Japan to determine the degree of interest in cake mixes. The results were encouraging: the Japanese enjoy eating cakes. Concluding that there was no reason why Japanese consumers would not want to buy ready-made cake mixes, the company proceeded to get Japanese supermarkets to carry its product. The sales were extremely disappointing. Did the Japanese interviewed mislead the manufacturer? Or did the manufacturer fail to ask enough or the right questions?
8. As a researcher, you have just been asked to do marketing research in order to make recommendations on how to market coffee in a number of Asian, European, and South American countries. What questions do you need to ask in order to understand the various buying motives, consumption habits, and uses of this particular product?

CASE 8–1
ONE WORLD, ONE AD?

Standardized advertising, the practice of using the same advertisement everywhere in the world, is a highly controversial issue. For decades, the debate has been heated, and it shows little likelihood of abating anytime soon. Standardized advertising is based on an assumption of consumer homogeneity. That is, peoples, regardless of race or ethnic origin, have the same needs and desires and thus can be motivated in the same ways. One advertisement for all, then, should suffice.

One study conducted by Boote investigated the psychographic dimension of the homogeneity assumption. He compared the "values" of 1,500 women, 500 each from the former West Germany, the United Kingdom, and France. Exhibit 1 provides the results of how twenty-nine value items were ranked by each of the three groups. T-tests were performed on the mean ratings of each scale item. Boote also did factor analysis on each group's responses, resulting in two value groups for West Germany, three groups for France, and four groups for the United Kingdom. He concluded that the two Germany groups were similar qualitatively to two of the British groups because of the groups' sharing of some but not all statements. As a result, he concluded that his findings seemed to support both standardized advertising and localized advertising. "On balance," he wrote, "the findings provide tenuous evidence in support of mounting a common advertising campaign in these three countries."

Questions
1. Study the table as well as the other information provided in the case. Do you agree with the researcher that there is some evidence to support the use of standardized advertising?
2. What are your recommendations to management concerning the use of standardized advertising?

EXHIBIT 1 Means and ranks of scale items by country and pairwise evaluation by T-test

| | | Means and Ranks of Scale Items | | | | | | Statistical Significance of Differences Based on T-Tests | | |
| | | Germany | | United Kingdom | | France | | Germany vs. U.K. | Germany vs. France | U.K. vs. France |
		Rank	Mean Rating	Rank	Mean Rating	Rank	Mean Rating			
1.	Having a familiar routine.	1	1.2633	10	2.1973	23	3.5433	Z	Z	Z
2.	Having people admire your possessions.	26	3.5933	26	3.7729	27	4.4400		Z	Z
3.	Being assured an appliance is easy to operate before you buy it.	5	1.6067	2	1.4314	2	1.3067	Y	Z	X
4.	To have possessions like those of your friends.	28	4.2533	28	4.3645	29	4.6467		Z	Z
5.	Having something good happen unexpectedly.	11	1.9967	7	2.0368	5	1.7267		Z	Z
6.	Being able to plan all activities in advance.	18	2.4033	18	2.6823	22	3.4333	Y	Z	Z
7.	Having fashionable possessions.	22	2.6700	25	3.4716	25	3.7867	Z	Z	Y
8.	Having distinctive possessions.	12	2.0033	24	3.3010	18	3.0367	Z	Z	X
9.	Learning about ways to save money on household expenses.	8	1.6833	8	2.0602	8	1.9867	Z	Z	
10.	To be among the first of my friends to own a new kind of product.	29	4.3733	29	4.3779	28	4.6100		Z	Z
11.	Having a modern, up-to-date home.	25	3.3267	20	3.0234	21	3.1733			
12.	Having an orderly way of life.	14	2.0567	11	2.2441	15	2.7200	Y		
13.	Having expensive-looking possessions.	27	3.7333	27	3.8562	26	4.2800		Z	Z
14.	To be with people who have up-to-date ideas.	16	2.2833	21	3.1538	24	3.7767		Z	Z
15.	Having products which work as expected.	2	1.4267	1	1.2676	1	1.2067	Z	Z	Z
16.	Having household appliances which are easy to carry.	4	1.5600	3	1.5686	3	1.3767	Z	Z	
17.	Having something to keep you busy.	21	2.6067	6	1.8963	6	1.7367		Y	Z
18.	Learning about something new for your home.	13	2.0300	13	2.3779	12	2.1767	Z	Z	X
19.	Having beautiful things in your home.	3	1.5467	17	2.6656	9	1.9900	Z		X
20.	Having products which are uncomplicated.	7	1.6500	5	1.8027	4	1.4433	Z	Z	Z
21.	Devoting most of your time to the home.	20	2.4933	15	2.5987	14	2.6733	X	Z	Z
22.	Having many outside interests other than your job or your home.	19	2.4733	15	2.5987	13	2.1933	Y	Z	
23.	Staying at home rather than going out.	24	2.9133	23	3.1806	20	3.1700	Y	Y	
24.	Doing things slowly and deliberately.	17	2.3733	22	3.1706	17	3.0167	Z	Z	
25.	Spending a lot of time on household tasks to get them done properly.	23	2.7567	19	2.7659	19	3.0400		Y	Y
26.	Being able to get domestic tasks done as quickly as possible (to do other things).	10	1.8733	12	2.2876	11	2.0600	Z	X	X
27.	Having things tidy and neat wherever you are.	9	1.7233	9	2.1204	7	1.9400	Z	Y	X
28.	Having appliances which are good-looking.	15	2.2167	14	2.5619	16	2.7833	Z	Z	X
29.	Saving money whenever possible.	6	1.6300	4	1.6488	10	2.0567		Z	Z

Scale: 5 Points   1 = Extremely Important; 5 = Not At All Important   *Code for T-Test Results*   X ≤ .05; Y ≤ .01; Z ≤ .001

Source: Alfred S. Boote. "Psychographic Segmentation in Europe," *Journal of Advertising Research* 22 (December 1982/January 1983): 19–25. Reprinted with permission of the Advertising Research Foundation

CASE 8–2
THE BEST FROZEN FOODS COMPANY

ALLAN R. MILLER
Bentley College

F. Rozen, president of the Best Frozen Foods Company, was reviewing the latest sales figures for his company. He noticed that the greatest profit margins came from sales in the military commissary system in Europe. The commissary system encompasses food stores run by the U.S. Army to serve military personnel and their dependents assigned to Europe. Most of the commissaries, as well as most of the personnel, are located in Germany. Only those military and American civilians connected with the U.S. government can shop at these stores. A local person cannot shop at the commissary unless he or she is a dependent of an authorized shopper.

The commissaries are essentially no-frills American-type supermarkets that sell grocery products that Americans want and need. Product selection is essentially the same as an American supermarket, but brand selection per product is limited.

F. Rozen called his vice-president, N. E. W. Market, into his office and said, "Our frozen foods are making profits in the German commissaries, especially with our giant family-size meals. As in America, our frozen corn is the best seller. Family meals with corn as a vegetable are outselling meals that have vegetables other than corn. Sales of frozen corn have exceeded our highest expectations. However, I remember that when I served with the Army in Germany you could not get frozen foods. This will make a great market for us to expand our frozen food line. Since our warehouse and transportation networks have been established, additional distribution costs are negligible.

"Whenever expanding our marketing area, we have used a massive television campaign, going with our successful theme "Better than Fresh." Since the German population drinks a lot of beer, let's use local actors drinking a cold beer while eating a meal. I envision a theme of frozen food with an ice-cold beer. I want you to go to Germany, get the shelf space, arrange the television advertising, promotion, and everything else involved in introducing the frozen food line in Germany. The food will be shipped next week and will be available for shipment to the stores in three months."

N. E. W. Market left for Germany the next day. Three weeks later, he sent the following report back to F. Rozen: "I have observed the following problems. First are the cultural differences between the United States and Germany. One difference involves shopping. Americans tend to do grocery shopping once a week; they buy their food for the week, and they want convenience. Meals are to be prepared and consumed as quickly as possible. Shopping is done as quickly as possible also. But in Germany, food shopping is a social occasion, especially in the smaller cities. Most of the local employees are off from noon till two. They go to the local shop and buy the food they need for the evening meal. In other words, they don't have the need to plan meals days in advance as Americans do. Fresh meats and other foods are readily available to the local population. Corn is not eaten by Germans; it is used as animal food.

"In the United States, refrigerators are larger and have very large freezer compartments. Many Americans even own separate freezers. The typical Germany refrigerator is smaller, about the size of a small office refrigerator. There is little room for frozen foods, if any. Germans are not used to frozen foods and even drink their beer warm. You have to request ice in a restaurant. Germans seem very conscious of having food available. There were food stands in front of the grocery markets, department stores, and just about everywhere else. These are quick food stands that sell sausages and french fries. Grocery stores have many fresh products. A lot of products, such as meat, fish, cheese, are sold by counter help. There is plenty of help in shops, and many people give out samples or conduct demonstrations. But, there is little refrigerator and almost no freezer space.

"I showed the package to potential customers. We have forgotten to print the package instructions in German. In fact, most packaging is printed in four or five languages, including German, English, French, and Spanish. People said the instructions didn't make sense and were difficult to follow. They also weren't sure how large a pound or ounce was."

The report also noted some advertising problems. "A major problem exists with television advertising. The only advertising occurs between 6:30 and 7:00 P.M. There is an all-advertising show that is one of the most popular shows. But when you can get space on the show, it must be bid for at least 18 months in advance. There is no guarantee when the commercials will be shown throughout a year and in what position commercials will be shown. Any kind of comparative advertising cannot be used. The food industry has told me that they will sue us if we use our theme Better than Fresh. This is considered derogatory to the fresh food industry, and therefore, illegal.

"I cannot find shelf space for our product. Stores do not have freezer space, nor do they want an untried product. Please advise on what action I should take. What should I do with the product, which is arriving soon?"

Questions

1. Summarize the problems involved in marketing frozen foods in Germany.
2. What should F. Rozen advise N. E. W. Market to do?
3. Should this product be introduced?
4. What suggestions would you have if the product is introduced?

NOTES

1. S. Tamer Cavusgil, "Guidelines for Export Market Research," *Business Horizons* 28 (November/December 1985): 27–33; S. Tamer Cavusgil, "Differences Among Exporting Firms Based on Their Degree of Internationalization," *Journal of Business Research* (June 1984): 195–228.

2. Anthony C. Koh, "An Evaluation of International Marketing Research Planning in United States Export Firms," *Journal of Global Marketing* 4 (no. 3, 1991): 7–25.

3. Kazuo Kobayashi and Peter Draper, "Reviews of Market Research in Japan," *Journal of Advertising Research* 30 (April/May 1990): 13–18.

4. E. H. Demby, "ESOMAR Urges Changes in Reporting Demographics, Issues Worldwide Report," *Marketing News,* 8 January 1990, 24–25.

5. Gerald Zaltman and Philip C. Burger, *Marketing Research: Fundamentals and Dynamics* (Hinsdale, IL: Dryden Press, 1975).

6. "Supplying Inside Story on Foreign Markets," *Chicago Tribune,* 17 March 1985.

7. See Cavusgil, "Export Market Research"; also see Susan P. Douglas, C. Samuel Craig, and Warren J. Keegan, "Approaches to Assessing International Marketing Opportunities for Small- and Medium-Sized Companies," *Columbia Journal of World Business* 17 (Fall 1982): 26–31.

8. Leonard M. Fuld, "How to Gather Foreign Intelligence without Leaving Home," *Marketing News,* 4 January 1988, 24, 47.

9. United States Postal Service, *International Direct Marketing Guide* (Alexandria, VA: Braddock Communications, 1990), 10–14.

10. Mark W. Plant, "The National Trade Data Bank: A One-Year Perspective," *Business America* 23 September 1991; Melissa Malhame, "The National Trade Data Bank: A Valuable Resource for Exporters," *Business America,* 112 (no. 2, 1991): 13–14.

11. Teri Flynn, "Information Brokers: Finding the Facts Business Needs," *Business America,* 23 December, 1985, inside front cover.

12. Janet Cawley, "Winnipeg's Tastes Are Continental," *Chicago Tribune,* 19 March 1986.

13. Charles S. Mayer, "Multinational Marketing Research: The Magnifying Glass of Methodological Problems," *European Research* 6 (March 1978): 77–83.

14. Uma Sekaran, "Methodological and Theoretical Issues and Advancements in Cross-Cultural Research," *Journal of International Business Studies* 14 (Fall 1983): 61–72.

15. Kazuaki Katori, "Recent Developments and Future Trends in Marketing Research in Japan Using New Electronic Media," *Journal of Advertising Research* 30 (April/May 1990): 53–57.

16. Charles F. Keown, "Foreign Mail Surveys: Response Rates Using Monetary Incentives," *Journal of International Business Studies* 16 (Fall 1985), 151–53.

17. David Jobber, Hafiz Mirza, and Kee H. Wee, "Incentives and Response Rates to Cross-National Business Surveys: A Logit Model Analysis," *Journal of International Business studies* 22 (no. 4, 1991): 711–21.

18. "Japan's Building Motor City II in S. California," *San Jose Mercury News,* 11 May 1990.

19. Naresh K. Malhotra, "Administration of Questionnaires for Collecting Quantitative Data in International Marketing Research," *Journal of Global Marketing* 4 (no. 2, 1991): 63–92.

20. "Learning about Competition—Creatively," *Marketing News,* 13 September 1985, 40, 47.

21. Demby, "ESOMAR."

22. Kazuo Kobayashi and Peter Draper, "Reviews of Market Research in Japan," *Journal of Advertising Research* 30 (April/May 1990): 13–18.

23. "About Marketing Overseas: Hazards and Opportunities," *Direct Marketing* (October 1985): 128.

24. "Hungary…How Capitalistic!" *Chicago Tribune,* 23 February 1986.

25. "A Phone Deal with China Could Cause Lots of Static," *Business Week,* 25 June 1990, 42.

26. Jonathan Kozol, *Illiterate America* (Garden City, NY: Anchor/Doubleday, 1985).

27. Susan P. Douglas and C. Samuel Craig, *International Marketing Research* (Englewood Cliffs, NJ: Prentice Hall, 1983), 91.

28. Attila Yaprak and Ravi Parameswaran, "Reliability Measurement in Cross-National Survey Research: An Empirical Evaluation," in *International Marketing Management,* ed. Erdener Kaynak (New York: Praeger, 1984), 172–93.

29. Harry L. Davis, Susan P. Douglas, and Alvin J. Silk, "Measure Unreliability: A Hidden Threat to Cross-National Marketing Research?" *Journal of Marketing* 45 (Spring 1981): 98–109.

30. Ravi Parameswaran and Attila Yaprak, "A Cross-National Comparison of Consumer Research Measures," *Journal of International Business Studies* 18 (Spring 1987): 35–49.

31. Carlos E. Garcia, "Hispanic Market Is Accessible, If Research Is Designed Correctly," *Marketing News,* 4 January 1988, 46.

32. Nancy J. Adler, Nigel Campbell, and Andre Laurent, "In Search of Appropriate Methodology: From Outside the People's Republic of China Looking In," *Journal of International Business Studies* 20 (Spring 1989): 61–74.

33. James Sood, "Equivalent Measurement in International Market Research: Is It Really a Problem?" *Journal of International Consumer Marketing* 2 (no. 2, 1989): 25–41.

34. Sekaran, "Cross-Cultural Research."

35. Mayer, "Multinational Marketing Research."

36. Bernie Whalen, "Reynolds' Research Plans Go Up in Smoke in Beirut," *Marketing News,* 17 September 1982, 9.

37. "Bank of America Rushes into the Information Age," *Business Week,* 15 April 1985, 90.

38. Robert E. Sweeney and Dan Alan Boswell, "Obey '10 Commandments' When Designing Marketing Information System," *Marketing News,* 16 April 1982, 16.

39. "Nielsen Issues 'Commonized' European Data," *PROMO,* March 1991, 61.

40. "U.S. Mailers Could Be Hamstrung by Proposed European Data Rules," *DM News,* 20 August 1991, 1, 7.

41. Ronald E. Yates, "Japan Rails at Criticism in Defending Trade Stance," *Chicago Tribune,* 18 June 1985.

A merchant, it has been said very properly, is not necessarily the citizen of any particular country. It is in great measure indifferent to him from what places he carries on his trade; and a very stifling disgust will make him move his capital, and together with it the industry which it supports, from one country to another.

Adam Smith

Market Analysis and Foreign Market Entry Strategies

9

CHAPTER OUTLINE

MARKETING ILLUSTRATION
There's More than One Way to Skin a Cat

IBM, once known for rigidly following a policy of doing business through its wholly owned subsidiaries, has done an about-face. To cope with the fast-moving computer market, IBM's game plan now consists of a portfolio of strategies. It has eighteen plants outside the United States. In Europe, it uses joint ventures, cooperative projects with governments and competitors, and long-term supply relationships. As an example of IBM's global strategy, it has formed an alliance with STET, Italy's state-owned maker of telecommunications and factory equipment.

In Japan, IBM has also transformed itself from being an autonomous operator to being a partner in order to regain the leadership position it lost to Fujitsu. The U.S. company has teamed up with a number of powerful Japanese companies. IBM's personal computer and low-cost, high-volume products, tailored by IBM for Japan, are manufactured by Matsushita, a company known for high quality, mass production, and marketing skills. Mitsubishi is a potential partner for the software and hardware product lines in the telecommunications market. IBM has formed a joint venture with Orient Leasing (the largest leasing company) and Morgan Guaranty International Finance to buy and sell IBM computers in order to compete with the government-backed Japan Electronic Computer. Another joint venture has been formed with Kanematsu-Gosho, a leading electronics distributor, and the venture has signed up thirty dealers to sell small computer systems. In addition, IBM, Kanematsu-Gosho, and Computerland have created another joint venture to market IBM's 5150 personal computer.

Source: "IBM Abandons Its Go-It-Alone Stance," *Business Week,* 14 March 1983, 41

IBM has demonstrated that no matter how mighty a company may be, it is not a practical strategy to enter all markets with a one-track mind and a single entry method. Even a large multinational corporation, with all its power, has to adapt its operating methods and formulate multiple entry strategies. The dynamic nature of many overseas markets makes it impossible for a single method to work effectively in all markets.

This chapter begins with a discussion of an economic analysis of foreign markets in order to compare and determine market opportunities. Most of the chapter is devoted to a coverage of the various market entry strategies. Some of these techniques—such as exporting, licensing, and management contracts—require no investment overseas. Other techniques, however, require varying degrees of foreign direct investment. These foreign direct investment methods range from joint venture to complete overseas manufacturing facilities, with such strategies as assembly operations, turnkey operations, and acquisition falling somewhere in between. These strategies do not operate in sequence, and any one of them can be appropriate at any time. And the use of one strategy in one market does not rule out the use of the other strategies elsewhere. The methods vary in terms of risk accepted and, to a certain extent, the degree of commitment to the foreign market.

Another purpose of the chapter is to discuss the advantages and disadvantages associated with each method of market penetration. Factors that have an impact on the appropriateness of entry methods are covered in order to provide guidelines for the selection of market entry strategies. The chapter ends with an examination of free trade zones, which can be used to complement most entry strategies.

MARKET ANALYSIS

Marketing opportunities exist in all countries regardless of the level of economic development. To assume that only developed countries offer more market potential is a misconception similar in nature to the so-called *majority fallacy*. A particular market may initially seem attractive because of its potential demand and size in terms of the number of consumers or their purchasing power. Yet the market may be attracting more than its share of competition. Since the market is thus crowded by many competitors, it may not be especially attractive after all. As a result, LDCs may provide a better return on investment because competitive expenditures can be significantly less when sophisticated and expensive marketing techniques are not necessary.

A marketer usually discerns far more market opportunities than a firm's limited resources permit to be pursued. Therefore, a marketer must develop a priority system so that available resources will not be spread too thin for the needed impact. Countries or markets must be screened based on certain relevant criteria for comparing opportunities. Such criteria may include market potential, economic growth, political risk, available natural resources, available labor, and trade barriers. Latin America, as a region, has rich natural resources and a dense population. Yet it has strong trade barriers as well as a lack of hard currencies, making the region generally unattractive as a market opportunity.

In assessing marketing opportunities, there is no single ideal criterion. A marketer must therefore employ a set of criteria that is relevant to the market opportunity under consideration. Economic variables that should be considered include GNP, population, GNP/capita, income, and personal consumption. Most countries are unlikely to meet all such requirements effectively. Canada, for example, performs poorly on the criterion of population density, since its density is less than one-tenth the density in the United States and is the lowest of any industrialized country. The strength of the Canadian market, however, lies in its per capita income ($13,670), which is the ninth highest in the world. The top eight countries in terms of per capita income are United Arab Emirates ($19,120), Brunei ($17,580), Liechtenstein ($16,900), the United States ($16,400), Switzerland ($16,380), Qatar ($15,980), Kuwait ($14,270), and Norway ($13,890).[1] Based on this criterion, there are several small but attractive countries.

Gross national product (GNP) is a measure of the value of all the goods and services produced by a nation. As such, GNP in effect measures the size of the economy. GNPs range from a mere $30 million for the Maldives to $2 trillion for the United States. This criterion favors the United States as the most important market on Earth. Although a higher GNP is generally regarded as an indicator of a better market, GNP alone does not accurately reflect market potential. India's GNP of $126 billion is almost twice as large as Austria's $65 billion; yet the larger number does not necessarily mean that India is a better market. A better indicator can likely be derived by considering GNP together with population. By dividing a country's GNP by its population, the result achieved is the **GNP/capita,** which measures *market intensity.* This figure can help a company establish country priorities since it is a measure of the richness of a market (i.e., degree of concentrated purchasing power). A country with a higher GNP/capita generally has a more advanced economy than a country with a lower figure. In the case of Austria and India, Austria has an $8,600 GNP/capita and thus is much more attractive in terms of wealth than India, whose GNP/capita is only $190.

Another general indicator of market size is a country's **population.** On this score, China is the foremost market because its population exceeds 1 billion. Because of China's strict birth control program, there is a chance that in the future India may take this distinction away from China. According to the private, nonprofit Population Reference Bureau, by the year 2025, 83 percent of the world's population will live in Africa, Asia, and Latin America.

Population size is a good indicator of market opportunity for low unit-value products or necessities. Much like GNP, a larger population generally indicates a more attractive market. Still, population by itself, not unlike GNP, can be misleading, especially when high-priced products or luxuries are involved. Switzerland's 6.3 million population does not seem impressive at first when compared to the 104 million population of Bangladesh. But GNP/capita reveals a totally different picture. Switzerland, as a market, becomes far more attractive because its GNP/capita of $14,240 is more than 100 times greater than Bangladesh's $100. Therefore, a large population does not necessarily indicate a better market opportunity.

Since markets are dynamic, one must observe market growth and population trends. About three-quarters of the world's 4.9 billion people live in developing countries, underscoring the importance of such markets. The world's population is projected to grow to 6.2 billion by the year 2000. Of course, not all regions or countries will grow at the same rate.[2] Mexico's population is expected to increase 42 percent by the end of the century, and Mexico City, already the world's largest city, will surpass Tokyo-Yokohama as the largest urban area. Other than in Africa, population growth rates have declined since 1970 in all regions. In contrast, sub-Saharan Africa, with a 3 percent annual growth, has a growth rate twice as high as that of the rest of the world. Nigeria may soon replace Japan as the seventh most populous country. On the one hand, Nigeria's population growth presents business opportunities. On the other hand, if there is no corresponding increase in resources and income, potential market rewards may be overshadowed by social problems.

It is inadequate to assess markets by relying only on each country's total population without considering its land area. From the marketing standpoint, the level of **population density** should be examined. Whereas total population indicates the overall size of a market, population density determines the ease in reaching that market. As the population in a certain area becomes dense or more concentrated, the efficiency of distribution and promotion increases as well. In this regard, the Java area of Indonesia is an ideal market. In addition to Indonesia's large total population, two-thirds of the more than 160 million Indonesians live on Java, an island that constitutes only 7 percent of the country's land area.[3] Java's population density is 740 persons per square kilometer—a big difference from the country's average density of 83 persons. In another case, Canada has a vast land area and a relatively small population, suggesting that the country would not be an attractive market. A closer examination, however, reveals that Canada's population density is actually a positive attribute since its three largest cities—Toronto, Montreal, and Vancouver—contain 29 percent of the population, which controls 33 percent of the country's buying power.[4] As a point of reference, the largest cities in the United States (New York, Los Angeles, and Chicago) have only 11 percent of the country's population and 12 percent of its buying power.

One trend identified in a United Nations study is that more and more people are becoming city dwellers (see Exhibit 9–1). By 2010, half of the world's population, up from the 42 percent of the 1980s, will live in urban areas. This trend should increase the level of population density. By the end of the century, all but three of the world's twenty largest cities will be in LDCs. The impact of this trend is that cities will experience increasing difficulties in providing decent health and housing for the poor. A positive effect is that the trend may spur social and economic development.

Another indicator of a country's wealth is the **personal income** of its citizens. Income can reflect the degree of attractiveness of a market because consumption generally rises as income increases. Income, however, should not be strictly considered in absolute terms. Consumers in LDCs may have low incomes but may still have ample buying power, because costs of living in such countries may be relatively low because of low food and heating costs. As a result, consumers in these countries can still have adequate disposable or discretionary income. Tables 9–1, 9–2, and 9–3 compare selected countries in terms of price level, wage and salary levels, and purchasing power, respectively.

How the income is spent will provide another clue to market potential. If a large portion of a person's income must go toward purchases of essentials, market opportunity for luxuries may be limited. Food costs, for example, are so high in Japan that the Japanese are forced to spend 25 percent of their disposable income on food. Their American counterparts, in contrast, are much more fortunate, spending only 15 percent of their income and leaving them with more discretionary income to be spent on nonessentials.

Income should never be considered by itself as a determinant of market attractiveness. China, for example, is the ninth largest economy in the world. Yet its per capita income is only $350, a figure that does not differ much from that of either Haiti or Guinea. Again, population size should be taken into account with income in order to get a better measure of the market.

One problem with **per capita income** is the assumption that everyone gets an equal share of the nation's income (see Exhibit 9–2). To overcome this weakness, a marketer should examine the distribution of income. When income is evenly distributed across the various population segments, a firm's product is likely to be suitable for all individuals. In contrast, the product may be unsuitable for certain segments if income varies significantly from one group of consumers to another. In the industrial nations and communist countries, income is somewhat evenly distributed. In many other countries, especially those less developed, **dualism** or a **dual economy** exists. In general, a declining share of national income by the

WORLD ECONOMY IN TRANSITION
The Urban Explosion

Total and urban population growth - world and selected regions, 1970–2000 *(In millions)*

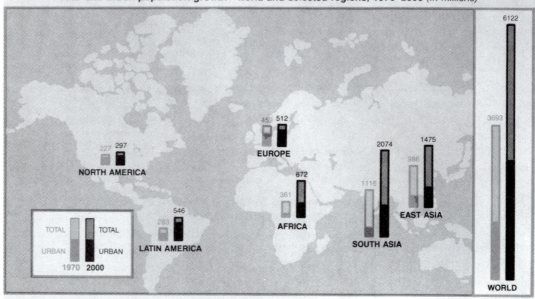

25 Mega Cities, 1970–2000[1] *(In millions)*

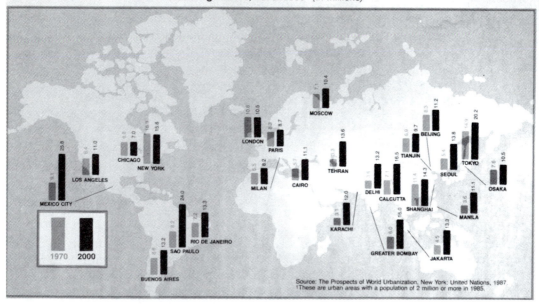

Source: The Prospects of World Urbanization, New York: United Nations, 1987.
[1]These are urban areas with a population of 2 million or more in 1985.

EXHIBIT 9–1   The urban explosion

Source: Finance & Development (December 1989): 47

416

TABLE 9-1 Price level in 52 major cities throughout the world

City	Price Level excl. Rent[a] Zurich = 100	Price Level incl. Rent[a] Zurich = 100	City	Price Level excl. Rent[a] Zurich = 100	Price Level incl. Rent[a] Zurich = 100
Tokyo	158.6	194.4	Montreal	67.9	69.3
Oslo	115.1	113.3	Luxembourg	66.9	69.1
Helsinki	110.5	106.2	Sydney	66.9	66.7
Stockholm	104.1	97.2	Singapore	66.5	82.7
Copenhagen	102.1	95.5	Panama City	61.2	69.7
Geneva	101.1	102.3	Los Angeles	60.5	67.9
Zurich	100.0	100.0	Athens	60.2	62.0
Dublin	80.5	78.3	Hong Kong	57.4	75.1
London	80.2	88.2	Lisbon	55.6	57.4
New York	79.9	93.1	Caracas	53.9	57.4
Vienna	79.4	76.6	Nairobi	53.7	52.9
Chicago	79.1	88.8	Lagos	52.9	50.1
Madrid	77.3	80.6	Istanbul	51.8	53.4
Düsseldorf	76.5	78.6	Nicosia	51.2	49.2
Paris	76.2	81.0	Bangkok	49.1	55.1
Frankfurt	76.1	75.6	Cairo	49.0	46.1
Abu Dhabi	75.2	83.6	Manila	48.5	50.4
Milan	74.5	75.3	Jakarta	47.8	48.3
Jeddah	73.7	78.8	Kuala Lumpur	47.5	46.3
Brussels	73.0	75.8	Johannesburg	47.4	45.0
Manama (Bahrain)	71.6	73.9	Bogotá	47.3	47.5
Toronto	69.7	82.4	Buenos Aires	47.0	45.9
Tel Aviv	69.5	66.6	São Paulo	45.5	49.3
Houston	68.6	66.9	Mexico City	44.0	42.7
Amsterdam	68.4	68.4	Rio de Janeiro	43.5	46.2
Seoul	68.2	77.2	Bombay	43.0	47.6

[a] Costs of a basket of more than 111 goods and services, including three rent categories, weighted by consumer habits. Order is according to index value.

Source: Prices and Earnings Around the Globe, 1988 ed. (Union Bank of Switzerland, Economic Research Department, 1988), 4

poorest 20 percent of the population is accompanied by a rise in dualism. According to the U.S. Bureau of the Census, the top 12 percent of the U.S. population accounts for 38 percent of the national wealth, and the poorest 26 percent accounts for only 10 percent of the income. In Brazil, dual economies are much more pronounced because the top 20 percent of the population has accumulated 61.5 percent of the nation's income, leaving only 3.5 percent of the income for the poorest 20 percent. For the Philippines, Peru, Mexico, and Turkey, the poorest 20 percent of these countries, according to the World Bank, hold less than 5 percent of the nation's income. In such cases, most consumers are simply not in a position to buy high-priced luxury products.

Exporters should pay attention to the **income elasticities of imports and exports** of target countries, because these coefficients indicate how imports and exports are influenced by consumers' income changes in each country. The income elasticity for U.S. exports is 0.99. The problem for the United States is that its income elasticity of import demand is 1.7, meaning that each 1 percent increase in American

TABLE 9–2   Wage and salary level in 52 major cities throughout the world

City	Salary (Wage)[a] Level: Gross Zurich = 100	Salary (Wage)[a] Level: Net Zurich = 100	City	Salary (Wage)[a] Level: Gross Zurich = 100	Salary (Wage)[a] Level: Net Zurich = 100
Zurich	100.0	100.0	Madrid	28.7	30.5
Geneva	92.6	89.4	Tel Aviv	26.1	24.0
Copenhagen	84.4	61.5	Johannesburg	24.2	24.1
Oslo	74.5	44.6	Jeddah	23.8	29.7
Los Angeles	73.1	71.1	Nicosia	23.8	25.2
Frankfurt	72.7	58.9	Hong Kong	19.5	23.4
New York	67.9	59.2	Seoul	18.8	21.2
Brussels	67.3	56.4	Panama City	17.7	19.4
Tokyo	67.2	70.1	Abu Dhabi	17.4	21.7
Chicago	65.0	59.2	Singapore	15.5	14.2
Düsseldorf	64.9	54.0	Caracas	14.8	18.0
Montreal	64.7	58.1	Istanbul	14.1	12.0
Stockholm	64.5	53.4	Lisbon	13.3	13.8
Toronto	61.8	55.9	Bogotá	9.7	11.3
Houston	60.6	60.4	Buenos Aires	9.7	10.1
Amsterdam	60.2	48.0	Kuala Lumpur	8.4	9.9
Luxembourg	59.7	58.4	São Paulo	8.0	7.9
London	57.9	52.4	Bangkok	7.1	8.6
Helsinki	57.8	51.0	Rio de Janeiro	7.1	7.8
Vienna	57.7	51.4	Nairobi	6.4	6.7
Milan	51.8	47.7	Jakarta	4.6	5.7
Sydney	46.7	44.3	Mexico City	4.4	5.3
Paris	43.9	43.3	Bombay	4.1	5.0
Dublin	42.2	37.0	Manila	3.7	4.3
Athens	—	—	Lagos	3.0	3.5
Manama (Bahrain)	30.5	35.4	Cairo	2.9	3.3

[a]Actual hourly earnings in twelve different occupations, weighted according to occupational distribution; net after deducting taxes and social insurance contributions

Source: Prices and Earnings Around the Globe, 1988 ed. (Union Bank of Switzerland, Economic Research Department, 1988), 5

consumers' income will result in a 1.7 percent growth in U.S. imports.[5] For each unit increase in income in the United States, U.S. imports will grow much faster than U.S. exports, leading to a deterioration of the country's balance of trade. Furthermore, a calculation by the Bank of Japan revealed that a decline of 1 percent in the value of the U.S. dollar will result in only a drop of 0.4 percent in real U.S. imports.

The income elasticity of U.S. import demand can be computed to see how U.S. imports from each of its trading partners will change in relation to income growth in the United States. Japan has the highest elasticity, followed by Australia, Germany, Great Britain, Denmark, and Sweden.[6] Not only are the income elasticities for imports from these countries relatively high, but the income elasticities for U.S. exports to these countries are also relatively low. Therefore, even if incomes in the United States and these countries rise in the same proportion, U.S. imports will still grow at a faster rate than U.S. exports. This is good news for those exporting to the United States, but not something that should excite U.S. exporters.

Income often dictates the extent of consumption because income and consumption are positively related. Although the effect of income is moderated by cultural

TABLE 9–3 Domestic purchasing power in 52 cities

City	Domestic Purchasing Power[a]		City	Domestic Purchasing Power[a]	
	gross Zurich = 100	net Zurich = 100		gross Zurich = 100	net Zurich = 100
Los Angeles	120.8	117.6	Manama (Bahrain)	42.6	49.3
Zurich	100.0	100.0	Tokyo	42.4	44.2
Frankfurt	95.5	77.3	Tel Aviv	37.5	34.5
Montreal	95.3	85.6	Madrid	37.2	39.4
Brussels	92.2	77.3	Hong Kong	34.0	40.7
Geneva	91.6	88.4	Jeddah	32.3	40.3
Luxembourg	89.2	87.3	Panama City	28.9	31.7
Toronto	88.6	80.3	Seoul	27.5	31.1
Houston	88.3	88.1	Caracas	27.4	33.3
Amsterdam	88.1	70.2	Istanbul	27.1	23.1
New York	85.0	74.1	Lisbon	24.0	24.8
Düsseldorf	84.9	70.6	Singapore	23.3	21.4
Copenhagen	82.7	60.2	Abu Dhabi	23.1	28.9
Chicago	82.2	74.8	Buenos Aires	20.6	21.6
Vienna	72.6	64.7	Bogotá	20.5	23.9
London	72.2	65.4	Kuala Lumpur	17.7	20.8
Sydney	69.8	66.2	São Paulo	17.6	17.4
Milan	69.5	63.9	Rio de Janeiro	16.2	18.0
Oslo	64.7	38.8	Bangkok	14.5	7.6
Athens	—	—	Nairobi	11.9	12.6
Stockholm	62.0	51.3	Mexico City	10.1	12.0
Paris	57.6	56.8	Jakarta	9.6	12.0
Dublin	52.4	46.0	Bombay	9.6	11.6
Helsinki	52.4	46.2	Manila	7.6	8.8
Johannesburg	51.1	51.0	Cairo	6.0	6.6
Nicosia	46.5	49.3	Lagos	5.7	6.6

[a]Gross and net hourly earnings divided by the costs of the total basket, excluding rent

Source: Prices and Earnings Around the Globe, 1988 ed. (Union Bank of Switzerland, Economic Research Department, 1988), 7

preferences, it still indicates the degree of consumption for many products. Thus, a marketer should also observe per capita consumption for each product under consideration since it can vary greatly from market to market (see Table 9–4). In the United States, there are 572 cars, 650 telephones, and 621 TV sets for each 1,000 persons. In Brazil, all figures are much lower: there are 76 cars, 90 telephones, and 184 TV sets for each 1,000 persons.

In planning export activities, it is also useful to estimate geographical/customer concentration. The geographical concentration index is obtained by dividing the value of the country's merchandise exports to its main customers by the value of its total merchandise exports. The higher the index, the greater is the concentration of exports to the main export markets. Any adverse changes in those markets can thus seriously impair the country's exports. These concentration indexes generally work well in assessing the creditworthiness of LDCs but may not be so useful in the case of industrialized countries, which have well-diversified economies and export markets.

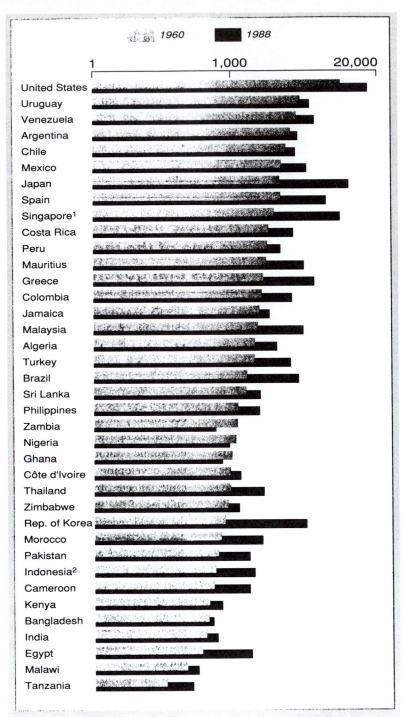

Note: A logarithmic scale is used to facilitate comparison of countries with high and low per capita income. Countries were selected, based on data availability, to provide a balanced sample in terms of population size and regional distribution.
[1] Data are for 1960 and 1985.
[2] Data are for 1962 and 1988.

Data: *World Development Report*, 1991

EXHIBIT 9–2   Per capita income (1985 dollars), 1960 and 1988

Source: IMF Survey, 29 July 1991, 231

TABLE 9–4 Countries leading the good life

	Automobiles per 1,000	Telephones per 1,000	TVs per 1,000	Daily Calories per Capita	Population per Physician	Infant Mortality (per 1,000 live births)
Bulgaria	120	200	96	3,642	280	15
Czechoslovakia	173	226	122	3,448	280	13
German Democratic Rep.	209	211	119	3,814	440	9
Hungary	145	134	275	3,569	490	18
Poland	105	118	85	3,336	490	18
Romania	11	130	—	3,373	570	25
Yugoslavia	125	122	175	3,563	550	25
U.S.S.R	42	115	300	3,399	480	25
Germany, Fed. Rep. of	446	641	377	3,528	380	8
Japan	235	535	250	2,864	660	6
United States	572	650	621	3,645	470	10
Argentina	127	100	213	3,210	370	32
Brazil	76	90	184	2,656	1,080	63
Mexico	65	90	108	3,132	1,240	47
Korea, Rep. of	16	294	—	2,907	1,170	25
Malaysia	84	—	—	2,730	1,930	24
Taiwan, Province of China	54	277	104	3,050	850	—
Greece	127	373	158	3,688	350	13
Ireland	206	235	181	3,632	680	7
Spain	252	381	256	3,359	320	10

Data: **Institute of International Finance**, *Building Free-Market Economies in Central and Eastern Europe: Challenges and Realities*

Source: *IMF Survey*, 7 May 1990, 135

Another useful indicator of a country's ability to endure the balance-of-payments problem is its **compressibility of imports.**[7] A compressibility index is the value of a country's nonessential imports divided by the value of its total imports of goods and services, and this index measures the amount of nonessential imports. A high index indicates that too much foreign exchange is being spent on nonessential imports. The country should then be able to compress its import bill in order to reduce the outflow of foreign exchange, since unnecessary imports can be curtailed so that foreign exchange can be diverted to other items more important to the survival of the economy. Brazil's declining compressibility index is a reflection of its effort to conserve foreign exchange. The significant increase of Mexico's index, in contrast, has been viewed with alarm since that increase in turn increases investment risk, especially when consumption is high but savings are low. Mexico's revenues are likely to be inadequate to service debts and pay for imports. It is therefore inevitable that foreign exchange controls must be imposed and imports of nonessential goods restricted. This can pose a serious problem to manufacturers of luxury goods wanting to sell to Mexico.

EXPORTING

Most international marketing textbooks essentially define **exporting** as a strategy in which a company, without any marketing or production organization overseas, exports a product from its home base. The exported product is fundamentally the same as the one marketed in the home market. As such, product modification for foreign markets is virtually nonexistent. The leading U.S. exporters (with export sales and exports as percent of sales in parentheses) are General Motors ($8.3 billion, 8.14 percent) (see Exhibit 9–3), Boeing ($7.3 billion, 44.86 percent), Ford ($7.2 billion, 11.55 percent), General Electric ($4.3 billion, 12.35 percent), and IBM ($3.0 billion, 5.97 percent).[8]

EXHIBIT 9–3   Exporting strategy

Source: Reproduced with permission of General Motors Corporation

The main advantage of an exporting strategy is the ease in implementing the strategy. Risks are minimal because the company simply exports its excess production capacity when it receives orders from abroad. As a result, its international marketing effort is casual at best. This is very likely the most common overseas entry approach for small firms. Many companies employ this entry strategy when they first become involved with international business and may continue to use it on a more or less permanent basis.

The problem with using an exporting strategy is that it is not always an optimal strategy. A desire to keep international activities simple, together with a lack of product modification, make a company's marketing strategy inflexible and unresponsive. As shown by a study by Cooper and Kleinschmidt, "the manufacturer who is content merely to sell his domestic product abroad, essentially unaltered, and pays little heed to the nature and selection of segments within his foreign markets, is likely to achieve a below average export performance, particularly in terms of export growth."[9] For a better strategy, it is essential that the product be variable and not fixed.

The exporting strategy functions poorly when the company's home-country currency is strong. In the 1970s, the Swiss franc was so strong that Swiss companies found it exceedingly difficult to export and sell products in the U.S. market. Swiss companies discovered that they had to resort to investing abroad in order to reduce the effects of the strong franc. During the first term of the Reagan administration, the U.S. dollar had also gained an extremely strong position. U.S. firms not only found it extremely difficult to export U.S. products but they also had to contend with a flood of inexpensive imports that became even more inexpensive as the dollar became stronger. A currency can remain strong over a stretch of several years, creating prolonged difficulties for the country's exports.

LICENSING

When a company finds exporting ineffective but is hesitant to have direct investment abroad, licensing can be a reasonable compromise. **Licensing** is an agreement that permits a foreign company to use industrial property (i.e., patents, trademarks, and copyrights), technical know-how and skills (e.g., feasibility studies, manuals, technical advice, etc.), architectural and engineering designs, or any combination of these in a foreign market. Essentially, a licensor allows a foreign company to manufacture a product for sale in the licensee's country and sometimes in other specified markets.

Examples of licensing abound. Some 50 percent of the drugs sold in Japan are made under license from European and U.S. companies. *Playboy* used to take licensed materials from France's *Lui* for its *Oui* magazine, which was distributed in the U.S. market. *Playboy*'s more common role, however, is that of a licensor, resulting in nine *Playboy* foreign editions. *Penthouse* magazine, likewise, has Japanese and Brazilian versions under license in addition to those in Spain, Australia, and Italy. German-speaking countries account for *Penthouse*'s largest overseas edition. One of the most well-known overseas licensed products is Pac-Man, which provides its licensor with many millions of dollars in royalties received from some 300 products bearing this trademark.

Between 1971 and the 1980s, U.S. receipts of royalties and related management and service fees from the licensing of patents and technologies grew by approximately 130 percent, from $2.4 billion to $5.5 billion.[10] This amount is almost ten times the amount U.S. firms pay as license fees to foreign companies. One of the leading U.S. licensors is McDonald's, whose stores abroad accounted for almost half of the company's all new openings as well as one-fifth of the company's sales.

Licensing is not only restricted to tangible products. A service can be licensed as well. Chicago Mercantile Exchange's attempt to internationalize the futures market led it to obtain licensing rights to the Nikkei stock index. The firm then sublicensed the Nikkei index to the SIMEX for trade in Singapore in 1986 and anticipated licensing the index for the Chicago Mercantile Exchange floor at some point in the future.

In spite of a general belief that foreign direct investment is generally more profitable and thus the preferred scheme, licensing offers several advantages. It allows a company to spread out its research-and-development and investment costs, while enabling it to receive incremental income with only negligible expenses. In addition, granting a license protects the company's patent and/or trademark against cancellation for non-use. This protection is especially critical for a firm that, after investing in production and marketing facilities in a foreign country, decides to leave the market either temporarily or permanently. The situation is especially common in Central and South America, where high inflation and devaluation drastically push up operating costs.

There are other reasons why licensing should be used. Trade barriers may be one such reason. A manufacturer should consider licensing when capital is scarce, when import restrictions discourage direct entry, and when a country is sensitive to foreign ownership. The method is very flexible because it allows a quick and easy way to enter the market. Licensing also works well when transportation cost is high, especially relative to product value. Although Japan has banned all direct investment and has restricted commercial loans in South Africa, Japan's success there is due to licensing agreements with local distributors. In 1987 Toyota sold 87,000 cars to South Africa by allowing locally owned companies to import and assemble parts from Japan. More than thirty Japanese corporations have similar ties to South African firms.[11]

A company can avoid substantial risks and other difficulties with licensing. Most French designers, for example, use licensing to avoid having to invest in a business. In another example, Disney gets all of its royalties virtually risk-free from the $500 million Tokyo Disneyland theme park owned by Keisei Electric Railway and Mitsui. The licensing and royalty fees as arranged are very attractive: Disney receives 10 percent of the gate revenue and 5 percent of sales of all food and merchandise. Moreover, Disney, with its policy of using low-paid young adults as park employees, does not have to deal with the Japanese policy of lifetime employment.

Nevertheless, licensing has its negative aspects. With reduced risk generally comes reduced profit. In fact, licensing may be the least profitable of all entry strategies.

It is necessary to consider the long-term perspective. By granting a license to a foreign firm, a manufacturer may be nurturing a competitor in the future—someone who is gaining technological and production knowledge. At some point, the licensee may refuse to renew the licensing contract. To complicate the matter, it is anything but easy to prevent the licensee from using the process learned and acquired while working under license. Texas Instruments had to sue several Japanese manufacturers to force them to continue paying royalties on its patents on memory chips.

Another problem often develops when the licensee performs poorly. To attempt to terminate the contract may be easier said than done. Once licensing is in place, the agreements can also prevent the licensor from entering that market directly. Japanese laws give a licensee virtual control over the licensed product, and such laws present a monumental obstacle for an investor wishing to regain the rights to manufacture and sell the investor's own product.

Inconsistent product quality across countries caused by licensees' lax quality control can injure the reputation of a product on a worldwide basis. This possibility explains why McDonald's goes to extremes in supervising operations, thus ensuring product quality and consistency. McDonald's was successful in court in stopping a franchisee from operating the franchises in France because the franchisee's quality was substandard. Anheuser-Busch, likewise, requires all licensees to meet the company's standards. The licensees must agree to import such ingredients as yeast from the United States.

Even when exact product formulations are followed, licensing can still sometimes damage a product's image—that is, psychologically. Many imported products enjoy a certain degree of prestige or mystique that can rapidly disappear when the product is made locally under license. The Miller brewery became aware of this perception problem when it started brewing Lowenbrau, a German brand, in Texas.

In some cases, a manufacturer has no choice at all about licensing. Many LDCs force patent holders to license their products to other manufacturers or distributors for a royalty fee that may or may not be fair. Canada, owing to consumer activism, is the only industrialized nation requiring compulsory licensing for drugs. Drug firms must license their products for a 4 percent royalty. Such countries as Belgium and Lebanon have no provision for compulsory licensing. But compulsory licensing is possible after a patent has been issued for three years in Canada and the Netherlands and at any time in Germany. In Nigeria, compulsory licensing may be enforced four years after a patent application is filed or three years after the patent is granted if the patent is inadequately "worked" (utilized).

Licensing, in spite of certain limitations, is a sound strategy that can be quite effective under certain circumstances. Farok J. Contractor questions the generalization that MNCs prefer "internalization" through direct investment to licensing, and he has identified specific conditions that make licensing a superior strategy.[12] Furthermore, Contractor adduces some empirical evidence that shows the level of licensing activity to correlate positively with company size and patent incidence.[13] Larger and more international companies, as well as those with more patents, are likely to do more licensing.

Licensing terms must be carefully negotiated and explicitly treated.[14] For example, Chinese understanding of the licensing arrangement can differ significantly from the usual practice in the United States. Since the Chinese insist on "complete" documentation of the licensed technology, a U.S. licensor must define what it means. Otherwise, the U.S. firm may be surprised to learn that it must spend a great deal of time preparing unnecessary documents or, even worse, that it is required to provide nonexistent materials.[15]

In general, a license contract should include these basic elements: product coverage, rights licensed under the contract, territorial coverage, tenure or term of contract, extension and renewal clauses, protection of rights subject to license, future rights and options, merchandising and management assistance, quality control, grantback and cross licensing, royalty rate and structure, service charges, royalty-free licenses, terms and conditions of payment, reporting and auditing requirements, equity participations, currency control, choice of law, know-how and trade secret protection, plant visits, commercial arbitration, taxes, termination provisions, and terminal rights and obligations.[16]

The license contract should include a provision for mandatory deposits in local currency in the licensor's name in order to minimize any problem associated with restrictions on fee remittances or foreign exchange control. Moreover, since license fees are based on sales price, it is necessary to agree on the price to be used. One royalty base commonly used is net sales price, which is invoice price less trade discounts, returns, duties and taxes, packing charges, and transportation and insurance costs. Depending on product and technology, royalty rates for licensing agreements range from a fraction of 1 percent to 50 percent, with 5–6 percent being an average rate.[17]

Research evidence has shown that four factors are basic to the structure of an international transfer of technology:[18]

The locus of decision making and control

The level of personal interaction in the transfer process

The level of the supplier's initial involvement

The stability of the relationship between the technology supplier and recipient

Supplier control, always desired by the supplier, can usually be increased only at significant costs to the recipient. Personal interaction, critical for sophisticated technologies, is not as important for simple or routine technology. It is necessary to specify the degree of participation of each party in preliminary activities (e.g., feasibility studies and personnel training). Finally, the stability of the relationship is affected by the shift in power of the parties, usually with the recipient firm gaining strength as it becomes more knowledgeable of the technology in question. These four basic variables, essential to both the short-term and long-term success, should be explicitly addressed in the agreement.

A U.S. licensor must pay attention to antitrust considerations. Certain license terms that restrict free use of the subject of the license are so-called *per se* violations (i.e., considered unlawful in themselves without any need to prove anticompetitive effects). Examples of *per se* violations under the U.S. laws are the following: a tie-in arrangement, requiring a licensee to purchase unpatented items; package licensing, requiring the licensee to acquire other unwanted patent rights; resale price maintenance; and exclusive grantback (i.e., cross-licensing). Other kinds of trade restraints (e.g., territorial restrictions) are tested under the antitrust *rule of reason*. That is, certain practices are unlawful if (1) these acts occurred and (2) they had an unreasonable anticompetitive effect. The Antitrust Division of the U.S. Department of Justice usually views license arrangements that prevent independent companies from selling in the United States in competition with the licenses as being highly suspect under the antitrust laws. For antitrust reasons, many licensors, instead of asking for cross licenses, prefer to have a separate agreement covering any reciprocal license grants.

When licenses are to be granted to European firms, a firm must consider the antitrust rules of the EC, specifically Article 85 of the Rome Treaty. This article prohibits those licensing terms (with some exemptions) that are likely to adversely affect trade between EC countries. Such arrangements as price fixing, territorial restrictions, and tie-in agreements are void.

A prudent licensor does not "assign" a trademark to a licensee. Far better is to specify the conditions under which the mark can or cannot be used by the licensee. From the licensee's standpoint, the licensor's trademark is valuable in marketing the licensed product only if the product is popular. Otherwise, the licensee would be better served by creating a new trademark to protect the marketing position in the event that the basic license is not renewed.

Licensing should be considered a two-way street because a license also allows the original licensor to gain access to the licensee's technology and product. This is important because the licensee may be able to build on the information supplied by the licensor. Unlike American firms, European licensors are very interested in grantbacks and will even lower the royalty rate in return for product improvements and potentially profitable new products.[19]

American licensors, usually to their misfortune, tend to look down on foreign technical development and show no interest in grantbacks or cross-licensing. Actually, there are many examples of important technical feedback to the United States (e.g., the Norwegian Sloderberg System for aluminum production, the British Pilkington process for producing plate glass, the German Wankel rotary combustion engine, and the Czechoslovak contact-lens technology).

The significance of cross-licensing is illustrated by the experience of Texas Instruments (TI). TI accused Japanese semiconductor makers of infringing on its chips patents by selling DRAMs (dynamic, random-access memories) in the United States when the licenses granted by TI expired in 1986. TI attempted to seek bigger license fees rather than cross-licensing agreements, but those firms resisted. The Japanese companies, however, were not without hope, since they have developed their own proprietary technology. TI itself was licensed to use those firms' technology. The result was that each company came to hold patents to which the others were not licensed. As can be expected, Hitachi, NEC, and Toshiba countersued TI for infringing on their patents, probably hoping to settle for the customary cross-licensing status quo. Thus, an intelligent practice is always to stipulate in a contract that licenses for new patents or products covered by the return grant are to be made available at reasonable royalties.

Finally, the licensor should try not to undermine a product by overlicensing it. For example, Pierre Cardin diluted the value of his name by allowing some 800 products to use the name under license. Subsequently, he created Maxim's as the second brand for restaurants, hotels, and food items. Neither extreme of overlicensing nor underlicensing is desirable. Underlicensing results in potential profit being lost, whereas overlicensing leads to a weakened market through overexposure. Over-licensing can increase income in the short run, but it may in the long run mean killing the goose that laid the golden egg.

JOINT VENTURE

The **joint venture** is another alternative a firm may consider as a way of entering an overseas market. A joint venture is simply a partnership at corporate level, and it can be domestic or international. For the discussion here, an international joint venture is one in which the partners are from more than one country. Exhibits 9–4 and 9–5 describe such ventures.

It's such universally sound advice, it can be offered in any tongue and followed in any land: work with the best in the business. In Indonesia, where executives of the Timur Jauh company faced the task of creating the first health care insurance system in the world's fifth most populous nation, the strategy was "bekerja dengan mutu yang tinggi dalam bidang bisnis"—find the best in that business. They found Ætna. Across the South China Sea in Hong Kong, the Bank of East Asia sought a joint venture to market life insurance. Their partner? Ætna. Why Ætna? Same rationale, although in Chinese (that's it at the top of this ad) it has a character all its own. In Spain, where Ætna's partner is Banco Hispano Americano, the logic runs "trabaje siempre con lo mejor de la industria." In every language, the bottom line is the bottom line.

WORK WITH THE BEST IN THE BUSINESS

Ætna

Ætna Life Insurance Company
Ætna Life Insurance and Annuity Company
151 Farmington Avenue, Hartford, CT 06156

EXHIBIT 9–4   A joint venture

Source: Reprinted with permission of Aetna Life Insurance Company/The Aetna Casualty and Surety Company

Much like a partnership formed by two or more individuals, a joint venture is an enterprise formed for a specific business purpose by two or more investors sharing ownership and control. Sony, for instance, has formed joint ventures with PepsiCo to sell Wilson sporting goods, with Prudential to sell insurance, and with CBS to sell phonograph records in Japan.

Joint ventures, like licensing, involve certain risks as well as certain advantages over other forms of entry into a foreign market. In most cases, company resources,

How BMW set a track record in Southeast Asia

Sime Darby, Southeast Asia's largest multinational company, reports on this successful partnership and on what they can offer your company, too.

BMW has clearly established its leadership throughout Southeast Asia.

With Sime Darby, the ultimate driving machine has found a partner that is as concerned with quality as it is with profitable performance.

Sime Darby believes Malaysia offers an ideal manufacturing base in Asia Pacific.

Take a holiday from taxes

The Malaysian Government welcomes foreign investment and offers many incentives including a tax holiday for five to ten years.

More and more companies are setting up operations in the country. Why? Natural resources are ample and skilled labour is easily available. The infrastructure is well-developed with excellent communications and reliable, efficient transport.

Record-breaking performance

Sime Darby knows how to set the pace, too. The last financial year ended with a show of record-breaking results. A success made possible only by the Group's corporate philosophy of honest, hard work with strength through diversity.

For over 80 years, Sime Darby has set high standards of efficiency and integrity over a wide range of activities. From plantations to property development, insurance and trading to manufacturing.

Successful partnerships

BMW is only one of many profitable partnerships with European, U.S. and Asian companies. In Malaysia, successful partnerships include established names like Berger, Inax, Shell, Michelin, Ford, Hyundai and Caterpillar.

Other ventures in Singapore, Philippines, Hong Kong and Australia include motor distribution, trading, packaging, furniture, tyres, and electrical and mechanical systems for buildings.

Tap into growing markets

Intra-regional trade is expanding rapidly to satisfy the increasingly affluent markets of the region.

Sime Darby has the financial strength, management expertise and connections to help you tap into these buoyant markets.

To find out more, write to Sime Darby. This could be the beginning of a new, rewarding relationship for your company.

Sime Darby

SOUTHEAST ASIA'S LARGEST MULTINATIONAL COMPANY

For a fact-filled brochure about Sime Darby, Asia Pacific and Malaysia, write to: **Sime Darby London Ltd.**, Hibernia Chambers, London Bridge, London SE1 9QX, England. Telex: 884541 SDTLL G and 8811529 SDTLL G. **Head Office:** Sime Darby Berhad, Wisma Sime Darby, Jalan Raja Laut, 50350 Kuala Lumpur, Malaysia. Telefax: 03-298 7398.

EXHIBIT 9–5 Country's investment climate and joint ventures

Source: Courtesy of Sime Darby Berhad

circumstances, and the reasons for wanting to do business overseas will determine if a joint venture is the most reasonable way to enter the overseas market.

Marketers consider joint ventures to be dynamic because of the possibility of a parent firm's change in mission or power.[20] Furthermore, the characteristics of joint ventures in developed countries differ from those in developing countries.[21] Root has a checklist for joint venture entry, and this list requires potential partners to consider the following points: purpose of joint venture, partners' contribution, host government's role, ownership shares, capital structure, management, production, finance, marketing, and agreement.[22]

There are two separate overseas investment processes that describe how joint ventures tend to evolve. The first is the "natural," nonpolitical investment process. In this case, a technology-supplying firm gains a foothold in an unfamiliar market by acquiring a partner that can contribute local knowledge and marketing skills. Technology tends to provide dominance to the technology-supplying firm. As the technology part-

TABLE 9–5 The top twenty Soviet joint ventures (as of mid-1990)

Name and place of registration	Number and date of registration	Charter capital (millions of rubles)	Founder countries' equities (percent)	Specialization
1. International Moscow Bank	No. 1,000 20/10/89	100	USSR-40 Italy-12 FRG-12 Australia-12 France-12 Finland-12	Crediting of JVs, Soviet and foreign organizations, institutions and banks, operations with securities, consulting and other services
2. Vikintrans, Lipetsk	No. 1,209 14/12/89	83.3	USSR-85 Sweden-15	Construction and running of food production and marketing facilities
3. Rasskazovo-invest, Tambov	No. 1,160 04/12/89	71.7	USSR-95.6 Yugoslavia-4.4	Production and marketing of leather for shoe-making and other goods
4. Intermetanol, Novomoskovsk, Tula region	No. 1,239 22/12/89	67.5	USSR-83.62 Bulgaria-16.38	Methanol production and marketing
5. Soreal, Moscow	No. 608 26/06/89	51.6	USSR-51 France-49	Production and marketing of cosmetics, personal hygiene products and household chemicals
6. Lomos, Moscow	No. 669 28/06/89	50.5	USSR-41 Finland-59	Exports, imports, investments abroad
7. Krovtech, Moscow	No. 509 29/05/89	48.1	USSR-51 USA-49	Design and construction of a factory to produce roofing and water-proofing materials, adhesive and sealing compounds
8. Khomatek, Moscow	No. 6 16/07/87	47.7	USSR-68 FRG-32	Manufacture of lathes, machining systems, robot facilities, sensor and laser equipment
9. Ceosil, Tallinn	No. 293 09/03/89	42.6	USSR-51 Yugoslavia-49	Production of zeolites for detergents and their marketing in the USSR and abroad

Source: Copyright *Delovie Lyudi*

ner becomes more familiar with the market, it buys up more or all equity in the venture or leaves the venture entirely. A contributor of technology, however, is not likely to reduce its share in a joint venture while remaining active in it. The second investment process occurs when the local firm's political leverage, through government persuasion, halts or reverses the "natural" economic process. The foreign, technology-supplying partner remains engaged in the venture without strengthening its ownership position, the consequence being a gradual takeover by the local parties.[23]

There are several reasons why joint ventures enjoy certain advantages and should be used. One benefit is that a joint venture substantially reduces the amount of resources (money and personnel) that each partner must contribute. Frequently, this strategy is the only way, other than through licensing, that a firm can enter a foreign market. This is especially true when wholly owned activities are prohibited in a country. Centrally planned economies, in particular, usually limit foreign firms' entry to some sort of cooperative arrangements (see Table 9–5).

TABLE 9–5 *(continued)*

Name and place of registration	Number and date of registration	Charter capital (millions of rubles)	Founder countries' equities (percent)	Specialization
10. Alyuminiyevy Zavod, Erevan	No. 252 10/02/89	40.9	USSR-75 France-25	Aluminium foil production and marketing
11. Usolyefari, Usolye-Sibirskoye, Irkutsk Region	No. 48 20/05/88	40.0	USSR-58.3 Bulgaria-41.7	Organic synthesis product making
12. Sovbutital, Tobolsk, Tyumen Region	No. 141 20/05/88	40.0	USSR-70 Italy-30	Synthetic rubber production
13. Gamos, Moscow	No. 1,282 29/12/89	35.45	USSR-51 Italy49	Industrial and consumer goods production, leasing, services
14. Khora, Moldavia	No. 1,148 01/12/89	35.0	USSR-71 Poland-29	Wine and juice making, farm produce processing
15. Falcon, Moscow	No. 627 20/06/89	34.0	Soviet-Danish Chelek JV-30 USA-70	Construction and running of hotels camping sites and sports facilities, tourism, consumer goods production and marketing
16. MKTS-Herschel, Moscow	No. 725 1989	32.2	USSR-90 FRG-10	Production and marketing of hard-alloy products
17. Sovpoliplas, Moscow	No. 114 01/11/88	28.6	USSR-51 Yugoslavia-49	Production and marketing of goods from polymer materials
18. Technopark, Moscow	No. 1,277 29/12/89	28.0	USSR-80 Italy-20	Innovation activities
19. Eksian, Khabarovsk	No. 780 07/08/89	26.0	USSR-50 North Korea-50	Production of pharmaceuticals from medicinal plants, medical services
20. Moscow-McDonald's	No. 159 14/12/88	14.952	USSR-51 Canada-49	Creation and running of fast-food restaurants

Since the failed Soviet coup in August 1991, there have been a number of U.S.-C.I.S. business deals. Philip Morris will make and sell cigarettes in the Russian republic under a joint venture with two Russian firms. Coca-Cola has formed a joint venture to bottle soft drinks in Ukraine. A review of U.S.-C.I.S. joint ventures reveals that early entrants have focused more on service than on manufacturing activity. The review states that equity investment and the involvement of many small- and medium-sized U.S. companies are relatively low.[24]

Because of the situational risks peculiar to a socialist country's centrally planned economy, in which contextual and transactional environments are blurred, MNCs manage risks by structuring joint venture sharing arrangements. An MNC's share in a joint venture within a centrally planned economy (e.g., China) is inversely correlated with the number of uncertainties and risks and also with the dependency that the venture must maintain in the contextual and transactional relationships of the host country.[25] Chinese authorities reported the establishment between 1979 and 1986 of some 272 Sino-American joint ventures, representing a financial commitment of $1,598 trillion by American firms in China. As far as U.S. executives were concerned, each joint venture was painstakingly negotiated under difficult conditions.[26]

Sometimes social rather than legal circumstances require a joint venture to be formed. When Pillsbury planned to market its products in Japan, it considered a number of options, ranging from exporting and licensing to the outright purchase of a Japanese company. Although foreign ownership laws had been relaxed, Pillsbury decided to follow traditional business custom in Japan by seeking a good partner. It thus got together with Snow Brand to form Snow-Brand/Pillsbury.

Joint ventures often have social implications. The familial and tightly knit relationship between suppliers and middlemen is prevalent in many countries. In Japan, this relationship is known as *keiretsu,* which means that familylike business groups are linked by cross ownership of equity. Such customs and business relationships make it difficult for a new supplier to gain entry. Even in the event that the new supplier is able to secure some orders, the orders may be terminated as soon as a member of the family is able to supply the product in question. A joint venture thus provides an opportunity for the foreign supplier to secure business orders through the backdoor. This is the process that Paradyne followed to gain entry into the Japanese computer market. Paradyne, a data communications manufacturer, formed a joint venture with Computer Services Corp., a Japanese software services company, to market PIX II, which provides a link between a central mainframe and remote terminals. This strategy became a practical necessity because Japanese users often ignore the best or most expensive product in order to buy from companies in their *keiretsu.* Although Computer Services Corp. is not a member of a *keiretsu,* it develops software and maintains computers for 510 major corporations across most of the major *keiretsu.* This business relationship was thus responsible for providing the initial foothold in a very large and lucrative market opportunity for Paradyne.[27]

A joint venture can also simultaneously work to satisfy social, economic, and political circumstances since these concerns are highly related. In any kind of international business undertaking, political risks always exist, and a joint venture can reduce such risks while it increases market opportunities. In this sense, a joint venture can make the difference between securely entering a foreign market or not entering at all. Mexico, for example, has stringent "Mexicanization" rules requiring majority local ownership. Although Mexico has allowed systematic and selective foreign control of new companies in nine industrial sectors and has even granted Apple a permit for 100 percent ownership, Apple prudently set up a joint venture anyway in order to minimize risks. Not only are political risks reduced but the political influence of a local partner can make it easier to sell to the government. In the case of Apple, its well-connected Mexican partners give Apple a marketing edge in selling to the government and state-run companies.

Joint ventures are not without their shortcomings and limitations. First, if the partners to the joint venture have not established clear-cut decision-making policy and must consult with each other on all decisions, then the decision-making process may delay a necessary action when speed is essential. Fujitsu, Japan's largest computer maker, formed a joint venture in 1980 with TRW, the largest U.S. independent computer-service company, to market Fujitsu's small computers and terminals. As it turned out, TRW's POS (point-of-sale) terminal business and sales organization was not ready for the product adaptation required for the joint effort to move ahead effectively. Fujitsu finally bought out TRW's 49-percent ownership in order to have sole possession of the decision process in this fast-moving market.

Whenever two individuals or organizations work together, there are bound to be conflicts because of cultural problems, divergent goals, disagreements over production and marketing strategies, and weak contributions by one or the other partner. Although the goals may be compatible at the outset, goals and objectives may diverge over time, even when joint ventures are successful. Dow-Badische was set up in the United States with BASF providing the technology to make chemical raw materials and fibers and Dow supplying the marketing expertise. A split eventually occurred despite good profits when BASF wanted to expand the fiber business—Dow felt that the venture was moving away from Dow's mainstream chemical business. BASF ultimately bought out Dow and made the business its wholly owned subsidiary.[28]

Another potential problem is the matter of control. By definition, a joint venture must deal with double management. If a partner has less than 50 percent ownership, that partner must in effect let the majority partner make decisions. If the board of directors has a 50-50 split, it is difficult for the board to make a decision quickly or at all. Dow's experience with its Korea Pacific Chemical joint venture illustrates this point. When prices plunged, the joint venture lost $60 million. To stem the loss, Dow wanted to improve efficiency but was opposed by its Korean partner. The government-appointed directors boycotted board meetings and a decision could not be reached. Both sides eventually ended up bringing lawsuits against each other.

Firms wanting to create a joint venture need to consider antitrust implications. Potential joint ventures are confronted with six basic antitrust laws: (1) Section 5 of the Federal Trade Commission Act, (2) Section 1, Section 2, and Section 6a of the Sherman Act, (3) Section 7 of the Clayton Act, (4) the Hart-Scott-Rodino Antitrust Improvements Act of 1976, (5) the National Cooperative Research Act (NCRA) of 1984, and (6) Title III of the Export Trade Company (ETC) Act of 1982. To ascertain whether a proposed joint venture may violate U.S. antitrust laws, the parties may request the U.S. Department of Justice under its business review procedures to state in advance its enforcement intentions with respect to the proposed activity. The Federal Trade

Commission also has similar procedures. In addition, the parties may apply for an export trade certificate of review under the ETC Act. They can also file a notification under the NCRA.[29]

Reich and Mankin assert that it is unwise for a U.S. company to form a joint venture with a Japanese partner because the former may be giving away a portion of its market franchise.[30] By relying on the Japanese company for manufactured products, the U.S. firm unknowingly brings in a Trojan horse and encourages new competition. This is so because the U.S. partner's contribution is in the area of sales and distribution, which has little concrete value and is potentially replaceable. This view, however, is likely overstated. If a Japanese manufacturer can so easily replace a U.S. marketer, the U.S. marketer can probably replace the Japanese partner just as easily, because for many products marketing costs exceed production costs. Moreover, the U.S. company may have a valuable brand name, and it can easily switch suppliers and avoid any losses owing to fixed costs associated with production.

Connolly points out the value of having a joint venture formed and operated by one firm from an advanced nation and one firm from an LDC.[31] The advantages that the Third World firm offers include lower labor and management costs, lower input costs, and an understanding of the environment of the Third World nation. However, Third World firms lack capital, up-to-date and improved technologies in manufacturing, and management and marketing skills, and they are subject to exchange controls—all of which are the ingredients that can be supplied by firms in advanced nations. Together, both parties have complementary assets and can provide an effective market entry.

According to a survey of 1,100 joint ventures involving 170 U.S. MNCs, about one-third of the ventures ended in dissolution or in an increase in the U.S. partner's power.[32] Reynolds's study was concerned with only 52 Indian-American equity joint ventures, but the findings seem to support the conclusions of a widening divergence in goals and change in partners' power.[33] Even though the partners' initial objectives were reasonably congruent, the partners became less compatible over time, accompanied by a changing locus of power. Commonly, regard for the objectives of the U.S. partner is reduced, and the joint venture's fit becomes less comfortable than it was at the outset. The implication is that joint ventures are dynamic and both partners should periodically review their individual goals and those of the joint venture they have formed.

MANUFACTURING

The **manufacturing** process can be employed as a strategy involving all or some manufacturing in a foreign country. IBM, for example, has sixteen plants in the United States and eighteen more in other countries. One kind of manufacturing procedure, known as **sourcing**, involves manufacturing operations in a host country, not so much to sell there but for the purpose of exporting from that country to a company's home country or to other countries (see Exhibit 9–6). This chapter is concerned more with another manufacturing objective: the goal of a manufacturing strategy may be to set up a production base inside a target market country as a means of invading it. There are several variations on this method, ranging from complete manufacturing to contract manufacturing (with a local manufacturer) and partial manufacturing. Sears, for

Mercedes-Benz excellence means more than just outstanding cars.

As the world automobile industry celebrates the 100th anniversary of the automobile, the Mercedes-Benz three-pointed star has achieved universal recognition as a symbol of undisputed technological advancement and excellence.

This high standard of excellence applies also to Mercedes-Benz trucks throughout America. The three-pointed star gives assurance that Mercedes-Benz trucks provide value:
- Proven product reliability
- A full range of 126-250 HP engines for both tractors and straight trucks to handle the most demanding jobs
- The only guaranteed parts-availability program in the industry
- 18-months unlimited warranty
- A nationwide dealer network for support
- American craftsmanship: Mercedes-Benz trucks are assembled in a modern, state-of-technology plant in Hampton, Virginia, by workers whose record for quality is the finest anywhere.

The Mercedes-Benz three-pointed star stands for excellence of each and every Mercedes-Benz truck in America. The majority of parts and components for these trucks are sourced from Mercedes-Benz do Brasil, the largest producer of trucks over six tons in the southern hemisphere.

Mercedes-Benz do Brasil S.A.

EXHIBIT 9–6   Sourcing and assembly operations

Source: Reprinted with permission of Mercedes-Benz do Brasil S.A.

example, avoids fixed investment with the use of contract manufacturing by enlisting local manufacturers to produce private-label products to specifications. Exhibit 9–7 describes the fact that Kikkoman Corporation has production facilities overseas.

There are several reasons that a company chooses to invest in manufacturing facilities abroad. One reason may involve gaining access either to raw materials or to take advantage of resources for its manufacturing operations. As such, this process is known as *backward vertical integration*. Another reason may be to take advantage

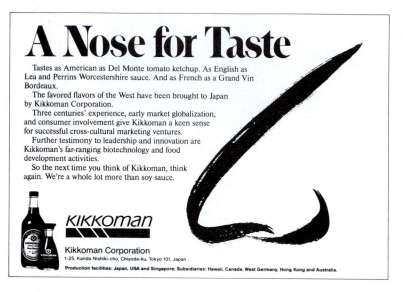

EXHIBIT 9–7   Overseas production facilities

Source: Courtesy of Kikkoman Corporation

of lower labor costs or other abundant factors of production (e.g., labor, energy, and other inputs). Hoover was able to cut its high British manufacturing costs by shifting some of its production to France (see Exhibit 9–8). The strategy may further reduce another kind of cost—transportation. British publishing firms have begun to do more printing abroad because they can save 25–40 percent in production and shipping costs.

Manufacturing in a host country can make the company's product more price competitive because the company can avoid or minimize high import taxes, as well as other trade barriers. Honda, with 68 percent of its car sales coming from exports and 43 percent from the U.S. market, has good reason to be sensitive to trade barriers. In order to avoid future problems of this nature, it set up plants in Ohio.

For automakers to be able to sell cars in Mexico, they must manufacture cars there, and each manufacturer is limited to a single product line. Since the 1960s, Mexico has banned automobile imports. As a result, GM has transferred its small-truck assembly from Texas to Mexico. In 1981 the government enacted more-severe legislation dealing with component part imports and ordered manufacturing companies to earn back hard currency or leave the country. In another case, Ford planned to build plants that would primarily export automobiles to the U.S. market. And Chrysler expanded shipments to the Middle East and Latin America.

A manufacturer interested in manufacturing abroad should consider a number of significant factors. Product image is one such factor. Although Winston cigarettes are made in Venezuela with the same tobaccos and formula as the Winston cigarettes in the United States, Venezuelans still prefer the more expensive U.S.-made Winston cigarettes.

Invest in France
The Hoover Company believes in it.

"The Hoover Company has been in France for 54 years. In 1981, we invested $11 million for the modernization of our Dijon plant and, at no time, have we regretted our decision: in the last two years, we have doubled our work force and quadrupled our production.

We are proud that our French company has become the largest exporter of vacuum cleaners in France and continues the high tradition of producing quality products for the home in the growing French market."

Merle R. Rawson, *Chairman of the Board and President*, THE HOOVER COMPANY, North Canton, Ohio.

When Planning Your Next European Venture, Consider France.

For information and assistance, contact:

THE FRENCH INDUSTRIAL DEVELOPMENT AGENCY

New York	Chicago	Los Angeles	Houston
610 Fifth Avenue	401 North Michigan Ave.	1801 Avenue of the Stars	2727 Allen Parkway
New York, New York 10020	Chicago, Illinois 60611	Los Angeles, Calif. 90067	Houston, Texas 77019
(212) 757-9340	(312) 661-1640	(213) 879-0352	(713) 526-1565

EXHIBIT 9–8   Manufacturing entry strategy

Source: Reprinted with permission of the French Industrial Development Agency

Competition is an important factor, since to a great extent competition determines potential profit. Another factor is the resources of various countries, which should be compared to determine each country's comparative advantage. The comparison should also include production considerations, including production facilities, raw materials, equipment, real estate, water, power, and transport. Human resources, an integral part of the production factor, must be available at reasonable cost.

Manufacturers should pay attention to absolute as well as relative changes in labor costs. A particular country is more attractive as a plant's location if the wages there increase more slowly than those in other countries. The increase in labor costs in West Germany led GM's Opel to switch its production facilities to Japan and led Rollei to move its production to Singapore. Several Japanese firms have been attracted by the $1 hourly wage rate in Mexico, a rate even lower than the hourly pay in Singapore and South Korea. A manufacturer must keep in mind, however, that labor costs are determined not just by compensation but also by productivity and exchange rates. Mexico's labor costs, already absolutely low, become even lower because of the country's falling exchange rate, but this advantage is offset somewhat because Mexican workers are relatively unskilled and thus produce more defective products.

The type of product made is another factor that determines whether foreign manufacturing is an economical and effective venture. A manufacturer must weigh the economies of exporting a standardized product against the flexibility of having a local manufacturing plant that is capable of tailoring the product for local preferences. For capital-intensive products that rely on volume production to keep costs down, it is more advantageous to produce the product in one central location (e.g., in the home country or in an advanced nation) and ship it into markets.[34] Freight-cost-intensive products, such as snack foods and soft drinks, take up large amounts of space and have high transportation costs in relation to unit value. For such products, it may be better to manufacture them in several locations, preferably near or within their markets. Of course, a middle ground is possible. The 3M company manufactures many products in semifinished or bulk form in order to secure the advantages of low-cost volume production before shipping the products to foreign markets for conversion and packaging.

Taxation is another important consideration. Countries commonly offer tax advantages, among other incentives, to lure foreign investment. Puerto Rico does well on this score. In addition, there are no exchange problems since the currency is the U.S. dollar. Exhibit 9–9 is an advertisement that extolls the advantages of having direct investment in Puerto Rico.

Just as important as other factors is the investment climate for foreign capital. The investment climate is determined by geographic and climatic conditions, market size, and growth potential, as well as by the political atmosphere. As mentioned earlier, political, economic, and social motives are highly related, and it is hardly surprising that countries, states, and cities compete fiercely to attract foreign investment and manufacturing plants.

In the United States, the different states use a variety of aggressive tactics to get their share of the 300,000 new jobs and $10 billion in capital that foreign businesses annually bring to the U.S. economy.[35] Exhibit 9–10 examines incentives in New Jersey. Maryland has some 440 foreign-owned companies, which create 45,000 jobs. A routine incentive is the willingness of a state to issue industrial-revenue bonds at low interest rates. In addition to companies' fundamental concerns for financing and tax breaks, firms seek a great deal more, and politicians offer such incentives as personal touch, skilled work force, low wage rates, government-financed job training, location, and assistance in obtaining visas and enrolling children in schools. Great Britain's BOC Group PLC got the training at South Carolina's expense for prospective

WHAT MAKES THESE CEOs MORE IN THE KNOW THAN OTHERS?

Kenneth H. Olsen, President, CEO, Digital Equipment Corporation   Vernon R. Loucks, Jr., Chairman, CEO, Baxter Travenol Laboratories, Inc.   Jim P. Manzi, Chairman, CEO, Lotus Development Corporation

Robert A. Breakstone, President, CEO, Health-Tex   D. Wayne Calloway, Chairman, CEO, PepsiCo, Inc.   Sidney W. Swartz, President, CEO, The Timberland Company

NO QUOTAS.
NO HIGH LABOR COSTS.
NO SHIPPING DELAYS.
NO LANGUAGE BARRIER.
NO HIGH RENT.
NO IMPORT DUTIES.

Not a yes man in the bunch. Yet every one of these industry leaders gave the nod to Puerto Rico for expansion of their production facilities.

And not just for all the wonderful things Puerto Rico doesn't offer. In a most revealing survey of executives of parent firms with plants in Puerto Rico, 77% attributed their company's success to the labor force and native Puerto Rican management.

This is not to say that substantial federal tax credits, local tax incentives, proximity to the U.S. market, factory space starting at $1.25/sq. ft./yr., and government-subsidized training programs didn't factor in their decisions. But once they noted the direct correlation between impressive quarterly results and their workers' commitment to excellence, these leaders of American industry all had basically the same thing to say: "We came to Puerto Rico for the taxes, but we stayed for the people." No wonder these guys are smiling.

For specific information on the advantages of Puerto Rico for a company in your industry, mail in the coupon or call 212-245-1200, Ext. 437. No obligation, of course.

NAME_____ TITLE_____
COMPANY_____
ADDRESS_____
CITY_____ STATE_____ ZIP_____
TELEPHONE (____)_____ PRODUCT or SERVICE_____
☐ Current expansion project   ☐ Future expansion planning   BW11287
Mail to: COMMONWEALTH OF PUERTO RICO
Economic Development Administration   Or call 212-245-1200, Ext. 437
1290 Avenue of the Americas
New York, N.Y. 10104-0092

PUERTO RICO
The climate is right.

EXHIBIT 9–9   Puerto Rico's incentives

Source: Reprinted with permission of the Commonwealth of Puerto Rico, Economic Development Administration

439

EXHIBIT 9–10   New Jersey's incentives

Source: Reprinted with permission of the New Jersey Department of Commerce and Economic Development

employees. Michigan's winning bid for Mazda's $700 million plant and 3,500 jobs includes sending some workers to Japan at state expense to learn Mazda's production system. Even quality of life is an important factor. Fujitsu shifted its operations from California to Oregon because of Oregon's abolition of the unitary tax and because the climate of Oregon is similar to that of Nagano. In addition, golf is popular among the Japanese, and Oregon is attractive because Japanese employees can play golf year-round. Historic and cultural reasons can also play a role in site selection. Most Japanese companies are well entrenched on the West Coast, British firms are on the East Coast, and German and Scandinavian companies are in the Southeast and upper Midwest.

Empirically, market size (in terms of the number of manufacturing establishments in a state) is strongly associated with the locational decisions of foreign manufacturers in the United States. However, with time, foreign manufacturers tend to become more like their domestic counterparts.[36] Regarding market selection, service firms behave like their manufacturing counterparts in the sense that less experienced service firms tend to enter foreign markets that are similar to their home country and that they choose less similar markets after gaining more experience. Concerning the choice of market entry mode, "the relationship between experience and desire for control may be actually U-shaped. Service firms demand high-control modes in the early and late stages of their international evolution."[37]

ASSEMBLY OPERATIONS

An **assembly** operation is a variation on a manufacturing strategy. According to the U.S. Customs Service, "Assembly means the fitting or joining together of fabricated components." The methods used to join or fit together solid components may be welding, soldering, riveting, gluing, laminating, and sewing.

In this strategy, parts or components are produced in various countries in order to gain each country's comparative advantage. Capital-intensive parts may be produced in advanced nations, and labor-intensive assemblies may be produced in an LDC, where labor is abundant and labor costs are low. This strategy is common among manufacturers of consumer electronics. When a product becomes mature and faces intense price competition, it may be necessary to shift all of the labor-intensive operations to LDCs. Atari has, for example, moved the assembly of video games and home computers to Hong Kong and Taiwan. Many manufacturers of digital watches, calculators, and semiconductors had done exactly the same thing several years earlier.

An assembly operation also allows a company to be price-competitive against cheap imports, and this is a defense strategy employed by U.S. apparel makers against such imports. As far as pattern design and fabric cutting are concerned, a U.S. firm can compete by using automated machines, but sewing is another matter altogether, since sewing is labor-intensive and the least-automated aspect of making the product. To solve this problem, precut fabrics can be shipped to a low-wage country for sewing before bringing them back for finishing and packaging. Warnaco and Interco save on aggregate labor costs by cutting fabrics in the United States and shipping them to plants in Costa Rica and Honduras to be sewn. The duties collected on finished products brought back are low. Concerning the importation of articles assembled abroad from U.S. components, subheading 9802.00.80 of the Harmonized Tariff Schedule of the United States (HTSUS) is of interest to those in the import/export business who wish to qualify for partial duty exemption. Subheading 9802.00.80 involves a deduction from the total duties owed, not a different rate of duty.[38]

Under the terms of the *maquiladora* program, foreign corporations can establish wholly owned subsidiaries in Mexico to produce almost exclusively for export. Unlike other foreign direct investment operations, *maquiladora* plants focus on assembly activities. The production components are imported into Mexico in-bond (duty-free), assembled, and then exported. The *maquiladora* program is attractive because of Mexico's proximity to the U.S. market and the comparatively lower cost of labor in Mexico. Furthermore, the provisions of Chapter 98 of the U.S. tariff schedule (formerly items 806.30 and 807.00 of the Tariff Schedule of the United States) allow such assembled goods into the United States with the tariff being assessed only on the value added abroad.[39]

Assembly operations also allow a company's product to enter many markets without being subject to tariffs and quotas. The extent of freedom and flexibility, however, is limited by local product-content laws. South American countries usually require that 50–95 percent of components used in products be produced domestically. Note that as the percentage of required local content increases, the company's flexibility declines and the price advantage erodes. This is so because domestic products can be sheltered behind tariffs walls, and higher prices must be expected for products with a low percentage of local content.

In general, a host country objects to the establishment of a "screwdriver assembly" that merely assembles imported parts. If a product's local content is less than half of all the components used, the product may be viewed as imported, subject to tariffs and quota restrictions. The Japanese, even with joint ventures and assembly operations in Europe, keep local content in foreign production facilities to a minimum while maximizing the use of low-cost Japanese components. British Leyland's Triumph Acclaim is one such example. Made in the United Kingdom under license from Honda, Acclaim contained over 55 percent Japanese parts. Italy considered Acclaim as a Japanese, not a European, car. Since the EC's rule of thumb seemed to be at least 45 percent local content, Italy asked the European Commission to decide what percentage of local content a product must have to be considered "made in Europe." An assembly manufacturing operator must therefore carefully evaluate the trade-off between low-cost production and the process of circumventing trade barriers.

MANAGEMENT CONTRACT

In some cases, government pressure and restrictions force a foreign company either to sell its domestic operations or to relinquish control. In such a case, the company may have to formulate another way to generate the revenue given up. One way to generate revenue is to sign a **management contract** with the government or the new owner in order to manage the business for the new owner. The new owner may lack technical and managerial expertise and may need the former owner to manage the investment until local employees are trained to manage the facility. In past years, Sears has transferred a great deal of technology to Latin America. The Andean Pact's "fade-out" rules subsequently forced Sears to sell 80 percent of its share to local investors in Argentina. Sears then secured management contracts in order to retain some of the profits it had formerly earned.

Management contracts do not have to be used only after a company is forced to sell its ownership interest. Such contracts may be used as a sound strategy for entering a market with a minimum investment and minimum political risks. Club Med, a leader in international resort vacations, is frequently wooed by LDCs with attractive financing options because these countries want tourism. Club Med's strategy involves having either minority ownership or none at all, even though the firm manages all the resorts. Its rationale is that with management contracts Club Med is unlikely to be asked to leave a country where it has a resort.

TURNKEY OPERATIONS

A **turnkey operation** is an agreement by the seller to supply a buyer with a facility fully equipped and ready to be operated by the buyer's personnel, who will be trained by the seller. The term is sometimes used in fast-food franchising when a franchisor agrees to select a store site, build the store, equip it, train the franchisee and employees, and sometimes arrange for the financing. In international marketing, the term is usually associated with giant projects that are sold to governments or government-run companies. Large-scale plants requiring technology and large-scale construction processes unavailable in local markets commonly use this strategy. Such large-scale projects include building steel mills; cement, fertilizer, and chemical plants; and those related to such advanced technologies as telecommunications.

Owing to the magnitude of a giant turnkey project, the winner of the contract can expect to reap huge rewards. Thus, it is important that the turnkey construction package offered to a buyer is an attractive one. Such a package involves more than just offering the latest technology, since there are many other factors important to LDCs in deciding on a particular turnkey project. Financing is critical, and this is one area in which U.S. firms are lacking. European and Japanese firms are much more prepared to secure attractive financing from their governments for buyers. Another factor for consideration involves an agreement to build a local plant. All equipment must be installed and tested to make certain that it functions as intended. Local personnel must be trained to run the operation, and after-the-sale services should be contracted for and made available for the future maintenance of the plant.

ACQUISITION

When a manufacturer wants to enter a foreign market rapidly and yet retain maximum control, direct investment through **acquisition** should be considered (see Exhibit 9–11). The reasons for wanting to acquire a foreign company include product/geographical diversification, acquisition of expertise (technology, marketing, and management), and rapid entry. For example, Renault acquired a controlling interest in American Motors in order to gain the sales organization and distribution network that would otherwise have been very expensive and time-consuming to build from the ground up. To enter the Thai market, Heinz acquired a 51 percent interest in Win-Chance Foods Company, Ltd. and renamed it Heinz Win Chance, Ltd. The three partners who began the business continued the operation owing to their understanding of the market and their familiarity with Thailand's laws and government.[40]

Acquisition takes many forms. According to Root, acquisition may be "horizontal (the product lines and markets of the acquired and acquiring firms are similar), vertical (the acquired firm becomes a supplier or customer of the acquiring firm), concentric (the acquired firm has the same market but different technology or the

HOW A SMALL COLORADO COMPANY BECAME A GLOBAL PLAYER.

Intellistor, Inc. is a small high-tech company in the foothills of the Colorado Rockies. With a staff of some 130 engineering experts, it designs and develops some of the world's most sophisticated storage systems for high performance computers.

Its products are sold all over the globe, and this is a source of great pride to Intellistor. And also kind of a surprise; when it was founded as a start-up back in 1983, it had no idea that it would become a global player. None whatsoever. Its biggest ambition had been to carve out a small market niche for itself in America. But then it met Fujitsu.

GLOBAL GIANT

Fujitsu is a global computer and communications giant, an enormous force in the worldwide high-tech revolution. With 115,000 employees and projects completed in more than 100 countries, it is working to promote local economies through global distribution of products and services.

Fujitsu discovered the genius of Intellistor in 1985, when it contracted with the company to develop an intelligent storage system for some of its computers. Intellistor did such a fast, efficient and creative job that Fujitsu came back for more. And more. And soon a very special relationship developed between the two companies—a relationship that resulted in marriage.

BRILLIANT BUT STRUGGLING

Like many high-tech start-ups, Intellistor was brilliant but struggling, starving for capital. For its part Fujitsu was at a point where it needed Intellistor; it could use the company's freewheeling, high-spirited entrepreneurial drive.

In 1987 Fujitsu acquired Intellistor. And since then Intellistor has doubled its employment, and developed a whole string of remarkable new products—which are finding their way to the global marketplace. And this is only the beginning. The future is bright for both sides. That's what you get when you put together the best of two different worlds.

Lew Frauenfelder, president of Intellistor. Mr. Frauenfelder founded Intellistor in 1983, met Fujitsu in 1985, and joined forces with the company in 1987. "Our relationship with Fujitsu," he says, "has brought only good. It has enabled us not only to survive but to double our employment and concentrate on doing what we do best: develop world-class products." For the full details of the Fujitsu-Intellistor story call (303) 682-6539.

FUJITSU

The global computer & communications company.

EXHIBIT 9–11 Acquisition

Source: Courtesy of Fujitsu America, Inc.

same technology but different market), and conglomerate (the acquired firm is in a different industry from that of the acquiring firm)."[41]

Acquisition is viewed in a light different from other kinds of foreign direct investment. A government generally welcomes foreign investment that starts up a new enterprise (called a *greenfield* enterprise), since that investment increases employment and enlarges the tax base. An acquisition, however, fails to do this since it displaces and replaces domestic ownership. Therefore, acquisition is very likely to be perceived as exploitation or a blow to national pride—on this basis, it stands a good chance of being turned down. There was a heated debate before the United Kingdom allowed Sikorsky, a U.S. firm, to acquire Westland, a failing British manufacturer of military helicopters. That episode caused the Thatcher government to halt its negotiation with Ford concerning the acquisition of British Leyland's Austin-Rover passenger-car division.

Because of the sensitive nature of acquisition, there are more legal hurdles to surmount. In Germany, the Federal Cartel Office may prohibit or require divestiture of those mergers and acquisitions that could strengthen or create market domination.[42] In general, a merger may be disallowed under these conditions:

A company with annual sales of more than DM 2 billion merges with any company that has domination of its market.

A company with annual sales of more than DM 2 billion merges with an enterprise that operates in a market consisting of medium-size companies.

Combined enterprises have total annual sales of DM 12 billion and at least two of the combining enterprises have annual sales more than DM 1 billion each.

A merger results in a 50 percent market share in an (already) oligopolistic market.

Other than legal and political complications, social reasons may also prevent the use of acquisition as a strategy to enter a market. Japan is a prime example. Foreign companies rarely attempt to enter Japan by acquiring existing Japanese companies.[43] Japanese firms themselves do not view acquisition with high regard—being acquired is like having to sell one's family. Not surprisingly, sound companies available for acquisition are difficult to find.

ANALYSIS OF ENTRY STRATEGIES

Exhibit 9–12 shows the extent of direct foreign investment by five major industrial countries. Table 9–6 describes transnational operation firms' reasons for foreign direct investment. To enter a foreign market, a manufacturer has a number of strategic options, each with its own strengths and weaknesses. Many companies employ multiple strategies. The IBM case cited earlier is an example of a multiple entry strategy. Another example involves Anheuser-Busch, which dominates the U.S. market with 34 percent market share. Anheuser-Busch has made plans to enter the huge overseas beer market—three times the size of the American market—by employing multiple entry strategies.[44] It has licensed foreign brewers in the United Kingdom, Japan, and Israel to produce, market, and distribute Budweiser beer, while excluding Bud Light from this arrangement. It has also used an exporting strategy by exporting beer from the United States to 10 foreign countries. Anheuser-Busch has recently made plans to go another step forward by having direct foreign investment through the acquisition of foreign breweries.

One would be naive to believe that a single entry strategy is suitable for all products or in all countries. For example, a significant change in the investment climate can make a particular strategy ineffective even though it worked well in the past. There are a number of characteristics that determine the appropriateness of

EXHIBIT 9–12   Direct foreign investment
Source: IMF Survey, 15 July 1991, 217

entry strategies, and many variables affect which strategy is chosen. These character-istics include political risks, regulations, type of country, type of product, and other competitive and market characteristics.

A host country's market size affects the decisions on manufacturing direct for-eign investment.[45] In addition, such decisions are influenced by certain classes of po-litical events in certain groups of countries. Although internation conflict adversely affects decisions to invest in both LDCs and developed countries, the effect of in-tranation conflict is different from LDCs when compared to developed countries. Conflictive intranation events are viewed as promoting instability in LDCs, and such instability could adversely affect foreign investors' business goals and profit. These events consequently decrease manufacturing direct foreign investment. Such events, however, are not a concern when the host nation is a developed country.

Foreign investment is without a doubt affected by a host country's investment regulations. The Andean Code, for instance, requires partial fade-out of ownership and sets limits on profit remittance and capital reinvestment. According to one study, the code has significantly influenced MNCs' activities in the region.[46] Because of in-creased business costs, the code discourages corporate activities within code-adopting countries by directing MNCs to choose foreign direct investment location in other countries.

Markets are far from being homogeneous, and the type of country chosen dictates the entry strategy to be used. One way of classifying countries is by the degree of control exerted on the economy by the government, with capitalism at the one extreme and communism at the other. Other systems are classified somewhere in between depending on the freedom allowed of private citizens in conducting their business activities. In free-enterprise economies, an MNC can choose any entry strategy it deems appropriate. In controlled economies, the options are limited. Until recently, the most frequent trade entry activity in controlled economies was exporting,

TABLE 9–6 Foreign direct investment motives

Motive	No. of Mentions	Mean Score	Dominant Motive
Part I—Institutional and Legal			
Technical standards and certification; Trademarks and patent law considerations	51	0.5	4
Administrative barriers, including customs procedures and VAT collection arrangements; national transport policies	12	0.2	0
Public procurement	69	1.0	43
Part II—Scale of Operations			
Capital requirements	24	0.37	14
Economies of scale	93	1.43	51
Spreading of risk	46	0.55	9
Part III—Internalization of Overseas External Advantage			
Lower factor costs	22	0.34	11
Transport costs	37	0.60	25
Labor relations	4	0.06	4
Specialist location advantages	46	0.74	21
Direct presence in market	203	3.76	169

Note: Companies may mention more than one of the categories. In those cases where the motives were interdependent, it was impossible to isolate a single dominant motive. Dominance has thus been ascribed to each of the interdependent motives.

Source: Andrew I. Millington and Brian T. Bayliss, "Non-Tariff Barriers and U.K. Investment in the European Community," *Journal of International Business Studies* 22 (no. 4, 1991): 705

followed by licensing for Eastern Europe, and importing and exporting without a linking contract for the Soviet Union.[47]

The country *temperature gradient* is another meaningful classification system. Countries can be classified as hot, moderate, or cold markets based on a number of factors, including level of economic development and trade barriers. Hot countries are dynamic markets receptive to new distribution ideas, whereas cold countries do not easily accommodate changes. This classification serves a useful purpose by suggesting proper market entry modes. Based on a study of 250 U.S. manufacturers, Goodnow and Hanz calculated the frequency distribution of market entry modes for each country. The findings indicate that as companies move from hot countries toward cold countries, they depend more on export entry and less on local production investment. For hot countries, of all entry modes, exporting accounted for 47.2 percent, local production for 28.5 percent, and other modes for the remaining balance. In stark contrast, cold countries deal in exporting for 82.6 percent and local production for only 2.9 percent.[48]

Market entry strategies are also influenced by product type. A product that must be customized or that requires some services before and after the sale cannot easily be exported to another country. In fact, a service or a product whose value is largely determined by an accompanied service cannot be practically distributed outside of the producing country. Any portion of the product that is service-oriented must be created at the place of consumption. As a result, service-intensive products require particular modes of market entry. The options include management contract to sell service to a foreign customer, licensing so that another local company (franchisee) can be trained to provide that service, and local manufacturing by establishing a permanent branch or subsidiary there.

A product that is basically a commodity may require local production in order to reduce labor and shipping costs. For a value-added or differentiated product, a firm can depend on the exporting mode because of the higher profit margin. Furthermore, local manufacturing may destroy the product's mystique and thus diminish a previously existing market.

When MNCs choose among full equity ownership, licensing, or a combination, the reasons for the preference for investment over licensing are threefold, and the type of technology is one of those reasons.[49] Initial considerations are the transferability of the technology and the cost for doing so. If the technology is complex or uncodified in a patent, the cost is less when the licensor transfers the technology to its own foreign affiliate than to an independent and unsophisticated licensee. The next consideration is the licensee's assessment of the value of the technology—a licensee has a tendency to offer relatively low payment. The final consideration involves opportunity costs, since the licensee may become a competitor in third countries.

Certain market characteristics, such as the economics of plant and marketing operations, affect entry strategies. Davidson and McFetridge studied 1,226 technology transfers in order to identify key characteristics in the choice of market entry mode.[50] The choice between licensing and direct investment was strongly affected by the characteristics of the individual technology and parent corporation. Public policy variables also played a role in the choice. Screening procedures and equity controls reduced the probability of internal transfer. The relationship between the host country's characteristics and the choice between licensing and direct investment received mixed support. Social factors such as religious and language similarities were positively related to direct investment levels, but economic conditions showed no consistent pattern for technology transfer. Market size and market sophistication also did not appear significant in affecting the choice. Since previous studies showed that both market size and market sophistication were positively related to levels of direct investment, the two variables were apparently related to levels of licensing in the same manner.

Other competitive characteristics are also determinants of entry choices. Statistical evidence from a Sleuwaegen study supports the proposition that the kind of monopolistic advantage held is decisive in whether exporting or local production is to be used as a market entry strategy. High selling costs favor local production abroad and discourage exports to nonaffiliates. "The other monopolistic advantages, based on product differentiation, as well as firm size and human capital, play an important role in determining which form of foreign involvement will be chosen."[51]

A study of foreign direct investment entries in the United States found that 65 percent entered the United States through acquisitions and that joint ventures and greenfields accounted for 9 percent and 26 percent respectively. Foreign acquisitions of American firms were more likely to fail than foreign greenfield investments.

Foreign-controlled firms failed less often than domestically owned firms.[52] Using time-series (the years to 1973–1986) and cross-sectional data (twenty nations), one study found that U.S. manufacturing firms used exporting instead of licensing as a hedge against repatriation risk in LDCs.[53]

There are two schools of thought that explain how multinational corporations select ownership structures for subsidiaries. The first has to do with *what the firm wants,* and MNCs want structures that minimize the transaction costs of doing business abroad (e.g., whole ownership). Factors affecting what the firm wants include the capabilities of the firm, its strategic needs, and the transaction costs of different ways of transferring capabilities. The second school of thought, related to *what the firm can get,* explains that what it wants may differ from what it can get (e.g., joint venture). In this case, ownership structures are determined by negotiations, whose outcomes depend on the relative bargaining power of the firm and that of the host government. The statistical analysis supports the bargaining school, in that attractive domestic markets increase the relative power of host governments. However, there is no support for the prediction that firms in marketing- and R&D-intensive industries have more bargaining power than others. MNCs prefer whole ownership when they have a lot of experience in an industry or a country, when intrasystem sales of the subsidiary are high, or when the subsidiary is located in a marketing-intensive industry. The joint venture is the preferred mode when MNCs rely on local inputs of raw materials and skills.[54]

FREE TRADE ZONES

When entering a market, a company should go beyond an investigation of market entry modes. Another question that should be asked is whether a **free trade zone** (FTZ) is involved and needs consideration. The decisions concerning market entry and FTZs are somewhat independent. An FTZ can be used regardless of whether the entry strategy is exporting or local manufacturing.

According to federal regulations, a free trade zone is "an isolated, enclosed, and policed area, operated as a public utility, in or adjacent to a port of entry, furnished with facilities for lading, unloading, handling, sorting, manipulating, manufacturing and exhibiting goods, and for reshipping them by land, water, or air. Any foreign and domestic merchandise . . . may be brought into a zone without being subject to the customs laws of the United States governing the entry of goods or the payment of duty thereon; . . . the merchandise may be exported, destroyed, or sent into customs territory from the zone, in the original package or otherwise. It is subject to customs duties if sent into the customs territory, but not if reshipped to foreign points."

From this description, one can see that an FTZ is a secured domestic area in international commerce, considered to be legally outside a country's customs territory. It is an area designated by a government for the duty-free entry of goods. It is also a location where imports can be handled with few regulations, and little or no customs duties and excise taxes are collected. As such, goods enter the area without paying any duty. The duty would be paid only when goods enter the customs territory of the country where an FTZ is located.

Variations among FTZs include free ports, tariff-free trade zones, airport duty-free arcades, export processing zones, and other foreign grade zones. FTZs are usually established in countries for the convenience of foreign traders. The zones may be run by the host government or by private entities. FTZs vary in size from a few acres to several square miles. They can be located at airports, in harbor areas, or within the interior of a country (e.g., Salt Lake City).

Worldwide, FTZs experienced nearly a threefold increase in numbers during the 1970s. By the mid-1980s, there were more than 400 zones located in eighty countries.[55] About $160 billion of the $1.7 trillion world trade was processed through FTZs, a rate of close to 10 percent of the world's trade.

For the United States, the goal of the Foreign Trade Zones Act of 1934 was to establish 300 cities as FTZs within the United States. The law was virtually ignored for its first forty years, and only 10 FTZs were actually in place by 1972. To improve the situation, a U.S. law of 1980 removed duty on the value added to imported goods by labor in U.S. FTZs and gave tax breaks to manufacturers, banks, and insurance companies.

A small percentage of international trade within the United States is accounted for by free zones, and only 30 percent of MNCs using them are U.S. firms. This relatively little use may in part occur because foreign governments have run FTZs much longer, thus making their companies more experienced in generating business through these outlets. The poor showing of U.S. firms demonstrates that there is a great need for these firms to better understand the operations of FTZs so they can take advantage of the tremendous benefits available.

There are about 172 FTZs (general-purpose zones), with additional subzones, throughout the United States. Subzones are special-purpose facilities for companies unable to operate effectively at public zone sites. The number of approved zones and subzones increased from 75 in 1980 to over 370 in 1990, and shipments received at these facilities jumped from $2.6 billion to over $90 billion.[56] Exhibit 9–13 shows a drastic jump in the volume of merchandise received by U.S. FTZs.

The benefits of FTZ use are numerous. Some of these benefits are country-specific in the sense that some countries offer superior facilities for lower costs (e.g., utilities and telecommunications). Other benefits are zone-specific in that certain zones may be better than others within the same country in terms of tax and transportation facilities. Finally, there are zone-related benefits that constitute general advantages in using an FTZ. A model proposed by McDaniel and Kossack incorporates the following zone-related benefits:

A lower rate of theft because of the required extra security by U.S. Customs

Lower insurance costs

Nonpayment of inventory tax

Excise taxes not paid on goods while stored in the FTZ

Delay of payment of taxes on goods to be imported into the U.S. Customs territory

Avoidance of fines for improper labeling

Avoidance of duty on goods to be reexported when the use of duty drawback, temporary import bond, or bonded warehouse is not an alternative

Savings of duty-drawback cost and trouble

Savings of the cost of temporary import bond

No duty payment on waste or shrinkage

Reduced duty on by-products of manufacturing processes

Ability to select in advance the lowest possible tariff

Advantage of the pipeline effect based on shorter time for customs processing, which reduces inventory in transit[57]

One popular misconception about FTZs is that they are used basically for warehousing. Although goods can be stored for an unlimited length of time in an FTZ, any gain from doing so is small when compared to the alternative of a bonded warehouse, which allows temporary storage without duty. Actually, the future of FTZs lies in manufacturing (product manipulation), not storing. Many activities can be performed in FTZs. According to Calabro, a company can "store, stockpile, manufacture, assemble, break-up, manipulate, mix, pack-repack, clean, repair, salvage, discard, destroy, inspect, sample, test, grade, weight, sort, mark/remark, label/relabel, display, exhibit, distribute, sell, and reexport."[58]

FTZs offer several important benefits, both for the country and for companies using them. One benefit is job retention and creation. When better facilities and grants are provided to attract MNCs, FTZs can generate foreign investment and jobs. For example, the Buffalo, New York, FTZ was able to attract a Canadian automobile

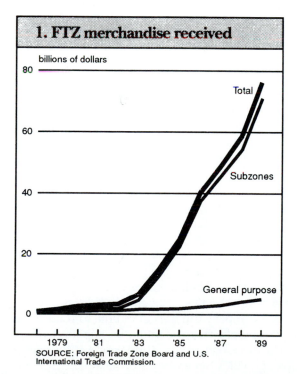

1. FTZ merchandise received

billions of dollars

SOURCE: Foreign Trade Zone Board and U.S. International Trade Commission.

EXHIBIT 9–13 Foreign trade zone merchandise received

Source: Chicago Fed Letter, August 1991

assembly operation and a Japanese camera importer to establish operations there. Nationwide, FTZs employ some 29,000 American workers.

Companies can derive several benefits from FTZs. The use of an FTZ improves the cash flow for a company since an FTZ eliminates the need to pay duty immediately on docking. An FTZ can eliminate the waiting period for the arrival of a product from an overseas firm. The firm can hold goods in an FTZ until the quota opens up, making it possible to move the goods immediately into the market at the earliest opportunity.

FTZs also provide a means to circumvent import restrictions. By having assembly operations in FTZs, products are removed from such restrictions. Japanese automakers assemble cars in U.S. zones to take advantage of tax reductions and customs duty exemptions; at the same time, these firms overcome self-imposed quotas. Honda produces 50,000 cars a year in the Marysville, Ohio, FTZ. Nissan, likewise, manufactures 60,000 trucks annually in the Smyrna, Tennessee, FTZ.

FTZs provide a means to facilitate imports. Imported merchandise can be sent into FTZs without formal customs entry and duty payment until some later date. Both foreign and domestic goods can be moved into FTZs and remain there for storage, assembling, manufacturing, packaging, and other processing operations. Goods that were improperly marked or cannot meet standards for clearance can be remarked and salvaged. Moreover, goods can be cleaned, mixed, and used in the manufacturing of other products. One Swiss cosmetics company imports in bulk and employs U.S. labor to repackage its goods for retailing. In fact, importers can even display and exhibit merchandise and take orders in FTZs without securing a bond. For retailers, benefits derived by using FTZs include the sorting, labeling, and storing of imports.

FTZs can not only facilitate imports but also facilitate export and reexport, though the gain from this practice is small when compared to the alternatives of duty drawback and temporary import bond. Still, domestic goods can be taken into an FTZ and are then returned free of quotas and duty, even when they have been combined with other articles while inside the zone. Sears uses the New Orleans FTZ to inspect foreign cameras it subsequently ships to Latin America. Seiko Time Corporation of America opened a 200,000-square-foot facility in the New Jersey FTZ to store and ship watches to Canada and Latin America. One European medical supply firm that makes kidney dialysis machines uses German raw materials and American labor in a U.S. FTZ for assembly purposes, and then it exports 30 percent of the finished product to Scandinavia.

Lower production costs can thus result from doing some production work in an FTZ. The use of an FTZ allows a company to take advantage of the comparative advantage in another country without having to go through unnecessary import-export paperwork and formalities. Form-O-uth, a Texas firm, has a factory in an FTZ in El Salvador. Cloth pieces cut in the United States are shipped to El Salvador for sewing because seamstresses there earn only 65 cents an hour. Once the sewing is completed, the finished pieces are shipped back to the United States for sale to Sears.

Finally, FTZs greatly reduce both duties and freight charges. These reductions are achieved in several ways. First, payment of duties, state and local taxes, and inventory taxes can be deferred. Second, a company can import in bulk to reduce the shipping space required and reduce the freight charges. Later, the imported goods can be processed in the FTZ according to market needs. Third, some FTZs offer a special tax break. Panama, for example, provides foreign investors tax-free status and the right to import technology and raw materials without duties. It may not be a coincidence that the FTZ operated by Panama happens to also be the largest one in the Western Hemisphere.

Fourth, the materials can be processed to a condition or product that is assigned the lowest-duty classification. Therefore, local assembly saves taxes since certain finished products are taxed at a lower rate than components and parts. Olivetti of Italy won the right to set up a special zone in Harrisburg, Pennsylvania, to assemble typewriters from components imported from abroad. By doing so, Olivetti was able to save 88 percent of the normal duty on imported components and only pay the rest of the duty when its finished products were shipped outside the zone. AMC provides another example. Its plant in the Kenosha, Wisconsin, FTZ combines domestic and foreign components. The duty on cars assembled in the zone is less than the duty charged on imported car parts.

Fifth, foreign assembly can be used if assembly costs are lower in a foreign FTZ. The entire Mexico border along the United States frontier functions as an FTZ. Some 650 American firms operate factories in Mexico, using cheap Mexican labor to assemble products before shipping them back to the United States. Import duties are applied only on the value added within the Mexican plant. Between 1970 and the mid-1980s, the number of Mexicans employed in this zone has increased sevenfold to about 150,000.

Finally, FTZs can prevent an overpayment of duties. In the movement and transport of goods, product contents commonly are lost because of evaporation, leakage, breakage, and other causes. Using an FTZ makes it possible to avoid paying tax on unrecoverable waste, whereas any recoverable waste is dutiable only on the condition and quantity entered. The product contents can be remeasured in an FTZ so that no duty is charged on any portions that have been lost. The same principle applies to damaged goods. These can be removed to avoid any tax being levied on the portion damaged.

CONCLUSION

When a company considers marketing in foreign markets, it needs to analyze such economic characteristics as GNP, income, and population in order to compare market opportunities. Once a particular market is chosen, management needs to decide on the market entry strategy. Additionally, the company should consider the feasibility of operating all or some of its international business in a free trade zone, since such a zone can complement many of the market penetration options.

If the company wants to avoid foreign direct investment, it can export its product from its home base, it can grant a license permitting another company to manufacture and market its product in a foreign market, or it can sign a contract to sell its expertise by managing the business for a foreign owner. If a firm is interested in making direct foreign investment, it can either start its business from the ground up or acquire another company. The acquisition, however, may receive a less-than-enthusiastic response from the foreign government. If the company decides to start a new business overseas, it must consider whether a sole venture or joint venture will best suit the objective. Sole ventures provide a company with better control and profit, whereas joint ventures reduce risk and utilize the strengths of a local partner. Regardless of whether a sole venture or joint venture is used, the company still must decide whether local production is going to be complete or partial (i.e., assembly). Finally, foreign sales to governments often take the form of giant turnkey projects that require the company to provide a complete package, including financing, construction, and training.

　　　　Each market entry strategy has its own unique strengths and weaknesses. In most circumstances, the strategies are not mutually exclusive. A manufacturer may use multiple strategies in different markets as well as within the same market. No single market penetration method is ideal for all markets or all circumstances. The appropriateness of a strategic option depends on corporate objectives, market conditions, and political realities.

QUESTIONS

1. Explain how the following variables are useful for the analysis of market potential: population density, per capita income, and GNP/capita.
2. Explain how a dual economy may affect a company's marketing plan.
3. What are the income elasticities of imports and exports? What are their implications?
4. What is a country's compressibility of imports? What are its economic implications?

5. Briefly explain these market entry strategies: exporting, licensing, joint venture, manufacturing, assembly operations, management contract, turnkey operations, and acquisition.
6. What is cross-licensing or grantback?
7. What are the factors that should be considered in choosing a country for direct investment?
8. What is an FTZ? What are its benefits?

DISCUSSION ASSIGNMENTS AND MINICASES

1. What are your criteria to evaluate and compare countries in terms of market opportunities? Is Canada an attractive market based on this set of criteria?
2. According to *Beverage Digest,* the 1986 per capita consumption of soft drinks in gallons is as follows: the United States (42.1), Germany (18.5), the United Kingdom (13), France (7), Italy (6.9), and Japan (1). What is your interpretation of this information in the light of your marketing of a brand of soft drink?
3. According to *Fortune* magazine, IBM's foreign subsidiaries imported less U.S.-made components in 1986, resulting in IBM's 12 percent decline in exports. Yet IBM was happy with the development. Why?
4. Since exporting is a relative risk-free market entry strategy, is there a need for a company to consider another market entry strategies?
5. Can a service be licensed for market entry purposes?

6. In spite of the advantages of free trade zones, American firms have so far failed to utilize them effectively. What are the reasons? Can anything be done to stimulate U.S. firms' interest?
7. One of the most celebrated joint ventures is NUMMI (New United Motor Manufacturing, Inc.), a joint venture between General Motors and Toyota. It seems surprising that the two largest competitors would even think of joining forces. GM is the number one manufacturer in the United States as well as in the world. Toyota, on the other hand, is number one in Japan and number two worldwide. NUMMI is a 50-50 joint venture with the board of directors split equally between the two companies. The venture was to manufacture the Toyota-designed subcompact, and the name chosen for the car was Nova. What are the benefits each partner can expect to derive from the NUMMI joint venture? Do you foresee any problems?

CASE 9–1
HOW TO EXPORT HOUSES

Prefabricated houses are not new. Some well-known mail-order retailers started selling such houses in the United States decades ago. One advantage of this type of housing is quick assembly—only a few days are needed. Another buying incentive is the lower price achieved through mass production. Another advantage of the assembly-line approach is better quality control. The major disadvantage is, of course, the product's image. There is no prestige in living in a prefab house, and the uniform look does not enhance consumer perception. Although mass production has generally negative connotations, it does not appreciably hurt such durables as refrigerators, automobiles, and sound equipment. Yet, for housing the negative image is quite overwhelming.

In Japan, where land and housing costs are outrageous, prefab houses are a necessity to many. One Japanese firm that has acquired technical know-how in manufacturing prefab houses is Misawa Homes. One of its popular designs is House 55. This model has ten capsules, requiring five large "containers" for transportation. The model's advantage is that rough assembly can be accomplished in just two hours. Another strength is its price—20 percent lower than conventional prefab houses and 30 percent less than wood houses. The model was exhibited at trade fairs in Europe and received a great deal of interest. Encouraged, Misawa Homes wanted to export its House 55 houses to Europe and the United States.

Questions

1. Do you think that such prefab houses as House 55 can gain consumer acceptance in the United States and Europe?
2. Even supposing the absence of U.S. consumers' negative reactions, are there any factors that pose no problem in Japan and yet would create difficulties in the United States?
3. What would be Misawa's strategy to enter overseas markets with the product?

CASE 9–2
GTECH CORPORATION

FRANCINE NEWTH
Providence College

Overview

GTECH Corporation can best be described as a technology company dedicated to the soft gaming sector of the public gaming industry. GTECH designs, produces, installs, and supplies networks for government-sponsored or licensed lottery jurisdictions and wagering organizations. The company was incorporated in Delaware in 1980 and, on March 1, 1981, acquired Datatrol's Gaming Systems Division, which consisted of related assets and on-line lottery contracts for Michigan, Rhode Island, and Connecticut. This acquisition led to the beginning of substantial success with on-line lottery networks. By 1987, GTECH was the recognized leader in the implementation and operation of such on-line networks installed on five continents: North America, South America, Australia, Asia, and Europe (see Exhibit 1).

The Industry

The gaming industry is divided into two sectors: (1) the hard gaming sector, such as casinos and racetracks, and (2) the soft gaming sector, which includes both off-line and on-line sale of tickets with randomly selected numbers.

The on-line soft gaming sector of the gaming industry is highly competitive; there are only about 500 customers worldwide, namely governmental authorities and government-licensed organizations. Lotteries are highly regulated and are operated by governmental lottery authorities, such as a lottery commission. Legislatures usually establish certain features of a lottery, such as the percentage of gross revenues, which must be paid back to players in prize money. The lottery commission, however,

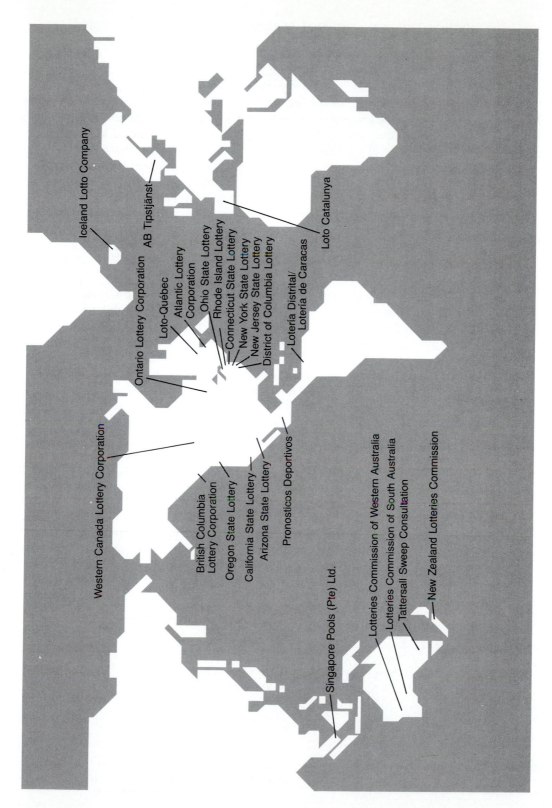

EXHIBIT 1 GTECH lottery contracts

Iceland Lotto Company

AB Tipstjänst

Loto Catalunya

Ontario Lottery Corporation

Loto-Québec

Atlantic Lottery Corporation

Ohio State Lottery

Rhode Island Lottery

Connecticut State Lottery

New York State Lottery

New Jersey State Lottery

District of Columbia Lottery

Lotería Distrital/
Lotería de Caracas

Western Canada Lottery Corporation

British Columbia
Lottery Corporation

Oregon State Lottery

California State Lottery

Arizona State Lottery

Pronosticos Deportivos

Singapore Pools (Pte) Ltd.

Lotteries Commission of Western Australia

Lotteries Commission of South Australia

Tattersall Sweep Consultation

New Zealand Lotteries Commission

generally exercises significant authority in determining the types of games played, the price, and the selection of the suppliers of tickets, equipment, and services.

Lottery contracts are usually awarded in a competitive procurement process in the form of a request for proposals (RFP). The most significant factors influencing the award of lottery contracts are the following: the ability to optimize lottery revenues through technological capability and applications knowledge; the quality, dependability, and upgrade capability of the network; the experience, financial condition, and reputation of the contractor; the ability to satisfy any other requirements and qualifications imposed by the lottery authority; and the price of the network.

The major competitors in the on-line lottery network business include GTECH; Control Data Corporation (CDC); Syntech International, Inc.; CSEE, a French company; International Totalizator Systems (ITS), Inc.; Scientific Games (SciGames), Inc., a subsidiary of Bally Manufacturing Corporation; and AmTote (see Exhibit 2 and Exhibit 3).

Domestic lottery contracts involve installing and operating a company-owned lottery network for a specified term, usually two to five years, subject to extension at the lottery authority's option. These domestic contracts are typically referred to as "operating contracts." Payments under operating contracts are based on a percentage of the lottery sales provided by the network. The percentage is usually based on specified volumes of sales and/or number of terminals in operation.

Foreign lottery contracts usually require companies to sell, deliver, and install a turnkey network for a fixed price, though some foreign contracts are now being negotiated as operating contracts. Companies may also be required to provide ongoing software and/or hardware maintenance, repair or update services, management consultation, or other services relating to the operation of the network. Payments of foreign lottery contracts are usually made in foreign currencies and are subject to the risks associated with fluctuations in exchange rates. Lotteries outside the United States are customarily operated by governmental authorities or by private parties licensed by the government. Many of the major countries have some kind of lottery operation, many of which are off-line. On-line lottery networks have been established in Australia, Canada, France, Singapore, Hong Kong, Israel, Spain, Sweden, Venezuela, Mexico, and New Zealand.

EXHIBIT 2 On-line Lottery Suppliers—Terminals Installed and On-line (as of December 1987)

Supplier	Number	Percentage Share
GTECH	40,170	57.3
CDC	12,015	17.1
AmTote	6,130	8.7
Syntech	4,300	6.1
SciGames	3,540	5.1
CSEE	2,500	3.6
ITS	1,500	2.1
Terminals	**70,155**	**100.0**

EXHIBIT 3 On-line Lottery Suppliers—Lottery Jurisdictions Contracted (as of December 1987)

Supplier	Number	Percentage Share
GTECH	26	60.5
CDC	6	14.0
SciGames	5	11.6
AmTote	3	7.0
Syntech	1	2.3
CSEE	1	2.3
ITS	1	2.3
On-line Jurisdictions	**43**	**100.0**

The industry's worldwide gross sales of on-line systems is approximately $16 billion. Typically, the lottery authority will allocate the gross receipts as follows: 50 percent to prizes, 35 percent to government/lottery authority, 10 percent to administration, and 5 percent to agent's commission.

GTECH

GTECH and its subsidiaries are engaged primarily in the design, production, implementation, operation, sale, and service of computer-based networks and network components. The purpose of these networks is to collect, process, and disseminate information rapidly. The systems are particularly designed for high-transaction-rate environments. The main application of GTECH's networks has been in on-line lotteries operated both domestically and internationally.

GTECH's technical know-how, its integrated on-line systems and speed of implementation, and the creative skills of its personnel are the elements that have contributed most to its success. The company maintains substantial ongoing research-and-development efforts in order to compete successfully in the technologically dynamic networking business. In fiscal 1987 the company spent $8,025,000 on R&D, as compared to $6,350,000 in fiscal 1986 and $3,685,000 in fiscal 1985. As of February 28, 1987, GTECH had 106 employees engaged full-time in research and product development. The company has 994 full-time employees.

GTECH's marketing efforts consist primarily of making presentations of its services and products to the lottery authorities of jurisdictions in which contracts are coming up for procurement or for network expansion. The company derives substantially all of its revenues from the rendering of services and the sale or supply of computerized on-line networks and components to government-authorized lotteries (see Exhibit 4).

Unlike many of its competitors, GTECH will provide a lease option of the terminals over a negotiated time period. This option is particularly attractive in that it reduces start-up costs considerably. GTECH will also install a system faster than its competitors, thereby generating lottery revenues quicker.

Islensk Getspa

In 1985 the prime minister of Iceland requested that the Sports Federation, the Handicapped Federation, and the Youth Federation work together to establish a lotto system in Iceland. These three federations made an agreement to work together for that purpose. On May 2, 1986, the Icelandic Parliament issued law 26/196, which allowed the minister of justice to give the three federations permission to operate number games. On July 8, 1986, the three federations established a new organization known as *Islensk Getspa,* the Iceland Lottery Company, which is a tax-exempt nonprofit organization.

The representatives of *Islensk Getspa* started investigating the organization of lotto in various countries. They soon identified firms manufacturing on-line equipment that had gained a dominant position worldwide.

On June 15, 1987, the management of GTECH, along with several other competitors, received a telex communication from representatives of *Islensk Getspa*

EXHIBIT 4   GTECH corporation and subsidiaries—financial information

(Dollars in thousands, except share data)	February 28 1987	February 22 1986	February 23 1985	February 25 1984	February 26 1983
Results of Operations					
Revenues from:					
Sales of product	$ 70,334	$ 45,640	$26,550	$25,687	$17,490
Services	57,734	34,727	19,120	7,814	13,418
Gross Profit:					
Sales of products	30,878	16,956	12,787	13,347	8,461
Services	13,895	11,074	8,160	1,112	6,073
Net Income	7,687	1,973	4,310	2,579	5,410
Earnings Per Share	$0.81	$0.21	$0.47	$0.30	$0.73
Weighted Averaged Shares Outstanding	9,460,686	9,230,280	9,110,814	8,510,754	7,415,400
Year-End Data					
Working Capital	$ 13,502	$ 28,772	$13,866	$12,561	$ 2,631
Total Assets	171,719	126,500	86,461	54,733	19,724
Long-Term Debt[a]	72,062	63,183	32,255	10,110	4,624
Shareholders' Equity[b]	46,007	35,141	30,977	26,139	6,733

[a] Includes capital lease obligations less the current portion of debt outstanding
[b] No dividends have been declared or paid by the Company during any of the fiscal periods presented

announcing that they were coming to visit them to discuss on-line lottery systems. The chairman of *Islensk Getspa,* Thordur Thorkelsson, and the managing director, Vilhjalmur B. Vilhjalmsson, brought with them a copy of their recent lottery law (see Exhibit 5), which essentially indicated that *Islensk Getspa* was ready to operate its lotto. Thorkelsson and Vilhjalmsson were going to collect enough information from these on-line lottery systems manufacturers to properly identify the necessary requirements for inclusion in their request for proposals (RFP). The process of requesting and negotiating proposals normally takes at least one year. As indicated earlier, the RFP is the standard procedure, given the complexity and the cost involved with on-line systems. The *Islensk Getspa* was very concerned about the start-up costs, which it would be compelled to raise.

GTECH estimated that the weekly gross receipts for *Islensk Getspa* would be approximately $100,000.

Questions

1. Does GTECH have any other strategic options than to submit a proposal to *Islensk Getspa?*
2. Develop a plan for a market entry strategy.

May 2nd 1986

PUBLIC LAW
regarding Numbers Lotteries.
KEEPERS OF THE POWERS OF THE PRESIDENT OF ICELAND
acc. to Par 8 of the Constitution

The Prime Minister, The Speaker of the Althing
and The President of the Supreme Court,
make known: The Althing has passed this law and
we have ratified it with our consent.

Par. 1

The Minister of Justice is permitted to grant The Iceland Sports Federation (*Iþróttasamband Islands* or *ISI*), The Icelandic Youth Association (*Ungmennafélag Islands* or *UMFI*) and The Icelandic Federation of the Handicapped (*Ör-yrkjabandalag Islands* or *ÖBI*) a licence to operate together, in the name of a Company which the Organizations will form, a lottery that will be conducted thus that a series of numbers and/or letters is listed or selected on a special form of ticket.

This permission will be in force until the end of year 2005.

Par. 2

The Company which will operate the lottery according to Par. 1, shall be governed by a Board of five persons which shall be appointed for a single year at a time. The Iceland Sports Federation shall appoint two of these, The Icelandic Federation of the Handicapped two, and The Icelandic Youth Association one. Reserve members shall be appointed in the same manner. The Parties appoint a Chairman alternately, for two years at a time, according to their agreement, but otherwise the Board itself shall decide on its Officers.

The Parties shall otherwise make an agreement which shall be approved by the Minister of Justice about the Company's operations, among other things about its liabilities and division of profits.

Par. 3

The Minister of Justice, having received the recommendations of the Board, decides the charge for participation in the lottery (ticket price).

Par. 4

The Minister of Justice, having received the recommendations of the Board, decides the total of the prizes, either as a proportion of the total ticket sale at each time which shall be paid in prizes, or the amount of individual prizes.

The Lottery prizes shall be exempt from all official charges other than property tax for the year in which they are won.

Par. 5

The profits of the lottery operation shall be employed to promote amateur sports among member clubs of The Iceland Sports Federation and The Icelandic Youth Association and to pay the initial cost of apartments for handicapped people on behalf of The Iceland Federation of the Handicapped or to fund the Federation's other activities for the benefit of handicapped people.

(continued)

EXHIBIT 5

Par. 6

The Minister of Justice, having received the Board's recommendations, shall issue a Regulation with more precise specifications regarding the lottery operations and he shall, otherwise, supervise the operations.

Par. 7

Other than the aforementioned Company of The Iceland Sports Federation, The Icelandic Youth Association and The Iceland Federation of the Handicapped are not licenced to operate a lottery of the kind described in Par. 1.

The licence of The Icelandic Football Pools—Islenskar getraunir—to operate a numbers lottery acc. to Passage 2 of Par. 1 vis. Par. 10 of the law about football pools No. 59 of May 29th 1972 shall be cancelled while the licence according to this law is in effect.

Par. 8

Violation of this law shall be subject to fines.

Par. 9

This law shall take effect immediately.

<u>Done in Reykjavik, May 2nd 1986.</u>

Steingrímur Hermannsson   Þorvaldur Garoar Kristjánsson

Magnús P. Torfason

(L.S.)

This is a true and accurate
translation of the original
document submitted this day.

Seltjarnarnesi, Dec. 18th 1986.

HERSTEINN PALSSON
CHARTERED TRANSLATOR
& INTERPRETER

EXHIBIT 9–5   *(Continued)*

Source: GTECH Corporation *Annual Report;* GTECH Corporation 10-K Form; correspondence from *Islensk Getspa;* interviews with GTECH executives.

CASE 9–3
PERSONAL COMPUTER POWER, INC.

DIRK WASSENAAR
San Jose State University

Personal Computer Power, Inc. (PCP, Inc.) is a five-year-old high-tech company that designs and produces personal computers and personal computer software. The original product of the company was a very powerful general-purpose software package developed for the IBM PC. This product, called Magic 1, was comparable to the well-known Lotus 1-2-3 program. It was a big success when it was introduced in early 1987 and achieved first-year sales of $2.3 million. Sales for later years are shown in Exhibit 1.

During the testing of Magic 1, some of the founders of the company felt that the IBM PC was not the most suitable machine to run this software. More important, they felt that a much more powerful, faster personal computer could be developed that would be fully compatible with the IBM PC. Within a year, they had succeeded in designing and producing a prototype of such a computer, and late in 1989 this

EXHIBIT 1 PCP, Inc. Sales: 1987–1990

	Magic 1	New Era 90
1987	11,500 units	0
	$2.3 million	
1988	27,200 units	0
	$4.9 million	
1989	61,250 units	0
	$9.8 million	
1990	74,600 units	8,500 units
	$11.2 million	$24 million

new machine, called New Era 90, was introduced. Initial sales were somewhat disappointing. Although the product performed well and received excellent reviews, the company faced several problems; among them were the following:

1. The up-scale domestic PC market was in a slump during the latter part of the 1980s. Estimates showed that, in contrast to the high growth rates of earlier years, the U.S. sales of PCs were maturing.
2. Distribution for the product proved difficult to establish. Many stores, facing lower sales and earnings, were slashing inventories and were concentrating on well-known, established brands.

In view of the problems, it was not too surprising that initial computer sales for 1990 had failed to meet the forecast of 24,000 units. Actual sales for calendar year 1990 were approximately 8,500 units (see Exhibit 1).

Recently Alex Brown, the president of PCP, Inc. read an article about the personal computer market in Western Europe. The article mentioned that this market tended to lag the U.S. market by two to three years. It also stated that the long-range opportunities in this market were excellent, because the Common Market countries alone had a population in excess of that of the United States and a purchasing power comparable to the United States market. Some other facts Mr. Brown remembered from the article were that U.S. computer companies together have over 70 percent of the personal computer market in the EC and that U.S. companies are the perceived and actual technological leaders in the market.

During a recent seminar dealing with the importance of foreign markets for U.S. business, the speaker had also mentioned the attractiveness of the EC market. However, he stressed the rapid economic growth in many Pacific Basin countries and the already existing and very large Japanese market.

Because of the slow sales of the Magic 1 and the discouraging near-term outlook for the U.S. personal computer market, Mr. Brown decided to investigate the foreign computer markets more closely. He called his Marketing VP to ask for the name of a person who could do an initial market study.

Questions

Assume you were assigned to do the market study.

1. Identify the six most attractive foreign target markets for this company and rank them in order of importance.
2. Identify and comment on the unique problems/opportunities that this company may encounter in trying to market its personal computer and software in the target markets identified above.
3. What marketing strategy would you recommend to PCP, Inc. for possible entry into the (a) European market(s) and (b) the Japanese market?

Source: Dirk Wassenaar, San Jose State University. Copyright 1990. Adapted with permission.

NOTES

1. *U.S. News and World Report,* 22 June 1987.

2. *The State of World Population* (New York: Fund for Population Activities, United Nations, 1986).

3. *Investment in Indonesia* (Kantor Akuntan Sudjendro and Peat Marwick, 1985), 12.

4. Allan B. Yeates, "Americans, Canadians Similar But Vive La Difference," *Direct Marketing* (October 1985): 152 ff.

5. "Will It Take Recession to Close the Trade Gap?" *Business Week,* 8 December 1986, 24.

6. Alex O. Williams, *International Trade and Investment: A Managerial Approach* (New York: Wiley, 1982), 23.

7. Ibid., 108.

8. "America's Leading Exporters," *Fortune,* 20 July 1987, 72–73.

9. Robert G. Cooper and Elko J. Kleinschmidt, "The Impact of Export Strategy on Export Sales Performance," *Journal of International Business Studies* 16 (Spring 1985): 37–55.

10. Joseph M. Lightman, "Foreign Patent Protection: Treaties and National Laws," in *Foreign Business Practices* (Washington, D.C.: International Trade Administration, Department of Commerce, 1981), 45.

11. "Japan's Embarrassment of Riches in South Africa," *Business Week,* 1 February 1988, 44.

12. Farok J. Contractor, "The Role of Licensing in International Strategy," *Columbia Journal of World Business* 16 (Winter 1981): 73–83.

13. Farok J. Contractor, "Technology Licensing Practice in US Companies: Corporate and Public Policy Implications," *Columbia Journal of World Business* 18 (Fall 1983): 80–88.

14. For a useful licensing checklist, see *Foreign Investment and Licensing Checklist for U.S. Firms* (Washington, D.C.: International Trade Administration, Department of Commerce, 1983).

15. *Doing Business with China* (Washington, D.C.: International Trade Administration, Department of Commerce, 1983), 7.

16. Vincent D. Travaglini, "Foreign Licensing and Joint Venture Arrangements," in *Foreign Business Practices* (Washington, D.C.: International Trade Administration, Department of Commerce, 1981), 75–85.

17. Ibid., 78.

18. Shidan Derakhshani, "Negotiating Transfer of Technology Agreements," *Finance & Development* (December 1986): 42–44.

19. Vincent D. Travaglini, "Developing a Product as Licensee of Foreign Company," in *Foreign Business Practices* (Washington, D.C.: International Trade Administration, Department of Commerce, 1981), 91–97.

20. Kathryn R. Harrigan, "Joint Ventures and Global Strategies," *Columbia Journal of World Business* 19 (Summer 1984): 7–16.

21. Paul W. Beamish, "The Characteristics of Joint Ventures in Developed and Developing Countries," *Columbia Journal of World Business* 20 (Fall 1985): 13–19.

22. Franklin R. Root, *Foreign Market Entry Strategies* (New York: AMACOM, 1982).

23. Linda Longfellow Blodgett, "Partner Contributions as Predictors of Equity Share in International Joint Ventures," *Journal of International Business Studies* 22 (no. 1, 1991): 63–78.

24. Douglas Nigh, Peter Walters, and James A. Kuhlman, "US-USSR Joint Ventures: An Examination of the Early Entrants," *Columbia Journal of World Business* 25 (Winter 1990): 20–27.

25. Weijian Shan, "Environmental Risks and Joint Venture Sharing Arrangements," *Journal of International Business Studies* 22 (no. 4, 1991): 555–78.

26. David K. Eiteman, "American Executives' Perceptions of Negotiating Joint Ventures with the People's Republic of China: Lessons Learned," *Columbia Journal of World Business* 25 (Winter 1990): 59–67.

27. "NTT Gives Another Inch to the U.S.," *Business Week,* 24 January 1983, 42.

28. "Are Foreign Partners Good for U.S. Companies?" *Business Week,* 24 May 1984, 58–60.

29. Robert H. Brumley, "How Antitrust Law Affects International Joint Ventures," *Business America,* 21 November 1988, 3–4.

30. Robert B. Reich and Eric D. Mankin, "Joint Ventures with Japan Give away Our Future," *Harvard Business Review* 64 (March–April 1986): 78–86.

31. Seamus G. Connolly, "Joint Ventures with Third World Multinationals: A New Form of Entry to International Markets," *Columbia Journal of World Business* 19 (Summer 1984): 18–22.

32. Lawrence G. Franko, "Joint Venture Divorce in the Multinational Company," *Columbia Journal of World Business* 6 (May-June 1971): 13–22; J. Peter Killing, "How to Make a Global Joint Venture Work," *Harvard Business Review* (May-June 1982): 120–27.

33. John I. Reynolds, "The 'Pinched Shoe' Effect of International Joint Ventures," *Columbia Journal of World Business* 19 (Summer 1984): 23–29.

34. "Global Marketing Success Is Contingent on a Solid Bank of Foreign Market Intelligence," *Marketing News,* 23 December 1983, 1, 12.

35. "The $10 Billion Sweepstakes: How States Woo Foreign Investment," *Business Week,* 20 May 1985, 152, 156.

36. Paul M. Swamidass, "A Comparison of the Plant Location Strategies of Foreign and Domestic Manufacturers in the U.S.," *Journal of International Business Studies* 21 (no. 2, 1990): 301–17.

37. M. Krishna Erramilli, "The Experience Factor in Foreign Market Entry Behavior of Service Firms," *Journal of International Business Studies* 22 (no. 3, 1991): 479–501.

38. *Foreign Assembly of U.S. Components,* U.S. Customs Service, Department of the Treasury, Washington, D.C., 1990.

39. Tim Gilman, "Mexico's Maquiladora Program: An Option to Retain Competitiveness," *Business America,* 4 December 1989, 13.

40. Anthony J. F. O'Reilly, "Establishing Successful Joint Ventures in Developing Nations: A CEO's Perspective," *Columbia Journal of World Business* 23 (Spring 1988): 65–71.

41. Root, *Market Entry.*

42. *Investment in Germany* (Peat Marwick, 1983), 62–63.

43. *Investment in Japan* (Peat Marwick, 1983), 5.

44. "Bud Is Making a Splash in the Overseas Beer Market," *Business Week,* 22 October 1984: 52–53.

45. Douglas Nigh, "The Effect of Political Events on United States Direct Foreign Investment: A Pooled Time-Series Cross-Sectional Analysis," *Journal of International Business Studies* 16 (Spring 1985): 1–17.

46. Robert Gross, "The Andean Foreign Investment Code's Impact on Multinational Enterprises," *Journal of International Business Studies* 14 (Winter 1983): 121–31.

47. Robert D. Hisrich and Michael P. Peters, "East-West Trade: An Assessment by US Manufacturers," *Columbia Journal of World Business* 18 (Winter 1983): 44–50.

48. James D. Goodnow and James E. Hanz, "Environmental Determinants of Overseas Market Entry Strategies," *Journal of International Business Studies* 3 (Spring 1972): 33–50.

49. Contractor, "Technology Licensing Practice."

50. W. H. Davidson and D. G. McFetridge, "Key Characteristics in the Choice of International Technology Transfer Mode," *Journal of International Business Studies* 16 (Summer 1985): 5–21.

51. Leo Sleuwaegen, "Monopolistic Advantages and the International Operations of Firms: Disaggregated Evidence from U.S.-Based Multinationals," *Journal of International Business Studies* 16 (Fall 1985): 125–33.

52. Jiatao Li and Stephen Guisinger, "Comparative Business Failures of Foreign-Controlled Firms in the United States," *Journal of International Business Studies* 22 (no. 2, 1991): 209–24.

53. Sam C. Okoroafo, "Effects of Repatriations Risk on the Choice of Entry Modes Used by U.S. Manufacturing Firms in LDCs," *Journal of Global Marketing* 3 (no. 2, 1989): 25–41.

54. Benjamin Gomes-Casseres, "Firm Ownership Preferences and Host Government Restrictions: An Integrated Approach," *Journal of International Business Studies* 20 (no. 1, 1990): 1–22.

55. "Free Trade Zoning Mushrooms, Gives Boost to Global Economy," *Chicago Tribune,* 26 February 1984.

56. John J. Da Ponte, Jr., "Updated Rules for Foreign-Trade Zones Reflect Big Increase in Zone Activity," *Business America,* 4 November 1991, 9–13.

57. William R. McDaniel and Edgar W. Kossack, "The Financial Benefits to Users of Foreign-Trade Zones," *Columbia Journal of World Business* 18 (Fall 1983): 33–41; See also *Importing into the United States* (Washington, D.C.: U.S. Customs Service, Department of the Treasury, 1985), 79–80.

58. Pat J. Calabro, "Foreign Trade Zones—A Sleeping Giant in Distribution," *Journal of Business Logistics* 4 (March 1983): 51–64.

PART FOUR
INTERNATIONAL MARKETING DECISIONS

□ **PART OUTLINE**

Because of the level of reliability and confidence consumers have in a certain [brand] name, they would expect to pay more within reason.

Allen Vangelos, vice-president, Marketing/Customer Relations,
Castle & Cooke's Fresh Foods Division

Product Strategies
Basic Decisions and Product Planning

10

CHAPTER OUTLINE

MARKETING ILLUSTRATION
East is East and West is West

Harris Ranch, attempting to please its Japanese customers, feeds the cattle barley instead of the customary corn. According to the Japanese, barley produces a whiter fat in the marbling and makes the meat taste better.

A U.S.-built refrigerator designed for a kitchen well-removed from American bedrooms is a disturbance in Japan when in the middle of the night it turns itself on a few feet away from its Japanese owners' sleeping mats. Sony, the distributor, spent five years asking its American supplier for a model with a quieter, vibration-free cooling fan and a motor that could run on Japan's 110-volt electricity.

Penthouse and its Hungarian partners introduced *Penthouse* as the first Western men's magazine in Eastern Europe. *Penthouse* planned to emphasized locally generated stories and investigative reporting, while toning down its nude photography so as not to be too shocking.

When Apple Computer Inc. was designing its PowerBook notebook computer, the firm's studies found that consumers associated darker colors with richness and value. Although black at first appeared to be appropriate as the choice of color for the case, Apple instead decided to go with dark gray. A black computer does not meet Europe's contrast and reflectivity standards.

Sources: "California's Classy Crop Cornucopia," *Fortune*, 6 June 1988, 91; "He's Ga-Ga about His Baby—and He's Not Alone," *Business Week*, 11 November 1991, 142, 144.

Just because a product is successful in one country, there is no guarantee that it will be successful in other markets. A marketer must always determine local needs and tastes and take them into account. Some products have universal appeal, and little or no change is necessary when these products are placed in various markets. But for every so-called universal product, there are many others that have a narrower appeal. For products in this category, modification is necessary in order to achieve acceptance in the marketplace. It is generally easier to modify a product than to modify consumer preference. That is, a marketer should change the product to fit the need of the consumer rather than try to adjust consumers' needs to fit product characteristics. An awareness of application of this marketing concept in an international setting would provide definite advantages to an international merchant. Although the principle has been universally accepted in domestic marketing, it has often been ignored in international marketing.

The purpose of this chapter is to study *product* in an international context. The discussion focuses on the meaning of product and the necessities of market segmentation and product positioning. Other topics include product development and services. There is also a critical look at the controversial issue of product standardization versus product adaptation, as well as the theory of international product life cycle and that theory's marketing implications.

WHAT IS A PRODUCT?

A **product** is often considered in a narrow sense as something tangible that can be described in terms of physical attributes, such as shape, dimension, components, form, color, and so on. This is a misconception that has been extended to international marketing as well, because many people believe that only tangible products can be exported. A student of marketing, however, should realize that this definition of product is misleading since many products are intangible (e.g., services). Actually, intangible products are a significant part of the American export market. For example, American movies are distributed worldwide, as are engineering services and business-consulting services. In the financial market, Japanese and European banks have been internationally active in providing financial assistance, often at handsome profits. Even when tangible products are involved, insurance services and shipping are needed to move the products into their markets.

In many situations, both tangible and intangible products must be combined to create a single, total product. This is clearly illustrated by the Klockner group of Germany, which packages turnkey projects in the United States and exports them to Latin American and Third World countries. The tangible aspect of this product is the heavy input of U.S. equipment, which is well regarded and thus utilized on projects in Latin America. The intangible aspect of the package is the management expertise provided by Klockner.

Perhaps the best way to define a product is to describe it as *a bundle of utilities or satisfaction*. Warranty terms, for example, are a part of this bundle, and they can be adjusted as appropriate (i.e., superior versus inferior warranty terms). Purchasers of Mercedes-Benz cars expect to acquire more than just the cars themselves. In hot and humid countries, there is no reason for a heater to be part of the automobile's product bundle. In the United States, it is customary for automatic transmission to be bundled with other standard automobile equipment.

One marketing implication that can be drawn is that a multinational marketer must look at a product as a total, complete offering. Consider the Beretta shotgun. The shotgun itself is undoubtedly a fine product, quite capable of superbly performing its primary function (i.e., firing shotgun ammunition). But Beretta also has a secondary function in Japan, where the Beretta brand is perceived as a superior status symbol. Not surprisingly, a Beretta can command $8,000 for a shotgun, exclusive of the additional amount of a few thousand dollars for engraving. In this case, Beretta's secondary function conceivably overshadows its primary objective. Therefore, a complete product should be viewed as a satisfaction derived from the 4 Ps of marketing (product, place, promotion, and pricing)—and not simply from the physical product characteristics. Exhibit 10–1 shows Japan Air Lines's bundle of utilities.

NEW PRODUCT DEVELOPMENT

There are six distinct steps in new product development. The *first step* is the *generation of new product ideas*. Such ideas can come from any number of sources (e.g., salespersons, employees, competitors, governments, marketing research firms, customers, etc.). A 3M company chemist, after spilling some liquid on her tennis

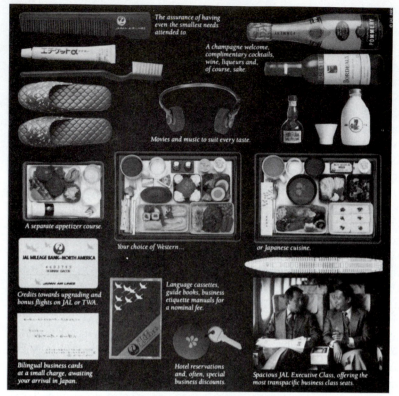

The special considerations of JAL Executive Class.

Preflight, inflight, postflight, no other airline
shows more consideration to business travellers.
Find out how we can make your next business
trip to the Orient a more profitable experience.
Call (800) 835-2246, Ext. 145 in the Continental
U.S. for your free "JAL Executive Service" guide.

JAPAN AIR LINES

Consideration. With us, it's a tradition.

EXHIBIT 10–1   Japan Air Lines's bundle of satisfaction

Source: Reprinted with permission of Japan Air Lines.

shoes, found that they had become capable of repelling water and dirt, and that is
how Scotchgard fabric protector was born. In another example, Toru Iwatami was
daydreaming at his desk one day just before lunch. His hunger led him to visualize
little round shapes devouring smaller ones—Pac Man—and the rest is history.[1]

The *second step* involves the *screening of ideas*. Ideas must be acknowledged
and reviewed to determine their feasibility. To determine suitability, a new product

concept may simply be presented to potential users, or an advertisement based on the product can be drawn and shown to focus groups to elicit candid reactions. As a rule, corporations usually have predetermined goals that a new product must meet. Kao Corporation, a major Japanese manufacturer of consumer goods, is guided by the following five principles of product development: (1) a new product should be truly useful to society, not only now but also in the future, (2) it should make use of Kao's own creative technology or skill, (3) it should be superior to the new products of competitors, both from the standpoint of cost and performance, (4) it should be able to stand exhaustive product tests at all stages before it is commercialized, and (5) it should be capable of delivering its own message at every level of distribution.[2]

The *third step* is *business analysis,* which is necessary to estimate product features, cost, demand, and profit. Xerox has small so-called product synthesis teams to test and weed out unsuitable ideas. Several competing teams of designers produce a prototype, and the winning model that meets preset goals then goes to the "product development" team.

The *fourth step* is *product development,* which involves lab and technical tests as well as manufacturing pilot models in small quantities. At this stage, the product is likely to be handmade or produced by existing machineries rather than by any new specialized equipment. U.S. firms are often far removed from the market because of a tendency to use outside marketing research firms to conduct consumer surveys, unlike Japanese employees, who visit customers at home to identify product problems. Ideally, engineers should receive direct feedback from customers and dealers.

The *fifth step* involves *test marketing* to determine potential marketing problems and the optimal marketing mix. Anheuser Busch pulled Budweiser out of West Germany after a six-month Berlin market test in 1981. Its Busch brand was another disappointment in France, where this type of beer did not yet correspond to French tastes.

Finally, assuming that things go well, the company is ready for *full-scale commercialization* by actually going through with full-scale production and marketing.

The first three steps can be combined and called the *homework phase.* This phase has received relatively less attention than the development and commercialization steps. Many companies have begun to realize that they must pay more attention to the homework phase, as evidenced by a 10–20 percent increase during a ten-year period in the cost of bringing out a new product.[3] The spending on the development phase remained constant during that same period, but spending declined from 60 percent to 40 percent for the commercialization stage. The shift in expenditure percentage reflects the desire to identify winners early (i.e., in the homework stage) rather than wasting money later on poor performers in the commercialization phase. The goal of many companies is to end up with an equal split among the three stages.

Production methods vary even among industrialized nations. In the United States, the tradition of individualism results in the common concept of involvement of rank-and-file workers in shop-floor decision making.[4] In Germany, the emphasis is on *ergonomics*—the biotechnological approach to increased efficiency by designing workplace to reduce physical and mental stress. Since dissatisfaction increases when cycle time for a task is less than 1.5 minutes, there is a concerted effort to lengthen the work cycle by enlarging typical assembly jobs (i.e., adding more complex tasks). Siemens' employees, in assembling electronics products, used to perform repetitive, simple tasks that lasted less than a minute as each unit passed on a belt conveyor. Now, the company's workers learn several jobs and work in a group at a well-designed work island. Boredom is thus avoided because workers can rotate jobs, socialize, work in longer cycles, and adapt quickly to product changes. GM's new plants seem to be based on the same principle. The assembly line has been replaced with hundreds of motorized, unmanned carriers (automated guided vehicles) to carry a car through the assembly process, and groups of workers can perform logical blocks of work instead of simplistic, repetitive tasks. These carriers should increase flexibility and allow different car models to be made at the same plant. Japan, however, shows little concern with ergonomics or work teams. The Japanese workplace is heavily engineered, and 24-second cycles are common. The only conclusion that can be made, then, is that work humanization has taken divergent approaches in different cultures.

MARKET SEGMENTATION

Market segmentation is a concept to which American marketers and academics like to pay a great deal of attention. All conceivable possibilities for segmenting the U.S. market have been thoroughly studied. Yet on the international scale, American marketers are prone to treat market segmentation as an unknown and unfamiliar concept, and they apparently leave their knowledge about market segmentation at home when they go abroad. More often than not, there is hardly any serious or conscious attempt by American businessmen to segment a foreign market. This phenomenon probably derives from an assumption that by going abroad geographic segmentation has been implemented. But geographic segmentation, an obvious choice, is often overemphasized and is usually inappropriate. Marketers fail to realize that the purpose of segmentation is to satisfy consumer needs more precisely—not to segment the market just for the sake of the segmentation.

Another mistake American businessmen make in foreign countries is attempting to capture the total market at once. The resulting disappointment in market performance demonstrates that two major problems have been overlooked. First, consumers in a foreign country are unlikely to be homogeneous. Usually, marketers must distinguish urban consumers from rural consumers. Even in largely homogeneous Japan, American Express found it necessary to segment Japanese consumers. It introduced the luxury gold yen card for the affluent segment and the green card for the middle-income segment.

Second, a "total market" strategy places the company in head-to-head competition with strong, local competitors. The success of Japanese products in the United States and in many other countries can be explained in part by the explicit and conscientious attempt by the Japanese to segment the market. Japanese firms usually pick their targets carefully, avoiding head-to-head competition with major U.S. manufacturers in mature industries. Starting at the low end of the product spectrum, a Japanese firm establishes a reputation for product excellence, and eventually gets customers to trade up over time. This strategy has worked exceedingly well in the automobile and consumer-electronics industries. Japanese computer makers have used the same market strategy in breaking into the U.S. computer market. Japanese firms market commodity products such as personal computers, disc drives, printers, and other peripherals before attempting to trade up with their customers to the larger systems, which have the highest profit margins. This strategy makes a great deal of strategic sense because the marketer does not arouse the U.S. giants early in the game. U.S. toolmakers' strategic mistake was their emphasis on large machines for big users, while leaving room at the low end for entry to foreign competitors with product lines at the $150,000 price level.

The most important reason behind the utilization of market segmentation is market homogeneity/heterogeneity. Based on the national boundary, homogeneity can be vertical (i.e., homogeneous within the same country) or horizontal (i.e., homogeneous across countries). Therefore, two countries exhibiting the lack of vertical homogeneity within their borders, may still be homogeneous horizontally when a particular segment of one country is similar to an equivalent segment of another country.[5] This is what Hassan and Katsanis call global market segment, and they derive it through "the process of identifying specific segments, whether they be country groups or individual consumer groups, of potential consumers with homogeneous attributes who are likely to exhibit similar buying behavior." They feel that the global elite and global teenager segments are particularly amenable to global segmentation.[6]

The value of market segmentation has been empirically demonstrated by a study of the export strategies of high-tech electronics firms. During one three-year period, firms electing a world marketer strategy (i.e., practicing both product adaptation and segmentation for the world market) realized a 130 percent annual export growth compared to only 26 percent for those adopting the selling orientation (i.e., no product adaptation nor segmentation).[7]

Nevertheless, market segmentation is not always necessary or desirable. This is especially true when either consumer needs within a country are largely homogeneous or a mass market exists. Kikkoman, in entering the U.S. market, understood that its target could not be restricted only to Japanese-Americans.[8] Noticing that U.S. occupation troops in Japan sprinkled soy sauce on everything from hamburgers to pork chops, Kikkoman made an intelligent decision in defining its market as the entire U.S. population. After studying the U.S. market repeatedly, it then set out to educate American consumers about the versatility of soy sauce and how American the product could be.

PRODUCT POSITIONING

Product positioning is a marketing strategy that attempts to occupy an appealing space in a consumer's mind in relation to the spaces occupied by other competitive products. The mind is like a computer in that it has slots or positions, and each bit of information is placed and retained in the proper slot. The mind screens and accepts information according to prior experience.

The target market of Polaroid's One-Film is that of amateurs in the United States who are overwhelmed by choices. Polaroid, however, decided not to sell One-Film in Europe, because European consumers are sophisticated enough to know that One-Film is essentially a conventional, moderately fast (ASA 200) film that is positioned in the market as a versatile film for different light situations.

Much like market segmentation, product positioning is frequently ignored by American marketers in selling abroad. In the international marketplace, there appears to be no serious effort to position products in any meaningful way. When American products occupy attractive positions at all, it is usually by chance and not by design. Foreign firms generally seem to understand the concept of international product positioning better than their American competitors. For example, the success of Perrier, the French sparkling mineral water, has largely been the result of positioning the product as a chic beverage with a snob appeal. In automobiles, Mercedes-Benz is for the wealthy, and BMW tries to maintain a uniform international image by appealing to the racy.

A marketer determines the perceived position of a product as well as the ideal position in a number of ways. One way is to use focus groups to explore possible alternatives. Another positioning method is to rely on perceptual and preference mapping. Respondents compare brands based on perceived similarity and in relation to their ideal brands. The statistical technique of multidimensional scaling (MDS) can then be used to determine the number and type of dimensions and to transform similarities into distances. Attributes can later be examined to see how each attribute is associated, more or less, with a particular brand. Exhibit 10–2 shows a perceptual map of various brands of automobiles.

Philip Morris, by constructing a two-dimensional map based on brand image, was able to learn a great deal about Brazilian smokers' perception both of its brands and its competitors' brands.[9] The firm discovered that British Tobacco had a virtual monopoly, with four brands strategically positioned in four middle-price categories. The Arizona brand was the cheapest and employed Marlboro's appeal to preempt Marlboro. The big brands of Continental, Hollywood, and Minister were in the upper-right quadrant. Philip Morris's Galaxy was in an unlikely position at the bottom of the vertical axis. After successfully adjusting the marketing mix, a new map revealed that Galaxy had moved closer to the mainstream brands considered respectable, upper-class, and attractive.

How a product is positioned may be determined by local regulations. This is the problem experienced by Pfizer in marketing Mecadox, a feed supplement-plus-antibiotic for hogs, in Europe. The product was approved only as a feed supplement in certain countries, as an antibiotic in others, and as both in some markets.[10]

A product must be positioned carefully. Mazda erred in its initial attempt to sell its rotary-engine automobile as an economy car, when in fact it is a performance car. A company may possibly use dual and even triple positioning. Beecham has positioned Aqua Fresh as (1) toothpaste, (2) breath freshener, and (3) plaque remover.

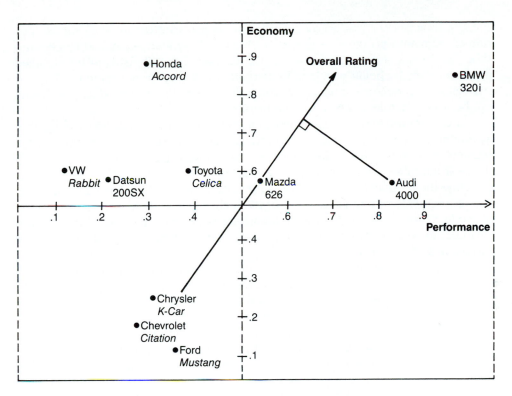

EXHIBIT 10–2 Automobile space map with preference vector (United States)

Source: Johny K. Johansson and Hans B. Thorelli, "International Product Positioning," *Journal of International Business Studies* 16 (Fall 1985): 59.

When a product has been incorrectly positioned or the original position loses its appeal, a firm should reposition the product. Beecham has been successful in repositioning several of its mature brands. Its Ribena brand, a black-currant juice sold to children for a half-century, experienced an impressive increase in sales after single-portion packs and new flavors were added to attract adult drinkers and toddlers. Canada Dry has repositioned its club soda as a stand-alone drink, a departure from its original position as a mixer. Arthur C. Bell, a British firm, was able to turn its Blended Scotch Whiskey into the best-selling Scotch in Britain by convincing drinkers that Scotch could be used with mixers.[11] Bell's campaign worked so well that it increased the number of British women Scotch drinkers to 40 percent of the total. Later, the company turned its attention to the U.S. Scotch market, which was hurt by "clear" spirits. Its appeal to women, younger people, and other non-Scotch drinkers was that Scotch should be taken "not neat but sweet."

When a market is segmented and a marketer decides to be in more than one segment, the product frequently, but not always, must be physically modified for each segment. Nike, once it had ascertained that its high-performance end of the U.S.

running-shoe market was no longer growing, began to diversify from the serious runner segment into other segments, such as children's shoes, nonathletic-leisure shoes, and work shoes. In other cases, the product may only have to be modified psychologically by being positioned differently for the different segments. The two strategies are at once complementary and independent, because product positioning can be used regardless of whether the market is segmented or not.

In theory and in practice, segmentation and positioning should be used together to reinforce each other. A particular product may be needed in a selected market segment, but such a match does not necessarily mean that different products with different attributes are always needed for different segments. The best approach is to define the product broadly enough so that its image can be adjusted to suit each market segment, without necessity of physical change. This is where the application of product positioning can be used to advantage, because positioning allows physical attributes to be kept constant while formulating different psychological attributes for various market segments.

Renault, for example, does not use the same product-position strategy in all countries. In France, it uses a small supercar image, a car that is fun to drive. In some European countries, the common perception is that an automobile purchase is a serious matter, and this necessitates a different product position. As a result, Renault emphasizes safety, modern engineering, and interior comfort in Germany. In Finland, Renault focuses on solid construction and reliability, whereas in Holland Renault is known for a small, high-quality, expensive automobile.[12] In another case, Volvo has the reputation of economy, durability, and safety both in Sweden and the United States, as indicated by Exhibit 10–3. More recently, Volvo has wanted the American public to view its product as an import with the comfort of a U.S. car. Some marketers view Volvo admiringly as a "strategic chameleon."

Although positioning varies from country to country and from product to product, international marketers should bear in mind that a "high quality" or "snob" position is generally appropriate in developing countries. Michelin's high-quality image has made it possible for Michelin radial tires to command a premium price in many international markets.

In general, products should not initially be positioned as low-cost or low-quality products because foreign-made goods are usually perceived as being products of quality and prestige. If products are positioned incorrectly, consumers have no incentive to buy the foreign-made goods, and potential purchasers will buy locally made products instead.

Another factor many American marketers overlook is that consumers in most countries pay a great deal more than their American counterparts for gasoline and electricity. Thus, convenience or bigness becomes secondary when compared with operational efficiency and economy. A marketer is unwise to emphasize how large and spacious an automobile is when foreign consumers are looking for durability and fuel economy. It makes no sense to boast about how roomy a refrigerator's freezer compartment is when consumers routinely shop every day or complain about their electricity bills. In the final analysis, consumer needs must determine how products

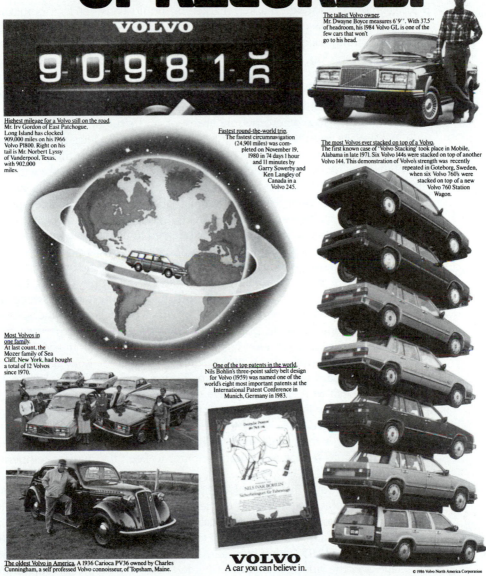

THE VOLVO BOOK OF RECORDS.

The tallest Volvo owner. Mr. Dwayne Boyce measures 6'9''. With 37.5'' of headroom, his 1984 Volvo GL is one of the few cars that won't go to his head.

Highest mileage for a Volvo still on the road. Mr. Irv Gordon of East Patchogue, Long Island has clocked 909,000 miles on his 1966 Volvo P1800. Right on his tail is Mr. Norbert Lyssy of Vanderpool, Texas, with 902,000 miles.

Fastest round-the-world trip. The fastest circumnavigation (24,901 miles) was completed on November 19, 1980 in 74 days 1 hour and 11 minutes by Garry Sowerby and Ken Langley of Canada in a Volvo 245.

The most Volvos ever stacked on top of a Volvo. The first known case of 'Volvo Stacking' took place in Mobile, Alabama in late 1971. Six Volvo 144s were stacked on top of another Volvo 144. This demonstration of Volvo's strength was recently repeated in Goteborg, Sweden, when six Volvo 760's were stacked on top of a new Volvo 760 Station Wagon.

Most Volvos in one family. At last count, the Mozer family of Sea Cliff, New York, had bought a total of 12 Volvos since 1970.

One of the top patents in the world. Nils Bohlin's three-point safety belt design for Volvo (1959) was named one of the world's eight most important patents at the International Patent Conference in Munich, Germany in 1983.

The oldest Volvo in America. A 1936 Carioca PV36 owned by Charles Cunningham, a self professed Volvo connoisseur, of Topsham, Maine.

VOLVO
A car you can believe in.

© 1986 Volvo North America Corporation

EXHIBIT 10–3 Volvo's product positioning

Source: Reprinted with permission of Volvo North America Corporation.

are to be positioned. Kellogg's, once discovering that its Rice Krispies are consumed in large quantities as snacks in Mexico, changed its promotional message to reflect that consumer need.

PRODUCT ADOPTION

In breaking into a foreign market, marketers should consider factors that influence *product adoption.* As explained by diffusion theory, at least six factors have a bearing on the adoption process: relative advantage, compatibility, trialability/divisibility, observability, complexity, and price. These factors are all perceptual and thus subjective in nature.

For a product to gain acceptance, it must demonstrate its *relative advantage* over existing alternatives. Products emphasizing cleanliness and sanitation may be unimportant in places where people are poor and struggle to get by one day at a time. Wool coats are not needed in a hot country, and products reducing static cling (e.g., Cling Free) are useless in a humid country. A sunscreen film attached to auto windshields to block out sunlight may be a necessity in countries with a tropical climate, but it has no such advantage in cold countries. Dishwashing machines do not market well in countries where manual labor is readily available and inexpensive. A study of eighty-two Canadian industrial goods firms found that, in judging a new product's export potential, what they referred to as "relative improvement" (i.e., relative advantage) had a potent, positive influence on foreign performance.[13]

A product must also be *compatible* with local customs and habits. A freezer would not find a ready market in Asia, where people prefer fresh food. In Asia and such European countries as France and Italy, people like to sweep and mop floors daily, and thus there is no market for carpet or vacuum cleaners. Deodorants are deemed inappropriate in places where it is the custom for men to show their masculinity by having body odor. Dryers are unnecessary in countries where people prefer to hang their clothes outside for sunshine freshness. Kellogg's had difficulties selling Pop Tarts in Europe because many homes have no toaster. Unlike American women, European women do not shave their legs, and thus have no need for razors for that purpose. The Japanese, not liking to have their lifestyles altered by technology, have skillfully applied technology to their traditional lifestyle. The electrical *kotatsu* (foot warmer) is a traditional form of heater in Japan. New kotatsu are equipped with a temperature sensor and microcomputer to keep the interior temperature at a comfortable level.[14]

If a new product has several competing and incompatible systems, such systems will serve only to confuse consumers. Videodisc is a good example. RCA used the stylus-in-groove approach to read data electronically; Pioneer relied on the contactless, optical system of using a laser to read picture and sound information; and JVC employed the VHD (video high-density) system. Given the lack of any perceived advantage over the video cassette recorder and saddled with the incompatibility problem, the videodisc ended up a flop.

A new product has an advantage if it is capable of being divided and tested in small trial quantities to determine its suitability and benefits. This is a product's *trialability/divisibility* factor. Disposable diapers and blue jeans lend themselves to trialability rather well. Nondairy coffee creamer, likewise, has not found great resistance in replacing sweetened condensed milk in many countries. But when a product is large, bulky, and expensive, consumers are much more apprehensive about making a purchase. Thus, washers, dryers, refrigerators, and automobiles are products that do not lend themselves well to trialability/divisibility. This factor explains one reason why foreign consumers do not easily purchase American automobiles, knowing that a mistake could ruin them financially. Many foreign consumers therefore prefer to purchase more familiar products, such as Japanese automobiles, that are less expensive and easier to service and whose parts are easier to replace.

Observation of a product in public tends to encourage social acceptance and reinforcement, resulting in the product's being adopted more rapidly and with less resistance. If a product is used privately, other consumers cannot see it, and there is no prestige generated by its possession. Blue jeans, quartz watches, and automobiles are used publicly and are highly observable products. Japanese men flip their ties so that the labels show. Refrigerators, on the other hand, are privately consumed products, though owners of refrigerators in the Middle East and Asia may attempt to enhance observability (and thus the prestige) by placing the refrigerator in the living room, where guests can easily see it. In any case, a distinctive and easily recognized logo is very useful.

Complexity of a product or difficulty in understanding a product's qualities tends to slow its market acceptance. Perhaps that factor explains why ground coffee has had a difficult time in making headway to replace instant coffee in many countries. Likewise, 3M tried unsuccessfully in foreign markets to replace positive-acting printing plates with presensitized negative subtractive printing plates, which are very popular in the United States. It failed to convert foreign printers because the sales and technical service costs of changing printers' beliefs were far too expensive. Computers are also complex but have been gradually gaining more and more acceptance, perhaps in large part because manufacturers have made the machines simpler to operate. Ready-made software can also alleviate the necessity of learning computer languages, a time-consuming process.

The first four variables are positively related to the adoption process. Like complexity, *price* is negatively related to product adoption. Before 1982, copiers were too big and expensive. Canon then introduced personal copiers with cartridges that customers could change. Its low price (less than $1,000) was so attractive to consumers (but not to competitors) that Canon easily dominated the market.

THEORY OF INTERNATIONAL PRODUCT LIFE CYCLE

Product life cycle is a well-known theory in marketing. But its international counterpart, **international produce life cycle (IPLC),** is relatively unknown. The theory, developed and verified by economists to explain international trade in a context of comparative advantage, has been covered rather briefly in some international economics and international marketing texts and in a few marketing articles.[15]

The IPLC theory describes the diffusion process of an innovation across national boundaries. The life cycle begins when a developed country, having a new product to satisfy consumer needs, wants to exploit its technological breakthrough by selling abroad. Other advanced nations soon start up their own production facilities, and before long LDCs do the same. Efficiency/comparative advantage shifts from developed countries to developing nations. Finally, advanced nations, no longer cost-effective, import products from their former customers. The moral of this process could be that an advanced nation becomes a victim of its own creation.

One reason that IPLC theory has not made a significant impact is that its marketing implications are somewhat obscure, even though it has the potential to be a valuable framework for marketing planning on a multinational basis. In this section, the IPLC is examined from the marketing perspective, and marketing implications for both innovators and imitators are discussed.[16]

Stages and Characteristics

There are five distinct stages (Stage 0 through Stage 4) in the IPLC. Table 10–1 shows the major characteristics of the IPLC stages, with the United States as the developer of the innovation in question. Exhibit 10–4 shows three life-cycle curves for the same innovation: one for the initiating country (i.e., the United States in this instance), one for other advanced nations, and one for LDCs. For each curve, net export results when the curve is above the horizontal line; if under the horizontal line, net import results for that particular country. As the innovation moves through time, directions of all three curves change. Time is relative, because the time needed for a cycle to be completed varies from one kind of product to another. In addition, the time interval also varies from one stage to the next.

TABLE 10–1   IPLC stages and characteristics (for the initiating country)

Stage	Import/Export	Target Market	Competitors	Production Costs
(0) local innovation	none	USA	few: local firms	initially high
(1) overseas innovation	increasing export	USA & advanced nations	few: local firms	decline owing to economies of scale
(2) maturity	stable export	advanced nations & LDCs	advanced nations	stable
(3) worldwide imitation	declining export	LDCs	advanced nations	increase owing to lower economies of scale
(4) reversal	increasing import	USA	advanced nations & LDCs	increase owing to comparative disadvantage

Source: Sak Onkvisit and John J. Shaw, "An Examination of the International Product Life Cycle and Its Applications within Marketing," *Columbia Journal of World Business* 18 (Fall 1983): 74.

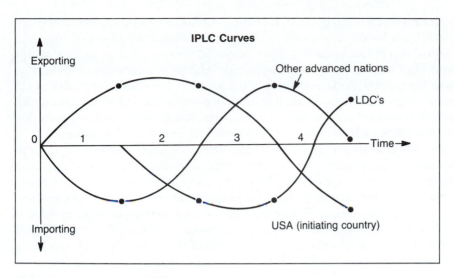

EXHIBIT 10–4   IPLC curves

Source: Sak Onkvisit and John J. Shaw, "An Examination of the International Product Life Cycle and Its Application within Marketing," *Columbia Journal of World Business* 18 (Fall 1983): 74.

Stage 0—Local Innovation   Stage 0, depicted as time 0 on the left of the vertical importing/exporting axis, represents a regular and highly familiar product life cycle in operation within its original market. Innovations are most likely to occur in highly developed countries because consumers in such countries are affluent and have relatively unlimited wants. From the supply side, firms in advanced nations have both the technological know-how and abundant capital to develop new products. Developed countries, in addition to being the original place where innovations take place, in all likelihood will be the place where such new products are first introduced to the public. Introduction occurs there because marketers are familiar with local desires and market conditions, making them believe that the risks in introducing a new product at home, rather than somewhere else, are smaller. Furthermore, it is common for a new product to have technical problems even after market introduction and acceptance, perhaps necessitating significant modifications. Products sold overseas may have to be adjusted to be suitable for their intended markets. All of these considerations together may be too complicated for innovating firms to deal with at the beginning. Thus, it is easier and more logical for a firm to concentrate its efforts in its home market before looking to overseas markets.

Many of the products found in the world's markets were originally created in the United States before being introduced and refined in other countries. In most instances, regardless of whether a product is intended for later export or not, an innovation is initially designed with an eye to capture the U.S. market, the largest consumer nation.

Stage 1—Overseas Innovation   As soon as the new product is well developed, its original market well cultivated, and local demands adequately supplied, the innovating firm will look to overseas markets in order to expand its sales and profit. Thus, this stage is known as a "pioneering" or "international introduction" stage. The technological gap is first noticed in other advanced nations because of their similar needs and high income levels. Not surprisingly, English-speaking countries such as the United Kingdom, Canada, and Australia account for about half of the sales of U.S. innovations when such products are first introduced overseas. Countries with similar cultures and economic conditions are often perceived by exporters as posing less risk and thus are approached first before proceeding to less familiar territories.

Competition in this stage usually comes from U.S. firms, since firms in other countries may not have much knowledge about the innovation. Production cost tends to be decreasing at this stage because by this time the innovating firm will normally have improved the production process. Supported by overseas sales, aggregate production costs tend to decline further because of increased economies of scale. A low introductory price overseas is usually not necessary because of the technological breakthrough; a low price is not desirable because of the heavy and costly marketing effort needed in order to educate consumers in other countries about the new product. In any case, as the product penetrates the market during this stage, there will be more exports from the United States and, correspondingly, an increase in imports by other developed countries.

Stage 2—Maturity   Growing demand in advanced nations provides an impetus for firms there to commit themselves to starting local production, often with the help of their governments' protective measures to preserve infant industries. Thus, these firms can survive and thrive in spite of relative inefficiency. This process may explain the changing national concentrations of high-technology exports and the loss of the U.S. share to Japan, France, and perhaps the United Kingdom.[17]

Development of competition does not mean that the initiating country's export level will immediately suffer. The innovating firm's sales and export volumes are kept stable because LDCs are now beginning to generate a need for the product. Introduction of the product in LDCs helps offset any reduction in export sales to advanced countries.

Stage 3—Worldwide Imitation   This stage means tough times for the innovating nation because of its continuous decline in exports. There is no more new demand anywhere to cultivate. The decline will inevitably affect the U.S. innovating firm's economies of scale, and its production costs thus begin to rise again. Consequently, firms in other advanced nations use their lower prices (coupled with product-differentiation techniques) to gain more consumer acceptance abroad at the expense of the U.S. firm. As the product becomes more and more widely disseminated, imitation picks up at a faster pace. Toward the end of this stage, U.S. export dwindles almost to nothing, and any U.S. production still remaining is basically for local consumption. The U.S. automobile industry is a good example of this phenomenon. There are about thirty different companies selling cars in the United States, with several on the rise. Of these, only four are U.S. firms, with the rest being from Western Europe, Japan, South Korea, Taiwan, Mexico, Brazil, and Malaysia.

Stage 4—Reversal   Not only must all good things end, but misfortune frequently accompanies the end of a favorable situation. The major functional characteristics of this stage are *product standardization* and *comparative disadvantage*. The innovating country's comparative advantage has disappeared, and what is left is comparative disadvantage. This disadvantage is brought about because the product is no longer capital-intensive or technology-intensive but instead has become labor-intensive—a strong advantage possessed by LDCs. Thus, LDCs—the last imitators—establish sufficient productive facilities to satisfy their own domestic needs as well as to produce for the biggest market in the world, the United States. U.S. firms are now undersold in their own country. Black-and-white television sets, for example, are no longer manufactured in the United States because many Asian firms can produce them much less expensively than any U.S. firm. Consumers' price sensitivity exacerbates the problem for the initiating country.

Validity of the IPLC

Several products have conformed to the characteristics described by the IPLC. The production of semiconductors started in the United States before diffusing to the United Kingdom, France, West Germany, and Japan. Production facilities are now set up in Hong Kong and Taiwan, as well as in other Asian countries. Similarly, at one time the United States used to be an exporter of typewriters, adding machines, and cash registers. But with the passage of time, these simple machines (e.g., manual typewriters) are now being imported, while U.S. firms export only the sophisticated, electronic versions of such machines. Other products that have gone through a complete international life cycle are synthetic fibers, petrochemicals, leather goods, rubber products, and paper.[18] The electronics sector, a positive contributor to the trade balance of the United States for a long time, turned negative for the first time ever in 1984 with a massive $6.8 billion deficit. A deficit also occurred at the same time for communications equipment, following the trend set by semiconductors in 1982. Exhibit 10–5 shows foreign penetration of U.S. markets.

The IPLC theory has been shown to have some explanatory relevance for the United States, Japan, and the United Kingdom but less so for the former West Germany.[19] As the theory predicts, nonstandardized products with growth potential usually experience an increase in export volume, whereas mature, standardized products tend to face import competition. The IPLC may not be applicable for all kinds of products—empirical evidence shows that commodities occasionally fail to behave in the predicted manner.[20]

The IPLC is probably more applicable for products related through an emerging technology. These newly emerging products are likely to provide functional utility rather than aesthetic values. Furthermore, these products likely satisfy basic needs that are universally common in most parts of the world. Washers, for example, are much more likely to fit this theory than are dryers. Dishwashing machines are not useful in countries where labor is plentiful and cheap, and the diffusion of this kind of innovation as described in IPLC is not likely to occur.

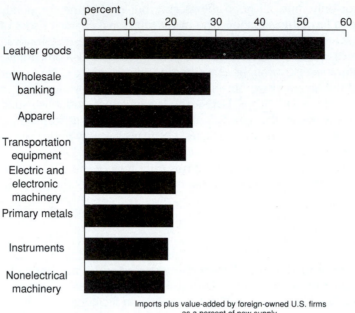

EXHIBIT 10–5   Foreign penetration of U.S. markets

Source: Herbert L. Baer, "Foreign Competition in U.S. Banking Markets," *Economic Perspectives* (May /June 1990): 23.

Marketing Strategies

For those U.S. industries in the worldwide imitation stage (e.g., automobile) or the maturity stage (e.g., computers), things are likely to get worse rather than better. The prospect, though bleak, can be favorably influenced. What is critical is for U.S. firms to understand the implications of the IPLC so that they can adjust marketing strategies accordingly.

Product Policy   The IPLC emphasizes the importance of cost advantage. It would be very difficult for U.S. firms to match labor costs in low-wage nations since costs are only 8 cents per minute in Japan, 2 cents in South Korea, and 0.5 cent in China. Still, the innovating firm must keep its product cost competitive. One way is to cut labor costs through automation and robotics. IBM converted its Lexington (Kentucky) plant into one of the most automated plants in the world. Likewise, Japanese VCR manufacturers are counting on automation to help them meet the challenge of South Korea.

Another way to reduce production costs is to eliminate unnecessary options, since such options increase inefficiency and complexity. This strategy may be critical for simple products or those at the low end of the price scale. In such cases, it is desirable to offer a standardized product with a standard package of features or options included. This is what Chrysler's Liberty project is supposed to achieve through so-called decomplexing.

To keep costs rising at a minimum, a U.S. firm may use local manufacturing in other countries as an entry strategy. The company not only can minimize transportation costs and entry barriers but also can indirectly slow down potential local competition from starting up manufacturing facilities. Another benefit is that those countries can eventually become a springboard for the U.S. company to market its products throughout that geographic region. In fact, sourcing should allow the American innovator to hold U.S. labor costs down and hold on to the original market as well. Ford Tracer is built by Ford in Taiwan for the Canadian market and in Mexico for the U.S. market. Similarly, stereo components sold in the United States are made in Japan, Taiwan, and South Korea.

Manufacturers should examine the traditional vertical structure in which they make all or most components and parts themselves, because in many instances outsourcing may prove to be more cost-effective. **Outsourcing** is the practice of buying parts or whole products from other manufacturers while allowing a buyer to maintain its own brand name. For example, Ford Festiva is made by Kia Motors, Mitsubishi Precis by Hyundai, Pontiac Lemans by Daewoo, and GM Sprint by Suzuki.

A modification of outsourcing involves producing various components or having them produced under contract in different countries. That way, a firm takes advantage of the most abundant factor of production in each country before assembling components into final products for worldwide distribution. IBM's PC system consists mostly of components made in low-cost countries—monochrome monitor in South Korea; floppy disk drives in Singapore; and graphics printer, keyboard, power supply, and semiconductors in Japan. Only the semiconductors, case, and final assembly are undertaken in the United States. American firms need to take advantage of this strategy more extensively.

Once in the maturity stage, the innovator's comparative advantage is gone, and the firm should switch from producing simple versions to producing sophisticated models or new technologies in order to remove itself from cut-throat competition. Japanese VCR makers make 99 percent of the machines sold in the United States and 75 percent of all machines sold worldwide, but they still cannot compete with low-wage Korean newcomers strictly on price, because labor content in VCRs is substantial. To retain their market share, the Japanese rely on new technology, such as 8 mm camcorders.

Procter and Gamble's problem in Japan results from its loss of the technological lead.[21] After single-handedly creating a disposable diaper market there in 1977, the company grew complacent and ignored the fact that its Pamper brand was nothing but a simple product. Soon, Japanese competitors placed better products on store shelves. Uni-Charm studied European and American buying habits in addition to polling 300 Japanese mothers three times each on opinions of foreign diapers. The responses led that company to add leg gatherings and reusable adhesive closures, to reshape diapers for better fit, and to introduce a leak-resistant panty-type diaper. Uni-Charm's highly absorbent, granulated polymer, which soaks up wetness and holds it in the form of a gel, was so popular that the company captured almost half of the market. Procter and Gamble, however, did not introduce polymer Pampers until 1985 and saw its market share plummet from 90 percent to 15 percent in the meantime. To make the matter worse for Procter and Gamble, a price war was another problem. Uni-Charm brought out a cheaper version of polymer-packed diapers for thrifty mothers. And Kao, another competitor, introduced the less-expensive "Q-size" for infants and another second-tier product costing 18 percent less.

For a relatively high-tech product, an innovator may find it advantageous to get its product system to become the industry's standard, even if it means lending a helping hand to competitors through the licensing of product knowledge.[22] Otherwise, there is always a danger that competitors will persevere in inventing an incompatible and superior system. A new system will at least confuse consumers; at worst, it may even supplant the innovator's product altogether to become the industry's standard. Sony's strategic blunder in guarding its Betamax video system is a good case to study. Matsushita and Victor Co. took the world leadership position away from Sony by being more liberal in licensing its VHS (Video Home System) to their competitors. Philips and Grundig did not introduce their Video 2000 system until VHS, which is used in two out of three VCRs in the world, was just about to become the industry's standard in Europe and the world. By that time, despite price cutting, it was too late for Video 2000 to attract other manufacturers and consumers. The problem was so bad that Philips' own North American subsidiary refused to buy its parent's system. Ironically, Sony itself had to start making VHS-format machines in 1988.

Pricing Policy   Initially, an innovating firm can afford to behave as a monopolist, charging a premium price for its innovation. But this price must be adjusted downward in the second and third stages of IPLC to discourage potential newcomers and to maintain market share. Anticipating a Korean challenge, Japanese VCR makers cut their prices in the United States by 25 percent and were able to slow down retailers' and consumers' acceptance of Korean brands. IBM, in comparison, was slow in reducing prices for its PC models. The error in judgment was the result of a belief that the IBM PC was too complex for Asian imitators. This proved to be a costly error because the basic PC hardly changed for several years. Before long, the product became nothing but an easily copied, standardized commodity suitable for intensive distribution—the kind that Asian companies thrive on. In addition to such brands as Daewoo's Leading Edge and Seiko's Epson, ComputerLand even produced its own private brand. Inevitably, commodity pricing soon determines the market.

In the last stage of the IPLC, it is not practical for the innovating firm to maintain low price because of competitors' cost advantage. But the firm's above-the-market price is feasible only if it is accompanied by top-quality or sophisticated products. A high standard of excellence should partially insulate the firm's product from direct price competition. U.S. automakers failed in this area—high prices are not matched by consumer perception of superior quality.

Promotion Policy   Promotion and pricing in the IPLC are highly related. The innovating firm's initial competitive edge is its unique product, which allows it to command a premium price. To maintain this price in the face of subsequent challenges from imitators, uniqueness can only be retained in the form of superior quality, style, or services.

The innovating marketer must plan for a nonprice promotional policy at the outset of a product diffusion. Timken is able to compete effectively against the Japanese by offering more services and meeting customers' needs at all times. For instance, it offers technological support by sending engineers to help customers design bearings in gearboxes.

One implication that can be drawn is that a new product should be promoted as a premium product with a high-quality image. Brazil's Interbras, knowing that it cannot fight cheaper Asian imports, has been successful in promoting its Hippopotamus brand as high-fashion shoes. Its promotional goal is to sell image rather than specific shoes.

By starting out with a high-quality reputation, the innovating company can trade down later with a simpler version of the product while still holding on to the high-priced, most profitable segment of the market. One thing the company must never do is to allow its product to become a commodity item with prices as the only buying motive, since such a product can be easily duplicated by other firms. Aprica has been very successful in creating a status symbol for its stroller by using top artists and designers to create a product for mothers who are more concerned with style than price. The stroller is promoted as "anatomically correct" for babies to avoid hip dislocation, and the company uses the snob appeal and comfort to distinguish its brand from those of Taiwanese and Korean imitators. Therefore, product differentiation, not price, is most important for insulating a company from the crowded, low-profit market segment. A product can be so standardized that it can be easily duplicated, but image is a much different proposition.

Place (Distribution) Policy　A strong dealer network can provide the U.S. innovating firm with a good defensive strategy. Because of its near-monopoly situation at the beginning, the firm is in a good position to be able to select only the most qualified agents/distributors, and the distribution network should be expanded further as the product becomes more diffused. Caterpillar's network of loyal dealers causes difficulty for Komatsu to line up its own dealers in the United States. In an ironic case, GM's old policy of limiting its dealers from carrying several GM brands inadvertently encouraged those dealers to start carrying imports. A firm must also watch closely for the development of any new alternative channel that may threaten the existing channel.

When it is too late or futile to keep an enemy out, the enemy should be invited in. U.S. firms—manufacturers as well as agents/distributors—can survive by becoming agents for their former competitors. The tactic involves providing a distribution network and marketing expertise at a profit to competitors who in all likelihood would welcome an easier entry into the marketplace. American automakers and their dealers seem to have accepted the reality of the marketplace and have become partners with their Japanese and foreign competitors, as evidenced by General Motors' ventures with Toyota, Suzuki, and Isuzu (to produce Nova, Sprint, and Spectrum respectively),

American Motors' with France's Renault (before the subsequent sale to Chrysler), Chrysler's with Mitsubishi and Maserati, and Ford's with Mazda and the Korean Kia Motors.

Managerial Implications

Since no country or company can in the long run maintain a monopoly on product knowledge or product production, American firms must understand the IPLC and its stages. The serious problems encountered by many U.S. industries operating in international markets clearly provides evidence for this contention. U.S. firms could learn a great deal from their Japanese competitors. Japan, not known for innovative behavior, has an excellent reputation for being a very good imitator by refining and improving existing technologies developed by the United States and other nations. Japan's traditional strength lies in its efficiency for manufacturing and distributing commodity-type products. This strength in turn enables it to compete on the basis of quantity, price, and distribution. A case in point is the penetration of Japanese printers into the U.S. market. These printers are reliable but have no unique features and are produced in high volume on automated production lines. It will not be long before personal and business computers follow what historically has been the case in the printer and shoe industries in the United States.

Once a product is in the final stage of its life cycle, the innovating firm should strive to become a specialist, not a generalist, by concentrating its efforts in carefully selected market segments, where it can distinguish itself from foreign competitors. To achieve distinction, U.S. firms should either add product features or offer more services. For the alert firm, there are early warning signals that can be used to determine whether the time has come to adopt this strategy. One signal is the product that becomes so standardized that it can be manufactured in many LDCs. Another warning signal is a decline in the U.S. exports owing to the loss or narrowing of the U.S. technological lead. By that time, certain forms of market segmentation and product differentiation are highly recommended. Another major means of help to U.S. firms would be to create even more advanced products in order to make any imitation strategy adopted by LDCs very risky, because the imitated versions would rapidly become obsolete.

PRODUCT STANDARDIZATION VERSUS PRODUCT ADAPTATION

In assisting a foreign company to buy personal computers, a trade consultant of the International Trade Division of the U.S. Department of Commerce called a representative of the U.S. firm that is Apple's overseas distributor. The following conversation took place:

"Do you represent Apple overseas?" asked the trade consultant.

"Yes, we do."

"Do you modify your computer so that it can be used abroad?"

"No, we don't," said the firm's representative. "Foreign firms have to buy it as it is."

"Then how can you expect to sell it overseas?" asked the consultant. "When Japanese firms want to sell here, they modify their products. So why should foreign firms buy your product when it does not work in their countries?"'

"That's true, but at least they have our brand name on the product."

"That's crazy."

This conversation illustrates a controversial issue in international marketing: product standardization versus product modification. Within the United States, there is a tendency among firms to prefer universal distribution of standardized products. Product standardization means that a product originally designed for a local market is exported to other countries with virtually no change, except perhaps for the translation of words and other cosmetic changes. Revlon, for example, used to ship successful products abroad without changes in product formulation, packaging (without any translation, in some cases), and advertising. There are advantages and disadvantages to both standardization and individualization.

Arguments for Standardization

The strength of standardization in the production and distribution of products and services is in its simplicity and cost. It is an easy process for executives to understand and implement, and it also is cost-effective. If cost is the only factor being considered, then standardization is clearly a logical choice because economies of scale can operate to reduce production costs. Yet minimizing production costs does not necessarily mean that profit increases will follow. Simplicity is not always beneficial, and costs are often confused with profits. Cost reductions do not automatically lead to profit improvements, and in fact the reverse may apply. By trying to control production costs through standardization, the product involved may become unsuitable for alternative markets. The result may be that demand abroad will decline, which leads to profit reduction. In some situation, cost control can be achieved but at the expense of overall profit. It is therefore prudent to remember that cost should not be overemphasized. The main marketing goal is to maximize profit, and production-cost reductions should be considered as a secondary objective. The two objectives are not always convergent.

When appropriate, standardization is a good approach. For example, when a consistent company or product image is needed, product uniformity is required. The worldwide success of McDonald's is based on consistent product quality and services. Hamburger meat, buns, and fruit pies must meet strict specifications. This obsession with product quality necessitates the costly export of french fries from Canada to European franchises because the required kind of potato is not grown in Europe. In 1982 a Paris licensee was barred through a court order from using McDonald's trademarks and other trade processes because the licensee's twelve Paris eateries did not meet the required specifications.

Some products by their very nature are not or cannot be easily modified. Musical recordings and works of art are examples of products that are difficult to differentiate, as are books and motion pictures. When this is the case, the product must rise and fall according to its own merit. Whether such products will be successful in diverse markets is not easy to predict. Films that do well in the United States may do poorly in Japan. On the other hand, movies that were not box-office hits in the United States have turned out to be moneymakers in France (e.g., most of Jerry Lewis's films).

With regard to high-technology products, both users and manufacturers may find it desirable to reduce confusion and promote compatibility by introducing industry specifications that make standardization possible. In the case of the Japanese Posts & Telecommunications Ministry's proposal that all value-added networks (VANs) in Japan comply with an international standard known as X.75, the specification has been approved by the International Telecommunication Union and is widely used in many public data networks, including those of most European countries. Because most private networks sold by U.S. suppliers do not comply with X.75, they lamely accuse Japan of utilizing the standard to hurt the sales of their products.

A condition that may support the production and distribution of standardized products exists when certain products can be associated with particular cultural universals. That is, when consumers from different countries share similar need characteristics and therefore want essentially identical products. Watches are used to keep time around the world and thus can be standardized. The diamond is another example. Levi Strauss's attempt to penetrate the European market with lighter-weight jeans failed because European consumers wanted the standard heavy-duty American type after all.

Some products are able to remain unchanged and be successful despite changes of culture. *Reader's Digest* is a good example. The magazine has endured for decades, earning the distinction of being the only mass circulation, general-interest magazine that has survived the advent of television. *Reader's Digest* has always kept the same upbeat editorial format, with the same folksy illustrations for the magazine's back cover in all of its editions. The popularity of this standardized print medium is confirmed by the 100 million people who read the magazine's thirty-nine editions in fifteen languages.

One study confirms that the degree of strategic standardization is low. Three factors—corporate orientation, nature of ownership, and consumer characteristcs and behavior—underlie the degree of strategic standardization.[23] Yet another study finds that the majority (81 percent) of the U.S. respondents exported their products without any modification.[24] The contradictory result of the second study is understandable because it focused on industrial products which are less likely to be affected by users' tastes. Furthermore, it may simply imply that U.S. firms, and not necessarily MNCs in general, are resistant to the idea of product adaptation.

A study of U.S. multinationals operating in Latin America reveals that their standardization and adaptation practices differed from those of U.S. multinationals operating in Europe. In terms of the type of product, consumer nondurable goods demonstrated the greatest degree of adaptation to local conditions. Understandably, such products are most subject to differences in consumer preference. Consumer durables and industrial goods, on the other hand, were situated at the less-adapted end of the spectrum. An important discovery is that firms that produced more than 50 percent of their Latin American sales at local production facilities showed a greater commitment to the markets and adapted more elements of the marketing mix to local conditions. More technology-intensive firms standardized their marketing strategies more than did less technology-intensive firms, probably as a result of the high cost of adapting high-technology products. Moreover, the smaller markets of Latin America seemed to encourage the firms to adapt less there than in the larger and more important European markets.[25]

Arguments for Adaptation

There is nothing wrong with standardized products if consumers prefer those products. In many situations, domestic consumers may desire a particular design of a product produced for the American market. But when that product design is placed in foreign markets, foreign buyers are forced either to purchase that product from the manufacturer or not purchase anything at all. This manner of conducting business overseas is known as the "big-car" and "left-hand-drive" syndromes. Both describe U.S. firms' reluctance and/or unwillingness to modify their products to suit their customers' needs.

According to the **big-car syndrome,** U.S. marketers assume that products designed for Americans are superior and will be preferred by foreign consumers. U.S. automakers believe (or used to believe) that the American desire for big cars means that only big cars should be exported to overseas markets.

The **left-hand-drive** syndrome is a corollary to the **big-car** syndrome. Americans drive on the right side of the road, with the steering wheel on the left side of the automobile. But many Asian and European countries have traffic laws requiring drivers to drive on the left side of the road, and cars with the steering wheel on the left present a serious safety problem. Yet exported U.S. cars are the same left-hand-drive models as are sold in the United States for the right-hand traffic patterns. According to the excuse used by U.S. automakers, a small sales volume abroad does not justify converting exported cars to right-hand steering.[26] And as explained by GM's president "There's a certain status in having a left-hand steer in Japan." This is one good reason why American automobile sales abroad have been disappointing. A half-hearted effort can only result in a half-hearted performance. American exporters have failed time and time again to realize that when in Rome one should do as the Romans do. Japanese automakers have not shown the same kind of indifference to market needs; Japanese firms have always adapted their automobiles to American driving customs (see Exhibit 10–6).

Those American firms that have understood the need for product modification have done well even in Japan. Du Pont has customized its manufacturing and marketing for the Japanese market, and its design units work with Japanese customers to design parts to their specifications. Sprite became the best-selling clear soft drink in Japan after being reformulated—the lime taste was taken out because Japanese were

Back in 1957 we brought our first two cars to America. And took them home again.

They were the best cars we'd ever made. They'd been bestsellers in Japan. But how would they do in the bigtime — in America?

We didn't know. We couldn't know, until we brought them here.

We brought them in August, 1957. And showed them with great hope. And even greater fear. What would happen if America didn't like them?

As it turned out, America *didn't* like them; our cars, the critics said, were "overpriced, underpowered, and built like tanks."

We had to start all over.

The message was painful and very clear: if we wanted to sell cars in a place like America, we had to start all over. And make a better car.

So we started over. And worked very hard for many frustrating years.

We stretched our technology farther than we had ever stretched it before.

We tried out ideas that had never been tried before.

We made every mistake that we could possibly make.

And one day we did it: we made a better car.

And the rest, as they say, is history.

And now comes the future.

Toyota is now, and has been for years, America's leading auto import.

But soon this import will be made right here.

On May 5 we broke ground for a new Toyota manufacturing plant in Kentucky.

The plant will cost $800,000,000, will employ 3,000, and will produce 200,000 cars a year.

Site of Toyota's new $800,000,000 auto plant in Kentucky.

It's a major investment in the future of the American automobile industry, and in the future of the American economy.

It's also a down payment on our debt.

We owe a lot to America. America gave us a chance when we were small and scared. It gave us the challenge that helped us become who we are.

This is something we will never forget.

TOYOTA

EXHIBIT 10–6   Toyota's product adaptation

Source: Reprinted with permission of Toyota Motor Corporation.

494

found to prefer a purer lemon flavor.[27] Yamazaki-Nabisco's Ritz crackers sold in Japan are less salty than the Ritz crackers sold in America; similarly, Chips Ahoy are less sweet than versions sold elsewhere. Responding to the Japanese demand for quality, Ajinomoto-General Foods used a better grade of bean for its Maxim instant coffee.

Firms must assess how extensive or substantial product modification is to be. According to one study, MNCs' product strategies are influenced by the differences in the relative degree of urbanization of target markets in LDCs.[28] Products for urban markets require minimal changes from those sold in developed countries. More changes are necessary for products marketed in both urban and semiurban markets. And maximum adaptation is needed for products sold in national markets, since those products serve culturally diverse rural groups. MNCs, on average, make four changes per product when marketing their products in LDCs.[29] Only one out of every ten products is transferred to LDC markets without modification.

Firms must choose the time when a product is to be modified to better suit its market. According to the Conference Board, important factors for product modification mentioned by more than 70 percent of firms surveyed are long-term profitability, long-term market potential, product-market fit, short-term profitability, cost of altering or adapting (e.g., retooling), desire for consistency (e.g., maintaining a world image), and short-term market potential. These factors apply to consumer nondurable and durable products as well as to industrial products.

Product adaptation is necessary under several conditions. Some are mandatory, whereas others are optional.

Mandatory Product Modification The mandatory factors affecting product modification are the following:

Government's mandatory standards (i.e., country's regulations)
Electrical current standards
Measurement standards
Product standards and systems

The most important factor that makes modification mandatory is government regulation. To gain entry into a foreign market, certain requirements must be satisfied. Regulations are usually specified and explained when a potential customer requests a price quotation on a product to be imported. For example, starting in 1986, Switzerland banned the use of phosphates in detergents.[30] Zeolites and nitrilotriacetates may be substituted for phosphates, but the permissible amount of nitrilotriacetates is fixed at 5 percent to avoid harmful effects in drinking water. The new regulation also requires labels and packages to show the chemical composition of the product. Avon shampoos had to be reformulated to remove the formaldehyde preservative, which is a violation of regulations in several Asian countries. Food products are usually heavily regulated. Added vitamins in margarine, forbidden in Italy, are compulsory in the United Kingdom and Holland. In the case of processed cheese, the incorporation of a mold inhibitor may be fully allowed, allowed up to the permissible level, or forbidden altogether.

Frequently, products must be modified to compensate for differences in electrical current standards. In many countries, there may even be variations in electrical standards within the country. The different electrical standards (phase, frequency, and voltage) abroad can easily harm products designed for use in the United States, and such improper use can be a serious safety hazard for users as well. Stereo receivers and TV sets manufactured for the U.S. 110- to 120-volt mode will be severely damaged if used in markets where the voltages are twice as high. Therefore, products must be adapted to higher voltages. When there is no voltage problem, a product's operating efficiency can be impaired if the product is operated in the wrong electrical frequency. Alarm clocks, tape recorders, and turntables designed for the U.S. 60 Hz (60 cycles per second) system will run more slowly in countries where the frequency is 50 Hz. To solve this problem, marketers may have to substitute a special motor or arrange for a different drive ratio to achieve the desirable operating RPM or service level.

Some U.S. companies that want to sell communications equipment in the huge Japanese market complain that NTT (Nippon Telegraph & Telephone) requires them to adapt their products to lower voltages and also to provide Japanese manuals. Yet foreign switchboard makers have to meet the U.S. technical standards in such areas as operating voltage, number of wires per cable, and other operating features. Plessy Co., a British firm, was surprised to learn that American customers wanted their PBX automatically to route all outgoing long-distance calls through the least-expensive carrier—a peculiar requirement for a European supplier because in Europe each country has only one long-distance company.

Like electrical standards, measurement systems can also vary from country to country. Although the United States has adopted the English (imperial) system of measurement (feet, pounds, etc.), most countries employ the metric system, and product quantity should or must be expressed in metric units. Since 1989 the EC countries no longer accept nonmetric products for sale. Many countries even go so far as to prohibit the sale of measuring devices with both metric and English markings. One New England company was ordered to stop selling its laboratory glassware in France because the markings were not exclusively metric.

In 1982 Congress abolished the U.S. Metric Board as well as a voluntary program for conversion to the metric system in order to save $2 million. That decision was shortsighted. Metric demands adversely affect U.S. firms' competitiveness because many American firms do not offer metric products.[31] A Middle East firm, for example, was unable to find an American producer that sold pipe with metric threads for oil machinery. A European firm had to rewire all imported electrical appliances because the U.S. standard wire diameters did not meet national standards. It is difficult to find a U.S. firm that cuts lumber to metric dimensions. Fortunately, the new trade act now requires the U.S. government and industry to use metric units in documentation of exports and imports as prescribed by the International Convention on the Harmonized Commodity Description and Coding System. The Harmonized System is designed to standardize commodity classification for all major trading nations. The International System Units (Système International d'Unités [SI]) is the official measurement system of the Harmonized System.

As noted by one U.S. newspaper columnist, "We are the last civilization on earth to resist the decimal system. We would rather divide by twelve or sixteen to figure how far we are going and how much gas we need to get there."[32] Very, very few countries still cling to the obsolete nonmetric systems. Among them are the United States, Burma, Brunei, and Liberia. Robert Heller of the Federal Reserve Board of Governors made the following comment: "Only Yemen and India have as low an export-to-GDP ratio as the United States. Would it come as a surprise to you to know that the U.S. and Yemen share something else in common? They are the only two countries in the world that have not yet gone metric! If an American manufacturer has to retool first in order to sell his wares abroad, his incentive to do so is considerably reduced, and it makes his first step into export markets all that much more expensive."

The 1982 decision to abort the conversion program has been decried by many as a backward step in the progress that the United States should be making in learning about the international arena. Although conversion to the metric system involves educating the U.S. public, the metric system is widely considered a far superior system. Once conversion is instituted, the next generation would learn metric measurement without any great difficulty. Exhibit 10–7 provides metric facts.

American firms often cite nontariff barriers as contributing to their failure in establishing a foothold in the Japanese market. Some of these nontariff barriers used by the Japanese are intentionally designed to discourage imports. Yet the Japanese often point out that U.S. firms commonly refuse to modify their products. The importance of this refusal is often understated or underestimated. Japan's NTT is the second largest telecommunications company in the world, but U.S. firms insist on selling their products without any kind of modification, even though without modification their products are not compatible with NTT's system. The NTT cannot convert its elaborate system to accommodate American specifications and materials. When purchases fail to materialize, many U.S. firms are quick to cite NTT's discrimination against U.S. imports. Hewlett-Packard, for example, withdrew from its effort to sell oscilloscopes after learning that its inch-denominated front panel screws would have to be replaced with metric screws. The requirement of measurement conversion would inconvenience the seller, but a buyer cannot be expected to change complex business systems in order to accommodate the vendor's selling requirements. American products will have to be produced in the metric system if those products are to be integrated with equipment in other countries.

Some products must be modified because of different operating systems adopted by various countries. Television systems provide a good example (see Exhibit 10–8). There are three different TV operating systems used in different parts of the world: the American NTSC (National Television Systems Committee), the French SECAM (Système Électronique Pour Couleur Avec Mémoire), and the German PAL (Phone Alternating Lines). In 1941 the United States became the first country to set the national standards for TV broadcasting, adopting 525 scanning lines per frame. Most other nations later decided to require 625 lines for sharper image instead. In most cases, a TV set designed for one broadcast system cannot receive signals

---

METRIC FACTS FOR EXPORTERS

▢ Lack of metric product designs and labeling increasingly bars U.S. products from foreign markets. The European Communities may soon completely bar nonmetric imports.

▢ The Made in the U.S.A. label no longer overcomes global market prejudice against inch-pound products. Not conforming to international standards/codes and preferences handicaps U.S. exporters.

▢ Canada is metric. U.S.-Canada free trade will increase even further—if the U.S. can offer metric products.

▢ Nearly half the U.S. patents issued last year were to foreign inventors. Future products incorporating these inventions will be metric. Will U.S. manufacturers be capable of producing or supplying components for these products?

▢ The U.S. domestic market shows no reluctance to accept metric products, whether produced domestically or abroad. Therefore, U.S. firms can likely satisfy both the domestic and export markets with a metric product.

▢ U.S. manufacturers who phase in metric use with new products avoid any conversion cost penalty and avoid the cost of a separate export product line.

▢ New military weapon systems will be metric under stronger Department of Defense policy, opening new export opportunities to NATO and other metric allies for U.S. aerospace industries.

▢ The 1975 Metric Conversion Act encourages rapid development of metric engineering standards and "the retention, in new metric language standards, of those United States engineering designs, practices and conventions that are internationally accepted or that embody superior technology." There is new urgency for this essential element of U.S. strategy to regain global competitiveness. (For information, contact the U.S. Department of Commerce, Office of Metric Programs, Washington DC 20230; tel. (202) 377-3036.)

EXHIBIT 10–7 Metric facts for exporters

Source: Business America, 26 September 1988, 5.

broadcast through a different operating system. Videotex and HDTV (high-definition TV) are other examples of products that thus far do not have a universal system accepted by the industry. When differences in product operating systems exist, a company unwilling to change its products must limit the number of countries it can enter, unless proper modification is undertaken for other market requirements.

Optional Product Modification   The conditions dictating product modification mentioned so far are mandatory in the sense that without adaptation a product either cannot enter a market or is unable to perform its function there. Such mandatory standards make the adaptation decision easy: a marketer must either comply or remain out of the market. Italy's Piaggio withdrew its Vespa scooters from the U.S.

EXHIBIT 10–8 World television standards

NTSC	Antigua	Costa Rica	Jamaica	Puerto Rico
	Bahamas	Cuba	Japan	Saipan
	Barbados	Dominican	South Korea	Samoa
	Belize	Republic	Mexico	Surinam
	Bermuda	Ecuador	Netherlands	Taiwan
	Bolivia	El Salvador	Antilles	Trinidad
	Burma	Greenland	Nicaragua	Tobago
	Canada	Guam	Panama	United States
	Chile	Guatemala	Peru	Venezuela
	Colombia	Honduras	Philippines	Virgin Islands
PAL	Afghanistan	Gibraltar	Netherlands	Swaziland
	(Kabul)	Hong Kong	New Guinea	Sweden
	Algeria	Iceland	New Zealand	Switzerland
	Argentina	India	Nigeria	Tanzania
	Autralia	Indonesia	Norway	Thailand
	Austria	Ireland	Oman	Turkey
	Bahrain	Israel	Pakistan	Uganda
	Bangladesh	Italy	Paraguay	United Arab
	Belgium	Jordan	Portugal	Emirates
	Brazil	Kenya	Qatar	United Kingdom
	Brunei	North Korea	Saudi Arabia	Uruguay
	China	Kuwait	Sierra Leone	Yemen
	Cyprus	Liberia	Singapore	Yugoslavia
	Denmark	Luxembourg	South Africa	Zambia
	Finland	Malaysia	Spain	Zimbabwe
	Germany	Malta	Sri Lanka	
	Ghana	Monaco	Sudan	
SECAM	Albania	Guadeloupe	Madagascar	Russia
	Benin	French	Martinique	Senegal
	Bulgaria	Guyana	Mauritius	Syria
	Congo	Haiti	Mongolia	Tahiti
	Czechoslovakia	Hungary	Morocco	Togo
	Djibouti	Iran	New Caledonia	Tunisia
	Egypt	Iraq	Niger	Vietnam
	France	Ivory Coast	Poland	Zaire
	Gabon	Lebanon	Reunion	
	Greece	Libya	Romania	

market in 1983, choosing not to meet U.S. pollution control standards for its few exports.

A more complex and difficult decision is optional modification, which is based on the international marketer's discretion in taking action. Nescafe in Switzerland, for instance, tastes quite different from the same brand sold just a short distance across the French border.

One condition that may make optional modification attractive is related to physical distribution, and this involves the facilitation of product transportation at the lowest cost. Since freight charges are assessed on either a weight or a volume basis, the carrier may charge on the basis of whichever is more profitable. The marketer may be able to reduce delivery costs if the products are assembled and then shipped. Many countries also have narrow roads, doorways, stairways, or elevators that can cause transit problems when products are large or are shipped assembled. Therefore, a slight product modification may greatly facilitate product movement.

Another determinant for optional adaptation involves local use conditions, including climatic conditions. The hot/cold, humid/dry conditions may affect product durability or performance. Avon modified its Candid moist lipstick line for a hot, humid climate. Certain changes may be required in gasoline formulations. If the heat is intense, gasoline requires a higher flash point to avoid vapor locks and engine stalling. In Brazil, automobiles are designed to run on low-quality gas, to withstand the country's rough dusty roads, and to weather its sizzling temperatures. As a result, these automobiles are attractive to customers in LDCs, especially when the automobiles are also durable and simple to maintain. American automobiles can experience difficulties in these markets, where people tend to overload their cars and trucks and do not perform regular maintenance, not to mention the unavailability of lead-free gasoline.

Another local use condition that can necessitate product change is space constraint. Sears's refrigerators were redesigned to be smaller in dimensions without sacrificing the original capacity, so that they could fit the compact Japanese home. Philips, similarly, had to reduce the size of its coffeemaker. In contrast, U.S. mills, for many years, resisted cutting plywood according to Japanese specifications, even though they were told repeatedly that the standard Japanese plywood dimensions were 3 by 6 ft—not the U.S. standard of 4 by 8 ft. In a related case, Japanese-style homes have exposed wood beams, but U.S. forest-products firms traditionally allow 2-by-4 studs to be dirty or slightly warped, since in the United States these studs will most always be covered over with wallboard. The firms have refused to understand that wood grain and quality are important to the Japanese because an exposed post is part of the furniture.

Consumer demographics as related to physical appearance can also affect how products are used and how suitable those products are. Habitat Mothercare PLC found out that its British products were not consistent with American customs and sizes. Its comforters were not long enough to fit American beds, and its tumblers could not hold enough ice. Philips downsized its shaver to fit the smaller Japanese hand. One U.S. brassier company did well initially in West Germany but failed to get repeat purchases. The problem was that German women have a tendency not to try on merchandize in the store and thus did not find out until later that the product was ill-fitting because of measurement variations between American and German brassieres. Furthermore, German customers usually do not return a product for refund or adjustment.

Even a doll may have to be modified to better resemble the physical appearance of local people. The Barbie doll, though available in Japan for decades, became popular only after Mattel allowed Takara (which holds the production and marketing agreement) to reconstruct the product. Of sixty countries, Japan is the only market where the product is modified. Barbie's Western-style features are modified in several ways: her blue eyes become brown, her vividly blond hair is darkened, and her bosom size is reduced.

Local use conditions include user's habits. Since the Japanese prefer to work with pencils—a big difference from the typed business correspondence common in the United States—copiers require special characteristics that allow the copying of light pencil lines.[33] Exhibit 10–9 describes how WordPerfect has successfully utilized the strategy of "local customization."

Finally, other environmental characteristics related to use conditions should be examined. Examples are endless. Detergents should be reformulated to fit local water conditions. IBM had to come up with a completely new design so that its machine could include Japanese word-processing capability. Kodak made some changes in its graphic arts products for Japanese professionals, most of whom have no darkrooms and have to work in different light environments.

Price may often influence a product's success or failure in the marketplace. This factor becomes even more critical abroad because U.S. products tend to be expensive, but foreign consumers' incomes tend to be at lower levels than Americans' incomes. Frequently, the higher quality of American products cannot overcome the price disadvantage found in foreign markets. To solve this problem, American companies can reduce the contents of the product or remove any nonessential parts or do both. Foreign consumers are generally not convenience-oriented, and an elaborate product can be simplified by removing any "frills" that may unnecessarily drive up the price. This approach is used by General Motors in manufacturing and selling the so-called Basic Transportation Vehicle in less-industrialized nations.

One reason that international marketers often voluntarily modify their products in individual markets is their desire to maximize profit by limiting product movement across national borders. The rationale for this desire is that some countries have price controls and other laws that restrict profits and prices. When other nearby countries have no such laws, marketers are encouraged to move products into those nearby countries where a higher price can be charged. A problem can arise in which local firms in countries where product prices are high are bypassed by marketers who buy directly from firms handling such products in countries where prices are low. In many cases, because of antitrust laws, international marketers who wish to maintain certain market prices cannot ban this kind of product movement by threatening to cut off supply from those firms reexporting products to high-priced countries. Johnson & Johnson, for example, was fined $300,000 by the EC for explicitly preventing British wholesalers and pharmacists from reexporting Gravindex pregnancy tests to Germany, where the kits cost almost twice as much.

In spite of authorities' efforts to prevent companies from keeping lower-priced goods out of higher-priced countries, marketers may do so anyway as long as they do not get caught. Some manufacturers try to hinder these practices by deliberately varying packaging, package coding, product characteristics, coloring, and even brand

INDUSTRIAL INFRASTRUCTURE

WordPerfect Grows in Europe Through Dutch Headquarters And Local Customization

In 1978, Alan C. Ashton, a computer science professor at Brigham Young University in Provo, Utah, got together with the director of its marching band, Bruce W. Bastian, to produce software that created the band's marching patterns. Out of their next collaborations grew the world's largest private software company, WordPerfect Corporation of Orem, Utah.

WordPerfect began working in 1984 with a Dutch software distributor, which, in 1985, spun off a distributorship dedicated to WordPerfect products. In 1988, WordPerfect acquired the spin-off and renamed it WordPerfect Europe. WordPerfect Europe moved with WordPerfect Nederland into a new 38,500-square-foot facility near Rotterdam in October 1990 with some 90 employees. According to Mr. Ashton, Holland continues to play a role in the company's European success:

"Bruce and I were impresssed by the management skills and the quickness with which the Dutch people developed the technical expertise to sell WordPerfect. Dutch universities are graduating people with the know-how to help us grow our business, not only in the Benelux but also throughout Europe.

"Our Dutch operation became successful because we invested in creating Dutch translations of most of our software products and manuals and included a localized

WordPerfect CORPORATION

Alan C. Ashton, President
WordPerfect Corporation

Spell-checker, Hyphenation routine and Thesaurus for the WordPerfect product itself. We adhered to this strategy as we expanded. Complete packages have been localized into 12 languages besides U.S. English, with partial packages available in another six, and Russian, Czech and Greek in the works.

"About 20% of WordPerfect's global revenues now come from European customers.

"The Rotterdam office handles technical support and some product development for system configurations that are unique to Europe, such as various printer hardware and UNIX ports. It offers marketing, financial and general management support as needed to our offices in 11 European countries and distributors in another six.

"Through SoftCopy Europe, which was formed in 1988 about a mile from our headquarters in Rotterdam, WordPerfect and other software suppliers have their

master program disks reproduced and packaged with manuals in shrink-wrapped boxes, for shipment directly to customers.

"From our initial telephone call to the Dutch distributor who is now the head of our European operations, our experiences in Holland have been first rate. We always have felt that the Dutch want our business and will do what is necessary to ensure that we, too, are successful."

HIT THE GROUND RUNNING

For more information, contact the Netherlands Foreign Investment Agency in:
New York
Tel: 212-246-1434   Fax: 212-246-9769
San Mateo
Tel: 415-349-8848   Fax: 415-349-8201
Los Angeles
Tel: 310-477-8288   Fax: 310-312-0771
Ottawa
Tel: 613-237-5030   Fax: 613-237-6471

Netherlands Foreign Investment Agency

This material is published by Ogilvy Public Relations Group, which is registered as an agent of the Government of the Netherlands. It is filed with the Department of Justice, where the required registration statement is available for public inspection. Registration does not indicate approval of the contents by the United States Government.

EXHIBIT 10–9   Product adaptation

Source: Courtesy of the Netherlands Foreign Investment Agency and Ogilvy Adams & Rinehart.

names in order to spot violators or to confuse consumers in markets where products have moved across borders. Osborne had this problem with its portable computer. Its European distributors complained that some local firms were bypassing Osborne and were able to sell Osborne computers in Europe at a lower price by dealing through U.S. wholesalers. To eliminate the problem, Osborne started producing computers with special features designed exclusively for export, thus making the U.S. version less attractive abroad.

Perhaps the most arbitrary yet most important reason for product change abroad is because of historical preference, or local customs and culture. Product size, color, speed, grade, and source may have to be redesigned in order to accommodate local preference. Kodak altered its film to cater to a Japanese idea of attractive skin tones. Kraft's Philadelphia Cream Cheese tastes different in the United States, Great Britain, Germany, and Canada. In Asia, Foremost sells chocolate and strawberry milk instead of low-fat and skim milk. Asians and Europeans by tradition prefer to shop on a daily basis, and thus they desire smaller refrigerators in order to reduce cost and electrical consumption.

When products clash with a culture, the likely loser is the product, not the culture. Strong religious beliefs make countries of the Middle East insist on ha-lalled chickens. In soup-conscious Brazil, Campbell soups did not take hold because homemakers there have strong cultural traditions of a homemaker's role, and serving Campbell soup to their families would be a soup served not of their own making. As a result, these homemakers prefer dehydrated products manufactured by Knorr and Maggi, used as a soup starter to which the homemaker can add her own flair and ingredients. Campbell soups are usually purchased to be put aside for an emergency, such as if the family arrives home late.

Product changes are not necessarily related to functional attributes such as durability, quality, operation method, maintenance, and other engineering aspects. Frequently, aesthetic or secondary qualities must also be taken into account. There are instances in which minor, cosmetic changes have significantly increased sales. By changing a cabinet, Sharp was able to increase both the price and sales of its TV sets. Therefore, functional and aesthetic changes should both be considered in regard to how they affect the total, complete product.

One company that incorporates multiple features of product modification in appealing to local tastes is Pillsbury. In marketing its Totino's line of pizzas in Japan, Pillsbury found it wise to make several mandatory and optional changes in its product.[34] Japanese food standards ban many preservatives and dyes. The ban often necessitates an extensive redesign of a product just to get it into the Japanese market. Totino's pizzas are basically a "belly stuffer" in the United States, a confirmation of many foreigner's perception that Americans have pedestrian tastes in food. But the Japanese "eat" with their eyes, too—all foods have an aesthetic dimension. They perceive American foods as being too sweet, too large, and too spicy, making it necessary to alter the ingredients to suit the Japanese palate. Furthermore, the pizza size had to be reduced from the U.S. 12-ounce size to the Japanese 6.5-ounce size to fit into smaller Japanese ovens. In effect, Totino's frozen pizza and package were completely redesigned for the Japanese market, and Pillsbury's success confirms that its efforts were worthwhile.

Kentucky Fried Chicken provides another good illustration of the adaptation process. In Japan, it is necessary to have a Shinto priest periodically conduct mass funerals for the firm's millions of chickens. The restaurant's menu also has been changed. In addition to serving french fries instead of mashed potatoes and gravy, Kentucky Fried Chicken sells chicken sandwiches and fish and chips. Another one of its products is *yakitori* (chicken in broiled and skewered bite-size chunks). Several products require reformulation as well. The company cuts out half of the sugar from the salads, because the Japanese like their salads to be tart. The firm's corn-on-the-cob is a three-inch piece, which is two inches less than the U.S. version, in order to satisfy the local preference for a lot of little things. For the Malaysian market, the company has even had to change its cooking method. Because Malaysians consider firm chicken to be fresh and soft chicken to be frozen, Kentucky Fried Chicken cooks its chicken to firm texture instead of the standard soft texture.[35]

The discussion so far has focused on factors that necessitate a modification in a product. Yet there are no easy solutions to how the product should be modified, though there are some guidelines that may prove of use for marketing abroad.[36] When a product is to be used in a region where technical skills are low, the product should be simplified as much as possible. If the literacy level is also low, a simplification of the labeling and instructions may be needed. If the product is likely to be maintained infrequently or is difficult to service, tolerance and reliability improvements are likely necessary. When the local income levels are low, a firm may want to change product quality and price, as well as to eliminate unnecessary frills. Other environmental and product design factors might include climatic variations (product adaptation), differences in standards (resizing and recalibration of product), availability of other products (greater or lesser product integration), availability of materials (change in product structure and fuel), power availability (resizing and rewiring of product), and special conditions (product redesign or invention).

Neither product standardization nor adaptation is an either-or proposition. MNCs may want to employ both strategies simultaneously. Consider McDonald's. The company has highly detailed specifications and rules that must be strictly followed. In England, its high standard for coffee aroused the ire of a British coffee supplier, and the company built its own plant when it could not get quality hamburger buns. McDonald's provides assistance to Thai farmers for cultivation of Idaho russet potatoes. When suitable supplies are unavailable in Europe, the company does not hesitate to import french fries from Canada and pies from Oklahoma.

McDonald's Corp., often used as an example of Americanism (and globalization) owing to its strict quality control and worldwide success, actually permits flexibility and creativity on the part of its franchisees. In Southeast Asia, it serves durian-flavored milk shakes made from a tasty tropical fruit whose aroma is acceptable to Asians but is considered foul by Westerners. Coconut, mango, and tropic mint shakes can be found in Hong Kong. Menu changes are also necessary in Europe. McDonald's sells near beer, which does not require a liquor license in Switzerland, and chicken on the Continent (to head off Kentucky Fried Chicken). McDonald's on the Champs Elysées offers a choice of vin blanc or vin rouge, and the coffee comes in a tiny cup with about half-dozen spoonfuls of very strong black coffee. In England, tea is available and will have milk in it unless black tea is ordered. McDonald's Australian outlets formerly offered mutton pot pie; outlets in the Philippines, where noodle houses are popular, offer McSpaghetti. Likewise, in Mexico, McDonald's offers the *McPollo* chicken sandwich and jalapeño sauce as a hamburger condiment. Because eating the Midwest-American beef is like eating soft pebbles to the Japanese, McDonald's hamburger in Japan has different texture and spices. In many countries, consumers consider fast food to be primarily a snack rather than a regular meal.[37] Furthermore, its operating philosophy has to be altered as well. In order to attract foreign partners who are well-qualified and well-financed, McDonald's grants territorial franchises instead of the usual practice of granting franchises store by store.

In conclusion, marketers should not waste time resisting product modification. When U.S. firms have gone abroad, the marketing concept seems to have been left behind. The reluctance to change a product may be the result of an insensitivity to cultural differences in foreign markets. Whatever the reason for this reluctance, there is no question that it is counterproductive in international marketing. Product adaptation should rarely become an important issue to the marketer. A good marketer compares the incremental profits against the incremental costs associated with product adaptation. If the incremental profit is greater than the associated incremental cost, then the product should be adjusted—without question. In making this comparison, marketers should primarily use only future earnings and costs.

A MOVE TOWARD WORLD PRODUCT: INTERNATIONAL OR NATIONAL PRODUCT?

Product standardization and modification may give the impression that a marketer must choose between these two processes and that one approach is better than the other. In many instances, a compromise between the two is more practical and far superior than in selecting either procedure exclusively. Black and Decker has stopped customizing products for every country in favor of a few global products that can be sold everywhere. Such U.S. publishers as Prentice-Hall and Harper also have adopted the "world book" concept, which makes it possible for an English-language world book to have world copyrights. Publishers change, if necessary, only the title page, cover, and jacket.

World product and standardized product may sometimes be confused with each other. A **world product** is a product designed for the international market. In comparison, a **standardized product** is a product developed for one national market and then exported with no change to international markets. Zenith and RCA TV sets are standardized products, whereas a German subsidiary of ITT makes a world product by producing a "world chassis" for its TV sets. This world chassis allows assemblage of TV sets for all three color TV systems of the world (i.e., NTSC, SECAM, and PAL) without changing the circuitry on the various modules.

As pointed out by Jagdish Sheth, global competition is sometimes mistaken for global markets.[38] Global products may exist, but they are aimed at specific, not universal, segments. Although industrial raw materials and their production methods can be standardized, finished industrial products are still not homogenized because use varies across countries. The likelihood is for the globalization of such specialty products as televisions and refrigerators. In contrast, time, another scarce resource, shows more diversity. As a result, time-sensitive products are less likely to become global because the needs of time-rich nations and time-poor nations differ.

A move toward a world product by a company is a logical and healthy move. If a company has to adapt its product for each market, this can be a very expensive proposition. But without the necessary adaptation, a product might not sell at all. Committing to the design of a world product can provide the solution to these two major concerns faced by most firms dealing in the international marketplace. GE, for example, produces a numerical control system suitable in both metric and English measures. In addition, it has designed machines to operate under the wide differences in voltage among the different European countries. GE refrigerators are built in such a way that they can be used regardless of whether the frequency is 50 Hz or 60 Hz. This emerging trend toward world products is also attractive for items with an international appeal or for those items purchased by international travelers. Electrical shavers made by Norelco and portable stereo radios made by Sony and Crown are produced having a universal-voltage feature.

One might question whether a world product would be more expensive than a national or local product, since the world product may need multipurpose parts. Actually, the world product should result in greater saving for two reasons. First, costly downtime in production is not needed to adjust or convert equipment to produce different national versions. Second, a world product greatly simplifies inventory control because only one universal part, not many individual parts, has to be stocked.

A world product requires corporate commitment, as illustrated by Ford Escort. The car was designed in Europe as Ford's world car. The company's American executives, however, were skeptical of their European counterparts' business and engineering judgment. In the end, the U.S. version was so thoroughly redesigned that the only common part that remained was the water pump seal.[39] There is no question that American executives must become more outwardly oriented and less inwardly inclined.

The Japanese ministry requires thirty-two changes on most U.S.-built cars. Some changes are understandable: replacing headlamps that, because of left-hand drive, dip in the wrong direction; changing "sharp-edged" door handles; and replacing outside rearview mirrors. Other requirements are harder to comprehend. For example, the requirement to fill the space between the body and the rear bumper has been adopted to prevent catching the sleeves of kimono-clad women when such women hardly exist in modern Japan. Honda is able to sell its U.S.-made cars in Japan at relatively low prices because it produces the car ready for sale in Japan (see Exhibit 10–10). Because cars manufactured by GM, Ford, and Chrysler are built for the American market, they must undergo expensive alterations to meet Japanese regulations.[40]

The trend toward an international product and away from a national product will continue as MNCs become more aware of the significance of world marketing. The willingness of several companies to consider designing a universal product for the world market is indeed a good indicator that this trend will continue.

What's right with this picture?

You won't see very many Accord Coupes that look like this one. There is no question about that. Unless, of course, you happen to work at Honda's factory located in Marysville, Ohio. Or live in Japan.

Carefully built and assembled at one of the automotive industry's most advanced manufacturing facilities, the Accord Coupe is made only in America. But that's not the only place it's sold.

Thousands of new Accord Coupes are exported to Japan each and every year. Where they are prized for their engineering, craftsmanship and value. Just as they are here.

But the other reason the Japanese are fond of this car is because it comes

with right-hand drive. Which is fitting since they drive on the opposite side of the road in Japan.

Mind you, producing both right-hand and left-hand drive cars from the same assembly line takes a lot of extra effort. The fact that Honda is the only U.S. carmaker to do so speaks for itself.

It's this kind of innovation and true commitment to people's needs which makes Honda, well, Honda.

Because even though we sell more Accord Coupes in America, it's just as important to satisfy our customers in other parts of the world.

After all, when you look at the big picture, that's what it's all about.

HONDA

EXHIBIT 10–10   Built-in product adaptation

Source: Courtesy of American Honda Motor Co., Inc.

MARKETING OF SERVICES

The United States is the most service-oriented society on Earth. The services sector represents almost 70 percent of the U.S. gross national product and employs 74 percent of the labor force. Likewise, a large majority of workers in many countries owe their jobs to the service industries: Canada (75 percent), Belgium (74 percent), Sweden (72 percent), Great Britain (72 percent), Japan (66 percent), Brazil (54 percent), and South Korea (48 percent).[41]

Internationally, the "invisible" trade is responsible for nearly one-fifth of the value of world exports. World trade in commercial services—transportation, tourism, telecommunications, banking, insurance, and other professional services—rose to a new high of $680 billion in 1989.[42] The importance of the export of U.S. business services is well supported by these trade facts: (1) exports of U.S. business services are almost one-third as large as U.S. exports of merchandise—up significantly from one-fifth in 1984; (2) such exports totaled $120 billion in 1990 (up from $43.5 billion in 1984), resulting in a surplus of $39 billion; (3) these exports are about 2.8 percent of U.S. GNP; and (4) exports (receipts) of travel and related passenger fares account for about one-third of U.S. exports.[43]

There are two major categories of services: consumer and business services. Business services that are exported consist of numerous and varied types, including advertising, construction and engineering, insurance, legal services, data processing, and banking. Among the consulting and technical services are personnel training and supervision, management of facilities, and economic and business research.

Because of countries' varying and changing laws, MNCs need accounting and tax services. Therefore, significant opportunities exist for accounting firms to serve as tax consultants for MNCs' expatriate employees and to administer MNCs' compensation plans and expatriate tax programs in compliance with local regulations. Ernst and Whinney has an active marketing plan to identify U.S. companies with American employees abroad and to contact these companies' executives who are responsible for administering the expatriate program.[44] As noted by the company, "this work is desirable, profitable, and recurring." Since fees are typically more than $1,000 per expatriate employee and since corporations may have several U.S. employees abroad, annual fees commonly exceed $100,000.

One type of service that is in demand worldwide is the financial product. Exhibit 10–11 describes several financial products (services) typically offered by Citicorp and other international banks. Other financial products are securities that are traded on several international exchanges. Japanese investors are heavy buyers of U.S. Treasury notes and bonds. For American investors, there are several mutual funds that invest in foreign securities.

The worldwide demand of many financial products results in the mutual offset link by the Singapore International Monetary Exchange (SIMEX) to the Chicago Mercantile Exchange (CME), which allows a contract bought on one exchange to be sold on another. The interest in overseas stocks explains why the CME holds the exclusive rights outside Japan to create, market, and trade the Nikkei 225 Stock Average futures contract, as described in Exhibit 10–12. The Nikkei Averages are a Japanese stock index based on stocks of all the major publicly held Japanese corporations. The av-

CITICORP INVESTMENT BANK: THE GLOBAL EDGE.

In 76 countries and 34 currencies, Citicorp Investment Bank℠ raised $69 billion for our clients, did over $27 billion in swaps, traded $11 billion in securities daily, and processed over $4 trillion in securities. All in 1984.

Which, among other things, brought Citicorp Investment Bank's 1984 earnings to $160 million.

The fact is, our worldwide network of 2,500 investment banking officers

combines global power with local expertise in securities origination and trading, mergers and acquisitions, interest rate and foreign currency risk management, international private banking, venture capital, corporate finance, portfolio management, investment advisory, and securities brokerage services.

As well as corporate trust and debt agency services, American Depositary Receipts, corporate employee benefit services, and custody services.

All backed by Citicorp's global network in 92 countries—and total capital of $12 billion.

Citicorp Investment Bank. The global edge in investment banking.

CITICORP ✛ GLOBAL INVESTMENT BANKING

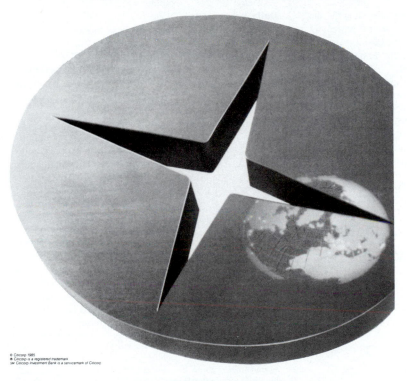

© Citicorp 1985
℞ Citicorp is a registered trademark
℠ Citicorp Investment Bank is a servicemark of Citicorp.

EXHIBIT 10–11 Citicorp's financial products/services

Source: Reprinted with permission of Citicorp Investment Bank.

erages are developed by NKS (Nihon Keizai Shimbun), which publishes the world's largest circulation daily business newspaper. The CME sublicensed its rights for the Nikkei 225 to the SIMEX for trading in the Asian time zone because too few Japanese stocks were being traded on U.S. security exchanges. On the CME floor, the popular stock index traded is the S&P 500 instead. Some believe that, in the future, that which is traded will be the averages based on stock prices of companies worldwide. One development in this direction is Morgan Stanley's granting the CME a license to trade futures based on the Morgan Stanley Capital International Europe, Australia, and Far East (EAFE) stock index. The EAFE index is a diversified portfolio on non-U.S. stocks that covers thirty-eight industries and represents 63 percent of the total market value

EXHIBIT 10–12 Nikkei futures contract information

Nikkei Stock Average[1] Futures	
Ticker Symbol	NK
Trading Unit	$5 × The Nikkei Stock Average
Price Quote	Index points
Minimum Price	.05 (5 index pts.)
Fluctuation(Tick)	($5.00/pt. = $25.00)
Daily Price Limit	Consult your broker or the CME Clearing House for specific information
Contract Months	Mar, Jun, Sep, Dec
Trading Hours (Chicago Time)	8:00 A.M.–3:15 P.M.
Last Day of Trading	First business day preceding the determination of the final settlement price, usually the business day preceding the 2nd Friday of the contract month.
Settlement	The final settlement price shall be the special opening quotation of the Nikkei Stock Average, used to settle the Nikkei Stock Average futures at the Osaka Securities Exchange, rounded to the nearest 1/10 of an index point.

[1]The Nikkei Stock Average is owned by and proprietary to Nihon Keizai Shimbun.

Options on Nikkei Stock Average[1] Futures	
Ticker Symbols	Calls: KN Puts: JN
Underlying Contract	1 Nikkei 225 futures contract
Strike Prices	500 point intervals, e.g., 23000, 23500, 24000
Premium Quotations	U.S. $ per index point
Minimum Price Fluctuation (Tick)[2]	5 index points = $25.00 per contract cabinet = $12.50
Daily Price Limit	None
Contract Months	All 12 calendar months[3]
Trading Hours (Chicago Time)	8:00 A.M.–3:15 P.M.
Last Day of Trading	March, June, September, December: usually the business day preceding the second Friday of the contract month.
Minimum Margin	No margin required for put or call option buyers, but the premium must be paid in full; option sellers must meet additional margin requirements as determined by the Standard Portfolio Analysis of Risk™ (SPAN™) margin system.
Exercise Procedure[4]	An option may be exercised by the buyer on any business day that the option is traded and, for the March Quarterly Cycle months, on the settlement day. To exercise an option, the clearing member shall present an exercise notice to the Clearing House by 7:00 P.M. on the day of exercise.

[1]The Nikkei Stock Average is owned and proprietary to Nihon Keizai Shimbun.

[2]A trade may occur at the value of a half-tick (cabinet) if it results in liquidation for both parties to the trade.

[3]Options on Nikkei 225 futures are listed for all 12 calendar months, with each exercisable into the quarter-end futures contract. For example, January, February, and March options are exercisable into the March futures contract, and the March futures price is relevant for the pricing of the three sets of options. At any point in time, you can choose from options that expire in the next three calendar months, plus the following two quarter-end expirations.

[4]Consult your broker for specific requirements.

Source: CME Futures & Options (Chicago: Chicago Mercantile Exchange, 1991), 28–29. Courtesy of Chicago Mercantile Exchange.

of these countries' stock exchanges. It is considered the performance benchmark of international market activity.

New service concepts are virtually unlimited. Mailflight, for example, is a British mailing specialist that can help American firms bypass the U.S. Postal Service. It will collect mail from anywhere if a client cannot deliver it to Mailflight's clearing center at JFK International airport, where mail is prepared with full documentation for same-day flights to the company's European centers. At those centers, mail sorting is done in accordance with the postal standards of the countries of destination, and mail can then be entered directly into the postal process within twenty-four hours.

It is difficult to distinguish a good from a service, since a tangible object provides services and a service can enhance the value of the tangible product. Although people buy foods from McDonald's, they are actually paying for the company's services and expertise. By the same token, a buyer of a business computer does not buy it for its physical attributes; the buyer expects performance. Furthermore, this may lead to a purchase of software, as well as a service contract. Of course, the software requires a physical floppy disk, and the repair and maintenance service still necessitates the use of parts and supplies. As a result, a distinction between a good and a service is increasingly blurred.

The automobile industry is a good example of how much product quality and service are intertwined. An automaker cannot be successful without adequate services. Toyota became successful by doubling and tripling its service budget after learning from its 100 studies that Volkswagen outsold other European cars in the United States because of superior service. The Customer Satisfaction Index subsequently rewarded Toyota with the second-best ranking, behind only Mercedez-Benz. Toyota's Lexus division took the top honor in 1991 and 1992.

Like merchandise trade, exports of services are influenced by changes in relative economic conditions and exchange rates. As shown by the travel industry, when the dollar was strong in the early 1980s, the increased buying power of the dollar made foreign travel by Americans a bargain. But when the dollar weakened, foreign travelers vacationed in the United States. The impact of the exchange rate, however, can be greatly moderated by such economic factors as inflation. Mexico's high inflation rate outpaced the rate of decline of the peso against the dollar. This explains a reduction in U.S. travel expenditures in areas experiencing high inflation rates (e.g., Mexico, South America, and the Eastern Mediterranean). Exhibit 10–13 examines international travel.

The primary competition for American service firms comes from Western Europe, with new challenges being mounted by Latin American and East Asian companies. Countries such as India view service as an infant industry that must be nurtured and protected. Not surprisingly, service exports/imports are subject to many nontariff trade barriers (e.g., local labor and content of service requirements, ownership restrictions, foreign exchange controls, and discriminatory taxation policies). A study of the Conference Board of twenty-three countries reveals these barriers: outright bans on investing in certain businesses (e.g., banking), employment bans (e.g., engineering and accounting), quotas, local standards (e.g., telecommunications), and discriminatory codes and tax systems (e.g., entertainment).[45] The U.S. advertising industry encounters such obstacles as controls of profit repatriation, restrictions on

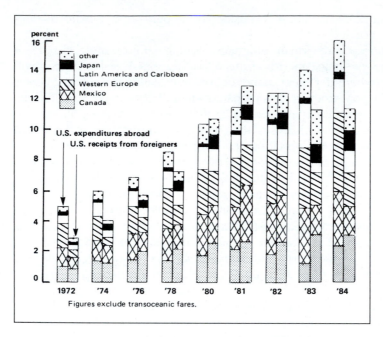

EXHIBIT 10–13   International travel—U.S. expenditures abroad and foreign expenditures in the United States

Source: Federal Reserve Bank of Chicago, "U.S. Expenditures on Foreign Travel Increase," *International Letter,* no. 549 (August 1985): 3. Courtesy of the Federal Reserve Bank of Chicago.

equity ownership, and limits on the number of nonlocal staff.[46] Foreign life insurers are not allowed to set up shop in South Korea. Germany's communication tariffs prohibit incoming information from reaching a third party without being processed in a data processing center first. American Express is thus required to process within the country data on German citizens.

Although service providers must abide by local laws, they may still want to try to change unfavorable laws or oppose proposed regulations that can adversely affect business activities. Since the move for fixed exchange rates will threaten the existence of the CME's currency contracts, the CME established the American Coalition for Flexible Exchange Rates to present the alternative point of view to that of the advocates of fixed rates. The Coalition is a nonpartisan league of noted economists, business leaders, and former government officials. Based on the belief that instability in foreign exchange markets is a symptom and not a cause of underlying economic problems, the group supports the idea that only a free functioning system of foreign exchange can achieve fair relative value of currencies.

Services have several unique characteristics; they are intangible, person-oriented, and perishable. Still, virtually all marketing concepts and strategies used to market tangible products are relevant to the marketing of services. Consider the concept of market segmentation. Because of consumers' varying demographics and heterogeneous needs for services, the market often has to be segmented. Qantas believes that the travel market, based on lifestyles, has six segments.[47] First, there is the "new enthusiast" group, consisting of inexperienced travelers who are young, fresh, eager, and hungry for experience, difference, and challenge. Second—almost the antithesis of the enthusiast—the "big spenders" are dedicated indulgers who are older, passive, and nonphysical. They are belongers, conformers, and a part of the establishment. Third, even worse than the big spenders are the "new indulgers." As experienced travelers, they are almost paranoid about their desire for the very best at all cost because travel is viewed by them as an opportunity to be pampered.

The fourth group is the "anti-tourist." Members of this group are nonconformist and distinctively experimental, and they disapprove of any tourist attitude and behavior. The next group, known as the "stay at home tourists," comprises those who are dependent, security minded, physically passive, and not adventurous. They do not enjoy difference or other cultures and want to speak their own language. As such, they want planning, familiarity, and bus tours. Many Americans would not be flattered to learn that these are generally American characteristics. Finally, the sixth group is exemplified by the "dedicated Aussy," a pragmatic, independent, self-reliant, nationalistic group that feels that overseas traveling is unnecessary. Members of this group, when going abroad, take their domestic minds with them.

Because of the varying needs across the six segments, an identical marketing mix for all groups is inappropriate. Some are more price-conscious than others. Those in the antitourist group may not exactly be budget-conscious, but they want to get value. That group's members, being rather impulsive, may respond well to a message that appeals to their mobility and feeling of "moving on."

Like a product, a company's service should also be defined broadly. American Express, for instance, does not look at itself as being in the credit-card business. Instead, the company is in the communications and information processing business, and its computer center in Phoenix processes a quarter million credit card transactions each day from all over the world. Exhibit 10–14, an advertisement for American Airlines, clearly shows that an airline's service is much more than simply selling a seat to take people from one place to another.

Services also require adaptation from time to time for foreign markets. Even movies distributed abroad, more often than not, must be packaged differently. The BBC's 1992 film production of *Lady Chatterley's Lover,* based on the novel by D. H. Lawrence, was shown on British TV. Because of its explicit scenes, it was repackaged for U.S. cinema showings. At the very least, movies distributed internationally require subtitles or overdubbing. Examples of modifications made by service providers for overseas markets include Wendy's (adding shrimp cake sandwiches in Japan), Shakey's (adding *chorizo* in Mexico and squid and cuttlefish in Japan), Arby's (deleting ham sandwiches), and Kentucky Fried Chicken (serving "chips" instead of fries in England and adding rice and smoked chicken in Japan).[48] Burger Queen changed its name in England to Huckleberry's to avoid insulting the Queen, and Kentucky Fried Chicken became (Colonel) Sanders in Brazil because of a pronunciation problem.

Although most of Disney's characters and attractions are culture-free, its stylized Main Street U.S.A. park entrance was not included in the Tokyo Disneyland. In spite of the aim of Tokyo Disneyland to give Japanese an American experience, Disney officials decided that Main Street is a concept that the Japanese cannot understand.[49] As a result, the entrance was replaced by World Bazaar instead.

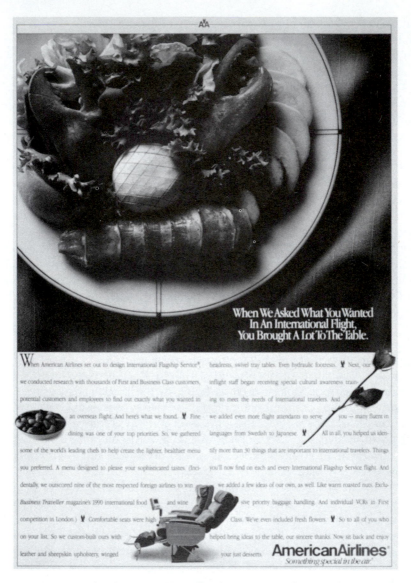

EXHIBIT 10–14   The service bundle of American Airlines

Source: Courtesy of American Airlines.

Service providers usually have more flexibility in providing services than prod-ucts because it is more difficult for consumers to ascertain and compare the quality of services among suppliers. Their prices still must be competitive, especially when the services offered are standardized. An examination of banking services should make this point clear. International banking services have long been a profitable business for U.S. banks, even though they have lately become significant problems because of nonperforming foreign loans. Increasingly, Japanese banks have been taking business away from American and European competitors. According to one estimate, Nomura, a Japanese securities firm, alone is responsible for the financing of nearly one-third of the entire U.S. national debt. Japanese banks have done particularly well in municipal bonds. Municipal bond issuers (local and state governments and agencies) use credit enhancements such as banks' letters of credit to increase the attractiveness of their securities to investors since banks are responsible for the issuers' debt if the issuers default in their debt service. The purchase of a letter of credit written by a strong bank enables the bond issuer to borrow at lower interest rates. The success of Japanese banks in the U.S. market is due in part to their more attractive prices or discounts. Still, these banks have to cope with U.S. politics. In the case of the City of Chicago, aldermen heatedly debated the merits of using Japanese banks to issue letters of credit, citing everything from patriotism to Pearl Harbor as reasons why the City should not use the banks, in spite of their lower fees.

U.S.-Canada trade in services was $31 billion in 1987. The U.S.-Canada Free Trade Agreement (FTA) sets precedents in the area of international services trade, as a result of the acceptance of several important principles. *National treatment* ensures that any new Canadian law or regulation must treat American service providers no less favorably than Canadian providers. The Agreement ensures that U.S. service providers have the *right to sell* across the border, making it feasible for them to provide a service from the United States without being forced to establish a commercial presence in Canada. This right should benefit such high-technology services as credit reporting and airline reservation, for which the normal means of delivery is over telephone lines to all customers from one central computer installation. Conversely, if a local presence is the preferred method of providing a service in Canada, the FTA guarantees the *right of establishment*. Service firms (e.g., retailers and wholesalers) often need a local commercial presence to produce the service in whole or in part where it is consumed. The United States and Canada have agreed to make publicly available (to make transparent) all laws and regulations. Because it is essential to know the rules of the game, such *transparency* enables U.S. service providers to participate with Canadian firms in the Canadian regulation process. Additionally, professional persons have the *right to cross the border* into Canada under streamlined documentational and procedural requirements.[50]

CONCLUSION

A product provides a bundle of satisfaction that the consumer derives from the product itself, along with its promotion, distribution, and price. For a product or service to be successful in any market, whether at home or overseas, it must therefore primarily satisfy consumer needs. In order to satisfy these needs more precisely, marketers should employ market segmentation, product positioning, and other marketing techniques. In the past, American marketers have been slow to realize that they must adapt their marketing practices when selling abroad. American marketers have overlooked the particular preferences and needs of customers overseas and have not adapted exported products, brands, and packages to meet these needs. For companies that have committed themselves seriously to their international market needs, performance can be very encouraging. Texas Instruments and Du Pont, for example, have done remarkably well in Japan, a market misunderstood by many, by assigning their best marketing personnel in that market. Du Pont, recognizing the importance of this market, maintains thirteen laboratories in Japan to work closely with customers in order to tailor products to meet customers' needs.

Although product modification for local markets is a necessity in many cases, it does not mean that all products must be changed. A standardized product designed for one market may fit many other markets as well. But this situation is relatively rare, and the standardized product that is suitable in many markets should be considered as a fortunate random occurrence. A world product, on the other hand, should be created with the world market in mind in order to maximize consumer satisfaction and simplify the production process in the long run. If a world product is not possible because of environmental diversity or other circumstances, a marketing manager should reexamine product characteristics and consumer needs. If there is a possibility that there is a convergence on the characteristics and needs, then it may be possible to standardize the product. When the characteristics and need variables do not converge, then it becomes a matter of changing the product to fit consumer needs, as long as the associated costs are not prohibitive. The time has clearly come for the export marketer to think less nationally and more internationally. It may in fact be as fundamental as determining that if the product can satisfy a need at a reasonable price, the product will sell itself in its international market. If the product cannot satisfy either requirement (i.e., need and price), then the export marketer should seek out alternative markets.

QUESTIONS

1. Explain how new product development in the United States may differ from that of other countries.
2. By marketing in a foreign country, must a firm automatically utilize geographic segmentation or other segmentation bases?
3. Explain (in the international context) how these product attributes affect product adoption: relative advantage, compatibility, trialability/divisibility, observability, complexity, and price.
4. Describe briefly the IPLC theory and its marketing implications.
5. Describe the factors that make it feasible to offer a standardized product.
6. Offer your arguments for product adaptation.
7. Explain the "big-car" syndrome and "left-hand-drive" syndrome.
8. Why do foreign governments erect barriers to U.S. exports of services?

DISCUSSION ASSIGNMENTS AND MINICASES

1. Provide examples of products for each of these IPLC stages: (0) local innovation, (1) overseas innovation, (2) maturity, (3) worldwide imitation, and (4) reversal.
2. Given the implications of the IPLC theory, how should U.S. innovating firms adjust their marketing strategies?

3. Why are U.S. manufacturers unwilling to modify their products for overseas customers?

4. Is it practical to offer a world product? (Note: this term should be differentiated from a standardized product.)

5. Do you think that the day may come when U.S. stock indices (e.g., Dow-Jones Industrial Averages, S&P 500) may be overshadowed or even replaced by a world or global stock index that represents the movement of stock prices worldwide?

6. Can standard marketing techniques (e.g., market segmentation and product positioning) be used to market services locally and internationally?

7. Some managers of McDonald's, buoyed by the success in Asia and Moscow, want to "McDonaldize" the world. Discuss the implications of this statement as related to standardization and adaptation.

CASE 10–1
GROTESQUE TOYS— Can We Market "Ugly" Internationally?

JEFFREY A. FADIMAN
San Jose State University

Children often annoy their parents—whether intentionally or not. In the United States, how to annoy one's parent is an art. It is no longer adequate just to put a toad in someone's pocket. Now there are gross toys. They are ugly and they are hot.

Slime has been around for quite some time. Technically speaking, Slime is a water-soluble gel laced with phosphorescents. Its practical purpose, however, is to make people sick with the way the sticky green stuff looks and feels. With many new repugnant toys, Slime is no longer unique and even pales by comparison. It is now joined in the gross corner by Worm Skull, Deathbreath, Sammy Sneeze, Slobulus, the Mad Scientist, and Madballs.

Madballs are plastic monster heads with hideous faces on one side to show partially exposed brains and dangling eyeballs. Mattel's Mad Scientist line includes the Monster Lab Playset, which lets children put monster bones together and sizzle off the monster flesh in a vat. The Dissect-an-Alien Playset, on the other hand, comes complete with an alien visitor's organs covered with "glow-in-the-dark alien blood." These organs can be pulled out and reinserted as desired.

According to Mattel's manager of marketing and public relations, the company makes no claim about its gross toys' educational or socially redeeming value. But she added that these toys might get children to learn how to control their fear of the unknown. Moreover, "it's an outlet; it's funny; it's not meant to be serious." Any alarm is undue alarm, and only the adults take these repugnant toys seriously.

Some adults, however, cannot disagree more. They have pointed out that ugly and violent toys teach intolerance and insensitivity. These hideous toys could give children nightmares and distort their sense of beauty. Also, many gross toys go beyond norms of decency and good taste. How can children then learn to respect their parents and others? Besides, children can always play with Barbie and Raggedy Andy dolls.

Questions

You have just been employed by a mid-size U.S. toy firm to develop its initial international promotion. You have been assigned to market the concept of "gross toys" to one foreign target market. You may want to visit a local toy store to see what is available.

Write a preliminary business memo (essay style) in which you respond to the following:

1. Why do you think this concept works so effectively among Americans? To which segments(s) of the market does it appeal? Why?
2. What objections would potential clientele within your target market have to this product, as currently promoted in the United States? Why?
3. Which segments of your target market might prove most receptive to this concept, if modified to reflect local expectations? Why?
4. Consider either one specific toy (e.g., Slime) or the concept as a whole (i.e., "gross toys"). How (in what ways) can you modify either the product itself (one toy) or the entire concept (gross toys), so as to make it acceptable to the target clientele you have selected? Consider modification of (a) the toy itself (or the entire concept), (b) the packaging, and (c) the image (purpose for which it is designed).
5. Why (after you have modified the concept) do you think it might be more effective within your target nation? Justify each modification.

CASE 10–2
SPERRY/MACLENNAN
Architects and Planners

MARY R. BROOKS
Dalhousie University

In August 1988 Mitch Brooks, a junior partner and director of Sperry/MacLennan (abbreviated as S/M), a Dartmouth, Nova Scotia, architectural practice specializing in recreational facilities, is in the process of developing a plan to export his company's services. He intends to present the plan to the other directors at their meeting in the first week of October. The regional market for architectural services is showing signs of slowing and S/M realizes that it must seek new markets. As Sheila Sperry, the office manager and one of the directors, said at their last meeting, "You have to go wider than your own backyard. After all, you can only build so many pools in your own backyard."

About the Company

Drew Sperry, one of the two senior partners in Sperry/MacLennan, founded the company in 1972 as a one-man architectural practice. After graduating from the Nova Scotia Technical College (now the Technical University of Nova Scotia) in 1966, Sperry worked for six years for Robert J. Flinn before deciding that it was time to start his own company. By then he had cultivated a loyal clientele and a reputation as a good design architect and planner. In the first year, the business was supported part-time by a contract with the Province of Prince Edward Island Department of Tourism to undertake park planning and the design of park facilities, from furniture to interpretive centers. A the end of its first year, the company was incorporated as H. Drew Sperry and Associates; by then Sperry had added three junior architects, a draftsman, and a secretary. One of those architects was John MacLennan, who would later become a senior partner in Sperry/MacLennan.

Throughout the 1970s, the practice grew rapidly as the local economy expanded, even though the market for architectural services was competitive. The architectural program at the Nova Scotia Technical College was graduating more architects wishing to stay in the Maritimes than could be readily absorbed. But that was not the only reason why competition was stiff; there was a perception among business people and local government personnel that, if you wanted the best, you had to get it from Toronto or New York. The company's greatest challenge throughout this period was persuading the local authorities that they did not have to go to Central Canada for first-class architectural expertise.

With the baby boom generation entering the housing market, more than enough business came their way to enable Sperry's to develop a thriving architectural practice, and by 1979 the company had grown to 15 employees and had established branch offices in Charlottetown and Fredericton. These branch offices had been established to provide a local market presence and meet licensing requirements during their aggressive growth period. The one in Charlottetown operated under the name of Allison & Sperry Associates, with Jim Allison as the partner, and, in Fredericton, partner Peter Fellows was in charge.

But the growth could not last. The early 1980s was not an easy time for the industry and many architectural firms found themselves unable to stay in business. For Sperry/MacLennan, it meant a severe reduction in staff, and it marked the end of the branch offices. Financially stretched and with work winding down on a multipurpose civic sports facility, the Dartmouth Sportsplex, the company was asked to enter a design competition for an aquatics center in Saint John, New Brunswick. It was a situation in which they had to win or close their doors. The company laid off all but the three remaining partners, Drew, Sheila Sperry, and John MacLennan. However, one draftsman and the secretary refused to leave, working without pay for several months in the belief that the company would win; their faith in the firm is still appreciated today.

Their persistence and faith was rewarded. In 1983 Sperry won the competition for the aquatics facility for the Canada Games to be held in Saint John. The clients in Saint John wanted to build a new aquatic center that would house the Canada Games *and* provide a self-supporting community facility after the Games were over. The facility needed to reflect a forward-thinking image to the world and act as a linchpin in the downtown revitalization plan. Therefore, it was paramount that the facility adhere to all technical competition requirements and that the design include renovation details for its conversion to a community facility boasting a new Sperry design element—the "indoor beach." The Saint John Canada Games Society decided to use Sperry's for the contract and were very pleased with the building, the more so since the building won two design awards in 1985: the Facility of Merit Award for its "outstanding design" from *Athletics Business* and the Canadian Parks and Recreation Facility of Excellence Award. Sperry's had gained national recognition for its sports facility expertise and their reputation as a good design firm specializing in sports facilities was secured.

From the beginning, the company found recreational facilities work to be fun and exciting. To quote Sheila Sperry, this type of client "wants you to be innovative and new. It's a dream for an architect because it gives him an opportunity to use all the shapes and colors and natural light. It's a very exciting medium to work in." So they decided to focus their promotional efforts to get more of this type of work and consolidate their "pool designer" image by associating with Creative Aquatics on an exclusive basis in 1984. Creative Aquatics provided aquatics programming and technical operations expertise (materials, systems, water treatment, safety, etc.) to complement the design and planning skills at Sperry's.

The construction industry rebounded in 1984; declining interest rates ushered in a short building boom that kept everyone busy for the 1984–87 period. Jim Reardon joined the company in 1983 and quickly acquired the experience and knowledge that would ease the company through its inevitable reexpansion. John MacLennan, by then a senior shareholder in the firm, wanted to develop a base in the large Ontario market and establish an office in Toronto. Jim Reardon was able to take over John's activities with very little difficulty, since he had been working very closely with John in the recreational facilities aspect of the business. Reardon became a junior partner in 1986.

With John MacLennan's move to Toronto in 1985, the company changed its name to Sperry/MacLennan in hopes that the name could be used for both offices. But the Ontario Association of Architects ruled that the name could not include "Sperry" because Drew Sperry was not an Ontario resident, and the Toronto office was required to operate under the name of MacLennan Architects. The Ontario office gradually became self-supporting, and the company successfully entered a new growth phase.

Mitch Brooks joined the practice in 1987. He had graduated from the Technical University of Nova Scotia in 1975 and had been one of the smaller number in his class to try and succeed in Halifax. The decision to add Brooks as a partner, albeit a junior one, stemmed from their compatibility. Brooks was a good production architect and work under his supervision came in on budget and on time, a factor compatible with the Sperry/MacLennan emphasis on customer service. The company's fee revenue amounted to approximately $1.2 million in the 1987 fiscal year; however, salaries are a major business expense and profits after taxes (but before employee bonuses) accounted for only 4.5 percent of revenue.

Now it is late August, and with the weather cooling Mitch Brooks reflects on his newest task, planning for the coming winter's activities. The company's reputation in the Canadian sports facility market is secure. The company has completed or has in construction five sports complexes in the Maritimes and five in Ontario, and three more facilities are in design. The awards have followed and, just this morning, Drew was notified of their latest achievement—the company has won the $10,000 *Canadian Architect* Grand Award for the Grand River Aquatics and Community Centre near Kitchener, Ontario. This award is a particularly prestigious one, as it is given by fellow architects in recognition of design excellence. Last week Sheila Sperry received word that the Amherst, N.S., YM-YWCA won the American National Swimming Pool and Spa Gold Medal for pool design against French and Mexican finalists, giving them international recognition. Mitch Brooks is looking forward to his task ahead. The partners anticipate a slight slowdown in late 1988 and economists are predicting a recession for 1989. With nineteen employees to keep busy and a competitor on the west coast, they decided this morning that it is time to consider exporting their hard-won expertise.

The Architecture Industry

In order to practice architecture in Canada, an architect must graduate from an accredited school and serve a period of apprenticeship with a licensed architect, during which time he or she must experience all facets of the practice. At the end of this period, the would-be architect must pass an examination similar to that required of U.S. architects.

Architects are licensed provincially, and these licenses are not readily transferable from province to province. Various levels of reciprocity are in existence. For this reason, joint ventures are not uncommon in the business. In order to "cross" provincial boundaries, architectural firms in one province often enter into a joint venture arrangement with a local company. For example, the well-known design firm of Arthur Erickson of Vancouver/Toronto often engages in joint ventures with local production architects, as was the case for their design of the new Sir James Dunn Law Library on the campus of Dalhousie University in Halifax.

In the United States, Canadian architects are well respected. The primary difficulty in working in the United States has been founded in immigration policies, which limit the movement of staff and provide difficulties in securing contracts. These policies will be eliminated with the Free Trade Agreement and with the reciprocity accord signed between the American Institute of Architects and the Royal Architectural Institute of Canada, a voluntary group representing the provincial associations.

Because architects in Nova Scotia are ethically prohibited from advertising their services, an architect's best advertisement is a good project, well done and well received. The provincial association (Nova Scotia Association of Architects—NSAA) will supply potential clients with basic information about licensed firms, their area of specialization, and so on. NSAA guidelines limit marketing to announcements of new partners, presentations to targeted potential clients, advertisements of a business card size with "business card" information, and participation in media events.

The provincial association also provides a minimum schedule of fees, although many clients view this as the maximum they should pay. Although architects would like to think that the client chooses to do business with them because they like their past work, the price of the service is often the decision point. Some developers prefer to buy services on a basis other than the published fee schedule, such as a lump sum amount or a per square foot price. Although fee cutting is not encouraged by the professional organization, it is a factor in winning business, particularly when interest rates are high and construction slow.

Since the "product" of an architecture firm is the service of designing a building, the marketing of the "product" centers on the architect's experience with a particular building type. Therefore, it is imperative that the architect convince the client that he or she has the necessary experience and capability to undertake the project and complete it satisfactorily. S/M has found with its large projects that the amount of time spent meeting with the client requires some local presence, although the design need not be done locally.

The process of marketing architectural services is one of marketing ideas. Therefore, it is imperative that the architect and the client have the same objectives and ultimately the same vision. Although that vision may be constrained by the client's budget, part of the marketing process is one of communicating with the client to ensure that these common objectives exist.

Architects get business in a number of ways. "Walk-in" business is negligible and most of S/M's contracts are a result of one of the following five processes:

1. By referral from a satisfied client.
2. A juried design competition will be announced. (S/M has found that these prestigious jobs, even though they offer "runners-up" partial compensation, are not worth entering except to win, because costs are too high and the compensation offered other entrants too low. Second place is the same as last place. The Dartmouth Sportsplex and the Saint John Aquatic Centre were both design competition wins.)
3. A client will publish a "Call for Proposals" or a "Call for Expressions of Interest" as the start of a formal selection process. (S/M rates these opportunities; unless they have a 75 percent change of winning the contract, they view the effort as not worth the risk.)
4. A potential client invites a limited number of architectural firms to submit their qualifications as the start of a formal selection process. (S/M has a prepared qualification package that it can customize for a particular client.)
5. S/M hears of a potential building and contacts the client, presenting its qualifications.

The fourth and fifth processes are most common in buildings done for institutions and large corporations. Because the primary buyers of sports facilities tend to be municipalities or educational institutions, this is the way S/M acquires a substantial share of its work. Although juried competitions are not very common, the publicity possible from success in landing this work is important to S/M. The company has found that its success in securing a contract is often dependent on the client's criteria and the current state of the local market, with no particular pattern evident for a specific building type.

After the architect signs the contract, there will be a number of meetings with the client as the concept evolves and the drawings and specifications develop. On a large sports facility project, the hours of contact can run into the hundreds. Depending on the type of project, client meetings may be held weekly or every two weeks; during the development of working drawings and specifications for a complex building, meetings may be as often as once a day. Therefore, continuing client contact is as much a part of the service sold as the drawings, specifications and site supervision and, in fact, may be the key factor in repeat business.

Developers in Nova Scotia are often not loyal buyers, changing architects with every major project or two. Despite this, architects are inclined to think the buyer's loyalty is greater than it really is. Therefore, S/M scrutinizes buyers carefully, interested in those that can pay for a premium product. S/M's philosophy is to provide "quality products with quality service for quality clients" and thus produce facilities that will reflect well on the company.

The Opportunity

In 1987 External Affairs and the Royal Architectural Institute of Canada commissioned a study of exporting opportunities for architects on the assumption that free trade in architectural services would be possible under the Free Trade Agreement. The report, entitled *Precision, Planning, and Perseverance: Exporting Architectural Services to the United States,* identified eight market niches for Canadian architects in the United States, one of which was educational facilities, particularly postsecondary institutions.

This niche, identified by Brooks as most likely to match S/M's capabilities, is controlled by state governments and private organizations. Universities are known not to be particularly loyal to local firms and thus present a potential market to be developed. The study reported that "postsecondary institutions require design and management competence, whatever the source" (p. 39). Athletic facilities were identified as a possible niche for architects with mixed-use facility experience. Finally, the study concluded that "...there is an enormous backlog of capital maintenance and new building requirements facing most higher education institutions..." (p. 38).

In addition to the above factors, the study indicated others that Brooks felt were of importance:

1. The United States has 30 percent fewer architectural firms per capita than Canada.
2. The market shares many Canadian values and work practices.
3. The population shift away from the Northeast to the sunbelt is beginning to reverse.
4. Americans are demanding better buildings.

Although Brooks knows that Canadian firms have always had a good reputation internationally for the quality of their buildings, he is concerned that American firms are well ahead of Canadian ones in their use of CADD (computer-assisted design and drafting) for everything from conceptual design to facility management. S/M, in spite of best intentions, has been unable to get CADD off the ground but is in the process of applying to the Atlantic Canada Opportunities Agency for financial assistance in switching over to CADD.

Finally, the study cautions that "joint ventures with a U.S. architectural firm may be required but the facility managers network of the APPA [Association of Physical Plant Administrators of Universities and Colleges] should also be actively pursued" (p. 41).

Under free trade, architects will be able freely to engage in services trade. Architects will be able to travel to the United States and set up an architectural practice without having to become qualified under the American Institute of Architects; as long as they are members of their respective provincial associations and have passed provincial licensing exams and apprenticeship requirements, they will be able to travel and work in the United States and to import staff as required.

Where to Start?

In a meeting in Halifax in January 1988, the Department of External Affairs had indicated that trade to the United States in architectural services was going to be one positive benefit of the Free Trade Agreement to come into force in January

1989. As a response, S/M has targeted New England for their expansion, because of its geographical proximity to S/M's home base in the Halifax and Dartmouth area and also because of its population density and similar climatic conditions. However, with all the hype about free trade and the current focus on the United States, Brooks is quite concerned that the company might be overlooking some other very lucrative markets for his company's expertise. As part of his October presentation to the Board, he wants to identify and evaluate other possible markets for S/M's services. Other parts of the United States, or the affluent countries of Europe where recreational facilities are regularly patronized and design is taken seriously, might provide a better export market, given their string of design successes at home and the international recognition afforded by the Amherst facility design award. Brooks feels that designing two sports facilities a year in a new market would be an acceptable goal.

As part of searching for leads, Brooks notes that the APPA charges $575 for a membership, which provides access to their membership list once a year. But this is only one source of leads. And of course there is the U.S. Department of Commerce, Bureau of the Census, as another source of information for him to tap. He wonders what other sources are possible.

S/M looks to have a very good opportunity in the New England market with all of its small universities and colleges. After a decade of cutbacks on spending, corporate donations and alumni support for U.S. universities have never been so strong, and many campuses have sports facilities that are outdated and have been poorly maintained. But Mitch Brooks is not sure that the New England market is the best. After all, a seminar on exporting that he attended last week indicated that the most geographically close market, or even the most physically close one, may not be the best choice for long-run profit maximization and/or market share.

Source: This case was originally prepared by Dr. Mary R. Brooks of Dalhousie University, as a basis for classroom discussion rather than to illustrate effective or ineffective handling of an administrative situation. The assistance of the Secretary of State, Canadian Studies Program in developing the case is gratefully acknowledged. © Mary R. Brooks

Questions

1. What types of information will Brooks need to collect before he can even begin to assess the New England market? Develop a series of questions you feel are critical to this assessment.
2. What selection criteria do you believe will be relevant to the assessment of any alternative markets? What preliminary market parameters are relevant to the evaluation of S/M's *global* options?
3. Assuming that S/M decides on the New England market, what information will be needed to implement an entry strategy?

NOTES

1. "E.T. and Friends Are Flying High," *Business Week,* 10 January 1983, 77.

2. Masashi Kuga, "Kao's Marketing Strategy and Marketing Intelligence System," *Journal of Advertising Research* 30 (April/May 1990): 20–25.

3. "Listening to the Voice of the Marketplace," *Business Week,* 21 February 1983, 90.

4. "Moving beyond Assembly Lines," *Business Week,* 27 July 1981, 87, 90.

5. Sak Onkvisit and John J. Shaw, "Standardization International Advertising: A Review and Critical Evaluation of the Theoretical and Empirical Evidence," *Columbia Journal of World Business* 22 (Fall 1987): 43–55.

6. Salah S. Hassan and Lea Prevel Katsanis, "Identification of Global Consumer Segments: A Behavioral Framework," *Journal of International Consumer Marketing* 3 (no. 2, 1991): 11–28.

7. Robert G. Cooper and Elko J. Kleinschmidt, "The Impact of Export Strategy on Export Sales Performance," *Journal of International Business Studies* 16 (Spring 1985): 37–55.

8. John E. Cooney, "Top Soy Sauce Brewer in Japan Shows How to Crack U.S. Market," *The Wall Street Journal,* 16 December 1977.

9. "Marketing Research Helped Philip Morris Penetrate the 'Impenetrable' Brazil Market," *Marketing News,* 17 September 1982.

10. Robert F. Roth, *International Marketing Communications* (Chicago: Crain Books, 1982), 5.

11. "Arthur C. Bell: A Campaign to Break the Ice in the U.S. Scotch Market," *Business Week,* 6 December 1982: 82 ff.

12. S. Douglas and B. Dubois, "Looking at the Cultural Environment for International Marketing Opportunities," *Columbia Journal of World Business* 12 (Winter 1977): 106–07; "Four-Point Marketing Strategy Keeps Renault in High Gear," *International Management* 36 (Fall 1984): 41–44.

13. Norman W. McGuinness and Blair Little, "The Influence of Product Characteristics on the Export Performance of New Industrial Products," *Journal of Marketing,* 45 (Spring 1981): 110–22.

14. Tohru Nishikawa, "New Product Development: Japanese Consumer Tastes in the Area of Electronics and Home Appliances," *Journal of Advertising Research* 30 (April/May 1990): 27–30.

15. Raymond Vernon, "International Investment and International Trade in the Product Cycle," *Quarterly Journal of Economics* (January 1967); Charles P. Kindleberger, *International Economics,* 5th ed. (Homewood, IL: Irwin, 1973), 62–67; Louis T. Wells, Jr., "A Product Life Cycle for International Trade?" *Journal of Marketing* 32 (July 1968): 1–6; H. Hoy and John J. Shaw, "The United States' Comparative Advantage and Its Relationship to the Product Life Cycle Theory and the World Gross National Product Market Share," *Columbia Journal of World Business* 16 (Spring 1981): 40–50.

16. This section is based largely on Sak Onkvisit and John J. Shaw, "An Examination of the International Product Life Cycle and Its Application within Marketing," *Columbia Journal of World Business* 18 (Fall 1983): 73–79.

17. Robert T. Green, "Changing National Concentration of High Technology Exports, 1974–1979," *Columbia Journal of World Business* 17 (Fall 1982): 72–76.

18. Kindleberger, *International Economics,* 65.

19. James M. Lutz and Robert T. Green, "The Product Life Cycle and the Export Position of the United States," *Journal of International Business Studies* 14 (Winter 1983): 77–93.

20. Alicia Mullor-Sebastian, "The Product Life Cycle Theory: Empirical Evidence," *Journal of International Business Studies* 14 (Winter 1983): 95–105.

21. "How P&G Was Brought to a Crawl in Japan's Diaper Market," *Business Week,* 13 October 1986, 71, 74.

22. Sak Onkvisit and John J. Shaw, "Competition and Product Management: Can the Product Life Cycle Help?" *Business Horizons* 29 (July-August 1986): 51–62.

23. Ishmael P. Akaah, "Strategy Standardization in International Marketing: An Empirical Investigation of Its Degree of Use and Correlates," *Journal of Global Marketing* 4 (no. 2, 1991): 39–62.

24. Anthony C. Koh, "An Evaluation of International Marketing Research Planning in United States Export Firms," *Journal of Global Marketing* 4 (no. 3, 1991): 7–25.

25. Robert Grosse and Walter Zinn, "Standardization in International Marketing: The Latin American Case," *Journal of Global Marketing* 4 (no.1, 1990): 53–78.

26. "The 'Left-Hand-Drive' Barrier to U.S. Sales," *Business Week,* 15 February 1982, 60.

27. Robert C. Christopher, *Second to None: American Companies in Japan* (New York: Crown, 1986).

28. John S. Hill and Richard R. Still, "Effects of Urbanization on Multinational Product Planning: Markets in Lesser-Developed Countries," *Columbia Journal of World Business* 19 (Summer 1984): 62–67.

29. John S. Hill and Richard R. Still, "Adapting Products to LDC Tastes," *Harvard Business Review* 62 (March-April 1984): 92–101.

30. "Western Europe Highlights," *Business America,* 25 November 1985: 16.

31. "Metric Transition: Help for U.S. Exporters," *Business America,* 26 September 1988, 2–5.

32. Bernie Lincicome, "In the Wake of the News," *Chicago Tribune,* 1 August 1984.

33. "Copier Firm Seeks Top Spot by Developing Dealer Network," *Marketing News,* 1 October 1982, 1, 13.

34. "Pillsbury Unlocks Japan by Doing as Japanese Do," *Chicago Tribune,* 11 February 1982.

35. David Zielenziger, "Fast Food Chains Flocking to Malaysia to Tap Expanding Consumer Market," *Asian Wall Street Journal,* 1 June 1981, 15.

36. Robert D. Robinson, "The Challenge of the Underdeveloped National Market," *Journal of Marketing* 25 (October 1961): 22.

37. "Goodbye Global," *Advertising Age,* 16 November 1987, 22, 36; Joanne Lipman, "Ad Fad: Marketers Turn Sour on Global Sales Pitch Harvard Guru Makes," *The Wall Street Journal,* 12 May 1988; Irwin Lowen, "Eyes on Europe," *Direct Marketing,* October 1990, 44 ff.

38. Alice Rudolph, "Standardization Not Standard for Global Marketers," *Marketing News,* 27 September 1985, 3–4.

39. "Now That It's Cruising, Can Ford Keep Its Foot on the Gas?" *Business Week,* 11 February 1985, 48 ff.

40. Lewis M. Simons, "For the Japanese, Ohio-Made Hondas Are Cheap Imports," *San Jose Mercury News,* 11 April 1988.

41. "Services Also Feeling Sting of Global Barriers," *Marketing News,* 13 February 1987, 18.

42. "Expansion of Global Output and Trade Continued in 1990, According to GATT," *IMF Survey,* 10 December 1990, 376–77.

43. "U.S. Trade Facts," *Business America,* 6 May 1991, 10.

44. *Preparing U.S. Income Tax Returns for U.S. Citizens Abroad,* 1986 ed. (New York: Ernst & Whinney, 1986).

45. "Global Barriers."

46. International Trade Administration, "Advertising," *1986 U.S. Industrial Outlook* (Washington, D.C.: U.S. Department of Commerce, 1986).

47. Derek Hollett, "Travel Discount Card Pulls Big Results in New Market," *Direct Marketing* (May 1985): 88 ff.

48. John D. Palmer, "Consumer Service Industry Exports: New Attitudes and Concepts Needed for a Neglected Sector," *Columbia Journal of World Business* 20 (Spring 1985): 69–74.

49. "Tokyo's Disneyland May Outdo Them All," Knight-Ridder Newspapers, 27 September 1982.

50. Merriam Mashatt, "The FTA Sets International Precedent in Service Trade," *Business America,* 30 January 1989, 8–9.

The protection of trade marks is the law's recognition of the psychological function of symbols.

Justice Felix Frankfurter, U.S. Supreme Court

Product Strategies
Branding and Packaging Decisions

11

CHAPTER OUTLINE

MARKETING ILLUSTRATION
The Name Game

The perfume industry is the business of fantasy. A popular brand can command a price more than forty times the cost of production. This is probably the only kind of business in which the actual product is much less important than its brand name. Samples of Paloma Picasso fragrance were distributed even before the final fragrance was selected. And it was proven in court that most people bought Chanel No. 5 because of the brand name, not its scent. The scent is not Chanel's significant product attribute.

In marketing a new perfume, the manufacturer first outlines the specifications in terms of "a certain population, for a certain price, at a certain date, often with a kind of scent and a predetermined name." The manufacturer must decide on the "rationale" of the product in such areas as prettiness, youth, sexiness, and the message to be ultimately conveyed in advertising. Fragrance firms are then asked to supply various formulas for selection. Unknown to most of the public, fragrance firms or perfumers "ghost-write" scents for such brands as Chloe and White Linen. Roure Bertrand DuPont, a suburban New Jersey firm, created Oscar de la Renta perfume, Opium by Yves St. Laurent, and L'air du Temps by Nina Ricci. The perfumes Opium, Y, Rive Gauche, Pour Homme, and Kouros all bear the name of Yves St. Laurent, yet he designed (created) the scent for none of them.

If the reality were known, it would destroy the romance, dream, and mystery associated with the brands. The public may imagine that fashion designer Oscar de la Renta has a small lab behind his office where he creates such perfumes as Ruffles. Actually, the product began simply as a name. A marketer of Parfums Stern noticed an unusual antique bottle with a top shaped like a ruffle and was reminded of de la Renta's preference in his designs for ruffles—conjuring an image of whimsical youthfulness and glamorous femininity for young, style-conscious women. The scent finally assigned to the Ruffles brand was probably the least important part of the whole product, since it was chosen only after the boxes and bottles had been designed. Ruffles's debut at $130 an ounce was a sellout, and it replaced Opium as the top-selling department store perfume.

Sources: Betsy A. Lehman, "Perfumers Need a Nose for the New." *Chicago Tribune,* 13 February 1985; "What Lies behind the Sweet Smell of Success," *Business Week,* 27 February 1984

The perfume industry provides a good illustration of the importance of the role played by brand name and packaging in the marketing of a product. Trademark and packaging decisions in the international context are often taken for granted and have received only scant attention in the literature. Often, articles and books simply give examples of package changes and of brand names that were misunderstood overseas. What should be emphasized is the advance planning necessary for the various branding and packaging strategies.

The purpose of this chapter is to acknowledge the strategic significance of branding and packaging and to examine some of the problems commonly faced by MNCs. Among the subjects discussed are brandless products, private brands, manufacturer's brands, multiple brands, local brands, worldwide brands, brand consolidation, brand protection, and brand characteristics. The strengths and weaknesses of each branding alternative are evaluated. The chapter also examines both mandatory and optional packaging adaptation. The emphasis of the chapter is on the managerial implications of both branding and packaging.

BRANDING DECISIONS

To understand the role of trademark in strategic planning, one must understand what a trademark is from a legal standpoint. In Thailand, **trademark** is legally defined to include "a device, brand, heading, label, ticket, name, signature, word, letter, numeral, or any combination thereof used or proposed to be used, or in connection with goods of the proprietor of such trademark by virtue of manufacture, selection, certification, dealing with, or offering for sale." According to the Lanham Trade-Mark Act of 1947, trademark in the United States "includes any word, name, symbol, or device or any combination thereof adopted and used by a manufacturer or merchant to identify his goods and distinguish them from those manufactured or sold by others." If a trademark is registered for a service, it is known as a **service mark** (e.g., Berlitz). Even though the two definitions vary somewhat from each other, the essential idea of branding remains the same in both.

A trademark can be something other than a name. Bibendum, the roly-poly corporate symbol, is Michelin's trademark. Nipper, the familiar fox terrier sitting next to a phonograph along with the phrase "his master's voice," is RCA's official symbol. Other easily recognized logos include Ralph Lauren's polo player and Goodyear's wingfoot. Exhibit 11–1 shows the logos of General Foods' well-known brands. Exhibit 11–2, in contrast, shows the trademarks of multinational firms that have direct investment in Cyprus.

In many countries, branding may be nothing more than the simple process of putting a manufacturer's name, signature, or picture on a product or its package. Many U.S. firms did precisely this in the old days, as illustrated by King Gillette's own portrait being used as a trademark for his Gillette razor blades.

The basic purposes of branding are the same everywhere in the world. In general, the functions of a brand are to (1) create identification and brand awareness, (2) guarantee a certain level of quality, quantity, and satisfaction, and (3) help with promotion. All of these purposes have the same ultimate goal: to induce repeat sales. The Spalding name, for example, has a great deal of marketing clout in Japan. In fact, a group of investors bought the company in 1982 because they felt that Spalding was the best-known name in sports in the free world and that the name was underutilized.[1]

For American consumers, brands are important. Overseas consumers are just as brand-conscious—if not more so—because of their social aspirations and the social meanings that brand names can offer. Eastern European consumers recognize many Western brand names, including some that are unavailable in their countries. Among the most powerful brand names are Sony, Adidas, Ford, Toyota, Volvo, BMW, and Mercedes. When International Semi-Tech Microelectronics Inc. acquired troubled SSMC Inc., the most important asset was probably the Singer trademark.

When a company is for sale, the remainder of the purchase price after deducting the fair value of the physical assets is called goodwill, "going concern value," or

EXHIBIT 11–1 General Foods's registered trademarks/logos

Source: Reprinted with permission of General Foods Corporation

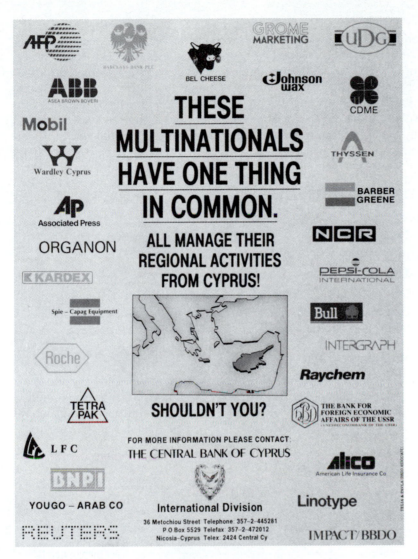

EXHIBIT 11–2 Trademarks and foreign direct investment

Source: Courtesy of Central Bank of Cyprus

an intangible asset. The value of intangible assets and percentage of net worth of the following firms are as follows: Fruit of the Loom ($908 million and 352 percent), Coca-Cola Enterprises ($2.94 billion and 188 percent), and IBM ($717 million and 2 percent). In the case of service businesses, nearly all of the purchase price that companies generate is considered goodwill.[2]

Taken into consideration the importance of branding as a marketing tool, one would expect that corporate headquarters would normally have a major role in brand planning for overseas markets. As a component of an MNC's marketing mix, branding is the area in which standardization appears to be relatively high. One study found a standardization branding rate of 82.5 percent among U.S. consumer goods manufacturers.[3] In comparison to the large U.S.-based industrial firms' European marketing strategies, these same firms' marketing mix strategies in Latin America appear to be more standardized. As expected, branding and product were least adapted, probably because of the relatively greater cost of adapting products and brands.[4] Westinghouse, for example, requires its Westinghouse *do Brasil* affiliate to use the common logo, resulting in all the MNC's Brazilian companies using the familiar circled W symbol in their promotion programs. Thus, centralization of trademark decisions is a common practice.

BRANDING LEVELS AND ALTERNATIVES

There are four levels of branding decisions:

1. No brand vs. brand
2. Private brand vs. manufacturer's brand
3. Single brand vs. multiple brands
4. Local brands vs. worldwide brand

Exhibit 11–3 shows an outline of the decision-making process when branding is considered. Exhibit 11–4 lists the advantages of each branding alternative.

Branding vs. No Brand

To brand or not to brand, that is the question. Most U.S. exported products are branded, but that does not mean that all products should be. Branding is not a cost-free proposition because of the added costs associated with marking, labeling,

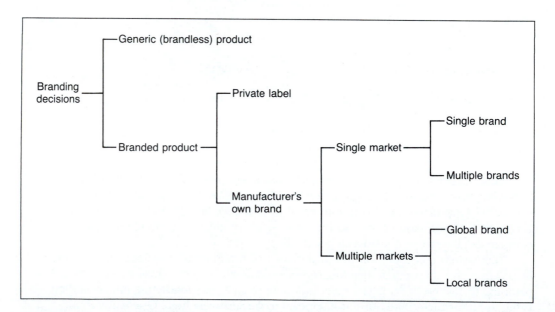

EXHIBIT 11–3   Branding decisions

No Brand lower production cost lower marketing cost lower legal cost more flexibility in quality and quantity control (i.e., possibility of less rigidity in control) good for commodities (undifferentiated items)	**Brand** better identification better awareness better chance for product differentiation better chance for repeat sales possible premium pricing (i.e., removal from price competition) possibility of making demand more price inelastic
Private Brand ease in gaining dealers' acceptance possibility of larger market share no promotional hassles and expenses good for small manufacturer with unknown brand and identity	**Manufacturer's Brand** better control of products and features better price because of more price inelasticity retention of brand loyalty better bargaining power assurance of not being bypassed by channel members
Multiple Brands (in single market) utilization of market segmentation technique creation of excitement among employees creation of competitive spirits avoidance of negative connotation of existing brand gain of more retail shelf space retention of customers who are not brand loyal allowance of trading up or down without hurting existing brand	**Single Brand (in single market)** better marketing impact permitting more focused marketing brand receiving full attention reduction of advertising costs because of better economies of scale and lack of duplication elimination of brand confusion among employees, dealers, and consumers good for product with good reputation and quality (halo effect)
Local Brands legal necessity (e.g., name already used by someone else in local market) elimination of difficulty in pronunciation allowance for more meaningful names (i.e., more local identification) elimination of negative connotations avoidance of taxation on international brand quick market penetration by acquiring local brand allowance of variations of quantity and quality across markets	**Worldwide Brand** better marketing impact and focus reduction of advertising costs elimination of brand confusion good for culture-free product good for prestigious brand easy identification/recognition for international travelers good for well-known designer

EXHIBIT 11–4   Advantages of each branding alternative (from manufacturer's viewpoint)

packaging, and legal procedures. These costs are especially relevant in the case of commodities (e.g., salt, cement, diamonds, produce, beef, and other agricultural and chemical products). **Commodities** are "unbranded or undifferentiated products which are sold by grade, not by brands." As such, there is no uniqueness, other than grade differential, that can be used to distinguish the offerings of one supplier from those of another. Branding is then probably undesirable because brand promotion is ineffective in a practical sense and adds unnecessary expenses to operations costs. The value of a diamond, for example, is determined by the so-called 4 Cs—cut, color, clarity, and carat weight—and not by brand. This is why DeBeers promotes the primary demand for diamonds in general rather than the selective demand for specific brands of diamonds.

On the positive side, a brandless product allows flexibility in quality and quantity control, resulting in lower production costs along with lower marketing and legal costs.

The basic problem with a commodity or unbranded product is that its demand is strictly a function of price. The brandless product is thus vulnerable to any price swing or price cutting. Farmers can well attest to this vulnerability, because prices of farm products have been greatly affected by competition from overseas producers. Yet, there are ways to remove a company from this kind of cutthroat competition.

Branding, when feasible, transforms a commodity into a product (e.g., Chiquita bananas, Dole pineapples, Sunkist oranges, Morton salt, Holly Farms fryers, and Perdue fryers). A **product** is a "value-added commodity," and this bundle of added values includes the brand itself as well as other product attributes, regardless of whether such attributes are physical or psychological and whether they are real or imaginary. The 3M company developed brand identity and packaging for its Scotch videotapes for the specific purpose of preventing them from becoming just another commodity item in the worldwide, price-sensitive market.

Branding makes premium pricing possible because of better identification, awareness, promotion, differentiation, consumer confidence, brand loyalty, and repeat sales. The value of branding was shown in a study of international product positioning. "Respondents tend to overrate the German cars (the BMW, the Audi, and even the U.S.-built V.W.) while underrating the American and the Japanese cars (the one exception being the slightly overrated Mazda)." As explained by the researchers, "the misperceptions evidenced in these perceptual maps are generally due to image factors such as brand name and country-of-origin stereotypes and are thus examples of both firm-specific and country-specific advantages."[5]

According to one Supreme Court decision (No. 649, May 4, 1942, *Mishawaka Rubber and Woolen Manufacturing Co. vs. S. S. Kresge*, 53 USPQ 323), "The owner of a mark exploits this human propensity by making every effort to impregnate the atmosphere of the market with the drawing power of a congenial symbol.... Once established, the trade mark owner has something of value." Exhibit 11-5 examines the importance of brand names.

Although branding provides the manufacturer with some insulation from price competition, a firm must still find out whether it is worthwhile to brand the product. In general, these prerequisites should be met:

1. Quality and quantity consistency, not necessarily the best quality or the greatest quantity.
2. The possibility of product differentiation.
3. The degree of importance consumers place on the product attribute to be differentiated.

As an example, Nike's unique designs (e.g., waffle sole) allowed the company to differentiate its brand from others and to become the top-rated brand among serious joggers.

How a Civil War general's name changed the face of Rock 'n Roll.

He didn't lead any legendary charges.

He didn't win any famous battles.

But while the names of more capable commanders are forgotten, his is practically a household word.

You could always pick Major General Ambrose Burnside out in a crowd. He was the one with the flamboyant line of bushy whiskers that ran from temple to chin.

The style caught on.

And before long, sporting "burnsides" was all the rage.

Over the years, "burnsides" be-

came sideburns. And once again, they became the rage. It's hard to imagine a rock star—or fan—of the '50s or '60s without them.

Names are important.

Hammermill knows. After all, we have the best-known name in paper.

We also know how important your company's name is.

That's why every single sheet of paper we make—and we make

a variety of business and printing papers as long as your arm—is designed to make your name stand out every time it appears in print.

We can't promise to make you a household word. But if you want people to remember your name, remember ours.

When it comes to paper, the name is Hammermill.

EXHIBIT 11–5   Significance of a brand name

Source: Reprinted with permission of Hammermilll Papers

Private Brand vs. Manufacturer's Brand

Branding to promote sales and move products necessitates a further branding decision: whether the manufacturer should use its own brand or a distributor's brand on its product. Distributors in the world of international business include trading companies, importers, and retailers, among others; their brands are called

private brands. Many portable TV sets made in Japan for the U.S. market are under private labels. In rare instances, Japanese marketers put their brands on products made by U.S. companies, as evidenced by Matsushita's purchases of major appliances from White and D&M for sale in the United States. The Oleg Cassini trademark is put on the shirts actually made by Daewoo.

Even though it may seem logical for a distributor to carry the manufacturer's well-known brand, many distributors often insist on their own private brands for several reasons. First, a distributor may be able to create a unique product by bundling or unbundling product attributes and then adjusting the price to reflect the proper value.

Second, a private brand is a defensive strategy that guarantees that a distributor is not bypassed by its supplier. For example, Ponder and Best, after losing the Rolleiflex and Olympus distributorships, came up with its own brand of photographic products, Vivitar.

Third, distributors can convert fixed production costs into variable costs by buying products made by others. Sperry's products are made by more than 200 manufacturers (e.g., Sperry's personal computer is manufactured by Mitsubishi). With this practice, Sperry is able to save cash and research-and-development expenses. Of course, it is important for a distributor with a private brand to have a reliable supplier.

Fourth and perhaps the most important reason for a distributor's insistence on a private brand is because of brand loyalty, bargaining power, and price. In spite of the lower prices paid by the distributor and ultimately by its customers, the distributor is still able to command a higher gross margin than what a manufacturer's brand usually offers. The lower price can also be attributed to the distributor's refusal to pay for the manufacturer's full costs. A distributor may want to pay for the manufacturer's variable costs but not all of the fixed costs. Or a distributor may want to pay for production costs only but not the manufacturer's promotional expenditures, because a distributor gets no benefit from the goodwill of a manufacturer's advertised brand. If a firm has any problem with the supplier (manufacturer), it has the flexibility of switching to another supplier to make the identical product, thus maintaining brand loyalty and bargaining power without any adverse effect on sales. RCA, for example, switched from Matsushita to Hitachi for its portable units of VCRs.

There are a number of reasons that the strategy of private branding is not necessarily bad for the manufacturer. First, the ease in gaining market entry and dealers' acceptance may allow a larger market share overall while contributing to offset fixed costs. JVC, for instance, is able to sell a great deal more VCRs by also manufacturing for Jensen, Kenwood, Akai, Sansui, and Tatung. Of the 100 or so VCR models under some 30 labels in the United States, all VHS brands are manufactured by only six manufacturers.[6]

Second, there are no promotional headaches and expenses associated with private branding, thus making the strategy suitable for a manufacturer with an unknown brand. Suzuki cars are sold in the United States under the GM Sprint brand name. Ricoh's facsimile machines are sold under AT&T's well-known name. Brother has had virtually no name recognition because it has marketed its many products under the private labels of U.S. major retail chains; to secure recognition, it has begun to mount a major campaign.

Third, a manufacturer may judge that the sales of its own product are going to suffer to a greater or lesser degree by various private brands. In that case, the manufacturer might as well be cannibalized by one of those private brands made by the manufacturer.

There are also reasons why private branding is not good for the manufacturer. By using a private brand, the manufacturer's product becomes a commodity, at least to the distributor. To remain in business and retain sales to the distributor, the manufacturer must compete on the basis of price, because the distributor can always switch suppliers. By not having its own identity, the manufacturer can easily be bypassed. Furthermore, it loses control over how its product should be promoted—this fact may become critical if the distributor does not do a good job in pushing the product. For example, Mitsubishi, which manufactures Dodge Colt and Plymouth Champ for Chrysler, felt that its products did not receive Chrysler's proper attention. As a result, Mitsubishi began to create its own dealer network and brand identity (e.g., Mitsubishi Mirage). Ricoh used to sell copiers in the United States only under such private brands as Savin and Nashua, whose sales lagged. After switching to its own brand name in 1981, Ricoh's sales increased tenfold to take second place in unit sales behind only Canon.

The manufacturer's dilemma is best illustrated by Heinz's experience in the United Kingdom, where consumer recognition for its brand is stronger than in any other country in the world. Whereas Campbell Soup and Nestlé's Crosse & Blackwell make some products under private labels to accommodate giant supermarkets' insistence, Heinz produces products only under its own brand because, as the largest supplier of canned foods there, it has the most to lose. To preserve its long-term market leadership at the expense of short-term earnings, Heinz has held down prices, stepped up new product introductions, launched big capital-spending programs, and increased advertising. Heinz does make private-label merchandise in the United States, where private brands account for 10 percent of its U.S. sales. Its logic is that the slow growth of U.S. private labeling does not pose a serious threat as in the United Kingdom, where private label sales in the 1980s made up 28 percent of packaged groceries sales, up from 20 percent in 1975.[7]

Clearly, the manufacturer has two basic alternatives: (1) its brand or (2) a private brand. Its choice depends in part on its bargaining power. If the distributor is prominent and the manufacturer itself is unknown and anxious to penetrate a market, then the latter may have to use the former's brand on the product. But if the manufacturer has superior strength, it can afford to put its own brand on the product and can insist that the distributor accept that brand as part of the product. For example, Kinishiroku had U.S. film sales derived primarily from some thirty original-equipment-manufacturer channels, such as mail order and drugstore film processors. Fotomat accounted for 70 percent of the company's original-equipment-manufacturer film sales. In the process of taking over Fotomat, Kinishiroku announced plans to expand from private-label manufacturing to direct distribution under its own brand name of Konica.

The hypothesis of the **"least dependent person"** can be quite applicable in determining the power of the manufacturer and that of its dealer. The stronger party is the one with resources and alternatives, and that party can demand more because it needs the other party less. The weaker party needs the other partner more because of a lack of resources and/or alternatives, and thus the weaker must give in to the "least dependent" party. In most cases, the interests of both parties are interdependent, and neither party may have absolute power. For instance, Kunnan, a maker of high-quality tennis rackets, lost some of its well-known customers when they began doing their own manufacturing. When those companies later discovered that they could not produce as well in terms of cost and quality, they came back to Kunnan for the private-brand manufacturing.

Private branding and manufacturer's branding is not necessarily an either/or proposition: a compromise can often be reached to ensure mutual coexistence. If desired, both options can be employed together. Michelin, for instance, is world renowned for its own brand, and most people do not realize that Michelin also makes tires for Sears, Ward, and Venture. Sanyo, another major international brand, is relatively unknown in the United States because it has relied heavily on private-label sales to Sears and other big companies. To rectify this identity problem, Sanyo has been pushing its own name simultaneously.

Single Brand vs. Multiple Brands

When a single brand is marketed by the manufacturer, the brand is assured of receiving full attention for maximum impact. But a company may choose to market several brands within a single market based on the assumption that the market is heterogeneous and thus must be segmented. Consequently, a specific brand is designed for a specific market segment. Exhibit 11–6 shows Anheuser-Busch's various brands for the U.S. market.

The watch industry provides a good illustration for the practice of using multiple brands in a single market for different market segments. Bulova, a well-known brand, also has the Accutron and Caravelle brands. Citizen, in its attempt to capture the new youth and multiple-watch owners market, traded down to include a new brand called Vega. Likewise, Hattori Seiko is well known for its Seiko brand, which is sold at the upper-medium price range ($100–300) in better stores; to appeal to a more affluent segment, the firm traded up with the Lassale name. Seiko's strategy is to deliberately divorce the Seiko and Lassale names, once used together, in the public mind, with the gold-plated Lassale line retailing for $225–750 and the karat-gold Jean Lassale line retailing for $675–35,000. Lassale watches have Seiko movements but are made only in the United States and Western Europe in order to curb parallel trading, and they are distributed only through jewelers and department stores.[8] The company also trades down, with Pulsar (the cheapest model at $50), Lorus ($12.95–49.95), and Alba ($9.95–19.95) for Asia.

Multiple brands are suitable when a company wants to trade either up or down because both moves have a tendency to hurt the firm's main business. If a company has the reputation for quality, trading down without creating a new brand will hurt the prestige of the existing brand. By the same rationale, if a company is known for its low-priced, mass-produced products, trading up without creating a new brand is hampered by the image of the existing products. Casio is perceived as a manufacturer of low-priced watches and calculators, and the name adversely affects its attempt to

EXHIBIT 11–6 Anheuser-Busch's multiple brands for a single market

Source: Reprinted with permission of Anheuser-Busch, Inc.

trade up to personal computers and electronic musical instruments. To overcome this kind of problem, Honda uses the Acura name for its sporty cars so that Acura's image is not affected by the more pedestrian Honda image.

Local Brands vs. Worldwide Brand

When the manufacturer decides to put its own brand name on the product, the problem does not end there if the manufacturer is an international marketer. The possibility of having to modify the trademark cannot be dismissed. The international marketer must then consider whether to use just one brand name worldwide or different brands for different markets or countries. To market brands worldwide and to market worldwide brands are not the same thing.

A single, **worldwide** brand is also known as an *international, universal,* or *global* brand. A Eurobrand is a slight modification of this approach, as it is a single product for a single market of twelve or more European countries, with an emphasis on the search for intermarket similarities rather than differences. Some analysts think that the concept of multimarkets as a homogeneous market will find wide acceptance in the future.[9]

A worldwide brand has several advantages. First, it tends to be associated with status and prestige. Second, it achieves maximum market impact overall while reducing advertising costs because only one brand is pushed. Bata Ltd., a Canadian shoe marketer and retailer in ninety-two countries, found out from its research that consumers generally thought Bata to be a local concern, no matter the country surveyed. The company thus decided to become an official sponsor of World Cup soccer in order to enhance Bata's international stature. For Bata and others, it is easier to achieve worldwide exposure for one brand than it is for multiple local brands. Too many brands create confusion and fragmentation.

Third, a worldwide brand provides a convenient identification, and international travelers can easily recognize the product. There would be no sense in creating multiple brands for such international products as *Time* magazine, American Express credit card, Diner's Club credit card, Shell gasoline, and so on.

Finally, a worldwide brand is an appropriate approach when a product has a good reputation or is known for quality. In such a case, a company would be wise to extend the brand name to other products in the product line. This strategy has been used extensively by GE. In another case, 3M perceived commonalities in consumer demographics and market development worldwide; in response, it devised a "convergence marketing" strategy to develop global identity for its Scotch brand of electronic recording products, whose design prominently displays the Scotch name and a globelike logo.

The use of multiple brands, also known as the *local* or *individual* approach, is probably much more common than many people realize. For instance, Unilever's low-lather fabric washing product is marketed under five different names in Western Europe. The automobile industry provides numerous examples. Ford's European Sierra is called Merkur in the United States. The Japanese strategy is to introduce a new car in Japan for one year before exporting it to the U.S. market under a different name. Toyota XX and Datsun Sunny, dubbed Toyota Supra and Nissan Sentra for the United States, are examples of this practice.

There are several reasons for using local brands. First, according to a study conducted by the United Nations Conference on Trade and Development, less-developed countries resent international brands because the brands' goodwill is created by an advertising budget that is much greater than research-and-development costs, resulting in no benefit derived from research and development for local economies.[10] In addition, local consumers are forced to pay higher prices for advertising and goodwill, benefiting MNCs but hindering the development of local competitive capacity. Such resentment may explain why India's ministries, responding to domestic soft drink producers' pressure, rejected Pepsi's 35 percent Pepsi-owned joint venture. Some governments have considered taxing international brands or limiting the use of such brands, as in the case of South Korea, which has considered placing restrictions on foreign trademarks intended for domestic consumption.

Second, when the manufacturer is unable to ensure uniform product quality across countries, it should consider local brands. Third, when an existing brand is difficult to pronounce, a new brand may be desirable. Sometimes, consumers avoid buying a certain brand when it is difficult to pronounce because they want to avoid the embarrassment of a wrong pronunciation. Wrigley had trouble with its Spearmint name in Germany until the spelling was changed to Speermint.

Fourth, a local brand is more easily understood and more meaningful for local consumers. By considering foreign tastes and preferences, a company achieves a better marketing impact. Post-It note pads made by 3M are marketed as Yellow Butterflies in France. Grey, an international advertising agency, worked with Playtex to create appropriate names for Playtex's brassieres in different languages. The result was Wow in England and Traumbügel (dream wire) in Germany. Translation can also make a brand more meaningful. This approach is sometimes mistaken for a single-brand approach when in fact a new brand is created. Close-Up (toothpaste) was translated as Klai-Chid (literally meaning "very close") in Thailand; the translation retained the meaning and the logo of the brand as well as the package design.

Fifth, a local brand can avoid a negative connotation. Pepsi introduced a noncola line under the Patio name in America but under the Mirinda name elsewhere because of the unpleasant connotation of *patio* in Spanish.

Sixth, some MNCs acquire local brands for a quick market penetration in order to save time, not to mention money, which otherwise would be needed to build the recognition for a new, unknown brand in local markets. Renault would have been foolish to abandon the AMC (American Motors) name after a costly acquisition. Thus, Renault 9, for example, became AMC Alliance in the United States. Chrysler subsequently bought AMC from Renault, one reason being AMC's coveted Jeep trademark.

Seventh, multiple brands may have to be used, not by design but by necessity, because of legal complications. One problem is the restrictions placed on the usage of certain words. Diet Coke in countries that restrict the use of the word *diet* becomes Coke Light. Antitrust problems can also dictate this strategy. Gillette, after acquiring Braun A.G., a German firm, had to sign a consent decree not to use the name in the U.S. market until 1985. The decree forced Braun to create the Eltron brand, which had little success.

Eighth and perhaps the most compelling reason for creating new local brands is because local firms may have already used the names that multinational firms have been using elsewhere. In such a case, to buy the right to use the name from a local business can prove expensive. Unilever markets Sure antiperspirant in the United Kingdom but had to test market the product under the Trust name in the United States, where Sure is Procter and Gamble's deodorant trademark. In an interesting case, Anheuser-Busch bought the American rights to the Budweiser name and recipe from the brewer of Budweis in Czechoslovakia; Budejovicky Budvar Narodni Podnik, the Czech brewer, holds the rights in Europe. Operating from the town of Ceske Budejovice, known as Budweis before World War I, this brewer claims exclusive rights to the Budweiser name in the United Kingdom, France, and several European

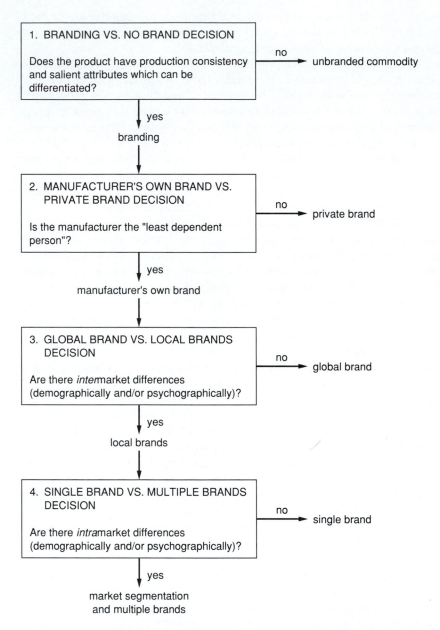

EXHIBIT 11–7 A branding model for decision making

Source: Sak Onkvisit and John J. Shaw, "The International Dimension of Branding: Strategic Considerations and Decisions," *International Marketing Review* 6 (no. 3, 1989): 29

countries. Courts have ruled that both companies have the right to sell in the United Kingdom, but Anheuser-Busch cannot sell Budweiser in Germany, Austria, and France, where the problem has not yet been resolved. Anheuser-Busch has to use the Busch name in France and the corporate name in other parts of Europe.[11]

Ninth, a local brand may have to be introduced because of price control. This problem is especially acute in countries with inflationary pressures. Price control is also one reason for the growth of the so-called gray marketers, as the phenomenon contributes to price variations among countries for the same product. Thus, instead of buying a locally produced product or one from an authorized distributor/importer, a local retailer can buy exactly the same brand from wholesalers in countries where prices are significantly lower. A manufacturer will have a hard time prohibiting importation of gray market goods, especially in EC countries where products are supposed to be able to move freely. Parallel trading can be minimized by having different national brands rather than just a worldwide brand.

The strategy of using a worldwide brand is thus not superior (or inferior) to using multiple local brands. Each strategy has its merits and serves its own useful functions. This is where managerial judgement comes in. Unilever, for example, considers consumer responses to a particular brand mix. It uses an international brand for such products as detergents and personal products because common factors among countries outweigh any differences. Food products, however, are another story. Food markets are much more complex because of variations in needs and responses to different products. The southern half of Europe mainly uses oil for cooking rather than margarine, white fats, or butter. The French more than the Dutch consider butter to be an appropriate cooking medium. German homemakers, when compared to British homemakers, are more interested in health and diet products. Soup is a lightweight precursor to the main dish in Great Britain but can almost be a meal by itself in Germany.[12] Under such circumstances of preferential variations, the potential for local brands is greatly enhanced.

Exhibit 11–7 provides a branding model for decision making.

BRAND CONSOLIDATION

Frequently, it is either by accident or by lack of coordination that multiple local brands result. Sony's Walkman initially lacked a global strategy, resulting in different packages and several local brands: Walkman (Japan), Roundabout (the United States), Stowaway (the United Kingdom), and Freestyle (Sweden). Once the product became popular, Sony decided to unify the brand name and adopt a single package design.[13]

Despite the advantages offered by the multiple-brand strategy, it may be desirable to consolidate multiple brands under one brand when the number of labels reaches the point of being cumbersome or confusing. National BankAmericard used to issue cards around the world under twenty-two names before consolidating them all under the Visa umbrella.

Another way of consolidating the brand franchise simply is to drop weak brands. Assuag-SSIH weeded out all but its most prominent watch brands. Its Eterna brand, for example, was never marketed in the United States, and that brand was eventually sold to another company.

When a marketer wants to change brands or consolidate them under one brand in order to unify all marketing efforts, the process on an international scale is complex and extremely costly. Although a unified brand across frontiers provides cost savings by eliminating duplication of design and artwork, production, distribution, communications, and other related issues, such a change is fraught with pitfalls and, if not well planned and executed, can cause more problems than it solves. Nestlé uses a gradual, evolutionary process in preparing its European brands for 1992. Its package design unification involves having the Nestlé name appear along with the local brand. The Nestlé name will be gradually enlarged over a period of four or five years until it replaces the local brand names entirely.[14]

Another kind of problem presents itself when a brand is well known but the corporate name is not, complicating communication for the company. In this situation, it is probably easier to change the corporate name to fit the better-known brand, a strategy used by Sony, Aprica, Olympus, and Amoco. Promotion for the creation of the Amoco name is shown in Exhibit 11–8.

Nissan's name change, in comparison, was risky because it followed an opposite route. Nissan's half-hearted entry into the U.S. market led to the use of the Datsun name to avoid embarrassment just in case the effort failed. But the company was later unhappy that the proud corporate name was not as widely recognized as its Datsun brand, which enjoyed an 85 percent recognition rate in the United States (compared to 10–15 percent for Nissan). The company decided to institute a world-wide brand by phasing out Datsun and phasing in Nissan. Some critics questioned the move because the change cost Nissan $150 million. Furthermore, years of goodwill gained from the Datsun name would be lost. To minimize this problem, both Nissan and Datsun names appeared together at first. Its initial television commercials and print advertisements emphasized that Datsun was a product of Nissan, as shown in Exhibit 11–9.

Despite Nissan's efforts and hundreds of millions of dollars on the new name, unfortunately, many American consumers thought that Nissan was a division of Toyota. Furthermore, not recognizing the names of individual cars, they thought that Pulsar was a popular watch brand and Maxima was an interest-bearing checking account.[15]

It is debatable whether the corporate name and the product's brand name should even be the same. When the name is the same, a brand that performs poorly or gains notoriety through bad publicity hurts the corporate image as well, as the images of the corporation and the product are so intertwined. The strategy is even riskier for fashion products because fashion comes and goes. Using the same name, however, is a relatively safe strategy and should work well if a firm has good quality control and the reputation of its non-fashion products has withstood the test of time.

BRAND ORIGIN AND SELECTION

Brand names can come from a variety of sources, such as from a firm's founders (e.g., Francois Michelin, Albert G. Spalding, Pierre Cardin, and Yves St. Laurent), places (e.g., Budweiser), letters and numbers (e.g., IBM), and coined words (e.g.,

Standard Oil Company (Indiana) is changing its name to Amoco Corporation

You already know our operating companies:
Amoco Production Company
Amoco Oil Company
Amoco Chemicals Corporation
Amoco Minerals Company.
Now, our entire corporate family is
proud to carry the Amoco name.
(Our new stock exchange symbol is AN)

Amoco Corporation

For more information, write: Amoco Corporation, 200 East Randolph Drive, Mail Code 3705, Chicago, Illinois 60601

EXHIBIT 11–8   A corporate name change

Source: Reprinted with permission of Amoco Corporation

Jordache, a modified acronym for the three brothers Joseph, Ralph, and Avi Nakash).
Sometimes it is easier simply to purchase an existing brand from another com-
pany. Hong Kong's Universal International bought Matchbox, a British toy car maker.
W. Haking Enterprises, another Hong Kong company, acquired the Ansco name from
GAF, and most Americans do not realize that the brand of Haking's low-priced cameras

EXHIBIT 11–9   Nissan's early efforts in phasing out the Datsun name

Source: Reprinted with permission of Nissan Motor Corporation in the U.S.A.

is actually a Hong Kong brand. North American Philips (NAP) bought the Schick shaver trade name. Underscoring the value of this name, Remington even filed a complaint alleging that the Schick name enabled NAP to avoid spending $25 million needed to launch a new shaver to supplement the Norelco line.

Brand selection is far from being an exact science, as illustrated by the origins of many successful brands. Gabrielle Chanel liked the scent of the fifth sampled bottle in 1921. Feeling that 5 was a pretty number, she named the perfume Chanel No. 5. No less exotic is the Toyota legend. Being told by a numerologist in 1937 that eight was a lucky number, the Toyoda family modified the company's name to Toyota, which required eight calligraphic strokes instead of ten.[16] The change did prove lucky—

Toyota is the biggest and most successful automaker of Japan. Preceding Toyota's historic move was the introduction of the Datsun line in 1914. "Dat" is the name formed from the initials of the three founding investors. A smaller version of the same car, dubbed "son of Dat," was launched in 1931.

More recently, brand selection has shifted away from being an art and is becoming more of a science. The name selection process consists of these steps:

1. Identifying objectives/criteria for brand names
2. Generating names
3. Screening for the appropriateness to the firm's image or its products' image
4. Researching consumers' choices/opinions
5. Searching for a trademark
6. Selecting the trademark[17]

There are several companies that specialize in creating brand and corporate names. One of them is NameLab, and its fee is $45,000. According to the company, the English language has some 150,000 words that consist of 6,200 word pieces or morphemes.[18] These morphemes are then combined phonically to create new words. When Nissan wanted a name for a new car that would avoid any implication that small cars are fragile, NameLab came up with Sentra, which connotes "sentry, someone who protects you, as well as central, which is mainstream."

Still, it must be pointed out that marketers often do not have the luxury of picking and choosing names that they like. Nor is it always feasible to conduct marketing research to investigate the appropriateness of a name. In Brazil Philip Morris chose the Galaxy name without marketing research because it happened to be one of the company's registered names. NUMMI's use of the Nova trademark for cars produced jointly by Toyota and General Motors was due in part to GM's ownership of the Nova brand name.

BRAND CHARACTERISTICS

A good brand name should possess certain characteristics, and such characteristics are thoroughly discussed in most advertising and marketing textbooks. In essence, a brand should be short, distinctive, easy to pronounce, and able to suggest product benefits without negative connotations. In the international arena, these qualities are also relevant. The importance of these criteria is confirmed by the results of a survey of executives of *Fortune* 500 firms.[19] The criteria and the percent of firms citing each criterion are as follows:

Descriptive of product benefits, 58.5 percent of the firms

Memorable, 46.3 percent

Fits with company image or other products' image, 46.3 percent

Trademark availability, 34.1 percent

Promotable and advertisable, 22.0 percent

Uniqueness in relation to competition, 22.0 percent

Length, 15.9 percent

Ease of pronunciation, 14.6 percent

Positive connotations to potential users, 13.4 percent

Suited to package, 6.1 percent

Modern/contemporary, 3.7 percent

Understandable, 2.4 percent

Persuasive, 2.4 percent

In selecting a brand name, a marketer should first find out whether a brand name has any negative connotation in the target market. Pajero, Mitsubishi's four-wheel drive vehicle, is a sexual insult in Spanish. The problem was discovered when the company promoted it in Latin America. Mack avoids using its bulldog symbol when selling in China, where dogs are not held in high esteem.[20] When Standard Oil of New Jersey discovered that its Enco was phonetically similar to the Japanese word for "stalled car," the company searched for a worldwide brand, using a computer to search for a word with no negative connotations in any language. The computer analyzed more than 550,000 four- and five-letter words based on the various vowel and consonant combinations. Finally, Exxon was chosen.

An international brand name should reflect the desired product image. Toward this end, consumer perception should be taken into account. For instance, worldwide consumers usually perceive French perfumes to be superior, and French-sounding names for this kind of product may prove beneficial. Likewise, good watches are perceived to be made in Switzerland, toiletries in the United States, machinery and beers in Germany, and so on. If appropriate, brands should reflect such images. Russian-sounding names can be used to position a vodka brand positively. Smirnoff originated in the Soviet Union but has been made in the United States for decades—a fact not known by many Americans.

One way of creating a desired image is to have a brand name that is unique or distinctive. Exxon has this quality. Aprica, a status-symbol stroller, is also unique in several respects. In choosing the name, Kenzo Kassai, the company's owner, wanted something cute like "apple" for his folding stroller. During a trip to Italy, he found *apri*—an appropriate name for something that opens and closes. As stroller in Japanese is said as "baby car," the *ca* syllable (for "car") is a natural ending. In effect, Aprica is a blend of English, Italian, and Japanese, meaning "open to the sun."[21]

A unique name often renders itself to graphic design possibilities, another desirable feature of a trademark. Exxon was chosen because of its distinctiveness, usefulness in world markets, and graphic design possibilities. After rejecting Hot-Line and Sound-About for not being appealing, Sony selected Walkman because of the distinctive logotype with two legs sticking out from the bottom of the letter *A* in *walk*.[22]

An international product should have international brand name, and this name should be chosen with the international market in mind. When possible, the name should suggest significant benefits. Although Emery Air Freight ships everything large and small anywhere in the world, its name gave no indication of this advantage. To overcome a secretary's fear of shipping a letter to foreign countries with a carrier specializing in freight, the corporate name was changed to Emery Worldwide. Not wanting the trademark to be closely identified with the United States, U.S. Rubber adopted Uniroyal to reflect its diverse businesses around the world. The former French-born chairman of Revlon viewed Amoresse as unsuitable for a fragrance for the international audience; consequently, the name was changed to Jontue.

One way of making a brand name more international is by paying special attention to pronunciation. Many languages do not have all the alphabets, and the English language is no exception. The Spanish alphabet does not include the letter *w*, and the Italian language has no *j, k, w, x,* or *y*.[23] Right Guard deodorant is practically unpronounceable in Italian. E-Z does not have any meaning outside of the United States because *z* is pronounced *zed* at places influenced by the British education system. Citibank was often pronounced *Shee-tee-bank* in Japan until the problem was overcome by choosing a Japanese written character that gave correct pronunciation. Exhibit 11–10 examines the vowels and consonants that pose pronunciation problems to the Chinese.

Stenographers can easily see why many American words are misunderstood overseas because shorthand notations are based on how a word is pronounced and not on the way it is spelled. In general, any prefix, suffix, or word containing such letters as *ph, gh, ch,* and *sh* invites difficulty. Phoenix sewing machines provide a good example—it is inconceivable to many foreign consumers how the brand can be pronounced *fe-nix* and not *pe-nix* or *fo-nix*. It is difficult to understand why the *o* and not the *e* is silent in this case. Also, if the *o* is silent, why should it be in there in the first place? By the same token, people in many countries do not make any distinction, as far

---

There are four romanized Chinese consonants that cause pronunciation problems. Here is a guide to pronouncing them accurately:

- □ c equals the *ts* of *ts*ar or i*ts;* thus cai (finance) sounds like tsai
- □ q equals the *ch* of *Ch*ina or *ch*ild; thus *Qin* (a Dynasty) sounds like *chin*
- □ x equals the *sh* of *sh*ine or *sh*eet; thus xi (west) sounds like *shee*
- □ zh equals the *j* of *J*im or *j*ig; thus *Zhang* (a surname) sounds like *Jang*

Chinese vowels are broader and longer than American vowels, otherwise they are very close in pronunciation, except for the Chinese *e* as in the names Hebei and Henan. The Chinese *e* is somewhat like the *o* of *other.*

Unless otherwise indicated, two Chinese vowels placed next to one another are pronounced as one sound, i.e. as a diphthong. The sister state of Illinois, Liaoning, is a two syllable word—*lyao-ning.*

Chinese surnames come first. The given names are not hyphenated in modern Chinese. Thus Huang Zhirong (the Chinese consul general) should be addressed as Mr. Huang.

Sometimes Chinese, especially those from Beijing, have a tendency to add an *r* sound at the end of certain words. Don't be confused by it. It is analogous to a Harvard *r.*

EXHIBIT 11-10 A brief guide to a pronunciation of romanized Chinese

Source: U.S. Department of Commerce

as pronunciation is concerned, for the following pairs: *v* and *w; z* and *s; c* and *z;* and *ch* and *sh*. A similar lack of distinction often exists with the trio of *j, g,* and *y.* The letter *c* in English words can be confusing because it can be pronounced like an *s,* as in the words *audience* and *fragrance,* or like a *k,* as in the words *cat* and *cost.* The letter *y* also poses some problems because it can sound like an *e* at one time and an *i* at another time. Consider the hair product Brylcream. Foreign consumers may think that the *l* is silent and that the *y* should sound like a long *i.* A simple test could have easily revealed any pronunciation difficulties. Exhibit 11–11 shows how Hoechst tried to overcome the pronunciation difficulty while producing a promotional message at the same time.

Finally, the legal aspect of branding definitely cannot be overlooked. A name that is similar to other firms' trademarks should be avoided. Sir Terence Conran had to use his own name when he exported Habitat to the United States in 1977 because the Habitat name had been registered by someone else. The original line of Interbras was called Stitches, which happened to be a U.S. trademark. In order to invade the U.S. market with its line of personal accessories, it borrowed Hippopotamus from Sao Paulo's disco and deliberately misspelled it in order to avoid legal problems.

Kunnan's branding problems provide a good illustration of various points.[24] Kunnan Lo, the head of a Taiwanese company, felt that the corporate name was inappropriate for its tennis rackets designed for the U.S. market because the name sounded too oriental. So he chose the American-sounding name Kennedy to suggest American-made quality, only to find that many tennis players were Republicans who did not like the Kennedy family. The brand name was thus changed to Kennex. The prefix Pro was latter added to eliminate the confusion with Kleenex. In addition to doing well in the United States, the brand is also popular in Europe and Japan where it is perceived as an American brand. Interestingly, this largest maker of high-quality tennis rackets also manufactures the product under private labels for such well-known firms as Prince, Wilson, and Spalding.

BRAND PROTECTION

The job of branding cannot be considered done just because a name has been chosen. The brand must also be protected. The first protective step is to obtain **trademark registration**. Because of the cost involved, it may be neither practical nor desirable to register the name in all countries, especially in places where demand seems weak. It is inexcusable, however, not to do so in major markets.

There are international arrangements that simplify the registration process. The Paris Convention (International Convention for the Protection of Industrial Property) is the most significant multilateral agreement on trademark rights because it establishes reciprocity, which allows a foreign trademark owner to obtain the same protection in other convention member countries as in the owner's home country. Although preventing discrimination against nonnationals, the degree of protection varies with individual national laws. In the case of the Madrid Convention, nationals of the participating countries can have simultaneous trademark filing among all member countries. The Trademark Registration Treaty (TRT) allows a company to file for trademark

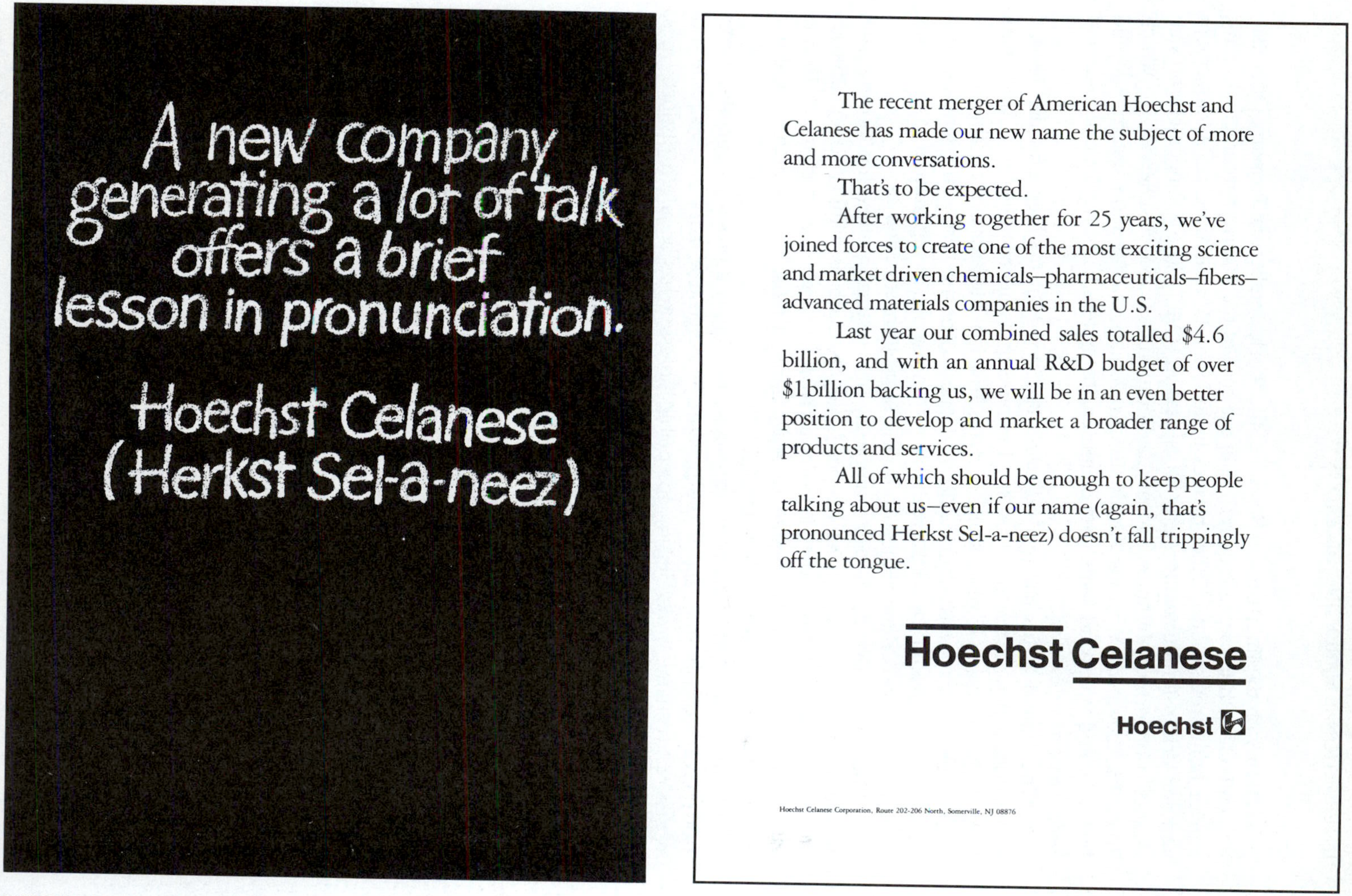

The recent merger of American Hoechst and Celanese has made our new name the subject of more and more conversations.

That's to be expected.

After working together for 25 years, we've joined forces to create one of the most exciting science and market driven chemicals–pharmaceuticals–fibers– advanced materials companies in the U.S.

Last year our combined sales totalled $4.6 billion, and with an annual R&D budget of over $1 billion backing us, we will be in an even better position to develop and market a broader range of products and services.

All of which should be enough to keep people talking about us—even if our name (again, that's pronounced Herkst Sel-a-neez) doesn't fall trippingly off the tongue.

Hoechst Celanese

Hoechst

Hoechst Celanese Corporation, Route 202-206 North, Somerville, NJ 08876

A new company generating a lot of talk offers a brief lesson in pronunciation.

Hoechst Celanese (Herkst Sel-a-neez)

EXHIBIT 11–11   Overcoming a pronunciation difficulty

Source: Reprinted with permission of Hoechst Celanese Corporation

protection with the International Bureau of the World Intellectual Property Organization (WIPO) without being required, as in the case of the Madrid Agreement, to have a prior home registration. Other treaties include the Central American Arrangement and the African Intellectual Property Organization (OAPI). The Arrangement of Nice [France] Concerning the International Classification of Goods and Services to Which Trade Marks Apply is the most widely used trademark classification system. Adopted by the United States and some sixty countries, the system has thirty-four product and seven service categories.

The United States has two registers. The Principal Register provides federal protection, a benefit not provided for by the Supplemental Register. A trademark owner who is unable to place a mark on the Principal Register may be able to do so later when the mark has acquired distinctiveness over the years. The Supplemental Register is still useful for a U.S. marketer who must obtain registration in the home country before becoming eligible to do the same in host countries.

The courts have developed a hierarchy of registration eligibility. Moving from highly protectable to unprotectable, these categories are "fanciful (Kodak), arbitrary (Camel), suggestive (Eveready), descriptive (Ivory), and generic (aspirin)."[25] In general, for a trademark to be eligible for registration, it must be "distinctive" or, if not, must be "capable of being distinctive."

Although a valid brand name can suggest or imply a product's benefits, it cannot merely describe the fact or the product. A suggestive mark is registrable, but a descriptive name is not legally acceptable unless it has acquired distinctiveness through long-continued exclusive use. Even if the descriptive mark might somehow have been registered, the mark can still be cancelled for lack of distinctiveness. Of course, it is not always easy to distinguish a suggestive mark from a descriptive mark. Weedless, as a lawn care product, may be either suggestive or descriptive.

The policy of the U.S. government is to contest applications for **generic trademarks** abroad (e.g., Wash-and-Wear or such foreign variants as Lava y Listo). If allowed to be registered, such trademarks could create significant problems in international trade.[26] A U.S. exporter, for example, will find it impossible to use common product names in advertising abroad without the risk of being sued for trademark infringement, or the exporter may find that the goods are refused entry into a foreign country altogether.

Apart from generic names, certain words or symbols are prohibited from registration by specific trademark laws. In Canada, "the adoption and use, without consent, of certain kinds of marks as trade marks is prohibited, i.e., royal, vice-regal and government arms, crests, flags; emblems of the Red Cross; national flags and emblems; scandalous, obscene matter; and portraits or signatures of living individuals. Such marks are also prohibited from registration. Also prohibited from registration are words that are primarily merely names or surnames; marks that are clearly descriptive or deceptively misdescriptive with respect to the character, quality, composition or source of the goods or services; marks that are the name of the wares or services; and marks that are confusingly similar to marks already registered."[27]

Most countries do not require the display of a trademark in a specific language or the translation of the trademark. Still, to be registered a foreign trademark may have to be written in a local language in such a way as to give the equivalent pronunciation. China requires a trademark to be displayed in Chinese characters. Coca-Cola, depending on a group of Chinese characters used, may have the right sound but the wrong interpretations. The original registered characters *(Koo-kah-koo-lah)*, when translated, mean either "a wax-fattened mare" or "bite the wax tadpole." The company then switched slightly to the new characters to read *Kah-koo-kah-lah,* which translate to "may the happy mouth rejoice."

Unlike patents, trademark registrations can be renewed indefinitely. To keep registrations in force, trademark owners are required to pay an annual tax or maintenance fee in most countries (though not in the United States). The technical requirements must also be observed. Some countries—such as Australia, France, Germany, Italy, South Korea, and Mexico—allow the fees to be paid by a foreign trademark owner residing abroad or by the owner's representative/agent in a third country. In other countries—such as Brazil, Greece, Japan, and the Netherlands—the fees can be paid by only a local or domestically domiciled representative/agent.[28]

Registration by itself does not offer automatic or complete protection. Other legal requirements must be met in order to maintain copyright. **Use** is a universal requirement. In China, publication, advertising, and exhibiting of a product with the trademark all constitute use. To establish use in most countries, a manufacturer must sell or make that product in the intended market.

The legal procedure to acquire and maintain a trademark varies from country to country. Exhibit 11–12 examines the trademark laws of selected countries. Whereas some countries recognize registration but not prior use, other countries do exactly the opposite. In most countries, a company can register a mark subject to cancellation if that mark is not used or continued to be used within a reasonable period of time. The failure to register, even with actual prior use, may force the company to forfeit its rights to another person who registers the same mark later but before anybody else. The first user can be held for ransom this way.

Going back as far as the 1870s, trademark rights in the United States were based on the "no trade, no trademark" premise. Until recently, the U.S. Patent and Trademark Office was practically alone in the world in requiring a potential mark owner to put the trademark into interstate or foreign commercial use first before it could even be registered. Registration in the United States was merely a formality because registration was optional. The problem with this practice is that more than one company may invest in an identical mark, not knowing that there are legal conflicts with others using or working on the identical or similar mark. A U.S. firm thus could not be certain that a proposed mark would still be available for registration when the product reached the consumer years after it was conceived. To solve the problem, American business has traditionally relied on "token use" by making a small-scale shipment of the product for purposes of filing a trademark application, even though the product might not be ready for full-scale commercial sale for years.[29]

The Trademark Act of 1946 (the Lanham Act) has been updated, and several changes have been made. One change involves intent-to-use trademark applications; the change permits companies to file an application based on projected future use. Now a declaration of a bona fide intent to use the mark in commerce is sufficient. A trademark registration is subsequently issued when the applicant files a statement showing evidence of actual use of the mark in commerce. To demonstrate use of the

□ **Argentina** First applicant entitled to registration. Registration valid ten years from registration. No use requirement.

□ **Australia** First applicant, as user or intended user, entitled to registration. Registration valid seven years from application filing date.

□ **Brazil** First applicant entitled to registration. Registrations valid ten years from issue date. Mark must be used within two years and not discontinued for more than two consecutive years. Mark registered more than five years immune from annulment action.

□ **Burma** No trademark law.

□ **Canada** Marks renewable every fifteen years. Person first to use mark in Canada or Paris Union country entitled to registration.

□ **Egypt** First applicant entitled to registration. Contestable on prior grounds for up to five years. Registrations valid ten years from application filing date.

□ **Indonesia** Exclusive rights to mark based on its first use in Indonesia. First applicant considered first user (i.e., registration establishes a presumption of first use). To preserve first user status, registrant must use mark within six months of registration date.

□ **Italy** First applicant entitled to registration. Prior user has contestability rights for five years if his prior use of mark was sufficient for it to be publicly known before contested mark's registration date. Registration valid twenty years from application filing date.

□ **Ethiopia** No trademark law.

□ **Germany** First applicant entitled to registration. Registration, not prior use, confers proprietary rights. Registrations valid for ten years from application filing date. Mark must be used within five years of registration date, otherwise subject to cancellation.

□ **Mexico** Trademarks registered for five years and must be used within three years of registration, otherwise subject to cancellation. Registration notice must appear on mark to be enforceable. Cancellation of registered marks may be sought on grounds that such marks are similar to a prior registration, are false indications of origin, or were applied for by local agent without prior permission of foreign owner. Mark may also be cancelled when government determines that owner has improperly priced or represented quality of product or service covered by mark to public detriment.

□ **Saudi Arabia** First applicant entitled to registration. Registrations valid ten years from application date and incontestable after five years. Person who can prove that he used mark for year before it was first registered can continue to use it. No compulsory use.

EXHIBIT 11–12   Trademark laws of selected countries

Source: Adapted from Joseph M. Lightman, "Foreign Trademark Protection: Treaties and National Laws," in *Foreign Business Practices* (Washington, D.C.: International Trade Administration, U.S. Department of Commerce, 1981), 61–73

mark, specimens in the form of containers, labels, tags, or displays associated with the goods must be filed. There is no penalty for reserving names that are never actually used. The second change is the constructive-use provision. For goods or services specified in the Principal Registration, an applicant receives a nationwide priority effect as though the applicant had used the mark throughout the nation as of the filing date. The definition of "use of the mark" has been changed to require that use be in the ordinary course of trade, and token use is prohibited. To reserve a mark, the intent-to-use application becomes the sole avenue. Finally, the term of federal registration has been reduced from 20 years to 10 years to clear out trademarks no longer used.

Although a single use of a mark may be adequate to register the mark, a company must exploit the mark commercially in good faith to prevent the loss of it.[30] The rationale is to prevent a company from abusing the law to its advantage when the owner has no intention of using the trademark other than to bar potential competitors with genuine interests from utilizing a competitive tool. An example is Snob perfume, a name owned in France by Le Galion, a French company, and in the United States by Jean Patou, an American company. Le Galion was able to challenge Patou's rights successfully because Patou (1) sold only eighty-nine bottles of Snob perfume in twenty-one years, (2) never supported the product with promotion, and (3) made only $100 in gross profit. Thus, Patou was suspected of registering the name just to bar a potential competitor from entering the market.

The quickest way to lose a trademark is by not using it. A failure to use a registered trademark for three years terminates all rights in China. In the case of South Korea, nonuse after a period of one year is grounds for cancellation of registrations.

The manufacturer may find that it is too expensive to keep on producing in such markets as Central and South America because of inflation and currency devaluations. But "ceasing all marketing activity in a country may result in the loss of a trademark. For example, Payot lost its trademark rights to a former licensee in Brazil after terminating operations there and allowing the mark to expire."[31] To avoid this costly problem, the trademark owner should consider some temporary licensing agreements with local manufacturers. By "parking products" with foreign firms, trademark owners can sustain their marks and brand awareness as well as have the flexibility of returning to resume their own production if the economy turns more favorable.

Another caveat is to make sure that the brand does not become so generic that it is identified with the product itself. A loss of trademark can occur if the name becomes part of the language; that is, when members of the consuming public use the brand name to denote the product or its common function rather than the producer of the product. Yo-yo (a foreign trademark), Roquefort cheese, and Champagne are proprietary names in France but generic names in the United States. The reverse is true of Ping-Pong, a U.S. registered trademark that is a generic name in China for table tennis. In Japan, there is no word for vulcanized rubber, and the Goodyear name is used to identify this product. Cyanamid has had to fight to keep Formica from denoting all plastic laminate or laminated wood. In Thailand, people think that *cola* (a generic name) is a brand name for Coca-Cola and order "cola" when they actually want Coca-Cola. This may provide other soft drink companies with a legal ground to challenge the trademark of Coca-Cola. Bayer's loss of the Aspirin trademark in the United States was due partly to the anti-German sentiment during World War II and partly to its failure to create a generic word for the product, whose chemical name is acetylsalicylic acid. Bayer would have been on more solid legal ground if it had established a generic term for household use (e.g., headache tablet or pain reliever tablet).

To avoid this problem of a brand name becoming a generic name, a firm must never use the brand name in a generic sense (i.e., using it as a verb or adjective to denote the product). Promotional materials should reflect the proper usage, and the public should be informed accordingly. Goodyear's policy, for example, is never to use the trademark in the context of a sentence in any printed material because (1) use requires the registration symbol (®) plus footnote "registered trade mark, the Goodyear Tire & Rubber Co." and (2) use violates registration description, which involves a particular letter style for the "GOOD" and the "YEAR."[32] Willy Motors, likewise, always emphasizes that Jeep is a trademark and uses an advertisement to inform consumers not to use Jeep as an adjective (e.g., jeeplike, jeepy, or jeep-type), a verb (e.g., jeep around or go jeeping), a plural (e.g., jeeps), or a generic without the capital *J*. In the Philippines, however, Jeep has become a generic name, and people there use privately owned small buses known as *jeepnies* for transportation. Jeep is now a registered trademark of Chrysler Corporation (see Exhibit 11–13).

It is not legally sound to combine trademarks.[33] It may seem remote that Honda will have trouble with its Honda Accord and Honda Civic marks, but the fact remains that the second mark (Accord, Civic) is in jeopardy through inference that it is the product's generic name. The public may thus assume that manufacturers other than Honda also make Accord and Civic cars.

Tabasco provides a good illustration of the various legal issues that have been discussed. Unlike Worcestershire sauce and soy sauce, Tabasco is a properly registered trademark. It is the name of a river and a state of southern Mexico. One may question how a geographical name could ever have been accepted for registration, as the name is not distinctive. The answer is that the name was capable of being distinctive and did become distinctive because it has been used continuously and exclusively by the manufacturer for a long time. Thus, the name has become associated with this particular company. Furthermore, Tabasco is the official botanical name of the hot red peppers, but those peppers were actually named for the sauce (i.e., product) and not the other way around. Tabasco is aware that consumers might use the brand to denote the product (i.e., hot sauce) rather than the maker of the product. It has thus hired two legal firms to police the world for any misappropriation of the trademark. Its vigorous enforcement enabled it to defeat B. F. Trappey Sons's legal bid for the right to use the word.

To hold the legal rights to a registered trademark is one thing, but to prevent others from illegally using it through counterfeiting is another matter altogether. In fact, counterfeiters, though acknowledging the illegality of the activity, may see nothing morally wrong with the activity. In China, the basic cultural values relevant to counterfeiting are neutral—it is not a violation to copy someone's ideas. Great artists' works for example, are copied as a sign of respect.[34]

EXHIBIT 11–13   Jeep: a registered trademark

Source: Courtesy of Chrysler Corporation

To prevent the importation into the United States of counterfeits and, to a lesser extent, gray market goods, a trademark owner whose mark is accepted for the Principal Register can register a mark with the U.S. Customs Service for the purpose of preventing entry of goods bearing an infringing mark. The Customs Service distinguishes colorable imitation from counterfeit trademark. A **colorable imitation** is a mark so similar as to be confused with a registered mark, whereas a **counterfeit trademark** is basically indistinguishable from a registered trademark. Colorable imitations are treated more leniently in that they can still gain entry as long as the objectionable mark is removed. But in the case of counterfeits, the Customs Reform and Simplification Act of 1978 allows the seizure as well as forfeiture to the government of any articles bearing a counterfeit trademark.

PACKAGING: FUNCTIONS AND CRITERIA

Much like the brand name, packaging is another integral part of a product. Packaging serves two primary purposes: functional and promotional. First and foremost, a package must be functional in the sense that it is capable of protecting the product at minimum cost.

If a product is not manufactured locally and has to be exported to another country, extra protection is needed to compensate for the time and distance involved. A country's adverse environment should also be taken into account. When moisture is a problem, a company may have to wrap pills in foil or put food in tin boxes or vacuum-sealed cans. Still, the type of package chosen must be economical. In Mexico, where most consumers cannot afford to buy detergents in large packages, detergent suppliers found it necessary to use plastic bags for small packages because cardboard would be too expensive for that purpose.

For most packaging applications, marketers should keep in mind that foreign consumers are more concerned with the functional aspect of a package than they are with convenience. As such, there is usually no reason to offer the great variety of package sizes or styles demanded by Americans. Plastic and throw-away bottles are regarded as being wasteful, especially in LDCs, where the labor cost for handling returnables is modest. Non-American consumers prefer a package to have secondary functions. A tin box or a glass bottle can be used after the product content is gone to store something else. Empty glass containers can be sold by consumers to recoup a part of the purchase price.

From the marketing standpoint, the promotional function of packaging is just as critical as the functional aspect. To satisfy the Japanese preference for beautiful packaging, Avon upgraded its inexpensive plastic packaging to crystalline glass. Similarly, BSR packs its product into two cartons, one for shipping and one for point-of-purchase display, because Japanese buyers want a carton to be in top condition. The successful campaign for Bailey's Irish Cream in the United States included a fancy gold foil box package that promotes this whiskey-based drink's upscale image.

In addition to functional and promotional functions, good packaging should also satisfy secondary criteria. A good design should have "impact, visibility, legibility, simplicity, consistency, versatility, and honesty."[35] Packaging does not have to be dull. Novel shapes and designs can be used to stimulate interest and create excitement.

MANDATORY PACKAGE MODIFICATION

A package change may be either mandatory or at the discretion of the marketer. A mandatory change is usually necessitated by government regulations. Consider the case of Dow Corning International. In one six-month period, it made ninety-six packaging changes to meet various regulations in Europe.[36]

The complexity of packaging regulations is very well demonstrated by the experience of R. J. Reynolds in marketing cigarettes, a relatively simple product.[37] The pack sold in the United States can be shipped to only three or four markets. The company has to employ more than 1,400 product codes for all its brands in all countries. Ethiopia requires the imprint "Ethiopia" on the cigarette paper in addition to a special closure seal on every pack indicating retail price in Ethiopian currency. In Australia, the number of cigarettes must be on the package front. Canada mandates bilingual health warnings, with a French warning on one side and an English warning on the opposite side. The package closure seal doubles as tax stamp in some countries and may contain some peculiar information, such as the picture of the country's ruler. The packaging problem caused by foreign governments' regulations seems to be getting more complex. The Winston brand had only 10–15 variations two decades ago and 50 variations a decade ago, but it now has to contend with 250 different packages altogether.

Several countries require bilinguality (e.g., French and English in Canada and French and Flemish in Belgium). This requirement may force the manufacturer to increase package size or shorten messages and product name, as a bilingual package must have twice the space for copy communications. In some cases, modification is dictated by mechanical or technical difficulties, such as the unavailability of certain typographic fonts or good advertising typographers.

In many cases, packaging and labeling are highly related. Packages may be required to describe contents, quantity, manufacturer's name and address, and so on in letters of designated sizes. Any pictorial illustration that is used should not be misleading. In Singapore, certain foods must be labeled to conform to defined standards. When terms are used that imply added vitamins or minerals (e.g., enriched, fortified, vitaminized), packages must show the quantities of vitamins or minerals added per metric unit. In addition, if the product is hazardous in any way, marketers should adopt the United Nations' recommendations for the labeling and packaging of hazardous materials.

Exporters of textile products must conform to countries' varying regulations. Spain has specific and extensive requirements concerning fiber content, labeling, and packaging. In addition to its flammability requirements, Sweden's labeling regulations include size, material, care, and origin. Venezuela requires all packaged goods to be labeled in metric units while specifically prohibiting dual labeling to show both metric and nonmetric units. Germany wants the description of fiber content to be in German, but labeling for Denmark must be in Danish or kindred. In the case of France, care labeling (if used) must meet an International Standardization Organization (ISO) directive.[38]

As discussed in a previous chapter, countries' different measurement systems may necessitate some form of product modification, and necessity applies to packaging as well. Products, toiletries included, cannot be sold in Australia in ounces. The Australian regulations require products to be sold in metric numbers, in increments of 25 mm. In Germany, liquid products must be bottled or packaged in standard metric sizes. Interestingly, the United States, a nonmetric nation, has the same requirement for liquor products.

Sometimes, packaging regulations are designed more for protection against imports than for consumer protection. Denmark requires returnable bottles for beverages and is thus able to prevent entry of French mineral water because the cost of returning bottles is prohibitive.[39] Belgium requires margarine to be distinguished from butter by requiring margarine to be sold in cubes. Intentional or not, this requirement has the effect of closing the Belgian market to foreign manufacturers of margarine with round or rectangular packaging.

There is no question that a marketer's packaging activities are complicated by various trade barriers whether such restrictions are by design or not. Still, these problems can be partially minimized. The problems faced by Paterson Jenks, an exporter of Schwaz spices and specialty food products, provide a good illustration.[40] Because of the various countries' product and packaging requirements, the company has to use 480 different pieces of artwork on packages and labels for its herbs and spices. Norway prohibits coloring in food products, and Finland requires bilingual labels for all imported goods to accommodate the 6 percent of the population that are ethnic Swedes. Another problem is that Paterson Jenks used 275 mm jars, but Germany will allow only the 100, 150, and 200 millimeter jars. To soften the impact of these market differences, the company planned to export in bulk and form joint ventures for local packaging arrangements.

OPTIONAL PACKAGE MODIFICATION

Optional modification of a package, although not absolutely necessary, may have to be undertaken for marketing impact or for facilitating marketing activities. Through accidents and history, users in many countries have grown accustomed to particular types of packages. Mayonnaise, cheese, and mustard come in tubes in Europe, but mustard is sold in jars in the United States. The popularity of tubes in Europe even led Lamy Lutti Candy Co., a French company, to package bubble gum in tubes several years ago.

In selecting or modifying a package, a marketer should consider local conditions related to purchasing habits. Products conventionally sold in packs in the United States are not necessarily sold that way elsewhere and may require further bulk breaking. This phenomenon is in part the result of lower income levels overseas and in part the result of a lack of unit pricing, which makes it difficult for buyers to see any savings derived from the purchase of a bigger package. Foreign consumers may desire to buy one bottle of beer or soft drink at a time instead of buying a six-pack or eight-pack. Likewise, one cigarette, not the whole pack, may be bought in a purchase transaction. As explained by Hill and Still, inexpensive, nonessential goods for personal use are usually sold in LDCs in packages smaller than those offered to the U.S. market.[41] Chiclets chewing gum, for instance, may come in two-piece packs in LDCs instead of the twelve-piece packs common in America. But products for family consumption (e.g., food) require larger sizes abroad because of larger families.

In addition to conditions of use, other cultural factors should be taken into consideration because such factors often determine and influence consumer preference. Although the UHT (ultra-high temperature) process for packaging milk and juices in unrefrigerated cartons has long been popular in Europe, it took quite a while for American consumers who were accustomed to fresh products to start accepting aseptic packaging.

Symbols and colors of packages may have to be changed to be consistent with cultural norms. If packages are offensive, they must be made more acceptable if the product is to be marketed successfully. For example, the controversial Jovan packages, with their sexual connotations, can prove to be too suggestive in some countries.

One helpful sign that should reduce packaging confusion is the European Community's standardization attempt. Changes in the EC's food packaging requirements should allow American food manufacturers and packaging agents to follow one unified EC regulation. Although size requirements differ by product, the EC has harmonized the sizes of sealed packages and containers. The uniformity assists consumers in comparing prices for the same quantity, thus abolishing the need for unit pricing. EC packaging regulations also help to promote conservation by decreasing the amount of paper utilized in packaging.[42]

CONCLUSION

A product is a bundle of utilities, and the brand and package are part of this bundle. There is nothing unusual about consumers' reliance on brand names as a guide to product quality. As shown by the perfume industry, the mystique of a brand name may be so strong as to overshadow the product's physical attributes. When practical and well executed, branding allows a commodity to be transformed into a product. In doing so with the aid of product differentiation, brand loyalty is created, and the product can command a premium price.

Branding decisions involve more than merely deciding whether a product should be branded or not. Branding entails other managerial decisions. A manufacturer must decide whether to use its own brand or that of its dealer on its product. A marketer must also determine whether to use a single brand for maximum impact or multiple brands to satisfy the different segments and markets more precisely. Regardless of the number of brands used, each brand name must be selected carefully with the international market in mind. Once selected, the brand name must be protected through registration, and other measures should be taken to prevent any infringement on that name.

Like the brand name, which may have to be varied from one country to another, packaging should be changed when needed. Mandatory modification of packaging should not be considered a problem because the marketer has no choice in the matter—if a marketer wants to market a product, the marketer must conform to the country's stated packaging requirements. Unilever, for instance, has to conform to the French requirement of selling cube-shaped packs, not rectangular packs, of margarine. Its descriptions for mayonnaise and salad dressing also have to vary from country to country.

Optional or discretionary packaging modification, in contrast, is a more controllable variable within a marketer's marketing mix. Usually, discretionary packaging is more related to product promotion, and it can take on the same importance as mandatory packaging. Soft drink containers are a good example of how packaging requirements must be observed. In many countries, bottles are manufactured in metric sizes because of government requirements. And the containers must be made of glass because consumers abroad regard plastic throw-away bottles as being wasteful. Therefore, both mandatory and optional packaging changes should be considered at the same time.

QUESTIONS

1. What are the requirements that must be met so that a commodity can effectively be transformed into a branded product?
2. Explain the "least dependent person" hypothesis and its branding implications.
3. When is it appropriate to use multiple brands in (a) the same market and (b) several markets/countries?
4. What are the characteristics of a good international brand name?
5. Explain these legal requirements related to branding: (a) registration, (b) registration eligibility, (c) use, (d) renewal, and (e) generic trademark.
6. Distinguish colorable imitation from counterfeit trademark.
7. Cite the factors that may force a company to modify its package for overseas markets. Discuss both mandatory and optional modification.

DISCUSSION ASSIGNMENTS AND MINICASES

1. Should U.S. farmers brand their exported commodities (e.g., soybean, corn, beef)?
2. Some U.S. retailers (e.g., Sears) and manufacturers (e.g., General Motors) place their trademarks on products actually made by foreign suppliers. Discuss the rationale for these actions by these U.S. firms and foreign manufacturers.
3. Discuss how certain English letters, prefixes, suffixes, syllables, or words create pronunciation difficulties for those whose native language is not English.
4. Is Hyundai a good name to use for an international brand? On what do you base your evaluation?
5. Go to the soft drink section of a supermarket. How many different types of soft-drink packages are there (in terms of size, form, and so on.)? Should any of them be modified for overseas markets?

CASE 11–1
MAJORICA S.A. VS. R. H. MACY

Majorca is a place well known for its pearls. One Spanish firm, Majorica S.A., has used Majorica, an ancient name for Majorca, since 1954 as its trade name as well as a brand name to describe its pearls.

Majorica was alarmed to learn that R. H. Macy, a major U.S. department store chain, was selling Majorca-labeled pearls that were made by Hobe Cie. Ltd., a competitor of Majorica S.A. Contacts with Macy produced no fruitful results in resolving the difficulty. Macy felt that it had the right to use the name in question because Majorca was the name of an island and because the pearls in question were indeed made there.

Subsequently, Majorica filed a lawsuit in a federal court, asking for a judgment to stop Macy from using the name. Majorica S.A. cited trademark infringement as the reason for seeking relief. It argued that Macy's action caused confusion among consumers as well as erosion of goodwill.

Questions

1. Is Majorica a valid brand name or just a generic trademark? Does the fact that it is the name of a place (i.e., island) affect the registration eligibility and legal protection of Majorica S.A.?
2. Was Macy's action legally defensible? Assuming that you are a federal court judge, do you think that Macy's use of the name could cause consumer confusion? Do you think that Macy's labeling constituted trademark infringement? Can the branding/labeling be somehow modified to prevent consumer confusion?

NOTES

1. "For Spalding the Name Is the Game," *Business Week,* 21 November 1983, 144, 148.

2. "Goodwill Is Making a Lot of People Angry," *Business Week,* 31 July 1989, 73, 76.

3. B. N. Rosen, J. J. Boddewyn, and E. A. Louis, "US Brands Abroad: An Empirical Study of Global Branding," *International Marketing Review* 6 (no. 1, 1989): 5–17.

4. Robert Grosse and Walter Zinn, "Standardization in International Marketing: The Latin American Case," *Journal of Global Marketing* 4 (no. 1, 1990): 53–78.

5. Johny K. Johansson and Hans B. Thorelli, "International Product Positioning," *Journal of International Business Studies* 16 (Fall 1985): 57–75.

6. Andy Wickstrom, "Who Made Your Recorder? You Can't Tell by the Name," *Chicago Tribune,* 20 November 1983, Arts section.

7. "Heinz Struggles to Stay at the Top of the Stack," *Business Week,* 11 March 1985, 49.

8. "Seiko to Split off Its Lassale Lines," *Jewelers' Circular-Keystone* (March 1985): G.

9. Dean M. Peebles and John K. Ryans, Jr., *Management of International Advertising: A Marketing Approach* (Boston: Allyn & Bacon, 1984), 13.

10. *The Role of Trademarks in Developing Countries* (Geneva: United Nations Conference on Trade and Development, 1979).

11. Ray Moseley, "This Bud's for You Chaps, Too, Busch Will Be Telling Britons," *Chicago Tribune,* 15 June 1984.

12. J. S. Downham, Presentation to the Annual American Marketing Association Conference, New York, May 1982.

13. R. Overlock Howe, "Japanese Stumble in Use of Corporate Identity," *Marketing News,* 25 October 1985, 7.

14. Janice Ashby, "European Unification in 1992 Challenges U.S. Export Packaging," *Marketing News,* 10 October 1988, 12.

15. "So Far, Nissan's Catch-Up Plan Hasn't Caught on," *Business Week,* 17 September 1990, 59 ff.

16. "Toyota: Can a 'Handshake' with GM Revive Its Slumping Export Sales?" *Business Week,* 2 August 1982, 50–51.

17. James U. McNeal and Linda M. Zeren, "Brand Name Selection for Consumer Products," *MSU Business Topics* (Spring 1981): 35–39.

18. Eileen Ogintz, "This Firm's Product? You Name It," *Chicago Tribune,* 28 March 1986.

19. McNeal and Zeren, "Brand Name Selection."

20. Ray Schultz, "Agency Helps Direct Marketers Cross Language, Cultural Barriers," *DM News,* 1 March 1986, 32.

21. "Aprica Kassai: A Fast Ride into the U.S. with Status-Symbol Strollers," *Business Week,* 21 January 1985, 117.

22. "The Selling of the 'Walkman,'" *Advertising Age,* 12 March 1982: M-37.

23. John D. Oathout, *Trademarks: A Guide to the Selection, Administration, and Protection of Trademarks in Modern Business Practice* (New York: Scribner's, 1981), 63.

24. "The 'Four Tigers' Start Clawing at Upscale Markets," *Business Week,* 22 July 1985, 136 ff.

25. Dorothy Cohen, "Trademark Strategy," *Journal of Marketing* 50 (January 1986): 61–74.

26. Vincent Travaglini, "Protection of Industrial Property Rights Abroad," in *Foreign Business Practices* (Washington, D.C.: International Trade Administration, U.S. Department of Commerce, 1981), 42.

27. *Doing Business in Canada: Patents, Trade Marks, Industrial Designs and Copyrights,* rev. 1979 (Industry, Trade and Commerce, Minister of Supply and Services Canada 1980).

28. Joseph M. Lightman, "Foreign Rules on Need for Agents to Pay Patents and Trademark Maintenance Fees," in *Foreign Business Practices* (Washington, D.C.: International Trade Administration, U.S. Department of Commerce, 1981), 87–90.

29. Vincent N. Palladino, "New Trademark Law Aids U.S. in Foreign Markets," *Marketing News,* 13 February 1989, 7.

30. Sidney A. Diamond, *Trademark Problems and How to Avoid Them,* rev. ed. (Chicago: Crain Books, 1981), 20–22.

31. Alan Breward, "Going International II: Central and South America" (meeting, Cosmetics, Toiletry and Fragrance Association, New York, 6 September 1984).

32. Peebles and Ryans, *International Advertising,* 102.

33. Oathout, *Trademarks,* 98.

34. Francis S. L. Wang, "Dealing with Infringement: The Underlying Factors," *East Asian Executive Reports* 7 (August 1985): 20–22.

35. "'Ten Commandments' Guide Multinational Packaging," *Marketing News,* 23 December 1983: 3, 5.

36. Robert F. Roth, *International Marketing Communications* (Chicago: Crain Books, 1982), 132.

37. "Tobacco Companies Face Special International Packaging Obstacles," *Marketing News,* 3 February 1984, 20.

38. Market Expansion Division. International Trade Administration, *Foreign Regulations Affecting U.S. Textile/Apparel Exports* (Washington, D.C.: U.S. Department of Commerce, 1986), 252–83.

39. "Global Marketing Success Is Contingent on a Solid Bank of Foreign Market Intelligence," *Marketing News,* 23 December 1983, 1, 12.

40. Nigel Piercy, *Export Strategy: Markets and Competition* (London: George Allen & Unwin, 1982), 37.

41. John S. Hill and Richard R. Still, "Adapting Products to LDC Tastes," *Harvard Business Review* 62 (March–April 1984): 92–101.

42. Don R. Wright, "The EC Single Market in 1991–Status Report," *Business America,* 25 February 1991, 12–14.

In a market system, all aspects of economic activity are interdependent, and the whole cannot function properly if any major element is not in its place.

Michel Camdessus, Managing Director, International Monetary Fund

Distribution Strategies
Channels of Distribution

12

CHAPTER OUTLINE

MARKETING ILLUSTRATION
A Place to Be (or Not to Be)

McDonald's makes few mistakes. Yet its first European venture proved to be one of those few. The firm put its first European fast-food outlet in a suburb of Amsterdam, thinking it would be the same as a suburb in Chicago. But in Europe, most people live in cities, and they are less mobile. Suburban shopping centers, which are good sites in the United States for fast foods, have not yet become popular in much of Europe. As a result, McDonald's had to move its original Amsterdam store into town.

Kentucky Fried Chicken learned the same lesson in Japan. It opened outlets in the Shinjuku entertainment district and at Expo '70 in Osaka. These suburban outlets were targeted at the driving public. But the Japanese still live in small houses with small yards and normally travel by train. Not surprisingly, the original outlets failed, and Kentucky Fried Chicken lost money for four years. Most of its outlets are now at central city locations and near railroad stations.

Johnson Matthey Ltd., after more than a century and a half, has become a very large British firm. It entered the U.S. market in 1981 with a mission: to become a leading jeweler in five years. Its strategy to accomplish this grand idea was to eliminate the traditional jewelry distribution system, which the firm deemed costly and inefficient. Operating primarily through ten large wholesalers, Johnson Matthey encouraged large orders with a generous consignment program that allowed customers to keep goods for six months for a modest carrying charge. The strategy backfired. The large volume caused many orders to be either delayed or unfilled. To make matters worse, distributors and retailers found it more desirable to push other manufacturers' products first because those orders were paid in cash. The problem of overordering and the lack of retailers' support together resulted in a return of 60 percent of the merchandise. Johnson Matthey then decided to get tough with its customers: the company limited return to no more than 35 percent and required payment for excessive returns. Predictably, it was sued by its distributors. Although distribution was not the company's only problem, it was the main reason for a loss of $90 million. Soon the company left the U.S. market.

Source: Russell Shor, "Johnson Matthey: Haste Made Waste," *Jewelers' Circular-Keystone* (August 1985): 364, 366

A good product may not be accepted by a market if it is not properly made available. All products need competent distribution. Nike, for example, developed shoes specifically for the European market, and yet it encountered difficulty in finding distributors. The problem was that existing dealers already carried such brands as Puma and Adidas. These dealers worried that they might be cut off by Puma and Adidas if they carried too many foreign brands.

A manufacturer can sell directly to end users abroad, but this type of channel is generally not suitable or desirable for most consumer goods. In foreign markets, it is far more common for a product to go through several parties before reaching the final consumer. Exhibit 12–1 shows how Sony, by acting as a middleman, offers its distribution expertise to help American firms market their products in Japan. The purpose of this chapter is to discuss the various channels of distribution that are responsible for moving products from manufacturers to consumers. Both international and domestic channels are examined.

SONY PLAZA WANTS MORE

U.S. PRODUCTS TO SELL IN JAPAN

"International trade requires efforts in importing as well as in exporting. There's an excellent market for American products in Japan. Our economy is strong. Japanese customers want diversity and are attracted by American brands. Sony has the sales force and knowledge of the Japanese market to help American firms find ready acceptance among Japanese consumers. This kind of trade will be beneficial both to Japan and to the American firms coming into the market."

A. MORITA SONY Chairman

With this philosophy, Sony Plaza Co., Ltd. was established by Sony Corporation, a Company known for it's own fine exports. Sony Plaza has made famous such names as Fieldcrest, Royal Copenhagen, Paddington Bear, Famous Amos, Goody, etc. in the Japanese market. And you? Sony Plaza wants to import yours.

If you're interested please talk to us. In the U.S. please write to: Ms. Michele Classe, Sony Corp of America, America Export to Japan Div., 9 West 57th Street, New York, N.Y. 10019. In Japan: Mr. Y. Maki, Sony Plaza Co., Ltd., Sony Bldg. 5-3-1 Ginza, Chuo-ku, Tokyo. 104, Japan.

EXHIBIT 12–1 Sony's distribution expertise

Source: Reprinted with permission of Sony Corporation of America

The chapter describes the varieties of intermediaries (i.e., agents, wholesalers, and retailers) involved in moving products between countries as well as within countries. The tasks and functions of the various intermediaries will be examined. It should be kept in mind that certain types of intermediaries do not exist in some countries and that the pattern of use as well as the importance of each type of intermediary varies widely from country to country.

A manufacturer is required to make several decisions that will affect its channel strategy, including the length, width, and number of distribution channels to be used. The chapter examines the various factors that influence these decisions. For an operation to be a success, a good relationship among channel members is vital. Johnson Matthey's failure in the United States can be attributed in part to the lack of such a relationship. McDonald's and Kentucky Fried Chicken, in contrast, were able to cultivate trust and gain cooperation from local foreign partners. Furthermore, as shown by these examples, there is no one single distribution method always ideal in all markets. Thus, the chapter examines channel adaptation.

DIRECT AND INDIRECT SELLING CHANNELS

Companies use two principal channels of distribution when marketing abroad: (1) indirect selling and (2) direct selling. **Indirect selling,** also known as the local or domestic channel, is employed when a manufacturer in the United States, for example, markets its product through another U.S. firm that acts as the manufacturer's *sales intermediary* (or middleman). As such, the sales intermediary is just another local or domestic channel for the manufacturer because there are no dealings abroad with a foreign firm. By exporting through an independent local middleman, the manufacturer has no need to set up an international department. The middleman, acting as the manufacturer's external export organization, usually assumes the responsibility for moving the product overseas. The intermediary may be a **domestic agent** if it does not take title to the goods, or it may be a **domestic merchant** if it does take title to the goods.

There are several advantages to be gained by employing an indirect domestic channel. For example, the channel is simple and inexpensive. The manufacturer incurs no start-up cost for the channel and is relieved of the responsibility of physically moving the goods overseas. Because the intermediary very likely represents several clients who can help share distribution costs, the costs for moving the goods are further reduced.

An indirect channel does, however, have limitations. The manufacturer has been relieved of any immediate marketing costs but, in effect, has given up control over the marketing of its product to another firm. This situation may adversely affect the product's success in the future. If the chosen intermediary is not aggressive, the manufacturer may become vulnerable, especially in the case where competitors are careful about their distribution practices. Moreover, the indirect channel may not necessarily be permanent. Being in the business of handling products for profit, the intermediary can easily discontinue handling a manufacturer's product if there is no profit or if a competitive product offers a better profit potential.

Direct selling is employed when a manufacturer develops an overseas channel. This channel requires that the manufacturer deal directly with a foreign party without going through an intermediary in the home country. The manufacturer must set up the overseas channel to take care of the business activities between the countries. Being responsible for shipping the product to foreign markets itself, the manufacturer exports through its own internal export department or organization.

One advantage gained in using the direct-selling channel is active market exploitation, since the manufacturer is more directly committed to its foreign markets. Another advantage is greater control. The channel improves communication because approval does not have to be given to a middleman before a transaction is completed. The channel therefore allows the company's policy to be followed more uniformly.

Direct selling is not without its problems. It is a difficult channel to manage if the manufacturer is unfamiliar with the foreign market. Moreover, the channel is time consuming and expensive. Without a large volume of business, the manufacturer may find it too costly to maintain the channel. Hiram Walker, a Canadian distiller, used to have its own marketing operation in New York City to distribute such brands as Ballantine Scotch, Kahlua, and CC Rye. Poor earnings finally forced the company to phase out its costly U.S. selling organization along with its New York City marketing operation.

Exporters who do not undertake international marketing research have a tendency to sell directly to a U.S. export agent. In contrast, those who undertake more formal international marketing research tend to be committed to exporting and invest resources in establishing a separate department to export their product directly to end users.[1]

A survey of exporting firms in the electrical, machine tool builders, food equipment, and fluid power industries found that firms that export industrial goods use distribution channel members identical to those used at home. The export distribution channels used most often by these industrial firms were sales representatives and export distributors. Although respondents appeared to be somewhat satisfied with their overall distribution system, they also showed relative dissatisfaction with trading companies in general. In the balance, firms that have been exporting for a while are happier with their distribution system than firms that have relatively little exporting experience.[2]

TYPES OF INTERMEDIARIES: DIRECT CHANNEL

There are several types of intermediaries associated with both the direct and indirect channels. Exhibit 12–2 compares the two channels and lists the various types of domestic and foreign intermediaries.

Foreign Distributor

A **foreign distributor** is a foreign firm that has exclusive rights to carry out distribution for a manufacturer in a foreign country or specific area. For example, when Don Wood returned to Detroit, he still remembered the MG sports car he drove in

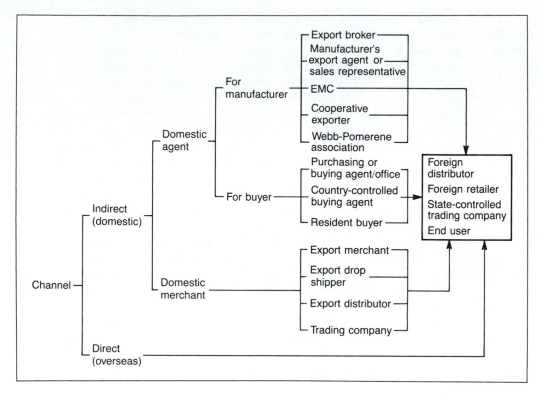

EXHIBIT 12–2   International channel of distribution

England during World War II. His letter asking MG's chairman to sell and ship one car to him brought the response that MG's policy was to sell only through authorized distributors. But MG was willing to appoint Wood its Midwest distributor if he would order two cars instead. Wood agreed to do so and went on to become a successful distributor.[3]

Orders must be channeled through the distributor, even when the distributor chooses to appoint a subagent or subdistributor. The distributor purchases merchandise from the manufacturer at a discount and then resells or distributes the merchandise to retailers and sometimes final consumers. In this regard, the distributor's function in many countries may be a combination of wholesaler and retailer. But in most cases the distributor is usually considered as an importer or foreign wholesaler. The length of association between the manufacturer and its foreign distributor is established by a contract that is renewable provided the continued arrangement is satisfactory to both.

In some situations, the foreign distributor is merely a subsidiary of the manufacturer. Seiko U.S.A., for example, is a distributor for its Japanese parent (Hattori Seiko), which manufactures Seiko watches. More frequently, however, a foreign distributor is an independent merchant. Charles of the Ritz Group has been the U.S. distributor for Opium, a very popular perfume made in France. A distributor may sometimes take on the name of the brand distributed even though the distributor is an independent operator and not owned by the manufacturer. Brother International Corp. is an independent U.S. distributor of Brother Industries, Ltd., a Japanese firm. Longines-Wittnauer Watch Co. distributes the Swiss-made Longines watch in the U.S. market. This distributorship is actually a subsidiary of the Westinghouse Electric Corp.

There are a number of benefits in using a foreign distributor. Unlike agents, the distributor is a *merchant* who buys and maintains merchandise in its own name. This arrangement simplifies the credit and payment activities for the manufacturer. To carry out the distribution function, the foreign distributor is often required to warehouse adequate products, parts, and accessories and to have facilities and personnel immediately available to service buyers and users. Still, the manufacturer must be careful in selecting a foreign distributor or it may end up with a distributor who is deficient in marketing and servicing the product. Apple Computer now does its own distribution in Japan because the services of Toray Industries, its former distributor, proved inadequate.

Foreign Retailer

If **foreign retailers** are used, the product in question must be a consumer product rather than an industrial product. There are several means by which a manufacturer may contact foreign retailers and interest them in carrying a product, ranging from a personal visit by the manufacturer's representative to mailings of catalogs, brochures, and other literature to prospective retailers. The use of personal selling or a visit, although expensive because of travel costs and commissions for the manufacturer's representative, provides for a more effective sales presentation as well as for better screening of retailers for the distribution purpose. The use of direct mail, although less expensive, may not sufficiently catch the retailers' attention.

For such big-ticket items as automobiles or for high-volume products, it may be worthwhile for a manufacturer to sell to retailers without going through a foreign distributor. In fact, most large retailers prefer to deal directly with a manufacturer. In Europe, for example, a number of retail food chains are becoming larger and more powerful, and they prefer to be in direct contact with foreign manufacturers in order to obtain price concessions.

State-Controlled Trading Company

For some products, particularly utility and telecommunication equipment, a manufacturer must contact and sell to state-controlled companies. In addition, many countries, especially those in Eastern Europe, have **state-controlled trading companies,** which are companies that have a complete monopoly in the buying and selling of goods. Hungary has about one hundred state trading organizations for a variety of products, ranging from poultry to telecommunications equipment and for both imported and exported products.

Being government sanctioned and controlled for trading in certain goods, buyers for state-controlled trading companies are very definitely influenced by their governments' trade policies and politics. Most opportunities for manufacturers are limited to raw materials, agricultural machinery, manufacturing equipment, and technical instruments rather than consumer or household goods. Reasons for this limitation include shortage of foreign exchange, an emphasis on self-sufficiency, and the central planning systems of the communist and socialist countries.

End User

Sometimes, a manufacturer is able to sell directly to foreign **end users** with no intermediary involved in the process. This direct channel is a logical and natural choice for costly industrial products. For most consumer products, the approach is only practical for some products and in some countries. A significant problem with consumer purchases can result from duty and clearance problems. A consumer may place an order without understanding his or her country's import regulations. When the merchandise arrives, the consumer may not be able to claim it. As a result, the product may be seized or returned on a freight-collect basis. Continued occurrence of this problem could become expensive for the manufacturer.

Customs regulations are generally a determinant of the practicality of direct selling to end users. U.S. publishers have no problem selling books and magazines in Canada. Because there is no duty collected for this kind of merchandise, orders from Canada can be fulfilled from the U.S. operations. Mail-order operators dealing in other kinds of merchandise, however, are not as fortunate. At one time, it was very difficult to ship merchandise across the border. A company hoped that its Canadian customers would cooperate by picking up parcels at customs and paying any taxes and duties. In such cases, it was necessary to have a fulfillment operation in Canada. Things brightened considerably for American direct marketers in 1986, when the Canadian Post Corp. announced that parcels from the United States would no longer be held for payment of duty charges. Instead, the new customs regulations allow such duties to be paid on the honor system. Canadian consumers thus can receive merchandise first before duty invoices are sent to them. Those with any past taxes unpaid will have any future shipments held at the border.[4]

To solicit orders, a manufacturer may use publications to attract consumers. Many U.S. magazines receive overseas distribution, and the advertisements inside are read by foreign consumers. Other U.S. magazines including *Time, Newsweek,* and *Business Week* facilitate the ordering process because they publish international editions. Of course, an advertiser can also place its advertisement directly with foreign publishers. This is the process many countries follow in order to promote the local tourism industry.

TYPES OF INTERMEDIARIES: INDIRECT CHANNEL

For a majority of products, a manufacturer may find it impractical to sell directly to the various foreign parties (i.e., foreign distributors, foreign retailers, state-controlled trading companies, and end users). Other intermediaries, more often than not, have to come between these foreign buyers and the manufacturer. This section examines the roles of those middlemen located in the manufacturer's country.

With an indirect channel, a manufacturer does not have to correspond with foreign parties in foreign countries. Instead, the manufacturer deals with one or more domestic middlemen, who in turn move and/or sell the product to foreign middlemen or final users. Although there are many kinds of local sales intermediaries, all can be grouped under two broad categories: (1) domestic agents and (2) domestic merchants. The basic difference between the two is ownership (*title*) rather than just the *physical possession* of the merchandise. **Domestic agents** never take title to the goods, regardless of whether the agents take possession of the goods or not. **Domestic merchants,** on the other hand, own the merchandise, regardless of whether the merchants take possession or not. An agent represents the manufacturer, whereas a merchant (e.g., distributor) represents the manufacturer's product. The merchant has no power to contract on behalf of the manufacturer, but the agent can bind the manufacturer in authorized matters to contracts made on the manufacturer's behalf.

Agents can be further classified according to the principal whom they represent. Some agent intermediaries represent the buyer; others represent the interests of the manufacturer. Those who work for the manufacturer include export brokers, manufacturer's export agents or sales representatives, export management companies, cooperative exporters, and Webb Pomerene associations. Agents who look after the interests of the buyer include purchasing (buying) agents/offices and country-controlled buying agents.

Export Broker

The function of an **export broker** is to bring a buyer and a seller together for a fee. The broker may be assigned some or all foreign markets in seeking potential buyers. It negotiates the best terms for the seller (i.e., manufacturer) but cannot conclude the transaction without the principal's approval of the arrangement. As a representative of the manufacturer, the export broker may operate under its own name or that of the manufacturer. For any action performed, the broker receives a fee or commission. An export broker does not take possession or title to the goods. In effect, it has no financial responsibility other than sometimes making an arrangement for credit. An export broker is less frequently involved in the export (shipping) of goods than in the import (receiving) of goods.

The export broker is useful because of its extensive knowledge of the market supply, demand, and foreign customers. This knowledge enables the broker to negotiate the most favorable terms for the principal. The broker is also a valuable associate for highly specialized goods and seasonal products that do not require constant distribution. An export broker may be thus used on a one-time basis by small manufacturers with limited financial resources who are selling in broad markets.

Manufacturer's Export Agent or Sales Representative

Because of the title of this intermediary, one might easily mistake an **export agent** or **sales representative** for a manufacturer's employee when, in fact, this is an independent businessperson who usually retains his or her own identity by not using the manufacturer's name. Having more freedom than the manufacturer's own salesperson, a sales representative can select when, where, and how to work within the assigned territory. Working methods include presenting product literature and samples to potential buyers. An export agent pays his or her own expenses and may represent manufacturers of related and noncompeting products. He may operate on either an exclusive or nonexclusive basis.

Like a broker, the manufacturer's export agent works for commission. Unlike the broker, the relationship with the manufacturer is continuous and more permanent. The contract is for a definite period of time, and the contract is renewable by mutual agreement. The manufacturer, however, retains some control because the contract defines the territory, terms of sale, method of compensation, and so on.

The manufacturer's export agent may present some problems to the manufacturer because an agent does not offer all services. Such services as advertising, credit assistance, repair, and installation may be excluded. An export agent may take possession but not title to the goods and thus assumes no risk—the risk of loss remains with the manufacturer. Finally, the manufacturer relinquishes control over marketing activities, and this can hurt a manufacturer whose volume is too small to receive the agent's strong support. The experience of Arthur C. Bell, a British firm, is a case in point. James B. Beam, its previous agent in the United States, neglected Bell because its salespeople had too many other products to handle. Bell switched to Monsieur Henri as its new agent. However, this hardly improved the situation because Henri also preferred to concentrate on larger accounts. As a result, Bell was left out of Christmas catalogs or dropped by many retailers. Bell thus contemplated acquiring a U.S. importer to have stronger control over its own marketing destiny.[5]

Under certain circumstances, it may not be justifiable for a small manufacturer to set up its own sales force and distribution network. Such circumstances include the following:

1. When the manufacturer has a geographically widespread market—the usual case in international marketing.
2. When some overseas markets are too thin.
3. When the manufacturer's product is new and the demand is uncertain.
4. When the manufacturer is inexperienced in international marketing.
5. When the manufacturer wants to simplify business activities.

A manufacturer can avoid fixed costs associated with having its own sales and distribution organization when it employs an agent, since the commission is paid only when sales are made. A manufacturer's export agent has extensive knowledge of specific foreign markets and furthermore has more incentive to work than the manufacturer's own salespersons. Additionally, the agent carries several product lines, and the result is that the expense of doing business is shared by other manufacturers. This arrangement allows the manufacturer to concentrate time, capital, and expertise on the product of goods rather than on having to deal with the marketing aspect. Of course, if the product is successful, the manufacturer can always set up its own sales force.

Export Management Company (EMC)

An **export management company (EMC)** manages, under contract, the entire export program of a manufacturer. An EMC is also known as a **combination export manager (CEM)** because it may function as an export department for several allied but non-competing manufacturers. In this regard, those export brokers and manufacturer's export agents who represent a combination of clients can also be called EMCs. When compared with export brokers and manufacturer's export agents, the EMC has greater freedom and considerable authority. The EMC provides extensive services, ranging from promotion to shipping arrangement and documentation. Moreover the EMC handles all, not just a portion, of its principal's products. In short, the EMC is responsible for all of the manufacturer's international activities. The United States, for example, has some 1,100 EMCs, accounting for about 10 percent of all U.S. export sales of manufactured goods.

Foreign buyers usually prefer to deal directly with the manufacturer rather than through a third party. Therefore, an EMC usually solicits business in the name of the manufacturer and may even use the manufacturer's letterhead. Identifying itself as the manufacturer's export department or international division, the EMC signs correspondence and documents in the name of the manufacturer. This may be an advantageous arrangement for small and medium-sized firms that lack expertise and adequate human and financial resources to obtain exports. This arrangement may be a good way for a firm to develop foreign markets while creating its own identity abroad. The EMC, on the other hand, faces a dilemma because of a double risk: it can easily be dropped by its clients either for doing a poor job or for making the manufacturer's products too successful.

EMCs are compensated in several ways. Frequently, compensation is in the form of a commission, salary, or retainer plus commission. Depending on the product, the commission varies from 7.5 to 20 percent of the wholesale distributor price. Some EMCs also become traders (i.e., export merchants). In such cases, they buy merchandise outright and thus take title to the goods. They are compensated by receiving discounts on goods purchased for resale overseas, and such discounts may be greater than what other middlemen receive for the domestic market. In a normal buy-and-sell arrangement, the EMC buys at the domestic net wholesale distributor price, less a certain percentage that is equivalent to the manufacturer's domestic sales overhead.[6] Furthermore, they may receive promotional allowances as well. The extent of the compensation paid is a function of the tasks and services involved. The commission for simple brokering is usually 10 percent or less. If the arrangements involved are rather complicated such as in setting up a unique channel of distribution, the compensation may be as high as 30 to 40 percent.[7] Some EMCs may require the manufacturer to pay for start-up costs, and these can range from $5,000 to $50,000.

There are several reasons why a firm uses an EMC. It has international marketing expertise and distribution contacts overseas. For the many services provided, an EMC's costs are relatively low because of the efficiencies of scale; that is, costs can be spread over the products of several clients. In addition, the EMC provides shipping efficiency because it can consolidate several manufacturers' products in one shipment. The orders are consolidated at the port and shipped on one ocean bill of lading to the same foreign buyer. By consolidating shipments of products from several principals, a company obtains better freight rates. Also, many EMCs provide financial services. By guaranteeing payments and collecting from overseas buyers, a manufacturer is assured of immediate payment. By providing all of these services, the EMC allows the manufacturer to concentrate on internal efforts and its domestic market.

Using EMCs, like using other types of intermediaries, does have its disadvantages. First, an EMC prefers new clients whose products complement the EMC's existing product lines. The EMC is very likely not interested in unknown products or new technologies that require too much time and effort in opening new markets overseas. A problem for a small manufacturer may be the extent of support it receives. If a firm seeks to do business with a large EMC, the EMC is not likely to give the small client adequate attention. If a small EMC is used, the EMC may be too small to give attention to all products of its clients. In general, most EMCs do put forth a serious effort and are willing and able to provide sufficient services for new clients. According to Brasch, a manufacturer should consider an EMC that

1. Specializes in its product type.
2. Has in place a well-organized and well-controlled worldwide distribution system.
3. Is well-financed and managed, and
4. Is willing and eager to devote significant amounts of managerial effort and money to launching a client's products.[8]

For assistance in locating EMCs, the manufacturer should contact NEXCO (the National Association of Export Management Companies), the only national organization of EMCs and export trading companies, as well as other regional EMC associations.

From one survey of 198 EMCs, several representative characteristics can be identified.[9] EMCs are generally small—only 7 percent have more than ten employees. About 25 percent have foreign branch offices. Most EMCs use outside freight forwarding firms. Some 85 percent accept credit responsibility. About 8 percent of EMCs never take title to a client's merchandise, but about 50 percent always take title. Even when an EMC does take title, it does not necessarily want to take possession. EMCs serve both large and small companies. With 63 percent representing manufacturers in three or more industries, EMCs are more market specialists than product specialists. A small number of EMCs do specialize both by geographic area and by industry (product). Thus, it is unreasonable to expect more than just a few to be experts in all foreign markets. A majority will accept exclusive rights for a single country or group of countries in the same continent. But only 16 percent of the EMCs want worldwide distribution rights on an exclusive basis.

Not all EMCs operate in the same manner. Based on a study done by Bello and Williamson, EMCs may have a variety of contractual agreements with manufacturers, ranging from formal contracts *(contractual channel)* to informal agreements *(administrative channel)* and independent operations *(conventional channel)*.[10] Consequently, EMCs differ in terms of export sales volume, number of product lines handled, and number of suppliers represented. Furthermore, operating arrangements may be different in terms of an EMC's export role, geographic market exclusivity, and annual sales requirements. Finally, EMCs' economic activities can be distinguished in terms of ordering procedures, pricing procedures, and promotion procedures. These variations must be considered by manufacturers in establishing distribution strategies. The conventional export channel is virtually risk free, since EMCs in this case are merchants who take title. "The likelihood that an EMC will act as an agent, possess market exclusivity, and have a sales quota imposed is reduced when the trading relationship is administered informally." The administrative channel is suitable for manufacturers that want some flexibility in penetrating world markets. When the contractual channel is used, the EMC tends to become the manufacturer's agent, with worldwide exclusivity and sales quotas. When both parties operate under contractual commitments over a long period of time, a contractual channel can provide important mutual benefits.

Cooperative Exporter

A **cooperative exporter** is a manufacturer with its own export organization that is retained by other manufacturers to sell in some or all foreign markets. Except for the fact that this intermediary is also a manufacturer, the cooperative exporter functions like any other export agent. The usual arrangement is to operate as an export distributor for other suppliers, sometimes acting as a commission representative or broker. Because the cooperative exporter arranges shipping, it takes possession of goods but not title.

The cooperative exporter's motive in representing other manufacturers primarily involves its own financial interests. Having fixed costs for the marketing of its own products, the cooperative exporter desires to share its expenses and expertise with others who want to sell in the same markets abroad. Because of these activities, a cooperative exporter is often referred to as a "mother hen," a "piggyback exporter," or an **export vendor.** Examples of cooperative exporters include such well-known companies as GE, Singer, and Borg-Warner. By representing several clients, the cooperative exporter is regarded as a form of EMC.

The relationship between the cooperative exporter and its principal is a long-term one. The arrangement provides an easy, low-risk way for the principal to start marketing overseas, and the relationship should ordinarily continue as long as unrelated or noncompetitive products are involved. A problem may arise if the principal decides to market a new product that competes directly with the cooperative exporter's own product or those of the exporter's other clients.

Webb-Pomerene Association

A **Webb-Pomerene association** is formed when two or more firms, usually in the same industry, join together to market their products overseas. The association constitutes an organization jointly owned by competing U.S. manufacturers exclusively for the purpose of export. It may seem strange for competing firms (rather than noncompeting firms) to cooperate, but experience has shown that joint export operations are not effective for unrelated products. The largest such association has almost 300 members, whereas the Northwest Dried Fruit Association has only 2 members.

Basically, a Webb-Pomerene association is an export cartel. Although cartels are illegal in the United States, this kind of cartel is allowed to operate as long as it has no anticompetitive impact on domestic marketing in the U.S. market. Although receiving no prior certification of antitrust exemption, the Webb-Pomerene Act provides the association with a qualified exemption. The only legal requirement is that the association must file with the Federal Trade Commission within thirty days after its organization.

Two court cases have proved useful in interpreting the Webb-Pomerene Act.[11] In 1950, a court prohibited four American members of a Webb-Pomerene association from jointly establishing factories in England, West Germany, and Canada because such activity does not constitute export trade. Firms' market positions are irrelevant as long as their activities conform to the specifics of the statute (i.e., a combination for engaging solely in export trade). Therefore, the government could not block American manufacturers of coated abrasives from combining to export exclusively through one corporation and from fixing prices and quotas abroad even though these firms collectively controlled 80 percent of the U.S. export trade in that commodity.

The Webb-Pomerene association performs several useful functions. It provides information to member firms, sets prices, allocates orders, and sells products. It arranges shipping of the merchandise by providing for freight consolidation, rate negotiation, and ship chartering or booking. The association thus takes possession of goods and makes all necessary arrangements but without taking title of the goods. As cooperative organizations, these associations tend to operate on a nonprofit or expense basis.

There are disadvantages in this type of long-term relationship. First, this type of arrangement is not available in the service sector because the act prohibits service firms from joining together. Second, convenient financing is not available because banks have not been allowed to participate in this type of commercial venture since the 1920s. Third, as expected for most partnerships, some opposition and disagreement among members is inevitable. If members fail to agree or cooperate, the association's effectiveness is seriously impaired. Finally, member firms lose individual identity because exports are done in the name of the association, making the arrangement somewhat more suitable for unbranded goods or commodities. Specialized products and popular brands are able to do their own exporting and thus do not want their brands replaced by a common association label or trademark. An unusual but possible arrangement is for members to retain individual identity (i.e., individual brand names); the machine-tool associations are a prime example. These associations were formed primarily to offer technical assistance and credit in markets too small to justify each exporter's own facilities.

Purchasing/Buying Agent

An export agent represents a seller or manufacturer; the **purchasing/buying agent** represents the foreign buyer. By residing and conducting business in the exporter's country, the purchasing agent is in a favorable position to seek a product that matches the foreign principal's preferences and requirements. Operating on the overseas customer's behalf, the purchasing agent acts in the interest of the buyer by seeking the best possible price. Therefore, the purchasing agent's client pays a fee or commission for the services rendered. The purchasing agent is also known by such names as *commission agent, buyer for export, export commission house,* and *export buying agent.* This agent may also become an export confirming house when confirming payment and paying the seller after receiving invoice and title documents for the client.

The buying agent is valuable for manufacturers because it seeks those firms out and offers them its services. However, since the agent operates on an order basis, the relationship with either seller or buyer is not continuous. This arrangement thus does not offer a steady volume of business for the manufacturer and neither does it offer any reduction in financial risk. In any case, the transaction between the manufacturer and the buying agent (or the agent's customer) may be completed as a domestic enterprise in the sense that the agent will take care of all shipping arrangements. Otherwise, the manufacturer will have to make its own arrangement.

Country-Controlled Buying Agent

A variation on the purchasing agent is a **country-controlled buying agent.** This kind of agent performs exactly the same function as the purchasing/buying agent, the only distinction being that a country-controlled buying agent is actually a foreign government's agency or quasi-governmental firm. The country-controlled buying agent is empowered to locate and purchase goods for its country. This agent may have a permanent office location in countries that are major suppliers, or the country's representative may make formal visits to supplier countries when the purchasing need arises.

Resident Buyer

Another variation on the purchasing agent is the **resident buyer.** As implied by the name, the resident buyer is an independent agent that is usually located near highly centralized production industries. Although functioning much like a regular purchasing agent, the resident buyer is different because it is retained by the principal on a continuous basis to maintain a search for new products that may be suitable. The long-term relationship makes it possible for the resident buyer to be compensated with a retainer and a commission for business transacted.

The resident buyer provides many useful services for a manufacturer. It can offer a favorable opportunity for a supplier to maintain a steady and continuous business relationship as long as the supplier remains competitive in terms of price, service, style, and quality.

For a foreign buyer, the resident buyer offers several useful services, one of which is the purchasing function. The resident buyer uses its judgment to make decisions for its overseas client, which does not have the time to send someone to visit production sites or firms or which cannot wait to examine samples. Another service provided by the resident buyer is the follow-up function. The resident buyer can make certain that delivery is made as promised. A late delivery can make the purchase meaningless, especially in the case of seasonable or fashion products. If the foreign client decides to visit manufacturing plants or offices, the resident buyer can assist by making hotel reservations, announcing the visit to suppliers, arranging vendor appointments, and so on.

Export Merchant

The intermediaries covered so far have certain factors in common: they take neither risks nor title, preferring to receive fees for their services. Unlike these middlemen, domestic merchants are independent businesses that are in business to make a profit rather than to receive a fee. There are several types of domestic merchants. Because they all take title, they are distinguished by other features, such as physical possession of goods and services rendered.

One kind of domestic merchant is the **export merchant.** An export merchant seeks out needs in foreign markets and makes purchases from manufacturers in its own country to fill those needs. Usually the merchant handles staple goods, undifferentiated products, or those in which brands are unimportant. After having the merchandise packed and marked to specifications, the export merchant resells the goods in its own name through contacts in foreign markets. In completing all these arrangements, the merchant assumes all risks associated with ownership.

The export merchant's compensation is a function of how product is priced. The markup is affected by the profit motive as well as by market conditions. In any case, the export merchant hopes that the price at which the product is sold will exceed all costs and expenses in order to provide a profit. An export merchant may sometimes seek extra income by importing goods to complement its export activities. The merchant may or may not offer a steady business relationship for his supplier.

Export Drop Shipper

An **export drop shipper,** also known as a *desk jobber* or *cable merchant,* is a special kind of export merchant. As all these names imply, the mode of operation requires the drop shipper to request a manufacturer to "drop ship" a product directly to the overseas customer. It is neither practical nor desirable for the shipper to physically handle or possess the product. Based on this operational method, the shipper's ownership of the goods may only last for a few hours.

Upon the receipt of an order from overseas, the export drop shipper in turn places an order with a manufacturer, directing the manufacturer to deliver the product directly to the foreign buyer. The manufacturer collects payment from the drop shipper, who in turn is paid by the foreign buyer.

Use of a drop shipper is common in the international marketing of bulky products of low unit value (e.g., coal, lumber, construction materials). The high freight volume relative to the low unit value makes it prohibitively expensive to handle such products physically several times. Minimizing physical handling reduces the cost accordingly.

One may question why a manufacturer does not simply deal directly with a foreign buyer, bypassing the drop shipper and saving money in the process—the shipping instructions would reveal the name and address of the foreign buyer. The answer is that the manufacturer can reduce the risk while simplifying the transactional tasks. It is a great deal easier for the manufacturer to call the export drop shipper in the manufacturer's own country instead of trying to sell to and collect from the buyer in a far-away destination.

There are also good reasons why the foreign buyer may not be able to or want to bypass the export drop shipper. The buyer may not have adequate product knowledge or supply knowledge, and the buyer's order may be too small to entice the manufacturer to deal directly. The drop shipper is thus valuable because this kind of merchant is highly specialized in knowing the sources of supply and markets. The drop shipper also has information and advice about the needed product and can arrange all details for obtaining it.

Export Distributor

Whereas export merchants and drop shippers purchase from a manufacturer whenever they receive orders from overseas, an **export distributor** deals with the manufacturer on a continuous basis. This distributor is authorized and granted an exclusive right to represent the manufacturer and to sell in some or all foreign markets. It pays for goods in its domestic transaction with the manufacturer and handles all financial risks in the foreign sale.

An export distributor differs from a foreign distributor simply in location. The foreign distributor is located in a particular foreign country and is authorized to distribute and sell the product there. The export distributor, in comparison, is located in the manufacturer's country and is authorized to sell in one or more markets abroad. Consider Mamiya, a Japanese manufacturer. J. Osawa is Mamiya's worldwide distributor (i.e., export distributor). Bell and Howell: Mamiya is in turn J. Osawa's exclusive U.S. distributor (i.e., foreign distributor).

The export distributor operates in its own name or that of the manufacturer. It handles all shipping details, thus relieving the manufacturer of having to pay attention to overseas activities. In other words, the sale made to the export distributor is just like another domestic transaction for the manufacturer. Because the export distributor, as a rule, represents several manufacturing firms, it is sometimes regarded as a form of EMC.

The export distributor usually sells the manufacturer's product abroad at the manufacturer's list price and receives an agreed percentage of the list price as remuneration. That is, the export distributor is either paid by commission or allowed a discount for its purchase. The manufacturer may bill a foreign buyer directly or may let the distributor bill the buyer to obtain the desired margin.

Trading Company

Those that want to sell and those that want to buy often have no knowledge of each other or no knowledge of how to contact each other. **Trading companies** have come into existence to fill this void. In international marketing activities for many countries, this type of intermediary may be the most dominant form in volume of business and in influence. Many trading companies are large and have branches wherever they do business. They operate in LDCs, developed countries, and their own home markets. Half of Taiwan's exports are controlled by Japanese trading companies. In Japan, general trading houses are known as *sogo shosha,* and the largest traders include such well known MNCs as Mitsubishi, Mitsui, and C. Itoh. The nine largest trading firms handle roughly half of Japan's imports and exports. Even large Japanese domestic companies buy through trading companies.

A trading company performs many functions; the term describes many intermediaries that are neither brokers nor import merchants. A trading company may buy and sell as a merchant. It may handle goods on consignment, or it may act as a commission house for some buyers. By representing several clients, it resembles an EMC, except for the fact that it (1) has more diverse product lines, (2) offers more services, (3) is larger and better financed, (4) takes title (ownership) to merchandise, (5) is not exclusively restricted to engaging in export trade, and (6) goes beyond the role of an intermediary (which provides only export facilitation services) by engaging directly in production, physical distribution channel development, financing, and resource development.

As the name implies, the trading company trades on its own account for profit. By frequently taking title to the goods it handles, its risks of doing business greatly increase. A trading company does not merely represent manufacturers and/or buyers, thus reducing risks, because increased risks are usually accompanied by increased rewards. In the case of WSJ International, which is a trader as well as a representative, profit margins gained on trading are about four times greater than margins on representative sales. It is thus not surprising that trading accounts for half of the company's revenues.

Manufacturers and buyers use trading companies for good reasons. The trading company gathers market information; does market planning; finds buyers; packages and warehouses merchandise; arranges and prepares documents for transportation; insurance, and customs; provides financing for suppliers and/or buyers; accepts business risks; and serves foreign customers after sales. It is, in short, a valuable entity in overcoming cultural and institutional barriers. Nanodata, for example, concluded that it was too expensive to reach unfamiliar and distant market areas. The company decided to hire TKB Technology Trading Corporation, a trading company, to identify good European markets for Nanodata's computer and to develop a distribution channel by choosing agents, distributors, or direct subsidiaries. TKB offered entry without expensive staff buildup until Nanodata was ready to do so on its own.

Like other intermediaries, however, the trading company must always face the possibility of being bypassed by its clients, and it thus must offer something of value to its customers. This holds true even for Mitsubishi, the world's largest trader with more than $70 billion in sales. Without its own production, this company could be squeezed out by Japanese clients that would set up their own marketing departments. Mitsubishi's solution in keeping old customers and getting new ones is to give buyers and sellers an incentive to do business with it. It has formed joint ventures with American and Japanese partners with an aim to acquire ownership influence with both its suppliers and customers. Furthermore, this firm cannot be easily replaced because of its long experience, expertise, and established networks.

Japanese Trading Companies   Because of the spectacular success of the huge Japanese trading companies, many companies—especially those in the United States—would like to emulate or duplicate them. Chew, however, points out that, since American manufacturers are much more involved with domestic and foreign wholesale transactions, the Japanese model is inappropriate unless the United States alters its domestic economic, social, and legal infrastructure—a very unlikely occurrence.[12]

Japanese trading companies have several distinct characteristics. They are supported by domestic Japanese business, from which they derive about one-half of their sales. They are particularly strong in the area of commodity and undifferentiated products. They are "characterized by high volume, low margins, liberal trade credit granting and low inventories, these factors combining to result in relatively low interest cost burdens despite high levels of debt outstanding."[13] Of the ten largest

Japanese trading companies, all are partners with groups of banks and other financial intermediaries.[14] This financial feature is important because it allows these companies to have easy, convenient, and almost permanent access to enormous amounts of capital and financing. Another contributing factor to the success of Japanese trading companies is a cultural one. Japanese manufacturers prefer to separate manufacturing from marketing, leaving the marketing function to trading firms, though a new breed of Japanese manufacturers prefers to have more marketing control and has been shifting away from this pattern of specialization.

Export Trading Companies   In the United States, the entities most resembling trading companies are Webb-Pomerene associations and EMCs, which together account for 12 percent of U.S. exports. Although EMCs and trading companies perform several similar functions, EMCs are different because they tend to be smaller, with just a few employees. EMCs also lack easy access to sources of financing and thus are usually undercapitalized. As a result, EMCs are less diversified in product and geographic area, and they restrict their business to exports with very little import focus. EMCs are thus not able to provide the complete range of services required by manufacturers.

Because of the limited success of EMCs and Webb-Pomerene companies (along with a concern over trade deficits), the United States has begun to turn to trading companies for a solution. The Export Trading Company (ETC) Act was passed in 1982. In Section 103 of the act, an **export trading company** is defined as a firm "which is organized and operated principally for the purposes of—(a) exporting goods and services produced in the United States; and (b) facilitating the exportation of goods and services produced in the United States by unaffiliated persons by providing one or more export trade services.... The term 'export trade services' includes, but is not limited to, consulting, international market research, advertising, marketing, insurance, product research and design, legal assistance, transportation, including trade documentation and freight forwarding, communication and processing of foreign orders to and for exporters and foreign purchasers, warehousing, foreign exchange, and financing, when provided in order to facilitate the export of goods or services produced in the United States."[15]

This act removed legal roadblocks that had impaired the effectiveness of EMCs and Webb-Pomerene associations. The two entities have not grown satisfactorily for two main reasons: lack of financing and antitrust restrictions. In the past, dealing with one of those two problems often involved getting into difficulty with the other. If firms tried to join together to strengthen their financial resources, they would be violating the antitrust laws. In trying to avoid antitrust problems, they remained resource poor.

For more than half a century, the Glass-Steagall Act of 1934 banned banks from engaging in nonfinancial activities and bank ownership of commercial enterprises. Title III of the ETC Act removed this ban, allowing banks to hold equity positions in export trading companies. An amendment to the banking regulations permitted banks to participate in ownership indirectly through bank holding companies, Bankers' Banks, or Edge Act cooperatives. Unlike nonbank investors, which do not have to register with the government, bank holding companies must file their applications with the Federal Reserve Board in order to start export trading companies, even though these holding companies do not enjoy antitrust protection. The act still bars any direct bank equity in ETCs, however. Also, unlike nonbank investors who can import freely, a bank-affiliated ETC must be either exclusively related to exporting activities or operated principally to facilitate U.S. exports. That is, revenue derived from export must be greater than 50 percent of the ETC's revenue.

The participation of banks in export trading is critical. The obvious benefit is financial resources, but banks have other strengths. They provide many of the services that ETCs do. They can reach out to small and medium-sized firms by using their foreign branches to identify foreign buyers and domestic branches in order to contact U.S. manufacturers. Because trading companies often take title to goods to expedite deals, the act has provided banks with an incentive to overcome their reluctance to take ownership. The banks are now in a position to derive higher profit margins than when they merely acted as agents.

The 1982 act provided a remedy for the antitrust problem as well. For decades, the Webb-Pomerene Export Trade Act of 1918 allowed firms to participate in joint export but may have discouraged participation unintentionally by granting antitrust exemption to only a limited degree. Title III of the 1982 act solved this problem by allowing domestic competitors to obtain binding antitrust preclearance for specified export activities. By granting prior antitrust immunity, the antitrust threat was removed, creating a favorable environment for the formation of joint export ventures. Such ventures, through large-scale operations and economies of scale, can now reduce cost and risk while promoting efficiencies. In order to be certified as not violating antitrust laws, a group of companies and banks that join forces for the purpose of export can obtain a Certificate of Review from the Department of Commerce (with the concurrence of the Justice Department) for certification as an ETC. This certificate functions as an antitrust "insurance policy." The ETC is then exempted from both criminal and civil antitrust activities and is immune from federal and state antitrust suits as long as the overseas cooperation does not filter back to affect competition and prices at home. When challenged, the certificate holder can recover legal expenses if the holder prevails.

Many hoped that the ETC Act would eventually attract some 20,000 new exporters and increase U.S. exports by 20 percent or $40 billion a year. If that projection would materialize, 640,000 jobs would be created. But results have been mixed. A survey conducted by Czinkota revealed that a majority of companies with some interest in international marketing were familiar with the act and expected it to improve the performance of U.S. export.[16] Czinkota nonetheless felt that those findings contradicted the actual business response to the act and that the federal government should undertake a large educational effort.

Within the first two years of the creation of the act, the Commerce Department had issued sixty-one certificates providing antitrust protection to twenty-three firms and individuals.[17] Whether the number is satisfactory is subject to individual interpretation. In any case, many of the companies applying for antitrust certificates were members of Webb-Pomerene associations, and they in all likelihood decided to obtain more comprehensive antitrust immunity.

The firms that have recently formed ETCs are from various backgrounds. Some are manufacturers with subsidiaries that have ready access to the parents' products. GE Trading Company, for example, has access to GE's 300,000 products. Other manufacturers include Rockwell International and GM, which have set up Rockwell International Trading Company and General Motors Trading Company, respectively. Retailers have also formed ETCs (e.g., Sears Roebuck Trading Company formed by Sears). Retailers such as Sears and Kmart have a great deal of bargaining power because of their enormous purchases, and this leverage serves them well in marketing U.S. exports through foreign retail chains. Other organizations forming ETCs are banks, which seem natural for this purpose. Because banks can own up to 100 percent of an ETC's stock, these ETCs are guaranteed to have adequate financial resources. In some cases, banks and other business firms may want to form a joint venture, as in the case of First Chicago and Sears World Trade, Inc.

One problem with ETCs is that the ETC Act is designed to promote only U.S. exports. Thus ETCs' import activities must take a secondary position, undertaken only when they are needed to promote exports. Consequently, ETCs may lack an efficient infrastructure for developing two-way trade. In this regard, ETCs differ greatly from Japanese trading companies, which achieve their efficiencies through domestic, foreign, and third-country trading activities. American ETCs may thus lack a comprehensive international perspective.

When selecting an ETC, the services offered must be taken into account. According to a study conducted by Bello and Williamson, "the importance of services provided by export intermediaries is influenced by the type of product exported, export role of the intermediary, and supplier's export sales volume."[18] With regard to the type of product, transaction-creating services were found to be more important for differentiated products, whereas physical-fulfilling services were not necessarily more important for undifferentiated products. As far as the export role is concerned, transaction-creating services were not more important for agents than for merchants, but some (not all) physical-fulfilling services were more important for merchants. There was some partial evidence, in the case of supplier's export sales volume, that transaction-creating services as well as physical-fulfilling services were more important for intermediaries with suppliers exporting over $1 million. Table 12–1 shows the service requirements for ETCs.

TABLE 12–1   Service requirements for American export trading companies

Suppliers Represented	Products Exported	
	Undifferentiated	Differentiated
Low export volume	Requires a less than average capability in promotion, market contact, and consolidation.	Requires an above average capability in promotion, but an average capability in market contact and consolidation.
High export volume	Requires a less than average capability in promotion, but an average capability in market contact and consolidation.	Requires an above average capability in promotion, market contact, and consolidation.

Source: Daniel C. Bello and Nicholas C. Williamson, "The American Export Trading Company: Designing a New International Marketing Institution." *Journal of Marketing* 49 (Fall 1985): 67. Reprinted from *Journal of Marketing*, published by the American Marketing Association

CHANNEL DEVELOPMENT

The suitability of a particular channel depends greatly upon the country in which it is used. A particular type of intermediary that works well in one country may not work well elsewhere or may lose effectiveness over time. This does not necessarily mean that each country requires a unique channel. But a company may find that a country classification system is useful, a system that can be used to determine how the distribution strategy should be set up from one group of countries to another.

Litvak and Banting suggest the use of a country temperature gradient to classify countries.[19] Their classification system is based on these environmental characteristics: (1) political stability, (2) market opportunity, (3) economic development and performance, (4) cultural unity, (5) legal barriers/restrictions, (6) physiographic barriers, and (7) geocultural distance. Based on these characteristics, countries may be classified as hot, moderate, or cold. A hot country is one that scores high on the first four characteristics and low on the last three. A cold country is exactly the opposite, and a moderate one is medium on all seven characteristics.

The United States generally falls in line with the characteristics of a hot country. So does Canada, even though its cultural unity is moderate (rather than high) and its physiographic barriers are moderate (rather than low). Germany, likewise, is a hot country in spite of some slight interference in the sense that its legal barriers and geocultural distance are moderate rather than low. Brazil, in contrast, largely conforms to a cold country's characteristics.

Goodnow and Hanz compared 100 countries on fifty-nine characteristics, and the findings yielded three clusters of hot, moderate, and cold countries.[20] Hot countries included the EC countries (except Ireland), Austria, Norway, Sweden, Switzerland, Canada, Australia, New Zealand, and Japan. Moderate countries included most Caribbean and Latin American countries, Finland, Hong Kong, Israel, Kuwait, Lebanon, Malaysia, Portugal, Ireland, Spain, South Korea, Taiwan, South Africa, and Yugoslavia. Cold countries included all African countries (except South Africa), most of the Middle East and Southeast Asia, India, Argentina, Bolivia, Haiti, Paraguay, Peru, and Greece.

It is a judgment call whether so many characteristics are necessary for the purpose of classifying countries. The level of economic development could be used as the sole indicator, but such a classification would be misleading because hot countries are not the same as industrialized countries. Still, one must question whether the refinement and improvement in the classification process justifies the extra effort necessary to wade through all relevant characteristics, especially since the level of economic development correlates well with these characteristics. For practicality, a shortcut appears to be desirable.

Classification is a means to an end, and the purpose of the country temperature gradient is to determine which intermediary should be used in a given country. The temperature gradient also indicates which kind of intermediary is likely to be functioning in a country. In a cold country, competitive pressures on institutional change are not dynamic. Legal restrictions, for example, can prevent or slow down new distribution innovations. Consider Egypt as an example. Only persons born of Egyptian fathers or Egyptian legal entities can represent foreign principals. Being "comfortably cold," middlemen see few threats to their existence.

For a hot country, environmental forces may be so hot that new institutional structures arise. Middlemen who fail to adjust will be bypassed and go out of existence. The survival of a channel member is thus a function of the ability to adapt to changing environmental conditions because the channel member cannot hide behind local regulations for protection. For example, in the United Kingdom, either the principal or the intermediary can terminate an agency relationship provided there is a reasonable notice. If the agent receives a weekly salary, a week's notice will suffice. If the agent receives a commission, the notice period may have to be extended to six months unless stated otherwise in the contract.[21]

The country temperature gradient has implications for all channel members. A foreign manufacturer can exercise maximum control over the evolutionary process in the distribution channel. The firm can initially rely on middlemen/distributors. If sales increase, the manufacturer can bypass the intermediary by setting up a sales branch or subsidiary. This is the trend being followed by foreign liquor suppliers in the U.S. market. These suppliers now very much control their own destiny by being responsible for their own distribution. E. Remy Martin & Co. took its cognac away from Glenmore Distilleries and became its own U.S. distributor through its Premier Wine Merchants. Distillers Co., a Scottish firm, did likewise by buying Somerset Importers from Esmark. Pernod Ricard and Monet-Hennessy adopted the same strategy by buying Austin Nichols and Schieffelin, respectively.

A local manufacturer should be alert to any new channel since the new channel may pose a threat to this existing channel. When possible, the manufacturer must preempt the competition from utilizing it. Xerox was successful and secure with its direct sales force channel—so secure that, when the Japanese competition entered the market, Xerox was totally unprepared. The Japanese invaded the U.S. market quickly and cheaply by using independent office equipment dealers, a channel that had been ignored by Xerox. The Japanese firms had their own direct sales force in large metropolitan areas, but they also supplied their machines to such U.S. firms as IBM, Monroe, and Pitney Bowes, thus exploiting these U.S. firms' extensive sales and distribution networks. Xerox was forced to experiment with such alternative channels as retail stores, direct mail, and part-time representatives.

Wholesalers, especially those involved in high-margin, low-volume operations, are particularly vulnerable to the threat posed by modern institutions. Wholesalers can easily be bypassed if they are successful in promoting their principals' products. Superscope, for example, lost the Sony franchise. On the other hand, if wholesalers do the job poorly, they are also likely to be eliminated or their authority and responsibility reduced. Mitsubishi was so unhappy with Chrysler's performance that the Japanese company developed its own independent dealer network in order to catch up with Toyota and Nissan.

Local retailers in a hot country are not exempt from innovations either. In Europe, computer makers have to depend on highly fragmented channels consisting of small retailers without financial resources for large inventories. Computerland has mounted an effort to change this distribution network by using its mass-marketing technique to duplicate its U.S. success in Europe. The company has opened several stores there.

Innovations tend to take place in a hot country before spreading to other hot countries and finally LDCs. Retailing innovations that conform to this description include self-service stores, discount houses, and supermarkets, all of which initially developed in the United States. Hypermarche, on the other hand, is a mass-merchandising method developed in Europe. This retail store is an enormous self-service combination of food and general merchandise, generally displayed in shipping containers. A single set of checkout counters is used. This innovation has had only limited success when introduced in the United States.

In another example, Apple has attempted to establish "Apple Centers" in the United States—a retailing concept utilized successfully in Europe. In 1985 Apple had few dealers and little public visibility in England. Apple thus developed the concept of "Apple Centers" as part of a strategy to improve its performance. The strategy involves having independently owned and managed retail outlets that are focused primarily on Apple products but also include software and peripherals from various manufacturers. The centers are offices that, under one roof, combine computer marketing, sales, training, support, and service. The concept was later extended to other European countries, resulting in more than sixty Apple Centers, which have helped the European unit become the biggest contributor to corporate profit. Because markets vary, Apple has made substantial adjustments in its Apple Centers to perform different functions in different markets.[22]

The success of an innovation is affected not only by the country temperature gradient but also by several other factors. A certain minimum level of economic development is required to support any form of outlet beyond simple retailing methods. General stores, a dying breed in the United States, are still very common in many countries. Firms' aggressive behavior will also be a determinant of the success of a new retailing method. Other cultural, legal, and competitive factors play an important role too. In LDCs, where there is plenty of low-cost labor and where people are accustomed to being waited on, self-service stores, discount houses, and supermarkets are slow in gaining widespread acceptance. In developed countries, by comparison, various factors work in the favor of large modern discount stores/supermarkets, including high population density, urbanization, literacy, and labor costs. Also, the high income level and relatively even income distribution make refrigerators and automobiles affordable and accommodate infrequent shopping trips and large purchases.

CHANNEL ADAPTATION

Because the standardized/globalized approach to international marketing strategy may not apply to distribution strategy in foreign markets, it is imperative that international marketers understand the distribution structures and patterns in those markets. Toward this end, comparative marketing analysis should be conducted.[23] A study of the degree of standardization in the marketing mix by large U.S.-based industrial firms in their Latin American business found that distribution was highly adapted to the different conditions in Latin America. The region's government regulation, a barrier to standardization, appears to force firms to adjust their prices, advertising, and distribution more than their products and brands.[24]

Some channel adaptation is frequently a necessity. Suspicion and privacy can limit the effectiveness of door-to-door selling or other direct-selling methods. Avon has had to develop other distribution methods in Japan and Thailand. Discount retailing may not be effective in countries where there are many middlemen handling small volumes of merchandise. A traditional distribution channel may seem inefficient, but it may maximize the utilization of inexpensive labor, leaving no idle resources.

A manufacturer must keep in mind that, because of adaptation, a particular type of retailer may not operate in exactly the same manner in all countries. Whereas a U.S. supermarket emphasizes low gross margin, its foreign counterpart may have a relatively high gross margin, emphasizing specialty goods and imported goods to a high degree. Furthermore, that foreign counterpart often operates a ready-to-eat food section. Interestingly, American supermarkets, especially those that have converted into superstores, have begun to do the same.

A particular distribution concept proven useful in one country may have to be further refined in another. Although 7-Eleven pioneered the convenience food store concept in Japan, the Japanese operation has evolved into being more sophisticated than the original counterpart in the United States. 7-Eleven Japan offers its customers steaming fish cakes, canned tea, and rice balls, while accepting payment for utility bills and accepting orders from the Tiffany's catalog. The 4,328 Japanese stores, viewing "slurpie" and ice drinks as passé, stopped serving them some years ago. To provide the most popular and latest products, about two-thirds of a typical store's 3,000 items will change in a year.[25]

CHANNEL DECISIONS

As in any domestic market, the international market requires a marketer to make at least three channel decisions: length, width, and number of channels of distribution. **Channel length** is concerned with the number of times a product changes hands among intermediaries before it reaches the final consumer. The channel is considered long when a manufacturer is required to move its product through several middlemen. The channel is short when the product has to change hands just once or twice. If the manufacturer elects to sell directly to final consumers, the channel is direct. U.S. and Japanese manufacturers of TV sets employ different strategies in the length of channel. Zenith uses a two-step distribution system, requiring retailers to buy from independent distributors. The system is unsuitable for video specialty stores, which prefer to buy directly from manufacturers. As a result, video specialty stores have turned to Japanese manufacturers who, in addition to having lower prices, are willing to distribute direct to these stores.

Channel width is related to the number of middlemen at a particular point or step in the distribution channel. Channel width is a function of the number of wholesalers and the different kinds that are used, as well as a function of the number and kind of retailers used. As more intermediaries or more types are used at a certain point in the channel, the channel becomes wider and more intensive. If only a few qualified intermediaries are needed to provide proper product support at a particular level or at a specific location, the channel is selective. The product, though perhaps not available everywhere, is still carried by at least a few qualified middlemen within the same area. Finally, the distribution becomes exclusive if only one intermediary of one type is used in that particular area.

The watch industry and its distribution strategies provide a good illustration of an industry with various channel widths. Timex, as a low-priced, mass-market product, is intensively distributed in the sense that any intermediary, no matter what kind, is allowed to carry the brand. Seiko is more selective. Seiko, as an upper-medium-priced brand, is sold through jewelry stores and catalog showrooms and is less likely to be found in discount or drug stores. Patek Philippe, in order to promote an image of elegance and exclusivity, limits its U.S. outlets to 100 meticulously selected fine jewelry stores.[26] Exhibit 12–3 shows that Patek Philippe chooses a channel that enhances an image.

Channel width is relative. Both Seiko and Omega employ selective distribution, though Omega is much more selective. Omega's tighter policy of selective, limited distribution results in the brand's being available only in top jewelry, specialty, and department stores. Because of the relative nature of channel width, it is inappropriate to compare width at the retail level with wholesale width. Because there are many more retailers than wholesalers, the issue of channel width applies only to a particular distribution level rather than through distribution levels. The degree of selectivity depends on the relative, not the absolute, number of intermediaries at a particular distribution level. As a product is moved closer to end users, the distribution channel tends to become broader. At a point closer to the manufacturer, the channel is not as broad. For example, at the distributor level, Brother International is the exclusive U.S. distributor for Japan's Brother Industries.

Another decision that concerns the manufacturer is the **number of distribution channels** to be used. In some circumstances, the manufacturer may employ many channels to move its product to consumers. For example, it may use a long channel and a direct channel simultaneously. The use of dual distribution is common if the manufacturer has different brands intended for different kinds of consumers. Another reason for using multiple channels may involve the manufacturer's setting up its own direct sales force in a foreign market where the manufacturer cannot remove the original channel (e.g., agents) because of strategic or legal reasons. Although Seiko, Lassale, and Jean Lassale are all made by the same Japanese firm, dual channels are used for these brands. Seiko and Lassale are sold through distributors in the United States, whereas Jean Lassale is sold by the manufacturer directly to retailers (jewelers).

DETERMINANTS OF CHANNEL TYPES

There is no single across-the-board solution for all manufacturers' channel decisions. Yet there are certain guidelines that can assist a manufacturer in making a good decision. Factors that must be taken into account include legal regulations, product image, product characteristics, intermediary's loyalty and conflict, and local customs.

Legal Regulations

A country may have specific laws that rule out the use of particular channels or middlemen. France, for example, prohibits the use of door-to-door selling. Although

A PATEK PHILIPPE DOESN'T JUST TELL YOU THE TIME.

It seems to us that there are certain unique qualities that can be found among the men and women who, over the centuries, have chosen to wear Patek Philippe watches.

Intelligence, for one thing. A delight in logic, for another. An appreciation of beauty. And perhaps most important, as great a respect for *internal* integrity as for *external* appearance.

Of course, we have the advantage of knowing the names of many of the great historical and contemporary figures who have been clients of Patek Philippe.

But we believe that even if you were to judge the watch solely on its own merits, without reference to some of its notable owners, you would come to the same conclusions about their characters as we have.

Here are some of the things that might guide your opinions. For esthetics, as well as function, every working part, down to the tiniest screw or the finest wheel, is microscopically rounded off and polished by hand, to a tolerance of no more than one-hundredth of a millimeter–a virtually frictionless state.

Cutting and pivoting the wheels and pinions alone involve 100 different operations, each one done by hand. And the pinions are lapped and polished on both sides.

In the Patek Philippe mechanical watch as well as the Patek Philippe quartz watch, many internal parts are plated with gold, again for function *and* appearance.

Our *horlogers complets*, complete watchmakers, mount the tiniest parts of a Patek Philippe by hand during the eight to nine month span that it takes to create each individual watch.

And once it is totally assembled, it is taken apart for further refinements.

During manufacture, each movement undergoes a total of 600 or more hours of testing, including testing for its response to cold, heat, humidity, and for wear, in five different positions. Actually, almost half the time of our watchmakers is spent on examination and re-examination of parts and final polishing.

Our quartz watch has only one-third fewer mechanical parts than our mechanical watch, and takes eight months to complete. Almost as long as our mechanical watch.

And the tiny 2.5mm Patek Philippe quartz movement comes from our own electronics factory, where we have been honing our skills in this twentieth century science of electronic timekeeping since 1952.

Ultimately, there is as much difference between a Patek Philippe quartz watch and other quartz watches as there is between a Patek Philippe mechanical watch and other mechanical watches.

For 144 years, our single-minded dedication to perfection has been the context for our company's existence–ever since the French watchmaker, Adrien Philippe, joined forces with the exiled Polish nobleman, Count Antoine de Patek–to create the world's finest watches.

Now that you know a little about the details of our meticulous timepieces, what do you think the ownership of a Patek Philippe, mechanical or quartz, might tell you about yourself?

Something very reassuring, perhaps?

The Patek Philippe pictured is self-winding, mechanical, with date. For a new and comprehensive presentation of Patek Philippe timepieces, please send $5–or for a brochure of current styles write–to Patek Philippe, 10 Rockefeller Plaza, Suite 629-B, NY, NY 10020.

IT TELLS YOU SOMETHING ABOUT YOURSELF.

EXHIBIT 12–3 Patek Philippe's channel of distribution

Source: Reprinted with permission of Henri Stern Watch Agency, Inc.

private importers in Iraq may choose to deal through commission agents, the Iraqi legislation prohibits state enterprises from dealing with third-party intermediaries (including commission agents) in obtaining foreign supplies.[27]

The overseas distribution channel often has to be longer than desired. In Bahrain, foreigners cannot own trading or marketing agencies, and all imports must go through a Bahrain agent.[28] Likewise, in Indonesia, foreigners are not allowed to import, export, distribute, or market locally manufactured products in the domestic market; neither are foreigners allowed to act as agents for local and foreign manufacturers. Only Indonesian persons and Indonesian domestic companies can obtain export licenses.[29] In addition, some government enterprises do business only with Indonesian entities. As such, a foreign company will find it necessary to go through a local agent/distributor.

Channel width may be affected by the law as well. In general, exclusive representation may be viewed as a restraint of trade, especially if the product has a dominant market position. In Germany, the Federal Cartel Office may intervene with exclusive dealing and distribution requirements. In other cases, the laws do the opposite, restricting the expansion of the distribution width. California and Illinois prohibit automobile showrooms of the same brand from being less than ten miles apart.

Due to the EC's 1992 program, geographic barriers between national markets have blurred, making it possible for consumers outside national sales territories to gain greater access to products and services. Therefore, EC antitrust authorities have increased their scrutiny of exclusive sales agreements. The Treaty of Rome prohibits distribution arrangements that affect trade or restrict competition (i.e., grants of exclusivity and restrictions of trade).[30]

When regulations are changed, the channel of distribution may also be affected. Consider the case of credit cards in Japan. Credit cards make up a kind of business that requires wide distribution, in the sense that it must be convenient for a card holder to use the card where a large number of banks and merchants accept or honor the cards. In Japan, banks were once discouraged from dealing with credit card transactions because the banks were prohibited from offering installment plans and charging interest, and thus merchants lacked access to an efficient nationwide credit authorization system. To squeeze out loan sharks who charge exorbitant rates (e.g., 100 percent or more) with little documentation, the Japanese government passed new legislation giving incentive for card holders, banks, and merchants to use or accept credit cards. Visa even negotiated with Japan's postal service organization to become its channel member so that Visa could attract those who had savings accounts with the postal service.

In some situations, regulations can be a trade barrier in disguise since regulations may have an uneven impact on domestic and foreign competitors. Japan claims a policy of open management in order to increase the number of licensed retail outlets handling foreign cigarettes from 14,000 to 20,000, yet that total is small when one considers that Japan's retail outlets are actually more than ten times that number. In addition, Japan Tobacco and Salt Public Corp., a wholesale monopoly before its abolition, had a 20 percent distribution charge that artificially boosted prices for foreign brands.

Product Image

The product image desired by a manufacturer can dictate the manner in which the product is distributed. A product with a low-price image requires intensive distribution. On the other hand, it is not necessary nor even desirable for a prestigious product to have wide distribution. Clinique's products are sold in only sixty-six department stores in Japan. And Waterford Glass has always carefully nurtured its posh image by limiting its distribution to top-flight department and specialty stores. At one time, it did not take on any new retail accounts for a period of a year. Its effort to create an air of exclusivity has worked so well that Waterford Glass commands a quarter of the U.S. market, easily making it the best-selling fine crystal.

Although intensive distribution may increase sales in the short run, it is potentially harmful to the product's image in the long run. This is a problem faced by Aprica as it moves its strollers beyond department and specialty stores into mass-market outlets such as JCPenney and Sears. Tiffany & Co. lost many upper-class customers when it broadened its clientele base. Cartier, trying to restore its esteem, has pared its retail distribution network, which had proliferated unwisely, by 50 percent in the United States and 25 percent worldwide.

Product Characteristics

The type of product determines how that product should be distributed. For low-priced, high-turnover convenience products, the requirement is for an intensive distribution network. The intensive distribution of ice cream is an example. Foremost's success in Thailand can be attributed in part to its intensive distribution and channel adaptation. Foremost tailored its distribution activities to the local Thai scene by sending its products (ice cream, milk, and other dairy products) into the market in every conceivable manner. Such traditional channels as wholesalers and such new channels as company-owned retail outlets (modern soda fountains) and pushcarts are also used. Pushcarts are supplied by the company and manned by independent retailers (i.e., sidewalk salesmen) who keep a 20 percent margin. However, traditional channels employing wholesalers, small stores, restaurants, hotels, and schools still account for a majority of sales.

For high–unit value, low-turnover specialty goods, a manufacturer can shorten and narrow its distribution channel. Consumers are likely to do some comparison shopping and will more or less actively seek information about all brands under consideration. In such cases, limited product exposure is not an impediment to market success.

One should always remember that products are dynamic, and the specialty goods of today may be nothing more than the shopping or even convenience goods of tomorrow. Consider computers, which were once an expensive specialty product that required a direct and exclusive channel. Since the early 1980s, computers have become more of a shopping good, necessitating a longer and more intensive channel. This change in the nature of the product serves to explain why such American computer makers as Nixdorf, ICL, and Philips were anything but successful when they persisted in using a direct sales force as their primary channel of distribution abroad. As an indication of how dramatically the distribution of computers has changed, Hyundai's personal computer for Blue Chip (a U.S. distributor) is sold like a TV set in such upscaled discount stores as Target and Caldor instead of through computer specialty stores.

Middlemen's Loyalty and Conflict

One ingredient for an effective channel is satisfied channel members. As the channel widens and as the number of channels increases, more direct competition among channel members is inevitable. Some members will perceive large competing members and self-service members as being unfair. Some members will blame the manufacturer for being motivated by greed when setting up a more intensive network. In effect, intensive distribution reduces channel members' cooperation and their loyalty as well as increases channel conflict. Michelin has been accused of undercutting its own dealers in the U.S. market by not only expanding its dealer network by 50 percent but also adding a direct channel to take national accounts away from dealers. Both actions increased price competition and reduced dealers' loyalty. Apple's problems in Japan owed in part to its addition of new channels even though it already had a big distributor.

One reason why Ricoh was able to become number one in unit market share in the United States was because of its commitment to the long term and to a strong dealer network.[31] Ricoh took three years to study and formulate its marketing plan. Based on the study, it found that manufacturers' deficiencies as identified by dealers were poor communication, insufficient quality control, erratic parts supply, too much competition, inconsistency in technical and sales training, and dealers' large inventory forced by manufacturer financing. Consequently, Ricoh granted exclusive territories for partnership and loyalty reasons. Moreover, it also allowed dealers to sell to major lucrative accounts rather than to reserve those accounts for Ricoh itself.

Business performance depends on the relationship between a manufacturer and his distributor. As confirmed in a study done by Rosson and Ford, the most successful manufacturer-distributor dyads are those in which both parties are nonstandardized in the sense that they are willing to adapt their roles and routines and that they have a commitment to developing business in the market in terms of contact and resource intensity. The successful dyads are generally more reciprocal in sharing decision making and exhibit lower levels of intercompany tension and conflict. Dyads facing high uncertainty "adhere more to established roles and routines, exhibit less joint decision making, and suffer from more frequent conflict. Each of these results is at variance with those for high performance relationships."[32]

Local Customs

Local business practices, whether outmoded or not, can interfere with efficiency and productivity and may force a manufacturer to employ a channel of distribution that is longer and wider than desired. Because of Japan's multitiered distribution system, which relies on numerous layers of middlemen, companies often find it necessary to form a joint venture with a Japanese firm, such as Pillsbury with Snow Brand, Xerox with Fuji, and Kentucky Fried Chicken with Mitsubishi. Japan's many-layered distribution system is not entirely unique in that part of the world, since the custom in many Far Eastern countries is to have multiple intermediary markups on imported goods. Yet the rule of thumb in Hong Kong is that there should be no more than two layers between a U.S. exporter of finished goods and Hong Kong consumers, usually consisting of an importer, agent retailer, or distributor.[33]

Domestic customs can explain why a particular channel is in existence. Yet customs may change or may be overcome, especially if consumer tastes change. For example, there are some 82,000 British pubs, 50,000 of which are owned by brewing companies; the problem they face is the trend toward beer consumption at home. The pubs have had to adjust by emulating trendy American bars, selling more wine and such food as hamburgers.

Power and Coercion

The "least-dependent-person" hypothesis, mentioned earlier in Chapter 11, states that the one party with resources and alternatives can demand more because it needs the other party less. As such, the least dependent member of the channel has more power and may be able to force other channel members to accept its plan. This hypothesis explains why it has been difficult for Japanese and Korean semiconductor manufacturers to recruit U.S. distributors to reach customers who are too small to buy directly from computer chip manufacturers. The major U.S. semiconductor manufacturers have long adopted a tacit policy of not allowing their distributors to sell Japanese competitors' products. Avnet Inc., the largest distributor in the United States, had to stop buying chips from Japan's NEC Corp. Samsung Semiconductor was initially happy when Arrow Electronics Inc., the nation's second-largest distributor of semiconductors, agreed to sell its products. Arrow abruptly terminated the agreement a few weeks later, citing changing business conditions. What happened was that Intel Corp. and Texas Instruments reduced the amount of business conducted with Arrow. It is thus not surprising that only one of the electronics industry's top ten distributors distributes Japanese or Korean chips.[34]

Contrary to a prediction made by reciprocal action theory, dealers in a developing country do not retaliate against the manufacturer's use of coercive influence strategies. Apparently, dealers in sellers' markets are so highly dependent on manufacturers that they have fewer equity concerns and higher tolerance than dealers in other channel contexts. In the industrial product channel, the model holds up very well in the empirical analysis.[35]

One must be careful in applying Western models overseas because their impact may differ in LDCs. The applicability of those models may vary from country to country as well. A survey of Japanese distributors of U.S. products examined how perceptions of influence affect control and conflict in the relationship. The findings indicated that aggressive influence evoked resistance and conflict but that more subtle influence strategies appeared to reduce conflict. Therefore, influence, as practiced in Western channels, may not be effective in relationships with Japanese firms.[36]

Control

If it has a choice, a manufacturer that wants to have better control over its product distribution may want to both shorten and narrow its distribution channel. In England, 75 percent of the beer is sold in pubs, most of which are owned by the big brewers who naturally push their own brands. To gain market entry, Anheuser-Busch licensed Budweiser to Grand Metropolitan PLC, a local giant. Unfortunately, Grand Met treated Budweiser as a follow-on in an effort to broaden its portfolio, which included the popular Foster's brand from Australia. Grand Met promoted Budweiser as a slightly exotic import for a niche market (the light-drinking yuppie set). Although

Grand Met owned 6,000 pubs, it was only able to place Budweiser in 3,000 of England's 82,000 pubs. Realizing that Grand Met's access to the market was quite limited, Anheuser-Busch took back full marketing control. After spending $20 million in advertising and promotional expenditures, Budweiser has managed to capture about 5 percent of the take-home lager sales in the south of the country.[37]

One study employed a model based on transaction cost analysis to explain exporters' vertical control selections. Exporters of specialized products should establish channel structures that require a greater commitment of resources. Such structures, however, require larger fixed costs. Conversely, in the case of a relatively competitive market with large numbers of buyers and sellers, an exporter may want to give up some control and switch to a looser structure by contracting in the marketplace for the provision of marketing functions.[38]

In conclusion, there are a number of factors that affect channel decisions. Some of these factors are interrelated. Empirically, it has been shown that overseas distribution channel choice is affected by culture and other product constraints.[39] In general, entering firms have a tendency to do the following:

Reinforce channel choices by adding new products to their current channel.

Erect a protective, restrictive governance structure around the distribution of complex, sophisticated products that require an investment in learning.

Integrate the distribution of products whose differentiation protects them from price competition.

Distribute substitutable products through independent intermediaries, which bear the brunt of the price competition common to such products.

Use intermediaries when introducing products to non-Western markets.

DISTRIBUTION IN JAPAN

One good way to understand how a foreign distribution system might differ from that of the United States is to examine Japan's complex distribution system. Japan's many-layered distribution system appears to be counterproductive. In modern societies where production is revered, Japan's distribution system seems ancient and inefficient. Employing 8.6 million people, the system consists of multiple layers of overstaffed intermediaries—overstaffed in part because of nepotism. The distribution network has more wholesalers and retailers per capita than any of the advanced industrial nations.

At the wholesale level, Japanese wholesalers perform the warehousing and financing functions in great detail. Because retailers are small and inadequately financed, the retailers shift warehousing and financing responsibilities to their suppliers by placing frequent but small orders. Wholesalers are expected to extend lengthy credit and accept the risk of selling on consignment. Wholesalers are also expected to stock an extensive assortment of goods and to provide rapid delivery. Supplier reliability and wholesaler ability to deliver with a short lead time outweigh any concern about price advantage.

Another distinctive feature of the Japanese wholesaling business is the close and frequent interaction among wholesalers. It is common business practice for wholesalers there to resell products to other wholesalers. Japanese wholesalers sell their goods to other wholesalers twice as frequently as do their U.S. counterparts. The figures show that they sell 38 percent of their goods to other wholesalers, 28 percent to industrial users, and only 22 percent to retailers. It should not be surprising then that geographically small Japan has 340,000 wholesalers, about the same as in the United States (i.e., some 370,000).[40] More startling is that Japan has thirty times the number of food wholesalers as there are in the United States. Most Japanese wholesalers are small and have less than nine employees. Only 5.6 percent of Japanese wholesalers have thirty or more employees.

The practice of retailing in Japan is no less cumbersome. With only one-third of the U.S. GNP and one-twenty-fifth of the U.S. land area, Japan's 1.6 million retail outlets exceed those in the United States by 6,000 stores. There is one retailer for every 69 persons and one wholesaler for every 323 persons—double the U.S. figure. The wholesale-to-retail ratio of Japan's sales is 5 to 1—a marked difference from the 1.3 to 1 ratio in the United States.[41]

Legal barriers pose a problem for distribution efficiency. The "large store" law, for example, prevents large department stores from modernizing the distribution system, and it is these large retailers who are most likely to carry imported goods. Foreign automakers have to contend with the high cost of opening dealerships in Japan. Japanese regulations prohibit local automobile dealers from sharing facilities with importers even though these dealers may sell products that have nothing to do with automobiles. In the United States, Japanese exporters have no difficulty in lining up American dealers to share their outlets.

In spite of the complex distribution system in Japan, many foreign firms have done well there by carefully selecting and adapting their distribution channels.[42] Schick controls 80 percent of the stainless steel razor blade market by relying on a powerful partner for consistent distribution, whereas Gillette's clout with retailers was dissipated because it used more than 150 distributors instead. Yet the distribution method does not always require large-scale adaptation. By ignoring the critics, Tupperware found that its party formula worked well in Japan, where social interactions are highly active. Disney, likewise, was successful despite its refusal to sell sake, a practice common in Japanese recreation parks.

The Japanese distribution system exists to serve social as much as economic purposes, and the social or societal goal sometimes overshadows economic logic. Channel members are not altogether different from family members, with all levels and members being tightly interlocked by tradition and emotion. It is a traumatic and sometimes tragic decision if channel members have to be dropped, and such members may be unable to bear the social consequence of losing face. Because of these social implications, small and/or inefficient channel members are retained and tolerated in order to maintain employment and income flows.[43]

The familial relationship of firms makes doing business easier, and it is customary for members of the same family unit to prefer sourcing from one another to sourcing on the outside. This tightly knit vendor-customer family relationship is perceived by some foreign firms as a trade barrier, but more likely these foreign manufacturers have failed to understand the system. As explained by Zimmerman, it is not as much a case of the Japanese versus foreign suppliers but rather a case of an insider against an outsider.[44] Any newcomer, Japanese or foreign, will have a difficult time penetrating the family unit's close organizational ties. The key to succeeding within this network is to work long and hard to become part of the family.

Compared to corporate groups in Germany, Spain, France, and Korea, the well-diversified industrial groups of Japan called *keiretsu* are similar but larger. There are six major *keiretsu* in Japan: Mitsui, Mitsubishi, Sumitomo, Fuyo, Sanwa, and Dai-Ichi. The *keiretsu* system has three major characteristics: (1) cross-ownership of equity (which allows the costs of a negative industry-specific shock to be shared by all other member firms from other industries), (2) close ties to the group's "main bank" (which provides the majority of the firm's debt financing), and (3) product market ties with the other firms in the group (which limit competition by discriminating against outside buyers/sellers.)[45]

In spite of the apparent rigidity which exists in Japan, it must be pointed out that Japan, as a "hot" country, is ripe for changes. Therefore, foreign manufacturers may want to experiment with alternative distribution channels in Japan. Like most American companies in Japan, Campbell Japan Inc. left the marketing of its Pepperidge Farm cookies to local distributors. Unfortunately, Campbell's distributors did a poor marketing job, and its Japanese importer was criticized for stocking stale cookies. Campbell then took exclusive control over the importing and storage of its products. Bypassing traditional Japanese importers and distributors, Campbell shortened its distribution channel by importing and delivering directly to one of 7-Eleven's wholesale suppliers.[46]

SELECTION OF CHANNEL MEMBERS

Because the success of a product depends so much on the efforts of channel members, a manufacturer must carefully screen all potential members. Most Hong Kong trading companies handle such a wide range of products that they may have inadequate time to devote to any additional product. To make matters worse, some agents in Hong Kong are known to take on a new product line for the sole purpose of denying it to other agents, knowing full well that they are not capable of being of much assistance to the new client.[47] Exhibit 12–4 lists the ten most common export mistakes, several of which have to do with distribution.

It is unwise to assume that a common Asian business mentality exists across Asian countries. A study of product retailers in Japan and Thailand found that, although seller's reputation, trust in the seller, and seller's reliability were important in both countries, these personal attributes were more important to the Japanese in buyer/seller relationships.[48]

Because it is difficult for a manufacturer to learn about distant potential dealers short of a personal and lengthy visit, there is a need to depend on other sources of information. Countries with export promotion programs usually have local offices

1. Failure to obtain qualified export counseling and develop a master international marketing plan before starting an export business.
2. Insufficient commitment by top management to overcome the initial difficulties and financial requirements of exporting.
3. Insufficient care in selecting overseas distributors.
4. Pursuit of orders from around the world instead of establishing a basis for profitable operations and orderly growth.
5. Neglect of export business when the U.S. market booms.
6. Failure to treat international distributors on an equal basis with domestic counterparts.
7. Unwillingness to modify products to meet regulations or cultural preferences of other countries.
8. Failure to print services, sales, and warranty messages in locally understood languages.
9. Failure to consider use of an export management company (EMC).
10. Failure to consider licensing or join-venture agreements.

EXHIBIT 12–4   The ten most common mistakes of potential exporters

Source: A Basic Guide to Exporting (Washington, D.C.: International Trade Administration, U.S. Department of Commerce, 1981): 84–85

in their major foreign markets that can provide information on how exporters may contact importers in such markets. Exhibit 12–5 illustrates how Hong Kong tried to attract U.S. importers.

One good source of information in the United States is the International Trade Administration, which has available trade lists by industry and country. For example, this agency has a list of Nigerian firms that are of questionable reliability. Furthermore, other information services of the Department of Commerce include the Export Trading Company Contact Facilitation Service, World Traders Data Reports (WTDRs), and Agent/Distributor Service (ADS).

The *Export Trading Company Contact Facilitation Service* is a computerized matching service that helps ETCs and other export support organizations (e.g., banks) find clients, and helps clients find them. Participants register in a central data base for matching by product interest. The information secured on the matched firms is provided to both parties. The cost in 1988 was $50 plus $5 per name for retrieval, but there was no registration fee.

World Traders Data Reports are background reports or descriptive trade profiles on individual foreign firms, containing information about each firm's business activities, its operating methods, its standing in the local business community, its creditworthiness, and its overall reliability and suitability as a trade contact. The information includes name, address, key contact, type of business, number of employees, year established, sales territory, products handled, general trade and financial reputation, and an assessment of the firm's suitability. These reports are designed to help American firms locate and evaluate potential foreign customers before making a business commitment.

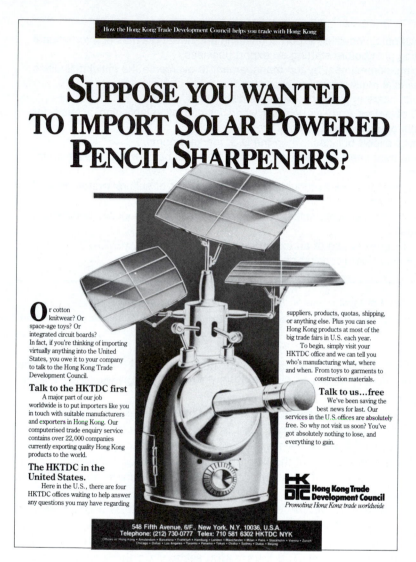

EXHIBIT 12–5   A trade inquiry service

Source: Reprinted with permission of Hong Kong Trade Development Council

The *Agent/Distributor Service (ADS)* is designed for firms seeking to identify potential foreign agents or distributors interested in a business relationship. It is a customized overseas search for interested and qualified foreign representatives on behalf of a U.S. client. Exhibit 12–6 reproduces an application form. U.S. commercial officers abroad conduct the search and prepare a report identifying up to six foreign prospects that have personally examined the U.S. firm's product literature and have expressed an interest in representing it. In 1988, the ADS charge was $90 per market or specific area.

Form Approved: OMB No. 41-R2710

FORM ITA-424P
(FORMERLY DIB-424P)
(REV. 4-80)

U.S. DEPARTMENT OF COMMERCE
INTERNATIONAL TRADE ADMINISTRATION

AGENT/DISTRIBUTOR SERVICE APPLICATION

"No request for the Agent/Distributor Service may be processed unless a completed application form has been received. (15 U.S.C. 171-197; 15 U.S.C. 1525-1527)"

GUIDELINE: For each territory for which an ADS search is to be made, submit four (4) copies of this form to the District Office nearest you.

Requestors Name/Title and Firm Name/Address:

George K. Jones
Export Manager
Compuscales, Inc.
1281 Poplar Road
Southmoore, Michigan 48870

District Office Address:

445 Federal Building
231 West Lafayette
Detroit, Michigan 48226

Signature:	TELEPHONE			Telex Number: 2-53471	Date Submitted:
	Area Code	Number	Extension	Cable Address: CSCALE, Michigan	7-15-80
	313	223-2112	3341		

SECTION A

1. **Your Firm's Activity**

   (a) [X] Manufacturer or Export Dept.　　(b) [ ] EMC/Manufacturer's Representative Distributor-Wholesaler　　(c) [ ] Other – (Describe) _____

2. **Export Sales:**

   (a) [ ] Product New to Export　　(b) [X] Product New to Market

3. **Number of Employees:**

   (a) [X] Less than 100　　(b) [ ] 100 – 500　　(c) [ ] Over 500

4. If you are presently represented for this product/service in this market, please list the representative's name and address.

   Name: Wells International Ltd.

   Address: P. O. Box 21, Lye, Stourbridge

   (a) Does this firm handle your product/service on an exclusive basis?　　[ ] Yes　[X] No

   (a) Has the firm been notified of your desire to obtain new representation?　　[X] Yes　[ ] No

   (An ADS cannot be undertaken without assurance that your present representative has been informed.)

5. If you have corresponded with any firm in this market regarding this proposal, please list their name and address and their reaction.

   Name of Firm: John Davies, Ltd.

   Address: 128 Crofton Square London

   Reaction: Has indicated preliminary interest. Continuing to negotiate.

SECTION B

1. **Type of Business Connection Desired:**

   (a) [X] Agent　　(b) [ ] Distributor

   Market: (City or Country) United Kingdom

3. **Product/service to be exported:** Electronic scales for weighing railroad cars and automotive vehicles, etc. Scales can be made available for metric standards. Readouts are displayed in lighted liquid crystal diodes, in various sizes, up to 10 cm. The smaller scales in our line are applicable to supermarkets, etc. use. (See details in brochure)

4. List special technical or other qualifications appropriate agents/distributors should have.
   Agencies handling electronic testing instruments, with servicing capabilities, and selling preferably to both private industry and to the government, are likely candidates.

5. Additional Comments:
   Agency should have servicing capability within the electronic field but does not need to have skills in servicing scales. We are willing to train the firm's personnel, bringing them to the U.S.A., if need be.

EXHIBIT 12–6 Agent/distributor service application

Source: The Agent/Distributor Service (Washington, D.C.: U.S. Department of Commerce, 1980), p. 5.

REPRESENTATION AGREEMENT AND TERMINATION

American firms often assume that, in the absence of provisions to the contrary, clauses appointing foreign distributors or agents are nonexclusive. Actually, the opposite is often the case. Indonesia prohibits a supplier from appointing more than one distributor or representative in the same territory. Columbia presumes that a sales agent's appointment is exclusive unless the agreement specifically states that the appointment is a nonexclusive one.

It may not be easy to terminate a representation agreement. In 1987, Mars/M&M made the following announcement in a Thai newspaper: "Effem Foods Co., an affiliate of Mars Incorporated Worldwide, has appointed East Asiatic (Thailand) Ltd. as its sole agent in Thailand." However, International Products (Thailand) Ltd. claimed that it had built the market and created outlets and that it was not concerned that the new sales agent was appointed. It insisted that it had substantial inventory and was still Mars's sales agent.

Based on the assumption that an agent or distributor often invests considerable effort and money to develop the local market for the principal, many countries have enacted **agency termination laws** to protect the interests of agents and distributors. Such laws have a tendency to penalize unilaterally foreign principals that have terminated the agency relationships. These laws often forbid a manufacturer from terminating its relationship with even incompetent channel members without a lengthy notice in advance or without an expensive settlement. For example, without just cause, Bolivia may not allow a principal's product to enter the country. In Abu Dhabi, an agent with a compensation claim pending can legally prevent the importation of the former principal's products.

Despite some variations, contract termination laws of various countries have several common characteristics.[49] First, these laws are constructed in such a way that they provide the agent with considerable leverage. The principal can terminate or refuse to extend an agency agreement without being penalized economically only upon a showing of just cause. For example, the reasons and situations under which the agreement may be validly terminated in Chile are (1) expiration of the contract term, (2) agent's resignation, (3) death, (4) bankruptcy or insolvency of either party, (5) legal incompetence of either party, (6) marriage of a woman agent, and (7) termination of the functions of the principal, if the agency was based on the exercise of such functions.

Second, the principal is obliged to compensate the agent when the relationship is terminated without just cause. If a fixed-term contract has run more than one year, Mexico sets the compensation at the value of six months' remuneration plus twenty day's remuneration for every year of service after the first year. In Austria, the damage payment may amount to between one year's and fifteen years' average commissions. Puerto Rico's required compensation in the event of unjust termination can be excessive, for it includes (1) actual value of expenses incurred by the agent in setting up and running the business, (2) value of the agent's inventories and stock, (3) loss of the agent's profits, and (4) value of the agent's goodwill. The agent may also claim an amount equal to the agent's profit experience for the previous five years or five times the average annual profit.

Third, the compensation and other rights granted to the agent may in some countries not be waived. Sweden, for instance, does not allow the agent to waive the termination notice requirements.

Fourth, the agency contract may not allow the parties to elect another country's law to govern the contract. Bolivia voids choice-of-law clauses since Bolivian law is the sole applicable law.

Fifth, the agent may be considered as an employee of the principal and is thus entitled to the protection of local labor laws concerning dismissal and compensation. The compensation may take the form of a pension.

Sixth, the principal may be required to give notice prior to termination, and the agent may have the right to contest the termination decision. Sweden stipulates that the notice term be three months when an indefinite-term agreement has been in effect for at least one year. In Switzerland, the law requires a two-month minimum period for termination notice after the first year, and the termination can be effective only at the end of each calendar quarter.

To minimize risk and problems, the principal should carefully structure the representation agreement. In general, certain contract terms must be included. The following advice should be followed. "The agreement will identify the parties and state the business of both the principal and the representative. It will state the residence or place of incorporation or formation of the parties. It will generally contain a time period during which the agreement will be operative and after which it will be deemed to have expired. In addition, there are a variety of contract terms which can be included to serve both parties' interests."[50]

MNCs should avoid **"evergreen contracts,"** which allow agreements to remain in effect or to be automatically renewed until terminated by one of the parties.[51] Such a contract may substantially increase the potential compensation obligations of the exporter under foreign laws on termination of distributors and sales representatives. Exporters should therefore have specific expiration dates in their foreign distributorship and sales representative agreements. Many countries regard the third or fourth renewal of even one- or two-year agreements as evidence of an evergreen contract. When renewing agreements, it is thus a good practice for the exporter to change the language of prior texts sufficiently in order to avoid creating the appearance of an evergreen contract. Another useful method of reducing or avoiding compensation payments is to include "just cause" termination provisions. The agreement should have the legally permissible grounds (just causes) for terminating distributors and sales representatives in the foreign country in question.

Finally, in making a contract, a firm should keep these points in mind:[52]

The agency agreement should be in writing.

The agreement should set forth the benefits to both parties.

A clear definition and meaning must be given to all contract terms, and there should always be an English version that is expressly allowed to prevail.

The rights and obligations of the parties should always be expressly stated.

If local laws allow, the contract should specify the jurisdiction to handle any legal disputes, thereby avoiding exposure in such conflicts to unfamiliar laws (e.g., "any dispute shall be litigated in the Courts of the State of Illinois or U.S. District Court for the District of Illinois").

Arbitration clauses should contain an identification of the arbitration body or forum.

The impact of foreign laws on the contract should be carefully considered to avoid including invalid clauses.

CONCLUSION

A product, no matter how desirable, must be made accessible to buyers. A manufacturer may attempt to use a direct distribution channel by selling directly to end users abroad. The feasibility of this channel depends on the type of product involved. Generally, the sales opportunity created by direct selling is quite limited. Intermediaries are usually needed to move the product efficiently from the manufacturer to the foreign user.

This chapter has discussed the roles of domestic and overseas middlemen. The manufacturer has the option of selling or assigning sales responsibility to intermediaries in its own country and letting them decide about reselling the product elsewhere. Another option for the manufacturer involves bypassing intermediaries and dealing directly with foreign buyers, assuming that the manufacturer has enough expertise, market familiarity, resources, and commitment. With the myriad of intermediaries available, it is impossible to prescribe a single distribution method ideal for all products and markets.

A number of factors—such as product type, regulations, customs, and intermediary loyalty—must be taken into account in designing and developing an international channel of distribution. These factors determine how long, how wide, and how many channels are appropriate. Ordinarily, those intermediaries that fail to add some value to the product as it moves through them are likely to be bypassed or dropped from the channel. But the manufacturer cannot afford to dictate terms, because an intermediary will carry a manufacturer's product only if the manufacturer minimizes channel conflict as well as provides some value to these sales intermediaries in return.

QUESTIONS

1. Distinguish between direct and indirect selling channels. What are the advantages and disadvantages of these channels?
2. Explain these types of direct-channel intermediaries: foreign distributor and state-controlled trading company.
3. Explain these types of indirect-channel agents: EMC, cooperative exporter, Webb-Pomerene association, and purchasing agent.
4. Explain these types of indirect-channel merchants: export merchant, export drop shipper, export distributor, and trading company.
5. Explain hot, moderate, and cold countries as classified by the country temperature gradient. What are the channel implications of this classification system?
6. What are the factors that affect the length, width, and number of marketing channels?

7. Explain these services of the U.S. Department of Commerce: Export Trading Company Contact Facilitation Service, World Traders Data Reports, and Agent/Distributor Service.

8. Why is it difficult—financially and legally—to terminate a relationship with overseas middlemen? What should be done to prevent or minimize such difficulties?

DISCUSSION ASSIGNMENTS AND MINICASES

1. Do you think that the U.S. ETCs can compete effectively with Japanese trading companies?
2. How should Japan be classified: hot, moderate, or cold? Do you think this classification may change in the future?
3. Should the distribution channels of Volkswagen and Porsche be the same?
4. Honda created a separate dealer network for its Acura brand. Is there a need for this expensive strategy?
5. Sony Corp. of America, in an effort to include retailing in its operations, runs its own licensed stores in Japan and Europe. In the United States, Sony has opened Sony Gallery of Consumer Electronics in Chicago. Inside the store, "boom boxes" and camcorders are displayed on pedestals as if they were art objects, and the Walkman is displayed on trendy mannequins. The gallery includes a life-size mock-up of an apartment with a built-in Sony home theater system. Some retailers are concerned that Sony might turn out to be both their supplier and competitor. How should Sony deal with this concern?

CASE 12–1
DARFILM/POLAROID

CEMAL A. EKIN
Providence College

Background

Darfilm, a medium-size company by Turkish standards, was founded by two partners in 1946. Specializing in film distribution, the company carved itself a niche in the 16-mm popular-movie market. Over the years, Darfilm expanded its operation to include 16-mm movie projectors and later added 35-mm movie theater equipment and all related supplies.

Because of the popularity of movies, the company prospered and sister companies emerged. Over the years, some of these companies became major corporations specializing in fields such as telecommunications. Later, a holding company was formed gathering all the companies under one umbrella.

In the meantime, Darfilm added various products to its product line, primarily in the audiovisual market. Overhead projectors, slide projectors, arc carbon for movie projectors, and similar products contributed significantly to sales. In 1960, Darfilm entered the photographic market by importing film, paper, and cameras.

By 1973, Darfilm had a product mix that was somewhat vulnerable to shifts in the movie market. The 16-mm movie market was shrinking, and some movie houses were switching to projectors that were not compatible with Darfilm's equipment, as well as newer equipment that did not use arc carbon at all. Trying to maintain a balanced portfolio, Darfilm commissioned a marketing research study of the photographic market. The research results were favorable, and Darfilm decided to enter the market with a stronger presence than it previously had. The existing lines of photographic equipment, film, and paper were expanded, new items were added, and more emphasis was placed on this side of the business.

Import restrictions were in place at the time, and some of the major brands were already being distributed by competitors. As a result, Darfilm was forced to import most of its goods from Eastern European countries, such as Poland, Czechoslovakia, and the former East Germany. The import regime imposed quotas on importers, and import procedures were rather involved. But Darfilm maintained a steady level of sales that were satisfactory to the company.

Distribution

Beginning in its early days, Darfilm developed a corporate distribution channel with approximately thirty branches located in major cities around the country. The branches serviced both Darfilm and such other sister companies as TurkTelefon, which was in the telecommunications market. Some of these branches later became independent companies in their own right, and currently there are only two branches outside of Istanbul—one in Ankara and the other in Izmir (the two next-largest cities after Istanbul).

Since 1980, Darfilm has relied on more traditional distribution channels, with which it has relatively good relations. In a speech given at the Polaroid Distributor Conference in Portugal in September, 1987, Ergun Melin (general manager) stated that the traditional channel consists of "fifty or so distributors and wholesalers, most of them located in a very busy part of the city [of Istanbul]. In addition, there are nearly two hundred wholesalers or major dealers outside Istanbul all over the country. We estimate that the number of photo studios exceeds ten thousand, located in proportion to density of population all over the country."

Promotion

Until 1978, there were no television broadcasts in Turkey, and newspapers served as the primary advertising medium. Even though some movie houses showed commercials, Darfilm did not make use of this medium. Darfilm's promotional campaigns were sporadic and primarily in the nature of announcements. When television commercials became available, these were viewed as expensive and unnecessary.

Turkish newspapers are primarily structured as a national medium with minor local content. They are printed at a few strategically located cities and distributed to the rest of the country overnight via private carriers. *Hurriyet* has the largest newspaper circulation, followed by the *Milliyet, Gunaydin, Tercuman*, and *Cumhuriyet*, as well as several minor papers. The editorial content of these papers varies from popular and eye-catching news in *Hurriyet* to the very serious and intellectual content of *Cumhuriyet*.

Pricing

Primary pricing policy at Darfilm is markup pricing with trade discounts. It is also customary in the photographic distribution channel to provide terms of sale that may extend to ninety days or more. Drafts and postdated checks are a widely accepted form of payment.

Polaroid

Polaroid, a major multinational corporation headquartered in Massachusetts, U.S.A., has been operating overseas for many years. In Europe, there are many Polaroid subsidiaries, including locations in Germany, Switzerland, Italy, the United Kingdom, and France. In some countries, such as Spain, Polaroid has chosen to use importers owned and operated by domestic companies.

Polaroid, widely known for its consumer photography cameras and films, also has many commercial products in its portfolio that contribute to its sales more than its amateur line of products. Its rich product mix includes Polaroid sunglasses, identification photography, technical and industrial photography, and many other product lines. According to Polaroid's 1986 annual report, the technical and industrial photography division "supplies instant imaging solutions for diverse needs of the workplace. Today, Polaroid markets more than 40 film types and more than 100 imaging systems designed to provide individuals in business, in commercial and professional photography, in medicine and science, in engineering, manufacturing, and quality control, and in teaching and the arts the ability to record, document, analyze, inspect, or present their work."

Until 1985, Polaroid equipment and film were imported to Turkey by a small company that did not have a significant market presence, and whose efforts did not go beyond importing small quantities of consumer photography products and distributing them to a very limited market. Polaroid decided to terminate its business relationship with that distributor and notified the Turkish company of its intention. Thus, Polaroid no longer had any presence in the Turkish market.

Darfilm was looking to expand its product line with suitable products. About this time, Polaroid approached Darfilm and offered it the exclusive right to become the official importer for Polaroid. The import-export regime had become much more liberalized, with red tape substantially reduced. General economic conditions in the country were in an upswing and offered an opportunity for Polaroid to enter the market in a significant way.

As noted by Ergun Melin, "Members of Darfilm and Polaroid were well aware of the huge potential that existed, especially in the document photography line. This is why we mutually agreed to give priority to this line from the very start." The use of document photographs in Turkey is much wider than in many other countries because of extensive bureaucratic procedures.

In July 1985, Darfilm started the Polaroid business with a team of four personnel, and by the end of the year the sales had reached the planned level with approximately ninety photographic studios. These studios had purchased Miniportrait cameras, which are used for ID photographs (similar to the passport photographs used in the United States, but slightly smaller in size). The price of a Miniportrait camera was 150,000 TL (Turkish lira). The appropriate film sold for 7,000 TL for a pack of eight films. The studios using Miniportrait cameras were charging 1,500 to 2,500 TL. Each Polaroid photograph contained four pictures on a single sheet. The traditional photographs carried a price tag of 800 TL for six black-and-white pictures and typically required from several hours to a couple of days for delivery.

Encouraged by this positive trend, objectives for 1986 were set to increase the number of existing Miniportrait studios to 350, to reach a sales volume of five times that of the previous year, and to participate in a government driver's license replacement project. By the end of 1986, Darfilm had tripled its personnel involved with Polaroid. Sales volume had reached one more time the planned volume for 1986, and there were five times as many Miniportrait studios across the country.

In December 1986, the Turkish government decided to undertake a project that would convert the driver's license from a booklet form to a credit card form. This meant the renewal of 4 million licenses and the issuance of 250,000 new licenses each year. Seizing the opportunity, Darfilm bid in this nationwide replacement program, along with a company from another country, to provide the driver's license replacements.

Polaroid already had extensive experience in producing driver's licenses, because its system had been, and still is, used extensively in the United States and other countries. The process involves photographing the person and the completed application form through one of the special Polaroid cameras, which essentially produces an instant Polaroid photograph. This is then laminated with plastic, producing the license.

The procedure proposed by the competitor company used a more elaborate system consisting of several layers of plastic. The necessary information is typed directly on two of the layers, one for the front and one for the back. An ID photograph is inserted into a cutout in one of the layers, and the whole package is heat bonded. In the opinion of the officials, this process produced a more rigid and more durable card than the Polaroid system, and the competitor was awarded the contract to supply the system.

Polaroid and Darfilm, however, did not leave this situation empty-handed. The process still required an ID photograph, and the government did purchase 150 Miniportrait cameras from Darfilm to be used at the license renewal stations. This consequently resulted in a steady stream of sales for the appropriate Polaroid film. Individuals who renew licenses can have pictures taken free of charge at one of these stations, provided they are willing to wait in line. They may also bring their own photographs, provided that the photograph is suitable for heat bonding and has a certain thickness.

Questions

1. Assess the situation from the viewpoints of Darfilm and Polaroid.
2. Should Darfilm and Polaroid have tried harder to get the driver's license contract?
3. What role, if any, should Polaroid play in the marketing of its products in Turkey?
4. What marketing strategy would you develop for Polaroid?
5. What marketing strategy would you recommend for Darfilm?

THE A.T. CROSS COMPANY

FRANCINE NEWTH
Providence College

The Legacy

As stated in the A.T. Cross Company 1986 annual report, "Everything begins with quality." Cross pens and pencils are known worldwide as standing for the ultimate expression of excellence. The story began in 1846 with the company's founder, Alonzo T. Cross. Mr. Cross, an immigrant, inventor, and craftsman, started his business in his Rhode Island home with a goal "to manufacture and market elegant, hand-tooled gold and silver filigree casings for wooden pencils." Today, the A.T. Cross Company is as devoted to design perfection and craftsmanship as Alonzo T. Cross was in 1846, which explains the enduring legacy of A.T. Cross. In fact, Cross offers a full perpetual warranty.

The Cross Profile

With ambition, vision, and a commitment to excellence, the A.T. Cross Company has grown into a major international manufacturer of fine writing instruments. The company has two plants, one in Lincoln, Rhode Island, and one in Ballinasloe, Ireland. Cross products are sold to the consumer gift market through selected stores (jewelry, department, stationery, gift, and bookstores). They are also sold to the business gift market through selected companies specializing in recognition programs.

The Industry

The fine writing instrument industry is truly an international industry with different market leaders in all parts of the world. The major international competitors are A.T. Cross, Schaeffer, Parker, Waterman, Pelikan, and MontBlanc.

Writing needs vary throughout the world. For example, fountain pens are very popular in Europe; in the Far East, most writing instruments must include fine-point cartridges. But packaging, advertising, and promotion truly constitute the major change elements in international markets rather than any change in the product per se.

Most international manufacturers of writing instruments have established either distribution networks of distributors or their own subsidiaries in charge of foreign distribution. Therefore, the distribution choices of a new entrant in a particular country are very limited.

International Expansion for A.T. Cross

In the early 1960s, the A.T. Cross Company began to receive several foreign inquiries concerning the availability of the Cross pens and pencils overseas. More specifically, businesses from Europe and the Far East were asking where, in their country, they could acquire Cross pens. These inquiries and demands for the fine writing instruments led the A.T. Cross Company to pursue the overseas marketplace.

A.T. Cross was particularly interested in distributing its products in Spain, France, the United Kingdom, and Germany. However, there were some strong existing competitors with well-established distributors in these countries. Furthermore, many distributors had exclusive arrangements with existing manufacturers.

Ideal foreign distributors should be small enough to want to take on a new manufacturer but large enough to advertise. Most European countries manufacture their own national brand of writing instruments. The following manufacturers of fine writing instruments had substantial market share in these countries: Inoxchrome (Spain), Waterman (national brand in France), Parker (national brand in the United Kingdom), and MontBlanc/Pelikan/Lamy (Germany).

There were also some other imported writing instruments within each one of these countries. As a result, the overseas marketplace was highly competitive. Regardless, A.T. Cross decided to enter these markets. At first, it could not find suitable distributors, so it began considering other distribution channels.

Questions

1. What should the company's distribution strategy be, faced as it is with strong existing competitors already represented by well-established distributors?
2. What would be the risks associated with the firm's setting up company-owned distribution subsidiaries?

NOTES

1. Anthony C. Koh, "An Evaluation of International Marketing Research Planning in United States Export Firms," *Journal of Global Marketing* 4 (no. 3, 1991): 7–25.

2. Bruce Seifert and John Ford, "Export Distribution Channels," *Columbia Journal of World Business* 24 (Summer 1989): 15–22.

3. Robert McElwaine, "Sales and Servicing of the Imports Provide $20 Billion Industry for U.S.," *Chicago Tribune.* 8 March 1983.

4. Jim Emerson, "Packages from the U.S. Will No Longer Be Held at the Canadian Border, Postal Officials Announce," *DM News,* 1 May 1986, 4.

5. "Arthur C. Bell: A Campaign to Break the Ice in the U.S. Scotch Marketing," *Business Week,* 6 December 1982, 82 ff.

6. International Trade Administration, *The Export Management Company: Your Export Department* (Washington, D.C.: U.S. Department of Commerce, 1981).

7. John J. Brasch, "Using Export Specialists to Develop Overseas Sales," *Harvard Business Review* 59 (May-June 1981): 6–8.

8. Brasch, "Export Specialists."

9. John J. Brasch, "Export Management Companies," *Journal of International Business Studies* 7 (Spring/Summer 1978): 59–71.

10. Daniel C. Bello and Nicholas C. Williamson, "Contractual Arrangement and Marketing Practices in the Indirect Export Channel," *Journal of International Business Studies* 14 (Summer 1985): 65–82.

11. Vincent Travaglini, "Webb-Pomerene Act: Overlooked by Exporter," in *Foreign Business Practices,* International Trade Administration (Washington, D.C.: U.S. Department of Commerce, 1981): 113–18.

12. Ralph H. Chew, "Export Trading Companies: Current Legislation, Regulation and Commercial Bank Involvement," *Columbia Journal of World Business* 16 (Winter 1981): 42–47.

13. Ravi Sarathy, "Japanese Trading Companies: Can They Be Copied?" *Journal of International Business Studies* 14 (Summer 1985): 101–19.

14. Chew, "Export Trading Companies."

15. For questions frequently asked about ETCs, see *Export Trading Companies, A Competitive Edge for U.S. Exports,* International Trade Administration (Washington, D.C.: U.S. Department of Commerce, 1985).

16. Michael R. Czinkota, "The Business Response to the Export Trading Company Act of 1982," *Columbia Journal of World Business* 19 (Fall 1984): 105–11.

17. Don Stow, "Export Trading Companies: An Update," *Business America,* 20 January 1986.

18. Daniel C. Bello and Nicholas C. Williamson, "The American Export Trading Company: Designing a New International Marketing Institution," *Journal of Marketing* 49 (Fall 1985): 60–69.

19. Isaiah A. Litvak and Peter M. Banting, "A Conceptual Framework for International Business Arrangements," in *Marketing and the New Science of Planning,* ed. Robert L. King (Chicago: American Marketing Association, 1968), 460-67.

20. James D. Goodnow and James E. Hanz, "Environmental Determinants of Overseas Market Entry Strategies," *Journal of International Business Studies* 1 (Spring 1972): 33–50.

21. Ovidio M. Giberga, "Laws Restrain Agency Agreement Terminations," in *Foreign Business Practices,* International Trade Administration (Washington, D.C.: U.S. Department of Commerce, 1981), 1–24.

22. Ron Wolf, "Bringing U.S. a Touch of Europe," *San Jose Mercury News,* 26 February 1990.

23. Bert Rosenbloom and Trina L. Larsen, "International Channels of Distribution and the Role of Comparative Marketing Analysis," *Journal of Global Marketing* 4 (no. 4, 1991): 39–54.

24. Robert Grosse and Walter Zinn, "Standardization in International Marketing: The Latin American Case," *Journal of Global Marketing* 4 (no. 1, 1990): 53–78.

25. "Seven-Eleven Woos Japanese Consumers by Staying a Step Ahead," *The Nation,* 26 July 1991.

26. Mike Schwartz, "Suppliers Tell Their Story," *Jewelers' Circular-Keystone* (September 1983): 63 ff.

27. Market Expansion Division, International Trade Administration, *Foreign Regulations Affecting U.S. Textile/Apparel Exports* (Washington, D.C.: U.S. Department of Commerce, 1986), 113.

28. *Bahrain* (New York: Ernst & Whinney International Series, 1983), 1.

29. *Investment in Indonesia.* (Kantor Akuntan Sudjendro and Peat Marwick, 1985).

30. Don Linville, "Marketing in Europe in 1992," *Business America,* 15 January 1990, 14–15.

31. "Copier Firm Seeks Top Spot by Developing Dealer Network," *Marketing News,* 1 October 1982, 1.

32. Philip J. Rosson and I. David Ford, "Manufacturer-Overseas Distributor Relations and Export Performance," *Journal of International Business Studies* 13 (Fall 1982): 57–72.

33. *International Trade Reporter: Export Shipping Manual,* publication no. 1413 (Washington, D.C.: The Bureau of International Affairs, February 2, 1982), 80:13.

34. Andrew Pollack, "Chip Makers Squeeze Asian-Line Distributors," *San Jose Mercury News,* 12 September 1988.

35. Gary L. Frazier, James D. Gill, and Sudhir H. Kale, "Dealer Dependence Levels and Reciprocal Actions in a Channel of Distribution in a Developing Country," *Journal of Marketing* 53 (January 1989): 50–69.

36. Jean L. Johnson, Tomoaki Sakano, and Naoto Onzo, "Behavioral Relations in Across-Culture Distribution Systems: Influence, Control and Conflict in U.S.-Japanese Marketing Channels," *Journal of International Business Studies* 21 (no. 4, 1990): 639–55.

37. "So Far, This Bud Isn't for the Brits," *Business Week,* 2 May 1988, 119.

38. Saul Klein, "A Transaction Cost Explanation of Vertical Control in International Markets," *Journal of the Academy of Marketing Science* 17 (Summer 1989): 253–60.

39. Erin Anderson and Anne T. Coughlan, "International Market Entry and Expansion via Independent or Integrated Channels of Distribution," *Journal of Marketing* 51 (January 1987): 71–82.

40. "The Distribution Knot Strangling Consumers," *Business Week,* 18 September 1978, 44, 49.

41. Mitsuaki Shimagushi and Larry J. Rosenberg, "Demystifying Japanese Distribution," *Columbia Journal of World Business* 14 (Spring 1979): 32–41.

42. Robert C. Christopher, *Second to None: American Companies in Japan* (New York: Crown, 1986).

43. Michael R. Czinkota, "Distribution in Japan: Problems and Changes," *Columbia Journal of World Business* 20 (Fall 1985): 65–71.

44. Mark D. Zimmerman, *How to Do Business with the Japanese* (New York: Random House, 1985).

45. Hesna Genay, "Japan's Corporate Groups," *Economic Perspectives* 15 (January/February 1991): 20–30.

46. "Campbell's Taste of the Japanese Market is Mm-Mm Good," *Business Week,* 28 March 1988, 42.

47. *International Trade Reporter.*

48. Raymond A. Jussaume, Jr. and Patriya Tansuhaj, "Asian Variations in the Importance of Personal Attributes for Wholesaler Selection: Japanese and Thai Marketing Channels," *Journal of International Consumer Marketing* 3 (no. 3, 1991): 127–140.

49. Ovidio M. Giberga, "Foreign Laws Governing Agency Agreements," in *The International Connection: A Guide to More Profitable Exporting* (AT&T, 1984): 16–21; Giberga, "Agreement Terminations."

50. Gil D. Messina, "Legal Aspects of Foreign Agency Agreements," in *The International Connection: A Guide to More Profitable Exporting* (AT&T, 1984): 25.

51. John T. Masterson, Jr., "Drafting International Distributorship and Sales Representative Agreements," *Business America,* 21 November 1988, 8–9.

52. Giberga, "Foreign Laws"; Giberga, "Agreement Terminations."

Imagine a world without lawyers, accountants, and insurance agents.

Murray L. Weidenbaum

Distribution Strategies
Physical Distribution and Documentation

13

CHAPTER OUTLINE

MODES OF TRANSPORTATION

CARGO OR TRANSPORTATION INSURANCE

PACKING

FREIGHT FORWARDER AND CUSTOMHOUSE BROKER

DOCUMENTATION

MARKETING ILLUSTRATION:
The Paper Chase

Any computer rated above 20 PDR (processing data rate) must be cleared by an interagency committee representing the U.S. State, Commerce, and Defense departments before it can be shipped out of the United States. The shipment must wait until an export license is issued, with the usual clearance time being three months. For some reason, the time required to process a license for a shipment to South Africa took considerably longer. Data General had to wait some sixteen months for an export license before being able to ship one machine to South Africa. In a further development, the Office of Export Administration issued a final ruling in late 1985 prohibiting the export of all computers, computer software, or technology to service computers in all apartheid-enforcing entities of the South African government. Validated export licenses are required for all exports to the South African military and police, though such exports can usually be made under general license to other parties in South Africa. These kinds of restrictions are maintained when the United States wants to further U.S. foreign policy or to fulfill its declared international obligation (e.g., to support the United Nations Security Council Resolutions).

The United States has an extensive set of regulations dealing with high-tech products. For such products, not only are export licenses needed, but these products are also prohibited from being reexported to a third country. In 1985, a U.S. judge fined L. M. Ericsson $3.1 million for transferring a restricted air-traffic-control computer system to the Soviet Union. ASEA, an electrical giant of Sweden that pioneered high-voltage transmission and robotics, was found to have violated U.S. export controls regarding computers that could have military applications. The computer in question, originally destined for a steel-mill project, was diverted to the Soviet Union via neutral Sweden. A similar incident involved shipping a computer to Czechoslovakia after its reexport application had been turned down by the United States.

When Technics Inc. applied for an export license to sell a piece of semiconductor equipment to Poland, months of review by the Commerce and Defense Departments followed. To obtain government approval, Technics's chief executive told the Commerce Department that his supposedly high-tech equipment was "no more technical than a frying pan with a lid." In addition, the basic manufacturing information, readily available in books, had been published more than twenty years earlier. To prove his point, he bought a $30 pressure cooker from a local department store and revamped it to cook a chemical coating on chips. The resulting machine worked almost as well as his much more expensive piece of equipment.

Source: Valerie Rice, "Recipe for East Bloc Trade," *San Jose Mercury News,* 2 May 1990.

Distribution is a necessary as well as a costly activity. According to one executive at Procter & Gamble, the average time required to move a typical product from "farm to shelf" is four to five months. Although it takes only about seventeen minutes to actually produce a product, the rest of the time is spent in logistical activities—storage, handling, transporting, packing, and so on.[1]

In the developed economies, the distribution sector typically accounts for one-third of the gross domestic product (GDP).[2] Furthermore, international logistics costs can account for 25 to 35 percent of the sales value of a product, a significant difference from the 8 to 10 percent for domestic shipment.[3]

Examples are endless that could demonstrate some of the difficulty in physically moving products overseas. U.S. firms can become easily frustrated by the physical distribution problems overseas. Port congestions coupled with the lack of efficient materials handling equipment can cause long delays. Even inland movements can be a problem, because some road networks cannot accommodate long containers and rail gauges vary across countries. China, for example, intentionally uses different rail gauges for security reasons (i.e., to prevent quick troop movement in the case of a foreign invasion). Not only must a company make arrangements for transportation, but it must also pay attention to how the product is packed for shipping. The process requires a great deal of paperwork throughout.

This chapter examines the various issues related to the process of moving a product from one country to another, beginning by comparing and contrasting the major transportation modes. The discussion then focuses on insurance and packing for export. Next, the chapter examines two kinds of intermediaries that, in the area of physical distribution, are virtually indispensable—freight forwarders and custom house brokers. Finally, a significant portion of the chapter is devoted to a discussion of documentation, including both shipping and collection documents.

MODES OF TRANSPORTATION

The availability of transportation is one important factor affecting a company's site selection, as noted in Exhibit 13–1. To move a product both between countries and within a country, there are three fundamental modes of transportation: air, water (ocean and inland), and land (rail and truck). Ocean and air shipments are appropriate for transportation between countries, especially when the distance is considerable and the boundaries are not joined. Inland water, rail, and highway are more suitable for inland and domestic transportation. When countries are connected by land (e.g., North America), it is possible to use rail and highway to move merchandise from locations, such as from the United States to Canada. In Europe, rail (train) is an important mode because of the contiguity of land areas and the availability of a modern and efficient train system.

The appropriate transportation mode depends on (1) market location, (2) speed, and (3) cost. A firm must first consider market location. Contiguous markets can be served by rail or truck, and such is the case when goods are shipped from the United States to Canada or Mexico. To move goods between continents, ocean or air transportation is needed.

Speed is another consideration. When speed is essential, air transport is without question the preferred mode of distribution. Air transport is also necessary when the need is urgent or when delivery must be quickly completed as promised. For perishable items, a direct flight is preferable because a shorter period in transport reduces both spoilage and theft.

Finally, cost must be considered as well. Cost is directly related to speed— a quick delivery costs more. But there is a trade-off between the two in terms of other

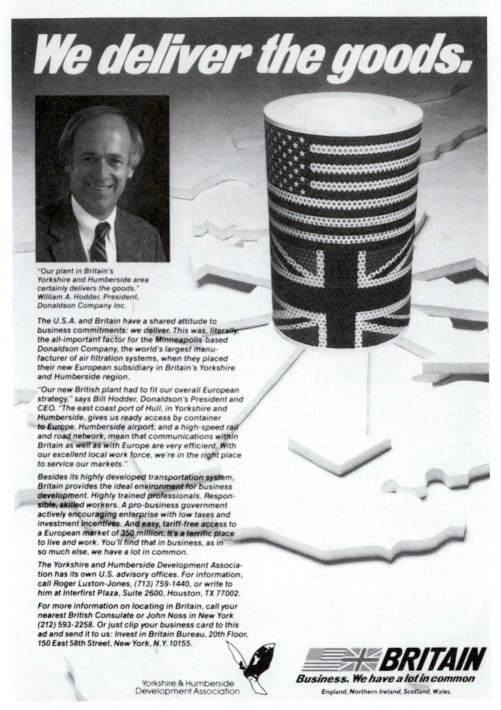

EXHIBIT 13–1 Transportation and site selection

Source: Reprinted with permission of Yorkshire and Humberside Development Association

kinds of savings. Packing costs for air freight are less than for ocean freight because for air freight the merchandise does not have to be in transit for a long period of time and the hazards are relatively lower. For similar reasons, the air mode reduces the inventory in float (i.e., in the movement process). Thus, there is less investment cost because the overall inventory is minimized and inventory is turned over faster.

A firm must understand that there is no one ideal transportation mode. Each mode has its own special kinds of hazards.[4] Hazards related to the ocean/water mode include wave impact, navigation exposures, water damage, and the various vessel motions (rolling, pitching, heaving, surging, swaying, and yawing). Hazards related to the air mode include ground handling and changes in atmospheric pressure and temperature. Hazards related to the rail and highway modes include acceleration/deceleration (braking), coupling impact, swaying on curves, and shock and vibration.

Of all the various transportation modes, air accounts for only 1 percent of total international freight movement. Yet it is the fastest-growing mode and is becoming less confined to expensive products. Air transport has the highest absolute rate, but exporters have discovered that there are many advantages associated with this mode. First, air transport speeds up delivery, minimizes the time the goods are in transit, and achieves great flexibility in delivery schedules. Second, it delivers perishables in prime condition. Harris Ranch uses a 747 jumbo jet to fly live cattle from the United States to Japan. A premium price commanded by high-quality beef in Japan makes it possible to use air freight.[5]

Third, it can respond rapidly to unpredictable and urgent demand. For instance, quick replacement of broken machinery, equipment, or a component part can be made by air. Fourth, it reduces to a minimum damage, packing, and insurance costs. Finally, it can help control costly inventory and other hidden costs, including warehousing, time in transit, inventory carrying cost, inventory losses, and the paperwork necessary to file claims for lost or damaged goods. These costs will increase as the time in transit increases. Furthermore, opportunity costs (e.g., lost sales and customer dissatisfaction) also adversely affect profit, especially in the long term. All of these costs can be minimized with air transport.

Traditionally, the appropriateness of air freight was determined solely by a **value-to-weight equation,** which dictated that air cargo should be confined to high-value products. One reason for that determination was that transport cost is a small proportion to such products' value. Another reason was that the amount of capital tied up for these products while in transit is high and should be released as soon as possible.

Recently, shippers have begun to shift the attention to the **freight rates— density effect,** which determines true costs rather than absolute costs of each transportation mode.[6] Air freight rates are usually quoted per unit of weight, and sea freight rates are usually quoted per unit of weight and volume (whichever yields more revenue for the steamship). For example, assume that the freight rates are $350/ton by air and $60/ton and/or cubic ft by sea. At first, it would appear that surface (sea) transportation is a great deal cheaper. But for a product that is 1 ton and 7 cubic ft, the cost of sea freight ($420) is actually higher than that of air freight ($350). Therefore, sea freight is very cheap when goods are very dense (i.e., low volume per unit of weight). But as density declines (i.e., the increase in bulk in relation to constant weight), the charge for sea freight rises rapidly. Consequently, air freight is quite competitive for such low-density goods as ladies' shoes, men's shoes, computers, color TV sets, refrigerators, and towels.

The dominant form of the international transportation of merchandise has always been ocean transport. Its main advantage is its low rate, though the savings achieved for many products are not necessarily greater than other transport modes on an overall basis. This helps explain why, when all the hidden costs related to ocean transportation are considered, air transportation is growing at a very rapid rate.

Quotations for ocean shipping can be obtained from a shipping company or a freight forwarder. Steamship rates are commonly quoted on weight and measurement. Goods are both weighed and measured, and the ship will use the method that yields a higher freight charge. Less-than-container shipments carry a higher rate than full-container shipments.

There are three basic types of shipping company: (1) conference lines, (2) independent lines, and (3) tramp vessels. An ocean freight **conference line** is an association of ocean carriers that have joined together to establish common rules with regard to freight rates and shipping conditions. Consequently, the operators in the group charge identical rates. The steamship conference has also adopted a dual rate system, giving a preferential treatment to contract exporters. A contract exporter agrees to ship all or a large portion of its cargo on a regular basis on vessels of conference member lines—in exchange for a lower rate than charged for a noncontract shipper. Nevertheless, the contract exporter is allowed to use another vessel, after obtaining the conference's permission, when no conference service is available within a reasonable period of time.

An **independent line,** as the name implies, is a line that operates and quotes freight rates individually and independently without the use of a dual-rate contract. Independent lines accept bookings from all shippers. When they compete with conference lines for noncontract shippers, they may lower their rates. In general, independent lines do not offer any special advantage for a contract shipper because they do not have significant price advantage. Furthermore, their services are more limited and not as readily available.

Finally, a **tramp vessel** is a ship not operating on a regular route or schedule. That is, tramp steamers do not have the established schedules of the other two types of carriers. Tramp vessels operate on a charter basis whenever and wherever they can get cargo. They operate mainly in carrying bulk cargoes.

In some circumstances, a shipper may not have an option on the vessel to be used. Because of certain laws enacted to protect a country's interests, mandatory use of a particular vessel is not uncommon. Brazil's shipping restrictions require goods imported for use by public or public-supported enterprises to be transported aboard vessels with a Brazilian flag.[7] All exported Japanese automobiles must be shipped on Japanese-owned ships, and the same restriction applies to all tobacco leaf imported to Japan. The United States has the Federal Cargo Preference Act, which supports and favors U.S. shipowners and maritime workers over foreign-flag vessels.

In general, the rates charged by U.S. conference lines are higher than the rates charged by lines of other nations. Foreign operators are able to charge lower rates because of the subsidies and support received from their governments. Soviet ships at one time were able to quote rates as much as two-thirds lower than U.S. conference lines' published prices. Subsequently, conference lines (e.g., Seatrain) decided to give illegal rebates to major customers in order to win back cargo shipments lost to the Soviets.

Recognizing both that nations have shipping interests and that subsidies cause problems, the UNCTAD proposed the UNCTAD Code of Liner Conduct. As a comprehensive regulatory and administrative framework to govern liner shipping, this code mandates a cargo-sharing scheme by reserving shipping to the national flag carriers of each trading partner. According to the UNCTAD code, each trading partner is allowed to reserve 40 percent of the total liner cargo for its national flag lines and to allocate 20 percent of the liner cargoes to third flag operators.[8]

CARGO OR TRANSPORTATION INSURANCE

Inland carriers generally bear the responsibility for any damage to goods while in their possession. The same thing cannot be said for ocean carriers. Their reluctance to accept responsibility is due to the numerous unavoidable perils found at sea. Such perils include severe weather, seawater, stranding, fire, collision, and sinking. As a result, ocean carriers refuse to accept any liability for loss or damage unless a shipper can prove that they were purposefully negligent—a difficult task indeed. To protect against loss or damage and to avoid disputes with overseas buyers, exporters should obtain marine insurance.

Marine cargo insurance is an insurance that covers loss or damage at sea, though in practice it also applies to shipments by mail, air, and ship (see Exhibit 13–2). It is similar to domestic cargo insurance but provides much broader coverage. The purpose of this insurance is to insure export shipments against loss or damage in transit. The insurance may be arranged by either a buyer or seller, depending on the terms of sale.

Types of Marine Insurance

There are two basic forms of marine insurance: (1) special (one-time) coverage and (2) open (blanket) coverage. A **special policy** is a one-time policy that insures a single specific shipment. One-time insurance is relatively expensive because the risk cannot be spread over a number of shipments. Nevertheless, it is a practical insurance solution if a seller's export business is infrequent.

An **open policy** is an insurance contract issued to a firm in order to cover all its shipments as described in the policy within named geographic regions. The policy is open in the sense that it is continuous by automatically providing coverage on all cargo moving at the seller's risk. The policy is also open in the sense that the values of the individual shipments cannot be known in advance. Under this policy, no reports of individual shipments are required, although the insured must declare all shipments to the underwriter. The underwriter agrees to insure all shipments at the agreed rates within the terms and conditions of the policy. Open marine cargo policies are written only for a specified time period. A single premium is charged for

EXHIBIT 13–2 Insurance

Source: Courtesy of CIGNA Companies

this time period, based on the insured's estimated total value of goods to be shipped under the policy during the term of the contract. The contract has no predetermined termination date, though it may be cancelled by either party.

Types of Risk

To protect cargo, an insurance policy must specify the kinds of protection desired. In providing coverage, the policy distinguishes between particular average and general average. Average, derived from the French word *avarie,* means loss or damage.

General average is a sacrifice made intentionally for the common good to diminish an impending peril. Any loss in a sea adventure is shared by all parties (i.e., all cargo owners and carriers). General average is thus a contribution by all parties to cover a loss sustained by one of the parties through a voluntary sacrifice made to save the ship and lives of those on board for the general benefit of all parties. To have a general average, the following considerations must exist: (1) a peril that threatens the whole adventure; (2) a sacrifice, either physical or in the form of unusual expenses incurred; and (3) a measure of success, for if nothing is saved there is nothing to contribute.

A merchant's protection with respect to general average assessments is largely dependent on the extent to which the merchant has insured the property. If the insured value equals or exceeds the CIF value (the contributory value), the underwriter will pay the general-average assessment in full. Otherwise, the merchant will be paid a pro-rata value in the amount borne by the insured as a proportion of the total assessed value. Such payments are not normally affected by any clauses dealing with a particular average.

Particular average is a partial loss of an accidental nature resulting from a peril against which there is insurance. Unlike general average, the loss is only experienced by the particular insured that is affected. In this case, only a shipper's insurer is liable, subject to the terms and conditions of the policy. For example, if the specified condition is F.P.A. (free of particular average), a partial loss is not covered, unless the loss is caused by the stranding, sinking, burning, or collision of the ship. In the case of W.A. (with average), a shipment is protected from partial damage as long as the damage exceeds 3 percent (or some specified percentage) of the total cargo value.

The coverage provided is determined by the perils to be insured against. The various types of coverage are as follows:

1. *Free of damage insurance.* This type of coverage is very limited, because it only covers total, not partial, loss of goods (i.e., actual or absolute total loss).
2. *Fire and sea perils.* Perils of the sea are the general words used in the Perils Clause to include losses caused by unusual forces of nature while operating in and about navigable waters. Examples of sea perils include the opening of seams caused by heavy weather resulting in seawater entering and causing damage to cargo, tempestuous action of the waves causing a vessel to be battered by the force of the sea, stranding on reefs, rocks, and shoals, and contact with floating objects such as logs or icebergs. When the insured has fire and sea perils coverage, claims are paid only when the vessel is stranded, sunk, burned, or in collision, and only if the damage is caused by fire or sea perils.

3. *Fire and sea perils with average.* This coverage is similar to fire and sea perils, but it is not necessary to show that the vessel has been stranded, sunk, burned, and in collision.

4. *Named perils.* This coverage includes fire and sea perils with average plus a number of additional perils that are named (e.g., freshwater damage, hook damage, nondelivery, breakage, assailing thieves, and barratry).

5. *All risk insurance.* This is the most complete type of coverage but applies only to physical loss of cargo or damage from an external cause suffered in transit. It excludes war, strikes, riots, costs of delay, and loss due to the inherent nature of goods. To establish a claim, it is not necessary for the insured to prove what caused the loss. It is usually sufficient for the insured to prove that a physical loss occurred, that the goods were in proper condition and properly shipped, and that the loss was not caused by the inherent vice of the goods.[9]

All of the above policies provide for general average and include salvage charges. A firm can also insure profit through a Valuation Clause in the cargo policy, which insures exports and contains a fixed basis of valuation. The following is an example of a typical valuation clause in a marine policy: "valued at amount of invoice, plus 10 percent."

PACKING

Packaging may be viewed as consisting of two distinct types: (1) industrial (exterior) and (2) consumer (interior). Consumer packaging is designed for the purpose of affecting sales acceptance. The aim of industrial packaging is to prepare and protect merchandise for shipment and storage, and this type of packaging accounts for seven cents of each retail dollar as well as 30 percent of total packaging costs.[10] Packing is even more critical for overseas shipment than for domestic shipment because of the longer transit time and a greater number of hazards. Consumer packaging is covered extensively in Chapter 11; this section concentrates instead on industrial packaging.

Packing Problems

There are four common packing problems, some of which are in direct conflict with one another: (1) weight, (2) breakage, (3) moisture and temperature, and (4) pilferage and theft.[11]

Weight   Overpacking not only directly increases packing cost but also increases the weight and size of cargo. Any undue increase in weight or size only serves to raise freight charges. Moreover, import fees or customs duties may also rise when import duties are based on gross weight. Thus, overprotection of the cargo can cost more than it is worth.

Breakage   Although overpacking is undesirable, so is underpacking because the latter allows a product to be susceptible to breakage or damage. The breakage problem is present in every step of ocean transport. In addition to normal domestic handling, ocean cargo is loaded aboard a vessel by use of a sling (with several items together in a net), conveyor, chute, or other methods, all of which put added stress and strain on the package. Once the cargo is on the vessel, other cargo may be stacked on top of it, or packages may come in violent contact during the course of the voyage. To complicate matters, handling facilities at an overseas port may be unsophisticated. The cargo may be dropped, dragged, pushed, and rolled during unloading, moving in and out of customs, or in transit to the final destination. In China, primitive methods (i.e., carts, sampans, junks, and so on) are used to move a great deal of cargo. Therefore, packing must be prepared to accommodate rough manual handling.

To guard against breakage, it may be desirable to use such package-testing equipment as vibration, drop, compression, incline-impact, and revolving drum. The cargo must not exceed the rated capacity of the box or crate. Attempts should be made to make certain that internal blocking and bracing will distribute the cargo's weight evenly. Cushioning may be needed to absorb the impact. Cautionary markings, in words and symbols, are necessary to reduce mishandling because of misunder-standing.

One universal packing rule is "Pack for the toughest leg of the journey." To accommodate this rule, cargo should be unitized or palletized, whenever possible. **Palletizing** is the assembly of one or more packages on a pallet base and the securing of the load to the pallet. **Unitizing** is the assembly of one or more items into a compact load, secured together and provided with skids and cleats for ease of handling. These two packing methods force cargo handlers to use mechanical handling equipment to move cargo.

Moisture and Temperature   Certain products can easily be damaged by moisture and temperature. Such products are subject to condensation even in the hold of a ship equipped with air conditioning or dehumidifying equipment. Another problem is that the cargo may be unloaded in the rain. Many foreign ports do not have covered storage facilities, and the cargo may have to be left in the open subject to heat, rain, cold, or other adverse elements. In Morocco, bulk cargo and large items are stored in the open. Mozambique does the same with hazardous, bulk, and heavy items. Cargo thus needs extra strong packing, containerization, or unitization in order to have some measure of protection under these conditions.

One very effective means of eliminating moisture is **shrink wrapping,** which involves sealing merchandise in a plastic film. Water proofing can also be provided by using waterproof inner liners or moisture-absorbing agents and by coating finished metal parts with a preservative or rust inhibitor. Desiccants (moisture-absorbing materials), moisture-barrier or vapor-barrier paper, or plastic wraps, sheets, and shrouds will also protect cargo from water leakage or condensate damage. Cargo can be kept away from water on the ground if placed on skids, pallets, or dunnage while having drain holes for crates.

There are several steps to ensure the proper way of packing to minimize moisture and breakage problems.[12] These steps are

1. Place water barrier material on interior of sides and roof.
2. Use vertical sheathing.
3. Block, brace, and tie down heavy items.
4. Use new, clear, dry lumber and provide adequate diagonals.

5. Unitize multiple similar items.
6. Use waterproof tape to seal fiberboard boxes.
7. Palletize shipping bags.
8. Use proper gauge, type, and number of straps.

Pilferage and Theft   Cargo should be adequately protected against theft. Studies have fixed such losses in all transportation modes in a range from $1 billion to in excess of $5 billion.[13] In the United States alone, the annual value of cargo stolen in transit exceeds $2.5 billion. Annual loss through theft is well over 100 million pounds in Great Britain, with employees' criminal activity being the main contributing factor.[14] Pilferage levels are consistently high in Bangladesh and substantial in India. There are a few techniques that can be used as deterrents. One method of discouraging theft is to use shrink wrapping, seals, or strapping. Gummed sealing tapes with patterns, when used, will quickly reveal any sign of tampering. Also, only well-constructed packing in good condition should be used.

Another area of concern is **marking.** The main purpose of marking is to identify shipments so that the carrier can forward the shipment to the designated consignee. Markings thus should not be used to advertise the contents, especially when they are valuable or highly desirable in nature. A firm is also wise to avoid mentioning the contents, trade names, consignees' names, or shippers' names on the package because these markings reveal the nature of the contents. Because markings are still a necessity, they should be permanent, though so-called blind marks should be used. To avoid handlers' becoming familiar with the markings, blind marks should be changed periodically. Bright color coding helps in spotting the pieces.

Packing alone should not be expected to eliminate theft. Packing should be used in conjunction with other precautionary measures. One of the most effective means of reducing exposure to theft, pilferage, and hijacking is to insist on prompt pickup and delivery. Another good idea is to avoid shipping the cargo if it will arrive at its destination on a weekend or holiday. One Chicago importer of jewelry found on Monday when he went to pick up his merchandise at the O'Hare airport that the cargo had already been claimed by someone else over the weekend.

Container

An increasingly popular method of shipment is **containerization. A container** is a large box made of durable material such as steel, aluminum, plywood, and glass reinforced plastics, examples of which are shown in Exhibit 13–3. A container varies in size, material, and construction. Its dimensions are typically 8 ft high and 8 ft wide, with lengths usually varying in multiples of 10 ft up to a maximum of 40 ft. A container can accommodate most cargo but is most suitable to packages of standard size and shape. Some containers are no more than truck bodies that have been lifted off their wheels and placed on a vessel at the port of export. These containers then are transferred to another set of wheels at the port of import for inland movement. This type of container can be put on a ship, or can become a barcar when placed on a railway flatcar, or can be made into a trailer when provided with a chassis. Containers are ordinarily obtained from either carriers or private parties.

EXHIBIT 13–3   Containers

Containers can take care of most of the four main packing problems. Because of a container's construction, a product does not have to have heavy packing. The container by itself provides good protection for the product against breakage, moisture, and temperature. Because breaking into a container is difficult, this method of shipment discourages pilferage and theft as well.

It is important to select the right container because containers come in varying sizes and types. Two basic types of container can be identified: (1) *dry cargo containers* and (2) *special purpose containers.* Some of the various types of dry cargo containers are end loading, fully enclosed; side loading, fully enclosed; and open top, ventilated, insulated. Special purpose containers come in different types for refrigerated, liquid bulk, dry bulk, flat rack, auto, livestock, and sea shed.

Exporters may have to plan for the return of secondary packaging or the container or both. Argentina's inefficient exports force those who do business with Argentina to ship most containers back empty.[15] One U.S. automaker, after experimenting with containers, resumed shipping parts in wooden crates instead. Japanese firms have partially solved the Argentina problem by using collapsible racking and shipping systems so that items can be more densely packaged for return shipment.

Shipments by air do not usually require the heavy packing that ocean shipments require. Standard domestic packing should prove sufficient in most cases. When in doubt, however, a company should consult the carrier or a marine insurance company for the best packing strategy. For a case in which a firm is not equipped to do its own packing, there are professional firms that package for export.

FREIGHT FORWARDER AND CUSTOMHOUSE BROKER

There are two intermediaries whose services are quite essential in moving cargo for their principals, across countries as well as within countries: freight forwarders and customhouse brokers. Their differing roles in the distribution process are shown in Exhibit 13–4. A **freight forwarder** generally works for exporters, whereas the **customhouse broker** generally works for importers. Because the functions are similar, freight forwarders sometimes act as customs brokers and vice versa.

A freight forwarder is a person responsible for the forwarding of freight locally as well as internationally. He or she is an independent businessperson who handles shipments for compensation. The kind of freight forwarder of concern here is the foreign or international freight forwarder who moves goods destined for overseas destinations.

A foreign freight forwarder is an exporter's agent who performs virtually all aspects of physical distribution necessary to move cargo to overseas destinations in the most efficient and economic manner. This freight forwarder can represent shippers in both air and ocean freight shipments because the procedures and documents required are very similar. The Department of Commerce makes the recommendation

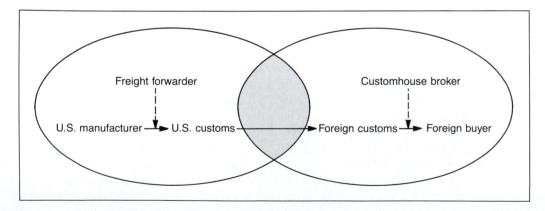

EXHIBIT 13–4   Intermediaries that facilitate physical distribution

that exporters use only those freight forwarders who are licensed by the Federal Maritime Administration.

The freight forwarder's major contribution to the exporter is his ability to provide traffic and documentation responsibilities for international freight movements. This middleman handles the voluminous paperwork required in international trade, and is highly specialized in (1) traffic operations (methods of shipping), (2) government export regulations, (3) overseas import regulations, and (4) documents connected with foreign trade and customs clearances. In brief, the freight forwarder arranges all necessary details for the proper shipping, insuring, and documenting of overseas shipments. An exporter's need for the freight forwarder's services varies according to the exporter's exporting effort or life cycle, as shown in Exhibit 13–5. As the exporter's business grows, the exporter tends to perform more of the forwarding function itself.[16]

The freight forwarder can assist an exporter from the very beginning in getting a shipment ready for overseas. Once the exporter receives an inquiry, it can turn to the freight forwarder for assistance in preparing its quotation. The freight forwarder can advise the exporter on freight costs, port charges, consular fees, cost of special documentation, insurance costs, and the forwarder's handling fees, as well as recommend the degree of packing needed or arrange to have the merchandise packed or have it containerized.

The freight forwarder also prepares ocean bills of lading and any special consular documents and reviews letters of credit, packing lists, and so on to ensure that all procedures are in order. After the shipment is made, the freight forwarder forwards all documents to the customer's paying bank with instructions to credit the exporter's account.

The freight forwarder can assist the exporter in other areas. This person can reserve space aboard an ocean vessel. He or she may consolidate small shipments into full container loads and, by doing so, can receive a lower rate from the carrier and pass on the savings to the shipper. The freight forwarder can arrange to clear goods through customs and to have the goods delivered to the pier in time for loading. This middleman then handles the goods from exit port to destination. If desired, the freight forwarder can further move goods inland in a foreign country through various affiliates.

The freight forwarder receives a fee from exporters. The service cost is a legitimate export cost and should be figured into the contract price charged to buyers. In addition, this person may receive brokerage fee and/or rebates from shipping companies for booked space. In such cases, the freight forwarder's commission is paid by the ship lines. Because freight forwarders control most of the smaller shipments and because the less-than-container (LTC) traffic accounts for 17–18 percent of the business, carriers woo freight forwarders with extra rebates.

The counterpart of the freight forwarder for an exporter is the customhouse broker for an importer. As an individual or firm licensed to enter and clear goods through customs, a customhouse broker is a person or firm employed by an importer to take over the responsibility of clearing the importer's shipments through customs on a fee basis. A licensed customhouse broker named in a Customs Power of Attorney can make entry. This broker is bonded, and the broker's bond provides the required

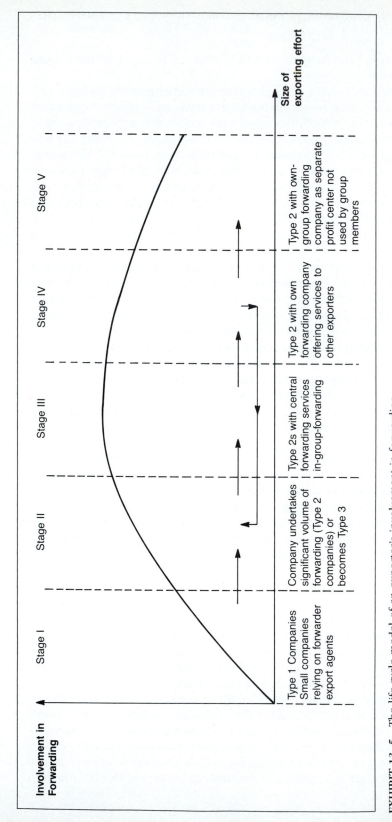

EXHIBIT 13–5 The life-cycle model of an exporter's involvement in forwarding

Source: G. J. Davies, "The Role of the Exporter and Freight Forwarder in the United Kingdom," *Journal of International Business Studies* 12 (Winter 1981): 106

coverage to carry on the responsibilities of the job. A customhouse broker may also act as a freight forwarder once the shipment is cleared. A customs broker must be licensed by the Treasury Department in order to perform these services.

The customhouse broker is indispensable in the receipt of goods from overseas. The services are valuable because the requirements for customs clearance are complicated. For example, U.S. Customs requires that entry documents must be filed within five days after the goods have reached the United States. To make entry, a person must have evidence of right to make entry (carrier's certificate), in addition to the commercial invoice, packing list, and surety. For infrequent entry, a single entry bond must be obtained from a U.S. surety company to cover potential duties and penalties incurred, but the surety may also be posted in the form of cash. Moreover, the person must fill out forms with regard to dutiable status and must also have the goods examined under conditions that safeguard the goods before they are released. Overall, entry is a two-step process—getting goods released and providing information for duty assessment and statistical purposes. The customhouse broker is in the best position to provide for these requirements.

DOCUMENTATION

It is not an exaggeration to say that "paper moves cargo." To move cargo, documentation is a necessity. American firms used to complain about the cost of documentation and shipping in the European Community. Documentation alone added 3 to 5 percent of the total cost of goods sold. Cabotage rules, for example, prevented a trucker from returning with a loaded truck after delivery.[17]

To facilitate cargo movement, nations have been working toward automated customs—paperless international customs procedures. The Customs Cooperation Council, representing more than 130 nations, has approved a plan by which customs administrations around the world can work toward electronic data interchange. The main standards body for international electronic messages is a United Nations-backed group called Edifact (Electronic Data Interchange for Administration, Commerce, and Transport). While Japanese companies do business with one another electronically, they use their own standards, which force outsiders wanting to establish computerized links to engage in expensive programming and translation efforts. Edifact, however, works everywhere. Japan has finally agreed to join with Singapore to create a regional Edifact board. By sending standardized digital messages at computer speeds, importers can bypass piles of bureaucratic paperwork. Use of paperless trading technology should significantly improve the speed and efficiency of data and global trade.

To fill out the required documents, a company must insert the proper identification number for its product. All products must be "shoehorned" into some kind of category. If a product is constructed out of several materials, it may be classified by the material that gives it its essential character. Prior to 1989, the Standard Industrial Classification (SIC) was the most common classification of products and services in the United States, and it was similar to the Standard Industrial Trade Classification (SITC) used by international organizations and a number of countries. On January 1,

1989, the Harmonized Tariff Schedule (HS) went into effect. The new system, designed to replace previous systems for classifying exports, contains logically structured nomenclature. There are twenty-one sections and ninety-nine chapters to arrange commodities according to general economic activity. The sections and chapters are arranged according to levels of processing, with primary commodities classified first, followed by the technically more complex products. The HS number consists of six digits, which are used by all participating countries. To meet each country's statistical and tariff requirements, the remaining digits are country-specific. Certain countries also use either alphabetical subdivisions after the six digits or combined alphanumerical systems. As an example, if the HS code for "widgets" is 12.34.56.78.90, the breakdowns are 12 (chapter), 12.34 (heading), 12.34.56 (subheading), 12.34.56.78 (tariff item), and 12.34.56.78.90 (HS Classification Number).[18]

There are many kinds of documents, and they can be grouped under two broad categories: (1) shipping documents and (2) collection documents. *Shipping documents* are prepared to move shipment through customs, allowing the cargo to be loaded, shipped, and unloaded. *Collection documents,* in contrast, are submitted to a customer or the customer's bank for payment.

Shipping Documents

There are several kinds of shipping documents. Such documents include export licenses and shipper's export declaration forms, among others.

Export License   An *export license* is a permit allowing merchandise to be exported. It is needed for all exports being shipped from the United States, except for shipments going to Canada and U.S. territories and possessions. International Harvester's sale to the Soviet Union of a $300 million industrial plant to make combines was thwarted when the company's license was revoked. This action was taken because of the United States' unhappiness with Soviet political involvement in Poland. Exhibit 13–6 shows a flowchart of the steps that make up the licensing procedure.

There are two kinds of export licenses: general and validated. A **general license** is a license for which no application is required and for which no document or written authorization is granted. It is a general authorization permitting the export of certain commodities and technical data without the necessity of applying for a license document. A general license allows the export through the Export Administration Regulations of all goods published in an authorization list and covers the export of nonstrategic goods (commodities not under restriction or control). Products that meet specific conditions can be shipped by merely inserting a correct General License symbol on the export control document known as a Shipper's Export Declaration. The various symbols and uses of general licenses are shown in Table 13–1.

If an exporter does not qualify for a general license, the exporter may apply for a validated export license which, in effect, is a formal authorization document. This license is secured by submitting a written license application (Form ITA-622P). The United States requires this kind of licensing for reasons of national security (strategic significance), short supply, or foreign policy.[19] National security controls were necessary to prevent the export of strategic commodities and technical data to the Soviet Union and other Warsaw Pact countries. Foreign policy controls, such

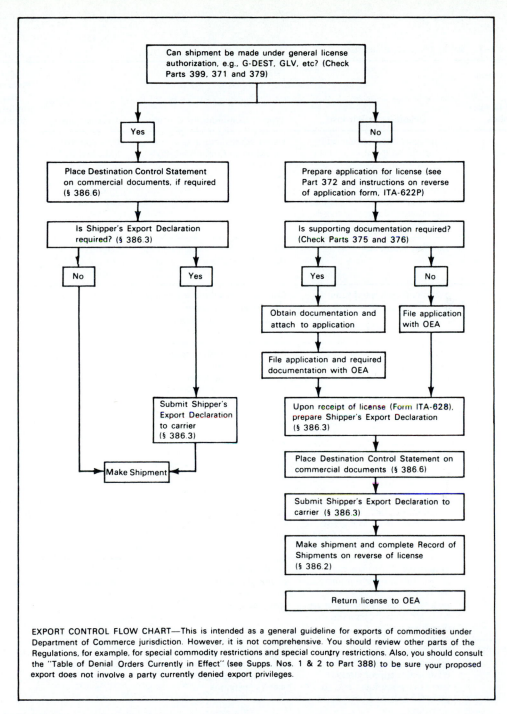

EXPORT CONTROL FLOW CHART—This is intended as a general guideline for exports of commodities under Department of Commerce jurisdiction. However, it is not comprehensive. You should review other parts of the Regulations, for example, for special commodity restrictions and special country restrictions. Also, you should consult the "Table of Denial Orders Currently in Effect" (see Supps. Nos. 1 & 2 to Part 388) to be sure your proposed export does not involve a party currently denied export privileges.

EXHIBIT 13–6 Export control flowchart

Source: Introduction to the Export Administration Regulations (Washington, D.C.: U.S. Department of Commerce, 1985), inside front cover.

TABLE 13–1 Table of general licenses

General License Symbol	Definition or Purpose	Type of Commodities Covered[a]	Destinations[b]	Specific Reference in Export Administration Regulations
G-Dest	Shipments of any commodity listed on the Commodity Control List to any destination for which a validated license is not required as indicated in the Commodity Control List column titled "Validated License Required."	Commodities indicated by information in Commodity Control List	Destinations indicated by information in Commodity Control List	§371.3
GIT	Intransit shipments	All commodities, except certain defined categories	Country Groups Q, T, V, and Cuba[c]	§371.4
GLV	Shipments of limited value	Commodities valued within the GLV dollar value limits specified in Commodity Control List	Country Groups Q, T, and V	§371.5
BAGGAGE	Shipments of personal and household effects, certain vehicles, and personally owned tools of trade	Commodities within defined general categories not identified by the code letter "A," "B," or "M" following the Export Control Commodity Number on Commodity Control List	All destinations	§371.6
		Commodities within defined general categories identified by the code letter "A," "B," or "M" following the Export Control Commodity Number on Commodity Control List	Country Groups T, and V[d]	§371.6
G-FTZ	Shipments of petroleum products refined from foreign origin crude oil in Foreign Trade Zones or Guam	Petroleum products listed in Supplement No. 2 to Part 377	All destinations	§371.7
SHIP STORES	Shipments of ship stores for use on outgoing and immediate return voyage of vessels; necessary equipment and spare parts for proper operation of departing vessel	Food, bunker fuel, and other commodities specified as ship stores and dunnage, with stated exceptions	All destinations[e]	§371.9
PLANE STORES	Shipments of plane stores for use on outgoing and immediate return trip of aircraft; necessary equipment and spare parts for proper operation of departing plane	Food, fuel, and other commodities specified as plane stores, and dunnage with stated exceptions	All destinations[c]	§371.10

TABLE 13–1 *(continued)*

General License Symbol	Definition or Purpose	Type of Commodities Covered[a]	Destinations[b]	Specific Reference in Export Administration Regulations
CREW	Shipments by members of crew of usual and reasonable kinds and quantities of personal and household effects under prescribed conditions	Clothes, adornments, medicine, toiletries, food, souvenirs, games, hand tools, and similar personal effects; furniture, household effects, and household furnishings; and their containers	All destinations	§371.11
RCS	Shipments to Canadian and U.S. vessels, planes, and airline installations or agents located abroad	Food, fuel, and other commodities needed for use by or on such carriers	Country Groups Q, S, T, V, W, and Cuba	§371.12
GUS	Shipments to members of U.S. Armed Services and civilian personnel of U.S. Government for personal use. Shipments to U.S. Government agencies for official use.	Commodities within defined categories	All destinations	§379.13
GTF-US	Shipments of commodities imported for display at exhibitions or trade fairs	Commodities imported for display at exhibitions or trade fairs, under stated conditions	Country Groups T and V[f]	§371.15
G-NNR	Shipments of certain non-naval reserve petroleum commodities	Commodities listed in Petroleum Commodity Group Q (see Supplement No. 2 to Part 377) with stated exceptions	All destinations except Country Groups S and Z	§371.16
GLR	Shipments of commodities returned to countries from which imported. Shipments of commodities returned to the country of manufacture or the country from which imported for servicing. Shipment for replacement of defective or unacceptable commodities.	Specified types of commodities	All destinations except country Groups S and Z, and Iran[g]	§371.17
GIFT	Shipments of gift parcels from individual donors to individuals or to religious, charitable, or educational organizations for use of donee or donee's immediate family.	Commodities not identified by the code letter "A," "B," or "M" following the Export Control Commodity Control List, up to a total of $200 in one parcel, ordinarily sent as gifts; such as food, clothing, medicines, toiletries, and drugs, with stated exceptions.	All destinations	§371.18

TABLE 13–1 *(continued)*

General License Symbol	Definition or Purpose	Type of Commodities Covered[a]	Destinations[b]	Specific Reference in Export Administration Regulations
GATS	Authorizes departure from United States of civil aircraft on temporary sojourn	Civil aircraft of foreign registry, under its own power	All destinations	§371.19(a)
		U.S. air carrier aircraft, under its own power	All destinations	§371.19(b)(1)
		Other civil aircraft of U.S. registry, under its own power	All destinations except S, W, Y, and Z	§371.19(b)(2)
GTDA	Shipments of generally available technical data	Technical data generally available to the public, scientific and educational data, and certain foreign origin data contained in an application for filing of a U.S. patent	All destinations	§379.3
GTDR	Shipments of restricted technical data	Technical data not exportable under General License *GTDA* but exportable subject to specified restrictions	Country Groups T and V[f]	§379.4
GTE	Temporary exports for use abroad and return to United States of certain commodities	Specified types of commodities	Varies	§371.22

[a] Except for exports made under the provisions of General License *GTDA* (see §379.3), no export related to nuclear weapons, nuclear explosive devices, or nuclear testing, as described in §378.1, regardless of type, and no export of any electronic, mechanical, or other devices primarily useful for surreptitious interception of wire or oral communications (see §376.13), may be made under the provisions of any general license.

[b] Country Groups are defined in Supplement No. 1 to Part 370.

[c] Exports or reexports from the United States under this general license are prohibited for commodities destined for the Republic of South Africa and Namibia and are permitted to Country Group S, W, or Y, only if the same exports may be made directly from the United States under a general license, and to Country Group Z (excluding Cuba) only if the same exports may be made directly from the United States to Country Group Y under a general license. Commodities identified by the code letter "A" following the export control commodity number on the Commodity Control List (Supplement No. 1 to §399.1) may not be exported to Country Group Q or to the People's Republic of China under General License *GIT*.

[d] Commodities identified by the code letter "A" or "M" may not be taken to the People's Republic of China under General License BAGGAGE.

[e] Under specified circumstances, exports under this general license are not permitted for use on vessels/planes registered in or under control of certain Country Group Q, W, Y, or Z countries or the People's Republic of China.

[f] Under specified circumstances, exports under this general license are permitted to Country Group Q, W, or Y.

[g] Under specified circumstances, exports under this general license are permitted to Country Group S or Z.

Source: A Summary of U.S. Export Administration Regulations (Washington, D.C.: U.S. Department of Commerce, 1985), 24–27.

as the restrictions placed on exports to South Africa and Namibia, are instituted by such licensing to promote U.S. foreign policy. In the case of short-supply controls, the licenses are granted with an eye to preventing the depletion of scarce materials (e.g., western red cedar and petroleum).

For control purposes, countries are classified as Q, S, T, V, W, Y, and Z (see Exhibit 13–7). Most free world countries are in the T and V groups, and most commodities can be exported to such countries under either a G-DEST or GLV general license. G-DEST also applies to most goods destined for communist countries.

Technical data is also subject to export control (see Exhibit 13–8). By definition, *technical data* is information that can be adapted for use in the design, production, manufacture, use, or reconstruction of articles or materials. All exports of such data require a validated export license unless the technical data can be exported under one of the two technical data general licenses—GTDA and GTDR. General License GTDA, applicable to all countries, allows the export of (1) technology generally available to the public, (2) scientific or educational data not directly and significantly related to industrial processes, and (3) certain types of patent applications. In the case of GTDR, this type of license permits the export of most unpublished data to free world destinations.[20]

To determine whether a product requires a validated license, an exporter should consult the Commodity Control List (CCL). This is a 700-page, fine-print, complete list of some 200,000 sensitive commodities controlled by OEA (Office of Export Administration).[21] If the code letter following the Export Control Commodity Number

---

Country Group Q
Romania

Country Group S
Libya

Country Group T
North, Central, and South America,
    Bermuda and the Caribbean, except
    Canada and Cuba

Country Group V
All countries not included in any other
    country group (except Canada, which
    is not in any group)

Country Group W
Hungary
Poland

Country Group Y
Albania
Bulgaria
Czechoslovakia
Estonia
Laos
Latvia
Lithuania
Mongolian People's Republic
Russia

Country Group Z
Cuba
Kampuchea
North Korea
Vietnam

EXHIBIT 13–7 Country groups

Source: A Summary of U.S. Export Administration Regulations (Washington, D.C.: U.S. Department of Commerce, 1985),10

| Do you have technical data or software within the meaning of §779.2(a) & (b)? | If no | See the regulations for the export of commodities. |

If yes

| Do you wish to remove the technical data (TD) or software (SW) from the US or release it to a foreign national? See def. of "export" at §779.2(c). | If no | See §787.4 for prohibited sales with reason to know a violation is about to occur. |

If yes

| Is the export for consumption or use in Canada? | If yes | See the exemptions to the prohibitions at §779.3(b). |

If no

| Under §779.4, is the TD or SW either
  Publicly available?
  Basic research?
  For foreign patent filing or educational material? | If yes | See GTDA at §779.4 |

If no

| Under §779.5(c) is your TD or software either
  Operation TD or SW
  Sales TD or SW
  Software updates
  Mass-market software | If yes | See GTDU at §779.5 |

If no

| Locate your TD on the Control List. See §799.1 on how to use the Control List. Remember, if your TD is described two or more places on the Control List, the most restrictive provision applies. |

Go to next question

| Is GTDU authorized under your ECN? | If yes | See GTDU at §779.5 |

If no

| Is GTDR authorized under your ECN for your TD to your destination? | If no | You must obtain a validated license or not export. |

If yes

| Is your export or reexport to South Africa or Namibia? | If yes | See §779.6(b)(1) for the GTDR limits and §779.6(d)(3) for written assurance requirements. |

If no

EXHIBIT 13–8 Decision tree for exporting technical data and software

| Is your TD classified under ECN 6398G? | If yes | See §779.6(d)(4) for the written assurance requirements and GTDR. |

If no

| Do you have in hand the written assurance required by §779.6(d)(2)? | If yes | See GTDU at §779.6 |

If yes

| You must obtain a validated license or not export. |

CAUTION: This decision tree is not a substitute for the provisions in the regulations, which you are fully responsible for reading and complying with. In the event of a conflict or ambiguity, the provisions of this regulation and the Control List prevail (not the decision tree).

EXHIBIT 13–8 Decision tree for exporting technical data and software *(continued)*

Source: Business America, 13 February 1989, 12

(ECCN) for a particular commodity is an A or B, the commodity is under validated license control to all countries except Canada. If the code letter is C, D, or E, the commodity is under validated license control to certain communist countries but not to free-world destinations.[22] In order to be granted a validated export license, an exporter must receive an order before making application. Special forms must be secured by the buyer or the buyer's government to support each order request. Care must be used in preparing the application form, which is a two-page, back-to-back document. One exporter's license application was denied because he submitted photocopies of each page on a separate sheet. Also, an exporter would be prudent to consult with a publication called *Denial Orders Currently Affecting Export Privileges.*

If all application forms are in order, a validated export license is issued by the OEA in response to an exporter's application for authorization to make a specific export. OEA's authority is provided by the Export Administration Act. OEA receives some 500 to 600 applications every working day, or a total of 125,000 to 140,000 license requests a year.[23] Of these, about 8 percent are for direct exports to communist countries, 71 percent for direct exports to noncommunist countries, 10 percent for authority to reexport U.S. commodities from one country to another, and 10 percent for an extension or amendment of a previously issued export or reexport authorization. For every commodity over which the Commerce Department has export control jurisdiction, the *Export Administration Regulations* provide for a special type of validated license that permits multiple exports with a single application.

Realizing the significance of quick approval, the U.S. government has been successful in reducing the time required to process an application. In 1988 a system of electronic processing was introduced, making it possible for an exporter to receive an export license electronically from Washington, D.C. Exhibit 13–9 describes the export license process.

Although OEA is the principal agency dealing with commercial exports, that agency works in conjunction with other government agencies. A review, for example, can be made by the Department of Defense, which maintains the Militarily Critical

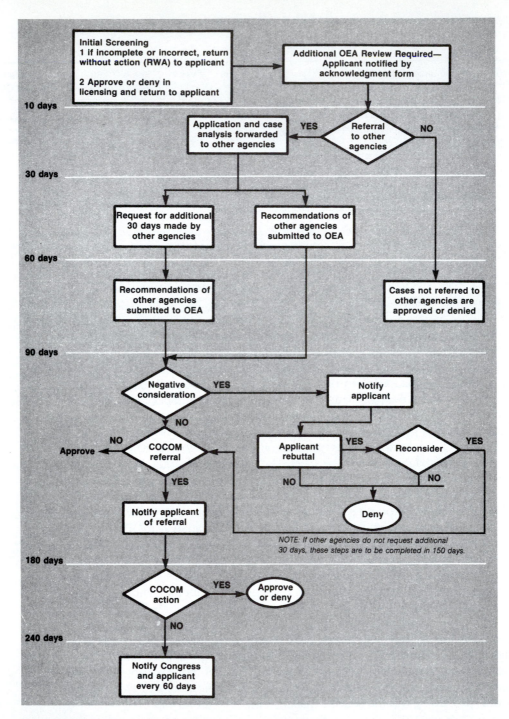

EXHIBIT 13-9 Export license process

Source: A Summary of U.S. Export Administration Regulations (Washington, D.C., U.S. Department of Commerce, 1985), 17

Technologies List for national security reasons. The Secretary of Defense, authorized by the Export Administration Act to review applications for exports to all Q, W, Y, and Z countries, reviews some 45 percent of all applications for export to communist destinations. An agreement may also have to be secured from the State Department, which may conduct reviews for foreign policy reasons. In cases of disagreement, the matter is referred to the president of the United States.

Other government agencies may be involved in the administration of export controls under other legislation. Consultations often take place in the Advisory Committee on Export Policy (ACEP) structure.[24] Members of ACEP include representatives from the departments of Commerce, Defense, State, Energy, Transportation (Maritime Administration), and Treasury, as well as representatives from the National Security Council, the Arms Control and Disarmament Agency, the National Aeronautics and Space Administration, the Central Intelligence Agency, and other agencies as appropriate (e.g., Justice Department—Drug Enforcement Administration, Nuclear Regulatory Commission, Interior Department, National Science Foundation, Agriculture Department, and Patent and Trademark Office). The ACEP structure primarily considers national security and foreign policy issues and license applications that are particularly complex. The system is designed to operate on a consensus basis when decisions are made.

Frequently, export controls are coordinated at the international level. Most of the export controls maintained by the United States are multilateral controls in the sense that they are maintained in cooperation with other countries. To coordinate export controls for security purposes, Western allies rely on an organization known as COCOM (Coordinating Committee on Multilateral Exports Control). COCOM, the most significant multilateral export control group, was created in 1949 to restrict the availability of strategic Western technology to controlled countries. Applications requiring COCOM approval are referred to COCOM after OEA's tentative approval (see Exhibit 13–9). Two more recent multilateral groups are the Missile Technology Control Regime (which coordinates controls on exports of missile technology) and the Australia Group (which coordinates controls on chemical weapons precursors).

COCOM consists of Australia, Japan, and the NATO allies (except Iceland)— Belgium, Canada, Denmark, France, Germany, Greece, Italy, Japan, Luxembourg, the Netherlands, Norway, Portugal, Turkey, the United Kingdom, and the United States. In response to the rapidly changing international political and military environment, COCOM agreed in 1991 to implement a new system of export controls for dual-use goods and technologies with significant military applications, resulting in a 50 percent reduction in existing export controls to a core list of militarily strategic technologies and goods.

In 1989 the U.S. government designated twenty-two technologies as critical to national security and "the long-term qualitative superiority of U.S. weapons systems." The technologies include biotechnology, laser weapons technology, and the manufacture of sophisticated composite materials that might be used in aircraft or elsewhere. The four criteria used for selection are an ability to enhance significantly the performance of proven types of weapon systems; a potential for creating new capabilities or systems; a potential for improving the reliability, availability, and maintainability of weapon systems; and affordability.

Sensitive items continue to require an individual validated license (IVL) for export to the West. The sensitive items include advanced computer equipment, certain underwater detection equipment, and cryptographic equipment. Items that are controlled for foreign policy reasons continue to require an IVL.[25]

On the other hand, in 1989 the Commerce Department removed unilateral export restrictions on a broad group of goods and technology. The new rule makes it possible to ship without prior approval many commonly available items that were controlled for national security reasons for more than twenty-five years. Decontrolled items include general industrial equipment, photographic equipment, servo-mechanical units and synchronous motors, and a broad range of industrial chemicals.

The Export Administration Act of 1979 requires the Commerce Department to remove licensing requirements for U.S. exports when items of comparable quality are freely available to East Bloc countries in sufficient quantities to render U.S. export controls ineffective. As a result, the Commerce Department has removed export restrictions on AT-compatible and similar desktop personal computers. The 1988 Omnibus Trade Act also requires lifting export controls on high-technology products already available to former Eastern Bloc nations from other sources. Seagate Technology Inc., the world's largest independent maker of disk drives, filed a petition with the Commerce Department in 1989 to remove small-capacity disk drives from long-standing export controls. Seagate demonstrated that a Bulgarian company, using its own technology, has been manufacturing comparable products. As a result, the Commerce Department stated that export licenses are no longer required for 3.5 inch and 5.25-inch drives with storage capacity up to fifty-five megabytes.[26]

Foreign and U.S. firms that illegally export U.S. products risk losing their export privileges. The Commerce Department denied all U.S. export privileges to Delft Instruments N.V., a Netherlands company suspected of illegally shipping U.S.-origin night vision gear to Iraq. The 180-day denial order was issued against Delft and its Belgian and German subsidiaries. The Commerce Department, in its first use of authority added to the Export Administration Act in 1988, denied U.S. export privileges for nine years to two West German firms (Chemco and Colimex) because of their "affiliation, ownership, control or portion of responsibility" to West German businessman Peter Walascheck. Walascheck was convicted of illegally reexporting a mustard gas ingredient to Iran and was denied all U.S. export privileges until 1998. Exhibit 13–10 describes how business firms can watch out for illegal export schemes.

Shipper's Export Declaration (SED) Form   SEDs are required to be filed for virtually all shipments, including hand-carried merchandise, and they must be deposited with an exporting carrier regardless of the type of export license. Exemptions apply to shipments to certain countries when the value is $1,000 or less and when the shipment is not moving under a validated export license. The information needed to fill out the form includes the name of the exporting carrier, port of loading, port of discharge, FOB value, forwarder's name, address, and FMC number, ECCN number (Export Commodity Control Number), and Schedule B number. An SED form is shown in Exhibit 13–11. For foreign merchandise that has entered the United States and that is being reexported, the form used is Form 7513—SED for in-transit merchandise.[27]

The following are some possible indicators that an illegal diversion might be planned by an export customer:

- □ The customer or purchasing agent is reluctant to offer information about the end use of a product.
- □ The product's capabilities do not fit the buyer's line of business: for example, an order for several sophisticated computers for a small bakery.
- □ The product ordered is incompatible with the technical level of the country to which the product is being shipped. Semiconductor manufacturing equipment would be of little use in a country without an electronics industry.
- □ The customer is willing to pay cash for a very expensive item when the terms of the sale call for financing.
- □ The customer has little or no business background.
- □ The customer is unfamiliar with the product's performance characteristics but still wants the product.
- □ Routine installation, training, or maintenance services are declined by the customer.
- □ Delivery dates are vague, or deliveries are planned for out-of-the-way destinations.
- □ A freight forwarding firm is listed as the product's final destination.
- □ The shipping route is abnormal for the product and destination.
- □ Packaging is inconsistent with the stated method of shipment or destination.
- □ When questioned, the buyer is evasive and especially unclear about whether the purchased product is for domestic use, export, or reexport.

EXHIBIT 13–10   Possible indicators of illegal export schemes

Source: U.S. Department of Commerce

The SED is a multipurpose document.[28] One of its purposes is to serve as an export control document. It declares the proper authorization for export by making reference to either a General License symbol or the license number of a validated license. The SED thus makes it possible to administer the requirements of the Export Administration Act.

Another purpose of the SED is to aid the Bureau of Census in compiling basic statistical information on export shipments. These data are compiled and published monthly and show the types of commodities exported and the countries that imported them.

Report of Request for Restrictive Trade Practice or Boycott (Form (ITA-621P)   The restrictive trade practice report is a form used to report illegal requests regarding boycott practices received from one country against another. This form must be submitted to the U.S. Department of Commerce when a company receives an illegal or legal reportable request regarding a company's business practices as outlined in the "Restrictive Trade Practices, Bulletin 369."

Certificate of Registration (Customs form 4455)   The certificate of registration is used to register a shipment with U.S. Customs. This registration is desirable for

SAMPLE COPY

U.S. DEPARTMENT OF COMMERCE — BUREAU OF THE CENSUS — INTERNATIONAL TRADE ADMINISTRATION

FORM **7525-V** (3-19-85)

SHIPPER'S EXPORT DECLARATION

OMB No. 0607-0018

1a. EXPORTER *(Name and address including ZIP code)*
Brown & Company
123 Samantha Rd.
Toledo, OH
ZIP CODE 43624

2. DATE OF EXPORTATION 7-8-85

3. BILL OF LADING/AIR WAYBILL NO. 000-1234-5678

b. EXPORTER EIN NO. 12-3456789

c. PARTIES TO TRANSACTION
☐ Related ☒ Non-related

4a. ULTIMATE CONSIGNEE
Kirk Sales LTD.
162 Belva Street
London, England

b. INTERMEDIATE CONSIGNEE
Bolden Service Company
3456 Fred Lane
London, England

5. FORWARDING AGENT
Sharyn Exports
P.O. Box XYZ
New York, NY 10047

6. POINT (STATE) OF ORIGIN OR FTZ NO. OH

7. COUNTRY OF ULTIMATE DESTINATION England

8. LOADING PIER/TERMINAL

9. MODE OF TRANSPORT *(Specify)* Air

10. EXPORTING CARRIER Fairway Air

11. PORT OF EXPORT Kennedy Airport

12. FOREIGN PORT OF UNLOADING Gatwick, England

13. CONTAINERIZED *(Vessel only)* ☐ Yes ☐ No

14. SCHEDULE B DESCRIPTION OF COMMODITIES, *(Use columns 15—19)*					VALUE (U.S. dollars, omit cents) *(Selling price or cost if not sold)* (20)
MARKS, NOS., AND KINDS OF PKGS. (15)	D/F (16)	SCHEDULE B NUMBER (17)	QUANTITY — SCHEDULE B UNIT(S) (18)	SHIPPING WEIGHT *(Pounds)* (19)	
B/1, B/2 2 boxes		Signal generators operating at frequencies over 1 GHZ, Model 525 sweep generator.			
	D	688.4010	2	146	$2,375
B/3 1 Box		Specially designed parts for Model 525 sweep generators, consisting of probes, tees, detectors, and detector mounts.			
	D	688.4060	X	68	$1,854

21. VALIDATED LICENSE NO./GENERAL LICENSE SYMBOL
A123456

22. ECCN *(When required)* 1529

23. Duly authorized officer or employee
H. Brown
The exporter authorizes the forwarder named above to act as forwarding agent for export control and customs purposes.

24. I certify that all statements made and all information contained herein are true and correct and that I have read and understand the instructions for preparation of this document, set forth in the "**Correct Way to Fill Out the Shipper's Export Declaration.**" I understand that civil and criminal penalties, including forfeiture and sale, may be imposed for making false or fraudulent statements herein, failing to provide the requested information or for violation of U.S. laws on exportation (13 U.S.C. Sec. 305; 22 U.S.C. Sec. 401; 18 U.S.C. Sec. 1001; 50 U.S.C. App. 2410).

Signature *R. Sharyn*
Title President
Date 7-8-85

Confidential – For use solely for official purposes authorized by the Secretary of Commerce (13 U.S.C. 301 (g)).

Export shipments are subject to inspection by U.S. Customs Service and/or Office of Export Enforcement.

25. AUTHENTICATION *(When required)*

This form may be printed by private parties provided it conforms to the official form. For sale by the Superintendent of Documents, Government Printing Office, Washington, D.C. 20402, and local Customs District Directors. The "**Correct Way to Fill Out the Shipper's Export Declaration**" is available from the Bureau of the Census, Washington, D.C. 20233.

EXHIBIT 13–11 Shipper's Export Declaration form

shipments that were originally imported and are now being returned to the country of origin for repair, replacement, alteration, or processing. If the shipment reenters the United States within one year of the date of export, it will reenter duty-free.

Hazardous Certificate   To export hazardous cargo, an exporter must use a shipper's certification or declaration of dangerous cargo. This document, required for all hazardous shipments, is used to describe the contents by providing the details and qualities of the items being shipped, their proper classification, required labels, and so on. This declaration must always be completed by the shipper (preferably on the shipper's letterhead) and signed by the shipper. There is no prescribed form for ocean shipments of hazardous materials at the present time. For all hazardous shipments moving via air freight, a shipper's declaration of dangerous cargo (air cargo) must be submitted to the airline.

Packing List   A packing list is a document that lists the type and number of pieces, the contents, weight, and measurement of each, as well as the marks and numbers. Its purpose is to facilitate customs clearance, keep track of inventory of goods, and assist in tracing lost goods. For insurance purposes, the packing list can be used in determining the contents of a lost piece. Furthermore, it is also useful in estimating shipping cost prior to export.

Shipper's Letter of Instructions   The shipper's letter of instructions is a form provided to the freight forwarder from the shipper giving all pertinent information and instruction regarding the shipment and how it is to be handled. When signed by the shipper, it also authorizes the forwarder to issue and sign documents on behalf of the shipper.

Dock Receipt   A dock receipt is proof of delivery for goods received at the dock or warehouse of the steamship line (see Exhibit 13–12). This document is required for shipments sailing from ports on the U.S. East and Gulf coasts. Six copies of the dock receipt must be lodged at the receiving warehouse before freight can be accepted.

Collection Documents

Before a seller can request payment, the seller must provide the buyer with a number of documents showing that the terms agreed upon have been complied with. The buyer requires such documents to protect itself and to satisfy its government's requirements.

Commercial Invoice   To collect payment, an invoice is needed. There are two kinds of invoices: (1) *pro forma* and (2) commercial. A *pro forma invoice* is an invoice provided by a supplier prior to the shipment of merchandise. The purpose of this invoice is to inform the buyer of the kinds and quantities of goods to be sent, their value, and important specifications (weight, size, and so on). The buyer may also need the pro forma invoice in order to be able to apply for an import license and/or a letter of credit.

A *commercial invoice* is a document that provides an itemized list of goods shipped and other charges (see Exhibit 13–13). As a complete record of the business transaction between two parties, it provides a complete description of merchandise,

DOCK RECEIPT

2. EXPORTER (Principal or seller-licensee and address including ZIP Code)		5. DOCUMENT NUMBER	5a. B/L OR AWB NUMBER
ABC COMPANY 84609 SOUTH LANE DETROIT, MICHIGAN U.S.A.	ZIP CODE 00000	BOOKING NO: DTI 435	

6. EXPORT REFERENCES

N7485

3. CONSIGNED TO	7. FORWARDING AGENT (Name and address — references)
	RADIX GROUP INTERNATIONAL P.O. BOX 66213 CHICAGO, IL 60666 FMC 232

8. POINT (STATE) OF ORIGIN OR FTZ NUMBER

MI

4. NOTIFY PARTY/INTERMEDIATE CONSIGNEE (Name and address)

9. DOMESTIC ROUTING/EXPORT INSTRUCTIONS

12. PRE-CARRIAGE BY	13. PLACE OF RECEIPT BY PRE-CARRIER	
14. EXPORTING CARRIER A VESSEL V.2	15. PORT OF LOADING/EXPORT NEW YORK	10. LOADING PIER/TERMINAL SHED 2180, PORT ELIZABETH
16. FOREIGN PORT OF UNLOADING (Vessel and air only) DAMMAM	17. PLACE OF DELIVERY BY ON-CARRIER	11. TYPE OF MOVE 11.a CONTAINERIZED (Vessel only) ☐ Yes ☒ No

MARKS AND NUMBERS (18)	NUMBER OF PACKAGES (19)	DESCRIPTION OF COMMODITIES in Schedule B detail (20)	GROSS WEIGHT (Pounds) (21)	MEASUREMENT (22)
AL MOOSA DAMMAM SAUDI ARABIA MADE IN U.S.A. NOS. 1/3	3	CARTONS: AUTO PARTS NOTE: DELIVERY CUT-OFF: 10/22/87 SAILING DATE : 10/24/87	540#	56'

DELIVERED BY:

LIGHTER _TRANSPORT INTL_
TRUCK

ARRIVED— DATE _10-21-87_ TIME _8:50am_

UNLOADED—DATE _10-21-87_ TIME _9:45am_

CHECKED BY _JB_

PLACED IN SHIP/ON DOCK LOCATION _29_

RECEIVED THE ABOVE DESCRIBED GOODS OR PACKAGES SUBJECT TO ALL THE TERMS OF THE UNDERSIGNED'S REGULAR FORM OF DOCK RECEIPT AND BILL OF LADING WHICH SHALL CONSTITUTE THE CONTRACT UNDER WHICH THE GOODS ARE RECEIVED, COPIES OF WHICH ARE AVAILABLE FROM THE CARRIER ON REQUEST AND MAY BE INSPECTED AT ANY OF ITS OFFICES.

FOR THE MASTER

BY _R. Smith_
RECEIVING CLERK

DATE _10-21-87_

ONLY CLEAN DOCK RECEIPT ACCEPTED.

EXHIBIT 13–12   Dock receipt

Source: Reprinted with permission of Radix Group International, Inc.

quantity, price, and shipping and payment terms. It is desirable that this invoice contain a breakdown of charges such as those related to inland transportation, loading, insurance, freight, handling, and certification. Because the invoice is required to clear goods through customs, all necessary information required by the buyer's government must be included. Exhibit 13–14 describes certain omissions and inaccuracies that may cause U.S. Customs to begin to ask questions and further inquire about a shipment in doubt.

The requirements of the exporter's country must be satisfied as well. The United States prohibits certain goods from being diverted to countries such as North Korea, Vietnam, and Cuba. Therefore, the invoice may have to be prepared so it includes an

```
┌──────────────────────────────────────────────────────────────────────┐
│         EXPORTERS ANONYMOUS                                            │
│         1331 BIRCH ST.                                                 │
│         CHICAGO, ILLINOIS 60666                                        │
│         U.S.A.                                                         │
│         TEL (312) 555-1234                                             │
├──────────────────────────────────────────────────────────────────────┤
```

YOUR ORDER NO.	CUSTOMER A/C	T.C.	S.C.	INSURANCE	INVOICE NO.	DATE
5903K	13804				4578	4/10/8X

SHIPPED TO.		VIA	OUR ORDER NO.
SAME		OCEAN FRT	1256

SOLD TO:
```
┌                    ┐        MARKS
  WILLIAMS CO PTY LTD.                WILLIAMS
  P.O. BOX 97                         SYDNEY
  SYDNEY NSW 2000 AUSTRALIA           NO.1/4
└                    ┘
```

CUSTOMS DECLARATION	TERMS
	OPEN ACCT/NET 60 │ CIF SYDNEY

PACKAGE NUMBER	QUANTITY	MODEL OR PART NO.	MERCHANDISE	PRICE	AMOUNT U.S. DOLLARS
1/4	10000	B236	AUTOMOTIVE GASKET B20	.90ea	9,000.00
			EX FACTORY		US$ 9,000.00
			INLAND FREIGHT		221.40
			FORWARDING FEE		93.50
			FOB VESSEL		US$ 9,314.90
			OCEAN FREIGHT		409.19
			INSURANCE		59.54
			CIF SYDNEY		US$ 9,783.63

```
CARRIER: A VESSEL V.1
LOS ANGELES/SYDNEY

4 CTNS: 2050#/930 Kgs

COUNTRY OF ORIGIN: U.S.A.


        WE CERTIFY THIS INVOICE TO BE TRUE
        AND CORRECT IN ALL PARTICULARS

        EXPORTERS ANONYMOUS   Mary Smith
```

These commodities licensed by U.S. for ultimate destination
AUSTRALIA. Diversion contrary to U.S. law prohibited.

INVOICE

EXHIBIT 13–13   A commercial invoice

Source: Reprinted with permission of Radix Group International, Inc.

antidiversion clause or destination control statement (see Exhibit 13–13). According to section 387.6 of the Export Administration Regulations, "No person may export, dispose of, divert, direct, mail or otherwise ship, transship, or reexport commodities or technical data to any person or destination or for any use in violation of or contrary to the terms, provisions, or conditions of any export control document, any prior representation, any form of notification of prohibition against such action, or any provision of the Export Administration Act or any regulation, order, or license issued under the Act."[29]

Foreign Customs Invoice   A customs invoice is a special format invoice required by customs officials in some countries in lieu of the commercial invoice, as those

The fundamental rule to be borne in mind is that the shipper and importer must furnish the Customs officers with all pertinent information with respect to each import transaction in order to assist the Customs officers in determining the tariff status of the goods. Examples of omissions and inaccuracies to be avoided are

- The shipper assumes that a commission, royalty, or other charge against the goods is a so-called nondutiable item and omits it from the invoice.
- A foreign shipper who purchases goods and sells them to a United States importer at a delivered price shows on the invoice the cost of the goods to the shipper instead of the delivered price.
- A foreign shipper manufactures goods partly with the use of materials supplied by the United States importer, but invoices the goods at the actual cost to the manufacturer without including the value of the materials supplied by the importer.
- The foreign manufacturer ships replacement goods to the customer in the United States and invoices the goods at the net price without showing the full price less the allowance for defective goods previously shipped and returned.
- A foreign shipper that sells goods at list price, less a discount, invoices them at the net price, and fails to show the discount.
- A foreign shipper sells goods at a delivered price but invoices them at a price FOB the place of shipment and omits the subsequent charges.
- A foreign shipper indicates on the invoice that the importer is the purchaser, whereas the importer is in fact either an agent who is receiving a commission for selling the goods or a party who will receive part of the proceeds of the sale of the goods sold for the joint account of the shipper and consignee.

EXHIBIT 13–14   Examples of omissions and inaccuracies

Source: Importing into the United States (Washington D.C.: U.S. Customs Service, Department of Treasury, 1982), 24

officials may not recognize the commercial invoice for customs purposes. A foreign customs invoice is shown in Exhibit 13–15. This type of invoice generally contains the same information as the commercial invoice and may also contain certifications with regard to value and origin of the shipment.

Consular Invoice   In addition to the regular commercial invoice, several countries, notably those in Latin America, require legalized or visaed documents that often include a special kind of invoice known as a consular invoice. A consular invoice is a detailed document prepared by a seller in the importing country's language on an official form supplied by the importer's government. Its purpose is to monitor merchandise and capital flows. Exhibit 13–16 lists those countries that require such documents.

A consular invoice must have an official stamp, seal, or signature affixed to it. This is the responsibility of the consulate general, who is a representative of the government of the importing country. The resident consul is supposed to verify the contents of the invoice (e.g., value, quantity, and nature of shipment) and to certify its authenticity and correctness. Usually, there is a fee for this service. Bolivia's consular fees for the notarization of invoices are 1 percent of the FOB value.[30]

COMMERCIAL INVOICE FOR THE **CARIBBEAN COMMON MARKET**		
SELLER (Name, Full Address, Country) ABC COMPANY 84609 SOUTH LANE DETROIT, MICHIGAN 00000 U.S.A.	INVOICE DATE AND NO. DATE: 10/1/87 NO: A495Z OTHER REFERENCES	CUSTOMER'S ORDER NO. PR8097
CONSIGNEE (Name, Full Address, Country) ANTIGUA WHITE SANDS MOTEL P.O. BOX 655 ST. JOHNS, ANTIGUA	BUYER (If Other Than Consignee) PRESENTING BANK XYZ BANK, ST. JOHNS COUNTRY OF ORIGIN OF GOODS UNITED STATES OF AMERICA	
PORT OF LADING MIAMI	TERMS AND CONDITIONS OF DELIVERY AND PAYMENT C AND F ST. JOHNS, ANTIGUA	
COUNTRY OF FINAL DESTINATION ANTIGUA	SHIP/AIR/ETC. CARICOM V.109	SIGHT DRAFT, DOCUMENTS AGAINST PAYMENT
OTHER TRANSPORT INFORMATION B/L NO. 185	CURRENCY OF SALE U.S. DOLLARS	

MARK AND NUMBERS	DESCRIPTION OF GOODS	GROSS WEIGHT(Kg.)	CUBIC METRES
A W S M ANTIGUA 1/2	RESTAURANT SUPPLIES	130 Kgs	1.354m3

NO. AND KIND OF PACKAGES	SPECIFICATION OF COMMODITIES (IN CODE AND/OR IN FULL)	NET WEIGHT (Kg.)	QUANTITY	UNIT PRICE	AMOUNT
2 CRATES	KITCHEN KNIFE A203	108 Kgs	50 DOZ	19.00/DZ	950.00
		PACKING			25.00
		FREIGHT INLAND OCEAN			35.00 120.00
		OTHER COSTS (Specify) FORWARDING FEE			50.00

IT IS HEREBY CERTIFIED THAT THIS INVOICE SHOWS THE ACTUAL PRICE OF THE GOODS DESCRIBED, THAT NO OTHER INVOICE HAS BEEN OR WILL BE ISSUED AND THAT ALL PARTICULARS ARE TRUE AND CORRECT.

J. Doe

J. DOE, Clerk 10/9/87 DETROIT
SIGNATURE AND STATUS OF AUTHORIZED PERSON DATE PLACE

INSURANCE
N/A

TOTAL INVOICE AMOUNT	
C&F ST. JOHNS	US$ 1,180.00

EXHIBIT 13–15 Foreign customs invoice

Source: Reprinted with permission of Radix Group International, Inc.

Near and Middle East Saudi Arabia Kuwait Lebanon Oman Jordan Bahrain Syria Yemen Iraq Iran United Arab Emirates **South America** Colombia (by request) Argentina Uruguay Paraguay	**Central America** Panama Nicaragua Honduras Guatemala **Far East** Philippines (by request) **Europe and Asia** Greece (by request) Spain (by request) Turkey **Africa** Libya **Caribbean** Dominican Republic

EXHIBIT 13–16   Countries that require a consular invoice

Source: Radix Group International, Inc.

It is significant to keep in mind that the consulate is not obligated to facilitate imports by approving the submitted documents quickly. Because the consul may take his or her time in returning the visaed documents, an exporter should allow reasonable time for the processing of a consular invoice. It can be a frustrating experience to rush the consulate for the documents while the shipment is waiting.

Because a consular invoice is a legal document, any errors noted later require special consideration. An exporter cannot simply make corrections on a consular invoice that has been certified. Such corrections are considered forgery, and the criminal penalty can be quite severe.

Although a consular invoice usually contains the same information as a commercial invoice, the actual information required by the consulate depends on where the shipping is to be made. The best way to find out what is specifically required is to speak directly with the consulate or consult one of the reference manuals available, such as Dun and Bradstreet or the International Trade Reporter of the Bureau of National Affairs (BNA).

Certificate of Origin   A certificate of origin is a document prepared by the exporter and used to identify or declare that the merchandise originated in a certain country. It assures the buyer or importer of the country of manufacture. This document is necessary for tariff and control purposes. Some countries may require statements of origin to establish possible preferential rates of import duties under the Most Favored Nation arrangements. This certificate also prevents the inadvertent importation of goods from prohibited or unfriendly countries. The forms can vary, ranging from a shipper's own letterhead certificate to a countersigning by the Chamber of Commerce

CERTIFICATE OF ORIGIN

2. EXPORTER (Principal or seller-licensee and address including ZIP Code)		5. DOCUMENT NUMBER	5A. B/L OR AWB NUMBER
SHIPPER OF AMERICA 1234 NORTH STREET CHICAGO, ILLINOIS U.S.A.	ZIP CODE 60000	6. EXPORT REFERENCES 9246	

3. CONSIGNED TO	7. FORWARDING AGENT (Name and address - references)
IMPORTER OF SAUDI ARABIA P.O. BOX 740 JEDDAH, SAUDI ARABIA	RADIX GROUP INTERNATIONAL P.O. BOX 66213 CHICAGO, ILLINOIS 60666 FMC 232

8. POINT (STATE) OF ORIGIN OR FTZ NUMBER
IL

4. NOTIFY PARTY/INTERMEDIATE CONSIGNEE (Name and address)	9. DOMESTIC ROUTING/EXPORT INSTRUCTIONS
GULF BROKERS LTD. P.O. BOX 2009 JEDDAH, SAUDI ARABIA	

12. PRE-CARRIAGE BY	13. PLACE OF RECEIPT BY PRE-CARRIER	
14. EXPORTING CARRIER A VESSEL	15. PORT OF LOADING/EXPORT NEW YORK	10. LOADING PIER/TERMINAL
16. FOREIGN PORT OF UNLOADING (Vessel and air only) JEDDAH	17. PLACE OF DELIVERY BY ON-CARRIER	11. TYPE OF MOVE 11.a CONTAINERIZED (Vessel only) ☐ YES ☒ NO

MARKS AND NUMBERS (18)	NUMBER OF PACKAGES (19)	DESCRIPTION OF COMMODITIES in Schedule B detail (20)	GROSS WEIGHT (Pounds) (21)	MEASUREMENT (22)
I.S.A. JEDDAH MADE IN U.S.A. NO. 1/4	4	BOXES: POWER TOOLS MANUFACTURER: SHIPPER OF AMERICA 1234 NORTH STREET CHICAGO, ILLINOIS 60000 U.S.A.	843#	97'

The undersigned......JANE DOE.................(Owner or Agent), does hereby declare for the above named shipper, the goods as described above were shipped on the above date and consigned as indicated and are products of the United States of America Dated at.....CHICAGO, IL...................... on the....10th. day of.....OCTOBER.................................19.87.

Sworn to before me this ...10th. day of......OCTOBER.............. 19.87.

Debra Uvelli
.....NOTARY PUBLIC..........

OFFICIAL SEAL
DEBRA UVELLI
Notary Public, State of Illinois
My Commission Expires 6/11/91

Jane Doe
SIGNATURE OF OWNER OR AGENT

The.....ANY TOWN ASSOCIATION OF COMMERCE AND INDUSTRY......................., a recognized Chamber of Commerce under the laws of the State of.......ILLINOIS..................., has examined the manufacturer's invoice or shipper's affidavit concerning the origin of the merchandise, and, according to the best of its knowledge and belief, finds that the products named originated in the United States of North America.

Secretary ....M. H. JONES.............................

EXHIBIT 13–17 A certificate of origin

Source: Reprinted with permission of Radix Group International, Inc.

(see Exhibit 13–17). In some cases, such forms must be visaed by an importing country's resident consul. The United Nations provides and recommends the use of Form A for this purpose. For international use, this document is generally notarized and chamberized.

Inspection Certificate An inspection certificate is a document certifying that the merchandise was in good condition immediately prior to shipment. Many foreign buyers protect themselves by requiring a shipper's affidavit or an independent inspection firm to certify quality and quantity and conformity of goods in relation to the order, as well as to ensure that the goods contracted for have actually been shipped.

This certificate is normally prepared by an independent firm other than the exporter, attesting to the quality or quantity of goods being shipped.

Special Purpose Documents As in the case of an inspection certificate, an importer may request other special documents, such as a certificate of weight/measurement and certificate of analysis in order to protect the importer's interests. A certificate of weight/measurement is issued by an independent party attesting to the weight or measurement of the merchandise to be shipped. A certificate of analysis contains an expert's report on the findings or grading of the substance or composition of the product shipped. The document assures the buyer that the goods are those that an exporter contracted for shipment.

Insurance Certificate A certificate of insurance is a negotiable document issued to provide coverage for a specific shipment. It briefly describes the transaction and its coverage. Usually, an insurance certificate is issued as an open-coverage policy to protect any and all shipments and transportation as long as a certificate is filed for each shipment. Generally, the policy will cover most losses sustained during transit. Not restricted only to ocean shipments is a marine insurance policy, which covers all modes of transportation.

Air Waybill An air waybill is basically a bill of lading issued by air carriers for air shipments. This transport instrument is not a negotiable document. As a result, a carrier will release goods to a designated consignee without the waybill.

Bill of Lading A bill of lading is a document issued to record shipment transportation (see Exhibit 13–18). Usually prepared by a shipper on the shipper's carrier's forms, this document serves three useful functions. First, as a document of title, it is a certificate of ownership that allows a holder or consignee to claim the merchandise described. Second, as a receipt of goods, it is issued by the carrier to the shipper for goods entrusted to the carrier's care for transportation. A bill of lading is thus proof of the carrier's possession of the freight. Third, as a contract of carriage, the bill of lading defines the contract terms between the shipper and his carrier. The conditions under which the goods are to be carried and the carrier's responsibility for the delivery are specified.

Bills of lading can be issued for inland (overland), ocean, or air transport. An inland bill of lading is issued by railroad or truck lines. It authorizes movement of goods from the shipper's warehouse to the port or point of export. An ocean bill of lading, in contrast, applies to goods shipped by water and is issued by steamship lines. When the document is issued by an air carrier, it becomes an air waybill. In the case of a so-called *through* bill of lading, shipment is provided for two or more transportation modes for delivery to a final destination. Another kind of bill of lading is the N.V.O.C.C., which is issued by a "nonvessel operator common carrier" that consolidates freight into a container for shipping by regular liner vessels.

According to the International Chamber of Commerce, the bill of lading is acceptable only when it is marked *clean* and *on board*. The bill of lading is clean when the carrier sees no evidence of damage to the packing or condition of the cargo. The cargo thus must be received in good order and condition without exception

UNION STAR LINE

SAMPLE BILL OF LADING

SHIPPER/EXPORTER	DOCUMENT NO.
SHIPPER OF AMERICA INC. 1234 NORTH STREET CHICAGO, ILLINOIS 60000 U.S.A.	**EXPORT REFERENCES** 9876

CONSIGNEE	FORWARDING AGENT — REFERENCES
OVERSEAS IMPORTS LTD. 5678 JOHN AVENUE D-2000 HAMBURG, WEST GERMANY	RADIX GROUP INTERNATIONAL P.O. BOX 66213 CHICAGO, IL 60666 FMC 232

	POINT AND COUNTRY OF ORIGIN IL

NOTIFY PARTY	DOMESTIC ROUTING/EXPORT INSTRUCTIONS
SAME	

PRECARRIAGE BY	PLACE OF RECEIPT CHICAGO	
VESSEL DAS BOOT V.01	**PORT OF LOADING** MONTREAL	ONWARD INLAND ROUTING
PORT OF DISCHARGE HAMBURG	**PLACE OF DELIVERY**	

PARTICULARS FURNISHED BY SHIPPER

MARKS AND NUMBERS	NO. OF PKGS.	DESCRIPTION OF PACKAGES AND GOODS	GROSS WEIGHT	MEASUREMENT
OVERSEAS IMPORT 9876 MADE IN U.S.A. NOS. 1/5	5	SKIDS S.T.C. 10 CARTONS: BOOKS	2000#	100'
		FREIGHT COLLECT	LADEN ON BOARD OCT 10 1987 *jws.*	

These commodities licensed by U.S. for ultimate destination WEST GERMANY.
Diversion contrary to U.S. law prohibited.

FREIGHT CHARGES PAYABLE AT   DESTINATION

	PREPAID	COLLECT

Received from the aforenamed shipper, the goods as described above by the shipper in apparent external good order and condition unless otherwise indicated herein or hereon to be transported in accordance with all of the terms printed, written, typed or stamped in or on this B/L of two (2) pages to which the merchant agrees by accepting this B/L any local privileges or customs notwithstanding.

In witness whereof, three (3) original BS-L have been signed, and if one (1) is accomplished by delivery of the Goods issuance of a delivery order or by some other means, the others shall be void if required by the carrier, one (1) original B/L must be surrendered, duly endorsed in exchange for the goods or a delivery order.

Dated at Port of Loading   **UNION STAR LINE**   *J.W. Smith*

10	10	1987	By J.W. SMITH
MO	DAY	YEAR	FOR THE MASTER

B L No
911999-01

EXHIBIT 13–18   A bill of lading

Source: Reprinted with permission of Radix Group International, Inc.

or irregularity. A bill of lading is *foul* when there is indication of damage to the goods received. For an on-board bill of lading to be issued, the cargo must be loaded aboard the named vessel on the specified date of loading. In comparison, even though a *received for shipment* bill of lading also mentions a particular vessel, this document only implies that the goods have been received by the steamship company. In such a case, because the goods are not yet loaded on board a particular vessel, it is possible that the goods may end up on another vessel instead.

In addition to being classified as clean or foul and by types of transportation carriers, a bill of lading can be *straight* or *negotiable*. A straight bill of lading, under international law, is nonnegotiable. It is consigned directly to a consignee rather than *to order*. As such, it allows delivery only to the consignee or party named on the bill. The carrier must be certain that the party receiving goods is actually the named party. To obtain possession of the shipment, the foreign buyer simply shows his proof of identity.

A shipper's order or negotiable bill of lading is a negotiable instrument that is consigned to order. When endorsed, it allows transfer of title to the holder of documents, and delivery can be made to a named party or anyone designated.

Both the straight and order bills of lading serve as collection documents. The buyer must pay for the goods, post bond, or meet other specified conditions before obtaining the bill of lading to claim the goods. The shipper endorses the bill and presents it to the bank for collection as evidence of satisfying the conditions stated in the letter of credit.

CONCLUSION

Moving cargo to an overseas destination is a much more complex task than transportation of freight locally. Other than the usual package designed to protect and/or promote a product while on display, packing (shipping package) is necessary if the merchandise is to be properly protected during shipment. Because of a greater number of hazards, the length of time during which the cargo is in transit, and a carrier's limited liability, the shipper should obtain marine insurance. In addition, the shipper should take necessary packing precautions to minimize any chance of damage. Containerization is one of several transportation modes that can achieve this goal.

Cargo cannot move without proper documentation. There are a great number of documents that must be filed to satisfy an exporter's government requirements and an importer's legal requirements. To compound the problem, the document requirements of the various countries are far from being uniform. The shipper, however, does not have any options—the shipper simply must submit all required documents if a cargo is to be moved and if the shipper is going to collect payment from the buyer. There are specialists in cargo movement who can facilitate the process for a fee. Freight forwarders and customhouse brokers work for the shipper and the importer respectively. They are capable of taking over all aspects of physical distribution and documentation. When the shipper wants to be relieved of these responsibilities, these intermediaries can help.

QUESTIONS

1. What are some of the hazards associated with the air, water, and land modes of transportation?
2. Explain how the freight rates–density effect can affect the choice of transportation.
3. Distinguish among conference lines, independent lines, and tramp vessels.
4. Distinguish between special coverage and blanket coverage.

5. When is an export license needed?
6. Explain these documents: SED, dock receipt, invoice (commercial, foreign customs, and consular), certificate of origin, inspection certificate, air waybill, and bill of lading.
7. Distinguish among these types of bill of lading: clean, foul, straight, and negotiable.

DISCUSSION ASSIGNMENTS AND MINICASES

1. Is there an ideal mode of transportation based on market location, speed, cost, and hazard criteria?
2. What products are suitable for air shipping?
3. Explain how containerization can solve the four packing problems of weight, breakage, moisture

and temperature, and pilferage and theft.
4. What are the functions of a freight forwarder and a customhouse broker? Is it worthwhile to use these agents?

NOTES

1. Gene R. Tyndall, "We Must Manage Change Before It Manages Us," *Marketing News,* 5 February 1990, 14.
2. Martin Christopher, *The Strategy of Distribution Management* (Westport, CT: Quorum Books, 1985), 3.
3. John F. Magee, William C. Copacino, and Donald B. Rosenfield, *Modern Logistics Management* (New York: Wiley, 1985), 193.
4. *Ports of the World: A Guide to Cargo Loss Control,* 13th ed. (CIGNA), 46–47.
5. "California's Classy Crop Cornucopia," *Fortune,* 6 June 1988, 91.
6. David Ross, "Air Freighting," in *Handbook of Physical Distribution Management,* 3rd ed., ed. John Gattorna (Aldershot, Hants, England: Gower, 1983), 223–37.
7. Market Expansion Division, International Trade Administration, *Foreign Regulations Affecting U.S. Textile/Apparel Exports* (Washington, D.C.: U.S. Department of Commerce, 1986), 26.
8. Reuben Kyle and Laurence T. Phillips, "Cargo Reservation for Bulk Commodity Shipments: An Economic Analysis," *Columbia Journal of World Business* 18 (Fall 1983): 42–49.
9. Ruel Kahler and Roland L. Kramer, *International Marketing,* 4th ed. (Cincinnati: South-Western, 1977), 211.
10. Charles A. Taff, *Management of Physical Distribution and Transportation,* 7th ed. (Homewood, IL: Irwin, 1984), 261.

11. International Trade Administration, *A Basic Guide to Exporting* (Washington, D.C.: U.S. Department of Commerce, 1981), 22.
12. *Ports of the World,* 51.
13. *Ports of the World,* 52.
14. John Wilson, "Security in Distribution," in *Handbook of Physical Distribution Management,* 3rd ed., ed. by John Gattorna (Aldershot, Hants, England: Gower, 1983).
15. Magee, Copacino, and Rosenfield, *Modern Logistics Management,* 196.
16. G. J. Davies, "The Role of Exporter and Freight Forwarder in the United Kingdom," *Journal of International Business Studies* 12 (Winter 1981): 99–108.
17. J. Michael Farren, "Opportunities and Challenges in the New European Market," *Business America,* 25 February 1991, 6–7.
18. United States Postal Service, *International Direct Marketing Guide* (Alexandria, VA: Braddock Communications, Inc., 1990), 7.
19. International Trade Administration, *A Summary of U.S. Export Administration Regulations* (Washington, D.C.: U.S. Department of Commerce, 1985), 3.
20. International Trade Administration, *Overview of the Export Administration Program* (Washington, D.C.: U.S. Department of Commerce, 1985), 15.
21. For information, see *Export Control of Technical Data,* International Trade Administration, U.S. Department of Commerce, 1985; *Enforcement and Administration Pro-*

ceedings, International Trade Administration, U.S. Department of Commerce, 1985; and *Index to the Commodity Control List,* International Trade Administration, U.S. Department of Commerce, 1985.

22. *Introduction to the Export,* ii.

23. *Overview of the Export,* 15.

24. *Overview of the Export,* 11.

25. "Fewer Licenses Required for Exports to the West," *Business America,* 2 July 1990, 20–21.

26. Ron Wolf, "Seagate Gets OK to Export to East Bloc," *San Jose Mercury News,* 15 May 1990.

27. See Bureau of the Census, *Correct Way to Fill Out the Shipper's Export Declarations* (Washington, D.C.: U.S. Department of Commerce, 1985).

28. *Introduction to the Export,* ii.

29. *Enforcement and Administrative Proceedings.* (Washington. D.C.: U.S. Department of Commerce, 1985), 3.

30. *U.S. Textile/Apparel Exports,* 22.

Everyone lives by selling something.

Robert Louis Stevenson

Promotion Strategies
Personal Selling, Publicity, and Sales Promotion

14

CHAPTER OUTLINE

MARKETING ILLUSTRATION
What's Up, Doc?

Monterey Stores, a department store chain located in Peru, launched a continuity promotion designed to increase repeat store traffic. Bugs Bunny and friends were used as the focal point of the program. The program featured a stamp album that was distributed free. The album held 336 stamps and 48 stickers which were associated with a participating brand. The stamps were sold in store; the stickers required a purchase of sponsored brands. Kids who filled up their albums received special premiums. The album also included coupons that served as entries into a sweepstakes. Record-breaking results followed.

Wanting women in El Salvador to achieve "liberation from the pad," Tambrands had to overcome women's preference of pads over tampons. Some women believed that the use of the tampon would cause them to lose their virginity. To educate consumers, Tambrands has used videotapes and booklets to describe what tampons are and how to use them properly. Additionally, nurses may be employed to provide information as well as samples to potential consumers.

Source: "'What's Up, Doc?' Sales at Monterey," *PROMO,* September 1991, 49

The examples in the marketing illustration provide clear evidence that a product must be promoted and that advertising is not the only means. A well-rounded marketing plan must include a proper promotion mix. This mix should not rely solely on advertising—personal selling, publicity, and sales promotion should also be included. This chapter examines the communication process in general as well as those promotional components other than advertising that are part of the process. Attention is given to the role of personal selling, internationally and locally. The pros and cons of employing local nationals for selling are also discussed.

A section is devoted to the treatment of publicity, examining the principles related to a sound publicity campaign, with an emphasis on how to deal with negative publicity. Another section investigates the use of sales promotion and the influence of local regulations on the various sales promotion techniques. Finally, discussion focuses on the promotion programs of the U.S. Department of Commerce.

PROMOTION AND COMMUNICATION

The purpose of **promotion** is both to communicate with buyers and to influence them. Effective promotion requires an understanding of the process of persuasion and how this proces is affected by environmental factors. The potential buyer must not only receive the desired information, but also be able to comprehend that information. Furthermore, the information must be sufficiently potent to motivate this buyer to react positively.

To communicate effectively with someone means that certain facts and information are shared in common with that person. **Communication** is basically a five-stage process consisting of source, encoding, information, decoding, and destination (see Exhibit 14–1). Encoding is a step that transforms the idea or information into a form that can be transmitted (e.g., written or spoken words). For a receiver to understand the coded information, that person must be able to decode these words.

The source can encode and the receiver can decode only through the experience each has had. The two large circles in Exhibit 14–1 represent the fields of experience of each party. If the two circles have a large common area, communication is relatively easy because both individuals have similar psychological and social attributes. Communication is more difficult if the overlapping area is smaller. Such is often the case with international communication. If the circles do not meet, communication is likely impossible; that is, the sender and the receiver have nothing in common, and they therefore have an extremely difficult time understanding each other. Moreover, "noise" (interference) can easily affect any one of the five stages, making the effect on the communication difficult to predict. Thus, the sender must be receiver-oriented. The message must consist of information that the receiver can relate to, and the information must be encoded with relevant images and words common to the receiver's experience and language.

It is not sufficient just for the receiver to be informed by the message; the receiver must also be persuaded to accept the information and to act as suggested. A promotional message thus must be designed in such a way that the purchaser reacts favorably. Effective motivation requires that the principles of mass persuasion be followed.[1]

The first principle is that the message must reach a person's sense organs. This may sound simplistic, yet frequently the message sent is not received by the intended audience. To ensure reception, the message must gain the attention of the

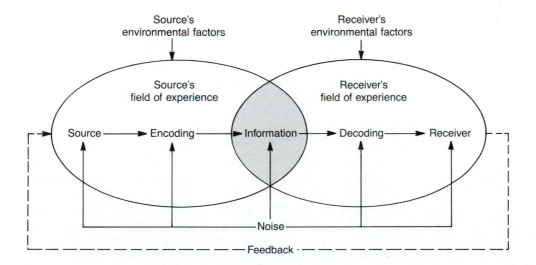

EXHIBIT 14–1 The process of communication

receiver. If the right media are not available or if the wrong message channel is used, the message may never get to the intended receiver. Furthermore, if the cue is not appealing, the receiver may never open his or her senses to the message because of a lack of interest. Note that what is interesting in one culture may not be in another. A message that refers to historical events in a home country (e.g., the 4th of July) may have little meaning in a host country.

The second principle requires that the message not contradict a person's cultural norms. It is possible, though not probable, that a message that is not consistent with the receiver's beliefs may sometimes be potent enough to make the buyer reevaluate traditional beliefs. In most cases, such a message is likely to be rejected, discarded, or distorted. The effective promotional message is thus one that is accepted as part of the receiver's attitude and belief structure. Understanding the principle is one reason that American Family Life Assurance Company was so successful in Japan with its "bank set sales." A premium was used in conjunction with banks' promotion because the Japanese have a favorable attitude toward saving. Banks simply deducted the cost of the premium from the interest in a policyholder's savings account.

The third principle requires that the sender create a message that arouses the receiver's need and that suggests a particular action that will enable the receiver to achieve a desired goal. If the suggested action results in several goals being realized simultaneously, the potency of the message correspondingly increases. An advertiser thus should identify relevant needs and motives. Motives can differ greatly among countries, even when the same product is involved. Consider the automobile. American car buyers usually replace their automobiles every few years, and styling is important to them. A typical British car owner, however, views the purchase as a lifetime commitment. For the Briton, the motive of function in terms of durability outweighs the emotional appeal of styling. Exhibit 14–2 shows that Volvo emphasizes safety as a buying motive.

The results of one study show that product quality, promotional effort, and service are the most important factors in winning sales in China. Competitors not having the highest quality levels should exert more-than-average promotional and service efforts. Table 14–1 provides means of the variables used to compare the six countries. The Italians seem to occupy the niche that demands lower-quality, lower-priced equipment. British firms appear to be in an undesirable place: middle quality, high prices, and weak promotional and service activities.[2]

The last principle suggests that the message must gain control of the receiver's behavior at the right place and time. The message should offer a well-defined path to reach the goal. If the purchaser is placed in a situation requiring action, the chances are increased that the buyer will take the suggested action. For example, Tokyo Toyopet, a division of Toyota, has done remarkably well by adhering to this principle. Its Toyota salesperson contacts a potential new-car buyer just after the latter's car has completed its "shaken," a mandatory inspection in Japan for a three-year old automobile. The timing is effective because this is when the car owner is most likely to think about trading in the old vehicle for a new one.

Infiniti's communication campaign to introduce the brand seems to largely contradict the principles of mass persuasion. Although novel, the promotion campaign was severely criticized for failing to directly communicate the features and benefits

EXHIBIT 14–2 Buying motive: safety

Source: Courtesy of Volvo North America Corporation

TABLE 14–1   Country comparisons (means of variables)

Variable	Germany	Switzerland	U.K.	Italy	Japan	France
Product quality	4.18	4.27	3.67	3.66	3.40	3.44
Price	4.19	4.34	3.74	3.35	3.44	3.45
PROM	3.26	3.19	2.76	3.13	3.44	2.48
Service	3.60	3.59	3.15	3.55	3.72	3.10
Technical transfer	2.98	2.80	2.73	2.99	2.59	2.55
Financial help	2.61	2.67	2.35	2.83	2.52	2.40
Barter	2.33	2.20	2.04	2.49	2.60	2.32
First to enter (reenter)	3.72	3.33	2.70	3.24	4.49	2.17
Percent of equipment in plant from country	28.41	24.48	20.95	33.33	37.50	14.67
Customer relationship	3.57	3.51	3.02	3.59	4.03	2.99
Customer preference	4.02	3.98	3.47	3.76	3.50	3.07

Note: All variables except the percentage of equipment installed in the plant range from a low of 1 to a high of 5.
Source: Norman McGuinness, Nigel Campbell, and James Leontiades, "Selling Machinery to China: Chinese Perceptions of Strategies and Relationships," *Journal of International Business Studies* 22 (no. 2, 1991): 197

of the Infiniti brand. The introductory TV spots and magazines advertisements did not show the product (i.e., car). Instead, they showed pictures of rocks, trees, hay, and so on. The TV spots included "Distant Leaves," "Misty Tree," "Delicate Branches," "Flock of Geese," and "Summer Storm." Infiniti dealers themselves were also upset.

PROMOTION MIX

To communicate with and influence consumers, several promotional tools are available. Advertising is usually the most visible component of promotion, but it is not the only component of promotion. The promotion mix also consists of three other distinct but interrelated activities: personal selling, publicity, and sales promotion.

The four promotional components are not mutually exclusive, and it can be difficult, at times, to determine which one of the four activities a particular promotional tool may be. Consider the common trade fair. Promotion for a trade fair can be viewed as advertising because a fair sponsor, as well as participating companies, generally uses direct mail and newspapers to advertise the event. Since the media receive both advertising orders and news releases, they may be willing to provide free publicity for the fair as well. Furthermore, staffing at a display booth is necessary, and there will be plenty of opportunity for a company's representative to use personal selling to make sales. Finally, it is not uncommon for fair participants to offer free gifts and special prices during the display, and these techniques are classified as sales promotion tools. This chapter concentrates on personal selling, publicity, and sales promotion.

PERSONAL SELLING

According to the American Marketing Association, *personal selling* is an "oral presentation in a conversation with one or more prospective purchasers for the purpose of making sales." Personal selling, more commonly known as salesmanship outside the

United States, is used at every distribution level. The cost of personal selling is high. According to a study by McGraw-Hill, it cost a company $229.70 in 1985 each time a salesperson was sent to make a call on an industrial customer, a drastic jump from the $9.02 of 1942.[3] In spite of the high cost, personal selling should be emphasized when certain conditions are met. Industrial buying or large-volume purchases, characterized by a large amount of money being involved, justifies personal attention. Personal selling has also proven to be effective when the market is concentrated or when a salesperson must develop a measure of confidence in the customer for the purchase. The effectiveness of personal selling is also a function of product type. In general, personal selling works well with high unit value and infrequently purchased products. Such products usually require a demonstration, are custom-made or fitted to an individual's need, or involve trade-ins.

In the Far East, Asian businesspeople do not like to discuss business deals with a foreigner who does not come highly recommended by some mutual acquaintance. Personal contact is important to selling in South Korea, not only because of the value placed on personal relationships but also because such contact serves to bring the end-user in touch with new processes and equipment. Because Japanese suppliers often visit their Korean customers, U.S. suppliers should (1) make visits to Korea to augment the efforts of the local representative; (2) hold more demonstrations, seminars, and exhibitions of their products in Korea, utilizing such facilities as the U.S. Trade Center in Seoul; (3) increase the distribution of technical data and descriptive brochures to potential buyers and industry associations; and (4) improve followup on initial sales leads.[4]

Note that not all salespersons are directly involved in selling. So-called missionary salespersons, for example, have the task of educating potential buyers about product benefits and promotional campaigns in order to create the goodwill that may result in subsequent sales. When Foremost first introduced milk and ice cream products to the Thai market in 1956, the company sent sales representatives (missionary salespersons) to educate people by giving talks on sanitation and nutrition in schools and by providing free samples to students.

Personal Selling versus Advertising

Personal selling is similar to advertising in the sense that both aim to create sales and that both must be understandable, interesting, believable, and persuasive. But advertising differs from personal selling in several aspects. Advertising relies on a nonpersonal means of contact and sales presentation. When compared to advertising, personal selling commands a much larger share of aggregate promotional dollars and accounts for several times more in terms of the number of personnel. This relationship exists in all countries. In fact, the abundant labor supply in LDCs makes it easy and inexpensive to employ sales personnel. Shoplifting problems also encourage the use of personal selling, making self-selection and self-service relatively rare.

The differences between advertising and personal selling can also be contrasted in terms of the communication process.[5] Advertising is a one-way communication process that has relatively more "noise," whereas personal selling is a two-way communication process with immediate feedback and relatively less "noise." Controlling the message is more difficult in personal selling than in advertising because sales-persons may react in unforeseen situations in such a way that may differ from the company's policy. Yet advertising is usually less persuasive because advertisements are prepared in advance by those with minimal contact with customers and because the message must be kept simple to appeal to a large number of people. Personal selling, on the other hand, is more flexible, personal, and powerful. A salesperson can adapt the message to fit the client at the time of presentation, and stimuli can be presented to appeal to all five senses.

Varying Quality and Style of Personal Selling

The quality of personal selling varies widely from product to product, from employer to employer, and from one target group to another. In general, salespersons selling for manufacturers are better trained and more qualified than those working for wholesalers and retailers. In terms of the target market, salespersons who sell to industrial users are more likely to be "order getters" and are generally aggressive, well-trained, and well-informed. Industrial salespersons, receiving high compensation, must be capable of mixing easily with top management. Those selling to wholesalers, retailers, and con-sumers, have a more routine selling job, and these salespersons are "order takers" and generally less aggressive in securing new business. Expensive products require a higher quality of personal selling than low-unit-value, high-turnover products.

Personal selling is not viewed as a prestigious occupation in most countries. It is often taught in trade schools or vocational schools rather than in colleges, and thus the quality of personal selling outside the United States is far from exemplary. In Brazil, for example, salespeople are not very well-trained by U.S. standards.[6] One bank offered a financial service for doctors, but the closure rate was very low because the bank did not feel it was necessary to train the salespersons in this new service. Another Brazilian company selling frozen fruit juice was able to get a 30 percent response rate from major companies to its advertisement. Yet the leads generated through that advertising became worthless because the company's salespersons were unable to close a single deal.

Selling styles differ significantly. In Japan, employers are agreeable to the practice of having salespersons call on their employees at the workplace. Japanese salespersons sell cars door-to-door. Subaru went one step further. With its image as a vehicle for outdoor types, Subaru equipped its door-to-door salespersons with Sportsman's Guide catalogs. Sportsman's Guide, a U.S. firm selling a proprietary line of sporting goods and accessories, was optimistic about this unique distribution channel.

In the United States, salespersons entertain clients at either breakfast or lunch. Overseas, it is much more common to meet for entertainment after business hours and to have sales discussions over dinner or in a nightclub. The after-hours business contacts are much more important overseas than they are in the United States. Clients expect attention to be given to social functions in addition to business functions, in-cluding golf, drinking, dining, and so on. Potential customers expect to be extensively wined and dined. A salesperson commonly takes customers to bars and nightclubs for social contacts with members of the opposite sex. Under such circumstances, salesperson must be prepared to be far more than order takers.

The personal-selling tactic may have to be modified in some markets. Avon is able to use door-to-door selling in the United States and Latin America, but it found that the practice is an anathema in some cultures. Asians, for example, are wary of strangers; as a result, Avon's sales representatives only stop at the homes of friends and relatives. Neighborhood parties sponsored by Avon are a modified promotional technique that seems to work well in Asia, and the technique has been tested in Germany as well. In France, the prohibition of door-to-door selling has compelled Avon to shift to direct-mail sales.

Personal selling must receive proper support in terms of training and information. Tokyo Toyopet has a training film it shows to its 1,200 door-to-door salesmen in how to handle objections and rejection.[7] The extremely high brand loyalty within the population makes it easy for a Toyota salesman to be welcome. The salesman can prepare an estimate of the trade-in value. By showing a well-made toy-size model of the new cars, he makes a showroom visit unnecessary. Since door-to-door selling is mainly used by sellers of inexpensive products, one may wonder about selling expensive products such as cars this way. Yet Tokyo Toyopet has been able to make a science out of the practice. The direct-selling strategy has worked well, and Tokyo Toyopet's sales have exceeded 70,000 units annually. For the country overall, door-to-door sales of new cars are a $26 billion business in Japan.

It is difficult for salespersons to be effective without advertising support. Advertising creates awareness and helps make customers more receptive. Tokyo Toyopet's advertising, for instance, does not take the form of direct-action advertising. Rather, it tells customers to be patient and to wait for one of the company's salesmen to call. Such advertisements are not product-oriented since the intent is to sell a company image. These advertisements are employed not to attract customers to the showroom but to aid in the salesmen's door-to-door sales activities.

Intercultural Negotiation

Successful negotiations require some understanding of each party's culture and may also require adoption of a negotiation strategy that is consistent with the other party's cultural system. One strategy is to rely on stereotyping. It is possible, for example, to use stereotyped preconceptions to identify the personality traits of negotiators from the different parts of China.[8] For example, the Northwestern and Eastern Mandarin, Gan, Minnan, and Huizhous peoples are considered business-minded. Whereas the Wu are supposedly adept at getting good deals, the Hakka are thought to be not so good at business. Whereas Southwestern Mandarin people are believed to be scheming, devious, and difficult to do business with, Northern Mandarin and Minnan peoples are supposed to be more cooperative. One may anticipate the Northwestern and Southwestern Mandarin peoples, and the Yue, Wu, Xiang, Gan, and Hakka to be stubborn, argumentative, and hot-tempered. On the other hand, the Northern and Eastern Mandarin peoples are thought to be at ease, content, and relatively unambitious, whereas the Wu and Minnan are more competitive, dynamic, and adventurous. Although stereotyping allows an easy label, it is also risky because generalization may lead one to believe that members of the group must share the same traits. These prejudices, if believed, may affect business negotiations and their outcomes.

A group of researchers observed 138 American, 54 Chinese, 42 Japanese, and 38 Korean businesspeople in a two-person, buyer-seller, intracultural-negotiation simulation. Negotiations between Americans involve the use of more problem-solving bargaining strategies that positively influenced negotiation outcomes. In negotiations between Chinese, better results were derived from more competitive strategies. In Japanese and Korean negotiations, buyers achieved higher economic rewards than sellers. In all four cultures, negotiators became more satisfied with negotiation outcomes if partners were rated more attractive.[9] Another laboratory simulation involved U.S., French, German, and British subjects. The American process of negotiation differs from that of the Europeans in several aspects. Negotiator characteristics play a key role in negotiations between French businesspeople, implying that sales representatives should be similar in background and personality to their French clients. Because German sellers appear to have dual goals of high individual profit and high buyer satisfaction, German negotiators need to make a trade-off between these two inversely related goals.[10]

International marketers are interested in the effects of cultural adaptation on intercultural communication. Compared to no adaptation as well as substantial adaptation, moderate adaptation was found to improve the adjudged attraction of the Japanese businesspeople. But a replication looking at American subjects' responses to Korean businesspeople's adaptive behaviors did not yield the same result.[11] Further studies should be conducted to identify conditions that make it desirable for businesspeople to adapt their behavior in response to the culture of the other party.

Motivation

Like other employees, salespeople need to be motivated. In many countries, Western firms find it difficult to retain and motivate salespeople.[12] The concept of individual recognition of sales representatives is at odds with Japan's team approach to business and its aversion to a compensation system that pays for performance. In Saudi Arabia, where selling is considered an undesirable occupation, qualified local sales representatives are hard to find because of a labor shortage. Because of India's various languages and social caste system, it is difficult for sales representatives to sell outside their own social level. In Brazil, the determination of sales force compensation and product pricing is affected by rampant inflation and national labor laws. It is thus a problem to pay someone less than the amount paid the previous year.

Based on a representative sample of the labor force in seven countries regarding what individuals seek from working, the two most dominant work goals are "interesting work" and "good pay," and these goals are consistent internationally, across different organizational levels, between the genders and among different age categories.[13] Although wage level has some explanatory value in predicting the compensation ratio, culture is a predominant factor that influences certain compensation patterns.[14]

Amway (Japan) Ltd., the subsidiary of privately held Amway Corp., is the corporation's top overseas affiliate as well as the ninth most profitable foreign company in Japan. Amway is able to bypass local retailers and wholesalers who often demand enormous markups. Amway does all its direct selling in homes through some 500,000 distributors (salespeople). Amway's cultlike corporate culture appeals to Japanese who prefer to identify strongly with their employers. As in the United States, Amway motivates salespeople by offering 30 percent commissions, bonuses, and trips abroad, and its pyramidal structure generously rewards distributors who bring new salespeople into their group. Distributors are attracted by the unusual brand of fraternal capitalism as much as potential earnings.[15]

Avon's joint venture with the Guangzhou Cosmetics Factory is the first foreign as well as Chinese company authorized to sell directly to Chinese consumers. Avon's concern about Chinese women's ability to understand the concept of direct sales quickly disappeared when local representatives told Avon to double the prices and sold one month's allocation of cosmetics in five days. Most representatives like the self-esteem, independence, and extra income (commissions).[16]

Telemarketing

Personal selling does not always require a face-to-face conversation. For instance, personal selling can be done over the telephone. Although telephone selling has been in existence for a considerable period of time, the growth of the direct-marketing field has pushed this method of selling to the forefront. This marketing practice, now known as **telemarketing,** has become very popular among sellers—but not necessarily with consumers, who feel they are being inundated with such calls. Because of the effective lobbying of telemarketing firms, U.S. lawmakers have been reluctant to pass laws, restricting the use of telemarketing. As part of the lobbying effort, the firms pointed out that legislators' own fund-raising efforts would be impeded by the proposed restrictions.

In overseas markets, telemarketing is not as far developed as it is in the United States. The limited availability of telephones for private households is one problem. The privacy laws are another obstacle. *Cold calling* (unsolicited sales calls) is receiving close scrutiny in the name of consumer protection and respect for privacy. A statutory cooling-off period may apply to sales closings over the telephone. In Finland, telemarketing is regarded as a form of door-to-door selling, and a consumer can cancel a purchase contract within seven days.[17] To avoid having a purchase contract nullified in Sweden, a seller must send a buyer a notice of consumer rights within three days of the purchase and must allow for a mandatory cooling-off period of one week. Germany is even more restrictive. It prohibits cold calls on the grounds of privacy invasion, and this ban even applies to an insurance salesperson's announcement of a visit. In Switzerland, Italy, Greece, the United Kingdom, France, Belgium, and the Netherlands, there is no specific legislation that restricts outbound telemarketing.

Expatriate Personnel

One controversial subject for which there is no definite solution is the nationality of the salespersons to be used in a market abroad. Some marketers argue for the use in a foreign market of *expatriate salespersons,* or those from the home country. Others take the opposite point of view by contending that the best policy is to use local nationals or those salespersons who were born in the host country. According to one study, the higher the interdependence between a branch office and headquarters, the more U.S. nationals are utilized in overseas operations to manage the inherent uncertainty.[18] However, though managerial behaviors are positively related to job performance for managers in the United States, they were not related to job performance for American expatriate managers in Hong Kong or job performance for Hong Kong Chinese managers (see Table 14–2).[19]

Expatriate salespersons are favorably viewed because they are already familiar with their company's product, technology, history, and policies. Thus the only kind of preparation they would need is a knowledge of the foreign market. Yet this may be the greatest obstacle for the expatriate salesperson. Whereas some may enjoy the challenge and adjustment, other expatriate personnel find it difficult to cope with a new and unfamiliar business environment. The failure to understand a foreign culture and its customs without question will hinder the effectiveness of an expatriate sales force. British managers, for instance, have difficulty in running retail stores in the highly competitive U.S. market, which is characterized by longer shopping hours and sizing differences. Learning from this experience, Sir Terence Conran decided to abandon his earlier practice of employing British managers and hired Americans for his top management team in running his new chain, Mothercare USA.[20]

Not only must an expatriate cope with new business conditions, but the expatriate's family must also share in the burden of making social adjustments. Life can be difficult both physically and psychologically for those who are unable to make necessary adjustments for an assignment that requires a lengthy relocation overseas. The expatriate may have second thoughts about accepting such an assignment, fearing that the distance from the headquarters may eliminate chances for promotion

TABLE 14–2 Significant differences between managerial behavior and job performance correlations for American managers in the United States and American expatriates in Hong Kong

Managerial Behaviors	American Managers in the United States	American Managers in Hong Kong	Level of Significant Difference
Representation	.19	.01	.10
Reconciliation	.33[a]	.10	.05
Tolerance for uncertainty	.13	.23	NS
Persuasiveness	.43[b]	.21	.05
Initiation of structure	.33[a]	.13	.10
Tolerance of freedom	.18	−.16	.01
Role assumption	.55[c]	.19	.01
Consideration	.46[b]	.19	.01
Production emphasis	.17	.19	NS
Predictive accuracy	.36[b]	.17	.10
Integration	.41[b]	.24[a]	NS
Superior orientation	.37[b]	.16	.05

[a] $p < .05$
[b] $p < .01$
[c] $p < .001$

Source: J. Stewart Black and Lyman W. Porter, "Managerial Behaviors and Job Performance: A Successful Manager in Los Angeles May Not Succeed in Hong Kong," *Journal of International Business Studies* 22 (no. 1, 1991): 109

or that the company may want to keep him or her abroad. Moreover, an overseas assignment may not be easy for American salespersons and their spouses because they may become frustrated with shopping, schooling, and the limited entertainment opportunities. Some may be driven by the boredom and frustration and may initiate an affair or begin to drink excessively. It is thus crucial that the personnel for overseas assignments be selected carefully. In fact, their families should also be interviewed to determine the suitability of their temperament for an overseas assignment. Tung has proposed a flowchart of the selection-decision process.[21] With regard to relevant variables or characteristics, Harvey provides a selection system for international candidates by examining their scores based on such variables as education/mental flexibility, communication skills, stability of marriage, adaptability of family, cultural empathy, language skills, curiosity and openness to uncertainty, openness to challenge, and absence of dogmatism.[22]

An examination of "the antecedents of spouse cross-cultural adjustment to interacting with host country nationals and to coping with the general, foreign environment" found spouse interaction adjustment to be positively related with firms that sought the spouse's opinion about the international assignment, the spouse's self-initiated predeparture training, and social support from family and host nations during the overseas assignment (see Table 14–3).[23]

Despite the problems associated with the use of expatriate personnel, local workers or the host country's own nationals may present another set of unique problems. Rather than having a multinational perspective, they may be more closely identified with their home country. They may also not possess an understanding of the headquarters' business cultures and objectives. Furthermore, they may be

TABLE 14–3 Multiple regression of spouse's general adjustment on antecedents

Variable	Beta	T
Anticipatory		
Previous experience	.05	.71
Pre-move visit	−.08	−1.11
Firm sought opinion	.16	2.29[a]
Favorableness of opinion	−.04	−.05
Firm-provided training	−.23	−3.18[b]
Self-initiated training	.10	1.42
In-Country		
Time in country	.02	.21
Social support (host-country national)	.03	.36
Family social support	.03	.39
Living conditions	.35	4.82[b]
Culture novelty	−.24	−3.24[b]

[a] $p < .05$
[b] $p < .01$
Adjusted $R^2 = .30$
$\quad F = 7.16 \ (p < .001)$

Source: J. Stewart Black and Hal B. Gregersen, "The Other Half of the Picture: Antecedents of Spouse Cross-Cultural Adjustment," *Journal of International Business Studies* 22 (no. 3, 1991): 473

geographically immobile in the sense that they may prefer staying in their own country rather than accepting a new position with more responsibilities abroad.

In all fairness, some disadvantages of using locals very likely apply to expatriates as well. More important is that these criticisms point out the problem of ethnocentrism. Companies that are truly multinational realize that good foreign personnel, though somewhat different in their thinking and approach, can be valuable and effective employees. Foreign personnel may also be able to provide knowledge and information that can be very valuable to American companies. Hewlett Packard is one example of an American multinational company that owes its success to the use of foreign personnel. Its European operations are run autonomously by Europeans. Local pools of technical expertise are tapped to develop products for worldwide distribution. New management ideas, such as flexible working hours and a program to introduce the company to school children, were first developed in West Germany before being adopted in the United States.

There are several advantages to be gained by an MNC in using foreign-born native personnel working in their own country. One advantage is that the company can avoid political, sensitive, or embarrassing situations. Since the government and the local community undoubtedly prefer that their own nationals be hired instead of outsiders, the MNC can avoid charges of exploitation while gaining goodwill at the same time. Visa's European organization has been staffed and directed by Europeans in an effort to dilute its image as an American company.

Another advantage to be gained is that the company can compete quite strongly for high-quality local personnel. An MNC can offer above-market pay, which may likely be still lower than the pay scale in the MNC's home market. This situation applies to Japan as well. The stigma associated with the Japanese working for foreign companies has recently been crumbling. In the past, the Japanese were reluctant to work for U.S. companies because they felt that it would be difficult to be promoted. They were also apprehensive about the role of politics within the organization. But younger Japanese are now more internationally oriented and are eager to join U.S. companies, since these workers resent the Japanese system of seniority, dedication, and loyalty.

When the host country's people are locally employed, expatriate relocation and travel expenses can be avoided. Tokyo is the world's most expensive city, and the costs of keeping expatriates there can be exorbitant. The rule of thumb with regard to the cost of keeping an American executive in Japan is based on the executive's salary plus at least $170,000 a year. One midlevel executive received a cost-of-living adjustment equal to half of his pay, plus $70,000 for house rent, $12,000 for a private school, $9,000 for an annual trip home, and $6,000 as a bonus for overseas duty. Since most additional compensation is taxable under the Japanese law, the company is forced to pay an additional one-third in taxes. The rent for a Western-style apartment jumped from $2,954 a month to $7,273 in just two years. The rent for an office is no less expensive: a 3,000-square-foot space costs $24,000 a month. Yet a company may have to wait a year for that space, unless a security deposit of $588,000 is provided to quicken the deal.[24]

The use of local personnel allows a company to proceed with its business more quickly since the adjustment period is eliminated. Language barriers and cultural difficulties are minimized. For example, it is difficult for an American salesperson to entertain his foreign clients without an understanding of the local culture. Without a knowledge of the local language, even simple or casual interaction such as telling a joke is a struggle. In Japan, a majority of business is conducted verbally in face-to-face interaction, whereas in the United States much greater emphasis is placed on correspondence and report preparation. Realizing that the American business culture is different, Ricoh uses American personnel to run its U.S. operations.[25] Furthermore, Ricoh recognizes that local nationals, being identified as part of the local scene, can be both efficient and effective since they have business and government contacts.

One answer to the question of the nationalities of personnel is that suitability can be determined in part by the distribution level. American salespersons can be used to contact overseas distributors, wholesalers, and large retailers. This international channel, however, is impractical at the consumer or local level. Most Japanese insurance companies and Avon, for example, use homemakers as part-time salespersons for door-to-door sales. American Family Life Assurance Company, likewise, uses no advertising in Japan but relies on a strong sales network and a full-time sales force selling group policies directly to companies.

When the personnel are examined in key positions and at headquarters, usually most American companies have only Americans. In a way, this is understandable because of the vast supply of local talent available to fill such positions. But some American MNCs are now realizing that a well-trained American may not be well-trained to work on a worldwide basis. American Standard has instilled a stronger global orientation into its corporate decision-making process by using foreign managers to run many of its important U.S. operations. For instance, eight of twenty-eight vice-presidential posts at headquarters are filled by foreign-born personnel. This practice makes such a company truly multinational, and that is an advantage over companies whose top management is of one nationality. Such heterogeneity provides a company with linguistic capabilities, exporting know-how, skills in negotiating with foreign governments, and an international flavor that many U.S. managers lack. The sales results for American Standard seem to support this conclusion. American Standard's international sales increased from 35 percent to 45 percent of its total revenues. More dramatically, the profit margins went from 0.8 percent to 4.8 percent.[26]

When local personnel are employed, an MNC must pay attention to the host country's labor laws. Such laws can temper the firm's decisions with regard to hiring and firing. This is especially true in socialist countries. China, for example, has become a hybrid of capitalism and socialism. The hiring rules there have been relaxed, making it possible for Chinese entrepreneurs to hire employees. MNCs, however, have to select employees from those sent to them by the state. The socialistic system, by guaranteeing jobs and security and by awarding bonuses equally among workers with no regard for performance, hampers efficient operations. As a result, workers are more concerned with a big bonus and not very interested in hard work. In any case, MNCs have recently gained more legal right to fire lazy or incompetent workers, though that right has not yet been extended to domestic enterprises. Nevertheless, MNCs should realize that a worker must be given many chances before that worker can be fired. In Indonesia, the normal practice is to engage employees for a three-month trial period, and firing is permissible during this period. A dismissal after the trial period may require the approval of the Department of Manpower, and this can prove to be a difficult undertaking. The procedure requires that the employee be given three written warnings prior to termination, but incompetence is not normally a valid reason for termination.[27] It is desirable to consider OECD's guidelines for employment and industrial relations.[28]

French law does not allow employers to restrict individual and collective liberties except when the restrictions are justified by the nature of the task to be accomplished and when the restrictions correspond proportionally to that end. Critics accused Walt Disney Co. of being insensitive to French culture, individualism, and privacy. The position of Euro Disneyland, in France, is that the appearance code is necessary to ensure product identification. Disney's rules require men's hair to be cut above the collar and ears; no beards and mustaches are allowed; tattoos must be covered. Women, in addition to wearing "appropriate undergarments," must have their hair in one "natural color" and can have only "limited use" of makeup. In addition, although the rules do not specifically require daily bathing, a video presentation for job applicants has a shower scene, and applicants are told that they are expected to show up for work "fresh and clean each day." The rules are in force also at Disney's amusement parks in the United States and Japan. Because of French individualism, Disney has relaxed its personal grooming code. Female employees may wear a brighter red nail polish than their counterparts in the United States. But Disney's facial hair policy still requires a clean-shaven, neat-and-tidy look.

PUBLICITY

The Nature of Publicity

Publicity is the nonpersonal stimulation of demand that is not paid for by a sponsor that has released news to the media. Advertising and publicity are quite similar in the sense that both require media for a nonpersonal presentation of the promotional message. One difference between the two is that with publicity a company has less control over how the message will be used by the media. Another difference is that publicity is presumed to be free in the sense that the media are not paid for the presentation of the message to the public. In practice, a publicity campaign is not cost free, because someone must be assigned to generate the publicity, and there are several direct and indirect costs. Still, the cost for publicity is minimal when compared to the benefit.

Publicity offers several advantages. In addition to the low cost, the material presented is not recognized as paid advertising *per se* because it appears in an editorial setting that makes it appear to have been generated by approval of the editorial staff. The material thus has more credibility, and consumers tend to accept it as news information rather than as advertising. This perception is particularly useful in countries where it is difficult to buy commercial time or advertising space.

Publicity should be used when a company advertises heavily, since advertising increases the likelihood that the media that have been used will reciprocate by using the company's news releases. Publicity is also effective when the editorial content can influence purchase, a point proven by Perrier. Publicity was the important part of Perrier's marketing program, because the company determined that it needed third-party endorsement by editors in news and lifestyle publications and broadcast media. Perrier therefore invited sixty editors and TV personnel to the mineral spring in France. The cost of $100,000 was more than offset by several positive articles that appeared later—which were worth several million dollars in publicity. Its other promotional vehicles were those associated with health and fitness, including marathons, road races, Perrier golfcourse openings attended by celebrities, and Louis Harris's *The Perrier Study: Fitness in America.*

There are several methods that can be used to gain publicity. Such methods include the following: contribution of prizes; sponsorship of civic activities; release of news about the company's product, plant, and personnel; and announcements of the company's promotional campaign, especially with regard to such sales promotion techniques as games and contests. Nike was able to overtake Adidas in the United States with effective publicity and sales promotion campaigns. In addition to asking athletes to help design shoes, Nike signed professional athletes to exclusive promotional contracts involving cash, free shoes, and promotion appearances. Shoes were given to top college teams, and the company gained additional exposure when these teams appeared on TV. Moreover, it sponsored running clinics, sporting events, and women's pro tennis events.

The Management of Publicity

Publicity is often viewed as a promotional component that is not possible to manage. News releases to the media may not be utilized by the media. If used, they may not be utilized in the manner intended. In reality, the problem is not so much that publicity cannot be managed but that publicity is usually managed in a haphazard way.

The Heinz company provides an example of how publicity should be managed. Heinz understands the need for good corporate citizenship, especially in nations once suspicious of Western economic influence. In China and Thailand, Heinz has worked closely with government officials and nutrition experts to give assurance that its presence is a benefit to the public health. In Zimbabwe, the Heinz Foundation and three other corporations donated over $200,000 to build and run a medical clinic. In addition, Heinz contributed $50,000 toward the construction of a hospital at the Kutama Mission.[29]

Proper management is required for all publicity campaigns. Every campaign must first have a well-defined objective. Without a precise objective, it is difficult to coordinate activities, and conflicting messages or items of little news value might be released. Confusion usually follows.

Much like the other three activities of promotion, the effectiveness of publicity must be measured. The effectiveness of publicity is not determined by the number of news releases or publication space and air time generated. Similar to advertising, personal selling, and sales promotion, the effectiveness of publicity should be measured by sales inquiries and changes in the attitude or response pattern of the public. Pepsi, a minor brand in Japan, wanted to become known as a major international brand. To achieve this objective, the company tied its promotion campaign to Michael

Jackson's thirteen concerts in Japan. Pepsi buyers could send proof-of-purchase seals to apply for tickets, jackets, T-shirts, and key chains. The publicity campaign went well, as evidenced by the high morale of the company's personnel as well as a 100 percent increase in summer sales.

A person responsible for a publicity campaign should keep the needs of the media in mind. Any request for information should be handled promptly because any requested information is likely to be used. In most countries, magazines have small editorial budgets and are understaffed. A publicity placement is more likely to be accepted if it is submitted in the form that is ready to be used. For example, photos and materials that are camera-ready relieve the publication of budget and time constraints.

Publicity is not a routine matter that can be held constant or managed in the same manner for all products and for all stages of a product's life cycle. The strategy developed for publicity changes with the various product life-cycle stages.[30] Press kits and news conferences are expensive and thus should be limited to the introductory stage, when they are most likely to gain attention. Routine news about personnel and the factory serve only as detractions and should be avoided for a new product. In the growth stage, items to be released to the media should concentrate on the past success of the product and its new useful applications. When the product reaches the maturity stage, the publicity effort should be held constant—not reduced. Any reduction should come only in the decline stage, when promotional expenditures in general are cut, and the reduction in publicity expenditures should be at the same rate as that of the overall promotional dollars.

Negative Publicity

Some publicity received can be far from being favorable. R. J. Reynolds encountered this problem in Japan when it had to disclose that its 16,000 cases of Winston Lights, used as samples, contained illegally high levels of the dicamba herbicide, higher than permitted by U.S. law. The poor publicity in quality-conscious Japan forced the company to call a press conference to allay fears of health hazards. Ajinomoto, a brand of monosodium glutamate, has been able throughout the company's history to dispel false rumors. A rumor was spread throughout Japan in the 1910s that Ajinomoto came from snakes. Another rumor, circulating in Islamic countries, was that Ajinomoto was processed from pig bones.[31]

No company wants negative publicity, but without the proper handling of publicity a situation may deteriorate. The adverse publicity generated by its powdered infant formula became a publicity nightmare for Nestlé. The company's idea of marketing a breast-milk substitute in LDCs to save babies from disease, malnutrition, and death backfired very badly. Church groups and consumer groups accused the company of promoting the product to those who could least afford it or were unable to use it properly. The poor handling of the animosity that developed engaged the company in a long and costly conflict.

Much has been learned from the Tylenol case, in which Johnson and Johnson was able to deal effectively with the contamination that occurred in its capsules. Marketers should carefully review how Johnson and Johnson was able to turn the negative publicity around and how it was able to regain sympathy and trust. Based on these experiences, there are several "do's" and "don'ts" that should be kept in mind.[32]

To begin, it is not wise to criticize the media for reporting unfavorable news. The criticism serves to alienate the media by inflaming the issue and prolonging the attention being given to it. It is also not wise to ignore adverse publicity. This behavior may give the impression of arrogance, and it wastes critical time that could be used to solve the problem if the problem is serious. A company should also avoid the "no comment" response because it conveys the impression of uncooperativeness and it implies guilt. If a full disclosure is not possible for security reasons, the company's spokesperson should say so and ask for understanding from the media.

When preparing to respond to inquiries about a newsworthy event, it is critical to review the facts, prepare news reports, and perhaps seek professional assistance. Personnel should be immediately organized to handle inquiries from consumers and reporters. Even when the problem is still unclear, contingency plans should be devised so that personnel can be put into action quickly. In fact, there should be a contingency crisis management plan that forces executives to think in advance about how to deal with unforeseen crises. According to one survey, 47 percent of firms surveyed do have some type of crisis communication plan in place.[33] In a more recent survey of 190 of 1,500 largest industrial and service firms in the United States, the percentage rose to 57%. Their plans covered such events as industrial accidents, natural disasters, merger and takeovers, and environmental problems.[34]

Those companies facing the greatest levels of industrial and environmental risk are more likely than others to have crisis communication plans. Such companies include those in the extractive industries and food and drug manufacturers. It is thus surprising that, given the nature of the business, Union Carbide failed to anticipate potential problems that could have occurred. As a result, the company was severely criticized for its handling of the devastating Bhopal (India) gas leak. Many inquiries in the early stages went unanswered, and at times the company appeared evasive when it did issue a response.

In dealing with the media, candor, preparedness, speed, and cooperation are all essential. If a company's guilt is undeniable, it is better to admit it at the outset so that attention can be shifted to the steps being taken to resolve the situation. Although a team effort is likely taking place, it is highly desirable that a top executive acts as the company's sole spokesperson so that inconsistencies can be minimized. The executive should be prepared to communicate quickly and professionally. He or she must possess accurate information and be ready to answer all questions. Since the media are eager to receive information, they can and should be accommodated, as well as exploited. The company can call news conferences that allow it to relay the information to the public through the media at no cost. At such conferences, the spokesperson can outline the steps being taken to protect the public interest. In effect, this tactic provides the company with free advertising and positive publicity.

If the product has serious potential ramifications, corporate image advertising can be used to reinforce the trustworthiness of the company and product. Marketing research can be valuable in tracking the public mood so that appropriate communication strategies can be adopted. Exhibit 14–3 shows how South Africa attempted to use advertising to deal with its country's negative image and bad publicity.

South Africa

Houses for sale: $16 000 and less

Imagine buying a four-roomed, State-built house for as little as $880. Or a five-roomed house for between $2 331 and $16 000. It's happening right now – in South Africa.

SHARING A BETTER QUALITY OF LIFE

South Africa is involved in a remarkable process of providing fair opportunities for all its population groups. The South African Government is committed to ensure that each of South Africa's many nationalities have the ability and resources to realize their social, economic and political aspirations.

Housing is a leading example of South Africa's development process. And as an integrated part of its drive towards home ownership for everyone, the South African Government has given the go-ahead for the sale of 500 000 State-financed homes at discounts of up to 40 % of their market value.

MEETING THE HOUSING CHALLENGE

South Africa's urban Black population is expected to rise from 9 million currently to around 20 million by the turn of the century. It is estimated that an additional 4.9 million housing units will have to be provided to accommodate this phenomenal urbanisation.

The housing challenge is being met by both the Government and the private sector. Government initiatives are directed mainly towards providing the machinery and support for self-help building projects, while private enterprise provides loans, subsidies and guarantees.

THE FUTURE – BETTER PROSPECTS FOR ALL

A recent survey indicated that 82 % of all employers were prepared to provide their Black staff with assistance to buy their own homes.

The facts on housing present only part of the picture. Many aspects of South African life have changed – and are changing at an ever-increasing rate. The future is exciting because we have the people, the dedication and a buoyant economy to enable us to keep on providing opportunities and improving the quality of life of all our people.

Because South Africa is a microcosm of so many of the world's sensitivities, it is often a contentious subject. If you are faced with a decision regarding South Africa, make sure you have all the facts.

For more information, simply complete the coupon below.

To: The Minister (Information),
The South African Embassy,
3051 Massachusetts Avenue,
Washington D.C., 20008 N.W.
Please send me more information on socio-economic and political developments in South Africa.

Name ....
Address ....
......................................Code ....

We're looking forward to the future.

DHiBern & Company 200422/USA/Rev

EXHIBIT 14–3   Management of negative publicity

Source: Reprinted with permission of the South African Consulate General, Washington, D.C.

The company should also be decisive. Its decision should be based on the public good rather than cost as an overriding motive. If product recall is warranted because a situation is potentially dangerous to the public, then recall should proceed immediately. A company should avoid vacillation or hedging. Procter and Gamble poorly handled a problem of contaminated cake mixes in California by making contradictory announcements about the product's recall. Jewel Foods' problem worsened because it delayed a recall of contaminated milk in Chicago. A decisive response does not mean, however, that product recall is always the preferred strategy. Gerber Foods took legal action against those states that wanted its baby food taken off the shelf because of broken glass found in some jars. The company's rationale was that the incident was an isolated one not related to its normal manufacturing process and that any recall would unduly alarm the public. Its position was subsequently supported by the results of an investigation.

SALES PROMOTION

The Nature of Sales Promotion

Sales promotion consists of those promotional activities other than advertising, personal selling, and publicity. As such, any promotional activities that do not fall under the other three activities of the promotion mix are considered sales promotion. Qantas, for example, offers its passengers Connection Cards that could be used to purchase London Fog coats wholesale. The trade often uses the term indiscriminately. Businesspersons may use the term *promotion* when they actually mean "sales promotion." In this book *promotion* is a broad term that encompasses sales promotion as well as the other three promotional activities.

The techniques of sales promotion are varied and numerous. The common ones used are coupons, sweepstakes, games, contests, price-offs, demonstrations, premiums, samples, money refund offers, and trading stamps. A combination of these can be used and sometimes is used in the same campaign. When Kelloggs expanded its business abroad, it had to enlighten consumers in South and Central America, the Middle East, and Asia about dry cereal and cold breakfasts. To instill this new eating habit, Kelloggs used samples and demonstrations in conjunction with a heavy advertising campaign. To regain market share in Japan, Procter and Gamble distributed 1.5 million diaper samples of improved Pampers. Each diaper box also had a picture of a little bear. Parents could get baby items by saving the required number of bears.

Coca-Cola and Pepsi provide a good illustration of how to use sales promotion to stimulate demand.[35] In Taiwan, Coca-Cola provided American coaches to conduct baseball and basketball seminars and sponsored concerts by pop artists such as Stevie Wonder. The company even asked the chef of the Taipei Hilton to create Chinese dishes using Coke (e.g., fried frog legs in a Coke-and-garlic sauce, braised spareribs in Coke and ketchup). In Asia, Coca-Cola gave beverage carts free of charge to small business owners on the condition that they sell only Coke products. Whereas Coca-Cola sponsored Chinese youth soccer, Pepsi supported international badminton championships and gave out Pepsi umbrellas to the Canton police. Pepsi-Cola (Thai) Trading Ltd. used comic books for children and sweepstakes to promote Mirinda and Mountain Dew. A child could exchange two bottle caps plus five baht for a comic book. The book had an entry form for the sweepstakes.

Sales promotion is temporary in nature. Not being self-sustaining, its function is to supplement advertising, personal selling, and publicity. To launch Budweiser beer in Great Britain, Anheuser-Busch employed the "American" theme. Its TV commercials on the 4th of July and Thanksgiving day were spots filmed in California with

American actors. To supplement its advertising effort, the company used a variety of sales-promotion techniques. It made posters, bunting, flags, pennants, T-shirts, and sweatshirts available to pubs and discos for promotional parties. Bud ashtrays, bar towels, coasters, football pennants, and similar items were offered for sale. Moreover, American disc jockeys were brought in to program American music nights.

Sales promotion is not restricted to the stimulation of demand at the consumer level. It may be used to gain middlemen's support as well. Moreover, the use of sales promotion is not limited to consumer products. It can be used with industrial selling too. Misawa Homes promoted its House 55 by sending samples to U.S. Homes and West Germany's Okal. Pfizer, like other drug firms, attracts drug wholesalers by sponsoring trips and other events. Gifts are given to doctors, and doctors' wives are taken on shopping tours.

The popularity of sales promotion has grown steadily both in the United States and overseas. A survey of executives conducted by *Stimulus,* Canada's leading advertising journal, revealed a shift from media advertising to sales promotion. Compared with five years ago, three of five firms had moved to spend more of their advertising budget on such nonmedia alternatives as trade shows, point-of-purchase displays, and publicity.[36] According to a POPAI (Point-of-Purchase Advertising Institute) and Du Pont study of shopping behavior in the United States, almost 70 percent of all non-food purchases in supermarkets are generated by in-store decisions. If the same decision-making pattern is prevalent outside the United States, sales promotion should prove to be just as indispensable.

Sales promotion is effective when a product is first introduced to a market. It also works well with existing products that are highly competitive and standardized, especially when they are of low unit value and have high turnover. Under such conditions, sales promotion is needed to gain that "extra" competitive advantage. A Japanese firm created a great deal of excitement in Thailand by including game cards in its detergent boxes, and consumers could not resist buying more and more in search of the winning cards. Likewise, most gas stations in Thailand at one time gave free washcloths with a gas fill-up. In Brazil, electrical products are treated as commodities, and Philips wanted to make electricians aware of its brand. Toward this objective, the company offered a free course, with a certificate and a tool kit as premiums. The course consisted of four lessons that had a great number of illustrations to accommodate the low literacy. The company's problem was the lack of a list of electricians, and there was also no vertical (trade) magazine such as *Electrician Today* for this purpose. Philips devised a list-builder program to get names for future contact by having a "take one" display in electrician shops. Since the course was too costly for an untargeted audience, the company qualified respondents by occupation. Middlemen were also allowed to participate in the sales-promotion program. Stores were informed of the display, and their salespeople or sales clerks were made aware of the program and benefits and asked to take the course, too.[37]

The effectiveness of sales promotion can be tempered by psychological barriers, and this fact is applicable to middlemen as well as consumers. Some foreign retailers are reluctant to accept manufacturers' coupons because they fear that they will not be reimbursed. Consumers, on the other hand, may review rebates, mail-in coupons, and money-back guarantees with suspicion, thinking that something must be wrong with the product.

International marketers need to confirm the validity of a statement concerning the effectiveness of a sales promotion technique. Sometimes, casual observation and hearsay have a way of making a particular claim become a statement of fact without support of empirical evidence. Such is the case with Hispanics' resistance to coupon use.[38] It is difficult to collect valid data on coupon use among Hispanics because for them the word *coupon (cupón)* is commonly associated with food stamps *(cupónes de alimentos)* or government handouts. Respondents' perception that coupons are not accepted by stores was the most frequently given reason for not using the coupons (see Table 14–4). The results did not support the hypothesis that Hispanic cultural values are incompatible with coupon use. When a cultural explanation for the lack of coupon use among Hispanic consumers becomes part of the folklore among marketing practitioners, it may become a self-fulfilling prophecy.

Much like many other marketing aspects, sales promotion methods may have to be modified. The techniques employed, to be effective, should be consistent with local preferences. Philips offered a set of dominoes as a premium in Brazil, where the

TABLE 14–4 Reasons that Puerto Rican residents gave for not using cents-off coupons

Reason[a]	Frequency	Relative Frequency[b] (percent)
Not accepted by stores	38	22.4
Lack of interest	30	17.6
Forget to bring them to store	19	11.1
Do not have the time	15	8.8
Little availability of coupons	15	8.8
It takes too much work	12	7.1
Do not know how to use coupons	9	5.3
Do not know that coupons can be used in Puerto Rico	9	5.3
Savings are too small	7	4.1
Cashiers do not know how to handle coupons	7	4.1
Consumer believes coupons must be mailed to United States for redemption	7	4.1
Coupons do not receive adequate promotion	6	3.5
Afraid of being embarrassed	6	3.5
Do not know which stores accept coupons	5	2.9
Short expiration dates	4	2.3
People do not use them	4	2.3
Coupons are printed in English	3	1.8

[a] No reasons are presented that were given less than three times.

[b] The relative frequency was calculated by dividing each frequency by the number of respondents who did not use coupons (170).

Source: Sigfredo A. Hernandez, "An Exploratory Study of Coupon Use in Puerto Rico: Cultural vs. Institutional Barriers to Coupon Use," *Journal of Advertising Research* 28 (October/November 1988): 42

game is the national pastime. A player holds the colored side up to prevent an opponent from seeing the dotted numbers side. Since the company's name was on the back of every domino, electricians were often reminded of the brand.[39]

Restrictions

Although sales promotion is generally received enthusiastically in LDCs, the activity is still largely underutilized, which may be due more to legal barriers than psychological barriers. European countries have a larger number of restrictions than the United States in this area. The legal requirements are so diverse that the European Association of Advertising Agencies (EAAA) decided that the standardization of promotion regulations was very unlikely in the near future.

Since it would be impossible to know the specific laws of each and every country, marketers should consult local lawyers and authorities before launching a promotional campaign. For example, Belgium requires a government tax stamp on window signs. The purpose of this section is to show how certain sales promotional tools might be affected by local regulations.

Premiums and Gifts   Most European countries have a limit on the value of the premium given. Colgate was sued by a local blade manufacturer in Greece for giving away razor blades with shaving cream. Austria considered premiums to be a form of discriminatory treatment toward buyers. In France, it is illegal to offer premiums that are conditional on the purchase of another product. In Finland, premiums are allowed as long as the word *free* is not used with them. A gift is usually subject to the same restriction as a premium. When Radio Shack duplicated its U.S. strategy by giving away flashlights, the company found itself in violation of Germany's sales law regarding premiums and gifts. Compared to the United States and the United Kingdom, which are very lenient, Belgium, Germany, and Scandinavia have strict laws concerning promotion owing to their desire to protect consumers from being distracted from the true value of a given product or service. Argentina, Austria, Norway, and Venezuela virtually ban the use of merchandise premiums. Other countries, being less restrictive, do not permit the value of the premiums to exceed more than a certain percent (e.g., 10 percent in Japan) of the value of a product that must be purchased so as to receive a premium.[40]

Price Reductions, Discounts, and Sales   Austria has a discount law prohibiting cash reductions that give preferential treatment to different groups of customers. Discounts in Scandinavia are also restricted. In France, it is illegal to sell a product for less than its cost. In Germany, marketers must notify authorities in advance if they plan to have a sale. Unlike in the United States, where there are all kinds of sales for all occasions (e.g., manager's sale, assistant manager's sale, buyer's sale, etc.), a sale in Germany is limited to such events as going out of business, giving up a particular product line, end of January (winter), end of July (summer), and a twenty-fifth anniversary. Both Austria and Germany are similar in the sense that special sales may be made only under certain circumstances or during specified periods of time (seasonal sales). Moreover, discounts for payment on delivery may not exceed 3 percent, and any quantity discounts must be within the applicable industry's usual numerical range.[41]

Samples   Germany restricts door-to-door free samples that limit population coverage as well as the size of the sample pack. The United States does not allow alcoholic beer to be offered as a free sample, and this law also holds for taste tests.

Sweepstakes, Games, and Contests   In Scandinavia, sweepstakes are illegal, and an ombudsman monitors for such activity.[42] In tightly regulated Germany, sweepstakes are legal as long as the sweepstakes promotion is separate from the order form. In Italy, the rule is reversed. Consumers can participate in a sweepstakes only if they order the product.

In the United States for a sweepstakes, game, or contest not to become an illegal lottery, a company must make certain that at least one of the three elements—chance, consideration, and price—is missing. Also, a state government's prior approval may be required. Florida, for example, requires advertisers to register the rules of a contest and prizes at least thirty days before launching the campaign. Without approval from the state's licensing division, the contest is termed an unlicensed lottery. British Airways promoted a sweepstakes but failed to notify the state that it would give away plane tickets and prizes. Consequently, Florida fined the company $2,000 and threatened prohibition of the "go for it America" campaign in that state.[43]

OVERSEAS PRODUCT EXHIBITIONS

One type of sales promotion that can be highly effective is the exhibition of a product overseas. This type of promotion may be very important because regular advertising and sales letters and brochures may not be adequate. For certain products, quality can be judged only by physical examination, and product exhibition can facilitate this process.

One very effective way to exhibit products abroad is to use trade fairs. Unlike trade shows in the United States, where the social or party atmosphere is prevalent, European trade fairs are an important part of the marketing mix that must be prepared with great care. These shows can account for one-third of a European firm's marketing budget.[44]

There are two main types of trade shows: *horizontal* and *vertical*. At one end of the spectrum are broad, well-established, annual affairs (horizontal trade shows). The Hamburg Fair, for instance, exhibits almost everything in both consumer and industrial goods. At the other end of the spectrum are specialized types for products in specialized industries (vertical trade shows). Electronica, annually held in Munich, is a vertical trade show.

There are more than 800 international trade fairs each year. *Business America* has an annual listing of international trade fairs where U.S. products can be exhibited. The listing is organized by country and includes date and name.

Misawa Homes promotes its prefabricated homes by displaying the technology at trade shows in Switzerland and the United States. Ecrevisse Acadienne exhibited its Louisiana crayfish (crawfish) at a huge international food show in France by serving it with champagne to more than 800 importers, chefs, and supermarkets. The food show was such a success that the company received firm requests for prices and shipping dates from France, the Netherlands, Sweden, and Italy.[45]

Trade fairs allow thousands of firms from many countries to setup "temporary stores or offices" right in the marketplace to display their products. A strong feature of a trade fair is that prospects are in a buying mood. Another advantage is that buyers are seeking out sellers at a central location. Obviously, a trade show presents a much easier contract situation for a salesperson because there is no travel to many diverse locations to call on potential buyers.

An exhibitor should investigate whether it is worthwhile to use a carnet for products that will be shipped or taken to the exhibition. A **carnet** is an international customs document that facilitates the temporary duty-free importation of product samples in lieu of the usual customs documents required to bring merchandise into several major trading countries. That is, a carnet is a series of vouchers listing the goods and countries involved where the product will be exhibited. For a fee based on the value of the goods to be covered, a carnet can be purchased in advance in the United States by American firms. Foreign firms can turn to their local carnet associations, which are members of the International Bureau of the Paris-based International Chamber of Commerce. By issuing carnets, these associations in effect guarantee the payment of duties that may become due on goods temporarily imported and not reexported. "A bond, letter of credit, or bank guaranty of 40% of the value of the goods is also required to cover duties and taxes that would be due if goods were not reexported and duties not paid by the carnet holder."[46]

There are several kinds of carnets. Some of these interrelated customs conventions are conventions on the (1) Temporary Importation of Professional Equipment, (2) Temporary Importation of Containers, and (3) Transport International Routier (TIR) Carnet for the International Transport of Goods. The TIR convention makes TIR carnets available so that exporters' road shipments to an interior destination will not be subject to payment or deposit of duties en route.

The other important conventions are the ECS Carnet for Commercial Samples and the ATA Carnet for Temporary Admission of Goods. ECS is derived from a combination of the French and English words *Echantillons Commerciaux/Commercial Samples;* ATA stands for a combination of the French and English words *Admission Temporaire/Temporary Admission,* and this convention provides for the recognition of carnets for temporary admission of virtually any type of goods.

At one time, the United States adhered to all five customs conventions. Since the ATA carnet is more comprehensive than the ECS Carnet, the ATA carnet has replaced the latter.[47] The United States allows ATA carnets to cover professional equipment, commercial samples, and advertising material. ATA carnets can be used in the following countries: Australia, Austria, Belgium, Bulgaria, Canada, Cyprus, Czechoslovakia, Denmark, Finland, France, Germany, Greece, Hong Kong, Hungary, Iceland, Iran, Ireland, Israel, Italy, Ivory Coast, Japan, Korea, Luxembourg, the Netherlands, New Zealand, Norway, Poland, Portugal, Romania, Senegal, South Africa, Spain, Sweden, Switzerland, Turkey, the United Kingdom, the United States, and former Yugoslavia.

Overseas exhibits are a costly form of promotion. There are costs related to the design and construction of a booth. There are also the transportation costs of the booth and products for display. Labor is required for setting up and later dismantling the booth. In addition to the rental costs of space and furniture, other costs include staffing and the transportation and accommodation of representatives.

There are a few suggestions that exhibitors at trade fairs should keep in mind. Space cost is only a small portion of the total cost. It is thus better to rent adequate space, since overcrowding discourages prospects from visiting the exhibit. Exhibit contents should be kept simple, and only the most important items should be displayed. To avoid having to set up the booth late and dismantle it early, a company may want to locate its booth away from the freight entrance area. Mailing lists of prospects should be obtained, and letters should be sent to them before the opening day. It is also important to have a qualified representative at the booth who can make sales decisions. This representative should arrive early and leave late. Early arrival also gives the representative time to become acclimated. Plenty of business cards and brochures should be kept on hand. Finally, the local traffic patterns should be taken into account. Unlike in the United States, where people are used to turning right and walking on the righthand side, many countries drive on the left side of the street and people thus walk on the left side of an aisle. An exhibitor may gain an advantage if it locates the exhibit on the left side of an aisle, since the visitors will traffic on that side.[48]

An exhibitor should notice and respect cultural differences in dress formality and the exchange of business cards. Trade shows overseas are serious affairs, and only businesspeople and buyers (not the general public) are admitted. Because most buyers want time to think about products, some serious follow-up after the show should be carried out. It may be worthwhile to spend a few extra days making calls on the most promising prospects. Later, the exhibitor should send letters with additional material or have a local representative call the visitors who stopped at the booth.[49]

A trade fair is not the only means of exhibiting products overseas. Companies can also rent space in trade centers to display merchandise on a more permanent basis. Vienna (Austria) and Taipei (Taiwan) are examples of two such trade centers located in two different parts of the world (see Exhibit 14–4).

Harrod's, a London retailer, often takes an unusual marketing approach. It sent the store to overseas consumers. Boats carrying crystal have been sent to New York and other major cities. Another of its unconventional tactics is to provide a trans-Atlantic 800 number (toll-free number) for telephone orders.[50] Its full-page advertisement in the Sunday *New York Times* offering three cashmere sales items brought Harrod's 2,500 U.S. orders totaling more than $300,000 in sales. These orders were more than enough to pay for the telephone cost of $30,000.

PROGRAMS SPONSORED BY THE U.S. DEPARTMENT OF COMMERCE

Because of the high cost of overseas exhibition, exporters should consult with the U.S. Department of Commerce (DOC). The Department can provide them with a number of valuable services and information. Table 14–5 lists these services, some of which are related to overseas promotion.

Exporters should select only those trade fairs that have the best potential. They should determine whether the Department of Commerce sponsors official U.S. participation in certain major international exhibitions.[51] The Department of Commerce

EXHIBIT 14–4 Trade center

Source: Courtesy of Far East Trade Service Inc.

TABLE 14-5 Services and information available from the U.S. Department of Commerce (DOC)

DOC Service	Potential Markets	Market Research	Direct Sales Leads	Agents and Distributors	Export Counseling	Export-Import Regulations	Overseas Contract Opportunities	Marketing Plans
Foreign Trade Statistics	X	X						
Global Market Surveys	X	X						
Market Share Reports	X	X						
Foreign Economic Trends	X	X						
Commercial Exhibitions	X	X	X	X				
Overseas Business Reports	X	X						
Overseas Private Investment Corp.		X						
New Product Information Services			X	X				
Trade Opportunities Program			X	X			X	
Export Contact List Services			X	X				
Agent/Distributor Service				X				
U.S. Commercial Service	X	X			X	X		
ITA Business Counseling	X	X			X	X		
Export Seminars					X			
U.S. Foreign Commercial Service	X	X	X	X	X	X	X	
International Economic Indicators	X	X						
Country Market Sectoral Surveys	X	X						
Office of Country Marketing	X	X	X	X		X	X	X
East-West Trade	X	X				X		X
Office of Export Administration					X	X		
Small Business Administration					X	X		X
Major Projects Overseas							X	
Worldwide Information and Trade System	X	X	X	X			X	
Product Marketing Service	X	X	X	X				

Source: Erik Wiklund, *International Marketing: Making Exports Pay Off* (New York: McGraw-Hill, 1986), 204. Reprinted with permission of McGraw-Hill Book Company

routinely arranges for *special solo exhibitions* of American products with good sales potential when suitable trade fairs are not available. A moderate participation contribution entitles a company to a full range of promotional and display assistance. Another kind of assistance is the trade mission. The Department of Commerce, for example, may send a boat full of merchandise to an overseas port. For example, one trip to Japan with a boat full of fresh produce and meat was quite a success.

An alternative to trade fairs is to use *U.S. Trade Center Exhibitions,* which are commercial showrooms operated by the U.S. government in major markets with high potential. Such showrooms can be found in Frankfort, London, Mexico City, Milan, Paris, Tokyo, Singapore, Sydney, Stockholm, Taipei, and even Moscow and Warsaw.

Several major product exhibitions are held annually at each center. A particular product theme is often used to reach an audience identified by marketing research. The immediate sales can run as high as $1 million with potential follow-up sales of $20 million over the first year. There are also technical seminars, often held in conjunction with exhibits that stimulate interest and sales further.

The Department of Commerce's Trade Center staff provides a number of services. A promotion campaign is conducted prior to exhibition. News announcements are released to selected media. Prospective customers, agents, and distributors are identified and contacted by either direct mail or personal calls. In addition to the design and construction of the exhibit, the Trade Center provides exhibit space, utilities, housekeeping services, hospitality, and lounge or meeting rooms for exhibitor-customer conferences. In return, the U.S. company makes a specified participation contribution and agrees to provide products, technical and promotional handout literature, and a qualified representative available at the booth.

U.S. firms can also test interest and locate agents or distributors by *catalog and video exhibitions* sponsored by the Department of Commerce and Foreign Service. Such exhibitions are held extensively in developing markets where opportunities for product exhibitions are more limited, and they allow for the presentation of U.S. product catalogs, sales literature, video tapes, and other graphic sales aids at American Embassies and Consulates.

Based on the belief that foreign sales of U.S. consumer products are best developed through *in-store promotion,* these DOC-sponsored events are designed to promote sales of consumer merchandise directly to consumers in major department stores and mail order houses from Finland to Hong Kong.

American exporters should investigate several other programs offered by the Department of Commerce. One is the "foreign buyer program." This program informs U.S. firms about foreign buyers visiting the United States. Appointments and plant visits can thus be scheduled. Another program is "products marketing service." This service is designed for small exporters who while traveling abroad need a temporary base of operations. The Department of Commerce's U.S. Export Development Offices can, for a modest fee, locate interpreters and secretaries, schedule appointments with prospects, and offer other helpful advice.

For companies with new products, the "new product information service" (NPIS) is very valuable.[52] This free export promotion service provides worldwide publicity by publishing short descriptions of new products in booklet form for distribution by the Department of Commerce's Foreign Commercial Service posts abroad. NPIS information is also disseminated through *Commercial News USA* monthly magazine and Voice of America radio broadcasts. This exposure enables foreign firms to be aware of new U.S. products, and it encourages contacts and sales. To qualify for this service, a genuinely new U.S. product must not have been sold in the United States for more than two years and must not have been exported to more than three countries on a regular basis.

CONCLUSION

A product, no matter how superior it is, should not be expected to sell itself. It must be promoted so that prospects can learn about the benefits provided by the product. The state of Pennsylvania, for example, had only one overseas office before 1980 but now has several to promote its exports. The state of Ohio has determined that, for each $1 spent to promote its exports, it derives $260 in export sales.

A product can be promoted in several ways—advertising, personal selling, publicity, and sales promotion. Although advertising is the most prominent technique, the other three methods are no less important. For promotion to be most effective, however, all four of the promotional techniques should be used and coordinated.

Personal selling usually commands the largest portion of the promotional expenditures. It is used internationally as well as locally at every distribution level and for all kinds of products. When expatriate sales personnel are to be employed, these personnel and their families should be screened for suitability before being given overseas assignments. For a variety of good reasons, qualified local nationals should be used whenever possible. If MNCs do not hire these qualified individuals, local progressive competitors are likely to quickly employ them.

With limited media time and space available in many countries, it is necessary to develop some rapport with media people in order to try to gain free publicity. Finally, the efforts in advertising, personal selling, and publicity activities should be supplemented and supported by sales promotion.

Two chapters are devoted to a discussion of the various aspects of promotion. This chapter has concentrated on the treatment of personal selling, publicity, and sales promotion. The next chapter is primarily concerned with international advertising.

QUESTIONS

1. Explain how personal selling overseas may differ from how it is used in the United States.
2. What are the requirements of a good publicity program?
3. What is a carnet?
4. What are the sponsored programs of the U.S. Department of Commerce that help U.S. manufacturers in exhibiting their products abroad?
5. Explain why standard sales promotion tools (e.g., premium, coupon) may not be applicable or effective abroad.

DISCUSSION ASSIGNMENTS AND MINICASES

1. Compare domestic communication with international communication. Explain why "noise" is more likely to occur in the case of international communication process in all five stages (source, encoding, information, decoding, and receiver).

2. Why is telemarketing not as widely used outside the United States?

3. Should expatriate personnel be used? What are some of the difficulties that they may encounter overseas? What can be done to minimize these problems?

CASE 14–1
CLUB MED

Phuket is an island in the southern part of Thailand. World-renowned for its beauty, the island attracts a large number of foreign tourists every year. A major resort operator there is Holiday Villages (Thailand) Corp., which operates Club Med Phuket. The resort has received a special investment status from Thailand's Board of Investment (BOI), making it eligible for governmental assistance and tax credits. Thai citizens as well as foreigners serve on the company's board of directors. Club Med Phuket began operation at the end of 1985.

Club Med's customers are primarily French and Japanese tourists who purchase the tour package abroad. Usually, customers pay a membership fee of approximately $15 for the first year and approximately $7.50 annually after the first year. In addition, customers are responsible for the expenses, which range from $112 a day per person in the peak traveling season to $77 a day during the regular season and $73 a day during the off season. On average, a typical customer spends about a week in Thailand—one to two days in Bangkok and the rest at Club Med Phuket.

In July of 1987, *Prachachat Business,* a financial newspaper, ran a story questioning the motives and business policies of Club Med Phuket. A former employee accused the company of being concerned only with profits, as well as of exploiting local labor.

It was also alleged that the company's foreign directors had adopted a policy of protecting the company's interests by not sharing the business available with other local and nearby firms. To achieve this objective, Club Med operates its own souvenir boutique and other service facilities in order to keep its customers from doing any shopping outside the resort. The company even goes so far as to coerce customers into using the dining facilities within Club Med.

According to the former employee, Club Med Phuket has now gone a step further in its pursuit of maximum profit by setting up its own tour operation. Wakong Siam Co., with an office at the Peninsula Plaza, has been created solely for the purpose of arranging tours for Club Med. Previously, the function was assigned to and performed by General Siam Co. However, Wakong made plans and began taking over that part of the operation in October. The result of this takeover is that Club Med is now able to control the employment of tour guides as well as the contracts with retailers and other service establishments. Those in the travel industry comment that the action amounts to an exploitation because the travel revenues generated are not shared with outsiders. When the income generated ends up in the hands of and is controlled by foreigners, it is like extracting local wealth and sending it overseas.

The charge of labor exploitation was based on the former employee's opinion that the salary for Thai employees was grossly inadequate. Club Med was alleged to take advantage of Thai personnel. For instance, a G.O. (Gentle Organizer) is paid an initial monthly salary of only $115. To make matters worse, the employee's employment period is for only three to six months without any written contract or guarantee of long-term employment. In the case in which the G.O. has completed an eighteen-month employment, the salary is increased to $270. This pay is still relatively low when compared with what a G.O. in other countries receives. In Malaysia and Singapore, those in the same employment capacity receive $385–460 per month.

The newspaper ended the article by implying that Club Med was in Thailand only to make money for expatriation.

Questions

1. Should Club Med ignore the negative publicity?
2. If not, how should Club Med respond to these charges?

CASE 14–2
THE INFANT FORMULA ISSUE
Nestlé Coordination Center for Nutrition, Inc.

The decade-long controversy surrounding the marketing of infant formula in developing countries ended formally on January 26, 1984, when Nestlé and several organizations concerned in the controversy announced that they had reached an agreement on interpretation of the World Health Organization Recommended Code of Marketing of Breastmilk Substitutes.

Media reports regarding the resolution of the controversy tended to oversimplify the realities of the very real health problems in developing countries and the company's efforts to implement the Code.

In order to understand what is happening in the present and the process involved in implementing the WHO Code, it is helpful to consider the circumstances and events leading to the adoption of the first international marketing guidelines.

Background

Henri Nestlé developed a milk-based infant food more than one hundred years ago to save the life of an infant who could not be breastfed, and Nestlé infant formula has been used to save lives ever since. It has been used by many major relief organizations, including the International Red Cross, to save the lives of thousands of starving infants, for example, in refugee camp situations and, recently, to assist in the crisis in Lebanon. No one has ever disputed the quality of Nestlé's infant formula.

If infant formulas did not exist, mothers would do what they did for centuries — and still do where infant formula is not available: use less nutritious local substitutes. A Third World mother considering use of a breast milk substitute is usually choosing between formula and such liquids as water, water mixed with starch or sugar, or fresh cow or goat milk that have been part of infant diets for centuries.

The appropriate role of infant formula in developing countries was debated for more than a decade by world health officials, members of the industry, health professionals, and corporate critics. One of the first and most extensive studies ever conducted on infant feeding—the five-year, nine-country collaborative study by the World Health Organization, which surveyed 23,000 mothers—revealed that breast-feeding is virtually universal in rural areas of the developing countries.

Questions raised about the safe use of the product, involving contaminated water, overdilution, and lack of refrigeration, apply to all water-based foods, that take up the traditional infant diet. And most scientific authorities agree that, keeping in mind these pervasive problems, infant formula is still the best alternative food for a baby when a mother cannot or chooses not to breast-feed. It is also valuable as a supplement to breast milk when the mother is indisposed to breast-feeding or when the infant reaches the age when breast milk no longer provides sufficient protein and calories for adequate growth.

The primary concern, then, has not been the product quality or its value, but appropriate marketing that avoids glamorizing the product.

The Origins of the Controversy

The infant formula controversy began, formally, in November 1970 at a United Nations sponsored meeting on infant feeding in Bogotá, Columbia. The meeting was one of a series called by the Protein Advisory Group (PAG) at which nutritionists, pediatricians, health care administrators and representatives of the food industries gathered to discuss different aspects of world hunger.

In July 1972 the Protein Advisory Group issued a policy document, PAG Statement 23, that provided a broad framework for cooperative action by the industry, the health care profession and national governments.

Although the groups involved with these initial meetings were appropriate to consider the implications of marketing infant formula in the Third World, some of the participants felt that more public attention should be focused on the matter. Media reports soon charged that the sale of infant formula was responsible for an increase in infant malnutrition and mortality in the developing world.

Derrick B. Jelliffe, then Director of the Caribbean Food and Nutrition Institute, who had participated in the PAG meetings, even claimed that ten million cases of infant illness and death were due to bottle-feeding. Although Dr. Jelliffe later admitted that this figure was symbolic, his charges touched a raw nerve around the world, contributing to the very emotional nature of the controversy. And in 1977 a group based primarily in the United States singled out Nestlé, the world's oldest and largest manufacturer of infant formula, for a boycott.

In 1978 the U.S. Congress held hearings, chaired by Senator Edward Kennedy, to investigate the controversy. Later, acting on a suggestion by industry, Senator Kennedy approached the World Health Organization about the possibility of an international standard for governments, health professionals, and industry to use as a guideline for the marketing of infant formula in the Third World.

A year later, the WHO held preliminary meetings to begin the development of guidelines and, in May 1981, the WHO Code of Marketing of Breastmilk Substitutes was adopted.

The WHO Code is Adopted

Nestlé was one of the main parties recommending the creation of a code, for without a code Nestlé's practices would continue to be the focus of controversy. The company also worked for a clear, unambiguous code, for with ambiguities there would be controversy.

Once the WHO Code was passed, Nestlé announced it would support the Code and waited for individual countries to pass national codes, which could then be put into effect. Unfortunately, very few such codes were forthcoming. (By the end of 1983 only 25 of the 157 member nations of the WHO had established national codes.)

Accordingly, Nestlé management determined it would have to apply the Code in the absence of national legislation and in February 1982 issued instructions to marketing personnel, delineating the company's best understanding of the Code and what would have to be done to follow it.

In addition, in May 1982 Nestlé formed the Nestlé Infant Formula Audit Commission (NIFAC), chaired by former Senator Edmund S. Muskie, and asked the Commission to review the company's instructions to field personnel to determine if they could be improved to better implement the Code and to monitor the company's application of those instructions. At the same time, Nestlé continued its meetings with WHO and UNICEF to try to obtain the most accurate interpretation of the Code.

NIFAC recommended several clarifications for the instructions that it believed would better interpret ambiguous areas of the Code and in October 1982 Nestlé accepted those recommendations and issued revised instructions to field personnel.

Other issues within the Code, for example, the question of a warning statement on labels, were still open to debate. Nestlé consulted extensively with WHO before issuing its label warning statement in October 1983, but there was still no universal agreement on it. Acting on WHO recommendations, Nestlé consulted with firms experienced and expert in developing and field-testing educational materials, so that it could ensure that those materials met the Code.

When the International Nestlé Boycott Committee (INBC) listed its four points of difference with Nestlé, it again became a matter of interpretation of the requirements of the Code. Here, meetings held at UNICEF with Nestlé, NIFAC, and INBC proved invaluable, in that UNICEF agreed to define areas of differing interpretation—in some cases providing definitions differing from both Nestlé's and INBC's interpretations.

It was the meetings with UNICEF, in early 1984, that finally led to a joint statement by Nestlé and INBC on January 25th. At that time, INBC announced its suspension of boycott activities, and Nestlé pledged its continued support of the WHO Code.

Source: Reprinted with permission of Nestlé Foods Corporation

Questions

1. What are the benefits, if any, of infant formula (a milk-based infant food)?
2. Given such benefits, why is (or was) there a concern over the sale of this product in LDCs—but not in Western Europe or the United States?
3. What were the reasons behind the Nestlé boycott?
4. Given that the controversy dragged on for a decade, what did Nestlé do (or what should it have done) in its handling of the negative publicity?

NOTES

1. Wilbur Schramm, ed., "How Communication Works," in *The Process and Effects of Mass Communication* (Urbana, IL: University of Illinois Press, 1961), 3–26.

2. Norman McGuinness, Nigel Campbell, and James Leontiades, "Selling Machinery to China: Chinese Perceptions of Strategies and Relationships," *Journal of International Business Studies* 22 (no. 2, 1991): 187–207.

3. "Cost of an Industrial Sales Call," survey LAP report #8013.8. (Laboratory of Advertising Performance, McGraw-Hill).

4. "Tips on Doing Business," *Business America,* 13 March 1989, 7–8.

5. Harold C. Cash and W. J. E. Crissy, "Comparison of Advertising and Selling," *The Psychology of Selling,* vol. 12 (Personnel Development Associates, 1965).

6. "About Marketing Overseas: Hazards and Opportunities," *Direct Marketing* (October 1985), 128 ff.

7. Kenneth F. Englade, "A Sales Pitch on the Front Porch," *Chicago Tribune,* 15 August 1985.

8. Lauren A. Swanson, "The Twelve 'Nations' of China," *Journal of International Consumer Marketing* 2 (no. 1, 1989): 83–105.

9. John L. Graham et al., "Buyer-Seller Negotiations Around the Pacific Rim: Differences in Fundamental Exchange Processes," *Journal of Consumer Research,* 15 (June 1988): 48–54.

10. Nigel C. G. Campbell et al., "Marketing Negotiations in France, Germany, the United Kingdom, and the United States," *Journal of Marketing* 52 (April 1988): 49–62.

11. June N. P. Francis, "When in Rome? The Effects of Cultural Adaptation on Intercultural Business Negotiations," *Journal of International Business Studies* 22 (no. 3, 1991): 403–28.

12. "Native Sales Staffs Pose Problems for U.S. Firms," *Marketing News,* 8 May 1989, 7.

13. Itzhak Harpaz, "The Importance of Work Goals: An International Perspective," *Journal of International Business Studies* 21 (no. 1, 1990): 75–93.

14. Anthony M. Townsend, K. Dow Scott, and Steven E. Markham, "An Examination of Country and Culture-Based Differences in Compensation Practices," *Journal of International Business Studies* 21 (no. 4, 1990): 667–78.

15. "Amway's Big, Happy Family Is All Smiles—in Japan," *Business Week,* 4 September 1989, 47–50.

16. "Avon Comes Calling in a Big Way in China," *San Jose Mercury News,* 30 June 1991.

17. Steven M. Schiffman, "European Governments Are Troubled by Outbound Telemarketing; Many Pass Laws," *DM News,* 15 January 1985, 17, 42.

18. Nakiye Boyacigiller, "The Role of Expatriates in the Management of Interdependence, Complexity and Risk in Multinational Corporations," *Journal of International Business Studies* 21 (no. 3, 1990): 357–81.

19. J. Stewart Black and Lyman W. Porter, "Managerial Behaviors and Job Performance: A Successful Manager in Los Angeles May Not Succeed in Hong Kong," *Journal of International Business Studies* 22 (no. 1, 1991): 99–113.

20. "Sir Terence Conran: A 'Teddy Bear with a Steel Backbone,' " *Business Week,* 25 November 1985, 108, 110.

21. Rosalie L. Tung, "Selection and Training of Personnel for Overseas Assignments," *Columbia Journal of World Business* 16 (Spring 1981): 68–78.

22. Michael G. Harvey, "The Executive Family: An Overlooked Variable in International Assignments," *Columbia Journal of World Business* 20 (Spring 1985): 84–92.

23. J. Stewart Black and Hal B. Gregersen, "The Other Half of the Picture: Antecedents of Spouse Cross-Cultural Adjustment," *Journal of International Business Studies* 22 (no. 3, 1991): 461–77.

24. "Now It's the Land of Rising Rent," *Business Week,* 7 July 1986, 43.

25. "Copier Firm Seeks Top Spot by Developing Dealer Network," *Marketing News,* 1 October 1982, 1.

26. "American Standard's Executive Melting Pot," *Business Week,* 2 July 1979, 92–93.

27. *Investment in Indonesia* (Kantor Akuntan Sudjendro and Peat Marwick, 1985), 28.

28. See Richard L. Rowan and Duncan C. Campbell, "The Attempt to Regulate Industrial Relations through International Codes of Conduct," *Columbia Journal of World Business* 18 (Summer 1983): 64–72.

29. Anthony J. F. O'Reilly, "Establishing Successful Joint Ventures in Developing Nations: A CEO's Perspective," *Columbia Journal of World Business* 23 (Spring 1988): 65–71.

30. David P. McClure, "Publicity Should Be Integrated in Marketing Plan," *Marketing News,* 10 December 1982, 6.

31. Kelichi Koseki, "Marketing Strategies as Adopted by Ajinomoto in Southeast Asia," *Journal of Advertising Research* 30 (April/May 1990): 31–34.

32. See "Tylenol Restaging Was Made Possible by Firm's Solid Research and Consumer Trust," *Marketing News,* 28 October 1983, 1, 12; Rick Atkinson, "Anatomy of Tylenol Case—A Corporate Calamity," *Kansas City Times,* 14 November 1982; and Michael L. Millenson, "For Tylenol Maker, the Horror Lingers," *Chicago Tribune,* 1 May 1983.

33. Kevin Higgins, "Advance Planning Needed to Cope with Crises," *Marketing News,* 26 April 1985; "Survey: 47% of Firms Have Crisis Communication Plans," *Marketing News,* 26 April 1985.

34. "Disaster Plans Lagging at 43% of USA Companies," *USA Today,* 4 November 1987.

35. "In Asia, the Sweet Taste of Success," *Business Week,* 26 November 1990, 96.

36. "Has Canada-Media Romance Cooled Off?" *POPAI News* 9 (no. 1): 1, 7.

37. "Electricians in Brazil Respond to Learning with Premiums," *Direct Marketing* (August 1985): 52 ff.

38. Sigfredo A. Hernandez, "An Exploratory Study of Coupon Use in Puerto Rico: Cultural vs. Institutional Barriers to Coupon Use," *Journal of Advertising Research* 28 (October/November 1988): 40–46.

39. "Electricians in Brazil."

40. United States Postal Service, *International Direct Marketing Guide* (Alexandria, VA: Braddock Communications, Inc., 1990), 39.

41. *Investment in Austria.* Peat Marwick, 1985, 55; *Investment in Germany.* Peat Marwick, 1982, 61–62.

42. Stan Rapp, "Doing Business Overseas," *DM News,* 15 March 1985, 13.

43. "Florida Hits British Airways with $2,000 Fine for Violations of Its Contest Rules," *DM News,* 15 June 1986, 7.

44. Joachim Schafer, "Foreign Trade Shows Are a Timely Way to Cut Trade Deficit," *Marketing News,* 20 November 1987, 12.

45. Ray Moseley, "Crawfish Could Be Cajuns' Cash Crop," *Chicago Tribune,* 5 July 1984.

46. International Trade Administration, *A Basic Guide to Exporting* (Washington, D.C.: U.S. Department of Commerce, 1981), 69–70.

47. Brant W. Free, "Carnets Simplify Carrying of Commercial Samples," in *Foreign Business Practices,* International Trade Administration (Washington, D.C.: U.S. Department of Commerce, 1981), 25–26.

48. For useful advice, see *How to Get the Most from Overseas Exhibitions,* International Trade Administration (Washington, D.C.: U.S. Department of Commerce, 1984).

49. William F. Kane, "Trade Fairs, Shows: Good Tools to Build International Markets," *Business America,* 17 July 1989, 5–6.

50. "Come in London," *Direct Marketing* (March 1986): 14.

51. *Guide to Exporting,* 72–77.

52. For information and requirements, see *New Product Information Service,* International Trade Administration (Washington, D.C.: U.S. Department of Commerce, 1981).

Worldly wisdom teaches that it is better for reputation to fail conventionally than to succeed unconventionally.

John Maynard Keynes

Promotion Strategies
Advertising

15

CHAPTER OUTLINE

THE ROLE OF ADVERTISING

PATTERNS OF ADVERTISING EXPENDITURES

ADVERTISING AND REGULATIONS

ADVERTISING MEDIA

STANDARDIZED INTERNATIONAL ADVERTISING

CASE 15–1: The Marlboro Man—Should We Modify His Image Overseas?

CASE 15–2: Toilet Advertising—Can We Modify the Medium Overseas?

MARKETING ILLUSTRATION
Sell Sizzle, Not Steak

The Brazilian firm that marketed the Hippopotamus brand wanted its calico hippo to represent what the alligator symbolized for LaCoste. The Brazilian firm carefully thought out its marketing objectives, and the firm's success in the United States owed much to its low-cost but sophisticated advertising campaign, using TV and billboards among other media. To avoid stirring up any protectionist sentiment, the campaign did not mention the shoes' origin. The emphasis was to sell an image rather than a specific shoe.

Chrysler has tried to attract American buyers by appealing to their sense of patriotism. Ford, on the other hand, has decided to promote an international image. Wanting to promote its car as a world car, Ford used advertisements depicting a drapecloth consisting of the flags of the major car-producing countries in order to show that Ford had utilized the best technology from all over the world. Ford did, however, downplay the British flag because British cars were perceived as having lower quality.

Although Anheuser-Busch and its foreign partners customized their foreign advertisements for each national market, they emphasized American themes. In Japan, where the positive American images are those of being young, spacious, easy, and sometimes macho, billboard advertising featured an enormous can of Budweiser with pictures of the Grand Canyon and New York City in the background. In Israel, the company employed the themes of rock-and-roll and cowboys. For the British market, its TV commercials showed U.S. army recruits drinking Budweiser after basic training because the British admire the achievement of the United States.

Source: "Bud Is Making a Splash in the Overseas Beer Market," *Business Week,* 22 October 1984, 52–53

The examples in the marketing illustration emphasize the need to communicate with buyers and to endow a product with a distinct image. A product must not only be physically superior but must also be psychologically desirable. Frequently, a product's psychological attributes are even more important than its physical characteristics. To convince consumers that a product is psychologically superior, a company uses advertising. A product has to be differentiated from competitive brands, and the differences can be either real or imagined.

The marketing of Budweiser overseas underscores the necessity for the adaptation of communication. To advertise internationally, a firm cannot simply repeat the same message indiscriminately in all markets. A message that elicits a favorable response in one country can easily fail to communicate with an audience in another country. To complicate the matter, there are constraints on advertising that preclude the use of certain kinds of media in certain countries.

The purpose of the chapter is to examine the advertising practices in countries other than the United States. The variations in advertising practices are discussed, as well as particular problems associated with the utilization of advertising media abroad. Finally, the chapter closely analyzes the most controversial subject in international advertising—standardized advertising. Some practical guidelines are offered that may be useful in resolving the controversy.

THE ROLE OF ADVERTISING

LDCs and socialist/communist countries, emphasizing production and distribution efficiency, usually attack advertising as a wasteful practice whose primary purpose is to create unnecessary wants. Yet advertising serves a very useful purpose—consumers everywhere, irrespective of their countries' political systems and level of economic development, need useful product information. Since the 1950s China has prohibited foreigners from advertising there because advertising was considered politically inappropriate. In the 1980s, however, China changed its policy in order that the Chinese population could be informed of products available, just as in a modern industrial society.[1] Virtually all media are now available for advertising: billboards, department stores' display cases, telephone books, newspapers, magazines, and journals. Even radio and TV time is available and can be purchased. TV advertising is quite a bargain, since a sixty-second spot for the nationally broadcast China Central Television I network costs only $5,000. Chinese viewers generally enjoy watching the commercials shown.

In one study, Chinese managers reacted favorably to the role of advertising on economic development, its use as a business tool, and its effects on competition. However, regarding the social effects of advertising, these managers did not view advertising as an information source that benefits consumers. They felt that there were too many commercials and that advertising made consumers buy things they did not need.[2]

According to the Galbraithian argument, disposable income and industrial development inevitably lead to advertising, which in turn leads to consumption. A reexamination of the relationship between advertising and national consumption, using cross-national annual data collected on fifty-three nations, however, found that income appears to lead to consumption, which in turn leads to advertising.[3]

A correlation has been shown to exist between advertising expenditures and a country's GNP and level of economic development. As a country becomes more industrialized, the level of advertising expenditure tends to increase as well. The United States is highest in per capita advertising spending at $424.07 per person. In fact, the United States spent more money on advertising in 1986 than all other nations combined. Starch INRA Hooper Inc. and the International Advertising Association reported that the United States spent about $102 billion, while all other nations in the survey had a combined total of $71 billion. Other big spenders included: Japan ($18.3 billion), the United Kingdom ($8.2 billion), West Germany ($8.1 billion), Canada ($4.8 billion), and France ($4.5 billion).[4]

Many of the largest advertisers in the United States also advertise heavily overseas. Procter & Gamble and General Motors, for example, are among the largest advertising spenders in France and Canada. Local firms in markets outside the United States often view this kind of expenditure as an unfair trade practice. They fear that American firms could easily overwhelm local firms in terms of advertising dollars.

PATTERNS OF ADVERTISING EXPENDITURES

In one 1989 study, advertising-to-sales ratios varied across fifteen countries, with ratios ranging from 0.95 for Yugoslavia to 7.62 for Australia. These ratios were not

TABLE 15–1   Methods of budgeting by country

Budgeting methods	Percentage of respondents using this method[a]	Major differences	
		Lowest percentages	Highest percentages
Objective and task	64	Sweden (36%)	Canada (87%)
		Argentina (44%)	Singapore (86%)
Percent of sales	48	Yugoslavia (22%)	Brazil (73%)
		Germany (31%)	Hong Kong (70%)
Executive judgment	33	Finland (8%)	USA (64%)
		Germany (8%)	Denmark (51%)
		Yugoslavia (13%)	Brazil (46%)
			Great Britain (46%)
All-you-can-afford	12	Argentina (0%)	Sweden (30%)
		Israel (0%)	Germany (25%)
			Great Britain (24%)
Matched competitors	12	Denmark (0%)	Germany (33%)
		Israel (0%)	Sweden (33%)
			Great Britain (22%)
Same as last year plus a little more	9	Israel (0%)	
Same as last year	3		
Other	10	Finland (0%)	Canada (24%)
		Germany (0%)	Mexico (21%)
		Israel (0%)	

[a] Total exceeds 100% because respondents checked all budgeting methods that they used.

Source: Nicolaos E. Synodinos, Charles F. Keown, and Laurence W. Jacobs, "Transnational Advertising Practices: A Survey of Leading Brand Advertisers in Fifteen Countries," *Journal of Advertising Research* 29 (April/May 1989): 46

related to population size, number of directly competing brands within the firm, or number of directly competing brands outside the firm.[5] Tables 15–1, 15–2, 15–3, and 15–4 provide information on budgeting methods, media allocation, measures of advertising effectiveness, and compensation methods.

The relationship between advertising expenditure and sales generated has been well documented. Some critics, however, contend that in saturated markets there is reciprocal cancellation of brand advertising. A study by Leeflang and Reuijl showed that advertising had an influence on the primary demand for cigarettes.[6] Annual, bimonthly, and monthly statistical observations of the former West German market revealed that advertising had a significant impact on sales in industry, even though the influence declined over time. One reason for the decline in influence may be that, after the introductory stage of a product, advertising efforts generally are shifted from the promotion of primary demand to the promotion of selective demand (i.e., brand advertising).

Certain variables determine the size of the advertising budget as well as the size of the overall marketing budget. According to the ADVISOR models, the size of an advertising budget is a function of: sales (+), number of users and other DMU participants (+), customer concentration (−), fraction of sales made to order (−),

TABLE 15–2 Allocation of advertising budget by media

Advertising media	Frequency of use (percentage)[a]	Standard deviation	Major differences	
			Lowest percentages	Highest percentages
Television	44	38	Denmark (0%)	Australia (72%)
			Sweden (0%)	Great Britain (68%)
			Israel (1%)	USA (68%)
Newspaper	19	26	USA (3%)	Sweden (43%)
			Brazil (4%)	Singapore (41%)
			Denmark (40%)	
Magazine	19	25	Australia (5%)	Germany (45%)
			Singapore (6%)	Denmark (43%)
			Argentina (7%)	Sweden (38%)
Radio	6	13	Denmark (0%)	Mexico (17%)
			Sweden (0%)	
			Finland (0%)	
Billboard	5	10		Israel (18%)
Cinema	1	5		Israel (11%)
Transit	1	5		
Other	6	16	Germany (0%)	Mexico (14%)
			Australia (1%)	Denmark (12%)

[a] Percentages do not add to 100% exactly because of rounding.

Source: Synodinos, Keown, and Jacobs, "Transnational Advertising Practices," 47

stage in life cycle (−), and product plans (+). The size of a marketing budget is a function of: prospect-customer attitude differences (−), proportion of direct sales (+), and product complexity (−).

When the ADVISOR models were applied to industrial marketing expenditures in the United States and Europe, the overall relationship between advertising and marketing as dependent variables and their corresponding independent explanatory variables were not significantly different between the U.S. sample and the European sample.[7] Strategic variables seemed to affect spending levels in both groups in essentially the same way. But there were variations in the two samples with regard to how individual independent variables explained the varying behavior of the independent variables. An implication is that the importance of particular predictor variables is not uniform across countries.

It is important to note variations in the various kinds of marketing expenses—when expressed as a percentage of sales—across countries and product categories. A study conducted by Zif, Young, and Fenwick examined marketing expenses as a percentage of sales for firms in the United States, Canada, Great Britain, and various European countries.[8] There are substantial differences in the ratio of marketing expenses to sales among the four geographic areas. The percentage variations across countries are higher for consumer goods than for industrial goods. The implication is that the promotional approach and spending levels for industrial products are relatively uniform across countries. For example, firms favor specialized publications over mass media. When compared to other kinds of marketing expenditures, the

TABLE 15–3 Measures of advertising effectiveness

Measure of effectiveness	Percent of respondents using this method[a]	Major differences	
		Lowest percentages	Highest percentages
Sales	82	Germany (56%)	Australia (96%) Israel (94%)
Awareness	66	Israel (6%)	Australia (92%) Hong Kong (84%)
Recall	45	Israel (13%) Mexico (13%) Yugoslavia (17%)	Germany (67%) Australia (65%)
Executive judgment	35	Finland (10%) Israel (13%)	Brazil (62%) Great Britain (54%)
Intention to buy	27	Argentina (8%) Great Britain (14%)	Australia (42%) USA (39%) Israel (38%)
Profitability	21	Israel (6%) Hong Kong (7%) Argentina (8%)	Finland (53%) Yugoslavia (39%)
Coupon return	15	Argentina (0%) Brazil (0%)	Denmark (27%) Hong Kong (25%) Sweden (25%)
Other	18	Yugoslavia (4%) Denmark (5%) Israel (6%)	Finland (50%) Mexico (34%)

[a] Percentages do not add to 100% because respondents checked all measures of effectiveness that they used.
Source: Synodinos, Keown, and Jacobs, "Transnational Advertising Practices," 47

TABLE 15–4 Compensation to advertising agencies

Compensation method	Frequency of use (percentage)[a]	Standard deviation	Major differences	
			Lowest percentages	Highest percentages
Commissions-from-media	49	46	Sweden (10%) Finland (13%) Yugoslavia (17%)	USA (79%) Brazil (79%) Singapore (75%)
Fee for service	30	43	Brazil (7%) Argentina (10%) Great Britain (15%) Singapore (15%) USA (16%)	Sweden (71%) Yugoslavia (50%) Finland (49%)
Cost-plus-a-fixed-percentage	9	26	Singapore (1%) Argentina (1%) USA (1%)	Hong Kong (23%)
Barter or trade	2	12		Argentina (17%)
Other	6	23		Finland (36%) Yugoslavia (17%)

[a] Total is only 96% because some respondents did not sum their categories to 100%.
Source: Synodinos, Keown, and Jacobs, "Transnational Advertising Practices," 49

variation across countries is much smaller for the ratio of sales force expenses to sales. Somewhat surprising is that there seems to be a significantly lower level of spending in the United States than in the other three regions, each of which is smaller in terms of population. This lower spending may be due in part to economies of scale resulting from a given amount being spent on advertising. Although the findings are derived from only industrialized nations, the variations in the marketing expense ratios indicate that executives should be careful when they approach advertising budget decisions in other cultures.

ADVERTISING AND REGULATIONS

Advertising can be affected in several ways by local regulations. The availability of media (or the lack of it) is one example. When and how much media time and space are made available, if at all, is determined by local authorities. Belgium prohibits the use of electricity for advertising purposes between midnight and 8:00 A.M. Greece and South Korea ban the erection of new signs. Furthermore, nationalism may intrude in the form of a ban on the use of foreign languages and materials in advertising.

Canada and Mexico are among those countries that have preclearance require-ments for advertisements on health-related products.[9] In effect, an advertiser must provide the burden of proof that its advertisement is truthful—it is even insufficient to make a true statement that may give a false impression without full disclosure of vital information. Advertisements must be handled carefully and tastefully if and when they are aimed at vulnerable or disadvantaged groups (e.g., children, elderly people, ill people, and uneducated consumers).

The legitimacy of comparative advertising has not been fully settled in many countries. The Draft Directive of the EEC Commission on Misleading and Unfair Advertising has proposed that "comparative advertising shall be allowed, as long as it compares material and verifiable details and is neither misleading nor unfair." In effect, this directive would require Austria, Belgium, France, Italy, and Luxembourg to remove present bans. Certain products are banned altogether from certain media or from advertising in certain countries. Table 15–5 lists some of the major advertising issues advertisers should be careful with when advertising in certain countries.

According to the World Health Organization, nations with complete bans on cigarette advertising are Norway, Finland, Italy, Iceland, Mozambique, Algeria, Jordan, Sudan, Bulgaria, Czechoslovakia, Hungary, Poland, Romania, Russia, Yugoslavia, Singa-pore, and French Polynesia. Those with partial bans include Senegal, Bolivia, Cyprus, Canada, Egypt, Belgium, Denmark, France, Germany, Ireland, Sweden, Great Britain, Australia, New Zealand, and the United States.

Interpreting the law creatively, R. J. Reynolds attempted to circumvent Norway's ban on cigarette advertising by advertising "Camel boots" instead. The advertisement used the same model, trademark, and the lettering in the word *Camel* as those used in Camel's cigarette advertisements. After a protest, the advertisement was eventually withdrawn. Advertisements in France are limited to a picture of a cigarette package with no "seductive imagery." To overcome this restriction, cigarette makers

TABLE 15–5   Major issues and countries to watch

Major Issues, Countries, and Organizations	
Advertising to children	Canada, Scandinavia, United States
Class action by consumer associations	EEC Commission, United States
Comparison advertising	EEC Commission (encouragement), France (possible relaxation), Philippines (ban), United States (encouragement)
Corrective ads	United States, EEC Commission
Feminine hygiene commercials (mandatory prescreening)	Canada (British)
Infant formula promotion	World Health Organization/UNICEF (severe restriction)
Privacy protection and transborder data flows	France, Norway, Sweden, United States
Reversal of the burden of proof on the advertiser	EEC Commission, Scandinavia, United States
Sexism in advertising	Canada, Netherlands, Scandinavia, United Kingdom, United States
Use of foreign languages in advertisements	France, Mexico, Quebec Province
Use of foreign materials, themes, and illustrations	Korea, Muslim countries, Peru, Philippines
Wording used in food and drug ads	Belgium, European Community, United States

Source: J. J. Boddewyn, "Advertising Regulations in the 1980s: The Underlying Global Forces," *Journal of Marketing* 46 (Winter 1982): 27–35

create products such as Marlboro cigarette lighters and Pall Mall matches that are purposefully made to resemble cigarette packages because there is no restriction on how such products can be advertised. In Sudan, Philip Morris advertised by having the Marlboro cowboy hold a Marlboro lighter.

The advertising approach taken is influenced by management's view of the market, consumers, and regulations. This assertion is supported by results from a study conducted by Samiee and Ryans of the views of German and Swiss advertising executives. Generally, the executives of the two countries hold similar attitudes about most advertising issues. The notable differences are that the Germans preferred more complex and informative advertisements and that they favored self-rule as a means of advertising regulation. These attitudes may account for the increase in confrontation and regulations found in the German market. In contrast, the Swiss are more aware of the influence of consumer organizations on advertising regulation, and they are insistent that corrective advertising should be used to control misleading advertisements. As a result, "the Swiss have been more successful in avoiding the higher degree of regulation found in Germany."[10]

ADVERTISING MEDIA

International advertising is the practice of advertising in foreign or international media when the advertising campaign is planned, directly or indirectly, by an advertiser from another country. To advertise overseas, a company must determine the availability (or unavailability) of advertising media. Media may not be readily available in all countries or in certain areas within the countries. Furthermore, the techniques used in media overseas can be vastly different from the ones employed in the United States, as examined in Exhibit 15–1.

Television

For Americans, television is taken for granted because it is available everywhere and in color. Outside of the United States, even in other advanced nations, it is a different story altogether. This difference may explain why U.S. advertisers spend $20 billion each year on TV commercials, four times the amount European advertisers spend.

In most countries, television is not available on a nationwide basis because of the lack of TV stations, relay stations, and cable TV. Color television, for the poor, is a rarity. Nevertheless, the viewing habits of people of lower income should not be underestimated because of the "group viewing" factor. For example, a TV set in a village hall can attract a large number of viewers, resulting in a great deal of interaction among the villagers in terms of conversation about the advertised products.

In many countries, TV stations are state controlled and government operated because of military requirements. As such, the stations are managed with the public welfare rather than a commercial objective in mind. The programming and advertising are thus closely controlled. The programs shown may vary widely and are usually dubbed in the local languages. European governments particularly abhor the U.S. private-broadcast model with its degenerate mass programming. More recently, however, European restrictions have been reduced on featuring films with frequent interruptions from advertisements. This reduction is due in part to an attempt by European countries such as France to end the government monopoly on media and to privatize the broadcast business by making available private broadcasting franchises.

Commercial TV time is usually extremely difficult to buy overseas. This is true even in Europe and Japan, where television is widespread. The usual practice in Tokyo is to use TV advertising to bombard the market, but the challenge for the marketer is to get air time. There are several reasons why television advertising time is severely limited. Most countries only have a few TV channels, which do not schedule daytime television or late-night programs. With less broadcast time comes less advertising time. Some countries do not allow program sponsorship other than spot announcements. Belgium, Denmark, Norway, and Sweden ban advertising on television altogether. Some governments permit advertising only during certain hours of operation. In Germany, advertising on television is permitted only between 6:15 and 8:00 P.M. (except Sundays and holidays) for a total advertising time available of twenty minutes. That same number of commercial minutes also applies to Switzerland. The problem of getting a fraction of the available television time was so severe for Unilever that the firm had to make adjustments in media strategy by relying more on other media. In most countries, the situation is such that an advertiser is fortunate to get air time at all.

RADIO

Often government owned; listener's loyalty is a function of program announcers, who may be independent and may work for several stations

Advantages   Leading medium for all social strata; viewed by listeners as a portable, up-to-date, free, and entertaining medium

Limitations   Frequent changes (as often as every half hour) of program format; clutter and some availability problems

TELEVISION

Almost always owned and operated by a government; black-and-white TV sets still dominate

Advantages   Immensely popular; group viewing is a common phenomenon

Limitations   Unavailable in rural areas; severe clutter, premium cost; lack of time availability partly owing to lack of daytime and late-night broadcast except for weekend

NEWSPAPER

Emphasis on sensational news; usually no evening paper; English-language papers appeal to those with affluence and influence

Advantages   High pass-along rate

Limitations   Lack of specialized sections for preferred positions; lack of space due to mechanical problems, resulting in a fixed, predetermined number of pages

MAGAZINE

Emphasis on newsstand sales rather than subscription sales

Advantages   Readily available space for advertising; selectivity

Limitations   Lack of reliable circulation figures

CINEMA

Resemble old-time, elegant movie houses in the United States; reserved seat system; ticket price depends on seat location and type of cinema (i.e., first run or second run); show slides and commercial before main feature

Advantages   Good impact due to size, sight, and sound; social event

Limitations   Patrons often not punctual because they are aware advertisements are presented at the beginning of a show

EXHIBIT 15–1   Asian media and their characteristics

Source: Sak Onkvisit and John J. Shaw, "A View of Marketing and Advertising Practices in Asia and Its Meaning for Marketing Managers," *Journal of Consumer Marketing* 2 (Spring 1985): 14

There are at least two tactics an advertiser can employ to overcome the problem of lack of broadcast time for advertising. One is to use shorter commercials. In the United States, the thirty-second spot is the norm and the use of the fifteen-second commercial is limited; but in Japan the fifteen-second spot is the standard. Advertisers there have learned to achieve simplicity and clarity in using this type of commercial: "Japanese commercials demonstrate that developing a strong, recognizable hook is the key to a successful 15."[11]

Although disputed in the United States, fifteen-second spots have become the norm in some countries. Spots shorter than thirty seconds are an overwhelming majority in France (71 percent), Japan (79 percent), and Spain (80 percent). As a matter of fact, the Japanese even have 8-second spots that function almost like billboards on TV and yet are graphically compelling.[12]

Another tactic is to purchase TV time well in advance. With a waiting list of 100 companies, TV advertising time in the Netherlands must be booked with a year's notice. Those advertisers able to get air time still face other advertising hurdles. For example, commercial interruptions can be long and frequent, creating a severe problem of clutter.

Advertisers sometimes use television stations in one country to reach consumers in another country. Canada is a prime example. More than 75 percent of Canadians are clustered within 100 miles of the U.S. border, and 95 percent are within 200 miles. Thus, nearly all Canadians are within the broadcast range of U.S. stations. U.S. advertisers often use U.S. TV stations to communicate with Canadian consumers. In fact, Canadian advertisers themselves make it a practice of using U.S. stations at the border (e.g., Detroit, Spokane, and Buffalo) to air commercials aimed primarily at the Canadian market. Reasons for this practice are that American TV stations have higher program ratings than Canadian stations and that the Canadian audience in total spends some 26 billion hours a week viewing U.S. shows—the equivalent of 78 percent of the total hours spent watching Canadian English-language TV programs.

New technology may allow advertisers to solve some of the problems related to TV time and government regulation (e.g., a ban on the advertising of certain products or to certain groups). Cable TV is now available in Western Europe. Commercial programs, for example, can be beamed from the United Kingdom to cable networks in Norway, Finland, and Switzerland. Retransmitting the signal, however, is still illegal in Norway. Satellite TV may present another solution and is gaining wider acceptance. McDonald's and Mars have begun to funnel some advertising dollars to the Sky Channel satellite network. McDonald's has used special commercials promoting safety in order to placate those European countries that restrict product advertising aimed at children. The problem with this new technology has been that, when an advertisement is aired, consumers in all countries are exposed to an identical message. But improved technology may in the future allow advertisers to beam particular advertising versions to different countries.

Radio

Radio is no longer king of the media in the United States, but it retains its status in many countries as the only truly national medium. In Mexico, for example, radio provides coverage for 83 percent of the country. It is popular for several reasons.

A radio set is inexpensive and affordable—even among poor people. It is virtually a free medium for listeners: the programs are free and the costs of operating and maintaining a radio set are almost negligible. Furthermore, illiteracy poses no problem for this advertising medium. As a communication medium, radio is entertaining, up-to-date, and portable. The medium penetrates from the highest to the lowest socioeconomic levels, with FM stations being preferred by high-income and better-educated listeners. Not surprisingly, radio commands the largest portion of advertising expenditures in a great number of markets.

In order for radio stations in the United States to survive and counter the threat of television, they have adopted the "magazine" format by specializing in a particular type of programming. Advertisers must not assume that stations have adopted this same approach abroad. In many countries, radio stations have not become specialized in a particular program format and see no need to be selective in order to attract the listening audience. Radio stations commonly vary their programming format throughout the day, sometimes as often as every half hour. An audience shift should thus be expected, and a consequence of this practice is that it may not be easy to reach the target market effectively.

Unlike U.S. stations, which do their own programming and hire their own announcers or disc jockeys, overseas stations are quite liberal in selling air time to outside operators. This is true in spite of the fact that for security reasons most overseas stations are owned, controlled, and operated by the government. Once the air time has been sold, the program format is determined by the sponsor or independent disc jockey. A certain disc jockey might even buy air time to broadcast from a number of stations, promoting his or her identity by frequently mentioning his or her name or title of show, by playing a particular theme song to begin and end the program, and by soliciting calls and letters from the audience. Listeners' loyalty is thus not so much to the station but to the disc jockey, who may roam from one station to another throughout the day.

Although air time for commercials is usually available, advertisers should still expect certain problems. The availability of a radio network is generally limited, and an advertiser must use many stations to blanket the entire market. Mexico's low program ratings also make it necessary for an advertiser to use many stations and spots to achieve impact. Also, many stations terminate their broadcast at an early hour each day. Because of these conditions, clutter is a tremendous problem. Program breaks are frequent and commercial minutes are so numerous that listeners have adopted the habit of constantly changing stations.

The measurement of audience size and impact is far from being standardized across countries. To measure gross rating points, a four-week time period is used in the United States. In Germany the norm is spots per month, whereas in the United Kingdom weekly ratings are the rule.[13]

Newspaper

In virtually all urban areas of the world, the population has access to daily newspapers. In fact, the problem for the advertiser is not one of having too few newspapers but rather one of having too many of them. In the United States, large cities can rarely support more than two dailies. In other countries, a city may have numerous newspapers dividing the readership market. Lebanon, with a population of 1.5 million, has some 200 daily and weekly newspapers, with the average circulation per paper of only 3,500.

Newspapers in communist countries are controlled by the government and are thus used for propaganda purposes. China's newspapers, for example, tend to carry news items that the government deems to express some moral and social value.

Believing that sensational news attracts readership, most non-U.S. newspapers in the free world are set up in a sensational news format. It is a rule rather than the exception for these newspapers to concentrate on murders, robberies, scandals, and rapes. Even the United Kingdom, where the citizens are known for their reserved manner, is not exempt from this practice. World news and nonscandalous political news often take a back seat to the more sensational news. As a result, non-U.S. newspapers look more like such weekly U.S. tabloids as the *National Enquirer* and *Star.* A newspaper that concentrates on news of substance and quality (i.e., unsensational news) must pay for this in terms of low readership.

Although local-language newspapers generally attempt to attract the masses, some papers segment the market based on readers' demographics and political ideology. In France, there are eight nationally distributed newspapers, each editorially connected to a certain political party or ideology. The political connection is reflected in the published news stories. The popular *Liberation,* for example, has a white-collar profile because it is for leftist-oriented yuppies.[14] Its reporting approach can be highly unusual. An issue might devote the first five pages to an analysis of the controversial film *Year of the Dragon,* or have a big and bold four-inch "War and Peace" headline for the Reagan and Gorbachëv summit, or distribute incense-scented newsprint for the arrival of Pope John Paul II.

Many countries have English-language newspapers in addition to the local-language newspapers. The English-language newspapers are patterned more like the traditional American paper, with an emphasis on world, government, and business news. This vehicle would be appropriate for an advertiser to reach government and business leaders, educated readers, upper-class people, and those with affluence and influence. The aim of the *Asian Wall Street Journal* is to supply economic information in English to influential businesspersons, politicians, top government officials, and intellectuals. It was not designed to be a newspaper for mass readers. Exhibit 15–2 shows a number of English-language newspapers in Asia, each carrying *World Paper,* an international news supplement.

Some countries have nationally distributed newspapers, as shown in Exhibit 15–3. But it is difficult to find a true national newspaper because almost every newspaper tries to be somewhat local in nature. Even in the United States, before *USA Today,* the closest thing to a national newspaper was perhaps the *New York Times,* with the *Washington Post* in second place. Clearly, it is even more difficult to have an international newspaper. Those papers distributed internationally include the *International Herald Tribune* (see Exhibit 15–4) and such financial newspapers as the *Wall Street Journal* (with the *Asian Wall Street Journal* for Asian countries) and the United Kingdom's *Financial Times.* As might be expected, these newspapers are not

EXHIBIT 15–2	English-language newspapers

Source: Reprinted with permission of *WorldPaper*

available everywhere, and the circulation is low. *Financial Times,* a century-old daily covering British business, international business, and economic and political news, has a worldwide circulation of about 230,000, with only 6,000 sold in the United States and Canada. Still, the *Financial Times* offers U.S. advertisers access to upscale readers in Europe and other parts of the world.

EXHIBIT 15–3 A nationally distributed newspaper

Source: Reprinted with permission of the *Globe and Mail*

There are several problems associated with advertising in foreign newspapers. The purchase of space is a monumental problem. The general unavailability of space is the result of overseas newspapers' having a fixed and small number of pages for each edition, including the Sunday paper. This may seem strange to American advertisers, who are used to getting newspaper space at anytime with just a few days' notice. American advertisers are often puzzled about why overseas publishers do not add more pages to accommodate advertisements that would bring in revenue. The answer is that equipment is limited and so is paper. Japanese newspapers, which

EXHIBIT 15–4   An international newspaper

Source: Reprinted with permission of the *International Herald Tribune*

experience these production complications, are limited to only sixteen to twenty pages a day. Because newspapers may have to ration and turn away advertisers, marketers may need special arrangements to buy space on short notice.

American advertisers are accustomed to having separate editorial sections in American newspapers and are often frustrated by foreign papers. A twenty-page newspaper may still have sections for sports, entertainment, fashion, business, and science, but each section may be only one page. It thus becomes difficult for an advertiser to match the product to the proper section or environment (e.g., tire and automotive products in the sports section) in a local newspaper.

Furthermore, with so many newspapers dividing a small market, it is expensive to reach the entire market. There are some three hundred eighty and eight hundred newspapers in Turkey and Brazil, respectively. With advertisements in just one paper, the reach would be quite inadequate. Advertising in several papers, on the other hand, is also impractical. It is fortunate for advertisers that people often read or subscribe to two or more dailies and often share newspapers. Despite a small circulation, readership may still be high. Usually, the pass-along rate in foreign markets is much higher than that in the United States. But reliable estimates of circulation of overseas newspapers are difficult to obtain. The figure provided by the newspaper publisher may be highly inflated, and there is no meaningful way, at least for advertisers, to measure or audit the circulation figures.

Magazines

Nowhere else in the world are there so many and varied types of consumer magazines as there are in the United States. Because U.S. magazines segment the reading market in every conceivable manner, there are magazines for the masses as well as for the few and select. This makes it possible for advertisers to direct their campaigns to obtain *reach* (the total number of unduplicated individuals exposed to a particular media vehicle at least once during a specified time period) or *frequency* (the intensity or the number of times within a specified period that a prospect is exposed to the message) or both. Foreign magazines are generally not highly developed in terms of a particular audience. They do not segment their readers as narrowly as U.S. magazines do, and they do not have the same degree of accurate information about reader characteristics. In Brazil, there are very few magazines, and people read all three or four of them. This results in a 60 percent *duplication* which can be a waste of promotional effort unless *frequency* is the objective.[15]

Marketers of international products have the option of using international magazines that have regional editions (e.g., *Time, Business Week, Newsweek,* and *Life*). In the case of *Reader's Digest,* local-language editions are distributed. Allen-Edmonds, a shoe company, was able to increase its foreign sales by advertising its shoes in the international editions of such magazines. For technical and industrial products, magazines can be quite effective. Technical-business publications tend to be international in their coverage. These publications range from individual industries (e.g., construction, beverages, textiles, etc.) to worldwide industrial magazines covering many industries. A trade magazine about China, for example, is a suitable vehicle for all types of industrial products of interest to the Chinese government. In Europe, the number of business publications is seven times as high as that in the United States. For an educated population of 230,000 in the Scandinavian countries, there are 1,200 technical and trade journals.[16] Canada, in contrast, does not have a large number of trade magazines. Unlike the United States, which has several competing trade publications, Canada usually has only one trade magazine for each market segment, making it easier to cover the entire Canadian market.[17]

Local (i.e., national) business magazines are a good vehicle to reach well-defined target audiences. *Nikkei Business* is one such magazine in Japan (see Exhibit 15–5). In some cases, a magazine may be designed almost exclusively to carry advertising

JAPAN'S BUSINESS LEADERS ALL LOOK ALIKE.

It's easy to spot business leaders in Japan. There's a Japanese business leader lurking behind every copy of NIKKEI BUSINESS.

NIKKEI BUSINESS is exclusively for Japan's corporate crème de la crème — a very choice body of 200,000 subscribers selected by NIKKEI BUSINESS' own publishers: Nikkei-McGraw-Hill.

To our readers, we're a valued cover-to-cover information source for international business, with a wealth of informed articles written exclusively by an in-house staff of experts.

To our advertisers, we're unparalleled advertising effectiveness. 100% on-target. With no spillover.

And no wastage.

So get behind NIKKEI BUSINESS and put NIKKEI BUSINESS behind you. And follow Japan's leaders right to the top.

Subscriptions: 202,677 (as of Aug. 5, 1985 issue)
Net paid circulation is regularly audited and certified by Japan ABC.
186,830 (1984)
For further information write to Yoshihiko Shimada, Advertising Manager, 1-14-6 Uchikanda, Chiyoda-ku, Tokyo 101, Japan Tel. (03)233-8031 Telex: J29902 NKMCGRAW

日経ビジネス
NIKKEI BUSINESS

Nikkei-McGraw-Hill, Inc., Publishers of Nikkei Business

North American Sales Network: New York Tel. (212) 997-2806, Chicago Tel. (312) 751-3716, Los Angeles Tel. (213) 480-5221, Houston Tel. (713) 462-0757, Toronto Tel. (416) 259-9631

EXHIBIT 15–5 A national business magazine

Source: Reprinted with permission of Nikkei-McGraw-Hill, Inc.

rather than much editorial content. For example, American suppliers may want to use *Product USA* to communicate through advertising with foreign middlemen.

Unlike the U.S. market, which has an organization such as the ABC (Audit Bureau of Circulations) to audit the circulation figures for most magazines, the circulation figures of overseas magazines are somewhat unreliable. Furthermore, overseas magazines tend to depend more on newsstand sales than on subscription sales, making it difficult to calculate consistent volume or to predict the size of readership in advance.

Because many magazines are unaudited, either by choice or by lack of an audit bureau, it is not sensible to exclude unaudited publications from the media schedule. Even when publications are audited, the information given may not be adequate. The English ABC provides minimum information, whereas the German IVW audit is very thorough.

Direct Mail

Confusion usually arises when such terms as direct mail, direct advertising, direct marketing, and mail order are discussed. It is important to understand that **direct marketing** is a broad term that encompasses the other related terms. According to the Direct Marketing Association (DMA), direct marketing is "the total of activities by which products and services are offered to market segments in one or more media for informational purposes or to solicit a direct response from a present or prospective customer or contributor by mail, telephone, or personal visit." This is a more-than-$1-billion business in the United States. As a system, direct marketing has two distinct components: (1) promotion and (2) ordering/delivery (see Exhibit 15–6).

Direct marketers can promote their products through all advertising media. They can solicit orders by making announcements on television or in magazines

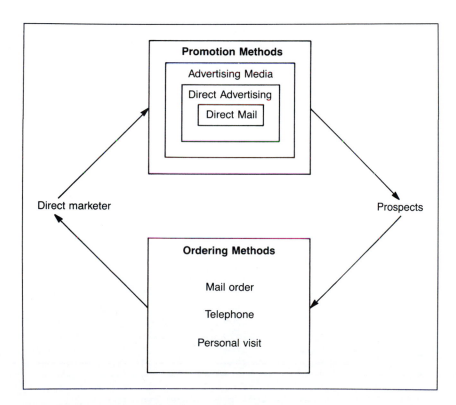

EXHIBIT 15–6 Direct marketing

(usually with coupons or order forms). Frequently, however, marketers rely on **direct advertising** in media created for that purpose. These media consist of direct mailings and all forms of print advertisements distributed directly to prospects through a variety of methods (i.e., advertising materials distributed door to door, on the street, or inside the store or those placed inside shopping bags and on auto windshields). **Direct mail** is thus only one kind of direct-advertising medium, which is in turn a part of general-advertising media or the promotional methods of direct marketing. Of course, the use of direct mail is not limited to just direct marketing. The Direct Marketing Association annually publishes a breakdown of direct-marketing expenditures by media in selected countries.

With regard to ordering, buyers can place orders by telephone (often with a toll-free number), through a personal visit, or by mail. An order that is sent in by mail and fulfilled by mail delivery is called a **mail order.** Thus, mail order is not a medium; rather it is just one of several means that can be used to place and handle orders. An ordering method consists of one of the two components of the direct-marketing system. Table 15–6 shows the ten largest mail-order companies. Table 15–7 shows mail-order direct marketers in two categories, U.S. firms marketing abroad and non-U.S. firms marketing in the United States.

For this discussion, direct mail and direct marketing are considered together. There are several reasons for doing so. Direct mail generally accounts for a major portion of direct-marketing advertising expenditures. Also, many reports on direct-marketing campaigns do not provide a detailed breakdown of the advertising dollar accounted for by media other than direct mail.

Direct mail is largely undeveloped in many countries. This is especially true where labor is cheap and abundant and where it is just as easy to use a salesperson to make sales calls. Furthermore, for countries with high illiteracy, this medium is not suitable for promoting consumer products.

TABLE 15–6   Ten Leading Mail-Order Companies Worldwide

Rank	Company Name	Country	Year of Data	Sales (US$ millions)	Type of Merchandise
1.	Sears, Roebuck & Company	United States	1984	2,966	General
2.	Great Universal Stores	United Kingdom	1984	2,717	General
3.	Otto Versand[a]	West Germany	1982	2,690	General
4.	Schickedanz	West Germany	1982	2,000	General
5.	J.C.Penney	United States	1984	1,774	General
6T.	United Automobile Association Services	United States	1984	1,420	Insurance
6T.	Mobil	United States	1984	1,420	General
8.	Time, Inc.	United States	1984	1,203	Publishing
9.	Reader's Digest Association	United States	1984	1,175	Publishing
10.	Colonial Penn	United States	1984	1,111	Insurance

[a] Includes Spiegel 1984 sales

Source: Arnold Fishman, "International Mail Order—Severe Handicap, High Costs, Tough Regulations," *Direct Marketing* (August 1985): 59

Without doubt, the United States is the most developed market for the advertising medium of direct mail. Foreign marketers as well as American marketers have a wide selection of buyer lists that permit them to contact the intended target audience with minimum waste.

European marketers are far behind the United States in exploiting the medium of direct mail. A total volume of 8.5 billion direct mail pieces mailed in Europe may seem high.[18] Actually, this figure is low by U.S. standards. A U.S. household receives 224 items of business mail a year, compared to only 38 for a European. Furthermore, one study found per-capita mail-order sales in eleven European countries plus three other countries to be $66, a figure much smaller than the $228 per-capita figure in the United States.[19]

Mail-order sales between 1988 and 1989 for the United States were $164.5 million or 10.9 percent of retail sales. The former West Germany came in second, recording $11.5 million in mail-order sales or 4.9 percent of retail sales. Mail order in Spain recorded $143,000 in sales and represented 0.2 percent of retail sales. Italy's $852,000 in mail order sales represented 0.6 percent of retail sales.[20]

In one study, the growth rate of direct mail was shown to not be uniform, as evidenced by the average number of direct-mail pieces received per person by residents of the various European countries: Switzerland (56), former West Germany (52), Sweden (52), Holland (50), Belgium (45), Finland (41), Norway (33), France (32), Denmark (29), the United Kingdom (22), Portugal (6), and Ireland (3).[21] The Swiss, Swedes, Germans, Dutch, and Belgians all received more than twice as many direct-mail pieces as the British. Nevertheless, the United Kingdom had the largest growth potential. It is interesting to observe that, although Ireland had only 3 pieces per person, the country led Western Europe in volume growth.

The growth and importance of direct mail is underscored by the extent of its use. Furthermore, the use of direct mail and direct marketing is growing rapidly in many countries. Approximately 82 percent of the principal German industries

TABLE 15–7   Global Mail-Order Direct Marketing, U.S. and Non-U.S.

U.S. Direct Marketing Offshore	Non-U.S. Direct Marketers Active in U.S.
Ambassador	Aer Rianta
American Express	Artis Orbis
Avon	Bertelsmann
Citibank	Foto-Quelle
CBS	Moore Ltd.
Encyclopaedia Britannica	Patrimonium
Franklin Mint	Quelle
Grolier	Otto Versand
K-Tel	
Reader's Digest	
Time, Inc.	

Source: Arnold Fishman, "International Mail Order—Severe Handicap, High Costs, Tough Regulations," *Direct Marketing* (August, 1985): 60

use direct-marketing techniques. In addition, about 35 percent of all Scandinavian advertising funds are spent on direct marketing.[22] Table 15–8 provides mail-order direct-marketing statistics of selected countries.

Direct mail is the leading business-to-business advertising medium in Belgium, Finland, Ireland, the Netherlands, Portugal, Sweden, Switzerland, Great Britain, and Germany. In second place are magazines, followed by trade directories and newspapers. Switzerland is the leader in the use of business-to-business direct mail offers, followed by Finland and Germany.[23]

Some marketers use direct marketing to reach potential customers across the seas. Collin Street Bakery, a firm located in Corsicana, Texas, uses overseas mail as well as newspaper and magazine advertisements, and it has been able to extend its fruitcake business to 194 foreign countries.[24] Normally, however, international direct mail is used to market industrial products rather than consumer products. The Scottish Development Agency, for example, was able to use direct mail to attract 9,443 jobs, sixty-nine projects, and $1 billion in investment in 1985. It has spent $1.5 million annually on direct-response advertisements and even more on direct mail in the United States.[25]

U.S. practices in using direct mail require some modification when taken abroad. Exhibit 15–7 describes the differences between U.S. and European mail-order requirements. There is difficulty in making a direct transposure of a U.S. mailing piece without change into a European mailing kit because of various weight rules and other unique regulations.[26] Population direct-mail lists are another serious problem since foreign list owners do not trust renters and brokers. List generation and management is still primitive abroad. American list owners enhance their lists with such information as buyers' frequency, recency, and dollar value, but direct marketers used to those practices can become frustrated with list brokers in Europe (except in Germany) because basic selection criteria are not even provided. Also, privacy laws are more restrictive abroad than in the United States. For example, Germany allows only two unique selection criteria per order when renting a list.

Foreign privacy laws have also seriously hampered list criterion and development. France and Sweden regulate the transborder flow of mailing lists and of personal data about their nationals. Japan restricts the compilation of computerized mailing lists. Privacy laws are especially strict in Germany and Austria, very likely as a consequence of the Hitler years.[27] Personal information on age, financial and credit background, political and religious affiliation, credit-card information, and drinking and sex habits may not be divulged for direct-mail purposes. When lists are rented, mail-order firms are not allowed to provide information on their customers' purchases, frequency of purchase, or any personal data. Although direct marketers have been lobbying for the law to be relaxed, most Germans and Austrians feel that the present laws are already too loose. Direct marketers must understand the countries' differing regulations of business mailing lists. Table 15–9 examines regulations of business mailing lists in a number of countries.

In Asia, the use of direct mail is also on the rise. With the emergence of local list brokers in Asia, a marketer can now purchase reasonable lists for the Asian market. In the past, direct-mail advertisers wanting to reach Asian businessmen and affluent consumers had to rely on either international lists held in the United States and

TABLE 15–8 International Mail-Order Direct-Marketing Statistics

	Sales (US$ billions)	Year	Retail Sales (percent)	Growth Rate[a] (percent)	Inflation Rate (percent)	Population (millions)	Per Capita Sales	Credit Card Penetration Percent of Eligible Population	Cards per Person	Advertising Growth Rate (percent)	Direct Mail Share of Advertising Expenditures	Direct Mail Volume per Household[b]
Europe												
1. Austria	.400	1984	1.5	3.0	6.0	7.5	53	23	1.1	—	—	—
2. Belgium	.269	1984	1.0	15.0	5.4	9.9	27	33	1.4	—	18.0[c]	125
3. Denmark	.102	1985	1.4	5.5	4.5	5.1	20	13	1.4	—	33.1[c]	71
4. Finland	.339	1984	2.5	10.0	6.2	4.9	69	2	1.3	—	11.6[b]	111
5. France	3.338	1985	2.5	7.3	4.7	55.0	61	66	1.5	9.0	8.7[b]	87
6. Italy	.607	1985	0.5	17.4	8.6	57.1	11	9	1.3	15.8	—	—
7. Netherlands	.490	1985	1.6	-1.0	1.7	14.5	34	18	1.3	5.0	33.1[c]	132
8. Sweden	.609	1985	2.0	12.0	5.7	8.3	73	57	1.9	—	27.5[c]	128
9. Switzerland	.576	1985	2.3	9.5	3.4	6.5	89	11	1.5	—	16.5[b]	146
10. United Kingdom	3.784	1985	3.4	10.6	5.7	56.4	67	59	3.0	8.4	7.4[c]	60
11. West Germany	7.788	1985	4.8	0.6	2.2	61.0	128	31	1.3	2.0	11.9[b]	123
Total Europe	18.302		—	—	—	286.2	64	—	—	—	13.8[b]	99
Non-Europe												
12. Canada	3.515	1985	—	39	3.8	125.4	138	—	—	8.5	—	—
13. Japan	5.913	1985	1.6	13	2.8	120.7	49	—	—	4.0	—	—
14. Australia	2.000	1985	—	25	3.9	15.6	128	—	—	3.5	—	—
Total Non-U.S.	29.73		—	—	—	447.9	66	—	—	—	—	—
United States	58.65	1985	2.8	10	3.3	239.0	245	85	5.8	8.8	16.4	—

Sources: Canada: Canadian Direct Marketing Association (12)
Association Europeene de Vente Par Correspondance(5–11)
Japan: Yano Research Institute (13)
Australia: Australian Direct Marketing Association (14)
Groupement De La Vente Par Correspondance (2)a
Daelle Varehas
Svenska Postorderföreningen
Verband des Schweizerischen Versandhandels (9)
Evans Dewar Sidaway (10)
Mail Order Trader's Association of Great Britain (10)
Syndicat des Enterprises de Vente Par Correspondance (5–7,10)
Services Postaux Europeene (last 3 columns)

[a]In native currency
[b]1983 data
[c]1984 data

Source: Arnold Fishman, "1985 International Mail Order Guide," *Direct Marketing* (August 1986): 43

- Media:
  - Limited media availability.
    - Limited list rentals.
    - Limited TV channel and commercial time availability.
- Regulatory:
  - Tighter regulation of promotional claims, copy content, competitive comparisons.
  - Tighter product safety approval requirements.
- Delivery systems:
  - Generally higher post rates.
  - Variability in postal rates (60 : 1 ratio between United Kingdom and Austria).
- Payment systems:
  - Low credit card penetration.
  - Variability in payment systems sophistication between countries.
- Business organization:
  - Mail-order holding companies rather than financial or consumer product conglomerates with mail-order holdings.
- Catalog operations:
  - Catalog operations often are agent-based with agents for the catalog company distributing catalogs, aggregating and paying for their customer's orders after deducting their commission and assuming responsibility for collecting from their customers (most common in United Kingdom and Germany.)
- Sales concentration:
  - Lesser development of specialty mail order and greater concentration of sales by catalog general merchandisers.
- Market fragmentation:
  - Marketing expansion internationally in Europe from national market bases hindered by:
    - Differences in population structure, lifestyle, fashion trends.
    - Differences in legal and technical regulations.
    - Differences in taxes.
    - Differences in post office regulations.
    - Differences in credit sales legal regulations.
    - Existing custom formalities.
    - Possible changes in currency parities during duration of fixed price offers.
    - Obstacles in merchandise return across national frontiers.
    - Obstacles in providing after-sales customer service across national frontiers.
- Merchandising:
  - Lower proportion of high-end items.
  - Product quality consciousness.
- Graphics:
  - Color fidelity essential in catalog merchandising.

EXHIBIT 15–7   European versus U.S. mail order: major differences

Source: Arnold Fishman, "International Mail Order—Severe Handicaps, High Costs, Tough Regulations," *Direct Marketing* (August 1985): 60

TABLE 15–9 Regulation of Business Mailing Lists (*continues through page 726*)

	Australia (B)	Austria (A)	Belgium (B)	Canada (Quebec B)	Denmark (A)	Finland (B)	France (A)	Germany (A)	Hong Kong (B)
1. Must permission be obtained from a gov't. agency before a private business firm can create and maintain a mailing list?	No (NSW)	Yes	No	No	No	No	No (but gov't. must be notified)	No	No
2. Must a business firm obtain the permission of a potential customer before his or her name can be added to the firm's mailing list?	No	No	No	No	No	No	No	No (if name and address only are stored)	No
3. Are there limitations on the type of consumer information that may be obtained and maintained by a private business firm?	No	Yes*	No	No	Yes*	No	Yes*	Yes*	No
4. Are there limitations on who else may have access to consumer information maintained by a private firm?	No (NSW)	Yes*	No	No	Yes*	No	No answer	Yes*	No
5. Must a private firm, at the request of a customer, provide the customer with a copy of the information kept on him or her?	No (NSW: in the absence of a court order)	Yes	No	Yes	Yes	No	Yes	Yes	No
6. Does a consumer have the right to require that a private firm correct erroneous information concerning that customer?	Yes (if a court order is obtained)	Yes	No	Yes	Yes	No	Yes	Yes	No
7. Does a consumer have the right to require that a private firm remove his or her name and other information from the firm's records?	No (NSW)	Yes	No	Yes	No	No	Yes	Yes	No
8. Does a consumer have the right to require that a private firm limit the use of information about the consumer to less than what the law allows the private firm to do with the information?	No (NSW)	No	No	Yes	No	No	Yes	Yes	No

TABLE 15–9 (continued)

	Australia (B)	Austria (A)	Belgium (B)	Canada (Quebec B)	Denmark (A)	Finland (B)	France (A)	Germany (A)	Hong Kong (B)
9. Does your gov't. make available to private business firms information about individuals that is maintained by various gov't. agencies (marriages, births, drivers' licenses, etc.)?	Yes (NSW)	No	Yes	No	Yes	Yes	No	No	Yes
10. If Yes (to number 9): Do such lists remain in the possession of the gov't. agency?	Yes (NSW)	—	No	—	No	Yes	—	—	Yes
11. Must a private firm obtain permission from a gov't. agency before transferring information concerning individual consumers from your country to another?	No (NSW)	Yes[b]	No	No	Yes[b]	No	No	No	No
12. Are there limitations on transferring information about individual consumers from one part of a private firm to another part in another country?	No (NSW)	Yes[a]	No	No	Yes[a]	No	Yes[a]	Yes[a]	No
13. Would the answer to number 12 be different if the information maintained within your country was only about consumers located in another country?	No (NSW)	No	No	No	Yes (no limitation when info. maintained solely for electronic processing)	No	No	No	No

(A) Countries having mandatory data protection laws.

(B) Countries without mandatory data processing laws.

[a] See full IAA report for listing of limitations.

[b] Information regarding the name of the gov't agency that must be contacted to obtain permission and requirements is listed in the full IAA report.

TABLE 15—9 *(continued)*

	Italy (B)	Japan (B)	Luxembourg (A)	Norway (A)	Spain (B)	Sweden (A)	Switzerland (B)	United Kingdom (B)	U.S.A. (B)
1. Must permission be obtained from a gov't. agency before a private business firm can create and maintain a mailing list?	No	No	Yes	No	No	Yes	No	No	No
2. Must a business firm obtain the permission of a potential customer before his or her name can be added to the firm's mailing list?	No	No	No	No	No	No	No	No	No
3. Are there limitations on the type of consumer information that may be obtained and maintained by a private business firm?	Yes*	No	Yes*	Yes*	No	Yes*	Yes*	No	No
4. Are there limitations on who else may have access to consumer information maintained by a private firm?	No	No	Yes*	Yes*	No	Yes*	No	No	No
5. Must a private firm, at the request of a customer, provide the customer with a copy of the information kept on him or her?	No	No	Yes	Yes	No	Yes	Yes (if that person demonstrates the info. affects privacy)	No	No
6. Does a consumer have the right to require that a private firm correct erroneous information concerning that customer?	No	No	Yes	Yes	No	Yes	Yes	No	No
7. Does a consumer have the right to require that a private firm remove his or her name and other information from the firm's records?	No	No	Yes	No	No	Yes	Yes	No	No
8. Does a consumer have the right to require that a private firm limit the use of information about the consumer to less than what the law allows the private firm to do with the information?	No	No	No	No	No	No	No	No	No

TABLE 15–9 *(continued)*

	Italy (B)	Japan (B)	Luxembourg (A)	Norway (A)	Spain (B)	Sweden (A)	Switzerland (B)	United Kingdom (B)	U.S.A. (B)
9. Does your gov't. make available to private business firms information about individuals that is maintained by various gov't. agencies (marriages, births, drivers' licenses, etc.)?	No	No	No	No	No	Yes	Yes	Yes	Yes (but varies from state to state)
10. If Yes (to number 9): Do such lists remain in the possession of the gov't. agency?	—	—	No answer	—	—	No	No	No	No
11. Must a private firm obtain permission from a gov't. agency before transferring information concerning individual consumers from your country to another?	No	No	No answer	Yes[b]	No	Yes[b]	No	No	No
12. Are there limitations on transferring information about individual consumers from one part of a private firm to another part in another country?	No	No	Yes[a]	Yes[a]	No	Yes[a]	No (unless the transfer can be regarded as a prohibited transfer of intelligence)	No	No
13. Would the answer to number 12 be different if the information maintained within your country was only about consumers located in another country?	No	No	No	No	No	No	No	No	No

(A) Countries having mandatory data protection laws.

(B) Countries without mandatory data processing laws.

[a] See full IAA report for listing of limitations.

[b] Information regarding the name of the gov't agency that must be contacted to obtain permission and requirements is listed in the full IAA report.

Source: "International Direct Marketing," *1983 Fact Book on Direct Marketing* (New York: Direct Marketing Association, 1983): 174–77

Europe or on locally compiled lists.[28] Rental costs for lists can be high, with an average of $140 for 1,000 names. Such list owners as *Time* and *Newsweek* charge as high as $250 for 1,000 names. It is common to mail materials from Singapore because of competitive printing services, availability of professional letter mailing firms, and discounts on airmail postage rates. Surface mail costs about $45 per 1,000 pieces in Singapore and Malaysia, with the cost being around $75 elsewhere. Indonesia is one of the most responsive markets to direct mail-outs, with Malaysia being a close second in that part of the world. Direct-mail users must expend special efforts in Hong Kong and Singapore because of the attitude there toward "junk mail." For Thailand, Taiwan, South Korea, and Japan, potential language problems must further be taken into account.

U.S. companies using direct mail to contact customers abroad may find "remailing" useful and economical. U.S. regulations prohibit remail operations, making it difficult if not almost impossible for other companies to take business away from the U.S. Postal Service (USPS)—at least within the United States. Mailers can bypass the restriction only (1) if quicker delivery (i.e., by noon the next day) is necessary to avoid loss of value on the piece and (2) if a mailer must pay a "premium" price or at least $3 for the delivery.[29] The USPS has interpreted the second requirement to mean a minimum of $3 for each individual piece, whereas others have contended that the premium price applies to a "package" of any number of pieces. Remailers thus challenge the USPS's monopoly on overseas mail deliveries. They ship packages, stuffed with letters intended for foreign destinations, to post offices outside the United States for remailing. Countries that are popular for this purpose include Australia, Canada, the United Kingdom, the Netherlands, Singapore, and Switzerland. Interestingly, the USPS, after receiving no legal support for its interpretation, entered the remailing business itself.

There are three basic ways to move a marketer's promotional materials from the United States. First, the ISAL (International Surface Airlift) system was designed by the U.S. Postal Service to use a combination of air and surface transportation. This is the least expensive way of moving materials for bulk mailers and publishers. After being received at ISAL's acceptance points, the material is airlifted to selected distribution points around the world where it merges with other surface-mail pieces. Second, mailers who do not want to bother with ISAL's requirements can pay a surcharge to ISAL consolidators, which are private companies that will sort, bag, and transport the material to an ISAL gateway city. Finally, remailers are private distribution services that provide a turnkey system and negotiate private rates with airline cargo divisions (see Exhibit 15–8).[30]

Outdoor

Outdoor advertising includes posters, billboards, painted bulletins, roadside and store signs, and electric spectaculars (large illuminated, electric signs with special lighting and animated effects). Given the great impact and impressiveness of size and color, outdoor advertising serves well as reminder promotion for well-known products.

Outdoor advertising is frequently used overseas because of the low cost of labor in painting and erecting such displays. In addition, this is considered a free

EXHIBIT 15-8 An advertisement for a remailing service

Source: Reprinted with permission of Johnson & Hayward Inc.

medium, because an advertiser can simply place its posters on any available wall, bus-stop shelter, tree, or fence without paying for it. The practice also encourages one advertiser to replace other advertisers' posters with one of its own.

Unlike most media, outdoor advertising is one medium in which the United States seems to lag behind other countries in terms of per-capita advertising expenditures and sophistication. This is an advanced and dominant medium in Europe and Canada. Outdoor advertising is also very important in countries without commercial TV (e.g., Belgium). In Saudi Arabia, outdoor and transit posters account for 27 percent of all media spending, in stark contrast with the mere 2.8 percent in the United States.[31]

Outdoor advertising does not have to be uninteresting. One advertiser changes its outdoor illustration and message frequently—with the model removing an item of clothing each time the poster board was changed. Another advertiser made it appear that the billboard was gradually being eaten away by termites.

New technologies have added such design options as backlighting, projection, Day-Glo paints, three-dimensionals, extensions, reflective disks, bows, and cutouts. Fiber optics may eventually replace neon because fiber optics are much more energy efficient and weigh less than neon glass tubing. Some advertisers have turned to video billboards that can show a twenty-second commercial repeatedly.

When using outdoor advertising, certain rules should be followed. Illustrations should be large, and words should be kept to a minimum. A rule of thumb is to say "what *must* be said" and not "What *can* be said." Simple, contrasting colors should be used: white on black or red seems to work well. The right typeface is critical; certain typefaces are difficult to read. Having all letters in capitals can be equally as difficult and should be avoided.

Screen (Cinema)

In virtually all countries, the cinema is a favorite activity for social gathering. People are avid moviegoers because of the limited television broadcasting and because of people's natural desire to go out to a place of social gathering. Cinemas (or theaters, as they are called in many parts of the world) are classified as first-class or second-class and sometimes even third-class, depending on how soon new films are shown there. Theaters usually open at noon during the weekdays and earlier on weekends, and they usually operate on a reserved-seat basis, with advance reserve bookings being highly encouraged. In Japan, the lack of theaters allows theater operators to pick and choose films and to book only those that will be heavily promoted months before the actual showing, preferably with repeated announcements in prime time on TV.

Much like outdoor advertising, the cinema is a very popular advertising medium outside of the United States. Cinemas sell commercial time to agencies or advertisers. The usual practice is for a theater to begin its program with a showing of slides of advertised products, and this slide show is followed by commercials. The theater may then proceed to show newsreels and documentaries that may contain paid news items such as a store opening. Then, just before the showing of the main feature, there are short promotional films or teaser trailers of coming attractions. An intermission can present another opportunity for advertising.

Cinema advertising has several advantages. It has the impact of outdoor advertising without the drawback of being stationary. It has sight and sound like television but with better quality. Furthermore, cinema advertising has a true captive audience. A disadvantage is that some moviegoers may resent having to watch commercials. But such resentment is likely a minor problem, since moviegoers are usually in a positive and receptive mood. The more serious problem is that patrons, knowing that there will be some commercials shown first, take their time in showing up and may be wandering into and about the theater until the main feature begins.

Directories

Directories are books that provide listings of people, professions, and institutions. The yellow-page telephone directories, with a listing of various types of companies, are a prime example. Directories may be sold or given away free of charge. Because the telephone is not widely available in many areas and the information is not accurate, this medium has been underutilized outside of the United States. In some countries, governments and private entities publish trade directories of local exporters and their advertisements.

Rural Media

In marketing to LDCs, marketers must understand the use of rural media. Mobile units, for example, can be sent to areas lacking access to mass media. Such vehicles can play recorded music and advertising messages over amplifiers or loudspeakers attached to the vehicles' rooftops. A marketer can also attract an audience by arranging for some type of festival advertising held at a temple or school. A free outdoor movie can be shown during the festival while advertising is broadcast through loudspeakers to the captive audience. In a way, such rural media are not much different than the traveling "medicine" shows of the American past.

Stadium

Stadium advertising is also appropriate, especially in soccer stadiums, because soccer (i.e., "football") is the most popular and passionate sport in the world. Signs can be displayed on stadium walls, and the advertising rules for outdoor advertising should be applied. During the 1986 World Cup soccer games, multinational advertisers could purchase two signs at a cost of $7 million. The two signs were displayed at all twelve stadiums in Mexico and during the 117 preliminary and final games over the four years between cup championships. The objective of this advertising is not so much to communicate with soccer fans who attend the game but rather to communicate with TV viewers. With a camera following the non-stop action on the field, each of the two signs showing a corporate logo on the stadium wall was seen an average of 7.5 minutes per game by 12 billion worldwide viewers.[32] Although NBC (which broadcast the finals to the United States) had to cut away from the action to broadcast commercials, non-U.S. broadcast networks were able to continue showing the entire game by simply showing logos or brief advertising messages on the edges of the screen—at the top, bottom, side, or all around, with the game being shown in the middle part of the screen.

Cigarette marketers are major sponsors of sports and cultural events (e.g., billiards, horse racing, rugby, and symphony orchestras) in England because these events receive extensive TV coverage. In effect, the prominent display of names and logos allows companies to associate their brands with glamor, health, vitality, and success.

Other Media

There are several other advertising media that are traditional and common in LDCs and elsewhere. Some of these media are *advertising specialties,* a variety of inexpensive items (e.g., pens, calendars, letter openers) carrying the advertiser's name, address, and a short sales message. In spite of the cost, such items are relatively durable. Because of their attractive appearance and low production cost, Ajinomoto's

TABLE 15–10   Percent of advertising expenditures (1980) allocated to various media in selected countries

Media	West Germany	United States	Japan	Brazil
Cinema	1	—	—	1
Radio	3	7	5	13
TV	10	21	35	32
Print	65	38	37	25
All others outdoor, direct, etc.	21	34	23	29

Source: World Advertising Expenditures (Mamaroneck, NY: Starch/INRA/Hooper, 1981)

calendar-type products are an effective display in Japan and other Asian countries. A charming, attractive young girl (Miss Ajinomoto) serves as an "eye-catcher" to help advertise products. Ajinomoto provides three-ounce bottles to restaurants as toothpick holders or seasoning containers. In addition to using the traveling cinema, a popular form of entertainment, Ajinomoto also uses the traveling cooking school, which combines the expertise of a cook and a nutritionist, to provide instruction and education to many institutions such as schools. Moreover, the company uses "exhibitions," or public-service advertising, to promote total company image and technical expertise, such as with the anticancer medicine Lentinan and the sugarless sweetener Aspartame.[33]

Media Mix

There is no one single advertising medium that is suitable for all countries and products. The media mix thus has to vary from one target market to another. Table 15–10 examines expenditure allocation in various countries. Nevertheless, the basic principles of media selection apply in all markets. In general, an advertising medium should be selective and cost-effective in reaching a large number of the intended audience. It should deliver the kind of reach, frequency, and impact desired, assuming that there are no particular legal restrictions.

Tokyo Toyopet provides a good illustration of how advertising media are selected to promote cars—in this case, Toyota cars. Newspapers and magazines, due to their national circulation in Japan, are unsuitable because this division of Toyota only concentrates on the Tokyo market. TV time is not readily available and much too expensive. As a result, radio advertising is the clear-cut choice. Not only is radio very popular among Japanese consumers, but it also allows Tokyo Toyopet to reach the target market at the right time. Drivers stuck in the terrible traffic of Tokyo are very receptive to advertising messages suggesting that they trade in their old, uncomfortable vehicles.[34]

STANDARDIZED INTERNATIONAL ADVERTISING

Standardized international advertising is the practice of advertising the same product in the same way everywhere in the world. The controversy of the standardization of global advertising centers on the appropriateness of the variation (or the lack of it) within advertising content from country to country. The technique has generated a heated and lively debate for more than twenty years and has been both praised and condemned—passionately.

Doing research is difficult in this area because of the ambiguous definition of standardization itself. Strictly speaking, a standardized advertisement is an advertisement that is used internationally with virtually no change in its theme, copy, or illustration (other than translation). More recently, a new breed of advocates of standardization has claimed that an advertisement with changes in its copy or illustration (e.g., a foreign model used in an overseas version) is still a standardized ad as long as the same theme is maintained. This new and broadened definition can cloud the issue even more with the added element of subjectivity. Because standardization is a matter of degree rather than an all-or-nothing phenomenon, a more precise definition of standardized advertising, conceptually and operationally, would go a long way toward solving the confusion created by contradictory claims.

Dewar's advertising is a good example of how difficult it is to state with certainty whether a certain advertisement is a standardized advertisement or not. After twenty years, the highly regarded U.S. "Profiles" campaign for Dewar's Scotch whisky was tailored to markets around the world. The format is the same in every country: it provides biographical information, hobbies, and philosophies to portray the successful lifestyle of an entrepreneurial "life-achiever" who also happens to be a typical and famous Dewar's drinker (see Exhibit 15–9). Previously, Dewar's overseas advertising used translations of American advertisements, but research revealed that the use of local personalities would communicate a stronger message. The localized profile advertisements used in Spain featured profiles of a Spanish author and a 29-year-old Spanish flight instructor and former hang-gliding champion. The Australian campaign gave Dewar's profiles of a 33-year-old Melbourne entrepreneur, a jewelry designer, and a photojournalist. In Thailand, the advertisement featured a Bangkok architect. These campaigns were handled by the local Leo Burnett offices.[35]

The issue of advertising standardization, without doubt, has far reaching implications. If it is a valid strategy, international business managers should definitely take advantage of the accompanying benefits of decision simplification, cost reduction, and efficiency. On the other hand, if the premise of this approach is false, the indiscriminate application of standardized advertising in the marketplace will cause more harm than good since it can result in consumers misinterpreting the intended message. Consequently, the important function of advertising to facilitate a consumer's search process can be seriously impaired.

There are three schools of thought on the issue of standardized advertising: (1) standardization, (2) individualization, and (3) compromise. The standardization school, also known as the *universal, internationalized, common,* or *uniform* approach, questions the traditional belief in the heterogeneity of the market and the importance of the localized approach. This school of thought assumes that better and faster communication has forged a convergence of art, literature, media availability, tastes, thoughts, religious beliefs, culture, living conditions, language, and, therefore, advertising. Even when people are different, their basic physiological and psychological needs are still presumed to remain the same. Therefore, success in advertising depends on motivation patterns rather than on geography. This belief is held by

EXHIBIT 15–9 A standardized advertisement?

Source: Reprinted with permission of Schenley Industries, Inc.

Elinder, Roostal, Fatt, Strouse, and Levitt, among others.[36] British Airways's image advertisements, which were designed by Saatchi and Saatchi to trumpet the newly sleek British Airways, have been cited as an example of a successful standardized campaign.

The opposite view of the standardization school is the individualization school, also know as the *nonstandardization, specificity, localization,* or *customization* approach. This conventional school of thought holds that advertisers must particularly make note of the differences among countries (e.g., culture, taste, media, discretionary income). These differences make it necessary to develop specific advertising programs to achieve impact in the local markets. Authorities sharing this view include Nielsen, Lenormand, Lipson, and Lamont.[37]

A good illustration of the importance of individualization is the Shiseido case. That company, the world's third largest cosmetic company, did poorly in its first attempt to penetrate the U.S. market because its advertisements featured only Japanese models. Another example is Levi Strauss. Although world renowned, Levi Strauss nonetheless created local promotional campaigns. Its European TV commercials employed the super-sexy appeal. In England, the message was that Levi's was an American brand, and the advertisements showed the all-American hero (cowboy) in fantasy Wild West settings. The company could not use the same tactic in Japan, however, because local jean companies had already positioned themselves as American. To differentiate itself from local competitors, the company stressed that Levi's was "legendary," and its "heroes wear Levi's" theme featured James Dean and other cult figures. This campaign was so successful that brand awareness there shot up from 35 to 95 percent. In Australia, the company built awareness and emphasized product benefits by using these lines: "fit looks tight, doesn't feel tight, can feel comfortable all night" and "a legend doesn't come apart at the seams." The Brazilian market, on the other hand, posed a problem because this market was influenced more by European fashion trends than by trends in the United States. Levi's made the necessary adaptation, filming its advertisement in Paris showing young people looking "cool" amidst a wild Parisian traffic scene.[38]

Between these two extreme schools is the compromise school of thought. While recognizing local differences and cautioning against a wholesale or automatic use of standardization, this middle-of-the-road school holds that it may be possible, and in certain cases even desirable, to use U.S. marketing techniques under some conditions. Those with this moderate view include Dunn, Keegan, Peebles, Ryans, and Vernon.[39]

Jain has proposed a framework for determining marketing program standardization. Standardization is more practical and effective under these conditions:[40]

1. Markets are economically alike.
2. Worldwide customers, not countries, are the basis for identifying the segments to serve.
3. Countries have similar customer behavior and lifestyle.
4. The product has cultural compatibility across countries.
5. There is a great degree of similarity in the firm's competitive position in different markets.
6. The firm competes against the same adversaries with similar share positions in different markets.

7. Product is industrial or high-tech (versus consumer product).
8. Home market positioning strategy is meaningful in the host market.
9. Countries have similar physical, political, and legal environments.
10. There are similar marketing infrastructures in the home and host countries.
11. Firms possess key managers who share a common world view.
12. Strategic consensus exists among parent-subsidiary managers.
13. Authority for setting policies and allocating resources is centralized.

Keegan provides a set of guidelines that can help in determining when it is appropriate to use standardized advertising. According to Keegan there are five international product and promotion strategies.[41] The choice of strategy depends on such factors as cost, need, and use conditions. A particular product can be extended (i.e., unchanged) if use conditions are uniform across markets. Likewise, a promotional campaign can be standardized or extended if consumer need for this particular product is universal. As a company moves from the first strategy toward the last, there is a corresponding increase in cost.

The first of the five strategies is *one product, one message, worldwide.* This strategy is feasible if both the need and use conditions are uniform across countries. Not many products satisfy these conditions, though Coke and Pepsi are often cited as examples. Other examples include diamonds, Chivas Regal scotch, and BMW automobiles. Mentioned in jest by some authorities are products that may even be more truly global, such as Israeli Uzi submachine guns, French Exocet missiles, Russian Kalashnikov rifles, and nuclear weapons.

The second of the five strategies is *product extension-communications adaptation.* A product may be extended to other countries because of uniform use conditions, but the promotional message very likely must be changed because needs vary. Toothpaste is used in the same manner everywhere but often for different reasons. People in the north of England and in the French-speaking areas of Canada use toothpaste primarily for breath control, making the appeal of fluoride toothpastes rather limited. Anheuser-Busch and its partners market the same beer in many countries but customize their advertisements (based on American themes) for each national market.

Product adaptation-communications extension is the third strategy. When use conditions differ but need remains constant across markets, modification of product but not promotion is necessary. Black and Decker, although wanting to globalize its power tools, must make several product adjustments to fit certain markets. The tools everywhere look the same on the outside. But inside it is another matter, especially for markets in which the variations in electrical outlets and voltages require different circuits and cords. Likewise, people everywhere use a word processor for essentially the same reason. Therefore, only the machine itself has to be modified for local use conditions. For example, the Japanese-language word processor is quite complicated because the keyboard must accommodate more than 2,000 kanji characters and two 48-character kana phonetic alphabets.

Interbras, a Brazilian firm, had to accept returns of more than 100,000 pairs of shoes sold to the former Soviet Union because it failed to adapt its flimsy tropical footwear to the harsher climates in that northern country. Chevrolet Malibus were mechanically unfit for Iraq's heat and dust. Their air filters tended to clog with dust, and the cars labored in the heat and traffic. Clark Copy International's copier worked poorly in China. The high heat and humidity caused the paper to jam, in addition to other reliability problems.

Dual adaptation is the fourth strategy. Both the product and promotion have to be changed for a foreign market owing to variations in need as well as use conditions in various countries. Refrigerators made for the United States, for example, must be modified to accommodate 220-volt and 50 Hz electricity overseas. The large refrigerator and its large freezer compartment do not appeal to people in countries where shopping for fresh food is done daily and where a refrigerator is used mainly for short-term storage. Additionally, with the high cost of electricity in virtually all markets outside the United States, the advertising appeal must be based on low electricity consumption, durability, reliability, and compactness.

Product invention is the last strategy. This strategy may have to be used if the existing product is too expensive for foreign consumers. A brand new product with different features may have to be designed in order to make it affordable. For generations, Indians have called *dhobis* to collect dirty laundry from middle-class neighborhoods and wash it upon the rocks at the river. Seeing this as an opportunity for product invention, Whirlpool Corp. has appealed to young professional Indian couples who want Western-style automatic washing machines by offering what it calls the World Washer. Whirlpool's compact washers have specially designed agitators that do not tangle saris, the flowing outfits worn by a large number of Indian women. Variations of the World Washer are also manufactured and sold in Brazil and Mexico, and there are plans to export them to other Asian and Latin American countries. Except for minor variations in the controls, the three versions are nearly identical and sell for $270 to $650. The World Washer is a simple, affordable, bare-bones washer that does only eleven pounds of wash, or about one-half the capacity of the typical U.S. model.[42]

Keegan's guidelines, although useful, are quite general. Thus, one must consider other relevant factors and treat them explicitly. For an international advertising manager, the decision is affected by his or her perception of whether it is "feasible" and "desirable" to implement standardization. In some cases, it may be feasible but not desirable to use a standardized advertisement; in other cases, it may be desirable but not feasible to do so. The applicability of advertising standardization is a function of these two conditions.

The *feasibility* issue has to do with whether environmental restrictions or difficulties may prohibit the use of a standardized campaign. Three common problems are local regulations, media and agency availability, and literacy (for print advertisements). Japan, for example, did not allow foreign cigarette brands to be advertised on TV until a few years ago. Even then, the ban was lifted only for new brands. Some countries restrict the import of message materials. In India, customs regulations impose duty on sales literature in loose sheets but not those in book form. Also, many countries have laws that place restrictions on the nature, content, and style of advertising messages. Germany's emphasis on fair competition results in the prohibition of slander against competitors. As a result, the advertiser must be wary of using comparatives (e.g., better, superior) and superlatives (e.g., best, most durable). The Marlboro cowboy was banned in England on the grounds that cowboy worship among children might induce them to take up smoking. Philip Morris's replacement of the cowboy with only a saddle and riding gear still proved unacceptable to the British government. In the end, the company had to use noncowboys driving around Marlboro country in a Jeep.

A multinational advertiser wishing to use a standardized advertising campaign needs to rely on an advertising agency with a worldwide network to coordinate the campaign across nations. Unfortunately, almost no agencies, regardless of size, are in a position to control local agencies overseas. A survey examining the extent to which American firms use the same agency to advertise abroad and in the home market found that only about one-third of the brands are handled by the same agency both at home and abroad. This proportion is relatively constant regardless of advertising budgets, product class, or whether the brand is standardized or non-standardized.[43] Most media purchasing is done by agencies from the specific target countries, that are most familiar with their own domestic media. True international advertising represents a small fraction of advertising activity and is directed at an upscale group of business executives who are the target market for travel-related products/services, business products, and upscale consumer products.[44]

Because illiteracy adversely affects the comprehension of advertising copy, the text portion of an ad must frequently be minimized or replaced with pictures. Although pictures may appear to be an effective means of communicating with nonliterate market segments, there are problems in pictorial perception, and certain types of pictures are likely to fail to communicate with nonliterate markets in developing countries. Therefore, international marketers should research their markets before attempting to communicate with them through pictures.[45]

Degree of feasibility varies from country to country, facilitating the implementation of standardization in some countries while creating problems in others. Furthermore, an environment may change, permitting either more or less opportunity for standardization in the future. Therefore, feasibility is dependent on the situation and does not offer solid support for either of the two extreme schools of thought.

Two major criteria exist to judge the degree of *desirability* of a standardized advertisement. One of these is the amount of cost savings that might be achieved. Thus, standardization is desirable only when the derived saving in production cost of this type of advertisement is significant.

Another criterion of desirability is consumer homogeneity, a major assumption of the uniform approach. If consumers were indeed homogeneous across countries, the debate would be resolved, since consumers could then be motivated in exactly the same way. Are consumers homogeneous? The proponents of each school of thought have offered real-life examples that are subjective and highly judgmental. Consumers would be better served if the collection of empirical data were based on research designs that eliminate the effect of confounding factors. The results of the literature review of management responses, consumer characteristics, and consumer responses indicate that there is no theoretical or empirical evidence to support the standardization perspective in its present form.[46]

Examinations of advertisement content have repeatedly found that, in practice, the content or message of advertisements varies significantly from one market to another. A study of the information content of U.S. and British TV commercials found that advertisements for high-involvement and rational products contain the most information, with generally higher levels in the United States than in England.[47] Because Chinese incomes are low and Chinese are inexperienced consumers, they tend to seek information on product attributes. Moreover, because they highly value performance and quality in their products, appropriately practical appeals—not "symbolic" advertising appeals commonly found in the West—should be used.[48] A study of automobile advertisements that appeared in business magazines in Brazil and in the United States found that Brazilian advertisements used urban themes more frequently but that American advertisements used leisure themes more frequently. Brazilian and U.S. advertisements were about equal in using work themes. Because values differ between the business culture of Brazil and that of the United States, advertisers considering a standardized advertising theme should carefully research each national market.[49]

In Japan, magazine advertisements were found to be generally more informative than American advertisements, although specific content varied cross-culturally.[50] Another study found that Japanese advertisements contained at least as many information cues as U.S. advertisements. In any case, Japanese advertisements were more emotional and less comparative than American advertisements.[51]

The lack of consumer homogeneity explains why advertising approach varies from country to country. As concluded by Dentsu, a large and well-known Japanese advertising agency, Western advertising is more verbal, direct, and logical. Japanese advertising, in contrast, tends to be emotional, indirect, and suggestive, and the use of soft music, beautiful scenery, and soft voices enhances the emotional appeals.[52] Such nonverbal elements inspire inference rather than direct understanding.

Many American advertisers do not appreciate the Japanese advertising approach, labeling it as art rather than as a sales tool. They criticize Japanese advertising as having mood but no concept. Japanese consumers, on the other hand, generally view American advertisements as being pushy and offensive, not unlike walking into their homes with shoes on.[53] To the Japanese, style and manners are important, and it is appropriate to use subdued mood and tone as well as subtlety of message. Therefore, advertising in Japan should be less personal, emphasizing the product rather than the consumer. For example, it is improper to talk about the consumer having bad breath or a dirty shirt. More appropriately, the message should emphasize how well the product works.[54]

In practice, the degree of standardization of the marketing mix by large U.S.-based industrial firms in their Latin American businesses was found to vary across individual elements. Branding and product were least adapted, whereas price and advertising were most adapted. In comparison with the same firms' marketing strategies in Europe, advertising, brand, and product were more standardized in Latin America.[55] Another study found that food, drink, and pharmaceuticals tend to adapt sales platforms more than do cosmetics or general consumer goods, but that there were no significant differences among creative context adaptation.[56] An analysis of print and TV advertisements for American products appearing in the United States, Germany, and Japan found that, regardless of product category, highly standardized messages contain significantly fewer amounts of consumer information cues than highly specialized messages (see Table 15–11).[57]

One study found that firms that advertise internationally utilize the following strategies: a combination of localized and standardized advertising (56 percent), all localized advertising (36 percent), and all standardized advertising (8 percent). The majority felt that it was important to adapt advertising components (language, models, scenic backgrounds, and product attributes) to blend with the culture. Regarding transfer, the acceptance of trademarks/brand names was the most important factor.[58]

After having seen or experienced difficulties in implementing the standardization concept, most international advertisers today have had second thoughts about standardization and have moved toward some degree of localization.[59] Saatchi and Saatchi touted the virtue of the "world brand" concept without having a single solid example of it (except for some of the ideas used in the worldwide British Airways

TABLE 15–11 Number of information cues in highly standardized and highly specialized messages for all products

Product	Similarity Rating[a]	Cues
Highly standardized messages		
Mars Bar: US/G-TV	1.00	1
American Express: US/J-TV	1.00	2
Marlboro Cigarettes: US/G-Print	1.63	1
Pan American Airlines: US/G-Print	1.78	2
Marlboro Lights: US/G-Print	1.78	0
Johnsons Baby Oil: US/J-Print	2.27	1
Polaroid Camera: US/G-TV	2.50	3
Coca Cola: US/J-TV	2.60	0
American Express: US/G-TV	2.75	2
[a]Mean: 1.33		
Highly specialized messages		
American Express US/G-Print	4.00	1
Visa: US/J-Print	4.00	5
Maybelline: US/J-Print	4.10	2
TWA: US/J-Print	4.10	3
Diners Club: US/G-Print	4.11	2
Exxon/Esso: US/J-TV	4.11	1
Ford Escort: US/G-Print	4.13	6
TWA: US/G-Print	4.22	3
Welch's: US/J-Print	4.54	2
Camel: US/G-Print	4.55	1
[a]Mean: 2.60		
[a]$(F(1,17) = 3.75; p = .07)$		

[a]Based on a five-point scale, ranging from 1 ("very similar") to 5 ("not similar at all").

Source: Barbara Mueller, "An Analysis of Information Content in Standardized vs. Specialized Multinational Advertisements," *Journal of International Business Studies* 22 (no. 1, 1991): 35

account). The Saatchis only owned a few of their agencies outright around the world and were not in a position to control local agencies. As Procter & Gamble's international chief has pointed out, although "technology" (e.g., gel toothpaste) is global, other aspects such as taste, coloring, packaging, and advertising of the technology are usually local.

Parker Pen Co. launched an ambitious "one world, one voice" program in 1984 to sell writing instruments all over the world. The effort was unsuccessful because the firm ignored national differences while force-feeding uniform promotional practices to local managers who doubted their wisdom. Parker's new European owners later reversed the strategy. By again tailoring advertisements to local markets, the company has turned losses into sizable profits. Coca-Cola Co., often a prime example of the practice of global marketing, allowed local flavor to be incorporated in its "General Assembly" campaign, which shows a thousand children singing the praises of Coke. Because each McCann office had permission to edit the film to include close-ups of a youngster from its market, at least twenty-one different versions of the spot existed.[60]

All forms of advertising standardization should not be ignored by the marketer. This technique may be appropriate on a modest scale, though definitely not on a worldwide basis. A limited homogeneity does exist in many cultures around the world. It is thus a good idea to find out when and where this limited scale of homogeneity exists so that some level of standardization can be considered.

For decision-making purposes, market segmentation can provide a practical framework for standardizing advertising, as shown in Exhibit 15–10. If the world is treated as one whole market, a standardized advertisement can then be used. But if the world is divided into several segments (i.e., regions or countries), each segment probably requires its own custom-made marketing mix (i.e., a localized advertisement).

A market should be segmented when five requirements are met: identification, accessibility, differential response, segment size, and cost/profit. Each country (or region) should be considered a distinct segment if the following conditions are met:

1. The marketer can identify the country's unique demographic characteristics.
2. The country is accessible through available selective advertising media with minimum promotion waste.
3. The responses to a unique marketing mix of customers in the country will be favorably different from those of other countries.
4. The country's population size is large enough to justify the specially designed marketing campaign.
5. Incremental cost as a result of the segmentation is less than incremental profit.

When all these segmentation criteria are met, market segmentation is applicable but advertising standardization is not.

There is no question that the United States is a market segment of its own because of its unique characteristics and responses, media availability, market size, and great profit potential. As such, Asian marketers and European firms (including those from the United Kingdom) as a rule design advertisements specifically for the U.S. market. In contrast, these marketers are more likely to introduce in, say, Asian

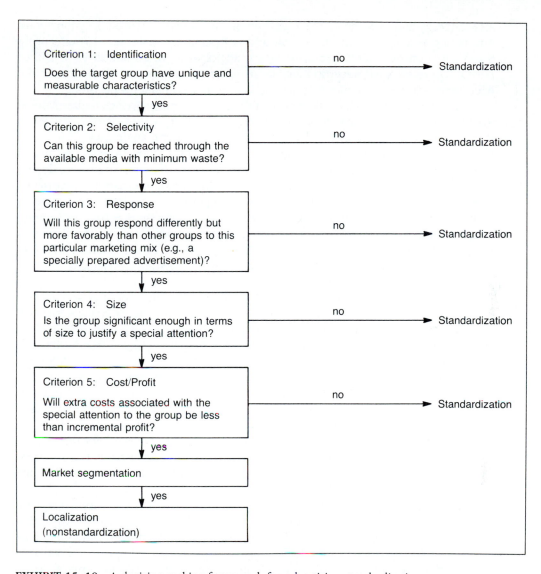

EXHIBIT 15–10   A decision-making framework for advertising standardization

Source: Sak Onkvisit and John J. Shaw, "Standardized International Advertising: A Review and Critical Evaluation of the Theoretical and Empirical Evidence," *Columbia Journal of World Business* 22 (Fall 1987): 53

countries (except Japan) the advertisements that they have already used in their own countries. This action may be due to their belief that these other markets are either similar or are not economically significant enough to justify nonstandardized advertising.

Marketers should understand that standardization is not a universal tool that can be automatically used without proper consideration. It makes no sense to forge worldwide uniformity and conformity for management's convenience if consumers seek diversity and individuality. Standardization and advertising are not synonymous. Advertising is supposed to (1) inform and (2) persuade customers (3) effectively. Standardization may fail to perform any (or all) of these three objectives. It is thus critical to pretest each advertisement in an international context to determine the effectiveness in terms of attention getting, comprehension, and persuasion.

As explained by Farley, it is important to do copy testing: "In fact, if international markets are the same, our meta-analysis should show that worldwide responsiveness is exactly the same— and that is clearly the exception rather than the rule."[61] In Accra, Ghana, a firm launched a major introductory campaign for a new hygiene product. At the center of the campaign on all advertising materials was a drawing of a family prepared by a Ghanian free-lance artist for the local office of an international advertising agency. A one-day copy test organized by stopping people on the street unexpectedly found that they thought the product was meant for the Nigerian expatriot community. The artist had, for whatever reason, drawn the women with hairstyles that Ghanians recognized as foreign. The account executive, an upscale urban Ghanian who had trained in Nigeria, also missed the inconsistency. Copy testing is critical to support entry into unfamiliar markets.

Criticisms of myopic standardization should not be interpreted as an endorsement for a polycentric approach, which requires custom-made campaigns for each individual market. Localization, practiced for its own sake, can be just as myopic. What is desirable is a kind of geocentricity, which is not the same thing as standardization.

Standardization is basically a campaign designed for one market but exported to other markets regardless of justification. In contrast, a geocentric campaign requires an advertisement to be designed for the worldwide audience from the outset in order to appeal to shared common denominators while allowing for some modification to suit each market. The geocentric approach combines the best of both worlds (i.e., the cost-reduction advantage of standardization and the advantages of local relevance and effective appeal of individualization). For example, Levi Strauss has switched from all localized advertisements to a pattern advertising strategy that provides the broad outlines, but not the details, of the campaign.

Devising a global advertisement is anything but easy. Playtex's experience with this type of campaign makes it plain that there can be a great deal of frustration and difficulty involved.[62] Once employing forty-three different advertisement versions throughout the world, Playtex decided to run a worldwide campaign for its Wow bra for two main reasons. First, cost of preparing commercials for only a dozen countries amounted to only $250,000 (versus $100,000 just for a single advertisement designed for the U.S. market alone). Second, the product's comfortable underwire was presumed to have a universal appeal.

To achieve its objective, Playtex first had to gain the cooperation and trust of local managers, who were afraid that the centralized approach would diminish their authority and job prestige. Videotapes of dozens of models had to be shown to foreign managers for approval before they agreed on one blonde and two brunettes whose looks were supposed to have universal appeal. Next, the company went to Australia to film the various versions of the commercial because only commercials produced there could be broadcast in that country. This requirement necessitated shipping 150 bras into Australia, and the explanation for having so many bras had to be given to

Australian customs officers. Many bras were required because of the variation of style preference across countries. For example, French women prefer lacy bras, whereas their American counterparts like the plainer, opaque styles.

Playtex also had to contend with various government regulations and industry standards. At that time, the television standards in the United States and South Africa did not permit women to be shown modeling bras, and the commercials for those two countries had to use fully clothed models showing a bra on a hanger. The editing of the commercial was another problem, because the length had to vary from twenty seconds to thirty seconds. Likewise, some versions of the commercial were required to have no sound for one second at the beginning. It is interesting that, although the advertising message was standardized, the company had no plan to standardize its bras because it was impossible to standardize such physical features as chest cavities, back sizes, and frame sizes of women of different countries.

IBM's advertising practices provide a good demonstration of how advertisers can strive for a proper balance of consistency and economy on the one hand and regional relevance on the other hand. The company has two types of promotion: international and national (local). A local IBM subsidiary may have its own advertising program based on local objectives, and it can (with cause) reject promotional materials supplied by the headquarters.[63] This approach forces the subsidiary to justify its decision while providing feedback to the headquarters. No subsidiary, however, may reject IBM's international programs since such programs are used both for corporate-type campaigns with international and corporate objectives and for new product introductions. These campaigns rely on inputs of managers of local subsidiaries and those in area headquarters as well as broad concept approval of major overseas subsidiaries. Still, IBM's approach is flexible in the sense that each international program provides several advertisements from which local managers can make their selection.

CONCLUSION

In LDCs, advertising is often viewed as something wasteful. In socialist/communist countries, it may be seen as incompatible with political objectives. It is undeniable that certain advertising practices are misleading, deceptive, and wasteful. Just as undeniable, however, is that advertising serves a useful function by providing consumers with relevant information for intelligent decision making. Although the U.S. style of advertising is not necessarily suitable for all other countries, it does make a significant contribution to the high standards of living in the United States.

U.S. advertisers need to realize and understand that foreign media are not always readily available. Many of the media, especially the broadcast media, are government operated and controlled for security reasons. Broadcast media are considered sensitive instruments because the equipment can be used for espionage or for supporting a coup attempt. It is a common practice for revolutionaries staging a coup to seek control of radio and TV stations for psychological warfare.

Even when foreign media are available, American advertisers must appreciate their different style and approach. Such media as outdoor, cinema, and rural advertising are used extensively outside the United States. Moreover, advertisers in many parts of the world rely more on a repetitive effect than on sophistication within a message. Direct-action advertising and the hard-sell approach may have to give way to an indirect-action approach, emphasizing the reputation and image of a company or brand name even though this usually does not result in immediate sales.

Because of the variations found in advertising regulations, media availability, media approaches, and consumer characteristics, there is a high degree of risk in employing standardized advertising on a worldwide basis. Although a global advertisement may have the advantage of lower cost, cost reduction should not always be the overriding motive. Advertisers need to be less ethnocentric and to show more consideration and regard for foreign consumers. All advertisements, standardized or not, should be tested for suitability for the intended audience before being utilized in the marketplace.

QUESTIONS

1. Cite some foreign regulations that restrict the use of either advertising in general or certain advertising practices in particular. Also, offer the rationale of these regulations.
2. Why is it difficult in most countries to buy (a) TV time and (b) newspaper space?
3. Outside of the United States, why is radio probably the closest thing to a national medium of communication?
4. Although the United States is well known for the creation of many new media, what are some media that are more popular overseas than in the United States?
5. Offer the arguments for each of the three schools of thought: standardization, individualization, and compromise.
6. Is there any empirical evidence supporting standardized advertising (or its homogeneity assumption)?
7. Are standardization and market segmentation compatible strategies?

DISCUSSION ASSIGNMENTS AND MINICASES

1. Does advertising serve any useful purpose in LDCs and socialist/communist countries?
2. Explain how the programming approach of the U.S. television industry may differ from those used in other countries.
3. Do you think that there is a market for a world or international newspaper?
4. Many American consumers consider direct mail to be junk mail, a term that is offensive to the direct-marketing industry. At present, this medium is largely underdeveloped outside of the United States. What is your assessment of the future of direct mail overseas?
5. As an advertising manager, would you plan to use a standardized advertisement?
6. Harman Kardon audio and video products are aimed at the high-end segment of the market.

According to a story appearing in the October 15, 1986, issue of *DM News,* Harman Kardon decided to advertise its products with the same graphic throughout the world. By producing basically one advertisement in six languages (English, Dutch, French, German, Italian, and Japanese), the company expected to save at least $200,000. The Zagoren Group was assigned the duty of coordinating the cooperative effort. The U.S. full-page version appearing in *Audio* and *Stereo Review* showed a Harman Kardon amplifier on a grand piano with a black background and "The Components of High Performance" as the headline. For this advertisement to be used overseas, must there be any changes necessitated by production and other requirements?

CASE 15–1
THE MARLBORO MAN
Should We Modify His Image Overseas?

JEFFREY A. FADIMAN
San Jose State University

The downfall of Winston was due in part to the broadcast ban on cigarette advertising. R. J. Reynolds had a difficult time adapting Winston's appeal to the print media. In contrast, Marlboro did not have this problem, and Philip Morris was able to use magazines and other print media to promote its Marlboro brand effectively. Overtaking Winston in 1976, Marlboro is now the undisputed leader in both the United States and worldwide.

Marlboro's success was quite spectacular. It was responsible for the transformation of Philip Morris from a small tobacco company to the number-one cigarette company in the United States. But it was not an overnight success. Initially introduced in a soft box with, among other filters, a red-cork tip, Marlboro had a female image, which made the brand unpopular among men. The company decided to make a few changes, which included the neutral-cork tip and the addition of a flip-top, crushproof box. Perhaps the most important change was the advertising theme. Marlboro's advertisements featured rugged-looking men, tattooed laborers, and cowboys "who came up the hard way." These virile men usually told something about their he-man lives and explained why they chose Marlboro. Philip Morris was extremely successful in creating a unique image that allowed a man to project himself through the cigarettes he smoked. Winston, on the other hand, could not acquire this distinct image.

The Marlboro cowboy is now a legend. Most U.S. consumers (including many others in all parts of the world) are accustomed to seeing the Marlboro Man. All advertisements of the Marlboro line (full-flavored Marlboro, Marlboro Lights, Marlboro Menthol, Marlboro Mediums, Marlboro 25s, and Marlboro 100s) have one thing in common—the cowboy. He may ride a horse or he may sit at a campfire. He may be alone or he may be with other cowboys. But he is always in the advertisements. The image is so strong that the copy needs only a few words, as shown in Exhibit 1. Yet the message is readily understood.

Questions

Consider the Marlboro advertisement and select a certain country as your target market. Write a formal business memo to a chief executive officer of a small international advertising agency in which you submit suggestions about:

EXHIBIT 1   The Marlboro man

Source: Reprinted by permission of Philip Morris U.S.A.

1. How you would modify the advertisement in order to make it more attractive to a selected target clientele (identify) within the country you have chosen.
2. Why each change you suggest would help the product image to conform more closely to their expectations.

Note: Rough sketches would be nice but are not necessary. Word-pictures can be drawn with equal skill. Simply show each change that you are making. It is the originality, imagination, and effectiveness of each suggestion, not your artistic skill that will count.

CASE 15–2
TOILET ADVERTISING
Can We Modify the Medium Overseas?

JEFFREY A. FADIMAN
San Jose State University

Do people have the right to privacy—in the restrooms? Well, not anymore. In the mid-1980s, a nightclub in a suburb of Chicago created quite a controversy by installing sound equipment above the urinals in the men's restroom. The tape for each unit started when a male patron stepped up to the urinal. While being there, he was insulted by a humorous message.

If a toilet message could be used for fun, it can also be used to make money. Before long, a few bathroom advertising agencies sprang up. One San Francisco agency put the commercial messages in toilet stalls and above the urinals. The 18-by-24-inch advertisements to be mounted to bathroom walls and stalls were enclosed in a plexiglass frame to discourage graffiti. Businesses paid a minimum of $276 per year per advertisement, while a building owner could earn about $2,000 per floor by renting the space.

Toilet advertising was found to offend a few people who wanted to decide on when and where to read. Still, this advertising medium offers several advantages. It has a captive audience, and message recall is good. According to one marketing research study, office workers visit the restroom, on average, three or four times a day, spending approximately four minutes per visit or the total of twelve minutes per day glancing at the advertisements. Of course, this medium is not appropriate for all products, with food and lingerie being prime examples.

Questions

You have just been employed by a small U.S. advertising firm with a keen interest in international promotion. You have been assigned to market the concept of bathroom advertising to a particular country.

Write a preliminary business memo, in essay style, in which you respond to the following questions:

1. Why does this concept work so effectively in the United States?
2. What objections, if any, would the people (rural? urban? other?) have to this type of advertising as it is currently promoted in the United States?
3. Which, among the various potential target clienteles within your chosen country, do you feel might prove most receptive to this type of advertising?
4. How (in what ways) could you redesign various aspects of the concept in order to make it more acceptable to members of your selected target clientele?
5. Why, after you have modified the concept, do you feel it will (or will not) work effectively in your target nation?

NOTES

1. International Trade Administration, *Doing Business with China* (Washington, D.C.: U.S. Department of Commerce, 1983), 27–28.
2. Richard J. Semenik, Nan Zhou, and William L. Moore, "Chinese Managers' Attitudes toward Advertising in China," *Journal of Advertising* 15 (no. 4, 1986): 56–62.
3. Robecca Colwell Quarles and Leo W. Jeffres, "Advertising and National Consumption: A Path Analytic Re-Examination of the Galbraithian Argument," *Journal of Advertising* 1 (no. 2, 1983): 4–13.
4. "U.S. Outspends the World in Ads," *Marketing News,* 29 February 1988, 22.
5. Nicolaos E. Synodinos, Charles F. Keown, and Laurence W. Jacobs, "Transnational Advertising Practices: A Survey of Leading Brand Advertisers in Fifteen Countries," *Journal of Advertising Research* 29 (April/May 1989): 43–50.
6. Peter S. H. Leeflang and Jan C. Reuijl, "Advertising and Industry Sales: An Empirical Study of the West German Cigarette Market," *Journal of Marketing* 49 (Fall 1985): 92–98.
7. Gary L. Lilien and David Weinstein, "An International Comparison of the Determinants of Industrial Marketing Expenditures," *Journal of Marketing* 48 (Winter 1984): 46–53.
8. Jehiel Zif, Robert F. Young, and Ian Fenwick, "A Transnational Study of Advertising-to-Sales Ratios," *Journal of Advertising Research* 24 (June/July 1984): 59–63.
9. J. J. Boddewyn, "Advertising Regulations in the 1980s: The Underlying Global Forces," *Journal of Marketing* 46 (Winter 1982): 27–35.
10. Saeed Samiee and John K. Ryans, Jr., "Advertising and the Consumerism Movement in Europe: The Case of West Germany and Switzerland," *Journal of International Business Studies* 13 (Spring/Summer 1982): 109.
11. "Emotional Impact Can Cut Clutter of 15-Second Spots," *Marketing News,* 5 December 1986, 12.
12. Wayne Walley, "Have :15s Hit Their Peak?" *Advertising Age,* 13 November 1989, 16.
13. Robert F. Roth, *International Marketing Communications* (Chicago: Crain Books, 1982), 262.
14. Jacques Neher, "Liberation of Paris Sets Tradition Free," *Chicago Tribune,* 2 February 1986.
15. "About Marketing Overseas: Hazards and Opportunities," *Direct Marketing* (October 1985): 128.
16. Roth, *International Marketing Communications,* 178.
17. Terry Seawright, "Canadians Require True Understanding," *Marketing News,* 29 August 1986, 16.
18. "International DM Conference in Montreux Draws 3,000 People," *DM News,* 15 May 1986, 51.
19. Arnold Fishman, "International Mail Order—Severe Handicap, High Costs, Tough Regulations," *Direct Marketing* (August 1985): 58–60.
20. "U.S. Retains Highest Mail Order Penetration: Kobs & Draft Study," *DM News,* 15 November 1989, 18.
21. Stan Rapp, "Creative Ideas from Great Britain," *DM News,* 15 September 1985, 14.
22. "International DM Conference."
23. "Ireland Leads Western Europe in Direct Mail Growth, Study Says," *DM News,* 15 May 1986, 9.
24. Dan Abramson, "Bakery Sold 1.5 Million Cakes by Mail in 45 Days," *DM News,* 15 February 1985, 21.
25. Marlene Nadle, "Scotland Attracts $1-Billion in U.S. Dollars Mostly by Using Direct Mail and DR Space Ads," *DM News,* 15 December 1985, 17.
26. Stan Rapp, "Doing Business Overseas," *DM News,* 15 March 1985, 13.
27. Emanuel Soshensky, "Direct Marketing in Austria is Expected to Grow Despite Harsh Privacy Restrictions," *DM News,* 1 December 1985, 6.
28. "Direct Mailers Now Finding Asia More Accessible," *Direct Marketing* (May 1985): 98.

29. Jim Emerson, "Federal Express and United Parcel Fight Proposed Rules on Remailing," *DM News,* 1 January 1986.

30. Richard Miller, "How to Get Your Mail Shipped to Europe," *DM News,* 23 December 1991, 26, 37.

31. Kevin Higgins, "Often Overlooked Outdoor Advertising Offers More Impact and Exposures Than Most Media," *Marketing News,* 22 July 1983, 1, 10.

32. "The Selling of the Biggest Game on Earth," *Business Week,* 9 June 1986, 102–03.

33. Kelichi Koseki, "Marketing Strategies as Adopted by Ajinomoto in Southeast Asia," *Journal of Advertising Research* 30 (April/May 1990): 31–34.

34. Kenneth F. Englade, "A Sales Pitch on the Front Porch," *Chicago Tribune,* 15 August 1985.

35. David Murrow, "Dewar's Profiles Travel Well," *Advertising Age,* 14 August 1989, 28.

36. Erik Elinder, "How International Can European Advertising Be?" *Journal of Marketing* 29 (Spring 1965): 7–11; Erik Elinder, "International Advertisers Must Devise Universal Ads, Dump Separate National Ones, Swedish Adman Avers," *Advertising Age,* 27 November 1961, 91; Ilmar Roostal, "Standardization of Advertising for Western Europe," *Journal of Marketing* 27 (October 1963): 15–20; Arthur C. Fatt, "The Danger of 'Local' International Advertising," *Journal of Marketing* 31 (January 1967): 60–62; Arthur C. Fatt, "A Multi-National Approach to International Advertising," *The International Advertiser* 5 (September 1964): 17–19; Norman H. Strouse, "The Internationalization of the Ad Man," *Columbia Journal of World Business* 1 (Winter 1966): 115–20; Theodore Levitt, "The Globalization of Markets," *Harvard Business Review* 61 (May-June 1983): 92–102.

37. Arthur C. Nielsen, Jr., "Do's and Don't's in Selling Abroad," *Journal of Marketing* 23 (April 1959): 405–11; J. M. Lenormand, "Is Europe Ripe for the Integration of Advertising?" *The International Advertiser* 5 (March 1964): 14; Harry A. Lipson and Douglas F. Lamont, "Marketing Policy Decisions Facing International Marketers in the Less-Developed Countries," *Journal of Marketing* 33 (October 1969): 24–31.

38. "Exporting a Legend," *International Advertiser* (November/December 1981): 2–3.

39. S. Watson Dunn, "The Case Study Approach in Cross-Cultural Research," *Journal of Marketing Research* 3 (February 1966): 26–31; John K. Ryans, Jr., "Is It To Soon to Put a Tiger in Every Tank?" *Columbia Journal of World Business* 4 (March-April): 69–75; Warren J. Keegan, "Multinational Product Planning: Strategic Alternatives," *Journal of Marketing* 33 (January 1969): 58–62; Dean M. Peebles, John K. Ryans, Jr., and Ivan R. Vernon, "Coordinating International Advertising," *Journal of Marketing* 42 (January 1978): 28–34.

40. Subhash C. Jain, "Standardization of International Marketing Strategy: Some Research Hypotheses," *Journal of Marketing* 53 (January 1989): 70–79.

41. Keegan, "Multinational Product Planning."

42. "A Little Washing Machine That Won't Shred a Sari," *Business Week,* 3 June 1991, 100.

43. Barry Nathan Rosen, Jean J. Boddewyn, and Ernst A. Louis, "Participation by U.S. Agencies in International Brand Advertising: An Empirical Study," *Journal of Advertising* 17 (no. 4, 1988): 14–22.

44. David W. Stewart and Kevin J. McAuliffe, "Determinants of International Media Purchasing: A Survey of Media Buyers," *Journal of Advertising* 17 (no. 3, 1988): 22–26.

45. Judy Cohen, "Pictorial Perception and International Marketing Communications," *Journal of International Consumer Marketing* 2 (no. 3, 1990): 49–75.

46. Sak Onkvisit and John J. Shaw, "Standardized International Advertising: A Review and Critical Evaluation of the Theoretical and Empirical Evidence," *Columbia Journal of World Business* 22 (Fall 1987): 43–55.

47. Marc G. Weinberger and Harlan E. Spotts, "A Situational View of Information Content in TV Advertising in the U.S. and U.K.," *Journal of Marketing* 53 (January 1989): 89–94.

48. Marshall D. Rice and Zaiming Lu, "A Content Analysis of Chinese Magazine Advertisements," *Journal of Advertising* 17 (no. 4, 1988): 43–48.

49. Richard Tansey, Michael R. Hyman, and George M. Zinkhan, "Cultural Themes in Brazilian and U.S. Auto Ads: A Cross-Cultural Comparison," *Journal of Advertising* 19 (no. 2, 1990), 30–39.

50. Charles S. Madden, Majorie J. Caballero, and Shinya Matsukubo, "Analysis of Information Content in U.S. and Japanese Magazine Advertising," *Journal of Advertising* 15 (no. 3, 1986): 38–45.

51. Jae W. Hong, Aydin Muderrisoglu, and George M. Zinkhan, "Cultural Differences and Advertising Expression: A Comparative Content Analysis of Japanese and U.S. Magazine Advertising," *Journal of Advertising* 16 (no. 1, 1987): 55–62.

52. William Lazer, Shoji Murata, and Hiroshi Kosaka, "Japanese Marketing: Towards a Better Understanding," *Journal of Marketing* 49 (Spring 1985): 69–81.

53. George Fields, *From Bonsai to Levi's: Where West Meets East* (New York: Macmillan, 1983).

54. Pete Hoke, "Wunderman's View of Global Direct Marketing," *Direct Marketing* (March 1986): 76 ff.

55. Robert Grosse and Walter Zinn, "Standardization in International Marketing: The Latin American Case," *Journal of Global Marketing* 4 (no. 1, 1990): 53–78.

56. John S. Hill and William L. James, "Consumer Nondurable Products: Prospects for Global Advertising," *Journal of International Consumer Marketing* 3 (no. 2, 1991): 79–96.

57. Robert E. Hite and Cynthia Fraser, "International Advertising Strategies of Multinational Corporations," *Journal of Advertising Research* 28 (August/September 1988): 9–17.

58. Barbara Mueller, "An Analysis of Information Content in Standardized vs. Specialized Multinational Advertisements," *Journal of International Business Studies* 22 (no. 1, 1991): 23–39.

59. Dennis Chase, "Saatchis' 'World Brand' Future Didn't Materialize," *Advertising Age,* 23 October 1989, 69; "P&G Goes Global by Acting Like a Local," *Business Week,* 28 August 1989, 58; "Goodbye Global," *Advertising Age,* 16 November 1987, 22, 36; "Ad Fad: Marketers Turn Sour on Global Sales Pitch Harvard Guru Makes," *The Wall Street Journal,* 12 May 1988.

60. "Goodbye Global."

61. John U. Farley, "Are There Truly International Products—and Prime Prospects for Them," *Journal of Advertising Research* 26 (October/November 1986): 17–20.

62. "Playtex Kicks off a One-Ad-Fits-All Campaign," *Business Week,* 16 December 1985, 48–49.

63. Roth, *International Marketing Communications,* 62.

Overseas operations should be told never to forget three no's. Never get involved in legal issues, never allow the formation of labor unions, and never fail to collect accounts receivable.

Takashi Kiuchi, general manager of planning and administration,
International Operations Group, Mitsubishi Electric Corporation

Pricing Strategies
Basic Decisions

16

CHAPTER OUTLINE

THE ROLE OF PRICE
PRICING DECISIONS
ALTERNATIVE PRICING STRATEGIES
DUMPING
PRICE DISTORTION
INFLATION
TRANSFER PRICING
CASE 16–1: Pricing for Profit?

MARKETING ILLUSTRATION
The Price Is Right

The pricing of consumer electronics in the U.S. market by foreign manufacturers provides a good illustration of how the relevant factors are identified and taken into consideration. Korean companies, establishing Samsung and Gold Star as their leading brands, did not want to use bargain basement pricing for their VCRs because they wanted to polish their somewhat questionable image. The companies therefore decided to establish VCR prices at slightly below the better-featured Japanese models' everyday prices but higher than Japanese brands' close-out prices. Prices were also kept higher to avoid an antidumping suit that had earlier been filed against Korean color TV sets. American dealers, on the other hand, expressed some reluctance in handling the Korean brands because the prices were not significantly lower than Japanese products to justify the expected lower quality. Japanese companies, anticipating lower Korean prices, had prepared and were ready to offer their own low-priced VCRs to meet the new challenge.

Another example of what factors should be considered in pricing is provided by Laker Airways. Laker Airways started the simple, original Skytrain concept in 1977. The pricing strategy called for a cut-rate price, which was made possible by the unbundling of the product (i.e., a walk-on, walk-off discount flight that charged for food and frills). Sir Freddie Laker blamed the bankruptcy of his company a few years later on a conspiracy by other carriers. Regardless of the merits of this charge, one contributing factor in the demise of Laker Airways was the abandonment of its original mission. By introducing several types of fares and introducing frills just two years after the original product, Laker became just another full-service airline but with no price advantage over competitors. Passengers felt that they were no longer flying "cheap and cheerful" and that they could get the same price and service from the better-known airlines.

The cases described in the marketing illustration demonstrate the complexity of pricing decisions. In the case of the Japanese, the need to adjust their prices was derived from an attempt to neutralize any threat from newcomers. For the Korean manufacturers, the strategy of offering lower prices was to penetrate the U.S. market and to compensate for the unknown quality of their goods. The low prices, however, still allowed the Korean manufacturers to make sufficient profit margins because of their lower labor costs. In both cases, the pricing strategies were somewhat constrained by host-country regulations, such as the antidumping laws. Finally, as demonstrated by Laker's success and failure, a product's price must reflect its proper value in the eye of the consumer.

This chapter examines pricing decisions in an international context. The chapter begins with a discussion of the role of price in general. It proceeds to cover the various factors that can affect price, with special attention given to certain variables that are unique to international marketing (e.g., foreign exchange rate, dumping, and price control). Methods for dealing with a foreign country's hyperinflation and transfer prices will also receive some attention.

THE ROLE OF PRICE

Price is an integral part of a product—a product cannot exist without a price. It is difficult to think or talk about a product without considering its price. Price is important because it affects demand, and an inverse relationship between the two usually prevails. Price also affects the larger economy because inflation is caused by rapid price increases. Price, however, is not any more important than the other 3 Ps. One should not forget that price should never be isolated from the other parts of the marketing mix. Price should never be treated as an isolate factor.

Price is often misunderstood, especially by many executives. Consumers do not object to price. What they object to is the lack of relationship between the perceived value of the product and the price being charged. They want a fair price, and a fair price can be either high or low as long as it reflects the perceived value of the product in question. Too high a price makes consumers resist making a purchase, because the value is not there. Many consumers have such a perception about American cars. On the other hand, a low price may not help a product that lacks value. Laker Skytrain was unable to attract businesspersons for the New York-London route even with lower prices primarily because baggage transfers were not available.

Price can be absolutely high from a cost standpoint yet relatively low from a demand standpoint, in relation to its value and other features. Therefore, price must be lower than the perceived value or exactly reflect the perceived value. For example, a markdown may be needed for damaged or obsolete goods. But a "high" price may appear to be quite reasonable when extra value is added to a product. Consumers around the world do not mind a high price if they indeed "get what they pay for." However, this too often is not the case. Chinese buyers of machinery do not appear to be influenced by price cutting and special terms. Instead, they want prices to reflect the quality being offered while having some flexibility on matters such as technology transfer and countertrade (see Table 16–1).[1]

Asia Cable illustrates the point about price and perceived value. *Asia Cable* is a newsletter providing economic, political, and cultural news about the Far East. When the initial price was set at $59, the publisher found out that no one wanted to subscribe. *Asia Cable* then discovered that a higher price may do better in the specialized corporate world. As a result, the price was changed to $495 a year. As noted by the publisher, "It is a matter of perceived value."[2]

PRICING DECISIONS

Pricing is one area of marketing that has been largely overlooked. Of all the 4 Ps of marketing, pricing is probably the one that receives the least attention, especially in an international context. A study of the marketing mix by large U.S.-based industrial firms in their Latin American businesses found that the degree of standardization varied across individual elements, with branding and product being least adapted. Perhaps because of government regulations, price and advertising elements were most adapted. In comparison with the same firms' European and Latin American strategies, price was similarly adapted in both regions.[3]

TABLE 16–1   Correlations of each variable with the preference rating of each country

Independent Variable	Germany	Switzerland	U.K.	Italy	Japan	France
Product quality	.40[a]	.41[a]	.49[a]	.40[a]	.39[a]	.47[a]
Price	.22[a]	.09	.23[a]	.05	−.03	.27[b]
Promotion	.16[b]	.33[a]	.35[a]	.31[a]	.13[c]	.30[a]
Service	.25[a]	.32[a]	.40[a]	.23[a]	.29[a]	.49[a]
Technical transfer	−.01	.12	.14	−.05	.19[b]	.13
Financial help	.17[c]	.14	.09	.21[c]	.21[b]	.05
Barter	.06	.10	.03	.29[a]	.18[b]	.37[a]
First to enter (reenter)	.27[a]	.38[a]	.39[a]	.26[a]	.01	.23[c]
Percent of equip. in plant from country	.10	.15	.57[a]	.24[b]	.10	.06
Plant size	.19[b]	.16[c]	.04	.14[c]	.15[c]	−.06
Percent of plant output exported	.03	.22[b]	−.16	.17[c]	−.10	.15
Customer relationships	.33[a]	.31[a]	.36[a]	.37[a]	.13[c]	.28[a]

[a] Significance of correlation ≤ .01
[b] Significance of correlation ≤ .05
[c] Significance of correlation ≤ .10

Source: Norman McGuinness, Nigel Campbell, and James Leontiades, "Selling Machinery to China: Chinese Perceptions of Strategies and Relationships," *Journal of International Business Studies* 22 (no. 2, 1991): 201

One problem with an investigation of pricing decisions is that theories are few and vague. Most of the theories that do exist reduce the large number of pricing variables to a discussion of demand and supply. Because the few theories are inadequate, many pricing decisions are based on intuition, trial and error, or routine procedures (e.g., cost-plus or imitative pricing).

Supply and Demand

The law of supply and demand is a sound starting point in explaining companies' price behavior. A common practice is to reduce the large number of pricing factors to two basic variables: demand and supply. In an efficient, market-oriented economy, demand is affected by competitive activity, and consumers are able to make informed decisions. Price, as a measure of product benefit, acts as the equilibrator of supply and demand. On the supply side, suppliers compete for consumers' limited funds by constantly cutting costs and enhancing product value. On the demand side, any increase in demand is followed by a higher price, and the higher price should in turn moderate demand. The higher price, however, usually induces manufacturers to increase the supply, and more supply should lead to a reduction in price which will then stimulate demand once again. For example, in 1982 Japanese manufacturers of VCRs seemed to lose control over inventories, and Europe was flooded with VCR sets. Consequently, a stockpile of unsold VCRs forced prices to fall dramatically.

The demand-supply model of pricing seems to work best with commodities under a monopoly situation. OPEC, an oil cartel, once controlled the supply of oil so tightly that the cartel was able to push oil prices up sharply. The demand remained high for a period of time because consumers were unable to adjust their driving habits immediately. In the long run, however, high prices curbed excessive demand, and oil prices tumbled during the mid-1980s. The law of supply and demand, in this circumstance, operated in the predicted manner. The moral could be that even a monopolist cannot keep on increasing prices without eventually reducing demand.

The twenty-two-nation International Tin Council, a tin cartel, experienced a similar fate. Initially, the cartel was successful in setting a floor price by buying up excess tin. At the time, Malaysia, Thailand, Indonesia, and Nigeria controlled 80 percent of world production. As the price rose, nonmembers increased their production and gained 40 percent of the market, and some consuming nations not willing to pay the higher prices switched to lower cost materials. After twenty-nine years, the Tin Council failed in its attempt to use export quotas and production cuts to keep the price stable and finally ran out of money in its effort to stockpile tin to support the price. The collapse of the cartel forced the London Metal Exchange to close, and tin trading was suspended. The tin price of $11,721 per ton plummeted. The experience of the Tin Council is not uncommon; commodity agreements in sugar, rubber, cocoa, and coffee have all experienced similar problems.

However, this pricing model based strictly on demand and supply is oversimplified. The straightforward relationship between supply and price can be affected by several factors. Numerous products have been so differentiated that supply alone as a factor is essentially irrelevant. If a product has a distinct, prestigious image, price may become secondary in importance to image. For such a product, supply can be reduced and price can be increased without curtailing demand. Waterford Glass became the best-selling fine crystal in the United States by carefully nurturing its "posh image" as well as by controlling the supply. Waterford held down volume while maintaining premium prices. According to the company, there is no advantage in owning a product that anyone can buy.

Because demand-and-supply analysis can only broadly explain companies' price behavior, it is necessary to consider other relevant factors that affect demand or supply or both and that ultimately influence pricing decisions. When asked to rate the factors important in price setting, American and Canadian international businesses provided the following answers based on a five-point scale (with an average rating in parentheses): total profits (4.7), return on investment (4.41), market share (4.13), total sales volume (4.06), and liquidity (2.19).[4]

Cost

In pricing a product, it is inevitable that cost must be taken into account. British Airways at one time blindly matched the competition's prices without carefully considering its cost structure. By instituting carefully considered restrictions on discount seats, the company was able to increase its yield significantly.

The essential question is not whether cost is considered but rather what kind of cost is considered and to what extent. For one school of thought, the thinking is that

full cost should be used in pricing a product for the overseas market. All costs—including domestic marketing costs (e.g., sales and advertising expenses, marketing research costs) and fixed costs (e.g., research, development, and engineering)—must be paid for by all other countries. As such, the company begins with a domestic price and then adds to it various overseas costs (e.g., freight, packing, insurance, customs duties). This pricing practice, with its high degree of centralization, is also ethnocentric. In effect, with an allowance for transportation costs and tariffs, the same price prevails everywhere in the world. Although the method is simple and straightforward, it is far from being ideal, because it is easy for the price to end up being too high.

Other international marketers use **marginal-cost pricing,** which is more polycentric and decentralized. This pricing method is oriented more toward incremental costs. An implicit assumption is that some of the product costs, such as administration costs and advertising at home, are irrelevant overseas. Also, it is likely that research-and-development costs and engineering costs have already been accounted for in the home market and thus should not be factored in again by extending them to other countries. The actual production costs plus foreign marketing costs are therefore used as the floor price below which prices cannot be set without incurring a loss. Japanese companies often rely on this type of pricing strategy to penetrate foreign markets, as well as to maintain market share. For the Japanese, breaking even is regarded as a success. The Japanese are thus willing to sacrifice profit in order to keep their factories going, a point illustrated by the chaotic pricing practices associated with their 35-mm cameras. At one time, their prices were much below the levels set a few years earlier, and the margins were squeezed to 5 percent or less.

The incremental cost method has the advantage of being sensitive to local conditions. Subsidiary or affiliate companies are allowed to set their own prices. A potential shortcoming in using this method is that because research-and-development costs and the costs of running the headquarters' operation must be borne solely by the home-country market, full cost may not be adequately taken into account by overseas subsidiaries.

In the long run, it is dangerous to be price competitive without being cost competitive. Grundig, for example, tried to gain market share in the VCR market by lowering its higher-priced product model, only to realize that it was losing $40 for every unit sold. There is, however, a possible solution for firms with high costs resulting from high tariffs, transportation costs, and high manufacturing costs at home. They have a choice of either producing their products in the overseas market or granting licenses to local producing firms there.

If a company is unable to control costs or to price its product sufficiently high to cover costs, sooner or later the company will be forced to leave the market. Sinclair, for example, was compelled to withdraw its Timex Sinclair computer from the U.S. market after the competition forced it to drop price to $29, a clearly unprofitable level.

Whether price should be uniform worldwide is a subject of much debate. One school of thought holds that from the management's viewpoint there is no reason for an export price to differ from the home price. Also, economists believe that arbitrage will eliminate any price differential between markets. The second school of thought, however, argues that export price should be lower than home price because the home market actually gains in its overhead expenses by spreading these costs over an expanded production volume. Yet others argue that export prices should be higher because price controls in some countries have kept prices artificially low at home.

Because it is unlikely that any school of thought always provides a suitable answer for all occasions and markets, it is desirable to identify conditions relevant to establishing a uniform price. According to Piercy, "Uniform pricing is likely to be favoured where there are no demand differences between markets; products are identical with those of competitors and easily substitutable; products can be bought and moved across market boundaries; customers can find out worldwide prices; customers may buy in a cheap market and re-sell to others in a more expensive market; or public authorities are monitoring prices." On the other hand, "Price differentiation is likely to be preferred and possibly operated where there are exploitable price differences between markets; products are differentiated and not easily substitutable with those of competitors; there are barriers to the transfer of products across national boundaries; it is not easy for customers to find out what is being charged elsewhere; and prices are not given great attention by authorities or the media."[5]

Elasticity and Cross Elasticity of Demand

Because of the elasticity and cross elasticity of demand, a company does not usually have the option of changing or holding its price steady, independent of action taken by the competitors. Ford, thinking that its number-one position in England was insurmountable, moved unilaterally to end price wars by eliminating discounts and incentives. This action proved to be a strategic error because competitors did not follow suit, and Ford's dominant market share dropped from 32 percent to 27 percent. Always remember that it takes only one company to start or continue a price war.

To be competitive does not mean that a company's price must be at or below the market. A superior or unique product can command a higher price. U.S. beef, generally from grain-fed cattle, sells better in Japan than does lower-priced Australian and New Zealand beef, because cattle in those countries are raised on grass and yield leaner meat. A product with a desirable image can also hold its price above the market. This has always been Sony's strategy, and Sony has stayed away from price wars that might damage its image. But Sony has on occasion been forced to lower prices when, as a result of competitors' price cuts, the price gap between it and other competitors has widened too far. Mazda, though not having a negative image, has a neutral image. Its marketing strategy during much of the 1980s was to position itself as a lower-priced Japanese alternative to Honda and Toyota. The Mazda MX-5 Miata was Mazda's attempt to create a distinct image by stressing feelings over features and performance over price.[6]

A company can insulate itself against cutthroat pricing to a certain extent by cultivating a unique and desirable image. A prestigious image allows a firm to act more or less as a monopolist and to gain additional pricing freedom. Cartier takes full advantage of its reputation. A watch made by its subcontractor for $125, for example, was sold by Cartier for almost five times that amount.

A 1979 study of exporters in France, West Germany, and Great Britain revealed interesting results. Many firms felt that it was impractical and even dangerous to compete on a price basis. Export price competitiveness was viewed as a "crude" form of competition, and price competition was used for simple products but not for products of quality and technological refinement. According to the report, "Only the primitives sell on price as a continuing policy."[7]

Exchange Rate

One pricing problem involves the currency to be used for billing purposes. As a rule, a seller should negotiate to bill in a strong currency, and a buyer should try to gain acceptance in a weak currency. European firms can also minimize exchange risk by using ECU in place of an individual currency for quotation and billing (see Chapter 19). But local regulations must be observed. Greece has strict foreign exchange control. All contracts involving payments in favor of a person in Greece may only be concluded in drachmae. Any provision in a contract to circumvent the requirement will void the contract. Greek law also prohibits the price to be determined in accordance with the rate of exchange of a foreign currency at some future date.[8]

The exchange rate is one factor that generally has no impact in domestic marketing but is quite critical in international marketing. Since March 1985, a severe drop in the dollar value against other major currencies has caused the earnings of U.S. MNCs to jump, because their overseas profits when repatriated brought extra dollars after exchange. In contrast, the devalued dollar brought nothing but displeasure to Japanese exporters. Because of the upward spiral of the yen, Komatsu was forced to raise its prices three times in 1985 and 1986. Komatsu's loss of price advantage forced the company to open a plant in the United States in 1986. Other companies such as Nissan, Honda, and Toyota also had to increase their prices several times. The largest price increase was in a market virtually controlled by the Japanese (e.g., expensive consumer electronics such as CD players and fancy VCRs). Their ability to increase price was, however, more limited at the low end of the market, where the Koreans were right on their heels.

Domestic manufacturers cannot expect to gain competitive advantage solely because of the drop of their home currency. Since its peak in 1985, the foreign exchange value of the U.S. dollar had dropped more than 50 percent by 1987. This significant decline should have dramatically reduced—but did not—the deficit in U.S. international trade. Instead, the deficit in U.S. merchandise trade rose at a record rate, to end 1987 in excess of $170 billion. Explanation ranged from the J-curve to the dollar's strengths against the currencies of Canada and many newly industrialized countries.

Even though dollar prices of imports to the United States indeed increased substantially, a depreciating dollar by itself cannot close the trade gap. A falling dollar, although making imports more expensive, has little meaning if prices for domestic substitutes increase to allow imports to maintain a price advantage. The potential price effects on trade resulting from an exchange-rate change require taking into account the domestic price developments for competing goods. One must examine how importers, exporters, and domestic producers price their products in terms of the falling dollar.

The real issue is the relationship between import prices and prices for domestically produced competitive goods. These exchange rate/price relationships are basic in measuring the impact of an exchange-rate change on countries' actual trade balances. As prices for foreign cars went up, American producers, being preoccupied with restoring profits rather than recovering market share, chose to increase prices as well. It is thus not surprising that the value and volume of automobile imports continue to increase. In contrast, prices of imported and domestic consumer durable goods (e.g., consumer electronics) provided a different and more favorable picture (see Exhibit 16–1). Unless American manufacturers realign their priorities, they should expect difficulty in reestablishing a competitive position for their products in the U.S. market against imports.[9]

Caterpillar's U.S. markets collapsed after the 1982 recession, resulting in a loss of almost $1 billion for Caterpillar from 1982 to 1984. The firm responded by closing old plants, reducing payroll by 30 percent, and expanding its product line. With the help of the dollar's decline, Caterpillar resisted the temptation to raise prices and recaptured market share from Komatsu.

Turnover

Turnover has a significant effect on price level: there is an inverse relationship between these two factors. A company generally is not averse to having a lower markup when the turnover is or will be high. There are several reasons for the existence of this relationship. Because high-turnover items are frequently purchased, buyers tend to develop a keen price awareness and sensitivity. Also, such items tend to have lower opportunity costs because they occupy floor space for only a short time. Moreover, selling costs are less because these items can be sold with a minimum of sales effort. Nevertheless, a decision maker should not automatically reach the conclusion that turnover is a causal factor. It is quite possible that turnover may turn out to be the effect instead. That is, lower prices result in high turnover, but the reverse is not always true.

Turnover is also highly related to the so-called **learning curve effect** or **forward pricing.** This method of pricing is based on the assumption that a large volume of sales, either at present or anticipated, will reduce manufacturing costs and that the reduced costs justify the adoption of a low initial price. The cost reduction is possible because of better economies of scale at a higher level of production and because of the higher efficiency derived from the ability of workers to learn how to use their machines to accelerate production. In effect, the formula requires the introductory price to be determined more by future volume, not present volume. This process is responsible for the transformation in two decades of the gigantic computer that cost several hundred thousand dollars into a small portable unit that costs only a few hundred dollars. Texas Instruments's success and failure were both due to this pricing and production system. TI was able to reduce price steadily as higher and higher levels of output were achieved. But several times during this process, TI reduced prices at a faster rate than the reduction in production costs, and the losses finally forced the company to withdraw from the digital wristwatch and home computer markets.

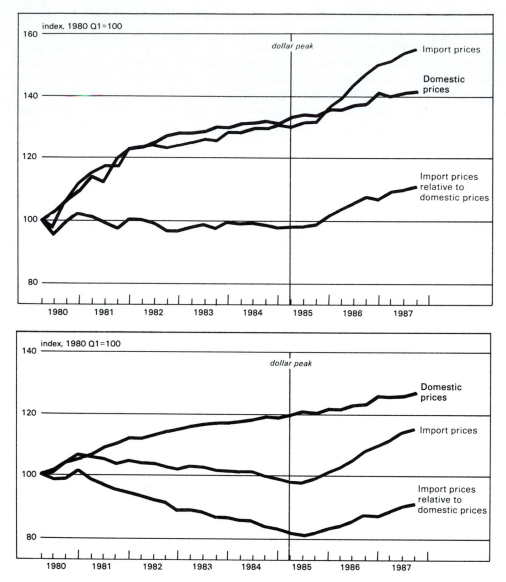

EXHIBIT 16–1   Import prices relative to domestic prices: top graph—auto prices; bottom graph—consumer durables

Source: Jack L. Hervey, "Dollar Drop Helps Those Who Help Themselves," *Chicago Fed Letter,* March 1988

Market Share

Highly related to both turnover and forward pricing is market share. A high market share provides pricing flexibility because the company has the advantage of being above the market if it so chooses. The company can also choose to lower its price because of the better economies of scale derived from lower production and marketing costs. Market share is even more critical for late entrants, because market share acts as an entry barrier. That is, without market share a company cannot achieve the high volume necessary to improve its efficiency. This explains why Hyundai was willing to sell personal computers under the Blue Chip label in the United States at a price that yielded little, if any, profit. The company's plan was to buy market share first to allow it to offer more expensive models later.

Market share can be bought with a very low price at the expense of profit. Michelin, for example, instigated price cutting because it felt that it was not getting sufficient volume. It became the supplier of tires for new Ford Escort and Mercury Lynx automobiles because of its low price. But this price was so low that Michelin lost money for every tire sold. In another example, GM's German subsidiary (Adam Opel) and British subsidiary (Vauxhall) used aggressive pricing to undercut its rival European carmakers. This strategy was necessary to gain market share, but it was not very good for profits. GM's sales did go up, but losses in profit resulted. Therefore, too strong a preoccupation with market share can be damaging and even disastrous for a company.

Various hypotheses explain the differences in pricing behavior between U.S. and Japanese firms, and they range from the dollar's dominant international role and the substantial market power of U.S. goods to the large size of the U.S. domestic market, which permits insensitivity to exchange rate fluctuations. Another explanation is a model based on differences in planning horizons and hysteresis.[10]

Hysteresis is a type of market inertia that says the relationship between two or more variables critically depends on past history. Hysteresis can occur when a firm has increasing returns to scale or when consumers are loyal to particular brands, making it very difficult for new entrants to sell their products at the same level of profit as established firms. In a hysteretic environment, when there is a differentiated shock (i.e., something that temporarily changes costs for some but not other producers), those firms facing higher costs must either raise prices to maintain profits in the short term and risk losing market share in the long run or raise prices less sharply to keep market share in the long run and maximize long-run profits. Japanese price behavior may thus be a rational strategy for long-run profit maximization rather than a predatory, single-minded obsession with market share.

Because U.S. manufacturers usually do not practice price discrimination between domestic and foreign customers, a change in the value of the dollar appears to be reflected entirely in the foreign-currency price of U.S. exports (i.e., complete pass-through of the change rate change). Japanese manufacturers, on the other hand, have a tendency to maintain stable yen prices domestically while keeping their export prices fairly stable by absorbing a significant part of yen fluctuation in the form of flexible profit margins. This pricing behavior, reflecting incomplete pass-through, generates "dumping" when the yen appreciates and lower prices domestically than abroad when the yen depreciates.

Tariffs and Distribution Costs

As a rule, when dumping and subsidies are not involved, a product sold in a host country should cost more than an identical item sold in a manufacturer's home market. This is the case because the overseas price must be increased to cover tariffs and extra distribution costs. In Japan, both tariffs and quotas combine to restrain imports and force the prices of imported goods upward. Also, the long distribution channel (i.e., many middlemen) common in many countries around the world is responsible for price escalation, often without any corresponding increase in distribution efficiency. Foreigners in Japan may be shocked to find that an order of plain toast (without coffee) can cost a few dollars.

Culture

U.S. manufacturers should keep in mind that neither the one-price policy nor the suggested list price will be effective in a number of countries. In the United States, a common practice is for retailers to charge all buyers the same price under similar buying conditions. In most other countries, a flexible or negotiated price is common practice, and buyers and sellers often spend hours haggling about price. Thus, price haggling is an art, and the buyer with the superior negotiating skills can be expected to do better on price than those unfamiliar with the practice.

ALTERNATIVE PRICING STRATEGIES

Pricing involves more than simply marking up or down, and a price change in terms of an increase or decrease is not the only answer to moving a product. There are several other alternatives available for making price changes that should be considered. These strategies include the timing of the price change, number of price changes, time interval to which price change applies, number of items to change, use of discount and credit, and bundling and unbundling. U.S. automakers have become rather ingenious in employing these strategies. They change the price by small amounts a number of times over the year. By increasing price significantly at the end of the current model year and then doing it again for the new model year one month later, the company can claim that the price increase for the new model is small because the calculation of the increase is based on the last price of the current year's model. Not surprisingly, GM saves the heftiest price increase for the end of the year in order to facilitate high sticker prices on the new models that are shortly introduced.

The effect of price can be masked and greatly moderated by financing or credit terms. Airbus, a European consortium jointly owned by four companies from France, Germany, the United Kingdom, and Spain, assembles and markets airplanes as an alternative for carriers that prefer not to buy American. In its eagerness to penetrate the U.S. market, the consortium provided export financing that subsidized Eastern Air Lines by more than $100 million. For Boeing, the consortium engaged in predatory export financing just to get sales. Frank Borman, then president of Eastern, found it such a good deal that he commented, "If you don't kiss the French flag every time you see it, at least salute it."

Discounts (cash, quantity, functional, and so on) can be used to adjust prices indirectly. Large buyers are in a position to command a larger discount if it can be granted legally. Although a quantity discount may provide an incentive for dealers to work harder, it often discriminates against smaller middlemen. Ricoh, concluding that it was not a sound practice to compete on price, decided to ignore tiered pricing that rewarded dealers with large orders. Ricoh uses only flat-rate prices, and small dealers pay the same price as large dealers.[11]

Another method used to moderate the price effect is to bundle or unbundle the product. The price reflects the bundling or unbundling of the product. Bundling usually has three objectives: add value, keep cost increments small, and increase prices a little or not at all for added value.[12] This is the strategy used by Japanese automakers, who increase the base price of their cars just enough to cover actual costs. The Japanese also sell cars in the United States with more standard equipment and fewer options. The strategy makes sense because their vehicles must be shipped from overseas factories, and any custom orders would only serve to delay production and shipment. Moreover, the price charged covers a "bundle" of standard equipment and represents a good value for buyers. Exhibit 16–2 examines Nissan's product bundling.

Detroit takes the opposite route. U.S. automakers keep price low by offering a base price for a bare-bones product. Any other equipment is optional and at an added cost. U.S. automakers thus offer a car with several hundred options. By letting a buyer choose any equipment combination at extra cost for each option, a fully equipped U.S. car can become quite expensive, as Detroit charges and seeks to make profit from each additional item in the option combination.

Ford has begun to experiment with the bundling approach by making available three levels of trim (bundling), each containing many items as standard equipment. The approach provides several benefits. It simplifies the production-and-assembly system while cutting costs and speeding up delivery time. Without having to stock a large and confusing number of options, better inventory control is achieved. With fewer combinations available, quality control should also be improved. Also, the method provides a clearer market image for the brand.

It cannot be said that a bundling strategy is always superior or inferior to an unbundling strategy. Bundling offers a buyer more product for less money while simplifying production and marketing activities. The overall bundle, of course, is not likely to match the buyer's need completely. On the other hand, a product can be unbundled so that the buyer does not have to pay for any extras not wanted. In effect, the price can be made more affordable by unbundling the product.

When a company faces escalating export prices because of the addition of transportation charges, customs duties, extra packing costs, and so on, it should consider strategies to moderate the impact of price escalation. According to Becker, there are several appropriate approaches. First, it may attempt to shorten the international distribution channel to reduce the number of times that certain marketing functions are repeated. This approach may also increase the degree of control over final market prices. Second, it can reduce its export price by using variable costs as a floor price. This strategy is appropriate only so long as there are no problems with dumping and additional countervailing duties. Third, it should consider modifying its product (e.g., lower quality, less frequent model changes, reduced options, and simplified designs) so that a lower price can be derived. Finally, the company may want either to export parts for overseas assembly or establish production facilities abroad. This last strategy, by decreasing the import content of labor and materials, thereby reduces export price escalation.[13]

EXHIBIT 16–2 Price and product bundling

Source: Reprinted by permission of Nissan Motor Corporation in U.S.A.

Korean buyers regard U.S. goods as being of good quality and performance but also as being too expensive. Because Koreans are very price-conscious, American exporters should consider (1) adapting their products for the Korean market, (2) taking into account in their price quotations the repeat business generated by the demand for spare parts and components and auxiliary equipment, (3) emphasizing the idea that the superior quality of U.S. products ultimately results in lower production costs, and (4) investigating possible warehousing arrangements in Korea that would allow larger shipments and less expensive freight for the trans-Pacific voyage.[14]

DUMPING

Dumping, a form of price discrimination, is the practice of charging different prices for the same product in similar markets. As a result, imported goods are sold at prices so low as to be detrimental to local producers of the same kind of merchandise. Boeing and McDonnell Douglas, for example, accused Airbus of receiving $9 billion in subsidies from the government consortium, enabling the company to price each airplane at some $15–20 million less than the true cost. Dumping also applies to services. Japanese banks in California were accused of dumping money in the U.S. market by pricing their loans at an interest rate lower than what U.S. banks charged.

Types of Dumping

There are several types of dumping: sporadic, predatory, persistent, and reverse. **Sporadic dumping** occurs when a manufacturer with unsold inventories wants to get rid of distressed and excess merchandise. To preserve its competitive position at home, the manufacturer must avoid starting a price war that could harm its home market. One way to find a solution involves destroying excess supplies, as in the example of Asian farmers dumping small chickens in the sea or burning them. Another way to solve the problem is to cut losses by selling for any price that can be realized. The excess supply is thus dumped abroad in a market where the product is normally not sold.

Predatory dumping is more permanent than sporadic dumping. This strategy involves selling at a loss to gain access to a market and perhaps to drive out competition. Once the competition is gone or the market established, the company uses its monopoly position to increase price. Some critics question the allegation that predatory dumping is harmful by pointing out that if price is subsequently raised by the firm that does the dumping, former competitors can rejoin the market when it becomes more profitable again.

Hitachi was accused of employing predatory pricing for its EPROM (electrically programmable read-only memory) chips. A memo prepared by the company urged U.S. distributors to "quote 10% below competition (until) the bidding stops, when Hitachi wins." The Justice Department, after a year-long investigation, dropped the probe because it found that there was insufficient evidence to prosecute.

Zenith has long accused Japanese television manufacturers of using predatory dumping. It charged in its antitrust suit that major Japanese manufacturers, through false billing and secret rebates, conspired to set low, predatory prices on TV sets in the U.S. market with the purpose of driving U.S. firms out of business in order to gain a monopoly. Both the Japanese and U.S. governments defended the Japanese firms' cooperation on the grounds of "sovereign compulsion." In other words, the defendants' cooperation was the result of a compliance with the Japanese government's export policy. After sixteen years of legal maneuvering, the Supreme Court dismissed the conspiracy theory but ordered a trial concerning the dumping charge.

Persistent dumping is the most permanent type of dumping, requiring a consistent selling at lower prices in one market than in others. This practice may be the result of a firm's recognition that markets are different in terms of overhead costs and demand characteristics. For example, a firm may assume that demand abroad is more elastic than it is at home. Based on this perception, the firm may decide to use incremental or marginal cost pricing abroad while using full-cost pricing to cover fixed costs at home. This practice benefits foreign consumers, but it works to the disadvantage of local consumers. Japan, for example, is able to keep prices high at home, especially for consumer electronics, because it has no foreign competition there. But it is more than willing to lower prices in the U.S. market in order to gain or maintain market share. Japanese consumers, as a result, must sacrifice by paying higher prices for Japanese products that are priced much lower in other markets.

The three kinds of dumping just discussed have one characteristic in common: each involves charging lower prices abroad than at home. It is possible, however, to have the opposite tactic—**reverse dumping.** In order to have such a case, the overseas demand must be less elastic and the market will tolerate a higher price. Any dumping will thus be done in the manufacturer's home market by selling locally at a lower price.

Legal Aspect of Dumping

Whether dumping is illegal or not depends on whether the practice is tolerated in a particular country. Switzerland has no specific antidumping laws. Most countries, however, have dumping laws that set a minimum price or a floor on prices that can be charged in the market.

Illegal dumping occurs when the price charged drops below a specified level. In 1987, the U.S. Department of Commerce determined that the color picture tubes from Japan, South Korea, Singapore, and Canada were dumped in the U.S. market at below fair market prices, and the agency imposed penalty duties.

What is the unfair or illegal price level, and what kind of evidence is needed to substantiate a charge of dumping? Exhibit 16–3 lists the factors used by the International Trade Commission to compare prices in order to determine whether imports are being sold at less than fair value.

The case of Melex golf carts from Poland illustrates the difficulty in determining a fair price. The success of Melex in the United States led to an accusation of dumping. The Treasury Department was unable to ascertain whether Melex's U.S. price was lower than prices at home in Poland because Poland has no golf courses and thus no demand for such a product. The cost of production was unsuitable for determining its fair price. Poland, as a socialist economy, does not let market forces fully dictate the costs of factors of production. For this reason, the 1974 Trade Act does not allow production costs in a communist/socialist country to be used for comparison purpose.

1. The determination as to whether merchandise is being sold to purchasers in the United States at less than fair value is ordinarily based upon a comparison between the net, FOB factory price to a United States importer and the net, FOB factory price to purchasers in the home market. If the sales to the United States are a CIF delivered basis or an FOB seaport basis, the necessary deductions are made in order to arrive at an FOB factory price.

2. If such or similar merchandise is not sold in the home market, or if the amount sold in the home market is so small (normally less than 5 percent of the amount sold to third countries) as to be an inadequate basis for comparison, then comparison is made between the prices to the United States and prices for exportation to third countries.

3. If the merchandise is sold only to the United States or if the merchandise sold in the home market or to third countries is not sufficiently similar to the merchandise sold to the United States to furnish a satisfactory basis for comparison, then comparison is made between the price to the United States and the constructed value, as defined by the Trade Agreements Act of 1979. Constructed value is the sum of
   a. the cost of materials, labor, and fabrication;
   b. the usual general expenses, such as factory and administrative overhead, and the usual profit realized in the manufacture of merchandise of the same general character; and
   c. the cost of packing and other expenses incident to preparing the merchandise for shipment to the United States.

   The statute provides that the amount added for general expenses must be at least 10 percent of the cost under item a and that amount added for profit must be at least 8 percent of the sum of such costs and general expenses.

If a relationship exists between the shipper and the United States importer other than that of seller and buyer (for example, if the importer is the agent or subsidiary of the shipper), then comparison is made between the home consumption or third country price and the exporter's sales prices, which is the price at which the importer resells the merchandise in the United States, less (1) transportation costs and duty, (2) the amount of any selling commission and selling expenses in connection with the sale of the merchandise in the United States, and (3) any costs incurred from further processing performed on the imported merchandise before its resale.

In comparing prices to the United States with prices in the home market or to third countries, allowance is made for differences in price which are wholly or partly due to differences in the quantities sold or to differences in the circumstances of sale. The Commerce Regulations set forth a general rule which in the ordinary case would govern whether a particular quantity discount would be acceptable for the purpose of granting a quantity discount allowance.

Differences in circumstances of sale for which allowance will be made are limited, in general, to those circumstances which bear a direct relationship to the sales which are under consideration, such as differences in credit terms, guarantees, warranties, technical assistance, servicing, assumption by a seller of a purchaser's advertising or other selling costs, or commissions.

In making comparisons using exporter's sales price, reasonable allowance will be made for actual selling expenses incurred in the home market up to the amount of the selling expenses incurred in the U.S. market. Allowance will generally not be made for differences in advertising or other selling costs, unless such costs are assumed on behalf of the purchasers; for example, advertising of a type designed to reach the purchasers', rather than the sellers', customers. Nor will allowance generally be made for differences in production costs, except in those cases where the merchandise being compared is not

(continued)

EXHIBIT 16–3   Dumping: bases for comparison

identical. In this case, allowance will be based primarily on the differences in cost of manufacture but, when appropriate, the effect of such differences upon the market value of the merchandise may also be considered, if it is established that the amount of any price differential is wholly or partly due to such differences. Differences in costs of producing merchandise with identical physical characteristics as end products will not be allowed.

When comparing the purchase price paid by the United States importer (or the exporter's sales price) with the home consumption price, the amount of any tax which is imposed upon home market sales, or which is refunded because of exportation, is added to the purchase price (or exporter's sales price).

In most cases a shipper should be able to satisfy himself that he is not making sales to the United States at less than fair value by the simple expedient of comparing his net, FOB factory prices to the United States with the net, FOB factory prices in the home market or to third countries.

EXHIBIT 16–3 *(continued)*

Source: Importing into the United States (Washington D.C.: U.S. Customs Service, Department of the Treasury, 1982), 34–35

To determine fair costs, the Treasury began to use a small Canadian manufacturer's costs as reference prices, only to see the Canadian firm stop making golf carts. Also, Poland protested that the Canadian firm's production costs were too high and unsuitable for comparison. The Treasury's next step was to rely on reference prices of a comparable product from free-market countries. Mexico and Spain were chosen because they were considered to be similar to Poland in terms of their level of economic development. Even though Mexico and Spain do not produce golf carts, they were used anyway to determine what their production costs would be if they produced such a product. After much review and discussion, the ruling was that the "constructed" value did not differ appreciably from Melex's actual price.

One item of evidence of dumping occurs when a product is sold at less than fair value. The Department of Commerce ruled in 1986 that Japanese semiconductor manufacturers had indeed dumped the EPROM chips, 256K DRAMs, and 64K DRAMs in the U.S. market. NEC was found to be a leading violator, selling its chips at 108 percent and 188 percent less than fair value.

Another example of dumping evidence is a product sold at a price below its home-market price or production cost. The United States relies on the official U.S. trigger price, which is designed to curb dumping by giving an early signal of an unacceptable import price. In the case of steel, the trigger price sets a minimum price on imported steel that is pegged to the cost of producing steel in Japan. According to the General Accounting Office, some 40 percent of all imports at one time were priced below the trigger price.

To provide relief, the Antidumping Act requires the Department of Commerce to impose duties equal to the dumping margin. The antidumping duty is based on the amount by which the foreign market value or constructed value exceeds the purchase price or an exporter's sale price. In the case of TV sets, the Treasury Department found in 1971 that dumping of Japanese products was taking place. This led to an agreement with twenty-two importers who were assessed $77 million for sets imported through March 31, 1979. The Commerce Department accepted $66 million as settlement of antidumping claims against more than 100 companies that imported $2.5 billion worth of Japanese sets at prices below the Japanese home market between 1971 and 1979. Zenith, contending that the penalty did not go far enough, challenged the ruling, but the Supreme Court declined to consider the appeal. Exhibit 16-4 explains antidumping investigation procedure, and Exhibit 16–5 lists antidumping terms.

How to Dump (Legally and Illegally)

Dumping is a widespread practice. Exporters and their importers insist on its use, when necessary, and will find ways to conceal the practice. One can learn from the Mitsui case. Mitsui was responsible for generating the largest dumping case and pleaded guilty to all twenty-one counts involving kickbacks and the falsifying of documents to customs officials in order to sell steel below trigger prices.[15] Mitsui attempted to conceal its dumping activities through several means. It hid the origin of the Japanese steel products by disguising them as U.S. made (e.g., wire rope imported to Houston). It submitted false documents to conceal the true merchandise value and backdated invoices to avoid trigger prices. Furthermore, it gave its U.S. customers a rebate equal to the difference between the nominal exchange rate and the actual exchange rate, and the calculations were made after product entry. These illegal rebates totaled $1.3 million between 1978 and 1981. Another deceptive method involved the use of damage claims. Mitsui honored false claims that goods were damaged during shipment and granted credits of $22,676 for damaged Korean wire nails without investigating or reporting these losses to its insurance company. In spite of these ingenious methods, Mitsui was exposed and paid heavy fines for dumping and fraud.

Sears was similarly indicted for conspiring with Sanyo and Toshiba to file false customs invoices involving the importation of Japanese TV sets between 1968 and 1975. To avoid customs penalties on low-priced Japanese sets whose prices were below Japanese market prices, Sears certified the purchase prices to be higher than what was actually paid. For two of those seven years, Sears overstated Toshiba's price by $1.66 million and Sanyo's prices by $7 million.

To prevent Japanese firms from dumping their EPROM chips in the U.S. market, the United States and Japan have established "fair market values" or minimum prices for these chips. But American chip makers asserted that the Japanese violated the trade agreement by dumping chips in Hong Kong, Taiwan, and Singapore and by selling chips to Korean users at fair market value but with rebate. The problem was that these chips could find their way to the U.S. market or that U.S. semiconductor customers might move their manufacturing operations to these other markets to take advantage of lower chip prices.

Without doubt, dumping is a risky practice that can cause a great deal of embarrassment, in addition to the payment of large financial penalties. Thus, a preferable strategy is to use other means to legally overcome dumping laws. One method that can help avoid charges of dumping is to differentiate the exported item from the item being sold in the home market. By deliberately making the home product and its overseas version incomparable, there is no home-market price that can be used as a basis for price comparison. This may be the reason that Japanese automakers market their automobiles under new or different names in the United States.

FILING AN ANTIDUMPING OR COUNTERVAILING DUTY PETITION

The Department of Commerce has the authority to initiate its own investigations, but usually an "interested party" starts an investigation by filing petitions simultaneously with the Department's Import Administration (IA) and the International Trade Commission (ITC). The following items must be included in an antidumping petition. Countervailing duty requirements are similar.

- Name and address of petitioner.
- Identification of the industry on whose behalf the petitioner is filing, including its names and addresses of other firms in the industry.
- A statement indicating whether the petitioner has filed for import relief under other sections of various trade acts.
- A detailed description of the relevant merchandise, including its technical characteristics and uses. The current U.S. classification number should also be included.
- The name of the foreign country from which the imports originate.
- The names and addresses of each company the petitioner believes is selling dumped merchandise and the proportion they represent of total exports to the United States during the most recent twelve-month period.
- All relevant factual information that is needed to calculate the U.S. price of the merchandise and the foreign market value of the actual (or similar) merchandise.
- The volume and value of imports from the country named in petition during the most recent two-year period and any other period the petitioner believes to be representative.
- The name and address of each company the petitioner believes imported, or is likely to import, the merchandise.
- Information regarding material injury, threat of material injury, or material retardation.

It may appear that filing a petition is a complicated, time-consuming, and costly procedure. However, the Import Administration provides pre-petition counseling for any potential filer. The ITC also offers assistance concerning the injury requirement of the petition. For information, contact the Office of Investigations, Import Administration, U.S. Department of Commerce, Room 3099, Washington, D.C. 20230; tel. (202) 377-5403.

Sequence for Antidumping (AD) and Countervailing Duty (CVD) Investigations

Day	Event
0	Petition filed
20	Decision on initiation
45	Preliminary injury determination by ITC*
AD 160 CVD 85	Preliminary determination by ITA
AD 235 CVD 160	Final determination by ITA*
SAD 280 CVD 205	Final injury determination by ITC*
AD 287 CVD 212	Publication of order

*If the determination is negative, the investigation is terminated.

EXHIBIT 16–4 Antidumping petition and investigation

Source: Business America, 5 November 1990, 3–4

Administrative Review—On the anniversary date of the publication of an order, the Commerce Department will review and determine the amount of any antidumping duty, if an interested party requests such a review.

Antidumping Duty—A duty assessed on imported merchandise that is subject to an antidumping duty order.

Antidumping Petition—A petition filed on behalf of an affected U.S. industry alleging that foreign merchandise is being sold in the United States at "less than fair value' and that such sales are causing or threatening material injury to, or materially retarding the establishment of, a U.S. industry.

Constructed Value—A means of determining fair or foreign market value when sales of such of similar merchandise do not exist or, for various reasons, cannot be used for comparison purposes.

Dumping Margin—Amount by which the imported merchandise is sold in the United States below the "fair value." For example, if the U.S. purchase price is $200 and the fair value is $220, then the dumping margin is $20. The margin is expressed as a percentage of the U.S. price, so in this example the margin is 10 percent.

Fair Value—The reference against which U.S. sales prices of imported merchandise are compared during the investigation. It is generally expressed as the weighted average of the exporter's home market prices, prices to third countries, or constructed value during the period of the investigation.

Final Determination—A determination rendered after it has been determined that goods are being sold at "less than fair value."

Foreign Market Value—The price, as defined in the Act, at which merchandise is sold, or offered for sale, in the principal markets of the country from which it is exported. If foreign home market sales are not usable, the foreign market value is based on prices to third countries or constructed value.

Preliminary Determination—A determination announcing the results of an investigation within 160 days after a petition has been filed or an investigation has been self-initiated.

Suspension of an Investigation—A decision to suspend an antidumping investigation if the exporters who account for the majority of the merchandise agree to stop exports to the United States within six months after the suspension date or agree to revise their prices promptly to eliminate any dumping margin.

Tariff Act of 1930, Title VII (the ACT)—Authorizes antidumping duties to be assessed against imported merchandise being sold in the United States at "less than fair value" if such sales cause or threaten material injury to a U.S. industry. The Assistant Secretary for Import Administration is responsible for making the fair value determination and the International Trade Commission is responsible for making the injury determination.

United States Price—The price compared to foreign market value in order to determine whether imported merchandise is sold at less than fair value.

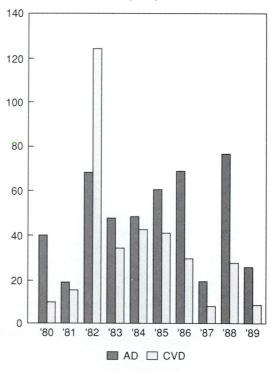

Cases Initiated by Import Administration

EXHIBIT 16–5   Antidumping terms

Source: Business America, 5 November 1990, 5

Another method used to circumvent dumping laws is to make competitive adjustments in nonprice items when negotiating with affiliates and distributors. For example, the creative use of credit can have the same effect as a price reduction.[16]

The dumping problem can also be overcome if the production of a product, rather than its importation, is carried out in the host country. This option has become necessary for Japanese manufacturers, who have no desire to lower prices in Japan because they do not have to contend with foreign competitors. The high prices at home, however, work to the disadvantage of Japanese manufacturers because it is easy to prove that they are engaged in dumping in the U.S. market. For Japanese VCR manufacturers, there is a dilemma: they cannot make their U.S. prices too low without violating dumping laws and yet the prices charged cannot be so high as to encourage Korean firms to move in and take market share away. One solution may be to manufacture the sets in the United States. To minimize the higher costs prevailing in the United States, Japanese firms could import as many components and parts from Japan as practical.

PRICE DISTORTION

Dumping laws are not the only cause of price variations. The power of the market force in setting prices can be moderated by a government's price policy. Few governments allow the market to set prices completely on its own accord. Exhibit 16–6 describes the role of markets and how prices are set in selected countries. When

---

Brazil
Relative prices are affected by exchange-rate policy and protective tariff and nontariff barriers to trade. Tax and credit incentives are frequently used to direct private sector investments.

Kenya
In general, prices do not reflect resource availabilities. They are distortive in agriculture, and manufacturers are protected from foreign competition. Direct controls, such as production licensing, limit the operation of markets.

Singapore
Singapore has always taken its price signals from international markets. Price distortions, introduced in the 1960s when Singapore was briefly a member of the Malaysian Federation, have been removed.

Thailand
The economy is essentially market-oriented. There are many distortions, however, in the form of production taxes and protection for manufacturing, but these are of relatively minor importance and are often not even binding.

EXHIBIT 16–6   The role of markets and prices

Source: Helen Hughes, "Private Enterprise and Development—Comparative Country Experience," *Economic Development and the Private Sector* (Washington, D.C.: The World Bank, 1983), 36–39. Reprinted with permission of the World Bank

a government is actively involved in buying and selling local and foreign goods, price deviations usually and readily follow. Because of the political influence of the agricultural sector in Japan, Japanese rice farmers were able to price their rice at several times more than U.S. prices, resulting in Japanese consumers paying double or triple the world price. Table 16–2 shows how automobile prices differ greatly from country to country. A medium-priced car in Singapore can cost about three times as much as a comparable car in Jeddah. Exhibit 16–7 explains the operation of the European Community's CAP (Common Agricultural Policy) price support mechanism.

On most occasions, a government sets the price artificially high in order to discourage the domestic consumption of imported products. U.S. wheat, for example, was sold in Japan at twice the price of what Japan paid for it. Japan Tobacco and Salt Public Corporation, a state monopoly, marked up foreign cigarettes so high (500 percent) that they cost 50 percent more than domestic brands. As would be expected, foreign cigarettes held only a 2 percent share of the market.

A government's licensing policy and patent enforcement can affect market prices indirectly at the very least. Canada has compulsory licensing and allows distributors to import duplicates of high-priced drugs in order to stimulate price competition. Such drugs are priced far below proprietary brand names, making it easy for generic drugs to win market share. The government further requires pharmacists to use generic drugs when the prescription is being paid for by the government. As a result, Valium's price in Canada was lowered from 74 percent of the U.S. price to a mere 6 percent.

Often, government policy is to keep prices artificially low, as in the case of necessities that are essentially for public welfare. Standard Oil (Indiana) pulled its Amoco Italia subsidiary out of Italy after a loss of $112 million in the first ten months of 1981 because of the price controls. The Italian government fixes most oil prices, and such prices often do not keep pace with market-generated prices elsewhere in Europe. In the case of the Netherland Antilles, in addition to very strict price controls over basic foodstuffs, the government also participates in setting rates for transportation and nongovernment-owned utilities. Furthermore, if an enterprise receives tax or other concessions, it is required by the government to (1) charge a fair price, (2) meet quality standards, and (3) guarantee delivery.[17]

Inflation is often the primary cause of price controls. Inflation affects public welfare and encourages workers to demand higher wages. To protect consumers and help control inflation, Greece has imposed price controls on a wide range of essential products and services. The control takes the form of either a maximum permitted selling price or maximum allowed profit margin.[18] Mexico also sets a controlled, subsidized price for the tortilla (corn flour pancake), which is a Mexican staple. This price, although rising, does not reflect the real cost of producing and marketing the tortilla.

To control inflation in Israel, Brazil, and Argentina, each of these countries employed indexation of the exchange rate (through the crawling peg system) and indexation of wages (by linking wages to past price increases). Brazil, for example, adjusted its exchange rate on a daily basis. Instead of containing inflation, however, indexation tends to perpetuate it instead. To prevent acute, chronic inflation from becoming full-blown hyperinflation, all three countries adopted stabilization

TABLE 16-2 Automobile purchase prices and maintenance costs

Medium-Priced Automobile[a]		Price[a] (dollars)	Taxes[b] (dollars)	Checkup[c] (dollars)
Abu Dhabi	Mazda 929 de Luxe	10,800	15	136
Amsterdam	Opel Kadett 1.6	13,800	204	100
Athens	Seat Ibiza 1.500	22,300	923	74
Bangkok	Toyota 1600 SE limited	18,000	55	14
Bogotá	Mazda 323, 1500	16,200	378	78
Bombay	Premier Standard	10,300	25	9
Brussels	VW Golf Diesel, 1600	12,100	175	21
Buenos Aires	Peugot 505	19,500	486	141
Cairo	Fiat Regatta 1500	18,800	63	9
Caracas	Ford Sierra, Modell 300	11,900	6	12
Chicago	Oldsmobile Cutlass Supreme	16,500	50	83
Copenhagen	Opel Kadett 1600	19,900	226	168
Dublin	Ford Sierra GL 2000	21,700	379	55
Düsseldorf	Audi 80	14,400	183	83
Frankfurt	VW Golf 1600	11,100	206	149
Geneva	VW Golf 1600 GL	13,700	159	123
Helsinki	Saab 900	27,100	—[d]	139
Hong Kong	Ford Laser 1,5 Ghia	14,900	353	192
Houston	Ford Tempo	12,800	63	82
Istanbul	Murat 131 Dogan	12,200	65	108
Jakarta	Toyota Corona AT 151	24,600	144	29
Jeddah	Mazda 626	9,000	320	134
Johannesburg	Honda Ballade	13,100	19	35
Kuala Lumpur	Proton Saga 1,5 Aeroback	10,200	90	16
Lagos	Peugeot 504	11,600	21	81
Lisbon	Renault 21 GTS	18,000	21	651
London	Ford Sierra 1600L	15,200	184	79
Los Angeles	Ford Escort	8,500	157	80
Luxembourg	VW Golf 1600C	9,600	68	55
Madrid	Renault 21 GTS	18,300	40	62
Manama (Bahrain)	Mazda 323, 1500	14,000	53	21
Manila	Nissan California 1500	15,900	48	18
Mexico City	Jetta Equipado	16,100	178	52
Milan	Alfa Romeo 1600	16,300	82	89
Montreal	Pontiac Sunbird	9,700	145	48
Nairobi	Datsun Nissan E23	26,400	117	18
New York	Ford Escort GL	9,700	35	142
Nicosia	Mazda Hatchback 323, 1300	13,500	99	22
Oslo	Ford Sierra 2.0	27,500	159	181
Panama City	Toyota Corona	11,300	27	46
Paris	Peugeot 405 GR	13,300	64	88
Rio de Janeiro	Chevrolet Monza 4P SLE 1.8	14,500	74	161
São Paulo	General Motors Monza 1.8	12,900	74	138
Seoul	Hyundai Stella GX	8,800	330	52
Singapore	Honda Accord 1.6	32,200	299	45
Stockholm	Citroen 16 TRX	16,100	90	94
Sydney	Toyota Camry	14,600	9	82
Tel Aviv	Ford Sierra 1600	24,400	241	140
Tokyo	Corona 2000 FXR	14,600	463	555
Toronto	Mecury Topaz L	9,300	44	119
Vienna	Ford Orion CL 1.6	13,800	183	136
Zurich	VW Golf 1800	15,100	297	152

[a] Purchase price (incl. sales tax) of a popular medium-sized make; price refers to 4-door standard model

[b] Road tax (license plate fee) per year or annual registration fee

[c] Average labor costs (not including price of spare parts, if needed, and oil change) for a 15,000 kilometer (approx. 9,000-mile) checkup

[d] No tax

Source: Prices and Earnings around the Globe, 1988 edition (Union Bank of Switzerland, 1988), 20

HOW THE CAP OPERATES:
PRICE SUPPORTS AND FINANCIAL COMPENSATION

Both nonprice measures and an elaborate system of price supports are used to implement the objectives of the CAP. The most common forms of nonprice support are subsidies for storage, consumers, and inputs, as well as deficiency payments and production premiums, which currently account for only a small fraction of total spending.

An elaborate system of price support is in place for most of the products—accounting for 91 percent of the output—covered by the CAP. The system is generally based on three prices, which are, in descending order,

- ☐ The *target price* is the upper end of the range within which producer prices are left to fluctuate. This term is used in the price support system for cereals, sugar, milk, olive oil, and grape and sunflower seeds. Because of technical differences, the same concept is defined by the term "guide price" for bovine meat and wine; "norm price" for tobacco; and "basic price" for pork.

- ☐ The *threshold price* is the lowest price at which imports may be purchased. This term is applied to cereals, sugar, dairy products, olive oil, and grape and sunflower seeds. A parallel concept is defined by the term "sluice-gate price" for pork, eggs, and poultry and by "reference price" for fruit, vegetables, wine, and certain fishery products.

- ☐ The *intervention price* is the lowest price at which public bodies may buy commodities to support the market. This price is generally the minimum price guaranteed to producers, even though the importance of intervention purchases has diminished.

    The intervention price does not, however, guarantee a minimum income to producers. For some products, producers must finance part or all of the disposal of excess supplies by paying what are called coresponsibility levies. They may be entitled to CAP benefits on only a limited volume (production quotas), or benefits may be reduced,

with a time lag, when a specified volume of output has been exceeded (known as guarantee thresholds).

To help European products compete against cheaper imports, various levies on imports are used to make imports more expensive than domestic products. At the same time, a system of variable subsidies (called refunds) generally serves to help exporters overcome the handicap of lower world prices.

To reduce the risk of trade distortions within Europe, one principle of the CAP is to maintain a uniform system of support prices, or a common price level, expressed in ECU terms. In principle, a country whose currency appreciates should reduce its prices, and one with a depreciation should increase its prices. In practice, countries have been unwilling to make instantaneous adjustments when their exchange rates have changed. This unwillingness is mainly related to inflation and income distribution concerns, according to the authors of the Fund study.

In response to this problem, a system of monetary compensatory amounts (MCAs) was designed in 1969 to prevent distortions in trade. When a country experiences an appreciation in its currency, positive MCAs are applied, which permit the country to delay lowering its agricultural prices without being flooded by imports from abroad. These MCAs act as the equivalent of import levies and export subsidies. In contrast, when a country experiences a depreciation, negative MCAs serve as the equivalent of import subsidies and export levies. In 1983, for example, the countries with positive MCAs were the Federal Republic of Germany, the Netherlands, and the United Kingdom. In 1984, the EC decided to change to a system of only negative MCAs so that currency realignments would give rise only to price increases. This was largely achieved—although not completely for the Federal Republic of Germany—by switching the reference point for the calculation of MCAs to the strongest currency, the deutsche mark. The switch to what became

(continued)

EXHIBIT 16–7 How the CAP operates: price supports and financial compensation

known as the Green ECU from the ECU gave an upward tilt to the common price level.

Financing for the CAP is provided by the European Agricultural Guidance and Guarantee Fund (EAGGF) and by national authorities. The study notes that the EAGGF covers most of the appropriations for agricultural expenditures from the EC's common budget. Although the CAP generates some revenues—through import levies, for example—these are considered part of the EC's budget revenues, with the exception of coresponsibility levies, and are not used for agricultural expenditures.

EAGGF expenditures are divided into a Guarantee section (more than 90 percent of expenditures) and a Guidance section. The Guarantee section includes the expenditures for price stabilization, incurred by market organizations in member states, which arise from export refunds and from the cost of intervention (calculated as the revenues from sales of stocks less the costs of intervention purchases and stockpiling). The Guidance section finances structural measures, including schemes for individual farmers or general programs to modernize agriculture. The study stresses that the expenditures of the Guarantee section are based on the interaction of policies in force under the CAP and

market prices, whereas those of the Guidance section are fully controlled by the EC budget.

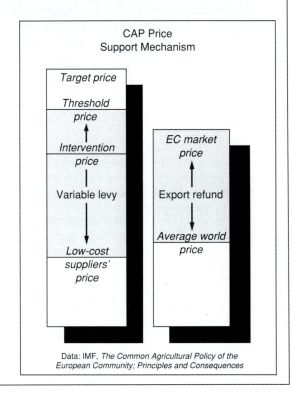

Data: IMF, *The Common Agricultural Policy of the European Community; Principles and Consequences*

EXHIBIT 16–7   *(continued)*

Source: IMF Survey, 20 February 1989, 60–61

programs based on a combination of orthodox measures (e.g., devaluations, restrictive monetary and fiscal policies, and partial deindexation) with innovative or heterodox measures (e.g., monetary reform, wage and price controls, and fixed exchange rates).[19] Brazil replaced its old currency with the cruzado, and Argentina did the same with the austral. These programs seemed to work initially, but their effectiveness was subsequently questioned.

Brazil's inflation was 366 percent in 1987 and reached at least 800 percent in 1988. The cruzado, created in 1986, lost value against the U.S. dollar at a rate of more than 1 percent a day. Increasingly, day-to-day transactions have switched from the cruzado to a treasury note called the OTN, which is adjusted for inflation. Prices of clothing and used cars were often set in OTNs. Based on the Finance Ministry's projection, inflation would reach an annual rate of close to 2,000 percent.

Following a military defeat in 1983, the civilian government of President Raúl Alfonsín was unable to achieve radical reform, and Argentina suffered an economic and political collapse. By the time the Alfonsín government fell in 1990, inflation was running at 200 percent a month. The next administration (President Carlos Menem) began privatization, reduced public expenditures, reduced tariffs, and backed the austral by gold or foreign exchange. By 1992 inflation was brought down to 1.5 percent a month.

Price controls are a common practice in communist and socialist countries that have state planning. China is a typical example. Its price system in the final analysis causes a distortion in the operation of the market. The state deliberately keeps the price of coal and other raw materials low while pricing some consumer durables well above the true market value. In several cases, production plants are trapped between artificially high prices for material inputs and artificially low prices for factory outputs. As a result, the plants may choose to stop producing inexpensive, everyday items because of low profit margins. These price distortions encourage some plants to produce such high-priced goods as washing machines, watches, bicycles, and sewing machines, even though these goods are too costly for consumers to purchase and are thus stored in warehouses that are already full of this kind of merchandise. Therefore, a poorly managed factory can show a hefty profit, at least on paper, because of the distortion that exists between profit incentive and centrally planned prices.

In an attempt to solve the problem, China has experimented with the free market method, which emphasizes material incentive, free enterprise, market-oriented prices, profits, and bonuses. Farmers were allowed to plant crops on private plots and sell their surplus in a "free market" at market prices for profit. The result of this experiment was that output almost doubled. The experiment was later extended to 6,600 factories in various large cities. State enterprises have been allowed to function as independent companies in determining profit and production. Certain factories have been permitted to keep a portion of their profits for reinvestment in new capital equipment or distribution to workers. Once the quota is filled, the companies can diversify into new products or market the surplus directly, and managers can reward and punish workers. Realistic prices should help market excess or unpopular items as well as goods that are in short supply. Prices of unsold durables should fall, whereas the prices of popular but unavailable refrigerators, for example, should increase.

Even when the government does not set prices, its other restrictive practices can still affect price. Quotas, for example, reduce supply and force prices to go up. Japan, when it voluntarily imposed a quota on its cars exported to the United States in 1981, was able to manipulate the quota so well that profit remained intact. The high demand coupled with the limited supply allowed Japanese automakers to raise prices several thousand dollars within the first few years without losing sales. That strategy was also to encourage customers to trade up to the more expensive models.

When a situation of price distortion exists, a company must devise a strategy to deal with it. In 1985 Argentina was experiencing an inflation rate of 1,000 percent. Merchants knew that price controls were inevitable, and they increased prices rapidly and drastically in order to circumvent the restrictions when price controls were implemented. Brazil's anti-inflationary Cruzado Plan was so disruptive to the flow of auto parts that even Ford and Volkswagen, which together had 60 percent of the market, had to merge their operations into Autolatina Ltd. to overcome price controls.

Another method of dealing with price controls involves the creation of a "new" product that is not subject to old or existing prices. Philip Morris's Galaxy brand serves as a good example.[20] In Brazil, more than 100 cigarette brands exist, and these are placed into eleven price categories and regulated by the government. Once a brand is established, it is exceedingly difficult to change its retail price by moving it into a different category. New packaging, however, can be used to circumvent the price controls. Philip Morris thus introduced a flip-top box for Galaxy in order to move its price up one level. Later, by adding a 100-mm version of this cigarette, the price was allowed to move up two price categories.

INFLATION

Table 16–3 shows inflation in sub-Saharan Africa.

Once price is set, it must still be adjusted periodically because of the impact of inflation. During 1985 the runaway inflation in Argentina made it easy to see that prices had to be adjusted upward on a sharp and continuous basis. Supermarkets there adjusted prices twice each day, and restaurants marked their prices in pencil to make easy daily changes. Argentine consumers rushed out to purchase goods as soon as they were paid, as a one-day delay could cost them dearly in terms of higher prices. Consumers were also sufficiently astute to realize that by using credit cards at the end of each month (accounting period), they could wait for a month or more before receiving invoices, which could then be paid off with depreciated money.[21]

In Brazil, it is difficult to offer products that are purchased over an interval of time.[22] Consumers cannot afford to commit themselves in terms of agreeing to buy a twenty-volume book series or a set of chinaware over a one- or two-year period. For a supplier, difficulties are experienced because it is unable to maintain its prices for more than a three-month period. Likewise, catalog houses face a dilemma because they cannot afford to print new catalogs frequently. On the other hand, they often cannot honor the prices printed in the catalogs because the prices have had to be changed while the current catalogs are available for distribution. Hermes, a Brazilian catalog company, tried to solve the inflation problem by switching from two catalogs a year to three catalogs. It later switched back to two catalogs. Using a new approach, "items are overpriced in a newly issued Hermes catalog with its normal six-month price validity. As currency value erodes, items that were initially overpriced become fairly priced, underpriced after four months and cheap after six. When a new catalog is issued, the price cycle resumes."[23]

When a marketer operates within a highly inflationary environment, it must think like its customers in order to protect itself. There are several strategies that can be devised for this purpose. First, merchants must collect their accounts receivable quickly. To protect itself, American Express requires its Argentine cardholders to pay their charge account purchases even before the bills are sent. Second, a product can be modified by reducing the quantity or eliminating extra frills so that an affordable price can be achieved. Third, sometimes it may be better not to make a sale. Some

TABLE 16–3   Inflation in sub-Saharan Africa: 1975–89 (percent, annual average)

	1980–1989	1975–89	Highest recorded
Industrial Countries	5.0	6.4	
Asia	7.9	7.3	
Sub-Saharan Africa	17.2	16.7	
More than 20 percent			
Ghana	43.7	52.2	122.9
Sierra Leone	63.7	43.9	178.7
Somalia[a]	41.1	32.9	91.2
Sudan[a]	33.1	25.1	64.7
Tanzania[a]	30.5	24.1	35.3
Uganda	104.6	—	238.1
Zaire[b]	58.8	62.1	238.1
Zambia[a]	30.8	24.5	55.6
Between 10–20 percent			
Botswana	10.5	11.0	16.4
Burundi	7.6	10.1	36.6
Gambia	17.9	15.1	56.7
Kenya	10.4	11.3	20.4
Lesotho	13.6	13.9	18.0
Madagascar[a]	17.2	14.3	31.8
Malawi	16.6	—	33.9
Mauritius	7.6	10.8	42.0
Nigeria	20.5	18.9	40.9
Swaziland[a]	13.9	13.7	20.8
Zimbabwe	13.5	12.3	23.1
Less than 10 percent			
Burkina Faso	4.1	6.4	30.0
Cameron	9.4	9.8	17.2
Central African Republic[b]	3.9	—	14.6
Congo	8.0	8.5	17.4
Ivory Coast	5.3	9.5	27.4
Djibouti	4.2	—	18.1
Ethiopia	4.3	8.3	28.5
Gabon[a]	7.7	9.8	28.4
Liberia[a]	4.3	6.1	19.5
Niger	2.4	6.7	23.5
Rwanda	4.4	6.8	31.1
Senegal	6.5	6.6	31.7
Togo	4.0	6.3	22.5

[a]For these countries, averages are for 1980-88 and 1975-88.
[b]For these countries, averages are for 1981–89.
Source: IMF Survey (March 1991): 29

Argentine retailers and distributors felt that they would come out ahead by closing their stores for a month instead of making sales because their inventories would greatly appreciate in value over the interval.

Fourth, the marketer can insulate itself against the declining value of a depreciating local currency by posting its prices in terms of an appreciating hard currency.

In Argentina, individuals switch out of pesos into dollars as soon as they are paid and convert the money back into pesos only when purchases are made. Sellers also play the same game. Real estate, automobiles, and big-ticket items are priced in dollars. Brazilian orange growers made an enormous mistake in 1983 by negotiating their crate price in cruzeiro rather than the dollar, thinking at the time that inflation in Brazil would be 70 percent. The actual inflation rate turned out to be several times higher than 70 percent, and value received for the oranges turned out to be very little compared to what was expected.

Another means of protection is through the accounting system. A company has the option of valuing its inventory and costs of goods sold based on either the **FIFO** (first in, first out) or **LIFO** (last in, first out) basis. During a period of stable prices, it may not matter much which method is used. But in a country experiencing high inflation, it may turn out to be a matter of survival for a marginal company as to which accounting inventory valuation method is used.

The FIFO method will understate the cost of goods sold during a period of high inflation, and this will result in excessive paper profits that are subject to the payment of higher taxes and dividends. The problem is made more difficult because there is less cash available for the replenishment of inventory, which when purchased is acquired at much higher prices. Thus, a firm is wise to adopt the LIFO system, which will improve the amount of cash flow. By assuming that the last item bought at a higher price will be the first item to be sold, the cost of goods sold is overstated, resulting in less profit being generated. Subsequently, less tax and dividend will be paid, and there are more funds remaining for the purchase of new inventory. Anderson Clayton, for example, uses the LIFO method to reduce its tax liability in Mexico. The improvement in cash flow reduces the need to borrow funds in that uncertain monetary environment.

Although LIFO would be preferred for a firm operating in a country with high inflation, there may be legal obstacles in the use of the LIFO method. For nonresident corporations in Germany, for example, inventory items are required to be valued at the lower of cost or market value. Use of either the FIFO or the LIFO method is not allowed unless it can be demonstrated that the method reflects the actual processing of goods.[24] In Brazil, companies that have an integrated cost system are required to value inventory for tax purposes on either the average cost or the FIFO basis. Direct cost and LIFO methods cannot be used.[25]

In an inflationary environment, a firm's price may be constrained on the one hand by government price controls and on the other hand by competitors who may operate under different cost conditions and who may not be willing to pass along the full inflationary increase to buyers. Nevertheless, it is still possible to take certain steps to mitigate the effects of high price and/or income elasticity in generating higher nominal prices.[26] One method can involve increasing prices frequently but in small increments to reduce the trauma of a large price increase. Another means of reducing the impact of higher prices is to have a strong promotional effort to stimulate demand while at the same time alleviating any inherent resistance to the higher prices. Finally, frequent but minor product changes may make consumers feel that they are getting something new or extra in the product.

TRANSFER PRICING

A common practice is for an MNC's many subsidiaries to trade among themselves or with the parent firm. Initially, it may seem that any price charged should be acceptable because the sales are among subsidiaries. If the selling price is relatively low, the profit is made by the buying unit. If the price is relatively high, the profit is made by the selling subsidiary. In the final analysis, the same amount of profit is still made by the parent firm whichever the case. This situation, however, is complicated by taxation. The transfer prices used, therefore, must be carefully considered.

There are four basic methods used to determine transfer prices. The first method involves transfers at *direct manufacturing costs*. The problem with this method is that when a buying subsidiary acquires merchandise at a very low price it has no incentive to hold down expenses or to maximize profits. The selling unit is also likely to be unhappy for not showing profit, feeling that it is subsidizing an affiliate of the firm's operations.

The second technique involves a transfer at *direct manufacturing cost plus a predetermined markup to cover additional expenses*. Profit is thus produced and added at every stage. The disadvantage with this method is that the price generated may be too high because market conditions are given secondary consideration to the markups taken.

The third course of action involves the use of a *market-based transfer price*. The price, though competitive, may end up being too low for the selling subsidiary because production cost may not be considered.

The fourth and final process employs an *arm's length price* as a basis for determining transfer price. This price would be the price that unaffiliated traders would agree on for a particular transaction. The problem with using this method occurs when the product has no external buyers or is sold at different prices in different markets.

The selection of a proper transfer price should be primarily based on acquiring maximum profits. Indeed, a survey conducted by Yunker revealed that profit maximization is generally the most important criterion in selecting a particular transfer pricing system.[27] In the case of German, Dutch, Belgian, and Swiss managers, there is no particular preference in the transfer price method used. For the French and Italians, the primary objective is tax minimization because of the French government's benign neglect in collecting taxes and Italy's confusing tax determination and collection procedures. These circumstances provide companies doing business in France and Italy with a great deal of opportunity for tax avoidance. Furthermore, non-U.S. MNCs' transfer price methods, in addition to being more market-oriented than those of U.S. firms, have been found to be less complex, considering only half as many factors in determining transfer prices.

Transfer pricing decisions are affected by several factors. A study of sixty-two U.S. MNCs revealed that the three most important factors were market conditions and competition in the foreign country as well as the affiliate's profit expectations. Next in order of importance were U.S. income taxes, foreign economic conditions, import restrictions, customs duties, price controls, foreign taxes, and exchange controls. The factors deemed least important were U.S. export incentives, floating exchange rates, management of cash flows, and other U.S. taxes.[28]

Another study involved MNCs' transactions with affiliates in Korea, Malaysia, the Philippines, Taiwan, Brazil, Colombia, Mexico, and Peru. Of the nine factors considered, profit repatriation restrictions and exchange controls were most important for pricing relations with subsidiaries because MNCs' primary concerns were to use transfer pricing to circumvent restrictions (i.e., use of a high transfer price as a cover to send home high profits or dividends). Next in terms of importance were joint-venture constraints and tariffs. The least important factor was credit status of a U.S. parent and its foreign subsidiary.[29]

Cost-plus and market-based pricing were the most popular methods used both in MDCs (more developed countries) and LDCs (less developed countries). The findings show that size and legal considerations (e.g., compliance with tax and custom regulations, antidumping and antitrust legislations, and financial reporting rules of host countries) are influential in the use of market-based transfer pricing. However, the extent of economic development in host countries and economic restrictions (e.g., exchange controls, price controls, restrictions on imports, and political and social conditions) are either unimportant or secondary determinants of a market-based transfer pricing strategy. Treasury Regulation 1.482 prescribes the following transfer pricing methods: the uncontrolled price method, the resale method, the cost-plus method, and some other appropriate method when none of the methods described above is applicable. U.S. multinationals appear to closely abide by U.S. tax regulations.[30]

Ordinarily, the parent firm should attempt to maximize its income in low-tax countries and minimize profit in high-tax markets. To minimize the income of a buying subsidiary in a high-tax country, use of the arm's length price is appropriate. In fact, any permissible costs should be added so that the price charged will be so high that it leaves the buyer with only a small profit subject to tax.

On the other hand, if the buying subsidiary is located in a low-tax country, its income should be maximized. This can be achieved by using a transfer price based on only direct production costs. In this case, the buyer will acquire the product for resale or use at a very low price. Its high profit is, however, subject only to low tax rates in this market. Although Cartier's corporate home is in low-tax Luxembourg, it wisely prices its watches so that most of the markup is collected by its lower-taxed Swiss subsidiary.

It is important to note that an MNC may not have complete freedom in choosing a transfer price method. According to Section 482 of the IRS code, a government can allocate gross income, deductions, credits, or allowances between related firms where arbitrary pricing or allocation is used to evade taxes. Eli Lilly attempted to sell products to its domestic subsidiary, which in turn sold them to a Western Hemisphere Trade Corporation (WHTC) at cost, resulting in profit being concentrated with the WHTC. The reallocation scheme was discovered and a demand rendered for $4 million in back taxes.[31] If the IRS attempts to enforce this rule, the burden of proof will be shifted to the company that will have to make an appeal for a refund. It will have to prove that the reallocation by the IRS of the sales and revenues was arbitrary and inconsistent.

Section 482 of the Internal Revenue Code requires arm's length dealings between related parties. An *arm's length price* or *charge* is defined as the amount or price that would be charged or would have been charged for the same product or service if independent transactions with unrelated parties under similar conditions were carried out. This requirement applies to (1) loans; (2) both goods and services (e.g. performance of marketing, managerial, technical, or other services for an affiliated party); and (3) possession, use, occupancy, loan, and assignment of tangible and intangible property.

If the IRS finds that adjustments are needed to correctly reflect a company's income, it is empowered to distribute, allocate, or apportion gross income, deductions, credits, or allowances among related organizations regardless of whether they are organized in the United States.[32] The purpose of the Internal Revenue Code is to prevent a low intercompany transfer price that shifts income away from the United States. At the same time, the application of the code is intended to be certain that the transfer price of a sale from a foreign company to a related U.S. company is not so high as to result in a small income being realized in the United States. The U.S. Customs Service, however, has a different perspective—it keeps an eye out for low transfer prices, which in turn reduce customs duties and which may result in dumping.

The IRS employs several methods to determine an arm's length price. When available, comparable uncontrolled sales must be used. When such sales do not exist, the resale price method is the next alternative to be used. When the first two methods are not applicable, it is permissible to use the cost-plus method. Any other appropriate pricing method can be used only when it is reasonable and when the first three methods are not relevant.

When possible and applicable, a company should consider locating a tax haven to shelter and maximize its income by using the tax haven to collect royalties, fees, dividends, and so on. A tax haven should include these characteristics: low tax on foreign investment or sales income, stable convertible currency, well-developed support facilities (telecommunications, financial services, and qualified workers), low taxes (property, stamp duty, personal income, death, and estate), and receptive sociopolitical climate.[33] To prevent American firms from escaping U.S. taxation, U.S. laws require U.S. firms to pay tax on their subsidiaries' income just as if such income had been remitted to U.S. parent firms.

In addition to the use of a tax haven, there are other techniques that can be used to maximize foreign tax credits.[34] Foreign tax credit can be used to reduce U.S. income tax. Companies should possess excess foreign tax credits up until they reach the excess limit and before crediting all foreign taxes paid. This situation often develops when companies do business in countries with high tax rates. Those U.S. firms operating in low-tax countries often end up with an excess limit situation because they have used all their foreign tax credits before reaching the excess limitation. The five strategies that can be used to deal with excess foreign tax credits are

1. Pass title overseas on export sales.
2. Create an offshore sales subsidiary.
3. Convert foreign investment interest income to "business" income.
4. Maximize fees (e.g., foreign subsidiary royalties, technical assistance fees for services performed outside of the United States, interest, and similar payments) paid by foreign subsidiaries.
5. Finance foreign operations from the United States.

Strategies that can deal with an excess tax limitation include

1. Elect to reduce foreign subsidiaries' pretax earnings.
2. Turn dividend into a loan in order to utilize foreign exchange losses.
3. Take advantage of effective foreign tax rates and rules.
4. Instruct any British subsidiaries to alternate dividends and loans.
5. Elect consent dividends from highly taxed foreign subsidiaries.

CONCLUSION

To set price, the concerns of all affected parties must be addressed. A manufacturer needs to make a profit. So do resellers, who demand adequate margin for their services. Moreover, competitors' reactions in terms of their price responses must be anticipated. Finally, it is necessary to take into account both consumers and the value they place on the product.

Several factors must be taken into consideration in setting price, including cost, elasticity of demand, supply, product image (prestige), turnover, market share/volume, product life cycle, and the number of products involved. The optimum mix of these ingredients varies by product, market, and corporate objectives.

Price setting in the international context is further complicated by such factors as foreign exchange rates, relative labor costs, and relative inflation rates in various countries. Other important considerations are export packing costs and charges, transportation costs, tariffs, tax laws, and profit remittance restrictions.

QUESTIONS

1. Explain how exchange rate and inflation affect the way you price your product.
2. What is dumping? When does it become illegal? What can a seller do to circumvent antidumping regulations?
3. What methods can be used to compute a transfer price (for transactions between affiliated companies)?

DISCUSSION ASSIGNMENTS AND MINICASES

1. How should U.S. farmers price their products?
2. To protect itself, how should a marketer price its product in a country with high inflation?
3. Price haggling is an art. Discuss how you can haggle effectively.
4. Explain why U.S. automakers prefer to use the "unbundling" approach in pricing their cars whereas their foreign competitors tend to use the "bundling" pricing approach.
5. DeBeers controls the supply of diamonds to a large degree. Its usual practice is to invite companies for "sight" where they are offered a certain quantity at a specified price. Price haggling is not allowed. Companies do not have to buy what is offered, but they will not be invited back for another "sight." Evaluate DeBeers' pricing practice.

CASE 16–1
PRICING FOR PROFIT?

U.S. firms pioneered the semiconductor industry but soon found themselves under a great deal of pressure from Japanese competitors. American firms felt that the Japanese market was closed to them while they were undercut at home and elsewhere by Japanese firms' unfair and below-the-cost prices. Whatever the reason, American firms lost some $500 million over two years.

Contending that Japan exported unemployment to the United States by dumping its chips, the United States was successful in forcing Japan to sign a five-year semiconductor trade agreement in 1986. The agreement required Japan to stop selling semiconductors at prices below cost.

The historic agreement soon turned sour. The United States accused Japanese manufacturers of continuing to dump their products elsewhere. In third countries such as Singapore, Japanese chips were available at low prices, and those chips found their way to the U.S. market. In its defense, Japan explained that it could not control all but major manufacturers. Also, it could not prevent gray market dealers and brokers who came to Japan and left with suitcases full of chips. The gray marketers' clients included American consumer-product manufacturers.

The violation of the trade agreement led the United States to impose penalties in 1987 against Japanese products. Tariffs of 100 percent were imposed on a minimum of $135 million and up to $300 million of Japanese goods. The products singled out for sanction included all black-and-white and some color television sets, automobile tape players, blank tape, refrigerators, computers, cash registers, and communications satellites. The U.S. government claimed that there should be no major price increases because the targeted products could be obtained from non-Japanese manufacturers. In reality, it was inevitable that consumers had to pay more for Japanese electronics goods.

Japanese electronics companies seemed to face more hurdles than other Japanese companies. In addition to the phenomenal rise in the value of the yen, which made exports difficult, the electronics industry had other problems. Because of the dumping charges and subsequent agreement, the Japanese firms had to agree to export products at prices mandated by the U.S. Department of Commerce. The additional penalty duties resulting from the semiconductor violation worsened the situation even more. Initially, Japanese electronics firms did not fare well and exports dropped a record 11 percent in 1986. Since then, the strong ones have become leaner and stronger.

Questions

1. Does the U.S. government's action to force up the prices of semiconductors serve a useful purpose?
2. Should semiconductors be considered products or commodities? How does the classification affect the pricing of semiconductors?
3. How should Japanese electronics companies react to quotas and duties? What should be their pricing and other strategies?

NOTES

1. Norman McGuinness, Nigel Campbell, and James Leontiades, "Selling Machinery to China: Chinese Perceptions of Strategies and Relationships," *Journal of International Business Studies* 22 (no. 2, 1991): 187–207.
2. Marlene Nadle, "Newsletter on Asian Affairs Sees Mail as Best Targeting Tool," *DM News,* 15 November 1984, 11.
3. Robert Grosse and Walter Zinn, "Standardization in International Marketing: The Latin American Case," *Journal of Global Marketing* 4 (no. 1, 1990): 53–78.
4. "Factors that Influence Pricing Decisions," *International Management* (June 1981): 3.
5. Nigel Piercy, *Export Strategy: Markets and Competition,* (London: George Allen and Unwin, 1982), 174.
6. "Mazda Rolls Out a Poor Man's Maserati," *Business Week,* 26 June 1989, 66.
7. ITI, *Barclays Bank Report on Export Development in France, Germany and the United Kingdom* (London: Barclays Bank International Limited, 1979).
8. *Investment in Greece* (Peat Marwick, 1983), 67.
9. Jack L. Hervey, "Dollar Drop Helps Those Who Help Themselves," *Chicago Fed Letter,* March 1988.
10. "Fund-Supported Programs Help Improve Macroeconomic Stability," *IMF Survey,* 2 July 1990, 199–200.
11. "Copier Firm Seeks Top Spot by Developing Dealer Network," *Marketing News,* 1 October 1982, 1.
12. "Panelists Offer Pricing Strategy Advice for Consumer and Industrial Products," *Marketing News,* 1 February 1985, 1 ff.
13. Helmut Becker, "Pricing: An International Marketing Challenge," in *International Marketing Strategy,* rev. ed., ed. Hans Thorelli and Helmut Becker (New York: Pergamon Press, 1980), 206–17.
14. "Tips on Doing Business," *Business America,* 13 March 1989, 7–8.
15. "The Federal Spotlight on Mitsui," *Business Week,* 13 April 1981, 44.
16. Warren J. Keegan, *Multinational Marketing Management,* 3rd ed. (Englewood Cliffs, NJ: Prentice Hall, 1984), 347.
17. *Investment in the Netherland Antilles* (Peat Marwick, 1985), 27.
18. *Investment in Greece,* 62.
19. Peter T. Knight, F. Desmond McCarthy, and Sweder van Wijnbergen, "Escaping Hyperinflation," *Finance & Development* 23 (December 1986): 14–17.
20. "Marketing Research Helped Philip Morris Penetrate the 'Impenetrable' Brazil Market," *Marketing News,* 17 September 1982.
21. "Chasing the Peso Leaves Argentines Breathless," *Business Week,* 10 June 1985, 66.
22. "About Marketing Overseas: Hazards and Opportunities," *Direct Marketing* (October 1985): 128.
23. Emanuel Soshensky, "Hermes of Brazil Reports Sales Gain Despite Delivery and Import Problems," *DM News,* 15 October 1987, 60, 74.
24. *Investment in Germany* (Peat Marwick, 1983), 22.

25. *Brazil* (New York: Ernst & Whinney International Series, March 1982), 5.

26. Laurent L. Jacque and Peter Lorange, "Hyperinflation and Global Strategic Management," *Columbia Journal of World Business* 19 (Summer 1984): 68–75.

27. Penelope J. Yunker, "A Survey Study of Subsidiary Autonomy, Performance Evaluation and Transfer Pricing in Multinational Corporations," *Columbia Journal of World Business* 18 (Fall 1983): 51–64.

28. Jane O. Burns, "Transfer Pricing Decisions in US Multinational Corporations," *Journal of International Business Studies* 9 (Fall 1980): 23–39.

29. Seung H. Kim and Stephen W. Miller, "Constituents of the International Transfer Pricing Decision," *Columbia Journal of World Business* 14 (Spring 1979): 69–77.

30. Mohammad F. Al-Eryani, Pervaiz Alam, and Syed H. Akhter, "Transfer Pricing Determinants of U.S. Multinationals," *Journal of International Business Studies* 21 (no. 3, 1990): 409–25.

31. Anthony P. David, "The Western Hemisphere Trade Corporation: The Bountiful Tax Accident," in *Multiple Business Operations,* vol. 4, ed. S. Prakash Sethi and Jagdish N. Sheth (Pacific Palisades, California: Goodyear, 1973), 107.

32. *Investment in the United States* (Peat Marwick, 1983), 35–37.

33. V. H. Kirpalani, *International Marketing* (New York: Random House, 1984), 337.

34. *Ten Tips for Maximizing Foreign Tax Credits* (New York: Ernst & Whinney, 1983).

Money often costs too much.

Ralph Waldo Emerson

Pricing Strategies
Terms of Sale and Payment

17

CHAPTER OUTLINE

COUNTERTRADE

PRICE QUOTATION

METHODS OF FINANCING AND MEANS OF PAYMENT

CASE 17–1: Countertrade: Counterproductive?

MARKETING ILLUSTRATION
Marketing Without Exchange of Money: An Old Practice in a New World

In exchange for operating in the Soviet Union, PepsiCo made an agreement with Soviet trade companies decades ago to take Stolichnaya vodka. Fortunately, the firm has been quite successful in selling Stolichnaya vodka in the United States. The hard currency earned from selling vodka was used to finance Pepsi's syrup sales and to establish new bottling plants. A more recent transaction involved PepsiCo and its partner (the Norwegian-owned shipping firm Framshipping), which agreed to sell seven Soviet-made ships in the West. Another $3 billion barter agreement later involved PepsiCo using hard currency derived from ship sales to expand Soviet bottling plants and open two Pizza Hut restaurants in Moscow.

Estee Lauder made an arrangement with several Soviet ministries and third countries to use revenue from the Estee Lauder store in Russia to buy Soviet chemicals and other goods that were then traded for hard currency in the West. Soviet authorities set prices for Lauder's products; a large bottle of perfume carried a retail price of 140 rubles or about two weeks' average pay there.

Following the breakup of the Soviet Union, plans were made in 1992 to let the ruble become partially convertible. In practice, because the ruble has not been directly convertible into Western currencies and because the hard currency of the countries of the former Soviet Union is limited, barter arrangements are still often necessary to make profits.

Sources: "For shipbuilders, It's Full Speed Ahead," *Business Week,* 9 July 1990, 56, 58; Peter Gumbel, "Perfumer Follows the Scent of Dollars along Twisted Path," *The Wall Street Journal,* 17 November 1989

Many Eastern European countries and less developed nations lack hard currency and resort to alternative pricing mechanisms. PepsiCo and Estee Lauder illustrate the fact that money is not the only means of payment. A successful transaction can take place by arranging for an alternative form of payment. A section of this chapter is devoted to the examination of countertrade as an alternative method of trading; the various types of countertrade are discussed. Another section deals with pricing terms used in international quotation. The chapter ends with a review of payment methods.

COUNTERTRADE

Countertrade, one of the oldest forms of trade, constitutes an estimated 5 to 30 percent of total world trade. Countertrade is a government mandate to pay for goods and services with something other than cash. In short, a goods-for-goods deal is countertrade.

Unlike monetary trade, suppliers are required to take customers' products for their use or for resale. In most cases, there are multiple deals that are separate yet related, and a contract links these separable transactions. Countertrade may involve several products, and such products may move at different points in time while involving several countries. Monetary payments may or may not be part of the deal.

There are three primary reasons for countertrade: (1) countertrade provides a trade financing alternative to those countries that have international debt and liquidity problems, (2) countertrade relationships may provide LDCs and MNCs with access to new markets, and (3) countertrade fits well conceptually with the resurgence of bilateral trade agreements between governments.[1] The advantages of countertrade cluster around three subjects: market access, foreign exchange, and pricing. A study of managers' opinions revealed that the disadvantages of barter and countertrade are in the areas of profitability; pricing; product quality; risk; and the added time, costs, and complexities.[2] Table 17–1 lists potential motives for countertrade.

Countertrade offers several advantages. It moves inventory for both a buyer and a seller. The seller gains other benefits, too. Other than the tax advantage, the seller is able to sell the product at full price and can convert the inventory to an account receivable. The cash-tight buyer that lacks hard currency is able to use any cash received for other operating purposes.

Types of Countertrade

There are several types of countertrade, including barter, counterpurchase, compensation trade, switch trading, offsets, and clearing agreements.[3] Exhibit 17–1 provides a classification of countertrade.

Barter **Barter,** possibly the simplest of the many types of countertrade, is a one-time direct and simultaneous exchange of products of equal value (i.e., one product for another). By removing money as a medium of exchange, barter makes it possible for cash-tight countries to buy and sell. Although price must be considered in any countertrade, price is only implicit at best in the case of barter. For example, Chinese coal was exchanged for the construction of a seaport by the Dutch, and Polish coal

TABLE 17–1   Potential motives for countertrade

	Types of Countertrade				
	BT[a]	CA/ST[b]	CP[c]	BB[d]	OF[e]
Avoids using foreign exchange	Yes	Yes	No	Rarely	No
Avoids repayment of external debt	Yes	Yes	No	No	No
Hides price discounts	Yes	Yes	No	No	No
Shifts risk	Yes	Yes	Yes	Yes	Sometimes
Substitute for foreign direct investment	No	No	Yes	Yes	Yes
Political factors dominant	No	Yes	No	No	Yes

BT   Barter
CA/ST   Clearing arrangement/switch trading
CP   Counterpurchase
BB   Buyback
OF   Offset

Source: Jean-Francois Hennart, "Some Empirical Dimensions of Countertrade," *Journal of International Business Studies* 21 (no. 2, 1990): 248

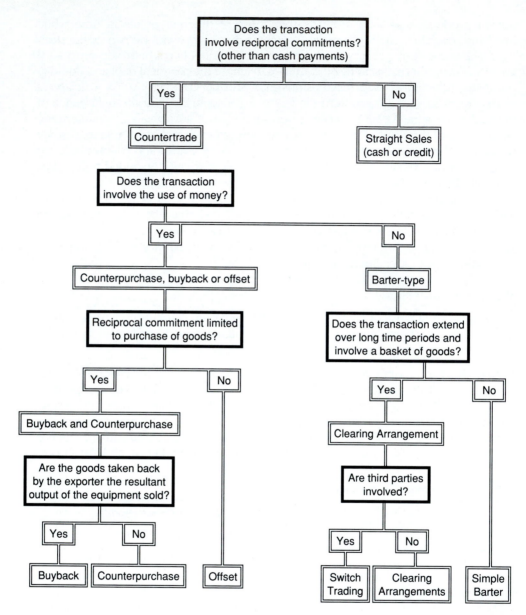

EXHIBIT 17–1   Classification of forms of countertrade

Source: Jean-Francois Hennart, "Empirical Dimensions," 245

was exchanged for concerts given by a Swedish band in Poland. In these cases, the agreement dealt with how many tons of coal were to be given by China and Poland rather than the actual monetary value of the construction project or concerts. It is estimated that about half of the U.S. corporations engage in some form of barter, primarily within the local markets of the United States.

Counterpurchase (Parallel Barter)   **Counterpurchase** occurs when there are two contracts or a set of parallel cash sales agreements, each paid in cash. Unlike barter, which is a single transaction with an exchange price only implied, a counterpurchase involves two separate transactions—each with its own cash value. A supplier sells a facility or product at a set price and orders unrelated or nonresultant products to offset the cost to the initial buyer. Thus, the buyer pays with hard currency, whereas the supplier agrees to buy certain products within a specified period. Therefore, money does not need to change hands. In effect, the practice allows the original buyer to earn back the currency. GE won a contract worth $300 million to build aircraft engines for Sweden's JAS fighters for cash only after agreeing to buy Swedish industrial products over a period of time in the same amount through a counterpurchase deal. Iraq persuaded the New Zealand Meat Board to sell $200 million worth of frozen lamb for a purchase of the same value of crude oil. Brazil exports vehicles, steel, and farm products to oil-producing countries from whom it buys oil in return.

Compensation Trade (Buyback)   A **compensation trade** requires a company to provide machinery, factories, or technology and to buy products made from this machinery over an agreed-on period. Unlike counterpurchase, which involves two unrelated products, the two contracts in a compensation trade are highly related. Under a separate agreement to the sale of plant or equipment, a supplier agrees to buy part of the plant's output for a number of years. For example, a Japanese company sold sewing machines to China and received payment in the form of 300,000 pairs of pajamas.

Switch Trading   **Switch trading** involves a triangular rather than bilateral trade agreement. When goods, all or part, from the buying country are not easily usable or salable, it may be necessary to bring in a third party to dispose of the merchandise. The third party pays hard currency for the unwanted merchandise at a considerable discount. A hypothetical example could involve Italy having a credit of $4 million for Austria's hams, which Italy cannot use. A third-party company may decide to sell Italy some desired merchandise worth $3 million for a claim on the Austrian hams. The price differential or margin is accepted as being necessary to cover the costs of doing business this way. The company can then sell the acquired hams to Switzerland for Swiss francs, which are freely convertible to dollars.

Offset   In an **offset,** a foreign supplier is required to manufacture/assemble the product locally and/or purchase local components as an exchange for the right to sell its products locally. In effect, the supplier has to manufacture at a location that may not be optimal from an economic standpoint. Offsets are often found in purchases of aircraft and military equipment.

Clearing Agreement   A **clearing agreement** is a clearing account barter with no currency transaction required. With a line of credit being established in the central banks of the two countries, the trade in this case is continuous, and the exchange of products between two governments is designed to achieve an agreed-on value or volume of trade tabulated or calculated in nonconvertible "clearing account units." For example, the former Soviet Union's rationing of hard currency limited imports and payment of copiers. Rank Xerox decided to circumvent the problem by making copiers in India for sale to the Soviets under the country's "clearing" agreement with India. The contract set forth goods, ratio of exchange, and time length for completion. Any imbalances after the end of the year were settled by credit into the next year, acceptance of unwanted goods, payment of penalty, or hard currency payment. Although nonconvertible in theory, clearing units in practice can be sold at a discount to trading specialists who use them to buy salable products.

Problems and Opportunities

Although countertrade is a common and growing practice, it has been criticized on several fronts. First, countertrade is considered by some as a form of protectionism that poses a new threat to world trade. Such countries as Sweden, Australia, Spain, Brazil, Indonesia, and much of Eastern Europe demand reciprocity in order to impose a discipline on their balance of payments. In other words, imports must be offset by exports. Indonesia links government import requirements in contracts worth more than Rp. 500 million to the export of Indonesian products, other than oil and natural gas, in an equivalent amount to the foreign-exchange value of the contract. Mexico took a hard line in 1981 against foreign automakers by ordering them to earn back hard currency if they wanted to stay in business with Mexico. As a result, VW de Mexico had to purchase and export Mexican coffee. Nissan Mexicana agreed to accept coffee, horsemeat, chickpeas, and honey. Brazil enacted a similar requirement and was able to extract agreements from foreign-owned automobile and truck makers to export nearly $21 billion worth of vehicles and other products in return for the right to import duty-free parts for their Brazilian plants. Despite this charge, there is evidence that countertrade does not necessarily restrict the overall trade volume.

Second, countertrade is alleged to be nothing but "covert dumping." To compensate any supplying partners for the nuisance of taking another product as payment, a countertrading country frequently trades its products away at a discount. If the countertrading country discounts directly by selling its goods itself in another market instead of through a foreign firm, dumping would clearly occur. But according to an International Trade Commission study, the practice does not seem to be harmful to the United States. Countertrade activity actually results in U.S. exports always greatly exceeding the value of imports. It would thus appear that many products that U.S. firms agree to take from their customers for overseas marketing are not dumped back in the U.S. market.[4]

Third, countertrade is alleged to increase overhead costs and ultimately the price of a product. Countertrade involves time, personnel, and expenses in selling a customer's product—often at a discount. If another middleman is used to dispose of the product, a commission must also be paid. Because of these expenses, a selling company has to raise the price of the original order to compensate for such expenses as well as for the risk of taking another product in return as payment. The fact that the goods are saleable—either for other goods or, in the end, for cash somewhere else—means that additional and probably unnecessary costs must be incurred. As explained by Fitzgerald, "Countertrade requirements, like any trade restrictions, increase the cost of doing business. These costs cannot be passed into the international market but must be borne within the country imposing the requirements."[5]

Related to this charge of increasing costs is the problem of marketing unwanted merchandise that may remain unsold. A company may have to take on the added job of marketing its customer's goods if it does not want to lose business to rivals who are willing to do so. GE lost a major sale of CAT scanners to Austrian hospitals after Siemens agreed to preserve 4,000 jobs by stepping up production of unrelated electronic goods within its Austrian plants. McDonnell Douglas was able to secure a contract to sell 250 planes to former Yugoslavia only after agreeing to market such Yugoslav goods as hams and other foods, textiles, leather goods, wine, beer, mineral water, and tours. The company had a difficult time selling the $5 million worth of hams and finally did so to its own employees and suppliers. With regard to the Yugoslavian tours, the best the company could do was to offer the trips as incentives to employees.

Financing, essential in virtually all types of conventional transactions, becomes more complicated in the case of countertrade. This is especially true when the sale of one product is contingent on the purchase of an unrelated product in return. Understandably, banks may hesitate to provide credit for such a deal because of their concern that the exporter may not be able profitably to dispose of the product given to the exporter as payment.

When a company is unable or does not want to be concerned with disposing the product taken from its customer, it can turn to companies that act as intermediaries. The intermediaries may agree to dispose of the merchandise for a commission or they may agree to buy the goods outright. The Mediators is one such middleman organization that operates a $500 million a year business globally.[6] Another well-known specialist in barter is Atwood Richards, Inc. Its clients include GE, Shell, and *Newsweek*.[7] As a true merchant bank, Atwood Richards trades in just about any kind of marketable product. It sold Jamaican bat manure for surplus mayonnaise, which in turn was exchanged for accommodations on a cruise line. Even TV time has been bartered by the company. In all deals, the firm takes title to gain leverage, though its clients warehouse the bartered goods while it looks for a trade. Atwood Richards rarely pays cash to buy goods and only converts inventory to cash for operating costs. This practice is based on the belief that when something is sold for cash, its value ends there. But goods can be leveraged up in exchange for other goods at cost, and those other goods continue the process of building up leverage.

The results of one study dispel some widely held views about countertrade (see Exhibit 17–2). First, the relationship between a country's credit rating and its propensity to countertrade is not as strong as commonly believed. Second, buyback and counterpurchase are substitutes to foreign direct investment. Third, there is a surprisingly large volume of countertrade between developing countries themselves. Fourth, each countertrade type seems to have its own separate motivation (see Table 17–1). Barter allows exchange without the use of money and explicit prices. Barter is therefore useful in order to bypass: (1) exchange controls, (2) public or private price controls, and (3) a creditor's monitoring of imports.[8]

Those firms that tend to benefit from countertrade are the following: (1) large firms that have extensive trade operations for large, complex products; (2) vertically integrated firms that can accommodate countertrade takebacks; and (3) firms that trade with countries that have inappropriate exchange rates, rationed foreign

☐ H1: Countertrade, in all of its forms, is undertaken to shift the risk of fluctuations in export receipts and will be disproportionately undertaken by centrally planned economies (CPEs).

Partial support; important, but not dominant, role played by CPEs.

☐ H2: Barter will be mostly used for goods, the price of which is fixed above market-clearing levels by domestic price supports, cartels, or commodity agreements.

Support; low number of barters between OPEC members, and between developed countries.

☐ H2a: The proportion of exports subject to barter should be greater for foods, raw materials, and fuels, than for manufactures.

Mixed; food, raw materials, and fuels make up a larger percentage of all bartered products than manufactures for OPEC and developing countries, but not for CPEs.

☐ H3: The relationship between debt (as proxied by creditworthiness) and countertrade should be greater for barter than for counterpurchase and buy back.

Support; the percentage of BTs undertaken by countries with a low credit rating is greater than that of CPs and BBs.

☐ H3a: Barter will be disproportionately used in commerce between heavily indebted countries.

Support; the most common form of barter is that between two middle-income developing countries.

☐ H4: The proportion of buy back contracts that involve a product from SITC 7 will be greater than the proportion of counterpurchase contracts that involve a product from SITC 7.

No support; no statistically significant relationship between countertrade type and product group in the case of CPEs.

☐ H4a: Buy back will be used more often for manufactures than for food, raw materials, and fuels.

Mixed: relatively high proportion of commodities sold by CPEs under BB.

☐ H5: Buy back will be disproportionately imposed by countries that ban incoming FDI.

Support; overwhelming proportion of BBs are imposed by CPEs; the proportion of BBs imposed by countries with high barriers to incoming FDI is significantly greater than their share of world trade.

☐ H5a: Buy backs will be more commonly used for the extraction of natural resources than for manufacturing.

Mixed; the proportion of BB involving food, raw materials, and fuels is greater than that involving manufactures in the case of developing countries, but not in that of CPEs.

☐ H6: Counterpurchase will be disproportionately used by countries that ban incoming FDI.

Support; the proportion of CPs imposed by countries with high barriers on incoming FDI is significantly greater than their share of world trade.

☐ H6a: Counterpurchase will be more extensively used for the export of manufactures than for that of fuels, raw materials, and food.

Support; CP disproportionately used to export manufactures.

☐ H7: Countries that impose offsets are likely to be small developed countries.

Partial Support; OFs are overwhelmingly imposed by developed countries on other developed countries.

EXHIBIT 17–2 Empirical findings

Source: Jean-Francis Hennart, "Empirical Dimensions," 266

exchange, import restrictions, and importers inexperienced in assessing technology or in export marketing. In contrast, firms whose characteristics are the opposite of those just enumerated are likely to encounter significant barriers to countertrade operations and to receive few benefits.[9]

There is no question that countertrade is a cumbersome process. Yet a firm is unwise not to consider it. Much like other trade practices, countertrade presents both problems and opportunities. More often than not, problems of countertrade are more psychological rather than real obstacles. Problems can be overcome. One need only remember that in the final analysis all goods can be converted into cash.

PRICE QUOTATION

A **quotation** describes a specific product, states the price for that product as well as a specified delivery location, sets the time of shipment, and specifies payment terms. When a company receives an inquiry from abroad, the quotation must be very detailed in terms of weight, volume, and so on because of the customer's unfamiliarity with foreign products, places, and terms. Also the *pro forma* invoice may have to be prepared and supplied with the quotation. Since the time of shipment is critical, the prepared quotation should specify whether the time mentioned is from the factory or the port of export and whether it includes the estimated inland transit time.

Terms of Sale

The quotation must include terms of sale. In the United States, it is customary to ship FOB factory, freight collect, or COD. Such terms, however, are inappropriate for international business, and other terms such as ex works, FAS, FOB, C&F, CIF, ex Dock, and DDP should be used instead.[10] Table 17–2 describes the point of delivery and risk shift for these different terms of sale. These terms are discussed next.

Ex Works (EXW) or Ex—Named Point of Origin   *Ex* means *from,* and the price quoted is calculated from the point of origin. There are several variations of this term, and they include *ex factory, ex warehouse, ex works, ex mill, ex plantation,* and *ex mine.* Under these terms, the seller makes goods available for the buyer at a specific time and place, usually at the seller's place of business or warehouse. The buyer takes delivery at the seller's premises and bears all risks and expenses from that point on.

FAS—Named Port of Shipment   FAS stands for *Free Alongside Ship.* Under this term, the price includes delivery of goods along side the vessel or other mode of transportation, and the seller pays all charges up to that point. This term does not include the cost of loading. It is customary to use the port of export as the point of origin for this transaction. The seller's legal responsibility ends once it has obtained a clear wharfage receipt.

TABLE 17–2   Point of delivery and where risk shifts from seller to buyer

	EXW	FAS	FOB	C&F	CIF	Ex Dock	DDP
Supplier's warehouse	X						
Export dock		X					
On board vessel			X	X	X		
Import dock						X	
Buyer's warehouse							X
Main transit insurance risk on	buyer	buyer	buyer	buyer	seller	seller	seller

FOB—Named Point FOB stands for *Free On Board*. Like the other terms within the quotation, the point where the price is applicable must be mentioned. There are a number of classes, and the point in question may be any one of these: the named inland carrier at the named inland point of departure, the named inland carrier at the named point of exportation, the named port of shipment, and the named inland point in the country of importation.

Nevertheless, the point used for quotation is usually the port of export. In such a case, the price includes local delivery and loading. The seller's responsibility does not end until goods have actually been placed aboard the ship and a bill of lading issued. The buyer arranges for overseas transportation and bears all costs and risks from the time the goods are placed on board (i.e., passes the ship's rail).

C&F—to Named Point of Destination C&F stands for *Cost and Freight*. Usually, this term will name the overseas port of import as the point in question. The price generally includes the cost of transportation to the named point of debarkation. The buyer, in turn, is expected to pay for insurance. Like FOB, the risk of loss or damage to the goods is transferred from the seller to the buyer when the goods pass the ship's rail.

CIF—to Named Point of Destination CIF stands for *Cost, Insurance, and Freight*. Again, the point used for quotation can be any location. But the International Chamber of Commerce recommends that this point should be the destination. The CIF price includes the cost of goods, insurance, and all transportation charges to the point of debarkation (destination). The delivery costs are thus extended beyond the country of export. Although the price covers more items or activities than FOB, the seller's obligations still end at the same stage (i.e., when goods are aboard or loaded). The seller pays for insurance, and the seller's insurance company assumes responsibility once the goods are loaded.

Ex Dock—Named Port of Importation Ex dock means from the dock at the import point. The variations of this term include *ex quay* (EXQ), *ex pier,* and *ex ship* (EXS). Ex dock goes one step beyond CIF and means that the seller is responsible for placing goods on the dock at the named overseas port with the appropriate duty paid, if any. Although used principally in the U.S. import trade, ex dock is seldom, if ever, used in American export practice, and its use in quotations for export is not recommended.[11]

DDP—Delivered Duty Paid An example of this kind of quotation is "duty paid landed U.S." With the payment of this price, the seller undertakes the delivery of goods to the place named in the country of import, most likely the buyer's warehouse, with all costs and duties paid. The seller obtains an import license if required and arranges for an overseas customhouse broker to clear the merchandise through customs and to act as a freight forwarder by forwarding the goods locally to the final destination.

Quotation Guidelines

Although the potential buyer will probably specify the terms to be used, the seller should make certain that the quotation or price is meaningful when specific terms are not requested. It is unwise for a company in a suburb of Chicago to quote a price as "FOB Evanston, not export packed." The buyer may have no way of knowing that Evanston is a suburb of Chicago. Even if the buyer does know where Evanston is, that firm would have difficulty determining how much the local transportation or freight charges would be to move the goods from Evanston to the Chicago port. Moreover, the buyer would surely be interested in knowing what the packing costs for export are, since the merchandise would have to be packed for export. Without a meaningful quote, it is difficult to receive serious consideration from a potential buyer.

Whenever possible, the exporter should quote CIF. Better yet, the quote should include a breakdown for the C(ost), I(nsurance), and F(reight). The buyer is then aware of all the relevant costs needed to get the product to the port in its country, and the buyer can decide whether it should arrange for the insurance and/or freight. If the seller needs assistance, a freight forwarder would be helpful in determining the CIF price.

Although the CIF price yields the greatest amount of information for the buyer, terms other than CIF may prove more appropriate under certain circumstances. If the exporter needs to conserve cash, the exporter should not quote CIF or any terms beyond it (e.g., delivered duty paid). If currency convertibility is a problem, FOB terms may be more desirable for both parties. That is, the buyer pays freight in its own currency or arranges to use a ship from its own country. China, for example, controls shipping arrangements for imports and exports in order to preserve foreign exchange and retain the insurance business. The country's foreign trade corporations (FTCs), responsible for most foreign trade, prefer selling on CIF terms while buying FOB in order to underwrite all freight charges and insurance themselves.[12] One potential problem encountered in this case is that ships arranged for the Chinese FTCs have been known to arrive considerably late, incurring high interest and warehousing costs for American firms. Moreover, delays at Chinese ports are another problem, and that can hold up the payment even more.

METHODS OF FINANCING AND MEANS OF PAYMENT

There are several payment methods. Some methods provide financing to buyers, whereas other methods assure sellers of prompt payment.[13] Table 17–3 compares these payment methods.

Consignment

When **consignment** is used, goods are shipped but ownership is retained by the seller. This means that the product is furnished on a deferred-payment basis, and when the product is sold, the seller is reimbursed by the consignee. In effect, the seller is providing full financing for the consignee. The problem with consignment sales is that a high degree of risk prevails. First of all, it is costly to arrange for the return of merchandise that is unsold. In addition, because of the distance involved, the seller has difficulty keeping track of inventory and its condition. Certain safeguards are thus necessary. For example, the contract should specify the party responsible

TABLE 17–3 Methods of payment

American firms involved in international trade face a unique set of problems. Ultimately, the goal of any exporter is to make a sale and be paid. In return, the importer wants to receive the agreed-on goods. Factors such as distance, time, language, culture, and country regulations must be taken into consideration by the respective parties, if their needs are to be satisfied.

The importer or exporter should answer the following questions before selecting the most appropriate method of payment.

- ☐ How reliable is the exporter?
- ☐ How long has the exporter been shipping?
- ☐ Is the exporter's product subject to inspection?
- ☐ How creditworthy is the importer?
- ☐ Has the importer demonstrated the ability to pay promptly?
- ☐ Can the importer count on getting the goods on time?
- ☐ What credit terms are offered by the competition?
- ☐ What are the political and economic conditions within the importer's and exporter's countries?
- ☐ What is the value of the goods?
- ☐ Is this a one-time shipment or does the possibility exist for additional orders?
- ☐ Is the product standardized or specialized, and is it resaleable?

After carefully evaluating the above questions, the importer or exporter is now prepared to select the proper payment method:

Method	Payment	Goods Available to Buyer	Risk to Exporter	Risk to Importer
Cash in Advance	Before shipment	After payment	None	Relies on exporter to ship goods as ordered
Letter of Credit	When goods shipped and documents comply with letter of credit	After payment	Little or none depending on letter of credit	Relies on exporter to ship goods described in documents
Sight Draft, Documents Against Acceptance	On maturity of draft	After payment	Buyer can refuse goods	Same as letter of credit unless the importer can inspect goods before payment
Time Draft, Documents Against Acceptance	On maturity of draft	Before payment	Relies on buyer to pay draft	Same as above
Open Account	As agreed	Before payment	Relies completely on buyer to pay account	None

Source: International Workbook (Chicago: UnibancTrust, 1985), 1. Reprinted with permission of UnibancTrust

for property insurance in the event there is damage to the merchandise while in the possession of the consignee. Because of these problems and difficulties, the method is not widely used by American exporters. Consignment, however, can be a satisfactory arrangement when the sale involves an affiliated firm or the seller's own sales representative or dealer.

Open Account

With an **open account,** goods are shipped without documents calling for payment, other than the invoice. The buyer can pick up goods without having to make payment first. The advantage with the open account is simplicity and assistance to the buyer, who does not have to pay credit charges to banks. The seller in return expects that the invoice will be paid at the agreed time. A major weakness of this method is that there is no safeguard against default, since a tangible payment instrument does not exist. The lack of payment instrument also makes it difficult to sell the account receivable. To compound the problem, the buyer often delays payment until the merchandise is received—a standard practice in many countries.

Because of the inherent risks of an open account, precautions should be taken. The seller must determine the integrity of the buyer by relying on prior experience, or through a credit investigation. Toward this end, there are several organizations that can provide some assistance in terms of credit information. First, there are commercial credit agencies such as the International Dun and Bradstreet's American Foreign Credit Underwriters Corp. Second, such organizations as chambers of commerce and trade associations can be contacted. Additionally, commercial banks and their overseas branches or correspondent banks usually have some useful credit information. Finally, government sources can also be valuable. World Traders Data Reports, for example, has a great deal of information on foreign firms.

Cash in Advance

The seller may want to demand cash in advance when

1. The buyer is financially weak or an unknown credit risk.
2. The economic/political conditions in the buyer's country are unstable.
3. The seller is not interested in assuming credit risk, as in the case of consignment and open account sales.

Because of the immediate uses of money and the maximum protection, sellers prefer cash in advance. The problem, of course, is that the buyer is not eager to tie up its money, especially if the buyer has some doubt about whether it will receive the goods as ordered. By insisting on cash in advance, the seller shifts the risk completely to the buyer, but the seller may end up losing the sale by this insistence.

Bill of Exchange (Draft)

A means of financing international transactions is through a *bill of exchange* or *draft,* which is a request for payment (see Exhibit 17–3). The request is an unconditional order in writing from one person (drawer) requiring the person to whom it is

U.S. $ 1,180.00 — OCTOBER 1 19 87

AT SIGHT------------------- of this *FIRST* of Exchange (Second unpaid)

Pay to the Order of ABC COMPANY

ONE THOUSAND ONE HUNDRED EIGHTY AND 00/100 ----------------- United States Dollars

for Value received and charge the same to account of

To ANTIGUA WHITE SANDS MOTEL
P.O. BOX 655
ST. JOHNS, ANTIGUA

ABC COMPANY

J. Doe
J. DOE
Authorized Signature

No. A495Z

SAMPLE 1

10/1/87
Date

Gentlemen:

We enclose Draft Number A495Z and documents listed below

☒ for collection,
☐ for
☐ for payment / negotiation under L / C

BILLS OF LADING	B/L COPY	COMM. INV.	INS. CTF.	CTF. ORIG.	CONS. INV.	PKNG. LIST	WGT. CTF.	OTHER DOCUMENTS
2/3	2	3				3		3 Customs Invoices

Please handle in accordance with instructions marked "X"

☒ Deliver all documents in one mailing.
☐ Deliver documents in two mailings.
☒ Deliver documents against payment if sight draft, or acceptance if time draft.
☒ All charges for account of drawee.
☒ Do not waive charges.
☐ Protest for non-payment / non-acceptance
☒ Do not protest.
☐ Present on arrival of goods.
☒ Advise non-payment / ~~non-acceptance~~ by airmail / ~~cable~~ giving reasons
☒ Advise payment / ~~acceptance~~ by airmail / ~~cable~~

IN CASE OF NEED refer to:

Name

Address

who is empowered by us:

a ☐ To act fully on our behalf, i.e., authorize reductions, extensions, free delivery, waiving of protest, etc.

b ☐ To assist in obtaining acceptance or payment of draft, as drawn, but not to alter its terms in any way.

OTHER INSTRUCTIONS:

PLEASE REMIT PROCEEDS TO OUR ACCOUNT NO. 12B452 AT FIRST AMERICA BANK, DETROIT

Please refer all questions concerning this collection to:

☒ Shipper : ABC COMPANY

☐ Freight Forwarder:

ABC COMPANY

J. Doe
J. DOE
Authorized Signature

EXHIBIT 17–3 A bill of exchange (draft)

Source: Reprinted with permission of Radix Group International, Inc.

addressed (drawee) to pay the payee or bearer on demand or at a fixed or determinable time. The drawer, usually the exporter, is the maker or originator of the draft requesting payment. The drawee, usually the buyer, is the party responsible for honoring or paying the draft. The payee may be the exporter, the exporter's bank, the bearer, or any specified person. In short, a draft is a request for payment. It is a negotiable instrument that contains an order to pay a payee. As noted by John Stuart Mill, the purpose is to save expense and minimize the risk of transporting precious metals from place to place as payment of imports. The bill of exchange simply allows banks to make adjustments by debiting or crediting accounts maintained in buyer or seller names with other banks.

The transaction process occurs in this way. The drawee accepts the draft by signing an acceptance on the face of the instrument. If the buyer does not accept (sign) the bill, the buyer is not given the attached documents to obtain goods from the steamship company, since the shipment is made on the negotiable order bill of lading. In practice, banks are responsible for payment collection. The original order bill of lading is endorsed by the shipper and sent to the buyer's bank along with the bill of exchange, invoices, and other required documents (e.g., consular invoice, insurance certificate, inspection certificate). Once notified by the bank, the buyer pays the amount on the draft and is given the bill of lading, which allows the buyer to obtain the shipment.

There are two principal types of bill of exchange: sight and time. A *sight draft,* as the name implies, is drawn at sight, meaning that it is paid when it is first seen by the drawee. A sight draft is commonly used for either credit reasons or for the purpose of title retention. A *time (usance or date) draft,* is drawn for the purpose of financing the sale or temporary storage of specified goods for a specified number of days after sight (e.g., thirty, sixty, ninety days, or longer). It specifies payment of a stated amount at maturity. As such, it offers less security than a sight draft since the sight draft demands payment prior to the release of shipping documents. The time draft, on the other hand, allows the buyer to obtain shipping documents to obtain merchandise when accepting the draft, even though the buyer can actually defer payment.

At first thought, it may seem that a time draft is not really different from an open account, since the goods can be obtained or picked up by the buyer before making payment. There is one crucial difference, however. In the case of the time draft, there is a negotiable instrument evidencing the obligation. Since this document can be sold to factors and discounted immediately, the seller can obtain cash before maturity. In the United States, factors are financial institutions that buy accounts receivable from manufacturers.

There are other variations of this kind of draft. If bills of lading, invoices, and the like accompany the draft, this is known as *documents against payment* (D/P). If financial documents are omitted to avoid stamp tax charges against such documents or if bills of lading come from countries where drafts are not used, this type of collection is known as *cash against documents.* Frequently, the draft terms may read "90 days sight D/A" or *documents against acceptance.* "Upon accepting this draft, the buyer is permitted to obtain the documents and the merchandise, while not being obliged to make payment until the draft matures."[14]

Bankers' Acceptance

A *bankers' acceptance* assists in the expansion of credit financing. In 1974 only 13 percent of U.S. trade was financed through acceptances, but the percentage increased to 28 percent of U.S. export-import trade in 1982 at a time when world trade was contracting.[15] A bankers' acceptance is a time draft whose maturity is usually less than six months. The draft becomes a bankers' acceptance when the bank accepts it; that is, the bank on which the draft is drawn stamps and endorses it as "accepted." Drafts drawn on and accepted by nonbank entities are called *trade acceptances.*

An acceptance becomes the accepting bank's obligation, and once accepted it becomes a negotiable instrument that can be bought or sold in the market like a certificate of deposit (CD) or commercial paper. Daily newspapers usually list the daily prices of bankers' acceptances in the financial section. The acceptance commission is the reason that a bank lends its name, integrity, and credit rating to the instrument. The discount charge is computed at the current prime bankers' acceptance rate from date of purchase to maturity. The bank has primary responsibility for payment to the acceptance holder at maturity. But the draft originator still has secondary liability in case the accepting bank does not honor the claim. Table 17–4 describes the characteristics of bankers' acceptances.

Letter of Credit

An alternative to the sight draft is a sight *letter of credit (L/C)*. As a legal instrument, it is a written undertaking by a bank through prior agreement with its client to honor a withdrawal by a third party for goods and services rendered (see Exhibit 17–4). The document, issued by the bank at the buyer's request in favor of the seller, is the bank's promise to pay an agreed amount of money on its receipt of certain documents within the specified time period. Usually, the required documents are the same as those used with the sight draft. In effect, the bank is being asked to substitute its credit for that of the buyer's. The bank agrees to allow one party to the transaction (the seller, creditor, or exporter) to collect payment from that party's correspondent bank or branch abroad. Drafts presented for payment under the L/C are thus drawn on the bank. The importer can repay the bank by either making an appropriate deposit in cash or borrowing all or part of the money from the bank. The drawee (buyer) is usually responsible for the collection charges by banks at home and overseas. Exhibit 17–5 examines the process involved in a letter of credit.

Several banks may be involved in the process. The *issuing bank,* as a rule, issues letters of credit for its present customers only, even if collateral is offered by someone else. In contrast, the *advising bank* is the bank that notifies the exporter that an L/C has been issued. The issuing bank forwards the L/C to the advising bank (its foreign correspondent), which is usually selected for its proximity to the beneficiary. In the case of a *confirming bank,* the same services are performed as the advising bank but also the confirming bank becomes liable for payment.

There are several types of letters of credit, including revocable, irrevocable, confirmed, unconfirmed, standby, back-to-back, and transferable.

Revocable Letter of Credit With a revocable L/C, the issuing bank has the right to revoke its commitment to honor the draft drawn on it. Without prior warning or notification to the seller, the bank can cancel or modify its obligation at any time before payment—even after shipment has already been made. Since the bank's commitment is not legally binding, the protection to the seller is minimal. Exporters generally do not want to accept a revocable L/C.

Irrevocable Letter of Credit This type of L/C is much preferred to the revocable letter of credit. In this case, once the L/C is accepted by the seller, it cannot be amended in any way or cancelled by the buyer or the buyer's bank without all parties' approval.

TABLE 17–4 Bankers' acceptances—characteristics governing eligibility, reserve requirements, and aggregate acceptance limits

	Federal Reserve System Treatment			
	Eligible for discount[1]	Eligible for purchase[2]	Reserve requirements apply if sold[3]	Aggregate acceptance limits apply[4]
Bankers' acceptance categories				
1. Specific international transactions				
a. U.S. exports or imports				
Tenor—6 months or less	yes[5]	yes	no	yes
6 months to 9 months	no	yes	yes	no
b. Shipment of goods *between* foreign countries:				
Tenor—6 months or less	yes[5]	yes	no	yes
6 months to 9 months	no	yes	yes	no
c. Shipment of goods *within* a foreign country:				
Tenor—any term	no	no	yes	no
d. Storage of goods within a foreign country—*readily marketable* staples secured by warehouse receipt issued by an independent warehouseman:[6]				
Tenor—6 months or less	yes[5]	no	no	yes
6 months to 9 months	no	no	yes	no
e. Dollar exchange—required by usages of trade in approved countries only:				
Tenor—3 months or less	yes	no	no	yes
more than 3 months	no	no	yes	no
2. Specific domestic transactions (i.e., within the U.S.)				
a. Domestic shipment of goods:[8]				
Tenor—3 months or less	yes[5]	yes	no	yes
6 months to 9 months	no	yes	yes	no
b. Domestic storage—*readily marketable* stables secured by warehouse receipt issued by independent warehouseman:[6]				
Tenor—6 months or less	no	yes	yes	no
6 months to 9 months	no	yes	yes	no
3. Marketable time deposits (finance bills or working capital acceptances) not related to any specific transaction				
Tenor—any term	no	no	yes	no

Notes: This table is an adaptation from a table presented in an unpublished paper from the 7th annual CIB Conference at New Orleans, October 13, 1975, by Arthur Bardenhagen, Vice President, Irving Trust Company, New York.

[1] In accordance with Regulation A of Board of Governors as provided by the Federal Reserve Act.

[2] Authorizations for the purchase of acceptances as announced by the Federal Open Market Committee on April 1, 1974

[3] In accordance with Regulation D of the Board of Governors as provided by the Federal Reserve Act.

[4] Member banks may accept bills in an amount not exceeding at any time 150 percent (or 200 percent if approved by the Board of Governors of (as defined the Federal Reserve system) unimpaired capital stock in FRB, Chicago Circular No. 2156 of April 2, 1971). Acceptances growing out of domestic transactions are not to exceed 50 percent of the total of a bank's total acceptance ceiling.

[5] The tenor of nonagricultural bills may not exceed 90 days at the time they are presented for discount with the Federal Reserve.

[6] As of May 10, 1978, the Board of Governors issued the interpretation that bankers' acceptances secured by field warehouse receipts covering readily marketable staples are eligible for discount. Readily marketable staples are defined, in general, as nonbranded goods for which a ready and open market exists. There is a regularly quoted, easily accessible, objective price-setting mechanism that determines the market price of the goods.

[7] Proceeds from the sale of an eligible for discount dollar exchange acceptance are not specifically exempted from reserve requirements under Regulation D, Section 204.2a (vii) (E) effective November 13, 1980, of the Board of Governors as are other acceptances that meet the condition of Section 13(7) of the Federal Reserve act. However, the Federal Reserve Board's legal staff issued an opinion January 15, 1981, stating that the proceeds from the sale of eligible dollar exchange acceptances are exempt from reserve requirements.

[8] Prior to the amendment to Section 13(7) of the Federal Reserve act (October 8, 1982) domestic shipment acceptances required documents conveying title be attached for eligible for discount to apply.

Note: Tenor refers to the duration of the acceptance from its creation to maturity. An eligible for discount acceptance must be created by or endorsed by a member bank, according to Section 13(6) of the Federal Reserve Act.

Source: Jack L. Hervey, "Bankers' Acceptance Revisted," *Economic Perspectives*, Federal Reserve Bank of Chicago (May-June 1983): 296. Reprinted with permission of the Federal Reserve Bank of Chicago.

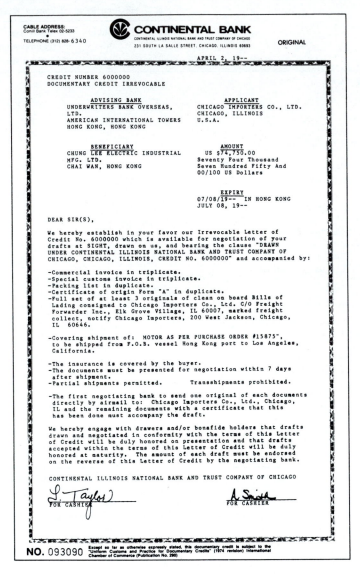

EXHIBIT 17–4   Import commercial letter of credit

Source: Reprinted with permission of Continental Illinois National Bank and Trust Company of Chicago

It is possible, however, for the buyer who receives proper documents but unsuitable goods because of fraud to obtain an injunction preventing the banker from paying the fraudster.[16] When Worlds of Wonder, a U.S. toy company, filed for bankruptcy protection, four Hong Kong creditors/suppliers were able to use irrevocable letters of credit to collect $16.5 million from an undisclosed bank. Another Hong Kong manufacturer, Applied Electronics, could not recover any of its debt since it held no outstanding letters of credit.

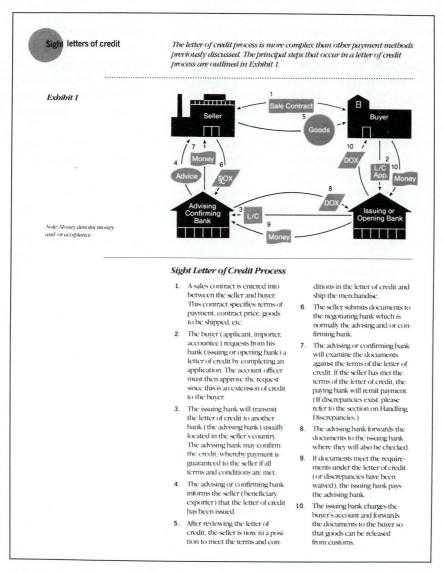

Sight letters of credit

The letter of credit process is more complex than other payment methods previously discussed. The principal steps that occur in a letter of credit process are outlined in Exhibit 1.

Exhibit 1

Note: Money denotes money and/or acceptance.

Sight Letter of Credit Process

1. A sales contract is entered into between the seller and buyer. This contract specifies: terms of payment, contract price, goods to be shipped, etc.

2. The buyer (applicant, importer, accountee) requests from his bank (issuing or opening bank) a letter of credit by completing an application. The account officer must then approve the request since this is an extension of credit to the buyer.

3. The issuing bank will transmit the letter of credit to another bank (the advising bank) usually located in the seller's country. The advising bank may confirm the credit, whereby payment is guaranteed to the seller if all terms and conditions are met.

4. The advising or confirming bank informs the seller (beneficiary, exporter) that the letter of credit has been issued.

5. After reviewing the letter of credit, the seller is now in a position to meet the terms and con-

ditions in the letter of credit and ship the merchandise.

6. The seller submits documents to the negotiating bank which is normally the advising and/or confirming bank.

7. The advising or confirming bank will examine the documents against the terms of the letter of credit. If the seller has met the terms of the letter of credit, the paying bank will remit payment. (If discrepancies exist, please refer to the section on Handling Discrepancies.)

8. The advising bank forwards the documents to the issuing bank where they will also be checked.

9. If documents meet the requirements under the letter of credit (or discrepancies have been waived), the issuing bank pays the advising bank.

10. The issuing bank charges the buyer's account and forwards the documents to the buyer so that goods can be released from customs.

EXHIBIT 17–5 Process involved in a sight letter of credit

Source: International Workbook (Chicago: UnibancTrust, 1985), 3. Reprinted with permission of UnibancTrust

Confirmed Letter of Credit For the exporter, it is highly desirable for the L/C to be confirmed through a bank in the exporter's country because the exporter then receives an additional guarantee of payment from a second bank (i.e., the confirming bank). The advising bank sends a cover letter along with the original L/C to the exporter, stating that the L/C has been confirmed. A U.S. exporter is in a much better position if there is a U.S. bank that accepts the responsibility of paying the letter of credit in case of refusal to do so by the buyer and/or the buyer's bank (i.e., issuing bank in a foreign country). In the early 1980s, the political crisis in Iran, for example, made it impossible for many American sellers to enforce the payment terms specified in unconfirmed letters of credit. Naturally, a confirmed L/C is more desirable when payment is guaranteed by two banks instead of one, especially if there is some doubt about the issuing foreign bank's ability to pay. Moreover, since the confirming bank is located in the same country as the exporter, the exporter is able to receive payment more readily by presenting documents to the confirming bank (rather than the issuing bank abroad) to show that all obligations have been completed.

Honesty is a virtue that cannot be taken for granted in international trade. A seller may, for example, ship unordered or inferior goods while collecting payment. A buyer may refuse to pay for goods received. It must be emphasized that a marketer can never be too cautious or careful when dealing in international trade. In the case of a confirmed letter of credit, the seller should not accept a statement from a bank that "confirms the existence of an L/C" because to confirm the existence of something is not the same thing as to confirm an L/C. A confirmed L/C requires the bank's engagement (i.e., taking obligation). Also, the bank that confirms the L/C must be financially sound, and the exporter should specify that "the confirming bank must be acceptable to the seller."

Unconfirmed Letter of Credit   When the L/C is not confirmed by a bank in the seller's country, the certainty is less and the payment slower. An unconfirmed letter of credit may still be acceptable as long as the foreign bank that issues it is financially strong. In fact, some multinational banks are so well known that they prohibit letters of credit issued by them to be confirmed because they believe that confirmation would tarnish their prestige. However, letters of credit can still be confirmed confidentially.

It is also possible to combine the several types of L/C. A letter of credit can be revocable and confirmed, irrevocable and unconfirmed, and so on. For maximum security and earliest payment, the seller should ask for an irrevocable and confirmed L/C. Japan's MITI, for example, requires irrevocable letters of credit before it will issue insurance coverage for exporters to Brazil.

Standby Letter of Credit (Bid or Performance L/C)   Unlike the purpose of a commercial L/C, which is trade-related, the purpose of a standby L/C (special purpose, or bid or performance L/C) is to guarantee a seller's obligation under a contract or agreement. It is used for such purposes as a performance bond, bid bond, surety bond, and loan agreement. In this case, it is the buyer that requires the seller to open an L/C naming the buyer as a beneficiary, instead of the other way around. The reason for this arrangement is that the subsequent failure of the seller to fulfill the agreement can be quite damaging to the buyer, since a period of time has elapsed and the buyer has to seek a new supplier all over again. Because of the possibility of a loss of profit as a result of a delay or failure of the seller, the buyer needs to be assured that the seller is indeed capable of delivering goods or completing the project as promised. A standby L/C is thus a bank's guarantee to the beneficiary that a specific sum of money will be received by the beneficiary under certain conditions. If the beneficiary is the buyer, the firm can draw under the standby L/C only when the applicant (seller) fails to meet its obligations. On the other hand, the beneficiary can also be the exporter, which can ask for full or partial payment as the project progresses. Thus, the seller is assured of payment for sales made on open account. The buyer draws by presenting the seller's draft with unpaid invoices, and the bank then releases all or part of the money to the seller.

Back-to-Back Letter of Credit   When the seller is a trading firm or middleman who must pay a supplier before asking the supplier to deliver goods to a foreign customer, the middleman may have to obtain an L/C naming the supplier as the beneficiary. This can become a problem if the middleman has inadequate resources to obtain a loan or an L/C from a bank. What the intermediary can do is to use the commitment of the customer's issuing bank (i.e., the customer's L/C) to collateralize issuance of the second L/C by the intermediary's bank in favor of, say, the supplier. This is an entirely separate transaction from the original or master L/C. The intermediary (seller) assigns the proceeds of the original L/C to its bank, which in turn issues the bank's own L/C in favor of the supplier for an amount not exceeding the original L/C.

Because a back-to-back L/C is a transaction entirely separate from the original or master L/C, the bank issuing back-to-back credit is liable for payment to the supplier even if there is a failure to complete the requirements of the original credit. Not surprisingly, many banks are reluctant to be involved with back-to-back transactions, preferring to handle the transferable credit option instead.

Transferable Letter of Credit   Again, when the seller is an agent or broker for the supplier of the goods, it is difficult for the agent to have an L/C issued to the supplier if the agent's credit standing is weak or unknown. To solve the problem, the agent or broker may request a transferable L/C from the buyer. This type of L/C allows the beneficiary (i.e., agent) to transfer *once* rights in part or in full to another party. The agent as the first beneficiary requests the issuing or advising bank to transfer the L/C to his supplier (second beneficiary). The transferring bank receives a commission for doing so. A reduction in the amount, unit price, shipment period, and validity period are allowed. Since the agent receives a fee or commission for the selling effort, the bank will pay the supplier based on the supplier's invoices for the transferred (lesser) amount. The agent then receives the difference between the full price (the agent's own invoice) and the lesser amount (the supplier's invoice). The transferee (supplier), after making the shipment, submits documentation to receive payment. After this is completed, the original beneficiary (agent) obtains a commission by substituting its invoice with any other documents evidencing price for the total value of the sale. The beneficiary presents a draft for the difference between the supplier's draft and sales value covered under the credit.

The dilemma for the agent is that, unlike a back-to-back L/C, there is a possibility that the transferable L/C may reveal the identify of the supplier to the agent's customer and vice versa. Once the buyer learns of this identity, the buyer may elect to contact the supplier directly in the future to avoid paying a commission to the agent.

If the original beneficiary (agent) does not want the buyer to be identified, the beneficiary's name or a neutral (forwarder's) name may be substituted for the buyer's name. The failure of the agent to provide the bank with substitute documents immediately will defeat the whole purpose, since the bank has the right to deliver the transferee's documents to the issuing bank.

Advantages and Disadvantages of Letters of Credit   The letter of credit offers several advantages. First, it offers security while minimizing risk. The bank's acceptance of the payment obligation is a better credit instrument than a bill of exchange that has been accepted by the buyer. An L/C creates a better relationship with the buyer since all terms are specified and both parties are protected. In addition, the exporter can receive payment before maturity by discounting the L/C. An L/C can be discounted at a lower rate because it offers greater security than a bill of exchange. The discount charge is usually computed at the current prime bankers' acceptance rate from date of purchase to maturity.

For the buyer, the L/C also offers several benefits even though the buyer may have to bear the burden of financing. First, the buyer can buy now and pay later. Second, the L/C offers the assurance of prompt delivery. There is also an expired date for credit, and no payment is made until the goods are placed in the possession of a transport carrier for shipment. In addition, the seller must complete the terms specified in the L/C before payment is released. Third, the buyer may receive a better price since the seller does not have to adopt unnecessary safeguards or to sell the L/C at deep discount. The buyer, as a result, may even qualify for the seller's cash discount.

It is imperative that the seller carefully examine the L/C terms to make certain that he or she understands them and can meet the requirements. The seller must examine such items as the description of the merchandise, trade terms, price, delivery date, required documents, the party responsible for insurance, departure and entry points, and so on. The seller must also determine whether the L/C received is confirmed and irrevocable if requested as such. The seller should not accept an L/C requiring that the inspection certificate be signed by a particular individual because if that individual, because of death or other reasons, cannot sign the certificate, the exporter is unable to fulfill all the requirements and cannot collect payment. A precautionary measure may be to insist that the certificate be issued by a particular inspection company rather than a specific person associated with the company.

In spite of the many advantages, the L/C does have disadvantages as well. The instrument lacks flexibility, is cumbersome, and is the most complex method of obtaining payment. Any changes in the terms require an amendment to the L/C. Although suitable for a routine transaction, the L/C does not work well when the transaction is unusual and requires flexibility. It can also be expensive for the buyer if the government requires a prior deposit before establishing the L/C. For example, Lebanon requires banks to have their customers make a 15 percent deposit on documentary letters of credit on goods to be sold in Lebanon.[17]

Another reason why the L/C can be a burden to the buyer is that it entails credit exposure. As such, the buyer's credit must be approved in advance by the buyer's bank. This is understandable because the L/C is issued on an unsecured basis, and the buyer-applicant only pays when the issuing bank is called on to make payment. Without a satisfactory credit standing, the bank may require cash or other collateral for its own protection. In fact, a cash deposit may not even be acceptable if the importer has financial difficulties or an unknown credit reputation, since prior creditors may later lay claim to that amount of money in the event of the importer's bankruptcy. As a result, the bank will treat a request for an L/C as a request for a loan or line of credit.

CONCLUSION

The exporter must make an effort to quote a meaningful price by using proper international trade terms. When there is doubt about how to prepare a quotation, freight forwarders should be consulted. These specialists can provide valuable information with regard to documentation (e.g., invoice, bill of lading) and the costs relevant to the movement of goods. Special financial documents such as letters of credit, however, require a bank's assistance. International banks have international departments that can facilitate payment and advise clients regarding pitfalls in preparing and accepting documents.

QUESTIONS

1. Explain these terms of countertrade: barter, counterpurchase, buyback, offset, clearing agreement, and switch trading.
2. Explain these terms of sale: ex works, FAS, FOB, C&F, CIF, ex dock, and delivered duty paid.
3. Explain (a) bill of exchange and (b) bankers' acceptance.
4. Explain these types of letter of credit: revocable, irrevocable, confirmed, unconfirmed, back-to-back, and transferable.

DISCUSSION ASSIGNMENTS AND MINICASES

1. Given that countertrade is a fact of life that is not going to go away, is there any valid argument from a *theoretical* standpoint for this method of doing business?
2. Assume that you are a U.S. manufacturer being asked to submit a quotation to a potential buyer. How are you going to prepare your quotation in regard to (a) terms of sale and (b) terms of payment?

CASE 17–1
COUNTERTRADE: COUNTERPRODUCTIVE?

In modern times barter and its numerous derivations, which have conceptually been gathered together under the rubric "countertrade," have gained renewed stature in international trade. This has occurred despite the fact that international money and credit markets have attained unparalleled levels of sophistication.

Where readily acceptable forms of money exchange and viable credit facilities are available, markets shun cumbersome and inefficient barter-type transactions. But, international liquidity problems and government restrictions on the operation of markets have prompted many less developed countries (LDCs) and nonmarket economies (NMEs), as well as industrial countries, to promote "creative" trade transactions that circumvent the normal exchange medium of modern markets.

The *shortcomings* of countertrade include the following:

1. Countertrade has a high inherent transaction cost.
2. Countertrade limits competitive markets.
3. Countertrade contributes to market distortions that lead to inappropriate economic planning.

Inefficiency in Transactions Costs

The underlying weakness of countertrade as a mechanism of trade and exchange is its inefficiency. The indivisibility of goods made barter inefficient, for example, and forced those involved with such trade to search for a better way. Barter gave way to goods/services-for-money exchange, which permitted transactions to incorporate divisibility as well as time shifting. The opportunity for more convenient (i.e., efficient), multiparty trade became a reality.

A major factor in the expansion of world trade during the last half of the twentieth century has been the emergence of a few widely accepted currencies, especially the U.S. dollar, as settlement currencies for international transactions. The development of international credit markets to support trade depended on the fact that transactions could be entered into without undue concern by the parties involved as to the delivery of the specific quantity and quality of goods and the timeliness of payment. A key characteristic of this type of market is that the channels of communication and exchange are well defined and relatively simple.

As a consequence of this clarity and simplicity, such markets are efficient. Specifically, the direct and indirect costs involved in the process of exchange account for a relatively small portion of the total cost of the transaction.

Such efficiency is not present in the conditional transactions that make up countertrade. The inefficiency cost must be borne by one or more of the parties involved.

Many countertrade transactions are entered into because the importing country is unable to obtain financing in the international markets and is short of hard-currency reserves. The lack of access, or limited access, to the credit markets may be due to restrictions on the country, placed as a condition for specific new lending by the International Monetary Fund (IMF) or foreign commercial banks. In this environment countertrade is sometimes viewed by an LDC government as a means of engaging in trade without the cost of entering the international finance markets.

Whereas it is correct that countertrade may mean that the international financial markets may not have to be tapped, it is not correct to assume that there are no financing costs associated with a countertrade transaction. In fact, because of the complexity associated with carrying out a countertrade transaction, the cost is higher than if the LDC has had access to those credit markets. Moreover, countertrade may end up subverting the capital and austerity restrictions that in some cases are a part of an IMF/LDC lending agreement.

In countertrade the costs of financing are shifted. They become implicit rather than explicit. The seller may absorb this cost in the form of accepting the obligation to buy or use or resell goods it otherwise would not accept (thus reducing its return on the transaction). Alternatively, the seller may build the transaction's finance costs into the price the buyer must pay. The finance costs are there, though hidden.

Limiting Competition

There is another implicit cost when countertrade is required by the LDC or nonmarket economy (NME) buyer as a condition of the transaction. Countertrade limits the potential number of sellers in the market. Not every seller firm is willing or able to engage in countertrade, thus, an LDC or NME buyer that insists on countertrade as part of a trade package limits its potential for obtaining a competitive product, service, or price. The fact is that engaging in countertrade costs the LDC or NME economy more in terms of real resources than a straight commercial transaction.

Market Distortions and False Signals

Developing countries may not have well developed international marketing facilities. As a result they often find it difficult to break into international markets with goods and services that are nontraditional for their economy.

In other cases an LDC or NME may choose to develop a new domestic industry by buying the technology and plant from abroad. Domestic demand may not be adequate for an efficient plant size. In response, they may opt for a larger, more efficient (but possibly from a world supply view, redundant), plant with the expectation of placing the marginal production on the international market.

Under such conditions counterpurchase or buyback agreements may be sought by the LDC or NME to finance the importation of plant and equipment for a new industry (as in a buyback agreement) or general imports (as in a counterpurchase agreement). The LDC or NME also may be seeking a more knowledgeable partner to handle the international marketing of goods for which it does not have the expertise.

The difficulty with this approach is that countertrade may be used to get goods onto the international market that would not "make it" under usual conditions and will not be competitive once the buyback agreement expires. Further, the industrial country firm that accepted the countertraded goods may dump them, which would be disruptive to international markets. The result may be that the LDC or NME producer may falsely interpret the signals and overestimate the real market demand for the dumped goods as being stronger than a longer-term, unsubsidized, market can bear.

Moreover, the secondary consequences of countertrade transactions are not benign. The inefficiencies of countertrade—the false price signals that result in the building of redundant plant and equipment—tend to promote the establishment of bureaucracies within governments and private firms that have "bought into" countertrade. In turn, these bureaucracies have a vested interest in maintaining the economic distortions that undergird the growth in countertrade.

Summing Up

Countertrade is a significant factor in modern international trade. In its different forms it is used as a marketing tool, as a competitive tool, as a tool to restrict trade alternatives, and as a tool to tie the trade of one country to another country. Countertrade in a modern world economy with highly developed goods, capital, and financial markets appears on its face to be an incongruous development. Countertrade is a costly, inefficient, and disruptive anomaly. Yet observers of international trade suggest that the volume of countertrade is growing.

Countertrade takes place in a world of imperfection where the political and economic policies of government and industry distort the relationships between and within the goods, capital, and financial markets.

Source: This case was abbreviated and adapted from Jack L. Hervey, "Countertrade—Counterproductive?" *Economic Perspectives* (January/February 1989): 17–24

Questions

1. Discuss the pros and cons of countertrade as a form of trade.
2. As a manufacturing firm located in a developed country, you are interested in taking advantage of the Eastern European markets' movement toward market-oriented economies. However, your potential customers lack hard currency and have asked you to consider countertrade. Are you willing to engage in countertrade? Why or why not?

NOTES

1. Jack L. Hervey, "Countertrade—Counterproductive?" *Economic Perspectives* (January/February 1989): 17–24.

2. Sandra M. Huszagh and Hiram C. Barksdale, "International Barter and Countertrade: An Exploratory Study," *Journal of the Academy of Marketing Science* 14 (Spring 1986): 21–28.

3. Robert D. Dennis, "The Countertrade Factor in China's Modernization Plan," *Columbia Journal of World Business* 17 (Spring 1982): 67–75; "New Restrictions on World Trade," *Business Week,* 19 July 1982, 118–22; "How Carmakers are Trimming an Import Surplus," *Business Week,* 30 January 1984, 36–37. Michael Edgerton, "U.S. May Try to Counteract Countertrade," *Chicago Tribune,* 14 April 1983; Terry Atlas, "Why Widget Sellers Must Be Food Importers, Too," *Chicago Tribune,* 14 April 1983; James O'Shea, "U.S. Studies Barter System Tradeoffs," *Chicago Tribune,* 29 January 1984.

4. Edgerton, "U.S. May Try to Counteract Countertrade."

5. Bruce Fitzgerald, "Countertrade Reconsidered," *Finance & Development* (June 1987): 46–49.

6. Lynn G. Reiling, "Countertrade Revives 'Dead Goods,' " *Marketing News,* 29 August 1986, 1, 22.

7. "Raking in a Bundle in the Barter Business," *Business Week,* 3 September 1979, 101, 104.

8. Jean-Francois Hennart, "Some Empirical Dimensions of Countertrade," *Journal of International Business Studies* 21 (no. 2, 1990): 243–70.

9. Donald J. Lecraw, "The Management of Countertrade: Factors Influencing Success," *Journal of International Business Studies* 20 (Spring 1989): 41–59.

10. For a list of the various costs included in the different terms of sale, see Paul S. Bender, "The International Dimension of Physical Distribution Management," in *The Distribution Handbook,* ed. James F. Robeson and Robert G. House (New York: Free Press, 1985), 786–87. For other terms of sale, see *Ports of the World: A Guide to Cargo Loss Control,* 13th ed. (Philadelphia: CIGNA), 87.

11. *Uniform Customs and Practice for Documentary Credits* (New York: The International Chamber of Commerce, Publication No. 290, 1974).

12. International Trade Administration, *Doing Business with China.* (Washington, D.C.: U.S. Department of Commerce, 1983), 15–16.

13. Banks with international departments have publications that explain the various types of collection methods and documents. For example, see *International Workbook* (UnibancTrust, 1985) and *Guide to International Collections* (Continental Bank, 1981).

14. International Trade Administration, *A Guide to Financing Exports* (Washington, D.C.: U.S. Department of Commerce, 1985), 21–22.

15. Jack L. Hervey, "Bankers' Acceptances Revisited," *Economic Perspectives,* Federal Reserve Bank of Chicago (May/June 1983): 21–31.

16. Frank R. Ryder, "Challenges to the Use of the Documentary Credit in International Trade Transactions," *Columbia Journal of World Business* 16 (Winter 1981): 36–41.

17. Market Expansion Division, International Trade Administration, *Foreign Regulations Affecting U.S. Textile/Apparel Exporters* (Washington, D.C.: U.S. Department of Commerce, 1986), 147.

PART FIVE
SPECIAL TOPICS
FINANCIAL ENVIRONMENT
AND DECISIONS

☐ PART OUTLINE

Owe your banker a thousand pounds, and you are at his mercy. Owe him a million, and the position is reversed.

John Maynard Keynes

Sources of Financing and International Money Markets

18

CHAPTER OUTLINE

NONFINANCIAL INSTITUTIONS

FINANCIAL INSTITUTIONS

GOVERNMENT AGENCIES

INTERNATIONAL FINANCIAL INSTITUTIONS/DEVELOPMENT BANKS

INTERNATIONAL MONETARY FUND (IMF)

FINANCIAL CENTERS

CASE 18–1: Too Close for Comfort

MARKETING ILLUSTRATION
Money Is an Emotional Subject

In order to help their corporate citizens win foreign contracts, many governments provide official financial aid. For example, governments provide low-cost credits to business corporations even though the cost of this subsidy amounts to several billion dollars annually. French, Swiss, and German governments use MOUs (memorandums of understanding) that name specific companies as beneficiaries and guarantee government export financing. The benefit of this subsidy is so spectacular that these countries have virtual monopolies on the sales of hydroelectric, thermal electric, and coal gasification projects to Brazil, forcing the United States to follow suit in providing a subsidy.

The mission of the U.S. Trade and Development Program (TDP) is to help U.S. firms compete in markets for technology, equipment, and services and to contribute to the economic development of LDCs. Established in 1980, TDP aims to achieve its goals by financing feasibility studies and other planning services for significant projects. One such project is water management in Venezuela. It financed a $33,000 feasibility study for Westinghouse Medical Sanitation Systems' solid waste management project. TDP's effort was a successful one. The financial assistance resulted in a total of $68.2 million in contracts and equipment sales for Ford, Caterpillar, Dumster, Joseph Heil, Freightlines, Omnivac, International Harvester, and Hill Manufacturing.

Sources: *United States Trade and Development Program: Congressional Presentation Fiscal Year 1987* (Washington, D.C.: U.S. International Development Cooperation Agency), 8; see also the booklet *United States Trade and Development Program* (Washington, D.C.: International Development Cooperation Agency)

The examples in the marketing illustration demonstrate the critical role that financing plays in securing overseas projects. Financing is important to the operations of both importers and exporters. Importers seek financing for the purchase of merchandise. Exporters likewise need financing for the manufacturing of their products and the maintenance of their inventories. Furthermore, overseas buyers attempt to shift the financing function to their suppliers. If an exporter agrees to extend credit, the exporter must in turn obtain financing for this purpose. Financing is not a problem only for small firms. In fact, in the case of international multimillion dollar projects, sellers' financing is usually expected, and financing terms often separate winners from losers.

Trade finance arises from the export of goods and services, when the buyer and seller negotiate the amount, time, and terms of payment. "The financing needs of the seller and buyer almost always differ, and sometimes conflict."[1] Naturally, the buyer desires a competitive price and a payment arrangement that does not tie up one's credit line, whereas the seller wants a financing arrangement that offers quick payment and protection against default. The method of trade finance attempts to accommodate these differences. Trade finance can be supplied by parties in the private sector (e.g., the buyer's cash in advance payment) or by parties in the public sector (e.g., a bank's financing of the sale—see Exhibit 18–1).

TRADE FINANCE IS SIMPLE. IT'S BANKS THAT MAKE IT COMPLICATED.

Trade finance can be simple. As long as your bank has the expertise to keep it from getting complicated.

This is one talent you'll find well developed at HongkongBank. After all, we've been conducting international trade finance for over 124 years.

Consequently, we've learned to tailor your trade financing to the way your business actually runs. And that makes things much simpler.

Presently, as one of the 30 largest banks in the world, we have a trade finance network of over 1,300 offices, in over 50 countries, worldwide.

This means we aren't forced to rely on correspondent banks to expedite your trade finance requirements. So you don't run the risk of added complications that can occur when your documents change hands from bank to bank.

We can simplify your day-to-day trade finance work, simply because we maintain control.

What's more, our preeminence throughout the Pacific Rim gives us an unequaled knowledge of local market situations and trading opportunities.

This results in faster, more accurate decisions. So you stay ahead of things,

instead of getting tangled up in them.

So next time your bank tells you trade finance is complicated, simply call 1-800-CALL-HKB. And talk to the one bank that knows how to keep it simple.

HongkongBank

The Hongkong and Shanghai Banking Corporation Limited

Fast decisions. Worldwide.

EXHIBIT 18–1 Bank's trade finance

Source: Courtesy of Hong Kong and Shanghai Banking Corp.

The purpose of this chapter is to discuss the various aspects of financing. The chapter covers both the local and international sources of financing that are available to public and private buyers, including the various private and nonprofit financial institutions. The chapter also examines such offshore financial centers as the Euromarket and the Asian Dollar Market.

Any business, no matter how large or small, domestic or international, always requires some kind of financing for its operations. Because international financing must deal with financial and economic conditions in more than one country, this activity involves more uncertainty and complexity than domestic financing. The greater complexity of international financing, however, is accompanied by a greater number of financing options. In addition to the standard channels, there are also other sources available almost exclusively for international business.[2] These sources include

1. Nonfinancial institutions
2. Private financial institutions
3. International agencies
4. Government agencies
5. The International Monetary Fund (IMF)
6. The Euromarket

NONFINANCIAL INSTITUTIONS

There are several nonfinancial institutions that can provide financing. First, there is **self-financing,** because a business can use its own capital or can withhold dividends so that profits can be plowed back into the organization for further business expansion. Second, retailers and manufacturers alike may be able to seek trade credit and financial assistance from certain middlemen, such as export merchants and trading companies. Third, when joint ventures are formed, foreign partners can also lend a helping hand. Fourth, subsidiaries of MNCs may borrow from affiliated firms as well as from the employee retirement fund. Finally, the business may decide to raise equity capital by selling stocks, or it may depend on **debt financing** by selling bonds in either the United States or foreign countries, with Eurobonds as a prime example of the latter.

One method of financing is to borrow money from **credit clubs** or **rotating credit associations.** Such clubs, popular among Asians, have long existed in Asia, especially in villages or rural areas where banks usually do not exist. Probably originating in China some eight hundred years ago, the system later spread to other countries. The clubs are called *kye* (pronounced "kay") by Koreans, *tontines* by Cambodians, and *share* by Thais. Such clubs are attractive because they allow members to borrow money at a lower rate than what they pay banks while also allowing investors to receive a higher return than what they can get from their banks. These highly informal and sometimes secretive credit clubs rely on the honor system and allow members to get quick loans without collateral. Club members pool their money, each putting a set amount into a monthly pool. A club operates for as many months as there are members. Each month, a different member gets the pool. Members bid for the pool, which goes to the lowest bidder. Those who win the early pools contribute more to the club while also receiving less money than those receiving later pools.

Those who wait thus make more profits, though at a higher risk. Having no written contracts, members nevertheless usually consider their investments safe because they know each other. In reality, horror stories abound as it is a fairly common practice for early bidders to disappear with the pool. In the United States, rotating clubs have flourished because recent Asian immigrants, without a credit history, have difficulty obtaining conventional bank loans. Members may meet at homes or restaurants and use these social gatherings for the purpose of carrying out bids.[3]

Another source of financing is **venture capital.** Venture capitalists invest funds in a firm in exchange for a share of ownership. Although known for their investments in high-technology firms, venture capitalists have diversified their portfolios. There are about six hundred venture capital firms in the United States. Private investors, however, fund most ventures. Venture Capital Network in Durham, New Hampshire, is a nonprofit service affiliated with the University of New Hampshire. Attempting to match entrepreneurs with investors, the Network charges investors $200 a year and those seeking capital $500 annually for registration.

When self-financing is used, a company should take advantage of a tax shelter for its export profit. In the past, companies were able to form **domestic international sales corporations** (DISCs) for this purpose. The DISC allowed a company to defer taxes on up to half of its export income. GE, for instance, was able to save millions of dollars this way. Some 5,000 American exporters had export sales through 8,000 U.S.-based DISCs.[4] In 1970, a year before DISCs were created, only 9 percent of U.S. goods were exported. The percentage jumped to 19 percent in 1980, with 67 percent of exports done through DISCs. The deferral of tax cost the U.S. government $1.65 billion in revenue in 1981.

DISCs were largely and effectively abolished in 1984 because GATT ruled that these tax shelters were an illegal export subsidy. Only an "interest charge DISC," with more limited tax benefits, is available for small exporters. In place of DISCs, a new tax shelter known as a **foreign sales corporation** (FSC, pronounced "fisk") was created.[5] A FSC is a special kind of corporation in the eye of tax authorities, making it possible for a FSC to gain a corporate tax exemption from 15 to 32 percent of the earnings generated by the sale or lease of exported goods (50 percent U.S. content) and a limited number of services. A FSC has more stringent requirements than a DISC had, making it impossible to have a mere shell or paper corporation for tax-deferred income. Qualifications that must be met for a FSC are

1. The company must be incorporated in a foreign country or U.S. possession.
2. It must have the main office outside of the United States, and this office must keep one set of its books of account.
3. There can be no more than twenty-five shareholders.
4. There must be no preferred stock.
5. At least one director must not be a U.S. resident.
6. It must not be a member of a controlled group, which includes a DISC.
7. It must elect to be a FSC by filing an election with the IRS.
8. To get tax exemption on more than $5 million of export sales, it must perform certain foreign management and foreign economic activities outside the U.S. customs territory.

In general, a FSC must maintain a foreign presence. That is, it must have a foreign office maintaining books and records. The board and shareholders must meet outside the United States, and one of the directors must be non-American. Another requirement is foreign economic substance. The office must perform business activities that result in business income. A minimum percentage of orders for goods must be procured through the foreign office, which must carry out such normal business operations as billing. This office must also account for at least 50 percent of five of the direct transaction costs (i.e., advertising, order processing, transportation, invoicing, and credit risk assumption). Because foreign taxes paid on the FSC's revenue are not eligible for tax credit or deduction in the United States, the company will probably choose to locate in a country with minimal tax on foreign corporations. A company may elect to locate in the U.S. Virgin Islands, Guam, the Commonwealth of the Northern Mariana Islands, or American Samoa. Qualified countries in which a FSC can incorporate and locate its foreign office include Australia, Austria, Belgium, Canada, Denmark, Egypt, Finland, France, Germany, Iceland, Ireland, Jamaica, Korea, Malta, Morocco, the Netherlands, New Zealand, Norway, Pakistan, the Philippines, South Africa, Sweden, and Trinidad and Tobago. Beneficiary countries of the Caribbean Basin Initiative are also included.

With regard to other means of self-financing, it is a common practice for MNCs to use both equity and debt financing. A company can raise equity capital by selling stock, both in its own country and in foreign markets. U.S. stocks, for example, are traded in London. GSS Electronics Ltd. (Thailand), a manufacturer of electronic parts and assemblies for computer hard disk drives, was the first U.S.-owned high-technology company to be listed on the Securities Exchange of Thailand. The firm sought new funding to complete a large plant expansion.

American investors interested in buying foreign securities, instead of working through foreign securities firms and exchange currencies, should consider American Depository Receipts (ADRs). Issued by U.S. banks, ADRs represent ownership of a set amount of the respective security on deposit in a foreign branch. Benetton offers 8 million to 9 million (ADRs) worth approximately $150 million on the New York Stock Exchange.

Exhibit 18–2 shows how the Hawley Group, a British firm, can obtain capital outside of the United Kingdom by attracting American investors to buy its shares in the form of ADRs. In addition, the company's desire for its share capital to become a global security has resulted in the trading of its common shares in Bermuda, Canada, Australia, New Zealand, and Germany, with discussions for listing on the Paris and Tokyo securities exchanges.

Although many firms limit the listing of their securities to their domestic exchanges, the growing internationalization of capital markets suggests that more and more firms perceive that the benefits of listing their stocks on foreign exchanges outweigh the related costs. One investigation of the motives for listing abroad involved data on 481 multinationals. There is a significant correlation between the likelihood of listing abroad and a firm's relative size in its domestic capital market as well as its ratio of foreign to total sales. In general, the absolute size of firms (and their relative size), their main line of business, and their nationality affect the decision to list on foreign stock exchanges. Firms that are larger within their domestic capital markets

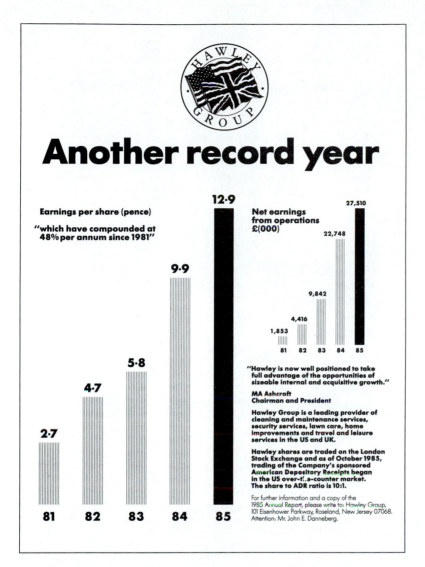

EXHIBIT 18–2 Equity financing and American Depository Receipts
Source: Reprinted with permission of the Hawley Group, Inc.

appear more likely to list abroad. Regarding the extent of a firm's dependence on foreign consumer and product markets, firms that generate a greater portion of their revenues abroad are more likely to list on a foreign stock exchange. Firms are willing to list on stock exchanges located in capital markets that are smaller than their own because of the positive relationship between foreign sales and listing abroad. Furthermore, listing abroad increases visibility in that country and provides free advertising.[6]

Exhibits 18–3, 18–4, and 18–5 illustrate the point that there are several attractive stock markets around the world, many of which have outperformed the U.S. market.

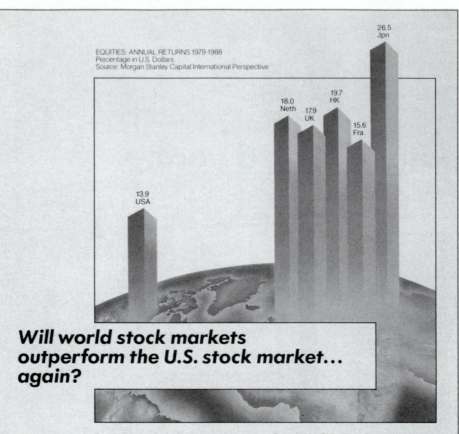

EXHIBIT 18-3 U.S. and world stock markets

Source: Courtesy of Swiss Bank Corporation

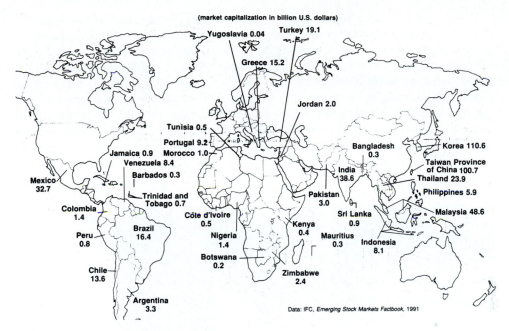

(market capitalization in billion U.S. dollars)

Yugoslavia 0.04   Turkey 19.1

Greece 15.2

Jordan 2.0

Tunisia 0.5

Portugal 9.2   Morocco 1.0
Jamaica 0.9
Venezuela 8.4
Barbados 0.3

Bangladesh
0.3

Korea 110.6

Taiwan Province
of China 100.7
Thailand 23.9

India
38.6

Mexico
32.7

Trinidad and
Tobago 0.7

Philippines 5.9

Pakistan
3.0

Malaysia 48.6

Colombia
1.4

Côte d'Ivoire
0.5

Sri Lanka
0.9

Peru
0.8

Brazil
16.4

Nigeria
1.4

Kenya
0.4

Mauritius
0.3

Indonesia
8.1

Chile
13.6

Botswana
0.2

Zimbabwe
2.4

Argentina
3.3

Data: IFC, *Emerging Stock Markets Factbook*, 1991

EXHIBIT 18–4   Emerging stock markets, 1990

Source: IMF Survey, 15 July 1991, 210

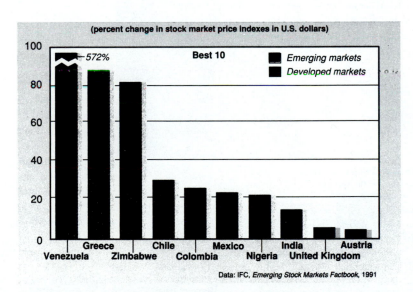

(percent change in stock market price indexes in U.S. dollars)

Best 10

■ Emerging markets
■ Developed markets

572%

Venezuela   Greece   Chile   Mexico   Nigeria   India   Austria
Zimbabwe   Colombia   United Kingdom

Data: IFC, *Emerging Stock Markets Factbook*, 1991

EXHIBIT 18–5   Emerging stock markets: top performers

Source: IMF Survey, 15 July 1991, 211

Because of various regulatory and traditional barriers to entry, stocks have historically played a relatively minor role in corporate financing in many European countries. In the case of German equity markets, for example, until recently, the largest banks that had a monopoly on brokerage effectively controlled access to the stock exchange. Small firms, being kept from issuing equity, remained captive loan clients. Additionally, the integration of banking and commerce in Germany has contributed to large German firms' traditional reliance more on bank credit and bonds than on equity to finance growth. German firms use their equity holdings to exert ownership control over industrial firms. As could be expected, stock exchanges were small, inefficient, and illiquid.[7]

EXCELLENCE THROUGH TEAMWORK

The Bankers Trust philosophy at work, for Procter and Gamble de Mexico.

Close teamwork among professionals at Bankers Trust recently made a most remarkable transaction possible.

Our client: Procter and Gamble de Mexico, a stand-alone subsidiary of the U.S. company. Our challenge: a multi-million dollar refinancing—at the very height of Mexico's financial crisis.

With the strong support of the Mexican government, we were able to match the company's need with Mexico's need to save foreign exchange. We helped them replace costly loans from other banks with a Bankers Trust specialty: commercial paper. (We were

The Bankers Trust team: Richard A. Price, Jr., Capital Mkts. Group (seated); Andrea Lamp Peabody, Relationship Mgr.; Johannes G. Derksen, Currency Management; Alok Singh, World Corporate Department in Mexico City.

EAGLES AEROBATIC FLIGHT TEAM

the first money center bank to act as agent for issuers of commercial paper. Our customers have some two *billion* dollars worth outstanding for which we are sales agent.)

The result: an innovative $44 million issue of commercial paper, brought to market by Bankers Trust.

The company will save millions in interest costs. Mexico saves large amounts of foreign exchange, and has once again seen a Mexican company's obligations successfully placed in the U.S. market.

A skilled Bankers Trust relationship manager coordinated the efforts of our

corporate finance experts in the U.S. and Mexico and our commercial paper specialists. Together, their efforts added up to nothing less than excellence.

The pursuit of excellence is unending at Bankers Trust. If it's a pursuit that's part of your philosophy, perhaps your company should be working with our bank.

Bankers Trust Company

An international banking network in more than 35 countries.
280 Park Avenue, New York, N.Y. 10015
MEMBER FDIC © BANKERS TRUST COMPANY

EXHIBIT 18–6   Selling commercial paper

Source: Reprinted with permission of Bankers Trust Company

In the case of debt financing, a company can opt to sell commercial paper, as discussed in Exhibit 18–6. Or a company can opt to sell bonds instead of stock. Some of the various kinds of debt financing are shown in Exhibit 18–7. Bond buyers or holders are the firm's creditors rather than its owners. U.S. firms can sell bonds in either the United States or foreign countries, with Eurobonds as a prime example of

EXHIBIT 18–7 Methods of debt financing

Source: Reprinted with permission of National Australia Bank Limited

the latter. Treasurers of U.S. firms must decide whether their bonds to be sold abroad are to be denominated in the dollar or in foreign currencies. In any case, it should be noted that debt financing requires the services of investment banks. Virtually every multinational bank and multinational brokerage house has a division that acts as an investment bank.

For a total perspective
to serve your financial world best...
Heller is the one.

The one that zeros in on creative solutions that answer all your needs. Get the Heller point of view for any or all of your financing needs, which include:

Asset-Based financing expertise to assist you in major acquisitions or mergers, meeting working capital needs or other types of financing. Professionals with the deal structuring expertise, funding capacity and service capabilities to serve your industry and market.

Factoring to provide specialized credit and collection expertise and working capital funds in marketing your products throughout the U.S. and around the world.

Equipment financing programs to facilitate the sale of equipment from the manufacturer to the end user. An integrated multi-service offering which satisfies financing requirements for each step in your distribution process.

Commercial Real Estate financing to support you in every phase of your project's development—from site development to permanent financing.

Heller wants to be involved in your financial planning process. As part of Heller International, there are 72 offices worldwide, staffed with professionals dedicated to a high level of performance. We've recently changed our name to Heller Financial emphasizing our commitment to set standards of excellence no one in the industry can match. We welcome you to test our commitment.

For more information and a copy of our 1984 Annual Review call: **1-800-458-4924.** (In Illinois, call: 1-800-621-2429. In Canada, call: 1-416-482-4012.)

Heller Financial

Asset-Based Financing • Factoring • Equipment Financing • Real Estate Financing
105 West Adams Street, Chicago, Illinois 60603.

Heller Financial, Inc. is an operating subsidiary of **Heller International Corporation.**
© Heller Financial, Inc. 1985

EXHIBIT 18–8   Factoring

Source: Reprinted with permission of Heller Financial

FINANCIAL INSTITUTIONS

International companies have several options in financial institutions that have the capability of dealing in international finance. The most common alternative is banks (and nonbank banks), both domestic and overseas. In addition to the well-known giant banks that operate globally, there are many medium-sized banks that have international banking departments. The multinational banks can make arrangements to satisfy all kinds of financing needs.

Other than making loans, banks are also involved in financing indirectly by discounting (i.e., factoring) letters of credit and time drafts. Some factoring houses buy accounts receivable with or without recourse at face value and then provide loans at competitive rates on 90 percent of the factors' acquired but not-yet-collected receivables. In general, *factors* help clients eliminate several internal credit costs by providing credit guarantee of receivables, by managing and collecting accounts receivable, and by performing related bookkeeping functions. The industry average factoring commission for these services is 1 percent. Factoring is a substantial part of the business for a company such as Heller International (see Exhibit 18–8).

In the United Kingdom, companies have a number of financial institutions to contact for loans. These institutions include foreign banks, British clearing banks, merchant banks (factor houses), finance houses, investment trust companies, pension funds and insurance companies, leasing firms, and development capital and other specialist venture capital organizations. In Germany, companies may be able to obtain short-term loans from German and foreign banks, usually by overdraft.

In 1978 four American banks ranked among the world's thirty largest banks and accounted for 16.4 percent of these banks' assets. Ten years later, only one U.S. bank remained on the list, and it accounted for only 2.4 percent of the top thirty banks' assets. Remarkably, Japan had the world's ten largest banks and also twenty of the world's thirty largest banks. The top ten banks are Dai-Ichi Kangyo Bank Ltd., Sumitomo Bank Ltd., Fuji Bank Ltd., Sanwa Bank Ltd., Mitsubishi Bank Ltd., Industrial Bank of Japan Ltd., Norinchukin Bank, Tokai Bank Ltd., Mitsui Bank Ltd., and Mitsubishi Trust & Banking Corp.

GOVERNMENT AGENCIES

It is not unusual for governments to provide **concessionary financing.** Such public loans, as a rule, carry lower-than-market interest rates, and their terms are more favorable than those of private financial institutions. Governments' role in financing can also be indirect but significant. Japan, for example, uses qualification for public loans as an inducement for private banks to cofinance. The qualification carries this significance by implying that any investment would be in the national interest and that the firm in question is financially sound.

The United States has several government agencies that provide financial assistance. One of them is the Small Business Administration (SBA). In addition to its regular SBA loans, this agency can assist small firms in their export activities through its Export Revolving Line of Credit Loan (ERLC), which is under the SBA's guarantee plan.

Another agency is the Overseas Private Investment Corporation (OPIC). Although best known for its Insurance Department's political risk insurance programs, OPIC also makes direct loans through its Finance Department. Its Direct Investment Fund (DIF) is for projects too small to interest large institutional lenders or for projects too short for institutional lending but too long for commercial banks. OPIC can participate in the cost-sharing financing of preinvestment surveys by small U.S. companies to investigate the feasibility of some opportunity. Furthermore, OPIC can guarantee up to 7 percent of repayment of loans to U.S. lenders. "Both the guarantee and DIF loan must be applied to a new facility, modernization or expansion of an existing plant, or new input of technology or services. The project must be commercially viable and must make a significant contribution to the host country economy."[8] Among OPIC's many services are political insurance, loan guarantees, direct loans, local currency loans, special project grants, reconnaissance survey and feasibility study fundings, and combinations of all these. OPIC's other services include investment missions, project brokering to American investors of known opportunities abroad, support of preinvestment feasibility studies, help in planning and structuring of projects, intercession with other U.S. and international financing sources, and guidance on investment climate and on "new mode" forms of nonequity investments.

The expansion of a manufacturer's facilities in Port-au-Prince and Jacmel (Haiti) was a typical OPIC project. OPIC granted a $300,000 loan to finance the expansion of the manufacturing of high-quality office furniture. The project met OPIC's loan criteria. Haiti, with a per capita income of $130, is the least developed country in the Western Hemisphere. With the creation of 400 new jobs at a unit cost of $750 of OPIC investment, the financing was cost-effective. Furthermore, the project allowed workers to use their traditional weaving skills while helping a small U.S. firm strengthen its market position.[9]

In the case of farm products, the U.S. Department of Agriculture's Commodity Credit Corporation (CCC) has the Export Credit Sales Program, which extends credit for exports of U.S. agricultural commodities. This is achieved by CCC's purchases of U.S. exporter's accounts receivable. Moreover, CCC has the Export Credit Guarantee Program, which protects American exporters against foreign banks' failure to pay.

A company seeking financing to fund a feasibility study for a development project in LDCs should contact the Trade and Development Program (TDP). The TDP promotes economic development in LDCs while promoting American goods and services at the same time. The criteria for TDP funding include development priority, U.S. export potential, funding availability, facilitative role, competition against U.S. exports, and some additional criteria. In 1982 TDP financed a $440,000 feasibility study of the Tiansheng Qiao hydropower project in China. The study resulted in U.S. equipment exports worth $20.3 million.[10]

A major source of funding for U.S. firms is the U.S. Export-Import Bank (Eximbank), which is responsible for the promotion of exports through financial assistance. Among its activities are direct loans, protective guarantees for banks' loans, and export credit insurance. Eximbank has several financial assistance programs. Its Working Capital Guarantee program allows exporters to obtain preexport financing by providing repayment protection for U.S. bank loans. Another kind of payment protection is through the Foreign Credit Insurance Association (FCIA) Export Credit Insurance policy, which protects those exporters that extend credit to foreign customers. Exim-bank also has other programs:

> Exporters may arrange competitive medium-term commercial bank financing with the help of three Eximbank programs. Eximbank's *Commercial Bank Guarantee* provides payment protection for the lender. The *Medium-Term Credit* program and the similar *Small Business Credit* program enable commercial banks to offer fixed-rate financing at the lowest interest rates permitted. The Medium-Term Credit program is available to assist exporters, regardless of size, who are facing officially supported foreign com-petition. The Small Business Credit program is available to companies who meet the Small Business Administration's definition of a small business. There is no need to show competition for the Small Business Credit program.
>
> Exporters competing for large export orders of heavy capital equipment items or for contracts related to major project development may request a *Preliminary Commit-ment* outlining the long-term financing support available from Eximbank if the bidder wins the order. The *Engineering Multiplier Program* offers medium-term, fixed interest rate direct loans to support preconstruction services by U.S. architectural and engineer-ing firms for a project with the potential to generate additional U.S. exports worth $10 million or twice the amount of the initial contract, whichever is greater. If the ex-porter is facing officially supported foreign competition, Eximbank may offer a long-term *Direct Loan* to the foreign purchaser, with interest fixed at the lowest level permitted. Eximbank may also offer a *Financial Guarantee* covering repayment of commercial financing denominated in U.S. dollars or other convertible currencies.[11]

In addition to providing direct loans, Eximbank may induce commercial banks to make loans by guaranteeing payment in case of default. The process is a simple one: An exporter applies to a bank for the financing of export sales, and the bank then applies to Eximbank for guarantee coverage of both commercial and political risks. In addition, Eximbank may buy the bank's export loans at a discount through its Discount Loan Program so that banks can acquire funds for further lending.

The U.S. Export-Import Bank has not been well supported by the U.S. govern-ment. Frequently, the loans are made at a rate that is not competitive, or funds may not be available at all. Consider the case of the U.S. nuclear power industry. The difference between the offers made by the U.S. Export-Import Bank and those made by its foreign counterparts was significant. South Korea was able to get France to fi-nance 85 percent of the cost of its project at 7.6 percent interest, whereas the United States could finance only 65 percent of the project at a 10.5 percent interest rate. For Taiwan, this interest differential amounted to $500 million in savings.[12] Not surpris-ingly, of ten overseas orders in 1980, U.S. firms got none. Because of this inability to obtain favorable financing for foreign buyers, American firms' international share of the nuclear power market has dropped from 70 percent to less than 50 percent.

To counteract the problem, the United States has urged European governments to increase their export credit rates and has reclassified borrowing countries in terms of their eligibility for rock-bottom credit rates. Countries are now classified as rel-atively rich, intermediate, and relatively poor. The Commonwealth of Independent States, Czechoslovakia, Israel, and Spain have been reclassified as rich countries, whereas Taiwan, Brazil, Mexico, South Korea, and Algeria have moved up to the intermediate category.

The effort of the United States was successful in pushing up the minimum export credit rates, with 9.5 percent as a floor rate, but did not work out as expected. European governments have been able to circumvent the restriction by offering **mixed** or **blended credit.** This type of financing package combines an official, conventional loan with either outright grants or foreign aid grants at below-market rates, in effect reducing the actual interest rate based on the condition that donor countries' products are bought. France, the heaviest user of this technique, won Malaysia's contract for a $200 million turnkey power plant by disguising its thirty-year loan at a 4.5 percent rate as an aid grant, which made up almost half of the financing package.[13] The magnitude of this type of concessionary financing is shown by the growth of such offers from the twenty-four-nation Organization for Economic Cooperation (OECD), which tripled from $2.1 billion in 1980 to $6.5 billion in 1984.[14] Mixed credit is particularly important in the sale of high-technology capital goods, and the indiscriminate use of this technique in foreign aid/export financing packages has fostered a built-in expectation for it on the part of buyers.

The United States, considering the use of mixed credit as unfair export credit subsidies, has again fought back by making financing more costly for OECD members. The new OECD guidelines, which took effect in July of 1988, require mixed credit to include at least 50 percent grants, up from the internationally agreed 25 percent. Furthermore, the United States has begun to play the same game by offering some unusually low-interest loans. For example, it assisted General Electric with a $30 million gas-turbine project in India with a 32.5 percent aid grant. GE had the lower bid, but credit assistance from Eximbank was nevertheless crucial in securing the project. In another case, the Eximbank offered a $100 million mixed credit line to Thailand for the purchase of U.S. high-technology products.

Another technique used to create a built-in disincentive for cheap credit is for the United States to retaliate against its European competitors with longer payback terms. Knowing that European governments have difficulty raising money for fifteen years even on a very selective basis, the U.S. Eximbank is able to win out over foreign competitors by simply offering fifteen- to twenty-year loans. The Europeans are no match for the United States in the maturity contest because the U.S. Treasury routinely borrows money for twenty or thirty years by auctioning Treasury bonds.

This discussion should illustrate to international marketers that a low price by itself does not necessarily provide advantages, especially in the case of expensive projects. Government financing is a necessity, and this involves more than just a low interest rate. The effective rate can be greatly moderated by the amount to be financed, outright grants, varying maturity dates, and other financing techniques.

INTERNATIONAL FINANCIAL INSTITUTIONS/DEVELOPMENT BANKS

One major source of financing is international nonprofit agencies. There are several regional development banks, such as the Asian Development Bank, the African Development Bank and Fund, and the Caribbean Development Bank. The primary purpose of these agencies is to finance productive development projects or to promote economic development in a particular region. The Inter-American Development Bank, for example, has as its principal purpose the acceleration of the economic development of its Latin American member countries. The European Bank for Reconstruction and Development (EBRD), located in London, is funded by thirty-nine countries and two European Community organizations. The United States, with a 10 percent share, is the largest single shareholder. The bank targets 60 percent of its loans for the private sector in Central and Eastern Europe.

In general, both public and private entities are eligible to borrow money from such agencies as long as private funds are not available at reasonable rates and terms. Although the interest rate can vary from agency to agency, these loan rates are very attractive and very much in demand. Exhibit 18–9 outlines the steps involved in procurement projects financed by these international agencies.

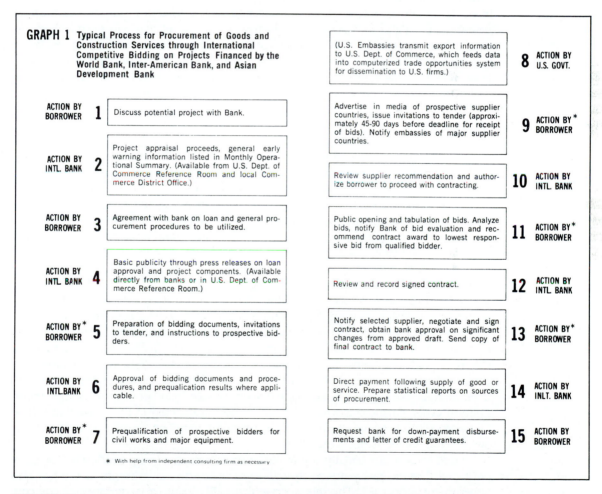

GRAPH 1 Typical Process for Procurement of Goods and Construction Services through International Competitive Bidding on Projects Financed by the World Bank, Inter-American Bank, and Asian Development Bank

ACTION BY BORROWER	1	Discuss potential project with Bank.
ACTION BY INTL. BANK	2	Project appraisal proceeds, general early warning information listed in Monthly Operational Summary. (Available from U.S. Dept. of Commerce Reference Room and local Commerce District Office.)
ACTION BY BORROWER	3	Agreement with bank on loan and general procurement procedures to be utilized.
ACTION BY INTL. BANK	4	Basic publicity through press releases on loan approval and project components. (Available directly from banks or in U.S. Dept. of Commerce Reference Room.)
ACTION BY* BORROWER	5	Preparation of bidding documents, invitations to tender, and instructions to prospective bidders.
ACTION BY INTL.BANK	6	Approval of bidding documents and procedures, and prequalification results where applicable.
ACTION BY* BORROWER	7	Prequalification of prospective bidders for civil works and major equipment.

(U.S. Embassies transmit export information to U.S. Dept. of Commerce, which feeds data into computerized trade opportunities system for dissemination to U.S. firms.)	8	ACTION BY U.S. GOVT.
Advertise in media of prospective supplier countries, issue invitations to tender (approximately 45-90 days before deadline for receipt of bids). Notify embassies of major supplier countries.	9	ACTION BY* BORROWER
Review supplier recommendation and authorize borrower to proceed with contracting.	10	ACTION BY INTL. BANK
Public opening and tabulation of bids. Analyze bids, notify Bank of bid evaluation and recommend contract award to lowest responsive bid from qualified bidder.	11	ACTION BY* BORROWER
Review and record signed contract.	12	ACTION BY INTL. BANK
Notify selected supplier, negotiate and sign contract, obtain bank approval on significant changes from approved draft. Send copy of final contract to bank.	13	ACTION BY* BORROWER
Direct payment following supply of good or service. Prepare statistical reports on sources of procurement.	14	ACTION BY INLT. BANK
Request bank for down-payment disbursements and letter of credit guarantees.	15	ACTION BY BORROWER

* With help from independent consulting firm as necessary

EXHIBIT 18–9 Steps involved in procurement through an international agency

Source: Export Opportunities for American Business through the International Development Banks (Washington, D.C.: Department of the Treasury, Office of International Development Banks, October 1976), 4–5

Of all the international financial organizations, the most familiar is the World Bank, formally known as the International Bank for Reconstruction and Development (IBRD). The World Bank has two affiliates that are legally and financially distinct entities, the International Development Association (IDA) and the International Finance Corporation (IFC). Exhibit 18–10 provides a comparison among IBRD, IDA, and IFC in terms of their objectives, member countries, lending terms, lending qualifications, and other details. All three organizations have the same central goal: to promote economic and social progress in poor or developing countries by helping to raise standards of living and productivity to the point at which development becomes self-sustaining.[15]

Toward this common objective, the Bank, IDA, and IFC have three interrelated functions, and these are to lend funds, to provide advice, and to serve as a catalyst in stimulating investments by others. In the process, financial resources are channeled from developed countries to the developing world. The hope is that developing countries, through this assistance, will progress to a level that will permit them, in turn, to contribute to the development process in other less fortunate countries. Japan is a prime example of a country that has come full circle. From being a borrower, Japan is now a major lender to these three organizations. South Korea is moving in a direction similar to that of Japan nearly a quarter century ago.

World Bank

The World Bank is owned by the governments of the 152 countries that have subscribed to providing its capital. Only countries that are members of the International Monetary Fund can qualify for World Bank membership. The United States, with 22.4 percent of the subscribed capital and 20.6 percent of the voting power, is the bank's largest shareholder. By tradition, the World Bank's president is an American. The members are quite diverse in their characteristics, ranging from China, the most populous, to Vanuata, which has a population of slightly more than 100,000, and from the United Arab Emirates, with a per capita GNP of more than $30,000, to Bhutan, which has a $180 per capita GNP.

The IBRD obtains most of its funds through borrowing in the capital markets of the United States, Europe, Japan, and the Middle East. The process is not unlike a private firm's seeking debt financing through the sale of securities. Such funds, in turn, are made available only to creditworthy borrowers, mainly for those projects that have high real rates of economic return. The bank's decisions are based on economic considerations only, and the political character of a member country is irrelevant. As a result, the World Bank does not make loans in support of military or political goals. Financial assistance is otherwise unrestricted in the sense that it may be used to purchase goods and services from any member country as well as from Switzerland, which is not a member.

IBRD loans are usually repayable over fifteen to twenty years, with a grace period of three to five years. Each loan must be made to, or be guaranteed by, the government concerned. The interest rate that IBRD loans carry depends on the cost at which the Bank raises funds in capital markets. For IBRD loans made before July

1982, the interest rate was fixed for the life of the loan. But by the early 1980s the interest rates on IBRD borrowings were so volatile that the adverse effects created could not be recouped by frequent changes in the interest rate charged on newly arranged fixed-interest-rate loans.

In order not to expose the World Bank to excessive interest rate risk, a pool-based variable-rate lending system was initiated in 1982. Interest charges applicable to the outstanding balance on all loans are uniformly adjusted every six months, up or down, in accord with the average cost of the pool of IBRD borrowings. Because the new lending system has added a potential element of volatility to borrowers' costs, the bank strives to find a point at which there is a balance between the susceptibility of the lending rate to change and the pursuit of the bank's other important objectives. In any case a degree of volatility is inevitable, though the World Bank attempts through its policies to reduce the impact of these variations.

In the process of applying for a loan, a borrowing country must follow the so-called *project cycle.* This unusual activity requires the bank to assist loan beneficiaries in preparing and implementing projects within the context of agreed development objectives. This framework thus creates a long-term working relationship between the bank and the borrower. The bank controls the progress of its projects as well as the quality of its outstanding loan portfolio by being involved in all necessary stages of the project cycle. Each step leads to the next step, and the final steps provide new ideas and new projects, making the cycle self-renewing.

There are six basic steps in the project cycle. The first step, called *identification,* assesses governments' proposed projects in terms of priority, based on economic and sector criteria as well as creditworthiness. *Preparation,* the second step, requires a project to be designed in such a way that the technical, institutional (managerial), economic, and financial alternatives can be compared. The third step, *appraisal,* involves a comprehensive review of all aspects of the project with the aim of obtaining a cost-benefit relationship compatible with the efficient use of scarce resources. Based on those findings, terms and conditions of the loan are recommended to achieve the most favorable results at the lowest possible cost. The fourth step involves *negotiations and approval.* During a board presentation, the bank and the borrower attempt to resolve outstanding issues to ensure the success of the project. The end result is a legally binding agreement that defines the objectives, actions, and obligations of the project. The fifth step is called *implementation and supervision.* Although the implementation of the project is the borrower's responsibility, the bank supervises the project by monitoring current operations to ensure their sound execution and by controlling disbursements of loans, typically over a six- or seven-year period. Finally, the *evaluation* step involves an *ex post* audit that is done independently by the Operations Evaluation Department in order to provide knowledge and information that, based on the bank's lending experience, is useful for future projects.

International Development Association (IDA)

Because very poor countries may have difficulty in borrowing on IBRD terms, the IDA was established specifically to assist such countries. By 1991 IDA had 138 nations

EXHIBIT 18–10 The World Bank and its affiliates

	THE WORLD BANK		International Finance Corporation (IFC)
	International Bank for Reconstruction and Development (IBRD)	International Development Association (IDA)	
Objectives of the institution	To promote economic progress in developing countries by providing financial and technical assistance, mostly for specific projects in both public and private sectors.		To promote economic progress in developing countries by helping to mobilize domestic and foreign capital to stimulate the growth of the private sector.
Year established	1945	1960	1956
Number of member countries (April 1983)	144	131	124
Types of countries assisted	Developing countries other than the very poorest. Some countries borrow a "blend" of IBRD loans and IDA credits.	The poorest: 80% of IDA credits go to countries with annual per capita incomes below $410. Many of these countries are too poor to be able to borrow part or any of their requirements on IBRD terms.	All developing countries, from the poorest to the more advanced.
Types of activities assisted	Agriculture and rural development, energy, education, transportation, telecommunications, industry, mining, development finance companies, urban development, water supply, sewerage, population, health, and nutrition. Some nonproject lending, including structural adjustment.		Agribusiness, development, finance companies, energy, fertilizer, manufacturing, mining, money and capital markets institutions, tourism and services, utilities.

	IBRD	IDA	IFC
Lending commitments (fiscal 1982)	$10,330 million	$2,686 million	$580 million
Equity investments (fiscal 1982)	IBRD and IDA do not make equity investments.		$32 million
Number of operations (fiscal 1982)	150	97	65
Terms of lending:			
Average maturity period	Generally 15 to 20 years	50 years	7 to 12 years
Grace period	Generally 3 to 5 years	10 years	An average of 3 years
Interest rate (as of April 1, 1983)	10.97%	0.0%	In line with market rates
Other charges	Front-end fee of 0.25% on loan. Commitment charge of 0.75% on undisbursed amount of loan.	Annual commitment charge of 0.5% on undisbursed and service charge of 0.75% on disbursed amounts of the credit.	Commitment fee of 1% per year on undisbursed amount of loan.
Recipients of finance	Governments, government agencies, and private enterprises that can get a government guarantee for the IBRD loan.	Governments. But they may re-lend funds to state or private organizations.	Private enterprises; government organizations that assist the private sector.
Government guarantee	Essential	Essential	Neither sought nor accepted.
Main method of raising funds	Borrowings in world's capital markets.	Grants from governments.	Borrowings and IFC's own capital, subscribed by member governments.
Main sources of funds	Financial markets in U.S., Germany, Japan, and Switzerland.	Governments of U.S., Japan, Germany, U.S., France, other OECD countries, and certain OPEC countries.	Borrowings from IBRD.

Source: The World Bank & International Finance Corporation (Washington, D.C., The World Bank, 1983), 5. Reprinted with permission of the World Bank

TABLE 18–1   Changing contributions to IDA (percentage of total contributions)

	Initial (1961–64)	IDA7 (1985–87)	IDA8 (1988–90)
United States	42.34	25.00	25.00
United Kingdom	17.33	6.70	6.70
France	7.00	6.60	7.30
Germany	7.00	11.50	11.50
Canada	5.00	4.50	5.00
Japan	4.44	18.70	18.70
Italy	2.40	4.30	5.30
Nordic Group	3.90	5.70	6.17
OPEC	0.49	4.20	3.47
Others[a]	10.10	12.80	10.86

Source: World Bank data

[a]The complete list of IDA8 donors, which includes some countries that borrow from the Bank, is as follows: Argentina, Australia, Austria, Belgium, Brazil, Colombia, Greece, Hungary, Ireland, the Republic of Korea, Luxembourg, Mexico, the Netherlands, New Zealand, South Africa, Spain, Turkey, and Yugoslavia

Source: Alexander Fleming and Mary Oakes Smith, "Raising Resources for IDA: The Eight Replenishment," *Finance & Development* (September 1987): 25

as members. Table 18–1 shows countries' contributions to IDA. By definition, a very poor country is generally one with an annual per capita GNP of $795 or less (in 1981 dollars), and approximately 50 countries fall under this classification. In practice, most of the IDA loans go to those countries that barely exceed half of the specified annual per capita GNP, and most of these countries are located in Africa south of the Sahara and in South Asia. These countries, though very poor, must still have sufficient economic, financial, and political stability to qualify for IDA loans.[16]

Whereas the World Bank makes "loans," the IDA provides "credits." These credits are made only to governments even though these governments routinely relend funds to their private and public enterprises. The credits must be repaid over fifty years, and there is a ten-year grace period before the beginning of the repayment of the principal. IDA credits carry no interest, but there is an annual commitment charge of 0.5 percent on the undisbursed portion and a service charge of 0.75 percent on the disbursed amount of each credit. These charges are intended to cover the administrative costs of running the IDA program.

International Finance Corporation (IFC)

Although the IDA shares the World Bank's staff, the IFC has its own operating and legal staff. Unlike the bank and the IDA, which have many operating aspects in common, the IFC works closely with private investors. In addition to providing convertible debentures, underwriting, and standby commitments, the IFC invests in commercial enterprises within developing countries and is able to take equity positions. By functioning in this area, the IFC complements the work of the World Bank by providing assistance in business areas that are impractical for the bank to operate. As of 1991 the IFC's total membership had become 135 countries.

The IFC's main function is to assist in the economic advancement of LDCs by promoting growth in the private sector of their economies and by helping to mobilize domestic and foreign capital for this purpose. The IFC provides financial, legal, and technical advice and contributes an element of confidence to the venture of the parties. Its special role is to mobilize resources on commercial terms for business ventures and financial institutions where a market-oriented approach is both applicable and preferable. It will not, however, provide financing if sufficient capital can be obtained on reasonable terms from other sources. Its lending criteria include foreign exchange earnings, increased employment, skill improvement and acquisition, higher productivity, and development of a country's natural resources on reasonable terms.

The International Finance Corporation has become more active in helping companies in developing countries raise financing through international offerings of investment funds and individual corporate securities. Toward this goal, the International Securities Group (ISG) was established in 1989 to provide investment banking services to corporate clients in developing countries.[17]

Multilateral Investment Guarantee Agency (MIGA)

The activities of the World Bank, IDA, and IFC are supplemented by those of a new affiliated international organization—the Multilateral Investment Guarantee Agency (MIGA). Established in 1988, MIGA has a specialized mandate: to encourage equity investment and other direct investment flows to developing countries through the mitigation of noncommercial investment barriers. To encourage international corporate investment so that developing countries can attract qualified investors, MIGA offers investors guarantees against noncommercial risks (especially risk of war or repatriation); advises developing member governments on the design and implementation of policies, programs, and procedures related to foreign investments; and sponsors a dialogue between the international business community and host governments on investment issues. Industrialized countries should also benefit from MIGA's augmentation of the existing capacity to insure their overseas investors, from its innovative types of guarantees, and from the efficiency derived from the free flow of investment resources.[18]

INTERNATIONAL MONETARY FUND (IMF)

During the Great Depression of the 1930s, many countries resorted to competitive currency devaluation and trade restrictions to maintain domestic income, resulting in lower trade and employment for everyone. Concern over these "beggar-thy-neighbor" policies led to a July 1–22, 1944, conference at Bretton Woods, New Hampshire, attended by delegates from forty-four countries. The IMF was born there on December 27, 1945, to institute an open and stable monetary system.[19]

The IMF is a cooperative apolitical intergovernmental monetary and financial institution. As a "pluralist" international monetary organization, its multiple activities encompass financing, regulatory, and promotional purposes. It acts as a source of balance-of-payments assistance-*cum*-adjustment to members, as a source and creator of international liquidity, as a reserve depository and intermediary for members, as a trustee, and as a catalyst. The use of the IMF's resources is based on balance-of-payments need, on equal and nondiscriminatory treatment of members, and on due regard for members' domestic, social, and political systems and policies.

Guided by its charter (Articles of Agreement), the IMF has six prescribed objectives:

1. To promote international cooperation among members on international monetary issues.
2. To facilitate the balanced growth of international trade and to contribute to high levels of employment, real income, and productive capacity.
3. To promote exchange stability and orderly exchange arrangements while avoiding competitive currency devaluation.
4. To foster a multilateral system of payments and transfers while eliminating exchange restrictions.
5. To make financial resources available to members.
6. To seek reduction of payment imbalances.

Exhibit 18–11 shows a growth in IMF membership. Membership in the IMF is open to any nation that controls its own foreign relations and is willing and able to fulfill the obligations of membership. Each member has a quota based on its subscription contribution to the fund. This quota determines the member's voting power and access to the IMF's financial resources. The IMF employs a system of weighted voting power that combines a basic allotment with a variable allotment. To recognize the sovereign equality of nations, each member has a basic allotment of 250 votes. To protect the interest of members with a greater magnitude of international trade and financial transactions as well as to account for the differences in subscriptions, variable allotment is used as well, resulting in one vote for each part of the member's quota that is equivalent to a *special drawing right (SDR)* of 100,000. The United States accounts for some 19 percent of the total. Table 18-2 provides a detailed breakdown of quotas for each member nation.

SDR

In former times, gold and foreign exchange were the major reserve assets, and there was some concern that an increase in the rate of such assets might not be adequate to sustain trade and maintain full employment. Furthermore, deficits in the balance of payments of reserve-currency countries could interfere with the confidence in the reserve currencies. In response to this apprehension, the First Amendment to the Articles of Agreement was created and took effect on July 28, 1969, and the special drawing right (SDR) was established.

Created by the IMF as a new asset, **SDR** is a composite fiduciary reserve asset to supplement existing reserve assets. It is the unit of account in which the fund expresses the value of its assets. The value was initially expressed in terms of gold,

Growth in IMF membership 1945-91

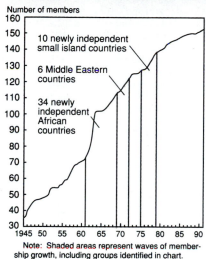

Number of members

10 newly independent small island countries

6 Middle Eastern countries

34 newly independent African countries

Note: Shaded areas represent waves of membership growth, including groups identified in chart.

EXHIBIT 18-11 Growth in IMF membership, 1945-91

Source: Marina Primorac, "How Does a Country Join the IMF?" *Finance & Development* (June 1991): 35

with SDR 35 being equivalent to one fine ounce of gold. From the middle of 1975 to the end of 1980, SDR was determined daily as the weighted average value of a "basket" of sixteen currencies corresponding to the relative share of each currency's issuing member in world exports. Given the commercial and financial importance of the U.S. dollar, it was assigned a weight of 33 percent.

For simplification, the size of the valuation "basket" was subsequently reduced at the beginning of 1981 to the currencies of the five countries with the largest share of world exports of goods and services. The SDR valuation basket was revised again on January 1, 1991, so that the weights would reflect changes in the relative importance of the five currencies in international trade and finance (see Table 18-3).

The term *special drawing rights* partly emphasizes the similarity with members' drawing rights on the General Resources Account, whereas *special* conveys the notion of SDR's uniqueness and difference from other existing drawing rights in the IMF. From a historical perspective, SDR is the first kind of an interest-bearing reserve asset created by international consensus. Unlike commodity money, the value of SDR as an asset is derived from the commitments of voluntary participants to hold and accept SDRs rather than from any intrinsic properties. SDR has been allocated to its members since 1970 in proportion to their respective quotas.

TABLE 18-2 Current and proposed IMF quotas

Member	Current[a]	Proposed[a]	Member	Current	Proposed	Member	Current	Proposed
Afghanistan	86.7	120.4	Guinea-Bissau	7.5	10.5	Peru	330.9	466.1
Algeria	623.1	914.4	Guyana	49.2	67.2	Philippines	440.4	633.4
Angola	145.0	207.3	Haiti	44.1	60.7	Poland	680.0	988.5
Antigua & Barbuda	5.0	8.5	Honduras	67.8	95.0	Portugal	376.6	557.6
Argentina	1,113.0	1,537.1	Hungary	530.7	754.8	Qatar	114.9	190.5
Australia	1,619.2	2,333.2	Iceland	59.6	85.3	Romania	523.4	754.1
Austria	775.6	1,188.3	India	2,207.7	3,055.5	Rawanda	43.8	59.5
Bahamas	66.4	94.9	Indonesia	1,009.7	1,497.6	St. Kitts & Nevis	4.5	6.5
Bahrain	48.9	82.8	Iran	660.0	1,078.5	St. Lucia	7.5	11.0
Bangladesh	287.5	392.5	Iraq	504.0	864.8	St. Vincent &	4.0	6.0
Barbados	34.1	48.9	Ireland	343.4	525.0	Grenadines		
Belgium	2,080.4	3,102.3	Israel	446.6	666.2	Sao Tome &	4.0	5.5
Belize	9.5	13.5	Italy	2,909.1	4,590.7	Principe		
Benin	31.3	45.3	Ivory Coast	165.5	238.2	Saudi Arabia	3,202.4	5,130.6
Bhutan	2.5	4.5	Jamaica	145.5	200.9	Senegal	85.1	118.9
Bolivia	90.7	126.2	Japan	4,223.3	8,241.5	Seychelles	3.0	6.0
Botswana	22.1	36.6	Jordan	73.9	121.7	Sierra Leone	57.9	77.2
Brazil	1,461.3	2,170.8	Kenya	142.0	199.4	Singapore	92.4	357.6
Burkina Faso	31.6	44.2	Kiribati, Repub-	2.5	4.0	Solomon Islands	5.0	7.5
Butundi	42.7	57.2	lic of			Somalia	44.2	60.9
Cambodia	25.0	25.0	Korea	462.8	799.6	South Africa	915.7	1,365.4
Cameroon	92.7	135.1	Kuwait	635.3	995.2	Spain	1,286.0	1,935.4
Canada	2,941.0	4,320.3	Lao People's	29.3	39.1	Sri Lanka	223.1	303.6
Cape Verde	4.5	7.0	Dem. Rep.			Sudan	167.7	233.1
Central African Rep.	30.4	41.2	Lebanon	78.7	146.0	Suriname	49.3	67.6
Chad	30.6	41.3	Lesotho	15.1	23.9	Swaziland	24.7	36.5
Chile	440.5	621.7	Liberia	71.3	96.2	Sweden	1,064.3	1,614.0
China	2,390.9	3,385.2	Libya	515.7	817.6	Syrian Arab	139.1	209.9
Columbia	394.2	561.3	Luxembourg	77.0	135.5	Republic		
Comoros	4.5	6.5	Madagascar	66.4	90.4	Tanzania	107.0	146.9
Congo, People's	37.3	57.9	Malawi	37.2	50.9	Thailand	386.6	573.9
Rep. of			Malaysia	550.6	832.7	Togo	38.4	54.3
Costa Rica	84.1	119.0	Maldives	2.0	5.5	Tonga	3.25	5.0
Cyprus	69.7	100.0	Mali	508.	68.9	Trinidad &	170.1	246.8
Denmark	711.0	1,069.9	Malta	45.1	67.5	Tobago		
Djibouti	8.0	11.5	Mauritania	33.9	47.5	Tunisia	138.2	206.0
Dominica	4.0	6.0	Mauritius	53.6	73.3	Turkey	429.1	642.0
Dominican Republic	112.1	158.8	Mexico	1,165.5	1,753.3	Uganda	99.6	133.9
Ecuador	150.7	219.2	Morocco	306.6	427.7	United Arab	202.6	392.1
Egypt	463.4	678.4	Mozambique	61.0	84.0	Emirates		
El Salvador	89.0	125.6	Myanmar	137.0	184.9	United Kingdom	6,194.0	7,414.6
Equatorial Guinea	18.4	24.3	Nepal	37.3	52.0	United States	17,918.3	26,526.8
Ethiopia	70.6	98.3	Netherlands	2,264.8	3,444.2	Uruguay	163.8	225.3
Fiji	36.5	51.1	New Zeland	461.6	650.1	Vanuatu	9.0	12.5
Finland	574.9	861.8	Nicaragua	68.2	96.1	Venezuela	1,371.5	1,951.3
France	4,482.8	7,414.6	Niger	33.7	48.3	Vietnam	176.8	241.6
Gabon	73.1	110.3	Nigeria	849.5	1,281.6	Western Samoa	6.0	8.5
Gambia	17.1	22.9	Norway	699.0	1,104.6	Yemen, Repub-	120.5	176.5
Germany	5,403.7	8,241.5	Oman	63.1	119.4	lic of		
Ghana	204.5	274.0	Pakistan	546.3	758.2	Yugoslavia	613.0	918.3
Greece	399.9	587.6	Panama	102.2	149.6	Zaire	291.0	394.8
Grenada	6.0	8.5	Papua New	65.9	95.3	Zambia	270.3	363.5
Guatemala	108.0	153.8	Guinea			Zimbabwe	191.0	261.3
Guinea	57.9	78.7	Paraguay	48.4	72.1			

[a] Million SDRs.

Note: Countries that became members after May 30, 1990 are not eligible for consent to quota increase.

Data: IMF.

Source: IMF Survey, September 1991, 6

TABLE 18–3 SDR valuation on August 26, 1991

Currency	1 Currency Amount	2 Exchange Rate on August 26	3 U.S. Dollar Equivalent
Deutsche mark	0.4530	1.74780	0.259183
French franc	0.8000	5.93500	0.134794
Japanese yen	31.8000	136.96000	0.232185
Pound sterling	0.0812	1.67980	0.136400
U.S. dollar	0.5720	1.00000	0.572000
SDR 1 = US$ 1.33456			1.334562
US$ 1 = SDR 0.749310			

Column 1: The currency components of the SDR basket.

Column 2: Exchange rates in terms of currency units per U.S. dollar except for the pound sterling, which is expressed in U.S. dollars per pound.

Column 3: The U.S. dollar equivalents of the currency amounts in Column 1 at the exchange rates in Column 2—that is, Column 1 divided by Column 2 except in the case of the pound sterling, for which column 1 is multiplied by column 2.

Note: The value of one U.S. dollar in terms of the SDR is calculated as the reciprocal of column 3, i.e., 1 ÷ 1.334562.

Source: IMF Survey, September 1991, 8

Functions

Among intergovernmental organizations, the IMF is unique in its combination of regulatory, consultative, and financial functions.

Regulatory Function Reflecting its objective of avoiding disruptive fluctuations and the rigidity of rates, the IMF administers a code of conduct with respect to exchange rate policies and restrictions on payments. Having the authority to influence some of its members' practices, the IMF must exercise firm surveillance over their policies. Toward this end, the fund has adopted three principles, spelled out in the document entitled Surveillance Over Exchange Rate Policies, to guide members in their conduct and to specify their rights and obligations. First, members are obligated to refrain from manipulating exchange rates to gain an unfair competitive advantage. Second, members must intervene if necessary to counter disorderly conditions that disrupt short-term movements in the exchange rates of their currencies. Last but not least, members should consider the interests of other members in their intervention policies.

To better achieve its goal in a changing financial world, the IMF incorporated the necessary reform into the Second Amendment of Agreement, which became effective on April 1, 1978. The amendment legalized some existing exchange practices while placing restrictions on others. A member is free to adopt an exchange arrangement of its choice but must notify the IMF promptly if it changes this arrangement. A member may peg the value of its currency to that of another currency or to the SDR or some other composite, but not to gold. The official price of gold was abolished, and the role of gold as an obligatory means of payment in transactions between the fund and its members was terminated.

Consultative Function A number of countries are handicapped in the effort to design suitable foreign exchange programs by the scarcity of reliable statistical data and of personnel with suitable skills in economic analysis and management. This is the area in which the IMF can be of assistance for such members. Because of the nature of the work, the IMF has built up a body of practical knowledge of balance-of-payments statistics, analysis, and policy, and of associated fields. The IMF's research in these topics makes it well qualified to offer advice.

The IMF can assist its members in at least three ways in designing programs to be supported with financial resources. First, it provides *training* for officials dealing with the compilation of statistics and the formulation and execution of policies related to the balance of payments. Second, it provides *technical assistance* in the fields of fiscal, monetary, and balance-of-payments policies; banking; exchange and trade systems; government finance; and statistics, as well as other information. Finally, the fund offers a wide range of *published materials* that cover descriptions and explanations of developments in the world economy and the IMF on the one hand and theoretical studies on economic behavior and policy on the other. By assisting members in these three areas, the fund provides consultations with member countries on a regular basis, and serves as a forum through which members can consult with one another on international monetary matters.[20]

Financial Function   The IMF's primary financial purpose, as set out in Article I, sections v and vi, is "to give confidence to members by making the general resources of the Fund temporarily available to them under adequate safeguards, thus providing them with opportunity to correct maladjustments in their balance of payments without resorting to measures destructive of national or international prosperity" and "to shorten the duration and lessen the degree of disequilibrium in the international balances of payments of members."

Although subscriptions constitute the main source of the fund's resources, they are supplemented by borrowing from official sources. Originally, 75 percent of a member's subscription was payable in the member's currency, with the balance payable in gold. Following the Second Amendment, gold was no longer used in obligatory payments to or by the IMF and was replaced by SDRs or the currencies of other members.

The IMF's financial resources are made available under a spectrum of policies and facilities that differ mainly in the type of balance-of-payments need and in the degree of conditionality. Access to resources is open to members in amounts related to their quotas, and the rules governing access apply uniformly to all members. Based on guidelines related to the economic indicators of the external position of a country, the fund assesses both a member's balance-of-payments need (the magnitude of financing) and the adequacy of measures to correct the underlying balance-of-payments disequilibrium (adjustment program). "Need" is a function of the member's balance-of-payments position, its foreign reserve position, and the developments in its reserve position. Even though the three elements are considered distinct and separate and each one alone can represent the member's need, it is the IMF's judgmental consideration of all three in combination with which it justifies that need.

The IMF's financial mechanism, designed to assist members in observing the code of conduct, is for the financing of temporary deficits only, not long-term debts. Because monetary resources are not intended for financing persistent deficits, the deficits must be self-correcting or they must be corrected through adopted policies. Brazil, for example, pledged to bring its annual inflation rate of more than 200 percent down to 170 percent. Mexico, likewise, was required by the IMF to ease restrictions on foreign investment and to reach agreement on macroeconomic policy, including inflation and trade-deficit goals, before banks will lend more money. As borrowing increases, so do the IMF's restrictions on the borrower's domestic and monetary affairs. During 1976 the British pound plunged in value to a record low. Lacking sufficient reserves to support the pound, the United Kingdom was forced to borrow every cent to which it was entitled. In return, the IMF demanded tighter control over Great Britain's money expansion. The British government's only bargaining chip at that time was that riots might result without the IMF's aid, leading to instability in Europe.

FINANCIAL CENTERS

MNCs have made it an increasingly common practice to raise capital offshore. There are four broad types of offshore financial centers: primary, booking, funding, and collection.[21] A **primary center** (e.g., London, New York) is an international financial center located in a highly developed industrial country. With financial systems highly developed, these centers serve worldwide clients by offering all kinds of financial services.

A primary center is at one extreme; a **booking center** (e.g., Nassau) is at the other. International banks may wish to take advantage of a country's highly favorable tax regulatory system by opening a "shell branch" there that may be nothing but one small room or a post office box. The purpose is to serve the financial needs of those outside the country by booking Eurocurrency deposits and international loans.

A **funding center** (e.g., Singapore) collects funds from outside a region for that region's internal use. A funding center can thus be characterized by inward intermediation of offshore funds. In contrast, outward financial intermediation is a characteristic of a **collection center** (e.g., Bahrain). This type of center has low absorptive capacity of the region's economies, resulting in excess savings accumulated in the collection center for international banks to invest.

According to the results of one study, the growing integration of major domestic and international offshore financial markets in the 1980s has resulted in an increase in the efficiency of international capital markets. However, structural changes in financial markets may have affected the effectiveness of monetary and fiscal policies, created new systemic risks associated with increased asset price variability, and reduced the certainty of developing country access to international capital markets.[22]

Euromarket

One place where governments and business can go to borrow money of a desired currency at a competitive rate is the *Euromarket*. This international market of foreign currency deposits in Europe has no fixed physical boundary, though London, as a hub, is its main location. Actually, the Euromarket is simply a telephone and telex network run by a few dozen international giant banks. Citicorp, for example, operates through its foreign branches in dozens of countries to provide global banking services to MNCs in any type of currency.

Unlike American banks, which accept nothing but U.S. dollars for deposit, European banks are relatively liberal and routinely accept all types of money, which do not have to be converted into any specific local currency. When a depositor needs funds and must withdraw them, no conversion is required, and the depositor will get back the same currency as deposited earlier.

Traded on the Euromarket are Eurocurrencies, which the world's major banks bid for and employ. *Eurocurrencies* are monies traded outside of the country of their origin. A Belgian franc becomes a Eurocurrency (i.e., Euro-Belgian franc) when it is traded anywhere outside Belgium. Despite the *Euro* prefix, a Eurocurrency is not necessarily restricted to denominations of European and American currencies. Representing a claim against North American, Asian, and Caribbean banks, the currency can be a Euroyen, for example, held by a Hong Kong bank in the Caribbean.

The Eurodollar, just one of many Eurocurrencies, is simply U.S. dollar deposited in banks outside of the United States (e.g., in Europe, Canada, and Japan). When Hong Kong or Singapore banks accept deposits and make loans in U.S. dollars, such dollars become Asian dollars. The Eurodollar once commanded more than 90 percent of the Euromarket, with the German mark in second place, holding about 10 percent of the Euromarket.

Eurocurrency deposits have continued to grow rapidly and reached a gross value of $4.5 trillion outstanding in 1987 and a net value of nearly $2.6 trillion (net of interbank claims). Eurodollar deposits, however, have not grown as rapidly and actually fell from over 80 percent of all Eurocurrency deposits outstanding in the early 1980s to only 66 percent by 1987. Because it is easier and cheaper than issuing corporate bonds in Japan, the Japanese are the biggest issuers of Eurobonds, accounting for 21 percent of all Eurobonds.[23]

One unique feature of the Euromarket is its stateless financial system. Although governments place restrictions on the operations of their national money markets, such restrictive measures do not apply to the Euromarket in spite of the fact that it shares the same locations and facilities as do the national markets. There is no central bank or control, and the Euromarket has no international authority to which it must answer. As an independent market of its own, it has its own interest rate structure, and anyone can invest or trade in it. Because it has no reserve requirements, it is able to offer high rates on deposits and also to make loans at lower rates. Exhibit 18–12 describes how certain companies raised capital in the Euromarket by issuing nondollar bonds.

There are several reasons why the Euromarket exists and why its growth has been so phenomenal. Communist countries preferred to deposit their U.S. dollars in Western Europe rather than in the United States for fear of having their money confiscated by the U.S. government. Also, since the end of World War I, many Europeans have held on to U.S. dollars as a hedge against inflation in the event that inflation reached an excessive rate in Europe.

Many Europeans still prefer to hold U.S. dollars in Eurobanks even though European interest rates on European currencies might be higher than the Euromarket rate for U.S. dollars. Furthermore, a few hours of simultaneous trading each business

Morgan Guaranty continues to manage issues in more currencies than any other underwriter

Progressive deregulation of financial markets and increased investor interest have accelerated the already rapid growth of the non-U.S. dollar capital markets. More than half the total number of this year's new issues in the international bond markets are in non-dollar currencies. And while 1984 new issue volume of non-dollar bonds in the Euromarket equaled $15.1 billion, in just the first eight months of 1985 total volume soared to $23.4 billion.

As this growth continues, more and more multinationals are turning to The Morgan Bank for non-dollar bond financing. In 1985, our subsidiary Morgan Guaranty Ltd has been lead manager of bond issues in more currencies than any other underwriter in the world.

With a unique set of capabilities, we are a truly global financial intermediary.

☐ As a major participant in the international securities markets—as well as the worldwide foreign exchange, government bond, and bullion markets—we have an exceptional ability to perceive and exploit market opportunities for our clients.

☐ Morgan is the leading counterparty that can act with equal proficiency as either principal or agent in interest-rate and currency swap transactions.

☐ Morgan's financial strength—nearly $5 billion in primary capital—lowers our clients' cost and risk in intermarket arbitrage.

Our clients find that using foreign currency bond markets broadens their investor bases and facilitates economic and accounting hedges of overseas investments. Through currency and interest-rate swaps we help them create dollar obligations at substantially reduced costs. We also identify opportunities to earn arbitrage profits in non-dollar markets.

Some examples of how Morgan has helped borrowers take advantage of new

Selected non-U.S. dollar issues lead-managed by Morgan Guaranty January–September, 1985

Bank of Tokyo	A$50 million
British Petroleum	¥ 17 billion
British Petroleum	£50 million
Chrysler Financial	SF 150 million
Chrysler Financial	NZ$65 million
Dresdner Finance	A$75 million
European Investment Bank	DKR 250 million
Gaz de France	FF 500 million
IBM France	FF 700 million
IBM World Trade	ECU 150 million
IC Industries	C$50 million
J.C. Penney	¥ 26 billion
Kingdom of Sweden	FF 500 million
Kredietbank	NZ$50 million
McDonald's	¥ 25 billion
Mobil	FF 500 million
Motorola	ECU 50 million
Nordic Investment Bank	DKR 200 million
Olivetti	SF 100 million
PepsiCo	SF 130 million
Peugeot	FF 500 million
R.J. Reynolds	ECU 125 million
R.J. Reynolds	SF 235 million
Security Pacific	ECU 100 million
Sterling Drug	£30 million

opportunities in non-dollar markets so far this year:

Swiss francs. Most recently our subsidiary Morgan Guaranty (Switzerland) Ltd launched as book-runner a SF 235 million issue which we combined with a currency swap to provide 15-year U.S. dollar financing for R.J. Reynolds. This was the largest Swiss franc offering to date by a U.S. company. In the Swiss public bond market we were also book-running lead manager for issues for PepsiCo and Olivetti.

ECUs. Morgan was lead or co-lead manager of ten ECU issues, including an ECU 125 million issue for R.J. Reynolds and an

ECU 100 million issue for Security Pacific Australia, both of which we swapped into U.S. dollar financing.

Sterling. We were book-running lead manager for Euro-sterling bond issues for British Petroleum and Sterling Drug. In addition, Morgan lead managed a $100 million issue for Minnesota Mining & Manufacturing that was the first dollar/ sterling dual-currency issue ever.

Yen. For J.C. Penney, we arranged U.S. dollar fixed-rate funding, at a cost below the yield on U.S. Treasury notes, through a Euro-yen bond issue and currency swap.

New Zealand dollars. This year we've led seven issues, including a NZ$65 million Chrysler issue which we swapped into floating-rate financing.

Deutschemarks. In Germany Morgan Guaranty GmbH is one of the few foreign-owned firms that German capital market guidelines allow to act as book-running lead manager of Euro-Deutschemark issues.

French francs. We were co-lead manager, with two French banks, of a Gaz de France issue that reopened the Euro-French franc bond market after a four-year lapse. Then we co-led franc issues for IBM France, the Kingdom of Sweden, Peugeot, and Mobil.

Danish krone. We were lead manager for the first two issues in the Euro-Danish krone bond market, which opened this year.

Measure our performance. Let us compete for your mandate. You'll find we deliver innovative services in the capital markets with the same high quality and skill that have long been hallmarks of all Morgan banking business.

Morgan Guaranty Ltd, 30 Throgmorton Street, London EC2N 2DT

Morgan Guaranty Trust Company, 23 Wall Street, New York, NY 10015   Member FDIC

The Morgan Bank

EXHIBIT 18–12   The Euromarket

Source: Reprinted with permission of the Morgan Guaranty Trust Company

day when European and U.S. banks are both open are extended by the operation of the London market, whose time zone makes it reasonably convenient for banks, investors, borrowers, and lenders across continents to contact one another. Even central banks find the Euromarket a convenient place to increase or decrease their reserves as well as the liquidity of their commercial banks.

The spectacular growth of the Euromarket has been greatly aided by government regulations. Restrictions on lending and borrowing practices in terms of ceiling rate, reserves, reserve requirements, taxes, and so on caused lenders to seek out opportunities abroad where they could earn higher yields. In the case of the United States, the major factor was the Federal Reserve System's Regulation Q, which fixed the low interest rates that were paid on time deposits of 1957, forcing investors such as Arab oil countries and MNCs to look elsewhere for higher returns on their idle dollars. As a result, London banks bid for dollar deposits and then reloaned them to New York banks. In addition to traditional time deposits and certificates of deposit, Eurobanks now attract dollar deposits with other investment opportunities, such as floating-rate certificates of deposit and floating-rate notes, with interest payments pegged to the cost of money—the London interbank offered rate (LIBOR) or the Singapore interbank offered rate (SIBOR). Also, global money managers may invest in such instruments as Eurobonds because of the dollar stability and security as well as the interest rate advantage over similar mark and franc securities. Moreover, the market gets more support from Rule No. 8 of the Financial Accounting Standards (FASB-8), which requires U.S. companies to translate gains or losses in foreign currencies onto their income statements in the quarter in which they occur. FASB-8 stimulates MNCs to trade frequently from one currency to another.

Much like lenders, borrowers with a good name and with large resources and demands have good reason to tap the Euromarket. When MNCs need free access to hard currencies such as dollars, the money may not be readily available in, say, the United States, or the process may be cumbersome and time-consuming (e.g., securing the SEC's approval for certain types of financing). Because of these encumbrances, the Euromarket can come to the rescue. When the Carter administration attempted to contain inflation by restricting credits and driving up interest rates, U.S. MNCs were able to circumvent these restrictions by borrowing in the Euromarket. In the case that the lending terms in the United States are not attractive, the Euromarket can be used as leverage because American companies can borrow there if the interest rate there is lower or if they can use that information to force banks in the United States to match that lower rate. A financial officer who wants to hedge against the interest rate swing in the Euromarket can use either a Eurodollar futures or options contract traded on the Chicago Mercantile Exchange for this purpose (see Table 18–4).

Despite its growth and usefulness, the Euromarket has attracted criticism. The lack of regulation generates some questions about the safety and stability of the market. Its high interest rate stimulates an outflow of funds from the United States, even though some of those funds are in turn reloaned to U.S. banks and businesses. The lack of regulations may create financial instability because MNCs, attempting to protect their profits, may make large and quick shifts of capital that can deplete a currency already in trouble. European and Japanese banks were unable to halt the dollar slide in 1977 even after spending some $35 billion in an effort to support the value of the currency. Therefore, exchange rates can move up or down drastically with no apparent justification. Also, as mentioned earlier, the Euromarket may contribute to inflation because it allows firms to bypass a country's anti-inflation measures, such as those imposed in the United States in the late 1960s and the late 1970s. The problem can become serious because the same dollar can change hands many times—limitless times, in theory. For these reasons, governments can be held "hostage" to activities beyond their control.

TABLE 18–4 Eurodollar futures

Eurodollar Time Deposit Futures		Options on Eurodollar Futures	
Ticker symbol	ED	**Ticker symbols**	Calls: CE
Trading unit	ED $1,000,000		Puts: PE
Price quote	Index points	**Underlying contract**	One ED futures contract
Minimum price	.01 (1 basis pt.)	**Strike prices**	$.25 intervals, e.g., 92.25, 92.50, 92.75
Fluctuation (tick)	1 basis point = $25.00 $(.0001 \times \$1,000,000 \times \frac{90}{360} = \$25)$	**Premium quotations**	U.S. $ per index point
Daily price limit	None	**Minimum price Fluctuation (tick)**[a]	.01 = $25.00 (cabinet = $12.50)
Contract months	Mar, Jun, Sep, Dec		
Trading hours[a] **(Chicago time)**	7:20 A.M.–2:00 P.M. Last day: 7:20 A.M.–9:30 A.M.	**Daily price limit**	None
		Contract months	Mar, Jun, Sep, Dec
Last day of trading	Second London business day immediately preceding the third Wednesday of the contract month	**Trading hours**[b] **(Chicago time)**	7:20 A.M.–2:00 P.M. Last day: 7:20 A.M.–9:30 A.M.
Delivery date	Last day of trading—cash settled	**Last day of trading**	Second London business day immediately preceding the third Wednesday of the contract month
		Minimum margin	No margin required for put or call option buyers, but the premium must be paid in full; option sellers must meet additional margin requirements as determined by the Standard Portfolio Analysis of Risk SPAN margin system.
		Exercise procedure[c]	An option may be exercised by the buyer up to and including the last day of trading. Exercise is accomplished by the clearing member representing the buyer presenting and Exercise Notice to the Clearing House by 7:00 P.M. on the day of the exercise

[a]Trading will end at 12:00 noon on the business day before a CME holiday and on any U.S. bank holiday that the CME is open.

[a]A trade may occur at the value of a half-tick (cabinet) if it results in position liquidation for both parties.

[b]Trading will end at 12:00 noon on the business day before a CME holiday and on any U.S. bank holiday that the CME is open.

[c]Consult your broker for specific requirements.

Source: Courtesy of Chicago Mercantile Exchange

Asian Dollar Market

Since inception in 1968, the *Asian Dollar Market* has grown at a rapid rate.[24] The need for this offshore financial market in Asia is the result of the time zone differences among East Asia, Europe, and the United States, making it difficult for Asian bankers to complete transactions within the same day. The growth was aided by the liberalization of regulations in Singapore.

The Asian Dollar Market is a group of banks in Singapore and Hong Kong that accept deposits and make loans in U.S. dollars. Their deposits are time, rather than checking accounts. The two major centers, though different, complement each other. Hong Kong serves as the major center for syndicated loans in the Far East, whereas Singapore dominates the funding side of the market. Put simply, Singapore gathers deposits from various sources while Hong Kong deploys them.

CONCLUSION

Any businessperson can surely appreciate the necessity of having adequate financing and cash flow. It is not uncommon for an importer to turn to its supplier for financial assistance. For the exporter to insist on cash in advance or the equivalent (such as a letter of credit), the sale may be jeopardized.

To finance operations, a company, in addition to selling securities, can turn to middlemen and various financial institutions for loans. Over and above the U.S. market, there are other important capital markets, such as the Euromarket and the Asian Dollar Market, in which financial resources can be secured. For a financial arrangement of significant value, government assistance can be requested from the U.S. Export-Import Bank, which has a variety of programs ranging from direct loans to participation arrangements with private lenders. It is rather unfortunate that the U.S. government is not as aggressive in this respect as are other governments.

As for the government itself, borrowing can occur with the IMF to support its currency and to finance temporary trade deficits, or borrowing can be initiated with the World Bank and its affiliates (IDA and IFC) to finance development projects. Private enterprises can thus benefit indirectly from the funds made available by the World Bank and IDA, or they can contact the IFC directly.

QUESTIONS

1. Name some of the financing sources for exporters.
2. What is FSC? How does it function as a source of financing for export?
3. Is it possible to raise capital by issuing stocks in a foreign country?
4. What are the functions (or services) of a factor?
5. What are some of the government agencies or quasigovernment agencies to which a U.S. exporter can turn for financing?
6. What is mixed or blended credit?
7. What are the goals and functions of the World Bank, the IDA, and the IFC?
8. What are the role and functions of the IMF?
9. What is SDR?
10. What are the Euromarket and Eurocurrencies?

DISCUSSION ASSIGNMENTS AND MINICASES

1. Is it worthwhile for a U.S. firm to form a FSC?
2. Given that foreign competitors through their governments' assistance are able to offer below-market interest rates for financing, how can U.S. firms fight back to remain competitive?
3. Since New York is the financial center of the world, is there any need for U.S. multinationals to use the Euromarket and/or the Asian Dollar Market?
4. The Hawley Group has plans to widen its shareholder base: "In addition to common share lists in the U.K. and Bermuda, and its sponsored American Depository Receipt (ADR) facility in the U.S.,

Hawley has recently obtained share listings in both Australia and New Zealand, imminently expects listing on the International Division of the Montreal Stock Exchange, and is holding active discussions in Frankfurt and Tokyo. These additional listings will broaden public awareness of the company and will allow Hawley to become a global, round-the-clock stock." The availability of Hawley stock through the ADR facility was launched in 1985 (see Exhibit 18–2). Is there any need for Hawley to be listed in so many markets?

CASE 18–1
TOO CLOSE FOR COMFORT

Because of the technology that allows intercontinental trading hookups and because of the existence of multinational investment banks, it is quite easy to trade stocks, bonds, currencies, futures, and options on a twenty-four-hour basis and move money across the world in minutes. Because of the industrialized world's laissez-faire approach, there is virtually no authority to control the flow of capital. As a result, for better or worse, some $2 trillion move around among securities markets every day. Although some people applaud the liberalization of world capital markets, just as many people would like to have more government supervision and control.

Bad news travels fast. In the case of financial markets, it can be a matter of seconds. The speed of information transmission was most evident on Black Monday of October 19, 1987. It was a day of financial meltdown. During the week preceding Black Monday, the Dow Jones Industrial Average (DJIA) stock index dropped 95 points and 108 points. When world trading resumed on Monday, Hong Kong recorded a 420-point drop. When the New York market opened, waves of selling began. At the end of the day, the DJIA had a record one-day decline of 508 points, which wiped out 23 percent of the index's value or the equivalent of $1.1 trillion. The plunge, when compared to the 1929 stock market crash, was worse in terms of percentage and speed.

Other markets soon followed the New York Stock Exchange—down. There were sell signals everywhere. Tokyo, the world's largest capitalized market, saw a drop in stock value of 14 percent of $400 billion in capital. The decline there of 3,836 points was four times the previous single-day drop of 831 points. Sydney lost 25 percent, or $39 billion of the value of Australian stocks. London followed suit, with a plunge of 250 points, or 12 percent of the Financial Times Index of 100 stocks, bringing the two-day loss to 500 points, or 22 percent. Sharp declines were recorded on exchanges in Taiwan, South Korea, Malaysia, Thailand, and Singapore. The same thing happened in Frankfurt and Dusseldorf, Amsterdam, Toronto, and Mexico City. The Hong Kong market was closed for the rest of the week.

The panic repeated itself the following week. On October 26, the Hong Kong market reopened and promptly lost 33 percent of the stock value. The losses elsewhere were as follows: Tokyo (5 percent), London (6 percent), and Frankfurt (6 percent). Then it was New York's turn—a loss of 8 percent or 156 points of the DJIA. The problem seemed to go around and around like an echo. In all, the world witnessed a loss of $1.6 trillion in global stock market value within days.

There is no question of the chain reaction, like knocking over domino pieces. Not so clear, however, were the causes of the panic. The various explanations were the Reagan administration's apparent willingness to let the dollar fall, the U.S. trade deficits, fear of global economic recession, mutual funds' massive selling, and computerized program trading.

Also unclear was whether the financial markets in the United States led the declines of the others or whether it was the other way around. Did New York lead Hong Kong, or did Asian markets influence European markets before affecting the New York and Chicago markets that would open later on the same day? At one time, the dominance of the United States was obvious. When the United States sneezed, others caught the cold. But today, Japan has the world's ten leading banks, and its own financial force allows it to act on its own. What is obvious is the interrelatedness of the various markets. They all can quickly act and react to the developments in other markets.

Another piece of the puzzle is the reactions of consumers and investors in the short run and long run. Consumers who lost their wealth on the stock markets may decide to curb their spending. The decline in consumption may then lead to a cut in production and employee layoffs. The group that took the immediate brunt, ironically, was the people employed in the securities industry.

Some experts think that the globalization of financial markets is inevitable because of the common denominator—money. The global economy has already been closely linked with the aid of technology. Consequently, each financial market is not and cannot be independent. In reality, it is more like a single, global securities exchange with branches in other countries. This reality provides investors and MNCs with more flexibility—so much flexibility that any individual country will find it exceedingly difficult to impose capital controls. The price of this flexibility is a greater degree of market volatility and perhaps chaos in global equities.

Questions

1. Can an event like that of Black Monday happen again?
2. At the time of those difficult weeks in October 1987, former West Germany was in better economic shape than the United States, which had record trade deficits and budget deficits. West Germany planned just before Black Monday to sell its 16 percent stake in Volkswagen. Should the crash of the U.S. markets have any impact on West Germany's plan?

3. Because of the globalization of financial markets, some financial experts predict that the international stock indices (based on stock prices of companies world-wide) may eventually replace such national indices as the DJIA and S&P 500 in representing the equity investment sentiment. The Salomon-Russell Global Equity Index and the Salomon-Russell Non-U.S. Equity Index are examples of this development (see Exhibit 1). Do you agree with the prediction? Why or why not?

FINALLY.
THE FIRST REALISTIC GLOBAL EQUITY INDEXES WRAPPED UP IN ONE NEAT PACKAGE.

Introducing THE SALOMON-RUSSELL GLOBAL EQUITY INDEX^{SM†} and THE SALOMON-RUSSELL NON-U.S. EQUITY INDEX.^{SM†}

In one highly effective package, Salomon Brothers Inc and Frank Russell Company bring global equity managers the first realistic picture of the universe of international equities available for foreign investment. These indexes are:

TRADEABLE

All closely-held, illiquid and restricted issues are eliminated.

CONSISTENT

The eighteen local indexes combined with the Russell 1,000 are weighted according to the market capitalization

actually available to foreign investors. So, they provide for standardized comparisons worldwide.

FLEXIBLE

Over 700 sub-indexes provide the ability to implement strategies derived from regional, country, or industry perspectives.

FULLY-DEVELOPED

The Salomon-Russell Indexes are accompanied by a data base of over 10,000 issues representing more than 40 equity markets worldwide.

The Indexes are supported by Salomon Brothers' research, capital commitment, and unparalleled execution capabilities in markets worldwide. For an overview of our approach to the global equity markets as detailed in our report, *International Equity Analysis*, contact Salomon Brothers.

Salomon Brothers Inc

Market Makers and Investment Bankers

One New York Plaza, New York, NY 10004
Atlanta, Boston, Chicago, Dallas, Los Angeles, San Francisco, Zurich.
Affiliates: Frankfurt, London, Tokyo.
Member of Major Securities and Commodities Exchanges/SIPC.

†Service marks of Salomon Brothers Inc and Frank Russell Company

EXHIBIT 1   Global equity indices

Source: Reprinted with permission of Salomon Brothers, Inc.

NOTES

1. "A Guide to Eximbank Programs," *Business America,* 5 November 1990, 10.

2. For some basic and useful information on financing, see *A Guide to Financing Exports,* U.S. and Foreign Commercial Service, International Trade Administration (Washington, D.C.: U.S. Department of Commerce, 1985).

3. See Steve Johnson, "Asians in U.S. Find It Harder to Bank on Their Credit Clubs," *San Jose Mercury News,* 22 July 1990.

4. "A Shakier Shelter for Exports," *Business Week,* 28 March 1983, 79–80.

5. For the discussion of DISC and FSC, see B. E. Lee and Donald R. Bloom, "Deficit Reduction Act of 1984: Changes in Export Incentives," *Columbia Journal of World Business* 20 (Summer 1985): 63–67.

6. Shahrokh M. Saudagaran, "An Empirical Study of Selected Factors Influencing the Decision to List on Foreign Stock Exchanges," *Journal of International Business Studies* 19 (Spring 1988): 101–27.

7. Christine Pavel and John N. McElravey, "Globalization in the Financial Services Industry," *Economic Perspectives* (May/June 1990): 3–18.

8. *Guide to Financing Exports,* 12.

9. *The Small Business Market Is the World* (Washington, D.C.: U.S. Department of Commerce), 26.

10. *United States Trade and Development Program: Congressional Presentation Fiscal Year 1987* (Washington, D.C.: U.S. International Development Cooperation Agency), 7.

11. *Guide to Financing Exports,* 10.

12. "The U.S. Nuclear Power Industry Cries for Help," *Business Week,* 31 August 1981, 102.

13. "On the Brink of an Export Financing War," *Business Week,* 9 April 1984, 46.

14. "The Ex-Im to Foreign Governments: Back Off," *Business Week,* 18 November 1985, 50.

15. For details, see Warren Baum, *The Project Cycle* (Washington D.C.: The World Bank, 1982); Eugene H. Rotberg, *The World Bank: A Financial Appraisal* (Washington, D.C.: The World Bank, 1981); *The World Bank Annual Report 1990* (Washington, D.C.: The World Bank, 1990); *The World Bank and International Finance Corporation* (Washington, D.C.: The World Bank, 1985).

16. Alexander Fleming and Mary Oakes Smith, "Raising Resources for IDA: The Eight Replenishment," *Finance & Development* (September 1987): 23–26.

17. Kumiko Yoshinari, "Accessing the International Capital Markets," *Finance & Development* (September 1991): 40–41.

18. Ibrahim F. I. Shibata, "Encouraging International Corporate Investment: The Role of the Multilateral Investment Guarantee Agency," *Columbia Journal of World Business* 23 (Spring 1988): 11–18.

19. See Anand G. Chandavarkar, *The International Monetary Fund: Its Financial Organization and Activities,* pamphlet series no. 42 (Washington, D.C.: IMF, 1984); *The International Monetary Fund: Its Evolution, Organization, and Activities,* 4th ed., pamphlet series no. 37 (Washington, D.C.: IMF, 1984); Joseph Gold, *SDRs, Currencies, and Gold: Sixth Survey of New Legal Developments,* pamphlet series no. 40 (Washington, D.C.: IMF, 1983).

20. For the various kinds of IMF assistance, see *Technical Assistance and Training Services of the International Monetary Fund* (Washington, D.C.: International Monetary Fund, 1985).

21. Y. S. Park, "The Economics of Offshore Financial Centers," *Columbia Journal of World Business* 17 (Winter 1982): 31–35.

22. "Capital Market Integration Has Benefits, but May Have Created New Risks," *IMF Survey,* 15 April 1991, 118–20.

23. Pavel and McElravey, "Globalization."

24. For a detailed discussion, see Kenneth Bernauer, "The Asian Dollar Market," *Economic Review,* Federal Reserve Board of San Francisco (Winter 1983): 47–62.

I don't distinguish between national and foreign capital. There is no flag on capital.

President Carlos Menem, Argentina

Currencies and Foreign Exchange 19

CHAPTER OUTLINE

MARKETING ILLUSTRATION
The Big Mac Index

Some people use the Big Mac Index as a convenient substitute for the purchasing power parity theory, which states that, although short-term factors may once in a while unduly affect exchange rates, purchasing power should be the same all over the world. The Big Mac Index simply looks at how much a Big Mac sandwich costs at McDonald's restaurants in different countries. For example, if a Big Mac costs $2.19 in New York City, but costs $2.78, or 27 percent more, in Tokyo, then the interpretation is that the Japanese yen is 27 percent overvalued compared to the U.S. dollar. Similarly, if a Big Mac costs $4.21 in Norway and 74 cents in Hungary, the krona is 92 percent overvalued, and the forint is 66 percent undervalued.

Source: George Anders, "What Price Lunch?" *The Wall Street Journal,* 23 September 1988

The Big Mac example serves as an introduction to the value of money as well as the impact of foreign exchange. All traders realize that volatility exists in the international financial market. For firms with international activities, foreign-exchange risk is inevitable and must be managed to keep it at a minimum.

The purpose of this chapter is to discuss the various issues related to international finance. First, it examines the meaning of money as a medium of exchange. Then it examines the effect of currency devaluation and appreciation. Next, the discussion focuses on an evaluation of the various systems of foreign exchange. Finally, some practical guidelines are offered about hedging options used to reduce foreign exchange risk.

MONEY

A hard currency is hard because of the solid trust that people have in the currency and not because of its gold backing. Business people must have faith that the country issuing the currency will fulfill its obligations.[1] For money to function as a store of value, there must exist something of value to store. Even though the former Soviet republics have gold, people have doubts about the ruble as a store of value.

An act of parliament does not make a currency international. Currencies become internationalized only because they meet the needs of official institutions and private parties more effectively than other financial assets can. An international currency fulfills three basic functions in the global monetary system: it serves as a medium of exchange, a unit of account, and a store of value. As a medium of exchange, private parties use an international currency in foreign trade and international capital transactions, whereas official agents use it for balance-of-payments financing and to intervene in foreign exchange markets. As a unit of account, private parties use an international currency for invoicing merchandise trade and for denominating financial transactions, whereas official agents use it to define exchange rate parities. As a store of value, international currencies are held by private agents as financial assets (e.g., in the form of bonds held by nonresidents) and by official agents (such as central banks) as reserve assets. For a currency to be used internationally, two sets of factors are essential. First, there must be confidence in the value of the currency and in the political stability of the issuing country. Second, a country should possess financial markets that are substantially free of controls. These markets should be broad (i.e., contain a large assortment of financial instruments) and deep (i.e., have well-developed secondary markets). The country should also possess financial institutions that are sophisticated and competitive in overseas financial centers.[2]

FOREIGN EXCHANGE

Foreign exchange transactions involve the purchase or sale of one national currency against another. The easiest way to understand this type of transaction is to view money as just another product that customers are willing to buy and sell. Like other products, money can be considered as branded, and the U.S. dollar, French franc, Japanese yen, and so on are simply some of the brand names for a money "product." Some of these brand names carry more prestige and are more desirable than others, much like other brand names.

People often wonder why it is necessary to have so many different currencies. Obviously, it would be preferable to have just one worldwide currency that could be used anywhere on Earth, similar to the U.S. dollar's being used and accepted in all fifty states. But a global currency is presently impossible because of two uncontrollable factors—national sovereignty and inflation.

Under normal circumstances, it is very rare for a country to adopt another country's currency as its own. One exception is Liechtenstein. It signed a customs treaty with Switzerland in 1923, making the Swiss franc its official currency. Moreover, Liechtenstein's customs affairs are administered by Switzerland.

Many Americans, knowing that the dollar is widely accepted, do not understand why the U.S. dollar cannot become a global currency and why other nations resist replacing their national currencies with the U.S. dollar. The resistance perhaps can be better understood if one imagines the tables being turned. Would the American public be willing to abandon the dollar and replace it with a new global currency? The fact that the United States is so unwilling to embrace the metric system in spite of its demonstrated superiority underscores this point clearly. Because of national pride, no nation wants to give up its identity and sovereignty, and this includes its national currency. National pride may also explain Great Britain's reluctance to allow the pound to join the European Monetary System (EMS), especially since the British believe that the pound has a more important role in the international financial world. Great Britain withdrew the pound from the EMS in 1992.

A less emotional but often uncontrollable issue is inflation, which reduces the value of money (i.e., purchasing power). And since it is impossible for all nations to have an identical inflation rate, the effect of inflation on the value of various currencies is uneven. In Argentina, the inflation rate was greater than 400 percent in 1984, and it accelerated to more than 800 percent later, forcing the government to adopt the austral as its new currency in 1985. Inflation in the United States at the same time was running in the single digits. In China during the 1940s, the currency had so little value that the Chinese had to cart their money around in wheelbarrows. After World War I, the value of German mark stood at 4 trillion marks to a dollar.

Israel abolished the lirot, the forerunner of the shekel, only to have to switch to the new shekel six years later because of inflation. On the first day of 1986, Israel dropped three zeros from its currency, thus making 1,000 old shekels worth one new shekel. Brazil did the same in creating the cruzado to supplement the cruzeiro. The Italian lira was so weak that the many zeroes needed to quote prices were more than the adding machines and computers could take.[3] The only debate was whether two zeroes or three zeroes should be dropped. To harden its currency, Italy introduced the new, de-zeroed lira in 1987, making it the equivalent of 1,000 old lire. To soften the emotional blow and allow time to print new bank notes, retailers were required to post two prices—one in the old lira and one in the new lira. In former Yugoslavia, one Slovenian organization asked in 1987 for the abolition of the 5,000 dinar bank note—the only one using the portrait of president Josip Broz Tito—because the inflation had devalued Tito's image.

These examples should make clear that it is impractical for any single currency to be used on a worldwide basis while maintaining constant value in all countries.

FOREIGN EXCHANGE MARKET

Firms needing to make payment for foreign business transactions never seem to have enough foreign currency on hand, and it is cumbersome for them to seek out those with adequate amounts to sell. There is thus a need for a *foreign exchange market* for all individuals and institutions in order that they may contact one another for this purpose. The foreign exchange market as it exists has no central trading floor where buyers and sellers meet. Most trades are completed by banks and foreign exchange dealers using telephones, cables, and mail. As a worldwide market, the foreign exchange market operates twenty-four hours a day.

The foreign exchange market facilitates financial transactions in three different ways. First, it provides *credit* or *financing* for firms engaged in international business. This can be achieved through a variety of means, such as letter of credit, time draft, forward contract, and so on. Second, it performs a *clearing* function similar to a domestic bank's clearing process for checking-account customers. Clearing is a process by which a financial transaction between two parties involving intermediation between banks is "settled." In the case of international clearing, the funds are transferred on paper from a commercial customer to his local bank, from there to a New York bank, and finally to a foreign bank abroad. The process allows payments to be made for foreign goods without a physical transfer or movement of money across countries.

Third, the market furnishes facilities for *hedging* so that businesses can cover or reduce their foreign exchange risks. **Hedging** is an activity that is used as a temporary substitute purchase or sale for the actual currency. This temporary transaction allows users to protect the price they secure from fluctuations because it establishes equal and opposite positions in the market.

The rationale for hedging lies in the exchange-rate fluctuation, which can move significantly and erratically, even within a short time. The Italian lira, for example, plunged by almost 20 percent against the dollar in a single day in 1985. Exhibit 19–1 provides a good illustration of the high degree of volatility in the foreign exchange market. Since it is common for a customer to take some time in accepting the quoted

EXHIBIT 19–1   Volatility of the foreign exchange rate

Source: Reprinted with permission of Daiwa Securities Company Limited

price, placing an order, and making payments, financial loss caused by exchange-rate movement can easily occur. Without a hedge, an American exporter selling to an Italian customer will suffer financially when the lira declines in value (or the dollar increases in value) because the lire paid, after conversion, will yield fewer dollars than first expected.

Some observers may conclude that though the danger of the falling lira to the U.S. exporter is real and serious, there is an equal opportunity for the lira to gain in value instead. Under this scenario, the exporter can increase the expected profit—once from the sale of the goods and again from the exchange gain. Based on this contention, the exporter would miss the windfall profit if the exporter had hedged. The problem with this idea, however, is that the exporter is in reality a mere amateur as far as the speculation game is concerned. He or she may be an expert in and have great knowledge in the manufacturing and selling of products. But the exporter is not in the business of making windfall profits and thus should concentrate on familiar trading operations rather than attempting to be a gambler in the unfamiliar and risky game of currency speculation. The caution applies to the Italian importer as well, especially when payment is to be made in dollars instead of lire.

The foreign exchange market provides a hedging mechanism needed to protect corporate profits against undesirable changes in the exchange rate that may occur in the future. For this purpose, the market has two submarkets—spot and forward. The two differ with respect to the time of currency delivery. The **spot market** is a cash market where foreign exchange is available for immediate delivery. In practice, delivery of major currencies occurs within one or two business days of the transaction, whereas other currencies may take slightly longer. A U.S. firm holding foreign currency can go to its bank for immediate conversion into dollars based on the spot rate for that day.

Exporters should also consider doing some hedging well before the arrival of foreign funds, and this is where the **forward market** becomes significant. Companies can protect themselves by selling their expected foreign exchange forward. A forward contract is a commitment to buy or sell currencies at some specified time in the future at a specified rate. By signing a forward contract of, say, forty-five days, a company has locked in a certain rate of exchange and knows precisely how many dollars, after conversion, it will get—even though payment, conversion, and delivery will not be made until later (i.e., forty-five days after).

It should be understood that the exchange rate specified in the forty-five day forward contract is not necessarily the same rate as the forward rate of the next day or the spot rate of forty-five days later. Both rates change constantly, fluctuating from day to day and even from minute to minute. The only rate that will stay unchanged is the one agreed on by the bank and the hedger as stipulated in the signed forward contract, even though subsequent forward and spot rates may move drastically the day after the signing of that contract.

One may wonder how the bank estimates in advance what the spot rate will be forty-five days later and whether the bank will suffer financially if the agreed-on forward rate turns out not to be as favorable as the spot rate when the forward contract expires. The answer is that the bank has no way of knowing what the spot rate will be a month and a half later, that it does not need to know, and that it receives neither financial gain nor loss regardless of what the spot rate is forty-five days later.

To understand the rationale in this answer, one must understand the operation of the forward market. The U.S. exporter, when it accepts the Italian importer's order worth 5 million lire to be paid for upon merchandise delivery forty-five days later, can cover its risk by signing a forty-five-day forward contract with the U.S. bank for the amount of lire in question. The U.S. bank, in turn, protects itself with an exchange that is a simultaneous buying and selling of a currency. The U.S. bank achieves this by borrowing 5 million lire from an Italian bank and converting the money into dollars immediately for its own use (e.g., lending or investing).

Once the Italian importer receives its merchandise, the importer does not have to be concerned with the exchange rate since it makes the payment in lire. The U.S. exporter then takes the lire to the U.S. bank for conversion at the rate agreed on earlier without having to concern itself with any rate fluctuations that have occurred over the time since the contract was signed. The last step in the process occurs when the U.S. bank returns the lire to the Italian bank for the loan it received. The Italian bank likewise experiences no financial risk, since it made the loan in lire and lire is what it is receiving. Because all parties knew precisely in advance the amount of the currency that they would receive or pay out, at no time were they affected by any swings that occurred in the exchange rate.

The U.S. exporter should realize that, in most cases, the spot rate is irrelevant for the preparation of price quotations and the determination of operational costs since foreign currency as payment is not received until a later day. Since there is no immediate conversion, the forward rate is the more appropriate one. The expectation in terms of interest rate inflation has already been factored into the agreed-on forward rate.

A question might be asked about whether the forward market leads the spot market or if the reverse occurs. There can be no definite answer to this question because the forward rate can either be higher or lower than its spot counterpart. Whether the forward rate is fixed at a premium or discount to the rate in the cash market depends on traders' expectations concerning the inflation and interest rates in the countries under consideration. One certainty, however, is that the two markets are separate but interdependent. Although the cash and forward prices do not usually move up or down exactly in parallel patterns, they do tend to move in tandem as they react to the same supply/demand factors in the market. The two rates will also converge as a particular forward contract approaches its delivery date and matures.

A study conducted by Batra, Donnefeld, and Hadar examined the effects of MNCs' reactions to uncertainty and risk aversion. According to these researchers, "It is shown that the presence of the forward market allows the firm to respond to changes in uncertainty and risk aversion by adjusting its transactions in the forward market while leaving its production and sales decisions unchanged. The forward market, thus, promotes stability with respect to the operation as opposed to the financial variables; and it also makes it possible to adopt decentralized decision making."[4]

FOREIGN EXCHANGE RATE

The foreign exchange rate is simply a price—the price of one national currency as expressed by the value of another. This exchange price, once established, allows currencies to be exchanged one for another. The exchange rate, however, is more than just a price of a currency. It affects the cost of imported goods and exported goods; the country's rate of inflation; and a firm's profit, output, and employment.

Much like the price of any other product, the price of a currency is determined by the demand and supply of that currency. When the currency is in demand, its price increases. But if a currency's supply increases without any corresponding increase in demand, its value declines. The purchasing power parity hypothesis, when combined with the quantity theory, attempts to predict exchange rates based on money supplies and production: "A nation with slower money supply growth and faster expansion in real capacity to produce should have a currency rising in relative value, whereas a nation with fast money growth and a stagnant real economy should have a depreciating currency."[5]

With excess imports comes an excess supply of money because a large volume of money must be generated to pay for all the imports. With excess money in circulation, the business community, as well as the general population, begins having doubts about its value, making the currency appear overvalued. In contrast, excess export results in too much demand for the exporting nation's currency, since foreign buyers require large amounts to pay for goods. The currency then becomes expensive because of its scarcity, and its real value increases.

The demand of a currency is determined by several factors. Some of these include the following:

1. Domestic and foreign prices of goods and services
2. Trading opportunities within a country
3. International capital movement as affected by the country's stability, inflation, money supply, and interest, as well as by speculators' perceptions and anticipations of such conditions
4. The country's export and import performance

During the first term of the Reagan administration, the demand for dollars was extraordinarily strong because of cheap land, huge markets, economic growth, low inflation, and a relatively high interest rate in the U.S. market. The perception that the United States was the most stable country was further bolstered by investors' confidence in former President Reagan. These favorable factors, operating in conjunction, were more than enough to push the dollar sky-high despite the huge trade deficits of the United States at the time.

Currency Equilibrium

A nation's currency is in *equilibrium* when its rate creates no net change in the country's reserve of international means of payment. The equilibrium rate operates to keep the nation's balance of payments in proper perspective over an interval of time by making imports equal to exports. When in equilibrium, the foreign exchange rate is stable, perhaps fluctuating slightly before returning to its parity position.

Despite most nations' desire to maintain currency equilibrium, currency has a tendency to get out of balance. The equilibrium is affected by the intensity of such fundamental problems as inflation and excess import. Both inflation and excess import are negatively related to the subsequent price of the currency. In theory, neither persistent trade surpluses nor deficits are desirable. Persistent trade surpluses are unwelcome because they make the surplus nation's currency too cheap and imported products too expensive, resulting in a loss of local consumers' buying power.

More serious than the surplus problem is the problem of persistent trade deficits. When this occurs, an adjustment of the disequilibrium is necessary to restore the equality of demand and supply. The adjustment can be achieved through several techniques. For instance, the disequilibrium within limits can be temporarily financed while waiting for the disequilibrium to reverse itself. Persistent deficits cannot be financed for long periods because the country would soon exhaust its reserves and credits in the effort to pay for imports. The country may opt to choose to control its money supply in order to correct the situation. Trade deficits eventually cause a country to take steps to tighten its money supply. By buying up excess supplies of money, the government makes money less available for imports, and the economy ultimately slows down.

There are other methods that can help in restoring equilibrium by shifting demand away from foreign goods. Trade restrictions such as tariffs and foreign exchange controls achieve this purpose by making imports more expensive. If all else fails, the government may resort to changing its exchange rate in order to alter the price relationship of goods traded between two countries. The new rate would reflect a new equilibrium, which would be reinforced by an increase in the cost of imported goods.

Effect of Devaluation

Devaluation is a reduction in the price of one currency in terms of other currencies. To the layperson, devaluation carries negative connotations. But countries that wish to stimulate exports normally want to devalue their own currency. To understand the effect of devaluation, one might consider two possible exchange rates: assume that the Japanese yen is going to be devalued from 130 yen to the dollar to 140 yen to the dollar. A question one might then ask is whether the new rate (i.e., 140 yen) is better than the old rate as far as Japanese exporters are concerned. The answer is a definite yes. One dollar now receives 10 more yen, meaning that a dollar spent in U.S. currency will purchase 140 yen worth of Japanese goods rather than 130 yen worth. In effect, it becomes attractive for others to buy from Japan because they essentially get 10 extra yen worth of merchandise for free. This effect helps to explain why Komatsu had a $20,000 price advantage at one time over Caterpillar on a $100,000 tractor. The explanation for the differential is that the dollar was too expensive in relation to the yen.

Another question one might ask is what effect devaluation will have on Japanese importers. This time, the effect is unfavorable because Japanese importers are required to spend 10 more yen to get the same amount of goods for each dollar as before. The yen devaluation therefore has made imported goods more expensive for Japanese importers and consumers.

The situation should also be examined for the United States. Which one of the two exchange rates would be the preferred rate in the United States? Just as in the case of Japan, the answer cannot be made without some qualifications. The desired rate will depend on the nation's particular objective. If the United States elects to pursue the goal of full employment, the 130-yen rate is preferred because this rate makes it easier for Japan to import more American goods without having to spend a relatively larger amount of yen. The demand for these relatively inexpensive U.S. products will increase in Japan, and this increase in demand is accompanied by a rise in employment in the United States.

But if the U.S. goal is to maximize consumer welfare, the 140-yen rate is better because American consumers can get more of the relatively inexpensive imported products without having to spend relatively more dollars for them. Yet this positive effect is countered by a negative one—the demand for imported goods reduces the demand for domestic products, and unemployment increases in the United States.

How well does devaluation really work? Although devaluation is supposed to expand exports and reduce imports, in practice the actual impact is often not as great as one might expect, especially in the short run. There are several reasons for this. Initially, the trade balance may worsen instead of improve. The country in difficulty often has a low marginal propensity to save, and buying habits and long-term contracts make it difficult in the short run to alter the physical trade volume.

Devaluation, instead of correcting the problem, can aggravate inflation—the very thing it is intended to control. Workers, seeing imported goods more expensive than before, often demand wage increases to compensate for their loss of buying power. To compound the problem, domestic industries usually take advantage of the situation by boosting their own domestic prices. This is the route frequently taken by the U.S. steel and automobile industries whenever import prices are driven up by devaluation or other restrictive measures. Therefore, devaluation cannot work in the long run because if these effects continue to cycle and recycle, a collapse of the economy is the result. Devaluation, in order to be effective, must be accompanied by a program to urge local firms to exert self-restraint and to encourage people to consume less and save more. In February 1989 the Sandinista government of Nicaragua devalued its currency (cordoba) and raised prices for petroleum products for the third time that year. The devaluation was designed to contain hyperinflation that had reached 20,000 percent in 1988.

One must also keep in mind that a substantial time lag occurs between the change in currency value and its impact on the physical flow of trade. The lag occurs because suppliers and buyers need time to adjust their habits and decisions before they start getting used to the new exchange rates. Furthermore, although devaluation makes imports more expensive, consumers may fail to curtail their purchases of those imports. This phenomenon is known as the *J Curve* because it takes quite a while for the economy to round the turn of the J. One should then expect a modest swelling of the trade deficit to occur after devaluation, before a sharp recovery can follow if the right steps have been taken. In general, economists believe that it takes some eighteen months before an increase in import prices can have significant impact on the volume of trade adjustment.

The findings of one study contradict a widely held belief that a depreciation of the home currency enhances the home country manufacturers' competitiveness. In the case of the world automobile and steel industries, firms' significant decline in their share of industry value is associated with the depreciation.[6]

If the economy is successful in expanding exports and reducing imports as intended, devaluation should increase the national income, which in turn will stimulate the volume of imports once again. Thus, the initial effect of devaluation can be reversed in the long run. Moreover, any deliberate devaluation carried on will result in a beggar-my-neighbor policy, which will export domestic unemployment to other countries. The deliberate practice of devaluation can easily provoke other trading partners to retaliate by lowering their own money value. Because of these consequences, the net gain from devaluation in the longer run is not going to be as large as its initial gain.

EXCHANGE-RATE SYSTEMS

There should be no doubt that an exchange rate can be quite volatile and that anyone who is unfortunate enough to make an incorrect decision about the rate's direction will pay for it dearly. Anyone having any doubts about the validity of this statement need only consider Argentina. In 1981 the Argentine peso plunged to only one-seventh of the value of what it had been at the beginning of the same year.

The concern over such a severe reduction in value has led economists and government officials into a heated and continuing debate over the best exchange-rate system. All existing systems have strengths as well as weaknesses, and there is likely no such thing as a perfect exchange-rate system. The major exchange-rate systems can be ranked in terms of increasing flexibility: fixed rate (gold standard and adjustable peg), semifixed (wide band and crawling peg), and flexible or floating rate. Exhibit 19–2 lists the prevailing exchange-rate systems.

Given that a perfect system does not exist, how does one go about evaluating existing systems? A system is acceptable when, given a certain rate of inflation in a country, the value of that country's currency is reduced in the international exchange markets by the same extent, while the value of the currency in a country with no inflation holds steady or moves up accordingly. The system being used should not allow countries to manipulate their rates to gain an unfair advantage over rival trading partners. In essence, a good system promotes stability, certainty, and inflation control.

Gold Standard

The gold standard was the start of modern exchange-rate systems. Gold was first developed as the standard of international exchange in the United Kingdom in the late 1700s, and many other nations had followed suit by the mid-1800s. In the case

□ *Peg single currency* (46). The country links its exchange rate to the value of a major currency—usually the U.S. dollar or the French franc—but does not change the rate frequently. About one half of all developing countries have such an arrangement.

□ *Peg currency composite* (40). A composite, or basket, is usually formed by the currencies of major trading partners to make the pegged currency more stable than if a single-currency peg were used. Currency weights may be based on trade, services, or major capital flows. About one-fourth of all developing countries have composite pegs.

□ *Flexibility limited in relation to single currency* (4). The value of the currency is maintained within certain margins of the peg. This system is currently used by four Middle Eastern countries.

□ *Flexibility limited cooperative arrangements* (10). This applies to countries in the exchange rate mechanism (ERM) of the European Monetary System (EMS) and is a cross between a peg and a float; EMS currencies are pegged to each other, but float otherwise.

□ *More flexible: adjusted to indicator* (5). The currency is adjusted more or less automatically to changes in selected indicators. A common indicator is the real effective exchange rate that reflects inflation-adjusted changes in the currency compared to those of major trading partners. This category also includes cases in which the exchange rate is adjusted according to a preannounced schedule.

□ *More flexible: managed float* (22). The central bank sets the rate, but varies it, sometimes frequently. Adjustments are judgmental, usually based on a range of indicators, such as international reserves, the real effective exchange rate, and developments in parallel exchange markets.

□ *More flexible: independent float* (27). Rates are market-determined. Most developed countries have floats—partial for the EMS countries—but the number of developing countries included in this category has been increasing in recent years.

EXHIBIT 19–2 Prevailing exchange rate regimes and their frequency (the number of countries in each category at end of March 1991 is shown in parentheses)

Source: David Burton and Martin G. Gilman, "Exchange Rate Policy and the IMF," *Finance & Development* (September 1991): 20

of the United States, the U.S. Coinage Act placed the dollar on the gold standard in 1873.[7]

Each country was required to link its currency value to gold by legally defining a *par value* based on a specified quantity of gold for its standard monetary unit. Thus, exchange rates had fixed par values as determined by the gold content of the national monetary links. A modification of this system occurred at a later date, and it became known as the gold exchange standard. Created in 1922, the modified system allowed countries to use both gold and the U.S. dollar for international settlement because the United States stood ready to redeem dollars in gold on demand.

In 1930 a dollar was defined as containing 23.22 grains of fine gold (with 480 grains in a troy ounce), whereas a British pound had 113 grains. In 1971 the gold content of the dollar was redefined from 0.888671 grams of gold to 0.73666 grams. The price of gold, being $20.67 per fine troy ounce in 1879, was later changed to $35 in 1933. The increase in gold price in effect devalued the dollar. Because each national currency had to be backed by gold, each country's money supply, in turn, was determined by its gold holdings.

Because of this common denominator (i.e., gold), all currencies' values were rigidly fixed. Although the values were fixed by law, that does not mean that these exchange rates could not fluctuate to some small degree in accordance with the demand and supply of a currency. The fluctuation had to be within the limits set by the costs of interest, transport, insurance, and handling of gold from one country to another.

Consider, by way of example, the case of the U.S. dollar in relation to the British pound, and assume that the par value of the pound as defined by the dollar when the gold standard was in effect was $4.86. If the cost of moving gold between the two countries was 2 cents per each British pound, the fluctuation limit would then be 2 cents either above or below that par value. That is, the value of the pound sterling could move either up to $4.88 or down to $4.84. The upper limit is known as the *gold export point.* The pound could not rise above the gold export point because the rate would then be greater than the actual cost of shipping gold. If the value of the gold export point were greater, a U.S. importer would find it more economical simply to buy gold with dollars and ship the gold as a payment to the British creditor instead of paying a higher price unnecessarily to buy pounds. It would be reasonable for the U.S. importer to pay $4.88 for each British pound but no higher than that price.

By the same token, the pound should not fall below $4.84—the lower limit known as the *gold import point.* If the pound fell below $4.84, a British importer would be better off converting pounds into gold for payment. The cost of shipping gold would be less than the high cost of buying dollars for payment. In doing so, the importer would export gold, and the United States would gain more gold for its reserves. In actual practice, governments always stood ready to buy and sell gold to make certain that the exchange rate would not move outside of the established limits.

The gold standard functioned to maintain equilibrium through the so-called *price-specie-flow mechanism* (or, more appropriately, the *specie-flow-price mechanism*), with *specie* meaning gold. The mechanism was intended to restore the equilibrium automatically. When a country's currency inflated too fast, the currency lost competitiveness in the world market. The deteriorating trade balance resulting from imports being greater than exports led to a decline in the confidence of the currency. As the exchange rate approached the gold export point, gold was withdrawn from reserves and shipped abroad to pay for imports. With less gold at home, the country was forced to reduce its money supply, a reduction accompanied by a slow-down in economic activity, high interest rates, recession, reduced national income, and increased unemployment. The onset of hard times would pressure inflation to be reduced. As domestic prices declined, demand for domestic products increased, and demand for imports declined. Price deflation thus made domestic products attractive both at home and abroad. The country's balance of payments improved, and gold started to flow into the country once again.

The price-specie-flow mechanism also restored order in the case of trade surpluses by working in the opposite manner. As the country's exports exceeded its imports, the demand for its currency pushed the value toward the gold import point. By gaining gold, the country increased its gold reserves, enabling the country to expand its money supply. The increase in money supply forced interest rates to go lower, while heating up the economy. More employment, increased income, and, subsequently, increased inflation followed. Inflation increased consumers' real income by overvaluing the currency, making it easier to pay for imports. It should be remembered that an inflated country with the exchange rate held constant is an advantageous place to sell products and a poor place to buy. With inflation, prices of domestic products would rise and become too expensive for overseas buyers. At the same time, foreign products would become more competitive, and the balance of payments would become worse. Next would come a loss of gold and the need to deflate, and the cycle would be repeated.

There are several reasons that the gold standard could not function well over the long run. One problem involved the price-specie-flow mechanism. For this mechanism to function effectively, certain "rules of the game" that govern the operation of an idealized international gold standard must be adhered to.[8] One rule is that the currencies must be valued in terms of gold. Another rule is that the flow of gold between countries cannot be restricted. The last rule requires the issuance of notes in some fixed relationship to a country's gold holdings. Such rules, however, require nations' willingness to place balance-of-payments and foreign exchange considerations above domestic policy goals, and this assumption is at best unrealistic. Thus, the operation of the gold standard was not as automatic or mechanical as the price-specie-flow mechanism might lead one to believe.

Because gold is a scarce commodity, gold volume could not grow fast enough to allow adequate amounts of money to be created (printed) to finance the growth of world trade. The problem was further aggravated by gold being taken out of reserve for art and industrial consumption, not to mention the desire of many people to own gold. The banning of gold hoarding and public exporting of gold bullion by President Franklin Roosevelt was not sufficient to remedy the problem.

Another problem of the system was the unrealistic expectation that countries would subordinate their national economies to the dictates of gold as well as to external and monetary conditions. In other words, a country with high inflation and/or trade deficit was required to reduce its money supply and consumption, resulting in recession and unemployment. This was a strict discipline that many nations could not force upon themselves or their population. Instead of having sufficient courage to use unemployment to discourage imports, importing countries simply insisted on intervention through tariffs and devaluations instead. Nations insisted on their rights to intervene and devalue domestic currencies in order to meet nationwide employment objectives. Because of the rigidity of the system, it was a matter of time before major countries decided to abandon the gold standard, starting with the

United Kingdom in 1931 in the midst of a worldwide recession. With a 12 percent unemployment rate at the time, the United Kingdom chose to leave the gold standard rather than exacerbate the unemployment problem. Monetary chaos followed in many countries.

Par Value (Adjustable Peg)

The need to restructure the international monetary system after World War II was the incentive for the delegates of forty-four countries to meet at Bretton Woods, New Hampshire, in 1944. The result of the meeting was the creation of the World Bank to finance development projects and the International Monetary Fund to promote monetary stability while facilitating world trade expansion. The IMF system, also known as the par value, adjustable, or Bretton Woods system, was created to overcome the problems associated with the gold standard. The inadequacy of gold as an international currency was overcome by turning to the U.S. dollar. As the other international currency, the dollar provides added reserves for stability as well as liquidity for gold and currencies.

The IMF required a fixed exchange ratio or par value. The agreement fixed the world's paper currencies in relation to the U.S. dollar, which was fully convertible into gold. Regarding the dollar as the acceptable store of value, countries were willing to receive it in settlement for international balances. Based on policies designed to avoid disruptive fluctuations and rate rigidity, members had to establish a par value for their currency, either directly in terms of gold or indirectly by relating the par value to the gold content of the U.S. dollar (within a margin of 1 percent on either side of parity). The IMF prohibits any unauthorized use of multiple exchange rates. Its policy is shown in Exhibit 19–3.

A correction of the par of exchange was possible in the case of a fundamental disequilibrium. The IMF was required to concur with a change from the initial par value through a cumulative amount of up to 10 percent. Any change in par value beyond this amount required the IMF's approval. However, there was difficulty in determining (1) when a fundamental disequilibrium existed, (2) whether the currency was over- or undervalued, and (3) the extent of the overvaluation or undervaluation.

To discourage speculation, the change in par value was kept infrequent, resulting in a late adjustment. Also, during a crisis, there was no time for mutual consultations as called for by the IMF's Articles of Agreement. In fact, mere rumors of pending consultations would probably be more than enough to encourage intense speculation. For instance, if the dollar sank in value to its lower limit but was not allowed to go further, no one would want to buy it at that point because its value was being kept artificially high. Its high price did not reflect its actual lower value. Speculators, knowing that devaluation had to follow soon and that the dollar had nowhere to go but down once devaluation took effect, would sell dollars first before buying them back at a new lower rate or price. With only sellers and no buyers, the resulting panic could force the financial markets to close.

One more problem with the par value system was the burden it placed on the dollar. The constant requirements for more and more dollars to finance the ever-expanding trade volume made foreign central banks and private holders nervous,

---

APPENDIX D. POLICY ON MULTIPLE CURRENCY PRACTICES*

The Executive Board has reviewed the Fund's policy with respect to multiple currency practices. The Fund shall be guided by the approach outlined in the conclusions set forth below.

1. Official action should not cause exchange rate spreads and cross rate quotations to differ unreasonably from those that arise from the normal commercial costs and risks of exchange transactions.

    a.   (i)   Action by a member or its fiscal agencies that of itself gives rise to a spread of more than 2 percent between buying and selling rates for spot exchange transactions between the member's currency and any other member's currency would be considered a multiple currency practice and would require the prior approval of the Fund.

        (ii)   An exchange spread that arises without official action would not give rise to a multiple currency practice.

        (iii)   Deviations between the buying and selling rates for spot transactions and for other transactions would not be considered multiple currency practices if they represent the additional costs and exchange risks for these other transactions.

    b.   Action by a member or its fiscal agencies which results in midpoint spot agency rates of other members' currency against its own currency in a relationship which differs by more than 1 percent from the midpoint spot exchange rates for these currencies in their principal markets would give rise to a multiple currency practice. If the differentials of more than 1 percent in these cross rates persist for more than one week, the resulting multiple currency practice would become subject to the approval of the Fund under Article VIII, Section 3.

        When difficulties are encountered in the interpretation and application of these criteria in specific cases, particularly concerning the nature of official actions, the staff will present the relevant information to the Executive Board for its determination.

2. The policy of the Fund on the exercise of its approval jurisdiction over exchange measures subject to Article VIII, as set forth in paragraph 2 of Executive Board Decision No. 1034-(60/27), adopted June 1, 1960, remains broadly appropriate. In accordance with this policy, the Fund will be prepared to grant approval of multiple currency practices introduced or maintained for

---

weakening their confidence in the dollar and heightening speculation. After starting strong, the dollar ended up being weak and unwanted, just as predicted by Gresham's law: Bad money drives out good money.

An analogy can be used to explain this problem. A man of wealth and reputation is able to obtain credit to buy anything he desires. But as he begins to overextend himself or as he prints his own money, the confidence of creditors in him and his money would severely erode. This analogy may serve to explain why Japan does not want its yen to become a reserve currency.

The consequent lack of confidence in the U.S. dollar drove creditors to turn to gold once again as an alternative. As the gold price rose, a gold pool was created in 1961 to stabilize its market price. When the pool sold gold to bring its price down, it had a negative impact on the dollar because 59 percent of the pool was a contribution of the United States. As the U.S. gold reserve shrank from $24 billion to $12 billion in 1970, the gold price remained stubbornly high, and confidence in the dollar further eroded. The pool was finally dissolved, and a two-tier gold price came into being.

balance of payments reasons provided the member represents and the Fund is satisfied that the measures are temporary and are being applied while the member is endeavoring to eliminate its balance of payments problems, and provided they do not give the member an unfair competitive advantage over other members or discriminate among members. The Fund will continue to be very reluctant to grant approval for the maintenance of broken cross exchange rates.

3. In accordance with the Fund's policy on complex multiple currency practices, as stated in Executive Board Decision No. 649-(57/33), adopted June 26, 1957, the Fund will not approve multiple currency practices under complex multiple rate systems unless the countries maintaining them are making reasonable progress toward simplification and ultimate elimination of such systems, or are taking measures or adopting programs which seem likely to result in such progress.

4. While urging members to apply alternative policies not connected with the exchange system, the Fund will be prepared to grant temporary approval of multiple currency practices introduced or maintained principally for non-balance of payments reasons, provided that such practices do not materially impede the member's balance of payments adjustment, do not harm the interests of other members, and do not discriminate among members.

5. To assist the Executive Board in reaching a decision concerning approval or nonapproval of a multiple currency practice subject to approval under Article VIII, Section 3, the reasons underlying the practice and its effects will be analyzed in reports on Article IV consultations or in other staff papers dealing with exchange systems. In all cases, consistent with the cycle of consultations under Article IV, approval will be granted for periods of approximately one year, in order to provide for a continual review by the Executive Board.

Decision No. 6790-(81/43)
March 20, 1981

EXHIBIT 19–3   IMF policy

Executive Board Decision No. 6790-(81/43), March 20, 1981, Selected Decisions of the International Monetary Fund and Selected Documents. Ninth Issue (Washington, 1981), pp. 225-27.
Source: Joseph Gold, *SDRs, Currencies, and Gold: Sixth Survey of New Legal Developments* (Washington, D.C.: International Monetary Fund, 1983), 107–8. Reprinted with permission of the International Monetary Fund

That is, central banks agreed to continue to buy and sell gold at the official price of $35 an ounce, but the free market price was allowed to seek its own level.

To many people, the adjustable peg lacks the certainty of the gold system as well as the flexibility of the floating system. In spite of the periodic growth in world trade, low inflation, and low interest rates under the IMF system, the problems created for the dollar were so great that President Richard Nixon finally severed the link between the dollar and gold in August 1971, thus ending the Bretton Woods international monetary system. Citizens of the United States were once again allowed to own or trade gold on December 31, 1974, and the dollar was permitted to float to seek its own value.

Crawling Peg (Sliding or Gliding Parity)

A cross between a fixed-rate system and a fully flexible system are the semifixed systems such as the crawling peg and the wide band. They differ from fixed rates because of their greater flexibility in terms of the exchange-rate movement. But they are not a floating system either because there is still a limit with regard to how far the exchange rate can move.

Because the infrequent adjustment of the IMF's par value system necessitated a large devaluation at a later date, the crawling peg rate was developed. The idea is to adjust the rate slowly by small amounts at any point in time on a continuous basis to correct for any overvaluation and undervaluation. The continuous but small adjustment mechanism (e.g., as little as 0.5 percent a month or 6 percent for the whole year) was designed to discourage speculation by setting an upper limit that speculators could gain from devaluation in one year.

The crawling peg system requires countries to have ample reserves for the prolonged process of adjustment, Also, the minor adjustments may not correct the currency's overvaluation or undervaluation. Consider the case of Brazil, which has been employing a form of a crawling peg to remedy its hyperinflation problem by devaluing its currency (cruzeiro) by a few percentage points each month. Usually, the devaluation of 2 percent each week takes place on Thursdays, as if it were some kind of a supermarket special. But even this annual adjustment total of more than 100 percent is not enough, and from time to time the 2 percent minidevaluations must be supplemented by a maxidevaluation. In December of 1979 and February of 1983, for example, Brazil suddenly chopped the value of the cruzeiro by 30 percent and 24 percent, respectively. Similarly, Mexico has devalued the peso at a controlled rate that proved too small to reflect the peso's proper value. In the first part of 1985 the peso lost more than 85 percent of its value against the dollar on the free market. In contrast to the official rate of 245 pesos to the dollar, the free market exchange houses charged 325 pesos, and the rates at the border were even higher. Considering that just a few years earlier the exchange rate was less than 100 pesos to the dollar, it might at first seem that the extent of the devaluation was dramatic. However, it was not enough. In mid-1986 the peso plunged a great deal more, resulting in each U.S. dollar fetching more than 700 pesos. Near the end of 1987, the peso lost as much as 59 percent in value in just a few days and ended the year at the rate of 2,200 pesos to a U.S. dollar. Such large devaluations are exactly what speculators wait for.

Wide Band

The purpose of the wide band is to compensate for the rigidity of the fixed rate systems. Similar to and yet different from the adjustable peg system, the wide band allows the currency value to fluctuate, say, 5 percent on each side of the par. Not primarily dedicated to exchange-rate changes, this system uses the more flexible movement to warn speculators of the more adverse consequences when their guess about the direction of the exchange rate proves to be wrong.

A group of European nations has been employing a particular form of the wide band. Exchange rate gyrations since the abolition of fixed rates created a special problem for European countries because of their dependence on trade within the bloc. The "snake" was thus created as a less formal system of stable but floating rates among their currencies. With the goal toward exchange-rate stability as well as unity and cooperation, West Germany, Benelux, and the Scandinavian countries in April of 1972 entered into a European Joint Float agreement known as the *snake*. The snake, as a system of stable but floating rates, is a currency band that links these countries' currencies, and their values are fixed against one another in a narrow band of 2.25 percent above and below the par values. The 4.5 percent limit for the joint twists of the snake, known as the "tunnel," provided this European monetary arrangement with the name of the "snake in the tunnel."

The snake was plagued with so many problems that it was difficult for it to achieve its goal. It was unable to protect the members' currencies from the dollar slump in the late 1970s. Currencies were forced out of the snake by divergent economic conditions in the member countries, recurring market pressures, and member countries' pursuit of independent objectives based on their economic policies. Devaluations and revaluations became a necessity.

To pursue the elusive goal of exchange-rate stability, the snake was subsequently replaced by the stronger and more elaborate European Monetary System (EMS). Italy elected to join the EMS in order to gain financial aid from West Germany and to impose more economic discipline, despite the risk of the government's being toppled by workers who were afraid of having to give up wage gains.

The EMS incorporates certain features in order to force member countries to make adjustments to correct their divergent economic conditions.[9] As a miniature-Bretton Woods system, the EMS employs the so-called grid parity system to link the members' currencies so tightly that they almost become a single currency. Like the snake, the EMS has a fixed exchange rate among members, and the participating currencies can fluctuate by up to 2.25 percent on either side of their bilateral "central rates" against other members, with the exception of the volatile lira's 6 percent fluctuation on either side. As the system's key currency, the strong mark was tightly bound to other currencies through government intervention. For this purpose, a common pool of money—the European Monetary Cooperation Fund (EMCF)—with gold accounting for 20 percent of the reserve backing was set up and is funded by governments in order to maintain parities. In this regard, the EMS with some $32 billion in dollars, gold, and the members' currencies in the pool, is like the pool of the IMF, and the EMCF has the potential of becoming the IMF's competitor. Exhibits 19–4 and 19–5 discuss the EMS in terms of its background and operation.

The EMS created a currency bloc known as the **European currency unit (ECU)** to provide a substitute as well as a complement to the U.S. dollar. The ECU is a composite of several national currencies. The weights for each currency are based on the relative GNP of each country and each country's share in intra-European trade. The weights are examined every five years or if the relative value of any currency changes by 25 percent.

Generally speaking, the ECU is worth about $1.30 (up from $0.85 in the 1980s). Originally used only for official settlements between central banks, the ECU has gained acceptance to the point that the private market offers depositors checking accounts denominated in ECU.

The ECU's role as an alternative currency for trade has been expanding. In 1988 the United Kingdom began selling large quantities of short-term government debt denominated in ECUs to replace some of the dollars it held as foreign exchange reserves. The former Soviet Union paid in ECUs for imports from Italy, France, Sweden, and Britain. Being used solely for settling international accounts, the ECU name does

Building on the European Coal and Steel Community formed in 1952, the Treaty of Rome of 1957 established the European Economic Community (EEC) and associated organizations, forming the European Communities (EC). The original EEC treaty did not contain policy commitments in the monetary or exchange-rate areas (the Bretton Woods system of fixed but adjustable par values was in effect at the time).

In the late 1960s, the stability of the international monetary system weakened. Among economies as intensely interwoven as those of the six EC countries at that time, reasonably stable exchange-rate relationships were essential. In December 1969 EC heads of state decided to pursue full monetary union. The Werner Plan, which studied the feasibility of this, was presented in 1970. It envisaged intra-EC exchange rates subject to gradually narrowing margins of fluctuation, with obligatory intervention at the margins. Within ten years, the Plan projected fixed intra-EC exchange rates, closely coordinated monetary policy supervised by a common monetary institution, and fully liberalized capital movements.

The Werner Plan was adopted by the EC Council of Ministers in early 1971. Soon, however, international monetary tensions led to the abandonment of the monetary union project. Instead, the European common margins arrangement (the snake) became operational in May 1972, with the six EC members and four other European countries participating. The reciprocal margins constituted obligatory intervention points, and the participants' central banks agreed to a system of unlimited, short-term financing of interventions. The operation of the arrangement was hampered by the new global uncertainties and the large oil shock of 1973–74. Inflation rates rose and grew more divergent. Several participants left the snake, some almost at its inception; only the Federal Republic of Germany and the Benelux countries (Belgium, the Netherlands, and Luxembourg) participated continuously in the arrangement.

At the 1978 EC summits in Copenhagen and Bremen, interest in monetary cooperation was revitalized with the creation of the European Monetary System (EMS). The goal was a European zone of exchange-rate stability through a lasting and effective system of close monetary policy cooperation. The main features of the system were established by the European Council and the EC Council of Ministers in December 1978. Following agreement among the participating central banks on the central rate grid (adjustable only by joint decision), fluctuation margins, rules for intervention, a short-term financing mechanism, and a new, basket-type European currency unit (ECU), the EMS and its Exchange Rate Mechanism (ERM) became operational in March 1979. The nine EC members all joined the EMS and all but the United Kingdom participated in the ERM. Later Greece, Portugal, and Spain, having acceded into the EC, joined the EMS, but like the United Kingdom, they stayed out of the ERM: on June 19, 1989, Spain became a participant in the ERM. There have been eleven exchange-rate realignments, most recently in January 1987.

The ECU serves as the numéraire (the legal tender) of the ERM; intervention-related credit operations can be settled in ECUs; and the finances of the EC, the European Investment Bank, and so forth, are denominated in ECUs. But the central banks participating in the ERM have preferred to intervene intra-marginally, using mainly balances of each other's currencies or U.S. dollars, so that the need for ECU balances has been less than expected.

In 1989 the EMS attained its tenth anniversary. The System has been anchored in practice in the deutsche mark, the strongest of the participating currencies—a development that had also characterized the snake in the 1970s. By fostering stability-oriented monetary convergence, the EMS has helped secure increasingly stable exchange rates within the ERM, thereby creating both favorable conditions for and renewed interest in further European monetary and economic integration.

EXHIBIT 19–4 Background to European monetary integration

Source: *IMF Survey,* 10 July 1989, 220

The institutional arrangements of the European Monetary System (EMS) include an exchange-rate mechanism with rules of intervention, a currency basket (the European Currency Unit, or ECU), and several credit facilities.

Exchange Rate Mechanism. The EMS is based on an exchange-rate mechanism (ERM) of fixed, though adjustable, exchange rates. The countries participating in the ERM are Belgium, Luxembourg, Denmark, France, Germany, Ireland, Italy, the Netherlands, and Spain. Each participating country has a central rate relative to the ECU. A grid of bilateral central rates with margins of plus or minus 2.25 percent (6 percent for Italy and Spain) has been established. At these margins, countries are obliged to intervene in unlimited amounts.

When a currency crosses a "threshold of divergence," a presumption arises that corrective measures will be taken, such as exchange market intervention or domestic policy responses. Thresholds are set at 75 percent of the maximum divergence spread and are set on the basis of a divergence indicator, which supplements the grid of bilateral central rates and fluctuation margins. The divergence indicator measures the position of each currency against the weighted average movement of the currencies included in the ECU basket. Realignment of some or all central rate relationships is permitted when ERM members and the Commission of European Communities determine that fundamental divergences

in economic performance of the members concerned have led to the emergence of sustained exchange-rate tensions.

ECU. The ECU is a basket of specified amounts of each currency in the EC, except for the Spanish peseta and the Portugese escudo. It serves as

- the *numéraire* of the EMS and of the ERM
- the reference point for the operation of the divergence indicator
- the unit of denomination for intervention debts and for credit ceilings
- a means of settlement of intervention debts among central banks

Credit Facilities. To facilitate compulsory intervention, ERM participants created a "very short-term financing facility" consisting of a reciprocal cash facility among their central banks. In addition, all EC members can use other credit facilities established before the EMS. The "short-term monetary support" is a quasi-automatic facility that provides short-term finance for temporary balance-of-payments deficits. Under the facility, each member is assigned a creditor quota that determines the extent of support it is expected to provide and a debtor quota that specifies the amount of assistance it can obtain. A "medium-term financial support" facility is also available for balance-of-payments assistance, but the use of its resources is conditional.

EXHIBIT 19–5   How the European monetary system works

Source: IMF Survey, 11 December 1989, 375

not appear on bank notes even though a new European Central Bank could issue real ECUs by 1997. According to Britain's Imperial Chemical Industries PLC, it could save $100 million a year or 1 percent of its annual European sales. European businesses, likewise, may be able to save $15 billion a year on foreign exchange commissions and currency hedging costs.[10]

One can easily see that the EMS is essentially the IMF's adjustable peg system, except that the EMS contains a wider band for exchange rate movement. One may wonder whether the EMS can accomplish what the IMF system was unable to accomplish. Whether it is a success or a failure depends on how one subjectively perceives the eleven exchange rate alignments that had occurred through 1987. Those who advocate the system are pleased that the system has been gaining popularity and that it has promoted stability, as the ECU has not fluctuated as wildly as some individual currencies. For advocates, eleven adjustments in this complex environment are not a large number. Others contend that eleven alignments are far too many, especially within such a short time after the EMS was organized in 1979. Furthermore, the problems associated with conventional fixed systems are apparently occurring again. Governments are not completely willing to give up their independent pursuit of reflationary or competitive devaluations. Belgium and Denmark, for example, rebelled against the strictures and sought devaluation at their trading partners' expense. The Belgian franc was devalued by 8.5 percent, and the Danish krone was devalued by 3 percent. Great Britain's refusal to support the round resulted in financial panic in 1992. Such actions could easily have provoked other members into competitive devaluations.

Under the wide band scheme, a country pursuing more inflationary policies will find the prices of its international goods going up, necessitating a depreciation program to correct the country's balance of payments in order to slow growth and curb inflation, while eventually risking recession. The country's exchange rate would then sink toward the floor under its par value. Once the fixed limit is reached (i.e., after hitting either the floor or ceiling), the country is back to the rigidity of the fixed rate all over again. Moreover, if a wide band is desirable because of the increase in flexibility, a country may be better off with no limit for movement at all.

Flexible (Floating) System

Under the fixed systems, excessive demand for gold developed and the United States was forced to suspend the sale of gold in 1968, except to official parties. But taking this action did not help, and by the late 1960s the dollar came under increasing pressure because of the prolonged and steep deterioration of the balance of payments. A crisis of confidence developed and foreigners' reluctance to hold dollars resulted in a change in the dollar's historic value. On August 15, 1971, the United States suspended the convertibility of the dollar into gold and other reserve assets altogether, and it floated the dollar to force a change in the parity as well as a review of the IMF. The subsequent Smithsonian Agreement resulted in a revaluation of other currencies and the devaluation of the dollar by 10.35 percent. In February of 1973, following a great deal of speculation against the dollar, the crisis renewed, and a second 10 percent devaluation followed. The crisis forced the official foreign exchange markets to close in Europe and Japan for about two and a half weeks. When these markets reopened, all major currencies were allowed to float.

After an initial period of remarkable stability, the dollar sank rapidly for seven weeks because of balance-of-payments deficits, Watergate revelations, renewed inflation in the United States, and a tightening of money abroad. Had the fixed systems been in effect, a traditional crisis would have resulted. Foreign exchange markets would have been closed, and large-scale adjustment of parities would have been necessary. With the dollar free to float, however, the beneficial effect was that speculative pressures were reflected in a sharp drop in the exchange value of the dollar without a closing of the market. The resultant devaluation, in turn, helped the United States to improve its trade performance.

In October of 1978 another crisis came along for the U.S. dollar. Concerns over inflation in the United States prompted a panic selling of the dollar, and the stock market plunged. In spite of the risk of recession, the Carter administration was forced to take drastic measures for several reasons: (1) the dollar decline reduced American consumers' purchasing power, (2) soaring prices hurt the anti-inflation program, (3) OPEC members' declining value of their dollar reserves encouraged them to boost oil prices, and (4) stock values lost more than $110 billion, resulting in a large-scale retrenchment of business investment plans. Among the measures taken were an increase in the Federal Reserve's discount rate, gold sale, and dollar buying. Initially, the magnitude of the action took the market by surprise. Gold prices dropped, and the bond market, stock market, and dollar all rose significantly. Yet by the end of the month, the strong anti-inflation policies themselves weakened the confidence in the government, and chaos ensued. Additional panic selling drove the dollar to record lows. Once again, by allowing the dollar to float, the traditional adverse consequences of market closings and official devaluation were averted.

Under a flexible or floating system, the market force, based on the demand and supply, determines a currency's value. A surplus in a country results in an appreciation of its currency, immediate higher prices, mass reserve, and opportunity costs. In addition, too much money on reserve leads to a loss of investment opportunities. On the other hand, a country's deficit will lower its currency value, making it easier to export more later.

In the absence of government intervention the float is said to be *clean*. It becomes *dirty* (i.e., managed) when there is a central bank intervention to influence exchange rates, which is a common action, especially by those with inflation and trade problems. A country experiencing inflation must reduce public spending and the money supply to cool its economy. But because of the delayed impact of devaluation on trade improvement, such restrictive measures need time to achieve their intended purpose before inflationary pressures work themselves back into the economy through higher import prices. The country must therefore continuously monitor and defend its currency over the time that the changes are taking effect.

Time is not the only reason, however, for government intervention. More often than not, the primary motive for intervention is to gain trade advantages so that a country can export its way out of a stalled economy. This deliberate and competitive devaluation can make the float quite "filthy." A weaker country, such as the United Kingdom, might exaggerate the value of its currency in order to make it fall beyond what is needed to compensate for inflation. In contrast, a strong country, such as Germany or Japan, usually prefers to intervene in order to retard appreciation of its currency in order to prevent the loss of its trade advantage.

Japan is often accused of buying dollars and selling yen—not to smooth out wild fluctuations in its currency but rather to keep the yen from appreciating. The result is an artificially favorable rate (i.e., overvalued dollar and undervalued yen). Some believe that Japan is able to manipulate the exchange rate so precisely that they can determine the desired exchange rate within a band of twenty yen. This effect is not achieved just by openly selling. The ministry of Finance and Bank of Japan also use other techniques. These two financial organizations hold discussions with banks and trading companies and instruct them on how to manage their money, whether to buy or sell the currency forward, and how to utilize their trade distribution systems for this purpose. Furthermore, the yen is also favorably affected by Japan's refusal to open up its capital markets and allow the yen to become a truly international reserve currency.

For importing countries, the objective of intervention is to keep a currency overvalued. Because of the political risk faced by increased unemployment, France and Italy are usually reluctant to apply strong domestic austerity measures. However, each is also unwilling to let its currency float freely to correct the problem. As a result, each intervenes periodically to break the spiraling circle of currency depreciation, higher import costs, higher inflation, and more currency depreciation. The former Soviet Union intervened in the past for another reason—profit. During a pending wheat deal, it dumped dollars so that those dollars could be bought back later at a lower rate of payment of the wheat purchase.

Interventions are unlikely to change a market trend. Central banks' combined resources are just not adequate to reverse a fundamental trend in the foreign exchange market. Consider the drastic measures taken by the United States in 1978 to rescue the dollar. Some of the actions taken were the following:

1. The activation of new lines of credit with foreign central banks for $15 billion worth of marks, francs, and yen to buy the dollar in the open market.
2. A sale of $2 billion of IMF SDRs to those central banks.
3. A temporary withdrawal of $3 billion worth of marks, francs, and yen from the U.S. reserve account at the IMF.
4. A sale in overseas markets of up to $10 billion worth of Treasury securities denominated in foreign currencies.
5. Additional gold sales.

Although the total amount seems mind-boggling, it should be noted that the turnover of money in New York alone on a single day is $40 billion. During the phenomenal rise of the dollar in the early 1980s, all experts and authorities agreed that the dollar was greatly overvalued, and yet nothing could be done to reverse the upward trend. The action of the G-5 countries (i.e., West Germany, France, Great Britain, Japan, and the United States) in the second half of 1985 succeeded in bringing down the value of the dollar only after the trend had already changed. Thus, the accusation concerning Japan's currency manipulation may not be totally justified. Subsequently, the drastic drop of the yen value from 265 yen per dollar to 120 yen in 1987 created significant trade problems for Japan, which stood by almost powerless. This plunge, however, probably vindicated Japan from the charge of currency manipulation.

EVALUATION OF FLOATING RATES

The fixed-rate and floating-rate systems have diverse natures and characteristics. Therefore, both of the systems cannot meet the same goals of certainty, stability, and inflation control. Advocates of the fixed-rate plan believe that the certainty and rigidity of exchange rates can promote economic efficiency, public confidence, and inflation control. In recent years, several U.S. public officials have been encouraging the return of some kind of gold standard. If this system could indeed work as intended, there would probably be no need to have more than one world currency.

Experience has shown that fixed rates do not work well for a prolonged period. Fixed rates were often said to have made for price stability from 1792 to 1971.[11] Actually, wholesale prices fluctuated quite widely throughout that period. The United Kingdom's wholesale price index is a good example. From the base of 100 in 1930, the index increased to 162 in 1946, 406 in 1956, 507 in 1966, and 1248 in 1976.[12] If inflation seemed to be controlled when the link between a currency and gold was restored, the effect took place only at the time of the action and was, at best, temporary.[13] Also, for fixed rates to work, the gold price must remain fixed to control inflation—a difficult if not impossible requirement.

Other problems associated with fixed rates include massive capital flows during a crisis and the closing of financial markets. According to Morgan Guaranty, between 1976 and 1985 citizens of Mexico and Venezuela sent $53 billion and $30 billion, respectively, out of their countries. Also, it is unrealistic to believe that the United States wants its money supply to be backed by gold and to be at the mercy of major gold producers such as South Africa.

If fixed rates were effective once, they are not now. As noted in an IMF publication, "The par value system and its adjustment mechanism appeared to be working well during the second decade of the Fund's operations. This was due mainly to high levels of employment and low and fairly uniform rates of inflation among the industrial countries, the willingness of members whose payments positions were strengthening during the period to accumulate U.S. dollars, and the ready adoption by countries of domestic measures to correct disequilibrium in their balance of payments."[14] Most, if not all, of the necessary conditions no longer exist today.

Critics of floating exchange rates contend that the system causes uncertainty, which discourages trade while promoting speculation. Actually, since 1973 the exchange markets have clearly demonstrated their resilience and their ability to maintain appropriate rates of exchange. As concluded in a study conducted by the IMF, "Exchange rate volatility since the early 1970s does not appear to have impeded world trade."[15] In fact, world exports climbed steadily for eight years after the float was put in place, and it is apparent that the system does not interfere with world exports.

The claim that uncertainty encourages investors to speculate and destabilize exchange rates is probably invalid. The fixed-rate system is more likely to encourage speculation by giving speculators a one-way, no-lose bet to make money, as the exchange rate can only move in one direction once the upper limit is reached. Whatever the fault of the floating rates, the fixed-rate regime is subject to the same fault, probably to a greater magnitude.

Because of a lack of the inherent discipline imposed by fixed rates, floating currencies are said to encourage inflation. In reality, the flexible-rate system makes the consequences of inflationary policies more readily apparent to the general public, labor, and employers in the form of a declining foreign value of the currency and an upward trend in domestic prices. This public awareness makes it easier to implement proper policies to correct the situation without reacting in a crisis atmosphere, as otherwise might occur. These countries are then able to pursue the mixture of unemployment and price objectives that they prefer and that are consistent with international equilibrium.

Member nations of the IMF can select from a number of exchange arrangements, including (1) joint floating, (2) independent floating, and (3) pegging to another currency, SDR, or a self-selected basket of currencies. From among these alternatives, exchange arrangements adopted by IMF members vary according to their perceived needs, as shown in Table 19–1. The exchange rates of various currencies are shown in Table 19–2. Exhibit 19–6 shows the movement of the exchange-rate indices of the five major currencies, and it should be noted that the rates did move under both the fixed and floating systems.

The floating system should be accepted with reservation. One problem occurs because of a high degree of short-term volatility and the large medium-term swings in exchange rates. Also, floating rates do not work well during recessions or through a faltering economic recovery. The float may exacerbate inflationary problems by quickly feeding higher import costs into local wages and prices. When Mexico devalued its peso in 1976, labor unions won a 23 percent wage increase, which only served to force the government to make a second devaluation just two months later.

The various exchange options have been studied by the Group of 10. The Group of 10 comprises Belgium, Canada, France, Germany, Italy, Japan, the Netherlands, Sweden, the United Kingdom, and the United States (Switzerland became an 11th member in 1983). The Group, though not a part of the IMF's formal structure, is linked informally with the IMF through (1) the General Arrangements to Borrow (GAB), (2) the nature of the issues with which the Group deals, and (3) the role the Group's members play in IMF policy decisions.

At a Tokyo meeting held on June 21, 1985, the Group of 10 announced the following conclusion: "A return to a generalized system of fixed parities is unrealistic at the present time" in this difficult and complex global environment. As explained by the finance ministers and central bank governors of these major industrial countries, "the existing exchange rate regime has shown valuable strengths. Exchange rate flexibility has made a positive contribution to external payments adjustment and to the maintenance of an open trade and payments system in a period of massive external shocks. It can help countries, especially the larger ones, to insulate their domestic price levels from inflation abroad, and can facilitate the pursuit of sound monetary policies geared more directly to domestic conditions. Furthermore, it is questionable whether any less flexible system would have survived the strains of the past decade."[16]

In spite of some limitations, the floating system was able to carry the world through the 1973–74 oil crisis smoothly. Since then, the floating system has proven itself through several periods of raging inflation, deep recession, and massive money movements from oil-consuming countries to oil producers. Many observers continue to find fault with it, but other systems have just as much, if not more, of the same flaws. At present, there does not appear to be a superior alternative that can be used.

TABLE 19–1 Exchange Rate Arrangements (June 1, 1984)[a]

Currency pegged to					Flexibility Limited in Terms of a Single Currency or Group of Currencies		More Flexible		
U.S. dollar	French franc	Other currency	SDR	Other composite[b]	Single currency[c]	Cooperative arrangements[d]	Adjusted according to a set of indicators[e]	Other managed floating	Independently floating
Antigua & Barbuda Bahamas Barbados Belize Bolivia Djibouti Dominica Dominican Rep. Egypt El Salvador Ethiopia Grenada Guatemala Haiti Honduras Iraq Lao P.D. Rep. Liberia Libya Nicaragua Oman Panama Paraguay St. Lucia St. Vincent Sierra Leone Sudan Suriname Syrian Arab Rep. Trinidad & Tobago Venezuela Yemen Arab Rep. Yemen, P.D. Rep.	Benin Cameroon C. African Rep. Chad Comoros Congo Gabon Ivory Coast Mali Niger Senegal Togo Upper Volta	Bhutan (Indian rupee) Equatorial Guinea (Spanish peseta) Gambia (pound sterling) Lesotho (South African rand) Swaziland (South African rand)	Burma Burundi Guinea Iran Jordan Kenya Rwanda Sao Tome & Principe Seychelles Vanuatu Vietnam	Algeria Austria Bangladesh Botswana Cape Verde China Cyprus Fiji Finland Hungary Kuwait Madagascar Malawi Malaysia Malta Mauritania Mauritius Nepal Norway Papua New Guinea Romania Singapore Solomon Islands Sweden Tanzania Tunisia Zambia Zimbabwe	Afghanistan Bahrain Ghana Guyana Maldives Qatar Saudi Arabia Thailand United Arab Emirates	Belgium Denmark France Germany Ireland Italy Luxembourg Netherlands	Brazil Chile Colombia Peru Portugal Somalia	Argentina Costa Rica Ecuador Greece Guinea-Bissau Iceland India Indonesia Israel Jamaica Korea Mexico Morocco New Zealand Nigeria Pakistan Philippines Spain Sri Lanka Turkey Uganda Western Samoa Yugoslavia Zaire	Australia Canada Japan Lebanon South Africa United Kingdom United States Uruguay

[a] Excluding the currency of Democratic Kampuchea, for which no current information is available. For members with dual or multiple exchange markets, the arrangement shown is that in the major market.

[b] Comprises currencies which are pegged to various "baskets" of currencies of the members' own choice, as distinct from the SDR basket.

[c] Exchange rates of all currencies have shown limited flexibility in terms of the U.S. dollar.

[d] Refers to the cooperative arrangement maintained under the European Monetary System.

[e] Includes exchange arrangements under which the exchange rate is adjusted at relatively frequent intervals, on the basis of indicators determined by the respective member of countries.

Source: The International Monetary Fund: Its Evolution, Organization, and Activities, pamphlet series, no. 37, 4th ed. (Washington, D.C.: International Monetary Fund, 1984), 76–77. Reprinted with permission of the International Monetary Fund.

TABLE 19–2 Exchange rates and exchange arrangements, March 31, 1992

Member (Currency)	Exchange Rate Pegged to[1]	Exchange Rate[1]	Exchange Rate Otherwise Determined[2,3]
Afghanistan (afghani)[2,16]	bskt		
Albania (lek)[4,16,20]	bskt	22.3508	
Algeria (dinar)[16]	$		
Angola (kwanza)[16]	$		
Antigua & Barbuda (EC$)[5]	$	2.70	
Argentina (austral)[16]	$	0.9925	
Australia (dollar)			1.3014
Austria (schilling)	bskt	11.556	
Bahamas (dollar)[7]	$	1.00	1.63597
Bahrain (dinar)[6]			0.376
Bangladesh (taka)	bskt	39.00	
Barbados (dollar)	$	2.0113	
Belgium (franc)[7]			33.79
Belize (dollar)	$	2.00	
Benin (franc)	F	50.00	
Bhutan (ngultrum)	Re	1.00	
Bolivia (boliviano)			3.8050
Botswana (pula)	bskt	2.1650	
Brazil (cruzeiro)[4]			1969.00
Bulgaria (lev)[4,6]			
Burkina Faso (franc)	F	50.00	
Burundi (franc)	SDR	273.07	199.30
Cameroon (franc)	F	50.00	
Canada (dollar)			1.1899
Cape Verde (escudo)	bskt	71.2450	
Central African Republic (franc)	F	50.00	
Chad (franc)	F	50.00	
Costa Rica (colón)	$		133.008
Cyprus (pound)[5]	bskt	0.466179	
Czechoslovakia (koruna)	bskt	29.03	
Denmark (krone)[7]	bskt		6.3725
Djibouti (franc)	$	177.721	
Dominica (EC$)[6]	$	2.70	
Dominican Rep.			12.96
Ecuador (sucre)[4]			1316.54
Egypt (pound)			3.31919
El Salvador (colón)[4]			8.17
Equatorial Guinea (franc)	F	50.00	
Ethiopia (birr)[4]	$	2.07	
Fiji (dollar)	bskt	1.49723	
Finland (markka)[11]	bskt	4.483	
France (franc)[7]			5.5675
Gabon (franc)	F	50.00	
Gambia (dalasi)			8.74891
Germany (deutsche mark)[7]			1.6427
Ghana (cedi)[4,16]			
Greece (drachma)			190.70
Grenada (EC$)[5]	$	2.70	
Guatemala (quetzal)			5.08446
Guinea (franc)			890.295
Guinea-Bissau (peso)[16]			
Guyana (dollar)			124.00
Haiti (gourde)[16]	$		
Honduras (lempira)			5.40
Hungary (forint)	bskt	80.02	
Iceland (króna)[4,10]	bskt	59.19	
India (rupee)[4]			25.89
Indonesia (rupiah)			2017.00
Iran (rial)[4]	SDR	92.30	67.2868
Iraq (dinar)[4]	$	0.310857	
Ireland (pound)[7]			0.616637
Israel (new sheqel)[13]	bskt	2.4040	
Italy (lira)[7]			1238.95
Ivory Coast	F	50.00	
Jamaica (dollar)			27.2672
Japan (yen)			133.20

TABLE 19-2 (continued)

Member (Currency)	Exchange Rate Pegged to[1]	Exchange Rate[1]	Exchange Rate Otherwise Determined[2,3]
Jordan (dinar)[4]	bskt	0.687995	
Kenya (shilling)[4]	bskt	30.0257	
Kiribati (dollar)[18]	A$	1.00	
Korea (won)			775.10
Kuwait (dinar)	bskt	0.29475	
Lao People's Dem. Rep. (kip)			717.00
Lebanon (pound)			1280.00
Lesotho (loti)[4]	R	1.00	
Liberia (dollar)[1]	$	1.00	
Libya (dinar)[19]	SDR	0.396429	0.289001
Luxembourg (franc)[7]			33.79
Madagascar (franc)[8]			1929.25
Malawi (kwacha)	bskt	3.3190	
Malaysia (ringgit)[12]	bskt	2.5847	
Maldives (rufiyaa)			9.91
Mali (franc)	F	50.00	
Malta (lira)	bskt	3.0914	
Mauritania (ouguiya)			81.740
Mauritius (rupee)	bskt	15.9611	
Mexico (peso)			3083.50
Morocco (dirham)[11]	bskt	8.8363	
Mongolia (tugrik)[4,16]			
Mozambique (metical)[8,4]			2153.66
Myanmar (kyat)	SDR	8.50847	6.2718
Namibia (rand)[4]			
Nepal (rupee)[4]	bskt	42.70	
Netherlands (guilder)[7]			1.8489
New Zealand (dollar)			1.82582
Nicaragua (new córdoba)[4]			25,000.00
Niger (franc)	F	50.00	
Nigeria (naira)[4,16]			
Norway (krone)[15]	bskt	6.4462	
Oman (rial Omani)	$	0.3845	
Pakistan (rupee)			25.0425
Panama (balboa)[4]	$	1.00	
Papua New Guinea (kina)[8]	bskt	0.95675	
Paraguay (guarani)[12]			1446.50
Peru (inti)[1]			0.96
Philippines (peso)			25.3830
Poland (zloty)			13,497.00
Portugal (escudo)			141.607
Qatar (riyal)[6]			3.64
Romania (leu)			198.00
Rwanda (franc)	SDR	171.18	124.930
St. Kitts & Nevis (EC$)[5]	$	2.70	
St. Lucia (EC$)[5]	$	2.70	
St. Vincent (EC$)[5]	$	2.70	
Sao Tome & Principe (dobra)			300.45
Saudi Arabia (riyal)[6]			3.745
Senegal (franc)	F	50.00	
Seychelles (rupee)[7]	SDR	7.2345	5.2800
Sierra Leone (leone)			476.19
Singapore (dollar)[4]	bskt	1.6605	
Solomon Islands (dollar)	bskt	2.87356	
Somalia (shilling)[4,16]			
South Africa (rand)[4]			2.87497
Spain (peseta)[7]			103.819
Sri Lanka (rupee)			43.25
Sudan (pound)			90.09
Suriname (guilder)	$	1.785	
Swaziland (lilangeni)	R	1.00	
Sweden (krona)[17]	bskt	5.977	
Syrian Arab Rep. (pound)[4]	$	11.225	
Tanzania (shilling)	bskt	290.00	
Thailand (baht)	bskt	25.60	
Togo (franc)	F	50.00	
Tonga (pa'anga)	bskt	1.3231	
Trinidad & Tobago (dollar)	$	4.260625	
Tunisia (dinar)			0.919250

TABLE 19–2 (continued)

Member (Currency)	Exchange Rate Pegged to[1]	Exchange Rate[1]	Exchange Rate Otherwise Determined[2,3]
Turkey (lira)[4]	bskt		6247.75
Uganda (shilling)[5]			1160.08
United Arab Emirates (dirham)[6]			3.671
United Kingdom (pound)[7]			0.574977
United States (dollar)			1.00
Uruguay (new peso)			2,774.00
Vanuatu (vatu)	bskt	111.83	
Venezuela (bolívar)[16]			65.05
Vietnam (dong)[16]	bskt	2.42307	
Western Samoa (tala)	bskt		
Yemen, Rep. of (rial)[16]	$		
(dinar)[16]	$		
Yugoslavia (dinar)[16]	DM	85	
Zaire (zaire)			142,312.42
Zambia (kwacha)[4,8]			133.690
Zimbabwe (dollar)	bskt	5.12558	

$	U.S. dollar	bskt	Currency basket other than SDR
F	French franc	Re	Indian rupee
R	South African rand	A$	Australian dollar
DM	Deutsche mark		

[1]Rates and arrangements as reported to the IMF and in terms of currency units per unit pegged to; rates determined by baskets of currencies are in currency units per U.S. dollar.

[2]Market rates in currency units per U.S. dollar.

[3]Under this heading are listed those members that describe their exchange rate arrangements as managed floating, floating independently, or as adjusting according to a set of indicators (see footnote 8), and certain other members whose exchange arrangements are not otherwise described in this table. In addition, U.S. dollar quotations are given for the currencies that are pegged to the SDR and for those that participate in the European Monetary System (see footnote 7)

[4]Member maintains exchange arrangements involving more than one exchange market. The arrangement shown is that maintained in the major market. A description of the member's exchange system as of December 31, 1990 is given in the *Annual Report on Exchange Arrangements and Exchange Restrictions, 1991.*

[5]East Caribbean dollar.

[6]Exchange rates are determined on the basis of a relationship to the SDR, within margins of ±7.25 percent. However, because of the maintenance of a relatively stable relationship with the U.S. dollar, these margins are not always observed.

[7]Belgium, Denmark, France, Germany, Ireland, Italy, Luxembourg, the Netherlands, Spain, and the United Kingdom are participating in the exchange rate and intervention mechanism of the European Monetary System and maintain maximum margins of 2.25 percent (in the case of the Spanish peseta and the pound sterling, 6 percent) for exchange rates in transactions in the official markets between their currencies and those of the other countries in this group.

[8]Exchange rates adjusted according to a set of indicators.

[9]Member maintains a system of advance announcements of exchange rates.

[10]The exchange rate is maintained within margins of ±10.0 percent on either side of a weighted composite of the currencies of the main trading partners.

[11]The exchange, which is pegged to the ECU, is maintained within margins of ±3.0 percent.

[12]The exchange rate is maintained within margins of ±2.25 percent.

[13]The exchange rate is maintained within margins of ±5.0 percent.

[14]Currency of Namibia is the South African rand, pending issuance of Namibia's own national currency.

[15]The exchange rate, which is pegged to the ECU, is maintained within margins of ±2.25 percent.

[16]Exchange rate data not available.

[17]The exchange rate which is pegged to the ECU is maintained within margins of ±1.5 percent.

[18]The currency of Kiribati is the Australian dollar.

[19]The exchange rate in maintained within margins of ±11.0 percent.

[20]The basic exchange rate of the lek is pegged to the ECU.

Data: IMF Treasurer's and Exchange and Trade Relations Departments

Source: IMF Survey, June 8, 1992, 185. Reprinted with permission of the International Monetary Fund.

Exchange rate indices of the five major currencies, 1970–85

1980 = 100

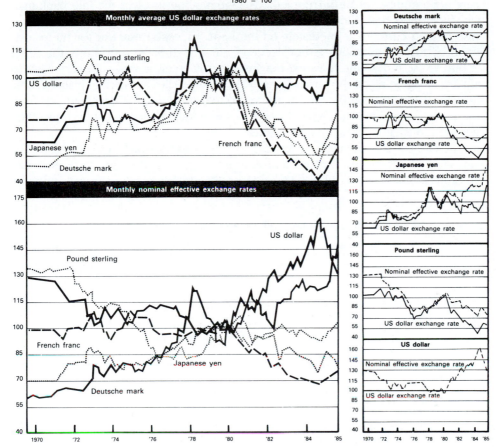

Source: IMF, *International Financial Statistics*

The two composite charts show, for each of the five currencies, monthly indices of the US dollar values of currencies and nominal effective exchange rates. Since these two indices are based on exchange rates expressed in terms of US dollars per unit of national currency, an upward movement indicates that the currency in question is appreciating while a downward movement indicates a depreciation.

The single currency charts present: (1) the monthly average US dollar value of the currency, expressed in terms of US dollars per unit of national currency, calculated relative to the currency's average values in the base year (*line ahx* in *International Financial*

Statistics); and (2) the nominal effective exchange rate (*IFS line amx*), which is a weighted index that combines the exchange rates between the currency in question and the currencies of 17 other industrial countries. The weights are derived from the Fund's multilateral exchange rate model (MERM) and each weight represents the model's estimate of the effect on the trade balance of the country in question of a 1 percent change in the domestic currency price of each of the other currencies. The weights, therefore, take account of the size and direction of trade flows as well as the relevant price elasticities and feedback effects of exchange rate changes on domestic costs and prices. The index is based on average market exchange rates in 1980.

EXHIBIT 19–6   Exchange rate indices of the five major currencies, 1970–85

Source: "World Economy in Transition," *Finance & Development* 23 (June 1986): 49

FINANCIAL IMPLICATIONS AND STRATEGIES

According to one study, there is a relationship between a written foreign exchange management policy and the relative size of foreign sales.[17] In practice, size is irrelevant because any prudent firm must manage foreign exchange risks. This section discusses the financial strategies to minimize exchange risks.

"Hedges protect yards from dogs and businesses from financial exposure."[18] There are a number of **hedging** methods. One method involves the interbank market, which offers both spot and forward transactions. An importer or buyer can purchase foreign currency immediately on the **spot** (or **cash**) **market** for future use. When the foreign exchange is not needed until sometime in the future, the seller (or buyer) can turn to the **forward market,** usually entering into a forward contract with a bank agreeing on the purchase and sale of currencies at a certain price at some future time. Smaller companies often have trouble obtaining forward contracts from their banks for two reasons. First, they are not well known. Second, their transaction sizes are too small to attract banks' interest.

Regardless of size, any company can use the **futures market** for hedging. The main difference between forward and futures contracts is the "standardized" sizes and delivery dates of the futures transactions. The standardization feature provides

TABLE 19–3   Comparison of the currency futures market with the interbank market

Characteristics	Futures Market	Spot and Forward Interbank Market
Size of Contract	Contract size is standardized in terms of currency amount.	Participants can trade any amount agreed upon between the buyer and seller. Contract size is tailored to individual needs.
Delivery Date	Standardized dates are used for all contract months, concentrating liquidity to produce maximum price competition.	Settlement of forward contracts can be at any date agreed upon between the buyer and seller. Delivery date is tailored to individual needs.
Method of Transaction	Trading is conducted in a competitive arena (on the exchange floor) by "open outcry" of bids, offers, and amounts.	Participants usually make two-sided markets (quoting two prices that indicate a willingness to buy at the lower price and sell at the higher price), for both spot and forward prices.
	Nonmember participants deal through brokers (Exchange members), who represent them on the trading floor.	Participants deal on a principal-to-principal basis, either directly or through brokers.
	Market participants usually are unknown to one another, except when a firm is trading its own account through its own brokers on the trading floor.	Participants in each transaction always know the other trading party
Accessibility	Participants include banks, corporations, financial institutions, individual investors and speculators. Qualified public speculation is encouraged. It is open to anyone who needs hedge facilities or has risk capital with which to speculate.	Participants are banks dealing with each other, and other major commercial entities. Access for individuals and smaller firms is limited. It is usually limited to very large customers who deal in foreign trade.
Commissions	A single, roundturn (in and out of the market) commission is charged. It is negotiated between broker and customer and is relatively small in relation to the value of the contract. Commissions are business expenses and generally are tax deductible.	No commission is charged if the transaction is made directly with another bank or customer. A commission is charged to both the buyer and seller, however, if transacted through a foreign exchange broker. The commission is set by "spread" between a bank's buy and sell price and is not easily determined by the customer. Commissions are business expenses and generally tax deductible.
Security Deposit	Margins (published small security deposit) are required of all participants.	Margins are not required by banks dealing with other banks, although for smaller, nonbank customers, margins or compensating bank balances may be required on certain occasions

market liquidity, making it easy to enter and exit the market at any time. But this same feature excludes the likelihood of meeting individual needs exactly. Table 19–3 lists the differences between these two hedging markets.

The most dominant futures market for foreign currencies is the International Monetary Market (IMM) division of Chicago Mercantile Exchange (CME) in Chicago (see Exhibit 19–7). On January 15, 1986, the ECU contract was added for trading (see Exhibit 19–8). These global commodities demand 24-hour attention. To meet this need, the LIFFE (London International Financial Futures Exchange) and the SIMEX (Singapore International Monetary Exchange), both patterned after the IMM, make 24-hour trading a reality. SIMEX is examined in Exhibit 19–9.

TABLE 19–3   *(continued)*

Characteristics	Futures Market	Spot and Forward Interbank Market
Clearing Operation (Financial Integrity)	The Exchange's Clearing House becomes the opposite side to each cleared transaction; therefore, demands of monitoring credit risk are substantially reduced.	Each counter party with whom a dealer does business must be examined individually as a risk, and credit limits set for each. As such, there may be a wide range of credit capabilities of participants. The handling of clearing operation is contingent on individual banks and brokers.
Marketplace	There is a central exchange floor with world-wide communications.	The market is over the telephone worldwide.
Economic Justification	The market facilitates world trade by providing a hedge mechanism. In addition, it provides a broader market and an alternative hedging mechanism via public participation.	The market facilitates world trade by providing a hedge mechanism.
Regulation	It is regulated under the Commodity Futures Trading Commission (April 1975).	It is self-regulating.
Frequency of Delivery	Theoretically, there should be no delivery in a perfect market. In reality, a small percentage (less than 1%) of all contracts traded results in actual delivery.	The majority (more than 90%) of trades results in delivery.
Price Fluctuations	Daily limit is imposed by the Exchange with a rule provision for expanded daily price limiits	There is no daily limit
Market Liquidity	There is public offset or arbitrage offset. All positions, whether long or short, can be liquidated easily.	Offsetting is with other banks. Forward positions are not easily offset or transferred to other participants.
Settlements	Settlements are made daily via the exchange's Clearing House. Gains on position values may be withdrawn and losses are collected daily.	Settlement takes place two days after the spot transaction (one day in the U.S. for the Canadian dollar and Mexican peso). For forward transaction, gains or losses are realized on the settlement date.
Price Quote	Prices are quoted in U.S. terms (dollar units per one foreign currency unit).	Prices are quoted in European terms (units of local currency to the dollar), except for British pounds, and some Commonwealth currencies.
Price Dissemination	Trading prices of currency futures are disseminated continuously by the Exchange.	Indicated bids and offers, as opposed to actual prices, are available throughout the Interbank market.

Source: Adapted from *Trading and Hedging on Currency Futures and Options* (Chicago: Chicago Mercantile Exchange, 1985), 19; and *Understanding Futures in Foreign Exchange* (Chicago: Chicago Mercantile Exchange, 1979), 6–7. Reprinted with permission of the Chicago Mercantile Exchange

Risk control for businesses that bruise easily.

When you ship $1.2 billion worth of bananas worldwide, a small flip in currency exchange rates could make a big difference in profits.

Chiquita, like many smart international companies, gets a good grip on those risks with currency options at the Chicago Mercantile Exchange. Hedging Deutschemarks, Pound Sterling and Yen, Chiquita has successfully guarded against financial bruising for years. And because 80% of all the exchange-traded currency worldwide was traded on the CME's International Monetary Market, they've found it easy to slip in and out of currency options quickly.

"The IMM is where all information that impacts foreign exchange prices comes together," says David Groelinger, Chiquita VP and Treasurer. "That's where the most efficient pricing takes place."

Even more efficient when Globex™ becomes available next summer. The new electronic system will operate after regular trading-hours, making it possible to trade around the world, around the clock.

If you're like the top bananas at Chiquita, and don't want your international earnings frittered away, the CME's currency futures and options should hold great appeal for you.

CHICAGO MERCANTILE EXCHANGE®
The Exchange of Ideas

1-800-331-3332 (US) 01-920-0722 (Europe) 03-595-2251 (Pacific)

EXHIBIT 19–7   Chicago Mercantile Exchange

Source: Courtesy of Chicago Mercantile Exchange

The CME's New ECU Futures: When Your Risk Is All Over the Map, Your Protection Should Be Too.

When you face exposure in more than one European currency, you need protection that covers a lot of ground. The European Currency Unit (ECU) futures contract at the Chicago Mercantile Exchange gives you the coverage you need. It's the newest addition to the currency-related futures contracts at the CME's International Monetary Market (IMM), where currency futures originated in 1972.

Here's how ECU futures can help you keep your foreign currency exposure—and even interest rate risk—within manageable boundaries.

ECU futures cover Europe 10 ways. The ECU is a unit of account whose price reflects the value and performance of 10 European Economic Community currencies, with the components weighted by the relative size of each country's economy. It is rapidly becoming a popular medium of exchange for European—and global—trade and finance transactions.

The free market determines the price at which the ECU trades against the dollar and other currencies, with the dollar price of the ECU approximating the total value of the dollar prices of the 10 individual components.

The ECU serves as a barometer of the value of European currencies. That means ECU futures can help you protect against—or take advantage of—changes in the performance of European currencies against currencies in other economic zones or against a single component currency.

Hedge currencies lacking futures and forwards. Because the CME's ECU futures contract is based on a basket of currencies, it has unique versatility. For instance, it offers the ideal hedge for many combinations of European currencies. No opinions on the relative strengths and weaknesses of individual currencies are required, and there's the added advantage of transaction cost savings.

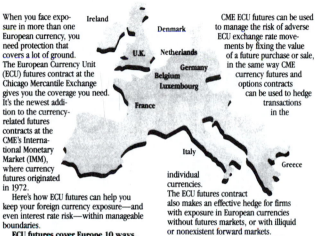

CME ECU futures can be used to manage the risk of adverse ECU exchange rate movements by fixing the value of a future purchase or sale, in the same way CME currency futures and options contracts can be used to hedge transactions in the individual currencies.

The ECU futures contract also makes an effective hedge for firms with exposure in European currencies without futures markets, or with illiquid or nonexistent forward markets.

In addition to hedging ECU-to-dollar exposure, the CME's futures contract can be used in conjunction with other CME currency contracts to hedge ECU price risk against other major world currencies such as the Japanese yen or the Swiss franc.

The ECU is now the third most popular unit of account for new Eurobond issues. With ECU futures, issuers and investors can hedge receipts or payments from ECU-denominated notes or bonds, as well as the purchase and sale of these instruments.

The ECU contract is even more than a flexible currency hedge, however. By spreading with the CME's Eurodollar contract, for example, lenders and borrowers can lock in attractive interest rates.

The CME covers the world. As the world's largest and most influential exchange for currency trading, the CME brings the advantages of liquidity and experience to ECU futures trading. The ECU futures contract's delivery cycles and other contract terms are similar to those of the CME's contracts such as Deutsche mark and Swiss franc futures, and it has attractive spread margins. That means ECU futures at the CME offer unparalleled arbitrage, spreading and trading opportunities.

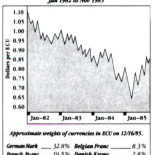

U.S. DOLLAR/ECU EXCHANGE RATE
Jan 1982 to Nov 1985

Approximate weights of currencies in ECU on 12/16/85.

German Mark	32.8%	Belgian Franc	8.3%
French Franc	19.5%	Danish Krone	2.8%
British Pound	14.5%	Irish Punt	1.2%
Dutch Guilder	10.4%	Greek Drachma	0.9%
Italian Lira	9.3%	Luxembourg Franc	0.3%

Protection that goes where you need it. For more information about how the new ECU futures can help you protect yourself anywhere in Europe, talk to your broker or call the CME, toll free, 1-800-331-3332.

CHICAGO MERCANTILE EXCHANGE®
FUTURES AND OPTIONS WORLDWIDE
International Monetary Market
Index and Option Market

30 South Wacker Drive Chicago, Illinois 60606
312-930-1000
67 Wall Street New York 10005 212-363-7000
27 Throgmorton Street London EC2N 2AN
01 920-0722

CONTRACT SPECIFICATIONS

Trading Unit:	ECU 125,000
Quotation:	U.S. $ per ECU
Ticker Symbol:	EC
Minimum Price Fluctuation:	$.0001 per ECU = $12.50 per contract
Price Limits:	None
Contract Months:	Mar, Jun, Sep, Dec
Trading Hours: (CST)	7:20 a.m. to 1:30 p.m.
Last Day of Trading:	Two business days before the third Wednesday of contract month
Last Trading Day Hours: (CST)	7:20 a.m. to 9:00 a.m.
Delivery:	Check with Clearing House for details

EXHIBIT 19–8   ECU futures

Source: Reprinted with permission of the Chicago Mercantile Exchange

Currency **options,** illegal in the United States until recently, provide another hedging alternative. The most important characteristic of options is likely an option buyer's ability to limit the loss, if the buyer's guess is wrong, to the premium paid. A buyer of a currency option acquires the right either to buy or sell a fixed amount of foreign currency at a set price within a specified time period, and the buyer can exercise this right when it is profitable to do so.

Both *futures* and *options on futures* significantly reduce risk. However, there are two key advantages of options on futures over futures. First, because a trader is able

The Exchange with foresight

SIMEX, the Singapore International Monetary Exchange, is an innovator in the financial futures market. As Asia's first international financial futures exchange, SIMEX has grown rapidly by developing new ways to meet the changing needs of participants around the world.

SIMEX was the first to introduce an unprecedented mutual-offset system with the Chicago Mercantile Exchange (CME); this allows investors to establish a position on one exchange and transfer it to or liquidate it on the other. Equally important, SIMEX has similar rules and trading systems as the CME's for safeguarding its market participants.

In response to the need for a way to hedge Japanese equities, SIMEX launched trading in Nikkei Stock Average Futures, the first exchange to offer a futures contract on what is now the largest stock market in the world. This offers more efficient and economical participation in the Japanese stock market together with greater flexibility.

It is innovations such as these and the efficient, well-regulated trading that keep SIMEX in the vanguard of futures trading.

Futures contracts currently traded on SIMEX include Eurodollars, Nikkei Stock Average, Deutschmark, Japanese Yen, British Pound, US Treasury Bond and Gold.

It's not surprising, therefore, that participants from all over the world have discovered the benefits of using SIMEX and have recognised its foresight in futures trading.

The Singapore International Monetary Exchange Limited

1 Maritime Square, #09-39 World Trade Centre, Singapore 0409. Tel: (65) 278 6363. Telex: RS 3800. Cable: SINMEX. Fax: 2730241

Call us today to discuss how SIMEX can play a part in your financial plans.

EXHIBIT 19–9   SIMEX

Source: Reprinted with permission of the Singapore International Monetary Exchange Limited

to take positions smaller than standard futures contracts, options on futures allow small businesses to hedge more effectively. Second, compared to futures, options on futures provide greater flexibility by allowing hedgers to cap their exposure.[19] Exhibit 19–10 shows how currency options can be used to minimize the volatility of a currency.

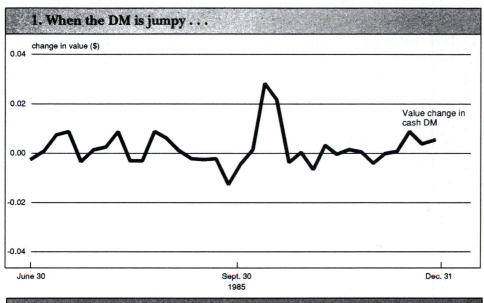

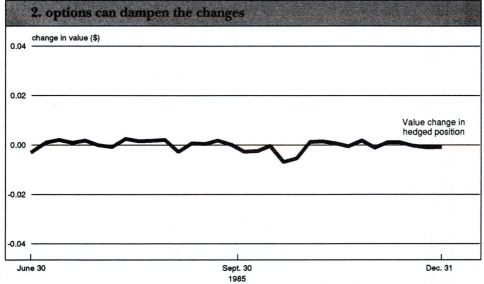

EXHIBIT 19–10   How options can neutralize the changes of currency value

Source: James T. Moser, "A Good Hedge Keeps Dogs Off the Yard," *Chicago Fed Letter* 27 (November 1989): 2

Although banks have been and are still the first choice of corporations seeking to manage foreign exchange risk, exchanges have devised new ways to attract firms or to get banks to work through exchanges. GAF Corp., a New Jersey specialty chemicals and building materials conglomerate with $1 billion in sales, works with either a bank or an exchange, depending on the dollar volume. It uses exchanges for most of its options transactions when they fall in the range of $5 million to $25 million because exchanges are more competitive in transactions of that size. When the amounts exceed $25 million, GAF uses banks instead.[20] Exhibit 19–11 provides a comparison of a variety of hedging methods.

Inflation discourages lending but encourages borrowing, because a loan when due can be repaid with less expensive money. A country with high inflation tends to have a weak currency, which is usually accompanied by high interest rates. The higher interest cost does not necessarily make it an undesirable place to take out loans.

In order to deal with the complexity of international trade, two strategies should be considered: **leading** and **lagging**. For an MNC with a network of subsidiaries, several techniques can be used to reduce foreign exchange. "Adjustments can be made in the speed with which one subsidiary pays off its accounts with another subsidiary. Subsidiaries with strong currencies could delay or lag the remittances of dividends, royalties, and fees to other subsidiaries of the multinational to decrease their liabilities. Those in weak currency countries could try to lead, or pay promptly, their liabilities and reduce their asset exposure."[21]

The currency to be used for the purpose of **invoicing** should be considered carefully. When the buyer is in a soft currency but the seller is in a hard currency, the invoice should use the seller's currency.[22] But the buyer's currency (or that of another selected third country) should be used for invoicing when the buyer is in a hard currency but the seller is in a soft currency. When both the buyer and the seller are in soft currencies, they should consider a third currency as an alternative. But if both are in hard currencies, it may not matter much whether the buyer's currency or the seller's currency is employed. Note that these invoicing strategies apply also to an MNC's subsidiaries that trade with one another. Furthermore, when the volume justifies the cost, the MNC should coordinate the invoicing activities by setting up a reinvoicing center.

Domestic firms should not expect to improve their performance solely on the basis of foreign competitors' misfortunes (i.e., appreciation of foreign competitors' currency). After all, foreign firms are still in a position to decide how much of the cost increase to pass on to buyers. Exhibit 19–12 shows the gap in percentage terms between the appreciation in the value of each country's currency measured in dollars and the price of their exports measured in dollars. Compared to other countries shown, Japan passed on far less of its currency-induced cost increases. Japan passed on only 53 percent of its currency-induced price increases and left a large 47 percent gap between the increase in its dollar-measured costs and the dollar price of its exports. In the case of the United Kingdom, it passed on more than the currency appreciation by 10 percent and almost exactly its labor-cost increases. Germany, in contrast, passed on 100 percent of its currency increases, resulting in a 0 percent

EXHIBIT 19–11 How foreign exchange products compare

Product	Who arranges	Credit line required	Margin required	Front-end premium	When valuation occurs	Extent of limitation of risk	Type of taxation	Minimum size	Ease of offset	Need for in-house supervision
Borrow the foreign currency	bank	yes	no	no	periodic	both directions (upside and downside)	ordinary	effectively none[a]	easy	yes
Foreign exchange forward	bank	yes	no	no	maturity	both directions	capital gains	effectively none[a]	difficult	no
Swap	bank	yes	no	no	periodic (settlement)	both directions	ordinary	effectively none[a]	difficult	no
Over-the-counter (OTC) option	bank	no	no	yes	maturity	one direction	(review)	effectively none[a]	easy	no
Hybrid: Buy one OTC option, sell another	bank	yes	no	no	maturity	within a range only, then unlimited	(review)	effectively none[a]	easy	no
Hybrid: Collar	bank	yes	no	no	maturity	risk within a range, then limited both directions	capital gains	effectively none[a]	difficult or easy	no
Exchange options:										
on physicals	exchange	no	no	yes	maturity	one direction	(review)	fixed by exchange	easy	possibly
on futures	exchange	no	no	yes	maturity	one direction	capital gains	fixed by exchange	easy	possibly
Futures	exchange	no	yes	no	daily	both directions	capital gains	fixed by exchange	easy	yes

[a]Although less than $1 million is rare

Source: Joe Stein, "Forex Products Treasures Like," *Futures* (December 1988): 35. Reprinted from *Futures* magazine, 219 Parkade, P.O. Box 6, Cedar Falls, Iowa 50613

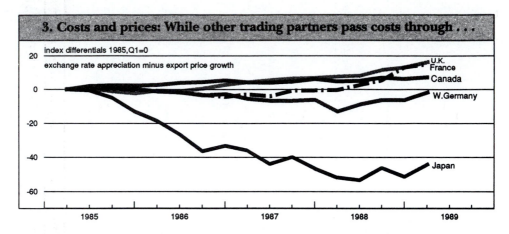

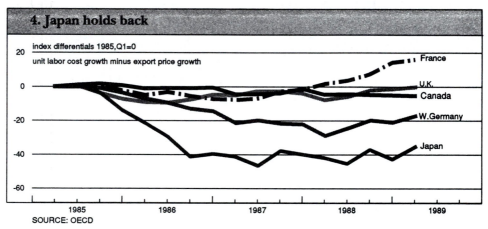

EXHIBIT 19–12   Passing on currency-induced cost increases

Source: Steven Strongin and Jack L. Hervery, "The Dollar Can Only Do So Much," *Chicago Fed Letter*, Octorber 1989

gap. However, Germany passed on 83 percent of its labor-cost increases, leaving a 17 percent labor-cost gap.[23]

According to Aggarwal and Soenen, traditional hedging techniques are not adequate in managing long-term exposure for foreign exchange risk.[24] Instead, firms should use marketing, production, and financial strategies. For example, when the home currency continues to strengthen, the firm should increase its purchases of material and components abroad. Another strategy is to shift production among foreign plants to hedge against foreign exchange losses.

Globalization offers protection from currency fluctuations. In the late 1980s Komatsu, was hit hard by the strong yen. To solve this problem, Komatsu, a Japanese firm, established strategic alliances overseas to shift production abroad. Komatsu has a joint venture with Dresser Industries in the United States while being linked in Europe with Hanomag, which has 20 percent of the German wheel-loader and bulldozer market. In addition to its ties with Korea's Samsung Shipbuilding and Heavy Industries, Komatsu imports sheet metal parts from its Indonesian joint venture and has a long-standing agreement with Robbins, a U.S. firm, on underground machinery.

CONCLUSION

This chapter, although somewhat technical in nature, has covered various financial circumstances related to international marketing. Borrowing money is one thing, but exchanging money is another matter altogether. There have been, there are, and there always will be dreadful accounts about how companies were caught short by the devaluation of a currency. For decades authorities have debated the merits of the various competing currency exchange systems. Although no single system is able to eliminate completely the volatility of rate movements, there is at present no superior alternative to the system of managed floating rates.

Regardless of the exchange rate system used, rate changes are almost always a certainty, and thus some degree of risk is inevitable. Because MNCs have no determination with regard to the exchange systems—fixed or floating rates—they must attempt to reduce their foreign exchange exposure. To hedge, multinationals can consider any one of the following markets: spot, forward, futures, options, and brokers' services. Other alternatives may include using adjustable prices and billing in strong currencies.

Because of the varying rates of inflation among countries, the impact of inflation on the value of the currency cannot be overlooked. For companies with assets in a high-inflation country, the value of their assets can be substantially and adversely affected. Yet MNCs can benefit from inflation if they know how to borrow money wisely. With regard to the timing of payment, money managers should lead in soft currencies and lag in stronger currencies. For an MNC with subsidiaries in many countries, reinvoicing is a well-advised strategy .

In spite of an increasing number of techniques believed to minimize foreign exchange exposure, it is premature to expect that the methods discussed here are all the techniques that corporate managers can employ. With trends indicating movement toward further deregulation in an increasingly complex world of financial activities, it is just a matter of time before new strategies are created to manage exchange risks.

QUESTIONS

1. Explain how inflation and nationalism make it impossible for a single global currency to exist.
2. Why do companies involved in international trade have to hedge their foreign exchange exposure?
3. Distinguish between the spot market and the forward market.
4. Should an exporter use the spot rate or forward rate for quotation?
5. Is devaluation good for exports and imports? Why is the impact of devaluation usually not immediate?
6. Explain how these exchange rate systems function: (a) gold standard, (b) par value, (c) crawling peg, (d) wide band, and (e) floating.
7. What are the EMS and ECU?
8. How does a clean float differ from a dirty float?

9. How can an MNC hedge or cover its foreign-exchange exposure?
10. How does the forward market differ from the futures and options markets?
11. How does inflation affect a country's currency value? Is it a good idea to borrow or obtain financing in a country with high inflation?
12. What are leading and lagging, and how should they be employed with regard to payment and collection?

DISCUSSION ASSIGNMENTS AND MINICASES

1. Should the world abolish all local currencies except the U.S. dollar, which would function as a global currency?
2. Should the world adopt a basket of the five or ten leading currencies (e.g., U.S. dollar, Japanese yen, Swiss franc, and so on) as a global currency for international trade?
3. Should U.S. firms insist on the U.S. dollar for all buying as well as selling transactions?
4. The United States has aggressively pursued the lower dollar value. Is this strategy good for the United States?
5. Should the United States abandon the float in favor of the gold standard or some other type of fixed or semifixed system?
6. Both fixed and floating rates claim to promote exchange rate stability while controlling inflation. Is it possible for these two divergent systems to achieve the same goals?
7. How should an MNC reduce its foreign exchange risks?
8. Honda was the first of the Japanese automakers to manufacture its cars in Ohio for the U.S. market. The success of its assembly plant in Marysville (Ohio) led to a plan to add a second Ohio plant. Honda also began exporting its cars from the American plant to Japan. Mazda and Mitsubishi followed suit. Other Japanese companies that export or plan to export products or components made in the United States to Japan include Hitachi, Yamaha, Fujitsu, and Sony. Politically and financially, what are the benefits of (a) manufacturing cars in the United States for U.S. consumption and (b) exporting cars to Japan?

CASE 19–1
UPS AND DOWNS
A Foreign Exchange Simulation Game

What goes up must come down. This applies to most currencies as well. The up and down movements greatly and eventually affect what consumers have to pay or are willing to pay for imported products.

For an international marketer, the effect of foreign exchange rate changes on operations and pricing is unavoidable. The marketer must estimate *how much* the value of a currency will go up or down and predict *when* the movement will occur. This, to say the least, is not an easy task, and it perplexes even the most experienced money manager. The marketer may be wrong about the direction of the move. Even if the guess is right, the timing may be off. The marketer thus may initiate a move too soon or too late. Without the right timing, the marketer may begin to question the decision concerning the direction. Assuming that the marketer got the right decisions on the direction and timing, he or she still has to consider the *magnitude* of change. Or the marketer may think that the currency has moved enough and then begins to hedge or remove the hedge. In other words, there are short-term and long-term trends. They may move together or move in the opposite direction. In effect, it is more than just making one basic decision. Every day (or even every minute) poses a new situation requiring a decision about whether the action is necessary.

Assume that you are going to export your products to both Japan and Germany, and assume that the value of the merchandise is $100,000 for each country. You will receive payments in Japanese yen and German mark in two weeks. Your net profit margin is 5 percent. Consult the exchange rates for today by looking up the information in a daily newspaper. One convenient method is to consider the currency futures tables that can be found in the *Wall Street Journal* and many daily newspapers. The *Wall Street Journal* and *New York Times* also provide options information (simply

903

EXHIBIT 1   Options contract specifications

	Options on Currency Futures[a]				
	British Pound	**Canadian Dollar**	**Deutsche Mark**	**Japanese Yen**	**Swiss Franc**
Option Coverage	One BP futures contract (BP 25,000)	One CD futures contract (CD 100,0000)	One DM futures contract (DM 125,000)	One JY futures contract (JY 12,500,000)	One SF futures contract (SF 125,000)
Strike Price Intervals	US 2.5¢	US .5¢	US 1¢	US .01¢	US 1¢
Months Traded	All 12 Calendar Months				
Ticker Symbols	Calls: CP Puts: PP	To be announced	Calls: CM Puts: PM	To be announced	Calls: SF Puts: PF
Premium Quotations	US ¢ per pound 1.00 = $250 ($.01 × BP25, 000)	US ¢ per C. dollar 1.00 = $1000 ($.01 × CD100, 000)	US ¢ per mark 1.00 = $1250 ($.01 × DM125, 000)	US ¢ per yen 1.00 = $1250 ($.0001×JY12, 500, 000)	US ¢ per franc 1.00 = $1250 ($.01 × SF125, 000)
Minimum Price Change	.05 = $12.50	.01 = $10.00	.01 = $12.50	.01 = $12.50	.01 = $12.50
Price Limit	Option ceases trading when the corresponding future locks limit				
Trading Hours (U.S. Central Time)	7:20 A.M. to 2:00 A.M.	7:20 A.M. to 2:00 A.M.	7:20 A.M. to 2:00 A.M.	7:20 A.M. to 2:00 A.M.	7:20 A.M. to 2:00 A.M.
Last Day of Trading	Two Fridays before the third Wednesday of the contract month				

[a]Contract specifications are subject to change. Check with your broker to confirm this information

NOTES COMMON TO ALL OPTIONS ON CURRENCY FUTURES:

Strike Prices

When a new contract month is listed for trading, there will be five put and call strike prices; the nearest strike to the underlying futures price, the next two higher, and the next two lower. For example, if the March DM price closes at $.3651 on the previous day, the strikes listed for March puts and calls will be 35¢, 36¢, 37¢, 38¢, 39¢.

A new strike price will be listed for both puts and calls when the underlying futures price touches within half a strike price interval of either the second highest or second lowest strike prices. As an example, if the March DM futures price touches 3751 after the options are listed as in the about example, then a new strike price at 40¢will be listed for puts and calls the next day. (No new options will be listed, however, with less than 20 calendar days until expiration.)

consider the nearby month as benchmark). Exhibit 1 provides options contract specifications. It should be noted that the sizes of these currency contracts are the same for both futures and options.

Questions

1. Because you will receive payments in two weeks, do you think there is any need to hedge your exposure?
2. Assuming that hedging is desirable, what is your hedging preference: cash, forward, futures, or options?
3. Do you want to hedge both the Japanese yen and German mark?
4. When do you want to hedge? (Note: You can hedge anytime within two weeks.)
5. Consider the exchange rates at the end of the two-week period and see how the profit from the sale of your products is affected by the rate changes as determined by your decisions.

NOTES

1. "What Makes a Modern Currency?" *Futures* (June 1990): 43.
2. George S. Tavlas, "International Currencies: The Rise of the Deutsche Mark," *Finance & Development* (September 1990): 35–38.
3. Uli Schmetzer, "Italy's New Lira to Zero out 'Millionaires,' " *Chicago Tribune*, 25 May 1986.
4. Raveendra N. Batra, Shabtai Donnenfeld, and Josef Hadar, "Hedging Behavior by Multinational Firms," *Journal of International Business Studies* 13 (Winter 1982): 59–70.
5. Peter H. Lindert and Charles P. Kindleberger, *International Economics*, 7th ed. (Homewood, IL: Irwin, 1982), 322.
6. Timothy A. Luehrman, "Exchange Rate Changes and the Distribution of Industry Value," *Journal of International Business Studies* 22 (no. 4, 1991): 619–49.
7. *Commodity Markets* (Chicago: Chicago Board of Trade, 1983), 56.
8. William L. Wilby, "Gold in the International Arena: How Automatic Is International Adjustment?" *Economic Perspectives*, Federal Reserve Board of Chicago (November/December 1981): 3–12.
9. Neil J. Pinsky and Joseph G. Kvasnicka, "The European Monetary System," *Economic Perspectives*, Federal Reserve Board of Chicago (November/December 1979): 3–10.
10. "One Big Currency—And One Big Job Ahead," *Business Week*, 23 December 1991, 40–42.
11. Jude Wanniski, "A Supply-Side Case for a Gold Standard," *Business Week*, 7 December 1981, 23, 27.
12. Roy W. Jastram, *The Golden Constant: The English and American Experience 1560–1976* (Salt Lake City: Wiley, 1977).

13. Amitai Etzioni, "From Nuggets to Dross: The False Gleam of a Gold Standard," *Business Week*, 8 February 1982, 16–17.
14. *The International Monetary Fund: Its Evolution, Organization, and Activities*, pamphlet Series no. 37, 4th ed. (Washington, D.C.: International Monetary Fund, 1984), 4.
15. "Fund Staff Study Examines the Impact of Protectionism," *IMF Survey*, 12 August 1985, 250.
16. "Report of the Deputies: The Functioning of the International Monetary System," *IMF Survey* (July 1985): 2–14.
17. Ike Mathur, "Managing Foreign Exchange Risk Profitably," *Columbia Journal of World Business* 17 (Winter 1982): 23–30.
18. James T. Moser, "A Good Hedge Keeps Dogs Off the Yard," *Chicago Fed Letter* (November 1989).
19. Moser, "Good Hedge."
20. Jon Stein, "Forex Products Treasurers Like," *Futures* (December 1988), 34–36.
21. Janice M. Westerfield, "How U.S. Multinationals Manage Currency Risk," *Business Review*, Federal Reserve Board of Philadelphia (March/April 1980): 19–27.
22. Mathur, "Managing Foreign Exchange Risk," 25.
23. Steven Strongin and Jack L. Hervey, "The Dollar Can Only Do So Much," *Chicago Fed Letter* (October 1989).
24. Raj Aggarwal and Luc A. Soenen, "Managing Persistent Real Changes in Currency Values: The Roles of Multinational Operating Strategies," *Columbia Journal of World Business* 24 (Fall 1989): 60–67.

SUBJECT INDEX

NAME INDEX

COMPANY AND TRADEMARK INDEX

COUNTRY INDEX